A Companion to the History of the Middle East

BLACKWELL COMPANIONS TO HISTORY

This series provides sophisticated and authoritative overviews of the scholarship that has shaped our current understanding of the past. Defined by theme, period and/or region, each volume comprises between twenty-five and forty concise essays written by individual scholars within their area of specialization. The aim of each contribution is to synthesize the current state of scholarship from a variety of historical perspectives and to provide a statement on where the field is heading. The essays are written in a clear, provocative, and lively manner, designed for an international audience of scholars, students, and general readers.

A Companion to International History 1900–2001
Edited by Gordon Martel

A Companion to Western Historical Thought
Edited by Lloyd Kramer and Sarah Maza

A Companion to Gender History
Edited by Teresa A. Meade and Merry E. Wiesner-Hanks

BLACKWELL COMPANIONS TO BRITISH HISTORY

A Companion to Roman Britain
Edited by Malcolm Todd

A Companion to Britain in the Later Middle Ages
Edited by S. H. Rigby

A Companion to Tudor Britain
Edited by Robert Tittler and Norman Jones

A Companion to Stuart Britain
Edited by Barry Coward

A Companion to Eighteenth-Century Britain
Edited by H. T. Dickinson

A Companion to Nineteenth-Century Britain
Edited by Chris Williams

A Companion to Early Twentieth-Century Britain
Edited by Chris Wrigley

A Companion to Contemporary Britain
Edited by Paul Addison and Harriet Jones

In preparation

A Companion to the Early Middle Ages: Britain and Ireland
Edited by Pauline Stafford

BLACKWELL COMPANIONS TO EUROPEAN HISTORY

A Companion to Europe 1900–1945
Edited by Gordon Martel

A Companion to Eighteenth-Century Europe
Edited by Peter H. Wilson

A Companion to Nineteenth-Century Europe
Edited by Stefan Berger

A Companion to the Worlds of the Renaissance
Edited by Guido Ruggiero

A Companion to the Reformation World
Edited by R. Po-chia Hsia

In preparation

A Companion to Europe Since 1945
Edited by Klaus Larres

A Companion to the Medieval World
Edited by Carol Lansing and Edward D. English

BLACKWELL COMPANIONS TO AMERICAN HISTORY

A Companion to the American Revolution
Edited by Jack P. Greene and J. R. Pole

A Companion to 19th-Century America
Edited by William L. Barney

A Companion to the American South
Edited by John B. Boles

A Companion to American Indian History
Edited by Philip J. Deloria and Neal Salisbury

A Companion to American Women's History
Edited by Nancy A. Hewitt

A Companion to Post-1945 America
Edited by Jean-Christophe Agnew and Roy Rosenzweig

A Companion to the Vietnam War
Edited by Marilyn B. Young and Robert Buzzanco

A Companion to Colonial America
Edited by Daniel Vickers

A Companion to 20th-Century America
Edited by Stephen J. Whitfield

A Companion to the American West
Edited by William Deverell

A Companion to American Foreign Relations
Edited by Robert D. Schulzinger

A Companion to the Civil War and Reconstruction
Edited by Lacy K. Ford

A Companion to American Technology
Edited by Carroll Pursell

A Companion to African-American History
Edited by Alton Hornsby, Jr

A Companion to American Immigration
Edited by Reed Ueda

BLACKWELL COMPANIONS TO WORLD HISTORY

A Companion to the History of the Middle East
Edited by Youssef M. Choueiri

A Companion to Japanese History
Edited by William M. Tsutsui

A Companion to Latin American History
Edited by Thomas Holloway

In preparation

A Companion to Russian History
Edited by Abbott Gleason

A COMPANION TO THE HISTORY OF THE MIDDLE EAST

Edited by

Youssef M. Choueiri

WILEY-BLACKWELL

A John Wiley & Sons, Ltd., Publication

This paperback edition first published 2008
© 2008 Blackwell Publishing Ltd

Edition history: Blackwell Publishing Ltd (hardback, 2005)

Blackwell Publishing was acquired by John Wiley & Sons in February 2007. Blackwell's publishing program has been merged with Wiley's global Scientific, Technical, and Medical business to form Wiley-Blackwell.

Registered Office
John Wiley & Sons Ltd, The Atrium, Southern Gate, Chichester, West Sussex, PO19 8SQ, United Kingdom

Editorial Offices
350 Main Street, Malden, MA 02148-5020, USA
9600 Garsington Road, Oxford, OX4 2DQ, UK
The Atrium, Southern Gate, Chichester, West Sussex, PO19 8SQ, UK

For details of our global editorial offices, for customer services, and for information about how to apply for permission to reuse the copyright material in this book please see our website at www.wiley.com/wiley-blackwell.

The right of Youssef M. Choueiri to be identified as the author of the editorial material in this work has been asserted in accordance with the Copyright, Designs and Patents Act 1988.

Library of Congress Cataloging-in-Publication Data

A companion to the history of the Middle East / edited by Youssef M. Choueiri.
    p.: maps; cm.— (Blackwell companions to world history)
  Includes bibliographical references and index.
  ISBN: 978-1-4051-8379-6 (paperback)
  1. Middle East—History. I. Title: Title on CIP data view: Companion to the Middle East.
II. Choueiri, Youssef M., 1948– III. Series.

DS62.C63 2005
956—dc 22

                                        2005002132

A catalogue record for this book is available from the British Library.

Contents

Illustrations

Plates

Figures

Maps

Tables

London (1997, 2001). He is currently working on a new project entitled *A History of Democracy in the Arab World*.

Fred M. Donner is Professor of Islamic History, the Oriental Institute and Department of Near Eastern Languages and Civilizations, University of Chicago. His publications include *The Early Islamic Conquests*, Princeton (1981) and *Narratives of Islamic Origins: The Beginnings of Islamic Historical Writing*, Princeton (1998) (*Studies in Late Antiquity and Early Islam*, 14).

Zouhair Ghazzal is Associate Professor of Middle Eastern History at Loyola University Chicago. He published *The Political Economy of Damascus in the Nineteenth Century* (in French, 1993), and completed a study on the Ottoman Syrian *'ulama* and judiciary, *The Grammars of Adjudication* (forthcoming). He is now working on the contemporary Syrian legal system.

Robert Gleave is Reader in Islamic Studies in the Department of Theology and Religious Studies, University of Bristol, specializing in Shi'ism and Islamic Law. He is author of *Inevitable Doubt: Two Theories of Shi'i Jurisprudence*, Leiden (2000) and editor of *Islamic Law: Theory and Practice*, London (1996), and *Religion and Society in Qajar Iran*, London (2004).

Ioannis N. Grigoriadis holds an MIA degree from the School of International and Public Affairs, Columbia University. He is currently a Ph.D. student in Turkish Politics at the School of Oriental and African Studies, University of London.

Gerald R. Hawting is Professor of the History of the Near and Middle East, SOAS. Among his publications are *The Idea of Idolatry and the Emergence of Islam*, Cambridge (1999); *The First Dynasty of Islam*, 2nd edition, London (2000); and two volumes (17 and 20) of the translation of *The History of al-Tabari*, Albany, NY (1989 and 1996). He is currently writing a chapter on Muslim rituals for an edited volume to be published by Ashgate as part of the Formation of the Classical Islamic World series (general editor, Lawrence I. Conrad).

Raymond Hinnebusch is Professor of International Relations and Middle East Politics at the University of St Andrews, Scotland. He has authored numerous books and articles on Syria, Egypt, and the international relations of the region including *Syria: Revolution from Above*, London (2000) and *The International Politics of the Middle East*, Manchester (2003).

P. M. Holt, M.A., D.Litt. (Oxon), Emeritus Professor of the History of the Near and Middle East, School of Oriental and African Studies, University of London, has published a number of articles on aspects of Mamluk history and institutions as well as *Early Mamluk Diplomacy (1260–1290)/Treaties of Baybaras and Qalawun with Christian Rulers*, Leiden (1995). He has also translated Peter Thorau's *Sultan Baibars I. von Agypten* as *The Lion of Egypt? Sultan Baybars I and the Near East in the Thirteenth Century*, London (1992).

Hugh Kennedy is Professor of the History of the Islamic Middle East at the University of St Andrews. His main publications include *The Prophet and the Age of the Caliphate* (1986), *Crusader Castles* (1994), *Muslim Spain and Portugal* (1996).

Alexander Knysh is Professor of Islamic Studies and chair of the Department of Near Eastern Studies, University of Michigan, Ann Arbor. He obtained his doctoral degree from the Institute for Oriental Studies (Leningrad Branch) of the Soviet Academy of

Notes on Contributors

Ali M. Ansari is Reader in the Modern History of the Middle East, University of St Andrews. He is the author of *Modern Iran Since 1921*, London, 2003, and *Iran, Islam and Democracy*, London, 2000.

Michael E. Bonine, Ph.D., University of Texas at Austin, is Professor of Geography and Professor and Head of Near Eastern Studies at the University of Arizona in Tucson, Arizona. He has written extensively on urbanism and urbanization in the Islamic Middle East, originally focused on Iran from fieldwork in the early 1970s. In 1982–9 he also served as Executive Director of the Middle East Studies Association of North America. His publications include: *Population, Poverty, and Politics in Middle East Cities* (ed.) (1997); with E. Ehlers, T. Krafft, and G. Stober, *The Middle Eastern City and Islamic Urbanism: An Annotated Bibliography in Western Languages* (1997); and M. E Bonine and N. R. Keddie (eds), *Modern Iran: Dialectics of Continuity and Change* (1981).

Michael Brett, BA Cantab, Ph.D. London, is Emeritus Reader in the History of North Africa, School of Oriental and African Studies, London. He is author of *The Moors: Islam in the West*, London (1980); *The Berbers* (with Elizabeth Fentress), Blackwell, Oxford (1996); *Ibn Khaldun and the Medieval Maghrib*, Aldershot (1999); *The Rise of the Fatimids: The World of the Mediterranean and the Middle East in the Fourth Century of the Hijra, Tenth Century* CE, Leiden (2001). He is currently engaged upon contributions to the *New Cambridge History of Islam*, and a history of Africa.

Simon Bromley is Senior Lecturer at the Open University. His research interests include theoretical developments in the field of international political economy and international relations. His publications include *Pacific Studies* (1994), *Rethinking Middle East Politics* (1991), and *American Hegemony and World Oil* (1991).

Michael Chamberlain is Associate Professor of History at the University of Wisconsin–Madison and the author of *Knowledge and Social Practice in Medieval Damascus*, Cambridge (1994). He is interested in problems relating to the social and cultural history of Egypt and Syria between 1100 and 1350.

Youssef M. Choueiri is currently Senior Associate Member, St. Anthony's College, University of Oxford. His publications include *Modern Arab Historiography*, London (2003), *Arab Nationalism: A History*, Oxford (2000), and *Islamic Fundamentalism*,

Sciences in 1986. Since 1991 he has lived in the United States of America. His research interests include Islamic mysticism and Islamic theological thought in historical perspective as well as Islam and Islamic movements in local contexts (especially Yemen and the Northern Caucasus). He has numerous publications on these subjects, including three books.

Metin Kunt is Professor of History at Sabanci University, Istanbul. Previously, he taught at Bosporus University, Istanbul, Cambridge University and, as visiting lecturer, at Leiden, Harvard and Yale. He is author of *The Sultan's Servants* and co-editor (with Christine Woodhead) of *Suleyman the Magnificent and his Age*.

Beverley Milton-Edwards is Reader in Middle East Politics at Queen's University, Belfast. Her main area of research has concentrated on two interrelated themes: dimensions of politics in the Middle East and Islamic politics. Recent publications include being co-author of *Conflicts in the Middle East* (2001), co-author of *Jordan: A Hashemite Legacy* (2001), *Contemporary Politics in the Middle East* (1999), and *Citizenship and the State in the Middle East* (1999).

Valentine M. Moghadam is Chief of Section, Gender Equality and Development, Division of Human Rights and Fight against Discrimination, UNESCO, Paris. Her previous position was Director, Women's Studies Program and Associate Professor of Sociology, Illinois State University. Among her publications are *Modernizing Women: Gender and Social Change in the Middle East* (1993/2003); *Women, Work, and Economic Reform in the Middle East and North Africa* (1998); *Patriarchy and Economic Development: Women's Positions at the End of the Twentieth Century* (1996).

Simon Murden received his doctorate from the University of Exeter in 1993 for work on international relations and political economy in the Gulf. He specializes in the study of contemporary globalization in the Middle East, as well as security issues in the region. He has been a lecturer in International Relations at the University of Plymouth and University College of Wales, Aberystwyth, and is the author of *Emergent Regional Powers and International Relations in the Gulf 1988–91*, Ithaca (1995) and of *Islam, the Middle East and the New Global Hegemony*, Boulder (2002). He is now a Senior Lecturer in the Department of Strategic Studies and International Affairs at Britannia Royal Naval College, Dartmouth.

Emma C. Murphy is a Senior Lecturer at the Institute for Middle Eastern and Islamic Studies, University of Durham. Her publications include: *Israel: Challenges to Identity, Democracy and the State* (co-authored, 2002) and *Economic and Political Change in Tunisia: From Bourguiba to Ben Ali* (1999). Current research interests include the contemporary political economy of North Africa and the history of the Palestine Mandate.

Tim Niblock is Director of the Institute of Arab and Islamic Studies at the University of Exeter, and Professor of Arab Gulf Studies. He has written widely on the politics, political economy and international relations of the Arab world. Among his books are: *Pariah States and Sanctions in the Middle East: Iraq, Libya and Sudan* (2001); *Class and Power in Sudan* (1987), *Iraq: The Contemporary State*, ed. (1982); *State, Society and Economy in Saudi Arabia*, ed. (1981).

Abdul-Karim Rafeq is William and Annie Bickers Professor of Arab Middle Eastern Studies and Professor of History. He received his Ph.D. from the University of

London in 1963. He was formerly Professor and Chair, Department of History, University of Damascus, and Visiting Professor at the Universities of Pennsylvania, Chicago and California at Los Angeles. His area of expertise is Arab Middle Eastern Studies. His publications include *The Province of Damascus 1723–1783,* Beirut (1966), *The Arabs and The Turks,* Beirut (1980) and numerous articles on social and economic history.

André Raymond, D.Phil. (1954), docteur d'Etat de Paris-Sorbonne (1972), is Professor Emeritus at the Université de Provence (Aix-en-Provence). He served as director of the Institut Français d'études arabes in Damascus (1966–75), and of the first Institut de recherches et d'études sur le monde arabe et musulman at Aix-en-Provence (1985–1989). His works include: *Artisans et commerçants au Caire au XVIIIème siècle* (1974); *The Great Arab Cities in the 16th–18th Centuries: An Introduction* (1984); *Grandes villes arabes à l'époque ottoman* (1985); *Le Caire* (1993); and *Le Caire des Janissaries* (1995).

Peter Sluglett, B.A. Cambridge, D.Phil. Oxford, is Professor of Middle Eastern History at the University of Utah, Salt Lake City. He has written extensively on the modern history of Iraq, and on the British and French Mandates in the Middle East, and is now working on the urban social history of Aleppo between the late Ottoman period and the end of the French Mandate.

Gareth Stansfield is Lecturer in Middle East Politics at the Institute of Arab and Islamic Studies at the University of Exeter, and Associate Fellow of the Middle East Programme at the Royal Institute of International Affairs (Chatham House), London. He recently co-authored with Liam Anderson *The Future of Iraq: Dictatorship, Democracy or Division?* (2004).

Paul Stevens was educated as an economist and as a specialist on the Middle East at Cambridge and the School of Oriental and African Studies; 1973–79 teaching at the American University of Beirut in Lebanon interspersed with two years as an oil consultant; 1979–93 at the University of Surrey. Since 1993, he has been Professor of Petroleum Policy and Economics at the Centre for Energy, Petroleum and Mineral Law and Policy, University of Dundee, Scotland (for details see web page www.cepmlp.org). Professor Stevens has published extensively on energy economics, the international petroleum industry, economic development issues and the political economy of the Gulf. He also works as a consultant for many companies and governments.

Lise Storm is a Ph.D. research candidate at the Institute of Arab and Islamic Studies at the University of Exeter, working on a project on democracy in the Middle East. She has been involved in the study of minorities for several years, focusing in particular on the situation of the Kurds and the Berbers. She has a B.Sc. and an M.Sc. in political science from the University of Copenhagen, Denmark, and the University of Leiden, the Netherlands.

Preface and Acknowledgments

Middle Eastern history is a vast field that no single work can realistically aspire to cover in all its periods, themes, and major events. Bearing in mind that this area is credited with introducing for the first time in human culture a huge number of inventions, instruments, tools and methods of organization, deemed necessary for launching enduring forms of civilization, all historical investigation ought ideally to revisit the earliest glimmerings of the dawn of history itself. Such an investigation would have to take account of agriculture, city planning, regular armies, market-places, temples, alphabetical systems of writing, monotheism, the wheel, empire building, tyranny versus accountable government, mathematics, geometry, astronomy and epic poetry, to mention only the most obvious Middle Eastern contributions to ancient as well as modern culture.

Although works of considerable erudition, the result of either painstaking arch-aeological explorations or diligent reconstruction of documentary evidence, have over the last two centuries been published, edited and continually updated, fresh discoveries are constantly being made and new theories are periodically advanced to throw light on a particular era or some material remains. Consequently, Middle Eastern historiography, or writings on the Middle Eastern past, be they in the form of narratives or theoretical treatises based on primary sources, has by and large been turned into an open field capable of receiving a steady stream of speculations and conjectures, without having to grapple with an ever-present threat of being swept away by the torrent of uncontrolled floodgates.

This volume was planned with all the above caveats, state-of-the-art contributions and latest scholarly efforts in mind. Our original plan, initially put forward by Tessa Harvey, Publisher of Blackwell History Division, was to produce a volume devoted to the modern history of the Middle East. However, further discussions and wider consultations with a number of colleagues convinced us to widen the scope of the historical treatment in order to offer a more solid analytical study of the formative and middle periods of Islam, on the one hand, and to allow readers and students to form a more informed judgement as to the continuities and ruptures in Middle Eastern historical development, on the other. I would like to thank in this respect the four anonymous readers who were first approached to offer their considered opinion on the feasibility of such a project as well as the need for its availability. Its main purpose remains to act as a companion to the study and understanding of the Middle East as a historical field of considerable human, strategic, and economic interest.

As our preliminary outline began to take shape, a more comprehensive picture started to emerge, so much so that it became imperative for us to pay equal attention to all the crucial and relevant episodes of Middle Eastern societies. These societies, driven as they are by both a global configuration of modernity and a sense of affiliation to local cultures tied to a long list of civilizations, historical memories, or symbols, have in the last few decades been forced to reassess their past achievements and legacies, be they inherited or imposed, and in a critical spirit, ranging from moderate debates in academic institutions to violent acts of defiance. Hence, both modernity and local habits of thought and practice have recently been subjected to scrutiny by a motley array of Middle Easterners, in an effort to find new ways of coping with the modern world with all its technological, economic, political and cultural complexities.

More importantly, while the rise of Islam ushered in a new turning point in the history of the region, it paved the way for the formation of distinctly developed forms and structures which were capable of undergoing a process of slow or abrupt changes. These changes brought about by a modern scheme of things, embracing the idea of industrial innovation together with an accountable form of governance and administrative efficiency, in addition to paying particular attention to the well-being of ordinary citizens, sum up the multifaceted dilemmas facing Middle Eastern societies under a new wave of globalism.

Thus, the final structure of the volume and its organization were the result of fruitful exchanges of ideas, dialogues and a willingness to revise or modify earlier versions and proposals. It is therefore with great pleasure and gratitude that I would like to thank all those whose direct or indirect contributions made the completion of this volume possible. I am grateful to Carl Petry, William L. Cleveland, Stephen Humphreys, Fred Donner, and Alexander Knysh for their support, advice, and inspiration. Although the final structure of the volume was my own, I wish to thank Nelida Fuccaro, Abdul-Karim Rafeq, Peter Sluglett, and Michael Chamberlain for convincing me to introduce new themes or allow more room for certain approaches.

Moreover, my thanks go to all the contributors, without whose diligence, positive responses and devotion to the world of scholarship, this volume would not have been possible. I would also like to thank James McDougall for offering to translate from French into English chapter 11 by André Raymond. To all the editorial staff at Blackwell I wish to extend my profound gratitude. I would like to thank, in particular, Helen Lawton, Angela Cohen, and Tessa Harvey. I would also like to single out Graeme Leonard for copy-editing the typescript with admirable thoroughness and meticulousness.

This book is dedicated to my daughter Hiba, both as a symbolic gesture of appreciation and an earnest attempt to reaffirm my belief in her generation as it prepares itself to meet the challenges of the twenty-first century.

A Note on Transliteration

The system of transliterating Arabic, Persian, and Turkish letters and words has been reduced to a minimum in most chapters. Under these circumstances only hamza or ' and 'ayn have been retained. However, in the first three chapters, in addition to chapters 5, 7, and 8, dealing as they do with classical Islam or featuring a number of technical Arabic terms, the Library of Congress transliteration system has been used.

Exeter, April 2005

Introduction

Youssef M. Choueiri

Modern Middle Eastern history is a relative newcomer to the academic field. Its emergence as an autonomous and legitimate field of study is closely connected with the Second World War, the onset of the Cold War, and the gradual decline of both Britain and France as colonial powers. For a long time, British, and to some extent French, diplomats and academics referred to this area as the Near East or *le proche-orient*, a designation which served to cover all cultures, histories, and languages of the region. Thus one could be a Near Eastern scholar studying Assyrian texts or researching the impact of the Industrial Revolution on native crafts in Syria. In other words, the old label was sufficiently flexible and generously commodious to allow ancient and contemporary eras to shelter under its wing. This flexibility is, however, denied the more recent label, which is a peculiarly American, and to some extent, Soviet invention.

Nowadays, to be a Middle Eastern specialist is, more often than not, a reference to someone whose scholarly, diplomatic, or journalistic interests are focused on the modern and contemporary aspects of the region.

Initially, both the Near and Middle East tended to coincide geographically, embracing the core countries of Iran, Turkey, Iraq, Greater Syria, Egypt, the Sudan, and Libya. With the passage of time and the emergence of the Arab world as a political block of states grouped under the umbrella of the Arab League, the designation widened to include North Africa as a whole. The Companion to Middle Eastern history will adopt this wider designation as its field of study.

As to the interpretations and theoretical schemes adopted to explain the long march of events or pinpoint significant changes of socio-economic structures, a number of conflicting paradigms have been adopted and expounded.

In its early scholarly stages, the trajectory of Middle Eastern history was often judged to be governed by one single overriding factor or cluster of factors. By the sheer presence of one underlying element, it was then assumed that the historical development of the Middle East tended to follow a lopsided, distorted, and invariably repetitive trajectory. All its societies and historical periods were, as a result, lumped together and deemed to obey a constant pattern of ironclad rigidity or a primordial essence. Whereas some scholars alluded to the universal aridity of its environment, others fastened on religion as a determinant that tended to rear its head, albeit under various guises, in almost all socio-political and economic upheavals. Yet others would underline the obfuscating patriarchal structures of its families as the most plausible explanatory device, conditioning and reproducing its regularly repeated series of violence or docility.

All these single-factor paradigmatic approaches were in the main meant to set apart the Middle East and treat it as a deviant cultural region, or as an unfortunate example of a frozen historical entity. Coinciding with the advent of modernity and European colonial expansionism, such arguments were explicitly or implicitly used to justify foreign intervention as the only agent capable of introducing the benefits of civilized norms of behaviour and governance. It is in this respect that modernity was denied a foothold in the Middle East except in its foreign incarnation or in the shape of marginal minorities anxious to overcome their lowly status.

However, these theoretical approaches have, since the 1980s, been subjected to wide-ranging critical assessments and shown to be affiliated with an outmoded Orientalist scheme of things. These assessments have consequently shifted the debate to a different level, whereby more sophisticated explanations came into play. Modernity, for example, was now assumed to constitute a universal character, which affects all cultures, albeit at an uneven pace of intensity. In other words, the Middle East has, in line with other societies, experienced the same wave of transformation and self-transformation and offered its own indigenous modes of responses and engagement. Hence, policies and programmes of nation building, modernization, democratic transformation, and a sustained level of development were considered to be intrinsic configurations of the region's landscape.

By placing the Middle East within the wider contours of world history, historical interpretations became attuned to the presence of a complex pattern of development. Such a pattern could henceforth indicate discontinuity as well as imaginative modes of linking the past to the present. Although no uniform theoretical treatment has so far received the tacit or explicit agreement of the majority of Middle Eastern specialists, it has become almost impossible to parade primordial or permanent factors to account for the multifaceted and multi-layered history of our region.

The *Companion to the History of the Middle East* is therefore planned to build on the achievements of this recent scholarship, expand its parameters and offer as far as possible a fresh account of the positive and negative aspects of its subject matter. While primarily focused on modern and contemporary periods, its scope is designed to include a number of chapters on the classical and pre-modern features of its institutions, economies, and cultures. Its purpose is to situate a variety of topics within a chronological framework capable of providing a lively and concise narrative.

The structure of the volume is divided into seven parts, together with an introductory chapter.

Part I introduces the Middle East as a historical entity by tracing its general development, with particular attention to the formative period of Islam and the subsequent emergence of an imperial Islamic domain and the establishment of the caliphate as a symbol of both unity and diversity. Whereas Gerald Hawting discusses in chapter 1 the rise of Islam through the perspective of the most recent scholarship, Fred Donner offers the reader in chapter 2 a nuanced interpretation of the Islamic conquests and the underlying motives of their leaders and organizers. By doing so, the image of Islam in both chapters becomes more complex and often far removed from familiar perspectives or received stereotypes. Hugh Kennedy traces in chapter 3 the emergence, development, and eventual decline of the caliphate as one of the most enduring and original Islamic institutions brought into being after the death of the Prophet Muhammad.

Part II delineates the consolidation of religious, cultural, and political traditions in response to the daily life and practical challenges faced by the new community. These include jurisprudence, Sufism and the integration of non-Muslims into the imperial structures of the caliphate. Shi'ism is also discussed as another response to the social and political upheavals following the elaboration of mainstream traditions. Zouhair Ghazzal demonstrates how the religious establishment in Islam, dominated by religious scholars or 'Ulama', developed over time in tandem with its own community in order to meet new needs or respond to different circumstances. Hence, the Sunni religious establishment in Islam is studied in its classical and modern contexts to delineate its varied functions in integrating both Muslims and non-Muslims into the wide world of Islamic culture (chapter 4). Robert Gleave completes this delineation by focusing in chapter 5 on the rise of Shi'ism as an Islamic movement straddling various schools of thought and sects. His account is based on a historical perspective that is conscious of past events and their contingent character, as well as more recent developments, particularly in the wake of the triumph of the Islamic revolution in Iran in 1979. Alexander Knysh in chapter 6 tackles a third theme which by its very chequered history has been of vital importance in both the middle Islamic period and the modern era. Thus, after surveying the various historiographical traditions developed over the centuries for the study of Sufism, he presents his own interpretations based on his original research into this lively subject.

Part III sets out to depict the process of transition to military rule or the militarization of Islam under a wide variety of dynasties. Ethnic origins, modalities of recruitment, and modes of economic management are highlighted as elaborate administrative structures designed to tackle a novel configuration of problems: declining revenues, the crusades and the threat of the Mongols. In chapter 7 Michael Chamberlain discusses these broad issues in relation to the Seljuks and the Ayyubids. It is also in this context that P. M. Holt in chapter 8 studies the Mamluk Institution in its widest significance and implications, with particular attention to its political and economic impact in the urban and rural areas. A similar cluster of problems are identified by Michael Brett in chapter 9, dealing with North African or Maghribi societies between 1056 and 1659.

Part IV ushers in a new type of Middle Eastern state: territorially based, yet imbued with an enduring imperial ethos. The Ottoman and the Safavid traditions of statecraft are seen as the last imperial experiments in an area becoming increasingly diversified as a result of momentous changes in the world at large. Metin Kunt in chapter 10 cogently highlights these two traditions of statecraft and institution building. It was also towards the end of this period that a certain type of Middle Eastern urban life matured and left its cultural imprint as a permanent legacy of city life down to the present time. André Raymond in chapter 11 demolishes the old paradigm posited by French Orientalists in their depiction of Middle Eastern or Islamic cities by delineating the multifaceted function of Middle Eastern cities in their public spaces and internal dynamism.

Part V concentrates on the rapid, internal and external, changes which cut across all countries of the Middle East. These included the commercial and the industrial revolutions, the emergence of European nation-states bent on a policy of overseas expansion and the first glimmerings of an internal drive for reform in the Ottoman world. In chapter 12 Abdul-Karim Rafeq plots the inexorable changes, which accompanied European imperial expansionism in both the eighteenth and nineteenth centuries. He also shows how a different balance of power was the end-result of an uneven relationship as the repercussions of the Industrial Revolution began to dominate Middle Eastern societies. On the other hand, Peter Sluglett in chapter 13 undertakes to weave the different strands of independence movements that emerged in the wake of the arrival of colonialism under varied guises and forms. By doing so he shows how the present system of national states came into being, highlighting at the same time its points of weakness and strength.

Part VI addresses the implications of colonial rule and the struggle for independence. These twin phenomena spawned a number of interdependent movements or political discourses: nationalism, Zionism, political parties, and modern armed forces. In addition, Middle Eastern political economies were subjected to structural and long-term changes as a direct result of the emergence of newly independent states. Whereas Emma Murphy in chapter 14 treats Zionism in all its shades and schools since its inception in the nineteenth century, the three principal nationalist movements in the Middle East – Arab, Turkish and Iranian – are discussed in chapters 15 (Youssef Choueiri) and 16 (Ioannis N. Grigoriadis and Ali Ansari). The pivotal function of political parties and trade unions is introduced by Raymond Hinnebusch in chapter 17. These organizations are discussed in their modern historical context and shown to be vehicles of long-term social and political changes. However, political parties were often sidestepped or hijacked by young military officers anxious to implement immediate radical policies of wealth redistribution or rapid industrialization. In chapter 18 Gareth Stansfield focuses his analysis on the various theories and historical narratives advanced by a number of scholars to explain or chronicle the intervention of Middle East military elites in political life. Simon Murden revisits in chapter 19 the various historical and theoretical accounts that sought to interpret the weak economic performances or achievements of most Middle Eastern states. His line of argument ranges over the inadequate analytical tools of these theoretical narratives by seeking to discover an indigenous bundle of cultural attitudes and political assumptions which have rarely been highlighted in their social and economic ramifications.

Part VII seeks to highlight issues and social movements that have surfaced and preoccupied historians and Middle Eastern specialists in the second half of the twentieth century, and are most likely to gain momentum well into the twenty-first. These range from oil and urban growth to the role of women and democratic human rights. In chapter 20 Michael Bonine seeks to situate the study of Middle Eastern urbanism and Islamic cities within a growing field of historical and social science disciplines concerned with the city as a unit of investigation. He highlights in particular the rapid urban development in all Middle Eastern states as well as the consequences for both the environment and their inhabitants, be they men, women or children. This is followed by oil and development (chapter 21), which tackles the industry of oil and its revenues in so far as they relate to internal domestic issues. Thus, Paul Stevens analyses the historical background of this vital industry and then proceeds to show its negative results in spite of the huge revenues it generates for a considerable number of countries in the region. Valentine Moghadam focuses attention in chapter 22 on gender issues, inequalities and relations of power in their Middle Eastern contexts. Her analysis accords full recognition to the political, social, economic, and cultural diversity of Middle Eastern women, while at the same time showing acute awareness of common characteristics born out of similar historical experiences. In politics and religion (chapter 23) Beverley Milton-Edwards brings out the significance of religion as a marker of identity, on the one hand, and the constant readjustments and constructs such an identity is subjected to in its journey to grapple with the upheavals of modernity, on the other. Her discussion embraces Jewish, Christian and Muslim religious experiences and their various historical endeavours to reinvent both politics and religion as part of a modern project. The fact that more space is given to Islamist movements and discourses than to Jewish or Christian ones, is a testimony to the vocal, and more often than not, strident character of these movements. Lise Storm in chapter 24 considers the question of minorities in their Middle Eastern contexts. Basing her analysis on a rigorous definition of ethnonational minorities while at the same time alluding to all other categories, including religious minorities, she concentrates on three conspicuous national groups: the Berbers, the Kurds and the Palestinians. The reactivation of religion, or the invention of religiously based discourses, is noted by Tim Niblock in chapter 25 in its original impulse to form part of a wider development sweeping across Middle Eastern countries in varying degrees of intensity and sustainability. Hence the rediscovery of civil society in conjunction with the advent of a new democratic drive is diagnosed, with a clear propensity to rehabilitate a wide range of social forces and institutions, formerly considered to belong to a bygone age. In chapter 26, Simon Bromley offers a panoramic view of the Middle East in its regional and international contexts. While his analytical approach contests the applicability of a geopolitical term that had its origins within European culture rather than the region designated as the Middle East, he traces the emergence of its states-system back to the imperial era following the First World War. Nevertheless, local social forces and political actors are also singled out for their specific roles in bringing about present-day Middle Eastern political order and its national/territorial states. The chapter also poses the question of a potential Middle Eastern unity based on either Islam or Arabism. More importantly, issues related to legitimacy, the increasingly visible role of the United States and the kind of reform programmes that are needed to achieve concrete development occupy the rest of the chapter.

The volume is, moreover, structured so as to respond to four major differentiated regional or political units: Iran, Turkey, Israel, and the Arab world. The Arab world itself is approached according to the local rhythms of its constituent parts: the Maghrib, the Nile Valley, the Arabian Peninsula, and the Fertile Crescent. However, in most cases the Arab world seemed to represent in its general historical transformations an evolving entity with common cultural and political affinities.

Another point we had to bear in mind was the desirability of treating certain topics as overarching entities that serve to throw light on the structure as a whole. Part VII is designed to serve such a purpose by allowing ample space to deal with common issues such as religion, oil and development, Middle Eastern women, politics and religion, democracy, urbanization, minorities and the states-system in its international context.

PART I

The Formative Period of Islam

CHAPTER ONE

The Rise of Islam

GERALD R. HAWTING

Introduction

Expressions such as 'the rise of Islam', 'the emergence of Islam', and 'the origins of Islam' are ambiguous and understood differently by different people. Commonly taken today simply as the name of a religion, historically Islam refers to something much bigger than what is generally understood now by the word religion. In pre-modern times, and in many places still, Islam implies a way of life involving such things as political, social, and economic norms and behaviour. An Islamic society may include groups that follow religions other than Islam. In that sense, Islam is a culture deeply affected by the religion of Islam but also by things which to modern eyes may appear to have little to do with religion, or to have sources that are not Islamic. To determine a precise point of origin for such a complex of ideas, practices and institutions is probably not possible. To decide a time at which its 'rise' or 'emergence' was over and when it existed in a state of maturity will involve a number of subjective judgements. Here the rise of Islam is envisaged as a process covering two to three hundred years, from approximately AD 600 to 900.

Islam has its own, not monolithic but broadly consistent, accounts of its origins and early history. Much reported in the Muslim traditional accounts is accepted as fact also by those who have tried to develop new understandings of what the emergence of Islam involved and how it occurred. It is the overall framework and different ways of looking at things that distinguish the more traditional versions of the rise of Islam from newer, academic ones. Beginning with a broadly traditional perspective should simplify the subsequent presentation of the ways in which academic scholarship has suggested new interpretations and approaches.

A Tradition-based Account

Muslims have presented Islam as the continuation of the true monotheist religion taught by Abraham (Ibrāhīm) and all the prophets sent by God to mankind before and after him. Abraham brought his religion to the Arabs of Arabia when he built the Ka'ba (literally 'cube'), the sanctuary of God, at Mecca, and established the rites of worship there. Abraham left his son Ishmael (Ismāʿīl) in Mecca, and Ishmael became the ancestor of the main branch of the Arab people. For some time the Arabs were faithful to Abraham's religion but following a pattern common throughout human history, they gradually fell away from the true path and lapsed into polytheism and idolatry. God then sent Muḥammad, the final prophet, to call them to Islam, which is identical with the religion of Abraham, and to make it supreme throughout the world. God's reasons for choosing Muḥammad as His prophet, and for sending him at the time and place He did, are inscrutable.[1]

Traditionally, the life of the prophet Muḥammad and the few decades after his death in AD 632 are seen as the time when Islam was established in a substantial sense as a religion, a state, and a society. For many, expressions like 'the rise of Islam' refer almost exclusively to the activities of the Prophet and his immediate successors. That is the time before Islam came out of Arabia.

Born in Mecca in western Arabia (the Ḥijāz) at a time given only imprecisely in the traditional biographies but generally taken to be about AD 570, Muḥammad, according to tradition, began to receive revelations from God when he was aged about forty. With some exceptions, his Meccan fellow townsmen rejected his teachings and his claims to be a prophet. At a date equivalent to AD 622 he and some of his Meccan followers left his native town in order to settle in the oasis town of Yathrib (later called Medina) about three hundred miles to the north. That event, known as the Hijra, is presented as the turning point in his fortunes. Subsequently (according to tradition seventeen years later), the year in which it occurred was chosen as the first of a new, Islamic era (the Hijri era, abbreviated AH).[2]

In Yathrib Muḥammad was successful in establishing a religious and political community and in overcoming various enemies. Prominent among them were the large Jewish community of Yathrib and the still pagan leaders of Mecca. The Jews, accused of conspiring with his pagan enemies, were removed from the scene by deportations and then executions. Two years before his death he was able to lead a band of his followers to Mecca and occupy the town without much bloodshed. Its sanctuary, the Kaʿba, was cleansed of idolatry and again dedicated to the worship of the one true God (Allāh) for which Abraham had established it.

God's revelations came to Muḥammad on many occasions throughout his prophetic career. The angel Gabriel (Jibrīl), brought the very words of God himself. In addition, God guided the Prophet's own words and behaviour, which his companions remembered and transmitted to later generations. Thus God made His will known in two ways, through His words (later to be collected in the Qur'ān) and through the Prophet's own words and deeds, collectively known as his Sunna. By the time of Muḥammad's death, the fundamental elements of Muslim belief and religious life (the so-called 'five pillars of Islam') had been fixed in their normative forms, the Islamic revelation was complete (although not yet committed to writing), and a state and society ruled by the Prophet from Medina and based on Islam established.[3]

Following his death, according to this view, there occurred a consolidation and extension of what he had achieved. From AD 632 until 661 the political and religious community founded by Muḥammad in Arabia was ruled by a succession of four caliphs, often called the 'Rightly Guided Caliphs'.[4] For many this was the Golden Age of Islam. God's words were collected from those who had memorized them or written some of them down, and the unchangeable text of the Qur'ān as we know it today was fixed in writing.[5] The institution of the caliphate was founded in order to provide succession to the Prophet's religious and political leadership (although prophecy had ended with his death). The first four caliphs, all of whom had been close companions of the Prophet, were in the best position to rule according to the norms and rules that God had established through him. The Muslim state was expanded under them, first over most of Arabia and then outside the confines of the peninsula in Syria, Iraq, Egypt and western Iran.[6]

Towards the end of this period of consolidation and expansion, however, there occurred what tradition calls the Fitna (656–61). Following the murder of the third caliph, 'Uthmān, by discontented warriors who had taken part in the conquest of Egypt, divisions among leading Muslims led to a civil war and the splitting of the community. There were two main rivals. 'Alī, Muhammad's cousin and son-in-law, was recognized by many as caliph in 656 in succession to the murdered 'Uthmān. He was opposed by Mu'āwiya, governor of Syria and a relative of the murdered caliph. Mu'āwiya claimed the right of vengeance against the murderers of his kinsman but 'Alī, many of whose supporters thought that the killing of 'Uthmān had been legitimate, would not hand them over.[7]

In the confused fighting and negotiations that resulted, a substantial number of those who had supported 'Alī abandoned him and opposed both him and Mu'āwiya. This group became known as the Khārijites. They accused 'Alī of having sinned by negotiating with Mu'āwiya, and they proclaimed that only God – not men – could decide the issues that divided the community.

Over the next century or so various groups that the tradition portrays as descended from the original Khārijites were involved in fighting against the caliphs, and they adopted some distinctive religious and political doctrines. Generally, they regarded only themselves as true Muslims; others were not really Muslims but unbelievers or at best hypocrites. The true Muslims had the duty of dissociating themselves from the others and – at least according to some of the extreme Khārijites – fighting and killing them. Eventually, Khārijism became a marginal movement within Islam but in the period of the rise of Islam it was very important. Not only were Khārijis frequently involved in revolts, their ideas stimulated religious and theological thought, and Khārijism provided a vehicle for the expression of discontent by groups within Islam who felt oppressed and downtrodden.[8]

With the death of 'Alī, apparently at the hands of a Khārijite, in 661 the caliphate fell into the hands of Mu'āwiya. He was the first of a series of caliphs who were all members of the same family, the Umayyads (661–750), who ruled from Syria. In the traditional accounts the Umayyads, with few exceptions, were worldly rulers who cared little for Islam. Islamic ideals were maintained mainly by the pious who transmitted the text of the Qur'ān and the details of the Prophet's Sunna but were generally excluded from positions of power or influence and often persecuted by the rulers.

From time to time opposition to the Umayyads flared up and was usually expressed in religious terms. As well as from the Khārijites, opposition often came from groups stemming from those who had supported 'Alī in his conflict with Mu'āwiya. They came to be classified generally as Shī'ites. They held that the only legitimate rulers were members of the family of the Prophet himself, and that usually meant someone who was descended from 'Alī.

The Umayyads are, nevertheless, given credit for continuing the policy of military expansion of the state. By the middle of the second/eighth century, the territory under at least the nominal control of the caliphate extended from Central Asia and north east India to Morocco and southern and central Spain.[9]

In 750 the Umayyads were overthrown by a religiously inspired military revolt, and the caliphate passed into the hands of the 'Abbāsids, who claimed descent from an uncle of the Prophet. They moved the centre of power to Iraq, where they began to build a new capital at Baghdad in 762. In the traditional view, although the 'Abbāsids were by no means perfect Muslims, their rule did represent something of a reversion to the ideals of the period that had preceded the Umayyads and a new and decisive period of consolidation began.[10] It was under the 'Abbāsids that the learning and tradition of Islam, especially the Prophet's Sunna and the interpretation of the Qur'ān, thus far transmitted mainly by word of mouth, came to be written down.

It is from around the end of the second/eighth century onwards that the earliest texts of the Muslim tradition that have come down to us, in various fields of learning, date. The earliest extant lives of the Prophet (*sīra*), the collections of reports about his words and deeds (the *ḥadith*s) that are the basis for knowledge of his Sunna, the works on the science and practice of law (*fiqh*), the commentaries on the Qur'ān (*tafsīr*), the books of history (*ta'rīkh*), the rules of Arabic grammar (*naḥw*), and the literature of other forms of Muslim learning, all date – in the form in which we have them today – from around AD 800 at the earliest. Much of the material such works contain was taken from earlier sources, either written, but now lost, or oral. Our knowledge of those earlier sources, however, depends entirely on the literature that begins to flow freely from about AD 800. Only the Qur'ān is an exception since that, according to tradition, had been fixed in writing under the Rightly Guided Caliphs.

At the same time, the religious scholars (the *'ulamā'*) who were the transmitters and interpreters of the knowledge and learning that came to be committed to writing, began to be recognized and respected in a way that had been denied them in the period of the Umayyad caliphs. They became the focus of Muslim religious life. Some of them were granted salaried positions by the caliphs, for instance as religious judges (*qāḍis*), while others preferred to keep their independence and refused to serve the state.

The fundamental theory of Islamic law (the Shari'a), that it is God's law known from the twin sources of the Qur'ān and the Prophet's Sunna, was given detailed written expression in the work of al-Shāfi'ī (d. 206/821). Then, during the third/ninth century and later, Sunnī Islam developed the institutions and texts that have remained characteristic ever since. Following the work of al-Shāfi'ī, which underlined the importance of knowledge of the Prophet's Sunna, attempts were made to distinguish authentic *ḥadith*s from the many dubious or false ones that had found their way into circulation. It was only from the authentic ones that the true Sunna could be known. Over time, the authority of six collections of *ḥadith*s regarded as authentic by their collectors was established among Sunnīs and their status became comparable to that of the Qur'ān itself.

At the same time minor differences of legal theory and religious practice among the Sunnīs were accommodated by the slow development of schools (*madhhab*s), in the sense of followers of a master. Groups of Sunnī legal scholars came to see themselves as followers of the doctrines of one among a number of important and influential master scholars active in the development of ideas about the law in the second/eighth and third/ninth centuries. The scholar (such as al-Shāfi'ī) seen as the master of the school came to be referred to as the Imam. Originally there were several such *madhhab*s, but eventually only four of them survived and extended toleration to one another. The idea developed that each individual Sunnī Muslim should hold allegiance to one of these four *madhhab*s and maintain it unless circumstances made it impossible.

At the heart of the Sunnī form of Islam is the idea that authority in matters of religious practice and faith belongs in the hands of the religious scholars (the *'ulamā'*). It is they who transmit and interpret the sacred and authoritative texts (the Qur'ān and its interpretation, the *ḥadīth*s and the law books). The caliph, on the other hand, was granted only a limited sphere of authority by the scholars and in some ways could be seen as merely a symbolic representative of the unity of the Sunnī community. In words attributed to the Prophet himself, 'the heirs of the Prophet are the religious scholars'. In other words, in the Sunnī tradition it is the religious scholars who guarantee the link between the Islamic community at any particular time and that of the Prophet.[11]

The pattern of authority in the Shī'ite tradition of Islam ended by appearing similar to that of the Sunnīs but in fundamentals is rather different.[12] Early Shī'ism is very diverse in character and has in common little more than opposition to the caliphate of the Umayyads and a belief that true authority belonged to a member of the Prophet's family. For most Shī'ite groups the Prophet's cousin and son-in-law, 'Alī, had a central role. He had been appointed, they believed, by the Prophet himself as his successor, but he had been cheated of his rights when the institution of the caliphate was invented on the Prophet's death. For most Shī'ites there were no Rightly Guided Caliphs but 'Alī. He had eventually succeeded to the caliphate in 656 (for the Sunnīs he is counted as the fourth Rightly Guided Caliph) only to suffer martyrdom and have the rights of his family usurped by the Umayyads in 661.

As the Prophet's son-in-law, 'Alī was the father of the only surviving line of male descendants of the Prophet (all of Muḥammad's sons are believed to have pre-deceased him). He came to be seen as the first of a line of Imams who, for their followers, were the only legitimate authorities in Islam. Neither the caliphs, given limited recognition by the Sunnīs, nor the Sunnī scholars, had true knowledge or authority, according to the followers of these Imams. The descendants of 'Alī, on the other hand, had a special relationship with God and possessed knowledge not available to ordinary mortals. For the Shī'ites true authority belonged to only one individual – the descendant of 'Alī who was recognized as the Imam of a particular generation – rather than in the scholars generally, as the Sunnī tradition held.

These Shī'ite Imams were rarely able to exercise their authority since they were continually watched by the (from their point of view) illegitimate wielders of worldly power, the caliphs. The history of the Imams, according to the Shī'ite understanding, is one of suffering and martyrdom. The defining event occurred in 61/680 when 'Alī's younger son Ḥusayn was persuaded to attempt to seize power from the Umayyad caliph Yazīd (680–3). The attempt ended in disaster. Ḥusayn and many members of his family were massacred at Karbalā' in Iraq and his head sent to Yazīd in Damascus where it was put on display. In the Shī'ite tradition this shedding of Ḥusayn's blood came to be given a significance not unlike the shedding of that of Jesus for Christians. The day when it happened, the tenth day of the first month of the Muslim year ('Āshūrā' day), became in time the major annual festival of Shī'ite Islam, marked by ceremonies and processions in its communities throughout the world.

However, Shī'ite groups from early on differed among themselves as to which particular descendant of the Prophet was the legitimate Imam in a particular generation, as well as on other issues such as the nature, extent and sources of the Imam's special characteristics. Following the 'Abbāsid seizure of the caliphate in 750 the attention and hopes of most Shīʿites turned to a line of Imams descended from the Prophet through ʿAlī and the Prophet's daughter Fāṭima. Their supporters clashed on several occasions with the ʿAbbāsids, whose own seizure of the caliphate had been justified by a claimed kinship with the Prophet. Attempted revolts, however, issued in bloodshed and repression.

Around 873 a descendant of ʿAlī in the twelfth generation who was recognized as Imam by one group of Shīʿites disappeared. According to his supporters, he had retired from the world to enter a state of occultation. He left behind no descendant, and his followers taught that the line of Imams descended from ʿAlī had come to an end. The last Imam will be absent in occultation until his return just before the end of the world when he will come back as the Mahdī and establish justice and righteousness in the world in preparation for the Last Day.

The idea of the messianic return of an Imam had been an ingredient of Islamic thought from a very early period, but the significant feature of it that emerged now was that his return was not to be expected imminently but at some remote time in the future. Meanwhile, his authority passed into the hands of religious scholars who functioned for their Shīʿite followers in much the same way as did theirs for the Sunnīs. The chief difference was that in the Sunnī tradition the ʿulamāʾ claimed authority in their own right, whereas for the Shīʿites they represented the authority of the absent Imam and they will return it to him when he comes back as the Mahdī.

This particular branch of Shīʿism is often referred to as 'Twelver (or, in Arabic, Ithnāʿasharī) Shīʿism' because it accepts a series of twelve imams beginning with ʿAlī. Eventually it became the dominant and most numerous branch of Shīʿism. Traditional Twelver Shīʿīs, naturally, understand the development of their tradition, which they see as the true form of Islam, as ordained by God from the start. Their Muslim opponents, equally naturally, see it as resulting from historical accidents. In particular they hold that the Twelfth Imam either died or never existed, and that it was simply impossible to extend the line of Imams further. The followers of these Imams, therefore, had to revise their doctrines and ideas about authority.

Just as in the Sunnī tradition, so too in Twelver Shīʿism, the elaboration of the idea that authority lay now in the hands of the religious scholars was accompanied by the emergence of a body of religious texts that came to be seen as authoritative. Following the occultation of the twelfth Imam, specifically Shīʿite collections of ḥadīths, commentaries on the Qurʾān, works of theology (kalām), books of law (fiqh), and other texts specific to the Twelver tradition came to be written and have remained definitive of that tradition until today. Eventually, therefore, for the biggest group within Shīʿism, authority was seen to reside in a textual tradition transmitted and interpreted by a body of learned religious scholars, just as it was in Sunnism.[13]

For traditional Sunnīs and Shīʿis the establishment of their respective systems of authority – which constitute for us the essence of the two traditions – was merely the consolidation and expression in writing of institutions and ideas established in the time of the Prophet. Although the authoritative texts (apart from the Qurʾān) were not written until later, the ideas in them and even many of their words represented a tradition faithfully transmitted from the time of the Prophet onwards. Even the ending of the line of Imams at a particular point was something predetermined by God. Unworthy and usurping rulers may have oppressed the believers and corrupted the religion from time to time, but Islam as it existed in the third/ninth and fourth/tenth centuries was the continuation of the Islam of the Prophet. That view emphasizes the continuity between the period before 656, when the centre of Islam lay in the Hijaz, and the later period, when the Hijaz, although it remained the holy land, was in most respects an unimportant backwater of the world of Islam.

Academic Reinterpretations

Since academic scholarship on Islam became firmly established during the second half of the nineteenth century, as a result of the work of scholars such as Ignaz Goldziher and Theodore Nöldeke, a number of different approaches and ideas, some more influential than others, have emerged. It is not possible here to do justice to all of them. Scholars, naturally, debate and dispute with one another and it would be misleading to suggest that there is one, dominant or even widely accepted under- standing of the rise of Islam among them. Some have attempted to divide contem- porary scholarship into 'radicals' and 'traditionalists', but that is inevitably a simplification of a more complex situation.

The following presents some important ways in which, in the author's view, academic scholarship has suggested new understandings of, or approaches to, the rise of Islam. Their cumulative effect is to encourage us to see it as an extended and complicated process, and to question what it means if we refer to the religion of the Arabs in, say, 650 as Islam.[14]

Arabia and the Rise of Islam

The traditional accounts present Islam as achieving a quite highly developed form within narrow geographical and temporal limits. It is presented as existing in a substantial way already by the death of the Prophet in 632, and then carried out of Arabia by the Arab Muslim conquests.[15] An alternative advocated by several academic scholars is to envisage it as the eventual outcome of a process occupying two centuries or more and involving the Middle East as a whole, not merely western Arabia.

Important in proposing such an approach was the German orientalist Carl Heinrich Becker. In several articles written in the first decades of the twentieth century he advocated the idea that Islam took shape in the lands outside Arabia following their conquest by the Arabs. Urging that Islam is more than just a religion, he argued that it was the outcome of the religious, political, social and economic conditions that developed in the Middle East following the conquests. The conquests, according to Becker and others, were not motivated by religion but by economic needs and desires. They established the political dominance of what must have been a relatively small number of Arab warriors over a larger and diverse non-Arab (and non-Muslim) population. Many of those conquered peoples were heirs to cultures and religious traditions of some antiquity, and it was the interaction between them and their military conquerors that led – eventually – to the formation of a new and distinctive Islamic religion and culture embracing both the Arabs and the subject peoples.

The new culture was dominated by Islam in the religious sphere and Arabic in the linguistic one. Over time the majority of the population became Muslims in religion and Arabs in language (although there remained important groups of non-Arabic speaking Muslims and non-Muslim Arabic speakers). In the evolution of this Islamic culture it was not only the conquered peoples whose religious and linguistic identity changed – so too did that of the Arab conquerors. Whatever the nature of the religion and language that the Arab conquerors brought with them, the Islam and the Arabic of the Islamic world around AD 900 is not a simple, straightforward, continuation of those brought out of Arabia in the seventh century. For Becker, the contribution of the non-Arab peoples was the more important.

The salient feature of Becker's approach is that it presents Islam as developing slowly outside Arabia. His primarily economic explanation of the Arab conquests is certainly questionable and difficult to square with the evidence of early non-Muslim sources, but his argument that the complex religious and cultural system of Islam cannot be understood simply as the product of Arabia before the Arab conquests has been influential.[16]

One difference between those who, with the tradition, identify the rise of Islam largely with the career of Muhammad, and those who, like Becker, see it as a process occupying a century and more, is the way in which they understand Islam. For the former, it seems to designate a basically straightforward, primarily religious, set of beliefs and practices. For many of them, Islam may even be understood as an ideal, distinct from the individuals and societies that have embodied it. It is made known through revelation and it is possible to ascertain what represents true Islam as distinct from corrupted or mistaken forms of it.

For a historian, on the other hand, a particular religion is not an abstract concept but something known from its diverse historical manifestations. Islam is the totality of what Muslims of different sorts have made it. It may be tempting to identify a particular idea or practice as 'not real Islam' or 'debased Islam', but when trying to understand it the academic observer has to take into account all of the ways in which Muslims have understood and practised it. Such things are usually, for historians, known from written and other evidence.

When Islam came out of Arabia, even according to Muslim tradition, there were no Muslim texts (even the Qur'ān was fixed in writing after the wars of conquest had begun), no mosques as we understand them today, and a relatively small group of people who may have regarded themselves as Muslims. There was virtually none of – or at least any way in which we might know about – the rich, diverse and contested complex of law, theology, ritual practices, ideas of authority, art and architecture, and other things that Islam means for us today. Even if we are willing to accept what tradition tells us, therefore, it is difficult for a historian to grasp what 'Islam' may have meant at that time. And on many important details (see below) academic scholarship has proposed different understandings of what tradition tells us.

Continuity and Change

Traditional accounts give the impression that the coming of Islam led to an almost complete break with the past in those places where it established itself. This impression results from several causes.

The central role of revelation in those accounts means that ultimately the coming of Islam did not depend on historical circumstances. In spite of the fact that the revelation occurred in a specific historical situation, the time and the place were of God's choosing and not determined by human activity. Furthermore, the primary purpose of the revelation was to rescue the Arabs from the condition of ignorance and barbarism (*jāhiliyya*) in which they were immersed.

According to Muslim tradition, the Jāhiliyya was the time in Arabia before the coming of Islam, and Islam is the complete antithesis of it. How historically accurate is the traditional image of the Jāhiliyya is certainly open to debate. It may be envisaged as an originally a-historical, disembodied concept of a society where the true religion of Islam was unknown. That abstract concept might then have been given a specific historical location by the early Muslim scholars who wished to stress the origins of Islam in a pagan Arab environment. In any case, the Jāhiliyya is so important to Islam's understanding of itself and its origins that it seems unlikely that the traditional accounts of it are a mere assortment of historical memories. The point of immediate relevance here is that in the short time between the beginning of the revelations to Muḥammad and the triumph of Islam throughout Arabia following his death, according to tradition, the Jāhiliyya was ended.

Similarly, outside Arabia the coming of Islam seems, in the traditional accounts, to bring down a rather opaque curtain on the past. Although it did not happen immediately, the majority of the subject peoples became Muslims and many of them became Arabic speakers. In the traditional perspective that is understood as the adoption by them of the religion and language of their conquerors. Even where some elements of pre-Islamic identity survived – as with the Persians, who became Muslims but continued to use their pre-Islamic language and drew on their pre-Islamic culture in various ways – the coming of Islam is seen as a decisive turning point, if not such a complete break with what went before.

This impression of discontinuity is not really created by explicit statements to that effect in the Muslim accounts of the rise and spread of Islam. Rather, it is that those accounts, which represent virtually the only detailed and continuous narratives of events in the lands conquered by the Arabs, focus entirely on the concerns of the Arab Muslims and say hardly anything about the non-Arab and non-Muslim peoples who were conquered. It is as if, with the coming of Islam and the Arabs, they virtually disappeared. From other evidence – including that of the literature that the conquered peoples continued to produce in the Islamic period – we know that that was not the case.

Academic historians are generally more aware of the importance of continuities. That major elements of classical Islamic culture – notably its philosophical and scientific learning – were continuations in Arabic of pre-Islamic Hellenistic, Persian, Indian and other traditions is obvious. It has also been demonstrated, especially on the evidence of papyrus documents that have survived from early Islamic Egypt, that the Arabs, when they established their control over the conquered lands, did not immediately change everything but continued to use many of the administrative institutions and personnel that they took over.

It was not until towards the end of the first Islamic century, in the 690s AD, that significant changes become visible. Muslim tradition and other evidence tell us that it was then that a distinctive Islamic coinage was introduced and languages like Greek and Persian began to give way to Arabic in the records of the administration. It has been persuasively argued that even things like the system of clientage, which facilitated the assimilation of the conquered people and the conquerors in the first century or so after the conquest, were adaptations by the Arabs of institutions found in the societies they conquered.[17]

Equally important in underlining the continuities between the pre-Islamic and Islamic Middle East and Mediterranean is the work of scholars outside the field of Islamic Studies. Those involved in the study of the period between the age of classical antiquity and that of classical Islam have defined it as the period of late antiquity. Naturally it is impossible to assign precise dates to it, but whereas it was once regarded as merely a period of, to use Edward Gibbon's phrase, 'decline and fall', modern scholarship has emphasized its innovative and dynamic characteristics. Two important themes are the triumph of monotheistic forms of religion and thought (notably, but not merely, Christianity) and the continuing importance and evolution of Hellenistic culture. Scholars, of course, do not always agree on the importance or the nature of the changes taking place but there is considerable agreement that in many ways Islam was heir to the world of late antiquity and the outcome of the religious, cultural, social and other changes of the period.[18]

Becker too supported the scholarly emphasis on continuities between the pre-Islamic and Islamic Middle East and Mediterranean worlds. In his view the conquered non-Arabs did not just accept a religious and linguistic identity that was brought ready formed to them. They played a part, probably the more important part, in creating their new identity. In doing so, naturally, they drew on much – ideas, vocabulary, practices, institutions, and many other things – which had nothing to do with Arabia.

Referring to the significant cultural unification of the Mediterranean world and the Middle East brought about by the conquests of Alexander the Great, Becker had remarked, 'Strange as it may seem, without Alexander the Great there would have been no Islamic civilisation.' In that perspective the Islamic caliphate broke down the ancient but essentially artificial political division of an area that already shared much culturally before the Arab conquests.[19]

Academic Reinterpretation of Some Fundamental Elements of Tradition

As well as suggesting broad perspectives from which the rise of Islam may be viewed in a different light to that of the traditional accounts, academic research has raised questions about some of the fundamental details of those accounts.

As we have seen, the Sunna of the Prophet, his divinely guided way of life and his decisions on questions put to him by his followers, known from thousands of *hadith*s, is one of the two main sources of Islamic law according to the traditional view. Each authentic *hadith*, according to the theory, has been transmitted from the time of the Prophet over several generations by a chain (the *isnād*) of scholars, each link in the chain being known by name. The traditional scholars recognized that not all of the *hadith*s could be genuine – for one thing, many of them contradict others – but they developed a science based on analysis of *isnād*s that, in their view, enabled them to distinguish between the genuine and the fabricated ones.

In the late nineteenth century, Goldziher's study of the *hadith*s challenged that view. Goldziher, it should be stressed, did not set out to prove a negative. His study of the *hadith*s was not merely concerned with the question of their authenticity but with an understanding of the phenomenon as a whole. One of his conclusions, however, was that many of them had been put into circulation in generations later than that of the Prophet, as individuals and groups within the developing Muslim community sought to capture his authority for their own diverse opinions and arguments. Goldziher left room for some authentic *hadith*s but his work implicitly puts the burden of proof on those who wish to use them as evidence for the time of the Prophet himself.[20]

Subsequently in the 1940s and 1950s, Joseph Schacht built upon Goldziher's work in this area to argue that the very idea that the Prophet's Sunna was, along with the Qur'ān, the main source of authority in Muslim law only began to emerge in the second/eighth century and only became widely accepted as a result of the advocacy of the idea by al-Shāfiʿī (d. 206/821). Schacht understood the vast majority of the *hadith*s as having been formulated and put into circulation in response to the growing strength of that idea. In the earliest period of Islam, he argued, law, when it had not simply been taken over from the societies conquered by the Arabs, was created in an ad hoc manner, largely by the caliphs and their governors. The *isnād*s, in Schacht's view were no guarantee of authenticity since an *isnād* could be made up just as easily as the text of a *hadith*. Neither Schacht nor Goldziher implied a fraudulent or cynical intention on the part of those who developed the theory of the Sunna or formulated the *hadith*s; they would simply have assumed that they were acting in accord with the intentions of the Prophet.[21]

The ideas of Goldziher and Schacht have been very influential. Some academic scholars have, indeed, found fault with some of Schacht's arguments and his interpretation of the evidence. Harald Motzki, for example, has argued that our relatively late texts nevertheless allow us to trace back into the first/seventh century certain *hadith*s and ideas that Schacht thought were late. On the other hand, it has been argued by Norman Calder that some books ascribed to important legal scholars of the late second/eighth and early third/ninth centuries only acquired the form in which we know them today some two or three generations later than their supposed authors. If that is so, it could indicate that Schacht's dating of the acceptance of the idea of the authority of the Prophet as decisive in matters of law was too early. At any rate, most scholars now recognize the difficulty of dating *hadith*s and those who think that it is possible to argue for a genuine continuity in the transmission of the Prophet's life and Sunna, now have to argue their case.[22]

The traditional accounts of how and when the text of the Qur'ān was formed have also been questioned by several academics. Until about the 1970s scholars generally accepted the traditional Muslim accounts, although many of them pointed out the inconsistencies and contradictions in them. In recent years different approaches to the study of the Qur'ān have been developed that propose different understandings of what was involved. John Wansbrough, starting from the Qur'ān's literary form and style and the development of the tradition of its interpretation, insisted that it was necessary not merely to focus on the compilation of the text as we know it but also on when and how that text came to be accepted as authoritative in Islam. He argued that we should understand both the formation of the text and the acceptance of its authority as an integral part of the gradual emergence of Islam itself. According to that view, the Qur'ān is not something there 'from the start', but develops along with all the other ideas, practices and institutions that go to form Islam as we know it from the third/ninth century on.[23]

The evidence of inscriptions and early Qur'ānic manuscripts has also come to be studied more and used by some scholars to support the view that the establishment of the fixed text of the Qur'ān was a slower process than the tradition allows for. In particular a manuscript apparently dating from around the beginning of the second/ eighth century and found by German archaeologists in the great mosque of Sanaa in the Yemen in the 1970s, has been interpreted as supporting the view that the text had still not been fixed in its canonical form at the time the manuscript was written. However, that and other manuscripts found in Sanaa have been difficult for scholars to access, and until they are more widely available (and probably even then) their significance will be hard to assess with certainty.[24]

In the sphere of the development of ideas of religious and political authority, the fundamental question at issue between the different 'sects' of Islam, Patricia Crone and Martin Hinds have argued that the Sunnī form is a relatively late and secondary development in the history of early Islam. In the Sunnī tradition, as we have seen, religious authority belongs to the religious scholars and not to the caliphs. Crone and Hinds argued that this was a radical departure from early Islamic concepts, according to which the caliph, as God's deputy on earth, was the sole authority over all aspects of the life of the Muslims. The Sunnī idea, according to that view, was not firmly established until after the middle of the third/ninth century following what was essentially a conflict about authority between the caliphs and the scholars (the *miḥna*).[25]

If Crone and Hinds are right, it follows that the concept of authority in Islam that is characteristic of the Shī'ite tradition – that it was contained in one person regarded as having a special relationship with God – is earlier than the Sunnī concept. Neverthe-less, the forms of Shī'ism known in classical Islam and surviving into the modern world may also be understood as relatively late developments from an earlier and more fluid situation. Twelver Shī'ism can be understood as the creation, out of earlier types of Shī'ism, of a religiously moderate and politically quietist form of the tradition in response to the growing dominance of Sunnī Islam in the first century of the 'Abbāsid caliphate. In this sense Twelver Shī'ism was an accommodation to the religious and political realities of the second half of the third/ninth century. The ending of the line of Imams, removing the need for struggle to establish his rule, and the transfer of authority from the Imam to the scholars, can, from this point of view, be seen as the crucial development in this direction.

Not all Shī'is, though, were prepared to follow this path, and others, such as the Ismāʿīlis, have also survived into modern times. Their different positions on who the rightful Imam is or was, on whether he is present in the world or in occultation, and on textual and human sources of authority other than the Imam, may also be understood as adaptations to historical circumstances during the formative period of Islam and later.

These are just some of the areas where research has called into question the understanding of Islam as something substantially developed in Arabia and brought out from there by the Arab conquerors. Evidently, not all of the views just summar-ized are accepted or strongly held by all academic scholars in the field. Those views involve interpretations of the available evidence, and different scholars may read the same evidence in different ways. Nevertheless, the arguments and suggested reinter-pretations of tradition, of which the above are only a selection, encourage us to see the two centuries or so following the Arab conquests of the seventh century AD as the decisive period for the rise of Islam. It was during that period that the elaborate complex of contested ideas, institutions and practices that we know today took shape.

In contrast, we find it hard to know what Islam might have been before the developments that followed the Arab conquests.

Evidence and Sources

Many academic scholars today are wary of committing themselves on the nature of Islam before the conquests, and especially on the life of the Prophet. The primary reason for that is an enhanced understanding that our sources for the Arabian period of Islam are more than just accounts of historical facts.

Muslim literary tradition (chronicles, biographies of the Prophet and others, commentaries on the Qur'ān, and many other types of traditional Muslim literature) is our only source for the rise of Islam in Arabia. As we have noted, in the form in which they are available to us, the works of Muslim tradition date from not earlier than about the end of the second Islamic century, about AD 800. Certainly they draw on and extensively cite, abbreviate or summarize, oral and written material from the first two centuries, but scholars are divided on how far it is possible to reconstruct the earlier development of the tradition on the basis of later texts.

For many, the work of Goldziher and Schacht on the *ḥadith*s and the legal traditions called into question too the value of the biographical tradition on the Prophet and the reports about the early history of Islam following his death. By the 1970s considerable scepticism had developed among scholars about the value of the traditional accounts as evidence for the events which they reported. This led to different approaches to those sources that still continue today.

One approach is to give up any attempt to reconstruct the early history of Islam in Arabia in the detailed and connected way in which the Muslim tradition itself does. Instead, the tradition is used to throw light on the way later Muslims, those responsible for collecting and composing the accounts which have come down to us, viewed the early history of their religion and culture. The relationship between their views and 'what really happened', it is argued, is not really knowable. Instead, the biographies of the Prophet and the accounts of the early history of Islam are analysed for what they can tell us about the aims and intentions, the needs and wishes, of those who compiled them. For example, it has been argued that much of the material in the traditional lives of the Prophet reflects the need of the developing Muslim community, in the face of polemic from its monotheist opponents, to develop an image of Muḥammad in accordance with then prevailing ideas about prophethood. The aim would be to justify the view of Muḥammad as a prophet sent to the Arabs.[26]

Another avenue is to seek to exploit as much as possible the evidence of sources other than the Muslim literary tradition – archaeological and similar materials, and the literary traditions of the peoples who had come under Arab rule. In their book *Hagarism* Michael Cook and Patricia Crone attempted to show what the rise of Islam might look like if based almost entirely on such materials. More usually scholars have tried to relate the archaeological and non-Muslim literary evidence to that of the Muslim literature and to use all the different sources in a critical manner. One effect of this approach has been to remind us just how much evidence there is outside the Muslim literary sources even though that evidence only allows us a fragmented and partial view of what was taking place. The evidence of sources other than the Muslim tradition has its own problems and it too does not really help us for the Arabian period of Islam. It does suggest, however, that from the start the various peoples who came under Arab rule regarded their conquerors as following a form of monotheism of their own.[27]

Thirdly, some scholars have sought to get back beyond the Muslim texts that are available to us and to recover from them earlier texts and documents. In this way, it is hoped, the tradition can be pushed back into the earlier centuries.[28]

Anyone working on the rise of Islam in a serious way has to accept that the main body of evidence has real problems as a source for what occurred in Arabia in the time of the Prophet and the first four caliphs. In a nutshell, the evidence as we have it comes from a later stage in the development of Islam and it reflects an internal perspective on events of fundamental importance for later Muslims. The danger is that the accounts of the earlier stages of the rise of Islam may represent a reading back of the ideas and understandings of Muslims living at the time when the new religion and culture was stabilizing.

There are various ways in which our lack of texts dating from before the end of the second century AH/eighth century AD may be explained: the transition from a predominantly oral culture to a written one, the loss of texts as a result of fire, political turmoil and other causes, the relative lack of cheap and easily available writing materials, etc. The fact that from about AD 800 onwards we see the production of a vast mass of traditional literature that has survived and been transmitted until today can suggest a different perspective, however. It may be taken to indicate that the formative period of Islam was coming to its end, that the religion and culture that had been developing in the Middle East following the Arab conquests a hundred and fifty years before was now showing signs of fruition. It too may be used to support the understanding of the rise of Islam as a gradual growth that reached maturity in the third/ninth century.

The Relationship of Islam to Pre-Islamic Middle Eastern Monotheism

The question remains of how we may envisage the start of the process that eventually led to the formation of Islam in a fully developed sense. Academic scholarship has generally agreed that in its origins Islam owes much to other forms of Middle Eastern monotheism, and that has often been expressed as Muḥammad being influenced by, or borrowing from, other versions of monotheism.

Most scholars have worked with the framework provided by Islam's own historical tradition. That presents the Prophet, before his move to Yathrib (Medina) in AD 622, as living in the overwhelmingly pagan setting of the Jāhiliyya. The people of Mecca, like the Arab tribes in the vicinity, worshipped many gods. The only thing that moderated that was a lingering memory of Abraham's building of the Ka'ba and his introduction of true monotheism to the Arabs. Under the influence of Abraham's religion, a small group of people tried to remain loyal to a form of monotheism distinct both from Judaism and Christianity and from the polytheism and idolatry of their contemporaries. These people are known in the tradition as Ḥanīfs.

The majority of the Arabs, on the other hand, are portrayed as having corrupted the religion of Abraham and turning it into a gross and primitive paganism, but even there a few remnants of Abrahamic religion survived. Most notably the Ka'ba, although it had become a centre of idolatry, was still regarded as more important than the many other shrines and holy places that were scattered throughout Arabia, and the god with which it was especially associated, Allāh, was honoured above the many other gods.

Most western scholars, unable to accept the historical reality of Mecca's association with Abraham, have nevertheless seen much of what tradition tells us about the society in which Muḥammad lived as based on facts. They have accepted the historical reality of the Ḥanīfs, for example, and interpreted them as evidence that the traditional paganism of the Arabs was already beginning to weaken in the period before Muḥammad. Similarly the predominance of Allāh and the Ka'ba over the other gods and sanctuaries has been seen as evidence that the old paganism was in decline and inklings of monotheism appearing.

In that light Muḥammad and his preaching have been portrayed as just the most prominent (and most successful) element in the emergence out of Arab polytheism of a monotheist form of religion. It was the fact that the society as a whole was already moving in that direction that facilitated his success. Some scholars thought that the rise of monotheism in Arabia could be explained in part by natural evolutionary trends – what they understood as the normal human progress from lower to higher forms of religion. More generally, though, it has been believed that the weakening of the traditional religion must have come about because of the impact of monotheist ideas on the pagan environment of the Jāhiliyya.[29]

The theory is that Muḥammad and many of his fellow Arabs, living in a still mainly pagan and polytheistic environment, came into contact with ideas, stories, practices and institutions coming from Judaism, Christianity or other related forms of monotheism. Islam was the outcome – a form of monotheism adapted to the needs and wishes of the Arabs. Much academic scholarship, therefore, has been devoted to the question of the sources and nature of those monotheistic ideas, and how they came to penetrate the remote area of inner Arabia where Muḥammad lived.

As for how those ideas reached Muḥammad and the people among whom he lived, various possibilities have been suggested. Many scholars, building upon the reports in the traditional lives of the Prophet that portray the Meccans as heavily involved in trade, have theorized that Mecca was on an international trade route and that religious and other ideas were carried along with trade goods. That theory has been weakened considerably by some of the arguments expounded by Patricia Crone in her *Meccan Trade and the Rise of Islam.*[30]

More academic energy has been expended on the issue of the nature and sources of the ideas. Since the German Jewish scholar Abraham Geiger published in 1832 his book on what he saw as Muḥammad's borrowings from Judaism there have been many studies arguing that Muslim ideas, practices and institutions are adaptations and reworkings of Jewish or Christian originals. The scholars concerned have often disagreed on whether Judaism or Christianity was the more important as a source for Islam, and during the twentieth century, as materials like the Dead Sea Scrolls from previously little known Jewish and Christian sects have become available, the hunt for the sources of Islam has widened.[31]

Muslim tradition itself contains material that might suggest that Islam was at one time much closer to Judaism than it subsequently became. It tells us that following his move from Mecca to Yathrib (Medina) in 622 Muḥammad and his followers fasted on the same day as the Jews (Yom Kippur, or 'Āshūrā' as it is called in the tradition) and prayed in the same direction, that is, towards Jerusalem. Only later in the Medinan period of his life, we are told, did these key practices change: Ramaḍān replaced 'Āshūrā' as the fasting period for Islam, and the direction of prayer (*qibla*) was turned from Jerusalem towards Mecca.

Such developments have been read by many scholars, beginning with C. Snouck Hurgronje and A. J. Wensinck, as symbolic of a break with Judaism. According to that reading, the Prophet did not understand his religion as a new one until he found himself rejected and scorned by the Jews. He then began to make Islam more distinctive by developing it as a specifically Arab form of monotheism. The most important feature of the transformation would be the elaboration of the idea that the pagan Ka'ba at Mecca had originally been founded by Abraham for the worship of the true God.

That has been the most influential of academic theories about the origins of Islam. It stresses the importance of the relationship between the Jews of Medina and the Prophet and of its deterioration. Some scholars have questioned the Qur'ānic evidence that Snouck Hurgronje used to support the theory, and recently there seems to have been some reversion to the older view, against which the Dutch scholar was protesting, that the Arabs already had a significant knowledge of the stories about Abraham before the time of Muḥammad.[32]

Whether it was Christianity, Judaism or some other form of Middle Eastern monotheism that is understood as decisive for the appearance of Islam, the process involved has usually been expressed in terms of 'influences' or 'borrowings'. However it happened, the Prophet and his Arab contemporaries are seen as coming under the influence of monotheist ideas and consciously adopting and adapting some of what came to them in order to elaborate a new and distinctive vision. In that view, a predominantly polytheist pagan society produced and adopted its own form of monotheism, largely as the result of the opening up of that society to monotheist influences.

There is, however, an alternative approach. The history of monotheism, like that of other religious traditions, has been marked by the emergence out of it of new sects resulting from disputes and debates among monotheists themselves. Some of those sects have then developed into distinctive and independent religions within the wider tradition. External influences and events in the political sphere, of course, are very relevant to how far an emerging sect will develop and spread.

Instead of seeing the religion that was to become Islam as the product of a pagan Arab society stimulated by ideas and materials from monotheist sources, then, it may be that we should be thinking of the growth of a sect within another form of monotheism. In other words, the origins of Islam could be understood as occurring in a way similar to that in which we understand the emergence of Christianity and Rabbinical Judaism out of ancient Judaism, or the modern forms of Catholicism and Protestantism out of mediaeval European Christianity. In that perspective Islam may be understood in its origins as a critique of existing monotheist ideas and practices as much as an attack on Arab paganism.[33]

One obvious difficulty, however, is that this approach seems to require an environment in which there was already a significant monotheist population diverse enough to generate internal arguments and debates. It is not impossible to imagine that such an environment existed in the Hijaz at the beginning of the seventh century AD, but that requires going considerably beyond the traditional evidence. Apart from the Jewish community of Yathrib, the tradition tells us nothing about the existence of communities of orthodox or sectarian Jews or Christians in the environment in which Muḥammad is reported to have operated. Those scholars who have suggested that there was in the Hijaz, for example, a community descended from that which produced the Dead Sea Scrolls, or a group of Samaritans, have done so entirely on the basis of what they see has significant parallels between features of Islam and those of the sect in question. The problem with ascribing to the Jews of Yathrib the status of the matrix of Islam is that tradition tells us that Islam began in Mecca.

One could, of course, take a more radical attitude to Muslim tradition about the very beginnings of Islam. It would be possible to read it, for example, as condensing into a limited chronological frame, and transposing onto an Arabian background, developments that took longer and occurred in a different geographical setting. The idea suggested by the tradition itself, that Islam arose from a conflict within some form of Judaism is not unlikely, and its presentation of itself as a form of monotheism especially associated with the Arabs and Arabia is so marked that it can be understood as a conscious and deliberate proclamation of a distinct identity, intended to mark it off from other forms of monotheism.

Conclusion

The academic study of the rise of Islam is an area of intense and often stimulating debate, marked by a diversity of approaches and theories and rather few uncontested facts or conclusions. To view it as a process extending over two centuries or so does greater justice to the richness and complexity of Islam than does the more traditional concentration on the life of the Prophet and the short time when it was confined to Arabia. Indeed, the evidence for the Arabian period, limited as it is to a tradition that is only available to us in texts dating from much later, makes analysis of the earliest period especially difficult. It is not possible to provide precise dates for the beginning and end of the process, but the third century of the Hijra (ninth century AD) was clearly of crucial importance.

NOTES

1 Cf. the ways in which Jews and Christians have presented their own traditions as descended – physically, spiritually, or both – from Abraham.

2 Hereafter, when relevant, dates will be given in the form 17/638, first/seventh century, etc. In the Islamic calendar a year consists of 12 lunar, rather than solar, months, and because no intercalation is permitted the months have no fixed relationship to the seasons. For a brief introduction to the Islamic calendar and tables of equivalence with the Christian calendar, see Freeman-Grenville, *The Muslim and Christian Calendars.*

3 For an account of the life of Muḥammad based on the traditional narratives see the article 'Muḥammad' in *Encyclopaedia of Islam*, 2nd edition (*EI2*). The earliest extant account of his life is the *Sīra* of Ibn Isḥāq (d. 151/768 in Baghdad) in the recension made by Ibn Hishām (d. 218/833 in Egypt).

4 The English 'caliph' derives from Arabic *khalīfa*. Traditionally, *khalīfa* is understood to mean 'successor' (of the Prophet) – *khalīfat rasūl Allāh*. The original sense of the title, however, is debatable; see the article "Khalīfa" in *EI2*.

5 For a discussion and summary of the traditions about the collecting and composition of the text of the Qur'ān, see Bell and Watt, *Introduction to the Qur'ān*, article 'Kur'ān' in *EI2*.

6   See, for example, Becker, 'Expansion of the Saracens'; Donner, *Early Islamic Conquests*.
7   On the Fitna, see the articles 'Adhruḥ', 'Alī b. Abī Ṭālib', 'Muʿāwiya b. Abī Sufyān' and
    'Ṣiffīn', in *EI2*; Hinds, 'Kūfan Political Alignments'; idem, 'Murder of ʿUthmān'; idem,
    'Ṣiffīn Arbitration Agreement'; idem, 'Banners and Battle Cries'; all are collected in
    Hinds, *Studies in Early Islamic History*.
8   See article 'Khāridjites' in *EI2*; P. Crone and F. Zimmermann, *Epistle*.
9   See the article 'Umayyads' in *EI2*; Wellhausen, *Arab Kingdom*.
10 On the ʿAbbāsid caliphate, see the article "Abbāsids' in *EI2*.
11 The Sunnīs are so called because of the importance of the Sunna of the Prophet in their
    legal theory. As a self-designation they often called themselves 'people of the Sunna and
    community' (*ahl-al-sunna waʾl-jamāʾa*). For the development of Sunnī legal theory, see
    Schacht, *Introduction*, especially ch.9. For further discussion, see Crone and Hinds, *God's
    Caliph*, Melchert, *Sunni Schools*, Zaman, *Religion and Politics*.
12 Arabic *Shīʿa* means 'party' and is in this sense short for 'the Party of ʿAlī' (*shīʿatu ʿAlī*).
13 See Kohlberg, 'From Imāmiyya to Ithnā-ʿAshariyya'; Bayhom-Daou, 'The Imam's Know-
    ledge'.
14 It has been noted that the earliest securely datable text to refer to the religion of the Arabs
    as Islam is the inscription inside the Dome of the Rock (72/691; Cook and Crone,
    Hagarism, 8 and n.49); the earliest securely datable text to use the word Muslims is a
    letter of 141/758 (Hinds, 'Letter from the Governor of Egypt', line 36 of the translation
    and the note thereto).
15 It should be noted that the understanding of the term 'Arabia' has varied considerably
    from time to time. For us today it tends to indicate the Arabian peninsula, the modern
    state of Saudi Arabia and its neighbours. In the period before the rise of Islam it often
    referred to a region or province attached to Palestine.
16 Becker, 'Islam als Problem'; idem, 'Expansion of the Saracens'.
17 Crone, *Roman, Provincial and Islamic Law*.
18 See, e.g., Bowersock, *Hellenism in Late Antiquity*, especially ch. 6; Cameron, 'Eastern
    Provinces'.
19 Becker, 'Islam als Problem', 15.
20 Goldziher, *Muhammedanische Studien* (English tr. *Muslim Studies*), vol. 2.
21 Schacht, *Origins*; idem, *Introduction*.
22 Motzki, *Origins of Islamic Jurisprudence*; idem (ed.), *Hadith: Origins and Developments*;
    Calder, *Studies*; Juynboll, *Muslim Tradition*.
23 Wansbrough, *Quranic Studies*; Rippin (ed.), *Formative Interpretation*.
24 Puin, 'Observations'.
25 Crone and Hinds, *God's Caliph*; article 'miḥna' in *EI2*.
26 Rubin, *The Eye of the Beholder*; idem (ed.); idem, 'Islamic Self-Image'; Wansbrough,
    Quranic Studies, ch. 2; idem, 'Res Ipsa Loquitur'.
27 Cook and Crone, *Hagarism*; Hoyland, *Seeing Islam*.
28 See, e.g., Schoeler, 'Foundations'; for some of the problems see Conrad, 'Recovering Lost
    Texts'.
29 The classic statement of the evolutionary approach is Wellhausen, *Reste*; in English see
    Nöldeke, 'Arabs (Ancient)'.
30 The best-known presentation of the 'trade route theory' in English is that of Watt,
    Muhammad at Mecca. Cf. now Crone, *Meccan Trade*.
31 Geiger, *Was hat Mohammed?*; The bibliography of works arguing that Muhammad
    borrowed from a particular version of the monotheist religion is too big to begin to list
    here.
32 Snouck Hurgronje, *Het Mekkaansce Feest*; Wensinck, *Muhammad and the Jews of Medina*;
    for some of the criticism of Snouck's use of the Qurʾān, see article 'Ibrāhim' in *EI2*.
33 Hawting, *Idolatry*.

FURTHER READING

Berkey, Jonathan: *The Formation of Islam: Religion and Society in the Near East, 600–1800*, Cambridge: Cambridge University Press, 2003

Bowersock, Glynn W. (ed.): *Late Antiquity: A Guide to the Postclassical World*, Cambridge, MA: Harvard University Press, 1999

Brown, Daniel: *A New Introduction to Islam*, Malden, MA, Blackwell, 2003

Brown, Peter: *The World of Late Antiquity: From Marcus Aurelius to Muhammad*, London: Thames and Hudson, 1971

Cameron, Averil: *The Mediterranean World in Late Antiquity: AD 395–600*, London: Routledge, 1993

Cook, Michael: *Muhammad*. Oxford: Oxford University Press, 1983

Cook, Michael: *The Koran: A Very Short Introduction*. Oxford: Oxford University Press, 2000

Coulson, Noel J.: *A History of Islamic Law*, Edinburgh: Edinburgh University Press, 1964

Donner, Fred McGraw: *The Early Islamic Conquests*, Princeton, NJ: Princeton University Press, 1981

Guillaume, Alfred (translator): *The Life of Muhammad: A Translation of Ibn Ishaq's Sirat Rasūl Allāh*, Oxford: Oxford University Press, 1955

Halm, Heinz: *Shiism*. Edinburgh: Edinburgh University Press, 1991

Hawting, Gerald: *The First Dynasty of Islam. The Umayyad Caliphate AD 661–750*. 2nd edition, London: Routledge, 2000

Hoyland, Robert: *Arabia and the Arabs: From the Bronze Age to the Coming of Islam*, London: Routledge, 2001

Kennedy, Hugh: *The Prophet and the Age of the Caliphates: The Islamic Near East from the Sixth to the Eleventh Century*. London: Longman, 1986

Madelung, Wilferd: *Religious Trends in Early Islamic Iran*, Albany, NY: State University of New York Press, 1988

Momen, Moojan: *An Introduction to Shi'i Islam*. Newhaven: Yale University Press, 1985

Morony, Michael G.: *Iraq After the Muslim Conquests*, Princeton, NJ: Princeton University Press, 1984

Rippin, Andrew: *Muslims, Their Religious Beliefs and Practices*, vol. 1: *The Formative Period*, London: Routledge, 1993

Robinson, Chase F.: *Islamic Historiography*, Cambridge: Cambridge University Press, 2003

Watt, W. M.: *Muhammad: Prophet and Statesman*, Oxford: Oxford University Press, 1961

CHAPTER TWO

The Islamic Conquests

FRED M. DONNER

Introduction

The term "Islamic Conquests" – sometimes also called, particularly in earlier scholarship, the "Arab Conquests" – is a loose designation for a far-flung and complex set of historical phenomena associated with the rise and spread of Islam in the Near East during the seventh and eighth centuries CE. At the center of these developments was the first appearance in western Arabia of the religion of Islam – or, more precisely, of its precursor in the Believers' movement launched by the prophet Muḥammad (d. 632) and his followers.[1] Closely associated with the Believers' movement occurred the crystallization and rapid expansion of a state whose leaders (the *caliphs*, or temporal successors to Muḥammad at the head of the Believers' community) identified with the new movement and took it as one of the main justifications for their expansion. It is this process of caliphal state expansion, which included military campaigns launched by the caliphs, that is usually called the "Islamic conquests."

The term "Islamic conquests" is itself derived from the Arabic–Islamic historical sources, the most important of which for this theme were literary compilations assembled during the second to fourth centuries AH (eighth to tenth centuries CE). These sources, produced by the Islamic community itself to describe in retrospect this crucial early chapter in the community's history, refer to it using the term *futūḥ* or *futūḥāt* (literally, "openings").[2] This term does not seem to have been used in pre-Islamic times; traditionally, raiding in pre-Islamic Arabia (usually undertaken for purely mundane purposes) was called *ghazwa*. In the new Muslim community, military raids to spread the faith or to defend the community were also called *ghazwa*, "raiding," not *futūḥ*, which was reserved for the broader process by which new territories were incorporated into the realm ruled by the caliphs. As a term, then, *futūḥ* definitely has a retrospective quality. The military dimension of the expansion process, however, has led to a tendency to translate *futūḥ* as "conquest" plain and simple, even though it might more idiomatically be rendered as "incorporation" or "integration" (that is, of new areas into the Islamic state). The term "Islamic *conquest*" may itself thus be considered slightly misleading, because it may emphasize too greatly the military aspect of the process. However, the term "Islamic conquest" is by now probably too deeply ingrained in Western scholarship to be discarded. When using it, however, we must be aware that it refers to far more than merely military victories and questions of tactics and military organization. While military action was an important part of the picture, we must recognize that the "conquest" raises as well such diverse questions as the role of religious proselytization, the crystallization and evolution of state institutions, the role of economic and other motivations in the expansion, the formation of a communal identity, linguistic change, and the ideological, political, social, and economic transformations effected by the conquests. The issue is further complicated by the uncertainty surrounding the changing meaning of *jihād* in the time of Muḥammad and his first followers, and its role in the expansion process: was it a religious call to "holy war," or a more general injunction to struggle for goodness in society and life that only occasionally required the use of force?[3] In the following sections, an attempt will be made to sketch out the main features of this complex of historical developments, including both the expansion of the state by military action and the broader social, political, and religious questions associated with this expansion.

The Islamic conquests can be roughly divided into two main phases, which we may designate the "charismatic" and the "institutional" phases. The first or charismatic phase lasted from the first decades until the middle decades of the seventh century CE. It began with the emigration of the prophet Muḥammad from Mecca to Medina in Arabia in 622 CE, and corresponded to the first burst of expansive energy that carried Muḥammad's community of Believers throughout Arabia and into the surrounding lands of Syria, Iraq, Egypt, and Iran. This initial phase was coterminous with a process of state formation – that is, with the crystallization of the new caliphal (or Believers') state, centered in an area (western Arabia) where there had been no state before – and raises many challenges of interpretation. These include: What was the exact nature of the initial impulse to expand? What was the relationship of this original expansionist impulse to the nascent state? What was the relative importance of ideological and material factors in the process of state formation? How did the new state institutionalize itself? etc. By the second or institutional phase, which can be dated from the middle of the seventh until the middle of the eighth century CE – roughly coterminous with the rule of the Umayyad dynasty (661–750), the caliphal state had assumed fairly well-defined institutional form, and the process of expansion and conquest was clearly the result of intentional state policy (that is, the conscious policy of the rulers, the Umayyad caliphs) realized by the institutional apparatus of the state.

Survey of the First or Charismatic Phase of the Conquests

Before proceeding further, it will be helpful to sketch the main events of the first phase of the conquest and expansion movement. The striking thing about this phase is its astonishing rapidity; for in a little over thirty years, the Believers appear to have established their hegemony over a vast region stretching from west of the Nile to eastern Iran.

The expansion of Muḥammad's community of Believers began already in his lifetime, following his emigration in 622 CE from his home-town, Mecca, to the small oasis town of Medina (Yathrib) in western Arabia. During his decade in Medina, Muḥammad gradually overcame internal opposition and began to launch raids (*ghazwa*) to extend the borders of the community to other towns and groups in western Arabia; by the last years of his life, he had forged alliances with many towns and pastoral groups in western Arabia, and also with some more distant groups in Yemen, Oman, eastern Arabia, and on the north Arabian fringes of Syria.

When Muḥammad died in 632, the Believers chose Muḥammad's confidant and father-in-law, Abū Bakr, to be his successor as temporal ruler of the community he had founded. (Later tradition called him *khalīfa*, caliph – "successor"). Muḥammad's death, however, caused some former allies to repudiate their ties with Medina, or at least to refuse to pay a tax that Muḥammad had ordained just before his death; in western Arabia, a few groups were even hoping to exploit the Believers' momentary disarray to plunder Medina. Abū Bakr therefore organized a series of campaigns whose goal was to defend Medina and to ensure payment of tax from all groups and to suppress any opposition. This opposition is indiscriminately called *ridda*, "apostasy," by the later Muslim sources, even though some groups in no way rejected the beliefs they had adopted in Muḥammad's day, but merely demurred on payment of tax; and, for convenience, the campaigns in which Abū Bakr subdued Arabia are usually simply called the "Ridda wars," even though they involved not only the disciplining of wayward former allies, but the outright subjugation of some Arabian groups that had had no prior contact with Muḥammad or the Believers' movement at all.[4]

Abū Bakr first stabilized the situation around Medina itself by sending troops to defeat the mutinous local groups; he also dispatched a small force, commanded by Usāma ibn Zayd, that Muḥammad had organized just before his final illness to raid southern Syria – a force that, after a quick foray to the north, returned to bolster the defenses of Medina. Abū Bakr then dispatched columns of troops under trusted commanders to bring all of Arabia under Medina's control, directing them against the most powerful opposition groups. He appointed the tactical genius Khālid ibn al-Walīd, commanding a force made up mainly of Meccans and Medinese, to subdue opposition in the Najd among the Asad, Tamīm, and other tribes, who had rallied around figures identified in the Islamic sources as "false prophets" – Ṭalḥa ibn Khuwaylid and the "prophetess" Sajāḥ, whom he chastised in the battles of al-Buzākha and al-Butāḥ. After gathering further tribal allies, Khālid marched on to deal with the most serious rebellion of all, that led by the "false prophet" Musaylima of the Ḥanīfa tribe in the rich oasis of al-Yamāma (the region around modern Riyadh). Musaylima's army was defeated in the bloody battle of "Aqrabā," and the Ḥanīfa tribe was placed under the supervision of a garrison. Meanwhile, Abū Bakr also dispatched a number of armies to confront other groups elsewhere in Arabia that either resisted or held aloof from the new state in Medina. One traversed the east Arabian coastal districts; another subdued 'Uman and the Mahra tribe (the latter in modern Dhofar province of southeastern Arabia); and others brought to heel the troublesome "false prophet" al-Aswad al-'Ansī in Yemen. Altogether, Abū Bakr dispatched eleven separate forces, which during the two years of his caliphate (632–4) brought the entire Arabian peninsula into obedience to Medina. These campaigns were of critical importance for the future of the Believers' movement, because they provided the caliphs with the manpower they needed to expand outside Arabia – particularly the hardy mountain villagers of Yemen and pastoral nomads of northern Arabia.

The prophet had shown a special interest in Syria, and had dispatched raiding parties in its direction several times during his life.[5] Abū Bakr also seems to have been interested in expanding the Believers' control into Syria, and organized four armies to invade it during the autumn of 633 CE, commanded by Yazīd ibn Abī Sufyān, 'Amr ibn al-'As, Shuraḥbīl ibn Ḥasana, and Abū 'Ubayda ibn al-Jarrāḥ. At first these forces concentrated on bringing under control the desert fringes of Syria, which were occupied with Arabic-speaking tribesmen, and avoided attacking Byzantine garrisons or major towns (with the exception of an early raid against Gaza). In time, however, the Believers began to attack the towns of southern Syria, including Bostra, Faḥl (Pella), Baysān (Scythopolis), Damascus, Ḥimṣ (Emesa), and Baʿlabakk (Heliopolis), in the reigns of Abū Bakr's successors ʿUmar (634–44) and ʿUthmān (644–56). The Byzantine emperor Heraclius organized a large army to re-take these areas, but in the pitched battles at Ajnādayn and Yarmūk (around 636 CE) the Byzantine forces were shattered, and Heraclius withdrew from Syria, leaving the region open as far as the Taurus foothills. By about 650 CE most towns, even coastal cities like Caesarea and Tripoli, had been reduced by siege or (more frequently) had signed a treaty with the Believers and capitulated. From Syria, campaigns were dispatched against northern Mesopotamia. ʿIyāḍ ibn Ghanm al-Fihrī led troops who overcame the cities of Edessa, Ḥarrān, Raqqa, Nisibis, Malatya, Raʾs al-ʿAyn, and others, and pushed into the mountains of Armenia by 646 CE.

At about the same time the Believers were engaged in the conquest of Syria, other forces made their way toward Iraq.[6] For reasons not stated in our sources, it appears that Iraq was considered by the early caliphs and their entourage to be a less important or desirable objective than Syria, at least at first. Following upon the *ridda* campaigns in northeastern Arabia, Khālid ibn al-Walīd proceeded toward the middle Euphrates to secure the submission of Arabic-speaking pastoral groups and towns in the region, such as al-Ḥīra. These were on the fringes of, or part of, the Sasanian empire. It is not clear whether this campaign was an effort to recapture the initiative that had been seized by local chiefs, such as al-Muthannā ibn Ḥāritha of the Shaybān tribe, who had begun to launch raids into Sasanian territory, or whether Khālid was the first to launch a foray in this area and co-opted leaders such as al-Muthannā once he got there. Having seized a few towns along the lower Euphrates and established the Believers' control among the pastoral tribes there, Khālid left the area in al-Muthannā's charge and, in response to orders from the caliph in Medina, made his way with a small force across the Syrian steppe to support the Believers' forces in Syria. The caliph ʿUmar dispatched a new army under Abū ʿUbayd al-Thaqafī to reinforce al-Muthannā in Iraq, but this force was destroyed by the Sasanians at the battle of the Bridge. ʿUmar therefore organized a new and much larger army, which marched to Iraq under the command of Saʿd ibn Abī Waqqaṣ, and which was periodically reinforced by additional recruits sent by ʿUmar as they became available. This force was able to defeat the Sasanians' main army decisively at al-Qādisiyya (ca. 636), after which most of central Iraq – breadbasket and unrivalled source of taxes for the former Sasanian empire – was occupied by the Arabian Believers, including the former Sasanian capital at Ctesiphon (Arabic al-Madāʾin). The last Sasanian monarch, Yazdagird III, withdrew to the Zagros region and attempted to mount a counter-strike, but was again defeated at Jalūlāʾ and Nihāvand (ca. 642); thereafter he fled to the Iranian plateau where he eventually met an ignominious end, and the Sasanian empire disappeared forever.

Southernmost Iraq formed a separate front; to it ʿUmar sent a small force led at first by ʿUtba ibn Ghazwān (later by Abū Mūsā al-Ashʿarī) who, joined by local tribesmen, siezed the town of Ubulla (Apologos) and routed Sasanian garrisons. With the collapse of Sasanian power farther north, follow-up campaigns were also possible in the south, and the district of Khūzistān was seized with its towns of Shustar, Ahwāz, and Sūsa. Troops from southern Iraq joined those from central Iraq in defeating Yazdagird at Nihāvand and began campaigning in the Iranian highlands.

With Sasanian power decisively destroyed, the Arabian conquerors in Iraq and their allies were able quickly to occupy much of the Iranian plateau (though some districts, such as the Elburz region, remained unsubdued for many decades to come, and most areas faced widespread tax rebellions or resistance by local potentates when the Believers were preoccupied with civil wars).[7] From central Iraq, troops took the whole Zagros region as far north as Azerbaijan, including Ḥulwān, Hamadhān, and Tabrīz. Some pushed into the corridor south of the Elburz, via Qazvīn and Qomm as far as Rayy (modern Tehran). Others occupied northern Mesopotamia or, pushing northward from Azerbaijan via Ardabīl, seized the Mughan steppe and the important town of Darband on the western shores of the Caspian Sea, situated near the main pass through the Caucasus mountains. Yet other forces, starting from Fārs province (Iṣṭakhr, modern Shiraz), passed through the southern Iranian provinces of Kirmān and Sīstān northwards into Khurasān where they occupied (ca. 650) the oasis of Marv, almost to the Oxus River on the fringes of Central Asia. In this area, the Believers made treaties with local feudal lords, leaving the social structure of Khurasān essentially intact.

While the conquest of Iran was taking place in the east, Egypt was being occupied in the west.[8] ʿAmr ibn al-ʿĀṣ, at the head of a contingent of troops in Syria, marched from Palestine (ca. 639) across northern Sinai into the Nile delta and seized Pelusium and Bilbays. Our sources disagree on whether this was done at the behest of the caliph ʿUmar, or on ʿAmr's own initiative, but the caliph soon sent another force directly from Medina to reinforce him. The combined force defeated the local Byzantine garrison and took the latter's fortress of Babylon (part of modern Cairo) after a siege; other contingents seized the Fayyum depression, passed through the western delta, and after defeating the Byzantines again at Nikiu, besieged Alexandria. Eventually, the Byzantine governor agreed to a treaty and handed Alexandria over as the Byzantine soldiers evacuated Egypt. By 642, all of Egypt, including the coastal towns and the Nile valley as far as the first cataract, was held by the Believers.

Traditional Views of the Charismatic Phase of Expansion

At the heart of the astonishing expansion just described was the religious movement begun by Muḥammad. Traditionally, this movement was viewed as the manifestation of a discrete confessional identity – that is, it was seen as a new and distinct religion, Islam, that was from the very beginning different from all other religions, even from other monotheisms such as Judaism and Christianity, with which it shared many common beliefs (one God, prophecy, revealed scripture, Last Judgment, afterlife in heaven or hell, etc.). This view is the one enshrined in the Arabic–Islamic sources themselves, written down mainly in the period from one to three centuries after the life of the prophet Muḥammad and the first expansion of his followers. Moreover, this conceptualization of Muḥammad's movement as a novel religion was until recently replicated by almost all western scholars.

Given their conviction that Islam already existed as a distinct confession, it was inconceivable to most scholars that the populations of the Near East, overwhelmingly adherents of other well-defined religious confessions such as Christianity, Judaism, or Zoroastrianism, should suddenly and voluntarily abandon those faiths for a new and different one, Islam. Both the traditional Muslim sources and the western scholarship that followed it in this interpretative path therefore portrayed the expansion of

Muḥammad's followers as a process of conquest (*futūḥ*) – hence the prominence of the term "Islamic conquest" (or "Arab conquest") as the rubric under which these events have usually been categorized (including in this volume). The victories over the Byzantine and Sasanian armies were seen as the work of soldiers inspired by and fighting in the name of the new religion, Islam; similarly, the absorption of the cities, towns, and rural districts of the Near East into the Believers' new state was also described as the result of military action – the product either of forcible subjection (*'anwa*) of non-Muslim populations by Muslim conquerors, or of siege followed by capitulation to the conquerors (*ṣulḥ*).[9] The presumed result of such capitulations was the creation of a new society in which the Arabian Muslims ruled, and all local populations, who were non-Muslim (usually Christian, Jewish, or Zoroastrian), constituted the lowly subject population. The "military model" of the expansion – that is, its conceptualization as the forcible imposition of a new religious and political order – seemed to provide the most obvious way to understand the rapidity of the new community's rise to ascendancy in wide areas of the Near East.

The "military model" of the conquests, however, raises in acute form the question: What were the forces that drove this movement in its first stage? Many historians, struck by the conquests' swift progress and vast scope, were puzzled by the fact that the conquests radiated from a place that lacked the elements usually considered essential to sustaining a rapid military expansion: an established state with well-developed military institutions and a significant base of economic resources on which to draw. Explaining the apparent energy and power of the early Islamic conquest movement, which exploded into the Near East apparently without any of these elements, emerged as a serious challenge for historians.

The oldest explanation for the dynamism that lay behind the Islamic conquests was that provided by the Muslim community itself, which saw it as the product of the new faith of Islam. This explanation took two forms. One was the belief that the conquests happened because of God's support for His faithful; in other words, it was God's will that the Muslims should be victorious on the battlefield against non-Muslim foes, often against overwhelming odds. According to this view – which historians who reject supernatural explanations cannot accept – the conquests are nothing less than a physical, historical sign of God's favor, and themselves constitute evidence for the truth of Islam as a faith-system.

The second aspect of this traditional Muslim view of the conquests emphasizes the early Muslims' zeal for their new faith, and attributes the success of the conquest movement in part to this deep commitment. Unlike the supernatural explanation, this is an explanation that any modern historian might embrace without difficulty, because the notion that religious commitment could be a powerful motivator of individual action should be unproblematic even to a historian of secular outlook.

Generally, however, western historians have been uncomfortable with religious explanations of the conquests, even those based merely on the idea of religious zeal as a contributing factor.[10] There were some exceptions,[11] of course, but most western scholars downplayed the force, or even denied the very existence, of the Believers' religious commitment. Some of them noted, for example, that the Believers did not require the Christians and Jews they "conquered" to embrace Islam, but rather allowed them to continue in their ancestral faiths as long as they paid taxes, and deduced from this that the conquerors were therefore not essentially motivated by religion.[12] The result of this was that some western scholars adopted a self-contradictory position on the conquests; on the one hand, they accepted the general notion that the expansion was somehow linked to the appearance of Islam, which they understood as a new religion, yet at the same time they wished to show that Islam, or religious zeal for it, was not really the cause of the expansion after all. Often these explanations took the form of reductionism – that is, explanations that tried to reduce the apparent causative force of Islam to other, more mundane, factors that were presented as the "real" causes. It is worth noting some of these reductionist arguments, at least briefly, and pointing out their shortcomings, because although most are discredited they are sometimes still advanced, even today.[13]

Perhaps the oldest reductionist theory, which appeared already in the nineteenth century, emphasized the conquerors' cupidity. Proponents of this view assumed that Arabian pastoral nomads were the dominant element in the conquest movement, the main motivation for which, they claimed, was the bedouins' desire to seize plunder. One summarized the motivations of the early conquests thus: "forthwith the whole Arabian people, both Town and Bedouin, were riveted to Islam by a common bond – the love of rapine and the lust of spoil."[14] Such a view, however, is predicated on assumptions rather than observable historical facts about the taking of booty, since little reliable evidence of the extent of plunder exists. More seriously, this interpretation completely fails to explain why the conquests should have happened when they did and as a sudden outburst – since the pastoralists and their presumed desire for plunder had been present for centuries. Likewise, this theory fails to explain why and how this latent desire for plunder, at one and only one crucial historical moment, took the form of an organized military, political, and religious movement. In this sense, the "plunder" argument simply begs the fundamental question of why the expansion took place when and as it did.

Another reductionist explanation provided by early western scholars of the conquests can be called the ecological or climatic hypothesis, according to which the conquests were sparked by the progressive desiccation of the Arabian peninsula in the years before the rise of Islam.[15] This supposed desiccation forced many Arabians to emigrate in waves from the peninsula into the surrounding lands, a popular migration that is disguised by the sources as a "conquest." Besides the fact that there is little or no convincing evidence for such a desiccation in the years immediately before the rise of Islam, the ecological hypothesis also fails to explain why the Arabians who moved into the Fertile Crescent in the seventh century appear not as a slow trickle of impoverished refugees, as one would expect if they had been forced out by dire circumstances, but rather as the sudden outburst of organized military forces. The ecological hypothesis also conflates the conquests and the "Arab migrations" – that is, it fails to separate the actual conquest of the Fertile Crescent, undertaken by military forces of decidedly small size, from the migration of larger groups of kinsmen into these areas, which the Arabic–Islamic sources reveal to have taken place only after the conquests; indeed, the migrations were made possible by the conquests, not the other way around.[16]

A number of more sophisticated hypotheses about the initial conquest movement, but ones that still contained a reductionist element, emphasized various economic factors as the crucial background to the Islamic movement. Early in the twentieth century, H. Lammens conjured up an image of Muḥammad's Mecca as the hub of a thriving trade in luxury goods connecting the Indian Ocean and Mediterranean basins, and argued that this provided the economic underpinnings of the conquest movement.[17] A half-century later, W. M. Watt built on Lammens's theory by hypothesizing that the disparities in wealth generated by this presumed trade created dislocations in traditional Arabian society (especially in Mecca) that Muḥammad's preachings were intended to remedy.[18] Marxist historians viewed the conquests as the product of the presumed exhaustion of the working classes in the Byzantine and Sasanian domains, which resulted in their capitulation to the arriving conquerors, and explicitly rejected what they termed "religious fanaticism" as a cause.[19] M. A. Shaban proposed that Muḥammad's career and the *ridda* brought trade in Arabia to a standstill, leading his followers to invade surrounding areas and thus to "unintentionally acquiring an empire" – religious motivations, he implies, were obviously not the real cause.[20] Numerous other students of Islam's origins (including the present writer) accepted the general outlines of the Lammens–Watt hypothesis of economic and social change in some form or other.[21] In recent years the notion that Mecca was an entrepot for an extensive luxury trade has been convincingly challenged by Patricia Crone,[22] but the existence of more modest commercial activity cannot be dismissed. Indeed, it has recently been proposed that Sasanian investment in Arabian trade and industry may have caused a wave of economic vitality in Arabia just on the eve of Islam.[23] It remains to be seen, however, just how this commerce and other economic activities, such as mining in the Ḥijāz, related to the rise of the conquest movement. The implication of all these theories, however, is that the expansion is the consequence of economic or social forces, rather than the result of a religious movement; statements in the sources suggesting a religious view of the conquests are often explained away as being merely the surface rhetoric masking the underlying social and economic forces – which are, by implication, "real."

Another reductionist approach to the early Islamic conquests chose to depict them as a kind of defensive proto-nationalism – a reaction of Arabians ("Arabs") against encroachment from the outside.[24] The rivalry between the Byzantine and Sasanian empires over Arabia, on the political, economic, and religious levels, was an undoubted fact, but whether the Believers' expansion can be identified as an Arabian "nativist" movement is questionable. The earliest documentary evidence available (including the Qur'an text as a kind of quasi-document) gives virtually no support to the notion that "Arabness" was a significant feature of the movement; on the contrary, it describes the movement overwhelmingly by means of religious terminology – using particularly the word *mu'min*, "Believer," and others related to it, as the crucial self-identifier. The domination of western thought by the nationalist idea[25] during the nineteenth and much of the twentieth centuries, however, made it almost inevitable that nationalist or nativist conceptualization should have been virtually all-pervasive in scholarship of the period.

A further problem inherent in the "military model" – particularly relating to the first, charismatic phase of the conquests – is to explain the causes of the conquests' success. This is because, as noted, the initial expansion movement radiated from a region – western Arabia – that lacked the base of natural and cultural resources one normally expects to find underpinning such an expansion, particularly a state expansion. How was it possible for people from this region to organize a movement that so quickly overcame vast areas of the Near East, even though those areas were home to two deeply institutionalized empires with well-established traditions of statecraft and tremendous resources based on an extensive agrarian base? And how was it possible for the new religion of Islam to establish itself so completely in an area where Zoroastrianism, Judaism, and Christianity had been deeply rooted for centuries and existed in highly sophisticated forms?

Scholars who adopted the more strictly military conceptualization of the conquests have tried in a variety of ways to explain their success in the face of perceived practical obstacles. One common theme was to emphasize not the strength of the Muslim armies, but rather the weakness of their foes, the Byzantine and Sasanian empires; according to this view, the rival empires were exhausted militarily, financially, and morally by over twenty years of bitter warfare, during which the Sasanians had occupied much of the Byzantine Near East only to be driven back again by the emperor Heraclius in the 620s.[26] In this view, the empires were unprepared for and unable to handle the unexpected military onslaught that came upon both of them from the south suddenly in the 630s.

Another explanation proposed by those favoring a military conceptualization of the conquests emphasized certain advantages held by the conquerors, rather than the weakness of the Byzantines and Sasanians. For example, some argued that the early Believers, when confronting the Byzantines' and Sasanians' southern flanks in Syria and Iraq, had the advantage of "inner lines of communication," which permitted the caliphs to shift troops from Iraq to Syria and vice versa in response to conditions. (They pass in silence over the fact that being wedged between two enemies and forced to fight both ahead and behind is normally considered a military liability.) Others have argued that the early Believers had superior weaponry or tactics, greater mobility, far better understanding of the desert fringes where most of the major battles against the Byzantines and Sasanians took place, or better leadership.[27] These possibilities may have some merit, but ultimately, such tactical advantages must all be linked to the fact that the Believers were putting together a new state, which enabled them to mobilize the social and other resources of Arabian society more effectively than before.[28]

A Revisionist View of the First or Charismatic Phase of the Conquests

As we have seen, the "military model" of the early Islamic conquests was rooted in the traditional sources' view that Muḥammad preached from the start a new religion, Islam, and we have seen the concomitant difficulties of interpretation that scholars attempted to eliminate by various reductionist approaches. Many of the difficulties of interpretation posed by the "military model" evaporate, however, if we adopt a somewhat different view of the nature of the religious movement Muḥammad started.[29] There is considerable evidence to suggest that Muḥammad and his earliest followers did not view their ideas as constituting a new religion, Islam, but were rather calling people to pious monotheist reform. We can most aptly call this the *Believers' movement* since, in the Qur'an and other early texts, participants in the movement are referred to, and refer to themselves, mainly as Believers (*mu'minūn*). That is, Muḥammad's religious movement emphasized belief in one God, and in the importance of righteous or pious behavior in accordance with God's revealed law. Former pagans who came to follow Muḥammad's preachings were expected to follow the law as revealed to Muḥammad in the Qur'an; those who were Jews or Christians, being monotheists already, did not need to give up their traditional faith to join the Believers' movement, but were expected to lead a righteous life in adherence to the teachings of the Torah or Gospels (Qur'anic *tawrāt, injīl*), which were accepted as earlier versions of God's revelation. One who did this was a Believer, regardless of whether he followed Qur'an, Torah, or Gospels. In other words, the Believers' movement was at the beginning non-confessional in the sense that it embraced righteous monotheists of whatever confession, whether Jews, Christians, or Qur'anic Believers. Although later Muslim tradition does its best to conceal the fact, there is some residual evidence showing that the early community of Believers did, indeed, include Jews and Christians as active members.[30] It also seems that the early Believers thought that the Last Judgment was imminent – that is, the Believers' movement was apocalyptic in character. This may explain the apparent dynamism and urgency of the movement; the conviction that the world is about to end and that one's ultimate salvation depends on what one does *now* could bring people to drop everything in their normal lives and get caught up in the enthusiasm of the cause.

Adopting such a view of the early Believers' movement changes significantly our perspective on the Believers' early expansion, and resolves a number of the puzzles associated with the more traditional "military model." Viewing the Believers' expansion into the lands adjacent to Arabia as the arrival of an ecumenical religious movement that preached monotheist reform and had as its goal the establishment of what the Believers saw as a God-guided, righteous political order, makes its ultimate success easier to grasp. For the Arabian Believers did not arrive as a new creed bent on suppressing existing religious communities in the name of their presumed new religion, much less on wooing them away from their former beliefs, but accepted many local Christians and Jews in the conquered lands as part of the movement.[31] To be sure, a new ruling elite of Believers was established that ruled over those who were not deemed adequately pious, and the dominant people in this elite were Believers of Arabian origin. But the ranks of the Believers also came to include many people of local origin; traditionally conceived scholarship identifies these people as *mawālī*, the Arabic term for clients of an Arabian tribal group, and treats them as "converts to Islam," but it is perhaps more appropriate to see them merely as Christians or Jews who had joined the Believers' movement. This ability of the early Believers' movement to incorporate many Christians and Jews (and some Zoroastrians) is presumably why the establishment of the Believers' hegemony seems to have occurred in most areas with relatively little trauma; for there is virtually no archaeological evidence of destruction or even of disruption to be found in the excavated sites dating from this period in Egypt, Syria, or Iraq.

This vision of the early expansion as a religious movement, however, does not require us to jettison all aspects of the traditional view of things; in particular, it does not preclude military activity on the part of the Believers. Although the Believers' contacts with most cities, towns, and rural districts may well have been generally more an exercise in persuasion than coercion, and resulted in negotiated submissions to the Believers' new kingdom, it seems likely that, much as the traditional narratives state, the Believers arrived in these areas in the first instance as organized armies or raiding parties – a fact that doubtless made their negotiators much more persuasive. Moreover, the Byzantine and Sasanian emperors surely would have sent armies to reclaim territories that had slipped under the Believers' control, or to dissuade additional localities from doing so. It seems plausible to assume that the Believers would have engaged these forces in pitched battles, not unlike the way they are described in the *futūḥ* narratives.

Furthermore, if we understand the initial goal of the Believers' movement to have been the establishment of a new, righteous kingdom run in accordance with God's revealed laws, it becomes possible to understand how a movement driven by religious zeal could nonetheless be largely free of pressure to "convert." For to talk of "conversion" becomes meaningless in the absence of a sharply defined identity as a separate, distinct religious confession. If a Jew or Christian could, by virtue of righteous behavior, also be reckoned among the Believers, there was no reason for him to "convert" to anything; he simply became a Believer, while remaining a Christian or a Jew. The Believers' movement, then, could establish itself readily in the Near East without requiring changes in a people's religious identity.

Like any vast historical phenomenon, the early expansion of the Believers must be viewed as the result of a variety of causative factors. These collectively provided a range of incentives to support the movement – regardless of how we decide to understand it – so that many different kinds of people found something appealing in it. Some participants in the Believers' movement doubtless were motivated by religious zeal and the desire to extend the realm subject to God's word. Others no doubt cared hardly at all for religious belief, nor troubled themselves with thoughts of the afterlife, but were drawn by the appeal of booty and earthly rewards. Still others may have sought commercial or financial opportunities, or political power, or just sheer excitement; and many people were doubtless drawn by a combination of factors. In this sense, many of the theories noted above may be seen as partial explanations of the nature of the conquests. However, most of them should be subsumed within the notion that the conquests are part of a process of state-formation ignited by a religious movement, because it was the new state that provided the context and organizing framework within which these other motivations could be effectively pursued.

Structural Developments during the First Phase of the Conquests

One of the crucial features of the first or charismatic phase of the conquest movement is the simultaneous development of various institutions of the state, including the army. Indeed, as we shall see, the army may have led the process of state institution-alization.

During Muḥammad's leadership of the Believers' movement in Medina (622–32 CE), there existed, as far as we can tell, no structured institutions of government of any kind, independent of his person (it was, to use Weberian terminology, still a thoroughly patrimonial regime). There was not yet even a standing army; although Muḥammad launched numerous raiding parties and several major military campaigns from Medina (for example, the campaigns against Khaybar in the north, or against Mecca in AH 8), these are described in each case as *ad hoc* assemblages of loyal supporters from Medina and allies from surrounding settlements or pastoral groups who had joined his community in some way.

The nucleus of a permanent army seems first to have materialized during the *ridda* wars that took place in Arabia during the two years following the death of Muḥammad in 632. At least some of the forces dispatched by the first caliph Abu Bakr (r. 632–4) were in the field for over a year of sustained campaigning, and their objectives seem to have been quite open-ended – both in marked departure from the limited objectives and *ad hoc* character of the armies of Muḥammad's time. The number and size of these permanent forces increased as Abu Bakr and his successor 'Umar (634–44) dispatched campaigns into Syria and Iraq. During this period the *dīwān* or regular army payroll was instituted, an event that can be said to mark definitively the creation of standing forces with expectations of regular campaigning.[32]

Several other institutions of the early Islamic state were closely linked to the institutionalization of the military during this period. One was the regular appointment of governors in various provinces of the vast areas the Believers' movement was rapidly acquiring in the middle decades of the seventh century – Syria, Iraq, northern Mesopotamia, Egypt, Iran.[33] In most cases, the first governor of a conquered district was, as one would expect, the commander of the army that had conquered and occupied it, who appears to have been in charge of regulating all aspects of life in that area – not only military campaigning and police matters, but also tax-collection and the adjudication of disputes. Fairly soon, however, we begin to read about regular dismissal of such military governors by the caliphs, and of their replacement sometimes by a team of officers, one to head the military forces of the province and another to handle the province's finances. We also sometimes read of increasingly regular (sometimes yearly) rotation of governors and provincial military commanders. Our chronicle sources for these matters in this early period are notoriously unreliable, but such reports seem to indicate a step forward in the rationalization of state administration. The earliest coin minting seems to have been linked to the existence of local authority in the hands of governors or military commanders in diverse provinces, who took over pre-existing Sasanian or Byzantine mints and personnel; it does not appear to have been centrally coordinated, and major changes in coinage types – still quite haphazard – did not begin until the time of the Umayyad caliph 'Abd al-Malik (r. 685–705), three-quarters of a century after the earliest conquests.[34]

Another institution linked to the military was the garrison town or *miṣr* (pl. *amṣār*), a number of which were founded during the charismatic phase in key locations in various provinces. Major ones were established at Baṣra in southern Iraq, Kūfa in central Iraq, and Fusṭāṭ in Egypt, and are described in the chronicles as army camps from which further campaigning was organized. In their early years, when the conquerors from Arabia were all clustered in these garrison towns, the *amṣār* clearly served not only key military functions, but also the vital ideological and sociopolitical one of preserving the cohesion of the Believers' movement. For, had the first Believers from Arabia settled in scattered localities throughout the vast provinces over which they took control, they would quickly have been overwhelmed by the cultural practices of local populations that greatly outnumbered them. The cultural isolation of the early *amṣār*, then, served as islands safeguarding the communal identity of the early Believers in a sea of non-believers.

The *amṣār* also became important foci of settlement for successive waves of Arabian migrants (often the families of the conquerors) who flocked to them once the province was "opened" – conquered. They grew rapidly into major cities with increasingly diverse populations, and became in time vibrant cultural centers in which was developed and from which radiated a new, synthetic Arabic–Islamic culture.[35]

In some areas – particularly, it seems, in Syria – the early Believers from Arabia appear to have settled in vacant quarters of existing cities such as Damascus and Hims. The latter town became the main military base of the early Believers in Syria for almost a hundred years after the conquests. This pattern of settlement in existing towns suggests that the major cities of Byzantine Syria had become partly depopulated on the eve of the conquests, probably from a combination of earthquakes and plague epidemics, as well as because of the impact of the last Sasanian–Byzantine war (603–30), all of which shattered the local economy and the fabric of urban life in early seventh-century Byzantine Syria. On the other hand, evidence from the excavations at

Ayla at the head of the Gulf of Aqaba have turned up remains of a modest new town founded during the conquest era just outside the gates of the Byzantine town (Ailana).[36] This suggests that in some localities in Syria, too, the Believers were creating new town foundations (even though Ayla itself is never mentioned in our sources as a *miṣr*).

We have little reliable information on the development of the tax administration the Believers established in the areas they conquered.[37] We must assume that there was one, for every state requires and aspires to secure a steady stream of revenue. But efforts to reconstruct what it was like must navigate a sea of contradictory information found in the Qur'an, in the Arabic–Islamic literary compilations about the conquests that often reflect systematizing efforts of later generations of legal scholars, and in the papyrus tax records of the early Islamic period, the advantages of whose documentary character is offset by the highly fragmented (and almost completely Egypto-centric) view they offer of the early tax system – if, indeed, it can be called a system at all. Much suggests that at first the Arabian Believers simply continued the bewildering profusion of local tax procedures they encountered in the districts they ruled, retaining the local administrators to apply them in the relevant local languages (Coptic, Greek, Syriac, Pahlavi). Only over the span of several generations was this local administrative personnel supplanted by Believers whose native language was Arabic – who by this time had themselves become sufficiently well established in these areas to be considered "locals." It seems that a true sytematization of the tax system was only fully conceived during the early 'Abbasid period, well over a century after the initial occupation of Syria, Iraq, Egypt, and Iran, and was never fully realized. Many texts shaped by the later, idealizing categories of the jurists describe conditions, even in early Islamic times, in terms of neat distinctions in taxation between Muslims and *ahl al-kitāb* ("peoples of the book", i.e., Christians, Jews, and Zoroastrians), between land-tax (*kharāj*) and poll-tax on non-Muslims (*jizya*), etc. But a glance at a rare text that seems to report actual conditions in northern Mesopotamia in the later eighth century[38] offers us a much messier picture: *jizya* on non-Muslims was a combined head and land-tax; taxes were collected three, and sometimes more, times per year instead of the prescribed once annually; the tax-collector for this Muslim regime in this district was a Zoroastrian; etc. It is, therefore, perilous to generalize too boldly about actual taxation practices, except to say that, particularly for the first century or more of the Believers' rule, they were very inconsistent and harked back to a variety of pre-existing practices.

Other aspects of what can be called the first state administration following the conquests are less well known. The caliphs early on created a *bayt al-māl* or central treasury, which may have represented a true public purse, that is, a fund for state expenses independent of the funding of the ruler himself, but we know more about the legal theory of it than we do about the actual history and functioning of the early *bayt al-māl*.[39] Perhaps on the model of the army *dīwān*, the caliphs also began to establish other ministries or bureaus (also called *dīwān*), particularly to handle the tax system. They also seem to have established a chancery to handle official correspondence in Arabic, but relatively few examples of its products survive, although its existence is noted in some literary sources.[40]

The adjudication of disputes in the Believers' realm seems to have been in the hands of local governors or military commanders, or their subordinate officials in specific localities, through the first century AH, at least if the Egyptian papyri are any indication. Although many idealizing reports speak of the very early appointment of *qāḍīs* or judges,[41] there is no documented evidence for the existence of independent judges before the early 'Abbasid period. More frequently mentioned is the institution of an official supervision of the *ḥajj* or annual pilgrimage ritual in Mecca. The pilgrimage was frequently headed by the caliph himself or by a high official designated by him. Doing so helped affirm both the Believers' religious traditions and the caliph's legitimacy as leader of the community of Believers, and so should be considered among the institutions intended to solidify the workings of the new state established in the wake of the conquests.

By the time of the first civil war (656–61), then, a rudimentary state administration had begun to crystallize among the Believers in the conquered lands. This administration was still crude in many respects, but it proved strong enough to provide a framework for the community of Believers to come together again at the end of the first civil war, and so allowed the community to resume its expansion in the second or "institutional" stage of conquests.

The Second or Institutional Phase of the Conquests

The first civil war or *fitna* (656–61) marked the end of the first or charismatic phase of the conquests, during which the expansion seems to have been sustained largely on the basis of an intense enthusiasm among the Believers for their collective mission of spreading the domain of God's word.[42] The first *fitna* was essentially a struggle within the Arabian (largely Meccan) ruling elite to determine who should lead the community of Believers in the aftermath of the murder of the third caliph, 'Uthman ibn 'Affan (r. 644–56), a question that was closely bound up with differing attitudes on *how* the community and state should be ruled.[43]

During the *fitna* the embryonic elements of state organization and institutions described in the preceding section remained in place, to the extent that they already existed, and were drawn upon in varying degrees by rival contenders for power. All serious claimants, especially 'Ali and Mu'awiya, drew on the military forces of the provinces they controlled, appointed provincial governors and subordinate officials, and attempted to assert their legitimacy by organizing official pilgrimage observances and other rituals.[44] When the *fitna* ended in 661 – following the assassination of 'Ali and the subsequent recognition as caliph of Mu'awiya, of the Umayyad family of Quraysh – it was possible, with internal peace restored, for the new ruler and his entourage once again to organize military campaigns of expansion. Now, however, the caliph could rely in doing so upon the institutions of the state: in particular, upon the standing armies, based in the garrison towns, sustained by regular taxation that was levied by the caliphs' provincial administration, which provided income some of which was distributed to the soldiers through a regular military payroll. We can probably assume that the standing armies were already by the early Umayyad period structured following an explicit chain of command, and that such matters as recruitment and terms of service were also regularized, although we have very little evidence of such organizational arrangements other than the names of some of the highest-level commanders who figure prominently in various events mentioned in the chronicle literature.[45]

During this second or institutional phase of the conquests, the bulk of the caliphate's military campaigns were pre-planned, even routine: the soldiers were usually mustered in the *amṣār* in Iraq, Egypt, or Syria during the late winter or spring months, and dispatched so as to attain their objectives in Iran, North Africa, or the Byzantine frontier during the summer "campaigning season." They retired in the autumn to their home bases, where they spent the winter "off-season" resting and preparing for the next season's hostilities. The routine, seasonal quality of campaigning in the institutional phase was perhaps most marked on the Byzantine frontier, so much so that the annual campaign into Anatolia was called in Arabic *al-ṣā'ifa*, literally "summering";[46] but on the whole a similar rhythmic quality is perceptible in campaigning elsewhere as well. The Syriac chronicle of Yohannan bar Penkaye, written during the late 680s in northern Mesopotamia, which provides one of our earliest descriptions of the Islamic state, describes how the armies of the Believers "used to go in each year to distant lands and provinces, raiding and plundering from all peoples under heaven. And from every person they demanded only tribute, and each one could remain in whatever faith he chose."[47] This valuable comment confirms the regular, annual nature of the military campaigns sponsored by the Believers in the late seventh century, as well as the non-confessional character of the expansion, which was essentially the political expansion of a state, notwithstanding the state's origins in a monotheist revival movement.

During the secondary phase, the conquests and expansion of the caliphal state encompassed even more distant territories than during the primary phase; their vast scope – from France to India – makes it impractical to provide more than the barest sketch of their outlines here.

During the primary phase of the conquests, as we have seen, the Believers had seized western Iran and many districts in the south and east of the country as well; during the second phase, those parts of Iran that were still in the control of independent local rulers were integrated more thoroughly into the Islamic state – particularly the rugged region south of the Caspian Sea.[48] From Khurasān in northeastern Iran, where the conquerors had established a garrison in 650, the whole area as far as the Oxus (Amu Darya) River was taken over in the last decades of the seventh century, as were parts of northern Afghanistan (Balkh). During the early eighth century, the area between the Oxus and Jaxartes (Syr Darya) Rivers was raided annually and finally seized, and some important towns beyond the Jaxartes, such as Shash (modern Tashkent) were subdued (741).[49]

The second decade of the eighth century saw the conquest of the lower Indus valley (Sind) as far north as Multan by a force dispatched by the Umayyad governor of Iraq, al-Ḥajjāj ibn Yūsuf, perhaps to punish the local ruler for sheltering pirates who had preyed on Muslim merchants. The leader of this campaign was a teenaged kinsman of al-Ḥajjāj, Muḥammad ibn al-Qāsim, who emerged as a heroic figure in later lore. Archaeological finds confirm the existence in the Indus valley of a continuing Muslim community with some commercial ties to Syria and other regions to the west, but the historical sources are virtually silent on this community and we know very little about it. It seems, however, to have remained a relatively modest presence in Sind for many centuries. The large-scale spread of Islam in Sind and elsewhere in India really began later, with the activities of the Ghaznavids and other dynasties based in Afghanistan in the eleventh century CE and later.[50]

The Believers had penetrated parts of Armenia and the Caucasus already during the first phase of the conquests and held these areas through the eighth century. During the ninth and tenth centuries, however, determined opposition on the part of the local Christian chiefs, backed by the Byzantines, frequent raids by the nomadic Khazars of the Volga region, and the activities of independent-minded Muslim warlords, slowly eroded caliphal control of these areas. By the late tenth century, Armenia and Georgia were again ruled by indigenous Christian kings.[51]

Farther west, the caliphs continued to launch regular summer campaigns into Anatolia, to which the Byzantines responded in kind, resulting in the emergence of a special frontier zone in Anatolia ravaged by continuous raiding on both sides. This continued into the ninth century; thereafter the collapse of 'Abbasid caliphal power and the Byzantine military resurgence pushed the border farther south, into northern Syria. The caliphs also mounted several campaigns which bypassed most of Anatolia and attacked the Byzantine capital at Constantinople (669; 673–8; 717–18; 783–5). Although these more than once posed a great threat to the city, they never succeeded in taking it.[52]

Egypt had served already during the first phase of conquest as a base for raids westward across North Africa into Libya and Ifriqiya (modern Tunisia). During the second phase, raids continued and were followed by consolidation of caliphal control: 'Uqba ibn Nafi' decisively conquered Ifriqiya in the 660s, establishing the garrison town of Qayrawan there in 670, and raided as far as the Atlantic in the 680s. Qayrawan, in turn, served as the focus for the radiation of Islamic culture and caliphal control in much of the Maghrib. Some Berber pastoralists and villagers of the Maghrib continued to resist the Believers' hegemony, however, even after the region was largely pacified by the forceful governor Musa ibn Nusayr in the early eighth century. Others, however, quickly joined the ranks of the Believers and became themselves important participants in the secondary phase of expansion.[53]

From North Africa, raids were launched into Visigothic Spain, which was apparently embroiled in a civil war; shortly thereafter, around 711, two armies crossed into Spain, one led by the Berber commander Tariq ibn Ziyad and the other by Musa ibn Nusayr. These forces defeated the last Visigothic King, Roderick, and quickly seized control of much of the peninsula as far as the Pyrenees, including the former capital at Toledo. The next century saw the immigration into Spain of significant numbers of Berber settlers and of some Arabs, particularly from Syria, as part of the ruling elite. We know little more about the history of Muslim rule in Spain until the fall of the Umayyad caliphate in the east (750) than the names of the Umayyads' governors, but during this period the Muslims consolidated their rule over all of the Iberian peninsula except for the mountainous north, which became the focus of small Christian kingdoms. From Spain, the Muslims pushed across the Pyrenees into southern and central Gaul; their defeat by the Frankish king Charles Martel near Poitiers in 732 marked their apogee in the west, and by 801 the cities north of the Pyrenees and even Barcelona were no longer under Muslim control.[54]

During their expansionist heyday of the seventh and eighth centuries, the Believers also took to the sea and seized various islands in the Mediterranean and a few outposts on that sea's northern shores. Cyprus became subject to shared Byzantine–Umayyad sovereignty in the seventh century, but generally the eastern Mediterranean remained a Byzantine lake, dominated by its powerful navy. In the western Mediterranean, however, the Aghlabid governors of Ifriqiya (Tunisia) built a powerful navy in the ninth century that seized Sicily from the Byzantines between 827 and 831, and Muslim raiders, many little more than freebooters, attacked many Italian coastal towns (Ancona, Naples, Rome) and established outposts in various localities in Provence, Switzerland, northern Italy, and southern Italy. The Balearic islands were conquered by forces from Islamic Spain; Crete was taken in 825 by a rebel and adventurer who fled Spain and put together a raiding party in Egypt.[55]

The regularity of the campaigning in the institutional phase was linked to a shift in the motivations for the conquests that had set in by this time. On the one hand, the Umayyad caliphs, as leaders of the community of Believers, doubtless aspired to extend the domain of the Believers' new, God-guided public order, and to displace as much as possible the older, in their eyes corrupt and sinful regimes of the past. That is, the Umayyad caliphs, like the first four caliphs who preceded them, continued to be impelled in part by what we may term religious motivations (even though this did not involve forcing people who were already monotheists – in particular, Christians and Jews – to embrace Islam). On the other hand, the Umayyad ruling elite also came to realize that campaigns were an effective way to raise revenue in the form of booty (including slaves). This was doubtless part of the reason why campaigns were sent out annually: raiding was, in effect, an alternative form of taxation, which was of course also undertaken on a regular basis. The revenues of the Umayyad state were not well distinguished from those of the ruling elite – the caliph and his immediate entourage; that is, the "public purse" and the "privy purse" were often one and the same, in practice if not in principle. Some caliphs used their revenues, whether from taxation or from the ruler's share of booty from military campaigns, not only for such state purposes as paying the army and bureaucracy, but also to secure, through patronage, the backing of important individuals such as powerful tribal chiefs; and sometimes they even employed them for personal purposes, such as to purchase properties as investments for themselves. The caliph Muʿawiya, for example, is reported to have possessed vast estates in eastern Arabia, worked by thousands of slaves who were probably part of his share of the booty.[56] The provision of captives as part of annual tribute (*baqt*) is mentioned in the treaty-agreement with Nubia, of which documentary evidence exists,[57] and campaigns of raid and conquest against Berber groups in North Africa seem especially to have aimed at securing slaves – a lucrative form of tribute.[58]

Besides the more routine annual campaigning, however, the Umayyad caliphs also organized exceptional campaigns with particular objectives. Most noteworthy of these were their several attempts to conquer the Byzantine capital, Constantinople. We can assume that the ultimate goal – or, perhaps, the fantasy – of the regular summer campaigns against Anatolia was to advance all the way to the Byzantine capital, but well-organized Byzantine resistance in Anatolia meant that the normal summer campaigns seldom got near Constantinople; instead, the Umayyad *ṣāʾifa* tended to joust with Byzantine forces in central Anatolia, whose various towns and districts were traded back and forth between the two empires year by year.[59] In any case, it became evident early on that Constantinople was probably too strong to be reduced by a land assault alone, because of the city's massive land defenses and its extensive coasts, which allowed it to be resupplied by sea. Twice, however, the Umayyad caliphs organized huge expeditions against Constantinople that were coordinated with naval expeditions so that the city could be subjected to combined land assault and sea blockade (674–80; 716–17). Similarly, a special naval and marine campaign was undertaken in 674 to Crete, and special forces dispatched in 711 to conquer Sind (in today's southern Pakistan).

In time – already by the later seventh century – the front had become so distant in east and west that the troops dispatched from the *amṣār* in either Iraq or Egypt spent much of the campaigning season simply getting to the land of the enemy. For this reason, new "second-tier" garrisons were founded as satellites of the original *amṣār* that had been established in the first phase of the conquests. In the west, Qayrawan was established in a fertile district in what is today central Tunisia in 670, and settled with a permanent force drawn from Fustat. In the east, the rich oasis region of Marw, conquered already in 651, was chosen as the base for a large garrison in 671; this was not a new city-foundation, as there had been some kind of urbanization in the oasis for at least a thousand years, but 671 marked the beginning of Marw's prominence as a *miṣr* from which the Muslims dispatched campaigns into easternmost Iran, Central Asia, and Afghanistan.

In sum, the basic feature of the conquests of the second or institutional phase, and what sets them apart from those of the charismatic phase, was that the caliphs could now rely on the increasingly developed institutional framework of the state. This meant that they could pursue campaigns of conquest on a regular basis as a means of revenue-extraction. A more bureaucratic motivation was thus added to the original motivation that impelled the charismatic conquests, namely the religiously based desire to extend the reach of the righteous community of Believers by expanding the state they had created.

Impact and Consequences of the Islamic Conquests

Finally, a consideration of the Islamic conquests – however one wishes to conceptualize them – must examine their historical impact and consequences for the societies of the Near East. In doing so, we need sometimes to adopt a retrospective view and try to identify long-range consequences, as well as changes that would have been visible to observers of the time.

First of all – and this is most definitely a retrospective perception – the conquests marked the decisive starting-point in the long historical process by which Islam became the dominant religion of the Near East and began to spread throughout the world. This is true even though the early Believers constituted, for at least several decades following the conquests, only a very small minority of the populations they ruled. It is also true even if we wish to see the Believers' movement of the time of Muhammad and the generation or two following him as not yet being exactly "Islam" in the usual sense, but rather as a religious movement emphasizing monotheism and piety that had an ecumenical and non-confessional character; for it was this movement that during the century following the Prophet evolved into Islam in the sense we usually use the term, that is, as a unique monotheistic confession whose distinctive markers are recognition of the prophethood of Muhammad and of the Qur'an as God's revealed word. The Believers' movement, if not yet "Islam" as people have understood that term for over a thousand years, represented the embryo or seed from which Islam emerged and spread throughout the world. In the Near Eastern context in particular, the Islamic conquests mark the beginning of the process by which Christianity, Zoroastrianism, and Judaism (along with other, non-monotheistic faiths) gradually lost out and ceased, and Islam came to be the dominant religious confession of the Near East.[60] The Believers' new political order thus provided the sheltering aegis under which, over several centuries, Islam (as it would increasingly be known) was adopted as the faith of millions of people from Central Asia and the Indus valley to Spain and North Africa.

Another change that came with the conquests, and one that was as obvious to observers at the time as it is to us today, was a political shift. The regions and peoples conquered or absorbed by the early Believers' movement were no longer subject to the Byzantine emperor or the Sasanian Great King, but were now ruled by the caliphs and their agents (usually military at first, then increasingly bureaucratic). The Sasanian state, indeed, ceased to exist entirely with the death of the last Great King, Yazdagird III, in 651. The Byzantine empire survived, but only in greatly truncated form, and the Byzantine emperors emerged as the longest-term rivals to the caliphs. The growth of new state institutions (sometimes borrowing freely from the institutions of their Byzantine or Sasanian predecessors) has already been noted. The larger change that these institutional developments articulated was a reorientation of revenues to the caliphs and their regime, and to the goals of the new regime, and away from the Byzantine and Sasanian regimes.

This political shift also meant the emergence of a new ruling elite. Although the Believers' movement came to include locals in the conquered areas, the new elite was, at first, overwhelmingly composed of Believers who were of Arabian origin and who spoke Arabic as their native tongue. Such people had been known in many of the conquered regions before the conquests – Arabian traders seem to have been known for many centuries, and the spread of Arabic language among the population of parts of Syria and Iraq is well attested on the eve of Islam. But these Arabic-speaking people (or actual Arabians) had been a politically marginal population in Byzantine–Sasanian times; the elites of Syrian or Iraqi society on the eve of Islam were, in Byzantine provinces, usually Greek-speaking, more rarely Aramaic- or Coptic-speaking, and in Sasanian provinces, Persian-speaking, more rarely Aramaic-speaking. The reorientation of revenues to the caliphs following the conquests meant that, through patronage and employment as part of the new regime, Arabic-speaking locals and immigrants from Arabia increasingly became the prosperous component of the population.

It is sometimes argued that, by sweeping away the old Byzantine–Sasanian border, the first phase of conquests created a new, unified, economic zone in the Near East, which (it is alleged) facilitated economic exchange and growth in the region. It is true that commerce after the conquests between, say, Egypt and Iran may have been facilitated in times of peace as compared with pre-Islamic times, because there was now no border, with its unavoidable tariffs, for merchants to cross. However, one must remember that the conquests created a new border between formerly Byzantine Egypt and Constantinople, so it might be more accurate to speak of a re-drawing of borders rather than creation of a "unified economic zone." This realignment of borders was probably not beneficial to the Byzantine empire, whose capital and central provinces were now cut off from the rich lands of the eastern Mediterranean, but whether it had a more general economic impact on the Near East, and exactly what that impact was, remains to be clarified.

Another consequence of the conquests for the Near East was an influx of Arabian immigrants, particularly to the new garrison towns in Iraq, Egypt, and to various districts and towns in Syria. As noted above, it would be completely misleading to see the conquests as a kind of *Völkerwanderung* driven by population pressure or the need for economic resources; for one thing, Arabia was (and remains) an area of low population density, so the post-conquest Arabian immigrants were probably relatively few. Yet, the Believers' success in absorbing into their new state vast lands adjacent to

Arabia – particularly Syria, Egypt, and Iraq – did open the way for some Arabians, whether settled townsmen or nomadic pastoralists, to move to these new areas (especially, at first, to the garrison towns).

The conquests also accelerated and extended the spread of the Arabic language into new areas at the expense of Aramaic, Coptic, Greek, Pahlavi (Middle Persian), and other languages. This was so partly because Arabic was the language of the conquerors and of new migrants, partly because it immediately served as the official language of the state, and partly because it was the language of the Believers' sacred book, the Qur'an. The process of Arabization is a highly complex one, however, and no simple relationship between it and the conquests (or the immigration of Arabians) should be drawn. Some areas that were conquered early on either never became Arabic-speaking (e.g., the Iranian highlands), or only became Arabic-speaking many centuries later, under the impact of other historical developments (e.g., much of North Africa).

In sum, the conquests set the stage for the birth and elaboration of a rich and diverse new civilization. Islamic civilization reworks and combines elements of older traditions – Judaic and Christian, Zoroastrian, Hellenistic, Iranian, Arabian – with the ethical and religious ideas of the Qur'an and Muḥammad's teachings to produce a coherent, dynamic new whole. The Believers' new political order provided the sheltering aegis under which, over several centuries, Islam (as it would increasingly be known) was adopted as the faith of millions of people from Central Asia and the Indus valley to Spain and North Africa.

NOTES

1   For clarification of the nature of the Believers' movement, see below.
2   On the term, see Conrad, "Futūḥ." The term *futūḥāt* (plural of a plural) is a neologism used mainly in modern scholarship. On the historiographical complexities of the traditional Islamic *futūḥ* literature see Donner, *Narratives of Islamic Origins*, esp. ch. 7, and Noth and Conrad, *Early Arabic Historical Tradition*. For a tabulation of the first works on the *futūḥ* theme, see Donner, *Narratives*, Appendix ("Chronological List of Early Texts"), 297–306.
3   See recently Simon, "Muḥammad and the Jihād"; Firestone, *Jihad*.
4   Shoufani, *Al-Riddah and the Muslim Conquest of Arabia*; Donner, *Early Islamic Conquests*, chapter 2; Jandora, *March from Medina*, ch. 2.
5   Donner, *Early Islamic Conquests*, ch. 3; Kaegi, *Byzantium and the Early Islamic Conquests*.
6   Donner, *Early Islamic Conquests*, ch. 4.
7   Zarrīnkūb, "The Arab Conquest of Iran"; Morony, "Arab Conquest of Iran"; Spuler, *Iran in früh-islamischer Zeit*, 3–21; Daryaee, "Collapse of the Sasanian Power"; Morony, "Conquerors and Conquered: Iran." Daniel, *Political History of Khurasan*, 19–22, notes the contradictory nature of the sources for Khurasan and the superficial quality of the initial conquest.
8   Butler, *Arab Conquest of Egypt*; Jarry, "L'Égypte et l'invasion musulmane."
9   On the *ṣulḥ-ʿanwa* terminology, Schmucker, *Untersuchungen*; Noth, "Zum Verhältnis von Kalifaler Zentralgewalt und Provinzen"; Simonsen, *Studies*.
10 This tendency is noted by Lewis, "The Significance of Heresy," 44, and Décobert, *Le mendiant et le combatant*, 46. See also Donner, "Orientalists and the Rise of Islam."
11 The Dutch scholar C. Snouck Hurgronje, although he never developed it carefully, always emphasized the importance of religious faith; see for example his "Islam," 29–30: "We

can find only in Islam an explanation of the planned procedure without which the foundations of the Arab world-empire would have been unthinkable." Bousquet, "Observations sur la nature et causes de la conquête arabe," concluded that religious commitment outweighed material and other inducements. See also Décobert, *Le mendi-ant*, 62–3, 65–6.

12 E.g., Arnold, *The Preaching of Islam*, esp. 45–6; Becker, "Die Ausbreitung der Araber."

13 A fuller discussion of these theories is found in Donner, *Early Islamic Conquests*, intro-duction, and idem, "Centralized Authority." See also Bousquet, "Quelques remarques critiques."

14 Muir, *The Caliphate*, 44.

15 Advanced by such varied scholars as T. W. Arnold, Hugo Winckler, Leone Caetani, Philip Hitti, Bernard Lewis, and Karl Butzer; see Donner, "Centralized Authority."

16 This point was already made by Becker, "Ausbreitung." A new "ecological thesis" has been proposed recently by Korotaev et al., "Origins of Islam." It argues that global climatic changes (including unusual wetness – not aridity – in Arabia) in the sixth century CE generated social changes in Arabia that prepared the way for the rise of Islam. Their arguments depend on many different orders of evidence – climatological, vulcanological, social, anthropological, religious, and historical – the linkages among which are poorly documented or undocumented, but they may repay further study.

17 Lammens, "La république marchande de la Mecque."

18 Most clearly presented in Watt, *Muhammad: Prophet and Statesman*, 46–55.

19 E.g. Belyaev, *Arabs, Islam, and the Arab Caliphate*, 129.

20 Shaban, *Islamic History, A.D. 600–750*, 14, 24–5.

21 E.g., Hodgson, *Venture of Islam*; Donner, *Early Islamic Conquests*; Ruthven, *Islam in the World*; Khalidi, *Classical Arab Islam*; Kennedy, *Prophet and the Age of the Caliphates*; Esposito, *Islam. The Straight Path*.

22 Crone, *Meccan Trade and the Rise of Islam*.

23 Morony, "The Late Sasanian Economic Impact on the Arabian Peninsula." On mining in the Ḥijāz and its possible economic and commercial impact, see Heck, "Gold Mining in Arabia."

24 Crone, *Meccan Trade*, esp. 247–50, and Bashear, *Arabs and Others in Early Islam*, have been the main recent proponents of the nativist theory; however, the hypothesis that the initial expansion of Islam was essentially an Arab identity movement resembles those of many earlier Western scholars who saw the conquests in ethnic terms (and hence tended to call them the "Arab conquests"). See for example, Arnold, *Preaching of Islam*, 46–8; Becker, "Ausbreitung der Araber," 69–70; Bousquet, "Observations sur la nature et causes," 48; von Grunebaum, "The Nature of Arab Unity Before Islam."

25 And, of course, by the concepts of racism that formed the rationalizing underpinnings for nationalism; for a bit more detail on this, see Donner, "Orientalists and the Rise of Islam."

26 For example, Canard, "L'expansion arabe," esp. 57–63.

27 Jandora, *March from Medina*.

28 Donner, *Early Islamic Conquests*, 268–9.

29 For a fuller explication of the revisionist hypothesis outlined in the next few paragraphs, see Donner, "From Believers to Muslims."

30 See Donner, "Believers to Muslims," for a survey of this residual evidence. The most obvious bit is the inclusion of the Jews of Medina in the *umma* document in which Muḥammad established the regulations for his new community; text in Ibn Isḥāq, *Sīrat rasūl allāh*, 34–46; English transl. Guillaume, *Life of Muhammad*, 231–5.

31 St. John of Damascus, high administrator for the later Umayyad caliphs, and the Umay-yads' Christian court poet al-Akhṭal, are among the more visible and better-known instances of this symbiosis.

32 See Donner, "The Growth of Military Institutions"; idem, "Formation of the Islamic State," esp. 285–6. On the *dīwān* or stipend-register, see Puin, *Der Dīwān von 'Umar ibn al-Ḥaṭṭāb*.

33 A list of governors is found in de Zambaur, *Manuel de généalogie et de chronologie*, part II (pp. 17–49). See also Blay-Abranski, *From Damascus to Baghdad: The Abbasid Administrative System*, 195–241; Crone, *Slaves on Horses*, 124–53.

34 On coinage see Bates, "History, Geography, and Numismatics"; idem, "The Coinage of Syria under the Umayyads"; Sears, *Monetary History of Iraq and Iran*.

35 Case-studies on the development of the *amṣār* as cultural centers: Pellat, *Le milieu baṣrien*; Djaït, *Al-Kūfa*; Kubiak, *Al-Fusṭāṭ*.

36 See Whitcomb, "Miṣr of Ayla," in Bisheh, *Studies in the History and Archaeology of Jordan* 5, 277–88.

37 On tax administration, see Simonsen, *Studies*; Schmucker, *Untersuchungen*; Blay-Abramski, 242–96; Donner, "Formation of the Islamic State," 286–8.

38 Studied in Cahen, "Fiscalité, Propriété, Antagonismes sociaux."

39 On it see Coulson, "Bayt al-Māl."

40 Some products of the Umayyad chancery are found in Abbott, *The Qurrah Papyri*.

41 See, for example, the extensive collection of reports on the "*qāḍī* Shurayḥ", supposed to have been appointed over Kufa from the time of the second caliph 'Umar onwards: Kohlberg, "Shurayḥ." Cf. on judges Blay-Abramski, 120–94; Donner, "Formation of the Islamic State," 288–9.

42 What the anthropologist Victor Turner would term a state of "communitas": *Ritual Process*, ch. 3.

43 The most detailed examination of the first civil war is now found in Madelung, *Succession to Muḥammad*, a work that is, however, characterized by an almost partisan (pro-'Alī) view of events.

44 See for example al-Ṭabarī, *Ta'rīkh*, i/3448 on conflicting reports of pilgrimage leaders sent by 'Alī and Mu'āwiya in AH 39/April 660.

45 The chronicles routinely mention the commander in charge of a particular foray, but seldom offer more detailed insights into the composition of his forces – how many subordinate units his force comprised, the names of his subordinate officers, the tactical specialization (if any) of various units, etc. The Nessana papyri may preserve a fragment of an actual payroll-list, although it is not clear whether this was for a military unit or for some other kind of levy, such as a civilian labor crew. See Kraemer, *Excavations at Nessana*.

46 On Byzantine border-warfare see Bonner, *Aristocratic Violence and Holy War*.

47 Mingana, *Sources Syriaques* I, 147, lines 1–6.

48 See Madelung, "Minor Dynasties of Northern Iran"; Morony, "Arab Conquest of Iran."

49 The classic study is Gibb, *Arab Conquests of Central Asia*. See also Bosworth, "Coming of Islam to Afghanistan"; Hasan, "Survey of the expansion of Islam into Central Asia"; Spuler, *Iran in früh-islamischer Zeit*, 29–34; Morony, "Arab Conquest of Iran," 209.

50 See Friedmann, "A contribution to the early history of Islam in India"; Gabrieli, "Muḥammad ibn al-Qāsim al-Thaqafī and the Arab Conquest of Sind."

51 Manandean, "Les invasions arabes en Arménie"; Kaegi, *Byzantium and the Early Islamic Conquests*, chapter 8; Laurent, *L'Arménie entre Byzance et l'Islam*; Dunlop, *History of the Jewish Kha'ars*.

52 Ahrweiler, "L'Asie Mineure et les invasions arabes"; Canard, "Les expéditions des Arabes contre Constantinople"; Bonner, *Aristocratic Violence*.

53 Taha, *Muslim Conquest and Settlement of North Africa and Spain*.

54 The murky history of the early Muslim presence in Spain, and the unreliability of a number of later Arabic accounts of its conquest, are discussed in Collins, *Arab Conquest of Spain*. See also Taha, *Muslim Conquest*. The classic study is Lévi-Provençal, *Histoire de l'Espagne Musulmane*; the conquest of Spain is covered in vol. 1, 1–89.

55   Ahmad, *History of Islamic Sicily*; Brooks, "Arab Occupation of Crete"; Lecam, *Les Sarra-zins dans le haut moyen-âge français.*
56   al-Balādhurī, *Ansāb* 11, 126–7, mentions 4,000 slaves (or families?) on Muʿāwiya's estates at al-Khaḍārim; cf. al-Askar, *al-Yamama in the Early Islamic Era*, 69.
57   See Hinds and Sakkout, "A Letter from the Governor of Egypt." Cf. also the report that the treaty with the city of Zarang in Iran required the city to hand over an annual tribute of 1,000 slave boys (Morony, "Arab Conquest of Iran," 207).
58   The evidence is summarized in Savage, *A Gateway to Hell, A Gateway to Paradise*, 72–5.
59   Cf. Bonner, *Aristocratic Violence.*
60   See Bulliet, *Conversion to Islam in the Medieval Period*; idem, *Islam: The View from the Edge*; Levtzion, *Conversion to Islam.*

FURTHER READING

As a general overview of the expansion of the early caliphate in its military dimension, the old essay by Carl H. Becker is still useful; it is found in English translation as "The Expansion of the Saracens" in H. M. Gwatkin et al. (ed.), *The Cambridge Medieval History* (Cambridge: Cambridge University Press, 1913), vol. 2, chapters 11 and 12. A useful overview of the general course of Islamic history in the early period is provided by Hugh Kennedy, *The Prophet and the Age of the Caliphates* (London: Longman, 1986). A detailed examination of the relationship between pastoral no-madic and settled peoples of Arabia and its impact on the formation of the earliest Islamic state is found in Fred M. Donner, *The Early Islamic Conquests* (Princeton: Princeton University Press, 1981). Documentary evidence for the early existence of the state is assembled in Fred M. Donner, "The Formation of the Islamic State," *JAOS* 106 (1986), 283–96. A brief introduction to the complexities of the Arabic conquest accounts is Lawrence I. Conrad, "*Futūḥ*," in Julie S. Meisami and Paul Starkey (eds.), *Encyclopedia of Arabic Literature* (London: Routledge, 1998), 237–40. A stimulating reconstruction of how conquered communities may have been assimilated into the Muslim community and state in the early Islamic era is Richard Bulliet, *Islam: The View from the Edge* (New York: Columbia University Press, 1994).

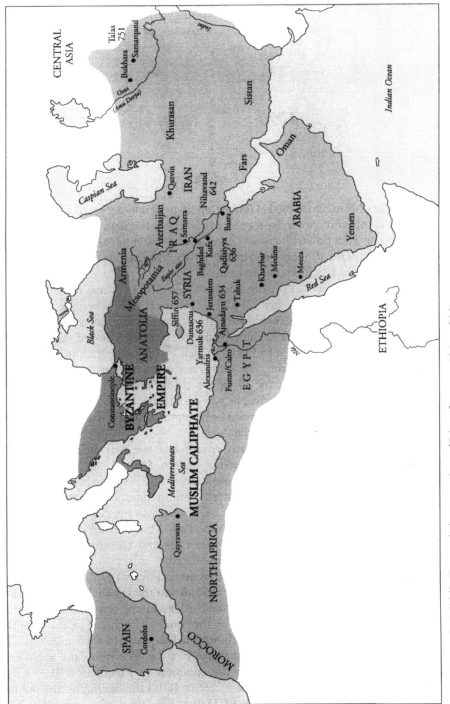

Map 2.1 The Middle East and the expansion of Islam from AD 634 to 800

Chapter Three

The Caliphate

HUGH KENNEDY

When the prophet Muḥammad died in 632 he left no generally accepted successor. The young Muslim community needed some sort of leadership but it was unclear who such a leader might be or what powers he would have. The Prophet himself had made it clear that he was the 'Seal of the Prophets' and that there would be no one after him who could claim his unique status. Decisions had to be made.

It is difficult to reconstruct the debates and the course of events which led to the appointment of Abū Bakr as the first caliph because these events became the subject of a vigorous polemic which has continued right down to the present day. Two main points of view emerged. The first of these held that Abū Bakr, one of the oldest and closest of the Prophet's associates, had been chosen by his other leading companions without any significant opposition. The other version, what can be described as a proto-Shi'ite reading, claims that the Prophet's cousin and son-in-law Ali was not present, because, as the nearest relative, he was preparing the body for burial. While engaged in this pious duty he was deprived of his rights since he had previously been designated by the Prophet as his true heir.

The different historical narratives neatly encapsulate the two different visions of how the leader of the Muslim *umma* should be chosen. On the one hand the choice of Abū Bakr was based on the rights of the most senior and respected of the Prophet's companions to choose the candidate they deemed most suitable. On the other hand there were those who supported Ali's claims because he was the closest relative of the Prophet and, they believed, his designated successor. The political debate is articulated in terms of the conflicting historical narratives and the three main ideas of designation, heredity and election were all articulated.

The debate was given added impetus by the fact that different groups in the nascent Muslim community supported the differing attitudes to the leadership. The death of the Prophet had brought into the open some of the latent tensions between the indigenous people of Medina now known as the *ansār* or 'helpers' of the Prophet, and the *muhājirūn* who had come with Muḥammad to settle in their midst in 622. The tension was exacerbated by the fact that many of the relatives of the *muhājirūn* had joined the Muslim community after the conquest of Mecca in 630 and now expected to have a powerful voice in Muslim affairs. From the beginning the political process was dominated by the Quraysh of Mecca, the Prophet's own tribe. They produced the first three caliphs, Abū Bakr, 'Umar, and 'Uthmān and they dominated the selection procedure. Though he himself was also from Quraysh, the supporters of

Ali came from the disenfranchised, those who believed that they had been deprived of their rights by the Quraysh of Mecca and their allies. The alliance of the Family of the Prophet, as represented by Ali and his descendants, with the subordinate and disadvantaged elements in Muslim society was established very early on. It is too soon at this stage to talk of Sunni and Shi'ite but the origins of later divisions can be found in the fast moving events of 632.

The choice of a title for the new leader was difficult. Clearly 'Prophet' was unacceptable. The earliest Muslims seem to have adopted two different titles. The first of these *Amīr al-Mu'minīn* meant Commander of the Faithful and represented the secular function of the ruler as ultimate commander of the Muslim armies. From the reign of 'Uthmān (644–56) if not before, the rulers were also styled *khalīfat Allah* or deputy of God on earth and it is from this that the English term 'caliph' is derived. This clearly meant that they laid claim to spiritual authority or, at least, to the authority to lead prayers and to make decisions on controversial matters of Islamic law and practice.[1]

The first four caliphs, Abū Bakr (632–4), 'Umar (634–44), 'Uthmān (644–56) and Ali (656–61) are conventionally described as the 'Rightly Guided' (*Rāshidūn*) because their rule is held by most Muslims to have been a golden age when the true principles of Islam were applied to government, for at least part of the time. Further lustre was attached to this era by the fact that it was the time of the great Muslim conquests in the Middle East, Syria and Iraq being conquered from 636, Egypt from 641 and much of Iran by 650. It was easy to link the success of Muslim armies with the piety of the rulers as a source of Allah's favour.

In reality the period of Rightly Guided Caliphs was much more fraught with tensions and anxieties than later tradition would have us believe. This is not a result of the failure of the political system but rather of the fact that it faced immense and probably unmanageable change.

The expansion of the territory ruled by the Muslims was accompanied by the equally impressive growth of those who claimed to be Muslims. Large numbers of Arabs and increasing numbers of non-Arabs who had never known Muḥammad and had converted too late to join the initial conquests now had to be integrated into the state. Three main, interconnected issues came to dominate the political life of the period. The first was how this enormous area should be governed, the second was the distribution of resources among the Muslims and the third was the choice of caliph and the powers the office should have.

Once again, two clear views emerged, although there was a continuum rather than a sharp break between them. There were those who maintained that the resources acquired at the time of the conquests belonged to those who had actually fought in the battles which had secured them, and to their descendants after them. They were forced to defend their gains from threats from two directions. At a local level there were later converts and recruits who bitterly resented the fact that they were excluded from the rewards enjoyed by other Muslims. From the other flank, the privileges of these early conquerors were challenged by caliphs and governors who wanted access to and control over the resources to establish an effective, even imperial system of government.

The method of choosing caliphs remained undecided. Abū Bakr had designated 'Umar as his successor and there seems to have been little opposition. These were very difficult times for the Muslim community. The death of the Prophet had been the signal for many Arabs to renounce their allegiance to Medina. Abū Bakr was forced to send out armies to defeat them and bring them to heel in a series of campaigns knowns the Ridda wars. These wars were hardly over when the first caliph died and the wars of conquest were only beginning to gather momentum. It was, in short, no time for a succession dispute. By the time that 'Umar died, assassinated by a Persian slave in 644, the position had changed out of all recognition; Syria, Iraq and Egypt were all conquered and Muslim armies were pushing rapidly through Iran. 'Umar had not designated a successor but he did make arrangements for one to be chosen. He appointed a group of six men, all well known figures in Quraysh who were to form a council or *shūra* to elect the new ruler. This was not really a representative body and large numbers of Muslims, including the *ansār* of Medina, were completely excluded. It was not surprising then, that the *shūra* chose one of its own number, the respected Qurashi 'Uthmān b. Affān as caliph.

The successions of 'Umar and 'Uthmān had, in fact, established two different precedents for choosing a caliph, designation by the previous caliph and choice by a electing council. The idea of hereditary succession had played no part in the debate.

The reign of 'Uthmān saw the beginning of serious dissension within the Muslim community. The fundamental cause of conflict was that 'Uthmān wanted to establish himself as a powerful ruler who could appoint and dismiss governors of the conquered provinces and collect any surplus revenue from these areas and have it taken to the capital in Medina. In order to put this policy into effect, he relied extensively on his kinsmen from Quraysh, some of whom had only joined the Muslim cause towards the end of the Prophet's life. He also emphasized the religious authority of his office by ordering the production of a standardized recension of the Qur'an and decreeing that all other recensions should be destroyed. There were not, it seems, great differences in the texts but, as with appointments and taxation, the real issue was the authority of the caliph.

These policies aroused considerable opposition, centred on a group of cities known as the *amṣār*, the most important of which were Kufa and Basra in the south of Iraq and Fustat or Old Cairo in Egypt. After the great conquests, 'Umar had decreed that the Arab tribes should not be scattered throughout the newly conquered lands but should be settled in new towns. Here they would live together and be paid pensions from the taxes collected from the subject peoples. This would mean that they would preserve their religious and cultural identity. It would also mean that the conquerors, most of whom came from Bedouin backgrounds, would become sedentary towns-people and so easier to contol and manage: becoming a good Muslim, it was made clear, meant abandoning the Bedouin lifestyle. The settlement in towns meant, of course, that these ex-Bedouin had lost their previous means of subsistence and were now very largely dependent on their pensions for their livelihoods. As conquerors and descendants of conquerors, they felt that they alone had the rights to the revenues of 'their' provinces and that they alone should choose the governors. They believed strongly that they were following the path of the pious 'Umar against the innovations of 'Uthmān and his Qurashi relatives.

In 656 these tensions came to a head and angry rebels, mostly from Kufa and Fustat marched on the caliph at Medina to demand reforms. There was a confrontation. Many of the notables of Medina kept their distance from 'Uthmān. Among them was Ali b. Abi Tālib, who was suspected by some of being in league with the dissidents. There were negotiations but the men of Fustat especially thought that the Caliph was acting in bad faith. In the end violence broke out and 'Uthmān was murdered sitting almost alone in his house reading the Qur'an.

The assassination of 'Uthmān was a traumatic event in the life of the Muslim community but it aroused many differing reactions. Among 'Uthmān's family, known as the Umayyads, there was a demand that the murderers be punished. Others in Kufa and Fustat thought that while the murder was regrettable, the murderers had been fighting to defend their rights and maintain the traditions established by 'Umar. In a sense, both parties had right on their side, but the two points of view were incompatible.

In the immediate aftermath of the disaster, Ali was chosen as caliph. He had been passed over when 'Umar and 'Uthmān had been chosen, partly at least because he was much younger than they were. Now his time had come and he finally became caliph. However what should have been the triumphant culmination of his career was marred by the circumstances of his accession. His attitude to 'Uthmān's assassination was, to say the least, ambiguous. His position was challenged almost immediately by two senior leaders of Quraysh, Talha and Zubayr, both well-regarded companions of the Prophet. Even more damagingly from Ali's point of view, they were joined by Muhammad's favourite wife, A'isha. They were determined that the leadership of the community should not pass out of the hands of Quraysh to the *ansār* and Ali's other supporters. They left Medina and went to Iraq, to try to gather support in the southern city of Basra. Ali was obliged to follow them. Talha and Zubayr failed to attract as many followers as they had hoped while the people of Kufa flocked to support Ali. Probably in December 656 there was a short decisive encounter in southern Iraq known to history as 'The Battle of the Camel' in which Talha and Zubayr were defeated and killed.

The Battle of the Camel had established Ali's position in the all important province of Iraq but it did not put an end to his problems. To achieve his victory Ali had been forced to leave Medina, which was never again to be the capital of the Muslim world, and base himself in Iraq. Furthermore, he had won his victory with the support of those militant elements in Kufa who had been implicated most strongly in the murder of 'Uthmān.

Many Muslims felt that Ali had been involved in the old man's death but none felt so strongly about it as 'Uthmān's family, the Umayyads. The Umayyads had owned estates in Syria before the coming of Islam and two brothers, Yazīd and Mu'āwiya, both sons of the Prophet's old enemy, Abu Sufyān, had played an important part in the Arab conquest of the area. First Yazīd and then, after his death, Mu'āwiya, had been governors of Syria. They had led expeditions against the Byzantines and had established close links with the leading groups of Syrian Arabs, both those who had lived there for centuries and those who had arrived at the time of the conquests. Mu'āwiya could count on their support in any encounter with the Iraqis.

Mu'āwiya did not reject Ali as caliph, but he did demand that the murderers of his kinsman 'Uthmān be brought to justice. This Ali simply could not do since he was dependent on their support. In 657 a military confrontation developed at a place called Siffin on the Euphrates in Syria between Ali and his followers, mostly from Iraq, and Mu'āwiya and his Syrians. A major battle was avoided when the Syrians appealed to the authority of the Qur'an, attaching leaves of the sacred text to their spears, and it was agreed that there should be arbitration between the two parties.

After the armies parted, Ali's position in Iraq began to deteriorate rapidly. Some of his erstwhile supporters left his camp in protest at the fact that he had accepted arbitration. Called Kharijites (those who go out) they developed a radical view of the caliphate and rejected the authority of both rivals. They believed that the caliph should be the most pious among the Muslims and that inheritance and membership of Quraysh were not to be taken into account. Some of them also held that those who sinned were not Muslims at all and should be killed with impunity. They became brigands, operating in small guerrilla bands and harassing both the Umayyads and their rivals.

By the time the arbitration took place, at Udhruh, now in southern Jordan, Mu'āwiya was strong enough to claim the caliphate for himself. Events moved swiftly: Ali was assassinated, for reasons unconnected with the dispute with Mu'āwiya in 661. Mu'āwiya moved into Iraq to assert his control.

The new Caliph took care to negotiate with the Iraqis. He made an agreement with Ali's eldest son Hasan that he would retire to Medina with a large fortune. He also made agreements with the *ashrāf* (pl. of *sharīf*), the chiefs of the main tribes settled in Iraq. They were allowed to rule the country as long as they accepted him as caliph. The *ashrāf* were powerful tribal leaders but their status owed nothing to Islam and everything to tribal custom. Many pious early Muslims believed that this was a reversion to the bad old days and that the elite should be chosen on religious merit. Iraqis were also given a free hand in Iran while Egypt was to be ruled by the man who had led the first conquest of the country, Amr b. al-As, who just happened to be a relative of Mu'āwiya's.

Mu'āwiya ruled with a light touch, relying on local elites to govern the provinces while he himself remained in Syria and led the *jihād* against the Byzantines. However, his death in 680 once more brought the question of the succession to the fore. He was determined that his own son Yazīd would succeed. As we have seen, hereditary succession was unknown in the caliphate and the proposal brought resentment against Umayyad rule to the surface. When Yazīd succeeded, he was faced by a challenge from Ali's younger son Husayn. Husayn was a son of Ali and Fatima and so a grandson of the Prophet himself. He had been staying in Medina when Mu'āwiya died but now marched across the desert with a few followers, heading for Kufa, where he hoped he could count on widespread support.

Before he could reach the city, he was met by troops sent out by the Umayyad, 'Ubayd Allah ibn Ziyād, governor, to intercept him. He and his small band were surrounded and soon massacred in October 680. The people of Kufa had not rallied to his support. This might have been just one more desert skirmish but because Husayn was his grandfather's grandson it had an impact which has lasted right down to the present day. Husayn became a symbolic figure, the holy martyr killed by impious oppressors. His sufferings are still commemorated among the Shi'a of Iran in passion plays and people still flagellate themselves as symbolic punishment for the people of Kufa who had failed to help him. The death of Husayn gave a powerful boost to all those who believed that political power should rest with the Family of the Prophet.

Yazīd only reigned for three years before dying of natural causes in 683. His death plunged the Umayyad regime into crisis and once again the Muslim community was bitterly divided about the choice of the new caliph. A number of candidates emerged, of whom the most impressive was Abd Allah son of that al-Zubayr who had been killed at the Battle of the Camel. He based himself in the Holy Cities while his brother Mus'ab went to Iraq. The supporters of the Umayyads were in complete disarray but eventually they decided on a man from another branch of the family, Marwān b. al-Hakam and his pious and talented son 'Abd al-Malik. At first Ibn al-Zubayr seemed to be well on the way to establishing himself as the generally accepted leader of the Muslims. However, it was once again social and political tensions in Iraq which undid him as they had undone Ali before.

In Iraq many of the indigenous people were starting to convert to Islam. They were often known as *mawālī* (sing. *mawlā*) meaning that they were clients of Arab tribes to whom they became attached on conversion. As Muslims they sought to take advantage of the privileges that older, Arab Muslims enjoyed, especially exemption from certain sorts of taxation. This was bitterly opposed by many of the old established Muslims who knew that their wealth and position were threatened. The *mawālī* in Kufa were encouraged to rebel against the government of Ibn al-Zubayr by one Mukhtār. Though Mukhtār came from a distinguished Arab family, he made the cause of the *mawālī* his own. He did not claim the caliphate for himself but encouraged them to acknowledge Muhammad, son of the Hanafite woman. The reference to his mother was important. Muhammad was a son of Ali but not by Fātima, so that, unlike his half-brother Husayn, he was not a direct descendant of the Prophet: descent from Ali was considered by some to be a good enough claim to lead the Muslim community.

Ibn al-Hanafiya took the title of *mahdi*, the first time it had ever been used in Islam. The word is often translated as Messiah and it implied one who came to inaugurate the rule of justice and true Islam. Mukhtār and his followers took over Kufa and Ibn al-Zubayr sent his brother to crush the rebellion which, in the end, in April 687, he did. Meanwhile the supporters of the Umayyads were picking themselves up and looking to re-establish their position. Under their new leader, 'Abd al-Malik, who took over on his father's death in 685, they first took Egypt with its rich resources. Then they embarked on the conquest of Iraq and in 691 the Syrian Umayyad armies led by the Caliph in person defeated Mus'ab ibn al-Zubayr at Dayr al-Jathālīq and entered Kufa in triumph.

The young Umayyad Caliph now began a series of reforms of government which were to have a profound effect on the administration of the Islamic world for centuries to come. He was aided in this by his right-hand man, the governor of Iraq and the East, al-Hajjāj ibn Yūsuf (d. 714). Under the Rāshidūn caliphs and Mu'āwiya the hand of central government had remained fairly light: the Muslims of the different provinces were more or less allowed to manage their own affairs as long as they pledged allegiance to the Caliph and forwarded a limited amount of money to him. 'Abd al-Malik put the Syrian army firmly in charge. In Iraq a new city was built for them at Wāsit, about half-way between the earlier garrison cities of Kufa and Basra. They were the effective policemen of Iraq and, to the fury of many of the Iraqi Muslims, they were paid out of Iraqi taxes. For the first time the caliphs had a standing army paid out of general taxation. The need to administer this new system led to the use of Arabic, to replace Greek and Middle Persian as the languages of administration. Everyone who wanted a government appointment now needed to be able to read and write in Arabic. Within a couple of generations, both Greek and Persian were in steep decline and even the Christians of Syria were using Arabic in their writings. The other main reform was the introduction of a new coinage, or rather, two new coinages, the gold dinar and the silver dirham. Both these were based on pre-Islamic Byzantine and Sasanian coinages but the old images were dropped. Almost all later Muslim coinages followed this example of having completely epigraphic coins without any images.

'Abd al-Malik's policies led to the development of a strong state, despite violent unrest in Iraq culminating in the major rebellions of Ibn al-Ash'ath in 700-1 and Ibn al-Muhallab in 720. Later Muslim writers sometimes accused the Umayyads of being impious but with the exception of the short lived caliph Walīd II (743–4) there is no real evidence of this and some caliphs, notably 'Abd al-Malik himself (685–705) and Hishām (723–43) were conscientious and God-fearing rulers. Their weakness was rather that they were dependent on the Syrian Arab army to maintain their rule and, in the end, it was not strong enough to sustain this role.

The Umayyads also presided over the last phases of the great Islamic conquests. In the west, Muslim armies conquered most of Spain and Portugal between 711 and 716. As in other parts of the Islamic world, the Muslim armies avoided the mountainous areas and the peoples of the Pyrenees and the mountains of Cantabria remained unconquered: it was from these regions that the Christian reconquest of Muslim al-Andalus was mounted. Instead, the Muslim armies went round the east end of the Pyrenees and raided deep into France. It was in central France that a Muslim expedition was defeated by the Frankish leader Charles Martel in 732 in what has become known as the Battle of Poitiers. In reality the defeat was far from decisive but it symbolized the end of Muslim expansion in Europe.

In the north east of the caliphate, the frontiers were extended beyond the Oxus. From their base at Merv (in Turkmenistan), Muslim armies led by the governor Qutayba ibn Muslim (705–15) set out to conquer Bukhara, Samarqand and the rich oasis of Khwarazm at the south end of the Aral Sea. The conquests were not easy and the Muslim armies were opposed by the Soghdian inhabitants of the cities and the Turkish nomads of the steppe lands. Nonetheless, by 913 Muslim armies had reached the Farghana valley (Uzbekistan) and the north eastern limits of the Muslim world were established. Transoxania remained frontier territory and it was from here that the Abbasids in the ninth century were to recruit their crack Turkish troops. At the same time, Muslim armies established some control over Sind (southern Pakistan) but this always remained a distant outpost, cut off from the rest of the Muslim world by the mountains and deserts of Afghanistan.

After Hishām's death in 743, resentments against Umayyad rule came to a head in many areas. In Iraq people still felt that the Syria-based regime had deprived them of their rights while in Khurasan, in the north east of the empire, many men, especially non-Arabs who had converted to Islam, felt that the Umayyads were distant and oppressive. The opposition crystallized around the old idea that if the caliph were to be a member of the Family of the Prophet then justice and a truly Islamic state would emerge. The question then arose of who would be included in the Family of the Prophet. The descendants of Ali were by now very numerous and it was by no means clear that any one branch had a better claim than any other. Then there were the descendants of other branches of the family, notably descendants of the Prophet's uncle al-'Abbās. In 740 Zayd ibn 'Ali, a great-grandson of Ali, led a rebellion in Kufa. As before, the Kufans failed to support the Alid claimant, the rebellion was easily defeated and the unfortunate Zayd was slain. However, the rebellion was important because of the arguments Zayd used to support his claim to the caliphate. He said that he was entitled to be considered as the true leader of the Family of the Prophet because he had seized the initiative and risen in revolt against the tyrants while other members of the Family had not. Some of his descendants were to pursue this claim in future generations and Zaydi imams established themselves in Yemen where they held power, intermittently, right down to the twentieth century.

The failure of the rebellion of Zayd ibn 'Ali meant that the initiative passed to another branch of the family, the descendants of al-'Abbās. Their claim to the throne was not without its problems, and when the Abbasids had come to power, they were obliged to restate and refine it continuously. They were not, of course, direct descendants of the Prophet and the original al-'Abbās had never himself converted to Islam, but as Muhammad's paternal uncle he was a senior member of of his kin. The Abbasids also claimed the succession on the grounds that the son of that Muhammad ibn al-Hanafiya who had been Mukhtār's *mahdi* had designated al-'Abbās's great-grandson, Muhammad ibn 'Ali as his successor. It was not really a very impressive claim because few Muslims accepted that Ibn al-Hanafiya's son was the true leader of the community and fewer still that his 'testament' was genuine. Later they justified their seizure of power by the Zaydi argument that they alone among the family of the Prophet had taken the initiative and been able to overthrow the Umayyads and avenge the deaths of al-Husayn and Zayd. This being the case, they deserved to be accepted as leaders by all supporters of the Family.

What was undoubtedly true was that the Abbasids had succeeded where all other members of the Family had failed. They were able to do this because of the support of the Muslims of Khurasan. While most people in Iraq seem to have held that blood descent from the Prophet was crucial, Muslims in Khurasan were more flexible. From about 720 small groups of people began preaching in the area in favour of 'a chosen one from the Family of the Prophet'. Spreading the word was a slow and dangerous process but in 747 open rebellion broke out in Merv, the capital of Khurasan. This was led by one Abu Muslim, who seems to have mobilized a large cross-section of the Muslims of Khurasan to support the cause. The rebellion seems to have been launched with the vague slogan of 'a chosen one' and it is not clear who, if anyone, knew that the Abbasids were involved.

The armies that Abu Muslim recruited among the warlike people of Khurasan were astonishingly successful. They rolled up the Umayyad forces in their home province and then drove them out of Iran. By the end of 749 they were in Iraq and had taken Kufa. It was at this point that the 'Abbasid family appeared. They had been in semi-exile in southern Jordan and now crossed the desert to meet up with their supporters. The exact sequence of events is obscure but it seems as if Abu Muslim's commanders in Kufa found the safe-house where the family were staying and took one of them, Abū'l-'Abbās to the mosque and proclaimed him as caliph with the regnal title of al-Saffāh. It was effectively a coup d'état which established the Abbasids and left all the other branches of the family of the Prophet out in the cold.

The proclamation of al-Saffāh also marked a change in the titulature of the caliphs. The Rāshidūn and the Umayyads had all reigned under their given names, 'Umar, 'Abd al-Malik etc. From the beginning the 'Abbasid adopted regnal titles, like Popes in the medieval west. The titles usually implied that the ruler was given victory of God (al-Manṣūr) or was a defender of the Faith. From the ninth century these titles were all active participles beginning with the syllable Mu which gives a confusing similarity to the names. These regnal titles remained in use down to the deposition of the last Abbasid Caliph of Cairo in 1517.

Al-Saffāh's position was confirmed by the swearing of oaths of allegiance in the mosque and the subsequent defeat and death of the last Umayyad Caliph Marwān II in 750. The 'Abbasids and their propagandists were adept at working out justifications for their seizure of power but the reality was that it had been accomplished by force. Just as the Umayyads had ruled through the Syrian army, so the early Abbasids ruled through the Khurasanis. They formed the garrisons which were stationed throughout the empire from Tunisia (Spain and the rest of the Maghrib were never part of the 'Abbasid caliphate) to Tashkent. The state they established looked very much like the Umayyad one with a new elite in charge and, while most Muslims accepted the new dispensation, a minority did not. Once again, dissent focused on the Family of Ali who many thought had been deprived of their rights to the caliphate just as Ali himself had been deprived by Abū Bakr and 'Umar after the Prophet's death. Much of the political debate of the first Abbasid century concerned relations between the ruling dynasty and their Alid cousins.

The first major confrontation came in 762 when the Alid Muhammad ibn Abd Allah, known as 'the Pure Soul', and his brother Ibrāhīm raised a revolt. Muhammad was something of a dreamer and hoped to follow the Prophet's example and establish an Islamic state based on Medina. The idea was hopelessly impractical. The Abbasid caliph al-Mansūr interrupted the routes which brought supplies to the Holy City from Egypt, many previously enthusiastic supporters deserted him and it only needed a small army to extinguish the rebellion and kill its leader. Ibrāhīm's revolt in Basra disintegrated when faced with the 'Abbasid regular troops. But the scale of support for the Alids had worried the 'Abbasids and the next caliph, who took the messianic title of al-Mahdī, made a serious effort to conciliate the Alids, offering them pensions and positions at court but not real power. Only a militant few who called themselves the Zaydiya after Zayd ibn Ali, resisted these blandishments.

The next Alid revolt in 786 was a much smaller affair and was easily put down by 'Abbasid troops, but it had long-term consequences. Two of the Alid leaders fled to outlying parts of the Muslim world to find refuge beyond the long arm of the 'Abbasid state. Yahya ibn Abd Allah went to Daylam, the mountainous land at the south-western corner of the Caspian Sea and his brother Idris went west to Morocco. Yahya was soon murdered by the 'Abbasids but the legacy of support for the Alid family remained strong in the area. Idris established a dynasty in Morocco who became the first independent Muslim rulers in the area. His shrine at Moulay Idris is revered to this day. Many adherents of the house of Ali made their peace with the 'Abbasids while still maintaining that real spiritual authority belonged to Ali's family. The Alid Ja'far al-Sādiq (d. 765), revered as the sixth Imam of the Shi'a, paved the way by teaching that following the doctrine of Ali did not necessarily entail armed uprising against the 'Abbasids. Ja'far's quietist teaching marked an important stage in the development of Twelver or Imami Shi'ism.

The reign of Harūn al-Rashīd (786–809) can be seen as the apogee of 'Abbasid power but it was followed immediately after his death by a prolonged and extremely destructive civil war between his sons, al-Amīn and al-Ma'mūn. This undermined the whole legitimacy of 'Abbasid rule. The execution of al-Amīn by his brother's followers spelt the end of the inviolability of the person of the caliph, their capital at Baghdad was laid waste by a long civil war and the Khurasani army was defeated and broken up.

Al-Ma'mūn showed his rejection of the old order by attempting to rule the entire caliphate from Merv in Khurasan, and faced with continuing opposition to his policies in Iraq, he made an even more radical move, adopting the Alid Ali al-Ridā as his heir apparent, so rejecting the 'Abbasid dynasty of which he himself was a part. There is no doubt that he hoped that this move would encourage popular support but he soon found that he was wrong. The 'Abbasids and the people of Baghdad were bitterly opposed while few of the Shi'a were convinced by this expedient gesture.

In the end lack of support in Iraq meant that al-Ma'mūn was forced to abandon this policy. In the autumn of 817 he decided to leave Merv. On the way his 'heir apparent', Ali al-Ridā was murdered near Tus by men who claimed they were obeying the caliph's orders. He was buried at a place which became known simply as Meshhed (Tomb) and his resting place developed into one of the great shrines of Shi'ite Iran. He was the only one of the Twelve Imams recognized by the mainstream Shi'a to be buried in Iran and, under the Persian form of his name, Ali Reza, has become almost the patron saint of the country.

In 817, however, that was all far in the future and al-Ma'mūn's renunciation of the Alid succession enabled him to re-establish himself in Baghdad, the home of his ancestors. The attempt at rapprochement with the Alids was not entirely abandoned, however. Mu'āwiya and the Umayyads were publicly cursed from the pulpits and the doctrine of the Mu'tazila was in some ways an attempt to bridge the gap between Sunni and Shi'i ideas of the caliphate. The main tenet of Mu'tazilism was that the Qur'an was created at a certain point in human history, the point when it was revealed to Muhammad. This was in opposition to those who held that the Qur'an had existed since the beginning of time but had only been revealed to Muhammad in his lifetime. This apparently obscure point of doctrine had serious implications. If the Qur'an was created at a certain point in time, it could presumably be interpreted by those with special authority and it was even possible that there could be a subsequent revelation which would modify it. Al-Ma'mūn claimed that as Imam as well as caliph (he was the first 'Abbasid to use the title of Imam), he and his successors were entrusted by God with making decisions about matters of Islamic law and practice. This was a position very close to that held by the Shi'ites, with the difference that they, of course, held that the Imam had to be a direct descendant of the Prophet. Clearly this view gave great religious authority to the Imam/Caliph.

This view was vigorously challenged by opponents who held that the Qur'an was inviolable and that matters of law and doctrine should be decided by reference to the Sunna of the Prophet, that is the record of his opinions and deeds as remembered and recorded in the multitude of Traditions which were lovingly collected and passed down. In this scheme of things, the power to make decisions lay effectively with the scholars, the 'ulamā' who collected and authenticated the Traditions and there was no role for caliph.

The issue might have remained one of academic debate if it had not coincided with the major fault lines in the Islamic state. Al-Ma'mūn and his successor al-Mu'tasim (833–42), no longer relied on the Khurasani troops settled in Baghdad to provide their elite forces. Increasingly their generals and favourites came from eastern Iran and their crack soldiers were recruited from the hardy Turkish nomad peoples of Central Asia, sometimes purchased as military slaves. The caliph al-Mu'tasim moved the capital from Baghdad to Samarra, some hundred miles to the north. Here he laid out a vast garrison city for his new army, far from the provocative and unruly people of Baghdad, and immense palaces for himself and his favourites. Meanwhile in the old capital, the Traditionists and the *ulamā* consolidated their hold on popular opinion, attracting support from those, notably the descendants of the old Khurasani army, who resented the fact that they had been supplanted and replaced.

Al-Ma'mūn attempted to enforce his theological views with an inquisition or *miḥna*. This examined all those who wanted any sort of public office to demand that they publicly accepted the createdness of the Qur'an. Most people accepted but a determined minority refused, even when faced with the threat of force. There were a few martyrdoms. It was the first time an Abbasid Caliph had openly asserted his right to make a binding decision about a major religious issue. In Western terms, he was claiming to be both Emperor and Pope. In the end, the Abbasids were obliged to abandon the attempt. The caliph al-Mutawwakil (847–61) gradually moved away from the position adopted by al-Ma'mūn and al-Mu'tasim. Mu'tazili beliefs were abandoned, the *miḥna* quietly dropped and the tombs of the Alid Imams were laid waste as the first three Caliphs were once more revered.

Al-Mutawwakil's change of policy went further than a change of ideology. He also seems to have tried to replace the Turks as the mainstay of his army and this was his undoing. In 861 he was assassinated, as he sat drinking with his intimate companions, by a group of Turks who felt that their influence was declining. They may or may not have been in cahoots with his son and heir al-Muntasir, who was also afraid that his position was being undermined.

It is hard to exaggerate the importance of al-Mutawwakil's assassination in the history of the caliphate. At the time of his death, the Abbasids were still as powerful as they had ever been. It is true that Khurasan and much of northeast Iran was effectively ruled by the Tahirid family but the Tahirids were inextricably bound up with the 'Abbasids. Apart from Khurasan, they ruled Baghdad and were important figures in the court at Samarra. Revenues were regularly sent from Khurasan to Iraq and were probably used to pay allowances and salaries in Baghdad. Under Tahirid rule, the province was more peaceful than it had ever been. It is also true that Spain and all of North Africa west of the modern Egypt–Libya border was now outside 'Abbasid control but Spain and most of the Maghrib had never been ruled by the dynasty and Tunisia had proved to be more trouble than it was worth. In the central Islamic lands, the grip of central authority was stronger than ever. In Egypt and Syria local elites had been replaced by Turkish cadres sent from Samarra. In Armenia and Azerbayjan recent campaigns had extended the rule of the caliphs into areas it had never reached before. The Byzantines were easily kept at bay.

In the nine years from 861 to 870 the power of the dynasty was almost entirely destroyed. In the late ninth and the beginning of the tenth century, the caliphs established themselves as regional powers in much of Iraq, Syria, and western Iran and even re-established a tenuous hold on Egypt for a time. But the caliphate was no longer a world power and everyone could see that the claims of the Abbasids to represent a universal caliphate were at best optimistic, at worst obviously absurd.

The long-term cause of the fall of the caliphate was the collapse of the rural economy of Iraq. According to ninth-century revenue lists, the alluvial lands of southern Iraq, from Baghdad to the Gulf, supplied the vast bulk of the revenues of the caliphs, four times as much as the next most productive province, Egypt, and five times as much as Syria and Palestine. By the ninth century, the Iraqi economy was in deep trouble. There may have been long-term factors to do with the salinization of the soil and other ecological changes but most of the damage was man-made. The long years of civil war which had followed the death of Hārūn al-Rashīd in 809 had seen bands of unemployed soldiers roaming the countryside, taking whatever they could lay their hands on, and warlords who moved easily from taxation to pillage. In these circumstances, no one was willing or able to undertake the long-term investments which the irrigation systems of southern Iraq required if the land was to remain productive. The restoration of 'Abbasid control by al-Ma'mūn may have halted the decline but it does not seem to have reversed it. After 861 different groups among the military were determined to get their hands on the resources of the area. In 865 there was a second, year-long siege of Baghdad when the supporters of the caliph al-Mu'tazz conquered the city and deposed al-Musta'īn. Both sides resorted to pillaging the countryside and breaching the irrigation canals to flood the land in order to prevent their opponents gaining military advantage. The re-establishment of a measure of stability by the caliph al-Mu'tamid and his brother al-Muwaffaq in 870 did not restore the position. Southern Iraq was ravaged by the long rebellion of the Zanj, slaves and others in the agricultural lands and marshes to the north of Basra. Despite some years of peace during the caliphate of al-Mu'tadid (892–902), the position deteriorated again during the chaotic reign of the caliph al-Muqtadir (908–932). The decay of the once flourishing lands of Iraq was typified by an incident in 935 when a military adventurer called Ibn Rā'iq, hoping to gain a temporary military advantage over a rival, breached the great Nahrawan canal which irrigated the flourishing towns and villages along the east side of the Tigris. The canal was never reconstructed and the settlements rapidly became what they have been ever since: dust blown ruins in a desolate landscape.

After al-Mutawwakil's death, there were five caliphs in nine years. Three of them were killed by the Turkish soldiers who were supposed to be their elite soldiers and guards. As different groups fought each other for control of the gradually diminishing revenues of the state, they humiliated and degraded the caliphs: in 866 al-Musta'īn had his head chopped off despite the fact that he had been given a clear and unequivocal amnesty and his body was buried at the roadside by passing strangers; in 869 al-Mu'tazz was tortured by being made to stand in the baking sun without any water before being locked in a small, airless chamber to die; in 870 al-Muhtadi was cut down by Turkish swords as he ran through the streets of Samarra trying to rouse the citizens to defend their caliph against the military. The prestige of the Deputies of God on earth never really recovered from this brutal onslaught and military leaders in the tenth century showed little compunction in following the example of their predecessors in deposing and murdering caliphs.

The Umayyads and early 'Abbasids had based their claims to leadership of the Muslim community on three main foundations. The first was the right they asserted to make decisions on matters of Islamic law and practice, the second was their role in leading the Muslims against the unbelievers, especially the Byzantines, and the third was providing leadership and protection to the *hajj*. Caliphs like al-Mahdi and al-Rashīd were careful to ensure the success of both *hajj* and *jihād* and to make sure that all the Muslims knew it. In the ninth century, these positions began to crumble. The ultimate failure to establish Mu'tazilism as the generally accepted Muslim creed spelt the end of the caliph's powers to decide questions of doctrine and these powers passed to the emerging *'ulamā'*. Al-Ma'mūn and al-Mu'tasim both led the *jihād* in person and made it clear that the campaigns against the Byzantines were a central part of their policies. Under al-Mutawwakil, 'Abbasid armies scored notable successes in Armenia, even though the caliph himself did not participate. The short-lived caliph al-Muntasir sent an expedition against the Byzantines immediately after his accession and expressed his intention of leading his armies in person. No subsequent 'Abbasid caliph led the Muslims against the ancient enemy. The leadership of the *hajj* was the last of the caliphal prerogatives to go. Hārūn was the last reigning caliph to lead the pilgrims in person, but throughout the ninth century the *hajj* was led by members of the ruling family appointed by the caliph. In the tenth century this changed suddenly. A group of Ismā'īli rebels called the Qarāmita (sometimes anglicized as Carmathians) drawn largely from the Bedouin of northern Arabia and Syria, attacked the pilgrim caravan on a number of occasions, massacring defenceless men, women and children. The caliphs seemed powerless to protect them. As a final indignity the Qarāmita stole the Black stone from the Ka'ba itself and took it back to their stronghold in eastern Arabia.

By the mid-tenth century the caliphate was in ruins. The material foundations of caliphal power had been destroyed and the ideological foundations of their position had been fatally undermined by their inability to perform the functions of the leader of the Muslims.

The decline of the Abbasid caliphate was hastened by the appearance of rival caliph-ates in the tenth century. There had, of course, been rivals for the caliphate before but these challengers had always intended to take over the universal caliphate, not to divide it between different caliphs. In 909, however, the Fatimid dynasty established them-selves in Tunisia and set up an alternative caliphate there. As their name implies, the Fatimids were, or at least claimed to be, descendants of Ali and Fatima and hence of the Prophet himself. In the late eighth century there had been a split among the supporters of the Alids after the death of the sixth Imam Ja'far al-Ṣādiq (d. 765). A minority claimed that one Ismā'īl was the legitimate successor and should rightly have succeeded his father. It is not clear how much support, if any, they had at the time but the memory of Ismā'īl was kept alive after his death and by the end of the ninth century a family in Salamiya in Syria were claiming to be his heirs. They were eventually forced to flee from their homeland and take refuge with the Berbers of Tunisia and Algeria who accepted their claims to political and religious leadership. With the support of these hardy pastoralists, they conquered Tunisia and proclaimed themselves caliphs.

The Fatimids' claim was based on hereditary right and they claimed God's support for what was essentially a semi-divine monarchy. They made it clear that they had inherited Ali's claims and his direct relationship with God. Although they were based in Tunisia, they claimed the universal caliphate, Tunisia was simply their temporary base until they conquered the rest of the Muslim world and established the rule of the Family of the Prophet throughout. In 969 they achieved the next stage of their programme when they conquered Egypt. Unlike Iraq, Egypt was a country of growing prosperity and the Fatimids benefited from the riches of the newly con-quered territory. Missionaries were sent out to Iraq and Iran to spread Fatimid propaganda and encourage Muslims to rise up against their existing rulers and proclaim their allegiance to the Fatimids. Some responded but the majority did not and there was never enough popular support to extend Fatimid authority over the eastern Islamic world.

Meanwhile a third caliphate emerged in al-Andalus, that is the areas of Spain and Portugal that were ruled by the Muslims. In 929 the Amir 'Abd al-Raḥmān III (r. 912–61) formally assumed the title of Commander of the Faithful. The caliphate of al-Andalus, or the caliphate of Cordova as it is more commonly known, did not, unlike the Fatimids, claim to be a universal caliphate but a regional one which acknowledged the legitimacy of other caliphates in other areas. 'Abd al-Raḥmān based his claim partly on the fact that his ancestors, the Umayyads, had been caliphs and he was simply reviving a title which had rightly belonged to his family. It was also a conscious rejection of the claims of the Fatimids in the Maghrib where the two powers competed for influence. 'Abd al-Raḥmān was in position to lead or protect the *ḥajj*, but he did fulfil other functions of the caliphate. In particular he made a point of leading the Muslims of al-Andalus in the *jihād* against the Christians of the north of the Iberian peninsula. Like the eighth and early ninth-century 'Abbasids, he too ensured that his leadership of the faithful was well reported in history and poetry. Like the Fatimids, he also began the minting of a gold coinage in his own name, something provincial governors and warlords did not do.

In the year 1000, then, there were three caliphates in the Muslim world, the 'Abbasids of Baghdad, the Fatimids, now installed in their new capital at Cairo, and the Umayyads in Cordova. The ideal of a single universal caliphate was a historical memory. The Fatimids and the Umayyads both ruled over substantial territories and the Fatimid caliphs of Egypt and Syria were certainly the richest and most powerful monarchs in the Muslim world. The 'Abbasids, in contrast, were mere shadows of their previous greatness. The military men who ruled the old 'Abbasid heartlands of Iraq and western Iran were Shi'ite Buyids. They made no effort to replace the 'Abbasids by members of the family of Ali but they certainly did not accept the spiritual authority of the 'Abbasids whose power now hardly extended beyond the walls of their Baghdad palace.

As Buyid power waned in the early eleventh century, the 'Abbasids began to reassert themselves, not as political leaders with armies to enforce their rule, but as spiritual heads of Sunni Islam. In 1029 the Caliph al-Qādir published a document known as the *Risālat al-Qādiriya*. In this he attempted, perhaps for the first time, to elaborate a Sunni creed. He asserted the legitimacy of the four orthodox caliphs, so countering the claims of the Shi'ites that Abū Bakr, 'Umar and 'Uthmān were usurpers who had deprived 'Ali of his rights. He rejected the Mu'tazilism of his own ancestors by condemning the doctrine of the createdness of the Qur'an. He also asserted that the traditions of the Prophet were to be accepted as the foundations of Muslim law. In taking this initiative, al-Qādir had reinvented the 'Abbasid caliphs as spiritual leaders of the Sunnis.

The political situation, on the other hand, became increasingly difficult for the 'Abbasids. In the 1050s the Fatimids seemed to be gaining ground in Syria and even in Iraq, where a military adventurer called al-Bassasīrī proclaimed his allegiance to the caliphs of Cairo. The 'Abbasid caliphate was only saved by the arrival of the Saljuq Turks. The Saljuqs, the leading family of the Ghuzz Turks, appeared in the Muslim world in the steppe lands of Kazakhstan at the beginning of the eleventh century. They were new converts to Islam and their first leader, Tughril Beg (d. 1065) seems to have embraced the Sunni faith with enthusiasm, perhaps encouraged by the hope that many people in Iran and further west would support him, barbarous Turk that he was, against the Shi'ite Buyids. He openly championed the cause of the Abbasids and his allegiance to them gave his power a legitimacy and a certain popular appeal which a Turkish nomad leader could never have received in his own right.

Tughril proclaimed himself protector of the caliphs and Sultan. The word sultan was commonly used in early Islamic times to mean 'the authorities' or 'the government,' an abstract noun. In the eleventh century Turkish rulers like the great Mahmud of Ghazna (998–1030) began to use it as a personal title, much as the English abstract noun 'Majesty' became the title of the person of the ruler. The assumption of this title allowed Tughril and his successors, notably the great Alp Arslan (1063–73) and Malik Shah (1073–92) to coexist with the 'Abbasid caliphs, the sultan representing secular power while the caliph provided legitimacy and an Islamic justification for Turkish power. It was now the Sultans who led the armies against the ancient enemy, the Byzantines, and more importantly against the heretical Fatimids.

In the twelfth century the power of the Saljuq Sultans declined, like that of the Buyids before them, and the 'Abbasids began to take advantage of the situation to reassert a measure of political power. The manifest failure of the Saljuqs to protect the Muslims against the invading Crusaders further undermined their credibility and the military men who inherited their power, like Nūr al-Din (d. 1174) and Salāh al-Dīn (Saladin) (d. 1193) looked to the 'Abbasids of Baghdad to give them titles and moral support. In this more relaxed political atmosphere, the 'Abbasid caliphs began to recover something of the secular power they had lost with the coming of the Buyids in 945. Caliphs like al-Muqtafi (1136–60) and al-Nāsir (1180–1225) created a small but viable state in central Iraq. It was a far cry from the glory days of Hārūn al-Rashīd but the 'Abbasids once more had an army to command and a state to rule.

All this was brought to an end with the Mongol conquest of Baghdad in 1258 when the city was sacked and the last 'Abbasid caliph wrapped in carpets and trampled to death by horses. It was the end to any hopes the ancient dynasty might have had to revive their power. The 'Abbasid name still had a certain resonance. In 1261 a surviving member of the dynasty was invited to Cairo by the Mamluk Sultan and the 'Abbasids were set up as religious dignitaries to give a veneer of legitimacy to Mamluk rule, as they had done to the Saljuqs before. The presence of the caliph helped the Mamluks to present themselves as the champions of Islam against he Crusaders and the Mongols. This time, however, there was no revival of their secular power. In 1517 the Ottomans conquered Egypt and the last 'Abbasid caliph, al-Mutawwakil III was carried off to Istanbul. It was later claimed that he had passed his rights on to the Ottoman Sultans who styled themselves as Caliphs as a result. They also took with them the insignia of the caliphate, including the mantle of the Prophet and the swords of the early heroes of Islam which can still be seen in the Topkapi Palace in Istanbul. The last Ottoman ruler Mehmet V Reshat abdicated as Sultan in 1922 but remained caliph until 1925.

The caliphs had lost their role as rulers of the Muslim world by the end of the ninth century. After 1258 they were no longer even local rulers. But the idea and the memory of the caliphs as supreme rulers who could unite the Muslim people under the banner of Islam remained a potent one, used by Arab nationalists in the nineteenth and early twentieth centuries and by Usāmah ibn Lādin in the twenty-first to inspire Muslims to recapture the glories of early Islam

NOTE

1   For a full discussion of the origin and implications of the title of caliph see P. Crone and M. Hinds, *God's Caliph* (Cambridge, 1986).

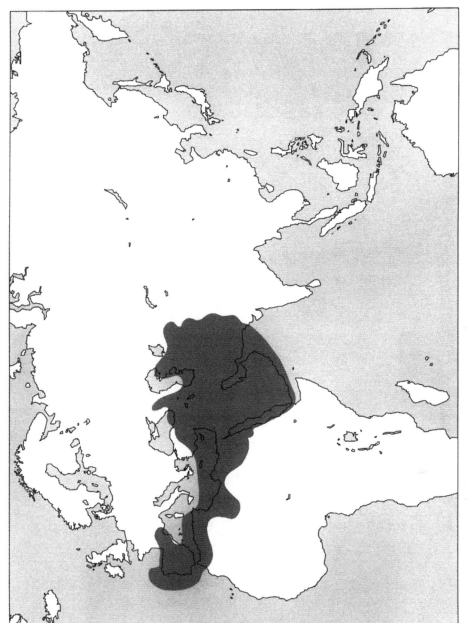

Map 3.1 The Middle East under the Umayyad Caliphate

PART II

Cultural Traditions and Social Structure

CHAPTER FOUR

The 'Ulama': Status and Function

Zouhair Ghazzal

Introduction: the Early Caliphate

The contention of this chapter is that the learned community in Islam ('*ulama*', s. '*ālim*) posited itself as a cohesive group only at specific historical junctures when new ruling dynasties came to power, dynasties which endeavored to rebuff the legitimate claims of old regimes, and used the ulama as a means to legitimate their political power. This strategy, however, materialized only at a high price: the ruling dynasty, whether claiming to be an inheritor of the venerable caliphate institution or not, had to relinquish all religious power to the body of specialists known as the ulama, and keep themselves restricted to the sphere of the political. This, however, represented a change from the more far-reaching power of the earliest dynasties. In effect, ever since the Umayyads took power in 661 amid the slaying of the fourth caliph 'Ali, both the early Sufyanids and late Marwanids, *pace* the Rashidun (the first caliphs and Companions of the Prophet), upheld a notion of the caliphate that was all encompassing: assuming both political *and* religious power. Indeed, the caliph was represented as *khalifat Allah* ("deputy of God on earth"). The early caliphs thus did not govern solely on the precepts of the prophetic *sunna* alone, but on *sunna tout court*, all kinds of acknowledged precedents and customs by the *umma*, the political Islamic community (Crone and Hinds 1986). By positing himself as God's representative on earth, relegating the prophet (with a small "p") to a secondary role, and claiming both religious and political power, the caliph enjoyed absolute power, one that sidelined the ulama to merely a consultative role. By the time of the late Marwanids, a body of "piety-minded" ulama begun to take shape, which was preaching for a universalistic Islam, one that was not based solely on its Arab tribal elements (Hodgson 1974, vol. 1). However, Umayyad caliphal polity could not afford relinquishing much religious power to the ulama, and kept them restricted to their own individual opinions, only for the purposes of consultation.

Even though the 'Abbasids (750–1258) did keep up with the official title of *khalifat Allah*, in practice the caliph's title subtly modified to that of *khalifat rasul Allah* ("deputy of God's messenger"), and both titles were kept in tandem in the literature. The change was indeed very subtle as it signaled a deep transformation in the institution of the caliphate. First, by positing himself as the "deputy of God's messenger," the caliph now was bound to the prophetic *sunna* (the sayings and doings of the Prophet and his Companions, what was to become the edited and textualized hadith). Second, knowledge (*'ilm*) of the sunna-cum-hadith became, by the first century of 'Abbasid absolutism, monopolized by the only legitimate religious body – the ulama – who originally, prior to their legal and juristic functions, were known as *ahl al-hadith* ("the people of the hadith"). And third, as religious power was relinquished de facto to the ulama, the caliph was rendered as caretaker of the political *umma*. In short, during the first century of 'Abbasid absolutism the division of labor between the political and religious began: while the caliph assumed the first, the ulama monopolized the latter.

My argument is that this polarization between politics and religion – the state and the ulama – became commonplace in Islamic history, and shaped polity as much as it shaped thought and praxis. Recognizing the polarization proves essential in understanding the nature of rebellious and oppositional movements to the legitimate caliphate, and the Sunni–Shi'i divide. The unification of the religious and political spheres remained an ideal guiding certain movements. For example, rebellious groups against the caliph (Kharijites, Imami Shi'is, Isma'ilis, Fatimids, etc.) usually came with their own lines of imams, or as was the case with the Kharijites, they thought that every Muslim had the legitimate right to become an imam. In other words, once the caliph was limited to his political role and relegated the religious to the ulama, he was challenged for not having assumed ultimate authority in both religion and politics, and imams emerged that endeavored to take both domains. The opposition to the legitimate caliphate relied on sunna and hadith – as the dominant ulama did – and interpreted them in such a way that would underscore their views. In short, the opposition – Shi'i or otherwise – went all the way back to the Rashidun and Umayyads, even though it seldom took them as models.

The polarization between religion and politics, and the concomitant autonomy of the ulama, was to be followed even among Shi'is. Thus, for instance, both the Safavids (1501–1722) and Qajars (1779–1925), and more recently, the Pahlavis (1926–79), all kept the ulama in their putative role of a "hierocracy," in the sense of a self-governed clergy that monopolized religion. Khomeini did no more than reclaim the non-separation of religion and politics in the persona of the juristic imam. In Shi'i mythology, however, the Twelver imams represented God's will on earth, while Khomeini's juristic faqih, who assumed both political and religious power, was no more than an intermediary between the Twelver imams and the umma.

Modern political movements such as Kemalism, Baathism, and Nasirism, either had to reduce the ulama's functions considerably (Turkey), or to bureaucratize them under the aegis of the state (Egypt and Syria). But in doing so, they inadvertently opened the way to radical Islamists in their claims for the "lost" caliphate of the Rashidun, which combined the political with the religious. In consequence, many of the radicals portray present-day Islamic societies as living in a *jahiliyya* ("ignorance"), while the praxis of the radical Islamist movements are portrayed in parallel to the secretive hijra ("migration") of the Prophet from Mecca to Medina in 622.

The 'Abbasid State and its Ulama

It is well known that in the first century of 'Abbasid absolutism many of the literary, legal, and artistic genres had taken shape and clustered around various rival schools of thought and *madhhabs* (legal schools). Such a global transformation ought to be seen in conjunction with caliphal authority ceasing to be the totalizing enterprise of the Umayyads, and that already in the first half century of 'Abbasid absolutism

(750–809), religious authority was a cooperative enterprise between the caliphs and the ulama (Zaman 1997). In effect, once the caliphate was stripped down to its mostly political functions, the ulama became openly in charge of the religious field. Apparently, the Umayyad caliphs could have enacted law (the so-called "caliphal law"), and decided which sunna and hadith to abide by; while the ulama might have been "consulted" whenever needed, but there was neither a joint venture between the caliphs and the ulama, nor did the latter institute a well defined corpus of scholarship.

If the shift towards the caliphal title of *khalifat rasul Allah* (deputy of God's messenger) had any significance, its effects could be perceived mostly in a re-centering of Islamic history around the persona of the Prophet and a de facto growth of the sharī'a-minded ulama. It was no coincidence therefore that the first systematic *siyar* (biographies of the Prophet) were drafted right after the 'Abbasid revolution in 750 by such figures as Ibn Ishaq (d. 768) and Ibn Hisham (d. 828). Furthermore, the hadith – whose quintessential art of selection (based on genuine *isnad* chains of transmission and authority) and editing pioneered by the legendary figures of Muslim (d. 875) and Bukhari (d. 870) – also began to be redacted in this period. The *sunna* of the Umayyad caliphs, which implied the canonization of *any* acknowledged customary practice by the community, and which might have proved crucial in the legitimation of the caliph's role, was subsequently narrowed down to the prophetic hadith. The sunna-cum-hadith, therefore, had to be compiled, edited and textualized systematically, for the purposes of both political power and the evolution of the law schools.

Legal and juristic reasoning, which by the first 'Abbasid century was under the ulama's monopoly, and provided legitimacy to the sharī'a-oriented state ideology, went through a parallel evolution to that of hadith. Thus, even though it is legitimate to speak of "caliphal law," no solid legal corpus materialized under the Umayyads. While formation of Islamic law goes back to the eighth and ninth centuries, according to recent scholarship, the dating of foundational legal sources, such as Abu Yusuf's *Kitab al-kharaj* and Malik's *Muwatta'*, has been shown to be different from the assumed time framework of the schools' founders, and their authorship has been questioned (Calder 1993). The leading foundational figures of the four Sunni legal schools (*madhhab*, pl. *madhahib*), such as Abu Hanifa (d. 767), Malik b. Anas (d. 795), Ibn Hanbal (d. 855), and Shafi'i (d. 820), all lived and taught in the first century of the 'Abbasid caliphate. The legal literature thus seems to have initially consolidated around the persona of the schools' "founding fathers," or the *a'immat al-madhhab* (the imams of the school), as they are often referred to. However, it was not until the tenth century that their opinions and sayings have been textualized by students and disciples, and canonized in the authorial texts that we are familiar with today. Again, recent scholarship has questioned the process of canonization of the schools, and their limitation to four only. In effect, a careful survey of the literature shows that the foundational texts – even those of the venerable Shafi'i – were neither of exceptional quality, nor were they necessarily more persuasive than others that were left at the margins and later forgotten (Hallaq 2001).

Be that as it may, what is of interest for our purposes is the *modus operandi* of the ulama's role, which became normative by the ninth/tenth century and which gave form and structure to the ulama's production of knowledge in the centuries that followed. We can understand this production of knowledge in terms of four observations.

First, the consolidation of the "proto-Sunni" ulama in the first half century of 'Abbasid rule defined the combination of hadith and fiqh (jurisprudence) as the two major activities of the ulama (Zaman 1997). In consequence, the corps of the ulama, now perceived as the only source of religious authority, gave political legitimacy to the 'Abbasid caliphs.

Second, "knowledge"-as-*'ilm* was to be limited to the combination of hadith and fiqh. Thus, even though the ninth/tenth centuries witnessed the flourishing of sufism, theology (*kalam*), interpretation of the Qur'an (*tafsir*), philosophy (*falsafa*), and the *belles-lettres* (*adab*) as autonomous traditions, nevertheless they were perceived as providing knowledge of another kind – *ma'rifa*. That kind of knowledge, *ma'rifa*, implied a mystical and/or philosophical knowledge of the divine, and a search of the inner truth (*bātin*) of being. While the knowledge of the ulama had originally been limited to hadith, when hadith became one of the four cardinal rules of the fiqh – together with the Qur'an, analogy (*qiyās*), and the consensus of the community of scholars (*ijma'*) – hadith compilation and interpretation could no longer be dissociated from the fiqh (Schacht 1950).

Third, it was crucial that the production of knowledge centered around acknowledged authorial traditions. That process began earlier in Sunni than Shi'i Islam, and clustered through the totemic figures of a madhhab's founders. Those were known as the "imams" of the school, a title that in Sunni Islam was generally restricted to leading religious and scholarly figures and had no political implications. The key point here is that by the tenth century the authoritative texts took almost exclusively the works of the founding fathers as their substantive starting point (*usul*, s. *asl*), while reducing the importance of the Qur'an and hadith, and establishing a hermeneutical tradition through the interpretation of the masters' opinions (Wheeler 1996). As layers upon layers of interpretations accumulated over the centuries, the ulama of the madhhab had to be categorized into *tabaqat* (s. *tabaqa*), sort of biographical categorizations of the ulama of the madhhab in terms of the importance (or lack thereof) of their contributions. The two broadest categories were the *mujtahid*s, or scholars who earned a reputation for independent reasoning, and the *muqallid*s, or the followers of the former. Gradually, the categorizations evolved into a complex "juristic typology," which by the Ottoman sixteenth century included seven hermeneutical layers of different brands of mujtahids and muqallids (Hallaq 2001: 14–17).

Finally, fourth, the cooperative enterprise between caliphs and ulama since the early 'Abbasids apparently prevented the ulama from addressing the issue of state power directly. As this cooperation survived under various forms up to the Ottomans, political representation remained limited to the caliphs, sultans, and princes whose dynasties took hold of state power, while the ulama maintained their monopoly over religious and legal affairs. Such an arrangement did not leave much room for alternative representative civilian bodies to emerge and create a counter-balance to the combined power of the state and the ulama. In consequence, no theory of state and "civil society" emerged in the political writings of Islamic civilizations, and the literature remained at a pre-theoretical level, preaching the virtues and symbols of caliphal/sultanic power (Azmeh 1997: 113).

In the wake of the Shi'i Buyid conquest of the 'Abbasid capital in 945, and the subsequent rise of the Seljuks in 1055, the caliphate disintegrated and officially came to an end amid the devastating Mongol takeover of Baghdad in 1258. However, both the Buyid "Shi'i century," and the Seljuk sultanate that followed, witnessed a revival and consolidation of the Sunni madhhahib, their schools (*madaris*, s. *madrasa*), and the foundation of sufi hostels (*khaniqat*). The ulama, who survived from their own endowments (waqfs) and stipendiary positions (*manasib*, s. *mansib*), acted independently of political authorities, and were reluctant to address public issues (Ephrat 2000: 8–9). By the time of the Seljuk sultanate (1055–1194), the process of the transmission of knowledge through the madaris and the authority of a teacher-cum-author became well instituted, even though it maintained all its informal qualities of master–disciples teaching: the personal authority of the individual scholar had more impact and meaning than any abstract body of knowledge; the *ijaza*, a personal certificate conferred by the teacher to his disciple, entitled the latter to teach a certain text; and, finally, the book (*kitab*) "represented a continuity and unbroken oral communication, transmitted even further by the author" (Ephrat 2000: 69).

The autonomy that the ulama maintained up to the Seljuks seems to have deteriorated in the middle Ayyubid (1175–1265) and Mamluk (1265–1516) periods. Amid the threat of the Crusades (1099–1299), the patrimonialism of the Ayyubids and Mamluks gave rise to the military patronage state. With the growth of the *amirs-a'yān* (military princes and notables) system, and at a time when "military households inserted themselves into the social life of the city [Damascus]," "Amirs and rulers made use of madrasas and dar-al-hadith for purposes that had little to do with education" (Chamberlain 1994: 54, 57). Thus, the militarization of the system meant that the stipendiary positions (manasib) of the ulama had to be patronized, if not feudalized (*iqta'*), by amirs and rulers. Needless to say, by the twelfth/thirteenth centuries, the evolution of Islamic societies and civilizations took a different direction from their European counterparts on the other side of the Mediterranean. In southern and western Europe, the literati that emerged in the public sphere of the Italian city-states and central France questioned the power of princes and state, and proposed remedies against abusive political power in order to protect "civil society."

To underscore that point I would like to briefly trace a comparison between Ayyubid and Mamluk military patrimonialism with southern and western Europe of the high Middle Ages. Recent research (Bartlett 1993; Moore 2000) provides indications of a "first European revolution" between ca. 950 and 1200 which restructured the early feudalism of the Carolingians under Charlemagne and his heirs. In effect, the early feudalism of duties and assignments of the year 1000 was still old-fashioned in that grants came from the imperial bureaucracy down to subdued feudal lords. It was the societal dynamism that erupted in the eleventh century, and in which the Crusades played a big role, which irreversibly modified the feudal system from one that was dominated by an imperial state and bureaucracy to one where various institutions – primarily the church – began a process of grant distributions. The newly formed groups and relations were institutionalized within legally protected systems of duties and hierarchies. The producers of knowledge – professors, scientists, jurists, artists and priests – were differentiated into categories and disciplines and their knowledge assessed along epistemologies and methods of inquiry within each discipline, which eventually led to the formation of the early "universities" of the high Middle Ages in the thirteenth century. Cities were chartered so as to attract more people, and the Italian city-states witnessed the growth of powerful merchants and bankers, and the foundations of modern political thought. More importantly, all such groups "connected" with one another in terms of their hierarchies, respective duties, and the knowledge that they produced. Such "connections" were to insure that there would be no abuse of power, and hence no arbitrariness, from the upper echelons of society. The mutual duties, ranks, hierarchies, landholding patterns, and offices gradually became institutionalized and legally protected the more Europe moved into a clearly differentiated system of groups and duties.

Thus, while in the Islamic Mediterranean military patrimonialism was the norm,

> A general characteristic of kingship in western and southern Europe in the twelfth century was the growth and intensification of the connections ... by which kings transmitted their will to local communities ... guidelines and measures passed on from above to competent agents at local level ... careers and interest groups formed at the beginnings and ends of these routes of administrative traffic ... were the means by which local societies could acquire statehood. Without such connections and without their local officials and advocates kingship was forced to remain distant and sporadic ... irrelevant for the mass of agricultural population. (Karl Lyser in Moore 2000: 194)

Populations had to be individualized, meaning that the individualities of the subjects (citizens) had to be recognized and legalized, disciplined, and subjected to power relations. The gradations of power had to find their place in respect to one another to eliminate arbitrary power and factionalism. By contrast, in the Islamic Mediterranean, populations were not individualized as in the European model, and thus the individualities of the subjects (citizens) were not recognized and legalized, disciplined, or subjected to power relations that would render military patrimonialism less abusive.

The Ottoman Reforms

The Ottomans, who adopted Hanafism as their main legal source, "bureaucratized" the ulama, created the function of Shaykh al-Islam, and had their trustworthy muftis draft fatwas in congruence with state policies. The major contribution of the Ottomans, however, was in their promulgation of a set of secular state laws known as the *qānūn* (often referred to as the regional *qānūnnāme*), and to which the ulama might have added significant contributions. By the seventeenth century the sultan's imperial household lost its old luster, and the *devsirme* system that supplied slaves to the imperial harem, bureaucracy, and military, became inefficient, while the old tax-farming *timār* system began a long process of disintegration, paving the way to the *iltizām*. Herein lie the crucial factors behind the ascendance of the *a'yān-ulama-multazim* class in the provincial cities.

It would not be incorrect to describe the eighteenth and nineteenth centuries as "the age of the a'yān," in which the ulama played a predominant role as scholars, jurists, judges, preachers and sufis. Those were the last two centuries of Ottoman rule in which the ulama maintained their classical functions: (1) surviving within informal networks of a'yān, merchants, and aghāwāt (rural notables), as in medieval times, the ulama were emasculated in their autonomy; (2) remaining part of the a'yān, the ulama survived from their waqfs and land grants, whether public or private; and (3) producing literature that was in continuation with the established canon, in particular the fiqh and sufism, the ulama did not bring major structural breakthroughs.

Throughout the Ottoman period the provincial urban ulama were networked to and competed with individuals and families who lived off various land grants and waqfs. Such patrimonial and prebendal networks did not function institutionally but on a personal and contractual basis. The ulama thus were not protected by any institutional framework as such – not even their own madrasas and various stipendiary positions – but had to compete for mansibs, land grants, waqfs, and privileges granted to the elites.

That was the ulama's *fin de siècle*. In the transition that brought the Fertile Crescent to colonial rule, a couple of points are worth underscoring. First, the 1858 Land Code brought "private property" semi-officially to many a'yān families. Paradoxically, however, the privatization of property only reduced the power of the a'yān by subjugating them to the policies of the imperial bureaucracy. In the old system, contractual settlements and property rights were manipulated within the jurisdiction of the sharī'a courts, providing judges and a'yān considerable room to ensure the transfer and devolution of their properties without much state interference. In the new system, however, ownership was controlled more thoroughly, and taxed accordingly. Second, the semi-official privatization of ownership went hand-in-hand with the bureaucratization of many of the a'yān's and ulama's key functions through the local councils of the Tanzimat reforms (1839–56), which, again, implied greater restrictions and a further loss of autonomy. Third, with the new nizami ("secular") courts and the restriction of the sharī'a courts to personal status matters, the ulama lost much of their power over the status of land and contractual settlements.

An Institution of Higher Learning: the Azhar

When the Baghdad caliphate was under the Buyids (945–1055), religious learning institutions in North Africa that were closer to colleges and "universities" than the regular madrasas flourished. In effect, religious institutions such as the Zitouna, founded in Tunisia in 734, the Qarawiyyin, founded in Morocco in 859, and the prestigious al-Azhar, founded in Fatimid Cairo ca. 950, were much larger than the regular madrasas of the Fertile Crescent and other parts of the Islamic world, and had broader and more demanding curricula (Zeghal 1996: 19). But the main difference probably resides in the fact that such institutions of higher learning were designed originally by the state bureaucracy, while the madrasas were for the most part autonomous from state interference. Such was the case of al-Azhar, which was designed by the Shi'i Fatimids in the mid-tenth century as a propaganda machine to foster the shift towards Shi'ism as the new state ideology. The Azhar only returned to Sunnism under the Ayyubids (1174–1252), and remained pretty much the same under the Mamluks (1252–1517). In all such instances, the Azhar continued as a powerful tool for state ideology, and provides an example of an institution of higher learning that was directly financed and monopolized by the state bureaucracy. Apparently, following the Ottoman occupation of Egypt in 1517, sultan Suleiman the Magnificent (the Lawgiver) (r. 1520–66) requested that the Azhar be headed by a Shaykh, and by 1522 the Egyptian judiciary, which the Azhar nurtured, became controlled by the imperial bureaucracy: a single Hanafi main judge replaced the traditional four madhhabs (Dsuqi 1980: 10–13). Overall, in the three centuries in which they ruled Egypt (1517–1798), the Ottomans had the ulama survive on their own through the ubiquitous waqf system, and the Azhar did no better.

After a brief Bonapartist interlude, Muhammad 'Ali (r. 1805–49), in line with his modernizing and centralizing policies, transformed the nomination of Shaykh al-Azhar into a direct prerogative of political power, a step that even the Ottomans with their so-called bureaucratization of the ulama had not dared. Such a step followed the disintegration of the traditional madrasas, which de facto implied more power to the Azhar. Nineteenth- and twentieth-century Egypt represents a major case of early modernization – which even preceded the first Ottoman Tanzimat (1839–56) – and which went hand-in-hand with the state control of religious institutions. To be sure, Egyptian religious modernization, though much less radical than the Kemalist reforms that swept Turkey in the 1920s, nonetheless represented both a precedent for the colonial and postcolonial Arab world, and a norm that was to be followed soon. From Muhammad 'Ali to Nasir (r. 1952–70), there was an overt state policy to assimilate the ulama into the state bureaucracy. That was not a bureaucratization of the ulama per se as much as a policy of keeping them at the mercy of statist institutions. It is as if the modern state, beginning with Muhammad 'Ali, considered semi-autonomous groups of ulama as a threat to its own existence. Such policies of assimilation, however, were more the outcome of the emergence of a modern secular public sphere, and had less to do with an internal evolution within the religious sphere. In effect, in the *ancien régime,* be it Mamluk or Ottoman, the ulama could act independently from the state, and more importantly, their thoughts and actions could not be scrutinized from other lay groups. With modernization, both state and ulama joined other parties competing for the public sphere and its discourses, and even under authoritarian regimes, they are the object of scrutiny and criticism. Moreover, ever since the appearance of militant and reformist Islamic movements, the religious field is beyond the official ulama's claim to hegemony. It would not be that far fetched, therefore, to perceive the modern association of the state and the ulama as a *mariage de raison:* the ulama hope to maintain that old privileged position as the sole spokesmen of religion and its genuine technicians, while the (secular) state would like to shade its reformist policies with religious coloring.

To be sure, the founding of the Muslim Brothers in 1928 by Hasan al-Banna, pushed the body of the traditional ulama, mostly associated with al-Azhar, into a slow process of fragmentation. A direct challenge confronted the Azhar in 1928 when the Muslim Brothers proposed a political reform based on the traditional notions of Islam. Soon, and side-by-side with the official ulama of al-Azhar, appeared on the public scene the lay intellectuals (*intellectuels laiques*) and those associated with the Muslim Brothers, both of whom raised accusations against the traditional ulama for their incapacity to renovate. In fact, under the Monarchy (1923–54), the Egyptian ulama were already such a sociologically diverse group, that the state found no better solution but to associate itself with the Azhar. But at the margins of the official ulama (mostly subsidized by the state) stood other groups of peripheral, oppositional, and militant ulama, some supportive of the Muslim Brothers or other related "societies."

Nasir, therefore, inherited a sociologically diverse group of ulama, which he thought ought to be addressed at two interrelated levels. On the one hand, he went much further than the toppled Monarchy in reforming the Azhar and subjecting it to more coercive statist policies. On the other, the Muslim Brothers, now under severe persecution from the state, had to go underground for several decades (1954–70), until Nasir's premature death in 1970, a situation that culminated in 1966 with the arrest and execution of their main ideologue, Sayyid Qutb.

Just after the Free Officers revolution in 1952, Nasir initiated a series of reforms that were intended to impose more state control over society: agrarian reforms imposed limitations on large properties; the abolition of the sharī'a courts in 1956 and the concomitant unification of the Egyptian legal system under a quasi-secular civil law; the abolition in 1952 of all private waqfs (*waqf ahlī*); and the nationalizations that swept the banking and industrial sectors by the late 1950s and early 1960s. All such statist measures, however, which for the most part were also adopted in Baathist Syria and Iraq, were a big gamble since they irreversibly damaged the consensus between the nascent bourgeoisie and the state, transforming the state into the largest capital holder. In the interim of the two Arab–Israeli wars of 1956 and 1967, such a heavy burden proved more and more impractical as the state was hit with one financial crisis after another. Nasir, therefore, was left with the dubious option of turning his state apparatus into a machinery that attempted to control society by force.

In parallel to the socio-economic reforms, the Nasirist regime sought an "Islamic legitimation" whose initial intention was not a "secularization" of society, but rather to assure a form of religious control by the state. Besides the abolition of the sharī'a courts and the family waqfs, the Azhar was the next target. Thus, statute 603 (1961) invalidated statute 26 (1936) that had prescribed the autonomy of al-Azhar and its related institutions. In consequence, the head of al-Azhar became a presidential appointee, and the resources of all Azharite institutions were directly tied to the state through the ministry of awqaf. As Shaykh Muhammad al-Bahī sarcastically observed, "It's the [Free Officers] revolution that has finally reformed the Azhar, because its Shaykhs did not want any reform" (Zeghal 1996: 28).

The Muslim Brothers flourished at the fringes of the traditional ulama, whether Azharites or otherwise. With the state seeking its own "Islamic legitimation" through the control of the traditional circle of the ulama, mosque preachers, shaykhs and saints of sufi turuqs, teachers and militants, rose to marginalize the official Azhar ulama. Besides operating within a different praxis, the peripheral ulama – for lack of a better term – are not limited to the interpretation of the sharī'a and knowledge of the fiqh. Indeed, their discourse is more like an exercise of "*bricolage*" and collage, which does not derive its legitimacy solely – as is the case in the conservative juristic discourse – from the madhhab's *modus operandi*. The Azharites are mostly from rural origins who aspire through their religious education for a higher status, and even though their education is no longer limited to theology and fiqh – and, more importantly, even though they do not necessarily graduate as shaykhs – they nevertheless remain socially perceived as the conservative group of ulama providing legitimacy to the state and ruling elite (Zeghal 1996: 99). By contrast, militant Islamic groups are not limited to the ulama and shaykhs, and recruit all kinds of preachers and lay intellectuals among their ranks. Profiting from the weakness of civil society and the ineffectiveness of the postcolonial nation-state, and receiving funds from multiple sources, the Islamists have manifested an ability to move swiftly from the private to the public, blurring the lines between civil society and the state. Having graduated for the most part from the state universities, the majority of Islamists feel free to mix the political doctrines of Ibn Taymiyya (d. 1328), Mawdudi, and Sayyid Qutb, with modernist doctrines from the social and natural sciences. Large factions of society thus are brought together through a militant discourse that ignores traditional distinctions between private and public, state and civil society, and gender and generational hierarchies.

Before closing this section on the Egyptian ulama, a brief comparison with their Algerian counterparts might be in order. The Algerian case represents both striking similarities and major differences from the Egyptian one. In Algeria's late and bloody revolutionary struggle for independence against the French colonizers in 1962, the ulama and its patron Shaykh 'Abdul-Hamid Ben Badis became de facto allies with the Front de Libération National (FLN), both of which heralded an Algerian nationalism. Then, with the independence in hand, the ideology of the FLN worked out a "nationalist" discourse of Islam, attempting to hijack political Islam from Ben Badis and his association. This nationalization of Islam went hand-in-hand with the nationalization of agriculture and industry, all of which were framed in terms of an anti-western and anti-liberal discourse (Labat 1995: 63). In contrast to Egypt, Algeria thus represents a different perspective in at least three respects. First, like most Arab societies, its body of ulama is not structured by well defined institutions that could be monopolized easily by the state. Second, its agrarian, industrial, and banking statist reforms came at least a decade later than Egypt, and directly affected the cohesion of the ulama whose traditional clients were both rooted within the urban bourgeoisie and the rural landed middle class. Third, the ulama, having fought for independence within the framework of the nationalist FLN ideology, invested some of their resources in the postcolonial state institutions, in particular in the educational field, and pushed for an Arabization of the curricula.

The main difference with Egypt, therefore, is that Algeria inherited a postcolonial situation where the state acted in association with a powerful group of "neo-reform-ist" ulama, who managed to infiltrate in the educational institutions, seeking a complete re-Islamization of society. Since the early days of president Houari Boume-dienne (r. 1965–78), a statist Islam came into being, supported by an official "clergy" trained in madrasas specifically designed to make explicit to the masses the broad state policies regarding Islamic nationalism, and the agrarian and industrial reforms. When Chadli Bendjedid came to power in 1979, he even opted for a re-centering of the state policies around basic Islamic values, to the detriment of the "socialist options" that formed the essence of his predecessor's program. However, the violence that pushed Algeria into a civil war since the late 1980s only reveals the failure of the state's efforts to dominate the Islamic discourse, as the unassimilated paramilitary Islamist groups have benefited largely from the non-cohesiveness of civil society. The "socialist" and "Islamist" state policies were by and large a gross failure.

The Iranian Shi'i Ulama

We have noted that in Sunni Islam the body of ulama, even though its origins go back to the late Umayyads, only coalesced in the first two centuries of 'Abbasid absolutism. For the Shi'is, however, the path proved more tortuous and uncertain. Having seen their first three imams – 'Ali (r. 656–61), and his two sons, Hasan (d. 669), and Husayn (d. 680) – slaughtered by the rival Sunni Umayyad clan, which later became the hallmark of Shi'i mythology, the Shi'is had to develop a religious theology that demarcated them from the dominant Sunnis, and that was reminiscent of a moving diaspora in exile. Unlike Sunni Islam, the "origins" of Shi'ism were to be modeled not around the Prophet's government between Mecca and Medina (622–32), but around the Twelvers' infallible imams. The disappearance of the twelfth imam in 873/4, said to live in a state of occultation (*ghayba*), has freed the Shi'i community from the need of a "visibly" present political and religious authority, bypassing possible fragmentations along rival political lines. Since the late ninth century, various doctrines emerged regarding the eligible authority that would assume the functions of the hidden imam, two of which predominated. The first, the Akhbaris, rejected the authority of a mujtahid imam – one who would deliver his own independent reasoning over crucial matters – as incompatible with the authority of the imams. The other, the Usulis, accepted the authority of independent reasoning (*ijtihad*) as essential for the survival of the community under the guidance of an imam. The Usulis thus have adopted a similar position to the rationalist Hanafis (the official legal school under the Ottomans) who acknowledged that their mujtahids shared that unique power to delve into the *usul* ("substance") of their doctrine.

For our purposes here, it is worth noting that the body of Shi'i doctrine, and the concomitant rise of the ulama, took shape at specific historical junctures when new ruling dynasties came to power. For instance, it was under the Shi'i Buyids (945–1055) that major Twelver jurists articulated their thought and elaborated themes of Shi'i fiqh (Choueiri 1990: 26), while under 'Abbasid absolutism the general Shi'i attitude was one of "denial of legitimacy with a quietistic patience and abstention from action" (Algar 1969: 2). More importantly, it was "from the Safavid period [1501–1722] onward that one may meaningfully talk about the evidence of a body of Shi'i ulama" (Algar 1969: 5). If this hypothesis is valid, the first body of Shi'i ulama was then formed more than six centuries after its Sunni counterpart, which underscores the main hypothesis of this chapter that the ulama as a group – as distinguished from individual scholars developing their own doctrine – only developed concerted forms of thought and action in conjunction with new dynasties needing their legitimation. It could be that the Safavids, who were originally rooted in sufi turuqs, thought to replicate the Ottoman Hanafi model of a body of ulama at the disposal of the state, hence their choice for an Islam that would differentiate them from their prestigious competitors.

Be that as it may, the ulama under the Safavids were faced with a dilemma, namely that Twelver Shi'ism, with its doctrine of the hidden imam, inherently contradicts the legitimacy of the state. The Twelvers believe that only through the return of the hidden imam will religious and political legitimacy reign in the world. Thus, and even though an official "hierocratic" clergy emerged as the outcome of Safavid rule, the ulama kept a low profile vis-à-vis the state. The Safavids for their part constructed an image of an absolutist ruler as the representative of the hidden imam, which de facto implied the domination of the ulama by the kingly power.

If the theocratic nature of the Safavid state eclipsed the power of the ulama, and relegated them to the dubious role of *conseillers du prince,* that was definitely not the case under the Qajars (1779–1925). The Qajars, who were of nomadic origin, badly needed the ulama as a source of religious legitimation. Eventually, the Usulis won, and the mujtahid jurist could construct the *ratio legis* of shari'a law and the fiqh through an independent process of reasoning (*ijtihad*). Like their Ottoman neighbors, the Qajars eventually managed a dual legal system in which the ulama had a significant role: while the latter were the interpreters of religious law, the state retained a parallel system of administrative justice based on custom (*'urf*), a duality that survived until the introduction of the first Civil Code in 1911.

Under the Qajars, the biggest debate that challenged and split the ulama (as it did among the Iraqi Shi'i ulama under Ottoman rule), was constitutional reform. The difficulty for the ulama in the Constitutional Revolution of August 1906 was the idea of constitutional checks and balances that the monarchy would be subject to through an elected body of representatives. Under the two Pahlavi shahs (1926–79) the relationship between the ulama and the state was more strained. However, in this case, the conflict was not so much over theological and juridical issues, as over the aggressive agrarian reforms, and their underlying liberalism, which were pursued systematically by the Pahlavis. Moreover, the Pahlavis had distanced themselves from Shi'i Islam and promoted a secular ideology whose discourse was articulated around pre-Islamic images of Persian (Zoroastrian) kingship.

Land ownership and reforms became crucial for both shahs. Mohammad Gholi Majd rebuffs Ann Lambton's argument that historically most of the land in Iran was owned by large landowners, and argues that "much of the agricultural land in Iran was the property of small landowners, whose numbers were far greater than has been realized" (Majd 2000: 8). In a nutshell, the Pahlavi shahs miscalculated the importance of small to medium landownership, and the links that the ulama had nurtured with rural land-owners, not to mention the clergy's own reliance on landownership, all of which led to the Islamic revolution of 1978–9 and the sudden end of 2,500 years of dynastic rule.

Beginning with the tormented rule of Reza Shah Pahlavi (1926–41), the ulama suffered a setback from the prestige they had painfully gained under the Qajars. They did not attempt any confrontation with the first Pahlavi shah, however, as they did decades later with his heir and son. To proceed with his agricultural reforms, Reza Shah began targeting both landowners and ulama, underestimating the alliance that was to be forged between the two. Even the predominant nationalism and liberalism that swept Iran in the interwar period up to the 1950s did not encourage any vast grassroots movement of ulama and small landowners, against the ruling dynasty. Instead, only the US-engineered coup against Mosaddeq's government in 1953 pushed the ulama and lay intellectuals alike to look for an alternative discourse.

Like his father, Mohammed Reza Pahlavi (1941–79) underestimated the coalition of forces, disenchanted by national liberalism and foreign interference, that in his case would topple his regime. In spite of the ulama's leading role in the Islamic revolution of 1978/9, it remains to be seen why and how Shi'i ideology attracted such large portions of the population. From the ulama themselves, to the landowners, merchants, army officers, and lay intellectuals, the social and political spectrum was very broad indeed. Why, then, did Iran, in less than a decade, shift from a modernist national liberalism towards a Shi'i ideology?

In hindsight the answer appears to be grounded in the decree of 9 January 1962, that prompted the redistribution of land and imposed limitations over large rural properties. Even though similar measures had been tried in Egypt during Nasir's 1952–61 land distribution program, and in the Baathist agrarian reforms in Syria and Iraq in the late 1950s and 1960s, Egypt's ulama had been much too subdued to the state to take any action. Moreover, the Egyptian Islamist movements neither had the prestige of the official ulama, nor were they linked close enough to the small and middle landowners to start any opposition of their own. By contrast, Iran inherited from the Safavids and Qajars a semi-official Shi'i clergy, which maintained its own independent channels for survival. Needless to say, the opposition of the ulama to the land reforms became of pivotal importance. Earlier, the Grand Ayatollah Borujerdi, the highest learned authority and the sole religious guide, had declared in 1960 his unequivocal opposition to land distribution. That was soon followed by Ayatollah Khomeini's fatwa: "Islam respects the principle of private ownership, and no authority has the right to confiscate someone's property, or transfer the property to another, without the consent and the free will of the owner" (Majd 2000: 205).

In the Iranian Shi'i tradition, beefed up by centuries of Usuli doctrine, the jurists (faqihs) were the ones to decide on legal and political matters through their own independent reasoning. Khomeini forged the notion of "the guardianship of the jurisconsult" (*wilayat al-faqih*) to buttress the other equally valid notion of "the source of religious knowledge" (*marja' al-taqlid*). Regarding land reforms, Khomeini argued in his fatwa that only the jurist holds that rightful authority to confiscate and distribute land. By undermining land distribution on both religious and national grounds, Khomeini initiated a strategy that would win the hearts of the clergy and laymen alike.

Even though the clergy had found itself under attack since the days of Reza Shah, "the ulama's political unity against the state was a post-1963 phenomenon" (Moaddel 1993: 5). That unity, however, does not alone explain the success of the Islamic revolution in 1978–9. Considering that lay intellectuals, merchants, bazaaris, landowners, army officers, all played a crucial role in advancing the Islamic Shi'i alternative to the Pahlavi monarchy, the "unity" of the revolutionary movement was indeed polymorphous—and, indeed, it is the Shi'i alternative, and the discursive consolidation that it enabled, which made Khomeinism possible.

The Iraqi Shi'i Ulama

Although the Safavids defeated the Mongols in 1508 and took control of Iraq, their rule did not last very long, and by 1534 it was the turn of the Ottomans who had already occupied Greater Syria and Egypt since 1516–17. There was, however, another Safavid interlude in Iraq in 1623–38, prior to the Ottoman comeback. The Ottomans lost power once more in 1704, but this time to the Mamluk Pashas, prior to re-establishing a full control over the Iraqi provinces in 1831. By that time, however, the Ottomans were determined to control Iraq through a process of "centralization" – a policy whose outlines became more manifest all over the Empire with the Tanzimat (1839–56, and 1856–76). Clearly, the Iraqi provinces posed more of a challenge to the Ottoman authorities than the rest of the Fertile Crescent. For one, the Shi'i population had grown considerably relative to the Sunni Kurds in the north and the Sunni Arabs in the middle, due to the massive conversion, late in the eighteenth century, of the southern tribes to Shi'i Islam. Shi'ism seems to have provided a better religious ethos for the tribal elements, which was connected to the accessibility of Shi'i sayyids in cities like Najaf and Karbala.

For another, Ottoman control over the Iraqi provinces since the defeat of the Mongols had been erratic and incomplete, leaving the southern Shi'i cities and their tribal elements at the mercy of their ulama and sayyids, who intermittently forged strong bonds with their Iranian counterparts. Under the Safavids, and more so with Qajar rule, the body of Iranian ulama had attained a degree of cohesiveness and organization hitherto unknown, which directly affected the Shi'i centers of learning in Najaf and Karbala. Only the Sunni ulama in cities like Baghdad had some loyalty to the Ottomans, and even that came with a cost.

For a long time, a similar theological and juridical division characterized the Iranian and Iraqi ulama. On the one hand, Akhbaris, with their belief of the supreme authority of the imams and their rejection of independent rational reasoning (*ijtihad*), left little room for the legitimacy of the state. For that reason alone, the weakening of the Safavids in the second half of the seventeenth century de facto implied the rise of Akhbarism. Once they were freed of the power of the state, the ulama could give more weight to the traditions of their imams, and perceive themselves as heirs and "representatives" to the imam. The ideal ruler "should be both a Sayyid and a senior jurisprudent" (Litvak 1998: 13). That leaves little room for rulers who did not grow from within the corps of the ulama. With the weakening of Safavid power, "the 'ulama' emerged as a hierocracy, that is, an establishment relatively independent of the state" (ibid.).

On the other hand, the Usulis, who were much closer to Hanafi rationalism in their belief in a juristic imam who could deliver opinions (*ahkam*, s. *hukm*) and fatwas based on his own independent reasoning (*ijtihad*), dominated in nineteenth-century Qajar Iran and had a tremendous influence on the Iraqi clergy. In effect, the Usuli doctrine, by limiting the imam to his juristic and religious duties, acknowledged the ruler as a political entity independent of the imams' jurisdiction. The Usulis were, therefore, very close to the proto-Sunni ulama of the first century of 'Abbasid absolutism in their cooperative division of labor between the rulers and the ulama. The main difference, however, is that Shi'is generally believe in the guardianship of the jurist (*wilayat al-faqih*), who represents the imam, and acts as an intermediary between the imam and the umma. That single designated jurist would have a greater authority than the ulama as-a-whole (Litvak 1998: 49). Shi'is also believe in a general guardianship of the ulama (*niyaba 'amma*), where the corps of the ulama represents the imam. Usulis portrayed the non-religious ruler as an intermediary figure between the imam and the jurist. By contrast, Khomeinism denies such a division, and combines the religious and political in the guardianship of the jurist, which is close to the notion of *khalifat Allah* that surfaced among the Umayyad caliphs and legitimized their political and religious authority.

Iraqi Sunni and Shi'i ulama protected themselves within endogamic systems of marriage, so that both would fit within the Weberian notion of status groups (*Stande*), which implies a group that lives *for* political privileges rather than *from* politics. If the Ottomans managed – at least until the Young Turks revolt in 1908–9 – to keep the loyalty of both a'yān and ulama (and at that time the two groups overlapped) through a gradual replacement of the iltizām grants with a semi-private property system (the *tapu*), the picture on the Shi'i side was altogether different. In effect, the Shi'is were also affected by the 1858 land reforms and their consequences, but very differently from their Sunni counterparts. The Shi'i ulama and sayyids of the four major southern religious Iraqi cities did not receive many grants from the Ottoman imperial bureaucracy and relied on their own internal system of religious taxes, the *khums*, one-fifth of a person's income.

Second, once the Ottomans attempted to weaken the tribal factions by granting lands to their leaders or by turning one against the other, the role of urban and tribal sayyids became more pronounced, so that since the adoption of Shi'ism by most of the tribal factions by the end of the eighteenth century, the sayyids gained accessibility to the tribes. Third, Shi'is considered the Ottoman sultan illegitimate and had their eyes open to neighboring Qajar Persia which, by the turn of the century, was going through its own constitutional crisis not much different from that of the Ottomans. Moreover, southern Iraq became the natural home of the Shi'i ulama once their Iranian counterparts gained more autonomy under the Qajars. By the end of the eighteenth century, southern Iraq thus hosted the bulk of Shi'i resistance whether from Arab or Persian origins, and Shi'ism, by contesting the legitimacy of both the Ottomans and the Qajars, was more radical than Ottoman Sunnism.

But while Sunnis looked with hostility at the Young Turks for fear of losing property rights and nobility status, the "liberal mujtahids" in Najaf played a pioneering role in the constitutional Persian crisis, and the Young Turks sympathized with the Persian constitutionalists. The Shi'i ulama reasoned on two interrelated principles: (1) the constitutional principles overlapped with Islamic shari'a law; and, (2) the ulama perceived themselves as the "general representatives" (*na'ib 'amm*) of the hidden imam. Those two principles undermined the rule of both Ottomans and Qajars as "unconstitutional." Thus, the ulama found a "natural" role for themselves as the legitimate representatives of the hidden imam, and hence created a role for themselves within a system of representations to which they identified (Luizard 1991: 272–3).

As the Iraqi views grew in tandem with the Iranian ulama, they were not that doctrinally different, throughout the twentieth century, from their Iranian counterparts. The only major difference was political: when Iran shifted to a Pahlavi regime, Iraq was under a British mandate that imposed a Hashimite monarchy (1920–58). Such a difference should not be underestimated, considering the sufferings that the Shi'is experienced since the demise of the monarchy by the military coup of 'Abdul-Karim Qasim (1914–63).

To begin, landownership and key governmental and bureaucratic positions were in the hands of the Sunni Arab minority. Such was the case under the Ottoman Tanzimat, and remained so with the British mandate and the Hashimite monarchy. While Iraq went through major land reforms only a couple of years before Iran, both's Shi'i clergy's arguments were almost identical. Having only small investments in waqf endowments in the shrine cities (Litvak 1998: 35), the Iraqi clergy received most of its funds either from landlords or from its own informal networks. In consequence, the land reforms were not received well among the Shi'i clergy, and the ulama "declared that land reform, because it involved confiscation of property, violated Islamic law" (Wiley 1992: 33). The six million donums, which by July 1959 had been redistributed to smaller landowners and peasants, tremendously affected the finances of the Shi'i ulama.

Some of the Shi'i ulama already were organized into political parties, probably as a preemptive measure to contain both the Iraqi Communist party (ICP) and the Muslim Brothers. The Hizb al-Da'wa al-Islamiyya ("call to Islam") was instituted in 1957 by Muhammad Baqir al-Sadr (1931–80), who like many other Shi'i ulama, after the return of the Baath in 1968, was persecuted and later assassinated in 1980, just a year after Saddam Husayn became president and the beginning of the Iran–Iraq War.

Under the Baathist regime the Shi'i community was targeted systematically, routinely tortured, assassinated, and exiled. In 1968 the Baathist regime confiscated what was left of the waqf endowments in the holy cities, and banned the traditional religious ceremonies. Another problem that the ulama faced was the large drop in their enrollments: from 12,000 students in the early 1900s, down to only 600 scholars and students in 1977 – even though such a drop cannot be solely attributed to the ruthlessness of Baathism, as only 6,000 students were enrolled in 1918, the first year of British rule, and 1,954 by 1957, right before the Hashimites were deposed by the military (Wiley 1992: 74).

Conclusion: the Pitfalls of the Modern Nation-state and the Ulama's Crisis

Islamic dynasties in all their historic and geographic variations did not manifest any willingness for a deep and structured control of "society." In fact, the state was an agency on its own whose ability to rule, collect taxes, rents, and surtaxes, determined its success for survival. Up to the later Middle Ages and the Ottomans, the relationships between military rulers, the bourgeoisie and the common people, were at the same time very loose and coercive. Various societal institutions, including those of the venerable ulama, persevered autonomously on their own without any "disciplinary" actions from the state. As Ira Lapidus has argued persuasively, the common people were left on their own, mired in violence and impotence (Lapidus 1984: 143).

The modern postcolonial state, therefore, has inherited an impossible situation where, on one side, society is organized along networks that protect it from the inefficiencies and coerciveness of a heavily bureaucratic system (Singerman 1995), while at the same time, modernization requires the nation-state gain full control of "civil society" through disciplinary techniques. While the western world was able to adopt those techniques centuries ago, it was not under a rationale of direct coercion that currently compels the Middle East (Giddens 1985).

The postcolonial state did no better than to coerce the public sphere, transforming the ulama into state employees. However, movements such as Baathism and Nasirism were short sighted in that, pace Kemalism, they were neither aiming at secularization per se, nor did they persuasively devise societal policies to address the long standing historical issue of the lack of cohesiveness of civil society. When opposition movements such as the radical Islamists began emerging in the colonial era of the 1920s, it was the new post-Ottoman civil society, with its middle-class professionals and national-liberal complacent élite, which was targeted. Realizing that Islam as an ideological system cannot be put aside, the nation-state tried a "nationalistic Islam" to beat the radicals at their own game. Thus, Numayri's Sudan, Sadat's Egypt, and Chadli's Algeria, all engaged major constitutional changes to the administration, the judiciary, and education system. The nation-state, however, strained with financial, economic, and political structural problems, has run out of steam; and the more it finds itself in a deadlock, the more it resorts to arbitrary coerciveness.

NOTE

I would like to thank Brian Appel, Mario D'Amato, Christopher Gilbert, and Peter Finocchiaro for comments on an earlier version.

CHAPTER FIVE

Shī'ism

ROBERT GLEAVE

The term Shī'ism covers a multitude of political and religious movements which have appeared at different points in Muslim history and had varying degrees of political and religious success.[1] The movements described in this chapter may all be called Shī'ite, but the political programmes, the religious doctrines and the extent of ideological coherence of each movement varies and any generalisation as to the character and constituent elements of 'Shī'ism' or 'Shī'ite' groups is far from simple. If there is one factor which all the movements described here share, it is probably best described as 'loyalty' to a member (or members) of the family of the Prophet Muhammad (*ahl al-bayt*). The loyalty Shī'ites profess may be political – that is, a descendant or relative of the Prophet Muhammad is proposed as the rightful political leader of the community; it may be religious – in the sense that one or more of the Prophet's relatives are believed to produce authoritative answers to questions of religious doctrine; or it may be devotional – in that the believer's experience of the divine is entirely identified with (or channelled through) a member of the *ahl al-bayt*. These different types of Shī'ite loyalty (political, religious and devotional) are rarely mutually exclusive. Most Shī'ite communities have, over time, combined elements of these different types of loyalty. The political, for example, has often been conjoined with the religious or devotional aspects of loyalty.[2] This hybridism makes Shī'ism a particularly varied historical phenomenon, and hence a particularly interesting aspect of Islamic history.

Both Sunnis and Shī'ites claim Prophetic precedence for their version of the ideal Muslim community, and hence the intra-Muslim polemic between these two traditions often centres on interpreting Muhammad's actions and statement. The basic issue tackled within the polemics concerns whether or not the Prophet Muhammad designated a successor, and if he did, whom he identified as this successor. Sunni polemicists and historians have, in general, adopted one of two positions. First, there are those who argue that Muhammad did not appoint a successor, though he did indicate a legitimate mechanism whereby an individual becomes the leader of the Muslims. This has some Quranic basis.[3] The mechanism was known as the 'oath of allegiance' (*bay'ah*), a quasi-sacred vow of fealty made to an individual by a tribe (or its leaders). Muhammad himself expanded the Muslim community through acts of fealty such as this, and for some Sunni writers, the *bay'ah* is the principal process whereby power becomes legitimate. Hence after the death of the Prophet, the leaders of the various tribal elements of the Muslim community came together at the meeting hall (*saqīfah*) of the Banū Sā'ida and pledged their allegiance to Abū Bakr.[4] Abū Bakr's political legitimacy flowed from this oath, though his worthiness for office flowed from his personal qualities (of piety and trustworthiness) and his close association with the Prophet Muhammad.

Other Sunni writers argue that some form of designation did take place, though the Prophet never simply declared his designated person. For example, when the Prophet on his deathbed was unable to lead the Muslims in prayer, he delegated the task to Abū Bakr. By doing so, it is argued, Muhammad was designating Abū Bakr not merely to lead the prayer: the delegation of this task was an indication of the Prophet's designation of Abū Bakr as his political successor.

Shī'ite writers also argue that there was clear designation before Muhammad's death. Muhammad, they argue, designated his cousin 'Alī b. Abī Ṭālib as his successor. The most famous occasion of designation is the 'event of Ghadīr Khumm' during the Prophet's farewell pilgrimage in 632. Muhammad took the hand of 'Alī and said, 'He to whom I am the patron, 'Alī is his patron also.'[5] This statement (or variants thereof) is found in both Sunni and Shī'ite sources.[6] Shī'ite writers deduce that the Prophet is expressing the pre-eminence of 'Alī, and designating 'Alī as his successor. Shī'ite writers cite this and other traditions of Muhammad's (such as his saying, 'I am from 'Alī and 'Alī is from me') as evidence of 'Alī's superiority. Non-Shī'ite writers, such as Ahmad b. Hanbal (d. 855), do not, in general, deny the historicity of the events of Ghadīr Khumm.[7] They argue, though, that the terms patron (mawlá) or even friend (walī) do not necessarily infer political succession.[8]

'Alī was not to gain political power until 656, and only after Abū Bakr, 'Umar and 'Uthmān had held the office of the caliphate (khilāfah). Sunnis recognise 'Alī as 'rightly guided' (rāshid), and of similar status to his three predecessors. Shī'ite writers declare the first three caliphs to be usurpers who denied 'Alī his rightful role. In so doing, they openly disobeyed the wishes of the Prophet. For them, loyalty to 'Alī is an element of 'true', 'original' Islam. By refusing to recognise 'Alī's primacy over all other Prophetic companions, the Sunnis have deviated from the message of the Prophet Muhammad.

'Alī eventually assumed the caliphate in the midst of controversy. 'Uthmān had been murdered by rebels in 655. Whilst 'Alī himself was not implicated in his murder, he was accused of not pursuing the criminals. His five-year reign as caliph was dogged by uprisings and rebellions against his authority.[9] Three in particular stand out as significant. First, 'Alī faced an immediate challenge from an alliance of the Prophet's companions, Talhah and al-Zubayr, and one of the Prophet's widows, 'Ā'ishah. The companions were probably angry at their exclusion from 'Alī's new administration, and 'Ā'ishah had always harboured a personal animosity towards 'Alī. 'Alī defeated their forces at the 'Battle of the Camel' in late 656.

The second opposition force was more serious. 'Uthmān's aggrieved relatives rose to challenge 'Alī's right to rule as caliph. Mu'āwiyah, 'Uthmān's cousin and governor of Damascus, had built a local power base in Syria. The two forces met at Siffīn, and after a standoff, the battle began. Troops on both sides wished to avoid excessive bloodshed; tribes and clans were divided between the two armies. 'Alī agreed to arbitration (taḥkīm). A group of 'Alī's own supporters objected to his decision to negotiate, and broke away. 'Alī had forfeited his right to be caliph by this decision, and they were no longer bound by their oaths of allegiance. These 'withdrawers' (khawārij, or 'Kharijites') posed a third threat to 'Alī's rule. The arbitration process became protracted; 'Alī was forced to deal militarily with the Kharijites at the Battle of Nahrawān (658). As 'Alī's power base drained away, his support was restricted to southern 'Irāq. He was eventually murdered by the Kharijite, Ibn Muljam, in the mosque at Kūfah in 661. There followed a period of unease as 'Alī's eldest son, al-Hasan, at first claimed the caliphate for himself, but later abdicated, reaching an agreement with Mu'āwiyah. For the following century, the caliphate remained within Mu'āwiyah's clan, the Banū Umayyah.

During al-Hasan's life the supporters of 'Alī did not rise in revolt. However, loyalty to 'the people of the house' – the descendants of the Prophet, or, more broadly, the descendants of the members of the Prophet's clan – gave rise to a series of later rebellions. Since the *ahl al-bayt* inspired both political and religious loyalty, Prophetic family members were believed to have insight into questions of religious doctrine and law. Some Shī'ah viewed particular members of the *ahl al-bayt* (usually termed Imams) as conduits for divine grace, inspiring a devotional loyalty amongst the Shī'ah.

The 'origins' of these different sorts of loyalty to the *ahl al-bayt* have been widely discussed. Within the Sunni historical tradition, one finds a popular motif that Shī'ism was invented by 'Abdallāh b. Saba'.[10] According to these accounts, Ibn Saba' was a converted Yemeni Jew. During 'Uthmān's caliphate, he was responsible (in part) for the forces which led to 'Uthmān's murder. He also propagated the idea that 'Alī had been designated by the Prophet as his legatee (*waṣī*). After 'Alī's death was announced, Ibn Saba' is reported to have expressed the belief that 'Alī was not dead, but would return (*raj'ah*) as a messianic figure. Such a story does demonstrate that Sunni historians felt the need to 'explain' the existence of heretical Shī'ism within the Muslim empire.[11]

The second explanation for Shī'ism is proposed by W. M. Watt. Watt argues that the list of 'Alī's supporters provide an 'origin' for Shī'ism. Most of 'Alī's early supporters came from Yemeni tribes. This contrasts with Kharijites who mostly came from 'northern' Arabian tribes. The northerners came from an environment of nomadic egalitarianism where 'all males of a tribe were roughly equal'[12]: Kharijite ideals of equality appealed to northerners. The Yemenis, however, 'came from South Arabia ... where for a thousand years kings had succeeded one another according to a dynastic principle and had been regarded as having superhuman qualities'.[13] Watt is not suggesting that there was any conscious attempt to 're-create a former polity'. Rather, the models of community organisation in the two areas of Arabia influenced the forms of loyalty in the early Muslim community. The basic ideas of Shī'ism were, then, encouraged to develop by the culture of pre-Islamic Yemen. Others have argued that Shī'ism was a reflection of ancient Iranian influence on early Islam.[14]

The most influential of recent scholars of early Shī'ism, Wilferd Madelung, argues that central Shī'ite ideas, such as the political and religious authority of the Prophet's family, are already indicated in the Qur'an. Previous prophets are described designating family members and kin to leadership roles. This, Madelung argues, was the preferred model of Muhammad himself. Shī'ite ideas formed part of the original Muhammadan (and hence Muslim) vision of society. Shī'ite themes were present in the comunnity during Muhammad's lifetime. Madelung's views have been criticised by several commentators following the publication of his influential *The Succession to Muhammad*.[15] 'Alī's conflict with Abū Bakr was 'political in the modern sense of the word'.[16] That is, whilst the idea of the political authority of the Prophet's family may

Plate 5.1 'Ashura, one of the most poignant anniversaries in the Shī'ite calendar, commemorating the murder in 681 CE of Husayn, the Prophet's grandson
Source: © *AlHayat* Newspaper, London

have been present in the earliest years of Islam, the more religious and devotional aspects of Shī'ite loyalty emerged only later in Muslim history.

Amir-Moezzi argues that early Shī'ism was an 'esoteric' doctrine of divine power, channelled through an Imām.[17] Amir-Moezzi argues that the rationalisation (and politicisation) of doctrine is a later development. For him, Shī'ism was originally characterised by a devotion to a saviour through whom one could gain knowledge of God. This individual, the early Shī'ites argued, was to be found amongst 'Alī and his descendants.

A number of Shī'ite rebellions are worthy of mention, not only because they exemplify the strength of Shī'ite feeling in the early Muslim community, but also because the doctrines espoused in some of these uprisings were later incorporated into the various expressions of Shī'ism, attaining doctrinal stability and surviving to the present day.

When 'Alī's son al-Hasan died in 669, most Shī'ah, it seems, shifted their hopes to al-Hasan's brother, al-Husayn. It was natural that the next Shī'ite leader should be al-Husayn rather than one of al-Hasan's children since they had both known the Prophet. After al-Hasan's death, a group of Kūfan Shī'ah wrote to al-Husayn in Madīnah asking him to lead them in their claim for justice against Yazīd, Mu'āwiyah's iyah's successor as the Umayyad caliph. Al-Husayn was, it is reported, hesitant at first,[18] though he eventually set off from the Hijaz to Kūfah. Yazīd, aware of his plans, sent a force to intercept al-Husayn's caravan. At Karbalā' in south 'Irāq, the two forces met and al-Husayn's small band of supporters were brutally killed in the battle.[19] The survivors were taken to Damascus in chains. The martyrdom of al-Husayn by Yazīd's forces at Karbalā' in 681 is commemorated each year at the festival of 'Āshūrā' (10th Muharram). The power of the story to move and inspire has inevitably led to certain embellishments, as it is told and retold. The principal elements of the story of al-Husayn, however, are not in doubt, and its effect on Shī'ite consciousness is of great importance for understanding modern Shī'ism.[20]

More serious attempts to destabilise Umayyad rule were launched in the following years. The Kūfan Shī'ah, racked with guilt over their failure to aid al-Husayn, gathered the following year. They visited al-Husayn's grave to weep and mourn and were about to set out to avenge al-Husayn's blood, when their camp was attacked. The attack on the 'penitent ones' (tawwabūn) seemed to further galvanise Shī'ite opposition to the Umayyads. Later, in 685, the Arab al-Mukhtār of Kūfah led a revolt in which he seized Kūfah for a period of two years. He claimed to be acting on behalf of Muhammad b. Hanafīyah. Ibn Hanafīyah was the third son of 'Alī, born of a Hanafite woman (and not of Fātimah). He was lauded by al-Mukhtār as al-mahdī (the 'rightly guided'), appointed by God as leader of the Muslims. Al-Mukhtār gained support from non-Arab clients (mawālī) through his call for equality between Arab and non-Arab. It is from al-Mukhtār's call that Shī'ism has been 'explained' as the Islamisation of Iranian ideas by Arab Sunni writers. Kūfah was a Shī'ite city state for two years, until the uprising was crushed in 687. The survivors of al-Mukhtār's rebellion, lead by Kaysān, went underground and began a period of intellectual gestation. The Kaysānīyah (Kaysān's followers) developed doctrines such as the occultation of the Imām (ghaybah).[21] They believed Muhammad b. Hanafīyah had not died, but had merely gone into hiding, and that he would return (raj'ah) to establish a messianic rule.

The leader of the fourth major Shī'ite rebellion of the Umayyad period, Zayd b. 'Alī, was a grandson of al-Husayn. He led a revolt in southern 'Irāq in 740. The rebellion was unsuccessful and Zayd was killed. His supporters later went on to form the Zaydīyya. His son Yahyá was to head another unsuccessful revolt in Khurāsān in 743. Yet another uprising occurred in 744 when 'Abdallāh, a descendant of 'Alī's brother Ja'far, was proposed as Imām by some Kūfan Shī'ites. His attempt to establish rule over Kūfah and other 'Irāqī cities was unsuccessful. He was forced to flee, first to Isfahān (in Iran, gaining some success), and eventually to Herat.

The major opposition to the Umayyads was, then, found amongst the followers of Muhammad's descendants and relatives (the Banū Hāshim). When Abū Muslim, a Shī'ite activist in eastern Iran, openly revolted against the Umayyads in 747, he did not immediately name his Imām. The movement gained military success and in 749 the forces entered Kūfah in a mood of messianic expectation. Most of the Banū Hāshim refused to accept the Imāmate when offered by Abū Muslim.[22] Eventually the descendants of Muhammad's uncle, al-'Abbās, accepted, and the forces proceeded to extinguish the remains of Umayyad power in the Middle East. The conquerors made their camp at the small village of Baghdad, making it the capital of the newly proclaimed 'Abbāsid empire. Though the 'Abbāsids had come to power with Shī'ite support, and their early propaganda emphasised the caliphs being members of the Banū Hāshim, they did not rely for long on Shī'ite ideas. The 'Abbāsid ideology shifted from Shī'ite Imāmate to dynastic caliphate.[23] They judged that the latter would provide greater long-term security.

During the 'Abbāsid period (749–1258) various strands of Shī'ism emerged as distinct doctrinal traditions. The stability of the 'Abbāsid period provided Shī'ites with the opportunity to develop a set of literary traditions, and the subsequent history of Shī'ism is the history of competing visions of the Imām.

By the end of the 'Abbāsid period (in 1258), only three of the competing branches of Shī'ism had survived in any organised fashion: the Twelvers (*ithnā' 'asharīyah*), the Ismā'īlīs (*ismā'īlīya*) and the Zaydīs (*zaydīya*). Other Shī'ite communities and traditions have survived into the modern period, but either they have not developed dogmatic definition and continuity, or they have separated from Islam altogether and are now considered a separate religious tradition (as in the case of the Druze).

The Umayyad period had been a time of Shī'ite experimentation. A number of different lineages from the Prophet were tested. This trend continued into the 'Abbāsid period. In 762, a great-grandson of al-Hasan was declared Imām by Kūfan Shī'ites. 'Al-Nafs al-Zakīyah' was declared *mahdī* by his father and, with his brother Ibrāhīm, proceeded to lead another unsuccessful Shī'ite rebellion. The rebellion was crushed in 763.

The recurrent failure of Shī'ite uprisings was undoubtedly one reason for the emergence of a politically quietist brand of Shī'ism which recognised the religious authority of the Imām, but also accepted that the Shī'ah were unable to gain power for him. The descendants of al-Husayn through his son 'Alī represented this trend. 'Alī b. al-Husayn (d. 681) had witnessed the battle at Karbalā', survived, been imprisoned, and eventually released and sent to Madīnah. The sources depict him as leading a quiet, pious life, teaching. He passed these qualities on to his son, Muhammad b. 'Alī al-Bāqir (d. 732 or 735). Al-Bāqir was recognised as an accomplished scholar in *hadīth* and law. As far as one can deduce from the sources, al-Bāqir's teaching included some ideas which became central for later Twelver and Ismā'īlī Shī'ite thought. The Imāmate, he argued, was passed from one Imām to the next by a process of designation (*nass*), performed by God but executed by the present Imām. With this doctrine, a line of Imāms from 'Alī and his sons was recognised. Al-Bāqir probably developed the notion that the Imām had to be drawn from a particular family line of descendants, and that each Imām had to 'designate' his successor. In view of this belief, it seems likely that al-Bāqir designated his son, Ja'far, as the next Imām.

Ja'far al-Sādiq ('the truthful one') was also a scholar of note.[24] His opinions are recorded in both Sunni and Shī'ite works of law. He inherited his father's disciples and held sufficient stature to retain authority, both as a religious teacher, and as the object of the devotional loyalty of his Shī'ah.

Many Shī'ite doctrines are traced to Ja'far. His learning, piety and political quietism during the momentous events of the 'Abbāsid revolution seem to have also preserved his reputation amongst Sunnis. When he died in 765, a discernible Shī'ite theological and legal tradition was emerging. His followers, however, were left in some disarray over his successor. Ja'far's eldest son, Ismā'īl, had (according to most sources) been designated as Imām. Unfortunately, Ismā'īl predeceased his father, raising a series of theological questions: could designation be rescinded once it had been given, and, if so, where might it then be placed? Why might God allow his Imām-designate to die? These theological problems led some Shī'ah to believe that Ismā'īl could not have died. He must, they argued, have gone into hiding to return as Imām at some future time. Others argued that the Imāmate must have passed through Ismā'īl to his son Muhammad b. Ismā'īl. These followers of Ismā'īl ('the Ismā'īlīs') were later to become a defined strand of Shī'ism. Those who believed the Imāmate could be rescinded once designated, and could be transferred to another descendant of the current Imām, believed that Jaʿfar's son Mūsa (d. 799 or 800) had been so designated. This group was known as the *Imāmīyah* (later to become the *Ithnā' ʿasharīyah*, or Twelvers).

The problematic nature of succession was to dog the simple transfer of the Imāmate in both the Ismāʿīlī and Twelver lines. The elements of the *imāmah* doctrine common to both traditions placed emphasis on the historical designation of leadership from the previous Imām. It also emphasised the knowledge and charisma of the future Imām. Both qualities of an Imām are, of course, subject to personal interpretation, and hence both groups were vulnerable to schisms.

The Imāmī or Twelver Shīʿites

The *Imāmīyah*, following Mūsa's line, divided once again when the eleventh Imām, al-Hasan al-ʿAskarī, died in 873; some believed he had not designated a successor at all; others said he had not died but was in hiding; yet others considered al-Hasan to have designated his brother Jaʿfar. None of these opinions seemed satisfactory. By the force of theological reasoning, the Imām could not fail to designate a successor; few were convinced he had gone into hiding; and Jaʿfar seemed a most inappropriate choice as Imām as he had schemed against his brother. Eventually it was proposed that al-Hasan had a son, named Muhammad b. al-Hasan, who had gone into hiding (or occultation, *ghayba*). This became subsequent orthodox doctrine. At first, this hidden Imām communicated with his Shīʿah through 'ambassadors' (*sufarā*). In 941, the fourth ambassador was, according to Twelver tradition, informed by the hidden Imām that he was the last, that the period of the lesser occultation (*al-ghaybat al-sughrā*) was over.[25] The world was now entering into the period of the greater occultation (*al-ghaybat al-kubrā*) and the Shīʿah were to wait until the Imām. On his return as a messianic figure, he would establish a rule of justice on earth. Generally speaking the twelve Imāms of the *Imāmīyah Ithrā' ʿasharīyah* (the 'Twelver' Imāmīs) adopted a politically quietist attitude. From this perspective, the Imāms had not seen political power as a principal element of their mission: only ʿAlī had held office; only al-Husayn had rebelled; the eighth Imām ʿAlī al-Riḍā was named as the successor to the ʿAbbāsid Caliph al-Maʾmūn in 816, but he was reluctant to accept, and in any case predeceased al-Maʾmān. Political ambivalence, and patient anticipation of the Imām's return (*intiẓār*) gave rise to a number of distinctive Twelver Shīʿite doctrines. First, anyone who attempted to take the Imām's rightful role as leader of the Muslims was, de jure, a usurper. The Shīʿah could not countenance accepting anyone who claimed to be Imām in place of the returning Twelfth Imām. This led to the oppression of the Shīʿah by Sunni caliphs. The Imāms had sanctioned dissimulation (*taqīya*) for their Shīʿah. The Shīʿah could take on the outward appearance of the current political or cultural milieu. If necessary, then, they could pretend to be Sunnis.

The Twelver theologians were generally quietist with regard to politics. However, Twelver Shīʿite themes did appear as part of subsequent propaganda. These rebellions appeared sporadically in Iran, both during the ʿAbbāsid period and after the Mongol invasion of 1258. Twelver Shīʿite themes were particularly prevalent in northern Iran. The Marʿashī Sayyid dynasty, which ruled Māzandarān from 1358 until the early fifteenth century, claimed descent from the fourth Imām and certainly based their legitimacy on their role as successors to the Hidden Imām.[26] Similarly, the Sarbadārid state, based in Sabzavār, was led by Twelver Shī'ites. One of the leaders of the state, Khwājah 'Alī (d. 1386), hoped to implement Imāmī law. Muhammad b. Makkī al-Āmilī (d. 1384), whilst not directly in the employ of the Sarbadārids, did write his famous legal compendium *al-Lum'ah al-Dimashqīya*, and sent it to Khwājah 'Alī.[27]

These early 'Twelver' dynasties were not sufficiently long lived to bring about any change in the Twelver Shī'ite emphasis on political quietism. However, one such movement did emerge in the late fifteenth century, and its military success, and subsequent sponsorship of Twelver Shī'ite learning, was to change the nature of Twelver thought permanently. The Safavīya were originally a Sunni Sufi order based around the descendants of Shaykh Safī al-Dīn al-Ardabīlī (d. 1334). The order was subsequently influenced by Shī'ism. It also developed a military wing, which had impressive military success in the late fifteenth century, resulting in 1501 with the capture of Tabriz, and the declaration of the Safavid dynasty by Shah Ismā'īl, the Safavid *murshid*. One of Ismā'īl's first decrees was to make Twelver Shī'ism the religion of the new Safavid Iran.[28] The subsequent history of the Safavids is one of consolidation and military success, leading to stability and wealth, and later decadence and collapse at the hand of Afghan invaders in 1722. During this period, Twelver Shī'ite scholars came to Iran and seminaries were established. Safavid Shī'ites have been responsible for the preservation and production of much Twelver literature. The Safavids, however, gave rise to a theological and legal problem. The traditional political quietism was now challenged by the existence of a 'Shī'ite' government. Theologically, Twelver thinkers were committed to the idea that the government of the Imām was the only legitimate rule. For some, the Safavids were simply illegitimate. For others, they were acceptable, but not ideal. Some Twelver scholars moved to Iran to receive the patronage of the new dynasty. Others either ignored Ismā'īl's invitation, or openly criticised those scholars who compromised their faith and worked with the Safavids. Those who supported the Safavids gradually gained the upper hand in the centres of learning, and nearly all the major Twelver Shī'ite theologians of the seventeenth and eighteenth centuries were either Iranians, or Arabs living in Iran.

Twelver Shī'ite communities outside of Iran lived a more precarious life. The (Sunni) Ottoman empire responded to the existence of Shī'ites within its borders with policies of, at times, acquiescence and, at other times, suppression. The Shī'ites were, at certain points, taken to be a 'millet' community (similar to the Christians and the Jews).[29] The Twelver communities of Syria and 'Irāq lived as 'minorities' in the Ottoman Empire. The Ottomans were often suspicious of the Twelvers, viewing them as a potential 'fifth column' for the Safavids. Where the Ottomans had less political control, Twelver Shī'ite communities settled and developed, particularly in eastern Arabia (Bahrayn and al-Hasā). Scholars from these areas, and from India, moved to the seminary and shrine cities of southern 'Irāq (Najaf and Karbalā').[30]

The Safavid dynasty collapsed in 1722 as the Sunni Afghans invaded and captured Isfahān. This led to a period of internal strife in Iran; as intellectual life in Iran waned, the seminaries of 'Irāq emerged as centres of learning. The scholars of the 'Atabāt (the 'Threshold' of the Imams) developed an institutional structure which could survive independent from government sponsorship. When the Qājar tribe re-established stability in Iran in the late eighteenth century, Shī'ite scholars had an autonomous structure that no longer required the patronage of Shahs and sultans.[31] The structure was funded by gifts from the faithful to the Shīʿite *ʿulamā*. The scholars had, quite ingeniously, developed a set of religious doctrines, and a series of social structures, which ensured that their role as community leaders was, to an extent, protected from any challenge by Qājār political power.[32]

Examples of the developing community 'prerogative' of the *ʿulamā* can be seen in a number of areas of Shīʿite thought. For example, when the Imāms were present, in theory no scholar need engage in personal reasoning (associated with terms such as *ijtihād, qiyās* and *raʾy*) in order to discover the correct interpretation or application of God's law (the Sharīʿah). Anyone who wished to know a legal ruling could refer to the Imām himself. The Imām's answer was, de jure, the law. This legal doctrine was, in turn, based on the theological doctrine that the Imām was the sinless (*maʿsūm*) embodiment of God's will, and was perfectly knowledgeable concerning the meaning of the Qurʾān and Sunnah of the Prophet Muhammad. When the Imām disappeared, however, the need to interpret the Imām's words and deeds (the *akhbār*) became essential, as these were the source of the Sharīʿah for the Twelver Shīʿites. The need for interpretation inevitably led to the need for expert interpreters, and hence the *raison d'être* of the *ʿulamā* was established. The Shīʿah need scholars who can exercise *ijtihād* (personal juristic reasoning) in order that the community might best understand the wishes of the Imāms.[33] Similarly, religious taxes such as *zakāh* or *khums*, could be given directly to the Imām when he was present. During his absence, however, the duty to give these taxes becomes problematic. Shīʿite thinkers at first recommended burying the money to await the Imām's return, or perhaps an individual Shīʿite could distribute it himself. In time, however, a more practical solution was found: certain reports from the Imāms were interpreted to imply that the Imāms had delegated (*niyābah*) the *ʿulamā* as their representatives in certain areas of the Law. One such area, it was argued, was religious taxes. The *ʿulamā* should receive and distribute the taxes as 'functional' Imāms.[34] Doctrines such as these not only legitimised the leadership role of the *ʿulamā* within the community; they also provided a source of financial income which could be used to fund scholarly activities.[35] In part, these doctrines, together with their practical implementation amongst the Shīʿite community, enabled the Shīʿite *ʿulamā* to establish an institutional structure with a high degree of autonomy from political power (unlike their Sunni counterparts). Shīʿite scholars did not 'need' the Qājār state for their legitimacy in the same way that Ṣafavid scholars had. The *ʿulamā* had to be wooed by the Qājār Shahs to provide religious justification for the actions of the Qājār state. This happened during the wars between Russia and Iran when the *ʿulamā* were requested to issue *fatwās* justifying the wars from a legal perspective, and declaring them to be *jihāds*.[36]

The independence gained by the *ʿulamā* also had disadvantages. The *ʿulamā* could less easily access the mechanisms of social control held by the state. During the Ṣafavid period, Twelver scholars had been able to suppress religious challenges such as Sufism or Sunnism through the organs of the state.[37] Under the Qājārs, activity such as this was greatly reduced. The *ʿulamā* were more independent, but they were also at first (politically) less powerful. A series of heterodox movements emerged in the early Qājār period, such as the Shaykhīs (a mystical philosophical movement founded by Shaykh Ahmad al-Ahsāʾī [d. 1826]).[38] Later in 1844, Sayyid ʿAlī Muhammad of Shiraz declared himself to be the *Bāb* ('gate') to the Hidden Imām, and began preaching against the religion of the established *ʿulamā*. It was only when his followers represented a threat to public order that the Qājār state got involved.[39] The Bābīs developed a significant military force, and were instigating rebellions across Iran. The Bāb himself was captured, executed and many of his followers were expelled. Some settled in Baghdad where one Mīrzā Husayn ʿAlī Nūrī (known as Bahāʾallāh) declared himself to be the 'one whom God has made manifest' – indicating his messianic status.[40] The Bahāʾī religion, based on his teaching, was born.

The independence of the *ʿulamāʾ* enabled them to criticise Qājār policy both from the seminary cities of ʿIrāq, and (more rarely) from inside Iran. In the late nineteenth century, western influence in Iran increased. The Qājār government, in desperate financial straits, began to sell concessions to western companies. The *ʿulamāʾ* joined forces with nationalists to protest at this sale of 'Muslim' assets to 'infidel' business-men. In 1890 the Qājār Shāh sold the right to sell and export tobacco from Iran. The protests against this included a boycott of tobacco, supposedly on the command of Mīrzā-yi Shīrāzī (the *marja ʿal-taqlīd* – 'source of imitation' for Shīʿites), resident in Sāmarrāʾ. The protests were so effective that the concession was rescinded. The *ʿulamāʾ* entered politics as an opposition force and had been instrumental in changing government policy. Ten years later they were to repeat the performance when the interests of the *ʿulamāʾ* and other (nationalist, secular) opposition forces coincided during the Constitutional Revolution (1906–9).[41] Many members of the *ʿulamāʾ* participated in the establishment of a constitution which guaranteed Iranians basic rights against the despotism of the Shāh. The battle over the constitution, in which Twelver Shīʿite scholars played a not insignificant role (on both sides of the argument), represents the *ʿulamāʾ*'s first ideological foray into the debates and issues of a modern nation-state. This involvement was to reach its height later in the twentieth century in the form of the opposition movement which led to the Iranian Revolution of 1979 (on which see below).

The Ismāʿīlīya

As mentioned above, the Ismāʿīlī Shīʿites followed the Imāmate line of Jaʿfar's first son, Ismāʿīl. Ismāʿīl, they argued, had been designated to take on the Imāmate, but had died (or according to some early Ismāʿīlīs, disappeared)[42] before Jaʿfar's death in 765. The reason for their dedication to Ismāʿīl is difficult to ascertain from the sources. It does not appear to have been on the basis of his personal qualities, which are rarely referred to in the sources. Rather, theirs seemed to be a principled belief in the nature of Imāmate designation: once given, a designation cannot be rescinded, for this would imply either that the designating Imām was ignorant of future events or the Imām's (or, perhaps more seriously, God's) decision was subject to change. If Ismāʿīl was the Imām after Jaʿfar, then, his son Muhammad b. Ismāʿīl, was to be Imām after him. In these disputes, one can see the theological conception of 'designated' Imāmate being theologically tested by various elements within the Shīʿah.

Little is known about Ismāʿīlī activity in the following century. In the late ninth century, however, historical sources record the spread of Ismāʿīlī doctrines through the work of missionaries (*dāʿīs*) in Kūfah, eastern Iran, Yemen and eventually north Africa and eastern Arabia.[43] There does not appear to have been extensive coordin-ation in these efforts, as the Ismāʿīlī movement in each area adopted distinctive characteristics. However, if it is possible to talk of an Ismāʿīlī institutional and doctrinal structure, it was based on the prevalent idea that Muhammad b. Ismāʿīl had disappeared and was to return in the near future as *mahdī*. In his absence, a certain individual was recognised as the representative or 'Proof' (*hujjah*) of the *mahdī*, and successive 'Proofs' commanded some measure of generalised authority across the Ismāʿīlī community.[44] The 'Proofs' were based in Salamīya in Syria, out of which the Ismāʿīlī mission operated. Ismāʿīlī missionaries appeared in various parts of the Muslim empire, either having been commissioned from Salamīya, or having emerged indigenously in other areas. A number of these missionary movements deserve special mention. In the late ninth to early tenth century, Ismāʿīlī missionary activity in central and eastern Iran was developed by a *dāʿī* called Khalaf. More significantly, in 877, the famous Qarmatian movement was founded by Hamdān Qarmat, aided by his brother, ʿAbdān, in Kūfah and its environs. Among Qarmat's doctrines was the standard Ismāʿīlī belief of the time concerning Muhammad b. Ismāʿīl's occultation and parousia. Converts to Qarmat's version of Ismāʿīlism had no need of the Sharīʿah, since they had transcended these regulations. Amongst Qarmat's followers was one Abū Saʿīd al-Jannābī who, in 899, founded a Qarmatī state in eastern Arabia. The Qarmatians (*qarmatīya*) are portrayed in Muslim literature as dangerous reprobates with a lack of respect for any divine ordinance.[45] Events such as the Qarmatian seizure of the black stone of the Kaʿbah in 930[46] only serve to exemplify the degeneracy of the Qarmatīya in the eyes of the (mainly Sunni) Muslim historical tradition.

Ismāʿīlī missionaries were also successful in Yemen through Ibn Hawshab (d. 914).[47] It was from Yemen that Abū ʿAbdallāh al-Shīʿī was dispatched to north Africa in 893. He established an Ismāʿīlī base upon which the north African Fāṭimid Ismāʿīlī state was built.[48] In 899, the 'Proof' in Salamīya, Saʿīd (later known as ʿUbaydallāh), claimed that he was the *mahdī*. He, or his later followers, presented a genealogy which linked ʿUbaydallāh first to Muhammad b. Ismāʿīl, and ultimately to Fāṭimah, the daughter of Muhammad (hence their name al-Fāṭimīya or Fāṭimids). The Qarmatians were most suspicious of this claim, and the Ismāʿīlīs divided over the question of Ubaydallāh's Imāmate.[49] Saʿīd embarked on a military campaign, linking up with the Yemeni missionary activity in north Africa, and eventually establishing the Fāṭimid state, which lasted from 909 to 1171. The Fāṭimid dynasty gave Ismāʿīlī Shīʿism a more secure institutional structure; all the major forms of Ismāʿīlism in existence today have their roots in the debates and discussions of the Fāṭimid period. Qarmatian Ismāʿīlism died out in the fourteenth century.

The sixth Fāṭimid caliph (or Imām) al-Hakam was declared a 'manifestation of God' and to have a 'divine nature' by some of his followers. Most Ismāʿīlī theologians rejected such 'extremist' (*ghālī*) claims. Two *dāʿī*s, named Hamzah and al-Darazī, separately claimed to be the representative of the divine al-Hakam.[50] On al-Hakam's death in 1021, the movement they had founded went underground, eventually leaving the area under Fāṭimid control. The secretive sect, called the Durūz (or Druze, after al-Darazī) survives today in Lebanon, Syria and Israel.[51]

After the death of the eighth Fāṭimid caliph, al-Mustanṣir, in 1094, the question of his succession divided the Ismāʿīlī community – both that under Fāṭimid control and elsewhere. Inside the Fāṭimid empire, the caliph's son al-Mustaʿlī, was generally recognised as Imām. Outside the empire, al-Mustanṣir's eldest son, Nizār, commanded much loyalty. The *dāʿī*, Hasan-i Ṣabbāh, had been active before al-Mustanṣir's death, propagating Ismā'īlism in Iran, establishing a number of Ismā'īlī military cells which had carried out attacks on the 'Abbāsid state. The Hashīshīya (the Hashish-users, from which the English word assassin is derived) as they were known, together with Hasan-i Ṣabbāh, supported Nizār's candidacy for Imām. The Nizārī Ismā'īlīs separated from the Fāṭimids and operated out of small castle outposts (the principal one of which was at Alamūt in the Elborz mountains).[52] The Nizārīs appear to have believed that either Nizār was in occultation (and in his place, there was a succession of *dā'īs* who represented him), or that Nizār's grandson was hiding in Alamūt. In time, the descendants of Hasan-i Ṣabbāh claimed to be descendants of Nizār, and hence Imāms.[53] The Nizārīs also experienced periodic internal disputes, usually over leadership. They were tolerated in eastern Islamic lands after Alamūt fell to the Mongols in 1257. They survived through the Ṣafavid period in Iran with their line of Imāms intact. In the early nineteenth century, the Qājār monarch, Fath 'Alī Shāh, accorded the title of Āghā Khān to the Nizārī Imām Hasan 'Alī.[54] The Imāmate was transferred to Bombay in the 1840s after Hasan 'Alī (the Āghā Khān) led a local rebellion against Fath 'Alī Shāh's successor, Muhammad Shāh.[55] Hasan 'Alī's descendants, each given the title Āghā Khān, have led the Nizārī community into the modern period.

Further schisms were to appear in the Fāṭimid line. Al-Musta'lī designated his son, al-Āmir as Imām, but he was killed in 1130 by Nizārī assassins. He left no obvious successor (his son Tayyib was only eight months old). Al-Āmir's cousin, 'Abd al-Majīd, claimed the Imāmate, calling himself al-Hāfiz ('the preserver'). The Ismā'īlīs in Yemen refused to recognise al-Hāfiz and established their own Tayyibī Ismā'īlī state. Tayyib himself had 'disappeared', and the faithful in Yemen, and in India, awaited his return. In his absence a 'Universal Missionary' (*al-dā'ī al-mutlaq*) led the faithful. Just as there were divisions over who should be Imām, amongst the Tayyibs there have been divisions over who is *al-dā'ī al-mutlaq*. The Sulaymānī and Dā'ūdī branches, which divided over questions of *dā'ī* succession in the sixteenth century, are both based in India today with little representation in the Middle East.[56]

The complex history of schisms and divisions within the Ismā'īlī movement was, in the main, played out in the Middle East until the fourteenth century. The transferral of the various Ismā'īlī branches to India (and later across the world) over the past five hundred years has meant that Ismā'īlī communities in the Middle East are now reduced to isolated collections of villages. Ironically, the largest group in the Middle East with Ismā'īlī roots are the Druze, who are recognised neither as Ismā'īlī Shī'ites nor Muslims.

The Zaydīya

The Imāmīya and the Ismā'īlīya placed great emphasis on the identity (and theological qualities) of the Imām, and this undoubtedly led to a pattern of schisms. There was, however, a Shī'ite tradition which avoided the technicalities of Imāmate designation and the theological issues of the Imām's infallibility (*'iṣmah*). The Zaydīya trace their origins to the revolt of Zayd b. 'Alī, the son of the fourth Imām. As with most early Shī'ite movements, Kūfah proved a fertile ground for Zayd's followers, and when Zayd led a rebellion against Umayyad rule in 740, it was in Kūfah that the movement based its operations. It was (as noted above) unsuccessful, though some of Zayd's supporters survived and developed a distinctive Shī'ite doctrine, first in Kūfah, and later in other parts of the Muslim empire.

The Zaydīs reduced the devotional loyalty to the *ahl al-bayt*. The supporters and companions of Zayd continued to propagate elements of his teaching following his death. Two elements of early Zaydī thought deserve special mention. First, Abū al-Jārūd Ziyād, whose followers were called the Jārūdīya, adapted the established Shīʿite position. As far as Abū al-Jārūd was concerned, ʿAlī had been designated by the Prophet, and the first three caliphs were usurpers. This position was opposed by the Batrīya Zaydīs, who were more moderate in their views. For them, ʿAlī was superior to the first three caliphs, but since he himself had recognised them, the Shīʿah should do so also. It was the Jārūdīya position which was to dominate later Zaydī Shīʿism.[57]

In the ninth century, theologians and jurists advocating the Jārūdī Zaydī position became influential in Kūfah and Madīnah. The Imāmate was to be conferred on the best (*afḍal*) of the descendants of the Prophet Muhammad, through ʿAlī and Fāṭimah.[58] Whether the Imām came from the Hasanid or Husaynid branches of the Prophet's descendants was, for most Zaydīs, unimportant. Any member of the *ahl al-bayt* could be Imām provided he fulfilled a number of conditions, the most important of which was that he 'rise up' (*khurūj*) with the sword and make a call (*daʿwā*) to the believers to recognise his Imāmate.[59] The Imām is generally not infallible (*maʿṣūm*), though in developed Zaydī theology, he should be a religious scholar (*mujtahid*) who happens to hold political power.[60]

After Zayd b. ʿAlī's failure in 740, the Zaydīya did not, it appears, stage any subsequent rebellions. The major Zaydī thinker, al-Qāsim b. Ibrāhīm (d. 860) developed the theological and legal doctrines of the Zaydī school during his travels in Arabia and Egypt. Zaydīs influenced by his teaching (which borrowed heavily from the Muʿtazilī rationalist school of theology) proselytised in Tabaristān on the Caspian sea coast.[61] They succeeded in establishing a series of short-lived coastal states in the late ninth and tenth centuries. Further west in Gīlān, a Zaydī state survived until the twelfth century. It eventually fell to the rising power of the Nizārī Ismāʿīlīs in the area. A most successful and long-lasting Zaydī state was based in northern Yemen. The grandson of al-Qāsim, Yaḥyā b. al-Husayn (d. 911), had endeavoured to gain power in Tabaristān. In the course of these efforts he was invited to mediate in a tribal dispute in Ṣaʿdah, Yemen. Through his success there, he was recognised as Imām by some tribes, and he named himself al-Imām al-Hādī ilā al-Haqq (the Imām Guide to the Truth). Yaḥyā's skills as both a scholar and a military leader established the usual Zaydī pattern for the Imām, and his writings (together with those of his grandfather al-Qāsim) are central to the Yemeni Zaydī tradition of scholarship. The descendants of Yaḥyā struggled to keep the Zaydī Imāmate alive, experiencing pressure from external enemies (mainly from Egypt and later Ottoman forces). In 1565, the Zaydī Imām waged war to expel Ottoman influence in north Yemen. By 1635 the campaign had been successful and the Zaydī Imāmate was (re)established. Despite continued external pressure in the nineteenth century (including the occupation of Ṣanʿā in 1872 by Ottoman forces), the Zaydī Imāms preserved their lineage. When Imām Yaḥyā al-Mutawakkil recaptured Ṣanʿāʾ in 1918, the Zaydī Imāmate in Yemen became fused with the political structure of the modern nation-state.

Shīʿism in the Modern Middle East

Shīʿism has contributed to political developments in the modern Middle East in two principal ways. First, some Shīʿite communities have espoused secular political doctrines, and produced leaders of secular (often Arab nationalist) movements. Second, Shī'ite thinkers (primarily Twelver jurists) have embarked on discussions concerning the nature of an Islamic state, and the means whereby it might be established. These discussions have, in turn, led to political movements which have played a role in the modern history of the Middle East (particularly Iran, Iraq and Lebanon).

Examples of the first phenomenon include some religious-ethnic communities whose historical roots can be found in *ghulāt* ('extremist') Shī'ism. This 'extremism' (*ghulūw*) is based on a devotional loyalty to the *ahl al-bayt* common to most Shī'ite groups. *Ghulāt* groups, however, express this loyalty through doctrines which attribute divinity to one or more of the *ahl al-bayt*.[62] The polemic between the major strands of Shī'ism often includes the accusation of *ghulūw*. Zaydīs accuse Twelvers of *ghulūw*, and Twelvers make the same accusation against Ismā'īlīs. Some Shī'ites, such as the Iranian Ṣafavids, were originally *ghulāt*, but later modified their doctrine to accord with 'orthodox' Twelver Shī'ism.[63] By definition *ghulāt* doctrines transgressed orthodoxy, and amongst the beliefs attributed to *ghulāt* groups were the divinity of the Imām, the transmigration of souls (*tanāsukh*) and the salvation of an elect few who had been initiated into the secret doctrines of the sect. Most *ghulāt* communities have not survived into the modern period, and those that have either adopted non-political, autonomous community existence, or non-exclusive secular political ideologies in which their Shī'ism plays a negligible role. Examples of the former trend include the Turkish Alevis (though they are becoming increasingly politicised) and the Kurdish Ahl-i Haqq. Examples of the latter are the Lebanese Druze and the Syrian 'Alawīs.

In the case of the Druze, the Fāṭimid caliph al-Hakam was considered divine. Although the Druze had a complex 'extremist' Shī'ite doctrine which could have been used to political effect, they have, in fact, participated in Lebanese politics primarily as an ethnic group, espousing no explicit 'religious' political agenda. In the Lebanese civil war, for example, the Druze militia defended Druze communities on a purely 'ethnic' basis. Druze leaders have espoused political programmes of various hues, being particularly influenced by Arab nationalism. The unacceptable nature of their doctrines to both Sunnis and Shī'ites has led the Druze to adopt an entirely secular (non-religious) political presence in the modern period.

A similar process has undoubtedly occurred with the 'extremist' 'Alawī community in Syria. The 'Alawīs – called Nusayrīs in pre-modern texts – trace their community origins to Ibn Nusayr, a companion of the tenth and eleventh Imāms of the Twelver Shī'ah. Ibn Nusyar preached the divinity of the Imām and intimated that he was himself the Imām-God's prophet. Whilst he and his followers were active in Kūfah and Baghdad in the early period, the community settled in Aleppo and eventually al-Lādhikīya on the Syrian coast. Here the community suffered various bouts of persecution from the Sunni authorities. In the late nineteenth century, the Nusayrīs promoted a new name for themselves – the 'Alawīya. This renaming was combined with a concerted effort on the part of some Nusayrī-'Alawīs to gain acceptance as orthodox Twelver Shī'ites. The French powers, to an extent, accepted them as such, granting them autonomous, and later federal, status, and staffing the law courts with Twelver judges. The orthodoxy of their doctrines, however, continued to be problematic, and so when 'Alawīs began to participate in Syrian politics (following independence in 1946), they were drawn to secular Arab nationalism, and did not develop any distinctly ʿAlawī political ideology. In particular, the Baʿthist movement in Syria dominated the political allegiance of the ʿAlawīs, and when the Baʿthists came to power in 1963, ʿAlawīs were well represented in the new elite. ʿAlawīs were particularly drawn to a radical military wing of the Baʿthists, and a coup in 1966 brought the ʿAlawī Ḥāfiẓ al-Asad to power. Asad, in general, favoured ʿAlawīs in the political structure,[64] and this has been maintained, to an extent, by his son Bashīr al-Asad who took over as president in 2000. Ḥāfiẓ al-Asad succeeded in persuading the Shīʿite cleric, Mūsā al-Ṣadr (d. 1978), to recognise the ʿAlawīs as orthodox Twelver Shīʿites,[65] but this recognition was linked more to Syria's role in the Lebanese civil war than to any doctrinal considerations.

The second manner in which Shīʿism has influenced modern Middle Eastern history is the use of Shīʿite ideas within a political ideology. At the end of the First World War, it was the Yemeni Zaydī Imāms who had the most success in establishing a Shīʿite state. The Zaydī Imāmate in North Yemen survived until 1962. The growing popularity of Arab nationalism amongst army officers led to a revolution after the death of Imām Ahmad, son of Imām Yahyā al-Mutawakkil.[66] His son, Muhammad al-Badr, was elected Imām, but was soon deposed by revolutionary forces and the Yemen Arab Republic was formed. Religiously speaking, this left the Zaydīs without an Imām, but this situation was doctrinally unproblematic. Zaydīs had survived before without an Imām, and since the Imām played no 'cosmic' role (as in Twelver and Ismāʿīlī Shīʿism), there was no necessity attached to the presence of an Imām. The Zaydīs still await the rising (*khurūj*) of their next Imām to political office. In the meantime, elements of Zaydī law, in modified form, continue to operate in the northern areas of the Republic of Yemen,[67] formed in 1990 through the unification of the (mainly Sunni) People's Democratic Republic of Yemen in the south with the Zaydī Yemen Arab Republic.

Twelver Shīʿism, on the other hand, has undergone a radical politicisation of its principal doctrines and seen an increase in political activity (amongst both *ʿulamāʾ* and laypeople). The *ʿulamāʾ* had become increasingly involved in the politics of the Qājār state as an opposition force.[68] This was also evident in the Iranian Constitutional Revolution (1906–9). After the First World War, the secularising government of Reżā Shāh (r. 1925–41) prevented the *ʿulamāʾ* from making further inroads into the political process.[69] Reżā Shāh excluded the *ʿulamāʾ* from power and gradually eroded their privilege. Religious endowments (*awqāf*) were confiscated, religious education came under state control and the role of the *ʿulamāʾ* in the legal system was minimised. These policies, combined with a close association with the USA, were continued by his son, Muhammad Reżā Shāh. The *ʿulamāʾ*'s reaction was first witnessed during Prime Minister Musaddiq's attempt to nationalise the Iranian oil industry in the early 1950s.[70] More significant were the demonstrations in the early 1960s, when religious students and others objected to the Shah's modernisation policies (his so-called 'White Revolution'). Amongst the scholars who had inspired and encouraged the demonstrators was Rūhallāh Khumaynī (Khomeini). Khomeini was expelled, and began to establish an opposition movement from exile in Iraq. He was probably the first Shīʿite thinker to develop a thoroughly Twelver Shīʿite political ideology.[71] In line with established tradition, he suggested that the *ʿulamāʾ* had been delegated certain tasks during the occultation of the twelfth Imām. However Khomeini, unlike his contemporaries, also included political rule, as well as community affairs (such as tax collecting and leading prayer) in this delegation. Since the *ʿulamāʾ* could only come to power through a revolutionary movement led by a scholar,

Khomeini argued that it was obligatory for all the *'ulamā'* to follow any scholar with the political ability to lead such a movement.[72] This scholar need not be the most learned as had been the case in the past (where learning dictated a scholar's position in the Shī'ite hierarchy). Instead this scholar needed only to have skills of political organisation and leadership. He called this theory 'the mandate of the jurist' (*wilāyat al-faqīh* or, in Persian, *velāyat-i faqīh*), employing common Shī'ite legal terms. In 1979, a popular movement in Iran succeeded in overthrowing the Shah, and Khomeini returned from exile as its leader. He soon succeeded in further enhancing his power by enshrining a version of *wilāyat al-faqīh* in the constitution of the new Islamic Republic of Iran.[73] Khomeini, as 'the jurist' (*al-faqīh*), was central to the Iranian Islamic project until his death in 1989. The factions fighting for control in modern Iranian politics, be they reformers or conservatives, are, in effect, battling for the right to claim Khomeini's legacy. A resolution of the debate concerning how to incorporate the concept of a *faqīh* into a modern nation-state has not yet been resolved.[74]

Partly inspired by Iranian success, Twelver Shī'ites outside of Iran have undergone a politicisation of both community and doctrine.[75] The Iraqi Twelvers, living in the poor south of Iraq, have suffered under secular rule since the Arab nationalist Ba'thists returned to power in 1968. This led to a call by some Iraqi dissident groups (such as the Da'wā organisation and the Supreme Council for Islamic Revolution in Iraq) for an Islamic republic. Khomeini's version of *wilāyat al-faqīh* has not gained great popularity amongst the Iraqi Shī'ah, who live in a state which is less religiously homogeneous than Twelver Shī'ite Iran. Thinkers such as Muhammad Bāqir al-Ṣadr (d. 1980) led a Shī'ite reformation, though his political programme was never as explicitly expressed as that of Khomeini.[76] The regime of Saddam Hussein, in power since 1979, systematically excluded the majority Shī'ite population from effective political participation.[77] Even though Shī'ites fought and died for Iraq in its war with Iran (between 1980 and 1989, with the religious problem of Shī'ite killing Shī'ite), their lack of political commitment to the Ba'thist regime was evident in the uprisings in the south which followed the 1990 First Gulf War. Following the collapse of the regime of Saddam Hussein in 2003, there continues to be vigorous debate amongst the *'ulamā'* of Karbalā', Najaf and the other Iraqi seminary towns on the appropriate type of Islamic government for Iraq.

In Lebanon, the Twelver Shī'ites also live in the poor south, bordering on Israel, and have suffered as a result of the tension between the Lebanese and Palestinian groups and the state of Israel. This led to the emergence of Shī'ite militias, such as Amal and later Hizballāh. Although Amal was, in part, founded by the famous, charismatic cleric Mūsā al-Ṣadr, it did not develop a particularly 'religious' ideology. Hizballāh, supported by Iran, pronounces a much more religious programme calling for a (vaguely defined) Islamic state in Lebanon. Shaykh Faḍl Allāh, the spiritual leader of Hizballāh, does not advocate a Khomeinist model, but instead states that one of his principal aims is to ensure the rights and well-being of the Shī'ah.[78] In both Lebanon and Iraq, Twelver Shī'ite movements have drawn on the fact that the Shī'ah live in relative poverty and their majority status is not recognised in the political structures. Any future systems of governance in either country will not, it seems, achieve stability, unless the needs of the Shī'ite constituency are recognised.

In general terms the modern period has seen a rise in the political activity of the Twelver Shī'ites, and an end to the political power of the Zaydī Shī'ite Imāms. The unification of north and south Yemen in 1990 has diluted the Zaydī character of the Yemeni state, making the re-establishment of any Zaydī Imāmate a distant prospect. This, and the removal of the Ismā'īlī Imāmate to India in 1843, has left the Twelvers as the principal Shī'ite political actors in the modern period. This dominance is such that the terms Shī'ah and Shī'ite are used almost exclusively to refer to the Twelvers by journalists and political commentators, though this chapter has demonstrated the extensive variety of Shī'ite doctrines and beliefs. In terms of the future of Shī'ite politics, the Twelvers have a distinct advantage in this age of political rationalisation: the Ismā'īlīs and the Zaydīs have to justify the rather 'irrational' proposition that only those who claim descent from the Prophet Muhammad can claim leadership of the community. The Twelvers' Imām, on the other hand, is in hiding and hence cannot interfere with the process of debate. This, perhaps, gives them a greater chance of constructing a governance structure that can be defended within modern political discourse.

NOTES

1 Nawbakhtī's *Firaq al-Shī'ah* outlines the variety of Shī'ite movements (see also Halm, *Shiism*).
2 Minorsky, 'Poetry', pp. 1026a–1027a.
3 (Q48.10 and 18, and Q60.13).
4 Ṭabarī, *Ta'rīkh*, vol. 1, pp. 1815–30.
5 Ibn Ḥanbal, *Musnad*, vol. 1, pp. 84, 118, 119; Ibn Mājah, *Sunan*, vol. 1, p. 43.
6 Majlisī, *Bihār al-anwār*, vol. 37, p. 137.
7 Ibn Ḥanbal, *Musnad*, vol. 1, *hadīths* 950 and 964.
8 See also Ibn Kathīr, *al-Bidāya*, vol. 5, pp. 208–14.
9 Madelung, *Succession*, pp. 141–310.
10 Ash'arī, *Maqālāt al-Islāmiyīn*, p. 15.
11 See Robinson, *Islamic Historiography*, see pp. 123–42.
12 Watt, *Formative Period*, pp. 43–4.
13 Ibid., p. 43.
14 Ibid., p. 40 and p. 54.
15 Patricia Crone (*Times Literary Supplement*, 7/2/1997); Ingrid Mattson (*Religion*, 78 (1998), pp. 321–3); Rockwell (*MELA*, 65–6 (1997–8), pp. 84–5).
16 Madelung, 'Shī'ism', pp. 14–15.
17 Amir-Moezzi, *Divine Guide*, pp. 61–9.
18 Ḥusayn Wa'iū Káshifī, *Rawāat al-shuhadā'*, p. 207.
19 Ṭabarī, *Ta'rīkh*, vol. 2, pp. 281–367; Ibn Shahrāshūb, *Manāqib*, vol. 3, pp. 206–72 and Mufīd, *Irshād*, pp. 197–253; Howard, *Guidance*, pp. 299–371.
20 Schubel, *Religious Performance*, 115–44.
21 al-Qāḍī, *al-Kaysānīyah*.
22 Halm, *Shiism*, pp. 24–6.
23 Nagel, 'Kalifat', pp. 101–9, pp. 153–64.
24 Ibn Khallikān, *Wafayāt*, vol. 1, pp. 327–8.
25 Ibn Bābūyah, *Kamāl*, p. 516.
26 Arjomand, *Shadow*, pp. 67–9; Calmard, 'Mar'ashīs', *EI²*, VI, pp. 510–18.
27 Melville, 'Sarbadārids', *EI²*, IX, pp. 47–9; Arjomand, *Shadow*, pp. 69–71.
28 Savory, 'Orthodoxy'; Morgan, 'Re-Thinking'.
29 Imber, 'Persecution of the Ottoman Shi'ites'.
30 Newman, 'The Myth of the Clerical Migration'.
31 Algar, *Religion and State*; Amanat, 'Madrasa and Marketplace'.

32   Momen, *Shi'i Islam*, pp. 197–207.
33   Calder, 'Doubt and Prerogative'.
34   Calder, 'Khums' and Calder, 'Zakat', Madelung, 'Authority' and Sachedina, *The Just Ruler*.
35   Litvak, *Shi'i Scholars*, pp. 179–82.
36   Gleave, *'Jihād* and the Religious Legitimacy'.
37   Arjomand, *Shadow*, pp. 109–21 and Babayan 'Sufis, Dervishes and Mullas'.
38   Cole, 'Casting Away the Self' and Cole, 'Shaykh Ahmad'.
39   Amanat, *Resurrection and Renewal*, particularly pp. 109–52.
40   Berger, 'Motif messianique'.
41   Martin, *Islam and Modernism*, pp. 113–38.
42   Nawbakhtī, *Firaq al-shī'ah*, p. 57.
43   Stern, 'The Early Ismā'īlī missionaries'.
44   Daftary, *The Ismā'īlīs*, pp. 127–8.
45   al-Nawbakhtī, *Firaq al-Shī'ah*, pp. 61–4.
46   Daftary, *The Ismā'īlīs*, p. 164.
47   Madelung and Walker, *The Advent of the Fatimids*, pp. 63–4.
48   Ibid., pp. 5–18.
49   Madelung, 'The Fatimids and the Qarmaṭīs', pp. 40–3.
50   Hodgson, 'Al-Darazī', p. 7.
51   Betts, *Druze*.
52   Ibn al-Athīr, *al-Kāmil*, vol. 10, pp. 215–20; Juwaynī, *Tārīkh*, vol. 3, pp. 186–216; Daftary, *Ismā'īlīs*, pp. 669–81.
53   Daftary, *Ismā'īlīs*, pp. 387–8.
54   Ghālib, *Ta'rīkh*, p. 269.
55   Algar, 'Revolt of Āghā Khān Maḥallatī', pp. 78–80.
56   Blank, *Mullas*, pp. 13–52.
57   Madelung, *Der Imam al-Qāsim*, p. 167.
58   van Ess, *Frühe*, pp. 56–8 (Arabic text).
59   Messick, *Calligraphic State*, p. 38.
60   Haykel, *Revival and Reform*, pp. 26–31.
61   Madelung, *Texts*, pp. 11–16 (Introduction).
62   Moosa, *Extremist Shī'ites*, pp. 311–81; Buckley, 'Ghulāh'.
63   Arjomand, *Shadow*, pp. 160–71.
64   Faksh, 'Alawi Community'.
65   Ajami, *Vanished Imam*, p. 159.
66   Dresch, *Yemen*, pp. 89–118.
67   Messick, *Calligraphic State*, pp. 135–200.
68   Keddie, *Religion and Rebellion*, pp. 72–80.
69   Faghfoory, 'Ulama–State Relations'.
70   Akhavi, 'The Role of the Clergy'.
71   Calder, 'Accommodation and Revolution'; Fischer, 'Four Levels'; Enayat, 'Iran. Khumayni's Concept'; Gleave, 'Khumayni and Khu'i'.
72   *Velāyat-e faqīh: Ḥukūmat-e Islāmī*, pp. 44–5.
73   Schirazi, *Constitution of Iran*, p. 22; Arjomand, 'Shi'ite jurisprudence'.
74   Roy, 'The Crisis of Religious Legitimacy'; Geiling, 'Marja'iyya'.
75   Momen, *Shi'i Islam*, pp. 246–99.
76   Mallat, *Islamic Law*, pp. 59–78.
77   See Nakash, *Shi'is*.
78   See Aziz, 'Fadlallah'.

FURTHER READING

Heinz Halm's *Shiism*, tr. Janet Watson (Edinburgh University Press, Edinburgh, 1991) is an excellent, short introduction to Shīʿism. Some of the most important articles on Shīʿism have been collected and edited by Etan Kohlberg (Shīʿism [Ashgate: Variorum, 2003]). Other collections of articles on Twelver Shīʿism include L. Clarke (ed.) *Shīʿite Heritage: Essays on Classical and Modern Traditions* (Global Publications, Binghamton, 2001), R. Ende and W. Brunner (ed.) *The Twelver Shīʿa in Modern Times* (Brill, Leiden, 2001) and L. Walbridge (ed.) *The Most Learned of the Shiʿa* (Oxford University Press, New York, 2001). Moojan Momen's *An Introduction to Shiʿi Islam* (Yale University Press, New Haven, 1985) is essential reading for anyone interested in Twelver Shīʿism. Wilferd Madelung is the most prominent and erudite modern scholar researching Shīʿite Islam and his various writings on Shīʿism are collected in *Religious Schools and Sects in Medieval Islam* (Variorum, London, 1985) and *Religious and Ethnic Movements in Medieval Islam* (Variorum Reprints, London, 1985).

The Institute of Ismaili Studies has revived the study of Ismāʿīlī Shīʿism. Farhad Daftary's *The Ismāʿīlīs: Their History and Their Doctrines* (Cambridge University Press, Cambridge, 1990) is the major reference work. Madelung's *Der Imam al-Qāsim bin Ibrāhīm und die Glaubenslehre der Zaiditen* (De Gruyter, Berlin, 1965) remains the only major study of early Zaydī thought. Madelung's many encyclopaedia articles for the *Encyclopaedia of Islam*, *Encyclopaedia Iranica* and the *Encyclopaedia of Religion* are extremely useful introductions. A list of Madelung's publications, including the encyclopaedia articles, is located in J. Meri and F. Daftary (ed.) *Culture and Memeory in Medieval Islam* (IB Tauris, London, 2003). The major English text for the study of the *ghulāt* has been Matti Moosa, *Extremist Shīʿites: The Ghulat Sects* (State of New York University Press, New York, 1988). The excellent Arabic study of the Kaysāniyya by Wadād al-Qāḍī (*al-Kaysāniyyah fī taʾrīkh waʾl-adab* [Dār al-Thaqāfah, Beirut, 1974]) remains very useful.

CHAPTER SIX

Historiography of Sufi Studies in the West

ALEXANDER KNYSH

Introduction

Libraries have been written on the phenomenon of "Islamic mysticism" or "Sufism" (Arab. *tasawwuf*) in the Muslim world, in non-Muslim Asia, and in the west. The definition of this term and its heuristic validity have been a matter of heated debates among western experts on Islamic studies.[1] In the meantime, as a contemporary western scholar has aptly remarked, "people end up taking up these terms to mean whatever they wish."[2] One can of course denounce this conceptual and terminological "free-for-all" as deeply misleading and deplorable (which, in a sense, it is), but one should bear in mind that the same lack of consensus applies to practically every analytical category deployed in the field of Islamic studies, including such critical ones as "Islam," "fundamentalism," "Wahhabism,"[3] "[Islamic] modernism/reformism," etc. All these and many other conceptions often mean different things to different people and their usage varies considerably depending on the context in which they are deployed. If we still insist on having a universally acceptable definition of Sufism, we'll have to concede that it is yet to be developed and agreed upon by western scholars. Does this imply that we should simply discard the notion of "Sufism," or, for that matter, all of the other analytical categories mentioned above? Interestingly, this is exactly what many Sufi masters of old encouraged their followers to do, citing the ineffability and uniqueness of mystical experience and its distinctness from one mystic to another. Yet, paradoxically, these same Sufi teachers have produced hundreds of volumes of mystical literature, which today constitutes the textual foundation of Sufi studies in the west.[4]

In the present chapter I will provide a survey of approaches to the study of Sufism's history in, first and foremost, western scholarship with special emphasis on the last one hundred years. My omission of modern Islamic scholarship on the subject implies no disrespect for its achievements. Surveying it would require a separate study due to the sheer wealth of studies of Sufism that has been produced in the Middle East and the Muslim world as a whole over the past several decades.

As any survey, my discussion of the vicissitudes of Sufi studies in the west is perforce selective, incomplete and guided, in part, by my own academic background and research competence. Despite my critique of certain trends in the academic study of Sufism, in the final analysis I take a positive view of western scholarship on the subject and argue that, over the past century and a half, western scholars have made great strides in furnishing a comprehensive understanding of its institutions, practices and teachings. At the same time, I will acknowledge the shortcomings of the study of Sufism in the west.

Western Studies of Sufism in a Historical Perspective

The study of Sufism in the west over the past century and a half is marked by a diligent quest for and accumulation of disparate facts and sources pertaining to the subject. This process usually went hand-in-hand with theory-building and conceptualization of the collected data, which led to the formation of influential explanatory models and academic "orthodoxies" that dominated western discourses on the subject for extended periods of time. Obviously, theory-building in any given historical epoch is conditioned by the overall intellectual climate of the age with its stereotypes, conventions, prejudices, classificatory models and other kinds of dominant intellectual assumptions. They inevitably impact academic and popular depictions of other societies and cultures, especially those of the "exotic" and "mysterious Orient."[5] While modern western views of the Far East or South Asia were, by and large, dictated by intellectual curiosity and pragmatic considerations (namely, trade and commerce, political control and profit), these geographical and cultural complexes were not perceived as sources of an imminent threat to western religious beliefs, ethical and moral values, and political fortunes. The Muslim world, on the other hand, had a long history of violent military and ideological confrontations with its Christian neighbors on both sides of the Mediterranean. Furthermore, unlike Buddhism and other "Oriental" religions, which rested on intellectual and spiritual premises alien to westerners, the religious foundations of Islamic societies were derived from a shared Judeo-Christian legacy. Muslim claims to this legacy were not only unwelcome, but also outright "insulting" to many members of the Christian clergy. This factor determined the righteous passion with which Christian scholars tried to counter Muslim "pretenses" to Abraham's legacy. Christian polemical agendas have insidiously penetrated and informed the mindsets of western students of Islam over the past century and a half. In general, the intellectual trajectory of Sufi studies in the west should be viewed against the background of European intellectual history in the nineteenth and twentieth centuries. A discipline that started as a first and foremost philological, text-centered exercise gradually evolved into a subdivision of "cross-religious" studies pursued by curious amateurs (diplomats, travelers, colonial officials), Biblicists, and area studies specialists, or "Orientalists." Since their activities coincided with Europe's colonial expansion in Central Asia, India, South East Asia, the Middle East, and North Africa, they did not remain immune from the colonial agendas of their respective nation-states.

Here it is not the place to enter the debate over the role of "Orientalism" in shaping the image of Islam among the western public at large that was initiated by the US scholar and literary critic Edward Said in the late 1970s. At the same time, one cannot avoid it altogether while dealing with the history of western study of Islam. According to Said, from the early nineteenth century on western academic approaches to Islamic societies were critically shaped by Europe's colonial ventures in the Middle East and beyond. Taking his cue from Michel Foucault (1926–1984), Said argued that these approaches were determined first and foremost by the dependent position of the Muslim world vis-à-vis European colonial powers. In Said's view, the entire body of knowledge and discourse about the Islamic Middle East generated by several generations of European Orientalists was implicated in the imperialist plot to subjugate and control Islamic societies. The "Orient" (and "Islam") of western scholarship was nothing but a series of blatant distortions and misrepresentations that was designed to justify and facilitate Europe's colonial policies in the Middle East. Said argued that any accurate and unbiased representation of the dependent colonial object by the colonizing subject was simply impossible.[6]

Finally, as with any other branch of humanistic scholarship the geopolitical realities outlined above (namely, western colonialism and the west–east power differential), one should keep in mind the so-called subjective factor, that is, the personality of the investigating subject with his or her personal inclinations (sympathies and antipathies), temperament, social upbringing, religious convictions, etc. The personal background of a scholar often colors his or her entire approach to his or her field of academic endeavor, in our case, to Islam and its civilization. The role of the subjective factor is even more pronounced when the scholar investigates the mystical tradition of Islam, which pertains to a highly personal and elusive aspect of human life. While some Western academics have attempted to trivialize the mystical experience behind Sufi teachings by treating it as any other human sensation or cognitive process, its deeply personal and intangible character is usually taken for granted and is seen as a complicating factor.[7]

The rich spiritual and intellectual legacy of Sufism may exert such an irresistible attraction upon its initially "unengaged" students that some of them may occasionally become totally transformed by it and, as it were, "sucked" into its world of fascination and mystery. Such scholars-turned-Sufis often choose to make the study and dissemination of knowledge about Sufism or a particular version of it their personal vocation. At the opposite end of the spectrum we find those who reject out of hand the reality and genuineness of mystical experience and declare it to be a deliberate sham on the part of "unscrupulous" Sufi masters seeking a higher social status and personal material gain through manipulating their credulous followers. This overly "skeptical" approach has until recently been the hallmark of Islamic studies in the Soviet Union.

Apart from these objective and subjective factors, a major challenge facing western students of Islamic mysticism is the vast geographical spread of Sufism and its institutions from West Africa to China (Xinjiang) and from the Volga region to South Africa. Sufi doctrines, practices and institutions have differed considerably from one region to another as they were determined by a myriad of local factors and conditions. Moreover, even within one and the same region they have changed, often drastically, over time.

Sufi Studies in a Historical Perspective

Although Europe's exposure to Sufism occurred already in the Middle Ages, the first serious attempts to address it in academic terms date to the seventeenth century.[8] Western scholars of that epoch were preoccupied with translating and analyzing the literary output of the "Soofees," especially, the works of such great Persian poets as Sa'di, 'Attar, Rumi, Jami and Hafiz.[9] A quite different image of Sufism emerges from travelogues and personal memoirs of western visitors to the Middle East and Central Asia in the eighteenth and nineteenth centuries. Produced for the most part by western travelers, colonial administrators and merchants, they emphasize Sufism's exotic aspects as manifested in the "erratic" behavior and "strange" practices of the "dervishes." In the works of this genre, literary concerns were often intertwined with a desire to provide a systematic and accurate account of various Sufi practices, doctrines, and communities. Despite their obvious fascination with the beauty of Sufi literature and the exemplary piety of individual Muslim mystics, authors of such works were reluctant to consider mystical propensities to be intrinsic to the Islamic religion. Wittingly or not, they viewed Islam as inferior to Christianity and therefore incapable of producing the vaulted spirituality and sophisticated theology they observed in Sufi texts. Yet, Western scholars were unable to furnish any conclusive evidence of Sufism's "foreign" origins in the absence of sources pertaining to its rise and early evolution. Practically all these scholars exhibited a gamut of anti-Islamic prejudices of their age. Typical in this regard is the work of Joseph Garcin de Tassy (1794–1878), whose admiration for Persian language and literature did not prevent him from paying tribute to the European anti-Islamic shibboleths of his time. For him, Islam was but "a grossly distorted [version] of Christianity," whose followers were similar to "Christian heretics" along the lines of the gnostic sect of the Adamites; Sufi teachings were a Muslim variant of "pantheism," which, however, should be distinguished from the "errors" of its Hindu counterpart.[10] However, despite the differences between the two, in the final analysis, they both lead their followers to "materialism, denial of human freedom [of action], lack of differentiation between [good and evil] actions and permission to engage in all manner of earthly pleasures."

Such views were shared by many European Orientalists of the age, who were usually trained as philologists or Biblical studies scholars. Their philological predilections are evident in their preoccupation with Sufi poetry, which they tended to treat in isolation from the tenets of Islam as a manifestation of "free-thinking" or even downright "libertarianism." The philological background of such western academics found an eloquent expression in their interest in various dictionaries of Sufi terms, which, in their judgment, provided the indispensable key to the understanding of masterpieces of Sufi literature. The distinguished German Orientalist Gustav Flügel (1802–1870) accomplished one of the earliest Latin translations of the dictionaries of Sufi technical terms by Abu 'Ali al-Jurjani (d. 816/1413) and Muhyi 'l-Din Ibn 'Arabi (d. 638/1240). Around the same time, Aloys Sprenger (1813–1893) a German scholar employed by the British colonial administration of India, published a critical edition of the Sufi dictionary by a famous commentator on Ibn 'Arabi, 'Abd al-Razzaq al-Kashani (d. 730/1329 or 735/1334). These works, together with the monumental collection of Sufi biographies by 'Abd al-Rahman al-Jami (d. 898/1492), which was edited in 1859 by the prolific British Orientalist William Nassau Lees (1825–1889), formed the foundation for the subsequent advancement of Sufi studies in Europe.

All major "histories of Islam" that appeared in Europe between the 1850s and 1890s contain at least a cursory discussion of Islamic mysticism. Their authors tended to draw a sharp distinction between Sufism and mainstream Islam (both Sunni and Shi'i) and to treat the former as a foreign importation from one or the other religious and philosophical system, especially Hinduism, Neo-Platonism, and the Christian monastic tradition.[11] In his influential *Geschichte der herrschenden Ideen des Islams* Alfred von Kremer (1828–1889) addressed Sufism in the context of his overall thesis regarding Islam's "dominant ideas." Although the main thrust of his work was formulated in opposition to the attempts of his predecessors to trace the specificity of Islamic civilization to the linguistic and racial characteristics of Muslim peoples, von Kremer displayed similar racial stereotypes in his discussion of Sufism. Thus, he consistently derived ascetic and mystical tendencies in Islam from extraneous sources, tracing the "ascetic aspects" of Sufism back to Christian monasticism and its "contemplative" element to the "Buddhist–Hindu" influences mediated by the Persian cultural milieu.[12] This latter influence eventually suppressed Sufism's "monastic" element and rendered it "contemplative" rather than "ascetic." This event marked the beginning of the "decline" and "degeneration" not only of Islamic mysticism but also of Islam as a whole. Such ideas informed western views of Sufism throughout the second half of the nineteenth century.

With European colonial expansion in the Middle East and South Asia in the early nineteenth century, western studies of Islamic mysticism acquired pragmatic dimensions. This pragmatic approach was dictated by the exigencies of colonial policy in Algeria for the French, in Indonesia for the Dutch, and in India and Egypt for the British. It was pursued primarily by European colonial administrators, who were concerned with Sufism's potential to rally the Muslim masses against colonial rule. Their intellectual endeavor, which a western scholar has dubbed as "police report scholarship,"[13] existed alongside academic Orientalism, whose practitioners were preoccupied with the recovery and translation of the intellectual and literary legacy of Islam's "golden age" (the ninth to eleventh centuries CE). The academics, for their part, were patently uninterested in the current condition of Islamic societies, which they viewed as one of "decay" and "stagnation," both socially and culturally. "Applied Orientalists," on the other hand, usually had a rather vague idea of the past glory of Islamic civilization and were concerned primarily with its "here and now." Many of them came from a military background – the earliest studies of Maghribi Sufism were undertaken by French army officers: Edouard de Neveu, Charles Brosselard, Henri Duveyrier,[14] and so on. This pragmatic trend in French Orientalist scholarship culminated in the influential book *Marabouths et khouan* (1884) by the French infantry captain Louis Rinn. In the introduction to his study, Rinn promised his readers a "comprehensive" and "impartial" discussion of the history and customs of North African Sufi brotherhoods.[15] However, in examining the antagonistic relations between members of the *sharifian* lineages (*marabouths*) and leaders of various Sufi brotherhoods he consistently advised his colonial superiors to avail themselves of this antagonism in order to consolidate French control over the colony.[16] In discussing the origins of Sufism, Rinn repeated the already familiar notion that it can be traced back to "ancient Indian philosophy," while also pointing out similarities between some key elements of Sufism in the Maghrib and Berber culture[17] – a tribute to the French view that the latter was incompatible with "Arab Islam" and developed its own version of the Islamic religion. On the other hand, his statistical data regarding the numerical strength and geographical location of various Maghribi brotherhoods is highly valuable.

The works of the Frenchmen Alfred Le Chatelier, Octave Depont and Xavier Coppolani are based on similar premises. The former examined the history and composition of eighteen Sufi brotherhoods that were active in the Hijaz (primarily in Mecca). In discussing the political and military potential of the powerful Sanusiyya brotherhood of Libya, Le Chatelier justified his intellectual endeavor by the fact the object of his study was a major obstacle to the French *mission civilisatrice* in the

African continent.[18] Le Chatelier's descriptions of his sojourn in Mecca bear a striking resemblance to an intelligence report from an undercover agent in an enemy camp. The French colonial anxieties over the Maghribi Sufi brotherhoods found a dramatic expression in the colossal book by the French colonial officials Depont and Coppolani, which summarized the results of several decades of French scholarship in France's North African colonies. Commissioned by the governor general of Algeria, it was intended to provide a panoramic picture of Sufism from its inception up to the end of the nineteenth century. In dealing with the problem of Sufism's origins, the authors sought to trace it back to Neo-Platonic ideas. At the same time, they identified other influences that left their imprint on Sufi doctrines and practices, including Berber "animism," the ancient Mithra cult, Manichaeism, and Christian monasticism.[19] While acknowledging the role of these and other "external influences," the authors nevertheless were careful to point out that mystical experience is shared by all human beings regardless of their association with any particular religious creed or philosophical doctrine. As with Rinn and Le Chatelier, Depont and Coppolani regarded Sufi brotherhoods as a major threat to French colonial presence in North Africa. Therefore, they insisted that any attempt at resistance on the part of their members should be immediately and forcefully suppressed.[20]

The usefulness of French colonial scholarship on the Maghrib has been a matter of academic disputes. Some western academics have argued that, if shorn of its colonial agendas, it can provide valuable first-hand data about the condition and structures of North African Sufi brotherhoods in the nineteenth and early twentieth centuries. Others, following Edward Said, insist that the faulty ideological premises of French colonial scholars have effectively rendered their works useless, for their biases determined the ways in which they selected and arranged their data.[21]

Given the importance of organized Sufism in Ottoman politics and social life, it is hardly surprising that it came under close scrutiny by western observers. Studies of Ottoman Sufi brotherhoods were undertaken by the American diplomat John P. Brown (1814–1872) and the German and British scholars Georg Jacob, Hans Joachim Kissling, Franz Babinger, Lucy Garnett, Frederick William Hasluck, to name but a few. In British India, the study of Sufism by colonial officers displayed the political concerns and anxieties similar to those of the French. In imperial Russia, interest in Sufism was sparked by Russia's colonial ambitions on its southern borders as well as its geopolitical rivalry with the Ottoman Empire. Contemporary Russian views of Sufism mirrored those of the French and the British. Among its various manifestations, Caucasian *miuridizm*[22] was viewed by Russian authors as particularly detrimental to Russian geopolitical aspirations. The negative tone of Russian academic and journalistic coverage of *miuridizm* was determined by the fierce resistance to the Russian conquest on the part of the mountaineers of Daghestan and Chechnya throughout the first part of the nineteenth century (the so-called "Caucasian War"). Russian writers depicted the leaders of the local branches of the Naqshbandi *tariqa* as calculating politicians who exploited the "blind fanaticism" of their misguided Sufi followers (Rus. *miuridy*) to further their political and military goals. The adepts of Imam Shamil (Shamwil), who belonged to the Khalidi branch of the Naqshbandi Sufi order, were portrayed by Russian scholars, military commanders and colonial administrators[23] as the instigators and backbone of the anti-Russian resistance. Similar apprehensions were expressed by Russian colonial officials in Central Asia, where at least one rebellion was attributed to the "agitation" of the local Sufi masters called *ishans*.[24]

The fears of the "rebellious nature" of Sufi brotherhoods expressed by some Russian and European scholars seem to corroborate Said's thesis regarding Orientalism's connivance and complicity in their countries' colonial projects. At the same time, colonial agendas were not nearly as strongly pronounced in the works of "armchair" academics, whose works evince biases of a different kind, namely, a conviction that Islam is incapable of producing a sophisticated spirituality associated with "philosophical Sufism." The link between this conviction and the European colonial project is not as straightforward, although it is certainly not unrelated to Europe's self-perception as the beacon of "progress." On the other hand, the substantial and sincere efforts by western academics to unravel the complex phenomenon of Islamic mysticism cannot be summarily attributed to their pragmatic desire to advance and justify the European colonization of the Muslim world.

The Founding Discourses

Great strides were made in the study of Sufism by scholars whose academic careers straddled the nineteenth and twentieth centuries. This was the time of the titans of European Islamology, whose intellectual legacy was destined to shape the subsequent development of this discipline. All these scholars were eager to identify the place of Sufi teachings, literature, and practices vis-à-vis "orthodox" Islam. They were less interested in Sufism's institutional and organizational dimensions, which was the logical outcome of their training as philologists. As with their predecessors, the question of Sufism's beginnings loomed large in their scholarship. Thus, in seeking to identify the provenance of mystical piety in Islam the great Hungarian scholar Ignaz Goldziher (1850–1921), advanced a thesis of the two principal sources of Sufism.[25] The first, characterized as "ascetic-practical," was, in his view, "indigenous" to Islam. It was inspired by the frugal and world-renouncing ways of the Prophet and some of his close companions.[26] The "mystic-speculative" trend in Sufism was a result of Islam's contact with the culturally and religiously sophisticated societies of the Middle East and South Asia. The "ascetic-practical" impulse was shaped by the "secularization" of the Muslim state under the Umayyads. The "mystic-speculative" impulse originated in Neo-Platonism and was later augmented by elements from other religious systems, especially those that emphasized the idea of love of God and union with him (e.g., Gnosticism). According to Goldziher, the idea of love between man and God reached its culmination in the teaching of al-Hallaj (d. 310/922), who deliberately sought martyrdom in order to reunite with his divine beloved. In his influential study of Islamic exegesis, Goldziher was the first western scholar to turn his attention to Sufi methods of Qur'an interpretation. In Goldziher's view, Sufi exegetes embraced the allegorical method of Qur'an interpretation, which set them apart from the "mainstream" Sunni commentators who focused on the historical, legal and philological aspects of the Muslim scripture. The Sufi fascination with the allegorical message of the scripture bears a close resemblance to (and was probably derived from) the Shi'i and Isma'ili "esoteric" concepts of the Islamic revelation[27] that focused on its hidden allusions to the special role of their imams against the background of Neo-Platonic emanationist cosmology. In Goldziher's opinion, in the eastern areas of the Muslim world Islamic mysticism came under the influence of Buddhism and Hinduism in both theory and practice.[28] In sum, Gold-ziher believed that from its beginnings in a simple renunciant piety (probably borrowed from Christian monasticism) Sufism evolved into a metaphysical doctrine of Neo-Platonic inspiration, which, in turn, engendered a pantheistic concept of the world – a notion reminiscent of, and partly derived from – the Indian religious traditions.[29] For Goldziher, the work of the great Muslim theologian al-Ghazali (d. 505/1111) marked the critical turning point in Sufism's history, because it "brought Sufism out of its isolation from the dominant conception of religion and established it as a standard element of the Muslim believer's life." Al-Ghazali's seminal work, the *Revivification of the Sciences of Religion,* was a bold attempt to reform Islam and, in Goldziher's words, "instill new life into the dry bones of the prevailing Islamic theology."[30] For him, al-Ghazali was a scholar of exceptional intellectual stature, whose great intellectual stature helped to integrate Sufism into the body of "official" Islam.

While Goldziher's investigations were based almost exclusively on the analysis of Sufi texts from various periods, his Dutch colleague Christiaan Snouck Hurgronje (1857–1936) combined archival work with field observations of "Islam in practice," which was made possible by his status as a high-ranking colonial officer in the service of the Dutch state. His awareness of sometimes dramatic discrepancies between the injunctions of normative Islam and the situation "on the ground" made him sensitive to the dangers of generalizing about the Islamic religion and its followers. Like Goldziher, Snouck Hurgronje considered Sufism to be a product of Islam's encounter with some pre-Islamic religious and philosophical systems, namely Neo-Platonism, Christianity, and, somewhat later, Hinduism and Buddhism. Snouck Hurgronje rejected Louis Massignon's attempts to derive Islamic mysticism exclu-sively from the Qur'an and the Sunna of the Prophet.[31] For him, Islam was first and foremost a "cross" between Judaism and Christianity, both of which contained mystical elements that contributed to the rise of Sufism. Snouck Hurgronje discerned several principal trends within mystical Islam: (1) "sensual," that is, derived from the personal experience of the deity by the mystic, who tended to couch it into bacchic or erotic symbols; (2) "moral and ethical," which impelled the Muslim to cleanse his soul of all mundane attachments and to prepare it for the contemplation of God through austere ascetic exercises, pious meditation and acts of self-abnegation; (3) "speculative," which developed under the influence of the Neo-Platonic doctrine of emanation and gradually evolved into a full-blown monistic metaphysics.[32] In ad-dressing the causes of the wide dissemination of ascetic and mystical tendencies among the Muslims Snouck Hurgronje cited the widespread Muslim disenchantment with the dry scholasticism of Muslim jurists and theologians. It was acutely perceived and eloquently articulated by al-Ghazali who, in Snouck Hurgronje's opinion, "rejected" the study of jurisprudence (*fiqh*) and speculative theology (*kalam*) in favor of the intuitive experiential knowledge espoused by the Sufis.[33] According to Snouck Hurgronje, by emphasizing God's immanent presence in this world Sufi doctrines inevitably clashed with the Qur'anic idea of God's absolute transcendence vis-à-vis his creation. This feature of Sufism, in his view, along with its tolerance toward other religions and beliefs, allowed it to overcome the intolerant and exclu-sivist spirit of "scriptural" Islam, making it a perfect forum for dialogue with other religious traditions.[34]

While both Goldziher and Snouck Hurgronje were, in the final analysis, sympa-thetic toward Sufism, the doyen of German Orientalism Carl Becker (1876–1933) was much less sanguine. For him, Sufism's fixation on the internal life of the individual amounted to "the barren gymnastics of the soul" and, in its extreme forms, to the religious "nihilism" which logically leads to "unbelief and pantheism." Sufism, in Becker's view, served no practical purpose, since it inculcated in its followers fruitless quietism and indifference toward the conditions of the world around them. Becker's low opinion of Sufism can be attributed to his Lutheran convictions as well as his political career and social stance: for several years he served as Germany's minister of culture.[35]

Another German scholar, Richard Hartmann (1881–1965), made Sufism his primary area of research. Focusing on what he regarded as the "classical" period of Sufism's history and its major representative Abu 'l-Qasim al-Qushayri (d. 465/ 1072),[36] Hartmann once again endeavored to resolve the problem of the origins of Sufism. His analysis of the work of al-Qushayri was informed by Becker's notion of Islam as "a [typical] sample of religious syncretism." In line with this premise, Hartmann sought to trace some principal Sufi concepts back to their "origins" in other religious and philosophical traditions, especially Hinduism, Manichaeism, Shamanism, and Mithra's cult. Since these belief systems enjoyed wide currency in the Muslim East, especially in Khurasan, which was al-Qushayri's homeland, the latter, in Hartmann's view, could not remain immune to them. Within Islam, Hartmann noticed some striking similarities between Sufi and Shi'i esotericism[37] – an idea that, as we shall see, was brought to fruition in the studies of Henry Corbin and Seyyed Hossein Nasr. At the same time, Hartmann acknowledged that these obvious parallels may, at closer examination, turn out to be mere coincidences. Hence his constant caveats and reluctance to pass a final verdict on the issue of Sufism's beginnings.[38] In the end, Hartmann proved to be incapable of breaking away from the dominant intellectual paradigm of his age, which encouraged scholars to regard similarities between religious teachings and intellectual paradigms as evidence of causal relations between them.

Hartmann's interest in the roots of Islamic mysticism was shared by many of his contemporaries. In his monumental *Literary History of Persia* the British scholar Edward Browne (1862–1926) outlined several approaches to this issue in the Orientalist literature of his time. One regarded Sufism as a natural development of the mystical elements inherent in the Qur'an and the teachings of the Prophet Muhammad. From this viewpoint, any quest for its external roots is meaningless. According to the other approach (Edward Palmer et al.), Sufism is an Indian and Persian reaction to the "Semitic genius" of the Arabs. The third thesis viewed Neo-Platonism as the principal source of mystical trends in Islam. Finally, the fourth thesis argued that Sufism arose as an "orthodox" trend within Islam only to be impregnated by "foreign" influences at the later stages of its evolution. The latter seems to have been Browne's own position,[39] although, like Palmer, he averred that Sufism had "its chief home, if not the centre and well-spring, in Persia."[40]

Taking his cue from von Kremer's monumental study of the history of Islamic ideas, the Scottish–American missionary and scholar Douglas Macdonald (1865–1943) proposed the following tripartite classification of the trends within Islamic mysticism: (1) the first trend evolved from the ascetic and quietist elements of Muhammad's teachings into an ascetic-mystical piety which was eventually accepted by the majority of Muslim scholars as "orthodox," especially following al-Ghazali's "reconciliation" of "official" Islam and Islamic mysticism;[41] (2) the "speculative" trend that developed under a strong influence of Neo-Platonism and Eastern Christianity (monasticism, the Pseudo Dionysius-Areopagite, Stephan bar Sudaili, etc.); (3) the "pantheistic" trend which was introduced into Islam by al-Bistami and al-Hallaj and which was totally "alien" to the Islamic doctrine of a transcendent God.[42] While this classification was rather standard for his age, Macdonald's attempts to consider mystical experience in Islam from the viewpoint of parapsychology (i.e., as an "auto-hypnosis" or "auto-suggestion" of sorts) were novel.[43]

An important contribution to the study of Islamic mysticism was made by the prolific British scholar, Reynold A. Nicholson (1868–1945). A man of unusual linguistic talents who mastered the three principal languages of "classical" Islam, he, through his study of the Sufi poetry of Jalal al-Din Rumi, came to the realization of the necessity to write an intellectual history of Islamic mysticism.[44] As a result, he undertook a life-long study of early Sufi literature that contained the "rudiments" of the later Sufi intellectual universe. In Nicholson's view, later Sufi ideas and literary conventions were simply incomprehensible to anyone who was not familiar with their antecedents, as explicated by the Sufi "classics" of the ninth and tenth centuries CE.[45] As with many of his predecessors and contemporaries, Nicholson adhered to the thesis of "multiple influences" and warned his readers against trying to derive such a complex phenomenon as Sufism from any single source, be it Eastern Christianity, Neo-Platonism, Gnosticism, Buddhism, etc. Yet, in his view, it was equally absurd to consider Sufism to be a native Islamic phenomenon that organically grew out of Qur'anic precepts and the prophetic Sunna.[46]

Similar hypotheses of the origins of mystical tendencies in Islam were advanced by Nicholson's colleagues, especially the Dutch Arendt Wensinck (1882–1939), the Swedish Henrik Nyberg (1889–1974), and the British Margaret Smith (1884–1970). Each of them recognized that the mystical movement in Islam can be traced to several "foreign" sources, yet each of them emphasized the role of one such source over the other. Their choice of this principal influence usually reflected their own academic background and intellectual predilections. Thus, Wensinck, who specialized in Eastern Christianity and Judaism (especially their Neo-Platonic elaborations), considered them to be the principal fount of Sufi ideas and practices. For him, Sufism was an Islamic variant of "Semitic[47] mysticism," which itself was a product of Neo-Platonic philosophy. As for "eastern influences" (namely, Hinduism and Buddhism), they were marginal,[48] because they went against the grain of the monotheistic spirit of the "Semitic mentality." Interestingly, he considered the interaction between the Christian (Aramaic) and Islamic (Arabic) variants of "Semitic mysticism" to be a two-way process. While in the beginning Muslim ascetics and mystics borrowed their theories and practices from the Christian monks of Syria and Iraq, by the thirteenth century CE Sufi ideas had come to serve as a source of inspiration for Eastern Christian mystics.

Margaret Smith's interest in Islamic mysticism was sparked by her study of Christian monastic movements in Egypt, Syria and Iraq.[49] As with Wensinck, she considered the rise of Sufism to be a natural continuation of the Christian mystical tradition in a new religious environment. Hence, various Sufi practices, such as the mortification of the flesh, night vigils, various kinds of vows and self-imposed strictures can be traced back to the monastic tradition of Eastern Christendom.[50] Smith's emphasis on the Christian roots of Islamic mysticism led her to question Nicholson's theory of its Neo-Platonic inspiration. In her opinion, Neo-Platonic influences were never direct;

rather, they were always mediated by the teachings and writings of the Church fathers and Aramaic-speaking monks from Syria and Iraq. One channel of Christian influences on early Islam was intermarriages between Arab conquerors and Christian women, who passed on their Christian values and ideals (including asceticism and mysticism) to their children.[51] The latter in turn disseminated them among the Muslim masses. Even "pantheism," which was adopted by some Sufi groups, was not borrowed by them from India and Central Asia, but from the writings of some Christian mystics, such as St. Clement of Alexandria, St. Basil the Great, St. Gregory of Nyssa, St. Macarius of Egypt, Aphraates the Monk, and Isaac of Nineveh.[52] Smith's occasional references to universal "age-old desire of the human soul for God and its longing to attain to communion with Him"[53] do not offset the obvious pro-Christian bias of her academic work. At the same time, her examination of the ascetic and mystical movements of the Hellenistic and early medieval Middle East in a comparative perspective was illuminating and timely.

The tendency to see Sufism as a trend in Islam most akin to Christianity found an enthusiastic exponent in the great Spanish Arabist Miguel Asin Palacios (1871–1944). For him, Sufi spirituality (which he admired) was, in essence, a borrowing from the Christian religion. In accord with this premise, the sophisticated mystical teaching of the great Andalusian–Arab thinker Ibn 'Arabi was but "Christianized Islam" (islam cristinanizado). In Asin Palacios's studies, Islam's thinkers of mystical slant such as al-Ghazali and Ibn 'Arabi were consistently compared to the great Spanish mystics San Juan de la Cruz and Santa Teresa of Jesus. At the same time, Asin Palacios was careful to emphasize that borrowing was not unidirectional; Islam, too, could occasionally influence Christian theology and culture (as was the case with Dante, whose portrayal of heaven and hell was, according to Asin Palacios, influenced by Muslim eschatological teachings[54]). Yet, in the final analysis, Islam's intellectual and spiritual vitality was an organic outcome of its appropriation of some key elements of the Christian religion.

The work of the French scholar Louis Massignon (1883–1962) marked a radical departure from the Orientalist obsession with the extraneous roots of Islamic mysticism. After analyzing the technical terminology of early Sufism (up to the fourth/tenth century), Massignon arrived at the conclusion that its origins can be found in the Qur'anic text itself and, therefore, one need not look any further. While the original meaning of the Qur'anic narrative was reinterpreted by the creators of the Sufi tradition in accord with their mystical experiences, this does not negate the fact that the principal Sufi ideas were based on a profound meditation on, and internalization of, the meaning of the Muslim revelation, not on any sources external to Islam.[55] According to Massignon, the fact of borrowing from such a source is difficult, if not impossible to prove, unless one can produce a decisive textual evidence to substantiate it. In most cases, such evidence simply does not exist. Why, then, not assume that certain similarities between Sufism and other mystical traditions are determined by the analogical workings of the human psyche. Hence, in Massignon's view, Sufism is essentially an "autochthonous" phenomenon within Islam that cannot be satisfactorily explained by references to "foreign" influences.[56] Ascetic tendencies in Islam emerged as a result of the intense "internalization" of the Islamic revelation by some otherworldly-minded Companions of the Prophet. Their ascetic propensities, gradually augmented by mystical ideas, found ready acceptance among the Muslims of Iraq and Khurasan. Such ideas were indigenous to Islam, as they were extracted from the Qur'anic text by means of an intense meditation on its esoteric dimensions. Gradually, there emerged in Sufism the "heretical" idea of the possibility of a union between the mystic and the divine, which was remarkably similar to the Christian doctrine of incarnation. It reached its ultimate expression in the preaching of the "mystical martyr" al-Husayn b. Mansur al-Hallaj (d. 310/922), whose life and death symbolize the apotheosis of mystical experience in Islam.[57] After his execution on charges of "incarnationism" (*hulul*), Sufism entered the period of "fossilization" and spiritual "decline" which was exemplified by the domination of the doctrine of "existential monism" associated with Ibn 'Arabi (d. 638/1240) and his school. Among the causes of that "decline," according to Massignon, was the impregnation of the "primeval" mystical experience symbolized by al-Hallaj with the "speculative" element artificially transplanted onto Islam from external sources, especially "Hellenistic philosophy."[58]

Massignon's vision of Sufi history and of various types of mystical experience in Islam have been detailed elsewhere[59] and need not be repeated here. I will limit myself to a few remarks about his overall approach to Sufism and its impact on subsequent western scholarship on the subject. While on the face of it, Massignon advocated the theory of the Qur'anic origins of Islamic mysticism, in his spirited and deeply sympathetic portrayal of al-Hallaj he implicitly drew a parallel between his martyrdom and the "passion" of Jesus Christ.[60] In a similar vein, al-Hallaj's theory of two natures, human and divine (*nasut/lahut*), which can be united in certain perfected human individuals, was, in Massignon's depiction, nothing but an Islamic version of Christology.[61] The fact that he elevated al-Hallaj over all other Sufis both before and after him betrays Massignon's Christian predilections[62] and his implicit (and perhaps unconscious) desire to "Christianize" the Sufi martyr. Thus, paradoxically, Massignon has found himself in the same camp as another Catholic student of Sufism, Miguel Asin Palacios. One should address, at least briefly, Massignon's method of reading mystical texts. According to him, the true cognition of a mystical phenomenon becomes possible only through a profound transformation of the cognizant subject by the object of his cognizance. By consistently re-living and internalizing the mystical experience of al-Hallaj, Massignon strove not just to explain it to his contemporaries, but also to participate in its "sanctity" and the "divine grace" associated with it.[63] In other words, Massignon's goal in his examination of Islamic mysticism was, among others, to enrich and deepen his own personal experience of the divine. As such, his work can hardly be described as strictly academic, although in the end one cannot deny that he has contributed in important ways to our understanding of al-Hallaj's controversial legacy and of early Sufism as a whole.

Not everyone was convinced by Massignon's insistence on the Qur'anic roots of Islamic mysticism. Among his opponents one should mention Max Horten (1874–1945), a distinguished German scholar who specialized in "Oriental philosophies." An expert on Indian systems of thought, he denied the Christian doctrine of Sufism's origins advanced by Miguel Asin Palacios, while at the same time disagreeing with Louis Massignon's "Qur'anic theory." As one would expect from a specialist of his background, he emphasized Indian (especially Vedantic) influences on Sufism, which he spotted in the teachings of al-Bistami, al-Junayd, and al-Hallaj. Thus, he claimed that in al-Hallaj we find a typical "Brahmanic thinker,"[64] whose teaching flew in the face of the standard Islamic notion of a transcendent God with its emphasis on God's immanent presence in the world and its natural phenomena.[65] To prove his point,

Horten undertook a thorough examination of the terminology of early Sufism, but arrived at opposite conclusions to those of Massignon. However, in the end, he failed to persuade the majority of his colleagues,[66] who found Massignon's thesis to be more convincing, even though they did not necessarily embrace it.

Massignon's examination of the formative period of Islamic mysticism was not unique. The Swedish bishop Tor Andrae (1885–1947) conducted a study of the first Sufi manuals and biographical collections by al-Sulami (d. 412/1021), Abu Nu'aym al-Isbahani (d. 429/1037), and al-Qushayri. Andrae's view of the origins of ascetic and mystical elements in Islam was rather ambiguous. As a student of the life of Muhammad and the early history of Islam, Andrae was aware of the presence of ascetic and mystical tendencies in the Muslim community from its very inception.[67] However, according to Andrae, Muhammad's teaching was itself a product of Christian influences. As for the earliest Muslim ascetics and mystics, their worldview was permeated by the ideas borrowed from the Christian monks and anchorites of Syria and Northern Arabia.[68] Like Massignon, Andrae considered the third/ninth and the fourth/tenth centuries to have been the period of an active creative elaboration of mystical theories and practices by a handful of talented pious individuals. It was followed by a gradual "decline" that occurred, at least in part, through the introduction into Sufism of speculative and metaphysical methods that were intrinsically "alien" to the irrational foundations of mystical experience.

To summarize, one can argue that by the 1960s the study of Islamic mysticism established its *Sitz im Leben* within the field of western (primarily European) Orientalism. By building on the foundations established by a handful of nineteenth-century pioneers, their twentieth-century successors generated a considerable body of academic literature that included both editions of – for the most part – early Sufi writings and analytical studies of individual Sufi masters as well as principal Sufi theories and practices. Their approaches to Sufism varied, often considerably, reflecting their diverse academic backgrounds and interests on the one hand and their personal intellectual and religious predispositions on the other. Yet, the problem of Sufism's origins and of "external influences" on its development remained at the center of academic attention. At the risk of oversimplification, one can say that there emerged two major approaches to Sufism in western scholarship. One, which can be characterized as "historicist," emphasized the concrete circumstances of Sufism's evolution across time and space, viewing it as an uninterrupted linear progression of individuals, concepts, and ideas.[69] Parallel to it we find a tendency to consider Sufism as a kind of "trans-historical" spirituality which, while not immune to its concrete social, economical, and political environment, enjoyed a certain degree of independence from it, thereby reflecting a set of "constants" of the human psyche (namely, the eternal human aspiration to a higher reality and to a unitive/monistic vision of the world). These approaches did not necessarily negate each other, as Massignon's masterful study of the Hallajian legacy finely demonstrated.

The pragmatic trend in Sufi studies, on the other hand, developed in response to the exigencies of European colonial politics in the Middle East and North Africa. Down-to-earth and sober, it left little room for the empathic appreciation in the Sufi tradition that characterized the work of Massignon or Asin Palacios. While calling it "police-report scholarship" is probably an exaggeration, the field data assembled by colonial administrators-cum-scholars was definitely shaped by their colonial and imperial presuppositions and anxieties. At the same time, it would be wrong to write their works off altogether, especially in view of the scarcity of "impartial" historical sources, assuming that such exist. Moreover, colonial scholarship that focused on the organizational and social aspects of Sufism felicitously offset the obsession with "classical" Sufi literature that we observe in the academic studies produced in European universities, seminaries, and scholarly societies. These two types of scholarship were intertwined and could sometimes be found in the work of one and the same scholar, Snouck Hurgronje being just one example of many.

Sufi Studies in Russia and the Soviet Union in the Twentieth Century

The vicissitudes of Russian studies of Islam in general and Sufism in particular were closely linked to the country's tumultuous political history in the twentieth century, namely, the Russian Revolution of 1917, the establishment of the Communist regime and the imposition of its ideology on all spheres of intellectual life in the Soviet Union. All these events had a profound impact on the popular and scholarly attitudes toward religion in Soviet Russia and its dominions. In the decades immediately preceding the Revolution, approaches to Sufism in Russian scholarship were similar to, and often derivative from, those of the western Orientalists discussed in the preceding sections. Their works were pored over by students at several "Oriental" departments of Russian universities located in Moscow, St. Petersburg and Kazan. Western Orientalist scholarship had a deep formative influence on Russian academic views of Islam and its various manifestations, including Sufism.

The two principal Russian authorities on Sufism in pre-Revolutionary Russia, Agafangel Krymskii (1871–1942) and Valentin Zhukovskii (1858–1919), specialized in classical Persian poetry. Like their European colleagues, they were well aware that it could not be properly understood and interpreted without at least a modicum of knowledge of Sufi theories and practices. Like many of his European colleagues, Krymskii considered Sufism to be essentially "alien," if not outright "hostile" to the spirit of Islamic revelation.[70] Sufism developed under the pervasive influence of Syrian Christianity and "Buddhist–Persian teachings." In Krymskii's view, "the Arab character was [inherently] incapable of mystical feeling." Hence, mystical teachings developed primarily in the Persian cultural and intellectual milieu and were vigorously opposed by the "nomocentric" Arabs.[71] The inequitable socio-economic conditions and political turmoil of the early Caliphate facilitated their adoption by the Muslim masses and subsequent blossom. In Krymskii's opinion, "the periods of Sufism's flowering usually coincide with the times of tremendous suffering of the common folk,"[72] when ordinary Muslims were forced to seek spiritual consolation in mysticism.

Krymskii's colleague Valentin Zhukovskii was reluctant to make such broad generalizations. He was more interested in the evolution of concrete Sufi concepts and literary topoi. For this purpose, he focused his attention on the earliest layer of Persian literature pertaining to Sufism, namely, the legacy of Abu 'l-Hasan al-Kharaqani (d. 425/1033), 'Abdallah al-Ansari (d. 481/1089), and Abu Sa'id b. Abi 'l-Khayr Mayhani (d. 441/1049). His painstaking edition and analysis of the first Persian treatise on "Sufi science" by al-Jullabi and Hujwiri (d. between 465/1072 and 469/1077) has retained its usefulness even today.[73]

The first Russian Arabist to undertake a serious study of Sufism was Aleksandr Shmidt (Schmidt). A student of Ignaz Goldziher, he dedicated his early research to the famous Egyptian scholar and Sufi ʿAbd al-Wahhab al-Shaʿrani (d. 973/1565). In his introduction to the study of al-Shaʿrani's *oeuvre*, Shmidt made some important remarks about the Sufi movement in Islam as a whole with special reference to the methods of the transmission of knowledge from the Sufi master to his disciples, which, at that time, was a little-known subject. For Shmidt, the popularity of Sufism can be attributed, at least in part, to the dire socio-economic conditions of late medieval Muslim societies, which impelled ordinary believers to seek consolation in God through the mediation of a charismatic Sufi master. However, unlike Krymskii who neglected to substantiate his "socio-economic" explanation of Sufism's popularity with any historical evidence, Shmidt provided a wealth of carefully selected historical facts about the plight of the Egyptian masses during al-Shaʿrani's lifetime. His portrait of the great Egyptian Sufi master was thus deeply grounded in historical and textual evidence, which makes it, in some respects, unsurpassed even today.[74]

Parallel to the academic study of Sufi Islam by Krymskii, Zhukovskii, and Shmidt, we find a substantial body of literature on various aspects of "everyday" Sufism, which was produced by Russian officials in Russia's colonial domains (primarily in the Caucasus and Central Asia). As we have already observed, this kind of literature had the tendency to focus on the political and social role of organized, or *tariqa*, Sufism with a view to gauging its potential to resist or undermine the metropolis's colonial designs. At the same time, by virtue of their presence "in the field" the authors of these works were able to furnish a wealth of information on how Sufism and its institutions (*tariqa*s, shrine complexes and other "holy places") functioned "in real life." As with western colonial scholarship, the Russian colonial literature of the late nineteenth to early twentieth centuries was shaped by the assumptions about Russia's imperial right to subjugate "uncivilized" peoples in order to impose upon them the fruits of western culture.

The Russian Revolution of 1917 ushered in the era of a drastic reassessment of pre-Revolutionary academic paradigms, resulting in the imposition in Soviet academia of a "class-based" paradigm of history and religion. While some leading Russian Orientalists (notably, Vladimir Minorsky and Vladimir Iwanov) chose to emigrate, those who remained in the country were forced to toe the Communist party line or, rather, to quote a famous Soviet witticism, "to fluctuate with its fluctuations." Throughout the 1930s to 1950s, practically the only serious Soviet expert on Sufism was Evgenii Berthels (1890–1957), whose volume of articles and essays titled *Sufism and Sufi Literature* was for several decades the only introduction to Sufism available to the Soviet reader. While Berthels's main focus in that volume was on Persian Sufi poetry, in a short introductory essay he addressed the history of Sufism as a whole, including the unavoidable problem of its origins. This essay exhibits his indebtedness to Massignon's "Qurʾanic theory," although he also agreed with Nicholson regarding the importance of Neo-Platonism in shaping the "speculative trends" in Sufism in the later period. Overall, however, most of Berthels's academic work dealt with the literary aspects of Persian poetry (both Sufi and non-Sufi) and did not address any broader issues pertaining to Sufism's history (e.g., Sufi institutions or Sufi epistemology and metaphysics). Practically all other studies of Sufism in the Soviet literature of the 1930s to 1970s were informed by a rather primitive interpretation of the Marxian doctrine of the role of the masses and class struggle in historical processes. As with other historical phenomena, Sufism was squeezed into the rigid Marxian dichotomy of "reactionary"–"progressive." No wonder that Sufi movements, which were seen by Soviet scholars as typical expressions of "religious ideology," were for the most part treated as "reactionary," despite some dissenting voices (especially in the Muslim republics of the Soviet Empire) which occasionally tried to depict Sufism as a vehicle of Islamic "free-thinking" or even incipient "materialism."[75] Those scholars who dared to depart from this Communist paradigm and to advance a dissenting view of Sufism and its institutions, were promptly accused of being "stooges of the world bourgeoisie" and barred from publishing their works. In the 1960s and 1970s, perceptions of Sufism among Soviet party functionaries and "ideological workers" (especially those based in the "Muslim" republics) were uniformly negative. Sufi orders (real or imaginary) were regarded by the official Soviet authorities as bulwarks of "religious obscurantism" and "retrograde" religious mentality which had to be overcome by all means necessary, including physical repression.[76] Such assumptions were duly replicated by scholars in Soviet academic institutions,[77] which had a profound deleterious impact on their heuristic value.

Sufi Studies in the Second Half of the Twentieth Century

It is extremely difficult to characterize Sufi studies in the west since the late 1950s due their vastness and diversity. Let us make a few general remarks.

First, the western scholars, whose work was surveyed in the previous sections (especially Goldziher, Macdonald, Asin Palacios, Andrae, Nicholson, Wensinck, Massignon, and Smith), laid solid textual and factual foundations for the study of Sufism in western academia. These outstanding scholars created a special branch of Islamic studies by providing careful critical editions of Sufi texts (which they identified as "essential"), while at the same time introducing and "sanctifying" a limited set of analytical methods, technical terms, and general assumptions about the nature of Sufism as well as about which Sufi writers should be regarded as its most authoritative exponents and which ones should be declared "marginal" or "inconsequential." These scholars trained a cohort of "native" Muslim scholars, who disseminated western perceptions and definitions of Sufism among their coreligionists, thereby providing an alternative reading of the Sufi tradition to that of traditional Muslim theologians.

Second, on the methodological plane, many western scholars of the 1950s and 1960s continued to rely primarily on philological methods and literary criticism in dealing with the written legacy of Sufism.[78] In addition to publishing original Sufi texts, these and other scholars of the period strove to spread their perceptions of Sufism among educated lay readers by translating what they regarded as major Sufi works into the European languages. These translations were instrumental in generating continuing interest in Sufism's history and literary legacy among both western academics and the public at large.

Third, in retrospect, one can say that Sufi studies have successfully survived the critique of western "Orientalism" launched in the 1960s and 1970s by Abdul Latif Tibawi and Edward Said, who indicted its representatives for their "complicity" with the western colonial project and the resultant "deliberate distortion" of Islam's image in the west. While Said's critique in particular has forced many western scholars to critically reassess their academic work and enhanced their awareness of their position as researchers, overall we find surprisingly little "soul-searching" among the western "Sufiologists" of the last decades of the twentieth century.

Fourth, throughout the first half of the twentieth century the bulk of western scholarship on Sufism was produced by European academics (especially those residing in Austria, Britain, France, Germany, Holland, Italy, Russia, and Spain). However, by the 1960s the national background of students of Sufism became more diverse. On the one hand, in the decades following the Second World War, the majority of western experts on Sufism were no longer based in Europe, but in North America. On the other hand, Europe's smaller nations (Finland, Norway, Sweden, Yugoslavia, Poland, etc.) established their own centers of Islamic studies, which often housed at least one or two experts on Sufism. In Israel, too, we find many scholars whose primary academic interests lay in the study of Sufism. Finally, a fresh crop of Sufiologists have grown in the Far East, especially in South Korea and Japan.

Fifth, the history of Sufi studies in the west can be seen as a string of academic continuities or even "intellectual dynasties," whose representatives have succeeded one another in (usually, but not always) an uninterrupted progression. Thus, in German-speaking academia, Hartmann was followed by Ritter and Meier, and, more recently, by Richard Gramlich and Bernd Radtke. In Britain, Nicholson found a prominent heir in Arberry, who, however, left no successor of his intellectual stature. In France, Massignon's magisterial work on al-Hallaj inspired his students Paul Nwyia and Henry Corbin[79] (as well as Georges Anawati and Louis Gardet), who were succeeded by a cohort of French academics, including Michel Chodkiewicz, Giles Veinstein, Marc Gaborieau, Eric Geoffroy, and others. In Russia, Zhukovskii's work was continued by Berthels, who was followed by Oleg Akimushkin and Natalia Prigarina, whose students endeavor to keep the tradition alive despite the economic hardships and social upheavals of the post-*perestroika* period.

Sixth, alongside academic studies of Islamic mysticism there has emerged a group of scholars who have made Sufism the object of their personal religious or intellectual commitment. Of these Henry Corbin is probably the most prominent (albeit quite unique) representative. His life-long fascination with Sufi/Shi'i esotericism and his profound impact on the perception of Sufism in twentieth-century Iranian society have been examined in detail in half a dozen studies,[80] which precludes the necessity of detailing it here. The same applies to the so-called "Traditionalist" school, which was discussed in a review article by Carl Ernst.[81]

Some Major Themes and Research Foci

Since the 1960s the major issues of Sufi studies outlined above have continued to attract the attention of Western researchers. Thus, Massignon's "Qur'anic theory" was elaborated by the Francophone Catholic monk Paul Nwyia, who undertook a thorough examination of the early Sufi exegetical tradition. Like Henry Corbin, who emphasized the "common roots" of Islamic esotericism,[82] Nwyia traced the roots of Sufi esotericism back to the esoteric intellectual entourage of the sixth Shi'i imam Ja'far al-Sadiq (d. 148/765).[83] To this end, Nwyia examined the allegorical commentary on the Qur'an attributed to the imam with a view to showing its close affinity with the exegetical methods pursued by some early Sufi masters. While Nwyia's thesis seems quite plausible and the texts that he furnished in support of it are convincing enough, it is not without a flaw. The problem is that Nwyia's textual evidence was collected by the seminal Sufi writer al-Sulami in his famous exegetical compendium titled *Haqa'iq al-tafsir*.[84] However, since al-Sulami throughout his life pursued a strong pro-Sufi apologetic agenda and since his attributions of exegetical dicta may have been determined by it, it is far from obvious that Ja'far al-Sadiq was indeed the real author of the exegetical logia attributed to him. Yet, the line of inquiry proposed by Nwyia is promising due to the centrality of Qur'anic exegesis to the Sufi world-view. Even more importantly, he should be given credit for his invaluable contribution to the study of Sufi technical terminology, which played such a pivotal role in the emergence of Sufism as a "free-standing" spiritual discipline and a specific lifestyle and worldview.[85]

Following in the footsteps of Nwyia, the German–American scholar Gerhard Böwering produced an excellent study of the life and work of one of the pillars of early Sufi exegesis, Sahl b. 'Abdallah al-Tustari (d. 283/896), which remains unsurpassed in its depth and precision. While Böwering agreed with Nwyia's opinion regarding the striking similarities between Sufi exegetical methods and those of the Christian Patristic tradition,[86] unlike his predecessor he was reluctant to see it as Sufism's principal source of inspiration and exegetical techniques. The presence of putative "external influences" in Sufi exegetical lore should not, in his view, be construed as evidence of a lack of creativity or slavish dependence on its Christian precursor. Böwering's superb analysis of the mechanism of the formation of elusive mystical associations and topoi in the mind of the Muslim exegete shows the latter to be by no means less imaginative or creative than his Christian counterparts. So, was there any causal relation between the two exegetical traditions? Böwering does not address this question.

The studies of Nwyia and Böwering contributed, perhaps against their will, to the old debate over the role of "foreign influences" in the shaping of Sufi theories and practices. This issue was revisited again in Bernd Radtke's critical examination of the intellectual universe of the early Sufi thinkers, Dhu 'l-Nun al-Misri (d. 245/860) and al-Hakim al-Tirmidhi (d. ca. 318/930), who are often seen by scholars as typical exponents of "Gnostic" and "Neo-Platonic" ideas in Islam. Radtke argues that the situation was much more complex and the direct influence of non-Islamic systems of thought on these and other early Sufi masters should not be automatically taken for granted. He has shown that both Dhu 'l-Nun and al-Tirmidhi were, in fact, relatively typical Muslim thinkers, whose anthropological, epistemological and cosmological views were quite in line with those of their peers.[87] The fact that certain "foreign" ideas were intricately interwoven into this shared intellectual universe does not necessarily imply that it was decisively shaped by Greek or Hellenistic ideas. In and of itself, their *Gedankenwelt* remained thoroughly and distinctively Islamic. Therefore, to view their mysticism as a simple conduit to Islam of unprocessed "foreign" influences is a gross oversimplification.

A critical reassessment of Massignon's "Qur'anic theory" was offered by the French scholar Marjan Molé, a member of the Dominican monastic order. While he agreed with Massignon that some pious Muslims may have developed their mystical ideas through meditating on the "inner" meaning of the Qur'anic revelation,[88] he insisted that the emergence of ascetic and mystical tendencies within early Islam could not be adequately explained without reference to the numerous Christian monastic communities of the Middle East. Monastic life and ideals were ubiquitous in Iraq, Iran, Egypt, and Syria, where Christian monks rubbed shoulders with Muslim ascetics and mystics. The latter, according to Molé could not remain immune to the appeal of monastic ideals and practices, such as those espoused by the Messalians, whose doctrine of the concealment of virtuous acts (*shituta*) may have contributed to the emergence of the Sufi "people of blame" (*al-malamatiyya*).[89] At the same time, Molé denied any "Eastern" influences – be they Buddhist or Hinduist – on Sufi theories and practices, including the much disputed contribution of Abu Yazid al-Bistami.[90]

A diametrically opposite view of the matter was held by the famous British expert on Indic religions Robert Charles Zaehner (1913–1974). Zaehner's argumentation rests on the already familiar notion that Sufism is "incompatible" with "orthodox" Islam and thus constitutes, in a sense, an "independent religion." Its "foreign" character, in Zaehner's view, is best attested by the teachings of Abu Yazid al-Bistami, who inherited his "pantheistic ideas" from a certain Abu 'Ali al-Sindi, whom Zaehner considered to be a Hindu convert to Islam.[91] According to Zaehner, al-Bistami's adoption of al-Sindi's "Hinduist" worldview marked a critical turning point in the evolution of Sufism from its monotheistic origins to an outright "pantheism" of Vedantic inspiration. Zaehner's thesis was greeted with skepticism: apart from the purported encounter between al-Bistami and al-Sindi, there was no historical or textual evidence to declare al-Bistami to be a proponent of Hindu-style "pantheism".[92] As Zaehner's critics pointed out, nothing that al-Bistami had said could not have been derived from the Qur'an and the Sunna.[93] This is not to say that there was no interaction and cross-pollination between Sufism and Indian religious traditions. However, such mutually enriching contacts took place much later, after the Muslim conquest of India and were much more complex than Zaehner's argument suggests.

With the emergence of Turkish nationalist ideology, some Turkish academics came to argue that Sufism found a particularly fertile and receptive environment among Turkic speaking populations, who were somehow "naturally predisposed" to mysticism and especially to the monistic doctrines of Ibn al-'Arabi and his followers.[94] Attempts were made to trace the origin of some Sufi concepts to ancient Turkic epos and mythology[95] and even to derive the very word "Sufism" (*tasawwuf*) from the Turkic word for "water" (*suv*).[96]

The "Iranian theory" of Sufism's origins found its most eloquent exponent in the great French scholar Henry Corbin, who traced them back to the esoteric milieu of early Shi'ism. His entire academic career was devoted to proving the affinity of these two strains of Islamic esotericism with special reference to the role of Persian thinkers in bringing the resultant intellectual universe to fruition. In Corbin's opinion, Sufism acquired its final shape and reached its full potential only after it had taken root among the Persians. Even though its most consequential exponent, Ibn al-'Arabi, was born and raised in al-Andalus, his eventual relocation from the Muslim west to the Muslim east symbolized the all-important shift of the center of Islamic mystical thought (which Corbin viewed as the pinnacle of intellectual and spiritual life in Islam) to Iran and the Persian-speaking parts of the Muslim world. Corbin did not view the relationship between Shi'ism and Sufism as a unidirectional process. At the early stages of its development Sufi thought was impregnated by Shi'i esoteric ideas. However, in time, the Shi'i tradition became "fossilized" and "dogmatized" only to be invigorated by the creative spiritual energies inherent in Sufi piety.[97] According to Corbin, the esoteric aspects of Sufism and Shi'ism, which had reached their apogee in the spiritual milieu of late medieval Iranian society, came to serve as effective safeguards against the "barren literalism" and "pettifogging mentality" of both "official" Sunnism and Shi'ism.

Corbin's "Iranian" thesis appealed to many famous Iranian intellectuals, such as Seyyed Hosain Nasr and 'Abd al-Husayn Zarrinkoob (Zarrikub), both of whom considered Sufism to be too great an achievement to be shared with any other Muslim nations and advocated the notion of Iran as the cradle of early Sufism.[98] Although at the beginning many Sufi ideas and practices were borrowed, at least in part, from Christian and Buddhist monks, Sufism's later development, according to them, was shaped almost exclusively by Persians, either Shiʿis or Sunnis with strong pro-Alid propensities. The affinity between the "Iranian spirit" and mysticism is best attested by the unprecedented flowering of Sufi poetry in the Persian language.[99]

To sum up, in the second half of the twentieth century, the issue of "Sufism's roots and origins" continued to loom large in western academic literature. As we could see, practically every scholar reviewed above considered it his duty to look for the roots of Islamic mysticism in the tradition he was best familiar with: for an Iranist, Sufism was a natural product of the sophisticated Iranian/Persian spirituality; for an Indologist it was a Muslim appropriation of Indian religious and philosophical systems, for a Turkologist it displayed an unmistakable affinity with "Shamanistic practices" and mystical propensities of the Turkic peoples, etc. Nevertheless, many western scholars have continued to view Sufism as a Muslim extension of the Christian monastic tradition, which in turn was impregnated by late Hellenistic wisdom.[100] This is hardly surprising given their, for the most part, Christian upbringing and their Christian audience, the expectations and interests of which they had to take into account.

At the same time, it is impossible to deny that the problem of "Sufism's origins" has served as a stimulus for western scholars to consider Islamic mysticism in a comparative perspective, thereby preventing them from secluding themselves within the narrow fields of their academic specialization. For some reason, such comparative studies rarely, if ever have addressed the issue of what should be considered "external influence," especially, to what extent our understanding of "authentic Arabian Islam" can serve as a useful benchmark to distinguish "Islamic" elements from "un/non-Islamic" ones. This problem was first raised by the great American scholar Marshall Hodgson, who pointed out the inadequacy of treating the "Arabic" intellectual and cultural elements of Islamic civilization as "genuine," while labeling its non-Arab components as "foreign importations" and "borrowings."[101] One can push Hodgson's caveat even further by arguing that this "Arabocentric" perspective is both static and a-historical as it treats the "Arabian" or "Qurʾanic" Islam as a self-sufficient and unchangeable entity, a "thing in itself" that was somehow immune from re-interpretation and re-assessment by its adherents, who came from a wide variety of educational, ethnic, cultural, and social backgrounds.

Another major issue of recent western scholarship on Sufism has to do with its perceived "blossom" and "decline." According to many western writers, the seventh/thirteenth century represented "the climax of Sufi achievement," whereupon Sufism entered the period of a protracted "decay" that has continued unabated throughout the rest of Islamic history and down to the present.[102] This purported "decay" found its expression in the growing indifference of individual Sufis to acquiring knowledge and creatively reinterpreting the classical Sufi legacy; the widespread and ostentatious forgoing of Islam's ritual obligations by many Sufis; the Sufi "obsession" with "cabbalism" and "witchcraft"; and, finally, the encouragement of popular saint cults and "vulgar superstitions" associated with it by Sufi leaders.[103]

Interestingly, this western notion of the purported "decline" and "degeneration" of later Sufism was informed, at least in part, by the constant complaints of medieval and modern Sufi writers about the rampant "debasement" of the originally high standards of Sufi piety at the hands of their contemporaries.[104] In addition, western proponents of the "decline thesis" may have been influenced by some early twentieth-century Muslim modernists and reformers, who considered Sufism to be a major cause of the intellectual and spiritual "paralysis" that had allegedly afflicted the world of Islam over the past several centuries.[105] Finally, the western proponents of Sufism's alleged "degeneration" were often blinkered by the old Orientalist fixation on the "golden age" of Islam, which, in their mind, came to an end around the sixth/ eleventh century, whereupon it sank into a protracted intellectual and cultural "stupor".[106] Finally, the notion of "decline" and "decadence" of later Sufism is, to some extent, a result of the nineteenth-century Orientalist fixation on texts, which often-times compels western scholars to privilege the earliest of them as "original" and "authoritative," while dismissing all later literary production as "unoriginal" and "epigonic." This preoccupation with the written legacy of Sufism has rendered many Orientalists oblivious of its political, economic and social functions, which are not explicitly addressed in Sufi literature, but which are certainly no less important in determining its vitality.

Thus, the issue is much more complicated than it appears at first sight. First, the notion of "decline," while convenient, is often summarily applied to all aspects of a given phenomenon (in this case, Sufism), which is rarely, if ever, the case in real life.[107] Nor is it ubiquitous, as a perceived or real "decline" in intellectual creativity and originality in, say, Egypt, may be counterbalanced by an intellectual "renaissance" in, say, the Indonesian Archipelago, where Sufism thrived during what is usually regarded by western scholars as the "dark ages" of Islam (from the tenth/ sixteenth century onward). Many Sufi leaders who lived in those "dark centuries" were both outstanding scholars and talented political and military leaders, whose achievements are quite commensurate with those of their predecessors who lived during Sufism's "golden age." In the social and political realm, later Sufism achieved particular prominence by dramatically expanding its teachings and practices among the Muslim masses from Central Asia to Africa. It did so by offering them a wide variety of intellectual and spiritual options and thereby accommodating a great range of potential followers from a humble villager to an urbane intellectual.[108] If worldly success is to be considered a criterion of vitality, then later Sufism definitely was more vigorous than its "golden age" predecessor, which was confined to a relatively narrow circle of "spiritual athletes" with little real political, economic or social influence. The role of post-"golden-age" Sufism in disseminating the message of Islam in the remote corners of the Muslim world from China to western Sahara should also not be forgotten.[109] Overall, the missionary activities of individual Sufis and Sufi brotherhoods in the later periods were quite successful, which one can hardly expect of a "moribund" movement described in some western studies of later Sufism.

A few other problems debated by western scholars of Sufism throughout the second half of the twentieth century deserve at least a brief mention. One is the relationship between various Sufi movements and individuals and the so-called "orthodox" or "official" Islamic establishment. Their perceived incompatibility is often based on the long-standing Orientalist assumption that Sufism is innately "alien" to "mainstream" Islam, whatever this term is supposed to mean, and, as such, suspicious in the eyes of the upholders of Islamic "orthodoxy."[110] However, in reality, there were no "pure jurists" and "pure theologians" locked in an uncompromising struggle with "heretical Sufis." Rather, many Muslim scholars often wore all these three hats (or turbans), and we are often dealing with internal politics and factional infighting within the Muslim scholarly community, in which Sufism was just one element out of many.[111] Even such famous critics of Sufism as Ibn al-Jawzi (597/ 2001), Ibn Taymiyya (d. 728/1328)[112] and Ibn Khaldun (d. 809/1406)[113] were not necessarily opposed to Sufism as such, only to certain manifestations of it which they considered detrimental to the community's well-being. This is not to say that there were no persecutions against individual Sufis or Sufi communities on the part of certain scholarly factions or state authorities. Such persecutions, however, were driven by a complex variety of factors, and one can hardly treat them as evidence of the perennial conflict between "Sufism" and "Islam". It is more appropriate to speak about clashes of personalities and vested economic interests (e.g., over the control of pious endowments and sinecures) and rivalry of scholarly factions. Furthermore, in many respects Sufism had much greater affinity with "traditionalist" Islam than with Islamic rationalism and philosophy.[114] The same applies to the complex relations between Sufism and Shi'ism, which are also characterized by similar ambiguity and which have changed dramatically over time.[115]

The last two decades have witnessed the growing interest among scholars in the history of Sufi institutions, especially brotherhoods or orders.[116] Collective monographs were dedicated to the Qadiriyya, the Naqshbandiyya and the Bektashiyya and their evolution in various parts of the Muslim world from Africa to China. Individual studies dedicated to a Sufi brotherhood are also numerous. Such studies are no longer carried out exclusively by historians and religious studies specialists, who rely primarily on written sources and archives. More and more researchers collect their data by interviewing members of various Sufi communities and by applying the methods and techniques of social and cultural anthropology.[117] Anthropological studies of Sufi organizations, however, are not without limitations, since even the best of them are "rarely very accurate or helpful in communicating the spiritual life and experience of the individuals [they] attempt to describe."[118] Despite such limitations, they provide a welcome alternative to the entrenched philological fixation on "normative" Sufi literature that has dominated the field over the past century and a half.

Conclusions

In sum, the study of Sufism in the west has come a long way since its inception at the beginning of the nineteenth century. Thanks to the efforts of several generations of European and American scholars (and, more recently, also their western trained colleagues in the Middle East and Asia) we now have a fairly comprehensive picture of the history and the present-day condition of Sufi movements in various parts of the Muslim world, although some geographical areas have received much more attention than others. As the study of Sufism increasingly becomes a "native" enterprise,[119] the western paradigms and assumptions presented above are being tested by scholars from the Middle East and Asia and, occasionally, found wanting. This "native" scholarship, in turn, is often informed by its practitioners' commitment to various religio-nationalist agendas, which oftentimes impel them to overplay the uniqueness of their "national" Sufi movements vis-à-vis those in the other parts of the Muslim world. In the end, there remains a critical and probably unbridgeable divide between those who approach the phenomenon of Sufism from outside in an attempt to investigate its social, political, economic and epistemological aspects and those who make a personal commitment to it and strive to live out its implications.

NOTES

1   Ernst Carl Ernst, *The Shambala Guide*, pp. ix–xix; cf. Mark Sedgwick, *Sufism*, pp. 5–8; and my articles "The *Tariqa* on a Landcruiser" and "Sufism as an Explanatory Paradigm."
2   Ernst, *The Shambala Guide*, p. xvii.
3   E.g., Knysh, " 'Wahhabism' as a Rhetorical Foil."
4   This field of intellectual inquiry, in turn, is very diverse. Western studies of Sufism range from spirited exercises in theosophical speculations to dry historicism aimed at describing the development of Sufi practices, teachings and institutions across the ages. For a typical example of the former, see Rushbrook Williams (ed.), *Sufi Studies*; for the latter, see my *Islamic Mysticism*.
5   Said, *Orientalism*, passim; cf. Clarke, *Oriental Enlightenment*, 22–8.
6   Said, *Orientalism*, pp. 272, 328, and passim.
7   Anawati and Gardet, *Mystique*, 14; Salim, "A Critical Approach," p. 56; Schimmel, *Mystical Dimensions*, 8–12; cf. Katz (ed.), *Mysticism*, passim ; cf. Hodgson, *The Venture*, vol. 2, 203–6.
8   Arberry, *An Introduction*.
9   E.g., Malcolm, *The History of Persia* (1815); Silvestre de Sacy, *Pend-nameh* (1819); Tholuck, *Blütensammlung* (1825); Rückert, *Sieben Bücher* (1837); Garcin de Tassy, *La poésie philosophique* (1860); Hammer-Purgstall, *Das arabische hohe Lied* (1854), etc.
10 Garcin de Tassy, *La poésie philosophique*, pp. 1, 2, 6, 10.
11 See, e.g., Dozy, *Essay*, 221, 239, 317, and so on.
12 Von Kremer, *Geschichte*, pp. xi, 65, 82–3, 130–1, etc.; cf. Nicholson, *The Idea of Personality*, pp. 26–7; another typical example of this academic attitude is the work of the British Orientalist Edward Palmer (1840–1882), for whom Sufism was "an Arian reaction" of the Persians to the "nomocentric" "Semitic genius" of the Arabs, *Oriental Mysticism*, p. xi.
13 Vikør, *Sufi and Scholar*, 11.
14 de Neveu, *Les khouanes*; Brosselard, *Les Khouan*; Duveyrier, *La confrérie*.
15 Rinn, *Marabouths*, p. vii.
16 Ibid., p. 19.
17 Ibid., p. 25 (*sufi*) and p. 64 (*wird*).
18 Triaud, *La légende noire*, passim.
19 Depont and Coppolani, *Les confréries*, pp. 83 and 93; 102–15.
20 Ibid., 279–89.
21 Burke, "The Sociology of Islam," p. 87–8.
22 From the Arabic *murid*, "Sufi disciple."
23 E.g., Khanykov, *O miuridakh* and Kazem-Bek, *Izbrannye sochineninia*; cf. Knysh, "Sufism as an Explanatory Paradigm."
24 See Nalivkin, "Ocherk," Mikhailov, "Religioznye vozzreniia," Veselovskii, "Pamiatnik"; for a recent reconstruction of a "Sufi-led" rebellion see Babajanov (Babadžanov), "Dukchi Ishan."
25 Goldziher, *Introduction*, pp. 116–66.
26 Ibid., 116–31.
27 Goldziher, *Die Richtungen*, pp. 180–309; idem., *Introduction*, pp. 138–40.
28 Goldziher, *Introduction*, pp. 140–4; Duka, "The Influence of Buddhism Upon Islam."
29 Goldziher, *Die Richtungen*, p. 180 and Waardenburg, *L'Islam*, p. 75.

30 Goldziher, *Introduction*, pp. 160–1

31 Snouck Hurgronje, *Verspreide Geschriften*, 746.

32 Ibid., pp. 741–5.

33 Ibid., p. 738; cf. Dallal, "Ghazali."

34 Snouck Hurgronje, *Verspreide Geschriften*, p. 742; Waardenburg, *L'Islam*, pp. 77–8.

35 Van Ess, "From Wellhausen," pp. 27–8; Batunskii, "Iz istorii."

36 Hartmann, *Al-Kuschairi's Darstellung*.

37 Idem, "Zur Frage," pp. 40–1.

38 Ibid., pp. 50, 59, 63, etc.

39 Browne, *Literary History*, vol. 1, pp. 418–19.

40 Smith, *The Sufi Path*, p. 14.

41 Macdonald, *The Religious Attitude*, 229–32.

42 Macdonald, *Development*, pp. 181–2.

43 Waardenburg, *L'Islam*, p. 160.

44 Nicholson, *Selected Odes*.

45 Idem. (ed.), *The Kitab al-luma'*, p. viii.

46 See, e.g., Nicholson, "A Historical Enquiry," passim; *The Mystics*, pp. 1–27.

47 By "Semitic" he meant Jewish, Aramaic and Arabic mystical traditions, since each of them expressed itself in a Semitic language.

48 Wensinck, *Bar Hebraeus's Book*, pp. lxxx and cx.

49 E.g., Smith, *Studies*, pp. 10–33 and 47–102.

50 Ibid., pp. 246–7.

51 Ibid., pp.112–13 and 141.

52 Ibid., pp. 47–102 and 256.

53 Ibid, p. 256.

54 Morris, "Ibn 'Arabi," pt. 1, pp. 542–3.

55 Massignon, *Essai*, pp. 26–7; cf. pp. 45–8 of the English translation.

56 Waardenburg, *L'Islam*, p. 154.

57 Massignon, *Essai*, pp. 309–14; cf. pp. 209–14 of the English translation.

58 Ibid., pp. 62, 285, 315–16; cf. pp. 35, 56, 185, 214 of the English translation.

59 Waardenburg, *L'Islam*, pp. 152–7 and passim.

60 Baldick, "Massignon," pp. 34–5.

61 Nicholson, *The Idea of Personality*, pp. 30–1.

62 Chodkiewicz, *Le sceau*, p. 103 note 3; cf. p. 81, note 15 of the English translation.

63 Waardenburg, *L'Islam*, p. 192.

64 Max Horten, review of Asin Palacios' *Abenmasarra* in *Der Islam*, vol. 6 (1916), pp. 106–10.

65 Idem, *Indische Strömungen*, pp. ix and 5.

66 Paret, *The Study*, p. 28.

67 *Islamische Mystiker*, pp. 13–14; cf. pp. 8–9 of the English translation (Andrae, *In the Garden*).

68 Ibid., pp. 9–15.

69 Waardenburg, *L'Islam*, 242–56.

70 Krymskii, "Ocherk razvitiia," pp. 28–9; idem, "Sufizm," p. 129.

71 Idem, "Ocherk razvitiia," p. 38.

72 Ibid., pp. 31 and 48.

73 Barthold, "Pamiati Zhukovskogo."

74 Shmidt, *'Abd al-Wahhab ash-Sharanii*.

75 Knysh, "Sufism as an Explanatory Paradigm," pp. 155–9; Rzakulizade, *Panteizm*; Ismatov, *Panteisticheskaia filosofskaia traditsiia*; cf. Zarrinkoob, "Persian Sufism," p. 210.

76 Yaacov Ro'i's *Islam in the Soviet Union*, passim.

77   See my review of Stepaniants, *Sufi Wisdom* in *Journal of Religion*, vol. 75/4 (October 1995), pp. 606–7.
78   E.g., Ritter, *The Ocean* and Meier, *Essays*.
79   Van den Bos, *Mystic Regimes*, pp. 33–9.
80   Idem, pp. 31–44; cf. Scarcia, "Iran ed heresia"; Adams "The Hermeneutics."
81   Ernst, "Traditionalism."
82   E.g., *Creative Imagination* and *En Islam*.
83   Nwyia, "Le tafsir."
84   See Böwering, *Minor Qur'an Commentary.*
85   Nwyia, *Exégèse* and *Trois oeuvres*.
86   Böwering, *The Mystical Vision*, pp. 135–42.
87   Radtke, "Al-Hakim"; idem, "Theologen und Mystiker"; idem, "Theosophie."
88   Molé, *Les mystiques*, pp. 4–5.
89   Ibid., pp. 9–12 and 18–22; for the *malamatiyya* see my *Islamic Mysticism*, pp. 94–9.
90   Ibid., pp. 7–8; cf. Arberry, *Revelation and Reason*, pp. 91–3.
91   Zaehner, *Hindu and Muslim Mysticism*, pp. 3. and 108–9.
92   Arberry, *Revelation and Reason*, p. 90; Hodgson, *The Venture*, vol. 1, p. 405 and Schimmel, *Mystical Dimensions*, p. 11.
93   Knysh, *Islamic Mysticism*, pp. 69–72.
94   Ülken, "L'école wujudite"; Schimmel, *Mystical Vision*, p. 11; Tadjikova, "Osobennosti sufizma."
95   Basilov, *Kul't sviatykh*, passim.
96   Aliev, "Zametki."
97   Corbin, *Histoire*, vol. 1, pp. 264–5; idem, *En Islam iranien*, passim.
98   Zarrinkoob, "Persian Sufism," pp. 182–4 and passim; cf. Nasr, "The Rise," passim; Damghani, "Persian Contributions", passim; cf. Lewisohn (ed.), *Classical Persian Sufism*.
99   Zarrinkoob, "Persian Sufism," pp. 139, 147 and 168.
100 E.g., Baldick, *Mystical Islam*, pp. 1–24.
101 Hodgson, *The Venture*, vol. 1, pp. 41–3.
102 E.g., Arberry, *Sufism*, pp. 119–23; cf. von Grunebaum, *Classical Islam*, pp.191–201 and Sourdel, *Medieval Islam*, passim.
103 Arberry, *Sufism*, pp. 120–2.
104 Arberry, *Sufism*, p. 121–2; cf. Schimmel, *Mystical Dimensions*, pp. 20–2, Meier, "Khurasan," 190–2 and passim; Harris (trans.), *The Risalah*, p. 16.
105 Al-Wakil, *Hadhihi hiya al-sufiyya*; Rahman, *Islam*, p. 146; Mubarak, *Al-Tasawwuf*, vol. 1, p. 136, etc.
106 E.g., Richards, *Islamic Civilization, 950–1150* and Grunebaum, *Classical Islam: A History 600–1258.*
107 Hodgson, *The Venture*, vol. 2, pp. 455–6.
108 Knysh, *Ibn 'Arabi*, pp. 49–58.
109 Meier, "Soufisme," p. 232; cf. Eaton, *The Sufis;* Fletcher, *Studies*, passim; Cornell, *Realm.*
110 E.g., Baldick, *Mystical Islam*, pp. 2–5 and 15–24.
111 Knysh, *Ibn 'Arabi*, pp. 273–5.
112 E.g., Makdisi, "The Hanbali School and Sufism" and idem, "Hanbalite Islam," pp. 240–51; Homerin, "Ibn Taimiyah's 'al-Sufiyah wa-l-fuqara' "; Meier, "The Cleanest About Predestination"; Ernst, *Words of Ecstasy*, passim; Sirriyeh, *Sufis and Anti-Sufis;* de Jong and Radtke (ed.), *Islamic Mysticism Contested.*
113 Knysh, *Ibn 'Arabi*, pp. 184–97.
114 E.g., Cooperson, "Ibn Hanbal"; Kinberg, "What is Meant"; and Melchert, "The Hanabila," passim.

115   E.g., Molé, "Les Kubrawiya"; Glassen, *Dies frühen Safawiden*; Babayan, *Mystics, Monarchs and Messiahs*; Bashir, *Messianic Hopes*.

116   E.g., Popovic and Veinstein (eds.), *Les Voies*; Buehler, Isin and Zarcone (eds.), *The Qadiriyya*; Gaborieau, Popovic and Zarcone (eds.), *Naqshbandis*; *Naqshbandis in Western and Central Asia*; Popovic (ed.), *Bektachiyya*;

117   E.g., Gilsenan, *Saint and Sufi*; idem, "Trajectories"; Crapanzano, *The Hamadsha*; Geertz, *Islam Observed*; Eickelman, *Moroccan Islam*; Turner, "Towards an Economic Model"; O'Brien, *The Mourides*; idem, *Charisma;* Hoffman, *Sufism;* Hammoudi, *Master*; Waugh, *The Munshidun;* Ewing, *Arguing Sainthood*, van den Bos, *Mystical Regimes*, etc.

118   Morris, "Situating Islamic 'Mysticism'," p. 320–1 note 16 and 319, note 14.

119   Eickelman, *The Middle East*, p. 277.

Part III

Imperial Structures and Dynastic Rule

CHAPTER SEVEN

Military Patronage States and the Political Economy of the Frontier, 1000–1250

MICHAEL CHAMBERLAIN

It is surprising to realize that in a period in which Europe lived in peace and prosperity unequaled until modern times, the Middle East suffered two major invasions of pastoralists, several minor ones, the Crusades, and the utter destruction of whole regions by the Mongols. Yet during this period a new set of social, cultural, and political institutions appeared in much of the world of Islam, one that put an end to the great variety, even exuberant hybridity, that characterized the immediate post-'Abbâsid period. These institutions formed the basis of the social and political order of the Middle East until the Ottoman period. Many of its cultural and social practices survived until the nineteenth century, and some, in altered form, until the present. The question that this chapter will address is how such an enduring set of institutions took hold in a period characterized by such disruption and disorder.

With the Seljuk invasion of Iran beginning in the early eleventh century, the Middle East experienced its first successful large-scale pastoralist invasions since the Arab conquests. While the Seljuk family ruled for a short time, the military patronage state, as the sum of their institutions is known to historians, was adopted by their successor states, and brought into regions the Seljuks could only dream of conquering. The Seljuk Turks first encountered Islamic culture and modes of political organization in the particular form these took in eastern Iran, selectively adopted the most portable and flexible among them, and disseminated them throughout the regions they conquered. In a case of path-dependence, the particular circumstances of a regional conquest became the basis for a universal set of institutions, so it is to the details of the Seljuk invasion that we now turn.

Pastoralist raiding was common, at times endemic, on the borders of the agrarian Islamic world. Pastoralists however did not frequently or easily form enduring states. Nomad chiefs could call on their followers to risk themselves for plunder or pasturage in settled areas; this is little more than the extension into the settled world of an outlook nomads adopt towards one another. Given a favorable geography, as on the eastern marches of China, pastoralists could construct something resembling a state if its purpose was to put plunder or tribute on a permanent footing. What they could not do without changing their way of life was rule directly over settled regions and keep them intact.

For this to occur there is an irreducible minimum of transformations that nomads must undergo. Perhaps most important is a change in worldview. Universal religion, and the sense of mission that it gives to individual lives, appears to have animated most if not all successful nomad conquests. Religion also gave chiefs the ideological edge they needed to transform themselves into commanders and rulers. The second transformation is a changed relationship towards animals: the moment a pastoralist horde abandons its flocks and becomes a full-time army it needs new institutions and forms of recruitment if it is to survive. And the third is in the nature of warfare itself, from the spontaneous, sporadic, and low intensity contests characteristic of pastoralists, to the ordered application of force for defined ends.

In the tenth century, the northeastern borderlands of Iran and Transoxania were occupied by Muslim Iranian and Turkish agriculturalists. In the steppes beyond, nomadic Turkish peoples were dependent on the agriculturalists for products they could not produce themselves, particularly cereals, arms and metal goods, as the agriculturalists in turn traded for their animals and animal products. Shamanistic in religion, tribal in their social and political organization, pastoralist Turks conducted raids and occasionally settled in small numbers. Some migrated into Iran and moved westwards, but their numbers were small and their impact slight. Even raiding was hazardous in historical terms. One reason for this was that the divide between the steppe and the settled world was also a religious frontier. Frontier warriors or ghazis, military brotherhoods that adopted as a mission the defense of Islam, could adapt their tactics to the steppe, maintaining light cavalry from fixed fortified settlements. This seems to have established a more secure barrier than anything settled states could provide. Pastoralist Turks were occasionally inducted into the service of Iranian monarchs, but they did not move into the region en masse.

In the tenth century, however, large numbers of pastoralist Turks were converting to Islam, and adopting for themselves the ghazi ethos that had so long kept them in check. Once they adopted Islam in its particular ghazi form, the border marches became a zone of political and economic instability, creativity, and, ultimately, fusion. The Turks who lived in it looked to Sûfî preachers and religious scholars as they once looked to shamans, with the difference that they now received an apprenticeship in Islam and the arts of settled living. Though short lived, the "organizational mode of the frontier," with its mobile wealth and labile social and political structures, was to have an effect on the developments that followed, and in time was to serve as something of a model for Turkish frontier society as it moved across western Asia.

In the tenth century the religious frontier that had long demarcated the ecological and political borders evaporated. The Iranian dynasties of the region fell to two new dynasties of Turkish Sunnî Muslims. The origins of the Qarakhânids and the Ghaznavids differed: the former arose on the steppe, while the latter was the work of a Turkish slave guard in Sâmânid service. In spite of their disparate origins, both adopted Persian forms of state organization, including notions of dynastic rule. However, even though they found imperial ideas and institutions useful, they never adopted them in a systematic or enduring way, even less did they exemplify such ideals in the eyes of their subjects. Thus the Qarakhânids were incapable of exercising much control over their far-flung domains; the Ghaznavids, happy enough to be called kings, had little interest in administration. Their occasional exhibition of ethical conduct excited more admiration for its Machiavellian charm than its sincerity.

The Seljuks appear in the historical record as members of the Qîniq, the leading tribe of the Ghuzz Turks (or Oghuz, called Turkoman by settled peoples), their pasture lands along the lower Syr Darya in the general region of Jand. Here they came into contact with settled modes of life, with Islam, and with producers of efficient weapons. Their eponymous and somewhat obscure leader Seljuk son of Duqaq converted to Islam in the last decade of the tenth century, and soon they began to conduct raids against pagan Turks as ghazis. Having established themselves as local powers, Seljuk's sons, who bore the intriguing names Mûsâ, Arslân Isrâ'îl, and Mikhâ'îl, together with Mikhâ'îl's sons Toghrîl-Beg and Chaghrî-Beg, began to contract their services to settled states. Fighting first on behalf of the Sâmânids in their losing struggle with the Qarakhânids, then on behalf of the latter, they received pastures in what had recently been an agricultural region of Transoxania. In this period they retained their pastoral mode of life, but mixed with settled peoples more than they had previously. It is possible that in this period they learned something of, without strictly adopting, orthodox Islam as practiced in northeastern Iran, the government of agrarian life, and the arts of war.

In the 1030s Toghrîl-Beg and Chaghrî-Beg, now in Ghaznavid service, moved or were dispatched to Khurasân, which they plundered. The Ghaznavids tried to bring the Seljuks to heel with promises of titles of honor and marriage into their house, but the Seljuks saw little point, and less profit, in abandoning plunder or pastoralism. Khurasân then experienced further misery as it watched the Ghaznavids attempt to subjugate the Seljuks and fail in the worst way. The Ghaznavid army, which suffered from a form of picturesque gigantism, lacked the Seljuks' mobility, and so could only plod around after them; while the Seljuks lacked the Ghaznavid's heavy forces, and so could not risk a decision on the battlefield. The ensuing stalemate ruined both the cities and the countryside. Despairing of the Ghaznavids, the notables of the cities came to terms with the Seljuks and opened the gates to them.

The brothers were now faced with a choice. They could consume their acquisitions through plunder and the expansion of pastureland, retaining a familiar mode of life at the cost of the ruin and depopulation of their new domains. Or they could recast themselves as territorial sovereigns, at the cost of alienating their tribal supporters and of giving their adversaries a fixed target. It appears that once they controlled the cities of Khurasân they determined to hold on to them, and from experience they knew how. They induced the 'Abbâsid Caliph to dub them "clients of the commander of the faithful" they flattered Sunnî scholars and Sûfîs; and they lured Persian courtiers, scribes, and literati into their service. These they set to work on the restoration of the apparatus of revenue collection, on articulating their ambitions and announcing their new grandeur to the world at large, and on making their court splendid. This began the process by which the Seljuks recast themselves as territorial sovereigns.

The Seljuks could not avoid or, given their ambitions, elude, a new Ghaznavid offensive. The Seljuk army was still capable of conducting a guerrilla defense based on maneuver and slow attrition, and in the event the Ghaznavid army exhausted itself in pursuit. When in 1040 the Seljuks gave battle at Dandânqân, the exhausted Ghaznavid army aroused itself only to be defeated and flee. Toghrîl now became the overall suzerain, while Chaghrî took over in the east.

Both brothers were careful to tailor their ambitions to their resources. Chaghrî took Khwârazm, and after a number of attempts to seize Ghaznavid territories in modern-day Afghanistan, contented himself with securing defensible borders. In the west Toghrîl seems to have been concerned with defending his position against potential adversaries, the Fâtimids in particular. He was able to tolerate Shî'î rulers, including the Bûyids and local Arab dynasts and amirs. But events in Iraq and western and southern Iran were to draw him out. The Turkoman migration was in full swell, as they moved with their animals into regions that could sustain pastoralism, including Azerbaijan, the Caucasus, Anatolia, Iraq, southern Iran, and northern Syria. Toghrîl was fearful of subjugating the Turkoman, conciliated them when necessary, and diverted them where possible. But he could not ignore rebellions against his authority, and in any case had to take a bow when the Turkoman subjugated local areas in his name.

How the Seljuks transformed themselves from pastoral chieftains to conquering warlords to agrarian monarchs has not been studied in detail, though its outlines are well known. The process itself was not strikingly novel, as there were a limited number of avenues by which pastoral chiefs, of ill-defined authority, few independent resources, and little or no guiding ideology, could become rulers. Neither chiefs nor rulers found it easy to disentangle themselves from their supporters and kin. But rulers were obliged to find new resources to balance their former supporters and to leverage their own households over their kin. By bringing in new men, including mamlûks and courtiers, the Seljuks began to replace a tribal form of decision-making and organization with one that made use of men who were dependent upon them.

As the Seljuks recast themselves as heirs to empires centered on the Iranian plateau, they began to adopt a strategic outlook seen in previous Iranian empires, though the term Iran itself was now dropped where it was not forgotten. They viewed the Ismâ'îlî Fâtimids as their principal adversary, thus recasting the ancient geopolitical rivalry between Iran and Egypt in religious and ideological terms. The strategic imperatives that this rivalry imposed on the Seljuks shaped their relations with other powers of the region. The regional politics of the 1050s and 1060s can thus be seen as an attempt by the Seljuks to secure their own position in Iraq and the Caucasus to free them to confront the Fâtimids in Syria and Arabia and to fend them off elsewhere.

The Twelver-Shî'î Bûyids had ruled Iraq for a century, permitting a humbled 'Abbâsid Caliphate to survive in Baghdad. Two immediate considerations seem to have shaped the Seljuks' relations with the Caliphate. First, the Seljuks adopted the Ghaznavids' religious strategies much as they inherited their geopolitical position. The Ghaznavids had long posed as the sole Sunnî power capable of defending the Caliphate from the Bûyids, a stance that was an important aspect of their claims to legitimacy and the ideological basis of their strategic ambitions. Second, once in control of western Iran, the Seljuks targeted the Fâtimid empire as their principal rival, and they had reason to fear Fâtimid designs on Iraq. Toghrîl invaded Iraq in 447/1055, claiming to desire to make the pilgrimage to Mecca and to fight off the Fâtimids. Arriving in Baghdad in Ramadan of that year, he deposed the last Bûyid ruler, and slowly began to win over the 'Abbâsid Caliph Al-Qâ'im (422–67/1031–75).

So began a new turn in the ancient dance by which an imposing semi-barbarian conqueror came to terms with a cultivated and revered figure, to the apparent – or at least publicly visible – benefit of both. Relations between the Caliph and the Seljuk ruler were from the outset marked by caution and uncertainty, although both professed to be gratified by events. The Caliph was pleased enough to confirm Toghrîl's legitimacy, but tried and failed to maintain his distance. It was not until

1058 that the Caliph received Toghrîl, and even then he tried to dismiss a request for his daughter's hand as impertinent. Nonetheless, whatever tensions may have existed between the two, and among their followers, both were strengthened by the alliance and each brought to the table what the other lacked.

Having countered Fâtimid ambitions in Iraq, Toghrîl now suppressed activist Shî'îs in Baghdad, and kept closer watch on the Shî'î Arab amirs of the region. Thus in the space of a generation, the Seljuks acquired the strategic depth that Iraq had long provided Iranian empires, and the ethno-linguistic topography, patterns of land use, and military balance of the region were permanently altered. The Seljuks now possessed an empire the contours of which the Sasanians would have understood and admired.

When the history of the region was written by scholars most interested in religion, these developments were taken as aspects of a "Sunnî revival," in which Sunnism as a historical actor reversed the gains of the long "Shî'îte century." And so it must have seemed to some. Shî'ism had receded from its high water mark, no longer threatened the Caliphate, and had lost much of its political verve and intellectual sheen. But historians today tend to distrust such dialectical approaches to history, and are warier of inferring motives from outcomes. The "revival" of Sunnî Islam, and the wide-spread adoption of the institutions and practices associated with it, is perhaps better understood through attention to how religion, social and cultural practices, and politics intertwined.

Upon the death of Toghrîl in 455/1063, rivalry over the succession erupted among Chaghrî's descendants (he had died in 452/1060), and was resolved in the end in the favor of Alp Arslân. Alp Arslân addressed himself to the issues that the rapid expansion of the empire had left open. The principal difficulties related to the Turkoman and to the distribution of power and rights of succession within the Seljuk ruling family. Having brought the Seljuks to power, the Turkoman were never reconciled to the sight of their former chiefs recasting themselves as monarchs. As Seljuk authority among the Turkoman still rested in part on conceptions of legitimacy derived from their shared tribal past, these two problems were related. An early incident in the reign of Alp Arslân shows how the sultanate drew on the imperial resources available to it to elevate itself above its tribal origins. Alp Arslân's uncle, Qutlumush b. Arslân, claimed leadership of the family (and thus rulership of the empire) by virtue of his standing as its eldest member, a claim that resonated with Turkoman deference to seniority. Alp Arslân countered these claims, and the military support upon which they rested, through the efforts of his Persian secretaries and mamlûk military units. To avoid a succession dispute among his descendants, Alp Arslân named his son Malik-Shâh heir apparent, using the Islamic term wâli 'ahd, and had the Caliph bless the succession.

As Seljuk ambitions in Iraq were initially modest and geopolitically motivated, their victory over the Byzantines at Manzikert (Malâzgird) in 1071 was not motivated in the first instance by a desire to spread Islam.[1] In the Caucasus and the northwest Alp Arslân sought to construct a system of alliances in order to free his hand against the Fâtimids. He invaded Armenia and Georgia in the 1060s to put an end to Byzantine influence there and to keep himself at the head of the Turkoman, but not to overthrow the existing Christian dynasties. Entering into a truce with the Byzantines soon thereafter, he now felt secure enough to move against the Fâtimids in Syria. However, Armenian and Georgian submission meant little to the Turkoman, and a diplomatic arrangement with the Byzantines even less. When in 463/1071 the Emperor Romanus assembled a large army and moved into Armenia, Alp Arslân felt obliged to respond to this threat to his zone of influence. He suspended operations against the Fâtimids, defeated Romanus at Manzikert, and set about restoring the status quo ante to his advantage. However, as long as Turkoman raiding continued unchecked, no stable state system could emerge and in time Anatolia was overrun and its turcization and Islamization commenced.

Malik-Shâh (465/1072–468/1092) was the first Seljuk ruler to be raised at court and it is in his reign that the resources of steppe, countryside, and city were most successfully employed. His succession to the sultanate was contested, as were most in the period: he had to suppress other claimants from within the Seljuk house, and having succeeded, was obliged to grant his relatives considerable freedom of action in their own territories. He continued his father's policy of consolidating the Seljuk hold on their provinces, of solidifying the eastern borders, and of forcing the Fâtimids back to Egypt. The Turkoman migration westwards made this process more complicated: they inserted themselves into local conflicts in the west much as the early Seljuks had done in the east, hiring themselves out to local powers including the Fâtimids. In 469/1076–7 Artuk, a Turkoman chief, defeated the Qaramites in Bahrayn, moving from there to Mecca, where in 468/1075 prayer was made in the name of the 'Abbâsid Caliph. Syria became a new theater of operations in 471/1079 when Tutush, a brother of Malik Shâh, took Damascus in the aftermath of a Turkoman invasion.

The relative unity of the Seljuk family did not survive the death of Malik Shâh. Exceptionally able or fortunate rulers continued to exercise power in particular regions. Sanjar (490/1087–552/1157), perhaps the most effective Seljuk after Malik Shâh, ruled Khurasân and the east as its nominal governor and then as ruler and overall sultan. But in time here as elsewhere, rivalries between commanders, Turkoman unruliness, and internal disputes within the Seljuk house contributed to the fragmentation of Seljuk power. By the middle of the twelfth century even states ruled by descendants of the Seljuk family should be considered successor states, as the power and authority of the greater Seljuk family had evaporated.

The Seljuks had long been in the habit of appointing senior amirs as tutors – atabeg or father-lord in Turkish – for their sons. This came to have a political dimension when atabegs became regents for young Seljuks following the deaths of their fathers. When the Seljuk family possessed a rough unity atabegs generally did what was asked of them. But once the Seljuk ruling family was incapable of acting collectively to preserve its common interests, atabegs began to assert their power independently, first as governors, then in their own names. Atabeg dynasties appeared in a number of regions, the best known in Mosul, Azerbaijan, Arrân, and Fars.

Another reason for Seljuk collapse was pressure from the northeast. The Khwâr-azm-Shâhs flourished in the Iranian northeast in part because their geographical marginality protected them from exciting the interest of potential rivals. Following the death of Sanjar they were able to exercise power openly and to expand to the south and southwest. At the end of the sixth/twelfth century they moved through Khurasân to the borders of Iraq, recapitulating the Seljuk conquests of the previous century. Though their empire was to be short lived, it was exceptionally destructive, and its inept politics in the steppe opened the Islamic northeast to Mongol invasion.

A final reason for the decline of the Seljuks was the increasing power of the Caliphate, whose temporal ambitions grew as Seljuk family unity waned. Following the deaths of Malik-Shâh and Nizâm al-Mulk, the caliphate acquired greater freedom of action in central Iraq, and in time began to field its own military forces there and further afield. By the middle of the twelfth century the caliphate had expelled the Seljuk governor from Baghdad, was conducting its own diplomacy, and entered the political and military fray on the same terms as other powers.

The Military Patronage State

The thirty-year period from the beginning of Alp Arslân's reign until the end of Malik-Shâh's was the Seljuk's Khaldunian golden age: the Seljuks benefited from a continuing if not always predictable sense of family solidarity. They were also able to draw on the resources of steppe and civilization and make political use of both. It is in this period that the constellation of institutions and practices of the "military patronage state" emerged, and to these we now turn.

The Seljuks faced a number of problems that were new to them but ancient in terms of pastoralist state formation. These can be summarized as the redefinition of the role of the ruling institution, the assertion of an imperial ideology, the organization of a court, the creation of a permanent army, the establishment of defensible borders, the adoption of principles within the ruling house to facilitate the succession, and the cultivation of existing elites to develop clienteles among them.

Seljuk rule was marked by tensions, never entirely resolved, among pastoralist and Turkish elements, Persian monarchical elements, and elements taken from Islamic forms of legitimacy, legality, and piety. By the time the Seljuks consolidated power and advanced a nuanced justification for it, they had four overlapping claims to legitimacy.

The sultanate was the principal locus of authority. The term sultan had long been a title of casual usage and imprecise meaning. Now it became a formal title that was struck into the coinage, its functions and jurisdiction defined by jurists and courtiers. The Seljuks advanced a claim to religious legitimacy by supporting the Caliph, from whom they received patents of investiture, and by inserting their names in the Friday sermon and on the coinage. They also claimed legitimacy in Islamic terms by establishing conditions favorable to the application of Islamic law and to cult, in particular prayer, zakât, and pilgrimage.

In spite of the attention paid to the sultanate by contemporary and later writers, it must be said that there was little in the relationship of the Caliphate to the sultanate that was new. For nearly two centuries Caliphs had been granting patents of investiture to local rulers, and Caliphs had long been asked to confirm outcomes of political contests. The new theory was therefore a way of grappling with an existing reality in juridical terms. But even if the theory of the sultanate was neither particularly new nor notably binding it was nonetheless a reflection of how the Seljuks asserted their legitimacy in Islamic and juristic terms. As such, it gave qâdîs, jurists, and supporters of the Caliphate the religious sanction they needed to work with them.

The Persian tradition of monarchical authority was a second dimension of Seljuk claims to legitimacy. The Seljuks and their followers would have been aware of this tradition through their contacts with the Ghaznavids and Qarakhânids, and as soon as they began to bring courtiers into their service they would have been instructed in its

details. Sonorous imperial titulature, center-of-the-world court culture, lavish patronage, and brilliant ceremonial became instruments of politics, or at least so the
Seljuks' supporters hoped.

The Seljuks were also tribal leaders, constrained by the obligation to rule in a
consultative manner but also buttressed by steppe loyalties. The primus inter pares of
the pastoral leader was long gone, but the Seljuks were careful to cultivate good
relations with their Turkoman followers and to advance claims to authority that made
sense to them. The Seljuks ignored the Turkoman at their peril, as these continued to
wield influence within the larger family, particularly in succession disputes, and were
capable of frustrating Seljuk policies if they could not determine them. Even such an
advocate of centralized administration as Nizâm al-Mulk recognized that the Turkoman had a legitimate claim, leading him to advocate that they be treated with favor
and honor. One way that Turkoman sensibilities could be squared with Islamic and
Iranian monarchical notions of legitimate power was through the exercise of the
sultan's prerogative to judge at court. This was conceived in Islamic terms as the
mazâlim or grievance court; to the secretaries he was giving justice as kings should,
and to the Turkoman he was ruling in a consultative manner.

And finally, at least in the period of their greatest success, the Seljuks were also
warlords, quick to display masculine virtue and careful to provide opportunities for
plunder. The most effective Seljuks had qualities that would have been familiar to the
war band. They had assertive and war-loving personalities, and were quick to act,
jealous in the possession of the initiative, fond of the hunt, and inclined to the
companionship of strong-willed men. Some of the less effective were killed by their
supporters.

Although such legal, imperial, pietistic, and lordly claims to authority were important to the Seljuk rulers, a specifically dynastic ideology seems not to have been
advanced. The transmission of power was conceived in vaguely pastoralist terms, or
at least terms that would have been understood on the steppe. Power was seen to
inhere in the Seljuk family at large, and was apportioned among its members. The
family could cooperate – in theory – to ensure that the sultan's designation of a
successor was honored. However, in the event most successions were contested, and
the various Seljuk households were jealous of their portion of the sovereignty invested
in the family as a whole. The notion that power rested in the family also makes it clear
that we should not think of the Seljuks as a unitary state, but rather as a collection of
powerful households kept in check by the head of the most powerful among them.
Seen in this light, the ruling household's adoption of monarchical and legal arguments for legitimate authority was one way of fending off the claims of the other
households within the ruling family.

The application of a tribal notion of collective control over land to a territorially
based state led to the practice of apportionment, whereby territories were parceled
out to various households within the larger family. Apportionment implied more an
assignment of the capacity to exploit than a permanent right. While Seljuk parcelized
sovereignties are conventionally characterized as an appanage system, the term should
be used only in the general sense of a resource granted to a member of a ruling
household. In contrast to the appanage of the Latin west, Seljuk objects of apportionment were not in theory or practice escheated to the ruling household upon the
death of the holder, their holders had no legally defined right to them or jurisdiction
within them, and no notion of primogeniture limited others' claims to them.

The central institution of Seljuk rule was the court (*dargâh*). Its organization and ceremonial were clearly based on Iranian antecedents, though it must be said that the glittery court culture of the previous era had been superseded by the throne rooms of some hard-hearted men. The principal members of the court were influential members of the ruling family, Turkoman chiefs, mamlûk amirs, and grand secretaries; the ruler had his own bodyguard, and his executioner reminded others of their place. The court was also where the vizier exercised power and presided over the court establishment and the dîwâns, though the latter were Persian speaking and were kept at some distance from the Turkish speaking court. Such unity as the Seljuk state possessed in the reigns of Alp Arslân and Malik-Shâh was in part due to the efforts of the famous vizier Nizâm al-Mulk. An Iranian whose family had been in the service of the Ghaznavids, Nizâm al-Mulk was in some respects a shadow ruler, and his family a shadow dynasty, whose success underpinned Seljuk power. It would be misleading to think of him as a bureaucrat or courtier, though the court was the principal institution through which he exercised power. He played a major role in military decisions and on campaigns, and kept up an army of mamlûks that rivaled those maintained by the lesser Seljuk rulers. He also exercised power as the head of a household upon which the Seljuks devolved considerable power and revenue sources. Today, best known for his treatises on government, he is also lamented by some scholars as the last chance for the reassertion of centralized bureaucratic control in a world in the process of fragmentation.

Once the Seljuks became territorial rulers they began to organize a permanent army. The Seljuk army never became a unitary hierarchical institution under a single command, nor do the Seljuks appear to have had a preconceived blueprint for its organization. Nonetheless, at a fairly early date, Seljuk rulers endeavored to transform a confederation of tribal peoples into a reliable instrument of warfare, one capable of the measured application of force through disciplined means for specific ends.

The transition from the horde organized for plunder and conquest to the permanent army was not achieved rapidly, evenly, or in the event fully. In contrast to the early Caliphate, the Seljuks permitted their original tribal supporters to retain their flocks, did not force them to settle in garrisons, and did not superimpose new levels of leadership over them. This may reflect in part their more limited ambitions, and in part the availability and diversity of other sources of military recruitment. In addition to the Turkoman, Alp Arslân also recruited units of Kurds, Armenians, Daylamis, and Georgians, largely sustained through booty and cash revenues. To balance both groups Alp Arslân, like Toghrîl before him, recruited mamlûks in ever-larger numbers, and soon slave soldiers constituted the decisive fraction of Seljuk military support.

Malik-Shâh appears to have desired to put the organization of the army on a more systematic basis. While recruiting larger numbers of mamlûks, he sought to organize the Turkoman under his command into smaller and more biddable units. He also tried to reduce his dependence on formations raised among other peoples, in large part due to the demands they made on his treasury, but also due to an appreciation that mamlûks, even more expensive, were more loyal. Nizâm al-Mulk, always careful to cultivate good relations with senior commanders, criticized this policy as incautious: it risked alienating the Turkoman, the origin if not the enduring basis of Seljuk power, as it created unhappy bands of demobilized soldiers. Since tribal peoples and freebooters are better controlled by enrolling them in an army than by chasing them with one, Nizâm al-Mulk's fears were borne out when Malik-Shâh was obliged to suppress revolts following the demobilization of the Armenians under his command.

There was considerable variety in the means by which the Seljuks exploited their revenue sources to sustain their military forces. In the east the Seljuks followed the Ghaznavid practice of supporting their armies through cash revenues, perhaps reflecting the previous situation in which plunder from India provided resources unobtainable elsewhere. In the west the Bûyid practice of 'iqtâ' was adopted and made to fit new situations, eventually to become the fundamental institution of the military patronage state.

The *'iqtâ'* was a temporary and revocable assignment of the usufruct of the land. Its origins were in the tax farm and can be seen as an attempt to moderate its pernicious effects. From the perspective of the center, the adoption of 'iqtâ' was a resignation to the fact that revenue could no longer pass through a central registry before being passed on to the army. 'Iqtâ' also seems to have fit itself into a pastoralist worldview that saw access to revenue sources in personal terms.

The 'iqtâ' holder or *muqta'* had no permanent or transferable right to his assignment, few if any administrative functions, and could be moved from one 'iqtâ' to another as his situation changed. Amirs constituted the most numerous recipients of 'iqtâ's, for which they were expected to provide military service, but 'iqtâ's were also granted to members of the ruling family and to powerful secretaries. Rulers themselves usually had the largest 'iqtâ's in their domains. It would be an error to think of the 'iqtâ' as a single institution universally applied. The 'iqtâ' itself took a number of forms and was in any case modified to fit local circumstances. Moreover, the 'iqtâ' did not supplant local revenue systems so much as penetrate them, creating institutions that derived from both local practice and the new institution. The result was considerable variety in the forms 'iqtâ' took as the Seljuks and their successors applied it in the regions under their control. But beneath the variety of its origins and applications, the 'iqtâ' reflected a new political-economic reality in which states were incapable of sustaining their military forces through centrally administered taxation.

Following their military success, the Seljuks found themselves in the possession of complex cities they were reluctant to govern, incapable of administering, and unable to make secure. The cities of Iran and Iraq had few if any city-wide municipal institutions beyond that provided by the mediating capacity of their religious scholars. They were held together more through informal ties of loyalty, obligation, and clientage than through such formal institutions as may have existed. Cities were often divided along factional lines that were understood in religious terms, as among others Shâfi'îs and Hanafis in Khurasân, and Hanbalis in Baghdad, had a social base, a communal expression, and a political stance. Many cities were periodically disordered by militias of young men who at times imposed a rough order within a political vacuum, and at times used their power to dominate and plunder.

In cities that were potentially chaotic and resistant to external control, the Seljuks learned to rule by making political use of practices that hitherto had been largely religious in nature. Of these the most important were the charitable foundations known as *waqfs*. Waqf in Islamic law means the immobilization of property for charitable ends. It had long been an expression of piety and a means by which individuals could pass on property to their descendants with some degree of legal protection. These uses of waqf did not end, but early on the Seljuks grasped the political utility of the institution. The waqf became both an instrument of governance and a means by which Seljuk households moved their unavowable private interests into the open and expected to be praised for it.

In Khurasân the Seljuks encountered the local institution of the *madrasa*, a place of teaching endowed through waqf to support a scholar and a number of students.[2] A related institution was the *khânaqâh*, a hostel for a Sûfî shaykh and his initiates. As the empire expanded, the Seljuks took these institutions with them, and in time madrasas and khânaqâhs appeared throughout their domains, eventually, under the successor states, making their way to Egypt. Some of the most important madrasas were founded by high ranking amirs, and Nizâm al-Mulk founded madrasas throughout the empire, including the famous Nizâmiyya of Baghdad. As the Seljuk empire was more a collection of powerful households than a unitary state, the households of powerful men and women made use of waqf to advance their own strategies. The Seljuk successor states also used madrasas as family tombs, which could become cultic centers of family power much like the ancestral residence of European aristocrats.

Perhaps more important than waqf's ideological luster and personal benefit was its political utility, most particularly in allowing the Seljuks to support the 'ulamâ'. The Seljuks relied on the 'ulamâ' for social and political tasks which they could not carry out by themselves or by other means. The 'ulamâ' moderated conflicts, mediated between the populace and the ruling institution, gave merchants and consumers the legal structure they required, and served as a channel of influence.

By endowing religious institutions through waqf, the Seljuks could win over existing elites while they brought in new men as alternatives to them, and urban elite politics henceforth took place in the domain of religion. The Seljuks supported qâdîs and other scholars by appointing them to madrasas, thereby tying prestigious religious scholars more closely to the new order if not the regime. Large landowners, pushed off the land when it was parceled out as 'iqtâ', might well have become dangerously alienated, but appointment to positions funded by waqf gave them a means of survival and advancement. Waqf also permitted a reshuffling of men with religious prestige throughout the cities of the empire, one that loosened up the aloof particularity of local notables. Itinerant scholars had long adorned the world of Islamic scholarship, but now the Seljuks appointed scholars to posts throughout the empire. These scholars should not be seen as their agents of the regime – they would have been horrified by the suggestion – but rather as counterweights to established interests. As such men possessed religious prestige, they were accepted in the cities in which they settled, married into local elite families, and acquired their own disciples. To the extent that such institutions supported such men for such purposes, the era of the Seljuk and Seljuk successor states can be said to extend into the nineteenth century, and its aftermath into the present.

As the early Caliphate ruled its subject Christians and Jews by granting considerable power and autonomy onto their religious leaders, the Seljuks ruled their cities by patronizing the 'ulamâ' and Sûfîs. These religious elites thus came to lead communities that sociologically (but not of course religiously or juridically) resembled the dhimmî communities following the Arab conquests. It is perhaps not a coincidence that where the practice of supporting scholars and Sûfîs through waqf was intensive, the sources pay much less attention to militias than elsewhere. As a means of filling the vacuum between rulers of distant origin and far-ranging preoccupations, and cities characterized by their variety and impenetrability, the employment of waqf as a political strategy would seem to have worked.

Overseeing the apparatus of revenue extraction were the registries called dîwâns. Dîwâns recorded revenue sources, revenue distribution, and revenue assignments; what they most emphatically did not do was administer by means of making use of revenue. Dîwâns had little administrative capacity, and the scribes and secretaries who worked in them were not bureaucrats in the Chinese or modern senses. They had little notion of autonomous bureaucratic power, nor did they see themselves as a distinct social type. Clerks and secretaries, rather, viewed themselves as clients of powerful households, and indeed all powerful households had their own dîwâns; the dîwâns of the sultan and a great amir were different in size, not kind. Though the names of offices throughout the period were various, there were several functions that rulers' dîwâns universally undertook. They recorded revenue sources and assignments, whether 'iqtâ', waqf, or stipends; they handled communications; and they funded the courts and domestic economies of powerful households. The dîwâns were more a means by which powerful households funded themselves and made use of revenue assignments for political ends than a bureaucratic dimension of state power.

The political economy of the military patronage state can be seen as one in which a new set of practices of revenue assignment penetrated the functional domains of land revenue, sovereignty, and urban life. The Seljuks ruled by parceling out power and revenue sources in packages to their dependants and clients. Apportionment, 'iqtâ', and waqf were each a means by which powerful households sustained themselves and their supporters. The politics of revenue assignment thus reflects a new relationship of politics to economy and society, one in which the practices of steppe and frontier penetrated an ancient agrarian and imperial world.

The Military Patronage State, 1100–1250

Between the fragmentation of Seljuk power in the early twelfth century and the appearance of the Mamlûk Sultanate of Egypt and Syria in the middle of the thirteenth, two larger trends shaped the otherwise disjointed and discontinuous political history of the period. In the east, Transoxania and Iran were increasingly affected, and in time utterly deranged, by developments originating in the distant steppe and China; while in Mesopotamia, Syria, and Egypt, Seljuk-derived practices of the military patronage state moved ever westward. By the end of the period Mongol invasions had wrecked Transoxania, Iran, and Iraq, while in the west the Mamlûks, the most successful military patronage state of them all, made use of the resources of Syria and Egypt to erect an enduring barrier to Mongol expansion and to assert a claim to the leadership of the world of Islam. By 1260 the geopolitical balance between Iran and Egypt had reasserted itself, with the difference that now Iraq, Iran, and Transoxania were ruled by non-Muslims. This process can thus be seen as the disappearance under steppe pressure of the frontier in the northeast and the migration westwards of forms of political and social organization that had originated in an earlier frontier.

The Qarakhânids and local Seljuk dynasts exercised power in the east until the 1140s, when events in North China made themselves felt in the region. These drew the Islamic northeast more inescapably into the orbit of steppe politics than before, and from this time it is difficult to discuss the broader history of the Middle East without reference to China, its borderlands, and the steppe. In northern China, between 1114 and 1122, the Manchurian Jurchen defeated the Khitan or (latterly) Liao dynasty and expelled their remnants, the "Black Cathay" or Qara-Khitai into Turkestan. There, the Qara-Khitai subjugated the Qarakhânids and in 1141 annihilated a Seljuk army near Samarqand, seizing Transoxania.

As mentioned above, a new power, the Khwârazm-Shâhs, arose in the twelfth century. Together with the Qarakhânids, they were vassals of the Qara-Khitai through the middle third of the twelfth century. In 567/1172 a new ruler, 'Alâ al-Dîn Tekish, took power, and in his long reign extended Khwârazm-Shâh power to the borders of Iraq and threw off allegiance to the Qara-Khitai. Following his death in 595/1200 his son Qutb al-Dîn Muhammad defeated the Qarakhânids and the Qara-Khitai, thus establishing conditions for a new empire. This, however, was cut decisively short by the culmination of the process by which Transoxania and Iran were brought into the world of the steppe, the Mongol invasion.

The Mongol invasions have generated a number of contrafactual speculations. Did the Caliphate bring them on by looking for allies against the Khwârasm-Shâhs? Could the Khwârâzm-Shâhs have prevented them by engaging in a more adept or at least less petulant diplomacy? Though the manner by which the Mongols entered the Middle East was shaped by Khwârazm-Shâh policies, it is probably safe to say that this was one invasion that was motivated by factors intrinsic to itself. Chingiz-Khân may have wanted to delay an attack on the Khwârazm-Shâh until he could deal with a number of problems on the steppe. But in 1218 the Khwârazm-Shâhs massacred a caravan of merchants arriving from Mongol domains, and soon thereafter attacked a Mongol army that was chasing down some Merkits in the Qipchak steppe. This was thought to be extremely foolish, not only by the Mongols, but by Muhammad himself. When Chingiz' army advanced on Samarqand in response, Muhammad reckoned he knew all he needed to know of Mongol military effectiveness, and deployed his army to protect his march to the rear. He was eventually chased by a Mongol detachment to an island in the Caspian, where he died soon thereafter in his bed. His son Jalâl al-Dîn Khwârazm-Shâh had a number of picaresque adventures while trying to avoid the Mongols, but accomplished little beyond keeping his foes amused and getting his troops killed.

Between 616/1219 and 620/1223 the Mongols applied themselves to the destruction of the cities of Transoxania and Khurasân and the massacre of their inhabitants. It is possible to try to view events from the Mongol perspective, by way of avoiding anachronistic or ethnocentric judgments, but why bother. Khurasân, whose material wealth and cultural weight rivaled Egypt and Iraq, became pasture, and its recovery continues today. In 620/1223 Chingiz returned to Mongolia, and the first wave of Mongol conquests of Iran came to a slow end, bogged down as much by internal disputes among Mongols as anything else.

Although the Seljuk invasions were the proximate cause of the pastoralization and Turcization of parts of Iran, their destructive effects were local in impact and limited in effect. In contrast, the new invasions were undertaken by armies of pastoralists who had little experience of settled life, who were non-Muslim, and who saw scant benefit in adopting Islamic or Iranian institutions. Though they had the military power to dominate large areas, within them their actions were wholly destructive.

In the west, the traditional line of division in the political history of the period is between the end of Seljuk dynastic rule and the beginning of the period of the atabegs. There is something to be said for this, as the power of the Seljuk house was undoubtedly ephemeral and most successor dynasties were founded by atabegs. Yet this periodization may collapse differences in the Seljuk period – the Seljuks were a very different ruling group once they abandoned their animals – while erecting a somewhat artificial distinction later. Though Seljuk rule was short lived, the Seljuks were succeeded by ruling households whose internal organization, modes of asserting power, and institutions of revenue extraction derived from Seljuk antecedents.

In the west, the atabeg successor states were organized on the same principles as the Seljuks themselves. As was the case of the Seljuks before them, the successor states recruited military forces where they found them or could attract them, tried to balance them with mamlûks, and supported them through a combination of 'iqtâ's and household revenues. As was true of the Seljuks, these ruling households relied heavily on secretaries – some on secretarial dynasties – and scholars whom they supported through waqf. The successor states also cast themselves as defenders of Islam, a role that the Crusades enabled the most successful among them to play. The broader history of Mesopotamia, Syria, and Egypt can be seen as a tension between, on the one hand, the tendency of states organized along the loose lines of their Seljuk antecedents to fragment, and on the other, the material and moral resources that frontier warfare concentrated in the hands of successful commanders.

One irony of this period was that the most successful of the Seljuk successor states appeared in regions in which the Seljuks had not ruled or ruled indirectly. The Seljukids of Anatolia came to power as a result of developments Toghrîl-Beg, Alp Arslân, and Malik-Shâh shaped but did not control.[3] For thirty years prior to Manzikert the Turkoman raided freely across much of Anatolia, though in relatively small numbers and generally fearful of being cut off from Azerbaijan. Some took up service with the Byzantines, but these were small in number and their local impact slight. While capable of raiding deep into Anatolia, the Turkoman hesitated to attack cities, and established no permanent fortified positions of their own. Following Manzikert, larger numbers of Turkoman entered and were determined to settle. These accelerated the process of Turcification and created a distinctive frontier culture that for a time owed little to orthodox Islam. During the 460s/1070s, members of a rival branch of the Seljuk family descended from Mikhâ'îl b. Seljuk arrived in Anatolia to lead bands of Turkoman ghazis, eliminating most of the Byzantine strongholds and playing a more adept role in regional politics. A member of this family, Sulaymân b. Kutlumush, took Nicea (Iznik), and established the Seljuk sultanate of Rum. Though its claim to constitute a distinct sultanate was resented by the great Seljuks, and rejected for some time by the Caliphate, there is no doubt that this was an enduring and in some respects remarkably successful state.

Syria had come into Seljuk possession in the 460s/1070s as a result of the now-familiar seizure of power by a member of the Seljuk house – Tutush, brother of Malik-Shâh – following a Turkoman invasion. After Tutush's death in 488/1095, the province broke up into smaller political entities based on individual cities and their hinterlands, while the coastal littoral remained under loose Fâtimid control.[4] Were it not for the Crusader invasion of 1097–9 Syria might well have remained a marginal patchwork of small states suspended between Iraq and Egypt. In time the establishment of the Crusader states (the kingdom of Jerusalem, the principality of Antioch, and the counties of Tripoli and Edessa) was to turn Syria into a new frontier region, with all the advantages that frontier warfare, particularly of an ideological nature, provided to enterprising state builders.

The Crusader invasion met with little sustained or organized opposition beyond that mounted by the powers directly attacked. One reason for this was that the Crusaders did not directly threaten the larger Muslim powers in the interior, particularly those centered on Damascus and Aleppo. Following their military success, the Crusaders fit themselves into the fragmented politics of the region without exciting much overt opposition. The Caliph, popular preachers, refugees, and some of the 'ulamâ' agitated for a collective response, but in the event local powers were too caught up in their own struggles to contemplate, much less to organize, a response. Moreover, most Sunnîs and Shî'a were too preoccupied with one another to give much thought to the invaders, whom they found possible to dismiss as Byzantine irredentists or, more commonly, barbarian Franks.

The counter-crusade began with the conquest of Edessa in 539/1144 by Zengî, a Turkish officer formerly in Seljuk service and atabeg to the local Seljuk ruler's sons. Edessa's independence was contingent upon the weakness of the Muslim states bordering it, as its economic base was weak and its geographical position vulnerable. When Zengî united Mosul and Aleppo, later adding to them Harrân, Hims, and Hamâ, Edessa could not hold off the new threat. Zengî's seizure of the county was not animated in the first instance by the desire to return it to Muslim rule; in fact he was said to have been flamboyantly impious and his relations with the 'ulamâ' were difficult. His victory, however, both inspired others and set in train a series of events that was to lead to the unification of Mesopotamia, Syria, and Egypt and the ultimate defeat of the crusader states.

The second crusade of 1147–8 failed to recover Edessa, its primary objective, and came to an end following a militarily incompetent and diplomatically disastrous siege of Damascus, hitherto allied to the crusader states. The principal consequence of the Crusade was unintended: in 549/1154 Zengî's son and heir Nûr al-Dîn picked off an isolated and enfeebled Damascus.[5] Unlike his father, Nûr al-Dîn saw the struggle against the Crusaders in religious and ideological terms. He was praised by his contemporaries for his personal piety, and frequented the 'ulamâ', who provided him with the justification he needed to subjugate or incorporate the smaller powers of the region. Zengî adopted the practices of the Seljuk military patronage state to good effect: he raised an army of mamlûks, ethnic contingents, and freebooters, supporting them with 'iqtâ's and household revenues; he advanced a political program based on Islam and jihad; he patronized scholars and Sûfîs, sustaining them with stipends and waqfs; and he recruited local scholars and officials to organize his court, oversee the apparatus of revenue extraction, and conduct his diplomacy.

A rough strategic balance now existed between the crusader coast and the Muslim interior, a rare geopolitical situation made possible only by Fâtimid debility. Both parties then vied to obtain a dominant position in Egypt, though the extent to which they aimed to rule the country directly is debatable. Between 558/1163 and 463/1170 the Fâtimids attempted to play the Crusaders and Zengî off one another, while each in turn tried to outflank the other in Egypt and to exploit Fâtimid internal rivalries.

Following a number of false starts, unexpected reversals, and difficult moments, Nûr al-Dîn's commanders secured a dominant position in Egypt. In 564/1169 the Fâtimid Caliph appointed Zengî's lieutenant Saladin (Salâh al-Dîn b. Ayyûb) as vizier.[6] Soon thereafter the Fâtimid Caliph was dead and Saladin toppled the local forces that stood in his way. In 566–7/1171 the Friday prayer in Cairo was made in the name of the 'Abbâsid Caliph, the Fâtimid Shi'ite religious establishment disbanded, and a Shafi'î jurist appointed as chief qâdî.

Nûr al-Dîn's satisfaction at this turn of events was tempered by alarm at the actions of his lieutenant, who now began to act as an independent ruler. Saladin assigned 'iqtâ's to his family and followers, to purchase his own mamlûks, to conduct his own diplomacy with the Franks, and to expand his domains, including an invasion of Yemen. Nûr al-Dîn recognized that what he had seen as insubordination had become rivalry just before his death in 569/1174. Saladin claimed to rule in the name of Nûr al-Dîn's son, atabeg to an atabeg dynasty, married his widow, and asserted himself in Syria and Mesopotamia. Soon he exercised power in his own name. He then attacked the Crusader states, but came to realize that success depended on the unification of Mesopotamia, Syria, and Egypt. Following a nine-year series of campaigns he turned his attention to the Crusaders, defeated them at the battle of Hattîn (583/1187), and took Jerusalem and most of the coast. The Third Crusade, launched to reverse the situation, ultimately failed in its objective of retaking Jerusalem, but succeeded in winning a truce for the reduced Crusader kingdom. By this point Saladin and his armies were exhausted and his Mediterranean fleet annihilated At the time of Saladin's death in 589/1193 his policy towards the Franks was limited to the maintenance of treaties and the fostering of trade.

The Ayyûbids, the family brought to power by Saladin, constituted an empire whose organization strongly resembled that constructed by the Seljuks.[7] Just as Seljuk unity under the authority of an overall sultan broke down following the end of the conquest era, resignation to the existence of the Crusader state meant that the frontier no longer countered the tendency of the Ayyûbid family to fragment. None of Saladin's successors could benefit from continuous frontier warfare, and no Ayyûbid sultan wielded the unchallenged authority that Saladin once possessed. Under the loose authority of the ruling sultan of each generation, it was the family itself, rather than a single line of descent within it, that claimed sovereignty; within the family power was exercised at the level of the individual households. Members of the family seized or were assigned provinces which they ruled more or less independently. Though fathers tried to transfer their power to their sons, successions were disputed and their outcomes unpredictable. To the extent that inter-Ayyûbid rivalries were moderated, it was to face common threats rather than to advance common interests.

As the Seljuks depended in the period of their greatest unity on a shadow ruling family headed by Nizâm al-Mulk, so the Ayyûbids depended on the Banû al-Shaykh, a family that served as viziers and commanders throughout their rule. It may not be a coincidence that Ayyûbid power came to an end following the death of the last member of the lineage. Also like the Seljuks before them, the Ayyûbid ruling households developed cadres of supporters through patronage of the learned, usually through waqf, and recruited military forces as they could attract them or purchase them, supporting them through 'iqtâ'.

The Ayyûbid devolution of revenue sources on clients meant that these did not act or see themselves as specialists within a hierarchical political system. Rather, it appears that they regarded themselves as lesser versions of great men themselves. These men asserted themselves openly and exercised power by devolving portions of their revenue sources onto their own clients. Thus the politics of revenue assignment again came to constitute a set of practices that cut across the functional distinctions of the ruling, the military and the learned, and cut through such hierarchies of rank as may otherwise have existed. Rulers ruled by playing off the dynamic tension of rival interests, rather than by asserting power through formal institutions. And their clients survived and advanced in like manner.

The relationship between the Ayyûbids and Crusaders in Syria and Palestine was necessarily difficult, but they appear to have tolerated one another, cooperated to keep one another in power, and ignored their subjects' bellicosity. During the sixty-year period of Ayyûbid rule, two crusades, the fifth (615/1218–618/1221) and the seventh (647/1249–648/1250), recognized that the road to Jerusalem led through Egypt, and disembarked at Damietta to attack in the direction of Cairo. In the event, Frankish fractiousness and tactical impetuousness undercut an otherwise sound strategic vision, and both were defeated.

As the second Crusade had the unintended effect of strengthening Muslim power in Syria, the fifth and seventh Crusades fortuitously reinforced power in the hands of those who fought them off. The fifth Crusade corresponded with an Ayyûbid succession crisis, one in which ambitious amirs and lesser Ayyûbid rulers seemed to be on the verge of dismembering such Ayyûbid unity as still existed. As the crusade represented a threat to the interests of all, the Ayyûbids and their amirs were obliged to cooperate, and a new sultan was able to assume power. The seventh Crusade also occurred in the context of a succession crisis, one that in the end was to put an end to Ayyûbid rule. The household of the deceased Ayyûbid sultan al-Sâlih tried to survive by concealing the fact of his death, and in disordered circumstances al-Sâlih's mamlûks, responsible for the defeat of the crusader army, seized power, first as unconvincing atabegs for a son of al-Sâlih, and finally in their own names.

In the first half of the thirteenth century, Syria was increasingly exposed to pressure from the distant steppe. At first this pressure was indirect, as raiders and movements of peoples pushed westwards by the Mongols washed up on Syrian territory, there to plunder or place themselves in the service of the lesser Ayyûbid households. But the lands west of the Euphrates and south of the Taurus were ultimately defensible. The scarcity of good horse pasture on the Syrian borders limited the numbers of invaders who could advance with their mounts, while the resources of Egypt meant that a strong defense could be mounted in Syria. When in 658/1260 the Mongols invaded Syria, they created for Egypt a new frontier that, as other frontiers had elsewhere, concentrated power in the hands of men who knew how to use it. Thus the Mamlûk sultanate, having originated in a succession dispute in the seventh Crusade, consolidated its power fighting off the Mongols. The Mamlûk sultanate became arguably the most successful and enduring military patronage state of them all.

Looking at developments in the Nile-to-Oxus region from the rise of the Seljuks to that of the Mamlûks, several overarching trends can be discerned. One is the process by which the steppe, near and distant, came to play a decisive role in the politics of the region. The period began with one pastoralist invasion and ended with another; the fortuitous irony is that the latter was eventually stopped by a form of political organization developed by the former. A second process was how the great variety that characterized the early post-'Abbâsid period came to an end, as the Seljuks and their successor states disseminated a new and universal set of practices. These derived from the encounter of the pastoralist army with eleventh-century Iran, Khurasân in particular, and were applied to myriad local contexts. But in spite of the variety of their origins and application, Seljuk institutions proved to be so militarily lethal, politically flexible, and adaptable to conditions elsewhere, that the major institutions of Egypt from the thirteenth century onward can be traced to eleventh-century Iran. The military patronage state gave rise to a new type of society, in which power and revenue sources were devolved on the military and the learned, who used it to create their own clienteles. This, in rough outline, survived many centuries and worked in many contexts.

To return to the comparison of the Arab and Seljuk conquests, both transformed collections of pastoralist peoples into standing armies, inspired them with a sense of mission on behalf of Islam, and used them to create an empire in the agrarian world. No Seljuk duplicated the feat of the Caliph 'Umar in controlling his military forces and creating a unitary state, even though the problems they faced were quite similar. The Seljuks permitted the Turkoman to retain their pastoral mode of life under their own leaders; 'Umar forced the settlement of the Bedouin in garrisons, rationalized their military organization, and superimposed his own leadership. The Seljuks never centralized the collection and distribution of revenue, instead devolving revenue sources onto their supporters; 'Umar, through the institution of the central dîwân of the early caliphate, ensured the unity of the state and its control over the far-flung armies. In one generation the Seljuks came to depend on their mamlûks to balance their tribal supporters, and soon thereafter were dominated by them; the early caliphate took two hundred years to lose power to its mamlûks, and even then the caliphate survived.

But this is not to say that the Seljuks failed where the caliphate succeeded. The caliphate conquered an imperial world, made adept use of imperial institutions that had long existed, and created the last great ancient universal empire before the Ottomans. The Seljuks entered a world in which military power was everywhere freeing itself from dependence on central bureaucracies, in which invasion from the steppe and the sea was unavoidable, and in which political power if not sovereignty itself was exercised at the level of the household. The military patronage state thus permitted the ideal of the universal cosmopolitan empire to survive within a political-economic context that tended towards fragmentation. Although individual dynasties were short lived, the practices that sustained them were enduring.

NOTES

1   This interpretation largely follows C. E. Bosworth, *The Cambridge History of Iran*, vol. 5, pp. 43–4. Claude Cahen argued that Alp Arslân intended to conquer Anatolia to fulfill the age-old Muslim ambition of subjugating Byzantium but later modified his views in the direction of Bosworth's: see C. Cahen, *The Cambridge History of Islam*, vol. 1A, P. M. Holt, A. K. S. Lambton, and B. Lewis (eds.) (Cambridge, 1970), p. 233 and C. Cahen, *The Formation of Turkey: The Seljukid Sultanate of Rûm: Eleventh to Fourteenth Century*, P. M. Holt ed. and tr. (Harlow, 2001), pp. 2, 3. The divergence of views may be due to Cahen's reluctance to distinguish between a general desire to shape events for the imperial benefit and a policy and plan of conquest.

2   On the institution of the madrasa see D. Brandenberg, *Die Madrasa: Ursprung, Entwicklung, Ausbreitung und kunsterliche Gestaltung der islamischen Mosche-Hochschule* (Graz, 1978); G. Makdisi, *The Rise of Colleges: Institutions of Learning in Islam and the West* (Edinburgh, 1981); G. Makdisi, "Muslim Institutions of Learning in Eleventh-Century Baghdad," *BSOAS*, 24 (1961), 1–56; G. Leiser, "The Madrasa and the Islamization of the

Middle East: the Case of Egypt," *JARCE* (1985); D. Ephrat, *A Learned Society in a Period of Transition. The Sunni Ulama of Eleventh-century Baghdad* (New York, 2000).

3   On the Seljukids see C. Cahen, *The Formation of Turkey.*

4   Bianquis, T., *Damas et la Syrie sous la domination fatimide (359–468/969–1076). Essai d'interprétation de chroniques arabes médiévales*, 2 vols. (Damascus, 1986–89).

5   The major study on Nûr al-Dîn, with an extensive bibliography, is N. Elisséeff, *Nûr al-Dîn, un grand prince musulman de Syrie au temps des Croisades 511–569 A. H./1118–1175*, 3 vols. (Damascus, 1967); later additions to the bibliography in N. Elisséeff, "Nûr al-Dîn Mahmûd b. Zankî," *EI* (2).

6   On Saladin the definitive modern biography, with full bibliography, is M. C. Lyons and D. E. P. Jackson, *Saladin: The politics of Holy War* (Cambridge, 1982).

7   On the Zengîds and Ayyûbids see C. Cahen, "Ayyubids," *EI* (2); J. C. Garcin, "Les Zankides et les Ayyubides," in J. C. Garcin et al. (eds.), *États, sociétés et cultures du monde Musulman médiéval, Xe–XVe siècle*, i: *L'évolution politique et sociale* (Paris, 1995), 233–55; R.S. Humphreys, *From Saladin to the Mongols: The Ayyubids of Damascus* (Albany, 1977); J. C. Garcin, *Un centre musulman de la haute-Égypte médiévale: Qûs* (Cairo, 1976); on the religious life of Ayyûbid Damascus, see L Pouzet, *Damas au VIe/XIIIe siècle. Vie et structures religieuses d'une métropole islamique* (Beirut, 1988); for an attempt to understand urban politics in Ayyûbid Damascus in a comparative context see M. Chamberlain, *Knowledge and Social Practice in Medieval Damascus* (Cambridge, 1994).

FURTHER READING

Few of the major works from the period have been translated. For Seljuk-period examples of the advice literature that Persian courtiers had long written for rulers see Nizâm al-Mulk, *The Book of Government or Rules for Kings: The Siyar al-Muluk or Siyasat–nama*, Hubert Darke tr., 2nd edn. (London, 1978) and Al-Ghazâlî, *Ghazali's Book of Counsel for Kings (Nasihat al-Muluk)*, F. R. C. Bagley tr. (London, 1971). For an example of the important genre of the biographical dictionary see Ibn Khallikan, *The Obituaries of Eminent Men*, 4 vols., M. de Slane tr. (London, 1871). A fine biography of Saladin is *Ibn Shaddad, The Rare and Excellent History of Saladin: or Al-Nawâdir al-sultâniyya wa'l-mahâsin al-yusufiyya*, D. S. Richards ed. and tr. (Aldershot, 2002). Two rare examples of medieval Islamic autobiographical literature date from this period: al-Ghazâlî, *Deliverance from Error: Five Key Texts Including his Spiritual Autobiography, al-Munqidh min al-Dalâl*, R. J. McCarthy tr. (Louisville, 2000) and Usamah Ibn Munqidh, *An Arab–Syrian Gentleman and Warrior in the Period of the Crusades*, P. K. Hitti tr. (Columbia, 2000). Reliable translations of important chronicles are rare and include, on the Mongol conquests, Juvainî, *The History of the World Conqueror*, 2 vols., J. A. Boyle tr. (Manchester, 1958); on Syria during the early Crusades, Ibn al-Qalânisî, *The Damascus Chronicle of the Crusades*, H. A. R. Gibb ed. and tr. (London, 1967); and on the entire period, Ibn al-'Ibri (Bar Hebraeus), *The Chronology of Bar Hebraeus*, vol. 2 (Oxford, 1932). Travelers' accounts include Naser-e Khosraw, *Book of Travels (Safarnama)*, W. M. Thackston ed. and tr. (New York, 1986); Benjamin of Tudela, *The Itinerary of Benjamin of Tudela: Critical Text, Translation and Commentary*, M. N. Adler tr. (New York, 1964); Ibn Jubayr, *The Travels of Ibn Jubayr*, M. J. de Goeje tr. (London, 2003).

CHAPTER EIGHT

The Mamluk Institution

P. M. HOLT

Introduction: The Development of Mamluk Studies

The beginning of Mamluk studies as a special field of historical enquiry was in the nineteenth century, when Etienne Quatrèmere (1782–1852) published his work on Ibn Faḍlallāh al-ʿUmarī (1838) and a partial translation of al-Maqrīzī's *al-Sulūk li-maʿrifat duwal al-mulūk* in his *Histoire des Sultans Mamluks de l'Égypte* (1837–45). For a wider readership Jean-Joseph Marcel (1776–1854) included two chapters on the Mamluk sultans in an account of Egypt from the Arab conquest to Bonaparte's expedition (which he had accompanied) in a volume entitled *L'Univers: Histoire et description de tous les peuples: Égypte* (1848).

The attitude of writers in Great Britain was less sympathetic. Humphrey Prideaux (1648–1724), dean of Norwich, the author of a highly successful and controversial book entitled *The True Nature of Imposture Fully Display'd in the Life of Mahomet* (1697), wrote to a friend, 'I could not say much of the *Mamalucs*, of whom I know no author, that has written in particular; neither did they deserve that any should. For they were a base sort of people, a *Colluvies* of slaves, the scum of all the *East* ... and, bating that they finished the expulsion of the *Western* Christians out of the *East* ... they scarce did any thing worthy to be recorded in History!'[1] The first British contribution to the subject appears to be Sir William Muir's *The Mameluke or Slave Dynasty of Egypt, 1260–1517* A.D. (1896), a brief account largely based on Gustav Weil's *Geschichte des Abbasidenchalifats in Egypten* (1860–2), which 'reveal[s] in discreet fashion the author's Christian standpoint'.[2] D. S. Margoliouth, then Laudian Professor of Arabic at Oxford, devotes 2 of the 160 pages of his *Lectures on Arabic Historians* (1930) to the Mamluk period.

A very marked development of Mamluk studies has taken place from about the middle of the twentieth century. At the start of this period in 1958, no paper on the Mamluk chroniclers was contributed to an international Conference on Historical Writing on the Near and Middle East held at the School of Oriental and African Studies in London. But during the following years there was a considerable output of Mamluk historical texts, which Arabophone historians took the lead in editing and publishing. Three outstanding examples are al-Maqrīzī's *al-Sulūk*, edited by Muḥammad Muṣṭafā Ziyāda and Saʿīd ʿAbd al-Fattāḥ ʿĀshūr from 1956, Ibn Taghrī-birdī's *al-Nujūm al-zāhira fī mulūk Miṣr waʾl-Qāhira* by Fahīm Muḥammad Shaltūt et al. from 1960, and Ibn Iyās, *Badāʾiʿ al-zuhūr fī waqāʾiʿ al-duhūr* by Muḥammad

Muṣṭafā from 1960. There also developed a new species of historical writing concerned with the critical investigation of aspects of institutions and culture. A prime exponent of this genre was David (Neustadt) Ayalon (1914–98), in his book *Gunpowder and Firearms in the Mamluk Kingdom* (1956) and numerous articles now collected in four volumes by Variorum Reprints (1977–94).

Contributions from North American writers have been numerous. Three examples may be taken from different kinds of historiography. Donald Presgrave Little produced a seminal work of source-analysis in *An Introduction to Mamlūk Historiography* (1970). R. S. Humphreys described the origination of the Mamluk sultanate from the preceding Ayyubid regime in *From Saladin to the Mongols* (1977) and accompanied this with two important articles on 'The emergence of the Mamluk army' in *Studia Islamica*, xlv, xlvi (1977). The biography of Qalāwūn, the second of the great Mamluk sultans, is treated by Linda S. Northrup, formerly one of Little's students, in *From Slave to Sultan* (1998).

Antecedents

The term *mamlūk* is one of a number of Arabic synonyms for 'slave', and has come to mean specifically a military slave. More commonly used in earlier times was the term *ghulām* meaning a boy or youth, with no original connotation of slavery. As a recognized military institution, Mamluk troops appear during the 'Abbasid caliphate in the first half of the ninth century. Muslim generals on the eastern frontier of the empire were then capturing large numbers of Turkish tribesmen in Transoxania, and these provided ideal recruits to the forces of their captors. As non-Muslims they could be enslaved, as strangers in an alien Islamic society their closest attachment was to their master, to whom their loyalty was unqualified. They were more dependable than freeborn Arab warriors, who were individuals proud of their tribal traditions. Although they were enslaved as non-Muslims, they were soon converted to Islam, whereby they acquired rights under the Sharī'a, and moreover Islam favoured the emancipation of a *mamlūk* on his master's death. The status of a *mamlūk* therefore offered opportunities to personal advancement in Muslim society, especially as the Arab component of military forces diminished.

A preference for Turkish troops was conspicuously displayed when the Caliph al-Ma'mūn (813–33) embodied them in large numbers in his army, and pursued what was virtually a systematic immigration policy by levying tribute from the eastern frontier provinces partly in slaves. His brother and successor, al-Mu'taṣim (833–42), a career soldier, purchased some 3,000 Turkish slave-troops to form an elite corps and his personal guard. In 836 he transferred them from the temptations and turbulence of Baghdad to a new city, 125 km north on the east bank of the Tigris. Sāmarrā' (officially *Surra man ra'ā*, 'The beholder is delighted') consisted essentially of the caliph's palace and the cantonments of his Turkish troops, but it inevitably superseded Baghdad as the administrative centre of the empire, and so continued until the closing years of the ninth century.

By that time the commanders of the Turkish forces were assuming political authority and dominating the civilian administrative officials in the provinces and at the centre. In Egypt, for example, two short-lived gubernatorial dynasties, the Tulunids (868–905) and the Ikhshidids (935–69), were both of Turkish Mamluk origin. Aḥmad b. Ṭūlūn, who ruled from 868 to 883, was said to be the son of a Turk

sent in the slave-tribute to al-Ma'mūn. Muḥammad b. Ṭughj, the descendant of
another Turk from Sāmarrā', took the old Iranian title of *ikhshīd* and ruled from
935 to 946. Similar developments took place elsewhere in the territories nominally
subject to the 'Abbasid caliphate. The Iranian Samanid state based in Transoxania was
dependent on Mamluk soldiery from the time of its greatest ruler, Ismā'īl (892–907).
One of these Mamluks, Alptigin, the former Samanid commander-in-chief, seized
Ghazna in Afghanistan, and his Mamluk, Sebüktigin, established a dynasty which in
the reign of Maḥmūd (998–1030) ruled from Transoxania to the Punjab.

In the eleventh century, when the 'Abbasid caliphate was long past its prime and
was under the protection and control of the Shī'ī Iranian Buyids, a new force entered
the lands of the Near and Middle East. These were Turcoman tribesmen from
Transoxania, who were seeking new pastures in Khurāsān and farther west. They
were headed by two brother chiefs from the family of Seljuk, Tughril Beg and
Chaghri Beg. While Chaghri Beg remained to rule Khurāsān, Tughril went on to
Iraq, overthrew the Buyids and entered Baghdad in 1055. As he and his people were
Sunnī Muslims, they were welcomed by the Caliph al-Qā'im (1031–75). Tughril
received the formal title of 'sultan', originally an Arabic word signifying 'power' in
the abstract. He was indeed the power behind the caliphal throne. He died childless
in 1063, and was succeeded by his nephew, Alp Arslan, who ruled for ten years. In
1073 Alp Arslan's son, Malik Shāh, became sultan. He was a young man, and was
only 37 when he died in 1092, but his reign, which was conducted under the tutelage
of his great *wazīr*, Niẓām al-Mulk, was the golden age of the Great Seljuk sultanate.
He was however challenged by a brother of Alp Arslan in accordance with the
Turcoman custom of succession by the eldest male of a family, and after his death
the sultanate was to be split by competitors for the throne.

By the time of Malik Shāh the sultan had clearly moved from being a tribal chief to
an autocratic ruler. He could no longer base his power on the Turcoman warriors
who had accompanied his forebears into the heart of the Muslim world – they were
too dispersed and too concerned with their own affairs as nomadic pastoralists to
form the military base of the Great Seljuk sultanate. In place of these freeborn
warriors Malik Shāh recruited Turkish slave-soldiers, i.e. Mamluks. These men,
utterly reliable because of their close personal ties with him, soon came to occupy
key posts in the administration. When in 1086 Malik Shāh brought his army into
Syria to impose a settlement on his brother Tutuş, who held the territory as an
apanage, he placed three of his Mamluks as governors of the chief cities: Aksungur
in Aleppo, Bozan in Edessa, and Yağısıyan in Antioch. Yağısıyan was killed in 1098,
when the First Crusade took Antioch. Tutuş, who had proclaimed himself sultan
after Malik Shāh's death, disposed of Bozan and Aksungur, who had revolted against
him, but Aksungur was to be the founder of a notable dynastic family, the Zangids,
which was to be at its zenith under his grandson, Nūr al-Dīn Maḥmūd b. Zangī
(r. 1146–74).

On the death of Tutuş in 1095 his apanage was divided between his two sons,
Riḍwān at Aleppo and Dokak at Damascus. It was a Seljuk custom, when a young
prince was appointed to an apanage, to place beside him a Mamluk guardian, who was
in effect the regent. He was known as the *atabeg*, i.e. father-commander, and might
strengthen his position by marrying the widow of his former lord. This is substantially
what happened in Damascus. The *Atabeg* Tuğtigin married the mother of Dokak, and
overshadowed the prince, who died in 1104. Tuğtigin appointed Dokak's brothers to

succeed him, but soon deposed them, and ruled in his own right. He was succeeded in 1128 by his son Böri, in Arabic Būrī, whence the dynasty is known as the Burids. Böri died after being wounded by an Ismāʿīlī assassin in 1152. The three sons and a nephew who succeeded him were of little consequence, and Damascus was taken in 1154 by Nūr al-Dīn b. Zangī, the *atabeg* of Aleppo. The term *atabeg* had by this time lost its original significance, and had become simply the title of a ruler.

Origins of the Mamluk Sultanate in Egypt and Syria

The climax of the Mamluk institution came in the century after Nūr al-Dīn b. Zangī with the emergence and development of the Mamluk sultanate in Egypt and Syria. The immediately previous rulers of this region were the Ayyubids, a Kurdish family and confederacy formed by the descendants and collaterals of Saladin (Ṣalāḥ al-Dīn b. Ayyūb), who died in 1193. Saladin, originally one of Nūr al-Dīn's freeborn retainers, had made himself the ruler of Egypt, and subsequently went on to usurp the Syrian possessions of Nūr al-Dīn's successors. After Saladin's death these were divided up among the members of his family. The political relations among the various branches of the Ayyubid clan were basically unstable, although a kind of paramountcy was held by the ruler of Egypt. The last of these, al-Ṣāliḥ Ayyūb, a great-nephew of Saladin, ruled from 1240 to 1249, and died during the crusade of King Louis IX of France.

During his father's lifetime al-Ṣāliḥ Ayyūb had built up a large force of Turkish Mamluks, which developed during his own reign into an elite corps known as the Baḥriyya, probably because they were quartered at Cairo on an island in the river Nile (Arabic, Baḥr al-Nīl) and a bodyguard, the Jāmdāriyya, literally 'the Keepers of the Wardrobe'. Thus the Mamluks, who had been of minor importance under the earlier Ayyubids, became a force of central significance, at first in the field as the spearhead of resistance to Louis IX, and after al-Ṣāliḥ Ayyūb's death in political affairs also.

The transfer of political power resulted from the circumstances immediately following al-Ṣāliḥ Ayyūb's death. This was at first aimed to prevent the demoralizing of the Muslim troops. The sultan had been attended on the campaign by his wife, Shajar al-Durr, formerly his Turkish concubine, i.e. a female Mamluk. In consultation with the army chiefs, she continued to issue in his name and with his forged signature orders and decrees for the soldiery, pending the arrival of his son and successor, al-Muʿaẓẓam Tūrān Shāh, from his residence in Ḥiṣn Kayfā, now Hasankeyf in modern Turkey. His arrival provoked trouble, although by this time the Crusaders were fortunately in retreat. Factional rivalry, a recurrent phenomenon in Mamluk politics, developed between the veteran Baḥriyya and the entourage of the new sultan. This was aggravated by Tūrān Shāh's disparagement of Shajar al-Durr, whom the Baḥriyya regarded as one of themselves. The upshot was a conspiracy of the Baḥriyya against Tūrān Shāh, who was murdered on 2 May 1250. They chose Shajar al-Durr to be their ruler, an event almost unique in Islamic history. She took the title of *Malikat al-Muslimīn*, 'Queen of the Muslims', and the throne-name of Umm Khalīl, 'the Mother of Khalīl', her deceased son by al-Ṣāliḥ Ayyūb, who was her link to legitimacy. Her reign was in fact short. Word came from Baghdad that the Caliph al-Mustaʿṣim disapproved of a female ruler, and the Mamluks thereupon chose one of themselves, al-Muʿizz Aybak al-Turkumānī, to be the sultan. Loyalty to the Ayyubids remained strong, and the Mamluks sought to satisfy this by appointing an Ayyubid boy as nominal sultan with Aybak as his *atabeg*. This however did not satisfy the Syrian

Ayyubids, and the two sides came to blows. There was in effect a balance of power between the Mamluks in Egypt and the Ayyubids in Syria, which was abruptly overthrown by the Mongol invasion of Syria in 1259–60. This destroyed the power of the Ayyubids, and when the Mongols were defeated at 'Ayn Jālūt on 3 September 1260 by the Mamluk chief, Baybars al-Bunduqdārī, the Syrian Muslim provinces fell into the hands of the Mamluk rulers of Egypt.

This was a turning-point of history when the Mamluks, hitherto an elite corps in the Ayyubid forces, seized political power. In place of the fragmented regime of the Ayyubids in Egypt and Syria they set up a single autocratic sultanate. This was firmly established by Baybars al-Bunduqdārī, the great survivor of the first decade of tangled political struggles. He became sultan by the murder of his predecessor and was enthroned in the Citadel of Cairo, probably in late October 1260. During his reign, which lasted until 1277 the essential institutions were developed from their less formalized Ayyubid prototypes. Baybars's work was carried forward by his former comrade-in-arms and eventual successor, Qalāwūn, who reigned from 1279 to 1290. Thereafter two successions of Mamluk sultans were to control Egypt and Syria. Their members were to be mainly of Turkish and Circassian origin respectively, and they are sometimes called the Baḥrī and Burjī Mamluks from the names of the corps in which they originated. The Mamluk sultanate was finally overthrown and its territories annexed in 1517 by the Ottoman Sultan Selim the Grim (1512–20).

Recruitment and Group-solidarity under the Mamluk Sultanate

The Mamluk sultanate depended originally on the purchase of Kipchak Turkish slave-boys in their homeland, the steppes of what is now southern Russia. This was a region harried by the Mongols, and many of the slaves were displaced refugees, as was Baybars himself. They were bought by slave-merchants, who had a privileged status in the Egyptian fiscal regime, and the trade was controlled by an official who was almost invariably a Mamluk amir. At the slave-market in Cairo they passed into the possession of the amirs or the sultan himself. Two anecdotes throw some light on the appraisal of potential Mamluk recruits. A young Ayyubid prince, who was about to purchase Baybars, was dissuaded by his mother, who said he had an evil eye – perhaps alluding to a defect in his eye. Qalāwūn by contrast bore the name of al-Alfī, 'the Thousander' as his master bought him for the high price of a thousand dinars (*ālf dīnār*). A Mamluk might have a series of masters; Baybars for example was first owned by one of al-Ṣāliḥ Ayyūb's own Mamluks, the amir Aydigin al-Bunduqdār (i.e. the Crossbowman), then by the sultan, under whom he was enrolled in the Jamdāriyya. The final master, who enfranchised the Mamluk was the most important, as loyalty to him was a primary duty.

Most information is naturally available about the Royal Mamluks who formed the sultan's military household. They were placed in barracks, where they received training directed to producing efficient mounted warriors, capable of using the lance and the bow. At the same time they underwent conversion, learnt the Qur'ān and the elements of Islamic law, theology and ritual. Some Mamluks of a scholarly bent went a good deal further than this. Sultan Qānsawh al-Ghawrī, who died in battle with the Ottoman invaders, used to hold frequent sessions with Egyptian scholars to discuss literary matters.

When the Royal Mamluks had finished their training, they were formally emanci-pated in groups, and each received a horse, arms and uniform from the sultan. They were permitted to grow beards as a token of their new status of freemen. Technically they were no longer *mamlūks*, although still so designated.

As already indicated, it was to the emancipating sultan that a Mamluk felt his primary loyalty. Underlying this was a basic sentiment of ethnic loyalty, whether Turkish or Circassian, as is instanced by the short reign of Sultan Kitbugha (1294–6), whose position was weakened by his origin as a Mongol prisoner of war. Again, the former Mamluk who became viceroy of Egypt after the Ottoman conquest, Khā'ir Bey, was known in a reproachful pun as *al-khā'in li-jinsihi*, 'the traitor to his nation'.

The loyalty felt by a group of Mamluks towards their emancipator created a bond among them. This loyalty was intensely personal, and was not transferred to the emancipator's successor. Hence until a sultan had built up his own group of Mamluks, known as *ajlāb* or *julbān* because they had been imported (*jalaba*) to Egypt, and placed them in positions of power, he was under a threat from the entrenched Mamluks of his predecessor, known collectively as *qarāniṣa*. This might lead to factional struggles or worse: we have seen how at the very beginning of this period the jealousy felt by the Baḥriyya towards the Mamluks of al-Muʿaẓẓam Tūrān Shāh led to the new sultan's murder in a revolt.

The group-solidarity of the *ajlāb* formed the second characteristic loyalty of Mamluks, and enabled them to exert pressure for the maintenance of their position. The greatest safeguard was to secure the sultanate for one of their group. This group-loyalty was known as *khushdāshiyya*, and its weakness was its particularity, that is to say as time passed and the *ajlāb* of successive sultans became *qarāniṣa*, they were fragmented into politically ineffective groups instead of forming a united body of veterans.

The Position of the Mamluk Sultan

The Mamluk sultan occupied a position of twofold significance. Originally he was the leader of a Turkish war-band, artificially formed from imported military slaves. In this respect he was regarded by the amirs as the first among equals, the chief among the People (*al-nās*), as the Mamluks were styled. On acquiring the sultanate he also became a traditional Islamic autocratic ruler, and was seen as such, especially by the non-Mamluk subject people, the 'herds' (*al-raʿāyā*), who formed the great majority of the population under his rule.

The Islamic legitimacy of the sultan's authority was originally secured by Baybars's installation of an ʿAbbasid prince as caliph after al-Mustaʿṣim, the last caliph of Baghdad, had been killed by the Mongols in 1258. This first ʿAbbasid caliph of Cairo, al-Mustanṣir, was solemnly installed on 13 June 1261, when Baybars took the oath of allegiance (*al-bayʿa*) to him. In return the caliph formally invested the sultan with 'the Islamic territories and whatever God might help him to conquer of the land of the infidels'. This signified that Baybars was appointed to a universal sultanate. In a great assembly on 4 July the head of the sultan's chancery read out the diploma of investiture at length. It served in fact as Baybars's manifesto for the conduct of his reign. The caliph died shortly afterwards in an ill-starred attempt to regain Baghdad. He was succeeded as caliph in Cairo by a kinsman, al-Ḥākim, who was to reign, but never to rule, for over forty years. The series of puppet-caliphs continued until the Ottoman conquest, after which it quietly lapsed. A writer who describes the structure and organization of the sultanate in the time of Jaqmaq (1438–53) devotes a very short chapter to the caliph, and says that 'occupation with learning is specifically appointed for him, and he is to have a library of books. He is to accompany the sultan for the benefit of the Muslims when he travels on business. He has many estates to meet his expenses, and handsome residences.' The phrase 'for the benefit of the Muslims' would seem to imply that the caliph acted as the keeper of the sultan's conscience, and might intervene if the ruler or his entourage acted wrongfully.

The recognition of a new sultan by the caliph remained an essential formality. As a sign of this, the sultan was invested by the caliph with the black robe which was the 'Abbasid livery. A second group of observances marked his accession as leader and first among equals of the war-band. There was first his election by a body of the leading amirs, or sometimes the leading conspirators of a usurper's faction. The electors would then take one or both of two oaths of allegiance. One was the traditional Muslim *bay'a* such as Baybars had taken to the Caliph al-Mustanṣir. This was essentially a recognition of the status and authority of the recipient of the oath. Alternatively there was the *ḥilf*, an oath of personal loyalty and support. The *ḥilf* might be taken reciprocally to the amirs by the sultan-elect, thus forming an embryonic social contract, but this tenuous symbol never hardened into a constitutional requirement. It might be hazarded that by the *bay'a* the amirs recognized the sultan-elect as a Muslim sovereign, by the *ḥilf* as the leader of the war-band, but the evidence is too scattered and disparate to allow of a firm conclusion.

At this point the sultan-elect would acquire a throne-name indicative of his new status. This would incorporate the royal title (*al-malik*) with a fulsome epithet. Baybars, for example, settled upon *al-Malik al-Ẓāhir*, 'the Manifest King', after his *wazīr*, 'an excellent historian', had pointed out several unpropitious precedents for his original choice of *al-Malik al-Qāhir*, 'the Conquering King'. Qalāwūn, who was to succeed him, took the title of *al-Malik al-Manṣūr*, 'the Divinely-aided King'. Apart from a very few early exceptions among the sons of Baybars, titles of this kind were held only by sultans, and here there was a marked divergence from Ayyubid usage, where such titles were held by all the princes.

The sultans were never crowned, the constitutive act on accession being the enthronement. When Baybars became sultan, irregularly as he had just participated in the murder of his predecessor, Quṭuz, on the army's return from liberating Syria, the place of the throne was taken by the sultan's cushion in the royal tent, although, as we have seen, a formal enthronement took place after his arrival in Cairo. The 'throne of kingship' is described as being a *minbar*, thus resembling the stepped pulpit found in a mosque. For ordinary court sessions, e.g. the hearing of petitions, the sultan would sit on a footstool (*kursī*) beside it.

Then the new sultan made his first appearance in a procession through Cairo to the Citadel. He rode on horseback by his dismounted amirs. An important item of the royal insignia, the *ghāshiya*, a gilded saddle-cover, was carried before him and displayed to the bystanders. This usage goes back through the Ayyubids to the Seljuk sultans. Under later sultans, at least from the middle years of the fourteenth century, the royal ride was curtailed to a procession within the Citadel, usually from an outer gate to the place of enthronement.

The Mamluks formed essentially a single-generation military and political elite. Their descendants, known as *awlād al-nās*, 'the sons of the People', were excluded from succeeding to their military rank and political authority. They were assimilated to the traditional Arabic-speaking Muslim society of Egypt and Syria, although they held a privileged social position and had an insight into the Turkish-speaking Mamluk community of their fathers or more distant ancestors. Two of the great chroniclers of the Mamluk period were *awlād al-nās*: Ibn Taghrībirdī (d. 1470), who wrote a history of Egypt from the Arab conquest to his own times, and Ibn Iyās (d. ca. 1524), whose work covered in detail the Mamluk sultanate from the mid-fourteenth century to its overthrow and the early years of Ottoman rule.

In the choice of the sultan this principle of the single-generation elite conflicted with the sultans' own desire to establish a hereditary monarchy. Baybars was followed briefly by two of his sons, the latter a mere child, from whom the throne was soon usurped by Qalāwūn (1279–90). Qalāwūn's own successful reign was followed by that of his son, al-Ashraf Khalīl (1290–3), who completed the extinction of the Crusader states. Khalīl was murdered by a conspiracy of his amirs, but the dynasty survived in his infant brother, al-Nāṣir Muḥammad, who, twice deposed and twice restored to the throne, finally came to the sultanate as a mature man and a skilled politician. In his third reign (1310–41) he remodelled the Mamluks, abandoning old standards of recruitment and training to increase their dependence on himself personally. On his death he was succeeded by three generations of his descendants, who were largely ineffective as rulers, for over forty years, until Barqūq, the first of the Circassian Mamluk sultans, usurped the throne in 1382. Barqūq was followed by his son Faraj, who held power (with a short break) until 1412. No later dynasty was established, although to prevent a lapse in administration a sultan's son was usually briefly installed on his father's death. What in fact appeared was a quasi-dynastic system, not of families but of Mamluk households. Barqūq was in due course followed by five of his own Mamluks. One of these, Sultan Barsbay (r. 1422–38), had a Mamluk named Qāyit Bay (r. 1468–96), whose own Mamluks were the last five sultans of Egypt.

The Fiscal System

The sultanate was supported by a fiscal regime with several sources of revenue. The first of these was a land-tax, the Islamic *kharāj*, paid in cash and kind by the peasant cultivators. In Egypt, where cultivation and tax-gathering depended on the annual Nile flood, every locality had its own body of village officials who were responsible for the surveying and allocation of the plots of land, and the collection of dues after the harvest. The greater part of the accruing revenue was alienated in assignments, each known as an *iqṭāʿ*, to maintain the Mamluk amirs and soldiery. The *iqṭāʿ* is sometimes misleadingly called a fief by European writers. Unlike the holder of a European fief, a *muqṭaʿ* was never the lord of the land, still less the lord of a rural manor. He lived in the capital or one of the provincial cities, and maintained himself and his personal contingent of Mamluks from the revenue of his *iqṭāʿ*. Under the sultanate, three grades of amirs became the norm: the amir of a hundred Mamluks, of forty Mamluks, and of ten Mamluks. The amir of Forty was also known as *amīr ṭablkhānah*, because an amir of this rank was entitled to maintain a personal military band (*ṭablkhānah*). These grades did not imply a chain of command or any kind of feudal vassalage, but an amir might rise through the ranks by a species of *cursus honorum*. Grants of *iqṭāʿ* were made directly by the sultan and were revocable; he might indeed revoke such grants to augment his own resources. It follows from this that an *iqṭāʿ* was not hereditary, at least in theory.

The sultan's own assignment of revenue, the fisc or privy purse, was known as *khāṣṣ al-sulṭān*, and from this he provided for the salaried officials of his household and administration. Twice during the Mamluk period the sultan endeavoured to enhance his own financial position through a new cadastral survey of the cultivable land, known as a *rawk*. It appears that the survey and consequent settlement made in Saladin's time (*al-rawk al-Ṣalāḥī*) was in force from 1176 to 1298, when a new survey was made by Ḥusām al-Dīn Lājīn, who had usurped the throne in 1296. This survey and settlement (*al-rawk al-Ḥusāmī*) assigned 9/24 of the landed revenue to the creation of a new standing army, which would of course be at the sultan's disposal, and it approximately halved the amount allotted to the amirs. Threatened by this strengthening of Lājīn's autocracy, the amirs revolted and killed the sultan. His *rawk* was never implemented. When al-Nāṣir Muḥammad was finally reinstalled as sultan in 1310, he resolved upon a new settlement. A preliminary *rawk* was carried out in Syria in 1313–14 as a pilot scheme, followed by *al-rawk al-Nāṣirī* in Egypt. For revenue purposes the cultivable land was divided into 24 shares (sing., *qirāṭ*, whence 'carat'). Under Saladin's settlement the *khāṣṣ* was allotted 4/24 of the revenue, while 10/24 had gone to the amirs and also to the *Ḥalqa*, i.e. the non-Mamluk military forces. Under al-Nāṣir Muḥammad's settlement his *khāṣṣ* shot up to 10/24, while the remaining 14/24 were allotted to the amirs and the *Ḥalqa* together. There was no later *rawk* in the Mamluk period, but significantly a cadastral survey of Egypt was made in 1526, within a decade of the Ottoman conquest.

Two other taxes came under the cover of Islamic law. One, known in Egypt as *Jawālī*, was the traditional *jizya*, the poll-tax levied on Christians and Jews living as *dhimmī*s under the protection of the Islamic state. It was important because of the large Coptic minority in Egypt, while Jews were found both there and in Syria. Owing to the nature of their occupations, this was largely an urban tax. Then there were customs duties, which were given a cover of legality as *zakāt* when levied on Muslims. Similar taxes were paid by *dhimmī*s and foreign traders. There were also internal trade and market taxes, which were essentially monthly payments for a licence to trade.

This leads on to the customary but uncanonical taxes (*mukūs*). When al-Nāṣir Muḥammad made his *rawk* he abolished a considerable number of these. They included, for example, a tax at the grain-wharf of Cairo, dues on ornamental belts, a prison due paid by all prisoners, the forced purchase of chickens, a due on sugar-cane and sugar presses, fees levied on weddings, and many other payments. None of these went directly to the government, but some were granted as a form of *iqṭā'*.

Household and Court Offices

The sultan's household and court were staffed at the highest level by a group of great Mamluk office-holders. Their establishment was one of Baybars's governmental reforms, and seems to have been based on Mongol practices, but some officers with similar titles had existed in earlier Islamic states. Ibn Faḍlallāh al-'Umarī (d. 1349) lists seven of these court offices 'in the presence of the sultan', the first of them being the vice-gerent or deputy sultan (*nā'ib al-salṭana*), who had 'absolute executive power in every matter referred to him concerning the army, finance and intelligence, i.e. the mail service'. But al-'Umarī wrote in the third reign of al-Nāṣir Muḥammad, who had abolished the vice-gerency as endangering his personal autocracy. Secondly, there was the post of chamberlain (*ḥājib*) or great chamberlain (*ḥājib al-ḥujjāb*), who before Baybars's reforms had been a mere doorkeeper, controlling access to the royal presence. While this remained one of his duties, he had assumed a public function as the arbitrator of military justice (not the Sharīʿa) among the Mamluks. His import-ance rose with the abolition of the vice-gerency. The third great officer was the *amīr jāndār*, who was essentially the lord high executioner. The title was used in this sense among the Turks of Central Asia, and in the Mamluk sultanate he was pre-eminently the sultan's head of security, supervising executions and imprisonment, and heading the forces which patrolled around the sultan. Fourthly, came the steward (*ustādār*, i.e. *ustādh al-dār*, 'master of the residence'), who had charge of the royal domestic offices, plenary powers of requisition on behalf of the domestic service, and also a security function as holding responsibility for the corps of tasters of the sultan's food and drink. An eminent court function was discharged by the fifth officer, the *silaḥdār*, the sword-bearer. His duties were more extensive than the title implies since he commanded a whole corps of *silaḥdāriyya* and was responsible for the state arsenal (*silaḥkhānah*). The sixth office, that of *dawādār* (literally, 'bearer of the inkwell') had precedents in the Seljuk sultanate, but it had been a lowly post held by an *ʿālim* until Baybars raised it to an office of great and increasing consequence in the Mamluk establishment. The *dawādār* was in charge of the sultan's communications both internally with the royal chancery and externally as the officer who presented the incoming mail (i.e. the intelligence reports) to the sultan. Significantly, the *amīr jāndār* as head of security was associated with him in this duty. Rather curiously, in the last decades of the regime Tūmān Bay (subsequently to be the last Mamluk sultan) led five military expeditions to Upper Egypt between 1509 and 1514 to collect taxes and suppress bedouin revolts. Clearly he owed this function to his personal character rather than to his post of *dawādār*. Finally, among the great officers there occurs the adjutant of the armies (*naqīb al-juyūsh*), whose somewhat limited functions were to parade the soldiery, and to produce (if necessary, to punish) individuals as required by his superiors. Al-ʿUmarī also mentions the office of master of ceremonies (*al-mahmandāriyya*) but does not expatiate on its functions.

The State Establishment

The official establishment during the Mamluk period was traditionally divided into three categories of officials: *arbāb al-suyūf*, literally 'the lords of the swords', i.e. the military, primarily the Mamluks themselves; *arbāb al-qalam*, 'the lords of the pen', i.e. the bureaucrats and other clerks serving the administration; and *arbāb al-waẓāʾif al-dīniyya*, 'the lords of the religious functions', i.e. those concerned with the cult of Islam and its institutions. With the exception of the first category, which has already been described, the establishment was drawn from the native Arabic-speaking sub-jects of the sultanate. These were in the great majority Muslims, but in Egypt Coptic Christians or converts to Islam played a great part in the financial administration. Seen historically, these Copts were the descendants of the bureaucrats who had existed in Egypt long before the coming of Islam. Although the Mamluks themselves were Turkish speakers, the official records were kept in Arabic.

The two chief branches of the central administration were the royal chancery and the financial departments. The head of the chancery, Fatḥ al-Dīn Muḥammad b. ʿAbd al-Ẓāhir, was promoted by Qalāwūn to be his confidential private secretary (*kātib al-sirr*), and thereby a new post was created which absorbed some of the functions of the omnicompetent Ayyubid *wazīr*. His father, Muḥyī al-Dīn ʿAbdallāh b. ʿAbd al-Ẓāhir, wrote a biography of Baybars, produced under the sultan's oversight. Muḥyī al-Dīn's nephew, Shāfiʿ b. ʿAlī, who was a chancery clerk, was also a writer, and takes some pains to display himself as a key figure in negotiations with the Franks. After the death of both Baybars and his uncle, he produced a sour revisionist biography of Baybars which served the interests of the usurper Qalāwūn and himself.

Among the additional functions of the confidential private secretary was to act as the official spokesman at sessions of the sultan's court for the redress of wrongs (*maẓālim*). This was the formalized function of a traditional Muslim ruler. Sessions were held twice weekly except in Ramaḍān. The sultan sat on the footstool beside the throne with the Sharīʿa judges on his right, the secretary and a body of clerks (*kuttāb al-dast*, 'the clerks of the bench') on his left, and the Mamluk grandees and others standing or sitting in due order. The petitions requiring decision were read by the secretary and his clerks. The sultan would consult the appropriate person present or decide according to his own discretion. The decision was noted by a clerk of the bench, and would pass to another group, the clerks of the roll (*kuttāb al-darj*) to be formally recorded.

The chancery was also involved in the administration of foreign policy, especially with the Frankish states. Shāfiʿ b. ʿAlī's interventions in these matters have been mentioned. He was always the advocate of realpolitik, and his supreme moment came in 1290, when Qalāwūn was considering the abrogation of his treaty with Acre and an attack on the Latin kingdom. He was delayed by the objections of the Mamluk grandees, who held that the oaths ratifying the treaty were sacred. The treaty was referred to the chancery so that the clerks could look for some reason for its abrogation. When both Fatḥ al-Dīn and Muḥyī al-Dīn failed to do so, Shāfiʿ declared, 'We serve the purpose of our lord the sultan. If he wishes to abrogate it, there is scope for abrogation. If it is not his purpose to abrogate it, its text does not require its abrogation.' On being told that the sultan would prefer its abrogation as the amirs had grown overbearing and lazy, he forthwith provided the necessary pretext. A further link between the chancery and foreign policy is indicated by the fact that senior members of the staff were commissioned as envoys. Muḥyī al-Dīn served in this way in negotiations with Bohemond VI of Tripoli and King Hugh of Cyprus and Jerusalem.

The loss of the Mamluk state archives, which must have been voluminous, has left only a handful of treaties, preserved in literary texts. Among these are eight treaties of Baybars and Qalāwūn with rulers of the Crusader states, and one between Qalāwūn and the envoy of the republic of Genoa, concluded in 689/1290. This is of particular interest as it demonstrates the meticulous procedure followed in the conclusion of a treaty. It arose from a specific problem. A Genoese corsair had captured an Alexandrian merchant vessel and seized the chattels of the traders. Qalāwūn thereupon arrested the Genoese in his ports, and closed his realm to Genoese trade. The Genoese republic sent its envoy to disavow the corsair and restore the commercial links. After due delay Qalāwūn agreed to make a settlement.

The documented procedure falls into five parts, the first comprising the actual terms of the treaty, the remaining four its certification. It is described as a truce (*hudna*), the traditional and technical term for a suspension of hostilities between Muslims and Christians for a fixed period. It opens with the oath of the envoy, Alberto Spinola, that he is bound to Qalāwūn (whose titles are given at length) and his son, al-Ashraf Khalīl, and proceeds with the decree of the republic of Genoa. This gives a guarantee of protection to all Muslims travelling to and from the sultan's realm with their goods and chattels to all territories in the present and future jurisdiction of the republic. All this is given in the most ample and specific terms, covering even Muslims falling into Genoese hands as a result of hostilities. Six Genoese witnesses to the act are named, as is also the clerk who wrote an interlinear version in 'Frankish', i.e. Italian. Then follows the signed testimony of Peter, the Melkite bishop of Old Cairo, who administered the oath to Spinola. The testimony of the witnesses to the oath-taking then ensues – three Oriental Christians and five Genoese. Next comes the oath itself *in extenso*. This is quite distinct from the oath with which Spinola introduced the truce. He specifically swears that he has concealed nothing of what was taken from the Muslims in the original incident with the corsair, and that he has not brought anything to compensate them except the actual sum realized from the sale of the captured ship and its cargo. A general testimony to the whole record by Bishop Peter ends the document.

The second group of departments served by *arbāb al-qalam* comprised a number of bodies concerned with the state finances, in which, as has been said, a predominant role was played by Copts. Since so large a portion of the revenue was alienated in the form of *iqtāʿs* to the Mamluk amirs and soldiery, an important department existed to deal with them. This was the so-called Army Department (*dīwān al-jaysh*), a term which describes its function, not its personnel, which was entirely civilian. Grants of *iqtāʿ* were almost entirely handled by this department, and were formally made in a document called a *manshūr*, i.e. a patent, drafted in the chancery. Amirs were granted the land-tax of one to ten villages according to their rank. Royal Mamluks were sometimes given that of a village but usually such revenue was shared between two or more troopers. The *Ḥalqa*, which had been the royal bodyguard in Ayyubid times but sank under the Mamluks to become the military organization for the *awlād al-nās*, received the revenue of a single village to provide the pay of a company, and similar *iqtāʿs* were granted to non-Mamluk auxiliaries. Such were the nomad Arabs of the Buḥayra and Sharqiyya provinces, who served the mail service (*barīd*) between Egypt and Syria.

The sultan's great personal holding, his privy purse, naturally required a department of its own, the *dīwān al-khāṣṣ*. Its head, the *nāẓir al-khāṣṣ*, usually a Copt or a convert, had a position of great affluence, influence and peril. There were two successive instances of this in the third reign of al-Nāṣir Muḥammad. Karīm al-Dīn al-Kabīr had been converted to Islam. He held office for thirteen years, but the weakness of his position was shown in March 1322, when the Royal Mamluks demonstrated because their pay was two months overdue. A little over twelve months later he was arrested and stripped of his great possessions. In the end he may have committed suicide. Another convert, al-Nashw, became *nāẓir al-khāṣṣ* in 1332. His worthy attempts to increase al-Nāṣir Muḥammad's revenue at first provoked only discontent among the subject peoples and merchants, and so could be ignored. But when in 1339 he began to threaten the finances of the amirs, the situation quickly changed. He was arrested and put to death. His personal wealth was seized and the site of his house was ploughed up in a search for hidden treasure.

When Barqūq usurped the sultanate, thereby initiating the Circassian Mamluk succession, he brought to the wealth of the sultanate that of the *iqtāʿs* he had previously acquired. To administer this new source of revenues a new department was set up entitled *al-dīwān al-mufrad*, 'the separate department'. It was not controlled by the *nāẓir al-khāṣṣ*, but by a Mamluk officer of the royal household, the *ustādār*. It was used for the payment of the Royal Mamluks. Another department, *dīwān al-amlāk*, also under the *ustādār*, was set up on the conversion of Barqūq's *iqṭā*'s into allodial properties (*amlāk*). By the end of the fourteenth century the old fiscal system had undergone great changes.

Where in all this was the state treasury as such? It was a department called the *dīwān al-wizāra*, which as the name indicated had originally been controlled by the *wazīrs* of the Fatimid and Ayyubid periods. Under the Mamluk sultanate the *wazīr* lost his power to other officials, and the post itself was abolished by al-Nāṣir Muḥammad. Although the wazirate subsequently revived, it was finally superseded by the *ustādār* when Barqūq set up his new treasuries. The *dīwān al-wizāra* incorporated the *bayt al-māl*, the original Muslim treasury, which in the Mamluk period drew its revenue chiefly in cash from Giza province. Manfalūṭ province in middle Egypt also contributed to the *dīwān al-wizāra*, chiefly in grain, which was sent to the royal storehouses in old Cairo. There were also contributions from various scattered estates in Upper Egypt. It is clear that in general the state treasury was inferior in wealth and importance to the *iqṭā*'s administered by the Army Office, the *khāṣṣ* controlled by its *nāẓir*, and Barqūq's personal treasuries under the *ustādār*.

The third category in the establishment, *arbāb al-waẓāʾif al-dīniyya*, the cult officials of Islam, need only a brief notice since they were similar to their counterparts in other Muslim states. The *qāḍīs* or judges of the Sharīʿa are however worthy of remark in two respects. In the first place, four chief judges (*qāḍī al-quḍāt*) were established in Egypt by Baybars in 1265 to deal with cases according to the Shāfiʿī, Ḥanafī, Mālikī and Ḥanbalī law-schools respectively. There had previously been a single Shāfiʿī chief judge. Baybars's action appears to have resulted from a dispute between the chief judge and a Mamluk grandee, although there was a distant precedent in the appointment of four chief judges for Muslim Syria by Nūr al-Dīn b. Zangī. In the second place, there existed in addition to the Sharīʿa a considerable body of secular law and legal decisions. The ruler's right and duty to hear and address wrongs was an ancient tradition, and the manner in which this was carried out has already been described. The institutionalizing of the practice is closely associated with Nūr al-Dīn b. Zangī of Syria, who organized a special House of Justice (*dār al-ʿadl*) for these sessions, first at Aleppo, then at Damascus. The Mamluks too had their House of Justice in Cairo. Baybars constructed one below the Citadel in 661/1262–3. It was superseded by one built by al-Nāṣir Muḥammad in the Citadel in 722/1322–3. Under Barqūq and later Circassian sultans such sessions were held in the royal stables. The jurisdiction practised was known in Egypt as *al-siyāsa*.

Apart from the sultan, one of the great officers of the royal household gradually acquired a judicial function. The great chamberlain at first exercised this function only among Mamluks, but subsequently, probably only from the time of al-Nāṣir Muḥammad, it was extended generally and to the detriment of the *qāḍīs*' jurisdiction. This was apparently an abusive extension of power, but it may have satisfied a popular demand for summary and effective justice. There is some evidence of resentment against the *qāḍīs*' courts in the fifteenth century

The Administration of Syria

While the hold of the sultan and the central administration over Egypt was close and immediate, Syria was controlled through a number of separate provincial governments, known collectively as *al-mamālik al-Shāmiyya*, 'the Syrian kingdoms'. After the elimination of the Crusader states and the absorption of their territory into the Mamluk provincial system, these were six in number: Damascus and Aleppo (the chief provinces of southern and northern Syria respectively), Ḥamāh, al-Karak, Tripoli and Ṣafad. Each was governed by a deputy (*nā'ib*) of the sultan, amongst whom the viceroy of Damascus enjoyed a pre-eminence of rank. He bore the title of *malik al-umarā'*, and maintained almost royal state, holding a solemn procession through the city twice a week, followed by a session in his residence for the hearing of petitions and a banquet for his amirs. At these sessions an empty throne, draped with yellow cloth and bearing a short sword, symbolized the sultan. The Mamluks had inherited yellow as the official colour of the regime from the Ayyubids. Similar ceremonies were practised at Aleppo, Tripoli and Ḥamāh, but without the symbolic throne.

Although a provincial governor was practically all-powerful within the area of his jurisdiction, he was nevertheless the creature of the sultan, and his power or ambition might be his downfall. Tengiz al-Ḥusāmī, governor of Damascus for nearly thirty years, was disgraced and brought to Cairo to die in 741/1340. This fundamentally precarious tenure of office may have instigated the unsuccessful attempts of two of his predecessors to declare their independence at the beginnings of the reigns of Baybars and Qalāwūn respectively. In addition, an important financial and military resource was denied to the governors. Although they could initiate grants of *iqṭāʿ*, these had to pass through the Army Office in Cairo for the sultan's signature before they were effective.

A contrasting picture of events is presented by the province of Ḥamāh. This had been an Ayyubid principality under Saladin's nephew, Taqī al-Dīn 'Umar, and his descendants. and this regime survived the growth of Mamluk power. Ever deferential to their Mamluk overlords in Cairo, the successors of Taqī al-Dīn retained the province until 1299, when the ruling prince fell ill and died, and a Mamluk amir was appointed as governor, to be followed by others for over a decade. In the meantime, a minor Ayyubid prince, Ismāʿīl Abu'l-Fidā', was born in 1273, and Qalāwūn's son, al-Nāṣir Muḥammad, in 1285. The two seem first to have become acquainted in 1310, when al-Nāṣir Muḥammad marched from Syria for his final accession to the sultanate. Friendship grew between the two men, and the sultan promised to make Abu'l-Fidā' the ruler of Ḥamāh. The first step was taken in the autumn of 1310, whn Abu'l-Fidā' donned the sultan's livery as governor of Ḥamāh. This was followed in August 1313 by a diploma granting him the autonomous state of Ḥamāh. Finally, his career was crowned in February 1320, when he went in procession to the Citadel of Cairo and received the title of sultan, borne otherwise only by the Mamluk ruler. He died in October 1331, and his son succeeded to his title and position. But al-Nāṣir Muḥammad died ten years later. In September 1341 this last Ayyubid sultan was transferred to Damascus with a military rank and a pension, and Ḥamāh was again placed under a Mamluk governor. Ironically, he was a Mamluk who had been presented by Abu'l-Fidā' to al-Nāṣir Muḥammad in 1310.

The Mamluks and the Indigenous Peoples

Although the Mamluks were an alien military and ruling elite, they did not form a closed group, completely dominating the indigenous communities of Egypt and Syria. With their Muslim subjects they shared their religion and a common way of life, and both groups were stirred by the idea of the *jihād*. The Mamluks were immigrants undergoing a process of assimilation, which was completed in the second and later generations by the *awlād al-nās*.

A distinction must be drawn between the relations with the urban and with the rural communities. From the latter they were both physically and socially distanced. The Mamluk holder of an *iqṭāʿ* was, as has been mentioned, not usually resident upon his *iqṭāʿ*, but lived in a city at the court of the sultan or a governor. The *iqṭāʿ* was merely a source of revenue in cash and kind, and the villagers were managed by the *muqṭaʿ*'s agent, his *wakīl*, with his staff.

Between the Mamluks and the indigenous townspeople, the links were of three main kinds. First of these were the economic links. The sultans and amirs accrued a considerable surplus from their grain revenues. This gave them a predominant share in the grain market, which they tried to control for their own profit. More sporadically, they intervened in commerce by enforcing the purchase of goods they had stocked. On the other hand, the great and wealthy Mamluk households were important as consumers of local commodities and patrons of local craftsmen. Merchants were employed as partners, bankers or agents of the sultan, e.g. in the monopoly of the spice-trade from the time of Barsbay in the fifteenth century.

Secondly, there were the political links between the Mamluks and the indigenous peoples. Here the *ʿulamāʾ* were of particular importance since they cemented together a society which was otherwise fragmented and acephalous. The Mamluks' formal deference towards the *ʿulamāʾ* was counterbalanced by the formal acceptance by the *ʿulamāʾ* of a regime with effective power. This is symbolized by Ibn Iyās, the last chronicler of Mamluk Egypt, in his regular record of the monthly visit of the caliph and the four chief *qāḍī*s to the sultan in the Citadel. At a very different social level, there developed in the late fifteenth century organized groups of youths known as *zuʿar*, partly gangs, partly an urban militia. They defended their quarters against abusive Mamluk demands, but they also used their strength to exploit their fellow-townspeople, and they were prepared on occasion to serve as clients and auxiliaries of the Mamluks.

Thirdly, social links existed between the two communities. The Mamluks had initial difficulties in surviving and establishing themselves in Egypt. As immigrants, they and their wives were peculiarly liable to a high mortality rate from locally prevalent diseases. The ravages of plague are particularly recorded, and there was probably also a high infant mortality. This may indeed be the reason for the continued recruitment of Mamluks from their countries of origin. There were however marriages between Mamluks and indigenous Egyptian women, while, as has been seen, the *awlād al-nās* became in effect a socially privileged section of the indigenous population.

Apart from the peasantry and the townspeople, a third category of the indigenous population was constituted by the Arab tribes. They were of two kinds. Sedentary or semi-sedentary tribes were established in frontier areas, as for example on the fringes of the Crusader states in Syria–Palestine, and in the Aswān region of Upper Egypt, the medieval frontier between Muslim Egypt and Christian Nubia. Here a tribal group, Banu'l-Kanz, had existed since Fatimid times, while arabized Berbers, the Hawwāra, were drafted there by Barqūq. Nomadic tribes populated the interior regions, especially in provinces fringing the Nile Delta and in Upper Egypt. The strength or weakness of the nomads reflected in an inverse relationship that of the Mamluk regime. Thus, there was a serious Arab revolt in 1253–4, when the Mamluks were barely established in control of Egypt and were confronted by the hostility of the Syrian Ayyubids. Again, when Mamluk power was in decline under Qānṣawh al-Ghawrī, virtually annual repressive campaigns were waged in Upper Egypt, as we have seen. Nevertheless there was usually a symbiosis between the Mamluks and tribal society. The tribesmen provided or transported some necessary commodities, and upon them depended the essential service of safeguarding the desert routes, notably for the annual Pilgrimage caravan and for the royal mail (*barīd*), the core of the intelligence apparatus. For these services the Arab chiefs like the Mamluk amirs were rewarded with *iqtā's*.

Conclusion

The Mamluk sultanate differed fundamentally from its predecessors in Egypt, the Fatimid caliphate and the Ayyubid sultanate, in that it was essentially a militarized Turkish state implanted on Egyptian soil. The first two effective sultans, Aybak and Qutuz, were little more than successful warlords. The true foundation of the state was the work of the two great sultans al-Zāhir Baybars and al-Mansūr Qalāwūn. For the somewhat lax governmental system of the Ayyubids, centred upon the omnicompetent civilian *wazīr*, they substituted an elaborate and highly centralized administrative machine. In some respects the Mamluk sultanate seems to be a prototype of its ultimate conqueror, the Ottoman Empire.

NOTES

1   Anon., *Life of Prideaux*, pp. 268–9.
2   Fück, 'Islam as an historical problem', p. 305.

FURTHER READING

The Mamluk sultanate is set in its context of Near Eastern history in P. M. Holt, *The Age of the Crusades* (Longman, London, 1986). Studies of individual sultans include (Baybars) Peter Thorau, *The Lion of Egypt*, tr. and ed. P. M. Holt (Longman, London, 1987); (Qalāwūn) Linda S. Northrup, *From Slave to Sultan* (Franz Steiner Verlag, Stuttgart, 1998); (al-Nāsir Muhammad b. Qalāwūn) Amalia Levanoni, *A Turning-point in Mamluk History* (E. J. Brill, Leiden, 1995); (Barsbay) Ahmad Darrag, *L'Egypte sous le Règne de Barsbay 825–841/1422–1438* (Institut Français de Damas, Damascus, 1961). The institutions of Mamluk society are most comprehensively described and analysed in the numerous articles of David Ayalon, now collected in four volumes: *Studies on the Mamlūks (1250–1517)* (Variorum Reprints, London, 1977); *The Mamlūk Military Society* (idem, 1979); *Outsiders in the Lands of Islam: Mamluks, Mongols and Eunuchs* (idem, 1988); *Islam and the Abode of War* (idem, 1944); also by Ayalon, *Gunpowder and Firearms in the Mamluk Kingdom* (Vallentine, Mitchell, London, 1956). A valuable study of urban society by Ira Marvin Lapidus, *Muslim Cities in the Later Middle Ages* (Harvard University Press, Cambridge, MA, 1967) is principally concerned with Damascus and Aleppo. Mamluk Syria as a whole is described by the Egyptian encyclopaedist al-Qalqashandī (1355–1418), and has been translated with an informative introduction by the French scholar M. Gaudefroy-Demombynes, *La Syrie à l'Epoque des Mamelouks* (Librairie Orientaliste Paul Geuthner, Paris, 1923). A feeling for life under the last Mamluk sultans is given by the diary of Ibn Iyās (an Egyptian of Mamluk descent) in *Journal d'un Bourgeois du Caire*, tr. and annotated by Gaston Wiet (2 vols., Libraire Armand Colin, Paris, 1955, 1960).

Chapter Nine

North Africa
State and Society, 1056–1659

Michael Brett

I

North Africa, consisting of modern Morocco, Algeria, Tunisia and Tripolitania, is geographically the bloc of the Atlas, a broad and blunt peninsula of Africa surrounded by the Atlantic to the west and the Mediterranean to the north and east. To the south is the Sahara, the first of three historical determinants. Physically and climatically, the coast and its hinterland are like Mediterranean Europe, enjoying cool wet winters and hot dry summers. Mediterranean Europe, however, is backed by the temperate zone of northern Europe, with its natural forest and good agricultural land making for dense settlement and economic growth. Mediterranean North Africa, a long and for the most part narrow ribbon of mountain and plain, is backed only by the Sahara, a barren region with a thin population at the upper limit of growth. Settlement has been limited to the oases; otherwise the population has been largely nomadic, and moreover, mainly tribal, that is, self-governing by customary rules. Tribal peoples of the desert have been joined by tribal peoples of the North African mountains to form a population that until recently has been beyond the pale of urban society and resistant to government by the state. Historically, the result has been economic, political and cultural division, most marked in the case of Roman Africa. The Romans colonised the Mediterranean coast, introducing the Roman city as an instrument of civilisation, and extending the area of cultivation down to the edge of the desert in eastern Algeria, Tunisia and Tripolitania for commercial agriculture. The mountains and the desert, on the other hand, were excluded with the help of a fortified frontier that divided the north and east from the south and west, separating the settled, civilised population from the tribal barbarians.

This was the historical setting for the second determinant, namely Islam: a religion; a way of life; and a civilisation. Beginning with the Arab conquests around 700 CE, the tribal barbarians of the Roman period became the Barbar or Berbers, a nation like the rest of humankind, with its own language and religion, in this case Islam. Once this national identity had been established in the course of the eighth century CE, the divisions of the Roman period were overlaid by Islamisation and Arabisation, which produced a cultural unity; by trade across the Sahara, which brought economic unity; and last but not least by native Berber conquerors, who imposed a political unity. Political unity, however, came at the cost of the third determinant for this purpose, namely war with Christian Europe, which began with the Arabs and endured down to modern times. That war was won from about 700 to 1000 CE, when the Muslim conquest of Spain and Sicily carried the frontier across the Mediterranean to create the Maghrib, the Muslim west, a civilisation on either side of the sea in which Muslim Spain, al-Andalus, took pride of place. From about 1000 to 1500 CE, however, the war was lost. Muslim Spain and Sicily were progressively conquered, until by the beginning of the sixteenth century the Portuguese and Spaniards had crossed the Mediterranean, and almost all the coastal cities of North Africa were in their hands. The tide only turned with the Ottoman conquest of North Africa up to the borders of Morocco, and the recreation of a Moroccan empire. War then degenerated into piracy, but ended in the nineteenth and twentieth centuries with the conquest of the whole of North Africa by Europeans, before the eventual return to independence since the 1950s.

In the middle of the eleventh century CE, all three of these factors; the desert, the faith and the war, combined to bring about a radical change in the balance of state and society in North Africa that had been established by the Arabs in succession to the Romans and Byzantines. The mosque had taken the place of the forum and the church at the centre of a commercial city, while the palace, the royal city, was home to the ruler who dominated the old Roman countryside with the help of tribal allies. But in the east, the pressure of warrior nomads brought about the collapse of the central government that the Arabs had installed in the former Byzantine province of Africa, comprising eastern Algeria, Tunisia and Tripolitania. At the same time in the west, in Morocco and western Algeria, other desert nomads created a new empire in the name of Islam. Meanwhile across the Mediterranean, Sicily was invaded by the Normans in 1060, and conquered by the end of the century; by which time the Christian advance in Spain had been checked, and al-Andalus itself brought under North African rule. These major events set the scene for the subsequent evolution of North Africa to the end of our period.

II

In 1052, at the battle of Haydaran to the south of Qayrawan (Kairouan) in modern Tunisia, the army of the Zirid sultan of Ifriqiya, Mu'izz ibn Badis, was routed by tribesmen of the Banu Hilal. These Arab bedouin had migrated into Tripolitania from the western desert of Egypt over the past fifty years, to be enlisted by Mu'izz as allies in an attempt to secure his southern borders against Berber unrest. His failure led to the disintegration of Ifriqiya, the former Byzantine province ruled by the Arabs from their garrison city of Qayrawan instead of Carthage. After 1052, the Zirids abandoned Qayrawan for Mahdia on the east coast, while their Hammadid cousins in eastern Algeria moved down to Bijaya on the north coast. A series of city states sprang up, mainly on the littoral; the plains of the interior were occupied by the tribes of the Banu Hilal; while the mountains became the retreat of the Berbers. The cities of the coast were left exposed to attack by the Normans of Sicily, whose King Roger II in the middle of the twelfth century seized all of them from Bijaya round to Tripoli, with the exception of Tunis.

The coming of the Banu Hilal, and their victory at Haydaran, was unrelated to the quarrel of the Zirids with the Fatimids, from whom they had inherited Ifriqiya when the latter moved to Cairo, in spite of the legend that the tribes had been sent from Egypt as a punishment for their disobedience. The quarrel that broke out in 1048, when Mu'izz changed his allegiance from Cairo to Baghdad, was important for a different reason. A product of the wider opposition between the Fatimids and the 'Abbasids, and between Shi'ism and Sunnism, his change of allegiance was a victory for the *'ulama'* of Qayrawan, the members of the Maliki school that had been established in the city since the ninth century. At the other end of North Africa, their militant Sunnism inspired the mission of Ibn Yasin to the Sanhaja Berbers of the western Sahara. Here, there was no central government. Over to the west of Ifriqiya, the Arabs had barely time to pass through Tlemcen and Tangier on their way to the conquest of Spain, before the great revolt of the Berbers in the middle of the eighth century led to the loss of all these lands to the Arab empire. They were not, however, lost to the world of Islam. While Spain became independent under the Spanish Umayyads, the route of the conquest through the old Roman Mauretania was colonised by Muslims from east and west, who created a cluster of little Muslim cities of which Fes, Tlemcen and Tahart were the most important. From these three capitals, routes went northwards into Spain, and southwards across the old Roman frontier to the Tafilelt and the Wadi Draa on the Saharan side of the Atlas, in search of the silver of the Anti-Atlas and the gold of the western Sudan. A fresh frontier was thus opened up in southern Morocco, far to the south of the old Roman lands to the north, on which war and trade went hand in hand. It was from here that Ibn Yasin set out to form the nomads of the desert into the Murabitun or Almoravids, a community of holy warriors for the victory of Sunni Islam over its enemies: pagans; bad Muslims; and finally Christians.

In the 1050s, the Almoravids conquered the western Sahara and took Sijilmasa in the Tafilelt for a capital. In 1070 they crossed the High Atlas and founded the city of Marrakesh. From Marrakesh their Amir, Yusuf ibn Tashfin, captured both Fes and Tlemcen to create a new Moroccan empire. In 1086, following the fall of Toledo to Castile in 1085, he crossed the Straits to halt the Christian advance, and to annex the whole of Muslim Spain by the time of his death in 1105. His empire-building was completed by the successors to the Almoravids, the Muwahhidun or Almohads, yet another militant community formed out of the tribes of the High Atlas by yet another prophet, the Mahdi Ibn Tumart. In 1147 the Almoravids were overthrown by 'Abd al-Mu'min, the Caliph of the Mahdi, who took over their dominions, and went on to recover Ifriqiya from the Banu Hilal on the one hand, the Normans on the other. By 1160, when the conquest of Ifriqiya was complete, the whole of North Africa, for the first and the last time before the French occupation, had been politically united.

The outcome was a historic reversal of roles. Since the time of Carthage, the centre of power in North Africa had lain along with the centre of civilisation in the far north east. Roman power had mapped that civilisation on the ground with the help of the *limes*, the fortified frontier that separated the citizen from the barbarian. The Arabs at Qayrawan had remained largely within this Roman boundary. But their identification of the Berbers as Muslims, and thus as members of their own religious and political community, had opened the way to the entry of these former barbarians into the new civilisation, until the point at which the tribesmen of the desert declared themselves its champions, and took over its government. As Ifriqiya disintegrated, the centre of power in North Africa was transferred to the Almoravid capital of Marrakesh in the far south west. There it remained for the next two hundred years in the hands of peoples far beyond the old Roman pale.

III

Looking back on these critical events from the end of the fourteenth century, Ibn Khaldun explained both the disintegration of Ifriqiya and the constitution of a great

North African empire in terms of tribalism, in particular the tribalism of the desert, where survival was at its most elementary, and self-reliance was at its most extreme. More fertile regions overrun by the tribesmen of the desert were quickly ruined by their way of life, in which cultivated land was treated as pasture, and buildings as a source of firewood; thus he famously compared the Banu Hilal to a swarm of locusts that devoured the land. Self-reliance, on the other hand, made them natural warriors, whose *asabiyya* or clan spirit gave them the will to power. In the case of the Almoravids, this was activated by religion, whose divine message drew an enthusiastic response from their simple hearts. Conversely, their *asabiyya* was essential to the success of the prophetic message, which otherwise would have come to nothing. The argument in both cases is circular; the Banu Hilal and the Almoravids inspired the theory of which they became the prime examples. Both as example and as theory, however, they have had a long afterlife in modern scholarship. The Banu Hilal have been held responsible for the poverty and weakness of North Africa in comparison with Europe in the nineteenth and early twentieth centuries. The warlike tribesman, on the other hand, has been used to explain the history of state formation in North Africa as one of recurrent conquest, in which peaceable townsfolk have been ruled by successive dynasties of tribal origin. Historically as well as sociologically, both propositions are at best half-truths that disguise the development of state and society over the six hundred years of our period.

Arab as well as Berber tribalism was far from elementary. Desert dwellers though they were, the Banu Hilal were from the outset the creatures of civilisation. They belonged, in the terminology of Ibn Khaldun, to the Arabs of the fourth generation, that is, to the generation after the conquerors who had left Arabia to create the Arab empire. While those conquerors had disappeared into the mass of the population of that empire, as subjects rather than rulers, the Arabs of the fourth had been left behind in their homeland to carry on with their traditional way of life, and emerge as a new nation outside the civilisation created by their predecessors. They were not, however, the archetypical savages he postulated at the root of human society. The Banu Hilal belonged within the mental and material orbit of Islam. Tracing their lineage to the North rather than the South Arabians, they shared in the culture of Arabism that pervaded the religion, the literature and the life of the medieval civilisation. In North Africa, their role was inseparable from government; as warriors, they formed an aristocracy in partnership with the state. As nomads, they did indeed bring about an extension of pastoralism. On the other hand they flowed into a settled rural population heavily dependent on the lords of the land, as Ibn Khaldun very well knew when he came to write the history of his own time.

The case of the Almoravids and Almohads is different, but equally complex. Fundamental as they were to the creation of a North African empire, as desert nomads the Almoravids were the exception to the rule of revolution that began with the revolt of the Berbers in the eighth century, and ended with the Almohads in the twelfth. The Kutama who had brought about the Fatimid revolution at the beginning of the tenth century were, like the Masmuda who formed the Almohad community, the relatively settled tribesmen of the mountains of eastern Algeria and southern Morocco. Their ways of life were correspondingly different; what they had in common was the same segmentary structure: the same division into clans and communities that commanded their loyalty in alliance and opposition. In all three cases, therefore, the conversion of these quarrelsome peoples into a disciplined army under the dictatorship of a prophet was achieved not by a simple appeal to their good nature, but through a murderous struggle for power. Apart from the call to arms in the name of God, the actual doctrine in whose name the call was made was irrelevant to its success. Observing the phenomenon, Ibn Khaldun was clearly correct to say that without the tribes and their *'asabiyya,* none of these missions could have succeeded; and equally, that without the missions, the *'asabiyya* in question would have remained a mere feature of tribal society. Without the doctrines, on the other hand, the missions could not have taken place. Not only were the doctrines in question very different from each other: Shi'ite Mahdism in the case of the Fatimids; Sunni legalism in the case of the Almoravids; and Qur'anic illuminationism in that of the Almohads. They were strongly, and consciously, opposed. The missions, in fact, were the product of doctrinal conflict in Islam as a whole, from the rise of the Fatimids at the beginning of the tenth century to the challenge thrown down by al-Ghazali's *Revival of the Sciences of Religion* at the beginning of the twelfth. Played out in North Africa, it was that conflict that brought the Berbers in from the margins to the centre of the new civilisation as masters of the Maghrib, the Islamic West.

IV

What then of the two propositions, that the economy of North Africa was ruined by the Banu Hilal, and that state formation has been the result of repeated tribal conquest? The Banu Hilal were part of a long-term structural change in the economy that began long before the Arab conquest with the decline of the economy of the Roman empire, accompanied by the appearance of camel nomadism in the northern Sahara in Late Antiquity. The Roman economy of North Africa within the imperial frontier was the result of systematic colonisation and intensive cultivation of wheat, olives and vines for a Mediterranean market; beyond that frontier, there was hunting for wild beasts for the games, and trade with the Garamantes of the Fezzan in the Libyan desert, but as yet no regular trans-Saharan trade. The export trade in cereals and olive oil may have survived at a lower level down to the Arab conquest and beyond, but from the eighth century onwards, their market was increasingly provided by the cities that sprang up in the wake of the conquest; the metropolitan city of Qayrawan, for example, depended upon the supply of grain from Beja to the north west. There was equally a market for dates from the oases of the Djerid to the south. As portrayed by Ibn Khaldun, the city was the fruit of the division of labour, increasing and diversifying production from the cultivator to the craftsman. He was well aware, however, that this was not a simple question of supply and demand. It depended heavily upon the redistribution of wealth by the state, which took its share of agricultural production in taxes to pay for the goods and services it required.

Many of those goods, as well as many of the people, came from abroad, from the east and from across the Sahara. From the eighth century onwards, North Africa was integrated into the intercontinental network of long-distance trade that sprang up within the Arab empire and reached out to China, the Indies and Tropical Africa. In that trade, the transport of the bulky commodities that had made the fortune of Roman North Africa was overtaken by the carriage of smaller quantities of more expensive items between widely separated 'islands of purchasing power'. Applied by Hopkins in his *Economic History of West Africa* to the royal courts of West Africa, the phrase is equally applicable to the capital cities of the Islamic world, spaced out across the deserts and mountains from North Africa to central Asia and northern India. It is especially true of those joined for the first time by routes across the Sahara, bringing slaves and gold from the Land of the Blacks in response to the demand of the Islamic world. The agents of such trade were merchants who worked particular sections of the network, either on their own account or on behalf of investors who provided them with their capital. Since the available wealth was largely concentrated in the hands of the rulers, these were the principal investors as well as the principal consumers, on whose behalf the merchants placed the redistributive economy of the state on a commercial footing. In the case of the Sahara, however, their business was not possible without the camel nomads who controlled the routes, provided the transport, and increasingly participated in the enterprise. The involvement of these nomads in this commercial enterprise, together with the settled populations of the oases and their cities, brought the desert into the world economy, and specifically into that of North Africa. Economic unity took the place of the economic division of the Roman period, underlying the political unification brought about by the Almoravids and Almohads. The Almoravids who initiated the process were themselves nomads who combined conquest with commerce, seizing control of the trade routes across the western Sahara, and demonstrating their wealth as well as their power and prestige in the gold of their coinage.

The arrival of the Banu Hilal in the course of the eleventh century was, in this perspective, no more than a reinforcement of the camel nomadism which had been established in the Sahara since the second or third century CE. The difference was that as newcomers, they were fighting for a place in the economic and political sun. Their success at Haydaran allowed them to move out of the desert into the interior of Ifriqiya, where they enjoyed a century of freedom before they were defeated by the Almohads, and incorporated into the Almohad state. Like the Zirids a century earlier, the Almohads sought to employ them as warriors, and brought selected bands as far west as the Atlantic plains of Morocco. In Tripolitania and Tunisia their place was taken by the Banu Sulaym, a further wave of bedouin from the east. But other tribes of the Banu Hilal moved across the northern Sahara into southern Morocco to the south of the Atlas, where by the end of the thirteenth century they had become the Banu Ma'qil, fighting for control over the oases. By the fifteenth century the Banu Ma'qil had entered the western Sahara as the Banu Hassan, who by the seventeenth century had taken the place of the Berber Sanhaja as the warrior tribes of the desert. Below them the Sanhaja from whom the Almoravids had sprung became men of peace, so-called clerical clans whose religious scholarship went hand in hand with trade. The same division into warriors and clerics appeared among the entirely Berber Tuareg in the triangle formed by the mountains of the Adrar, the Ahaggar and Air in the southern half of the desert: a clear indication of the way in which the successors of the Almoravids had settled into a specialised commercial routine. At the limit of their expansion to the west, the descendants of the Banu Hilal conformed to the structure of a society shaped by the trans-Saharan trade.

In North Africa itself, the effect of the bedouin influx in the century following the battle of Haydaran can be seen in the contrast between Ifriqiya and Norman Sicily that came to light in the 1130s and 40s as Roger II embarked on his conquest of the North African coast. Mahdia was then dependent upon the supply of Sicilian grain, for which the king required payment in gold. While Sicily, a land of Muslim peasants taxed by their Norman overlords, had a surplus for export, the North African city had been cut off from its sources of supply in the interior. On the other hand, it had gold, which argues for the continuance of trade. This certainly continued to flourish following the return of central government following the Almohad conquest, stimulated by the rapid growth of the European market. This took not only the products of North Africa but those of the Bilad al-Sudan, the Land of the Blacks: gold in the thirteenth century, and eventually slaves. European manufactures, such as velvet, in turn found their way into North Africa and across the Sahara, as merchants from the Balearics, Barcelona, Genoa and Venice established their factories in the principal ports under licence from the authorities. It is certainly significant that where in the Roman period the principal exports of North Africa had been agricultural, they were now the products of the pastoral economy: wool and leather, with their associated manufactures, leatherwork, cloth and carpets. But this was as true of Morocco as of Ifriqiya, where the Hilalian Arabs were few, and the Berber Marinids gave their name to the Merino sheep. The commercialisation of pastoralism was yet another sign of the integration of nomadism into the economy, irrespective of race.

Agriculture was by no means ruined, but was certainly affected. The arrival of the bedouin in Ifriqiya rendered the cultivation of marginal land unsafe, and drove settled Berber populations to withdraw to the security of the hills and mountains in fortified villages, many in caves in the cliffs. From the thirteenth century onwards, this retreat became an advance into the mountains of Greater Kabylia east of Algiers, which were colonised by a relatively dense population of hilltop villagers, whose *qaba'il* or tribes gave their name to the region. Out on the plains, high and low, the reconstitution of the Ifriqiyan state by the Almohads brought a measure of stability, but at considerable cost. The warrior tribes of Hilal and Sulaym became an arm of government, whose fiscality determined the character of the agricultural economy. As the warrior tribes closed their ranks, the less successful eked out a poor living from their flocks and herds, or turned to cultivation under the thumb of the landlord and the tax collector. As sharecroppers and taxpayers, such peasants provided the revenues on which the redistributive economy of the state was founded. While the political history continued to be violent, warfare endemic, and central government periodically at a discount, over the centuries this fiscal regime strengthened its grip on the society and the economy. In such circumstances productivity, especially of grain, is likely to have remained low. Favourable terms for sharecroppers might bring about an increase in land under cultivation, but there was little or no incentive for the peasant who kept no more than a fifth of what he produced. Where there was irrigation, on the other hand, and water rights regulated by custom, agriculture prospered in gardens around the cities or in the oases and the mountains. And everywhere it remained sufficiently buoyant to support a local market economy.

V

Right across North Africa, the fiscal character of the state gave it the name of *makhzan*, 'magazine' or treasury, instead of *dawla* or dynasty. Both concepts were well known to Ibn Khaldun, who combined them in the circular maxim current in the Islamic world, beginning and ending with the prince as the fountainhead of justice: no justice without the army; no army without taxes; no taxes without wealth; no wealth without justice. It was a maxim likely to be more honoured in the breach than in the observance, as Ibn Khaldun likewise knew when he warned against the folly of exorbitant taxation; the army of soldiers and secretaries had to be paid at whatever cost. The *ra'iyya* or 'flock' in the care of the royal shepherd was roughly shorn by the *khassa*, the elite of his servants who lived to tax and taxed to live. Such oppression was self-defeating; it undermined the dynasty and prepared the way for its overthrow, as had happened to so many dynasties in the past. Already by Ibn Khaldun's time, however, the landscape had changed, and the experience was at variance with the prediction.

The Almohads were the last in the line of religious revolutionaries that stretched back to the revolt of the Berbers in the mid-eighth century. Their successors were not driven by faith to create a new world order, but to recreate their empire after it fell apart in the mid-thirteenth century. As empire-builders the Almohads, like their Almoravid predecessors, were dedicated to the defence of Islam, the proof of their mission and the justification of their cause. But in 1212 they were shaken by defeat at the battle of Las Navas de Tolosa, followed by the accession of a minor to the Caliphate. A long-standing rivalry between the dynasty established by 'Abd al-Mu'min and the shaykhs of the community over the succession to the Mahdi in matters of faith, then became a struggle for power that culminated in 1229 in the massacre of the shaykhs by a new Caliph who repudiated the authority of Ibn Tumart altogether. It was the signal for secession. By 1250 the whole of Muslim Spain had been overrun by the forces of Portugal, Castile and Aragon, leaving only Granada as an independent kingdom. The governor of Ifriqiya, a great Almohad shaykh, had established the Hafsid dynasty at Tunis, which under his successor claimed the caliphate for itself in 1253. At Tlemcen a Berber chieftain, an erstwhile tribal ally, had founded the 'Abd al-Wadid or Ziyanid dynasty, while Fes had fallen in 1248 to long-standing enemies of the Almohads, the nomadic Berber Banu Marin from south-eastern Morocco. In 1269 the Marinids took Marrakesh, and put an end to their empire.

The next hundred years, however, down to the time of Ibn Khaldun, were spent by these three dynasties in attempts to claim that empire for themselves. As Almohads themselves, the Hafsids were the first to do so, but succession disputes towards the end of the thirteenth century left them weakened and divided between Tunis and Bijaya, and exposed like the Zirids before them to the attacks of the Aragonese in Sicily. The 'Abd al-Wadids at Tlemcen had no such pretensions to universal empire, only the ambition to take eastern Algeria from the Hafsids, and the determination to resist the Marinids, by far the most ambitious of the three. Having taken Marrakesh, the Marinids invaded Spain; laid siege to Tlemcen for seven years; and finally, in the middle of the fourteenth century, took not only Tlemcen but Tunis after a last disastrous expedition into Spain. But their conquests were fleeting; and succession crises throughout the rest of the century restricted their power in the fifteenth century to Fes, where they were succeeded in 1472 by their relatives the Wattasids. The 'Abd al-Wadids came back to Tlemcen only to suffer the same fate, and fall under the overlordship of the Hafsids at Tunis. These had recovered from the Marinid invasion, and in the fifteenth century, under two long-lived sultans, restored Ifriqiya to its former primacy. Not only Tlemcen but the Wattasids at Fes came to acknowledge them in a final, faint resurrection of the Almohad empire. Marrakesh, where the state system formed by the three dynasties had originated, sank to the level of regional capital, while the centre of political gravity returned to its former location in the north-east.

VI

At its inception four hundred years earlier, that system had been built by the Almoravids upon an alliance between the warriors of the desert and the scholars of the towns, with the men of letters, indispensable for the purpose of government, in third place. Despite all changes of personnel, these features remained constant. At its simplest under the Almoravids, the combination became much more sophisticated under the Almohads, who endeavoured to unite all three elements in a single echelon. Their tribal regiments were commanded by *mizwars*, commissars above whom were the shaykhs or elders of the community. Above them was the Caliphate of the Mahdi in the hands of 'Abd al-Mu'min and his descendants, who asserted their claim to superiority over the shaykhs, and sought to incorporate them into their own following by training up their sons as *huffaz*, 'memorisers', or *tulaba*, 'students'. These were educated in the arts of war and administration as well as religious scholarship, to serve as lieutenants of the caliph and mentors of his sons. The attempt collapsed with the empire, but not before the Almohads had made a serious endeavour to impose their faith on their subjects, directing the scholars who had been the chosen allies of the Almoravids away from the traditionalism of Maliki *fiqh* to the revolutionary radicalism of Ibn Tumart.

Such totalitarianism broke down in practice for want of the numbers required. To govern such a vast region as the Maghrib, the regime was of necessity eclectic. Like the Almoravid, the Almohad army incorporated black slave troops, Berber and Arab tribal horsemen, and even Christian mercenaries. Maliki jurists were in the majority, while the secretaries came increasingly from al-Andalus. When the empire disintegrated, and Muslim Spain was largely lost, this Andalusian immigration became a stream that contributed much of the administrative expertise of central government. The conspicuous example is that of Ibn Khaldun himself, born at Tunis to an immigrant family from Seville, who made his career in the service of all three dynasties before emigrating to Cairo. That service was typically divided into three: the army, the treasury, and the chancery, with precedence usually given to the army. In the case of the Hafsids, the heirs to the Almohad Caliphate at Tunis, the military hierarchy of the Almohads was reconstituted as the core of the army and the principal element of the royal council, while as at Marrakesh, the princes of the dynasty ruled the provinces under the guidance of a senior officer. The dominance of the shaykhs lasted down to the restoration of Hafsid power in the fifteenth century, when the prayer in the name of the Mahdi Ibn Tumart was finally discontinued. The much slighter dynasty of the 'Abd al-Wadids at Tlemcen retained its chieftaincy of a predominantly tribal army down to the beginning of the fourteenth century. The Marinids of Fes appointed their warriors as ministers in charge of all three services, although the work of the treasury and the chancery was performed by more literate and more numerate secretaries. The central importance of the treasury was evident at Tlemcen at the height of the dynasty's fortunes in the first half of the fourteenth century, when the Andalusians in charge took over the government as Wazirs. At Tunis, the Hajib or chamberlain of the palace took control of the chancery, and went on to take control of the state at the time of the Marinid invasions in the middle of the fourteenth century. Such prime-ministerial functions, however, were political rather than institutional. The office of Wazir never developed into a permanent feature of government. At Fes, indeed, *wazir* was a title given to all ministers, and eventually became a title of nobility. The competition of such ministers for power in the second half of the fourteenth century brought about the decline and eventual fall of the Marinids in the fifteenth.

However important the treasury might be, and however skilled its secretaries, there was no budgetary control over revenue and expenditure. Everything was taxable by the state under Islamic law, and beyond that by custom, particularly in the case of trade, which was a ready source of cash. Revenue from the countryside required armed expeditions that lived off the land and brought back produce to be sold on the market or used for payment in kind. Much was in any case collected in the provinces to pay the collectors, with no more than a proportion sent to the capital. Specific revenues from specific sources were allocated for specific purposes: a regiment of guards at Fes, for example, paid out of income for the gardens of the city, or the moneys from Biskra required to put the Dawawida Arabs into the field when summoned by the Hafsid sultan. They were granted to specific individuals, such as the Almohad shaykhs at Tunis, as payment for their services, or given away with the land to form the estates of the aristocracy, including tribal chiefs. They were conceded along with the right of collection to the warrior tribes who formed so large a part of the armies of all three dynasties, and in the vocabulary of a later period, 'ate' the taxpaying *ra'iyya*, the flock of subjects within the reach of their migration. And they were permitted to petty local rulers like the Banu Muzni at Biskra in return for some contribution in time of need. Such delegation of rights and powers created a wealthy and powerful aristocracy that in times of crisis usurped the treasury's own share of the fisc, and prompted the warnings of Ibn Khaldun of the danger to the dynasty from the greed of its servants. Meanwhile it was instrumental in bringing about the wider social changes of the period.

VII

Like the political changes at the beginning of the period, the social changes that followed were inseparable from religion. The great doctrinal controversy within Islam as a whole that had generated the three great revolutions of the Fatimids, the Almoravids and the Almohads in the Maghrib was over, leaving only the holy war against the foreign, Christian, enemy as a rallying cry. Mahdism, the messianic belief in a saviour sent from God that had achieved its greatest triumphs in North Africa, had dwindled into the forlorn hope of the poor and the oppressed. It was left to the Maliki school of the law to take its place as the undisputed orthodoxy of North Africa on behalf of the state, even under the Hafsids at Tunis. Both the *qadi*, the judge, and the *mufti*, the jurisconsult, were appointed by the state, and employed their skill and judgement to resolve the multifarious cases with which they dealt in the public as well as in the private interest of the parties. Their authority and influence was enhanced by their learning, which benefited from the patronage of rulers concerned to establish their credentials as legitimate successors to the Almohads. From the second half of the thirteenth century onwards, all three dynasties founded *madrasa*s or residential colleges in their capital cities for instruction in the sciences of religion, the Marinids in particular, who were anxious to create a broad class of educated servants. The result was the appearance of a North African intelligentsia, extending from Tunis through Tlemcen and Fes across the Straits to Granada, and like Ibn Khaldun, as skilled in literature as in law. Its members were involved on the one hand in politics, on the other in the rule and regulation of the society to which they belonged, extending outwards from the city into the countryside.

In the countryside, however, they encountered an unofficial rival in the saintly rather than scholarly figure of the *murabit*, who retained something of the zeal of Ibn Yasin and his fellow warriors in the way of God, but had largely turned from being a missionary dedicated to the reform of society, to a conservative who blessed the way of life of his community. Colloquially known, in French spelling, as the *marabout*, he survived down to the twentieth century as a charismatic individual whose tomb, likewise known as a *marabout*, sanctified the land and its occupants. But from the Almohad period onwards, his holiness acquired both doctrinal and institutional form from Sufism, which first took hold in the Maghrib in al-Andalus, and then in Morocco at the time when the Almohads were striving to introduce their own form of illuminationism. Sufism and Almohadism were indeed two aspects of the same phenomenon: the desire for the 'taste' of divinity that al-Ghazali had achieved in theory and in practice with his vision of Muhammad as the perfect man and the Qur'an as the source of light. But whereas the teaching of Ibn Tumart had been dogmatic and dictatorial, that of Sufism was simply attractive and persuasive; and where the one perished, the other survived. Frowned upon by the Almohads, Sufism nevertheless performed the task the Almohads had set themselves, broadening the base of Islam in the society they had come to rule, not compulsorily, by the state, but voluntarily, by the individual.

Sufism, as represented in the works of the Andalusian Ibn al-'Arabi at the beginning of the thirteenth century, was on the same high intellectual level as Almohadism. It took root when the mystic attracted disciples who followed his way, and gained a reputation as a saint who blessed the community at large. It did so, in other words, when he became a *marabout* in the growing tradition of the holy man. The first such Sufis in twelfth-century Morocco took up a range of positions from that of al-Dukkali, whose legalistic way was close to Almohadism, through the ascetic and scholarly Harzihum to the piety of Abu Ya'za, who spoke only Berber. But the institutional development of Sufism in North Africa took place in the second half of the thirteenth century, when it spread eastwards into Ifriqiya and beyond, through territories occupied by the Banu Hilal and the Banu Sulaym. It did so when the way of the Andalusian/Moroccan Abu Madyan was taken up in the first half of the thirteenth century by al-Dahmani, of a noble bedouin Arab lineage, who abjured the life of a warrior for that of a saint. The phenomenon is parallel to that in the tribal Sahara, where the dominant clans separated out into warriors and clerics. Arabs who followed the example of al-Dahmani colonised the cross-country routes in the manner of Sufis in the Muslim east, who had long established their *zawiyas* or 'corners' as refuges for travellers like themselves. Such *zawiyas* now sprouted across North Africa for the benefit of the wayfarer, but as centres of spiritual as well as material hospitality, and roots in the cultivation of the surrounding land. Many grew as a result to an impressive size, with a mosque, a school, a residence for the saints and their disciples, a hostelry and perhaps a hospital grouped around the tomb of the founder. Meanwhile they appeared in the cities, and began to cluster around the holy city of Qayrawan, for example, or in the southern Tunisian oasis of Nafta. Large-scale or small-scale, they were instrumental in the colonisation of the countryside by the holy man who 'brought the dead land to life'.

Thus constituted, the *zawiya* flourished away from the cities as a centre of government for local populations which looked to its saints for the peace, the protection and the settlement of disputes that the state, and the law, either could not or did not provide. For that reason it did not escape the attention of the state, which sought to enlist the services of the holy men by its patronage. By the fifteenth century in Ifriqiya the *zawiya* had become in consequence a wealthy institution, incorporated into the fabric of the Hafsid state. In Morocco, on the other hand, the decline of the Marinid state had freed the *zawiya* in the tribal countryside to develop into an autonomous centre of regional power and influence. Sufism itself, as Ibn Khaldun observed, remained suspect in the eyes of the law; but in the end its appeal to all classes of society, enhanced by the economic and political importance of the *zawiya*, meant that many Sufis were jurists, and many jurists Sufis, all members of the same broad intelligentsia. Membership was open to talent, but since scholarship and saintliness both ran in families, it was to a very large extent hereditary. In Morocco and western Algeria, indeed, class turned into caste with the rise of the *sharif*s or *shurafa'*, those claiming descent from the Prophet. The majority traced their ancestry in the Hasanid line, which was introduced into the region as far back as the eighth century by Idris, the founder of Fes. They multiplied under the Marinids, reinforced by immigrants from the Hijaz, and became particularly strong at Fes; in 1465, indeed, they seized control of the city, and put the last Marinid sultan to death. The *shurafa'* enjoyed not only prestige, but the presumption of authority for the faith on the strength of their illustrious ancestor. This gave their scholars and saints a coveted eminence in the profession of law and the calling of sanctity.

VIII

The formation of this composite elite was an important step in the formation of North African society within the framework established by the Almohad empire. It was important not only in itself, but for its contribution to social and political change in the population as a whole. The size of the population can only be guessed at some four to five million, fluctuating over the centuries, but never in any case rising above a low ceiling, and certainly depressed by the Black Death in the middle of the fourteenth century. Inputs would have made little difference to the total. Immigration into the cities from the countryside, for example, is likely to have been neutralised by a higher death rate. And the continual import of black slaves from the ninth century onwards simply replenished the supply of domestics and of agricultural labour in the Saharan oases. It introduced a new element into the make-up of the population without leading to an overall increase. Some local increase in northern Morocco may nevertheless be attributed to the steady influx of Andalusians, both Muslim and Jewish, that followed the loss of the greater part of Muslim Spain in the middle of the thirteenth century. Settling at Fes, they provoked a rivalry for control of the city and its *qaysariyya* or central market that contributed to the rebellion of the *shurafa'* in 1465.

If the *shurafa'* at Fes were in competition with their rivals, their multiplication in the Marinid period raises a second point, that within a static population, the growth of one sector would have taken place at the expense of another, perhaps to the point of extinction. This was clearly the case with Islamisation. The original Christian population of Ifriqiya shrank in face of the dynamic increase in the Muslim community, until it disappeared with the Almohad conquest. Within the Muslim community itself, Kharijism, which had been so popular in the eighth century in opposition to the Umayyads, failed to secure acceptance as the principal form of Islam. As Malikite Islam prevailed over its rivals, the Kharijites, becoming a sect, lost the hold they had secured on trans-Saharan trade, and survived into the post-Almohad period as a few isolated Berber communities in southern Ifriqiya and the northern Sahara. Only the Jews were successful in reproducing themselves in commercial and artisanal communities in town and countryside.

By far the most striking example of such changes in the later medieval period was the increase in the number of Arabic speakers at the expense of Berber speakers, with an accompanying sense of Arab as opposed to Berber identity. Arabisation had begun with the foundation of the new Muslim cities of North Africa in the course of the Arab conquest as melting-pots for their immigrant populations. It had proceeded with the establishment of Arabic as the language of literacy and learning, government and business, and been reinforced by the prestige of an Arab genealogy. The Berber dynasties of the Zirids and the Almoravids had both claimed Yemeni ancestry, while Ibn Tumart claimed descent from Muhammad long before the rise of the *shurafa'*. But it had taken the appearance of the Banu Hilal to introduce both the language and the genealogy into the mass of the population of the countryside, in the course of the far-reaching reformation of state and society with which the bedouin were associated. Nomadic peoples are their own melting-pots, dividing and combining to form new tribes with new names and new genealogies, new patron and new client clans. In the case of the Banu Hilal and the Banu Sulaym, the process was driven by the success of the warrior clans, who not only took over the territories of the nomadic Berber peoples of the Libyan desert: the Lawata, the Hawwara and the Mazata, but created a fresh population of more or less impoverished nomads excluded from their ranks. This radical restructuring of the population extended through Ifriqiya to the borders of Morocco. Warrior Arabs joined with warrior Berber nomads in the armies of the 'Abd al-Wadids at Tlemcen; more important was the way in which Berber villagers colonised the mountains to avoid both the Arabs and the tax-collector out on the plains, or fell under their domination along with the poorer bedouin, many of whom were driven to join them in the fields. In either case they fell under the influence of the *marabout*, who might lead their sporadic resistance, but in his *zawiya* gathered them into new communities and affiliations under his patronage and protection. In this new melting-pot, the *qaba'il* or tribes of the mountains from whom al-Qaba'iliyya or Kabylia is named became strongly Berber, while the plains were Arabised. The linguistic change was symptomatic of the social change, in which old identities had disappeared along with the original communities.

IX

With the evaporation of doctrinal conflict, and the reconstruction of tribal society under the pressures of religion and state, the age of revolution was past. As Ibn Khaldun observed, the *'asabiyya* required for the purpose was lacking among the victims of the new order, for whom Mahdism was no more than a pious hope, and the saint had taken the place of the prophet. When in the sixteenth century the age of revolution returned, it did so in two quite separate ways that divided rather than united the region: foreign conquest on the one hand, internal conquest on the other.

The common denominator was the third great factor in the history of the period, the holy war against the Christians of Portugal and Spain. That millennial conflict had flickered since the loss of the major part of al-Andalus in the thirteenth century, but flared up around the time of the fall of Granada in 1492 to determine the subsequent course of North African history. The capture of Ceuta by the Portuguese in 1415 was followed by the occupation of most of the main coastal cities from Agadir to Tripoli by the Portuguese and Spaniards between 1470 and 1510. This establishment of the infidel on the other side of the sea provoked the establishment at Algiers of the Barbarossa brothers from the Ottoman Aegean, out of which grew the Ottoman conquest of Algeria, Tunisia and Tripolitania by 1574. In Morocco it brought a return to Mahdism with the designation of a *sharif* by a *marabout* as the man born to be king. Muhammad al-Qa'im became the founder of the so-called Sa'dian dynasty that by the end of the century had restored the Moroccan empire. Between the Ottomans and the Sa'dians, the Wattasids, the 'Abd al-Wadids and the Hafsids all disappeared, and with them the political configuration of the past. Ifriqiya, the old Byzantine province that had survived the coming of the Banu Hilal, now finally ceased to exist. Tripolitania was joined by the Ottomans with Cyrenaica, which had previously been ruled from Egypt. Eastern Algeria was placed with western Algeria in a new province under the new Ottoman capital, Algiers. Tunis took second place as the capital of all that was left of the Hafsid empire. The border with Morocco remained contentious, but as it settled to the west of Tlemcen, the modern political divisions of North Africa were established, and the foundations of the modern states were laid.

The conflict of empires: Portuguese and Spanish, Ottoman and Moroccan, was invited by the disintegration of central government in North Africa that developed in Morocco and at Tlemcen from the beginning of the fifteenth century, and concluded at the death of the Hafsid sultan 'Uthman at Tunis in 1488. The Hafsid state, that had been so strong and influential throughout the century, collapsed in a dispute over the succession, so that right across North Africa, government outside the dynastic capitals came down to the level of cities, tribes and saints. Into this situation the Portuguese and Spaniards were drawn only partly by crusading zeal; the Portuguese took the Atlantic ports of Morocco en route to West Africa, the Spaniards the Mediterranean ports to stifle Muslim piracy. The Ottomans and the Sa'dians, on the other hand, seized the opportunity to conquer the interior. All four empires owed their success to the revolution in warfare brought about by the introduction of firearms, which enabled them to overcome North African opponents armed with traditional weapons. But the result of the conflict between Spain and the Ottomans was different from that between Portugal and the Moroccans. The Ottoman conquest grew out of the endemic piracy of previous centuries, a form of holy war that had been stimulated by the arrival of the refugees from Granada. It was achieved as much by sea as by land, by fleets that came to form part of the Ottoman navy as well as by the artillery and janissaries of the Ottoman army. And it confirmed the primacy of the coast over the interior with a return to the situation under the Romans, the incorporation of North Africa into a Mediterranean empire ruled from across the sea. The Sa'dian conquest, on the other hand, grew out of the politics of the interior, creating an empire that was centred like that of the Almoravids and Almohads, inland at Marrakesh. The coast was a frontier against the infidel.

The contrast is apparent in the conflict between the two empires. The Ottomans had to contend not only with the Spaniards but with local rivals, in particular with the saints who rose up in place of the old dynasties as contenders for power: the Shabbiyya at Qayrawan, the so-called 'kings of Kouko' in the mountains of Kabylia. The emergence of the *marabout* as a statesman had been prepared by the growing role of the *zawiya* in government, which stemmed from his authority in the eyes of the local population; the failure of the Hafsids and 'Abd al-Wadids left him as the only figure to command the community as a whole. Not without difficulty, however, he was beaten by the superior military strength of the Ottomans, and by their superior prestige as successful holy warriors under the command of the Great Ghazi or Holy Warrior at Istanbul. He was, however, equally influential in Morocco, where the limitation of Wattasid rule to the northern part of the country had left the south to its own devices. There, from the canyon of the Draa in the Anti-Atlas, the Sa'dians came to make good the claim of holiness to power over the faithful. The claim combined the inherited virtue of the *sharif* with the charisma of the *marabout* who designated the new Muhammad. But unlike Ibn Tumart and 'Abd al-Mu'min, there was no great new doctrine, nor any conversion to Islam. Muhammad al-Qa'im was appointed in 1510 to command the tribes who looked to Sidi Barakat for guidance in their dealings with the Portuguese at Agadir. His commitment to holy war was ambivalent, since he and his sons profited from the trans-Saharan trade with the infidel. But their appeal enabled them to create a *makhzan*, a government with an army based upon taxation, that overcame both political and religious opposition to confront the Ottomans at Algiers with a rival for the rule of the faithful in North Africa.

If the Sa'dians challenged the legitimacy of the Ottomans, they imitated their superior military and administrative organisation. By the end of the sixteenth century their greatest Sultan, Ahmad al-Mansur al-Dhahabi, had instituted at Marrakesh a central government on the Ottoman model. Claiming supreme religious as well as political authority, the Sultan gave audience from behind a curtain. Beneath him, a *wazir* acted as prime minister, with a council of ministers meeting twice a week, a chief *qadi* to hear complaints, a chancery, and a treasury whose tax collectors were commissioners from the ranks of the *'ulama'*. The army likewise was modelled upon the Ottoman, with a corps of musketeers resembling the janissaries, though made up of foreigners including European renegades. The court was nevertheless peripatetic: the vast *mahalla* or camp of the Sultan was a major instrument of government that sought to overcome the separatism of regions and peoples. And it broke down following the death of Ahmad in 1603 in the course of a succession dispute that rapidly brought the dynasty to its knees. There had been no time to establish the kind of institutional continuity in evidence in the Ottoman provinces, where the offices of state were filled on a regular basis by the servants of the distant Sultan.

X

The contrast was complete in the first half of the seventeenth century, when central government disappeared from Morocco but survived in the Ottoman provinces despite a struggle for power between the Pashas, the governors sent from Istanbul, and the military. At Tripoli the Bey, the commander of the army, gradually ousted the Pasha. At Tunis first the Dey, the commander of the janissaries, and then the Bey, the commander of the cavalry, took charge. At Algiers the Agha or commander of the janissaries, in concert with the captains of the corsair fleet, seized power from the

Pasha in 1659, before it fell into the hands of the Dey, an officer elected by the janissaries, in 1671. This frequently murderous progression towards provincial independence did not, however, undermine the state; it was more a sign of the way in which the three regimes had taken firm hold on the country. Janissary armies of a few thousand men recruited in Anatolia were the nucleus of a small ruling class partly constituted by their offspring, the *kuloghullari* or 'sons of the slaves (of the Sultan)', whose legitimacy was bolstered by the introduction of the Hanafite school of law by Turkish jurists who took precedence over the native Malikites. Through alliances with the Arabs of the plains, the Berbers of the mountains, the *marabouts* and other notables, this tiny minority kept the peace, and ensured that the state resumed its previous progress towards the constitution of a society ever more liable to taxation, ever more constituted into subjects.

In Morocco, on the other hand, the Sa'dians divided in 1610 between rulers at Marrakesh and Fes, and thereafter lost both power and authority before their final demise in 1659. Their place was taken by the great *marabouts* whom Ahmad al-Mansur had repressed as rivals to the dynasty. Three of them now contended for power at Marrakesh, two at Fes, until in the 1640s the *zawiya* of Dila' in the Middle Atlas extended its rule over most of the country as far as the High Atlas. Scholars and saints, the *marabouts* of Dila' represented the long-standing opposition within the religious establishment to the claims of the *sharifs* to primacy. But despite the failure of the Sa'dians, their identification of the state with the descendants of the Prophet was now so well established, that neither the charisma of Dila' nor its Berber forces were strong enough to overcome resistance to their rule. From 1659 their power crumbled in the face of opposition from Fes and the rise of yet another Sharifian dynasty, the 'Alawites, who came to power in 1668. The victory of the 'Alawites was final. The power of the *marabouts* was at an end, although the conflict between the authority of the Sultan and that of the scholars smouldered on. The place of the Ottoman model of central government was taken by a palatial household, a clumsy instrument that nevertheless succeeded where Dila' had failed to reconstitute the Moroccan empire. The country united beneath a Sultan committed to the defence of the faith.

The drawback was increasing isolation. Whether at Marrakesh, Dila', Fes or Meknes, the imperial capital was inland, away from the sea. At Sale the Hornacheros, Moriscos expelled from Spain in 1610, set up their own little republic to carry the war back to the Christian enemy at sea: the Sallee rovers whose voyages took them as far as Cornwall and Iceland. Dila' put an end to their independence, and their piracy continued thereafter as a lucrative arm of the Moroccan empire. But it accompanied a restriction of the trade with Europe from which the Sa'dians had profited in the sixteenth century. In the Ottoman dominions, on the other hand, the posture and the practice of holy war went hand in hand with commercial activity and commercial prosperity. From Algiers to Tripoli, corsairing not only flourished in the hands of the captains, many of them European renegades, who played an important role in government at Algiers. It developed commercially through the ransoming of captives, and the sale of captured merchandise to European merchants who came increasingly for more normal trade. Meanwhile the incorporation of Mediterranean North Africa into the Ottoman empire had opened up the markets of the eastern Mediterranean, for which Tunis developed the manufacture of caps and tiles. Such prosperity was very evident in the three capitals. Tunis in particular grew back to its former size after the warfare of the previous century, as did Tripoli. Algiers developed from a small port into one of the great cities of the empire, the Turkish style of its palaces and mosques in sharp contrast to the Andalusian style of Morocco.

Relations with the Sahara, that first factor in the history of North Africa, were no less important, and no less political. Over the centuries since the rise of the Almoravids and the appearance of the Banu Hilal, the evolution of an aristocracy of warrior nomads and clerical clans that ruled over a servile population of cultivators in the oases was complete in the west and south. To the north, the extensive Algerian and Libyan oases from Wargla and the Mzab to the Fezzan housed cities and states on a North African model. In the fourteenth and fifteenth centuries, the Fezzan had been ruled by the empire of Borno, evidence of the success of trans-Saharan trade in bringing the Sudan into the Islamic world. But in the sixteenth century it was ruled from Murzuq by the Awlad Muhammad, a dynasty founded by a Moroccan *sharif* and *marabout* who had been invited, in characteristic fashion, to settle the disputes of the population. Government was partly Bornoan but mainly Hafsid in character, relying heavily upon the grant of land to warrior Arab chiefs and *marabout*s, and strong enough to resist the Turks at Tripoli. As in Egypt, Ottoman ambitions reached towards the Bilad al-Sudan, but expeditions to the Fezzan succeeded only in gaining recognition and tribute. The connection was to the advantage of the Awlad Muhammad, who profited as middlemen from the trade of the Ottoman empire with Borno: guns and horses in exchange for slaves.

In the west, the *sharif*s themselves were the imperialists who clashed with the Sudanese empire of Songhay over the oases of Tuat and the salt mines of Taghaza, with very different results. Ahmad al-Mansur, the Conqueror (of the Portuguese in 1578), won the further soubriquet of al-Dhahabi, the Golden, for the victory at Tondibi in 1591, when his army of musketeers marched across the Sahara to rout the army of Songhay and bring down its empire. The aim was to lay hands on the gold of West Africa in the manner of the Spanish *conquistadors* in the New World, and was briefly successful. But the Moroccans at Timbuktu were unable to turn their triumph into an empire to compare with Mexico and Peru. Following the death of Ahmad in 1603, they lost contact with Marrakesh, and became the local rulers of a city that remained a focal point of Saharan society and trans-Saharan trade.

XI

What of that broad intelligentsia represented by Ibn Khaldun in the time of the Marinids, the ‘Abd al-Wadids and the Hafsids? The sixteenth century had been unhappy and unconducive to scholarship, which nevertheless survived into the seventeenth. The *marabout*s of Dila’ were the outstanding example in Morocco, but the literary culture is best displayed by al-Maqqari’s retrospective celebration of Muslim Spain after its final eclipse with the expulsion of the Moriscos in 1609. Inspired by the work of Ibn Khaldun’s contemporary, the Granadan Ibn al-Khatib, it is a vast compendium that reveals the familiarity of al-Maqqari’s generation with the immense repertoire of Arabic literature in the Muslim West. Composed at Cairo by a scholar from Tlemcen and Fes for friends at Damascus, it was copied in North Africa, in one case to the order of a Turkish grandee at Algiers. It is a tribute to both state and society in North Africa from the eleventh to the seventeenth century.

BIBLIOGRAPHICAL NOTE

The study of state and society in Islamic North Africa falls into two periods, before and after independence. French scholars of the colonial period collated the major sources and wrote the basic histories of the region (Julien 1970); of Morocco (Terrasse 1949; Le Tourneau 1949; Deverdun 1959); and of the eastern Maghrib (Brunschvig 1940–7; Idris 1962), but with the exception of Julien considered that Islamisation and Arabisation had led to economic, social and political decline. Since independence this judgement has been reexamined, with modest success pending further research: see Lacoste (1984) and Laroui (1977). The standard work of reference is the *Encyclopaedia of Islam*, 2nd edn. (1957 ff.), though the reader needs to be familiar with the Arabic form of names and subjects. Abun-Nasr (1987) is now the standard history. Relevant periodicals are *The Maghreb Review*, the *Journal of North African Studies*, the *Revue du Monde Musulman et de la Méditerranée* (previously the *Revue de l'Occident Musulman et de la Méditerranée*), and *Al-Qantara*. Brett and Fentress (1996) discuss the evolution of state and society. For the earlier part of the period, their work is supplemented by Norris (1982). Much of the interpretation has turned on the *Muqaddimah* of Ibn Khaldun (1967, 1986), variously discussed in Brett (1999), a collection of relevant studies. The structure of the state prior to Ibn Khaldun is treated by Hopkins (1958). Down to the fifteenth century, state and society in the eastern Maghrib are described by Idris and Brunschvig, above, followed by Daoulatli (1976). Brignon et al. (1967) is a useful history of Morocco, supplemented for the later mediaeval period by Le Tourneau (1961, 1969), Kably (1986), Shatzmiller (2000) and Powers (2002). Berque (1978, 1982) is of major importance for the centuries after Ibn Khaldun, though difficult; Hess (1978), reviewed in Brett (1999), looks at the sixteenth and seventeenth centuries from an Ottoman point of view. The Saharan dimension is covered by the *Cambridge History of Africa*, vols. 3 and 4. All the above refer in various ways to the role of religion in state and society; books on religion itself, however, are rare, and the periodical literature must be consulted. Bel (1938) is dated and incomplete. Cornell (1998) deals with Sufism in Morocco, while Geertz (1968) provides a final touch. The last word is with al-Maqqari (2002).

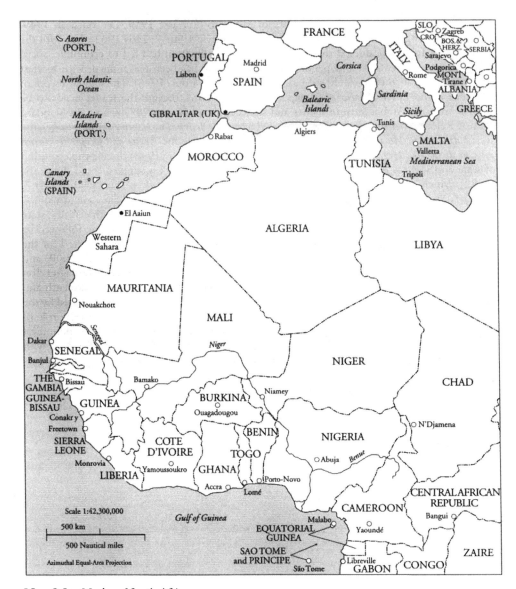

Map 9.1 Modern North Africa

PART IV

A New Middle Eastern System

CHAPTER TEN

Ottomans and Safavids
States, Statecraft, and Societies, 1500–1800

METIN KUNT

The period commonly styled as 'early modern' with reference to European history roughly coincides with an equally distinct era in Islamic history, one that might be termed the 'age of the great dynastic empires'. The grandest of these empires, most populous and prosperous though also the shortest lived, the Mughals of India, is arguably the best researched and best known perhaps because of its relevance to British history. Many features of Mughal India, from Turkic dynastic origins and Persianate political culture to the central place of Islam especially in terms of social organisation and legal practice, and its flourishing literary and visual arts, could be profitably studied in conjunction with Ottoman and Safavid polities. There was also considerable mutual and reciprocal influence between the Mughals and the other two empires: Mughal shahs contested the eastern marches of the Safavid domains and sought ways to wrest ideological leadership of the Sunni Muslim world from the Ottomans; they provided prosperous employment to artists and men of letters from Iran, architects and military experts from Ottoman lands. History, shared heritage and culture, continuing contacts and connections, especially intimate with the Safavids, all indicate that the Mughals should be viewed in the same context as their Muslim contemporaries, yet geography places the Mughal empire outside our purview. In the period under study, those regions and peoples of west Asia and north Africa (with the major exception of Morocco) which now come under the Eurocentric rubric 'Middle East' as it is commonly understood these days and provide the focus of the present volume were ruled exclusively by the Safavid and Ottoman empires.

Historians often refer to these polities as Safavid Iran and Ottoman Turkey. This practice is misleading for at best it falsely implies a predetermined territorial aim as well as an ethnic supremacy, or at least predominance in each case. Territorial and cultural if not ethnic 'Iranianness' of the Safavîs may be defended, but in the case of the Ottomans there is the additional and more serious problem that while Europeans may have referred to their domains as 'Turkey' none in the Islamic world nor any in Asia in general would have recognised the term; in the Turkish language itself the word 'Türkiye' had to be invented as a translation of European usage only around the turn of the twentieth century. Muslims and other Asians knew the Ottomans as 'Rûmî', that is to say 'Romans' since they conquered regions previously known as 'Rûm', Byzantine Rome. The lands ruled by these Turkish-speaking Muslim 'Romans' were the domains of the 'House of Osman', the Ottoman realm, never 'Turkey'. Unlike China or India or even Iran there was no historical Turkey, certainly not where the Ottomans held power. Ottoman lands did not constitute a historical entity except as the hinterland of Byzantium/Constantinople, the second Rome. The territorial expanse of Süleyman the Magnificent's sixteenth-century empire was very similar to that of Justinian a millennium earlier in the sixth century. There were exceptions in the two empires' reaches. Whereas Justinian held sway in Italy, Ottoman 'Romans' never succeeded in their half-hearted attempts to conquer it; on the other hand, in Hungary and lands around the Black Sea as well as to the east in Mesopotamia and to the south in Arabia and shores of the Red Sea Süleyman's domains were much more extensive. Essentially, however, Justinian's and Süleyman's rule from Constantinople/Istanbul extended over all that they could conquer far from that central, focal point. Rather than being seen as territorial entities, both the Ottoman and the Safavid powers should more usefully be conceived as dynastic empires.

The Emergence of Ottomans and Safavîs

The eponymous founders of the Ottoman and Safavid dynasties, Osman Bey (d. 1324) and Shayh Sâfî ad-dîn (d. 1336) were early fourteenth-century contemporaries, one a frontier chieftain in north-west Anatolia and the other a sûfî shayh in Ardabîl in Âzerbayjân near the Caspian coast. Osman Bey was one of dozens of chiefs who led bands of frontiersmen on the Saljukî–Byzantine marches along the rim of the central Anatolian plateau; victories in skirmishes against local Byzantine forces enhanced his reputation and stature among frontiersmen in Bithynia so that at his death people calling themselves Osman's men, Osmanli in Turkish, constituted a significant force, though still restricted in territory to Bursa and the region to the south east of the Marmara Sea. In the course of the fourteenth century Osman's descendants, still the Osmanli, succeeded in enlarging their domains both against Byzantium and against the other frontier emirates in west Anatolia. Two factors assured success to the Ottomans: the control of the passage to south-east Europe at the Dardanelles from the mid-century, and cutting off the hinterland of Anatolia from other emirates on the Aegean Sea. Even though utterly defeated by Timur (Tamerlane) in 1402, Ottoman power rose again due to their unrivalled position straddling the Dardanelles, controlling the passage of would-be frontiersmen to the Balkans and their booty back to Anatolia. Shayh Sâfî's descendants, on the other hand, consolidated the primacy of their order over other mystic brotherhoods in Âzerbayjân and extended their appeal into Anatolia.

Both Ottoman political power and Safavî religious appeal were based on a similar, almost identical, social reservoir, the Oghuz Turks, the 'Ghuzz' of Arab Muslim writers. The Oghuz branch of western Turks had moved to the eastern Caspian region in the tenth century and in the mid-eleventh had provided the military power of the Saljukî sultans. Oghuz tribesmen coming south into Iran had been encouraged by Saljukî central authorities to move on with their flocks to Âzerbayjân and eastern Anatolia where the mountain ranges and river valleys provided summer and winter pastures to their extensive livestock. While it was the Saljukî Sultan

Alparslan's defeat of the Byzantine emperor at Malazgirt (Manzikert) in 1071 that opened Roman Anatolia to Turkish power, it was the Oghuz who in fact settled the 'land of Rûm' and established the first local political entities. The Oghuz of Âzerbayjân and Anatolia were reinforced by other Turkish immigrants especially during the Mongolian upheaval of the thirteenth century: some displaced from Transoxania by the Mongol irruption, some as Mongol allies with a common inner Asian political and social ethos. The Oghuz of Anatolia lived in an uneasy relationship with the Saljukîs of Rûm, those of Âzerbayjân came under the sway of Ilkhanî Mongols; with the disintegration of the Saljukî state by the end of the thirteenth century and of the Ilkhanîs by the mid-fourteenth the movement of Oghuz to the west continued, to Rûm and later to the Balkans but by then under strict control and guidance of the Ottomans. Once Timur's grand design failed the Oghuz of eastern Anatolia and Âzerbayjân eventually created their own political formation, the Aqquyunlu federation, with the participation of Turkmen of northern Mesopotamia and western Iran. It was within the confines of the Aqquyunlu that the Safavî sûfî order flourished and came to provide the spiritual bond to Aqquyunlu subjects and court alike. The Safavî dynasty of shayhs forged marriage ties with the Aqquyunlu shahs; the rank and file of the order was also politicised and indeed militarised as Safavîs assumed leadership of Oghuz raiders in the Caucasus. The Ottomans had glorified their expansion into Byzantine, Bulgarian, and Serbian lands as 'ghaza', frontier fighting for the cause of Islam. By the late fifteenth century the Safavîs of Âzerbayjân, too, added ghaza to their spiritual claim to leadership of Oghuz tribesmen. The Ottoman polity had undergone a transformation to a centralised rule after the conquest of Constantinople in 1453; by the end of the century the Safavî shayhs effected a veritable revolution when they displaced the Aqquyunlu rulers and became shahs themselves.

Turko-Persian Polities

Ottoman ghâzîs had expanded their domains over two centuries with fairly constant fighting not only against non-Muslim neighbours to the west but also against other Turkmen emirates of Anatolia, at least when they failed to coerce them into submission. The Safavîs, on the other hand, displaced the Aqquyunlu dynasty and, all at once, became the rulers of a well-defined domain within the space of a single year in 1501. They inherited a polity which they of course changed to suit the new dispensation. But Safavî rule was not only a dynastic change, nor even the replacement of existing political cadres, it was the occasion of the greatest religious revolution since the emergence of Islam itself. Ghaza in the service of Islam had served as one aspect of Ottoman ideology as it expanded; a new religious basis for political rule was the much greater ideological impact of the Safavî dynasty when Shi'ism was enforced on Safavî subjects. To understand the necessity for such a drastic and unprecedented policy of mass conversion we need an evaluation of the main features of Muslim polities around 1500.

Since the Saljukî sultanate was established in the eleventh century, and even more firmly since Mongol Ilkhanî rule in the thirteenth, a new model of socio-political organisation had developed in central and eastern Islamic lands, one which has been termed 'Turko-Persian'. Simply put, the term refers to polities that emerged since the Ghaznavîs and Saljukîs in the eleventh century which were based on Turkish/Turkic military muscle and civilian administrators, mostly of Iranian stock, who glorified and revived the Sasanî heritage of politics and government. The presentation of the great Persian epic of kings, Shâhnâmeh, by Ferdowsî to the Turkish ruler Sultan Mahmud of Ghazneh in the early eleventh century may be taken as the beginning of this new style of government. The book of kings, with its accounts of the wisdom and valour, as well as the jealousies and failings of Sasanî shahs and heroes, set values and virtues of kingship. The Shâhnâmeh's version of the worldly and spiritual attainments of the exemplary universal ruler Alexander, Iskandar in Muslim usage, provided the highest standard later rulers were measured against and often attempted to emulate. The great Saljukî sultans, Ilkhanî shahs and other Turko-Persian rulers reigned in the ethos of the Shâhnâmeh and under the shadow of Iskandar. Persian heritage thus shaped the ideology of states and Iranian vazîrs and scribes provided the practical apparatus of government. On the other hand rulers and their armies were most commonly of Inner Asian origin or descent. The politics of the ruling house and the disposition of the army were imbued with this Turkic heritage. Rulers and military commanders spoke Turkish; Persian bureaucrats and authors provided the literary and artistic culture of the court and of the polity as well as its statecraft.

The Inner Asian heritage of ruling houses shaped dynastic politics even when they were established in predominantly sedentary regions of historical Iran and West Asia. The ruler reigned as the senior member, the great khan, of the dynastic clan; other male members of the family, brothers of the khan, his sons and nephews, shared political power as governors of regions. Succession was not by a generally accepted rule such as seniority but by acclamation by leaders of the polity of the most politically astute and militarily effective member of the ruling house. One might say that the rule of succession was that there should be no rule, but an eminent historian of Inner Asia has in fact borrowed a term from Celtic polities, tanistry, to define this process in the Turkic context. The importation of the term helps to create a comparative context but the comparison is inexact: tanistry in the Celtic case refers to the designation of an heir apparent whereas in Inner Asian history there was never such certainty of succession. Instead, the process of the candidates battling each other, sometimes metaphorically but often in reality, was expected to bring out the best possible great leader, a literal survival of the fittest to rule. This was such an important consideration that even at the risk of civil war the principle of a leadership struggle was maintained. The inevitable instability of political rule afflicted all post-Saljukî Turko-Persian polities.

The other main aspect of these political formations, the functional-ethnic division between Turkish military and Persian bureaucracy, worked well when kept in check by a strong ruler who could maintain the balance, but the inherent factionalism surfaced during leadership struggles. This division was also reflected in society: despite the fact that there were townsmen and peasants of Turkish background as well as Persian nomads, the main deep cleavage in society was between the nomadic Oghuz and sedentary Persian population. Political ideology derived from the Persian heritage and the military prowess of the Turks often failed to uphold the polity. The historical significance of the Ottoman and Safavî empires is that each in its own way and to a varying extent managed to overcome political and social divisions and create relatively durable political entities. The Safavî dynasty took over an existing state and imposed Shi'î Islam on its populace to transcend the Safavî brotherhood of Oghuz Turks and to subvert the Sunnî Islam of the majority of townsmen and peasants of its domains: the resulting bonding in Shi'ism of hitherto disparate social and political elements proved remarkably successful. The new Shi'i self-identity in fact survived Safavî rule itself and provided the basis of Iranian nationalism and patriotism in the twentieth century.

An Islamic revolutionary ideology could work as the cement of a Muslim society such as in Aqquyunlu-turned-Safavî lands, but in the Ottoman case Muslims, Turkish or others, sedentary or nomadic, were no more than half the population. The successful Ottoman frontier enterprise grew slowly, over many generations, incorporating non-Muslim Greeks, Bulgarians, Serbians, not only as conquered peoples but also at the ruler's court and in the military. Except in specific political and institutional circumstances there was no coercion to conversion to Islam. The Ottoman solution to endemic political and social instability was not so much through ideology but through institutional arrangements to strengthen the political centre around the sultan's household. Ottoman structures were so well-rooted and resilient that the Ottoman dynasty remained in power into the twentieth century even after its central power weakened from mid-eighteenth century on; when it finally disbanded in defeat after the Great War, along with the Austro-Hungarian and the Russian empires, it left behind no ideology to speak of. At its zenith, though, the effectiveness of Ottoman central authority was as remarkable as the success of the Safavî revolution. The epic clash between Ottoman military organisation and Safavî fervour provided the main backdrop to west Asian history from the fifteenth to the eighteenth centuries.

Ottomans vs. Safavîs: the Shaping of Modern West Asia

The stage of the Safavî revolution was Aqquyunlu lands in eastern Anatolia, Âzerbayjân, Mesopotamia and western Iran. The appeal of the Safavî order, however, had been much wider, also reaching Oghuz Turkmen groups elsewhere in Anatolia and Syria, in Ottoman and Mamluk domains. Before the order politicised and militarised Safavî adherents in Ottoman lands were treated the same as followers of any other sûfî order, as long as they did not create social disturbances. Safavî agents from Âzerbayjân regularly visited Ottoman subjects who were Safavî adherents and collected tithes for the shrine of Shayh Sâfî at Ardabîl. Once Shah Ismâ'il toppled the Aqquyunlu dynasty and called on all his adherents, wherever they may have been living, to join the movement, Ottoman Safavîs became a great danger to the Ottoman state. Anatolian Oghuz Turkmen had supported the Osmanli frontier enterprise but in the second half of the fifteenth century they felt increasingly hemmed in, even marginalised by Ottoman political intervention, taxation and humiliating regulation. With Shah Ismâ'il Anatolian Oghuz had a new opportunity to join a movement and help to establish a political order where they would have a proud and prominent place. Soon after Shah Ismâ'il's initial success many Ottoman Safavî adherents either pulled up tents and migrated to his domains or remained behind to stage uprisings. By 1510 the Ottoman government was in danger of losing control of Anatolia. 'Let the Ottomans keep Rumeli [Roman lands in the Balkans], this side [of the Dardanelles] will be Safavî-ruled' was the battle cry of Anatolian Oghuz. The Safavî ferment in Anatolia was suppressed with difficulty; many of the insurgents were deported to the Balkans, some from the southern port of Antalya by ship across the Aegean Sea, to place them beyond the reach of the call from Ardabîl. Finally in 1514 the full Ottoman army marched on the Safavî frontier and defeated Shah Ismâ'il's superb cavalry at Chaldiran. This was a victory of an army which at its core had the sultan's household troops with the musket-bearing janissary infantry supported by the household field artillery; the shah's valiant Turkish cavalry, invincible until Chaldiran, succumbed against this awesome firepower. In 1071, at a location very close at Manzikert the Byzantine army had failed in its attempt to stem the tide of Saljukî pressure on Roman Anatolia; had Sultan Selim's Ottoman army similarly failed at Chaldiran Anatolia would have come under Safavî rule even more easily than the Saljukîs captured it more than four centuries earlier. After all, the Turks of Anatolia in the early sixteenth century were much more amenable to Safavî rule than the Byzantine populace was to Saljukî invasion; many, indeed, were outright supporters of a new regime. Victory at Chaldiran assured Ottoman domination of Anatolia and eventually shaped the boundary between the two empires. Chaldiran was essentially a defensive battle for the Ottomans; after his victory Sultan Selim invaded Safavî heartlands in Âzerbayjân but could not hold this hostile territory nor its capital Tabriz, fiercely loyal to the Safavî cause. Western portions of what had been Aqquyunlu lands in eastern and south-eastern Anatolia, including the second capital Amid/Diyarbekr, were incorporated into the Ottoman realm; in later campaigns Sultan Suleiman also captured Iraq, but Âzerbayjân, again invaded and devastated, remained in Safavî hands though Qazvîn, further removed from Ottoman threat, replaced Tabriz as the main seat of the shah.

Thus cut off from western, Ottoman Oghuz, nor able to keep Mesopotamia, the Safavî movement resulted in an Iranian realm. Safavî expansion in the north east into Turkistan was also checked by the Uzbek khans of Central Asia. To the east, too, the Safavîs were blocked by Babur Shah's newly emerging Mughal power. Shah Ismâ'il's call had been heard far and wide but his edict was only obeyed in this land hemmed in by formidable Sunni rivals. Located in Iran it became the most Persianate of the new Muslim empires. Yet at the same time its power remained based on the original supporters of the call, the Oghuz of Anatolia and Âzerbayjân. In other ways, too, the Safavî realm was closer to the inner Asian roots of later Muslim empires, while the Ottomans effected an imperial organisation claiming for themselves the Sasani heritage. It is a further irony that when sixteenth-century Ottoman writers depicted contemporary west Asian politics with reference to the Shâhnâmeh they cast themselves as representing legendary Iran and the Safavîs as Turan.

After defeating Shah Ismâ'il, Sultan Selim next turned south toward the once powerful and prosperous Mamluk sultanate in Syria and Egypt, recently under pressure from Portuguese activity in the southern seas. This is another defining point in west Asian history but one where European maritime expansion had a great impact on regional power relations. When the Portuguese blockaded the Red Sea and cut off the lucrative spice trade which contributed hugely to Mamluk prosperity, the great Mamluk cavalry army was impotent to deal with this danger. They were simply not equipped with an adequate naval power, nor had they seriously adapted to gunpowder warfare. They sought help from their European partners in the spice trade, the Venetians, and even from the Ottomans. Until recently, as late as the 1480s, the Mamluks and Ottomans had been engaged in a struggle for mastery of Cilicia, south of Ottoman Anatolia. Now Mamluks needed Ottoman naval expertise and gunpowder know-how. In 1516 Sultan Selim, victorious over the Safavîs and secure in his eastern marches, decided to move south. He defeated the Mamluks north of Aleppo and captured Syria. The following winter his army, aided by the navy along the route in Palestine and Sinai, marched on Cairo itself. Early in 1517 he broke

Mamluk resistance outside the capital and brought the sultanate to an end. Full mastery over Egypt was a process that continued at least throughout the following decade, but at his death Sultan Selim left his son Suleiman a much enlarged empire. During his long reign from 1520 to his death in 1566 Sultan Suleiman continued the struggle against the Safavîs and wrested Iraq from their control. He also dealt with the Portuguese danger in the Indian Ocean by establishing a naval command at Suez and in the Arabian Sea; by mid-sixteenth century the Ottomans and the Portuguese had reached a modus vivendi which restored to the Ottoman Levant a healthy share of the spice trade.

Replacing the Mamluk sultans in Syria and Egypt also made the Ottoman sultans the rulers of the Hijaz, the birthplace of Islam and the setting of the holy cities of Mecca and Medina. Ruling Jerusalem directly as an Ottoman district and governing the Hijaz through the sharifs from their base in Jidda, the Ottomans became the pre-eminent power in Sunni Islam. In eastern Anatolia and in Iraq, captured from the Safavîs, the Ottomans had many Shi'î subjects but after the initial epic and vital clash gave way to periodic invasions of Safavî lands the Ottomans developed their imperial ideology to include leadership of the Islamic community and defence of the true faith against Safavî heretics and Habsburg Holy Roman emperors.

Institutions and Ideologies

Whereas the Safavî Oghuz, settled in Iran, conformed to the model of the Turko-Iranian polity, the Ottomans had the curious task of creating distinct military and civilian officers out of the human material they had available to them in Anatolia and in their European territories. Rising from the rough frontier instead of the more sophisticated, Persianised centres of culture in Anatolia, the Ottoman court as well as its periphery were Turkish speakers and remained so even when the dynasty attained great power and prestige. The ethnic-functional division between a Turkish military and a Persianised civilian administration simply did not happen to a full extent. The scribes of course maintained Persian traditions to an extent both in their book-keeping and in their literary efforts, but in the new capital Constantinople/Istanbul as well as in the flourishing Anatolian and Balkan urban milieu Turkish was established as a legitimate, eventually the preferred language of expression in history writing, literary efforts, and other products of high culture, hitherto considered the exclusive domain of Persian. Even the *ulamâ*, at least in Anatolia and the Balkan provinces, replaced Arabic with their native Turkish not only in such mundane tasks as keeping court records and issuing legal documents, but also in learned discourse.

While Turkish triumphed as the literary and spoken language of Ottoman Rome, ethnic Turks were limited in their political and military roles. Some just managed to receive revenue grants for military service but their holdings were not hereditary, their sons had to prove their own prowess to be granted revenues. For a Muslim-born Turk the way to join the ruling elite was rather through a madrasa education to serve as a member of the ulama or in the scribal profession. For the military-administrative elite, normally made up of ethnic Turks in the Turko-Persian model, the Ottomans created a new 'Roman' race, a new blend, Turkish-speaking and Muslim, but from non-Muslim, non-Turkish origins. The emergence of this 'rûmî' ethnicity was partly due to intermingling in the normal course of events in Anatolia and in the Balkans, especially in urban environments. But there was also a deliberate attempt in elite households: revenue grants to officers and even to relatively minor cavalrymen assumed that the holder would maintain an official household, a retinue proportionate to the amount of revenues. In the case of a cavalryman stationed in a village, collecting the local revenues made up of agricultural taxes as well as fees and fines charged in the course of his duties in keeping the peace, his retinue might consist of two or three local lads volunteering for military service. Higher ranking officers were expected to maintain military households numbering dozens of retainers. District governors and governors general of provinces fielded hundreds of warriors under their banners. As for the sultan himself, his revenues allowed him to maintain household troops in the tens of thousands.

Large-scale military households were a long-established feature of Islamic polities at least since Umayyad times and it might be said that the system reached its apogee in the Mamluk sultanate where the principle of dynastic succession was curbed in favour of a mamluk commander acclaimed as sultan. Such households were made up of slaves specially trained and groomed for military service and higher office; they were also deliberately alienated from the native population. Unquestioned personal loyalty to the master of the household, literally the owner of the mamluks, was the justification of the system. Mamluk slaves were outsiders, originally non-Muslim (for Muslims could not be enslaved though slaves would become Muslims), most, Turks and Slavs, from the Eurasian steppe. Removed from their original homeland and family ties, placed within a polity where they were deliberately kept apart from the society at large, these highly trained and effective military households formed the underpinnings of political power.

In Arab and Persian lands military slaves were mostly of Turkish origin and maintained a Turkish ethos. In Ottoman Rome the irony was that since ethnic Turks formed the dominant if not the majority element in language and society at large, slaves in military retinues, at least those in the sultanic and grandee households, had by definition to be from a non-Turkish background, though Turkified and Islamised after recruitment. The Ottomans utilised all the traditional sources of recruitment: captured in battle or raids, received as presents from tributary chieftains, or purchased. There also developed a uniquely Ottoman method, one descriptively called *devshirme*, gathering: these were young men on the threshold of puberty taken from their rural, Christian families in Ottoman domains and drafted into royal service. In classical Islamic law non-Muslims within an Islamic polity would have been classified as poll-tax (*jizya*) paying protected people of the book (*dhimmi*) and therefore exempt from this human levy. The origin of *devshirme* recruitment is obscure but it may have developed at first in the frontier zone where, in the shifting boundaries and loyalties, who was subject to Ottoman rule and who an outsider may have been difficult to determine. In any case, the legality of *devshirme* recruitment did not seem to have exercised Ottoman rulers; the *ulamâ* felt they had to justify it only a century after it was first practised.

The hand-picked *devshirme* boys stood apart from men captured in battle or in raids: frontier lords may have drafted such boys for a short time in earlier days but soon, in the first half of the fifteenth century, *devshirme* were destined only for the sultan's household and later in the century came to dominate the top offices of the realm both as higher-ranking provincial officers and in central government. Other slaves, some said to be 'volunteers' from Ottoman lands, some taken in the Mediterranean, or along the central or eastern European frontiers, formed the backbone of grandee households. Taken together these 'new Turks', so to speak, came to represent Ottoman Rome par excellence. European visitors, who conceived of the Ottomans as 'Turks' and their realm as the 'Turkish Empire', talked and wrote in undisguised surprise about meeting 'a Turk, but English born', or German, Russian, Italian, Greek, or Serbian. A Polish embassy to Istanbul had a young secretary who sought and was granted permission to talk to his brother who was by then 'a Turk' in the sultan's palace service. Often the wives of these 'new Turks' were themselves equally foreign-born young women who came out of palace service at the same time as their husbands to form a new Ottoman household at the young man's first appointment to independent office. By the mid-sixteenth century the Ottoman military-administrative elite was made up of these new Turkish-speaking Muslim officers who called themselves not Turkish but 'Roman' or 'Ottoman'; it was in this sense that Ottoman writers could comment that the 'Ottomans' took the best qualities of many nations and blended them into a new, superior race: they may not have known of expanding the gene pool, but they thought they observed the benefits. The Ottoman Romans distinguished themselves from ethnic Turks, functionally if the Turkish-born were fellow members of the elite as bureaucrats or *ulamâ* members, socially and politically from the urban and rural Turks, subjects of the Ottoman sultan as much as Greeks or Armenians or Arabs. The Ottoman dynasty, too, was as much a product of this new blend as their servitors. From the beginnings of the family of Osman, the beys made marriage alliances with neighbouring Byzantine or Serbian princesses. Later the sultans chose not to continue such marriages but sired their sons and daughters with harem favourites of various ethnic backgrounds brought up in the palace. The language of the dynasty as well as of the polity remained Turkish, but not, strictly speaking, as a mother tongue.

Ottoman dynastic power was based on this group of Ottoman Romans, many of whom received their education and training in the imperial palace. When they received independent office outside of palace service the sultan's servitors headed their own households formed, like the imperial palace, of slave servitors though not of *devshirme* origin. If, in one sense, the Ottoman state was the rule and reign of the sultans, in another, equally valid sense it can be said to have been the conglomeration of all the households, the sultan's as well as those of his great officers. The whole system can be defined as consisting of the sultan and all the independent office-holders with assigned revenue sources as livings, *dirlik* in Ottoman usage: the sultan, a few dozen vezirs and pashas, several hundred provincial officers, and tens of thousands of cavalrymen around the realm made up this Ottoman class.

In contrast, the Safavî empire was centred on a charismatic shah. The first shah, Ismâ'il, invincible until Chaldiran, was the anointed leader of his Turkoman followers, Âzerbayjanî and Anatolian alike. To achieve a greater degree of internal integration than the Aqquyunlu Turkoman sultanate had been able to, Shah Ismâ'il initiated a programme of converting all his subjects, town-dwellers, nomads and peasants, and of whatever ethnic background, to Shi'ism. Followers of the Safavî brotherhood had been close to the Shi'i version of Islam in any case, but for the Sunni majority in his realm this forced conversion was revolutionary. The fact that the programme was achieved within a generation or two is a truly remarkable historical phenomenon. Furthermore, this messianic movement was not specific to any particular region. The Safavî message and the call was for all Muslims. Once the transfer of power from Aqquyunlu to Safavî was accomplished the revolution was carried elsewhere, mainly to those areas where the natural constituents still lived: Ottoman Anatolia was the first target; Mamluk Syria was also threatened; areas of eastern Iran and Turkestan in Transoxania were invaded. Shah Ismâ'il and his successors were checked in their ambitions by Ottoman firepower in the west, stiff Uzbek resistance in Central Asia and by the rise of Babur's Mughals in Afghanistan. The movement meant to conquer and convert the Turko-Persian Islamic world was thus hemmed in in greater Iran and turned into a regional Shi'î empire, its messianic zeal curbed and spent.

The Turkoman adherents of the movement at its inception were reorganised into uymaq groupings based on provenance even more than on ancient Oghuz tribal affiliations. The uymaqs were settled in various parts of the Safavî realm, their leaders as governors. True to Turkish dynastic politics, as in the Ottoman case, princes were also sent out to provincial commands. But with ideological impetus gone the institutional weaknesses became apparent. The policy of 'Shi'ification' of the realm had been successful and gave Safavî society a considerable degree of cohesion, but the conception of the shah as messianic leader died with Shâh Ismâ'il in 1524. His son and successor Shâh Tahmâsb ruled with great authority but when his long reign came to an end in 1576 dynastic struggles plunged the realm into turmoil. The factional politics of princes and uymaq leaders, divisions in court and provinces reduced the earlier Safavî dream to ordinariness.

When, after a decade of faltering, Shâh Abbâs emerged as a strong ruler he had to reorganise his empire to strengthen its institutions. First he had to deal with the Ottoman threat. The Ottomans had followed up their initial defeat of the Safavîs by conquering Baghdad and Basra. After Tahmâsb's death the Ottomans reopened hostilities, this time marching in the north, through the southern Caucasus, invading Âzerbayjân, and gaining the silk production on Caspian shores. The Ottoman invasion allowed Shâh Abbâs to reunite his Turkoman forces. Although defeated and forced to retreat, accepting loss of his territories to Ottomans in 1590, he bided his time and renewed hostilities once he had dealt with the Uzbek threat to his lands and while the Ottomans were engaged in a long war against the Habsburgs. In a war that continued intermittently for the next four decades Shâh Abbâs first regained his losses in Âzerbayjân and Georgia, then he attacked Ottoman Iraq, capturing Baghdad after a century of Ottoman rule. The Ottomans soon recovered Baghdad but only after Shâh Abbâs's death. The 1639 treaty between the two empires concluded a war that had lasted intermittently since 1578; the boundary set in the treaty was merely a return to the status quo established by Sultan Suleyman and Shâh Tahmâsb in the middle of the previous century.

Reorganisation and Reorientation

Shâh Abbâs was able to take the struggle to the Ottomans because he set his rule on much firmer foundations. Shrewd enough to realise that with the founding ideology of his forefathers long diminished he had to strengthen his rule by other means, he decided to emulate the royal institution surrounding and supporting the Ottoman sultan. He needed his own household troops to balance the military power of the Turkoman commanders, so he drafted his slave-soldiers from the Caucasus, mainly from Georgia. He needed greater investment in firearms, muskets for his household troops and an effective artillery. To achieve this end he needed to bolster his royal revenues, not by appropriating revenue-grants allocated to provincial military, but by enhancing his revenue base. In both empires small-scale revenue-grants comprised agrarian revenues, collected mostly in kind. As the size of a revenue-grant increased so naturally did the community that provided its income. In towns and cities, the command and revenues of which were allocated to high-ranking officers, a greater proportion of the revenue came from commercial and industrial activities and so provided more cash to the holder. The ruler's own revenue sources included the most important cash sources in the realm, customs duties on international trade and commercial taxes. It follows that in both empires increase in foreign trade enhanced the ruler's revenues, hence the age-old tradition of building caravansarays, bridges, roads to facilitate trade and also providing security at mountain passes and river crossings. In the Ottoman case the sultan's revenues were greatly increased by the conquest of Mamluk lands and reviving the Indian Ocean trade through the Levant. As for the Safavîs, they looked to European partners to carry their silk, their most important cash export, south through the Gulf or north through the Caucasus.

Shâh Abbâs took great care to encourage silk production and exports. For their international expertise he patronised Armenian merchants. He had decided to move his capital further away from Ottoman threat to the heart of his realm, to the once-royal city of the Saljukîs, Isfahan. Shâh Abbâs rebuilt the city on a grand scale befitting the capital of his great empire as the symbol of his royal power. As part of his urban programme he resettled an Armenian community in Isfahan. In close proximity to the shah, the merchants of New Julfa enjoyed his protection; their rigorous engagement in international trade, especially in the export of Safavî silk in all directions, north to Russia, east to India, as well as to Europe, supplied the income with which Shâh Abbâs paid for his musket-bearing household troops and his new gunpowder empire.

If the Safavî shah learned from the example of his mighty neighbours, the Ottomans returned the compliment. As the Safavîs discovered ideology alone could not guarantee success, the Ottomans felt the need to hone the ideological basis of their empire. During the formative centuries of Ottoman polity, as a 'rûmî' identity had been forged, the sultans ruled over a population including large non-Muslim communities. The Ottoman sultan was the refuge of all his subjects regardless of religious identity; he projected justice as the foundation of his rule, and *qânûn* imperial law as the cornerstone of his justice. Ottoman political theory, mainly articulated in history writing, justified a powerful ruler and his *qânûn* law as necessary to keep the order of the world. Dursun Beg who wrote the history of Mehmed the Conqueror (of Constantinople) at the close of the fifteenth century argues that whereas God entrusts a prophet with divine, eternal law, *shar'ia*, he also supports a ruler who imposes his *qânûn* law in each age. 'Divine right of kingship' may have been a European theoretical construct but Dursun Beg's formulation comes very close to its spirit.

In the course of the sixteenth century Ottoman writers posited various ideological bases for sultanic rule. For a generation or two after the conquest of Constantinople 'caesar' was added to Ottoman imperial titles. Ottoman court historians evoked Alexander the Great and ancient Persian kingship and depicted the sultans as their rightful heirs. From the middle of the century they also brought out Islamic themes. Ottoman control of Islamic holy cities and their mastery over the annual hajj pilgrimage, as well as the demographic change in favour of Muslims as a consequence of southern expansion all played a part. The old Islamic ideal of a single *umma* community under the leadership of a single caliphal political authority had long since become a distant memory. Muslim political writers had long accepted the reality of many rulers in the world of Islam and thought righteous rulers all could be styled a caliph in their own realms. On that basis even in the fifteenth century Ottoman sultans had styled themselves 'commander of the faithful'. In the mid-sixteenth century a retired grand vezir, Lutfi Pasha, wrote a treatise confirming this view of the multi-caliphate but argued that Ottoman sultans could be called the greatest caliphs of the Islamic world. At about the same time Sultan Suleyman also wanted to make sure that his sultanic *qânûn* was fully in accordance with Islamic *shar'ia*; this was accomplished by the great jurisconsult Ebus'suud Efendi. By the end of the century the Ottomans routinely used Islamic terminology in reference to the sultan, his reign, and his armies, as the champions of Sunni Islam. The epic struggles against the Catholic Habsburgs, both in the Mediterranean and in central Europe may have played a part in the Islamisation of Ottoman ideology, but it was confronting the Safavî 'heretics' that truly established the Sunni Islamic nature of the polity.

Institutionally, too, there were changes. The Ottoman sultans had increased their household troops to such an extent that their pay, though not increased, nevertheless became a huge burden on the sultan's own treasury. Imperial revenues had increased considerably with cash sources in the Levant, Egypt, and further south. Yet the amount of silver in the realm was not sufficient for the degree of monetarisation necessary to support the pay for imperial expenditures. Restored trade in the south and increased trade in the Mediterranean brought much needed European silver (ultimately from Mexico and Peru by way of Spain and Italy), but much of it was expended on inconclusive warfare against the Habsburgs and the Safavîs and also for luxury imports, furs from Russia and jewels and fine textiles from India. Around 1600, therefore, the Ottomans too had their 'time of troubles' characterised by unrest among household troops and uprisings among provincial troops, especially in Anatolia. When these disturbances were finally brought under control and peace established along the borders, the administration of the empire was reorganised along new lines, according to new principles.

Earlier, 'classic', Ottoman rule was based on the principle of an egalitarian agrarian society, the peasants allocated plots of land large enough to support a family. The plots were equal not in size but in productivity; smaller plots were given in better-watered parts or with richer soil, somewhat larger in mediocre land and largest in stony, difficult areas. This conception of equality was carried into other spheres; money fines and non-Muslim per capita tax (*jizya*) were collected at the ratio of 1:2:4 from the poorest subjects, middling and better-off respectively. Land dues and share of production, as well as incidental dues and fines were paid to the revenue-grant holder, a cavalryman, an officer, pashas, vezirs, and the ruler himself. In the Ottoman realm there were about 50,000 cavalrymen and several hundred provincial officers with their own revenue sources, living close to the peasants and townsmen in their domains. The holders of larger revenue grants were of course much more distant, many of them, certainly the vezirs and of course the ruler, in the capital. Such officers sent officials from their own households to manage the revenue sources which, in the case of the sultan, were dispersed throughout the realm. The larger the revenue source, as a rule, the more distant the holder: this held true in both empires. The Safavîs had allowed their Turkoman commanders to hold large revenues in the provinces; the efficiency and the superiority of the Ottoman system was due to the large number of small-scale holdings.

Yet from around 1600 the need for cash in the sultan's treasury caused a shift away from smaller revenue grants to larger holdings; in this way, too, the Ottomans came to resemble the Safavîs. Revenues in large-scale holdings were often collected through tax-farming. Another change was to charge a collectivity, a village, say, or a community or a guild or a congregation, to be responsible for revenue collection within the community. The power and protection of the Ottoman state used to reach its individual subjects directly; from around 1600 corporate bodies, civic or ethnic or confessional, came to be addressed and held responsible. Such a system inevitably enhanced the role of local prominent men, Muslim *a'yân* notables, non-Muslim communal leaders, especially their clergy, and officials owing primary responsibility to a particular grandee rather than to a larger entity, a 'state'.

Ottoman and Safavî historiographical traditions treat the issue of 'state formation' very differently. Safavî historians see a twofold division of royal demesnes and the 'state' sector, state here comprising revenue sources allocated to officials and officers. This is a distinction between a 'privy purse' versus a 'public treasury' and is treated as the paradigm even in very recent analyses on Shâh Abbâs and his policy of royal power through trade and household-building. On the contrary, Ottoman historiography has analysed the emergence of state institutions, such as the imperial council and the central bureaucracy, from within the sultan's household. Beginning in the mid-sixteenth century, the central political problem was to determine the limits of sultanic power and the functioning of the imperial council under a policy-setting grand vezir. This tension was never resolved, even in the constitutional period at the end of the nineteenth century; how sultans and grand vezirs wielded power depended by and large on personal forcefulness and exigencies of particular periods. Yet the scribal bureaucracy, funded by the sultan's own household treasury until the seventeenth century, thereafter gained a degree of independence when many of them were allocated their own revenue sources. The civilian bureaucracy was strengthened even more when, as a result of defeat at the hands of a European coalition, eighteenth-century Ottoman government turned away from military conflict as chief instrument of foreign policy and adopted diplomacy as its main tool in dealing with European powers.

Perhaps the main distinction between the two empires, with important consequences to be felt to this day, was in the position of the *ulamâ* men of learning and religion and, by extension, the interpreters and administrators of Islamic law. In Safavî society the Shi'î *ulamâ* gained great power when the founding ethos of the polity forcefully converted its subjects to the Shi'î rite. Once the Safavî brotherhood lost its impetus, the *ulamâ* came to represent the religious conscience of the realm. Supported by generous pious foundations established by shahs and grandees, and wielding the power of interpreting and advancing *sharî'a* unmatched in Sunni society, they continued to exert great social influence independent of whatever political power the dynasty still held. Ottoman *ulamâ*, by contrast, had become state functionaries. An Ottoman *qâdî* magistrate was empowered by political authority; he administered not only *sharî'a* to Muslim Ottomans but *qânûn* law promulgated by sultanic authority to all subjects. Criminal and commercial law as well as administrative procedures and matters of taxation were all established by the sultan's firman. The *qâdî* magistrate was also required to oversee purely administrative matters and work closely with military-administrative provincial officials so that, in effect, they constituted a parallel administrative apparatus. Ottoman *qâdî*s, similar to other provincial officials, were shifted every year or so to a different location. Promotion to high office passed through many provincial appointments. True, some learned men preferred to stay in their hometowns. This was so especially in the Arab provinces. Such *ulamâ* families continued to play their traditional role as community leaders but however much they might be respected in their locality they could not achieve high office in the empire. In the eighteenth century Damascene *ulamâ* petitioned the sultan that they too wanted to be considered for positions at the centre of power. The sultan replied that they were by all means welcome to such consideration provided they learned Turkish and joined provincial rotation. Some, at least, took up the challenge; in the nineteenth century there were a growing number of Arabs-turned-Ottoman, if we can so designate them, holding high office in Istanbul.

When Ottoman military might faltered, defeated by technologically advanced European armies and navies, when central power was diffused and devolved to provincial and regional notables, the social fabric of the empire was held together by the scribal bureaucracy at the centre and by the magistrates throughout the realm. By the end of the eighteenth century, even before Napoleon invaded Egypt, the Ottoman centre decided that to survive it had to learn from the example of Europe. During the nineteenth-century programme of European-style modernisation it was the civilian administrators, from the scribal chambers as well as from among the *ulamâ*, who were at the forefront of reform. Their policies were successful enough that Ottoman central power once again extended to its provinces. There was, however, a cost. With Islam setting the ideological tone, with Muslims as the self-styled 'real Ottomans', with Muslim provincial notables wielding increasing power through the eighteenth century, non-Muslims were seen as the subject flock. *Rayah*, a term once comprising all subjects of the 'just sultan', came to refer only to the neglected, often ignored non-Muslims by 1800. At the dawn of modern history, in the age of revolutions, Ottoman internal developments coincided with the new European ethos of national liberation to goad non-Muslim subjects in Ottoman Europe to ever-louder demands for self-determination and autonomy.

While the Ottoman dynastic empire survived until the end of the Great War by reforming and reinventing itself, the Safavî dynasty collapsed at the beginning of the eighteenth century. Shâh Abbâs the Great left his successors a greatly enhanced royal authority but this was squandered in successive generations. The royal household, designed by Abbâs as a force with firepower, instead became bloated with sinecures. The shah's hold on his provinces weakened, Afghan tribesmen rose against Safavî rule and invaded Isfahan itself. Russia and the Ottoman empire both tried to exploit these disturbances by advancing on Safavî provinces in the Caucasus. Nadir Khan, a Turkoman supporter of the Safavî claimant, defeated the Afghans and fought the Russian and Ottoman invaders; wielding supreme power and following military successes he soon declared himself the shah. For all his military prowess Nadir Shâh was not able to establish a lasting political system and remains an interesting footnote in Ottoman–Safavî relations: he formally suggested to the Ottoman sultan and his *ulamâ* that Shi'î Islam should henceforth be considered not a major cleavage but merely a fifth interpretation of *sharî'a* law to be placed on the same footing as the four Sunni schools. He may have hoped for a better integration into the Islamic *umma*, but his suggestion was rejected; when he was assassinated in 1747 any semblance of territorial unity was lost. The former Safavî realm was resurrected and central authority was re-established fifty years after Nadir Shâh's death, when another Turkoman power, the Qajars, ascended the throne of Iran which they placed in Tehran, closer to their own tribal power base. The history of Qajar Iran is no less interesting, in its own distinct way, than the history of Ottoman reform in the nineteenth century. The seeds of their relative success and failure were already sown by 1800: Qajar Iran was able to keep its territories intact due to the Safavî cement of society even though it was made up of disparate ethnic elements and even when it came under immense foreign pressure. The Ottoman empire gradually adopted championship of the Sunni Islamic world, even resurrecting the conception of a universal caliphate now held by the House of Osman, a policy which integrated Muslim subjects closer but was unable to counter non-Muslim demands for autonomy and independence. Safavî social cohesion lived on after the dynasty collapsed; the realm of the House of Osman was divided, even before its demise, into many constituent ethnic parts.

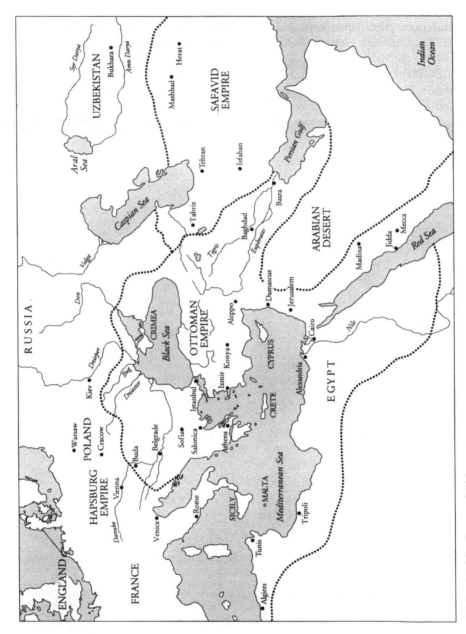

10.1 Middle East ca. 1600

CHAPTER ELEVEN

Urban Life and Middle Eastern Cities
The Traditional Arab City

ANDRÉ RAYMOND

From the 1920s onwards, a number of French Orientalist scholars, the principal creators of a significant body of research on the Arab cities of the Mediterranean, forged the concept of the 'Islamic' city. Stephen Humphreys has very properly emphasised this particularity in pointing out 'the great French tradition of Islamic urban studies' and in noting that, in this field, the period from the 1920s to the 1940s saw the development of 'a thin but steady stream of publications (the majority of them by French scholars) on various aspects of the topic.'[1]

An investigation in historical sociology might perhaps allow us to explain the marked interest shown by French scholars in this particular field. It is, of course, hardly unworthy of note that this trend in research, and its definition of an 'Islamic' city, emerged in North Africa, in what we might call the Orientalist school of Algiers. The important works of William Marçais ('L'Islamisme et la vie urbaine', 1928) and Georges Marçais ('L'Urbanisme musulman', 1939),[2] preceded and/or provided a framework for the publication of important monographs devoted to the great Arab cities of the Maghrib: Marrakesh, by Gaston Deverdun (1959), Rabat, by Jacques Caillé (1949), Fez, by Roger Le Tourneau (1949), and Algiers, by René Lespès (1930).[3] To this 'Maghribi' current was added what might be called the Damascus school, of which most notable works are those of Jean Sauvaget on Damascus and Aleppo (1934 and 1941) and Jacques Weulersse on Antioch (1934).[4] Marcel Clerget's book on Cairo (1934) naturally also belongs to this French tradition, and is all the more remarkable for being concerned with a city placed under British influence, in an Egypt still overcast by the imposing shadow of Cromer.[5] *A contrario*, the absence of any contemporaneous, basic study of Mosul or Baghdad in British-controlled Iraq, in itself an equally remarkable fact, confirms the pre-eminence of French scholarship at this time in urban studies of the Arab world. Nonetheless, the final formulation of the notion of the Islamic city was not reached until later, with Gustave von Grunebaum's article 'The Structure of the Muslim Town'. Published in 1955, this text effectively sums up the doctrine which had developed in French research from the 1920s to the 1950s.[6]

This body of work was developed in areas subject, at the time, to various forms of French authority – direct colonisation in Algeria, protectorates in Tunisia and Morocco, mandates in the Levant. There is thus nothing surprising in the fact that these texts clearly display the influence of a colonial spirit, a fact which doubtless partly explains the rather negative judgements they render on these traditional 'native' towns. The recourse of the first interpreters of Arab–Mediterranean urbanism to the epithet *'musulman'* in their description of the ancient cities they looked upon derived, also, from the Orientalists' propensity to describe all Islamised lands as totally conditioned by Islam. Islam, in their view, was a foundational and all-encompassing phenomenon; everything occurring within Islamic countries was therefore to be considered first and foremost as 'Islamic'. Robert Ilbert writes judiciously on this point that 'it is because most Orientalists posited a fundamental role for Islam in the structuring of space at the outset [of their studies] that they discovered it in their conclusions'.[7] We should not, then, be surprised to find Islam invoked in respect not only of religious institutions (obviously Islamic), political organisation and socio-economic activity, but also with reference to the physical structure of a town (for example, the configuration of a network of streets) or even the characteristics of a house – all of which could not be described as anything but 'Islamic'. Another major presupposition of Orientalist scholarship which strongly coloured this picture of the 'Islamic' city was the idea that all believers, as equals in religion before God, are held to constitute a unitary society within the bounds of the *umma*. This notion led scholars to posit the existence of a relatively homogeneous urban organisation, one that would minimise the importance of socio-economic stratification in urban struc-ture and habitat. The supposedly unitary character of the latter was stressed: 'the close vicinity of rich and poor families is the rule in Arab cities', wrote Antoine Abdel Nour . . . 'There was no real distinction in the city [of Aleppo] between rich and poor districts'.[8]

The Orientalist vision of the 'Islamic' city was, moreover, heavily influenced by the fact that French colonisation in both Maghrib and Mashriq developed in areas where ancient Greek and Roman civilisation had been expressed in admirable urban cre-ations, whose majestic remains, still visible from Volubilis to Palmyra via Timgad, Dougga, Leptis Magna and so many other sites, inspired an entirely comprehensible fascination. The scholars' admiration of an orderly urban system, one which deployed a rich civic and religious architecture and rested upon highly developed urban institutions, led them to cast a critical eye over Arab cities which seemed to them to have been conceived in precisely opposite terms: 'Nothing could be more alien to a Muslim town in the Maghrib than the rectilinear avenues of a Roman or modern city', notes Roger Le Tourneau with evident melancholy in a book devoted to the Muslim cities of North Africa.[9] The cultural shock provoked in the mind of someone like Jean Sauvaget by the comparison of ancient urbanism – whose traces in Syrian towns he sagaciously reads – with its 'Islamic' counterpart leads him to reconstitute, through a painstaking study of the contemporary street network, the probable structure of some of the great Greek and Roman metropolises: Laodicea (Lattakia), Beroea (Aleppo), Damascus.[10] This tendency to compare and contrast an urbanism of antiquity, with its omnipresent and prestigious achievements, with an Arab urbanism whose characteristics are so different, was all the more dangerous in that French colonisation was prone to present itself as taking up the inheritance of the Roman *imperium*. The return to a regular, orthogonal plan, which was endowed with an almost moral superiority over the supposed 'disorder' of Arab towns, appeared as the sign of a victory for civilisation and progress after an 'intermission' lasting some fifteen centuries; this is certainly the sentiment underlying the remark of Le Tourneau cited above, in which 'modern' (in this instance French) urbanism parallels that of Antiquity. Just as devastating was the comparison with the cities of medieval Europe, whose system of communes contributed to the rise of the west while the Muslim world began its slide into a long decline. Finding nothing in the works of the great theoreticians of urban society (Max Weber in particular) which might apply to the towns they were studying, specialists (of whom Jean Sauvaget is the clearest example) could only conclude that they were dealing with a type of urban life whose only definition was the woeful enumeration of *that which it lacked*: the regularity and institutions of Antiquity, the communal organisation of the European Middle Ages.

This moroseness was all the stronger for the tendency, generalised in French historiography at the time, to pass severe judgement on the 'Turkish' period which had everywhere (save Morocco) preceded French colonisation. This very negative view is naturally explained by the difficulties experienced by the Ottoman empire and the decline affecting it just as western imperialism began its dismemberment. It is also difficult to avoid thinking that, in blackening the memory of the 'pre-colonial' period, French academic specialists contributed, consciously or not, to the valorisation of Europe's salvific, civilising intervention. One could cite an abundance of negative considerations in respect of the Ottoman period; I will limit myself to two significant works, both of which are monumental contributions to urban history. Under the Ottomans, wrote Marcel Clerget, Cairo 'was slowly extinguished ... allowing the debris of its glorious past to crumble slowly ... Cairo was returned ... to the scattered habitations so much to the taste of the first Arabs ... Art, along with all other manifestations of intelligent and organised activity, died out'. In Aleppo, wrote Sauvaget, in conclusion to a book in which he had nonetheless recognised the dynamism and splendour of the city in Ottoman times, the 'factors of disaggregation are constantly renewed, their increasing momentum accelerating the dislocation of the urban centre. Aleppo of the Ottomans is but a visual trick (*trompe-l'oeil*): a sumptuous façade behind which lie only ruins'.[11]

These remarks sufficiently illustrate the negative characterisation of the 'Islamic' city as described by Orientalist scholars, a city defined more by that which it is not than by any positive features of its own. In physical appearance, it has lost the regularity of the ancient city, substituting for Greco-Roman orthogonal order a structure which apparently obeys no logical principle. Its streets follow a highly irregular pattern – worse, they frequently end in blind alleys. The reflections of Roger Le Tourneau on Maghribi towns are, in this respect, entirely characteristic of this school of thought: 'An aerial photograph of any Muslim town brings to mind Daedalus' labyrinth. Buildings, instead of being integrated into a preconceived whole, force communicating roads to bypass them, to thread their way as best they can around them. The result is an extraordinary multiplicity of blind alleys and roadways which are very rarely rectilinear'. Georges Marçais wonders, without proposing a response, about the idiosyncrasies which such disorder appears to reveal: 'It is not, besides, as if the Muslims, for all that they seem content with narrow roads, had not appreciated the advantage of a straight line as the route from one point to another.'[12] In the cities of Syria, the monuments of the Muslim town are nothing but the *degraded* image of a fine ancient order: 'The *suq*s, the *qaysariyya* and *khan* ... are merely the degenerate remains of the colonnaded avenue, the basilica, the agora', remarks Sauvaget, who furnishes a brilliant demonstration of the process by which the colonnaded street of antiquity was transformed into the Muslim *suq*.[13]

Scholars of the Syrian school, attentive observers of the imbrication of ancient remains in the 'Islamic' city, particularly emphasised the dislocation of a supposedly ill-articulated town, divided up into sectors, each turned in upon itself. Weulersse's work on Antioch describes a city deeply divided between its Turkish, Christian and Alawite communities. Immersed in an alien, Sunni rural world which it dominates and exploits without offering anything in return, the town is essentially 'parasitic'; it 'consumes without producing'.[14] The Algiers scholars appear to echo this conception in their insistence on describing a city inhabited by 'urbanites' (*baldi*) so foreign to the people beyond the walls that they can be described as a population apart. Pierre Boyer describes the 'Moors' of Algiers as an ethnic community, 'a population proud of its urban status, and which rejects any connection with Arabs or Berbers of the *bled* [countryside]. Indeed, their origins are sufficiently mixed among themselves so as to justify, in part, their pretensions'.[15] Sauvaget concludes vigorously: 'The Islamic city is no longer considered as an entity, as a complex and living being in itself; it is no longer anything but an assemblage of individuals and their contradictory interests.'[16]

The Islamic city was incapable of endowing itself with communal institutions, it lacked administration – but how could it be otherwise? 'The status of towns', notes Sauvaget, again, in his article on Damascus, 'is nowhere the object of any particular disposition of Islamic law. There are no longer any municipal institutions.' The Islamic city is a non-city, Muslim urbanism a non-urbanism. Sauvaget goes so far as to say, in the conclusion to his work on Aleppo, that the Islamic period 'brings no positive contribution ... One can attribute to it nothing but the dislocation of the urban centre'. The work of Islam 'is essentially negative'; the city, having become 'an inconsistent and inorganic assemblage of districts', is 'nothing so much as the negation of urban order'.[17]

It would be difficult to press further the negation of one's object of study, and one can see how, in their description of this non-town, essentially characterised by what it lacks, the Orientalist interpreters of the Islamic city find themselves rather short of positive material, labouring with difficulty to define its global configuration. Evoking 'the structure of the Muslim town', von Grunebaum mentions two 'focal' points, the great mosque (*jami*) and the market (*suq*); he is particularly concerned to define the institutional workings of a city to which Muslim law, in his view as in that of Sauvaget, 'does not concede a special status'.[18] In short, the Orientalists consider that this 'type' of city is characterised by a mosque situated in a central location, which is no specificity at all, since one could say as much of the cathedral churches of medieval cities that no one, in contrast, proposes calling 'Christian'. Its markets are closely linked to the mosque; Louis Massignon evokes the examples of the exchange (*sagha*) and spun-thread (*ghazl*) markets, and elevates to the status of a principle the notion of the invariable location of major markets, characterised by their spatial concentration and the strict specialisation of activities which take place there. The Islamic city has its public baths (*hammam*) whose function accompanies the ritual prayers, but this institution, too, existed in the ancient cities, in a technologically sophisticated and architecturally splendid form. The presence of a citadel and, perhaps, a palace of the prince, are hardly any more distinctive. The traditional house, with its interior courtyard, is similarly described as characteristically 'Islamic', although its archetypal pattern is found in every ancient Mediterranean civilisation. In such a town, again, function a certain number of Islamic institutions: justice dispensed by the *qadi*, censure of morals and markets by the *muhtasib* ... All of which boils down to saying that the 'Muslim' town is the place where the Muslims live, a tautology which is of no value whatsoever in constructing an analysis of the organisation of urban space.

Finally, let us observe that this 'Islamic' city is described within a geographical frame which is most often limited to *either* the Maghrib *or* the Mashriq, and is very rarely extended to encompass the whole of the Mediterranean Arab world. As regards its temporal location, the 'Islamic city' is timeless: Georges Marçais, in his 'L'Urbanisme musulman', refers, from one page to another, to the Fustat of the Fatimids, the Fez of the Marinid sultans, and the Algiers of the Ottoman deys to describe a city whose living, Maghribi models (which he had before his eyes) appear to embody, without differentiation, both the 'classical' and the modern town.

It would be tiresome to examine in detail the process through which this Orientalist concept of 'the Islamic city' has been subjected to thorough critique and revision. It will be enough to point out that it was towards the end of the colonial period, from the 1940s onward, that the framework within which these theses had developed was called into question. As the colonisers' self-assurance, and their tendency to nourish prejudices against the civilisation they studied, began to run out of steam, local scholars emerged who progressively transformed themselves from simple, more or less anonymous, informants (whose task was to provide 'raw data' to European specialists who alone were invested with the more noble office of interpretation) into researchers in their own right.[19] The perspectives of scholarship were thus modified, and the new attention paid to societies hitherto considered as backward contributed to the effort to understand, from within, traditional systems different to those familiar to Europeans. In the particular area which concerns us here, we can date the end of 'classic' Orientalism to 1957, the year in which the second volume of Gibb and Bowen's monumental *Islamic Society and the West* appeared. The title alone describes simultaneously an unachievable ambition (announcing a general 'survey' which was impossible at the time, given the state of knowledge of the sources) and its biased conception (a palpably Eurocentric enterprise).[20] The publication, in 1955, of Gustave von Grunebaum's article may then be considered the swan song of the Orientalist theory of the Islamic city, of which his paper is also the epitome.

Equally important was the rediscovery of Ottoman sources for the history of the Arab provinces of the empire, a development which followed the movement begun at the end of the 1930s for Turkey and the central imperial regions by Ömer Lutfi Barkan and his school. Stephen Humphreys, again, has rightly emphasised the importance of this revolution in the use of archival sources,[21] which enabled the development of a more detailed understanding of the administrative, social and economic conditions in which the last phase of the history of Arab cities took place before the great rupture of modernisation in the nineteenth century. The notion of an irremediable urban decay in the Ottoman period, and the conception which had been held of the cities' 'non-administration', were subjected to a re-examination which undermined a certain number of Orientalist assumptions. The interventions, in a field of study previously dominated by Arabists and Islamicists, of specialists from other disciplines – historians, geographers, sociologists and anthropologists, scholars like Claude Cahen and Eugen Wirth – also contributed to a revision of the fundamental Orientalist conception of 'the Islamic factor' as the unique key to the explanation of every phenomenon analysed.

Various Orientalist prejudices were thus critically re-examined. It is a well-known fact, although the Orientalists have sometimes appeared to forget it, that the 'Islamic' world constitutes an enormous and prodigiously varied whole, of which the Arab world is only the western promontory. Oleg Grabar, writing on artistic forms (but the logic is equally applicable to urbanism), points out the difficulty of employing a single qualificative concept, 'Islamic', to account for phenomena and production concerning countries with such varied historic and cultural traditions, such different natural characteristics, as those existing in the 'Muslim world' in its broadest sense, from Morocco to China, from central Asia to North Africa.[22] It thus appears indispensable to take account of specific regions within the wider Muslim world.

The idea that there exists an 'Islamic' city which one might study without taking into consideration the whole historical evolution from the Muslim conquest to the nineteenth century is just as problematic. Jean-Claude Garcin is entirely justified on this point when he observes that the development of a Muslim society over a period of twelve centuries must render problematic 'a *ne varietur* interpretation of "the Islamic city" '.[23] Consideration of chronology is indispensable for an understanding of the successive variety of 'Islamic' cities existing from the moment of their foundation through the classical and modern periods. Contrary to the expectations of the Orientalists, the ancient city whose remains we know and examine *is* the modern city, that is to say, in most cases, the 'Ottoman' city: the city of the 'classical' period cannot be reached save through a *reconstruction* achieved by reference to historical sources.

Progress in the understanding of the cities of late antiquity has, moreover, contributed to dissipating the illusion of a Roman and Byzantine urban ideal contrasted to the Arab city which was substituted for it, the degraded inheritor of a perfect patrimony. To take an example in Syria, where this problem of 'Arab succession' was a theme abundantly addressed in the work of Jean Sauvaget, the research carried out at Apamea by J.-Cl. Balthy has demonstrated that the weakening of the ancient order can be read in the plan of the city several centuries before the Arab conquest.[24] Consideration of progressive Arab migration into the towns, occurring well before the conquest itself, should also encourage us to address the problem of Arabisation in somewhat different terms. In fact, the discovery of a progressive degradation of the ancient order is not an entirely new fact to specialists of Arab cities; conscious of this, and as if moved by a final moment of remorse, Sauvaget wrote on the penultimate page of his *Aleppo* that the reduction of the framework of urbanised life to more rudimentary forms had begun under the Byzantines, but he did not draw the conclusions that his remark entailed.[25] Claude Cahen suggested in a more logical fashion, in 1958, that it was necessary to avoid viewing pre-Islamic urban history 'through a clichéd imagery of the impeccable ancient city ... The city which Islam inherits is no longer the city of antiquity'. This theme was repeated with convincing force by Samuel Stern ('The Constitution of the Islamic City') and most particularly by Hugh Kennedy in his article 'From Polis to Madina', where he observes that, in the urban communities of fifth and sixth century Syria, 'there was no classical town plan to affect later growth ... The "streets" were narrow, winding paths, there was no agora, no colonnades, no theatre'.[26] Many of the (negative) aspects which the Orientalists thought characteristic of the 'Islamic' city were, therefore, apparent in the 'ancient' city which preceded it, and resulted from three centuries' evolution of urban development. 'The late Roman cities in the East were evolving towards the model of the Islamic city which was characterized by the looseness of its structure and the absence of corporate municipal institutions', notes Liebeschuetz in conclusion to his work on the later development of Roman cities.[27] Moreover, the recently uncovered remains of Umayyad re-use of the ancient colonnades of Palmyra and Bet Shean (ancient Scythopolis), which illustrate Sauvaget's theory, also indicate that this development was gradual and long-term,[28] another consideration against positing an overly absolute opposition between the two urban types.

It seems appropriate, having gone through this re-examination of the Orientalist view of the 'Islamic city', to focus instead on what we might rather term the 'traditional' city, that is, the town as it existed before the great transformations of every kind produced by the nineteenth century. The 'traditional city' offers particularly favourable scope for research: we can observe it directly through the study of what remains of the old cities' centres (what geographers call *madina*s); information regarding it is especially abundant thanks to the archives of the Ottoman period; and it was the object of a scientific cartography whose first example, at the very end of the Ottoman period, is the plan of Cairo in the *Description de l'Égypte*. I think also that, since we are unable really to pinpoint the characteristics of an 'Islamic' city, a precise understanding of which is denied us by the state of research outside the Arab world and whose reality is, in any event, doubtful, we would do better to limit the area under consideration to the Mediterranean Muslim world, expanded to include Morocco, Iraq and the Arabian peninsula, an area about which we have adequate documentation and which is the only one for which it appears possible to define coherent characteristics. I would hope, then, to be able to define a 'traditional Arab-Mediterranean city' which might be found from Marrakesh to Baghdad and from Aleppo to San'a, and whose specificities might be compared to those of other cities found in other areas of the wider Muslim world, or belonging to earlier historical periods.

The Traditional Arab City in the Mediterranean Region

The principal error of the Orientalists was no doubt to suggest (or, in the case of Sauvaget, baldly to assert) that the 'Islamic' city was anomic, even anarchic. This was to neglect the fact, nonetheless blindingly self-evident, that, constituted as it is by the conglomeration of a large number of inhabitants, and site of highly specialised activities, a city cannot be anything but a complex system, one which enables the accomplishment of certain functions to the benefit of its population. The very idea of the possibility of urban anarchy is nonsense. The task is not to limit oneself to drawing a debilitating contrast with other urban systems (whether ancient or medieval European) which allows only deficiencies to appear, leading in consequence to a judgement on the 'Islamic city' as a non-city. It is rather to bring to light the specific elements which allow us to understand its constitution and functioning. In short, the traditional Arab city must also be considered as *an urban system* with its own originality, endowed with its own specific characteristics, whose structure must be analysed and whose workings understood, even though they may obey principles different to those with which we are familiar. It is to an analysis of the principal characteristics of this urban system, which may be only more or less specific but whose gathering together constitutes a distinctive whole, that the following discussion turns.[29]

The fundamental feature of the structure of the traditional Arab city is the very pronounced opposition between a 'public' centre, where religious, cultural and economic activities are concentrated, and a vast 'private' zone which is principally residential. The city's vigorous 'centrality' is revealed in the contiguity of the great mosque, where collective Friday prayer is said and which is often a centre of higher learning (al-Qarawiyyin in Fez, al-Zaytuna in Tunis, al-Azhar in Cairo, the Umayyad mosque in Damascus) to the zone of great markets (*suq*s) which are characterised by the professional and geographical specialisation of their activities. This market district can play a unifying role where the city is divided into sectors which are strongly individualised by religion or ethnicity; in Jerusalem, divided into Muslim, Latin and Armenian Christian, Jewish and Maghribi quarters, and in Antioch, with its Sunni Turkish, Christian and Alawite quarters, the markets constitute a sort of mediating space, permitting the whole population to pursue essential economic activities in some unity. The centres of political power are sometimes situated in this area, as with the citadels of Damascus and Aleppo, but this is neither a generalised pattern (the citadel of Cairo and the Bardo of the Muradids and Husaynids in Tunis are both located outside the centre) nor invariable (in Algiers, the centre of power was moved from the heart of the city to the Qasbah in 1817).

In the absence of precise information regarding pre-Islamic Arab cities, it is difficult to define the origins of this strict division of space[30] which appears, however, to be a long-standing feature. It appears clearly on city plans, in the presence around the principal mosque of the great *suq*s and, above all, the principal caravansarays (whose name varies from one region to another: *khan, funduq, wakala, samsara*), where the most essential commerce (wholesale and international trade) and particularly import-ant artisanal activities take place. Here we find a network of regular and relatively wide roads, connected via other streets more or less directly to the outskirts of the town. The most remarkable examples of these central arteries are the triple line of great markets in Aleppo (a legacy of the classical Roman era) and the Qasaba of Cairo (laid out by the Fatimids at the foundation of the city in 969). In Algiers, the 'lower city' near the waterfront corresponded to this centre; 75 per cent of its streets were open at either end, while the upper town, what we now think of as the 'Casbah' proper, contained only 40 per cent of open-ended streets (60 per cent being impasses). This relative regularity, which contradicts the stereotype of an anarchic 'Islamic' street-plan, was evidently indispensable for the development of the intense activity of the city's centre, which generated a large volume of traffic in the movements of both people and merchandise. This central district had such a strongly marked character that it was sometimes indicated by a particular name, as in the case of the *mdineh* (*madina*, 'city') in Aleppo and *al-rab'*, the covered markets of Tunis.[31] It is import-ant to note here the work of Baber Johansen, who has shown how the *fuqaha* (jurists) of the Hanafi school conceived of this division of the city, precisely into two regions, 'public' and 'private', in each of which the law was to be applied differently; the responsibility for unpunished crimes (*qasama*) fell in the former case to the public authorities and in the second to the residents themselves.[32]

The 'public' zone of the city lay around the great mosque, which also served as a centre of higher education boasting large numbers of masters and pupils; in the eighteenth century, al-Azhar is estimated to have had some three thousand *shaykh*s and students. Added to this were numerous other religious institutions and schools (*madrasa*s) which were also simultaneously places of prayer and of teaching. Eco-nomic activity often developed around the 'market halls' (in different regions called *qaysariyya* or *bedestan*), enclosed buildings accommodating trade in luxury commod-ities such as fabrics and imported goods. The Fez *qaysariyya*, situated between the sanctuary of Moulay Idris, the city's founder, and the Qarawiyyin mosque, and

Cairo's *Khan al-khalili* in the neighbourhood of the Qasaba and al-Azhar, are models of this kind of central economic infrastructure. Louis Massignon amply demonstrated how markets like the *sagha* (for the manufacture of, and trade in, precious objects, also the centre of exchange) were ordinarily situated in a very central spot, near the great mosque.[33] From the presence of a large number of caravansarays in this district – 19 in the Aleppo *mdineh*, for example, covering a total area of 4.3 hectares – we can trace the extent of this central zone, which varied with the importance of the city and its economic activity: 1.1 hectares in Algiers, 6 in Tunis, 8.7 in Damascus, 10.6 in Aleppo, 11.8 in Baghdad, but 60 in Cairo, the Ottoman empire's second city. In Cairo, the Qahira district founded by the Fatimids contained 229 caravansarays (of a total of 348 whose location is known); Cairo's central artery, the Qasaba, alone held 57 per cent of the fortunes of the city's artisans and merchants in only 1.2 per cent of its total area. This central zone was liable to develop by encroaching on the surrounding residential area – this was the case of the Aleppo *mdineh*, which grew from 6 hectares at the time of the Mamluks to 11 at that of the Ottomans, and of the centre of Cairo, which expanded from 30 to 60 hectares over the same period. This layout endowed the urban structure with a certain plasticity. The shape of the economic zone underwent continuous alteration with the development of the city and changes in the relative importance of different activities, with trades whose importance was increasingly moving closer towards the centre and declining ones being pushed out. Geographically, however, this zone tended to remain stable, no doubt thanks to the persistence of links between the great mosque and the markets. The case of Mosul, where this centre was displaced under the Ottomans from the heart of the city (around the Nur al-din mosque) to an exterior location (near the Tigris and the Ottoman citadel) is a very remarkable exception.

Around this 'hypercentre' lay the residential districts, which extended out to the city limits. It is here that one finds the 'quarters' (*hawma* in the Maghrib, *hara* in Egypt and Damascus, *mahalla* in Aleppo, Mosul and Baghdad) which were a characteristic feature of Arab cities. Each quarter formed a relatively closed unit, with one or several gates (*babs*) which were customarily closed at night to ensure security. A principal street (*darb*) ran through the quarter, subdividing into secondary lanes which generally ended in blind alleys. It is here that we enter the famous network of irregular streets and alleys without exits which some scholars have seen as a specificity of the whole city. In most cases, however, such impasses made up no more than 40 to 50 per cent of the total street network, concentrated in the residential zone. Understood within this context, the role of the impasse is perfectly clear. The life of the quarter was oriented towards the centre of the city, where its inhabitants went to work, to shop, and to fulfil their religious duties. It was via the centre that the residential zone communicated with the world beyond the city, not through the interior of the quarter itself – its limits were marked by the houses at the end of impasses, which backed directly onto buildings at the edge of the neighbouring quarter. Relatively isolated from the exterior, the quarter's residents lived as if in a village community, under the authority of their own *shaykh*. Each of the one hundred or so quarters of Cairo occupied an average surface area of two hectares, with a population of around one thousand – a small number, which facilitated local-level administration and allowed the development of personal relationships between residents obliged to submit themselves to a relatively strict system of mutual control. Entirely given over to residential use, the quarters had only a limited economic infrastructure, consisting of *suwayqa*s, unspecialised markets which supplied day-to-day necessities, and of which Jean Sauvaget provided a classic description in the cases of Aleppo and Damascus.[34] Besides these small shops, a quarter might also contain a small mosque, a public bath and a bakery. It was the scene of an intense collective life, with family celebrations (marriage, circumcision), religious ceremonies centred around a local saint, and communal festivals, of which the Damascus *'arada* is a remarkable example.[35]

The doubly radio-concentric structure of the city

This general structure underlies a doubly radio-concentric urban organisation, well illustrated by the range of economic activities which were laid out, broadly speaking, from the centre to the periphery following the descending order of importance of the various trades. The richest and most specialised commerce was located in the centre – fabrics, spices, precious metals, books. In Cairo, where the great Yemeni coffee trade appeared at a relatively recent date (during the seventeenth century), the 62 caravan-sarays involved were all established in the vicinity of the Qasaba. Further from the centre, one finds the less prestigious trades and, finally, at the edge of the city, trade in bulky produce from the countryside (cereals, vegetables, fruits, livestock), activities requiring open space (the manufacture of mats or ropes), along with unpleasant or polluting businesses such as ovens, abattoirs and tanneries. This classification appears so invariable that any significant change in the general scheme is likely to indicate the rise of a particular business (as it moves towards the centre) or its decline (as it moves further out). Such movement might, however, be connected to broader urban development: in Aleppo (ca.1570), Cairo (ca.1600) and Tunis (ca.1770), the removal of the tanneries (*madabigh*) to an external location can be explained by phases of urban expansion in the Ottoman period.[36]

This layout, in radiating circles, appears equally clearly in respect of residential areas, as can be seen for those cities where comprehensive studies have been carried out. The better-off naturally sought proximity to the centre, with its religious and commercial activities (*shaykh*s preferred the neighbourhood of the great mosque). The density of the centre, due to the intensity of its economic activities, meant that space in this area was at a premium, excluding the possibility of accommodation for the poor. The least privileged social strata were therefore ordinarily pushed out towards the periphery. In Tunis, the palaces and fine houses of the seventeenth and eighteenth centuries, studied by Jacques Revault, occupy an oblong area extending around the centre of the city.[37] A study of the size of building plots clearly shows the diminution of their area correlative to their distance from the centre; from areas of 410, 270 and 230 square metres in the central zone, we find others, towards the periphery of the *madina*, of 169, 147 and 122 square metres. This progressive reduction in space is evidently tied to the difference in socio-economic status of the inhabitants.[38] In the case of Cairo, Nelly Hanna has demonstrated, over the period 1738–44, the diminution in the average price of houses from the wealthy central district (20,684 *paras* – the *para* being local silver currency) through the more modest, 'average' dwelling (at 8,931 *paras*) to the poorer housing on the outskirts of the city (4,825 *paras*). The annual rent for a plot of land follows the same descending curve from one zone to another – 171, 76 or 17 *paras* for an area of one hundred *dira'* (cubits).[39] In the case of Aleppo, Jean-Claude David, studying the quality of housing, points to the existence of a zone of high-status residences near the *mdineh* and citadel, with houses occupying areas of between four and nine hundred square metres and whose interiors (numerous rooms, each with a specific function and sophisticated decoration) evince quality. Further from the centre, the size and quality of the houses diminish, and poor quarters extend along the periphery, in particular in the popular eastern suburb.[40]

The 'average' habitation is often simply a reduced version of the courtyard house, with a smaller area, less elaborate interior decoration, and a less developed specialisation of different rooms, but Nelly Hanna's work has also demonstrated the existence in Cairo of an 'atypical' house without a courtyard.[41] On the city's outskirts and in its faubourgs lived a more modest, and even impoverished, population, whose living standards are much less well known to us simply because the poorer house, being poorly constructed, degrades rapidly leaving no trace, in contrast to those fine houses which remain to us, but whose study can inform us only about the wealthiest fraction of the city's inhabitants. Somewhat paradoxically, the excavations of Scanlon and Kubiak at the Fatimids' Fustat (a site on the southern edge of modern Cairo, deserted since the mid-fourteenth century) give a good indication of what the poorer houses of the pre-modern city might have been like; one or two rooms, cheaply built and naturally without any of the characteristics of the 'traditional' courtyard house. The almost rural nature of these buildings can be traced to the frequently rural origin of their inhabitants – migrants from the countryside who established themselves on the fringes of the city and whose experience of urbanisation was somewhat brutal.[42] The exterior quarters of Fez and Tunis, with their straw-roofed huts of mud-brick (*nuwayl*), must have resembled, *mutatis mutandis*, the 'shantytowns' of today's metropolises. In this peripheral area one might also find collective housing, *hawsh*, composed of one-roomed apartments grouped around a central courtyard – the vigour of this kind of community life in these poorer areas can doubtless partly explain the popular unrest which frequently developed there.

This doubly radio-concentric spatial organisation was, of course, only very rarely materialised in actually concentric town plans – it is a tendency rather than a rule. Mosul, which did have the exceptional appearance of a 'circular' city, laid out around its great mosque, later saw its centre shift, as we saw earlier. In other cases, natural, historical, or social factors hindered development along such 'model' lines. Tunis, trapped between two lagoons, could not but develop northward and southward, into its two great faubourgs of Bab al-Suwayqa and Bab al-Jazira. Cairo, its expansion blocked by cemeteries to the north and east, by the hills (*tells*) of urban refuse accumulating to the north east, and by the Muqattam hills to the east, developed mainly to the south and west, giving rise to a layout in which the original central cell, the Fatimids' al-Qahira, is completely 'decentred'. The importance of the pilgrimage, and of the cereal trade linked to the Hawran, account for the development of the long Maydan faubourg which decentres Damascus towards the south. Aleppo, limited in its expansion to the south by cemeteries and to the west by the Quwayq river, developed its principal suburbs to the north and east.

The foregoing discussion has emphasised the importance of factors of socio-economic segregation. This idea of the classification of the urban population into social categories defined by status and wealth contradicts the traditional conception, strongly expressed by Antoine Abdel Nour, according to which social mixity was the rule in 'Islamic' cities.[43] This vision of things is of relative value only at the level of detail; it is shown to be inaccurate when one examines the problem in a global perspective and is, of course, at variance with the everyday experience of traditional cities, where the contrast between rich and poor zones is an almost palpable reality. There is a world of difference between the elegance of the rue des Andalous or Turbat al-Bey in the bourgeois centre of Tunis and the modest Ka'adin and Hajjamin streets in the Bab Suwayqa and Bab Jazira suburbs. In Aleppo, one is struck immediately by the contrast between the magnificent, bourgeois quarter of Farafira, near the citadel, and the Safsafa district in the eastern faubourg.

This is only logical. A careful study of local society in several major cities of the Ottoman period demonstrates the strength of a social inequality that only naturally found its expression in the separation of rich, middle-class and poor residential zones. Contrary to certain stereotypes, traditional urban Muslim society, far from expressing the egalitarian image of the spiritual *umma*, exhibited extreme inequalities in the Ottoman period. Research carried out in Cairo demonstrates that, in the first decades of the eighteenth century, the relationship between the most modest inheritance (that of a vegetable dealer in 1703) and the most spectacular (that of a major coffee merchant in 1735) was in the order of 1 to 60,000. In Damascus at the same time, the ratio was around 1 to 4,000. Social inequality, as measured by the Gini index (as a fraction of 1, where 0.00 represents perfectly equal wealth distribution, and 1 absolute inequality), stands at 0.74 for Cairo and Damascus, even 0.80 for Algiers at the end of the eighteenth century – an extremely high level expressing more significant social stratification than that of any contemporary society.[44]

Another well-known aspect of segregation at work in the Arab city was that organised by minority or ethnic communities. In all the cities studied, Jewish and Christian quarters constituted geographically separate areas. Jews were often housed a short distance from the centre of a city, first of all, because of their important role in the trade in precious metals and in currency exchange, which made them indispensable to the major businesses, and, secondly, because they were bankers to the janissaries, the key urban militia of the Ottoman period – this was particularly the case in Cairo. Such a central location also facilitated the authorities' control over the Jewish population. The concentration of the Jews of Tunis in their *hara* has been well documented by Paul Sebag, who shows that the majority of synagogues were located within this quarter, where Jews accounted for two-thirds of the population as late as the 1950s, at a time when the intermingling of different communities was well advanced in colonial Tunis.[45] We see the same concentration of population in the Christian quarters of Middle Eastern cities, although their location varies somewhat – the Christian district is very close to the centre in Baghdad, further removed in Damascus, and out in the suburbs of Cairo and Aleppo. In Aleppo, the Christian community had extended its share of the northern faubourg during the Ottoman era, progressively pushing out eastward a Muslim population which, obviously, had little desire to share urban space with the Christians. The population of the oldest parts of the quarter (the Judayda), was almost entirely Christian, with their proportion of the whole population diminishing regularly towards the east. In the case of Aleppo, we can clearly see how, more than a submission to an 'apartheid' imposed by the Muslims on their 'protected communities' (*dhimmi*s), as in most cities, urban dynamics displayed the desire among the Muslim majority as well as the Christian minority to live *entre eux*, among themselves, for the better regulation of the life of the community.

The minority Muslim communities obeyed a comparable principle of separation, at least where their 'foreignness' was highly visible. Thus was a Kurdish quarter established in Damascus in the medieval period. In Cairo, there was an unequal degree of concentration of 'foreign' Muslim communities – Syrians and Maghribis, by virtue of the common language they shared with the local Muslims, were relatively widely dispersed, while Turks, as a separate language community, were more strongly concentrated in certain neighbourhoods.

In this regard, Antioch was a textbook case, although the conclusions which can be drawn from it have no doubt been abusively generalised. In this city, studied by Jacques Weulersse in the early 1930s, the urban fabric was constituted by a sort of aggregate of individual towns. Three communities (Sunni Turks, Alawite Muslims and Christians) divided up the space between them in a manner illustrative of their respective political and social importance. The Turks, who until 1918 were the dominant partners, occupied the centre of the city. The Christian quarter was nearby. As for the Alawites, a poor and heterodox minority, their two quarters were thrown out onto the edges of the city, as if to exclude them from it. However, the market district, situated at the northern rim of Antioch along the Orontes, and laid out in such a way as to connect with three of the city's residential districts, constituted a sort of common ground on which the city's unity could be recovered – at the price of a further division of the *suq*s on a confessional basis. The situation of Antioch is accounted for by the somewhat exceptional imbrication of different communities in Syria. In any event, it ought not to give rise to entirely negative analyses which might permit the slide into a general theory of the 'disarticulation of the Islamic city'. The federating role of the markets and, as we shall see, the contribution which each community made to the administration of the city, were positive elements in this regard. Jerusalem, as we have seen, furnishes another example of this same complexity.[46]

We saw above how the Orientalists made a 'unitary' model of the courtyard house, a model inevitably described as timeless and universal. It is 'Islamic' because conceived for the protection of familial intimacy, a preoccupation considered to be essentially linked to religious prescriptions. This is a house turned in upon itself, its blank walls remaining opaque to any socio-economic analysis directed at it from outside. The importance of the central courtyard is not only functional (its contribution to the regulation of the temperature of the building) and social (its facilitation of family life); it has a symbolic, even religious, significance. Forty years after Georges Marçais, a Lebanese scholar writing on this point sounds a curious echo of his formulation of 1940: the house 'is aired and lit by its interior courtyard, which alone possesses its square of sky.' Even more markedly does Antoine Abdel Nour assign, in 1979, a quasi-metaphysical value to this domestic space: 'The courtyard, a celestial thing, as our texts so finely put it [this being a possible, but tendentious, translation of the Arabic *samawi*, "open to the sky"!] achieves, also, by this means, communication not with other men, but with the cosmos.'[47]

The remark of Oleg Grabar, on the tendency of scholars to describe as 'Islamic' anything and everything that appears in the world 'of Islam', is particularly cogent here: 'A typical example of this process is the courtyard house, frequently regarded as the typical Islamic house because it allows for the creation of private, semi-private and public areas. In reality that particular plan is not even usable in most of the tropical Muslim world or in the cold northern climes where Islam also penetrated. In other words, the climatic and thus regional significance of the courtyard house far out-weighs its potential adaptability to the social prescriptions of the faith.'[48] The so-called 'Islamic' courtyard house in fact belongs to a model which is easily identifiable in the ancient Mediterranean world from the earliest times to the Roman period. It is, moreover, a type of habitat which could hardly be appropriate to the greater part of the Muslim world where climatic conditions are so totally different to those which prevail around the Mediterranean.

On the other hand, if it is undeniable that the courtyard house was largely dominant in the great cities of the Arab world, from Marrakesh to Baghdad, which are our object here, and even in Iran and Afghanistan, we cannot, on the pretext of a formally identical arrangement, consider as a single, undifferentiated type everything from the rich, vast and sumptuously embellished houses of the grand quarters to the small and simple, almost rural, habitations of the popular districts. This is the error committed by a number of scholars who have considered princely and bourgeois residences – that is, the only houses to survive – as representative of the 'traditional' habitat of the *madina*.

Finally, to make the courtyard house the single archetype of housing in Arab cities is to neglect the existence of a large number of 'atypical' houses, examples of which exist in all the major cities of the Arab world which have already been noted. We can limit ourselves to mentioning, without going into detail, collective housing of the caravansaray type (*funduq, wakala, khan, samsara*) which, besides their commercial role, contributed to the provision of accommodation, not only for foreign and local merchants but also for thousands of soldiers and ordinary civilians. The *rab'*, a type of collective tenement block let for rent, seems to have existed only in Cairo, close to the centre. Estimates allow us to suppose that up to 10 per cent of the city's artisans and traders lived in such buildings, which allowed a large, more modest, population to reside close to the centre of Cairo, thus mitigating the otherwise exclusively bour-geois character of this zone.[49] Another type of middle-class dwelling has also been identified in Cairo, one whose features (the absence of a courtyard in particular) differentiate it entirely from the model of the 'traditional' house.[50] All around the Red Sea region, tall houses without a courtyard provided a highly original type of traditional habitation, notably at Rashid (Rosetta), Jeddah, Suwakin and in Yemen. We have already discussed the existence of modest housing of the *hawsh* type, which was present over a wide area – we find it mentioned in Cairo, Damascus, Aleppo and Medina. Finally, we may suppose that very basic, popular housing, such as that uncovered by the excavations of Scanlon and Kubiak at Fatimid Fustat, existed more or less everywhere, although it has now completely disappeared. In reality, then, there were numerous types of housing in the Mediterranean Arab world, varying according to the different needs of populations whose socio-economic status was highly diversified. It is only the lack of material and written evidence which has prevented us from fully appreciating this variety.

City administration

The Orientalist conception of the 'Islamic' city requires a thorough revision in one further, basic respect. Recent research on Arab cities shows that the supposed under-administration, even non-administration, of urban areas in the Ottoman period has been greatly exaggerated.[51] This conception never took proper account of the multiple elements which serve to explain why these cities did not collapse into anarchy.

The principal Arab cities of the Ottoman era, which were also the provincial capitals of the empire, were never entirely neglected by the central imperial authorities; the Sublime Porte frequently made its influence felt in their management. The Sultan wrote, in 1552, to the governor and the *qadi* of Cairo, instructing them to examine the question of the removal of the city's tanneries from their present location (which had become too central, the city having expanded around them) to a more peripheral site: 'The tanneries and slaughterhouses inside Cairo produce smells which incommode the small children of the Muslims … The people of the quarters near these tanneries complain and say: the existence of these tanneries is a cause of harm for our children.'[52] The tanneries were in fact removed, if several decades later. The correspondence between Istanbul and Aleppo, conserved in the *awamir al-sultaniyya* (Orders of the Sultan) collection of the Damascus archives, provides numerous examples of the central government's interest in the urban affairs of the city. 'On the ground', the governors (*pashas*) appointed from Istanbul played a not insignificant role, at least in the earlier period of Ottoman dominion; Muhammad Pasha, governor of Cairo in 1652–56, gained the popular surname of Abu 'l-Nur ('father of light') in the city, in recognition of his having ordered the city's mosques to be repaired and their stonework cleaned. Locally appointed officials – the *agha* of the janissaries, the *wali* and *muhtasib* – also participated actively in addressing the city's problems.

Although one can hardly consider them municipal officers, there were also responsible officials in the Maghribi capitals: a *shaykh al-balad* in Algiers, *shaykhs* of the *madina* and of the faubourgs in Tunis, a *shaykh al-bilad* and an assembly, the *majlis al-bilad*, in Tripoli,[53] and we must assume that they had a hand in local affairs. The study of court registers (*mahkama* records) shows how the intervention of judges (*qadis*) in the affairs submitted to them enabled the resolution of many of the problems concerning the towns' inhabitants. They regulated the quality of construction work, took action against impediments to the smooth flow of traffic and against annoyances of all kinds (the noise, smell and insalubrity produced by various artisanal activities), and arbitrated disputes between neighbours. A detailed picture of the judges' 'doctrine' can be deduced from the totality of decisions rendered, as Robert Brunschvig in fact suggested long ago.[54]

If Arab cities lacked true 'municipal institutions' as late as the second half of the nineteenth century, they were nonetheless amply supplied with communities (*tawa'if*) whose activities compensated at least in part for this absence.[55] In a way, they occupied the place of those institutions which, in other areas of the world, would constitute that 'civil society' whose supposed absence in the Muslim world has been much discussed by political scientists. The most important were the guilds of trades and professions, whose presence facilitated the administration of the city's central districts. There were 100 or so in each of Algiers and Tunis, 160 in Damascus and Aleppo, and around 250 in Cairo. This corporate administration was sometimes headed by a *shaykh al-masha'ikh* (in Damascus) or *amin al-umana* (in Tunis and Algiers). The communities of each quarter played a similar role in the residential districts; in each of Cairo's hundred or so *hara*s, the *shaykh* played an important role in the management and security of the quarter. The *shaykh*s of religious and ethnic communities had a similar function in the administration of their respective groups. It is thus hardly accurate to speak of the urban population as existing without any administration – what we see is, rather, that the town's inhabitants found themselves tied into a series of superimposed networks, each with a different competence and organising principle, which together exercised a quite strict personal and communal control and which the political authorities utilised in the administration of the city and its population.

Finally (and this is doubtless a fundamental point for the understanding of the properly urban administration of the city), we must give the greatest consideration to a well-known Islamic institution, the *waqf* (*habus* in the Maghrib), whose role in the organisation of urban development has perhaps been insufficiently emphasised.[56] The *waqf*, as a religious endowment whose revenue provided for the upkeep of religious or charitable monuments or institutions, could bring together around such institutions a significant number of commercial buildings (shops, markets, caravansarays, houses, *rab's*, *hammams*), whose revenues also contributed to their upkeep. In the Ottoman period, which saw a remarkable flourishing of *waqf*s, such religious foundations could also, according to their importance, contribute to local property developments for the renovation of a district, or even to developments at the level of the city itself. On the 'micro-urban' level, one might point, for example, to the works undertaken by Yusuf Dey in the central district of Tunis (after 1610), to those of Ipshir Pasha in Aleppo (1653), or of 'Uthman Katkhuda in the development of the Azbakiyya district of Cairo (1734). At the 'macro-urban' level we could mention the four great *waqf*s which enabled the remodelling and expansion of the Aleppo *mdineh* in the sixteenth century (around the Khusru Pasha mosque in 1544, the 'Adiliyya mosque in 1555, the *khan* al-Gumruk in 1574, and the mosque of Bahram Pasha in 1583). On a similar scale were the enterprises of Iskandar Pasha (ca. 1555), of Ridwan Bey (ca. 1640) and of Ibrahim Agha (1650) in Cairo, which marked the expansion of the city to the south. It would be no exaggeration to say that the *waqf*/*habus* was the principal instrument in the organisation of development in these cities. Taking account of this institution permits us to resolve one of the most intractable contradictions of the Orientalist conception of the 'Islamic' city: how a town apparently so poorly organised and ill administered was capable, not only of maintaining itself, but of undergoing the kind of major expansion that took place during the Ottoman era.[57]

Conclusions

The vigour of the organisation of urban space, with its multifunctional centre bringing together religious, cultural and economic activities, and the repartition of economic and residential activities from the centre towards the periphery, has a logic of its own which explains the success of a type of city which Sauvaget, Clerget and many others thought doomed to complete anarchy. This city was governed by institutions which, if not 'communal', were no less efficient for that. Justice and the *waqf* contributed respectively to ensuring its day-to-day management and to organising its expansion. The segregating factors which we have noted did not produce internal disaggregation but, paradoxically, contributed to the unity of the city by facilitating its administration. What we find, then, is a coherent and original *urban system* which explains the success of these towns, and their dynamism in the early modern period.

A number of questions remain unanswered, the first of which is that of the origin of this system, which must doubtless be looked for in the pre-Islamic period of the history of Arab societies around the Mediterranean. The second is that of the relationship between the Arab city and the ancient Mediterranean towns, regarding which the recent discoveries at Palmyra and Bet Shean have both contributed new information and posed new questions. The third is the question of the structure of the 'classical' Arab city and its possible specificities when compared to what we have here designated the 'traditional' (Ottoman-era) city which succeeded it. Finally, it will be necessary for parallel investigations to be carried out in other regions of the vast Islamic world, so that we might gain a better understanding both of the specificities of the Arab Mediterranean region and of the elements of an Islamic universalism that might be discerned in it.

NOTES

Translated by James McDougall, St Anthony's College, Oxford.

1   R. Stephen Humphreys, *Islamic History: A Framework for Analysis*, Princeton University Press, 1991, p. 228.

2   William Marçais, 'L'islamisme et la vie urbaine', reprinted in *Articles et conférences*, Paris, 1961; Georges Marçais, 'L'urbanisme musulman', reprinted in *Mélanges d'histoire et d'archéologie*, Algiers, 2 vols., 1957.

3   Gaston Deverdun, *Marrakech des origines à 1912*, Rabat, 2 vols., 1959–61; Jacques Caillé, *La ville de Rabat jusqu'au Protectorat français*, Paris, 3 vols., 1949; Roger Le Tourneau, *Fès avant le Protectorat*, Casablanca, 1949; René Lespès, *Alger, étude de géographie et d'histoire urbaine*, Paris, 1930 ... Only Tunis misses out in this distinguished list; it had to wait until 1998 for the appearance of *Tunis. Histoire d'une ville* by Paul Sebag.

4   Jean Sauvaget, 'Esquisse d'une histoire de la ville de Damas', *REI*, 4 (1934); *Alep, Essai sur le développement d'une grande ville syrienne*, Paris, 1941. Jacques Weulersse 'Antioche, Essai de géographie urbaine', *BEO*, 4 (1934).

5   Marcel Clerget, *Le Caire*, Cairo, 2 vols., 1934.

6   Gustave von Grunebaum, 'The Structure of the Muslim Town', 1955, reprinted in his *Islam*, London, 1961, pp. 141–58. Janet Abu Lughod, in 'The Islamic City', *IJMES*, 19, (1987) follows the chain of transmission (*isnâd*) of the authorities marking this theory, from its Founding Fathers to the final synthesis.

7   Robert Ilbert, 'La ville islamique, réalité et abstraction', *Les Cahiers de la Recherche Architecturale: Espaces et formes de l'Orient Arabe*, 10–11 (April 1982). See also Oleg Grabar, 'Reflexions on the Study of Islamic Art', *Muqarnas*, 1 (1983), p.8.

8   Antoine Abdel Nour, *Introduction à l'Histoire Urbaine*, Beirut, 1982, pp. 155, 165. This brilliant Lebanese scholar, killed by Israeli soldiers in Beirut in 1982, had made the conceptions of the Orientalist school his own.

9   Roger Le Tourneau, *Les villes musulmanes de l'Afrique du Nord*, Algiers, 1957.

10 Besides his work on Damascus and Aleppo, see (among other publications), 'Le plan de Laodicée sur Mer', *BEO*, 4 (1934).

11 M. Clerget, *Le Caire*, pp. 178–80; J. Sauvaget, *Alep*, p. 239.

12 Le Tourneau, *Les villes musulmanes*, p. 20. G. Marçais, 'L'urbanisme musulman', p. 227.

13 J. Sauvaget, *Alep*, p. 247.

14 J. Weulersse, *Paysans de Syrie et du Proche-Orient*, Paris, 1946, pp. 86–8. See also his 'Antioche'.

15 Pierre Boyer, *La vie quotidienne à Alger*, Paris, Hachette, 1963, p. 49.

16 J. Sauvaget, 'Esquisse', pp. 455–6; *Alep*, p. 248.

17 J. Sauvaget, 'Esquisse', pp. 455–6; *Alep*, pp. 247–8.

18 G. von Grunebaum, 'Structure', *passim*.

19 I am thinking here of Arab scholars such as Yusuf Ahmad and Khaled Moaz, who remained in the shadow of great *savants* like Max van Berchem and Jean Sauvaget.

20 H. A. R. Gibb and H. Bowen, *Islamic Society and the West*, Oxford, 2 vols., 1950–7.

21 S. Humphreys , *Islamic History*, p. 231.

22 O. Grabar, 'Reflexions', p. 8.

23 Jean-Claude Garcin, 'Habitat médiéval et histoire urbaine', in *Palais et maisons du Caire, vol. I. Epoque mamelouke*, Paris, 1982, p. 216.

24 See in particular J. and J.-C. Balty, 'Le cadre topographique et historique', in J. Balty (ed.), *Colloque Apamée de Syrie*, Brussels, 1969. See also on this subject the papers presented at the conference *La Syrie de Byzance à l'Islam*, edited by P. Canivet and J.-P. Coquais, Damascus, 1992. A recent overview is given in J. H. W. G. Liebeschuetz, *The Decline and Fall of the Roman City*, Oxford University Press 2001.

25 J. Sauvaget, *Alep*, p. 248.

26 Claude Cahen, 'Mouvements populaires et autonomisme urbain', *Arabica*, 5 (1958), p. 226; S. M. Stern, 'The constitution of the Islamic City', in A. Hourani and S. Stern (eds.), *The Islamic City*, Oxford, 1970; Hugh Kennedy, 'From Polis to Madina', *Past and Present*, 106 (1985), pp. 13–14.

27 J. H. W. G. Liebeschuetz, *The Decline and Fall*, p. 406. Of course, I do not subscribe to the remark on the character of the 'Islamic' city.

28 Khaled As'ad, 'Ikhtishâf ... sûq fî Tadmur', *Annales Archéologiques Arabes Syriennes* 37–8 (1991). Yoram Tsafrir and Gideon Foerster, 'Urbanism at Scythopolis-Bet Shean', *Dumbarton Oaks Papers* 51 (1997).

29 I addressed this problem in my 'Islamic City, Arab City', *BJMES* 21–1 (1994); 'Ville musulmane, ville arabe', in J.-L. Biget and J.-Cl. Hervé (eds.), *Panoramas urbains*, Fontenay/Saint-Cloud, ENS, 1995; and 'La structure spatiale de la ville', in M. Naciri and A. Raymond (eds.), *Sciences Sociales et Phénomènes Urbains dans le Monde Arabe*, Casablanca, 1997. I consider the conclusions of E. Wirth – who, at the end of a severe criticism of Orientalism, proposes the *suq* as the only true characteristic of a city which he proposes calling 'oriental' – to be excessively restrictive. ('The Middle Eastern City: Islamic City? Oriental City? Arabian City', lecture delivered at Harvard in 1982).

30 See the excavation notes of A. T. Ansary, published in *Qaryt al-Fau*, London, 1981, and his article 'Qaryat Dhat Kahl: al-Fau', in *Sciences Sociales et Phénomènes Urbains*.

31 See the recent analysis by Abdelhamid Henia in *Propriété et stratégies sociales à Tunis (XVIe–XIXe siècles)*, Tunis, 1999, pp. 239–46.

32 Among the works of Baber Johanson, see: 'The All-Embracing Town and its Mosques', *ROMM*, 32 (1981); 'The claims of men and the claims of God', in *Pluriformiteit en verdeling*, Nijmegen, 1980. This research clearly contradicts the thesis of Jean Sauvaget concerning the supposed ignorance of the *'ulama* about what a city is.

33 Louis Massignon, *Mission en Mésopotamie (1901–1908)*, Cairo, 2 vols., 1912; 'Enquête sur les corporations musulmanes d'artisans et de commerçants du Maroc', *Revue du Monde Musulman*, 58 (1924).

34 J. Sauvaget, 'Décrets mamlouks de Syrie, I', *BEO*, 2 (1932), pp. 29–30; 'Esquisse', pp. 452–3; *Alep*, p. 105.

35 See R. Lecerf and R. Tresse, 'Les 'Arada de Damas', *BEO*, 7–8 (1937–8). Nawâl al-Messiri Nadîm has studied the life of one quarter in Cairo in her 'The concept of the Hâra', *Annales Islamologiques*, 15 (1979).

36 A. Raymond, 'Le déplacement des tanneries à Alep, Le Caire et Tunis', *Revue d'Histoire Maghrébine* 7–8, 1977, reprinted in *REMMM*, 55–6 (1990).

37 Jacques Revault, *Palais et Maisons de Tunis*, Paris, CNRS, 4 vols., 1967–78.

38 A. Raymond, *Grandes villes arabes à l'époque ottomane*, Paris, Sindbad, 1985, map on page 335.

39 Nelly Hanna, *Habiter au Caire*, Cairo, IFAO, 1991, pp. 185, 207.

40 Jean-Claude David, 'Alep, dégradation et tentatives actuelles de réadaptation', *BEO*, 28 (1975).

41 N. Hanna, 'Bayt al-Istambulli', *Annales Islamologiques*, 16 (1980) and more generally her *Habiter au Caire*.

42 W. Kubiak and G. Scanlon, *Final report on Fustat C*, Cairo, 1989.

43 See above, and note 8.

44 A. Raymond, *Artisans et commerçants au Caire au XVIIIème siècle*, 2 vols., Damascus, 1974, II, p. 375. Colette Establet and Jean-Paul Pascual, *Familles et fortunes à Damas*, Damas, IFD, 1994. C. Establet , J.-P. Pascual and A. Raymond, 'La mesure de l'inégalité sociale dans la société ottomane', *JESHO*, 37, 1994. Tal Shuval, *La ville d'Alger vers la fin du XVIIIème siècle*, Paris, CNRS, 1998.

45 Paul Sebag, *La hara de Tunis*, Paris, 1959, p. 33.

46 J. Weulersse, 'Antioche essai de géographie humaine'.

47 G. Marçais, 'L'urbanisme musulman', p. 227. A. Abdel Nour, 'Types architecturaux et vocabulaire de l'habitat en Syrie', in D. Chevallier (ed.), *L'espace social de la ville arabe*, Paris, 1979, p. 83.

48 O. Grabar, 'Réflexions', p. 8.

49 A. Raymond, "Le rab", un habitat collectif au Caire à l'époque ottomane', in *Mélanges de l'Université Saint-Joseph*, 50 (1984).

50 See the work of Nelly Hanna ('Bayt al Istambulli' and *Habiter au Caire*).

51 J. Sauvaget, 'Esquisse', pp. 455–6.

52 This document, from the Topkapi library (KK 888 f. 324 r., no. 1407, first of sha'bân 959), was kindly communicated to me by Professor Gilles Veinstein; it is a pleasure to record my thanks to him here.

53 The institutions of Tripoli have been studied by Nora Lafi, *Une ville du Maghreb entre ancien régime et réformes ottomanes*, Paris, L'Harmattan, 2002, p. 105.

54 Galal al-Nahal, *The Judicial Administration of Ottoman Egypt*, Chicago, 1979; Robert Brunschvig, 'Urbanisme médiéval et droit musulman', *REI*, 1947.

55 A. Raymond, 'The Role of the Communities (*tawâ'if*) in the Administration of Cairo in the Ottoman Period', in N. Hanna (ed.), *The State and its Servants*, Cairo, AUC, 1995.

56 A. Raymond, 'Les grands waqfs et l'organisation de l'espace urbain', *BEO*, 31, 1980.

57 A. Raymond, 'La conquête ottomane et le développement des grandes villes arabes', *ROMM*, 27 (1979).

FURTHER READING

Auld, S. and Hillenbrand, R. (eds.), *Ottoman Jerusalem: 1517–1917*, London, 2 vols., 2000.

Bouhdiba, A. and Chevallier, D. (eds.), *La ville arabe dans l'Islam*, Tunis, 1982.

Brown, Carl (ed.), *From Medina to Metropolis*, Princeton, 1973.

Cohen, J.-L. et al. (eds.), *Alger: Paysage urbain et architecture*, Paris, 2003.

Cuneo, P., *Storia dell'urbanistica. Il mondo islamico*, Rome, 1986.

Mantran, R. (ed.), *Histoire de l'empire ottoman*, Paris, 1989.

Maury, B., Raymond, A., Revault, J. and Zakariya, M., *Palais et maisons du Caire. Époque ottomane*, Paris, 1983.

Panzac, D. (ed.), *Les villes dans l'empire ottoman*, Paris, 2 vols., 1991–4.

Raymond, A., *The Great Arab Cities in the 16th–18th Centuries: An Introduction*, New York, 1984.

Raymond, A., *Cairo*, Cambridge, 2000.

Raymond, A. (ed.), *Le Caire*, Paris, 2000.

Raymond, A., *Arab Cities in the Ottoman Period*, Aldershot, 2002.

Saadaoui, A., *Tunis ville ottomane*, Tunis, 2001.

Serageldin, I. and El-Sadek, S., *The Arab City*, Riyadh, 1982.

Serjeant, R. B. and R. Lewcock (eds.), *San'a': An Arabian Islamic City*, London, 1983.

Shuval, T., *La ville d'Alger vers la fin du XVIIIème siècle*, Paris, 1998.

Wirth, E., *Die Orientalische Stadt*, Mainz, 2 vols., 2000.

PART V

The Middle East and the New World Order

CHAPTER TWELVE

A Different Balance of Power
Europe and the Middle East in the Eighteenth and Nineteenth Centuries

ABDUL-KARIM RAFEQ

Introduction

The Middle East here refers to the Arab countries extending from Egypt eastward, in addition to Turkey and Persia (Iran). The Ottoman empire ruled most of the Arab lands included in the Middle East for about four centuries, from roughly 1516, when it conquered Syria, to 1918, when the Ottomans withdrew from Syria and the rest of the Arab world after their defeat in the First World War. Although the Ottomans defeated in 1514 Shah Isma'il, the Safavid ruler in Persia, who adopted Twelver Shi'ism as the official religion, they did not pursue their conquests in that country. Ottoman policy was to stabilize the borderline with Persia which constituted the historical, ethnic and cultural boundaries between Iraq and Persia.

The Ottoman state grew out of Turkoman tribes from central Asia who headed in the second half of the eleventh century towards the borderline separating Byzantine Anatolia from Arab–Muslim Syria and Iraq. The Turkomans intensified their raids on Byzantine territory, and a battle took place between them and the Byzantines at Menzikert, near Lake Van, in 1071. The Byzantine army was led by Emperor Romanus IV Diogenes and the Turkomans were led by the Seljuq Sultan of Baghdad, Alparslan. The Byzantines were defeated and the Turkomans swept over Anatolia establishing principalities one of which was the principality of 'Uthman (Otman) that was established in 1299.

The defeat of the Byantines comes a few years after the religious schism in 1054 between the Byzantine Orthodox church and the Catholic church in Rome over, among other things, the addition by the Pope to the Nicene Creed of 325 that the Holy Spirit proceeds from the Father and the Son. The Byzantine church and the Oriental churches had already agreed in the Council of Constantinople in 381 to add to the Nicene Creed that the Holy Spirit proceeds from the Father. The schism weakened Byzantium and contributed to its defeat which in turn instigated the Crusades in 1097. Those three important dates of 1054, 1071 and 1097 were to change the political map of the region.[1]

The Ottomans penetrated into the Balkans around 1350 conquering as far as Hungary and isolating the Byzantine empire. In 1453, the Ottomans conquered Constantinople and brought the Byzantine empire to an end. A new age began for the Middle East and for Europe. Not since the early Muslim conquests did Islam expand as it did in Anatolia and the Balkans under the Ottoman rule.[2]

The Ottomans followed two patterns in dominating the Middle East: conquest on the battlefield, as happened in conquering Syria in 1516, Egypt in 1517, Iraq in 1534 and Yemen in 1539; and imposition of their rule with the agreement of the local rulers, as happened in the Hijaz when the ruling sharif accepted Ottoman rule, and in North Africa, where the Turkish sea ghazis (pirates) in control of the coastal towns called on the Ottomans to defend them against attacks by Philip II of Spain.[3]

The conquest of the Arab lands provided the Ottomans with religious legitimacy as rulers of the holy cities and of the former capitals of Islam. The Ottomans also gained economic resources from the Arab countries, which they used to finance their conquest and their rule in Europe.[4]

The pattern of Ottoman conquest was to expand first in Europe and then in the Arab lands. When the Ottomans began to lose territory, they first lost territory in the Balkans and then in the Arab lands. After about six hundred years of expansion and loss, the Ottomans in 1918 went back to Anatolia from where they began their expansion in the 1350s. The legacy of Ottoman rule in the Balkans as well as in the Arab lands has yet to be assessed.

Symptoms of weakness in the Ottoman empire began to appear during the rule of Sulayman the Magnificent (1520–66). The devaluation of the silver unit of the Ottoman currency, the *aqche*, occurred in the second half of the sixteenth century, causing inflation while the importation of silver and gold from the New World (America) into Spain and Europe soon affected the Ottoman empire.[5] The devaluation of the currency weighed heavily on the salaried officials. The civilians accepted bribes to make both ends meet. The salaried troops imposed extra taxes on the people, especially in the countryside. When the government tried to stop the troops from enforcing extra taxes, they rose in revolt. A series of military revolts, caused primarily by inflation, occurred in Yemen in the 1560s, in Egypt between 1589 and 1609, in Syria between the 1590s and the 1660s, and in Baghdad in the early 1620s. The Baghdad revolt was exploited by the Safavids who occupied Baghdad in 1623 and kept it under their control until 1639. This great challenge to the Ottoman empire necessitated a great sultan in the person of Murad IV (1623–40) who was able to regain Baghdad from the Safavids in 1639. Revolts by the military also occurred in the capital Istanbul, and the rebellious troops killed the sitting Sultan 'Uthman II in 1622.

The change of the name of the silver currency from *aqche* into *para* in 1620, and then into *ghurush* (piastre) in 1680 did not improve the value of the currency. Losing confidence in their currency, the people in the Ottoman empire began to use European silver and gold currency.

Europe, the Ottomans and the Arabs in the Eighteenth Century

From being conquerors in the Balkans and central Europe in the fourteenth, fifteenth and sixteenth centuries, the Ottomans suffered defeats and loss of territory in the seventeenth and the eighteenth centuries. The Holy Roman empire under the Habsburgs twice repulsed the Ottomans' siege of Vienna in 1529 and 1683. After further defeats in 1687 and 1689, the Ottomans signed the treaty of Carlowitz with the Habsburgs in 1699. By virtue of this treaty, the Ottomans lost most of

Hungary, Transylvania and Podolia, which they had controlled for over three hundred years.[6]

On the Russian front, Tsar Peter the Great (1682–1725) made two attempts to gain control of the Sea of Azov, which would give him an outlet into the warm waters. He succeeded, however, in occupying the silk-producing territory in northern Persia in 1721–2. The occupation affected the flow of Persian silk to Aleppo and consequently damaged the business of the English merchants of the Levant Company that was established in Aleppo in 1581.[7] Under Catherine II (1762–96), who implemented the reforms advocated by the philosophers of the Enlightenment, Russia defeated the Ottoman empire in a protracted war that began in 1768 and ended in 1774 with the treaty of Kuchuk Kaynarja. Turkey surrendered its rule over the Crimea, which Russia annexed in 1783. This loss was more devastating to the Ottomans than the loss they had sustained in the treaty of Carlowitz. In the latter treaty the Ottomans lost territories inhabited by Christians, but in the treaty of Kuchuck Kaynarja they lost territory inhabited by Muslim Turks like them.[8] The occurrence of the French Revolution in 1789 divided Europe between those who opposed the revolution and those who supported it. The Ottomans were too weak to exploit Europe's preoccupation with the revolution.

The Safavid front also became active against the Ottomans in the eighteenth century. Sunni Afghan troops invaded Persia and deposed the Safavid Shah in the early 1720s. The Safavids, however, regained their throne in 1729 with the help of a Turkoman chieftain, Tahmasp Kuli Khan (the slave of the Safavid ruler Tahmasp). After Tahmasp Kuli Khan had established his power, he deposed his master the Safavid Shah in 1736 and ruled on his own under the name of Nadir Shah. Hostilities with the Ottomans were soon renewed when Nadir Shah laid an unsuccessful siege to Mosul in 1741. Nadir Shah was assassinated in 1746. A period of chaos followed until Karim Khan Zand (from the Zand tribe) established stability in Persia between 1763 and 1779. Karim Khan Zand occupied Basra from the Ottomans between 1775 and 1779.[9] Shortly afterwards, the Qajar dynasty ruled Persia from 1795 to 1925.

Politically, the Ottoman state still suffered in the eighteenth century from the same polarization of power in Istanbul between the Kizlar Agha and the Grand Vizier that had existed in the past century. The impact of this polarization on provincial politics and administration in the eighteenth century was more devastating than was the case in the previous century. Almost every provincial governor kept an agent in Istanbul who bought support for him either through the Grand Vizier or the Kizlar Agha.

Economically, the Ottoman state suffered far more than before from diminishing revenues due to the absence of conquests, the loss of territory and the embezzlement of taxes. The increasing numbers of salaried troops and officials constituted a major drain on the treasury. The partial diversion of caravan trade between Asia and Europe to the sea route around the Cape caused a loss of revenue for the state.

The cumulative effects of these factors on the Ottoman state were tremendous. The base of defiance in the provinces to the state had widened in the eighteenth century. Earlier salaried troops and local chieftains led the way in revolt. In the eighteenth century, however, several power groups challenged the state's authority. Families of notables emerged as governors of major provinces; Mamluks became de facto rulers in Egypt, governors in Baghdad and for a short period governors in southern Syria; the Bedouin became more insubordinate, and a religious challenge to the Ottomans and to the Sufi orders occurred in the heartland of the Arabian Peninsula championed by the Wahhabis-Saʿudis.

Provincial Governors of Local Origin

Unlike the sixteenth and the seventeenth centuries when most governors in the Arab provinces were appointed from among Turks, a new tendency of appointing local Arabic-speaking persons as governors appeared in the eighteenth century. As Ottoman authority declined in that century, influential local notables were able to buy provincial positions in Istanbul through an agent who put his money on either the Grand Vizier or the Kizlar Agha.

Members of the local ʿAzm family in Syria governed the province of Damascus and other Syrian provinces, sometimes simultaneously, for over sixty years at intermittent periods in the eighteenth century and the early years of the nineteenth. An agent in Istanbul called Khalil Efendi bought support for the ʿAzms through the Grand Vizier.[10] Some of the ʿAzm governors stayed in office for long periods contrary to the earlier practice when most governors were deposed after one or two years in office. Thus Asʿad Pasha al-ʿAzm was governor of Damascus for fourteen years (1743–57). The reason for this long tenure is that Asʿad Pasha had ensured throughout his rule the safety of the Damascene pilgrim caravan on its way to the Hijaz. In his dealings with the Bedouin along the caravan route, Asʿad Pasha either used force to subdue them or bought them off.[11] The security of the pilgrim caravan was of prime importance for the Ottoman sultan in his capacity as Protector or Servitor of the Two Holy Sanctuaries, especially after his military reputation had suffered defeats on the battlefield. For these reasons and to better ensure the security of the pilgrim caravan, the sultan entrusted its command regularly to the governor of Damascus in 1708.[12] The earlier commanders, mostly drawn from Janissary chiefs and Ottoman officials, failed to protect the caravan from Bedouin attacks. However, despite Asʿad Pasha's ability to ensure the security of the pilgrim caravan for fourteen years, the Ottoman authorities deposed him in 1757. One of the reasons for his deposition was the enmity of the new Grand Vizier, Raghib Pasha, to him. Urban–rural rivalry was strong at the time, and Raghib Pasha denounced Asʿad Pasha as 'peasant son of a peasant', after a deal between them had failed. Also, the Kizlar Agha in Istanbul happened to hate Asʿad Pasha because he did not take good care of him when he passed through Damascus on his way for the pilgrimage. The state was also interested in confiscating the wealth, which Asʿad Pasha had accumulated during his tenure in office. The confiscation of large amounts of specie hidden by Asʿad Pasha made the state revalue the currency. Asʿad Pasha was finally accused of having incited the Bedouin to attack the pilgrim caravan after he had been deposed. The caravan was almost annihilated in the attack that occurred in 1757.[13]

The significance of the rule of the ʿAzms is that they were part of a general phenomenon of local families of notables taking advantage of the decline of Ottoman authority to assume power in key Arab provinces. Thus, the governorship was the second Ottoman institution that the Arabic-speaking people in Syria had been able to penetrate after they had taken over in mid-seventeenth century the Janissary Corps in Damascus and turned it into a local corps known as the Yerliyya. The Sultan sent another military corps to Damascus in 1660, which became known as the Kapi Kullari Janissaries, meaning slaves of the sultan, or Imperial Janissaries, to maintain his authority.

In upper Galilee in Palestine, a local chieftain of Bedouin origin, Zahir al-'Umar al-Zaydani rose from the rank of tax farmer in the region of Safad–Tiberias to a local governor establishing for himself a small Arab principality based on the fortified seaport of Acre. Although still within the Ottoman establishment, Zahir defied the attempts of the Ottomans to depose him as tax farmer and self-appointed local ruler. He depended on Bedouin supporters, mercenary Maghariba (North African) troops, and fortresses he built to defy the Ottomans from the 1730s until his death in 1775.[14] After Zahir's death, a military officer in the Ottoman army, Ahmad Pasha al-Jazzar, sent to fill the power vacuum in the region, took power into his own hands and ruled the province of Sidon and occasionally Damascus in the period between 1775 and his death in 1804. With British help from the sea, Jazzar defended Acre against the attack of Napoleon Bonaparte in 1799.[15]

In Iraq, too, a local family, the Jalilis, monopolized the governorship of the province of Mosul from 1726 to 1834, with slight interruptions. The Ottoman sultan tolerated their rule because they were able to defend Mosul against attacks from Persia, such as the siege imposed on the city by Nadir Shah in 1743. The Jalilis rule came to an end in 1834 when the reforming Sultan Mahmud II (1809–39), with his new European-style army, put an end to the local power groups in the empire.

A family of Turkish origins, the Qaramanlis were able to rule Tripolitania in Libya from 1711 to 1836. They defended the country against attacks by pirates from the sea and by Bedouin from the interior. Another family of military Turkish origins, the Husaynids, ruled Tunisia from 1705 to 1957, and defended it from attacks by land and sea. It survived the French occupation of Tunisia in 1881.

Resurgence of Mamluk Power in the Eighteenth Century

The Mamluks, who stopped the advance of the Mongols at the battle of 'Ayn Jalut in northern Palestine in 1260 and put an end to the remnants of the Crusaders in 1295, established a sultanate of their own, based on Egypt and Syria, which lasted from roughly 1260 until 1517 when it was overthrown by the Ottomans.

The Mamluks were recruited as pagans from the steppes of Russia. Sold as slaves in Egypt and Syria, the Ayyubid sultans trained them in horsemanship and the handling of white armament, such as sword, spear and shield while on horseback, converted them into Islam, and emancipated them. Thus the Mamluk from being a slave becomes a free Muslim. His sons as free Muslims do not qualify to be Mamluks. Hence every Mamluk had to be imported as pagan, trained, Islamized and freed. As such, there was no dynastic rule among the Mamluks despite attempts by some Mamluk sultans to designate their sons as their successors.

Even though the Ottomans defeated the Mamluks on the battlefields in Syria in 1516 and in Egypt in 1517, they allowed the importation of Mamluks into Egypt and used them in the administration and in the army. After several attempts at revolt in Egypt in 1522, in 1589–1609 and in 1660–1662, the Mamluks whose ultimate aim was to re-establish the old Mamluk sultanate eventually became de facto rulers in Egypt in the second half of the eighteenth century. As holders of the military rank of Sanjaq Bey, the Mamluks were entrusted with the command of the Egyptian pilgrim caravan to the Hijaz, the command of military expeditions in support of the sultan and the command of the military convoy that carried the treasury from Egypt to

Istanbul. A Mamluk chief was appointed governor of the rich district of Sa'id in Upper Egypt, known as the granary of Egypt.

The paramount chief among the Mamluks in the 1760s and the early 1770s was 'Ali Bey, who was given the title of *shaykh al-balad*, implying that he was the actual ruler of the city alongside the Ottoman governor who had become a figurehead. 'Ali Bey was aware of the political and military problems of the Ottoman sultan who was embroiled in war with Russia (1778–84). 'Ali Bey intervened in the Hijaz in 1770 on behalf of the sultan to reinstate the deposed Sharif there. He also intervened in Syria against the Sultan in an attempt to reestablish the old Mamluk Sultanate. His troops occupied Damascus for ten days in June 1771 but then withdrew because the leader of the expedition 'Ali Bey's preferred Mamluk Muhammad Bey Abu'l-Dhahab was apparently in collusion with the Ottomans against his master 'Ali Bey. In 1773 Abu'l-Dhahab killed his master 'Ali Bey and was nominated by the Ottomans governor of Egypt. He then led an expedition into Palestine allegedly to fight the rebellious Zahir al-'Umar but he died after he had conquered Acre in June 1775. His Mamluk army withdrew to Egypt.[16]

The Mamluks continued as de facto rulers of Egypt until Napoleon Bonaparte defeated them in 1798. The English tried to recruit the Mamluks to work for them but failed. The new governor of Egypt Muhammad 'Ali Pasha put an end to Mamluk rule in Egypt by eliminating their chiefs in 1811–12 and stopping the importation of Mamluks into Egypt.

The Mamluks in Iraq were employed as military troops by the Ottoman governors of Baghdad Hasan Pasha and his son Ahmad Pasha during their rule between 1704 and 1747 to repel attacks from Persia. Recruited from Georgia (*Bilad al-Karj* in Arabic) and the Caucasus, the Mamluks monopolized the governorship of Baghdad, and occasionally Basra, from 1747 to 1831. Nine Mamluk governors ruled Baghdad during this period. Although the Mamluks defended Iraq against attacks from Persia, the Ottomans were unable to remove them from office.

Of the nine Mamluk governors, two stand out as powerful and reformers. Sulayman Pasha the Great, known as Büyük Sulayman Pasha (1780–1802) established his authority over the local Kurdish and Bedouin tribes, repelled the Wahhabi-Sa'udi attack on the Shi'i sites in Karbala in 1802, and introduced reforms in imitation of the reforms introduced by the Ottoman sultan. The last Mamluk governor of Baghdad Da'ud Pasha (1816–31) repulsed attacks from Persia against Baghdad in 1821, established a modern army after the Ottoman state had abolished the Janissaries in 1826, allowed British and French merchants to actively pursue business in Iraq, and introduced reforms in agriculture and industry with European aid. The two European figures established in Baghdad at the time were the Frenchman Rousseau who was consul in Basra in 1780 and then in Baghdad (1796–7) and the Englishman Rich who was British resident in Baghdad in 1808.

The significance of the Mamluk governors in Baghdad was that, together with the Jalilis in Mosul, they defended Iraq against attacks from Persia, ensured security, and prevented the Wahhabis-Sa'udis from gaining a foothold in Iraq. They also introduced reforms in agriculture and industry with European aid, and allowed European merchants and diplomats into the country. Like the reforming sultans in Istanbul, and Muhammad 'Ali Pasha in Egypt, the reforms introduced by the Mamluk governors were centred on the creation of a modern army and promoting the resources of the country. However, in his bid for centralization and the elimination of the power groups in the empire, Sultan Mahmud II, with his new army, put an end to Mamluk rule in Baghdad in 1831.

The Mamluks in Syria were initially in the service of Ahmad Pasha al-Jazzar who was sent with his troops to establish security in Syria after the death of Zahir al-'Umar in 1775. Jazzar was appointed governor of Sidon, but he made fortified Acre his seat. He was three times appointed governor of the province of Damascus in addition to Sidon. Up till his death in 1804, Jazzar was effectively in control of the whole of southern Syria. He benefited from the flourishing economy of the region and from the exportation of cotton to France. He tightened his control over the French merchants by enforcing a monopoly on exports and fixing the prices of products.

Despite Jazzar's cruelty which earned him the title of Jazzar (butcher), his Mamluks rose against him in 1798 but he quelled their revolt with ferocity. Upon his death in 1804, Jazzar was succeeded by one of his Mamluks who had taken part in the revolt against him. He was Sulayman Pasha, nicknamed al-'Adil (the just), in comparison with the cruelty of Jazzar. Sulayman Pasha ruled the province of Sidon from 1804 until his death in 1818. He depended on Mamluk troops in repulsing Wahhabi-Sa'udi raids into Syria. The Damascene pilgrim caravan was disrupted at the time because of the Wahhabi-Sa'udi threat. The end of Sulayman Pasha's rule marked the end of Mamluk rule in Southern Syria.

The predominance of Jazzar and Sulayman Pasha in southern Syria for about half a century coincides with the rule of Amir Bashir Shihab II (1788–1840) in Mount Lebanon. Amir Bashir's rule witnessed Napoleon's invasion of Syria in 1799 and Muhammad 'Ali Pasha's rule in Syria (1831–40). Amir Bashir was not sure that Napoleon Bonaparte would be able to establish his rule in Syria, and he therefore did not support him. His attitude was otherwise with Muhammad 'Ali who challenged the Ottoman Sultan, headed towards Istanbul and eventually ruled Syria for nine years. Amir Bashir supported Muhammad 'Ali Pasha with Maronite troops in quelling revolts against him. This eventually created tension between the Christians and the Muslims in Syria.[17]

The Mamluks in Syria never attained the status they had acquired in Egypt and in Iraq. However, the resurgence of Mamluk power in Egypt, Iraq and Syria, in the second half of the eighteenth century is significant. It represents the increasing weakness of the Ottoman empire and its need for reform of the army and the institutions of the state.

Growing Insubordination of the Bedouin Tribes

Another example of the weakening authority of the Ottoman empire in the eighteenth century was the growing insubordination of the Bedouin tribes. The Bedouin were always a thorn in the side of the urban authorities. They threatened the pilgrim and trade caravans and encroached on settled areas while seeking pasture. The Ottomans used a variety of methods in dealing with the Bedouin. They fought them when possible, bought them off if they were redoubtable and in control of strategic places on caravan routes, or played off one tribe against another, or even one clan within the same tribe against another clan. The government also appointed Bedouin chiefs to administrative positions and bestowed on them honorary titles to win them over.

Syria witnessed early in the eighteenth century the migration of the 'Anaza confederation of tribes from the Arabian Peninsula into the Syrian Desert (badiyat al-Sham). The 'Anaza replaced the fragmented tribes of the Mawali who were pushed into the periphery of the desert. The 'Anaza also pushed the Shammar tribe which migrated from the Arabian Peninsula into Syria about the middle of the eighteenth century into the border with Iraq along the Euphrates river. The 'Anaza thus controlled the trade routes between Syria and Iraq. Their seasonal movements in search of pasture pressured the smaller tribes on the periphery to penetrate deep into agricultural lands and also to threaten the pilgrim caravan.

In Iraq, the Muntafiq confederation of tribes controlled the region around Basra. The Mamluk governors of Baghdad occasionally extended their rule over Basra to control the Muntafiq. A positive role of the Muntafiq Bedouin, however, was their defence of the borders of Iraq in 1802 against the raids of the Wahhabis-Sa'udis. In Egypt, small tribes in the Delta (Lower Egypt) threatened communications, but they were controlled by the authorities. In the Sa'id (Upper Egypt), however, the Hawwara tribe predominated and controlled the trade of grain. A Mamluk governor was usually appointed governor of the Sa'id to control the trade in grain and ward off Bedouin attacks on agricultural land.

The activity of the Wahhabis-Sa'udis, who were established in central and eastern Arabia in the second half of the eighteenth century, pushed several tribes towards the western shores of the Persian/Arabian Gulf where they established with British aid a number of principalities. The Sabah clan established an Amirate in Kuwait (a diminutive form of Kut, meaning fortress) at the top of the Gulf which controlled access to the Gulf. The Khalifah clan was established in Bahrayn, the Thani clan in Qatar, and a combination of smaller principalities governed by Bedouin shaykhs, hence known as Shaykhdoms, spread along the southern coast. Most of these principalities engaged in navigation and fishing, but Bahrayn excelled in pearling. The shaykhdoms were accused of engaging in piracy[18] and fighting with each other. The British around 1820 signed treaties with the shaykhdoms prohibiting piracy and achieving peace through truces among them. The British later on imposed direct political domination over the Gulf principalities between 1869 and 1971. In 1970, Kuwait, Bahrayn and Qatar became independent, and the remaining shaykhdoms united to form the United Arab Emirates in 1971. Down the Gulf, Oman remained independent but torn by internal struggle between the coast governed by a sultan from Muscat and the interior governed by a religious Imam. In 1971, both parts were united under Sultan Qabus

In central Arabia in the meantime the Wahhabi-Sa'udi alliance was posing a major religious and political challenge to the Ottoman authorities. The major powers in western Arabia at the time were the Sharif in the Hijaz, who was under Ottoman control, and the independent Zaydi Imams in Yemen. Najd was under the control of two tribes: the Sa'udis in Dar'iyya and the Mu'ammars in 'Uyayna. Najd was flourishing at the time because pilgrims and traders from the Gulf passed through it on their way to the Hijaz.

Wahhabism was a reformist movement on the periphery of the Ottoman empire but in the heartland of Islam. It was founded by Muhammad Ibn 'Abd al-Wahhab (1703–92) who hailed from a family of Hanbali judges in 'Uyayna in Najd. Influenced by the Syrian Hanbali scholar Ibn Taymiyya (1263–1328), Muhammad Ibn 'Abd al-Wahhab called for a return to the practices of early Islam when it was pure and simple under the Arab ancestors, the *salaf*, hence the movement came to be known as salafiyya. It called for the abolition of the extreme Sufi practices and visitation to shrines, and emphasized that there should be no intercessor between God and the believer; hence its followers were known as *muwahhidun* (Unitarians).

Allying themselves with the Sa'udi tribe, the Wahhabis-Sa'udis attacked the Shi'i site of Karbala in Iraq in 1802 and raided Syria in 1810. They also conquered the Hijaz, including the two holy sanctuaries of Islam, Mecca and Medina. Muhammad 'Ali Pasha of Egypt was ordered by the Ottoman Sultan to oust the Wahhabis from Hijaz which he did between 1812 and 1818.[19] It took the Wahhabis-Sa'udis over one hundred years to regain control of the Hijaz and oust the Sharif family in 1925. Sharif Husayn at the time alienated the emerging Sa'udi Amir by declaring himself caliph after Mustafa Kemal (Ataturk) had abolished the caliphate in the Ottoman empire in 1924 and declared Turkey a republic.

European Mercantilism and Middle Eastern Traditional Economy and Society

The aim of European mercantilism was to strengthen the economy of the nation-state in Europe and its capacity to launch war by encouraging exports and limiting imports. Europe under mercantilism was basically interested in promoting its business relations with the rest of the world. The Ottomans on their part facilitated the spread of European trade in their lands by concluding with the European states commercial treaties known as capitulations which gave many privileges to European merchants including the right to be governed by the laws of their countries in cases of litigation in the Ottoman courts. The first capitulations were reportedly given by Sultan Sulayman the Magnificent in 1535 to Francis I of France who befriended the Ottomans against the common enemy, the Habsburgs of the Holy Roman empire. Other European states were later on granted similar privileges. In the course of time, the capitulations became a state within a state. The privileges initially provided by the capitulations to European merchants were extended to include their Middle Eastern protégés, most of whom were Christians and Jews.

Benefiting from the privileges given by the Ottomans to foreign merchants, the British established the Levant Company in Aleppo in 1581. The French established a consulate in Aleppo in the 1540s. The consular agents at the time were primarily representatives of commercial companies whose principal duty was to promote trade.

The French utilized the Chambre de Commerce de Marseille to promote their commercial interests world wide. French commercial activity increased tremendously in the Middle East during the rule of King Louis XIV (1643–1715) and his finance minister Jean Baptiste Colbert (1661–83). Colbert's commercial policy, which was known as Colbertism, was an integral part of mercantilism. Neither Zahir al-'Umar who carved for himself a small principality in upper Galilee in the eighteenth century, nor Jazzar, who succeeded him, would have been able to raise an army of mercenaries and Mamluks and to fortify Acre and other towns without the flourishing trade in the regions which they monopolized to their advantage.

The backbone of the traditional economies and societies in the Middle East was the guilds. Mercantilist Europe did business with the guild economy which served its interests. Capitalist Europe later on weakened the guild system and contributed to the economic and social instability of the region.

The origins of the guild system are still controversial. Guilds appeared in the Arab countries under Ottoman rule. Before that, there were crafts and craftsmen but no guilds. In matters of dispute, craftsmen referred their cases to the judge (qadi) or to the jurist (mufti) who found a solution to them.

The Ottomans apparently inherited the Byzantines' guild system and encouraged its application in the empire. As early as the sixteenth century, there are references in the court records in Syria to the formation of guilds. The guild system reached the peak of its organization and effectiveness in the seventeenth end the eighteenth centuries. Like Egypt[20] and the rest of the Ottoman empire as far away as Albania,[21] Syria had a highly sophisticated guild system. The terms used for guild in the court records of Syria are the standard one *ta'ifa*, meaning group, and the less-used Arabic term *sunf* (pl. *asnaf*) and the Persian term *kar* meaning occupation.

The guilds maintained the division of labour and engaged in three principal activities: production, marketing and services. Unlike European guilds which had to be authorized by the government, the guilds in the Ottoman empire were by and large autonomous. As autonomous bodies, the guilds had important economic and fiscal roles. They upheld the division of labour, regulated the distribution of raw materials among their members, guaranteed the quality of production, fixed the prices of commodities and levied taxes collectively imposed on their members, each in accordance with his work.

The guilds chose their heads (shaykhs), merged with each other or separated from each other by their own free will. Decisions taken by the majority of the members were enforced on all members. Representatives of the guild conveyed to the judge in the Islamic court the decisions taken by the guild. The judge accordingly legalized the decisions and wrote them down in the registers.

Like the European guilds, the guilds had three professional ranks: apprentice (*mubtad'i*), journeyman (*sani'*), and master (*mu 'allim* or *ustadh*, abbreviated into *usta*). Only the master could open a workshop and employ apprentices and journey-men if he could afford the cost involved in that. The master had to buy or rent the *gedik*, that is, the equipment necessary for his profession, and the *khilu* which is the right to use the equipment in the shop. Both the *gedik* and the *khilu* could be very expensive depending on the type of craft involved. A non-professional could buy the *gedik* and the *khilu* in part or in whole for investment. Their prices could be high depending on the type of the commodity. Looms in a textile shop, for example, cost a lot of money before the introduction of the European jacquard loom.

The workshops were small and run mostly by individuals. Partnerships among the masters before the impact of industrial Europe were rare. The judge considered partnership a violation of Islamic law and practice and ordered the guild members not to resort to it because it was harmful to the Muslims, as he put it. The reason apparently is that partnership encourages monopoly over a commodity, prevents competition and contributes to higher prices.

With the consolidation of the role of the guilds in urban economy, some guilds challenged the regulations that restricted their growth and expansion by resorting to *yamak* relationship. This means that a major guild would attach to it a junior but related guild which markets its by-products and contributes to the payment of its taxes. *Yamak* relationship, which falls short of a merger, is in effect an advanced economic organization that satisfies the interests of the members of both guilds and does not breach Islamic law and practice.[22]

A major aspect of the guild system is that it reflected the coexistence of the religious communities in real life. Several guilds had mixed memberships. There were guilds which included Muslim and Jewish members, such as butchers and druggists, guilds made up of Muslim and Christian members, like weavers and bleachers of cloth, and guilds which included members of all the three communities, such as bakers and tailors. Other guilds were limited to one community in which case the community tried to keep the secret of the craft for its members.

The delegations representing the guilds with mixed memberships before the Islamic court included representatives from all the communities that formed the guild. The criteria for joining the guild, rising through its professional ranks and representing it before the court were based on professional skills rather than on religious affiliation. During the ceremonies marking the promotion of a member from one professional rank to the next in the guilds with mixed membership, the appropriate religious rituals for each member were performed. For a promoted Muslim craftsman, the Fatiha (the opener of the Qur'an) was recited, for a Christian, the Lord's Prayer and for a Jew, the Ten Commandments. The guild thus maintained a high sense of work ethic and truly reflected religious tolerance in society as a whole.[23]

Unlike mercantilist Europe that coexisted with the traditional economies and societies of the Middle East, industrial Europe in the nineteenth century devastated those economies and societies. The flooding of the local markets in the nineteenth century with goods from Europe caused major strains in local economies and societies. Also, the reforms introduced by the Ottoman sultans in the late eighteenth and the nineteenth centuries brought about major dislocations in the local social and economic structures.

Reform in the Ottoman Empire

Suffering major defeats on the European, Russian and Persian fronts, the Ottoman empire was forced to introduce reform. The first reforming Sultan Selim III (1789–1807) established a new European-style army known as the *nizam-i jedid*. For the new army, he opened military schools and introduced conscription. He also sent the first diplomatic mission to Europe in 1792. The reforms antagonized the old Janissary army and the religious scholars ('ulama) who accused the sultan of imitating the infidels. They brought about his deposition in 1707, and his assassination in 1808.

Sultan Mahmud II (1808–39) succeeded in abolishing the Janissaries in 1826 for their poor performance in the Greek war for independence from Ottoman rule. He also controlled the 'ulama by depriving them of their control over the religious endowments (*waqfs*). He created a Directorate of Waqfs to administer the religious endowments and made the 'ulama salaried officials under state control. Sultan Mahmud also ended the rule of the provincial power groups, the Jalilis in Mosul, the Qaramanlis in Tripolitania, Libya, and the Mamluk governors.

The second phase of reforms, known as the Tanzimat (Regulations), was introduced in 1839 by Sultan Abdul-Majid, who issued the Khatt-i Sherif Gülkhane (Noble Rescript of the Chamber of Roses). The rescript advocated religious freedom for all the people in the empire regardless of their creed or race. It was likewise timed to win over the support of Europe, especially Britain, against Muhammad 'Ali Pasha who was in control of Syria. A second rescript known as Khatt-i Hümayun (Imperial Rescript) was issued by Sultan Abdul-Majid in 1856 restating equality for all subjects. But it also was not implemented. Its aim again was to placate the European powers who defended Turkey in the Crimean war against Russia (1854–6).

Other reforms organizing the provincial administration of the empire took place in the early 1860s. The peak of the reforms, however, was the declaration of a constitution and the convening of a parliament in 1876 by Sultan Abdul-Hamid II (1876–1909). These reforms were ascribed to the Grand Vizier, Midhat Pasha, who became known as the father of the constitution. Facing opposition by liberals and nationalists, Sultan Abdul-Hamid suspended the constitution, dissolved the parliament and dismissed Midhat Pasha in 1878. To strengthen his position and his appeal to Muslim public opinion, Sultan Abdul-Hamid declared himself caliph and called for pan-Islamism. This also was intended to threaten the European powers, notably France and Britain, who ruled over millions of Muslims in North Africa and Asia.[24] Germany, however, stood by Sultan Abdul-Hamid and endorsed his Islamic policy. In a speech delivered in Damascus in 1898, German Emperor Wilhelm II gave his full support to the Sultan's Islamic policy. He assured the three hundred million Muslims of Germany's total support of them.[25] The Zionists, headed by Theodor Herzl, had approached Wilhelm II to mediate on their behalf with the Ottoman sultan and obtain for them his approval for Jewish immigration to Palestine. But the sultan apparently rejected the idea.

The reforms introduced by the Ottoman sultans were primarily intended to strengthen their absolute rule. They paid lip service to equality among their subjects to placate the European powers and obtain their support at critical times. The reforms, however, created liberal opposition to the sultans' autocratic rule.

Demands for wider reforms were voiced by intellectuals, journalists, students and army officers most of whom were influenced by European liberal ideas and had studied either in Europe or in European-style schools in Turkey. In 1865 a clandestine Young Ottoman Society was established calling for Ottoman–Islamic solidarity under an enlightened sultan. Its slogans were justice, liberty and homeland, but not equality. It also supported the constitution of 1876. The society eventually foundered because of personal ambitions, social cleavages and inability to present a social and economic programme to attract the masses.

The Young Turks replaced the Young Ottomans in 1889. Being mostly military drawn from the middle and the lower middle class, they were more coherent professionally and as a social group. Accused of a coup in 1896 and banned, they went to Salonica, capital of Macedonia, where they operated clandestinely through the army. They eventually forced Sultan Abdul-Hamid to re-declare the constitution in 1908, and then deposed him in 1909. The Committee of Union and Progress (CUP) of the Young Turks then ruled Turkey alongside a weakened Sultan-Caliph. The Young Turks led Turkey into the First World War as the ally of Germany.[26]

European Capitalism and the Arab Middle East

The relationship between Europe and the Arab Middle East changed dramatically in the nineteenth century. The business relations and the coexistence that prevailed between mercantilist Europe and Middle Eastern economies and societies changed into military intervention, occupation and economic domination of the Middle East by capitalist Europe. Adjustment to the new conditions on the part of Middle Eastern peoples involved profound changes in the structures of local economies and societies.

Egypt between two European Conquests

Napoleon Bonaparte's expedition into Egypt in 1798 ushered in a new phase in the relations between Europe and the Arab Middle East. Expansion into the Middle East was a historic goal for France ever since French King Louis IX led the seventh and the eighth Crusades. His death in Tunis in 1270 was followed by his canonization by the Pope in 1297 on account of his piety and embodiment of Christian ideals. Louis's sainthood made him the symbol of French philanthropic work in the Middle East and throughout the French empire. French hospitals in the region, for instance, are still named after him.

The French merchants in Egypt complained of harassment at the hands of the Mamluks who were the de facto rulers of Egypt. The basic aim of the French expedition, however, was to disrupt British trade with India via the Red Sea and also via the land route across the desert.

The French conquered Egypt in 1798. The English in the meantime destroyed the French fleet in the Egyptian seaports. The British also offered support from the sea to Ahmad Pasha al-Jazzar, who was defending Acre against Napoleon's attack in 1799. Napoleon failed to conquer Acre during his Syrian expedition that lasted from 20 February to 20 May. Napoleon returned to France in 1799, and the British evacuated the French troops from Egypt in 1801. A later attempt in 1807 by the British to intervene in Egypt with the collaboration of a Mamluk faction was a failure.[27]

Egypt and the Middle East thus entered the zone of European influence and competition. The cultural impact of Napoleon's expedition into Egypt was tremendous. The discovery of the Rosetta stone by the French enabled French scholars to decipher the sacred hieroglyphic language of ancient Egypt with which its past history was written. An interest by Egyptians and others then developed in the ancient history of Egypt. The science of Egyptology began from that period. The other contribution of the expedition was the publication of a multi-volume work entitled *Description de l'Egypte* that studied in detail all aspects of Egypt's history and culture.

The power vacuum in Egypt caused by the withdrawal of the French and the failure of the British to replace them was filled by Muhammad 'Ali, an army officer sent to Egypt by the Ottomans at the head of Albanian troops to restore order to the country. Muhammad 'Ali was appointed governor of Egypt in 1805. He got rid of the Mamluk chiefs in 1811–12 and stopped the importation of Mamluks into Egypt that started about the middle of the thirteenth century, when the Mamluks established a sultanate in Egypt and Syria that lasted until 1517. The Ottomans, however, allowed Mamluk importation into Egypt to serve in the administration and the army until Muhmmad 'Ali stopped their importation and executed their leaders in 1811–12. After consolidating his power, Muhammad 'Ali Pasha removed the Mamluk tax farmers and appointed government officials in their place. He controlled the 'ulama by making them salaried officials and he established a state directorate to administer the waqfs.[28]

Muhammad 'Ali succeeded in his agricultural reforms by building dams and canals for intensive cultivation. But he failed in industrialization. This was due to the lack of local skills and industrial consciousness among the Egyptians, to the shortage of internal and external markets, and to intense European competition. The 1838 commercial treaty between Britain and the Ottoman empire that reduced customs duties on imported goods to the Ottoman empire to a mere 3 per cent flooded Middle Eastern markets with European goods and damaged local production.

Muhammad 'Ali's introduction of European-style industry financed by agriculture was influenced by the Saint Simonians (after Comte Claude de Saint Simon, 1760–1825), who considered Muhammad 'Ali an enlightened despot and experimented with their ideal society governed by science in Egypt. The Saint Simonians laid the foundation of Egypt's dependence on foreign loans and debts to finance industry which was a failure. Thus Muhammad 'Ali Pasha's jump from subsistence economy to industrial economy had failed. Egypt then reverted to an export-oriented economy which peaked during the American Civil War of 1861–5, which allowed Egypt to export its long-staple cotton to Europe.

The economic reforms introduced by Muhammad 'Ali were not an end in themselves but a means to build a strong army and establish an empire. Muhmmad 'Ali intervened in the Hijaz between 1811 and 1818 and succeeded in ousting the Wahhabis-Sau'dis from the Hijaz and the Holy Places of Islam for over a century, until 1925 when the Wahhabis-Sau'dis again conquered the Hijaz and ousted its ruler Sharif Husayn. Muhmmad 'Ali also conquered the Sudan between 1820 and 1824 hoping to conscript the Sudanese into his new army and obtain economic resources. He also supported the Ottomans in their war against the Greeks who were fighting for independence which they achieved in 1830.

Muhammad 'Ali's campaign into Syria in 1831–2 was the most important of his foreign ventures, perhaps more so for Syria than for Egypt. His loss of Syria in 1840 under pressure from Britain and other European nations marked the end of his dream for empire. His failure was due largely to European action against him. There was no war at the time to keep Europe busy.

The establishment of the Alexandria–Cairo railway that was undertaken by Britain in 1851 and completed in 1856 was followed by the construction of the Suez Canal in 1869. The expense of the canal further aggravated Egypt's debts. Britain bought Egypt's shares in the Suez Canal in 1875. British control over the lines of communication all the way to India enabled Queen Victoria to declare herself Empress of India in 1877. This also led to the British occupation of Egypt in 1882.

European Influence in Syria

Egyptian rule in Syria between 1831 and 1840 opened the country up far and wide to European influence. Muhammad 'Ali Pasha's son, Ibrahim Pasha, who was in control in Syria at the time, allowed European diplomats, missionaries and traders into the country. European consuls were established in Damascus where none had existed before. Catholic and Protestant missionary schools were also allowed to function.

Trade was the major area through which Europe dominated the Syrian economy at the time. In his report on the commercial statistics in Syria which John Bowring submitted to the British government in 1839, he gave ample information about the number of Damascene merchants, whether Muslim, Christian or Jewish, who were engaged in business relationships with Europe. Sixty-six Muslim commercial establishments in Damascus, according to Bowring, were involved in trade with Europe with a capital estimated at 20 to 25 million piastres (200,000 to 250,000 pounds sterling). There were twenty-nine Christian merchants in Damascus with a capital of 4.5 to 5.5 million piastres who were engaged in foreign trade. Twenty-four Jewish houses, with a capital estimated at from 16 to 18 million piastres, were occupied in foreign trade. A total of 107 shopkeepers retailed British goods in Damascus with a capital of 1,600,000 to 2,100,000 piastres. The extent of foreign trade with Syria and the establishment of foreign merchants in the country necessitated the establishment of mixed courts of commerce. The tribunal of commerce in Damascus, according to Bowring, was composed of twelve members, nine of whom were Muslims, two Christians, and one Jew.[29]

The influx of European industrial goods, mainly textiles, to the Middle East disrupted local manufactures and had a devastating impact on the guilds that manufactured and marketed these products. Modern transport facilities using steamships arriving at expanded seaports flooded the local markets with European goods. The seaport of Beirut, for example, was enlarged to accommodate steamships.[30] A carriage road was built between Beirut and Damascus in 1863 to facilitate the transport of goods into the interior of the country. Railways were built in the 1880s between select Syrian seaports and the interior to expedite the transfer of goods. The Ottoman commercial treaties with Britain and other European states in 1839 and later, reducing customs duties on imported goods, facilitated the influx of European goods into the markets of the Ottoman empire.

European goods were competitive on the local markets. They were cheaper, better, and appealing to the local taste. European fashions soon spread in the Middle East which in turn promoted the sale of European cloth that fitted them. Men, for instance, began to wear trousers. For lack of a word in Arabic for trousers, the Frankish word pantalon was and still is used in Arabic for trousers. Syrian women were fascinated with European cloth that carried European marks and labels.

Competition among European manufacturers further lowered the price of their commodities and made them even more competitive on the local markets. Local products suffered from the competition of European cloth and also from the increase in the price of cotton and silk produced locally. These cash crops were sold to Europe and some of them were exported into Syria as spun threads at high prices. The Syrian economy became a dependency economy linked to the world market.

The impact of European goods on the local textile industry was devastating. Sales diminished, workers' wages decreased, lay-offs occurred frequently and bankruptcies were reported to the courts. Clashes took place between journeymen and masters within the guilds over wages. The traditional hand looms that fetched high prices earlier were put on sale more frequently and at much lower prices than before because their products suffered from a decline in demand. A petition by a Damascene tax farmer, who collects taxes from textile guilds, to the Damascus authorities asks for a decrease in the amount of taxes because of the inability of the guilds to pay their dues. He blames the importation of European goods for the plight of the guilds.[31]

A disparity in wealth between the impoverished craftsmen, the majority of whom were Muslims, and the nouveaux riches, who were mostly Christians acting as entrepreneurs and agents for European manufacturers, became apparent. The Christian entrepreneurs became the target of the poor. The Jews, who also benefited from the trade with Europe, usually kept a low profile. Muslim merchants also made money from dealing with European merchants, but they were taken for granted. Only wealthy Christians were targeted by the mob in Aleppo[32] in 1850 and in Damascus[33] in 1860. Religious fanaticism was not the major cause for the riots even though it was used by interested parties to whip up the emotions of the masses.

Relations among the religious communities were already strained under Egyptian rule in Syria because of the many privileges granted to Christians. Christian missionaries were allowed to open schools and local Christian communities were authorized to build new churches. A large measure of freedom was given to the local Christians. The Catholic churches that split from the orthodox churches and were not recognized by the Ottomans were given official recognition under Egyptian rule. Ibrahim Pasha, the Egyptian governor of Syria, appointed a Christian as his man of affairs. However, the use by Muhammad 'Ali of the Maronite troops of his ally the amir of Mount Lebanon, Bashir Shihab II, to suppress Muslim insurgents in Syria in the years 1834 to 1838 increased religious tension among the communities. Also, the issuing of two imperial rescripts by the Ottoman Sultan Abdul-Majid in 1839 and 1856, calling for equality among all the subjects regardless of creed and race, which were difficult to implement, aroused religious suspicions among the Muslims towards the non-Muslims. The single issue, however, that alienated the communities from each other was the imposition of conscription on Muslims only. The Muslim poor were badly affected because the wealthy could pay money in lieu of military service.

The communal tension and the disparity in wealth between the poor and the rich triggered the socio-economic riots in Aleppo and in Damascus. Neither the poor Christians[34] nor the Jews were attacked by the mob, which indicates that the riots were not primarily motivated by religious fanaticism. No similar riots had occurred in Syria in the three preceding centuries under Ottoman rule. There was no breakdown in the traditional economic and social orders at that time to ignite similar riots. Mercantilist Europe did not exert any destabilizing pressure on the prevailing economic and social systems in the Middle East. In the nineteenth century, however, those systems broke down under the strong impact of their integration into the world market. The guild system, the backbone of stability and of orderly economic and social relations, was weakened under the impact of capitalist Europe. The riots in Mount Lebanon in 1860 also played a role in inflaming the riots in Damascus. Druzes and Maronites in Mount Lebanon were locked up in a deadly struggle between peasants seeking emancipation and feudal lords anxious to safeguard their positions. The struggle was further complicated by the exploitation by Europe, especially France under Napoleon III, of these events. Ottoman officials were also accused of complicity and were held responsible for not stopping the riots. Several Ottoman officials were executed at the time. To prevent the European powers from exploiting the situation further, the Ottoman authorities acted quickly and brought the riots to an end by punishing the instigators and compensating the victims.[35]

Local reaction to the impact of capitalist Europe and the riots was quick. The people soon put the riots behind them and returned to their cooperation across the religious divide. They pooled resources and engaged in partnership to measure up to the challenges of the world market. The Damascene manufacturers had already imported the jacquard loom from Europe and some of these looms had been destroyed in the 1860 riots. More jacquard looms were imported from Europe after 1860 and attempts were made to imitate European textile designs. The word 'jacquard' is still in use in Arabic in the Middle East when referring to textiles with figured patterns.[36]

To avoid similar riots and to strengthen the bond among the religious communities, the emerging proto-bourgeoisie in Syria and Lebanon which included Christians and Jews as well as Muslims evolved the ideology of Arabism which emphasizes the shared Arabic culture to which all the religious communities had contributed. To make Arabism more acceptable to Muslims, it was couched in religious terms. A saying attributed to the Prophet Muhammad which says 'Love of one's country is an act of faith' (*Hubb al-watan min al-iman*) appeared at the top of every issue of a Lebanese newspaper established in 1860 under the name of *Nafir Suriyya* (*The Clarion of Syria*). The newspaper was issued by the Lebanese literary figure Butrus Bustan, a Maronite convert to Protestantism. The *watan* (*patrie* or homeland) was the common denominator that brought the Arabs together regardless of their creed or race.

NOTES

1   For the early history of the Ottoman state, see: Claude Cahen, *Pre-Ottoman Turkey: A General Survey of the Material and Spiritual Cultures and History, c. 1071–1330*, translated from the French by J. Jones-Williams (New York: Taplinger, 1968); Paul Wittek, *The Rise of the Ottoman Empire* (New York: Burt Franklin, 1971); Cemal Kafadar, *Between Two Worlds: The Construction of the Ottoman State* (Berkeley: University of California Press, 1995).

2   For the expansion of Islam in Anatolia, see: Speros Vryonis, *The Decline of Medieval Hellenism in Asia Minor and the Process of Islamization from the Eleventh through the Fifteenth Century* (Berkeley: University of California Press, 1986).

3   Compare with Halil Inalcik, 'Ottoman Methods of Conquest', *Studia Islamica* II (1954), 102–29.

4   Halil Inalcik, 'Arab–Turkish Relations in Historical Perspective (1260–1914)', in *Studies in Turkish–Arab Relations*, Annual I, Istanbul (?), 1986, 148–57.

5   Fernand Braudel, *La Méditerranée et le Monde Méditerranéen à l'Epoque de Philippe II*, 2 vols. (Paris, 1949), translated into English by Sian Reynolds as *The Mediterranean and the Mediterranean World in the Reign of Philip II*, 2 vols. (New York: Harper and Row, 1972); Cemal Kafadar, 'Les Troubles Monétaires de la fin du XVIe Siècle et la Prise de Conscience Ottomane du Déclin', *Annales*, March–April, 1991, no. 2, 381–400.

6   On the significance of the treaty of Carlowitz, see: Bernard Lewis, *The Middle East: A Brief History of the Last 2,000 Years* (New York: Scribner, 1995), 276–7.

7   On the Levant Company, see: Alfred C. Wood, *A History of the Levant Company* (New York: Barnes & Noble, 1964); also Bruce Masters, *The Origins of Western Economic Dominance in the Middle East: Mercantilism and the Islamic Economy in Aleppo, 1600–1750* (New York: New York University Press, 1988).

8   Lewis, *A Brief History*, 179–80.

9   On chaos in Persia during this period, see: John R. Perry, *Karim Khan Zand: A History of Iran, 1747–1779* (Chicago: Chicago University Press, 1979).

10   On Khalil Efendi, the agent of the 'Azm family in Istanbul, see: Abdul-Karim Rafeq, *The Province of Damascus, 1723–1783*, paperback (Beirut: Khayats, 1970), 92–4.

11   Ibid., 160–207.

12   On the organization of the Damascene pilgrim caravan, see ibid., 52–76, Abdul-Karim Rafeq, 'New Light on the Transportation of the Damascene Pilgrimage during the Ottoman Period', in *Islamic and Middle Eastern Societies*, ed. Robert Olson (Battelboro, VT: Amana Press, 1987), 127–36; 'Damascus and the Pilgrim Caravan', in *Modernity and Culture: From the Mediterranean to the Indian Ocean*, eds. Leila Tarazi Fawaz and C. A. Bayly (New York: Columbia University Press, 2002), 130–43.

13   Rafeq, *Province*, 213–22.

14   Ibid., 126–31, 195–8, 214–49, 152–260, 302–8; see also Thomas Philipp, *Acre: The Rise and Fall of a Palestinian City, 1730–1831* (New York: Columbia University Press, 2002).

15 P. M. Holt, *Egypt and the Fertile Crescent, 1516–1922: A Political History*, paperback (Ithaca: Cornell University Press, 1985).

16 Ibid., 85–101.

17 Ibid., 232–8.

18 On the rebuttal of piracy, see: Dr. Shaykh Sultan Muhammad al-Qasimi, *The Myth of Arab Piracy in the Gulf* (London: Croom Helm, 1986).

19 Holt, 149–55, 179–80.

20 For the guilds in Egypt, see André Raymond, *Artisans et Commerçants au Caire au XVIIIe Siècle*, 2 vols. (Damas: Institut Français de Damas, 1973, 1974).

21 For the guilds in Albania for which the Arabic word *ta'ifa* is used in the Albanian court records, see: Zija Shkodra, *Esnafet Shqiptare* (Tirane: 1973), the book has a summary in French at the end; 'Les Esnaf ou Corporations dans la Vie Urbaine Balkanique des XVII–XVIIIe Siècle', *Studia Albanica*, 2 (1985), 47–76.

22 Abdul-Karim Rafeq, 'Craft Organization, Work Ethics, and the Strains of Change in Ottoman Syria', *Journal of the American Oriental Society*, 111 (3), 1991, 495–511.

23 Abdul-Karim Rafeq, 'Craft Organizations and Religious Minorities in Ottoman Syria (XVI–XIX Centuries)', in *La Shi'a Nell'Impero Ottomano* (Rome: Accademia Nazionale Dei Lincei, 1993), 25–56; 'Coexistence and Integration among the Religious Communities in Ottoman Syria', in *Islam in the Middle Eastern Studies: Muslims and Minorities* (Osaka: Japan Center for Area Studies. 2003), 97–131.

24 For the reform movement in Turkey, see: Bernard Lewis, *The Emergence of Modern Turkey*, 3rd edn. (New York and Oxford: Oxford University Press, 2002), chs. 4–6.

25 Descriptions of Emperor Wilhelm II's visit to Damascus and other cities in 1898 are given in Arabic by two journalists: Ibrahim al-Aswad, *al-Rihla al-Imbraturiyya fi'l-Mamalik al-'Uthmaniyya* (*The Imperial Journey in the Ottoman Realm*) (Ba'abda (Lebanon): al-Matba'a al-'Uthmaniyya, 1898) and Khalil Sarkis, *Rihlat al-Imbratur Ghalium al-Thani Imbratur Almanya wa-Qarinatuhu ila Filastin wa-Suriyya* (*The Journey of Emperor Guillaume II, Emperor of Germany, and his Wife to Palestine and Syria*), ed. Hasan Suwaydan, 2nd edn. (Damascus: Dar al-Farabi, 1997).

26 For the Young Turks, see Feroz Ahmad, *The Young Turks: The Committee of Union and Progress in Turkish Politics, 1908–1914* (Oxford: Clarendon Press, 1969).

27 Holt, *Egypt and the Fertile Crescent*, 155–63.

28 Afaf Lutfi al-Sayyid-Marsot, *Egypt in the Reign of Muhammad 'Ali* (Cambridge: Cambridge University Press, 1984).

29 John Bowring, *Report on the Commercial Statistics of Syria* (London: W. Cloves for H. M. Stationery Office, 1840), Reprinted (New York: Arno Press: 1973), 93–4.

30 For the development of Beirut in the nineteenth century, see: Leila Tarazi Fawaz, *Merchants and Migrants in Nineteenth-century Beirut* (Cambridge: Cambridge University Press, 1983).

31 Rafeq, 'Work Organization, Work Ethics', 509–11.

32 Bruce Masters, 'The 1850 "Events" in Aleppo: An Aftershock of Syria's Incorporation in the Capitalist World System', *International Journal of Middle Eastern Studies*, 22 (1990), 3–20; *Christians and Jews in the Ottoman Arab World: The Roots of Sectarianism* (Cambridge: Cambridge University Press, 2001), ch. 5.

33 Leila Tarazi Fawaz, *An Occasion for War: Civil Conflict in Lebanon and Damascus in 1860* (Oxford and London: Centre for Lebanese Studies and I. B. Tauris, 1994).

34 The poor Christians in the Midan neighbourhood in Damascus, for example, were not molested in the riots of 1860, see: Abdul-Karim Rafeq, 'The Social and Economic Structure of Bab al-Musalla (al-Midan), Damascus, 1825–1875', in *Arab Civilization: Challenges and Responses: Studies in Honor of Constantine K. Zurayk*, eds. George N. Atiyeh and Ibrahim M. Oweiss (Albany: State University of New York Press, 1988).

35 Abdul-Karim Rafeq, 'The Impact of Europe on a Traditional Economy: The Case of Damascus, 1840–1870', in *Economie et Sociétés dans l'Empire Ottoman (fin du XVIIIe–début du XXe Siècle*, eds. Jean-Louis Bacqué-Grammont et Paul Dumont (Paris: Centre National de la Recherche Scientifique, 1983), 419–32; 'New Light on the 1860 Riots in Damascus', *Die Welt des Islams*, 28 (1988), 412–30.

36 For local reaction to the European impact, see Nu'man al-Qaasatli, *al-Rawda al-Ghanna' fi Dimashe al-Fayha'* (*The Pleasant Gardens of Fragrant Damascus*) (Beirut, 1876) reprinted (Beirut: Dar al-Ra'id al-'Arabi, 1981).

FURTHER READING

Ahmad, Feroz, *The Young Turks: The Committee of Union and Progress in Turkish Politics, 1908–1914* (Oxford: Clarendon Press, 1969).

Fawaz, Leila Tarazi, *Merchants and Migrants in Nineteenth-century Beirut* (Cambridge: Cambridge University Press, 1983).

Hourani, Albert, *A History of the Arab Peoples* (Cambridge: Belknap Press of Harvard University Press, 1991).

Masters, Bruce, *The Origins of Western Economic Dominance in the Middle East: Mercantilism and the Islamic Economy in Aleppo, 1600–1750* (New York: New York University Press, 1988).

Perry, John R, *Karim Khan Zand: A History of Iran, 1747–1779* (Chicago: Chicago University Press, 1979).

Philip, Thomas, *Acre: The Rise and Fall of a Palestinian City, 1730–1831* (New York: Columbia University Press, 2002).

Rafeq, Abdul-Karim, *The Province of Damascus, 1723–1783* (Beirut: Khayats, 1970).

Raymond, André, *Artisans et Commerçants au Caire au XVIIIe Siècle*, 2 vols. (Damas: Institut Français de Damas, 1973, 1974).

Al-Sayyid-Marsot, Afaf Lutfi, *Egypt in the Reign of Muhammad Ali* (Cambridge: Cambridge University Press, 1984).

Vryonis, Speros, *The Decline of Medieval Hellenism in Asia Minor and the Process of Islamization from the Eleventh through the Fifteenth Century* (Berkeley: University of California Press, 1986).

CHAPTER THIRTEEN

Colonialism, the Ottomans, the Qajars, and the Struggle for Independence
The Arab World, Turkey, and Iran

PETER SLUGLETT

In the period between the mid-nineteenth century and the outbreak of the First World War, much of the Middle East and North Africa either was already, or subsequently came, under different forms of colonial rule, and most of those parts of the region which were not formally colonised were subject to the pressures of varying degrees of 'informal empire'.[1] In addition, with the exception of Morocco, the entire region either had been, or still was, nominally part of the Ottoman or Qajar empires. These two geopolitical units had been in existence, in the case of the Ottomans, since the late thirteenth century, and in the case of the Qajars, since 1779, and were to come to an end in 1924 and 1925 respectively. This chapter will discuss the imposition of European rule in the Middle East, the 'imperial legacy' of the empires which preceded it, and the various stages and forms of resistance to colonial rule from the colonised populations until the military coups of the 1950s.

New Political Dispensations in the Nineteenth and Twentieth Centuries in the Middle East and North Africa

Let us begin by making a brief *tour d'horizon* of the stages of the imposition of European colonial control, proceeding from west to east. In North Africa, France invaded and began to conquer Algeria in 1830, conquered Tunisia in 1881 and (together with Spain) imposed a protectorate upon Morocco in 1912. All three became 'colonial settler states', in the sense that a substantial proportion of the population (eventually as much as 15–20 per cent in the case of Algeria) were Europeans, mostly French (but also Italian) families, who came to live and work in North Africa, both on the land and in the cities, some of whose descendants remained there until forced out by the independence struggles of the 1950s and early 1960s (Prochaska, 1990). The same was true of Libya, albeit on a smaller scale; Libya was annexed by Italy in 1911, and attracted some 110,000 Italian settlers in the inter-war period, mostly from the impoverished rural south (Segre, 1974; Anderson, 1986).

In Egypt, following the rise of a nationalist movement which threatened to challenge the British and French administration of the public debt (put in place in 1876), British troops invaded in 1882, and occupied the country informally until the declaration of a British protectorate on the outbreak of the First World War.[2]

Although large numbers of foreigners resided in Egypt, they were generally neither 'settlers' nor '*colons*' in the French North African sense (since they lived mostly in the cities and engaged in commerce or in other service occupations) and most of them were not citizens of the occupying power. Thus of the 99,610 foreigners living in Alexandria in 1917 (19 per cent of the city's population of 444,617), 25,393 were Greek and 17,860 Italian; the British population (including troops) came to 10,658 and the French to 8,556 (Ilbert, 1996: II, 757–59). While Britain remained in political control of Egypt until and beyond 1914, France owned 40 per cent of the Egyptian public debt and about two-thirds of all Egyptian banking and mortgage companies before the First World War (Issawi, 1982: 62–71; Saul, 1997; Owen, 2004).

On the coasts of the Arabian Peninsula, Britain's concern to keep the route to India safe and open led to the signature of a series of treaties, beginning in 1820, with the rulers of Bahrain and of the area now roughly corresponding to the United Arab Emirates. In 1853 the rulers signed a Perpetual Maritime Truce (hence the 'Trucial States', as the United Arab Emirates were formerly known). In 1892, largely to counter possible French intrusion, Bahrain and the lower Gulf emirates (including, at this point, Muscat and 'Uman) signed further agreements with Britain under which they agreed not to grant or dispose of any part of their territories except to Britain, and to conduct their foreign relations exclusively through the British government. In 1899 and 1916 respectively, Kuwait and Qatar, which had not been parties to the earlier 'piracy' treaties, signed similar exclusive agreements with Britain, largely because of their rulers' desire to escape Ottoman and/or Saudi tutelage. To complete the picture, Britain annexed Aden in 1839, and turned it into a naval base. 'Exclusive' treaties were signed with the tribal rulers of the interior, and in 1937 the area was divided into the port and its immediate hinterland (Aden Colony) and the more remote rural/tribal areas (Aden Protectorate).

In the 'Levant', a form of colonialism of a rather different kind came into being after the defeat of the Ottoman empire by Britain and France at the end of the First World War. The former Arab Ottoman provinces were assigned to Britain and France as mandates from the newly created League of Nations, Britain taking responsibility for Iraq, Palestine and Transjordan, and France taking responsibility for Lebanon and Syria (Méouchy and Sluglett, 2004) the mandate system was that the states concerned should remain under the tutelage of the mandatory power, until such time as they were able to 'stand alone', a period which, although not specified, was viewed as not of indefinite length. In addition, 'the mandate regimes in the Middle East had the specific characteristic, one unusual for a colonial regime, that they took over from a relatively strong, relatively modern state – the late Ottoman empire' (Khalidi in Méouchy and Sluglett, 2004: 696).

Of the five states, Palestine was unique among its neighbours in that it was a settler state, since the text of the Palestine mandate included the terms of the Balfour Declaration (1917), in which Britain as mandatory power undertook to facilitate the setting up of a 'national home for the Jewish people'. In 1922, there were 93,000 Jews in Palestine and about 700,000 Arabs; in 1936, there were 380,000 Jews and 983,000 Arabs, and in 1946, about 600,000 Jews and 1.3 million Arabs; thus the Jewish population increased from 13 per cent to 31 per cent over a period of twenty-four years (McCarthy, 1990). It is probably true to say, at least initially, that Arab opposition to Jewish immigration was focused at least as much on the Jews' perceived character as European *settlers* (as in, say, Algeria) as on their religious affiliation.

As has been mentioned previously, the rest of the Middle East did not experience direct colonial control, although the Ottoman empire's borrowings from European sources, and a mounting trade deficit, led it to declare bankruptcy in 1875. Its finances were subsequently managed by the Ottoman Public Debt Administration, essentially a committee representing the interests of the European bondholders (Blaisdell, 1966).[3] After the collapse of the empire at the end of the First World War, and the loss of the Arab provinces, Anatolia was occupied by the armies of the victorious Allies (especially France, Greece and Italy), and, under the terms of the Treaty of Sèvres in August 1920, divided between them and partitioned into independent statelets in Armenia and Kurdistan. However, in the spring of 1920, the Ottoman general Mustafa Kemal took over the leadership of a national resistance movement, and set up a provisional government in Ankara. By the autumn of the same year the Soviet Union had taken over eastern Armenia, and Turkey had taken over western Armenia and Kurdistan, thus nullifying the provisions of the Treaty of Sèvres. By 1921–2 Kemal had extended his authority over most of the rest of Anatolia, expelling the Greek occupiers from Izmir, and on 1 November 1922 the Grand National Assembly in Ankara inaugurated the Turkish Republic. With some later adjustments, the present frontiers of Turkey were agreed upon under the terms of the Treaty of Lausanne in July 1923.

Iran was the object of British and Russian economic and political interest from the last decade of the eighteenth century until the signature of the Anglo-Russian Entente in 1907, the period of the so-called Great Game (Gillard, 1977). The British wanted to control Iran because of its proximity to India; at the same time the Russians were expanding their empire in Central Asia and also, or so the British made out, intent on gaining access to the warm-water ports on the Persian Gulf. In 1907 Iran was divided into British and Russian spheres of influence; both powers had been somewhat alarmed by the Constitutional Revolution of 1906–11, although it turned out that the people of Iran were obliged to wait rather longer for the end of autocracy than some Iranian intellectuals had envisaged in 1906 (Amanat, 1997; Keddie, 1999; Martin, 1980; Abrahamian, 1982). In addition, oil was discovered in considerable quantity in south-western Iran in 1908, and by 1914 the British government had bought a controlling interest in Anglo-Persian, the company responsible for exploiting it. The country endured a long period of chaos before and during the First World War. After the collapse of Tsarist Russia in 1917, Britain resumed its interference in Iranian affairs, subsidised the government, tried to reorganise the army, and attempted to set up a virtual protectorate in the form of the Anglo-Iranian Agreement of 1919, which the Iranian parliament refused to ratify. Eventually, Reza Khan, the head of the Cossack Brigade in Qazvin, with the encouragement of the British military commander in Iran, General Ironside (Keddie, 1981: 87), and with at least tacit approval from Ironside's superiors in London, marched on Teheran in February 1921, and obliged Ahmad Shah to accept his nominee as prime minister. In 1923, Ahmad Shah Qajar left Iran for Europe, and two years later Reza Khan manoeuvred the Iran parliament into ending the Qajar dynasty and giving him the imperial crown.

Finally, principally because of their remoteness and lack of major strategic importance, central Arabia and northern Yemen were never colonised. Both areas were intermittently part of the Ottoman empire; the Ottomans attempted to re-impose their authority on Yemen between 1871 and 1918, but the mountainous nature of the terrain and the lack of modern communications meant that their impact was fairly minimal. A number of factors (the end of the Ottoman empire, Anglo-Italian rivalry in the Red Sea area in the inter-war period, the waning of British power in the Middle East after the Second World War) combined to make the last two imams (Yahya b. Muhammad, 1904–48, Ahmad b.Yahya, 1948–62) much more powerful, and able to rule over a wider area, than almost any of their predecessors. Ahmad's rule was especially tyrannical, and after his death in September 1962, his son Muhammad al-Badr had few supporters left within the country. A coup organised by his Yemeni enemies, with Egyptian backing, initiated a civil war which put an end to the imamate and (after many vicissitudes) set up the Yemen Arab Republic in 1970. By this time the opposition seems to have concluded that its objectives could not be attained through the agency of a revivifying or reforming imam, a solution which the 'Free Yemeni' movement had considered in the 1940s (Douglas, 1987), and the Zaydi imamate, founded by Tarjuman al-Din al-Qasim b. Ibrahim Taba'taba' in 860, came to an abrupt end.

In central Arabia, the fortunes of the Sa'ud family, which had risen and fallen throughout the nineteenth century, were boosted by a combination of fortunate coincidences. These included the rise to power of the energetic 'Abd al-'Aziz ibn 'Abd al-Rahman (Ibn Sa'ud); his capture of Riyadh from the Sa'uds' principal rivals, the Rashids of Ha'il, in January 1902; growing Ottoman weakness, and Britain's concomitant desire to avoid a power vacuum in the peninsula. Between 1902 and the First World War, Ibn Sa'ud gradually consolidated his position in eastern and central Arabia. In February 1905, the Ottomans appointed Ibn Sa'ud *qa'immaqam* of southern Najd; early in 1906, a raiding party killed his main rival, 'Abd al-'Aziz ibn Mu'tib al-Rashid, and largely in consequence, Turkish forces withdrew from most of northern and north-western Najd (al-Qasim) by the end of that year. By 1913 Ibn Sa'ud had gained sufficient strength and confidence to expel the Ottoman garrison from al-Ahsa; in May 1914 he was recognised by the Ottomans as *wali* of Najd. With the First World War the political situation in the Arabian peninsula changed irrevocably in his favour (Leatherdale, 1983: 15, 369–70).

In December 1915 Ibn Sa'ud signed a treaty with Britain under which he was recognised as ruler of 'Najd, El Hassa, Qatif and Jubail' (no cessions of territory, and no economic concessions, to any foreign power). In return, he agreed, *inter alia*, to 'refrain from all aggression on, or interference with, the territories of Kuwait, Bahrain and the Shaikhs of Qatar and the Oman Coast, who are under the protection of the British Government' (Leatherdale, 1983: 372–3). In 1922, the Rashids were finally defeated and ousted from Ha'il; at this point Ibn Sa'ud and his followers began to look for fresh fields to conquer, both in the east and in the west. As early as May 1919, one of Ibn Sa'ud's lieutenants had attacked the camp of 'Abdullah ibn [Sharif] Husayn at Turaba (in the Hijaz, about 150 miles from Jidda) and put 'Abdullah to flight. Although not immediately obvious at the time, the event in fact marked the beginning of a process which culminated with the expulsion of the Hashimite family from the Hijaz (and the Arabian peninsula as a whole) in December 1925 and later with the formal establishment of the Kingdom of Sa'udi Arabia in 1932 (Sluglett and Farouk-Sluglett, 1982).[4]

In this way, after the enormous watershed represented by the First World War, the configuration of the modern Middle East lurched into being. Apart from the changes to the borders of Israel in 1948 and 1967, most of the territorial dispensations created by the time of the Lausanne conference in 1923 are still with us today.[5]

Plate 13.1 Sa'd Zaghlul, anti-colonialist Egyptian leader
Source: © *AlHayat* Newspaper, London

However, while the states continue, the forms of regime which govern them have changed almost beyond recognition, as the result of anti-colonial wars, civil strife, and above all of military coups, usually labelled 'revolutions', in the 1950s and 1960s. It is to the history of the anti-colonial struggle, both real and invented, that we shall now turn.

Nationalism in the Arab Provinces in the Last Decades of the Ottoman Empire

In 1990, Eric Hobsbawm noted that 'Nationalism requires too much belief in what is patently not so', and went on to quote Renan's lecture at the Sorbonne in March 1882, *Qu'est-ce que c'est une nation?*: 'L'oubli, et je dirai même l'erreur historique, sont un facteur essentiel de la formation d'une nation, est c'est ainsi que le progrès des études historiques est souvent pour la nationalité un danger' (Hobsbawm, 1990: 12). In the case of the contemporary Arab world, one quite stubbornly held belief in 'what

Plate 13.2 Mustafa Nahhas, Egyptian Prime Minister and founder of the Arab League
Source: © *AlHayat* Newspaper, London

is patently not so' is the notion that, in the immediate aftermath of the First World War, British and French imperialism simply replaced four centuries of Ottoman imperialism, division and despotism, and that the liberation of the Arabs, which had been that people's primary goal for 'several generations', was forcibly postponed for another half century or so. That European colonial or quasi-colonial rule retarded, or acted as a brake upon, 'Arab development' is a proposition that can legitimately be postulated, but it is as inaccurate to view the Ottoman empire as 'just another' variant of imperialism as it is to project the 'Arab national struggle' against the Ottomans very much further back than the early years of the twentieth century.

In fact, nationalism took some time to reach the Arab provinces of the Ottoman empire. There were two main, interconnected, reasons for this; first it was generally the case among the population of that region that identity was conceived of in religious, rather than ethnic, terms, and second, most of that population was Sunni Muslim, the same sect as the Ottoman Turks. Hence notions of 'oppressive rule by alien rulers' is anachronistic. Ideas of nationalism and self-determination had indeed surfaced in Greece early in the nineteenth century, in parts of [what was then still to become, but is now 'former'], Yugoslavia, and in the areas which are now Bulgaria and Romania, leading to their independence from the empire at various times in the nineteenth century (Jelavich, 1983). Of course, south-eastern Europe was predominantly Orthodox Christian, with a relatively small Muslim population, speaking a variety of local languages, which became the languages of the new states. In the course of the nineteenth century, the Ottoman government had promulgated a series of educational, legal and constitutional reforms, and in addition had tried to create something approximating to 'Ottoman national consciousness' (*Osmanlılık*), explicitly extending promises of good government and regular tax assessment, in the words of the Hatt-i Şerif of Gülhane (3 November 1839) to 'all our subjects, of whatever religion or sect they may be; they shall enjoy them without exception' (Anderson, 1970: 59–65). These promises were not, ultimately, sufficiently attractive to preserve or attract the loyalty of the peoples of the Balkans, but it is an interesting indication of the official thinking of the time, influenced, certainly, by mounting pressures for change from the European powers.

There is very little evidence of similar 'national' sentiments finding a wide echo in the Arab provinces. In fact, the Tanzimat reforms generally had the effect of bolstering (and also of helping to create) a group with strong ties to Istanbul.[6] 'Abd al-Hamid's social and religious conservatism, together with the very real advantages that the urban notables derived from supporting him, meant that opposition in, for instance, Syria, was largely confined to a few radicals and those Salafi ulama for whom the sultan's pan-Islamism was an inadequate substitute for more thorough-going Islamic reforms (Commis, 1990). In consequence, when the Committee of Union and Progress (CUP) came to power after the Young Turk Revolution in 1908, there was not all that much support for it in Syria.

In fact, it was only after the ousting of 'Abd al-Hamid and the counter-coup of April 1909 that the CUP's efforts at Turkification began to lose it most of the support which its earlier anti-absolutist ethos might have attracted. Hence in the five years between 1909 and 1914, the CUP's growing tactlessness and apparently headlong rush towards the promotion of Turkish rather than Ottoman nationalism began to have the effect of making public opinion in Syria increasingly at odds with the government in Istanbul (Kayali, 1997). Even so, the principal goal of the leaders of the 'Syrian opposition' appears to have been to restore a more palatable form of Ottomanism, reconstructed, certainly, in the general direction of a greater degree of administrative decentralization. With the defeat of the empire in 1918, of course, Ottomanism ceased to be an option. Until then, however, 'the empire, for most Muslims and even some Christians, was simply seen as the only remaining political force capable of forestalling European colonial ambitions' (Masters' 2001: 176).

From Colonialism to Independence in the States of North West Africa

To sum up, then, with the exception of Iran and Turkey, which were emerging as more or less independent states, and of Yemen and 'Sa'udi Arabia' whose importance at the time seemed rather limited, the whole of the Middle East and North Africa was under British, French, Italian or Spanish control by 1920, with Britain and France as the principal imperial powers. In brief, the states of North Africa were generally fairly quiescent until after 1945, although the colonial regimes, with their policies of widespread confiscation of tribal land for the benefit of a small and often highly stratified settler population, were deeply unpopular. In Morocco, the French were generally able to contain the movement for national independence which began to gain strength in the 1930s (Le Tourneau, 1962; Julien, 1978), but they precipitated a major crisis by exiling the Sultan, Muhammad V, to Madagascar in 1953. As a result, the rallying cry of the national movement became the return of the sultan from exile, which led in its turn to the sultan/king retaining his position as ruler after Morocco's independence in October 1956.[7] Although the Moroccan monarchy had been able to utilise its 'moral and spiritual capital' to obtain public support at various times in the past, the gradual transformation in the 1950s of the somewhat remote and shadowy figure of Muhammad V into a national hero cum charismatic leader, buttressed by notions of 'Islamic legitimacy' (Munson, 1993; Sluglett, 2002) is remarkable, especially given the Bonapartist tendencies in vogue elsewhere in the Muslim world at the time (as exemplified by Bourguiba, Nasser, Musaddiq and Sukarno in the 1950s).

Habib Bourguiba (1903–2000) took over the leadership of the Tunisian national movement after his release from prison in 1936. His neo-Destour party had about 110,000 members in 1954, and was closely linked with the labour movement. Bourguiba was imprisoned again in France between 1938 and 1943, and after the war a guerrilla movement was formed which attacked French farms and settlers. Probably because France could not take on anti-colonial wars in both Tunisia and Algeria at the same time, Tunisian independence was negotiated fairly smoothly in April 1955. Unlike its counterpart in Morocco, the Tunisian monarchy had been seriously compromised by its links with France, and did not survive independence. Bourguiba presided over a republican regime which became increasingly dictatorial until his removal in 1987 (Anderson, 1986: 158–77, 231–50).

Algeria's road to independence was far rockier than that of the other states of the Maghrib, in fact more so than any other state in the region, mainly because of the large numbers of French settlers in Algeria and of Algerian workers in France. The governments of the Fourth Republic attempted to incorporate Algeria into France, which appealed to the settlers but which was vigorously opposed by the great majority of the Arab population. In 1954 the Algerian resistance formed the *Front de la Libération Nationale* under the leadership of Ahmed Ben Bella, who was captured by the French in 1957 and only released at the end of the war. Some of his colleagues subsequently set up an Algerian government in exile in Tunis. The 'war of national liberation' (Horne, 1977)[8] which lasted until 1962, and in which between a million and a million and a half Algerians, and 27,000 French were killed, was intensely divisive, especially as 'more Algerian Muslims fought as soldiers or *harkis* on the French side than fought in the Algerian army' (Knapp, 1977: 53). The fundamental divisions in Algerian society, especially the ethnic divisions between Arabs and Berbers (perhaps 20 per cent of the total population but highly concentrated in certain areas), between francophones and arabophones, educated and uneducated, religious and secular, have severely affected Algerian politics since independence.

In Libya, Italian conquest and pacification between 1911 and 1932 had faced bitter resistance, involving major losses of life. However, given the isolated and fragmented

nature of Libyan society, this general hostility did not produce a nationalist movement. The country's liberation was carried out almost accidentally, by the Allied
armies in 1942; the British entered into a tentative alliance with the Amir Idris al-
Sanusi, head of the Sanusi order, an Islamic movement somewhat akin to Wahhabism
in Sa'udi Arabia, who was brought back from exile in 1944. After several years of
negotiations, Libya became independent under United Nations auspices early in
1952 and Idris became the new state's hereditary ruler. With the rise of Nasser
shortly afterwards, however, Idris' somewhat autocratic and paternalistic style became
something of an anachronism, and his regime, under which the first oil concessions
were granted and oil struck in 1959, was overthrown by a military coup in September
1969 while he was out of the country (Knapp, 1977: 174–91).

The Colonial Period in the *Mashriq*

In Egypt, Iraq, Lebanon, Syria and Transjordan – the situation in Palestine was of
course unique – the British and French set up, with varying degrees of alacrity,
enthusiasm and 'success', republics and constitutional monarchies. In all five states,
a relatively small group, whom it is convenient, if perhaps harsh, to describe as
'collaborators',[9] participated in administering the country with British or French
support. In a very limited sense, of course, the Arab states had achieved an important
part of the goal which the relatively small numbers of 'Arab nationalists' had sought
before and during the First World War, that is, the liberation of their territories from
Ottoman rule. Of course, those individuals had probably imagined, or at least
desired, a political order in which British and French tutelage would be very much
more limited than it actually became.

In the inter-war period the new political order was widely contested in the Arab
world. The mandate regimes were generally unpopular, especially in Syria and Palestine. Britain had invaded southern Iraq at the end of 1914, and continued to occupy
the country after the war. There was a widespread national rising in the summer of
1920, which took several months to quell. However, after having largely 'pacified' the
country and having set up a compliant government, the British felt able to make their
formal withdrawal in 1932, although real independence was not obtained until 1958
(Sluglett, 1976; Batatu, 1978). In Lebanon the French were welcomed by the
Maronites and other Catholic Christians, but by few others, since the new Lebanon
had been carved out of Syria (Salibi, 1988; Zamir, 1985, 1997). Thus it was not until
1936 that Lebanese Sunni politicians reluctantly came to the conclusion that the
separation between Syria and Lebanon was going to be a permanent if unsatisfactory
feature of the political landscape, and joined more fully in Lebanese politics (Johnson,
1986). In Syria there was a major national rising between 1925 and 1927 which the
French had considerable difficulty in controlling, although a notable-dominated
group, al-Kutla al-Wataniyya, emerged as the voice of moderate nationalism, with
whom, it seemed, the French might be persuaded to work. Expectations were raised
in 1936 with the victory of Léon Blum's Popular Front government in France,
although negotiations for independence ceased when it fell a year later, and Syria
remained under French control until 1945 (Khoury, 1987; Thompson, 1999).

Egypt had been under British tutelage since 1882 and more formally since the
declaration of the protectorate in 1914, and thus escaped the formal structures of the
mandate system. After the war a group of Egyptian politicians wanted to send a

delegation (*wafd*) to the Paris peace conference under the leadership of Sa'd Zaghlul (thereby indicating Egypt's status as an independent state), and when permission for this was refused, there was a widespread national rising. Britain eventually recognised a very limited form of Egyptian independence in 1922, under which it retained ultimate control over four 'reserved points', the security of the communications of the British empire, the defence of Egypt, the protection of the interests of minorities and foreign powers, and matters relating to the Sudan. The Wafd party under Zaghlul and his successor Mustafa Nahhas won an overwhelming victory whenever there were free elections, but was never free to implement popular demands. An Anglo-Egyptian treaty enabling Egypt to enter the League of Nations as an independent state was signed in 1936, but all but the third of the 'reserved points' remained, and there was a large British military presence up to and even beyond the moment when Neguib and Nasser seized power in 1952 (Botman, 1991).

The nature of the cul-de-sac in which the British found themselves in Palestine soon became uncomfortably clear. There was no obvious way of reconciling Zionist and local Arab interests, and the clashes became bloodier with the passage of time (Swedenburg, 2003). The Arab leadership was often implicated in the process of Zionist expansion, since, of course, all the land that the Zionists acquired before 1948 was bought, either from absentee landlords, Palestinian notables, or, in the 1930s and 1940s, from smallholders hit by the world downturn in agricultural prices (Stein, 1984). In addition, the Palestinian notables were deeply divided among themselves, some seeking accommodation with the British, some trying to placate the Zionists, and some fiercely rejecting any compromises. After the Second World War, Britain's straitened economic and military circumstances,[10] growing anti-British activity on the part of the Zionists, clear evidence that the United States was not prepared to 'share the burden' of governing Palestine, and the recommendation, by UNSCOP, the United Nations Special Committee on Palestine, for the eventual partition of Palestine into an Arab state and a Zionist state, brought Britain to announce, early in October 1947, that it would withdraw from Palestine in May 1948. After a series of military actions in the winter and spring of 1948, the Zionists were sufficiently confident of their capacity to resist the armies of the Arab states to declare the state of Israel on 15 May, although fighting continued until February 1949. As far as the Palestinians were concerned, the principal results of the fighting were 'the destruction of [their] society and the birth of the refugee problem' (Morris, 2001: 252), in fact the creation of some 700,000 refugees, who fled to what is now the West Bank and Gaza, Transjordan, Syria and Lebanon.

Some Characteristics of Middle Eastern Politics in the Inter-war Period

In general, the politics of the region underwent a series of sea changes in the inter-war period. In the first place, struggles for autonomy from Istanbul (which had in any case been waged neither consistently nor with any particular determination) now gave way to a more broadly based anti-colonial struggle. Secondly, political life underwent a complete change of direction, in that the centre of the local political universe shifted to the new national capitals. Mosul and Basra now looked towards Baghdad, and Aleppo looked towards Damascus, and local notables had to adjust their focus and their networks accordingly. Thirdly, the issue of Palestine gradually moved centre-stage in the 1930s, especially after the revolt of 1936–9 (Rubin, 1981). The 'anti-colonial struggle' in the Arab world was temporarily halted by the Second World War, in which the Arab states generally supported the Allies, particularly after the Soviet Union joined the Allies in 1941. In the decades after the war the influence of France and Britain in the region gradually declined, to be replaced by that of the United States and the Soviet Union (Louis, 1984).

Although Iraq became nominally independent of Britain in 1932 and Egypt in 1936, and Syria and Lebanon of France in 1945 and 1946, strong economic and military ties bound the various states to their former European rulers, especially the linkages between Britain and Egypt and Iraq.[11] The constitutional arrangements made in Egypt and the mandated territories were based on European models, but it was well-known that elections were rigged. Particularly in the Cold War period after 1945, the imprisonment without trial and torture of political offenders (for the most part those suspected of 'communism', but also members of Muslim fundamentalist groups, particularly in Egypt, where the Society of Muslim Brethren was founded in 1928) were not uncommon. The creation of national armies and wider access to education in almost all the states of the Middle East had the effect of creating a new and highly influential social group, many of whose members were imbued with notions of social justice and national independence (and, in time, anti-Zionism), and who also came to believe that only a revolutionary break with colonialism would bring about genuine independence.

The major exceptions in the region to these 'colonial' political structures were of course Turkey and Iran. Turkey became an independent republic, recognised as such internationally by the terms of the Treaty of Lausanne in 1923. The founder of the state, Mustafa Kemal (Kemal Atatürk) attempted with some success to create a European-style secular nation-state, a task which was facilitated by Turkey's relative ethnic homogeneity,[12] largely the result of the expulsion (or massacre) of most of the Greek and Armenian bourgeoisie between 1914 and 1924 (Keyder, 1987). Atatürk moved the capital to Ankara, abolished the caliphate, banned the fez, and replaced the Arabic script of Ottoman Turkish with the Latin alphabet. In addition he inaugurated a major programme of state-sponsored economic development, a policy usually described as *étatism*. The Turkish state was supposedly (and in many ways later became) democratic but was in fact ruled by its leader and a one-party structure until the elections of 1950, after which the opposition was voted peacefully into office. Turkey's foreign policy in the inter-war period and the Second World War 'can be characterised as cautious, realistic and generally aimed at the preservation of the status quo and the hard-won victory of 1923' (Zürcher, 1998). Relations with the former capitulatory powers (whose subjects had had extra-territorial rights in the Ottoman empire) remained somewhat prickly, but relations with the Soviet Union, with which Turkey shared a border, were generally cordial. Turkey virtually cut itself off from its neighbours to the south and east (Syria and Iraq), erecting tariff barriers which completely changed the economies of all three states, which used to trade freely with each other as part of a unitary economic system. A major point of contention between Syria and Turkey was the *sanjaq* of Alexandretta, assigned to Syria in 1920 (and thus part of France's Syrian mandate). There seems little doubt that the Turks made strenuous efforts to fabricate a Turkish majority, but as war became increasingly imminent and France was anxious not to drive Turkey into the arms of Germany and Italy, the area became the Turkish province of Hatay in June 1939. Whether or not as a consequence of this, Turkey remained neutral until 1945, when it symbolically declared war on Germany in order to qualify itself for membership of the United Nations.

Reza Khan took the throne of Iran in 1925, and created a new dynasty, the Pahlavis, which lasted until his son Muhammad Reza Shah's ouster in 1979 and the foundation of the Islamic Republic of Iran (Abrahamian, 1982). In many ways, Reza Shah's policies in the 1920s and 1930s closely resembled those of Atatürk; both men were avid centralisers, keen to modernise their countries through education and industrialisation, and to extend the authority of their state to its furthest corners. Reza Shah had the advantage of being able to rely on small but regular oil revenues, although these increased enormously under his son in the 1950s and 1960s. Again, both men were autocrats, and in Reza Shah's case his attempts at secularisation, or rather at making a visible separation between 'church' and 'state', which were continued by his son, ran up against a much more determined and more powerful clerical hierarchy than their contemporaries in Turkey. Reza Shah's pro-German leanings were sufficient to force his abdication in 1941 – the Allies were anxious to be able to supply their new ally, the Soviet Union, through Iran, and would brook no opposition. In 1941 Muhammad Reza Shah was only twenty-two, and for some time remained in the background. The sudden end of autocracy produced a flowering of political movements, and later in the 1940s the Soviet Union took upon itself to support autonomist movements in Azerbaijan and Kurdistan. By 1946 the central government and the army had re-established control, but opposition to the regime was widespread. In 1951, a democratically elected Prime Minister, Muhammad Musaddiq, announced, to almost universal acclaim within the country, the nationalisation of the Anglo-Iranian Oil Company, which had almost inexplicably refused a 50/50 profit-sharing arrangement with the Iranian government.[13] Britain announced a worldwide boycott of Iranian oil, and the economy collapsed. Musaddiq remained popular; the Shah left the country in August 1953, but a few weeks later Musaddiq was overthrown in a plot masterminded and financed by the CIA (Abrahamian, 2001). The Shah returned and reintroduced his father's style of modernising autocracy, which worked for some two decades but then gradually precipitated his own end.

During the inter-war period, national movements of varying strength and popularity developed in Egypt and the mandated states, though only to a limited extent in Transjordan, which had a population of less than half a million.[14] These movements generally survived beyond the more or less artificial grants of national independence to Iraq in 1932, Egypt in 1936, Lebanon in 1945 and Syria in 1946, even until the revolutions in Egypt in 1952, Iraq in 1958, and the comparable watershed in Syrian politics in 1961. These nationalist movements were generally uncoordinated and fragmented, and were only united in the reasonably clear knowledge of what they did *not* want, the continuation of the indirect rule of the former colonial power and its local agents or assistants.

Looking at the period between formal independence and the revolutions of the 1950s, the various components of the national movement in the region between Egypt and Iraq (and, to some extent, including the opposition to the Pahlavis in Iran) can be divided into five principal, though not watertight, typologies. Going from right-wing to left-wing, there were quasi-fascist groupings like Misr al-Fatat in Egypt, al-Qumsan al-Hadidiyya in Syria, al-Futuwwa in Iraq; various manifestations of the Arab nationalist movement in Iraq and Syria (Hizb al-Istiqlal in Iraq, the emergent

Ba'th Party in Syria); more or less 'tolerated' national independence movements like the Egyptian Wafd and the Syrian al-Kutla al-Wataniyya; social democratic groups like Jama'at al-Ahali and its successor the National Democratic Party in Iraq and the Liberation Movement of Iran, and finally the various communist parties in the region. To this should be added the Muslim Brethren in Egypt and its offshoots elsewhere, which introduced religion as activist ideology into the political arena. Needless to say, some of these groupings were far larger and/or more influential than others, and in addition, size, in the sense of numbers of members, was not always correlated with influence.

After the Second World War, the fascist or quasi-fascist parties generally dropped quietly out of sight, and their former members gravitated towards more palatable political organisations. Many were attracted to the new form of Arab nationalism which had begun to develop in the 1930s, which appealed to the glorious Arab past and to an Arab world now divided by British and French imperialism yet united by a common language and heritage, ideas which owed much to Italian and German ideas of the nation which were filtering through to the Middle East at the time. This rallying cry of 'Arab unity' was first sounded in the early writings of Sati' al-Husri (1882–1968) (Choueiri, 2000: 101–24; Tibi, 1981: passim). Of course the idea has little *historical* resonance, since the 'Arab world' had not been united under 'Arab rule' since well before the fall of the 'Abbasid empire in 1258. As has been mentioned already, ethnic, that is Arab, solidarity had not been a particularly significant political force in the Arab world before the revolutions of 1908–9.

As Director of Education in Iraq in the 1920s and 1930s, Sati' al-Husri was able to propagate his views of Arab history through school textbooks, an activity he continued in Syria after his expulsion from Iraq in 1941, and subsequently at the Arab League, where he became head of the Institute for Advanced Arab Studies in 1953. In general, al-Husri believed in the notion of a unitary Arab nation, and found Renan's view of the nation as a 'daily plebiscite' completely unacceptable. He also rejected Marxism for its 'cosmopolitanism', and, in spite of his claims to the contrary, was profoundly anti-communist all his life. Anti-Marxism and anti-communism are two of the hallmarks of pan-Arab nationalism; al-Husri also considered that the fact that the various Arab states were at widely differing stages of socio-economic development was ultimately irrelevant. Al-Husri was a polemicist, not a scholar, and his work is 'less important for its philosophical content or its methodology than for the extraordinary influence which it has exerted not only on the intellectual climate in the Arab countries, but also on political practice there' (Tibi, 1981: 124, 132). Al-Husri's *oeuvre* is not, therefore, a body of thought which needs to inspire a great deal of respect, but there is little doubt of the extent and insidiousness of its influence. Nasserism and Ba'thism, and the pan-Arabism of the 1960s and 1970s, closely follow the tradition he founded.

The more 'conventional' political opposition movements either became fossilised after the Second World War, were co-opted and/or corrupted by the various regimes, or otherwise proved incapable of providing viable leadership in the independence period. Both the Egyptian Wafd and the Syrian National Bloc ran out of steam in the 1940s and 1950s, as new generations of leaders with more radical ideologies emerged to challenge them (Botman, 1991; [Lutfi al-Sayyid] Marsot, 1977), while Lebanese politics remained, and to a remarkable sense still remain, confined within much the same confessional parameters as they did in the 1950s (Seale, 1965; Goria, 1986). In the same way, Iraqi cabinets in this period resembled an elaborate game of musical chairs, where the friends of so-and-so were more or less rapidly succeeded by the friends of such-and-such (Farouk-Sluglett and Sluglett, 2003; Batatu, 1978; Khadduri, 1960).

The social democratic groups did not, on the whole, become corrupt, but since they were not operating in a 'conventional' democratic environment where the opposition could become the government through parliamentary elections, their influence and ideology, though often highly respected and admired, largely remained on the margins of everyday politics. Some of their members gradually moved further to the left as time went on: 'Abd al-Qadir Isma'il of Jama'at al-Ahali became a member of the Iraqi Communist Party, and 'Ali Shari'ati's ideological positions in the late 1970s were somewhat to the left of those of Mehdi Bazargan, the leader of the Liberation Movement of Iran (Chehabi, 1990: chs. 1–5).

Some Middle Eastern communist parties exerted an extremely important influence during and after the Second World War, far greater than the number of their members might suggest. When the Soviet Union joined the Allies in 1941, communists could raise their heads cautiously over the battlements, especially in Iran, where three members of the Tudeh held cabinet posts briefly in 1946. The Iraqi Communist Party was a major factor in its country's politics between the 1940s and its decimation at the hands of the Ba'th and the Nasserists in 1963. The success and appeal of the Syrian Communist Party was a major reason for the Syrian Ba'th's somewhat hasty embrace of, or perhaps more accurately desperate plea for, union with Egypt in 1958. Of course, no Middle Eastern communist party came near to sharing power, let alone wielding it, but the notions and language of social and economic reform which the parties introduced in the various states were often appropriated, and sometimes put into practice, by their nationalist opponents when they came to power. In addition, large numbers of intellectuals, creative writers and artists embraced some of the ideas and ideals of Marxism–Leninism, although the expression of these ideas eventually became less and less tolerated under the conditions of the Cold War (Batatu, 1978; Botman, 1988; Beinin and Lockman, 1987; Budeiri, 1979; Abrahamian, 1982).

Finally, no survey of such movements would be complete without reference to the ideology of Islamic activism, which made its first major appearance on the political scene with the foundation of the Muslim Brethren in Egypt in 1928. Although the Ottoman and Qajar empires were 'Muslim institutions' the relationship between 'Islam' and 'the state' was generally limited to the notion that it was the function or duty of the state to create the political and social backdrop against which the good Islamic life should be lived, rather than promulgating, let alone advocating, anything which might be called *Islamic government*. There had certainly been movements of Islamic *renewal*, in various parts of the Islamic world in the nineteenth century, including Indonesia, the Indian sub-continent, west Africa, central Asia, and the Arabian peninsula, but these were more concerned with advocating a return to what their leaders imagined to be 'true Islam' than with an Islamic political programme or an Islamic state. Hasan al-Banna, who founded the Muslim Brethren, was born in 1906, and trained as a teacher in Cairo in the late 1920s. He then went to Isma'iliyya in the canal zone as a schoolteacher, which he remained for the rest of his life, teaching children in the day time and adult literacy classes in the evenings. In March 1928, he founded the Muslim Brethren, apparently at the behest of some members of his evening classes, poor day-labourers with a keen sense of their own powerlessness and humiliation, and the domination of Egypt by foreigners and their local supporters. The movement spread unobtrusively in the late 1920s and early 1930s, the years of the great world economic depression, which produced immense deprivation all over the third world as well as in Europe and North America. In 1932 al-Banna moved to Cairo, where he established his movement's headquarters. By the time of the outbreak of the Second World War, the *Ikhwan* became one of the most important contestants on the Egyptian political scene, recruiting members not only from among the poor and oppressed, but also students and civil servants. Its main proposals were the insistence on Islam as a total system, complete unto itself, and the final arbiter of life in all its categories, that is, an Islam formulated from and based on the Qur'an and Sunna, applicable to all times and to all places (Mitchell, 1969). After the Second World War the movement had a certain success in Syria (Reissner, 1980), but although its leaders (Banna was killed in 1949) generally welcomed Nasser and supported his programme at the beginning, rifts soon appeared, and after highly questionable accusations of involvement in an attempt to assassinate Nasser in October 1954 (six men were sentenced to death by a kangaroo court in December 1954), the Brethren were officially banned.

It is difficult to draw a neat line separating the 'colonial period' from what followed it. In an important sense the colonial period came to an end with the military coups which became revolutions in the 1950s, but of course Britain hung on in South Yemen until 1967, and, to the rulers' great chagrin, left what became the United Arab Emirates in 1971. Clearly, the structures which the British and French left behind in the mandated states were too fragile to survive their departure, and the neo-imperialism which followed, with the Soviets and the Americans jockeying for position, was a completely different, though perhaps equally insidious, form of political control. In general, the explosion of world demand for oil in the post-war period probably accounts for a large part of the chronic instability of the region, but, as I have noted elsewhere,[15] the cold war was especially responsible for encouraging the marginalisation of democratic movements, and the rise of religious fanaticism. The colonial period was not a happy period in the history of the Middle East, and we are still living with some of its less attractive consequences today.

NOTES

1   China, Latin America and the Middle East were the main focus of Britain's 'informal empire'. For a review of the literature, see C. M. Turnbull, 'Formal and Informal Empire in East Asia', Peter Sluglett, 'Formal and Informal Empire in the Middle East', and Rory Miller, 'Informal Empire in Latin America', in Robin W. Winks (ed.), *The Oxford History of the British Empire*, vol. 5, *Historiography*, Oxford University Press, Oxford, 1999, pp. 379–402, 416–36, and 437–49.

2   Since Egypt was still, at least nominally, an Ottoman province, and the Ottomans had sided with Germany and Austria-Hungary in 1914.

3   As mentioned above, Egypt was obliged to submit to a similar regime.

4   For a stimulating recent analysis of Sa'udi history, see Madawi Al-Rasheed, *A History of Saudi Arabia*, Cambridge, Cambridge University Press, 2002.

5   The major exceptions are the redrawing of the boundary between Turkey and Syria in 1939, giving the former '*sanjak* of Alexandretta' to Turkey, where it now forms the province of Hatay, and the merger between the Yemen Arab Republic and the People's Democratic Republic of Yemen in 1990.

6 'The notables were content to accept directives from the imperial capital and did their utmost to harmonise their aims with those of the dominant power group in Istanbul, which now included members of the Damascus elite.' Philip S. Khoury, *Urban Notables and Arab Nationalism: The Politics of Damascus 1860–1920*, Cambridge, Cambridge University Press, 1983, p. 53.

7 Spain withdrew from the northern part of the country at the same time, but maintained, and still maintains, its *praesidios* (Ceuta, Melilla and Alhucemas); 'Spanish Sahara' gained independence from Spain in 1974.

8 There is a useful map of the Algerian Civil War on p. 280 of the *Times Atlas of World History*, 4th edn., London, Times Books, 1993 (which, inexplicably, does not reappear in later editions).

9 For an interesting discussion of the implications of this word in the colonial context (with references to a variety of other colonial situations), see Keith Watenpaugh, 'Towards a new category of colonial theory: colonial cooperation and the Survivors' Bargain. The case of the post-genocide Armenian community of Syria under French mandate', in Méouchy and Sluglett, pp. 597–623.

10 In 1947, 100,000 British troops were stationed in Palestine, approximately one British soldier per eighteen inhabitants, at a cost of £40 million a year. See W. Roger Louis, 'British Imperialism and the End of the Palestine Mandate', in W. Roger Louis and Robert W. Stookey (eds.), *The End of the Palestine Mandate*, Austin, TX, 1986, pp. 19–20.

11 The French departure from Syria, in circumstances of considerable rancour, marked a fairly profound watershed in the relations between the two countries. Although considerable tensions surrounded the end of the mandate in Lebanon, relations remained reasonably cordial because of the strength of commercial relations and France's traditional role as protector of the Maronites, which it managed to maintain for several decades after Lebanese independence.

12 In the inter-war period, the 'Kurdish problem', although certainly present, was generally characterised more as a struggle between religious diehards and a modernising secular central state than as an ethnic conflict. In fact, the Kurds had played a key role in preventing 'the infidel, Greek, Armenian, French or British overrun[ing] the homeland' in the period immediately before the establishment of the state. David McDowall, *A Modern History of the Kurds*, London, I. B. Tauris, 1996, pp. 184–213.

13 'Almost inexplicably', because the US had arrived at the same arrangements with ARAMCO in Sa'udi Arabia a few months before. In fact, AIOC was to agree to this in 1954.

14 In any case, for much of the period before 1948, the tensions in Transjordan seem to have been rather less acute than those elsewhere. See Michael Fischbach, *State, Society and Land in Jordan*, Leiden, Brill, 2000.

15 Peter Sluglett, 'The Cold War in the Middle East', in Louise Fawcett (ed.) *The International Relations of the Middle East*, Oxford University Press, 2004.

FURTHER READING

Abrahamian, Ervand, *Iran Between Two Revolutions*, Princeton, NJ, Princeton University Press, 1982.

Anderson, Lisa, *The State and Social Transformation in Tunisia and Libya, 1830–1980*, Princeton, NJ, Princeton University Press, 1986.

Batatu, Hanna, *The Old Social Classes and the Revolutionary Movements of Iraq: A Study of Iraq's Old Landed Classes and its Communists, Ba'thists and Free Officers*, Princeton, NJ, Princeton University Press, 1978.

Botman, Selma, *Egypt from Independence to Revolution, 1919–1952*, Syracuse, Syracuse University Press, 1991.

Choueiri, Youssef, *Arab Nationalism: A History*, Oxford, Blackwell, 2000.

Farouk-Sluglett, Marion, and Peter Sluglett, *Iraq since 1958: From Revolution to Dictatorship*, 3rd edn., London, I. B. Tauris, 2003.

Issawi, Charles, *An Economic History of the Middle East and North Africa*, New York, Columbia University Press, 1982.

Keddie, Nikki R., *Roots of Revolution: An Interpretative History of Modern Iran*, New Haven and London, Yale University Press, 1981.

Khoury, Philip S., *Syria and the French Mandate: The Politics of Arab Nationalism, 1920–1946*, Princeton, NJ, Princeton University Press, 1987.

Louis, William Roger, *The British Empire in the Middle East 1945–1951: Arab Nationalism, The United States and Postwar Imperialism*, London, Oxford University Press, 1984.

Mitchell, Richard P., *The Society of the Muslim Brothers*, London, Oxford University Press, 1969.

Morris, Benny, *Righteous Victims: A History of the Zionist–Arab Conflict, 1881–2001*, New York, Vintage Books, 2001.

Sluglett, Peter, *Britain in Iraq 1914–1932*, London, Ithaca Press, 1976.

Sluglett, Peter, 'Formal and Informal Empire in the Middle East', in Robin W. Winks (ed.), *The Oxford History of the British Empire*, vol. 5, *Historiography*, Oxford University Press, Oxford, 1999, pp. 416–36.

Zürcher, Erik J., *Turkey, a Modern History*, London, I. B. Tauris, 1998.

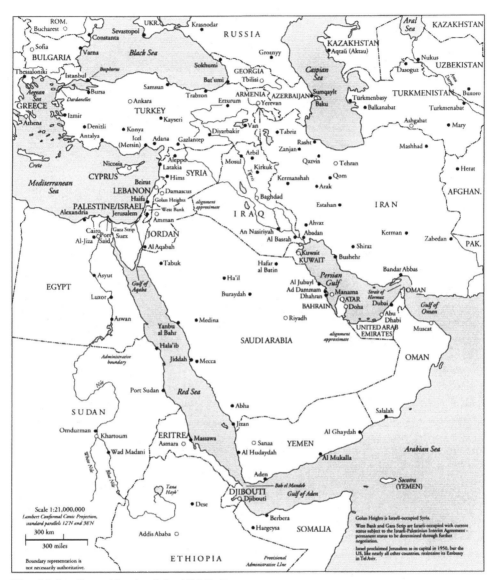

Map 13.1 Central lands of the Middle East

Independence and Nation Building

CHAPTER FOURTEEN

Zionism and the Palestine Question

EMMA C. MURPHY

Introduction

Zionism has been a mission-statement for the creation of the state of Israel. Simul-taneously it has been the justification for the dispossession of the Palestinian nation. In liberating one people from their diaspora, it has provided the logic for the creation of another. It has brought both salvation and despair, a historic recovery of land and a tragic loss. Conventional accounts of the origins of the 'Palestine problem' attempt to unravel this conundrum through an exploration of Zionism and its impact upon Palestine and the Palestinians. While this chapter utilises the same formula for establishing a narrative and accompanying critique, it does so with reservation. There is always a danger that an assessment of the Palestine question through the lens of the *march of Zionism* alone will reduce the Palestinian peoples, and their history, to reactionary or passive victimhood. The reader should constantly be aware of the dialectics of two nations and two nationalisms in conflict, rather than understanding this as a narrative of the content and consequences of one such national ideology alone. The chapter cannot do full justice in the allotted space to the complexities of this interaction but, while staying true to the standard format for assessing Zionism's place in the progression of the Palestine problem, it will try at critical junctures to signpost the reader to limitations in the utility of this orthodox approach.

Even the starting date of our story is a source of controversy. Those sympathetic to the Zionist cause – which at this point we may very loosely define as the belief in the necessary transfer of a significant proportion of the world's Jewish population into lands identified with a previous Jewish past and located along the eastern shores of the Mediterranean – are often eager to link the roots of modern Zionism to the historic longing of Jews to return to their biblical homeland. That previous existence came to an end following their expulsion after the failed Bar Kochba revolt against Roman rule in AD 134. A small Jewish community remained in Palestine throughout subse-quent Persian, Arab, Crusader, Mongol and Ottoman invasions and, though their fortunes fluctuated somewhat, they ultimately found themselves numerically limited, largely confined to religious cities and dependent on philanthropic contributions from the *diaspora*. The vast majority of Jews were to be found outside of the land which, according to biblical texts, was promised to – and paid for by – the Jews. The spiritual connection was never lost, however, with a return to Jerusalem being a core element of Jewish religious identity.[1] The subsequent centuries of persecution and resulting repeated migrations, ensured that the sense of non-belonging to anywhere other than the 'promised land' remained a constant in Jewish thought and identity. This group sentiment became mythologised and romanticised such that Zionist writers like Leonard Stein described it thus:

> Save in a few exceptional cases, it never occurred to them, any more than it occurred to their neighbours, that they had a place in the permanent fabric of the societies among which they dwelt. The part they were permitted to play in these societies might, in its degree, be useful or even dignified. But through good and evil days alike, Palestine remained the desire of their hearts.[2]

In reality *diaspora* Jewry understood the 'promised land' more as an abstraction than a practical programme. Jersualem was a spiritual rather than spatial homeland and the anticipation of a physical 'return' was limited to the personal piety of individuals.

To start our narrative of Zionism with the biblical origins of a Jewish state and the notion of Jewish continuity in the territory of Palestine raises a number of problems. Firstly, it elevates a religious text containing an uncorroborated account of the words of God, in promising the land to the Jews, to the status of 'fact'. Can the Bible be taken as a 'true' chronicle of events and can the moral weight of one religion outweigh the material implications for non-believers? Secondly, this version of truth prioritises the experiences of one people over others within the historical narration. Non-Jewish populations in Palestine during the period from the creation of the diaspora (or indeed pre-dating the Jewish presence there) to the creation of the Israeli state, are afforded no rights and no affinity to the land. They are observers of, or even obstructions to, Jewish history, but have no history of their own that recognises their fundamental connections to the land (be they through conquest, migration, or simply longevity of residence).[3] This is clearly a nonsense, although one perpetuated by the theological domination of study of the area's ancient history.

Finally, this starting point, although utilised extensively by political elites in subsequent nation and state-building processes, ignores the essentially secular nature of the political ideology which provided the foundations of the Israeli state in the late nineteenth century. The development of Zionism as a modern ideology was based on Jewish self-identification with nationhood rather than faith. Although spiritual, literal and sentimental attachments to Palestine were convenient for the purposes of identifying a territory to which the nation could relocate in order to reconstruct itself, religious tradition, myth, ritual and symbol was less a substantive element of the base than a rhetorical and legitimising aspect of the superstructure for the anticipated political entity.

The Forerunners of Zionism and the Failed Enlightenment

Alternative accounts of the history of Zionism begin with efforts to identify the early philosophical roots of the idea of a politically rather than spiritually motivated Jewish return to the 'land of the Hebrews', which surfaced in the nineteenth century.

Around 90 per cent of the world's two and a half million Jews lived in Europe in 1800, three-quarters of them in Russia and Poland, a part of which had been acquired by Prussia. Conditions for Jewish communities in what we may call east and west differed, with varying degrees of discrimination and persecution heaped upon Jewish communities by dominant non-Jewish populations, and with the 14 per cent or so of European Jewry living in the west enjoying considerably better conditions than their co-religionists in the east.

The century had started well for them. In 1807 Napoleon (whose oriental adventures had led him to invite the Jews of North Africa and Asia to rally to his flag) had emancipated the Jews of his empire. This came on the tails of the seventeenth-century European Enlightenment, which dismissed the dogma of religion in favour of the rationalism of science. Although writers like Voltaire and Diderot were even more despising of the Jewish religious traditionalists than they were of Christianity, the Enlightenment brought a new modernity to the public sphere in which individuals merited equality, liberal values replaced sectarian intolerance, and the state redefined its relations with citizens on the basis of emancipated participation. Jewish intellectuals were not slow to adjust to the new ideas and a specifically Jewish enlightenment, the *Haskalah*,[4] which sought to reform Judaism and reconcile it with the new modernity, began to take shape. Momentum for change accelerated with the French Revolution, as a result of which Jews were admitted to the full rights of citzenship in 1790, emancipation bringing new possibilities for assimilation. Prussia was soon to follow the French lead, with full legal emancipation being achieved by 1812. The legacy of the past remained, however, with Jews being disproportionately confined to certain professions and remaining socially disadvantaged. Despite the willingness of many to abandon the traditional modes of dress and behaviour which had marked them out as 'alien' in their host countries, they were still considered to have collective degenerate characteristics, their religious affiliations were thought to be backwards and irrational, and their ethnic exclusivism was deemed unhealthy. While they were to be emancipated as individuals, they were still to be rejected as a community.

It was not long before many of the concessions to emancipation were clawed back by European governments pandering to emerging state-centred nationalisms founded on notions of ethnic purity and on the need to mobilise nations behind the industrialising state. Ironically, as the western European Jews were seeking to assimilate and thereby weakening their own group cohesion, the tides of anti-semitism[5] were swelling around them. At the margins of Jewish political society, recognition of the limitations of their liberation prompted a number of intellectuals to reconsider the benefits of assimilation and to conclude that the future of the Jews lay elsewhere.

Mordecai Manuel Noah suggested in 1825 that an 'asylum' be created for all Jews in a free and powerful country where they might prepare themselves for the final 'restoration to their ancient heritage'. While Noah was writing in America, the prominent British Jew, Sir Moses Montefiore was pursuing an alternative scheme, funding small-scale Jewish colonisation in Palestine, and books and articles were being written suggesting that the Jews should seek refuge under an Ottoman ruler in Palestine. Non-Jews, like the authors, George Eliot, Sir Walter Scott and Benjamin Disraeli as well as prominent personalities of the day such as Edward Ashley (the seventh earl of Shaftesbury) and the diplomat, Laurence Oliphant, supported the notion of a homeland or safe-haven for Jews, based as much on a proto-Zionist Protestant evangelicalism as on a real sympathy with the ongoing misfortunes of the Jews. At the time, however, the poverty-stricken and marginal lifestyle of Jews in the crumbling Ottoman empire had little appeal for most bourgeois European Jews. Proto-Zionist notions of a return to Zion served rather to reinforce European expansionist ambitions in west Asia, with some politicians in Britain, France and Germany envisaging versions of a Jewish buffer state between Orient and Occident.

A more significant contribution to early western European Zionism was made by the socialist, Moses Hess (1812–75), the author of *Rome and Jerusalem, the Last Nationality Question*, published in 1862. Even in his early works, and unlike many of his contemporaries, Hess identified Jews in terms of their nationality rather than their religion. Nonetheless, as a people, they were marked out by what he perceived as the futility of a dead religion, past its useful life. Time was better spent promoting the needs of the proletariat in general rather than a minority attached to a futile and antiquated code. In 1852, Hess, who had worked with Marx and Engels, retired from active politics, and found himself returning to his spiritual roots, once again embracing his cultural identity. Through his study of natural sciences, and his observations of growing racism in western Europe, Hess had come to believe that his epoch would be characterised by nationalism. Unlike his fellow Marxists, he did not see a future in which classes were the principal social formations but rather suppressed nations seeking liberation. Having become profoundly conscious of the ingrained nature of anti-semitism he argued that the time was ripe for the Jews to seek a new future for themselves through the creation of a commonwealth in their historic homeland, Palestine. Assimilation was doomed to failure, not only because Jews would always 'remain strangers among the nations' but also because, without access to soil of their own, they were by definition a parasitic race. Reform of Judaism to make it more compatible with European cultural preferences was dangerously misleading in its assertion that the Jewish and gentile worlds could be reconciled harmoniously within Europe, while orthodox religious fanaticism was equally misguided in its failure to accept the virtues of modern science. In sum, he advocated a secular, nationalist approach to the resolution of the Jewish question, with Palestine being identified as the preferred destination.

While developments in Jewish intellectual thought in western Europe were propelled by the philosophical trends of the era, notably nationalism, socialism, Marxism, and bourgeois liberalism, their counterparts in Russia and Poland were forced to respond to more tangible events which threatened devastation of their communities.

Tsar Alexander II (1855–81) initiated a short-lived respite for the Jews from their forcible confinement to the *pale of settlement*,[6] their exclusion from urban or professional life and their ruthless subjection to taxation. His liberal reforms had enabled them to begin moving back into cities, to attend universities and to participate in local government. Jewish intellectuals responded with their own, all-too-brief attempt at a reformation. They encouraged Jews to move out of the ghettos, to adopt less distinctive styles of dress, to participate fully in Russian life, and to embrace the sciences and secular studies of Russian educational institutions. This was in sharp contrast to intellectual orientations before that time. Exclusion and persecution had previously forced Jewish communities to turn inwards upon themselves, to reinforce their own internal social fabric with a reliance on tradition and ritual, or – in the case of the Hassidim – with religious emotionalism and mysticism. In this repressed and fearful world, the orthodox Rabbis had held a particular status as vehicles for the perpetuation of an unchanging, untouchable belief, that redemption awaited the Jews if they could only make themselves deserving of it in the eyes of God. The power of this promise over the imagination of Russian Jewry was not eroded by the brief period of limited emancipation, and was to resurface quickly as the sky began to fall.

In 1881, the Tsar was assassinated and his Slavophile son, Alexander III, soon turned the forces of both the state and Russian society against ethnic and religious minorities, making of the Jews a particular scapegoat for Russian military and economic failures. They were subjected to the infamous May Laws of 1882, whereby Alexander appeased the Russian peasants by allowing them to drive Jews off the land, to expel them from cities, and to herd them into ghettos. The resulting massacres and destruction or seizure of Jewish property, the so-called *pogroms* of 1881–4 and 1903–5, brought a premature end to the nascent Jewish enlightenment.

Instead, eastern European Jews developed alternative strategies for communal survival. Large numbers fled the Pale, moving as refugees into the peripheries of western Europe, to the United States or South Africa if that was possible, or – in somewhat smaller numbers – to Palestine, comprising the first *aliyah*, or wave of Jewish immigration. It has been estimated that between 1882 and the outbreak of the First World War in 1914, some two and a half million Jews left Russia and eastern Europe.[7] By 1903, some 25,000 of these had reached the shores of Palestine.

The earliest arrivals were the Bilu'im and the Chovevei Zion,[8] members of small localised associations set up in Russian towns and cities. A combination of religious orthodox Jews and radical Jewish students, these associations frequently confined their activities to teaching classes in Hebrew, gymnastics or self-defence, but they also raised funds and provided volunteers for immediate migration to Palestine. The impetus for these early colonising efforts had come from the combined responses of both rabbinical and secular thinkers to the failure of Russia to accommodate its Jewish inhabitants.

Rabbi Judah Alkalai of Semlin (1788–1878), in his *Minhat Yehuda* (1845) suggested that the redemption of the Jews, although ultimately dependent on messianic intervention, should be preceded by a physical return of the chosen people to their promised land, where they should organise themselves under a representative assembly. In 1857 he called explicitly for the establishment of a Jewish state. Another rabbi, Zwi Hirsch Kalischer of Posen (1795–1874) also argued in his work, *Derishat Zion* (1862), that the Jews needed to take action to relocate to Palestine, after which God would reward them with their redemption. Through Alkalai and Kalischer, the nationalist spirit of the age (and the Jewish response to anti-semitism in Europe) was harmonised with the teachings of the Hebrew texts, suggesting that Jewish identity could be redefined from the passive traditionalism of the ghettos to a more active culture that was still within the framework of religious orthodoxy.

Secularists too began to abandon their belief in the promises of assimilation. In 1882, Leo Pinsker (1821–91) published *Selbstemanzipation* (*Autoemancipation*). Originally from an 'enlightened' Odessa family, Pinsker had been shocked by first the anti-Jewish Odessa Riots in 1871 and later the pogroms which started in 1881. Pinsker argued that the Jews would never be treated with respect in Europe because they lacked national equality in the form of a state of their own. The only solution lay in the establishment of such a national home, although he accorded no particular attachment to Palestine as being desirable above other destinations. German and West European Jews should take on the challenge of raising funds to enable themselves, but more importantly their poorer and more oppressed Russian counterparts, to purchase the homeland. Like Alkalai and Kalischer, Pinsker was advocating self-help for the Jews; he was identifying their dilemma as a national problem, but he was not attempting to resurrect a biblical past.

Unfortunately for the enthusiastic but naïve settlers they were unprepared for the harshness of rural life in Ottoman Palestine, and were frequently overcome by malaria, their crops ruined by pests and droughts. Coming from impoverished, mostly urban backgrounds, they were under-funded for the enterprise, had few agricultural implements, had no experience of handling livestock and found it hard to adjust to the climate. The Turkish rulers were suspicious, ultimately banning their immigration altogether, and even the *old yishuv*, the small existing community of indigenous Jews, were unwelcoming, believing the newcomers to be threatening for relations with the Arab population, to have potentially subversive political notions, and to be competitors for European philanthropic contributions. Pinsker and his contemporaries earnestly tried to organise the local Chovevei Zion groups into a central organisation that could collect funds and mobilise support from Russia and Europe, but although they were able to send funds and volunteers to a few small outposts near Haifa, Jaffa and in the Galilee, there was little organised response from Western Europe and their organisation soon found itself torn apart by the differences between the Rabbis' religious ambitions and Pinsker's secularism.

Theodor Herzl and the *New Yishuv*

The idea that the Jews formed a national rather than a religious community, and the logic for statehood in Palestine, were thus not new when Theodor Herzl (1860–1904) wrote his own manifesto, *Der Judenstaat* (*The Jewish State: An Attempt at a Modern Solution of the Jewish Question*) in 1896. Herzl had been born into a culturally assimilated family in Budapest, moving to Vienna to study law and then to Paris to practise journalism. As a bourgeois European, Herzl had internalised much of the cultural stereotyping of Jews prevalent in nineteenth-century Vienna – that they were 'inferior, cowardly, unmanly, preoccupied with money, bereft of idealism'.[9] He was nonetheless increasingly aware of the anti-semitism that was sweeping Austria and Germany at the time. In 1891 he covered the trial in Paris of Captain Alfred Dreyfus, a young Jewish army officer accused of treason. Dreyfus was crucified by the rest of the press on the basis of his Jewishness – he was labelled a turn-coat and a traitor because all Jews were ultimately so. Although he agreed with his socialist contemporaries that anti-semitism was an anachronism that would ultimately disappear with modernisation, events in Europe had shown Herzl that progress towards this end was too slow. In the meantime, the Jews were being corrupted by their internal exile. The ghetto mentality was passive in the face of persecution and dependence on philanthropy, and had weakened the Jews such that they needed to free themselves from this before civil freedoms could be meaningful.

Herzl argued that the means to eradicate anti-semitism was through recognition by the Jews that they constituted a nation and that when they lived in their own state they would be accepted by other nations instead of being reviled by them as unwelcome parasites. Such a state would be supported by the great powers, eager to expel the Jews from their midst. Although the basis of statehood was national, religion would play a role in that the Jewish faith had bound the community together throughout its history and could provide further cohesive logic. For this reason Palestine was a desirable, although not the only possible, location. The prospect of a 'return' to the 'promised land' would have a powerful mobilising effect on religious Jews and even secular Jews could not fail to be moved by the potent symbolism this would represent.

But above all, the new state was to be founded on liberal, bourgeois and modernist principles. His vision of statehood was essentially a recreation of European, industrial society; an aristocratic republic (they were not yet ready for democracy), with a mutualistic economy where private property coexisted with the collectivism needed to mobilise resources for the good of the community. It would be characterised by universal suffrage, free and universal schooling, welfare institutions – a utopia built on the capital of western European Jews and the labour of east Europeans.

The vision (laid out in a novel entitled *Altneuland*, published in 1902) was not quite so appealing for the indigenous Arab population of Palestine. Although he expressed a concern for their civil and human rights, he nonetheless dismissed their own claims to the land in a typically European colonialist manner. The Jewish state would be a bastion of civilisation, 'a portion of the rampart of Europe against Asia'. The Jews would bring 'cleanliness, order and the well-established customs of the Occident to this plague-ridden, blighted corner of the Orient'.[10] The inconsistencies in his humanist claims and his colonial mentality meant that, ultimately, the presence of a native people was only to be resolved by 'spiriting them across the border'.

Herzl's ideas may not have been wholly new, but they were promoted at a moment in time when the convergence of rising anti-semitism, the acknowledged failures of assimilation, and the evolution of new socialist, liberal, nationalist and humanist ideals served to make them supremely relevant to alienated and disillusioned Jews across Europe. Yet they were by no means universally popular.

One of his most notable critics was Asher Zvi Ginzberg (1856–1927), also known as *Ahad Ha'am*, an advocate of what became known as cultural Zionism. Ginzberg's critique was premised on Herzl's total neglect of what, in Ginzberg's view, made the Jews Jewish. There was nothing specifically Jewish about Herzl's proposed state, and therefore it would become a state for the Jews rather than a Jewish state. Herzl's ideal state was merely a manifestation of assimilation, having no Hebrew features and offering only a sterile material salvation. Having visited Palestine himself a number of times, Ginzberg was acutely aware of the existence of the Arab population and that mass Jewish colonisation and statehood could only result in domination over the Arabs, hardly a route for the replenishment of the Jewish soul after generations of cultural and spiritual impoverishment. While he supported the concept of a Jewish national movement and the relocation of Jews to Palestine, he believed that the priority lay less with statehood than with recovery of a Jewish identity through educational, linguistic, literary and professional revivals. Like Herzl, Ginzberg was a product of western philosophical thought, concerned with the crisis of the diaspora but not with religious revivalism. Unlike Herzl, he envisaged a peaceful and moral accommodation with the Arabs, a modernity in harmony with history and a settlement that served rather than replaced the diaspora.

There were also religious objections to Herzl's programme. Orthodox groups like *Agudat Israel* argued that political Zionism denied the Messianic aspect of Jewish redemption. Worse, the abandonment of religion as the defining pillar of Jewishness was the ultimate act of assimilationist betrayal. For other liberal and reform wings of the faith, political Zionism merely replaced segregation via the ghetto with segregation via the nation-state. A reformation of Judaism to internalise emancipation and modernity, a requisite for successful assimilation, was more desirable than further isolation from non-Jews. Moreover, universalist goals such as brotherhood, justice, truth and peace on earth were fundamental to Jewish spiritual fulfilment, and would be sacrificed in the effort to steal the land away from an existing Palestinian population. The mystical traditions of Hassidism provided yet another thread, suggesting that the 'Jewish question' had a spiritual diagnosis and that a revival of traditional Jewish values of pacifism, humanism and spiritual self-awareness would do more to repair the damage done to the Jewish body-communal than any political entity. Moreover, Jewish colonisation of Palestine could then be pursued in the context of peaceful, cooperative relations with the Arabs, and tortured diaspora relations with the gentiles could be set on the path to recovery.

Cultural and spiritual Zionism, as well as religious opposition to Herzl, reflected eastern European philosophical traditions. There was no dispute that a Jewish problem existed, the debate revolved around determining the nature of the connections between Jews and the importance of sovereign control to the Jews' ability to determine their own destiny.

Yet not all religious figures were opposed to Zionism. Rabbi Avraham Yitzhak Kook (1865–1935) emerged as the key figure in accommodating secular political Zionism and Orthodox Judaism when he argued in his teaching that political Zionism was an instrument of God and a part of the Messianic redemption of the Jews. It may have been secular in orientation but it was nonetheless inadvertently part of a greater divine plan. Kook believed that the political Zionists were the bearers of great energies whose practical activities ultimately served a spiritual purpose in preparing the way for the Messiah to restore Zion. Jewish statehood in Palestine, or the recovery of the land from the gentiles, would fulfil prophecy and should be encouraged and facilitated, the indigenous Arab population playing little part in his programme for the future.

A final major response to Herzl came from the socialist and Marxist intellectuals, who understood both the problem and the solution in materialist terms. Russian Marxists, most notably those in the Jewish Workers Association (the *Bund*) rejected their traditional Jewish culture and embraced instead the notion of universal redemption in the form of the rise to power of the proletariat. Herzl's political Zionism was to them a reactionary nationalist endeavour, thrusting Jews further into isolation and leaving them marginal to the historical forces of progress. In an attempt to reconcile classical Marxism and Zionism, Ber Borochov (1881–1917) argued in *The National Question and the Class Struggle* (1905) and *Our Platform* (1906) that, while Marxism was correct in identifying any form of nationalism as part of the superstructure of oppression by ruling classes, the oppression of whole nations by others created abnormal conditions under which the struggle for national freedom had to precede the broader class struggle. He advocated national emigration to Palestine as a means of establishing an independent Jewish economic order within which a Jewish proletariat could pursue the social revolution unfettered by adverse national conditions.

Not all Jewish socialists were comfortable with these ideas. Indeed a more pragmatic trend, Labour Zionism, fuelled the second *aliyah* of 1904–14, the foremost advocate being A. D. Gordon (1856–1922). Labour Zionists merged the populism and romanticism of Russian literary figures like Tolstoy with the socialist faith in productive labour, arguing that only a return to ownership of, and physical labour on, the land itself would redeem the Jewish people. Manual labour (which had so often been denied them) was essential for Jews to restore their individual and collective self-esteem, making them self-reliant, expunging bourgeois affectations and founding a Jewish economic infrastructure that would support the community.

Plate 14.1 Yassir Arafat, leader of the PLO and President of the Palestinian National Authority (d. 2004)
Source: © *AlHayat* Newspaper, London

Zionism was not just about political and economic transformation, but also about a psychological revolution which would undo the damage of centuries of exile, dispersal and dependence.

As long as Zionism remained a philosophical discourse, rather than a practical programme for colonisation, Palestine featured only marginally in its vision. Narratives of the development of Zionism which examine only the development of this discourse, neglect the importance of events within Palestine itself. The decline of the Ottoman economy, the introduction of land laws which fuelled rural landlessness and chronic peasant indebtedness, changes in social structures resulting from the Tanzimat reforms, and the encroachment of a European capitalist mode of production – all served to weaken the resistance of the region to subsequent colonisation and are equally deserving of detailed consideration in locating the roots of the Arab–Israeli conflict and the role that Zionism was to play within it. The period witnessed the emergence of an educated, urban Palestinian middle class, allied with traditional ruling families but sufficiently 'modernised' to respond to Turkish nationalism within the empire with a nascent home-grown Palestinian variety, linked in to, but not wholly convergent with, broader Arab nationalism. Representation in an Ottoman parliament, and the introduction of print-capitalism which favoured wider political discussion, inspired a distinct Palestinian identity which has usually been conveniently ignored in orthodox Zionist narratives which seek to argue the absence of a strong, competing claim to the land of Palestine.

Internationalists versus Pragmatists in the *Yishuv*

The first forty years of the twentieth century witnessed the transformation of Zionism from a philosophical discourse to a practical programme for the colonisation of Palestine. The second, third and fourth *aliyahs* brought 30,000 (1904–14), 37,000 (1919–23) and 70,000 (1924–8) new Jewish immigrants respectively. By 1929 the Jewish population of Palestine had risen to 154,000.[11] By far the greatest proportion of new immigrants came from Russia, Poland and Eastern Europe. Together they contributed the Labour Zionist elite which was to dominate the *yishuv* and later Israeli politics until 1977. Yet successful relocation to Palestine did not mean that the Jewish community enjoyed either internal harmony or peaceful relations with the indigenous Palestinian population.

Palestine at the time was experiencing still more upheaval. The First World War had provided Britain with the opportunity to occupy Palestine and, despite promises made to return it to independent Arab ownership,[12] at the end of the war this occupation was formalised through the award in 1922 of a League of Nations Mandate. The terms of the Mandate made specific reference to the Balfour Declaration, a letter sent by the then British Foreign Secretary to the leading British Zionist, Lord Rothschild on 2 November 1917, which publicly confirmed that Britain 'viewed with favour' the establishment in Palestine of a Jewish national home. In the letter itself, the Palestinian population was referred to only as 'non-Jewish communities' and only in terms of their civil and religious rights. In short, they were not a national entity in the eyes of the new rulers of Palestine and had no rights as such that might supersede the rights of any actual or potential immigrant communities.

British rule, which lasted until 1948, was subsequently characterised by the struggle to reconcile the need for orderly administration of its acquisition with the destabilising impact of large-scale Jewish immigration. Following the publication of Herzl's manifesto, European Jewry had rapidly organised itself under a World Zionist Organisation (WZO), with a Jewish Colonial Trust and Jewish National Fund being established to raise funds for this immigration and settlement. Now a new Jewish Agency was established to coordinate with the British and with the existing *yishuv* community in Palestine. While the shell-shocked Palestinians were still coming to terms with the British betrayal and the loss of traditional Ottoman diplomatic networks, the Zionist leadership was busy using the umbrella of British rule to shelter burgeoning colonies and facilitate the development of pre-state institutions. Although the Palestinians grew increasingly hostile to the growing Jewish presence, there was little they could do to prevent it. A divided and ineffective leadership of absentee landlord notables, out of touch with the grassroots and unable to coordinate their relations with the British, did little to promote the interests of the peasantry. Rural impoverishment and illiteracy meant that Palestinian agriculture was unable to compete with the modern technologies introduced by the Zionists, and the fragile local industrial base was under-capitalised and not sufficiently export-oriented to attract British contracts. While Britain did introduce some infrastructural, educational and welfare improvements to the benefit of the Palestinians, they paid for these out of intensive taxation which further eroded the economic capacity of the Arabs.

The growing tensions between communities soon erupted into spasms of violence. In 1929 a dispute over Jewish access to the Western Wall ignited into a wave of riots that spread across the country and in which 133 Jews and 116 Arabs were killed. Subsequent efforts to redefine British rule in recognition of Palestinian fears of spiralling Jewish immigration and land purchases restricted Jewish immigration, drawing the fury of Zionist leaders at a time when events in Europe were creating new momentum for the relocation of Jews to Palestine. Adolf Hitler's rise to power in Germany coincided with new American and British restrictions on Jewish immigration from increasingly anti-Jewish Europe. Consequently, and despite British efforts to limit immigration, by 1936 the Jewish population in Palestine had risen to 370,483 out of a total population of 1,336,518.[13]

In April 1936 the first Arab uprising began, a spontaneous swelling of resistance against British rule which began in the villages but which was later hijacked by the Palestinian leadership. The British response was harsh. Massive deployments of troops and a ruthless policy of arrests, executions and expulsions meant that by 1939 the uprising had been quelled, the peasantry disarmed and the leadership either exiled or killed. British policy subsequently sought once again to restrict Jewish immigration and to reassure the Arabs of their ultimate independence, concerned that wider Arab hostility on its colonial periphery would ill serve British interests as war in Europe loomed.

During the Mandate years, political Zionism did not remained unchanged. The experiences of organising and implementing large-scale immigration and the construction of a new Jewish community in Palestine, had created something of a rift between the leadership of the WZO – which continued to seek international endorsement for statehood – and elements of the new *yishuv* leadership which favoured practical settlement as the means to effectively establishing facts on the ground. The rift found its most painful expression in the form of a right-wing Russian orator and writer, Vladimir Ze'ev Jabotinsky (1880–1940). Since the issuance of the Balfour Declaration in 1917, the president of the WZO, Dr Chaim Weizmann, had argued strongly that the Zionists' interests were best served through the patronage of the British government, to the extent that he was at times prepared to delay the implementation of Zionist ideals in order to accommodate British strategic interests. Jabotinsky argued that it would be better to declare openly the desire for statehood and prepare for it through the creation of a strong Jewish army in Palestine. In 1925 Jabotinsky formed his own maximalist political party (*Zohar*) which sought Jewish majority rule over a territory to include both Palestine and what was then Transjordan. Inspired by a national socialism ironically not too dissimilar to that emerging in

Europe, he advocated direct military action to achieve these objectives, as well as a fatherland-type society based on discipline, adherence to a great leader, the notion of Jewish racial superiority, corporate political economy and aesthetic militarism. In his version of the Zionist state, the indigenous Palestinian Arabs would have equal rights as individuals but no rights as a national or cultural collective. From 1934, Jabotinsky's so-called Revisionists began to advocate a policy of non-cooperation with the British, a policy which brought them into opposition with the *yishuv* leadership.

The left-wing *yishuv* leadership were themselves divided between those who saw their fate as being linked to the broader forces of international communism and those who desired a more location-specific and practical brand of socialism. The former gathered themselves into a political party called *Poalei Zion* (Workers of Zion), considering themselves primarily a working-class Marxist body seeking political autonomy for the Jewish people in Palestine. The non-Marxist Labour Zionists formed *Hapoel Hatzair*, an alternative party which focused on practical aspects of colonisation such as Hebrew Labour (the notion that Jews should live off the fruits of their own labour, refusing to exploit the labour of others and therefore redeeming themselves through manual work and self-sufficiency).

The White Paper of 1938, which was considered by the Zionists to be a fundamental betrayal of their cause by the British government, inadvertently triggered a further development in Zionist logic. *Yishuv* leaders like David Ben Gurion abandoned their belief that Britain would provide the necessary sheltering umbrella while the Zionists established their nascent state. Instead, they re-focused their attentions on the United States of America, exhorting the American Zionist Emergency Council and associated American Zionists to exert pressure on the US government to take on that role.

American support was indeed to be forthcoming, although it was the horror of the European Holocaust that was ultimately to propel American political elites to see virtue in the Zionist cause. The persecution, expulsion and clinically ruthless extermination of Jews on an unprecedented scale virtually eradicated the traditional Jewish communities of Europe.[14] The end of the war saw 250,000 displaced European Jews residing in temporary refugee camps, many of whom were understandably unwilling to return to their countries of origin. The Holocaust, or Shoah, had provided them with the final evidence that assimilation was an impossible dream in the face of immutable European anti-semitism. Even when the exiles had little knowledge of Palestine, far less ambition to emigrate there, the Zionist networks were busy spreading the word of a 'land without a people for a people without a land'. As fast as they recruited potential immigrants, they utilised wartime smuggling and resistance networks to ship them to Palestine on every boat they could muster, breaking through a British naval blockade set up by a greatly weakened Britain desperate to maintain political stability in post-war Palestine. The United States' administration, unwilling to accept large-scale immigration of the refugees into its own heartland and eager to appease domestic Jewish voters, also attempted to pressure the British into easing restrictions on Jewish immigration. Despite coming to power with a distinctly pro-Zionist manifesto, the new Labour government was unable to reconcile the competing demands of the *yishuv* and its American ally on the one hand, and Palestinian nationalists demanding the fulfilment of British promises for independence on the other. The British sought to repress Zionist efforts to bypass their authority by first interning and then expelling unapproved immigrants. In response, the *yishuv* leadership began to actively work against the British forces in Palestine, sinking British naval ships that attempted to blockade immigrant boats, attacking British troops guarding internment camps in Palestine, and cooperating with the revisionist Zohar groups which had by now reformed into paramilitary groups, notably the Irgun Z'vai Le'umi (National Military Organisation) and an offshoot, the so-called 'Stern Gang'. In February 1947, the British government decided it could no longer carry the human, financial and political costs of continuing to station 80,000 troops in Palestine. The entire problem was referred to the United Nations, which subsequently established a Special Committee of eleven members,[15] spent five weeks in Palestine, and was feted by the *yishuv* leadership but virtually ignored by their Palestinian rivals. UNSCOP finished its report at the end of August 1947, recommending by a majority of seven members to three (with one abstention) that Palestine be partitioned into two states, one Arab and one Jewish, joined through economic union and with a separate Jerusalem–Bethlehem enclave coming under international supervision.

The Zionists generally favoured the report, since it offered them both statehood and unlimited immigration. Their reservations revolved around the impracticality of the proposed territorial divisions and the assumption that their stronger economy would subsidise the weaker Arab economy. The Palestinian Arabs rejected the proposals out of hand. The Jews of the *yishuv* comprised 31 per cent of the population of Palestine and owned less then 7 per cent of the land, yet the plan allocated to them 55 per cent of the territory, on which 45 per cent of Palestinian Arabs lived and worked. The Palestinians, by contrast, constituted 69 per cent of the population but would receive only 45 per cent of the land. The distribution itself was bizarre to say the least, with each national community receiving three chunks of land, connected only at narrow points and denying either state real territorial viability. The United Nations General Assembly nonetheless endorsed the partition on 29 November 1947 with Resolution 181 on the Future Government of Palestine.

The British announced their intention to leave Palestine in May 1948, leaving the Zionist and Arab communities to determine their own responses to the UN vote. The result was a frantic scramble to retrieve 'the key from under the door mat' before the other party. And thus we enter perhaps the most disputed narrative of all, the war for the control of Palestine.

The orthodox Zionist version of the events of this period rotates around the Arab refusal to accept even the principle of partition. This Arab 'intransigence' was compounded by the decision of the Arab armies to sweep into Palestine as the Mandate expired, attacking the fledgeling Jewish state with vastly superior forces. The new state fought heroically and ultimately successfully to repel the onslaught. The Palestinian Arabs, in contrast, either as a result of exhortations from their leaders to clear the battlefield or out of cowardice, fled their homes and became displaced refugees in wider Arab lands. Either way, their departure signified their loose attachment to the land, while the brave, Davidian stand of the Jews against the Arab Goliath indicated both their greater moral authority and the legitimacy of their claims to the soil.

Arab historians have argued that this is a largely fictional interpretation of events, recorded by partisan military and political figures with a vested interest in creating a glorious national myth to disguise an original sin. They argue that the Zionists used their superior military training and equipment, the result of both British support for the *yishuv* and simultaneous disarming of the Palestinians, to launch unprovoked attacks on Palestinian Arab areas that fell either within those areas allocated by the partition plan to the Jews, or within contiguous areas that would be needed to reinforce the territorial integrity of a new Jewish state. The actions took advantage of British protection in the final months of the Mandate and included the deliberate and violent expulsion of Palestinian Arab populations to prevent the emergence of a fifth column behind lines. When the Arab armies did finally attack, they were ill equipped, poorly trained, and uncoordinated, each working to its own political agenda and betrayed by King Abdullah of Transjordan who had reached a secret agreement with the Zionists for the carving up of Palestine. Zionist scholars point out that the Arab version lacks official documentation to support all its claims and relies heavily on the testimony of the 'victims' who have a vested interest in excusing their departure from Palestine.

In the 1980s a third narrative began to emerge, based on archival material newly released in Israel. The authors of this body of work, the so-called Israeli revisionist historiographers,[16] argued that many of the claims of the orthodox Zionist narrative were spurious, but equally that not all the arguments of the Palestinians held water. The critical re-examination of the founding history of Israel sought to acknowledge the wrongs done to the native inhabitants while locating them within an objective evaluation of a state-building process. Some of the refugees had indeed been voluntary economic migrants, while others had been swept before Zionist paramilitaries in a deliberate effort to clear the land for purposes of military necessity. Atrocities had been committed by both sides, the capabilities of the invading Arab forces had been far lower than Zionists would have us believe, Abdullah had indeed colluded with the Zionist leadership and the Zionist narrative had been polished up and sanitised for the purposes of nation-building.

There can be no argument, whichever narrative one ultimately plumps for, about the end-product of this brief but critical period in Palestine's history. Fighting broke out between the two communities as soon as the British announced their imminent departure, one result of which was the mass uprooting of a large part of the indigenous Palestinian population. On 14 May 1948, the State of Israel was declared to be in existence, some eight hours before the British finally took their leave of Palestine. Arab armies from Egypt, Syria, Lebanon, Transjordan and Iraq moved in and what had been an inter-communal struggle, only barely contained by British forces under attack from both national groups, became all-out inter-state warfare. Almost a year later the Israeli forces had managed to repel the Arab attacks and secure borders around some 77 per cent of Mandate Palestine, the rest falling under either Egyptian (the Gaza Strip) or Transjordanian (East Jerusalem and the West Bank) administrations. Some 360 Palestinian villages and 14 towns that fell within the new Israeli state had been destroyed and 85 per cent of the Palestinians living in those areas had either been expelled or had fled. There were now some 726,000 Palestinian refugees living either in neighbouring Arab states or in areas of Palestine still under Arab control. The Jewish state was a confirmed fact and the first major ambition of the Zionist movement had been accomplished.

Liberation Ideology or Colonialism?

While Israelis were celebrating independence, the Palestinians were mourning over *al nakhba* – the catastrophe. The subsequent efforts of the two sides and their sympathisers outside Israel and Palestine to comprehend the dimensions of what had happened resulted in two very different perspectives.

For Zionists, the achievement of statehood and Jewish sovereignty was the conclusion to the struggle for liberation that had its roots variously (depending on the particular Zionist philosophical tradition) in the enforced exile of the Roman era, the ghettos of central Europe, or the failures of efforts to assimilate into post-Enlightenment European society. Britain, from being a necessary sponsor of the Zionist cause, had become its imperialist oppressor and as Jews had redeemed themselves spiritually through the labours of the *yishuv* era, so they now liberated themselves politically from the yoke of imposed rule. Zionism became the ideology of liberation, the battle to transform the *yishuv* into a sovereign state being a war of independence for a nation, the identity of which is defined within, and by, Zionism itself.

To the Palestinians, to the wider Arab world, and to the leftist supporters of national liberation struggles in the post-colonial world, the creation of Israel was a manifestation of the opposite: a successful European colonisation of someone else's lands, sanctioned and supported by first the old imperialists (Britain and France) and now the new world power (the United States). The colonialist paradigm argued that the Israelis were no different from other European colonists, depending for their initial relocation upon (British) military occupation power, justifying their settlement on religio-civilisatory grounds, asserting their racial superiority over the indigenous peoples and exhibiting a common colonial mentality that stressed differentiated political rights. Territoriality and links to the land were crucial – access to the land was not enough; rather, they sought exclusive rights to this and other natural resources. The desire to break free of the mother-country, and the effort to expel rather than exploit the native population, are evidence of a particular colonial settler model, similar to that evidenced in South Africa, Australia, the United States and Algeria, and while the settlers might have initially paid, perhaps even over the odds, for the land they settled, they ultimately resorted to a violent expropriation and the wholesale political subordination of the remaining indigenous population.[17] From this perspective, Zionism should be understood as a fundamentally racist ideology which has justified the dispossession of one nation on the grounds of the superior moral, cultural and political claims of another.

The Zionist counter-arguments came from a number of quarters: one school of thought argued that the *yishuv* era was characterised by a duality of economic, political and social entities. The separation of the two national groups was not solely spatial, but was a result of the progressive and utopian aspects of Zionism that sought self-redemption rather than inter-communal exploitation. Ideology and leadership were the most significant factors in defining the relationship between the communities, suggesting that tensions between them were less a result of competition over resources than a cultural resistance to the ideals of the Jewish society by its wider environment. This argument has been undermined in recent years by a number of studies that have highlighted the nature and scope of the interaction between the communities, demonstrating a level of economic interdependence and political engagement hitherto ignored.[18]

A second school argues that Zionist settlement was fundamentally progressive. The concept of Hebrew Labour specifically abhorred the exploitation of non-Jews for Jewish profit. Land was purchased, often at grossly inflated prices, from Palestinian landlords who had themselves been ruthless and who had done nothing to develop either the quality of the land or the technology that could be used to enhance its productivity. Zionist settlers reclaimed uncultivated lands, making the infertile fertile and thereby gaining the normative advantage. While left-wing advocates of the colonial paradigm argue that Zionist settlement was in fact a capitalist encroachment on a pre-capitalist mode of production (and that Zionism was therefore the ideological superstructure for the exploitation of the periphery by the metropol), this school argues back that Zionism was a collectivist ideology which favoured the utilisation of private funds for public ends and which directed capital from the diaspora into Palestine rather than channelling profits back out.

Perhaps the most controversial of the claims of the colonialist school is the assertion that Zionism equates with racism. This argument achieved international sanction when the United Nations General Assembly passed Resolution 3379 on 10 November 1975. The resolution specifically determined that Zionism is a form of racism and racial discrimination. The UN resolution was viewed by Israel and its supporters as a politically motivated and essentially anti-semitic move, orchestrated by the Arab states. The supporters of the resolution pointed to the inequality of treatment of Jews and non-Jews in Israeli state laws, most notably in the Law of Return, which grants every Jew in the world the right to settle in Israel while the Palestinian refugees of 1948 and their descendants are permanently excluded from return. The comparison with the apartheid regime in South Africa was readily made. Even Israeli democracy, so prized by American advocates of the notion of the Israeli democratic outpost in a sea of authoritarian Arab regimes, was viewed as an ethnic democracy, reserved for one ethnic group but denied another.[19] As if to prove the politically opportunistic dynamics behind the resolution through repetition, it was ultimately revoked by the UNGA in 1991 as an international contribution to fostering a creative environment for renewed peace-making between Israel and the Arab world.

The colonial paradigm has metamorphosed in recent years as some Israeli scholars have accommodated the conceptual parameters while rejecting the normative implications. The sociologist, Baruch Kimmerling, has argued that Israel was indeed an immigrant-settler society, whose 'low frontierity' (the limited spatial aspects of the colonies) meant that the *yishuv* and subsequently Israeli society developed specific characteristics such as collectivism, nationalised land ownership, Hebrew labour exclusivism, coercive expropriation of land after 1948 and an ideological focus on the right to the land. While acknowledging that the state was founded by immigrant colonisers, he is not delegitimising their efforts or implying that retrospective justice needs to be done to the indigenous peoples, merely identifying the origins and determining characteristics of the polity.

All the narratives and analyses provided above of the *yishuv* and Mandate eras in Palestine, can be faulted on the grounds that Palestine's history has been subverted into a backdrop for the Zionist enterprise and that Palestinians have been located through their responses to that enterprise rather than the independent social, economic and political developments which contextualised their own history. A more robust narrative might examine the development of Palestinian identity and social evolution as part of the wider colonial experience, as one corner of a rapidly transforming Arab region, or even as a consequence of the articulation of the capitalist mode of production with a pre-capitalist environment. Such approaches deny the uniqueness of Zionism and are thus unacceptable to its advocates, but they offer a fairer deal to Palestinians in terms of the story's narration.

Similarly, one can argue that the focus on the Holocaust as the catalyst for international support for the transformation of the *yishuv* from community to state, directly or indirectly connects the persecution of the Jews in Europe to the legitimacy of the Israeli state. As Michael Prior has pointed out: 'One of the features of the *Shoah* as an *apologia* is that no attention is paid to the cost to the Palestinians.' The Zionist movement was established some fifty years before the Shoah and cannot therefore claim its legitimacy retrospectively. Moreover, the so-called 'Holocaust Theology' which demands that the perceived needs of Jews be considered as moral absolutes as a consequence of the uniqueness of their suffering, relegates the Palestinians to the level of sub-humans who are relevant only as far as they pose a threat or impediment to the satisfaction of those needs.[20]

Zionism Matures with Statehood

Once the Israeli state had been officially declared 'open for business', Zionism had to be refocused onto the primary missions of the new state, notably the facilitation and management of rapid immigration to build up the human resources of the state and consolidate its role as the epicentre of Jewish nation-building in all its forms. The nationalist component of Zionism was to take precedence over the liberationist element, construction over redemption.

The role played by David Ben Gurion, the first prime minister of Israel, has to be acknowledged here. Ben Gurion's roots were in the Marxist wing of Zionism, but once statehood had been achieved he all but abandoned his commitment to this ideological sub-culture in favour of the construction of a national political religion, *mamlachtiut*, or étatism. Ben Gurion was convinced that the various geographically derived cultures of the diaspora had to be harmonised into a single, Israeli, socio-political culture. Of course, this new Israeli culture was to be a repackaged version of Ben Gurion's, and his *yishuv* contemporaries', own European civilisational identification, although he was clear that the communal characteristics fostered by diaspora life per se included some degenerative traits which needed to be jettisoned. Mamlachtiut was premised on the notion of a shared national consensus over objectives. Particularistic diversity was to be avoided or at least not institutionalised. Democracy was good, but party politics should not be allowed to interfere with national leadership. Collective responsibility and broad government coalitions ensured inclusion rather than exclusion of as many interest groups as possible, but national leadership was to fall to the hands of chosen (rather than elected) protégés whose loyalty was less to political party bases and more to the person and ideals of Ben Gurion himself. The purpose was clear – to build up the political and institutional infrastructure, the economic base, and the ideological superstructure of the state. It would be an over-statement to argue that in becoming the official ideology of a nation-state under construction, Zionism lost its own internal diversity and even self-conflict. But it is fair to say that a new, predominant and largely consensus-driven nationalism arose out of the process.[21]

This consensus lasted throughout the first two decades of statehood, but gradually began to weaken as a number of unresolved features of the new state emerged. Not only was the new state unable to reconcile the formal and informal demands of democratic political life with its ethnic preference for its Jewish citizens; it was also unable to harmonise its Jewish communities within one cultural framework. The

1970s saw growing protests from oriental Sephardi and Mizrahi Jewish groups who felt marginalised and excluded from the new state.[22]

The real rupture of a consensual interpretation of Zionism came after Israeli forces occupied Palestinian lands in the West Bank, Gaza Strip and East Jerusalem in 1967. The prevailing Labour elite were unable to reconcile their desire to exploit the strategic and economic opportunities offered by the occupation, with their socialist rhetoric. As the national leadership prevaricated, opting for woolly compromises, they fell out of step with their own Zionist imperatives. If Israel did not have a legitimate claim to the biblical heartlands of Judea and Samaria, what claim did it have to Tel Aviv and Haifa? If the mission was to redeem the lands promised to the Jews through pioneering settlements, how could they pass up the opportunity to 'recover' the tomb of Abraham, the well of Joseph and – most importantly of all – the last remaining wall of the Second Temple in East Jerusalem? But, if Zionism was a national liberation ideology which rejected colonial exploitation, how could Israel exploit the land and labour resources of the Occupied Territories, deny the indigenous population political and national rights, and engage in violent strategies for repression.

The answers came in the form of a revival of the religious nationalism of Rabbi Avraham Yitzhak Kook in the *yeshivas* of Jerusalem, although a new twist was added in the form of an alliance with the secular aspirations of Israeli nationalists for territorial expansion and praetorian strength. The main religious political party, the Mafdal, was radicalised by the opportunities offered by the newly acquired lands, having been heavily penetrated by members of a new virulently pro-settlement religious movement, the Gush Emunim (Bloc of the Faithful), a founding figure of which was Kook's son, Rabbi Zvi Yehuda Kook. Mafdal transferred its coalition allegiance from the old Labour elite to the right-wing Likud bloc of parties, helping to sweep Menachem Begin to power in the electoral 'earthquake' of 1977.

The religious nationalists interpreted the victory of 1967 as a heroic fulfilment of prophecy which should not be reversed through an exchange of land for peace, but which should rather be consolidated through mass settlement, the expulsion of the Palestinian peoples, and the re-casting of Zionism as an eschatological mission-statement for the Israeli state. Their spatial vision of Eretz Israel was taken from the Bible, including the lands from 'the wilderness to Lebanon and from the River, the river Euphrates, to the Western Sea', coinciding closely with the strategic aspirations of secular nationalists. Settlement of the new areas was part of the process of messianic redemption, but it also revived the pioneering ethos of Israel's early years and struck a chord with Israelis who felt the country had lost its direction under the Labour leadership's surrender to materialism and permissiveness. Individuals like Rabbi Meir Kahane (founder of the Kach party which openly advocated anti-Arab violence and mass transfer) and Rabbi Moshe Levinger (another leading light of Gush Emunim) considered themselves the true heirs of Zionism, restoring its religious foundations but equally internalising the need to engage with the secular political discourse and co-opt secular political forces. They were eagerly welcomed into alliances by secularist right-wing nationalists, who were comfortable with the symbolism and legitimacy provided by religious invocations, but whose primary ambitions did not include transforming Israel into a theocracy.

This alliance has transformed Israeli domestic politics, not least through the revival of the liberationist aspects of Zionist philosophy and their synthesis with Torah diktats in a society where only one in four Israelis identify themselves as religious observants yet religious parties can determine a coalition or bring down a government. The religious revival has worked its way into mainstream Israeli politics, and religious parties – even those whose primary concern is not the reclamation of the full territory of biblical Israel – have gained ground in determining many aspects of Israeli life.[23] But if the consequences have been traumatic for secular Israelis who are struggling to stem the tide of religious encroachments on their civil and human rights, for the Palestinians they have been a disaster. Although some ultra-orthodox groups like Neturei Karta and the Satmar Hasidim continue to reject the State of Israel as an act of rebellion against God, for the most part religious political parties in Israel have denounced the peace process on the grounds that land won must not be ceded to non-Jews. The Palestinians are denied the status of equals, their national identity and rights are an irrelevance, their very existence on the land is an affront to divine authority. While secular nationalists may not share quite such an extreme perception, at least acknowledging the role of Palestinians as the 'other' in a struggle for sovereignty, they derive electoral strength from the religio-nationalist constituency which sharpens their position when it comes to (rejecting) negotiations with the Palestinian Authority.

Post-Zionist Possibilities?

There is, however, an alternative intellectual current which began to emerge in Israel in the 1980s and 1990s, although it has been obscured more recently by a popular shift in favour of hardline solutions to the current Palestinian Intifada. Referred to as a *post-Zionist* discourse, it draws in part on the gains made by Israeli revisionist historiographers in eschewing reliance upon pre-state history and iconography for the definition of the Israeli soul. But it is much more than this; it is the suggestion that Israeli society is maturing to a point where Israeli nationalism, as opposed to Jewish nationalism, is the predominant source of an individual's identification. Such an identification reinforces Israel's democratic credentials because it allows the perception of the nation to be inclusive of minorities, rather than exclusive. What matters is citizenship, not national or religious identity. Post-Zionism does not necessarily imply a rejection of Zionism, but rather a recognition that it has served its purpose and is now being succeeded by a democratic orientation more appropriate to modern times. To be fair, there is little systematic evidence that the Israeli public actually views itself as having moved to such a stage of self-evaluation (including Israeli Arabs who came into direct confrontation with government troops in 2000 over their continuing marginalisation and exclusion). Indeed, writers like Herbert Kelman[24] have admitted that post-Zionist discourse has a normative component that suggests this is where Israeli society *ought* to have found itself, rather than that it already has. But there are positive signs. When Israel celebrated the fiftieth anniversary of statehood in 1998, the national public TV channel aired a 22-part historical series entitled *Tkuma* (*Revival*) telling the story of Israel's birth and history from the perspective of both victor (Israel) and vanquished (the Arabs), giving voice to both the dominant, essentially Ashkenazi, narrative of statehood and the marginalised and disenchanted narrative of the 'oriental immigrants'. The theory was that Israel had come of age and should be able to review its own past with a critical eye. In practice, the series brought bitter criticism from the nationalist right wing, who saw it as whining self-flagellation that failed to celebrate the achievements of Zionism. Yet when the daily newspaper *Ha'aretz* asked readers 'Do you think Israeli society is ripe for a critical history', an overwhelming 70 per cent said yes![25]

Post-Zionism suggests that the mission of Zionism is all but complete. A militarily strong and resilient Israel has gathered in all the likely *aliyahs*. The state infrastructure has evolved into a bureaucratic, complex and at times chaotic entity much like any other. The melting pot of internal cultures is bubbling away, acknowledging the virtues of pluralism and rejecting the forced assimilation of the early state years. In almost every way, Israel has been 'normalised'. What does this mean? Tom Segev has argued cogently that it is both a combination of 'Americanisation' (or harmonisation with a global *Kulturkampf*) and a return to Jewish tradition, which is no longer cast aside in the search for collective renewal.[26]

Once Israel becomes home to the world's largest community of Jews and the flow of immigrants dries up to a thin trickle, the Law of Return will have no meaning. With an economy almost fully integrated into a globalised world, can Israel really continue to claim a separateness of the Jewish people from global *goyism*? Can Zionists continue to seek a collective spiritual redemption when the actions of the military and settler groups trample so emphatically on the basic human rights of the Palestinians living under Israeli ccupation? Ariel Sharon's government may have proclaimed upon its election the 'victory of Zionism over post-Zionism', and the collapse of the peace process may have pushed Israelis back into a siege mentality, but this is not the Zionism of Israel's founding fathers. Perhaps this is a temporary aberration reflecting the difficulties of a peace process which will ultimately necessitate Israel abandoning some of its 'sacred cows'. Ariel Sharon was not elected as prime minister because the majority of Israelis subscribed to his vision of Greater Israel: he owed the votes to demands for a tough line on security *within* Israel and to religious groups seeking to reverse Ehud Barak's 'civil revolution' which aimed to stem the tide of religious encroachment on everyday life. There are indications that Israeli society is slowly accommodating itself to the internal tensions of a post-Zionist era, but until peace with its Palestinian neighbours is achieved, Zionism is likely to remain the ideological lifeline which unites a large proportion of the world's Jews with one another and with the land of Israel.

NOTES

1   Hebrew scriptures make clear the connection between the Jewish people and the land of Israel, or Zion. Yahweh chose it as his dwelling place and from it would come deliverance. Jewish existence in Zion was dependent on the proper behaviour of its inhabitants and thus separation from the land was interpreted as a punishment for Jewish unfaithfulness to the covenant with Yahweh. However, a return was prophesied, subject to Yahweh's intervention once the people were deemed worthy to return.

2   Stein, *Zionism*, p. 20.

3   Arguments in this realm range from Henry Cattan's assertions regarding the inaccuracy of Biblical accounts, to Keith Whitelam's suggestion that the true ancient history of Palestine has been 'ignored and silenced by Biblical studies'. Cattan, *The Palestine Question*, and Whitelam, *The Invention of Ancient Israel*.

4   Notably associated with Moses Mendelssohn (1729–86)

5   A term first coined by Wilhelm Marr in the nineteenth century when he complained that Jewish influence had penetrated too far into German society, making 'slaves' of the latter.

6   A term given to a section of eastern Poland where the majority of Eastern European Jews lived in the eighteenth and nineteenth centuries, annexed by Russia but cordoned off from the heartlands. The Jews were restricted to these provinces, were subject to harsh controls, prevented from enjoying either a communal political life or participating in local government, were forcibly conscripted into the army and ruthlessly taxed.

7   See Walter Laqueur, *A History of Zionism*, p. 60.

8   The term Bilu is drawn from the words *Bet Yaakov lechu ve nelcha* – 'O house of Jacob – come ye and let us go', Isaiah II 5. Chovevei Zion can be translated as meaning 'Lovers of Zion'.

9   Kornberg, *Theodor Herzl: From Assimilation to Zionism*, p. 2.

10   Herzl, *The Complete Diaries* of *Theodore Herzl*, p. 343.

11   Figures from Sachar *A History of Israel: From the Rise of Zionism to Our Time*, various pages.

12   A series of letters had been exchanged with Sherif Hussain of Mecca during the war in which British officials encouraged Hussain to mobilise his own armies against the Ottoman and German troops in Arabia, in return for which he would be awarded a vaguely defined territory at the eastern end of the Mediterranean.

13   Anonymous source quoted in Fraser, *The Arab–Israeli Conflict*, p. 12.

14   Howard Sachar has provided the following figures for this annihilation in *A History of Israel: From the Rise of Zionism to Our Time*, p. 249. 'The statistics of the Final Solution numbered 2,800,000 Polish Jews, 800,000 Soviet Jews, 450,000 Hungarian Jews, 350,000 Rumanian Jews, 180,000 German Jews, 60,000 Austrian Jews, 243,000 Czechoslovakian Jews, 110,000 Dutch Jews, 25,000 Belgian Jews, 50,000 Yugoslav Jews, 80,000 Greek Jews, 65,000 French Jews, 10,000 Italian Jews – all liquidated by shooting, gassing, hanging, burning, or starvation and disease. The data of survival took longer to accumulate, for it was based on the number of Jewish "displaced persons" who gathered in the Allied occupation sectors of Germany.'

15   The United Nations Special Committee on Palestine (UNSCOP) included representatives from Sweden, the Netherlands, Czechoslovakia, Yugoslavia, Australia, Canada, India, Iran, Guatemala, Uruguay and Peru.

16   The early figures identified as such included Simha Flapan, *The Birth of Israel: Myths and Realities*; Benny Morris, *The Birth of the Palestinian Refugee Problem, 1947–49*; Ilan Pappé, *Britain and the Arab–Israeli Conflict, 1948–51* and Avi Shlaim, *Collusion Across the Jordan: King Abdullah, the Zionist Movement and the Partition of Palestine*.

17   Best-known proponents of this argument are Maxime Rodinson in *Israel: A Colonial Settler State*; Samih Farsoun, 'Settler Colonialism and Herrenvolk Democracy', in R. Stevens and A. Elmissiri (eds.) *Israel and South Africa: The Progression of a Relationship*, A.W. Kayyali (ed.) *Zionism, Imperialism and Racism* and G. Jabbour, *Settler Colonialism in Southern Africa and the Middle East*.

18   Examples of the dual society thesis would include N. Eisenstadt, *Israeli Society* and Dan Horowitz and Moshe Lissak's *Origins of the Israeli Polity: Palestine Under the Mandate*. For an example of the relational paradigm, see Zachary Lockman's *Comrades and Enemies: Arab and Jewish Workers in Palestine, 1906–1948*.

19   The classic text on this perspective is Uri Davis' *Israel: An Apartheid State*.

20   Prior, *Zionism and the State of Israel: A Moral Inquiry*, pp. 219–20.

21   Elizer Schweid has suggested that this consensus-driven Zionism can be understood as the Americanisation of Zionism, the creation of a mass culture, centred on youth and striving 'to obscure all unique characteristics of modern national identity'. 'Jewishness and Israeliness' in *Palestine and Israel Journal*, 2002.

22   Henriette Dahan-Kalev has argued that the Euro-centric leadership in Israel 'invented' the Mizrahi as a communal group in order to identify the 'other' within Zionism. The oriental, pre-modern character of the group was contrasted with the modernism and

progressiveness of the new Israeli-born *sabras*, justifying their social and cultural re-education within the process of creating a hegemonic Israeli culture. 'The "Other" in Zionism: The Case of the Mizrahim', in *Palestine and Israel Journal*, 2001.

23 Including definitions of who is a Jew, state enforcement of Sabbath observance, the status of religiously derived family law, food imports and sales, circumcisions, conversions and burials of immigrants, the status of Conservative and Reform rabbis and their access to state funds, the distribution of education funds and support for yeshivas, financial support for large (primarily Orthodox) families, exemptions from military service etc.

24 Kelman, 'Israel in Transition from Zionism to Post-Zionism', in *The Annals of the American Academy*, 1998.

25 'The Making of T'kuma: An Interview with Yigal Eilam', in *Palestine–Israel Journal*, 1998.

26 Tom Segev, *Elvis in Jerusalem: Post-Zionism and the Americanization of Israel.*

FURTHER READING

For information on Zionism before and during the Mandate, read Walter Laqueur (1972), *A History of Zionism*, New York: Schocken Books; Simha Flapan (1979), *Zionism and the Palestinians*, London: Croom Helm; or Shlomo Avineri (1981), *The Making of Modern Zionism*, New York: Basic Books. For recent discussions of the development of Zionism, see Michael Brenner (2003), *Zionism: A Brief History* (trans. Shelley Frisch), Princeton: Markus Wiener; Yoram Hazony (2001), *The Jewish State: The Struggle for Israel's Soul*, New York: Basic Books. For Jewish critiques of Zionism, see Michael Prior (1999), *Zionism and the State of Israel*, London: Routledge; and Boas Evron (1995), *Jewish State or Israeli Nation?*, Bloomington and Indianapolis: Indiana University Press. For discussion of Labour Zionism during and after the Mandate era, see Mitchell Cohen (1987), *Zion and State: Nation, Class and the Shaping of Modern Israel*, Oxford: Basil Blackwell. For discussion of secular right-wing Zionism, see Colin Shindler (1995), *Israel, Likud and the Zionist Dream*, London: I. B. Tauris. For post-Zionist discourse, see Laurence J. Silberstein (1999), *The Postzionism Debates: Knowledge and Power in Israeli Culture*, New York: Routledge. For a succinct summary of the main Israeli revisionist texts and arguments, see Ilan Pappé (1999), *The Israel/Palestine Question*, London: Routledge. For an interesting attempt to track both the rise of Zionism and Palestinian nationalism within Mandate Palestine, see Tom Segev (2000), *One Palestine Complete: Jews and Arabs Under the British Mandate*, London: Little, Brown and Co. For studies of the emergence and development of Palestinian nationalism, see Yezid Sayigh (1997), Oxford: Clarendon Press; Rashid Khalidi (1997), *Palestinian Identity: The Construction of Modern National Consciousness*, New York: Columbia University Press; David McDowall (1994), *The Palestinians: The Road to Nationhood*, London: Minority Rights Group; and Baruch Kimmerling and Joel S. Migdal (1993), *Palestinians: The Making of a People*, New York: Macmillan.

CHAPTER FIFTEEN

Nationalisms in the Middle East
The Case of Pan-Arabism

YOUSSEF M. CHOUEIRI

In the first half of the twentieth century, Middle Eastern nationalisms were lumped together and treated as part of an undifferentiated phenomenon sweeping across the entire length of the continents of Asia, Latin America and Africa. More importantly, these nationalisms were seen to be no more than political responses of western-educated elites to European expansionism and colonialism.

Moreover, French and British colonial scholarship tended to frown upon such nationalisms, deeming their emergence to be either unfortunate, or undesirable in both their aims and methods. By contrast, American scholarship tended, at least in the initial stages of its development, to be more charitable, assigning to nationalism positive cultural connotations and political significance, thereby holding it to denote an earnest desire to join the modern world of independent nations. The subtle, but problematic, European differentiations of various types of nationalisms, often introduced for purely political purposes, tended to be blurred or assigned no particular importance. Thus, the distinctions between liberal patriotism, territorial nationalism and ethnic allegiances were all placed along the same spectrum of positive human loyalties. However, by the early 1930s a more nuanced approach began to be deployed in order to account for the apparent persistence and growth of a number of Middle Eastern nationalist movements, be they Turkish, Iranian or Arab.

These movements centred on defined territories, and while addressing themselves to particular ethnic communities, desired to fashion modern nation-states out of countries that had been for centuries part of wider imperial domains. Moreover, their territorial and political spaces were also home to sizeable minorities with a different national agenda.

The Turkish heartland, for example, had been incorporated in the structures of the Saljukid and Ottoman empires before it was reconfigured to form a national territory in its own right. Persia – later to be designated Iran – had always formed, prior to its emergence as a national entity, the nucleus of an imperial structure, such as the Safavid imperial state, or an integral part of other empires, including the ʿAbbasid or the Umayyad. As for the Arabs, their territorial fatherland did not become clearly delineated until the first half of the twentieth century. Moreover, this fatherland in its modern history, unlike Turkey or Iran, has never been unified into a single state with the result that it has had to satisfy itself with a dual identity almost equally shared by a particular state and the entire Arab homeland at the same time.

Furthermore, the era of independence and nation-building was preceded by an unprecedented expansionist drive, undertaken by a number of European countries, bent on building colonial empires and fuelled by the Industrial and French revolutions.

Nationalism in the Middle East was thus conceived as an integral part of a wider movement springing out of the sudden political awakening of the Orient, or the east, as it tried to free itself from the shackles of colonialism. We thus find scholars of nationalism, such as Hans Kohn (1891–1971) and Carlton Hayes (1882–1964) articulating their interpretations of nationalism by reference to a worldwide movement stretching from Italy and Germany to India, China and the Islamic world. Such an approach culminated in the work of Rupert Emerson who published in 1960 a highly positive assessment of nationalism as a new political effort undertaken by the peoples of Asia and Africa to chart their own future on the basis of self-determination and national liberation (Rupert Emerson, *From Empire to Nation*, 1960).

However, this general scheme of organising the data and events of Middle Eastern nationalisms was based on an analytical framework conceived to consist of three successive waves of nationalist awakenings.

The first wave was firmly located in its western European background and context, with England playing a leading role in giving birth to a particular brand of nationalism. Often dubbed patriotism – a deliberate designation meant to highlight its softer edges as opposed to Continental nationalism – this English variety was said to have enjoyed a graduated development. Sprouting in the seventeenth century and continuing to grow over the next two centuries, it was characterised by a benign liberal outlook and a highly tolerant attitude towards the other. Hence, this wave was from the moment of its inception brimming with a plenitude of political diversity and displaying a firm belief in the autonomy of the individual. Clearly drafted laws and charters enshrining the rights of the individual as a living embodiment of the national spirit and its culture crowned all of this. These rights included liberty, freedom of speech, assembly and belief, religious tolerance, and an abiding commitment to uphold the rule of law. Hence, patriotism denoted loyalty to the fatherland as a national territory rather than allegiance to race or ethnicity (Hans Kohn, *Nationalism: Its Meaning and History*, 1946).

The second wave is assumed to have been generated by the first one, whereby Central and Eastern Europe is said to have acted as its main theatre of operation. This particular wave, although generated by the first, had its own characteristics, which shifted the national focus from the individual to the community. In other words, it was less concerned with individual liberty and more interested in creating strong bonds of political loyalty. Instead of centring allegiance on a clearly defined territory, it embraced the values of a particular race and its alleged unique qualities. In this sense, it projected a racial dimension that highlighted ties across international borders and adjacent nations and held blood and linguistic affiliations to be more essential and enduring than territorial bonds.

The third wave, although directly affected by the roaring tides of the first (mainly through the experience of colonialism), was more in tune with the Eastern European model. This was all the more so as a result of certain cultural affinities and shared political defects. Racial and linguistic bonds were now reworked and adopted as the emblem of ethnic groups and communities, often inhabiting the same territory and seeking to oust each other in ugly scenes of massacre and carnage. In both cases, the advent of a new revolutionary intelligentsia, motivated by an authoritarian drive for power, was held responsible for such an outcome (Elie Kedourie, *Nationalism*, 1960). Such a diagnosis becomes all the more intriguing when one recalls how the third wave swept over Asia, Africa or Latin America in response to the colonial policies of the representatives of the third wave. It was thus historically and causally linked to western European models, particularly in its first phase of articulation, as we shall see later.

It is in this context that a more historically accurate description of nationalism could be offered as a way out of the confusion that still reigns in its study. Such a model, based on the theoretical contributions of recent scholarship on the subject (Gellner, 1984; Breuilly, 1993; Anderson, 1993) envisages three types of Middle Eastern Nationalism: (1) *liberal patriotism*: a cultural and political movement that began to gather momentum by the end of the nineteenth century and culminated in its final phase in the struggle for independence; (2) *integral nationalism*: the achievement of independence gave way to a more radical phase whereby liberal policies were deemed incapable of creating a modern nation-state or a well-integrated society. This was particularly the case during the era of Ataturk and Reza Khan in Turkey and Iran, as well as in the Arab world under the leadership of Jamal 'Abd al-Nasir (Nasser); and (3) *territorial nationalism*: this particular trend, emerging into the political arena in the 1970s, combines a number of ingredients, chief amongst which figure democratic accountability, cultural diversity, and recognition of minority rights, gender equality and the encouragement of civil society organisations. Not yet fully articulated or developed across the Middle East, and buffeted by the rise of Islamist politics and the new age of globalisation, its survival is precariously poised. Moreover, the Arab case is further complicated by the clash of identities alternating between state patriotism and pan-nationalism.

These types are of particular relevance to Turkey, Iran and the Arab world, but do not exhaust all varieties of nationalism. Hence, ethnic nationalism cannot be completely excluded, particularly in the case of a number of national minorities, such as the Kurds (see in this respect chapter 24 on minorities).

Religion and Nationalism

Colonialism was accompanied by an internal movement of reform, which embraced the central states of the Middle East and had as its ultimate aim the creation of viable nation-states throughout the region.

It is generally agreed that in the nineteenth century Muslim thinkers and statesmen began to recognise the importance of reforming their religion and society as a result of the ascendancy of Europe in the military and economic fields. Hence, modern reform in Islam meant a clear realisation of relative decline in comparison with western societies, as well as an earnest endeavour to join the modern world with a newly recast belief-system.

This reform movement embraced the major Muslim states and their urban centres. Ottoman sultans and officials who were anxious to keep pace with European advances in the military fields first initiated it. However, this early attempt led in the process to lively debates within the ranks of the religious establishment itself, pitting reformists against conservatives. The repercussions of these debates engulfed the principal urban centres of the Islamic world, particularly in India, Persia, Egypt and North Africa.

Consequently, Islam was restated or reinterpreted in the light of the efforts of both Muslim statesmen and religious leaders.

Covering a wide spectrum of theoretical and practical issues, these debates ranged from the applicability of Islamic law in the modern world, to the viability of Islam itself within a new international order composed of independent states and secular forms of government.

Islamic reformers justified their undertaking by deploying a number of theoretical and methodological tools. Whereas the strategies pursued did succeed in achieving some of their stated aims, their partial success served to sow the seeds of more radical movements, such as nationalism, socialism and religious fundamentalism.

One salient outcome of these debates and endeavours seems to relate to the way reformist Islam gave legitimacy to the concept of nationality as a politically acquired right, closely associated with a certain territory as opposed to religious, sectarian or tribal affiliations.

To what extent did religion in its reformist phase facilitate the consolidation of nationalism?

Both religion and nationalism are more than mere ideologies or emotional states of mind. They represent social and intellectual movements, which seek to restructure both the material and cultural aspects of life. Moreover, they both provide collective identities, strive to change unjust situations and operate on the basis of sustained actions and rituals.

Religion is ancient, whereas nationalism is a modern phenomenon. Nevertheless, both exist in a state of constant flux, carried forward by social actors and agents, undergoing either evolutionary developments or sudden mutation. Consequently, one could say that religion as it is practised today has itself joined the world of modernity, or has been modernised despite its ancient origins. Moreover, it is a matter of great importance to realise that to belong to a particular religion or a defined nationality as a result of traditional ties of communal solidarity, is often the case in Middle Eastern culture.

But it is safe to assume at the outset that both have been subject to a process of slow or violent transformation. At the heart of this transformation stands the role assigned to the individual as an autonomous entity whose status in society is no longer ascribed but earned. However, this freedom in its modern embodiment has often served to sever organised religion from the state or to bring it under its direct control.

Until recently, the study of nationalism was bound up with charting the steady decline of religion. In fact, this depiction has by and large remained the general paradigm within which conceptual tools were deployed in order to account for the rise of nationalism or the decline of religion. Some scholars, seeing the upsurge of fundamentalist movements across the globe, have sought to resolve this tension between two contradictory social forces by conflating both, thereby trying to show how religion can easily replace nationalism or act as its surrogate mother. This approach depicts religion as a political agent capable of adapting its broad belief-system to a nationalist agenda by way of a selective memory and an imaginative or creative reading of its past (Gellner, 1992; Zubaida, 2002).

By doing so, these scholars bypass the absolute and timeless nature of religion. Hence, this theoretical operation confines itself to the task of tabulating the function of religion or nationalism in the modern world. It thus becomes much easier to discuss functionality than to wrestle with the intricate characteristics of substances and their enduring qualities. However, it must be admitted that the study of sub-stance, philosophically and historically, has now been discredited either as a tool of analysis or as a concrete entity. Having discarded substance as an absolute model of study, one is faced with a number of questions pertaining to the idea of function.

How does religion or nationalism function in society? What forms, rituals and practices are deemed necessary to sustain their presence and visibility? Apart from endowing individual lives with a meaningful direction, how do they both persist in a post-modern world or in the age of globalisation?

First of all, one could say that religion and nationalism do share certain common characteristics:

1. Both are considered to be spontaneous or involuntary responses to sociological factors and psychological dilemmas.
2. Both are universal, in the sense that all societies have had to adopt one or the other in their historical development.
3. Until recently, religions and nationalisms sought to sublimate 'male dominance', thereby turning women into subordinate subjects confined to the private, as opposed to the public, sphere of life.
4. Both are emotionally charged and often shot through with the energy of con-stant endeavour and self-sacrifice. The concept and practice of martyrdom often straddle their inner dynamics.

More importantly, their existence is justified and defended on the basis of a deep human need. To experience the loss of a particular object, prerogative, or state of being is said to account for their necessary presence. The idea of losing innocence, proximity to a loved one or national sovereignty explains in this context why certain events take place, or how individuals of a particular social group become alienated and committed at the same time to a religious or nationalist ideal. Thus, loss of national independence may be easily juxtaposed to the loss of a close relative whereby a heightened sense of impending disaster is recycled to re-emerge under a new label of utter devotion to a higher cause. Both religion and nationalism come to the rescue of the individual and society in order to compensate for such a loss and restore control over one's individuality.

Finally, nation-building, or the movement which culminated in the division of the world into nation-states, is said to embrace both, whereby high culture becomes the end product of a refined reinterpretation of religion, and nationalism provides the cement of a new industrial order (Gellner, 1984).

However, despite all these similarities in function or social contexts, the fact remains that religion and nationalism possess different characteristics, which often issue in dissimilar political and social outcomes.

This is all the more so when religion is politicised and turned into a movement of radical change. It therefore assumes an identity of its own and proceeds to create its own universe.

Political religion derives its fundamental principles from a divine text, which is rooted in a direct encounter with God as the ultimate arbiter. Nationalism, on the other hand, embraces the community as its source of legislation and legitimacy. Whereas religion posits God's laws to be a timeless and immutable set of rules to be obeyed and observed, nationalism relies on human reason to decide for itself its conduct and approach to various social problems. One is anchored in sacred traditions and the other is utterly secular in its judgement and strategic decisions. Although moral standards may overlap and appear to speak the same language, the relative values of nationalism are constantly questioned and undermined by absolute criteria considered to be in accord with a predetermined scheme of things.

Whereas religion uses a certain territory as a provisional launching pad for its ultimate aims, nationalism defines its very identity by espousing a delimited geographical area, endowing its history with a cherished national legacy.

Political religion abhors borders, decries national identification and tries to soar above human ties centred on defined territories. Moreover, its mission is driven by a system of classification that creates clear separate islands within the same national territory: believers and non-believers, men and women, God and the community of the select, the chosen and the true representatives of the divine will as opposed to a collection of errant groups of people.

In the Middle East itself the historical relationship between religion and nationalism has been more complex than these stark dichotomies may lead us to believe. However, religion has to a large extent been nationalised, or incorporated by various forms of nationalist movements and states, without, however, succeeding in obscuring the universalist appeal of religion. This universalism, be it mere piety, Sufism, the spirit of reformism, or the relentless drive of fundamentalist politics, is today under severe pressure to readjust itself, yet again, to the dictates of globalisation and the new world order.

At the turn of the century both Turkish and Arab writers vied with each other to demonstrate and flaunt the services their respective ethnic communities had offered Islam both as a religion and a state. Turkish intellectuals alluded to the glorious feats of Ottoman arms in expanding the frontiers of Islam and defending its heartland against foreign schemes of occupation and invasion. By contrast, the Arab educated elite singled out the pivotal role of their ethnic community in giving birth to Islam, supplying both its prophet and the language of its holy book, not to mention its early warriors and political leaders.

In Turkey, nationalism came into being in defiance of religion. It represented a violent abrogation of a religious past and present for the sake of a bright secular future. However, by the middle of the twentieth century, Turkish nationalism seemed to have reached a cultural and political accommodation with religion without sacrificing its secular credentials.

In Iran, this relationship has oscillated between two extremes, with each vying for a dominant position, but often settling on a tense compromise. The policies of the first two shahs between 1926 and 1979 tried to confine the religious establishment to a marginal position only to be confronted by a militant backlash which succeeded in placing religion at the centre of national life. Today Iran is still in the throes of an ongoing experiment with both religion and nationalism alternating as two driving forces, without clear victory for the one or the other.

In the Arab world, religion was enlisted in launching and sustaining national struggles for independence in an effortless and almost neutral approach to political life and constitutional governments. It was only when national struggles were aborted and neutrality violated that religion made its stand as an autonomous counterforce.

Israel represents a hybrid, which imported religion into disparate communities. This was made possible by using the Bible as a national charter and the persecution of the Jews throughout history as a unique national identity. Some responded, while others did not. However, both religion and nationalism in Israeli society are so entwined in a potentially explosive mixture that only the Palestinians can manage to read its daily effects as it grinds on without having resolved this fatal tension.

The following three sections, divided into chapters, chart the trajectory of Arab, Turkish, and Iranian nationalism in the Middle East.

Arab Nationalism

Arab nationalism emerged and developed as a series of overlapping cultural, political and social movements. It was initially both a movement of separation and unification, aiming at detaching the Asian part of the Arab world from the Ottoman empire and seeking at the same time to unify the constituent administrative units of this territory into one single state. This drive for both separation and unification found its political and military culmination in the 1916 Arab Revolt, led by Sharif Husayn of Mecca and immortalised by Lawrence of Arabia in his *Seven Pillars of Wisdom*. However, the legacy of the Arab Revolt, launched in alliance with Great Britain and to a lesser extent France, left Arab Asia severely and artificially divided into several states under direct or indirect European control. While Palestine was promised by Britain as the site of a new Jewish homeland, Iraq and Transjordan enjoyed a degree of self-rule under British supervision, and France carved out for itself a Syrian mandate under the auspices of the League of Nations. Moreover, the rest of the Arab world was also firmly placed under the rule of Britain (Egypt, the Sudan, in addition to Asian Aden and other Gulf shaykdoms), France (Tunisia, Algeria and Morocco) and Italy (Libya). Only Saudi Arabia, founded in 1932, escaped direct occupation and enjoyed, together with North Yemen, the status of a nominally independent state.

It was at this juncture that Arab nationalist ideas and programmes began to spread out from Syria and Iraq into the wider Arab world. Egypt was the first to join such endeavours at both the popular and official levels, particularly as it became aware of the advantages such a pan-Arabist stance would confer on her as the most populous and advanced Arab country or in the struggle to wrest its independence from successive British governments. By the end of the Second World War, the drive for Arab unity had gathered momentum and entered the political arena as a permanent feature for years to come. The League of Arab States, founded in 1945, expressed this new drive, albeit at its most loose and incoherent embodiment. It was also during this period that pan-Arabism, a general movement denoting the cultural and political ties that made cooperation between various Arab states a desirable and feasible enterprise, began to give way to a more radical and coherent movement dubbed Arab Nationalism.

Pan-Arabism was in this respect what Arab writers referred to as *'uruba*, a term which simply meant a general commitment to a common national identity based on bonds woven by language, culture (religion in particular), history and shared destinies. *'uruba* or *Arabism* could thus be marshalled to embrace wider connotations than a mere political movement, which Arab nationalism increasingly became and was perceived as such by both its adherents and opponents. Hence, all Arab states and citizens could proclaim their adherence to the Arab nation and its Arabism, while at the same time avoiding the stricter implications of having to adopt Arab nationalism and its drive for political unification.

In this sense, pan-Arabism did not always entail a proactive stance committed to the idea of Arab unity as the central aim of a well-articulated political programme. In other words, pan-Arabism evolved over time to form a cultural substratum, or a material underpinning upon which Arab nationalism could venture to erect various schemes of national regeneration.

Pan-Arabism was largely the product of the nineteenth century and its programmes of reform and modernisation. It was, however, restricted at this stage to a broad commitment to the idea of reviving Arab culture in its positive and glorious aspects. Such a revival consisted of revisiting certain historical episodes in order to lend them a novel interpretation designed to justify decline or preach the message of a new cycle of renewal.

Hence the destruction of the 'Abbasid caliphate by the Mongols in 1258 was said to have ushered in the rapid decline of the Arabs either as a military or a political force in the Islamic world. Moreover, the advent of new ethnic communities to positions of power in the Arab empire, such as the Persians and the Turks, and the services they rendered to Islam, were often obscured or readjusted to allow the Arabs to resume their natural function as custodians of both Islam and its sacred language.

It is for these reasons that once an Arab dynasty or personality established an autonomous principality, no matter how precarious or short-lived, signs of recovery were immediately cited and accorded a significant function in historical developments. In other words, movements that were built upon purely religious or local dynastic ambitions became auspicious portents of a general pan-Arabist revival. For example, the revivalist Wahhabi movement, which originated in central Arabia in the 1740s, was seen in this light (Antonius, 1938, pp. 20–38).

Named after its founder, Muhammad b. 'Abd al-Wahhab (1703–93), and adopted as a political ideology, by a local chieftain, Muhammad Ibn Sa'ud (d. 1765), it was based on puritan principles, calling for the absolute unity of God in opposition to the worship of saints or the veneration of holy men and Sufis. Nevertheless, it was deemed to have denoted a resurgence of Arab vitality by the mere fact that it was led by two Arab personalities who aimed at unifying local tribal groups under the banner of the original message of Islam. It also demonstrated an implicit drive for independence by the challenge it posed to the authority of the Ottoman sultans.

While it found some support in Central Arabia until its suppression between 1812 and 1818 by Muhammad 'Ali (1805–48), the governor of Egypt, it did not herald the birth of a new Arab movement. Tribally based, religiously motivated and geographically isolated from the main urban centres of the Muslim World, it nevertheless denoted the crystallisation of an Islamic revivalist trend in the face of internal decay and domestic upheavals.

Moreover, the confrontation between this rising power and Muhammad 'Ali's army was an early indication of the political orientations of regional powers in the Arab world as they entered the modern cycle of their history and became differentiated into nation-states. Although Egypt at the time was still nominally under Ottoman suzerainty, its dynamic ruler, Muhammad 'Ali, was in the process of launching one of the most comprehensive programmes of industrialisation and modernisation in the Arab world. His policies paved the way for the rise of indigenous elites that made the entertainment of an independent path of development a concrete possibility.

In Yemen, the Gulf regions of Arabia and Morocco, dynasties claiming autonomy or complete independence were also a prominent feature of this period. As the

Plate 15.1   Shukri al-Quwatly (second on the left), first President of independent Syria
Source: © *AlHayat* Newspaper, London

Ottoman empire underwent a process of reform in order to reverse its decline, particularly after 1792, local Arab dynasties had the opportunity to establish themselves on a more secure basis. These reforms, initiated by Sultan Selim III (1789–1804), and supported by a group of bureaucrats, army officers, diplomats and interpreters, gave the Arab subjects of the empire the opportunity to engage in a modern process aimed at regenerating the imperial fortunes of the Ottoman dynasty and its various nationalities. Cultural Arabism was thus born out of this tripartite encounter: Ottoman policies of modernisation, European schemes of expansion and colonial control, and imagined models of Arab achievements accomplished during the golden age of a flourishing civilisation. In this sense, cultural Arabism was largely a literary and ethnic movement that succeeded in reintroducing themes of national regeneration by revisiting former glories and cultural monuments in a creative act of ascribing modern connotations to past glories (cf. Smith, 1994, p. 3).

   This sense of cultural and ethnic Arabism emerged and consolidated itself in Arab countries that were the direct theatre of Ottoman reform or European expansion. This applies in the main to Egypt, greater Syria and Tunisia. Other Arab countries joined in this process at different levels or stages, a fact that explains the belatedness of political pan-Arabism in their historical development. This was particularly the case of Morocco, Algeria and the Arabian Peninsula. The absence of one factor, either Ottoman reform or direct European presence, accounts to a large extent for this uneven process of cultural Arabism.

Plate 15.2   Nasser: Egyptian President and charismatic symbol of Arab nationalism
Source: © *AlHayat* Newspaper, London

Nevertheless, the rediscovery of Arabic civilisation as a glorious golden age, coupled with an earnest desire to acquire knowledge of the modern European world, were the hallmarks of this cultural movement.

Thus, a configuration of social, institutional, economic and international events constitutes significant factors in the generation of Arabism. These historical conditions include the following:

1. The advent and consolidation of new Arab elite groups anxious to assert their interests and cultural credentials in a new political order.
2. Social and economic changes brought about or precipitated by a newly invigorated Europe. These changes, accentuated by European rivalry for the acquisition

of overseas possessions, and as a result of modern transformations embodied in the Industrial and French Revolutions, created in turn vigorous responses of resistance and a desire for emulation.

3. Persistent Ottoman policies of reform aimed at halting the decline of imperial power. Initially confined to military and administrative structures, these reforms encompassed by the mid-nineteenth century state institutions, landownership, religious laws and social practices.

Ethnicity and Language

One of the most enduring legacies of the nineteenth century was the introduction of a new notion of citizenship, whereby political loyalty was directed towards a particular territorial entity, such as Syria, Egypt or Tunisia. Cultural Arabism was in this respect more than a mere literary movement, embracing as it did in its worldview the twin structures of a general Arab community, be it in the past, the present or the future, and a particular territorial fatherland (Egypt, Syria etc.), with the Ottoman state acting as the ultimate guarantor of both.

Such an unprecedented opportunity was to be explored for its positive implications by three different social groups.

The first group consisted of religious scholars and prominent community leaders who claimed either direct descent from the Prophet Muhammad, or proper knowledge of religion and its sound historical representations. Members of this group were considered to be the natural representatives of their ethnic community, either by their function as competent interpreters of Islamic law or as custodians of Arab culture and values. Both tasks required knowledge of Arabic and all auxiliary sciences associated with it.

The second included members of a new Christian intelligentsia based in Syria and Lebanon. Embracing teachers, journalists, editors, doctors and translators, this group disseminated its ideas by forming literary associations, publishing newspapers, and founding schools on modern European lines. The literary association, the newspaper and the school formed novel networks of communication and inculcation, acting as the mouthpiece of a new generation imbued with a sense of pride in a rediscovered Arab culture, and an enthusiastic response to western achievements in the fields of science, technology and education.

The third comprised a new stratum of urban notables and landowners who entered the new institutions of a reformed Ottoman state either as civil servants, or representatives of their local communities. Members in this last group were destined to emerge in due course as leaders of political Arabism. In the meantime, the revivification of Arab culture enhanced their qualifications to assume wider responsibilities in an era of equality and fraternity.

These groups sought to demonstrate their adherence to the new order of reform and renewal by adopting a policy based on singling out the multifaceted achievements of the Arabs as an indication of their deep-rooted national credentials, on the one hand, and reinterpreting the contributions of their culture to the birth of modern notions of government, scientific discoveries and methodologies of experimental science, on the other. Arabic was, as a result, rehabilitated as a language not only of religion and law, but of administration, politics, philosophy and science as well. It was slowly to be readopted by various local dynasties as the official language instead of Ottoman Turkish, as in Tunisia and Egypt in the nineteenth century. Arab ethnicity as the repository and emblem of brilliant accomplishments became in its own right a topic to be approached with pride and a spirit of reverence. The reason for such practical and intellectual outcomes was not far to seek: both were meant to adumbrate an abiding ability by their bearers or owners to resume a similar role dictated by present circumstances.

A new literary Arabic language was consequently forged to represent an autonomous cultural identity, and capable at the same time of expressing the vocabulary and terminology of modern science and political life. The Arabic language was thus modernised and new terms were coined in order to convey the meaning of political ideas and institutions, or scientific innovations and philosophical concepts. Such a process could be seen, for example, in the attempt by Arab scholars to coin a term denoting the republican system of government in the wake of the French revolution, or the notion of democracy and parliamentary elections.

Hence, language was presumed to act as a national instrument of communication, refashioned to probe and cope with the intricate developments of the modern world, penetrate its hidden and apparent meanings, and gain access to its novel intellectual, scientific or institutional aspects.

This new language arose out of the joint efforts of Syrian, Egyptian and Tunisian writers. They were in the main teachers at newly established schools, editors of newspapers or journals, and civil servants working for modernising rulers.

In addition, new Arabic dictionaries were compiled in order to update and reinsert Arabic as part of a much wider cultural awakening.

In Egypt, the versatile writings of the reformist religious scholar, teacher and translator, Rifaʻa Rafiʻ al-Tahtawi (1801–73), set the stage for the adoption of a new style of expression. It was further developed and given a solid articulate form by the Egyptian religious reformer, Muhammad ʻAbduh (1849–1905), a disciple of Jamal al-Din al-Afghani (1838–97), one of the most prominent leaders of political Islam in the nineteenth century. By 1876, Egypt, in addition to Beirut, had become the foremost centres of Arabic literature, learning and journalism. It was thus in Egypt that the combined productions of Syrian and local writers endowed the Arabic language with its final and concrete modern form.

The emphasis on Arabic as an eloquent language embodied in literature, history, science and poetry went hand in hand with the rediscovery of the Arabs as an ethnic community in possession of cherished ideals and valid values. By doing so, these religious scholars and secular writers injected a new meaning into the notion of Arabism, widening its scope so as to include by the turn of the twentieth century all Arabic-speaking communities.

We see this process at work in the works of al-Tahtawi who served Muhammad ʻAli and his successors (Choueiri, 2003, pp. 27–8; al-Tahtawi, 1868, p. 549)

Claiming descent from the Prophet Muhammad, and proud of the special position accorded to him, al-Tahtawi mentions on more than one occasion the virtues of the Arabs, singling out their generosity, magnanimity, readiness to assist those in distress and fulfilment of obligations. According to him, these characteristics were to be found among pagan, Christian and Jewish Arabs, long before the advent of Islam (al-Tahtawi, 1868, p. 486).

By highlighting the ethnic virtues of the Arabs as a community of creative individuals and endeavouring to underline cultural achievements in the pre-Islamic and post-Islamic periods, this strand of thought grew into a wider pan-Arab current. It became the hallmark of a new style of political and historical argumentation, invading at the same time literary genres and debates. This current was adopted, with slight variations or nuances, by both Muslim and Christian members of the intelligentsia and the political elites, thus paving the way for the creation of a neutral cultural space to be shared by a single national community.

The fatherland and patriotism

While Arab ethnicity was highlighted irrespective of particular territorial locations, patriotic affiliations were often confined to a particular geographic unit, such as Egypt, Tunisia, Syria and Iraq.

It was in the first half of the nineteenth century, particularly after the formal inauguration of the Ottoman reform movement, that the concept of the fatherland as a territorial entity entered the public arena as part of political discourse in the Arab world. A new form of human and national organisation was to be undertaken, bolstered by a systematic and consistent plan of action. The fatherland, singled out as a particular Arab country, was fixed as a permanent marker capable of undergoing radical change, while affording its inhabitants a clear reference point. This was turned into an act of patriotism and a call to perform heroic feats of national proportions. The idea of *al-watan* or the fatherland, introduced by Ottoman officials or their local associates, spread into various parts of the Arab world, becoming a familiar and integral part of the political vocabulary of Muslim and Christian Arabs alike.

Political Arabism, 1900–1945

By the turn of the twentieth century, a new second phase, extending from 1900 to 1945, began to take shape with an eminently political character. In this phase the concept of the fatherland was developed further to include self-determination, national independence and active participation in the political process of one's country.

This process gained impetus with the collapse of the Ottoman empire at the end of the First World War. Although Ottoman collapse granted Arab nationalists the opportunity to implement their own programme, their efforts were often thwarted by external pressures or internal squabbles. Moreover, the peace settlement as envisaged by the victorious western powers robbed almost all Arab countries of the opportunity to achieve full independence, or devise viable political systems and sustainable economic growth. Indeed, within one single decade (1920–30), one Arab rebellion after another, and all directed against European colonialism, was either utterly defeated or achieved partial and ephemeral success. This was the case in Syria, Iraq, Egypt, the Sudan, Libya, Tunisia and Morocco. Moreover, the insistence of Great Britain on carrying through its promise, enshrined in the Balfour Declaration, to the Zionist leadership to use its 'best endeavours to facilitate the achievement' of 'a national home for the Jewish people' in Palestine, constituted one of the most controversial political acts, whose consequences were to reverberate across the region down to the present time.

It was in this period that notions of political Arab nationalism were refined and expounded. For example, the idea of the Arab nation as a political entity and its geographic scope were discussed with a view to offering clear definitions of their contents or history. Further, the duality of adhering to a notion of local patriotism, confined to a particular Arab country, and the loyalty to a higher sense of nationalism, embracing the Arab nation as a whole, entered the political arena as an enduring feature of the modern Arab world. This was particularly the case in the countries of the Fertile Crescent, recently freed from Ottoman rule but firmly placed under various methods of British and French control. One noteworthy development in this period was the emergence and proliferation of political parties embracing a wide array of ideologies, ranging from liberalism, to Communism and nationalism.

Articulation of Pan-Arabism

By the turn of the twentieth century, the concept of nationalism, *qawmiyya*, postulating the existence of a discrete national identity possessed by the Arabs, with a corresponding right to separate political institutions, began to be used as a normal term. The Syrian religious scholar and member of the new intelligentsia 'Abd al-Rahman al-Kawakibi (1849–1902), was one who did so by calling for the creation of a national community based on the joint efforts of all religious sects and groups, be they Muslim, Christian or Jewish.

In a book published in 1900, *Characteristics of Tyranny*, he articulated a new concept of the nation in Arab political theory, basing his premises on the active participation of the people as free individuals and citizens. His discussion of the nature of political oppression, with particular reference to the rule of Sultan 'Abdulhamid, displayed the maturation of Islamic reformism in its efforts to create a new paradigm whereby the original message of Islam is shown to be in conformity with concepts and notions put forward during the age of reason or the Enlightenment (Haim, 1954; Rossi, 1954). It is in this context that al-Kawakibi's remarkable contribution to an emerging pan-Arabist ideology should be underlined, and irrespective of his ultimate sources. He singled out the separate existence of an Arab nation bound together by ties of patriotism, and he called upon the Arabs as reborn citizens to take responsibility for their future, leaving aside their sultan, caliph or any other non-elected leader (al-Kawakibi, 1931). Thus, parliamentary democracy, accountable governance and the necessity of creating a new type of political organisation were introduced and entered the field of Arabism in its new stage.

However, al-Kawakibi's concept of a separate national existence did not at this juncture turn into an active endeavour seeking complete independence from the Ottoman state. The emerging movement for separation was temporarily postponed by the eruption of the Young Turk Revolution of 1908. This revolution forced Sultan 'Abdulhamid (1876–1909) to restore a constitutional form of government (first promulgated in 1876 and suspended in 1878) leading one year later to his abdication in favour of a more pliant sultan. Almost all Ottoman national communities welcomed such a development with open enthusiasm, looking forward to the creation of a new Ottoman state based on decentralisation, the rule of law, and the protection of minority rights by a constitutional government

Such high hopes were soon to be dashed as between 1908 and 1913 the Ottoman state lost virtually all its European dominions, and was forced to cede in the same period the Arab province of Libya to Italy. This prompted the Committee of Union and Progress (CUP), a political organisation dominated by the armed forces, to renounce decentralisation and reaffirm the necessity of instituting tighter central rule in order to protect the fatherland against foreign intrigues. One result of this orientation was the emphasis it placed on Turkish, to the exclusion of other languages, such as Arabic, as the only valid medium of national communication and government.

As a reaction, a number of Arab associations and organisations, consisting mainly of students, military officers and civil servants, were created, either clandestinely or officially. These cultural and political organisations, while not espousing independence or separation, redefined Ottomanism so as to become a partnership between two equal communities: the Turks and the Arabs. In North Africa, Moroccans, Algerians and Tunisians were arguing at the same time for greater equality between Arabs and French settlers, while Egyptians were divided into two camps: one calling for a better deal from Great Britain, and the other insisting on complete independence.

These demands laid the foundations of an ever-widening dichotomy between two ethnic communities in the Arab provinces of the Ottoman empire. In Egypt and North Africa, while Islamic or local overtones became more pronounced, there emerged an underlying principle based on a broad Arab culture. It was, however, in Greater Syria that Arabism was first articulated, as a modern political ideology.

In June 1913, an Arab Congress was convened in Paris to draw up a list of demands based on decentralisation and administrative reforms within the Ottoman empire. It was organised by the moderate Ottoman Administrative Decentralisation Party and Beirut Reform Committee, as well as the secret and radical party al-Fatat (the Young Arab Society). The Congress was dominated by Syrian representatives, particularly those resident in Beirut, Damascus and Cairo.

It was in this congress that the concept of pan-Arabism became less vague and acquired theoretical rigorousness, whereas its geographic limits were confined, for political and international reasons, to the Arabian Peninsula and the Fertile Crescent.

Theoretically, a Beiruti editor and publisher and a member of al-Fatat organisation, 'Abd al-Ghani al-'Uraysi (1850–1916), argued that the Arabs constituted a political community and a nation on the basis of five interrelated factors: language, race, history, customs and political aspirations. Geographically, the Syrian chairman of the Congress, 'Abd al-Hamid al-Zahrawi (1855–1916) conceded to an Egyptian attending the Congress as auditor, that Egypt was indeed an Arab country and an Ottoman province, but its particular grievances (British occupation) fell outside the jurisdiction of the Congress (al-Khatib, 1913, pp. 42–3, and 115). It is in this context that pan-Arabism in its Asian background is to be understood as largely a movement of Ottoman Arabs struggling against policies of Turkification. Their hopes were, moreover, pinned on British or French assistance.

This movement culminated in the Arab Revolt of 1916. It was led by the spiritual leader of Western Arabia and a descendant of the Prophet, al-Sharif Husayn, and in association with Syrian and Iraqi army officers. To the Allied powers (Britain and France), the revolt formed part of their military efforts to destroy the Ottoman state after its entry into the First World War on the side of Germany.

Although independence was promised as a reward to Arab forces for participating in the war, Britain and France established themselves, following the Paris Peace Conference in 1919, as mandatory powers in the Fertile Crescent. In Arabia, Sharif Husayn lost his newly established authority as king to the advancing forces of the Wahhabites, led by 'Abd al-'Aziz Al Sa'ud. In 1932 the Kingdom of Saudi Arabia came into existence. This was the only Arab state, together with North Yemen, to achieve a semblance of independence and escape direct European occupation.

Political Parties

Following the failure of various Arab revolts against European colonialism and mandatory systems between 1919 and 1932, the stage was set for the emergence of new political forces led by an educated young generation. The fact that certain Arab countries gained relative political independence – Saudi Arabia, North Yemen, Iraq and Egypt – encouraged these new parties to put forward programmes of action, deemed relevant to the Arab world as a whole.

The first public glimmerings of such an approach emerged in 1931 during the convention of a pan-Islamic congress in Jerusalem. As its name indicates, this was a political gathering convened to articulate Muslim anxieties regarding the threatened status and future of Palestine, with particular emphasis on the aggressive policies of Zionism. Almost all Arab countries sent delegates to attend. It was the first time that Arab delegates from the Maghrib, Egypt, the Arabian Peninsula and the Fertile Crescent had come together to tackle what was increasingly becoming a pan-Arab and pan-Islamic cause. These delegates held a separate meeting to deliberate purely Arab matters, and proclaimed a new pan-Arab covenant composed of three principal articles.

1. The Arab countries form an integral and indivisible unity. Hence, the Arab nation does not accept or recognise all forms of fragmentation that have befallen this unity.
2. All efforts in every Arab country are to be directed towards the achievement of total independence within one single unity; it being understood that every endeavour that aimed at confining political activity to local and regional issues is to be resisted.
3. Given that colonialism, irrespective of the identity of its principal representatives and the forms it may assume, is incompatible with the dignity of the Arab nation and its paramount purpose, it is to be rejected and resisted by the Arab nation with all the means at its disposal. (Zu'aytir, 1994, pp. 372–3)

The drive for Arab unity became entangled in this period with the question of reinstating the Islamic caliphate after its abolition by Ataturk in 1924. This question loomed larger than its practical importance in the rivalries of three Arab countries, each trying to assert a certain regional role. These countries were Iraq, Saudi Arabia and Egypt. Most Arab nationalists developed political and financial ties with one or the other, particularly Iraq and Saudi Arabia. It was also in this period that Egyptian writers, politicians and journalists began to adopt a more positive attitude towards pan-Arabism. Moreover, as demands for independence were increasingly voiced in North African countries, Egypt became a meeting place for Maghribi leaders, either fleeing persecution or seeking to mobilise Arab opinion in their favour.

In August 1933, the first pan-Arab political party, the League of Nationalist Action (LNA) was founded at a meeting in a Lebanese town. Its founding members, drawn from Greater Syria and Iraq, belonged to western-educated professional groups – lawyers, teachers, medical doctors, editors and journalists. Its constituent assembly, composed of over thirty representatives, issued a political programme which expanded themes briefly discussed by the pan-Arab covenant of 1931. Thus, the statement dwelt at length on the characteristics of colonialism and its nefarious schemes to combat Arab nationalism and turn Palestine into a Zionist entity, creating in the process a class of Arab collaborators and agents.

The League of Nationalist Action defined its two principal objectives as being: (1) the absolute sovereignty and independence of the Arabs; and (2) comprehensive Arab unity. It also stressed the necessity of carrying out a radical programme of socio-economic and moral reform. However, it left open the specific nature of the political or economic system it wanted to implement (Zu'aytir, 1994, pp. 529–34).

This party enjoyed a certain popularity amongst the young generation in the second half of the 1930s, and its leader, the Syrian lawyer 'Abd al-Razzaq al-Dandashi, was hailed as a symbol of a new type of Arab leadership. His early death in 1935 marked what turned out to be a prolonged period of internal disputes and lack of political direction. Moreover, it never managed to shake off its middle-class image, and was confined in the main to the urban centres of greater Syria. It did not survive as an organisation beyond 1945. Its lack of a well-defined strategy and internal squabbles made it an easy prey for the intrigues of the leaders of its local rival, the National Bloc.

Side by side with this organisation, there emerged two other similar, but clandestine, societies. These were the Arab Liberation Society and another, most commonly called the Arab Nationalist Party. Their membership, programme and areas of operation overlapped with the LNA. Both had a hierarchical structure designed to enable their members to infiltrate or control other parties and associations, and win them over to the cause of Arab unity. They met the same fate that befell the LNA. Their members went on to join other parties, or confined their activities to publishing articles and books on Arab nationalism.

All these parties and movements concentrated on articulating issues, demands and programmes, in addition to general pronouncements pertaining to the definition of Arab nationalism or the Arab nation. In this sense, they never managed to offer a coherent doctrine or political philosophy. This failure became apparent at a time when both fascism and communism were being propagated as comprehensive worldviews, capable of rescuing humanity from all its miseries.

Social Arabism, 1945–1973

The end of the Second World War, the intensification of the struggle for Palestine between Arabs and Jews, and the rise of the United States together with the Soviet Union as global powers, defined the main contours of this phase. Furthermore, social and economic issues long overshadowed by the issue of independence or political rights, came to the fore as dominant themes in the programmes of almost all new political parties. Hence, agrarian reform, industrialisation, employment, health and housing were some of the issues that could no longer be ignored and had to be addressed as essential elements in the building of a modern nation-state. It was also in this period that revenues and profits accruing to multinational companies from Arab oil fields became a bone of contention between local rulers or nationalist parties and western governments.

Politically, most Arab countries gained their independence between 1945 and 1962. They were all admitted to the League of Arab States as full members. Founded in 1945, and conceived as an agency of cooperation, this league reaffirmed the sovereignty and territorial integrity of each Arab state, while leaving the door open for a more advanced form of Arab unity.

Henceforth, there began to develop a new type of official pan-Arabism that was largely based on preserving the existing states system, while trying at the same time to coordinate its general approach to external challenges. Such a dominant pattern has persisted up to the present time in spite of numerous attempts to unite two or more Arab states with each other. So far no concrete or lasting unions have ever been achieved. The only exception was the unification of various Gulf shaykdoms in 1971 and that of South and North Yemen in 1989.

The most spectacular achievement of Arab nationalism was the brief union between Syria and Egypt, under the leadership of Jamal 'Abd al-Nasir (Nasser). Established in February 1958, it was dissolved in September 1961 as a result of Syrian secession. In 1963 there occurred another attempt to unify Egypt, Syria and Iraq. Political differences, economic disparities and divergent patterns of social development turned it into a stillborn endeavour.

However, in this third phase, Arab nationalism acquired widespread popular support and succeeded in implementing its own radical programme in the economic, social and cultural fields. Henceforth, Arab nationalism became associated with socialism, one-party rule and the liberation of Palestine. As it turned out, bureaucratic mismanagement limited capital resources and persistent external threats marred the implementation of socialism in its Arab version. The confrontation with Israel, an ever-recurring problem, as well as the constant interference of other western powers, added further complications, diverting much-needed resources, draining the national energy of entire communities, and culminating in disastrous military losses.

Although Arab nationalism asserted itself in this social phase as a popular movement, eclipsing in the process all other ideologies throughout the Arab world, particularly between 1956 and 1970, when Nasser (1918–1970), the Egyptian president, dominated in his policies, speeches and activities the Arab world, it failed to achieve its central aim of Arab unification. Apart from external pressures and military defeats, its political formula of one-party rule was one of its most spectacular misconceived projects as it became in the main a tool for suppressing its political opponents instead of being a dynamic channel for political participation and mobilisation.

Social Arab nationalism was represented at the political level by three main currents: Ba'thism, Nasserism and the Movement of Arab Nationalists.

Ba'thism and Nasserism

Ba'thism represents the ideology of the Arab Ba'th Party. This party was launched in 1941, but was not formally founded until 1947 by two Damascene French-educated schoolteachers, Michel 'Aflaq and Salah al-Din al-Baytar. It was renamed the Arab Ba'th Socialist Party in 1953 after its merger with the Arab Socialist Party of Akram al-Hawrani. The last championed the cause of the peasants against their landlords in the city of Hama and its environs. The Ba'th recruited among students, workers, peasants and minorities, acting as a well-organised party built on hierarchical lines: cells, sections, divisions, branches and regions. From its base in Syria, it spread to Iraq, Lebanon, Jordan, Palestine and the Arabian Peninsula. It did not establish a foothold in other Arab countries until the 1970s. Even then it had only a small organisation in Sudan and Tunisia, while Egypt, Algeria, Libya and Morocco remained outside its ambit. However, its ideology, based on Arab unity, freedom and socialism, was adopted, in one form or another, by a number of Arab parties, particularly the Arab Socialist Union (ASU), set up by Nasser in 1962 in the wake of Syria's secession from the United Arab Republic.

Nasserism grew out of the policies, political pronouncements and domestic or international activities of President Nasser and his colleagues. Initially confined to a set of policies (agrarian reform, evacuation of British military bases, building a strong army and social justice), its most articulate ideological outlook was embodied in the National Charter of 1962. The theoretical thrust of the Charter highlights the central function of socio-economic factors in determining the development of nations. It thus declares the socialist solution to be 'a historical inevitability imposed by reality, the broad aspirations of the masses and the changing nature of the world in the second part of the twentieth century' (Hanna, 1969, pp. 358-9). Moreover, Nasserism reversed the order according to which Ba'thism desired to achieve its goals, thereby turning socialism into a prerequisite of freedom and unity. By giving primacy to socialism, Nasserism after 1962 demarcated its own ideological territory within the Arab nationalist movement. Thus, with hindsight and the failure of union between Syria and Egypt, Nasserism underlined the importance of effecting internal transformations within each Arab country as a necessary prelude to achieving unity of purpose and aims. Democracy was moreover defined as 'political freedom', and socialism as social freedom. However, whereas both were deemed to form one organic unity, social justice was supposed to precede political freedom, thereby delaying its implementation until an undefined moment in the future. Nevertheless, Arab unity was to be achieved as the culmination of a long process of economic, social, political and cultural change, brought about by a new generation of Arab leaders, operating in the context of their own independent countries, and relying on organisations similar to the Arab Socialist Union of Egypt. Such a prospect came to an abrupt end with Nasser's death in 1970 despite the efforts of a number of Nasserite leaders to revive his legacy or update the National Charter to take account of a new regional and world order.

MAN

Apart from Ba'thism and Nasserism, Arab nationalism was adopted by the Movement of Arab Nationalists (MAN). This organisation was founded by a group of Palestinian, Syrian and Kuwaiti students at the American University of Beirut in the early 1950s. The spiritual leader of this movement was 'Ali Nasir Al-Din (1892–1974), a founding member of the League of Nationalist Action. The MAN was more distinguished by its stress on immediate action rather than subtle theoretical issues. Its leading figure was the medical doctor, George Habash, who was highly respected as an efficient organiser and a passionate orator with a strong popular appeal. His main aim revolved around the necessity of mobilising all available resources to confront the newly established Israeli state. However, most of its policies were a mere refined version of those pursued by pan-Arabists in the 1930s.

The political appeal of MAN was thus largely derived from its confrontation with colonialism and became as a result more relevant in Arab countries still wrestling with this particular aspect, as in Yemen, Kuwait, Jordan and Palestine. As it was being gradually superseded by the Ba'th party, it drifted towards closer ties with the leadership of Nasser as the new symbol of Arabism. Its ideology was never developed in a coherent or comprehensive fashion, thereby leaving the door open for individual interpretations or sudden shifts of emphasis. Organisationally, it had branches in Jordan, Iraq, Kuwait, Oman, Qatar, Bahrain, South Yemen, Syria and Lebanon. By 1963, and following Nasser's shift to a programme of socialist policies, its second-generation leaders, such as Muhsin Ibrahim and Muhammad Kishli, called for the adoption of quasi-Marxist notions of class struggle, armed insurrection and the building of a new type of political organisation. By 1966 its central organisation began to fragment into its regional constituent parts. Following a number of hastily convened conferences to address such a grave development, fragmentation continued apace splitting it into regional organisations centred on particular Arab states: Kuwait, South Yemen, Lebanon and Palestine. After the devastating defeat of the Syrian, Egyptian and Jordanian armies by Israel in 1967, most of MAN's cadres adopted different versions of Marxism–Leninism and renounced what they dubbed their former semi-fascist, petit bourgeois ideology. This was particularly the case of the Popular Front for the Liberation of Palestine (1967) headed by Habash, and the Popular Democratic Front for the Liberation of Palestine, which split off from the first, accusing it of right-wing tendencies and a reluctance to make a clear break with the past. This splinter group was led by the Jordanian Nayif Hawatimah (1969). Its branch in South Yemen, the National Liberation Front, seized power in 1967, but not before it had transformed itself into a fully fledged Leninist organisation. By January 1969, it had ceased to exist as a pan-Arab movement (Kazziha, 1975, chs. 4 and 5).

Relative Decline

After the defeat of 1967, the death of Nasser in 1970 and the apparent failure of various Arab states to achieve their stated goal of unity and national solidarity, Nasserism diminished in Egypt as a major political force to be reckoned with, or sufficiently capable of holding power. This was dramatically illustrated by the ease with which Nasser's successor, President Anwar Sadat, was able to create within a few years his own political set of policies, dissolving in the process the Arab Socialist Union, built by Nasser as the sole ruling party.

The Ba'th party in Syria, on the other hand, underwent a process of radicalisation, characterised by the influx into its ranks of rural, provincial and lower middle-class members. However, this trend of radicalisation was gradually reversed after 1970 and the advent to power of President Hafiz al-Asad. Following his death in 2000, Hafiz al-Asad was succeeded by his son Bashar, who promised to open up the system of government and liberalise the economy. Although some improvements have been introduced, particularly in the field of information and human rights, no qualitative changes have yet been implemented.

In Iraq, the Ba'th passed through its radical phase between 1958 and 1966. By 1968, and after several attempts, it had become the dominant force in Iraqi politics. After the triumph of Khumayni against the Shah in 1979, the Iran–Iraq War (1980–8), and the brief occupation of Kuwait in 1990–1, the Iraqi president, Saddam Husayn, began to adopt a new political discourse in which pan-Arabist and Islamist notions intermingled. Following years of sanctions and the gradual impoverishment of Iraq, a

combined Anglo-American force invaded Iraq in March 2003, leading to the removal
of the Ba'thist regime within a few weeks, as well as to the capture of Saddam Husayn
some months later (December 2003). The Ba'th party was banned and its leaders
pursued as war criminals.

Following the ascendancy of Saudi Arabia as a regional power after the rise of the
oil price in the aftermath of the 1973 war, coupled with the death of Nasser in 1970,
only three years after his military defeat by Israel in 1967, Arab nationalism entered a
new stage of relative decline. Such a decline was eagerly seized upon by various
regional and international powers, including the oil-producing Gulf states. The
Soviet invasion of Afghanistan in 1979, coupled with the triumph of Ayatollah
Khumayni as the leader of a new religiously based, Islamic republic in Iran, boosted
the prospects of the message of fundamentalist politics, with its stress on Islamic
values and concepts of governance, aided and abetted by the financial clout of
conservative oil-producing countries that dominated political and economic affairs.

Since the 1970s, Arab nationalism has been witnessing a steady erosion of its
political or social influence. Although pan-Arabism (as described above) has maintained its cultural hegemony both at the official and popular levels, such a hegemony
is being challenged by the rise of Islamic fundamentalism, on the one hand, and calls
for democratic reforms, on the other. Consequently, Arab nationalism has, as so often
in its past, been recast to meet or assimilate one or the other.

Today Arab Nationalism can be said to include a number of strands and programmes of action.

Such trends appeal to different constituencies and seem to be in a state of almost
permanent flux. These comprise the following:

1. An official trend represented by states which advocate ideas of pan-Arabism,
    while being extremely reluctant to enter into hasty or uncertain unions.
2. An Arab nationalist ideology tinged with either Marxist notions of class struggle,
    socialist construction and Leninist-type activities, or Islamist concepts and
    greater emphasis on the role of Islam in the formation of the Arab nation and
    its contemporary culture. However, the Marxist trend has been steadily moving
    towards the adoption of democracy as both a vehicle of struggle and a process of
    government, while neo-Arab Islamism has also undergone similar subtle and
    clear transformations. This has been particularly the case after the collapse of
    the Soviet Union in the early 1990s, and the pursuit of capitalist policies in the
    Republic of China since the 1980s.
3. A neo-Arabism that posits nationalism as an ideological instrument recast to
    achieve the gradual unity of the Arab world. The pursuit of this aim is informed
    by the diversity of the Arab world in its geographic, ethnic, economic and
    cultural aspects. It has also adopted democracy as one of its instruments of
    struggle and principal objectives, stressing in particular the need for multi-
    party politics, freedom of assembly and speech, and national sovereignty.

FURTHER READING

Arab nationalism had its first history in the work of George Antonius, *The Arab Awakening*.
Other studies built and amplified, or slightly modified Antonius's general account. These
include Zeine N. Zeine, *Arab–Turkish Relations and the Emergence of Arab Nationalism*

(Beirut: Khayat's, 1958); Albert Hourani, *Arabic Thought in the Liberal Age 1798–1939* (London: Oxford University Press, 1962; reprint, Cambridge: Cambridge University Press, 1983); C. Ernest Dawn, *From Ottomanism to Arabism: Essays on the Origins of Arab Nationalism* (Urbana, IL: University of Illinois Press, 1973); Philip S. Khoury, *Urban Notables and Arab Nationalism: The Politics of Damascus 1860–1920* (Cambridge: Cambridge University Press, 1983). A more historically rooted study and widely acclaimed in the Arab world is A. A. al-Duri, *The Historical Formation of the Arab Nation*, tr. Lawrence I. Conrad (London: Croom Helm, 1987). Slightly outdated and highly polemical is Bassam Tibi, *Arab Nationalism: A Critical Inquiry*, 2nd edn., tr. Marion Farouk Sluglett and Peter Sluglett (New York: St. Martin's Press, 1990). While Rashid Khalidi et al. (eds.), *The Origins of Arab Nationalism* (New York: Columbia University Press, 1991) traces the early emergence of Arab nationalism and its varied historical contexts from different perspectives, Youssef M. Choueiri, *Arab Nationalism: A History* (Blackwell, Oxford, 2000), offers a new approach to its study, emergence and development. Other useful books, ranging from scathing criticism to sober objectivity, include the following: Fouad Ajami, *The Arab Predicament* (Cambridge: Cambridge University Press, 1982); Maxime Rodinson, *The Arabs* (Chicago: University of Chicago Press, 1981); Israel Gershoni and James P. Jankowski, *Redefining the Egyptian Nation, 1930–1945* (New York: Cambridge University Press, 1995); Tawfic E. Farah (ed.), *Pan-Arabism and Arab Nationalism: The Continuing Debate* (Boulder: Westview Press, 1987); and Adeed Dawisha, *Arab Nationalism in the Twentieth Century* (Princeton, NJ: Princeton University Press, 2003).

CHAPTER SIXTEEN

Turkish and Iranian Nationalisms

IOANNIS N. GRIGORIADIS AND ALI M. ANSARI

Turkish Nationalism

Introduction

The seeds of nationalism, which spread from its western European cradle, found fertile soil in the Ottoman empire. In a region where multi-ethnic, multi-cultural empires had prevailed since antiquity, identities and affiliations were developed on non-national lines; religion and locality remained the determining factors in the formation of collective identities. Nationalism was the intellectual force that challenged existing allegiances, identities and states, resulting in a radical reinterpretation of the 'self' and the 'other'.

Turkish nationalism was among the last to rise in the declining Ottoman empire of the late nineteenth century. The preponderance of Islamic identity and the privileged position that Sunni Muslims[1] enjoyed had initially deterred the proliferation of nationalist ideas, which would be to the detriment of the cohesion of the multi-ethnic and multi-religious empire. Nonetheless, the rapid rise of nationalism within Ottoman Christian minorities, the formation of nation-states in former Ottoman provinces and imminent existential threat for the ailing empire resulted in the development of Turkish nationalism. Defensive in nature, Turkish nationalism soon succeeded in striking a chord among Ottoman Turkish intellectual and military elites.[2] The formation of a Turkish nation-state was seen as the only desirable choice, given the seeming inevitability of the empire's demise.[3] In the aftermath of the First World War the feasibility of the Turkish nationalist project was put into question,[4] yet the leadership skills of Mustafa Kemal (Atatürk)[5] in the crucial years 1919–23 guaranteed the establishment of a Turkish nation-state in Anatolia. This study will examine the official civic version of Turkish nationalism and will explore the impact of ethnic nationalism and Islam on it. It will also evaluate the success of the Turkish nationalist project and address challenges towards it. It will be argued that the official civic nationalism has been amalgamated with ethnic and religious elements that crucially affected its character. The Turkish nationalist project has been remarkably successful in homogenising Anatolian Muslim populations and creating a strong sense of Turkish national identity. Yet the whole conceptual framework of Turkish nationalism has most seriously been challenged by the emergence of Kurdish nationalism as well as by Turkey's prospective membership of the European Union. Kurdish nationalism questioned the ethnic homogeneity of the Anatolian Muslim population, while the European Union challenged with its accession criteria and supranational character the nationalist basis of the republican Turkish state.

Official civic nationalism

The application of the civic nationalism model in Turkey is inextricably linked with the programme of radical westernisation that Atatürk put forward in his effort to overcome Turkish political, economic and cultural underdevelopment.[6] In order for Turkey to converge with 'contemporary civilisation',[7] lessons from the decline and dismemberment of the Ottoman Empire should be utilised. Both pan-Islamist and pan-Turkist ideologies should be thoroughly abandoned, and a civic, territory-based model of national identity should be developed. In his famous address to the Turkish Assembly from 15 to 20 October 1927 (*Nutuk*), Atatürk elaborated on his effort to establish a civic Turkish national identity:

> I am neither a believer in a league of all the nations of Islam, nor even in a league of Turkish people. Each of us here has the right to hold his ideals, but the government must be stable with a fixed policy, grounded in facts, and with one view and one alone: to safeguard the life and independence of the nation within its natural frontiers. Neither sentiment nor illusion must influence our policy. Away with dreams and shadows! They have cost us dear in the past![8]

The French Jacobin model of civic territorial nationalism became a source of inspiration: Anatolia constituted the Turkish 'fatherland', the indivisible territorial unit, which would form the basis of Turkish nationhood.[9] Citizenship and common culture were crucial elements in the development of civic Turkish national identity. Equal citizen rights for all inhabitants of Anatolia would nurture 'a sense of solidarity and fraternity through active social and political participation', as Anthony D. Smith put it.[10] Regarding the common culture desideratum, warfare, massacres and population exchanges in the first quarter of the twentieth century had altered the multi-religious character of Anatolia, establishing an undisputed Muslim preponderance. The formerly strong Armenian and Greek communities had perished,[11] and Anatolia was inhabited by Turks and numerous other Muslim ethnicities. Kurds, Arabs, Lazes, Bosnians, Albanians, Circassians and other Caucasian peoples were only a few of the existing Muslim ethnicities in Anatolia, while a significant Muslim Alevi minority challenged the Sunni majority.[12] Although Turkish national identity was not embedded in all the Muslim populations of Anatolia, these populations were deemed to be suitable for becoming citizens of the Turkish republic, provided they opted for a fusion of their distinct ethnic and cultural features with the state-espoused Turkish national identity.[13] In his effort to establish Anatolia as the undoubted fatherland of the Turkish nation, Atatürk favoured archaeological and historical research that aimed at providing evidence of the antiquity and paramount significance of Turkish presence in Anatolia.[14] The Turkish History Thesis, launched during the First History Congress organised in Ankara in 1932, came to the point of claiming that the Turks were the descendants of the founders of all civilisations in Iraq, Anatolia, Egypt and the Aegean.[15] While such absurd allegations were eventually left to fall into oblivion, civic nationalism has remained the core of the officially endorsed version of Turkish nationalism. Ethnic and religious elements, however, maintained their importance in defining who a Turk is.

Ethnic nationalism

The model of ethnic nationalism found big resonance among Turkish nationalists in the later years of the Ottoman empire. Under the influence of German Romanticism, nations were seen as the natural division units of the human race, with their own distinct character, which its citizens must, as a duty, keep pure and inviolable.[16] The Turkish nation was thus seen as a single unit, ranging from the Adriatic Sea to the borders of China, whose political unification should be furthered. The spread of ethnic nationalism was boosted by the immigration of Russian-born Turkic intellectuals influenced by pan-Slavism.[17] The most prominent of them, Yusuf Akçura (Akçuraoğlu) addressed in his seminal treatise 'Üç Tarz-i Siyaset' the dilemmas of Turkish nationalism in the beginning of the twentieth century.[18] Ottomanism, the hammering of an ethnic- and religion-blind civic identity for all Ottoman subjects, was dismissed as a chimera, given that none of the Ottoman ethnic and religious communities was willing to substitute Ottomanism for its own identity. Pan-Islamism was also dismissed as unrealistic given the reaction it would cause in western powers, which ruled over large numbers of Muslim subjects. Pan-Turkism would antagonise the Russian empire, which ruled over the Caucasus and Central Asia, yet Akçura seemed to lean towards it. Pan-Turkism gained momentum in the last years of the Ottoman empire when Russian capitulation in the First World War raised hopes for Ottoman expansion towards the east. These hopes were, however, soon dashed, and republican Turkey denounced all pan-Turkist ideals, focusing on the formation of a civic Turkish national identity.

Despite official condemnation of ethnic nationalism, state policies asserted that ethnic nationalism had left its imprint on official state nationalism. Discriminatory policies against population groups on the basis of their ethnicity were a continuation of measures taken in the last years of the Ottoman empire and aimed at the same direction, namely minority assimilation or emigration.[19] The 1934 Resettlement Law (İskan Kanunu) and the 1942 Property Tax (Varlık Vergisi) exemplified these policies.[20] The importance of ethnic nationalism was also attested by the systematic exaltation of the Turkish nation[21] and language. The word 'Turk' should lose the demeaning connotations it carried throughout the Ottoman history[22] and become a source of national pride. Besides, the Sun Language Theory, coined in the 1932 First Language History Congress, attempted to prove that Turkish was the most ancient, accurate and beautiful language in the world and all the languages originated from it, while the Turkish Language Reform aimed at purifying Turkish from Arabic and Persian influences.[23] Anti-minority campaigns in the language field continued in 1937 with the launch of the 'Citizen, speak Turkish' (Vatandaş Türkçe Konuş) campaign for the exclusive use of Turkish in public.[24]

Ethnic nationalism never became a dominant ideological current in Turkish politics, although the state endorsed parts of its ideology. Pan–Turkist ideals briefly gained impetus during the Second World War at the time when Germany seemed to be winning the war against the Soviet Union.[25] In the 1960s Turkish ethnic nationalism found its political representative in the person of Alparslan Türkeş and the Nationalist Action Party (Milli Hareket Partisi–MHP). Since then the Cyprus and Karabagh conflicts, as well as the Balkan crisis have attracted some interest in ethnic nationalism, while the demise of the Soviet Union, which briefly raised hopes for close cooperation of ex-Soviet Turkic republics under Turkey's leadership, also mobilised some solidarity.[26] It was rather, though, through its covert impact on the official version of nationalism than through its political representatives that ethnic nationalism influenced Turkish national identity.

The role of Islam

The role of religion as identity badge in the Ottoman empire was institutionalised by the *millet* system. Although the term *millet* is usually related to non-Muslim communities of the Ottoman empire, it is true that the term referred to Muslims as well, anchoring the decisive role of religious affiliation in determining one's identity.[27] The identification of the Turkish nation with Islam was facilitated by the leading role of the Ottoman empire in the Islamic world[28] and its contribution in the expansion of Islam in Anatolia, central and south-eastern Europe. Conversion to Islam was not only an act of personal belief or expedience, but also a shift of identity, voluntary participation in the Islamic community of believers (*ummah*) and identification with the Ottoman political ideology and culture. Novel nationalist ideas later transformed religious communal into national identities. Ottoman Christian communities were the first to be influenced and were followed by Ottoman Muslims. It is the irony of history that the nation that submerged its identity the most into Islam was the first to attempt the radical dissociation of its national identity from religion.[29]

Early Turkish nationalists identified Islam in the mid-nineteenth century as one of the basic elements of Turkish identity and did not consider it to be incompatible with westernisation.[30] More radical views, however, soon appeared, blaming Islam for Turkish underdevelopment and championing secularisation of the state and society according to the French positivist model. The most influential Young Turkish thinker Ziya Gökalp attempted to compromise Turkish nationalism with modernity and Islam by differentiating between civilisation (*medeniyet*), culture (*hars*) and religion (*din*). He defined civilisation in technological and political terms, culture as the set of values and beliefs which define a people, and restricted religion into its essential content. The Turkish nation should adopt western civilisation and rediscover its own Turkish culture, which had faded under the influence of Arab culture.[31] Islam had to be dissociated from Arab culture and restricted to the private sphere.[32] Although many Young Turks did not see Islam as an essential element of Turkish identity, political conditions did not allow them to implement anti-Islamic policies. On the contrary, Islam was used as a political tool and mobilising force in the wars against western powers and adjacent Christian states. Atatürk followed the same policy in the years of armed struggle (1919–23), but disclosed his true intentions as soon as he was powerful enough to do so. On 17 November 1922 the last Ottoman Sultan, Mehmet VI Vahdettin, was forced into exile, while on 29 October 1923 the caliphate was officially abolished and the republic of Turkey proclaimed. Strict measures were taken in order to secularise the state and society.[33] The office of Şeyh-ül-İslam was abolished and his functions taken over by the Directorate of Religious Affairs in 1924. Religious orders (*tarikat*) were banned in 1926, while the remnants of the Islamic Law (*şeriat*) were replaced by the Swiss Civil and the Italian Penal Code. Meanwhile, existing Islamic courts and schools were abolished as well as religious education in public schools. At the symbolic level, of crucial importance was the adoption of the Latin alphabet, which broke a strong cultural bond between the Turkish nation and Islam. The breach with the Ottoman Islamic past was finalised when the clause of the 1924 constitution declaring Islam to be the state religion of Turkey was removed in 1928.[34]

Official secularisation policies intended to dissociate Turkish national identity from Islam; yet their success was only limited. At the elite level, Islam ceased to be an essential element of Turkish identity; at the grassroots level, however, the role of Islam as symbol of Turkish national identity remained intact.[35] Islam was the only unifying factor of the multilingual, multi-ethnic populations of Anatolia and the most tangible element of their Turkish identity.[36] Intensive state efforts to inculcate civic Turkish nationalism through the means of education and control of public and political Islam had only limited success. Islam eventually re-emerged in the public sphere during the rule of the Democrat Party (*Demokrat Parti*–DP) in the 1950s and claimed an active role in Turkish politics in 1970, when Necmettin Erbakan founded the National Order Party (*Milli Nizam Partisi*–MNP), the first Islamist party in the history of republican Turkey. Erbakan stressed the paramount importance of Islam as an essential element of Turkish national identity, despite long state efforts to eliminate it and defended a union of Muslim believers. His argument was followed by a group of conservative Kemalist intellectuals, the 'Hearth of the Enlightened' (*Aydı nlar Ocağ ı*), which argued for an Islamic revival as a means of strengthening Turkish nationalism against growing minority nationalist and leftist dissidence. These positions were elaborated into an ideological construction named 'Turkish–Islamic Synthesis' (Türk-İslam Sentezi–Tİ S).[37] Islam was thus seen not as a fully fledged political ideology, as in the case of Erbakan, but as an element that could revitalise Turkish nationalism.[38]

The military coup of 12 September 1980 acted as catalyst for the infusion of Islamic elements into official Turkish national ideology. Extreme secularist policies were held to be one of the reasons for the proliferation of radical leftist and rightist as well as Kurdish nationalist ideas, which resulted in civil strife and disorder with detrimental effects for Turkey's stability. Besides, state abstention from religious education had resulted in the increasing influence of legal and underground religious groups. In accordance with the views expressed by the 'Hearth of the Enlightened', religious instruction in Turkish primary and secondary schools became compulsory under article 24 of the 1982 constitution. The 'Turkish–Islamic Synthesis' constituted the ideological core of the new school curriculum.[39] The special relation between the Turkish nation and Islam was stressed and similarities between pre-Islamic Turkish and Islamic civilisations and values were emphasised.[40] Meanwhile, state funding of religious education and foundations exponentially increased. Islam was regarded as an essential element of Turkish national identity, and its public manifestation was tolerated to the extent that it respected the principles of republicanism and secularism. The return of Necmettin Erbakan into politics as leader of the Welfare Party (Refah Partisi–RP) polarised the debate on Turkish political Islam but did not disturb the balance set by the 1980 military regime. Islam was still viewed as the cementing factor in a society split by ideological and ethnic divisions.[41] Only the rise of the Welfare Party into power in the mid-1990s alarmed the Turkish military and secularist forces, which then initiated a campaign to deter increasing Islamisation of Turkish society.

The success of the Turkish nationalist project

Being a hybrid of civic nationalism with considerable influences from ethnic nationalism and Islam, Turkish nationalism has been remarkably successful in its mission.

The mosaic of Anatolian Muslim ethnicities was largely homogenised, a strong sense of Turkish national identity was forged and the consolidation of a Turkish nation-state in Anatolia became possible.[42] Although Islam was not fully purged from the public domain and retained its appeal to the majority of the population, the Turkish state preserved secularism and western-style parliamentary democracy[43] to an extent unforeseen in the Islamic world. The success of Turkish nationalism contrasted with that of other Middle Eastern nationalist movements, whereby political realities fell far short of objectives and expectations.[44]

The reasons for that difference can be traced in Turkish history and politics. In the aftermath of the Moudros Armistice, while western powers had already occupied Ottoman Arab lands, a significant part of the Anatolian interior remained inaccessible to western invasion. This fact facilitated the emergence of the Turkish nationalist movement, which secured Turkey's independence, while former Ottoman Arab territories were governed by western powers under the mandate regime.[45] Atatürk's absolute political power during the republican years was also *sine qua non* for the successful implementation of the Turkish nationalist programme. The extent of political and social reform caused friction in large segments of the Turkish society, which would have been insurmountable, had Atatürk been forced to negotiate with elite groups and compromise on his programme. Of vital importance was also the fact that the influence of Ottoman elites, which had sided with the Ottoman Sultan in his internal struggle against Turkish nationalists, was minimised in republican Turkey and could pose no serious obstacles to Atatürk's nationalist project. Tribal, religious and ethnic affiliations also faded under the impact of state education and urbanisation. It was virtually impossible for the millions of peasants that settled in Turkey's big cities in search of a better livelihood to preserve their distinct identity against the state-imposed model of Turkish national identity. Last but not least reason for the relative success of Turkish nationalism was the pragmatic character of Turkish nationalism. The civic version of Turkish nationalism that Atatürk espoused fell short of both pan-Islamism and pan-Turkism as far as ambitions and grandeur were concerned. Kemalist nationalism was characterised by a much more impassive perspective: defending Anatolia and establishing a Turkish nation-state there was a target that was not beyond the military and political capabilities of Turkish nationalists, and all efforts were focused on that. This realistic approach, which was absent in the case of Arab nationalism, greatly facilitated the consolidation of the Turkish nation-state and the forging of Turkish national identity. The Turkish nationalist project faced serious challenges from Kurdish minority nationalism and Turkey's prospective accession to the European Union.

The Kurdish challenge

The rise of Kurdish nationalism posed the first serious challenge to Turkish nation-alism as it contested its most fundamental assumption, namely the congruity of Islam with Turkish national identity in Anatolia. Ottoman Kurds had remained attached to their religious and tribal identities until the very last years of the Ottoman empire. Despite the formation of Kurdish nationalist groups, the vast majority of the Kurdish population remained loyal to the Ottoman rule and sided with the forces that opposed the partition of the Ottoman empire along ethnic lines. When Atatürk-led republican Turkey declared its intention to break its links with its Ottoman and

Islamic heritage and enforce a civic Turkish national identity, Turkey's Kurds had to choose between assimilation and resistance.

The first armed Kurdish rebellion against Kemalist secularisation and ethnic homogenisation plans took place in 1925. Under the leadership of Sheikh Said of Palu, a number of Kurdish tribes rebelled against Turkish rule. The character of the Sheikh Said revolt was two-fold, religious and ethnic: reaction against the forced secularisation of the Turkish state and society initiated by Atatürk's modernisation programme was matched with willingness to resist state efforts to forcibly homogenise Turkey's Kurdish population. Turkish armed forces succeeded in quickly suppressing the rebellion, which, nonetheless, became a watershed: large-scale purges against Kurdish and other dissident elements in Turkey followed shortly after. The Turkish state engaged in violent policy measures to suppress Kurdish resentment and subsequent uprisings, and also gave greater impetus to Atatürk's secularisation programme.[46]

The Kurdish issue came again to the fore in the 1960s, under the suitable political environment created by the 1961 Turkish constitution. The problems of Turkey's Kurds were articulated, and steps toward their representation in Turkish politics were made. The 1971 coup and constitutional amendments lifted some of the most liberal elements of the 1961 constitution; yet the emergence of the Kurdish question as one of the most important political issues in Turkish politics could not be prevented. Kurdish political groups were formed, addressing their agenda in a socialist or nationalist backdrop. Political turmoil and violence between radical leftist and rightist political groups, which characterised Turkish politics of the 1970s, played an important role in the radicalisation of Kurdish politics in Turkey. The Kurdish Workers Party (Partiya Karkaren Kurdistan–PKK) spearheaded radical Kurdish nationalists by organising guerrilla warfare in the Kurdish-inhabited provinces of eastern and southeastern Turkey and terrorist attacks in Turkey's urban centres. In the early 1990s the Democracy Party (Demokrasi Partisi–DEP) became the representative of moderate Kurds who opposed the use of violence but demanded respect of the human rights of Turkey's Kurds. Turkey's reaction was fierce, involving major military operations against the PKK, the closure of the DEP and arrests of its prominent members.[47] The PKK was effectively neutralised with the capture of its leader Abdullah Öcalan in 1998 and a series of successful Turkish military operations; the Kurdish issue had, however, already mobilised a big number of Turkey's ethnic Kurdish population.

Turkish national identity was shaken, and this aroused fear that other ethnic groups might follow the Kurds in searching for their distinct national identity.

The challenge of the European Union

The prospect of Turkey's membership of the European Union has set the second serious challenge to Turkish nationalism. Westernisation was a primary strategic and political choice of Atatürk and his successors at the start of the Turkish state, and nationalism was part of this project. Turkey sided with the western powers during the Cold War and participated in numerous western international organisations. This participation, however, was not impaired by Turkey's illiberal nation-building policies, as state-centred policies were still the norm in Europe.

The transformation of the European Union into a supranational political organisation in the early 1990s has, nonetheless, greatly affected the political dimension of its enlargement process. The European Union became a *sui generis* supranational organisation, requiring substantial sovereignty concessions from member states in favour of EU institutions and furthering the development of a common post-national European identity.[48] Through Turkey's EU-influenced, gradual political liberalisation, ethnic homogenisation policies were challenged. The ethnic composition of Turkey's population and the role of Islam and state in society came under re-examination. The ongoing deregulation of nation-states and national identities inside the European Union rocked the conceptual foundations of the Turkish nation-state.

The prospect of compromising Turkey's sovereignty and nation-building policies in favour of minority rights and a post-national European identity has met with the suspicion and opposition of a substantial part of the Kemalist elite.[49] According to its argument, the price of such a policy would be the disintegration of the Turkish national ideology and, possibly, state. The whole Turkish nation-building project would be endangered as latent ethnic divisions within the Turkish people could re-emerge and threaten national unity achieved in the republican years. On the other hand, there is no other visible political orientation as favourable for Turkey as its membership of the European Union, which is also seen as part of the 'Kemalist imperative'. Atatürk's nationalism was very much European in the 1920s, yet it is no more European at the advent of the twenty-first century. Nationalism has been discredited in its former cradle, and the success of Turkey's EU vocation will greatly depend on the redefinition of its national identity, not on the basis of state-based or selective[50] models, but according to liberal, citizen-based approaches open to the post-national challenge.

Iranian Nationalism

Introduction

Iranian nationalism in its various forms has been the determining ideology of modern Iran. Its centrality to the Iranian political landscape is indicated by its pervasive use in political discourse, both as a means of legitimising policy and deriding the positions of opponents. Yet it remains a difficult concept to define with any precision, and while its contested nature may provide it with a dynamic vigour and continuing social relevance, its essential ambiguity ensures that it remains a plural construction. Indeed many of the political debates in modern Iran revolve around the contestation between various definitions of Iranian nationalism and the determination to monopolise discourse by imposing an 'authentic' version. This synopsis will focus on the three main trends in nationalist thought in the modern era: *secular* nationalism; *dynastic* nationalism; and *religious* nationalism. These trends are by no means exclusive, but they do express the three main periods of ideological development.

Secular nationalism, appropriated from Europe, was the dominant form of nationalism in the era of the notables, determined by the intelligentsia and supported by the emergent professional classes, as well as industrial workers and coming to popular fruition during the oil nationalisation crisis of 1951–3. Despite the educational reforms under Reza Shah, literacy during the first half of the twentieth century remained low, and estimates were set at between 10 and 20 per cent of the population, with a higher proportion in the cities. Oral communication however remained dynamic and political activity was often vibrant. In 1943 for instance, Tehran, with a population of 750,000 could boast 47 newspapers. As the nationalisation crisis gripped the public, this figure rose to some 700 papers in 1951. With the fall of Mosaddeq in 1953 official ideology emphasised the dynasty, although this approach conflicted with the very real social and economic changes which were taking place. By the 1960s student numbers were growing exponentially with increasing numbers going abroad. At the same time, Iranians were being exposed to growing numbers of foreigners in Iran, and the dramatic growth in the mass media (television as well as radio) was obviating the need for literacy. Seasoned observers noted the growth of a 'middle-class' consciousness, much of which remained unfulfilled by the Shah's dynastic nationalism. For many young students the route to salvation was in the adoption of religious nationalism. They were to prove an important element in the ideological vanguard of the Islamic revolution. While a quadrupling of oil prices in 1973 allowed more money to be spent on the official dynastic nationalism, it also allowed an increase in education and travel. By the end of the 1970s some 100,000 students were entering higher education in Iran while an estimated 50,000 were studying abroad.

'Iran' and 'Persia'

One of the more obvious debates has revolved around the conflicting definitions of 'Iranian' and 'Persian' nationalism. For the purposes of this overview the term 'Iranian' will be used to look at the broad panoply of nationalisms under discussion, while 'Persian' will be limited to a particular understanding of Iranian nationalism, and the literary culture which developed around the emergence of the 'new Persian' language.

The roots of modern Iranian nationalism

The ethnic origins of Iranian nationalism are profound, and the construction of nationalism in Iran can rely on a rich reservoir of historical sources which provide a sense of continuity and identity. Language, literature and epic poetry which has emphasised the historical consistency of the territorial integrity of *Iranshahr*, have all proved essential to the modern development of nationalism. While the grand narrative of nationalist discourse may exaggerate the notion of continuity over change, there is little doubt that a sense of Iranian ethnic identity has existed to varying degrees over many centuries, and authors have commented on the existence of a 'cultural continuity' which arguably prevailed in the classical period, and certainly survived the period of the Arab/Islamic conquests in the seventh century.[51] Indeed the absorption of the ancient Iranian state into the Islamic caliphate harboured tensions which tended to accentuate the ethnic and cultural differences which existed between 'Arab' and 'Iranian', and the evidence suggests that political assimilation did not translate easily into the cultural sphere. Cultural and religious festivals such as the Zoroastrian new year (NowRuz) and the traditional harvest festival of *mehrigan*, proved difficult to eliminate from the Iranian calendar and were eventually tolerated by the Umayyad caliphs, while following the 'Abbasid Revolution' a more synthetic 'Islamic' cultural identity emerged which saw a fusion of Arab and Iranian norms. By the ninth century a more distinctive Iranian identity was manifesting itself through the re-emergence of 'new Persian' as the lingua franca of the eastern caliphate, and with it the emergence of a distinctive literature, which while undoubt-edly elitist, reflected the continuing tensions between 'Iranians' and their 'Arab' overlords.

Probably the most significant development as far as modern Iranian nationalism is concerned, was the composition of the *Shahnameh* (*Book of Kings*) by the poet Ferdowsi, which was completed at the turn of the eleventh century. Not only did the epic poem effectively resuscitate the Persian language, providing a valuable repository and reference for authentic Persian words (Ferdowsi deliberately avoided the use of non-Persian words where possible), but in committing the creation myth of Iran and its ancient kings to verse, Ferdowsi not only provided the terms of reference for a distinct 'national' memory, but an effective means for its social absorption and dissemination. It is important to remember nonetheless that political realities ensured that the revitalisation of Iranian identity remained essentially cultural rather than political, and indeed that the absence of the latter paradoxically facilitated a cultural diffusion beyond the recognised ethnic parameters of the 'Iranians'. Arguably, the apolitical nature of Iranian cultural identity ensured its durability through periods of political turmoil, and a succession of 'Turkic' dynasties in particular proved enthusi-astic consumers of the Iranian national myth.

While a case has been made for the origins of the 'modern' Iranian state in the foundations of the Mongol Il-Khanid dynasty in the thirteenth century, the fusion of cultural and political identities would have to await the emergence of the Safavid dynasty in the sixteenth century. Even now, concepts of Iranianness had to compete with powerful ethnic and religious identities, insofar as the Safavids derived much of their political legitimacy from the imposition and development of Shi'ism, and a reliance on Turkic military forces. Indeed, while the conventional nationalist nar-rative likes to see the origins of the Iranian 'nation-state' in the foundation of the Safavid empire, it is worth remembering that while the Ottoman Sultan composed poetry in Persian, his Safavid rival, Shah Ismail, was doing the same in Turkish. That said, it was not long before the radical Shi'ism of the early Safavids gave way to the elitism of Persian culture, language and literature.[52] This not only reflected the growing centrality of the Persian bureaucracy, but the very real cultural potency of Iranian mythic history. Shi'ism defined and distinguished Iranian identity and the Safavid state provided it with a renewed territorial integrity, such that when the Safavid empire finally collapsed in 1722, successive rulers sought both to emulate and re-establish it. Nader Shah Afshar, for example, could count among his motives a determination not only to emulate the Safavids (and indeed, the empire of Tamer-lane) but more intriguingly, the 'ancient empires'.

European influences

Modern Iranian nationalist discourse can be traced to developments in the Qajar state in the nineteenth century. Like its Safavid predecessor, as the Qajar state became more settled, sedentary and bureaucratised, so it adopted many of the formalities and rituals of Iranian kingship, including an increasing use of old Persian names (as derived from the *Shahnameh*), royal titles and representations. While the Qajar state defined itself in pluralistic or imperial terms – 'the Guarded Domains of Iran' – elite culture was distinctively Persian with a historical memory that was 'Iranian'. Euro-pean travellers commented on this keen sense of identity founded on a belief of former imperial greatness drawn from the *Shahnameh*.[53] They often contrasted it with their own appreciation of the Iranian imperial state as related through scripture and classical texts. This European understanding was reinforced by the development of scientific history and archaeology, which increasingly relegated the narrative of the *Shahnameh* to the realm of literary myth. The European political ascendancy of the mid to late nineteenth century combined with a stark appreciation of Iranian political impotence ensured that European traditions of 'nationalism' began to transplant indigenous narratives, particularly among the political and intellectual elite. The concept of Iranian nationalism which emerged by the end of the nineteenth century, therefore, was rich in secular and racial overtones acquired from the Europeans. Something of this influence can be seen in the writings of Mirza Agha Khan Kermani, who wrote in the 1890s:

> The root of each of the branches of the tree of ugly character of Persia [*sic*] that we touch was planted by the Arabs and its fruit [sprang from] the seed sown from the Arabs. All the despicable habits and customs of the Persians are either the legacy and testament of the Arab nation or the fruit and influence of the invasions that have occurred in Persia.[54]

Secular nationalism

European influence and in particular the development of the 'Aryan myth' determined that modern Iranian nationalism as an ideology of political action sought to emulate and imitate the logic of the west. The early ideologues of nationalism, such as Kermani (above) defined nationalism within the familiar parameters of secularism (which at times extended to a denigration of Islam) and an ethnicity understood in explicitly racial terms. As in other Middle Eastern states at the turn of the twentieth century, 'nationalism' was seen as the essential panacea for the ills of the state, the precursor to modernisation. National unity and uniformity were the hallmarks of this new nationalism, and while traditional Iranian identity had been culturally distinctive but politically ambiguous (and therefore inclusive in its approach), the new ideology of nationalism espoused centralisation, standardisation and rigorous definition. The inclusive ambiguity of identity gave way to the exclusive rigour of ideology, and while Iranian identity had been plural in its accommodation of regional variation, the new ideology was avowedly 'Persian' and determinedly monopolistic. In the words of one prominent intellectual, Iran was, 'one homogenous nation ... composed of one pure race, one culture, and one encompassing civilisation with one single historical heritage'.[55]

What had been the prerogative of the political elite was to be popularised, disseminated and imposed. Such radical approaches to nationalism remained limited among key members of the elite, and many found the antagonism with Islam to be distasteful or indeed impractical. During the period of the constitutional revolution (1906–9), activists argued forcefully for a constitution which would proclaim that sovereignty resided with the people, an entirely novel idea for Iran, and one which did not go down well with many members of the Shi'a *ulema*, and others sensitive to what were understood as national traditions. Indeed the constitutional revolution was arguably undone by the fractures in the movement created by disagreements over the precise meaning and direction of 'national' policy, ultimately leading to stagnation within government and the failure of the central state.

Unable to fulfil their ambitions through the Constitutional Movement, nationalists turned their attentions to the 'invention of a saviour', an autocrat who would be able to firmly impose a nationalist agenda. In the aftermath of the Great War, and the devastation which rival armies had inflicted upon the Iranian countryside, nationalist ideologues, disaffected with the impotence of the Qajars, sought an alternative and in 1921 helped orchestrate a 'coup' with the assistance of the leader of the Cossack Brigade (one of the few military organisations in existence), Reza Khan. Reza Khan quickly dispensed with his collaborator, the journalist Seyyid Zia Tabatabie, and rapidly moved through the political ranks, from commander in chief, to minister of war and then prime minister in quick succession. His personal ambition and rigorously nationalist approach to the political ailments of the Iranian state earned him widespread support among members of the intelligentsia who actively promoted him as the saviour of the nation. Lacking a tribe of his own, Reza Khan forcefully pushed through legislation which would expand the new Iranian armed forces, and began the process of effectively re-conquering the country from within in order to impose central administration. Not only did Reza Khan ensure the ratification of a conscription law, but also managed to secure vastly increased funds for the army, which he considered 'the soul of the nation'.[56] In addition, during the fifth parliament (1924), weights and measures were to be standardised, a new calendar was adopted dated from the Hijra but calculated according the Iranian solar year along with new months derived from Zoroastrian mythology. Finally, all Iranians were obliged to take family names. Reza Khan conspicuously took the surname 'Pahlavi'.

In adopting the name 'Pahlavi', Reza Khan, who in 1925 was made Reza Shah by a grateful and compliant Parliament, intended to associate himself and his new dynasty with ancient Iran, and by some colourful accounts, one of the great ancient aristocratic houses. This association was one of the central tenets of the secular nationalism as expressed by the Pahlavi state. It was 'secular' insofar as it sought to diminish the role of Islam within the Iranian cultural heritage, though its sacral aspects, inasmuch as it drew heavily on Zoroastrian precepts, were very much in evidence. This tied in effectively with the emphasis on 'Aryanism' which had been appropriated from western conceptions of the Aryan myth. At the same time, this was an Aryanism which was very much focused on the Medes and the Persians, to the exclusion of most other Iranian 'nations'. Such views were widespread among the intelligentsia as the following comments by the Marxist Taqi Arani reveal: 'All patriotic Iranians, especially the officials in the Ministry of Education, must do their very best to replace Turkish with Persian. We must send Persian journals, Persian newspapers, Persian textbooks, and Persian teachers to Azerbaijan – that ancient homeland of Zoroaster and of the Aryans.'[57] This rigorously 'Persian' Iranian nationalism was to be pursued through a purification of the language with the establishment of an academy intended to rid the language of 'foreign' (essentially Arab) imports, and a standardisation of grammar and spelling. Suggestions that the Arabic script could be replaced with the more authentically 'Iranian' Latin script (as in Ataturk's Turkey) were eventually shelved when it was realised that the process would be far too problematic.

In other areas, however, the new ideology was pursued with vigour, with the forced settlement of the tribes (nomadism was considered antithetical to the national project), and imposition of western dress, including the removal of the veil. This latter measure was justified on nationalist grounds with dubious claims that the 'European hat' had in fact originated in the Sasanian empire. Similarly extensive changes were made to the nomenclature of the new state, with 'ancient' names and titles being resuscitated, and allusions to non-Iranian sources being eradicated. Most conspicuously, 'Arabistan' was renamed 'Khuzistan', and in 1934, following prompting from the Iranian embassy in Berlin, Reza Shah instructed that henceforth foreign countries only use the term 'Iran' rather than 'Persia' when describing the country. The argument ran that 'Persia' was a foreign (Hellenic) construct which only reflected a part of the Iranian state (Pars/Fars). But implicit in the decision to insist on the use of 'Iran' was the view that 'Persia' carried with it negative semantic baggage denoting decadence and underdevelopment, whereas Iran, with its 'Aryan' associations, was modern and forward looking. This was ironic given the *Persianisation* of Iran which had been pursued, and was to be systematically deconstructed and challenged following the abdication of Reza Shah in 1941.

Indeed in the period 1941–53, 'secular nationalism' took on a more popular mandate as politicians competed to redefine Iranian nationalism, and to *popularise* it against the exclusive elitism which many politicians had characterised as nationalist policy under Reza Shah. Indeed in the absence of the imposing centralising authority of Reza Shah and the collapse of the Iranian army in face of the Allied invasion (1941), they began to deconstruct the dominance of centralisation and called for regional variation, especially where the tribes were concerned, limited decentralisation (though this did not last long), and a more inclusive interpretation of Iranian nationalism which de-emphasised the role of Persian and stressed cultural rather than ethnic (or indeed racial) homogeneity. In many ways, political liberalisation and dynamism led to the popularisation of nationalism through the development of a whole spectrum of nationalist parties ranging from the socialists to the right-wing pan-Iranists, as politicians competed for the loyalties of the emerging urban proletariat, which had appeared following the economic and educational reforms of the previous twenty years. This undoubtedly remained an elite-led process (despite a flourishing of the print media, literacy was estimated to stand at 20 per cent) but the period witnessed a dramatic rise in the growth of political consciousness, facilitated not only by debate, but through the development of technology.

The wireless radio, introduced with enthusiasm by Soviet troops eager to politicise the proletariat, was fundamental to the raising of political awareness, but it also performed the function of linguistic standardisation. For all the regional inclusivity of the new nationalists, the emergence of the mass media forced the pace of centralisation and the continued *Persianisation* of Iran. The strength of Iranian nationalism in this period took foreign powers by surprise, and the British in particular were unprepared for the vigour of the National Front movement led by the patrician politician, Dr Mohammad Mosaddeq. Mosaddeq was to become the supreme icon of modern Iranian nationalism (a position he holds to this day), on account of his opposition to the British and his determination to nationalise the Anglo-Iranian Oil Company. His brief period in power (1951–3) also highlighted other developments in nationalist discourse, especially the persistence of 'religious nationalism', as defined by Ayatollah Kashani who provided the National Front with much of its traditionalist constituency and arguably its most extensive social base. The social potency of religious nationalism was only to become apparent in 1979 following the emphatic failure of the other major narrative of nationalism, that of dynastic nationalism.

Dynastic nationalism

Dynastic nationalism had become increasingly prominent during the rule of Reza Shah, and indeed had been present from the inception of the dynasty and the desire of the intelligentsia to promote a national saviour. In the initial stages, however, Reza Shah was very much portrayed as the vehicle or means by which the nationalist project could be vigorously pursued. That is, he was seen as having a finite and specific function in the service of the 'nation-state'. As the reign progressed, however, Reza Shah's perception of his, and his new dynasty's, centrality to Iranian nationalism became more pronounced, and the argument was increasingly made that the nation-state was dependent on the continuation of the dynasty. This intimate association was crucial in legitimising a dynasty that many Iranian aristocrats regarded as *parvenu*, and indeed during the effective interregnum (1941–53), this view came under systematic attack by nationalists who argued for a strict de-personalisation of nationalist ideology. The monarchy may be an important national institution but it was very much an expression of the national will and not its master. Staunch monarchists however opposed this view and sought an ever closer association between the Pahlavi monarchy and the myths of nationalism. Much to the consternation of nationalists they succeeded in posthumously awarding Reza Shah the title 'Great', thereby associating his achievements with the Achaemenid Shahs, and the Safavid Shah Abbas. Of particular importance to the new king, the young Mohammad Reza Shah, were the associations with Cyrus the Great.

Dynastic nationalism nevertheless did not gather pace until the overthrow of the National Front government in 1953, and the gradual consolidation of Mohammad Reza Shah's rule. Indeed it took the better part of a decade and the growth of oil income before the new Shah was able to give political expression to his personal sentiments. Initially he had sought to legitimise himself by associating himself with democratic aspirations and the emergent professional middle classes, and in the aftermath of the white revolution in 1961 (formally launched in 1963), as a revolutionary monarch appropriating ideas from the Iranian left: an apparent contradiction which drew concern from many quarters. This contradiction was resolved by the Shah through the development of 'charismatic' kingship, in particular the traditions of Persian sacral kingship. Iranian nationalism had become a deeply personal affair. This new narrative drew an intimate connection between Iranian monarchy and the nation, which it was argued could be traced in a relatively unbroken line, back to Cyrus the Great, the founding father of the Iranian nation. The monarchy and the nation enjoyed a symbiotic, mystical relationship, which Mohammad Reza Shah fully endorsed and cultivated, such that it was argued that the health (and wealth) of the nation depended on the strength of the monarchy.

Where history, and indeed myth, tended to contradict this narrative, it was quietly airbrushed out. Thus for example, while the *Shahnameh*, as the name implied, emphasised the centrality of kings to the Iranian national consciousness, the relationship of the kings to the state was at times ambivalent, and occasionally wholly negative, resulting in regicide, a consequence which Mohammad Reza Shah obviously did not want to highlight. Indeed, in spite of the richness of monarchical discourses in Persian literature and political treatise, it remains remarkable how little of this resource was actually utilised by the dynasty's myth makers. Instead, the narrative was almost wholly adopted from western histories of the pre-Islamic imperial past, concentrating on the Achaemenids and even drawing on Herodotus to justify monarchy over democracy.[58]

Dynastic nationalism was given expression through the adoption of new titles such as the evocative title of *Shahanshah Aryamehr* (King of Kings, Light of the Aryans), the lavish celebrations for the 2,500 years of Persian monarchy celebrated with great pomp and circumstance in Persepolis and Pasargadae in 1971, where the Shah delivered a eulogy at the tomb of Cyrus the Great, and most controversially by the sudden and abrupt imposition of the 'imperial calendar' in 1976. Overnight, Iranians who were under the apparent misconception that they were living in 1355, discovered that it was actually 2535. The fact that Iranians had just celebrated 2,500 years of monarchy in 1971, led some to question from where the additional 30 years had emerged? A quick calculation would reveal that the '35' years corresponded exactly with the Shah's reign ensuring that his accession in 1941 coincided with the beginning of a new 2,500-year cycle, with himself rather than Cyrus the Great at the helm. A crucial aspect of the dynastic nationalism as defined by Mohammad Reza Shah was the importance of monarchy to the religious and spiritual well-being of the nation. Thus, in his book, *Towards the Great Civilisation*, Mohammad Reza Shah argued:

> An important point to note is the real meaning of the word *shahanshahi*, which cannot be explained in ordinary historical terms. When it is necessary to translate into a foreign language, it is normal to translate it as 'Imperial', but the meaning of the Western term Imperial is simply political and geographic, whereas from the Iranian perspective, the term shahanshahi has more than the normal meaning, it has a spiritual, philosophical, symbolic, and to a great extent, a sentimental aspect, in other words, just as it has a rational and thoughtful relevance, so too it has a moral and emotional dimension. In Iranian culture, the Iranian monarchy means the political and geographic unity of Iran in addition to the special national identity and all those unchangeable values which this national identity has brought forth. For this reason no fundamental change is possible in this country unless it is in tune with the fundamental principles of the monarchical system.[59]

Religious nationalism

Religious nationalism had been the predominant form of nationalism in Iran as it emerged from the nineteenth century. Iranian identity had, since the sixteenth century, been closely associated with Shi'ism; a legacy of the Safavid state. Secular nationalists, borrowing from European nationalisms, had ascribed to Islam all the ills of the nation and as such had sought to construct a nationalism divested of religious elements. This form of nationalism had been central to state policy for much of the Pahlavi period, despite allusions to the dynasty, and the importance of religious nationalist sentiment to the oil nationalisation crisis. Indeed the contribution of religious nationalism in both the constitutional revolution and the National Front movement was largely dismissed or ignored by nationalist historians of the period. However, the sacral aspects of dynastic nationalism as defined in the later Pahlavi period provided an unwitting framework for the return of religious nationalism to the forefront of the political stage.

The re-emergence of 'religious nationalism' as a central force in Iranian politics was in large measure determined, as with Arab nationalism, by the perceived failure of secular nationalism and the inability of the elites to relate effectively with the masses who in many ways retained traditional loyalties and were better able to relate and communicate through traditional Shi'a myths. For some Iranian ideologues, this was a consequence of the reality that 'secular nationalism' had been imported from the west and as such was an alien concept to most Iranians. More damningly, what authenticity it may have enjoyed had been diminished by its clear and obvious association with western culture, especially as expressed by its supporters and practitioners in Iran. An affection for all things 'western' seemed to contradict the major tenets of 'secular nationalism', and this position was passionately if contentiously argued by Jalal Ale Ahmad in his devastating critique entitled *Gharbzadegi* (*Westoxication*). This argument that secular nationalism lacked authenticity because of its enthusiasm for the west and denigration of Iranian culture was taken up by lay religious thinkers, in particular the highly influential Ali Shariati, whose colourful prose sought to convince a new generation of young and increasingly educated Iranians (many of whom were being educated abroad) that national salvation and social justice could only be achieved through the medium of Shi'a Islam.

A revived, purified Shi'ism was to be the means by which the nation could attain salvation and solve the myriad social problems which the ideology of secular nationalism had palpably failed to do. This attempt to restore the relationship of the nation to Shi'ism did not automatically imply an intimate link with the orthodox Shi'a *ulema*. Indeed Shariati had a problematic relationship with the *ulema* on account of his continued criticism of orthodox Islam and its institutions. But the implications of the association nonetheless served to sanctify the nation and by extension the role of the *ulema* in legitimising nationalism. In many ways the sacral aspects of dynastic nationalism can be seen as a method by which Mohammad Reza Shah sought to harness this trend to his own purposes. But his close association with the west in the eyes of many Iranians always gave this aspiration an air of vacuity. Few people could take the Shah's proclamations of divine right monarchy seriously, and much to that monarch's consternation, the mantle of sacral nationalism would be appropriated by one who neither he nor the staunch secular nationalists had considered.

Ayatollah Ruhollah Khomeini had been a middle-ranking cleric when he was thrust into national prominence because of his vociferous opposition to the reforms launched under the rubric of the white revolution in 1963. While the violent protests which resulted could be dismissed as the last gasps of reactionaries, Khomeini's subsequent protest was to prove much more damaging to the national credibility of the Shah, and ensure his own position as defender of the national honour. In 1964, Mohammad Reza Shah took the highly contentious step of accepting US demands that its governmental personnel (broadly defined) be granted extra-judicial rights while serving in Iran. The widespread perception that the Shah had sold out the country (a view reinforced by the immediate announcement of a $200 million loan) and reintroduced the very system of 'capitulations' his father had done so much to eradicate, caused widespread popular anger. In the absence of any credible opposition, it was left to Ayatollah Khomeini to effectively articulate the nation's outrage:

> I cannot express the sorrow I feel in my heart. My heart is constricted ... Iran no longer has any festival to celebrate; they have turned our festival into mourning ... They have sold us, they have sold our independence; but still they light up the city and dance ... If I were in their place, I would forbid all these lights; I would give orders that black flags be

raised over the bazaars and houses, that black awnings be hung! Our dignity has been trampled underfoot; the dignity of Iran has been destroyed.[60]

Khomeini's vitriolic condemnation resulted in his exile, but he had effectively seized the initiative from both secular nationalists and the Shah, as the popular choice to defend the national honour. That this role was treated with incredulity and contempt by his ideological opponents only allowed him to consolidate this position with minimal interference. In seeking to criticise his religious credentials, his opponents neglected to appreciate the gains he was making among nationalists who increasingly saw national salvation in the synthesis between religion and nationalism. Since he appeared to epitomise this synthesis it should come as little surprise that the national authenticity of Khomeini should so easily displace the perceived artificiality of the Shah during the revolution of 1978–9.

Contemporary developments

Critics regularly argue that the Islamic revolution in Iran resulted in the displacement of nationalist ideology by that of a broader pan-Islamic worldview, noting Khomeini's apparent ambivalence to his imminent return to Iran as evidence. Yet as indicated above, Khomeini was a far more complex character, attracting support from both traditional and progressive constituents, most of whom were strongly nationalist in their leanings. That they promoted a nationalism rich in Shi'a mythology was arguably simply a return to nineteenth-century conceptions of Iranian identity. There is little doubt that in the early stages of the Islamic revolution there was a much more frequent use of Islamic discourse to justify political action, but the limitations of a pan-Islamic discourse were already apparent, when Khomeini insisted that presidential candidates be native Iranians who could show that they had been born in the country. Furthermore, other changes which may have been expected from a state determined by Islamic ideology were not administered. The calendar, for instance, which had been reformed in 1924, was not touched, nor were the basic features of the Pahlavi state, or indeed the centrality of (Islamic) Iranian culture. The emphasis may have shifted from Cyrus the Great to Imam Ali, but even here religion was increasingly subservient to the needs of the nation. This became all too apparent with the onset of the Iran–Iraq War, when the demands of mobilisation meant that war rhetoric had to reflect popular sentiment and emotions. People may have fought for Islam but it was a distinctly Iranian Islam.

Indeed a strong case can be made that the Islamic Republic, and the institutions it established, facilitated a process by which Islam was *nationalised*. Ayatollah Khomeini occupied the new position of *velayat-e faqih* (Guardianship of the Jurist) with constitutionally mandated authority over other Shi'a jurists. He also acquired the title 'Imam', and while himself careful not to associate his title with that of the infallible Imams of Shi'a tradition, there is little doubt that among some of his more devout followers, the title implied much more than simple political authority. What this meant in practical terms is that Shi'ism was being defined in terms of the Iranian state. Indeed in the aftermath of the war, the relationship between 'religion' and 'nationalism' increasingly favoured the latter, as Islamic structures, such as *hejab* were even justified in nationalist terms; very much in the same vein as the adoption of western dress in the 1920s and 1930s. On a social and intellectual level, the changes were even more dramatic, as research into ancient Iran became more popular among students, and arguments were being effectively made for a more synthetic approach to Iranian identity which included not only Islamic and pre-Islamic influences, but significantly, that of the west. More intriguing has been the genuine growth of popular Iranian nationalism, marrying Persian narratives appropriated from western scholarship (the Achaemenids), with the powerful indigenous narratives of mytho-history as revealed in the *Shahnameh*.

> Mythology describes the spirit of various nations. And there is no nation or people whose history is free from myth. Of course, in conformity with the weight of civilisation and the history of a nation, the myth of the nation is deeper and more complicated. And civilised nations usually have myths. The ethical myth and the myth epic indicate the spirit of Iranians ... the Book of Kings [is] the symbol of Iran.[61]

Iranian nationalism, founded essentially on a *Persian* narrative has hitherto been a province of the elites, appropriated as it was largely from a western 'scientific' history. Despite the best efforts of the Pahlavi state, it proved difficult to effectively communicate this narrative to the mass of Iranians, who turned in the first instance to familiar Shi'a myths, and latterly to the national myths of the *Shahnameh*, which have enjoyed a political rehabilitation. This powerful combination of reinvigorated 'grand narrative', increasingly divorced from racial overtones, and instead married to the rehabilitated, cultural and inclusive 'meta-narrative', is likely to determine the direction of Iranian nationalism for decades to come. Its cultural and social relevance, combined with a dramatic growth in literacy and political awareness will likewise ensure its centrality to political action and legitimacy within Iran for the foreseeable future.

NOTES

1   Non-Sunni Ottoman Muslims (Alevi, Shi'ite, Druze) often faced severe discrimination.
2   Young Ottomans and Young Turks were the most prominent groups influenced by nationalist ideas.
3   Suna Kili, 'Kemalism in Contemporary Turkey', *International Political Science Review*, 1(3), 1980, pp. 382–3.
4   Following the Moudros Armistice of 31 October 1918, military forces of Entente states, severely restricting Ottoman sovereign rights, occupied large parts of Ottoman territory.
5   Surnames in brackets were adopted after 1934, when the Family Name Law was passed.
6   Exploring Atatürk's modernisation programme falls beyond the scope of this study. For more information, see Bernard Lewis, *The Emergence of Modern Turkey*, 2nd edn. (Oxford, London, New York: Oxford University Press, 1968), pp. 256–93 and Eric Zürcher, *Turkey: A Modern History* (London, New York: I. B. Tauris, 1998), pp. 194–203.
7   In Atatürk's words: 'We will raise our national culture up to the level of contemporary civilisation.' See Mustafa Kemal Atatürk, *Atatürk'ün Söylevleri Ve Demeçleri*, 4th edn., vol. I–III (Ankara: Atatürk Kültür, Dil ve Tarih Yüksek Kurumu, Atatürk Araş tı rma Merkezi, 1989), p. 318.
8   Mustafa Kemal Atatürk, *Nutuk* (Ankara: Kültür Bakanlı ğ ı Yayınları, 1980), pp. 6–7.
9   David Kushner, *The Rise of Turkish Nationalism 1876–1908* (London: Frank Cass, 1977), pp. 50–5.
10 Anthony D. Smith, *The Ethnic Origins of Nations* (Oxford, Malden, MA: Blackwell, 1988) pp. 134–6.

11 Nergis Canefe, 'Turkish Nationalism and Ethno-Symbolic Analysis: The Rules of Exception', *Nations and Nationalism*, 8 (2), 2002, pp. 145–6.

12 For a full account of Turkey's ethnic composition, see Peter Alford Andrews, ed., *Ethnic Groups in the Republic of Turkey* (Wiesbaden: Dr. Ludwig Reichert Verlag, 1989).

13 Kili, pp. 388–9.

14 Lewis, pp. 357–61.

15 Tekin Alp, *Kemalizm* (İstanbul: Istanbul Cumhuriyet Matbaasi, 1936), pp. 129–75 and Hugh Poulton, *Top Hat, Grey Wolf and Crescent: Turkish Nationalism and the Turkish Republic* (London: Hurst and Co., 1997), pp. 101–4.

16 Elie Kedourie, *Nationalism* (London: Hutchinson, 1966), p. 58.

17 Kushner, pp. 7–9.

18 Yusuf Akçura, *Üç Tarz-ı Siyaset*, (Ankara: Türk Tarih Kurumu Yayınları, 1976), pp. 19–36.

19 Tanıl Bora, ' "Ekalliyet Yı lanları": Türk Milliyetçiliğ i Ve Azı nlı klar', in *Milliyetçilik*, ed. Tanıl Bora, *Modern Türkiye'de Siyasi Düsünce* (Istanbul: Iletiş im Yayınları, 2002), pp. 911–13.

20 According to the 1934 Resettlement Law, the Jewish communities living outside Istanbul were forced to settle there. The 1942 Property Tax was almost exclusively levied on Istanbul minority merchants, aiming at their financial destruction. For more information, see Ayhan Aktar, *Varlı k Vergisi Ve 'Türkleştirme' Politikaları, Iletiş im Yayınları 599–Tarih Dizisi 4* (Istanbul: Iletişim Yayınları, 2000).

21 Cemil Koçak, 'Kemalist Milliyetçiliğin Bulanı Suları', in *Milliyetçilik*, ed. Tanı l Bora, *Modern Türkiye'de Siyasi Düsünce* (Istanbul: Iletiş im Yayınları, 2002), pp. 37–41.

22 Educated Muslim elites of the Ottoman empire preferred the term 'Ottoman' (*Osmanlı*) and attributed the term 'Turk' to the Turkoman nomads, or later, the ignorant and uncouth Turkish-speaking peasants of the Anatolian villages. See Lewis, pp. 1–3, Kushner, pp. 20–6.

23 Poulton, pp. 109–14.

24 Aktar, pp. 130–4.

25 William Hale, *Turkish Foreign Policy 1774–2000* (London and Portland, OR: Frank Cass, 2002), pp. 90–1.

26 Jacob M. Landau, *Pan-Turkism: From Irredentism to Cooperation*, 2nd edn. (Bloomington: Indiana University Press, 1995), pp. 221–4.

27 Lewis, p. 335.

28 The Ottoman Sultan had been invested with the title of Caliph (supreme political and religious leader of all Muslims) since the early sixteenth century.

29 Kushner, pp. 1–2.

30 Namık Kemal, one of the leading figures of Young Ottomans, is the most eloquent representative of this school of thought. See Niyazi Berkes, *The Development of Secularism in Turkey* (Montreal: McGill University Press, 1964) pp. 208–18.

31 Ziya Gökalp, *Türkçülüğ ün Esasları* (Istanbul: Kum Saati Yayınları, 2001), pp. 37–53.

32 Poulton, pp. 76–82.

33 Kili, pp. 383–92.

34 Zürcher, pp. 194–203.

35 Ayş e Kadı oğ lu, 'The Paradox of Turkish Nationalism and the Construction of Official Identity', *Middle Eastern Studies*, 32 (2), 1996, pp. 188–9.

36 A significant percentage of the Anatolian population were refugees from former Ottoman territories, which they were forced to flee on the basis of their Islamic religion, which identified them with Ottoman Turks.

37 Poulton, pp. 178–81.

38 Duygu Köksal, 'Fine-Tuning Nationalism: Critical Perspectives from Republican Literature in Turkey', *Turkish Studies*, 2 (2), 2001, pp. 64–5.

39 Poulton, pp. 181–7.

40   Kadı oğ lu, pp. 189–92.
41   Mühittin Ataman, 'Özal Leadership and Restructuring of Turkish Ethnic Policy in the 1980s', ibid. 38 (4), 2002, pp. 127–8.
42   The rise of Kurdish minority nationalism since the 1960s has outlined the limits of the success of the Turkish nationalist project, yet this should not lead to belittlement hammering a strong national identity in a country with forty-seven identified ethnic groups. See Andrews, ed., pp. 47–9.
43   Multi-party politics were first introduced in 1946.
44   Bassam Tibi, *Arab Nationalism: Between Islam and the Nation-State*, 3rd edn. (Basingstoke, Hampshire and London: Macmillan Press, 1997), pp. 22–5.
45   The *de facto* partition of Ottoman Arab territories gradually resulted in the development of local interests, which had stakes in the consolidation of the *status quo*.
46   Henri J. Barkey and Graham E. Fuller, *Turkey's Kurdish Question* (New York: Rowman & Littlefield Publishers, 1998), pp. 11–13.
47   Kemal Kiris çi and Gareth M. Winrow, *The Kurdish Question and Turkey: An Example of a Trans-State Ethnic Conflict* (London, Portland, OR: Frank Cass, 2003), pp. 136–51.
48   Jürgen Habermas, *The Postnational Constellation* (Oxford: Polity Press, 2001), pp. 17–19.
49   İhsan D. Dağ ı, *Batı lı laş ma Korkusu* (Ankara: Liberte Yayınları, 2003), p. 3.
50   Ibid., pp. 1–2.
51   See, for example, A. D. Smith, *The Ethnic Origin of Nations*, Blackwell, Oxford, 1986, p. 107.
52   See A. Soudavar, 'The Early Safavids and Their Cultural Interactions with Surrounding States', in N. Keddie and R. Mathee (eds.) *Iran & the Surrounding World*, University of Washington Press, Seattle, 2002, pp. 89–120.
53   See in particular Sir John Malcolm *The History of Persia from the Most Early Period to the Present Time*, John Murray, London, 2nd edn., vol. I, 1829, p. 475.
54   Quoted in S. Bakhash, *Iran: Monarchy, Bureaucracy & Reform under the Qajars: 1858–1896*, London, Ithaca Press, 1978, p. 345.
55   Hasan Taqizadeh, quoted in M. Reza Ghods, 'Iranian Nationalism and Reza Shah', *Middle Eastern Studies*, 27(1), 1991, p. 36; significantly, Taqizadeh was of Azeri descent.
56   D. Wilbur, *Reza Shah Pahlavi: The Resurrection and Reconstruction of Iran*, New York, 1975, p. 95.
57   Quoted in E. Abrahamian, *Iran between Two Revolutions*, Princeton, 1982, p. 156.
58   M. Honarmand, *Pahlavism – Maktab-e No* (*Pahlavism: A New Ideology*) Ordibehesht 1345/April/May, 1966, Tehran, p. 3.
59   M. R. Pahlavi, *Be Sooye Tamadun-e Bozorg*, Tehran, undated, p. 244.
60   R. Khomeini, 'The Granting of Capitulatory Rights to the US', 27 October 1964, reproduced in H. Algar (tr. and ed.), *Islam & Revolution: Writings and Declarations of Imam Khomeini*, Mizan Press, Berkeley, 1981, pp. 181–8.
61   President Khatami addresses Iranian Expatriates in USA, BBC SWB ME/3339 MED/1, dated 23 September 1998, New York 20 September 1998.

FURTHER READING

Turkey

Hugh Poulton's book *Top Hat, Grey Wolf and Crescent: Turkish Nationalism and the Turkish Republic* (London, Hurst and Co., 1997) is a very good study of Turkish nationalism. David Kushner also offers valuable insights in *The Rise of Turkish Nationalism 1876–1908* (London, Frank Cass, 1977). Jacob M. Landau's *Pan-Turkism: From Irredentism to Cooperation*, 2nd edn. (Bloomington: Indiana University Press, 1995) is recommended for those interested in

Turkish ethnic nationalism. General reference books such as the classic – but slightly outdated – work of Bernard Lewis, *The Emergence of Modern Turkey*, 3rd edn. (Oxford, Oxford University Press, 2001) and Eric Zürcher's *Turkey: A Modern History* (London, New York: I. B. Tauris, 1998) also contain precious information. For Turkish language speakers the volume *Milliyetçilik* (İstanbul: İ letiş im Yayınları, 2002) edited by Tanı l Bora is an indispensable source of scholarship and knowledge.

Iran

There is a growing and extensive literature in Persian on the concepts of identity and nationalism. In the English language, the mainstay of studies on the development of Iranian nationalism remains R. Cottam's *Nationalism in Iran*, Pittsburgh, 1964, which provides a rigorous analysis of the structure and development of Iranian nationalism as a real political force in modern Iran. A good introductory essay is Beeman, W., 'What is Iranian National Character', *Iranian Studies*, 9, 1976, pp. 22–48. For an overview of developments of the different interpretations of nationalism see A. M. Ansari, *Modern Iran since 1921: The Pahlavis and After*, London, Longman, 2003. For the cultural dimension of Iranian nationalism, see R. Behnam *Cultural Foundations of Iranian Politics*, Utah, 1986; while Jalal Ale-Ahmad's *Plagued by the West (Gharbzadegi)* tr. P. Sprachman, New York, 1981, now available in English translation, provides a good example of the growing identification of Iranian nationalism against Western cultural penetration. For a discussion and critique of nationalism under Reza Shah, see M. Reza-Ghods, 'Iranian Nationalism and Reza Shah', *Middle Eastern Studies*, 27 (1), 1991 pp. 35–45; and H. Katouzian, 'Nationalist Trends in Iran, 1921–1926', *International Journal of Middle East Studies*, 10, 1979 pp. 533–51. For an excellent collection of essays on the oil nationalisation crisis and its impact on the ideology of nationalism, especially the iconic stature of Dr Mosaddeq, and the role of the *ulema*, see Bill, J. and Louis, W. R. (eds.), *Musaddiq, Iranian Nationalism and Oil*, London, I. B. Tauris, 1988, pp 307–29. For elements of continuity between 'dynastic' and 'religious' nationalism, see G. Aneer *Imam Ruhullah Khumaini, Sah Muhammad Riza Pahlavi and the Religious Traditions of Iran*, Stockholm, 1985, while Ayatollah Khomeini's debt to the left is well documented in E. Abrahamian, *Khomeinism*, London, I. B. Tauris, 1993. For a useful antidote to excessively nationalistic interpretations of Iranian history and identity, see M. Vaziri, *Iran as Imagined Nation*, London, Parragon House, 1993.

CHAPTER SEVENTEEN

Political Parties and Trade Unions

RAYMOND HINNEBUSCH

The Literature on Political Association

Do parties and unions matter in the Middle East? Earlier modernization theory-inspired literature took parties seriously: thus, according to Halpern, once traditional legitimacy erodes, leaders find that only parties can bind them to the masses in an organized way for a common political aim.[1] For Huntington, the political party was the single most important key to political modernization, that is, to the institution-alization of political participation.[2] Party case studies proliferated. Deeb traced the history of one of the most successful independence parties, the Wafd. Several writers analysed ruling single parties, 'the modern form of authoritarianism'. Khoury traced the development of such parties as the outcome of revolutionary generations while several seminal studies, notably of the Neo-Destour in Tunisia and the ASU in Egypt, identified the functions that they performed.[3] At the same time, Marxist-inspired literature traced the rise of class conflict between capital and worker that provided the conditions of unionization and class-based parties.[4]

Yet, thereafter, the role of parties, unions and class politics was seemingly margin-alized in both the actual Middle East and the scholarly literature on it (except for writings on Turkey and Israel).[5] It is a fact that the region, with a disproportionate number of no-party, one-party or dominant-party states, seems to suffer from a deficit of the party competition associated with democracy. For what Richards and Waterbury call the 'failure of parties',[6] Bill and Springborg offer a 'political culture' explanation: the continued viability of traditional solidarity groups (kinship groups, *shillas*) and of clientelism as an alternative mechanism of elite–mass linkage, both of which deter and colonize broader forms of impersonal association. An alternative structural explanation points to the pre-emption of political space by the prior external imposition (and subsequent channelling of oil 'rent') through the bureau-cratic and military arms of the state, allowing it to subordinate or corporatize political structures, including parties and unions, which would otherwise have represented civil society or mobilized class conflict.[7]

In the 1980s, the literature focused on Islamic movements as alternative forms of association filling the political vacuum left by the failure of political parties to institutionalize participation.[8] Thus, while the state harnessed parties and unions as instruments of corporatist control to demobilize participation (from above), primordial society (whether *shillas* or Islamist movements) flourished in the political vacuum, acting as buffers against the state while colonizing its instruments (from below).

Symptomatically, the 1990s preoccupation with liberalization in the region led to no renaissance of literature on parties. It was dominated instead by debates over whether enough civil society (largely conceived as liberal-oriented NGOs and professional associations) had survived to 'civilize' both the authoritarian state and its Islamic antithesis and hence to drive democratization. The initial verdict on parties under early political liberalization experiments was that their dependence on personalities, un-democratic internal life and rapid proliferation and fragmentation rendered them unable to promote, support or hold accountable democratic governments.[9]

Political Parties in the Middle East

It is, however, myopic to write off the importance of political parties in the region. Organizations with a family resemblance to parties exist in two-thirds of Arab states and while their roles may be more marginal than in developed states, similar *structures* are unlikely to perform wholly dissimilar *functions* in a political system. Moreover, in important respects parties both reflect and affect the nature and development of politics and the state in the region.

First, parties reflect the inherited societal tradition. Thus, they do, indeed, reflect the power of sub-state identities and small group politics in their tendency to form and fragment around personalities, families and sects. But they also reflect the power of trans-state identities in the region: branches of parties such as the Muslim Brotherhood, the ba'th, Nasserites, the Arab Nationalist Movement and its Palestinian offshoots (the PFLP and DFLP) as well as communist movements spread across borders throughout the region.

Second, however, parties also reflect societal change, notably the development of the modern 'political technology' of impersonal association that both reflects and affects the formation and political mobilization of classes and other larger collectivities. Thus, as political mobilization expanded, parties evolved appropriately in their *composition, ideologies,* and *organizational capacity.* As, over time, party recruitment widened from the upper class to include activists of middle and even lower class origin, the ideologies of parties came to appeal to wider constituencies (normally, promoting more egalitarian or reformist programmes). Parties also evolved beyond personal factions and clientelist networks and assumed the bureaucratic forms of organization needed to incorporate larger numbers of participants from further down in the stratification system (in the first stage, branches appeared in the provincial towns, later, cells in factories and villages and a permanent staff at the centre). Thus, the same conceptual tools used to study parties elsewhere are usefully employed in understanding their development in the Middle East.

Thirdly, variations in the type of *party system* and of the consequent function of parties in the political system both reflected and affected the process of *state formation.* Thus, embryonic multi-party systems were a feature of the period of early (mostly oligarchic) pluralism; single party systems of the subsequent authoritarian-populist 'revolutions from above'; and dominant party systems of their 'post-populist' transition; while mature multiparty systems have been pivotal where democracy has been institutionalized. The following discussion traces this party development.

Early party pluralism

This stage spanned a period beginning around 1900, when political contestation emerged within a small oligarchic political arena, and usually ended in the 1950s or 1960s when the mobilization of middle class activism, insufficiently channelled by institutions, ended in either repression or regime overthrow.

The earliest precursors of political parties appeared in the late Ottoman period when groupings of officers, bureaucrats or professionals formed to press for modernization, constitutional rule (the Committee of Union and Progress) or Arab rights within the empire (*al-'Ahd*). The collapse of the empire led to a proliferation of nationalist parties seeking to fill the ideological vacuum, notably the *Fatat* party that backed the short-lived Faisal government in Damascus. Under western imperialism and early independence, *parties of 'notables'* dominated; parties were the instruments of small groups of wealthy and prestigious local leaders (*ay'an, zu'ama*), normally great landlords or merchants, whose extended families controlled certain urban quarters or villages. These parties were precipitated by the creation of parliaments where factions of deputies grouped together in 'conservative' or 'liberal' blocs supporting or opposing the government but seldom able to hold it accountable. Linked more by personal ties than ideology, they were ephemeral and vulnerable to factionalism. Able to count on the dependants of the notables, such as peasants on their estates or clients in urban quarters, to win elections, notable parties had little need for party cadres or organization. Classic examples of such parties were the Liberal-Constitutionalists of Egypt, the various court parties in Morocco and Jordan, and the National and Constitutional blocs in Lebanon. In the early Iranian *majlis,* caucuses (*maslaks*) of royalists and liberals appeared.

The main opposition provoked by the upper class notable parties were what might be called *'parties of new intellectuals'* formed by middle class professionals, often teachers and their students, professing liberal or radical ideologies, often organized around a political newspaper, and, in the 1930s, sometimes giving birth to fascist-inspired militant youth groups (Green Shirts, Blue Shirts). Such parties were often able to mobilize student demonstrations and influence educated political opinion but, lacking clientelist networks in an era prior to mass politicization, they were doomed to remain relatively small urban groups and were unable to win elections. Mustafa Kamil's National Party in Egypt, the Iraqi Istiqlal party, the Democrat Iran party, and the early ba'th party are good examples.[10]

Where nationalist agitation spurred political mobilization, certain early parties evolved into large-scale independence movements, normally combining coalitions of notables, groups of intellectuals and students mobilized by nationalist ideology, with elements of the lower classes brought in through street agitation or the clientele networks of the notables. Some became formidable electoral machines, able to win parliamentary majorities through a combination of nationalism in the cities and clientelism in the villages. The Egyptian Wafd and the Moroccan Istiqlal, Mossadeq's National Front in Iran, and the Syrian Kutla (National Bloc) all came close to representing the whole nation against the imperialist power. However, their mobilization of a socially heterogeneous base around the single issue of independence doomed most of them to fragmentation after independence when they tended to lose their intellectual activists and their mass bases (as happened to the Moroccan Istiqlal from which the National Union of Popular Forces seceded) or to factionalize (thus, the Syrian Kutla split into the Damascus-centred Watani and the Aleppo-centred Sha'b parties). The major exception was the Tunisian Neo-Destour Party whose charismatic leadership and exceptional organizational capacity enabled it to make the transition to a ruling single party.

As, from the 1940s to the 1960s, the educated middle class grew and politicization spread to the rural peripheries, several parties of intellectuals were able to develop and fill the vacuum left by the decline of notable parties. The key to this was an ability to bridge the middle class–mass and urban–rural gaps by propagating nationalist and populist ideology and developing formal organization with branches in the provincial towns. Similar to their prototype, the Turkish Committee of Union and Progress (Young Turks), they included several secular nationalist parties such as Egypt's Misr al-Fatat (Young Egypt, later the Socialist Party of Egypt), the Syrian Social Nationalist Party (SSNP),[11] the National Democratic Party in Iraq, the National Socialists of Jordan, and the Arab Socialist Ba'th Party in Syria and Iraq. All combined ideologies mixing nationalism and reformist socialism and support among middle class professionals, army officers and growing student populations with footholds in trade unions and peasant movements. At the same time, communist parties attempted to organize the emerging working classes, achieving temporary successes in Iran, Egypt and Syria; but they were quite vulnerable to ideological factionalism, state repression and delegitimation on nationalist grounds and in some cases remained too rooted in certain ethnic minorities. Finally, widely imitated across the region was the Muslim Brotherhood of Egypt which, attracting activists from religious students and support from the petite bourgeoisie (small merchants, artisans, clerks) and recent migrants to the city, demonstrated the ability of Islamic ideology and militants to build a well-organized mass base, including cooperatives, charities and paramilitary organizations.[12]

The ideological and organizational power of the Brotherhood, the communists and the Ba'thists was demonstrated by their ability to spread across state boundaries. Although still partly leader dependent (the Egyptian Ikhwan temporarily declined after the supreme guide was killed), their remarkable durability amidst state repression and generational change in leadership indicated considerable organizational and ideological institutionalization. However, in agrarian societies where notables and tribal chiefs kept much of the mass public encapsulated in their clientele networks, none of these parties were normally able to mobilize the electoral majorities needed to take power constitutionally (although some entered into coalition governments with parties of notables); and most therefore flirted with attempts to subvert and use the military to gain power.

Party development took somewhat different forms in different states. In the post-Second World War period when the Iranian political system was rapidly liberalized, a number of significant parties were founded. The Democrat Party, a catch-all party including both landowners and intellectuals and centred around the personality of veteran politician Ahmad Qavam al-Saltaneh, actually won a *majlis* majority in 1947. The Iran Party was a liberal grouping of intellectuals. The Marxist Tudeh Party, possessing both middle class and worker activists and the most disciplined organization, led the trade unionization of Iran's emerging industrial working class after the Second World War. Mossadeq's National Front (Jebhe-ye Melli), an umbrella movement of notable parties and middle class parties of intellectuals rather than an organized mass party, nevertheless dominated the *majlis* in the early 1950s on the strength of its nationalist programme and charismatic leader.[13] This pluralism was cut short by the 1953 re-imposition of royal autocracy.

In Iraq, middle class parties could not make breakthroughs into the notable-dominated parliament but developed outside and against it. These included the Istiqlal, followers of Arab nationalist veteran Rashid Ali al-Gaylani, and the liberal National Democratic Party, which grew out of the earlier Ahali group of intellectuals. After the 1958 revolution there was a dramatic expansion in participation as the now-tolerated Communist Party, recruiting from intellectuals, the working class and the Shi'a urban poor, rapidly grew to 25,000 members by 1959 while the Kurdish Democratic Party mobilized the Kurds, both tribal and intellectual, and the Ba'th Party incorporated lower middle class Sunnis. The degeneration of this pluralism into near-anarchy invited unstable military rule until the consolidation of the Ba'th Party regime after 1968.[14]

Lebanon is a limiting case where pluralism survived yet extreme societal fragmentation along sectarian, local and clan lines deterred the emergence of a mature party system in spite of the state's liberal political structures and the gradual political mobilization of both the middle and lower strata. Instead, earlier primitive proto-parties continued to dominate. These were the 'blocs' of notables (zu'ama), typically parliamentary caucuses linked to society through clientele networks rather than extra-parliamentary organization. To be sure, in parliamentary elections from 1951 to 1972, the representation of true party-affiliated deputies climbed from 10 per cent to 30 per cent of the seats, but, where successful, parties were almost always clan led and were only able to mobilize cross-class mass support by ideologizing a sectarian appeal. The most durable and organized such party was the Maronite Kata'ib (or Phalanges) led by the Gemayal clan, which mobilized the Maronite bourgeoisie, the petite bourgeoisie and parts of the peasantry, in opposition to other sects but also often against the main Maronite zu'ama. Other similar but less organized parties included the National Liberals (of the Maronite Chamouns), the Druze-dominated Progressive Socialists (of the Junblatts) and the Dashnak party representing Armenian Christians. The Muslims were represented by zu'ama blocs inside parliament, and outside it were regionally fragmented into urban quarter-based Nasserite or Sunni Islamic groups. Even the Communist Party factionalized along sectarian lines between Orthodox Christian and Shi'a factions. During the civil war, party militias, pushing aside the zu'ama, ruled 'cantons' and collected taxes, with the Lebanese Forces, a Kata'ib offshoot, controlling most Maronite regions and the Shi'a militias, Amal and Hizbollah, emerging to dominate the Muslim regions. In the post-Taif 1992 elections, however, zu'ama domination revived with only 39 of 108 parliamentary deputies being party affiliated; this election did, however, register the post-civil war change in the sectarian balance of power: the Shi'a Hizbollah and Amal, re-invented as parties, won 12 seats, the largely Orthodox Christian SSNP 4, the Dashnak 4 and the Progressive Socialists 4, with the Maronite parties self-excluding themselves.[15]

Single party systems

In a second phase of party development middle class political leaders, variously originating in middle class parties and/or the military, established single party systems as instruments of 'revolution from above' in the 1950s and 1960s. According to Huntington, the single party system originates in a bifurcation between the revolutionary regime and 'traditional' society (or the old oligarchy), its function to both *concentrate* power in the hands of the revolutionary elite (and exclude the oligarchy from power) while *expanding* power by mobilizing a mass constituency. The revolutionary struggle substitutes for party competition in keeping the party dynamic and the ruling elite responsive; where there is little such struggle, the single party tends to be weaker and as conflict with the old oligarchy declines, so does the party's responsiveness to its constituency. Indeed, as the party elite becomes part of a new upper class, the party starts to change from an instrument of revolution into a patronage machine (through which clients seek favours and careerists upward mobility) and finally into an instrument of mass de-mobilization.[16]

Single parties aspired to be mass parties penetrating the peripheries and organizing the masses, but they varied widely in their ability to do so. What Owen calls 'rallies and unions' were relatively weak parties established by military leaders from above (such as the Liberation Rally and National Union in Egypt, the Arab Liberation Movement of Syrian dictator Adib Shishakli and the Arab Socialist Unions (ASU) established by military leaders in Egypt, Iraq, Sudan and Libya). In these parties, ideological commitment was unimportant and nominal membership was extended to virtually the entire population except for active opponents of the regime; this made these organizations vulnerable to infiltration by many contradictory vested interests, even those unsympathetic to the regimes' reform programmes. Such parties were not elite recruitment mechanisms, with the military and bureaucracy remaining the career paths to the top. On the contrary, party offices at the centre and province were staffed by ex-military officers and bureaucrats 'on loan' rather than by political activists; the top layers of the party hierarchy were thus a mere auxiliary of the bureaucracy, incapable of channelling participation or aggregating interests. Harik calls this sort of organization a 'collaboration movement' because at the local level it co-opted notables (and their clientele networks) who were allowed a relatively free hand in their locales in return for acquiescence in the regime but had no say in national policy; as such, these parties were also crippled as mobilizational instruments. Those leaders who wanted to carry out a revolution in the village soon became dissatisfied with and tried to transform such organizations. Thus, Nasser tried to reinvigorate the ASU by recruiting a cadre of young militants on ideological grounds to displace or balance the village notables but abandoned the effort after the 1967 war. In Libya Muamer Qaddafi attempted to invigorate his mass organization by encouraging a 'cultural revolution' against the bureaucrats and tribal leaders and by recruiting ideological militants into 'revolutionary committees' meant to 'guide' the wider mass membership.[17]

Stronger single party regimes resulted when the party, through a history of grassroots struggle, acquired a cadre of militants and some roots in the population prior to the assumption of power. Subsequently, party leaders normally adopted a 'Leninist' strategy of party building from top down, in which ideological militants recruited from plebeian strata established party cells in villages, factories, and schools, while creating or taking over labour, peasant and youth unions. The ruling party acquired a full time professional apparatus, and a pyramid of congresses, partly elected, partly co-opted, linked base and centre. The party might share power with a charismatic leader and/or the military, but the sign of its 'strength' was its greater centrality in the performance of political functions than in the 'rally' form of single party. Thus, the party organization was a major ladder of recruitment into the political elite, its top congress, representing the regime elite assembled, had some role in policy making, the party normally subordinated and supervised the government bureaucracy in the implementation of policy and, at the local level, party militants played a key role in social reforms, notably land reform. The Destour Socialist Party in Tunisia, the Yemen Socialist Party (Previously National Liberation Front) in former Democratic Yemen, and the ruling ba'th parties in Syria and Iraq approximated this model. The decline of the party tended to be accompanied by its displacement from policy making, by the ascendancy of the military over it (as in Syria under Asad), by its transformation into a creature of personal rule (as in Iraq and Tunisia) or by its degeneration into personal and tribal factions (as in former Democratic Yemen where the party violently self-destructed).[18]

The Syrian Ba'th case is representative of the more highly developed kind of single party system. The Ba'th Party had a long history of political contestation and enjoyed certain roots in the villages, unions and campuses prior to its power seizure via an army coup; subsequently, however, a Leninist-type party apparatus was built from the top downward, linking up with and expanding the ba'th's pre-existing bases, notably in rural society. Though reduced after 1970 to but one arm of Hafiz al-Asad's presidential regime, the party nevertheless remained at the centre of governance in Syria.

The party hierarchy (as it stood in the 1980s) rested on a base of 11,163 cells grouped in 1,395 'basic units' located in villages, factories, neighbourhoods and public institutions; these formed 154 sub-branches at the district (*mantiqa*) or town level; and these constituted 18 branches in the provinces (*muhafazat*), big cities and major institutions (such as a university). A parallel structure existed inside the army. Each level of organization had its own assembly and executive 'command' (*qiyada*) – headed by an *amin* (secretary). At the national level, the party bases were represented in an elected party congress of 771 delegates which in turn elected the 21-member politburo (or regional command).

Party congresses were, in principle, the supreme policy making body in Syria. In fact, before Asad's 1970 takeover, party congresses laid down ideological doctrine and long-range programmes, decided between or reconciled competing ideological (moderate and radical) factions or legitimized changes of course resulting from major regime splits. Even after 1970, when the presidency concentrated much policy making power, party congresses, in bringing together party apparatchiki, senior army commanders, ministers, governors and interest group leaders, were the political elite assembled and hence arenas in which rival bureaucratic interests and intra-elite conflicts were reconciled. Although congresses ceased to reflect open ideological struggle, their resolutions did tend to have a statist policy bias, arguably expressive of a certain institutionalization of Ba'th party ideology and potentially at odds with the periodic presidential-sanctioned moves toward liberalization promoted by technocratic ministers. These congresses were also occasions of vociferous criticism by delegates of members of the party and government leadership over corruption and incompetence, some of whom were then removed in elections to the regional command that followed. Whether this reflected the party 'bases' holding leaders accountable, feuding elite factions using the peccadilloes of their rivals to bring them down, or Asad's use of such arenas to put some limits on corrupt practices, party congresses arguably functioned as a limited accountability mechanism. However the absence of a congress between 1985 and 2000 vitiated this mechanism and was a sign of a relative decline of the party in the political system.

The party's politburo (or regional command) operated as a middle level policy making and implementation organ under the presidency and within the guidelines of congress resolutions. It was politically superior to and officially nominated the governments that the president appointed, with the members of the command keen to insert clients in ministerial positions. The command, through its array of specialized offices (bureaux for peasants and agriculture, economy, education, workers, youth, etc.), coordinated the work of ministerial officials and interest group (professional, peasant and labour union) leaders in the implementation of the party's policy. A separate 'national command' was responsible for party ideological indoctrination and relations with ba'th party branches outside of Syria.

The 500,000 member bases of the party organization incorporated and, to an extent, empowered the regime's constituency, a middle- to lower-class 'populist alliance'. More than 60 per cent of members were from the lower (worker and peasant) classes and only 2 per cent from upper/upper middle strata. Equally important in a fragmented society, the party recruited across and hence helped to bridge the urban–rural and sectarian cleavages in Syrian society. Moreover, the party was a ladder of upward political mobility through which plebeian elements continued to be recruited into the elite. This and the need of the party elite to sustain its bases of support tended to constrain regime departures from the statist and populist policies that apparently favoured its constituency. Finally, the local party organization gave the regime roots at the base of society; at the village and district level, the party and its auxiliaries, notably the peasant union, were typically made up of educated youth, the local schoolteacher, and middle peasants in the cooperatives. On behalf of such constituents, the local party intervened with the bureaucracy to redress grievances, place clients in jobs, and generally to lubricate the creaky workings of the bureaucratic state.[19]

The Algerian case is mid-way between the weak and the strong types of single party systems. Algeria's struggle for independence gave birth to a succession of mass parties that expressed the dominant nationalist and Islamo-populist political culture; yet these parties did not effectively institutionalize the participation and ideology of their constituencies.

The Algerian People's Party founded by Messali Hadj was a mass movement seeking independence through demonstrations and strikes. When this failed, the FLN (Front de Libération Nationale), an elite guerrilla organization, mounted armed insurrection; the FLN evolved into an umbrella embracing autonomous guerrilla clans and absorbing almost all pre-existing political groups, including the People's Party. In this process, the FLN was factionalized and after independence, its constituent parts were absorbed into the army and bureaucracy or went into opposition, leaving it a moribund shell subordinated to the military. In the 1970s, President Boumediene revived the FLN as a bureaucratic apparatus with 10,000 party workers, controlling the mass organizations and charged with carrying out his 'agrarian revolution'. Its congress was, moreover, the formal arena in which the succession of President Chadli Ben Jedid was brokered.

When, however, the FLN was perceived to deviate from the dominant populist ideology, it lost mass support and the opposition FIS (Front Islamique du Salut) took over the expression of the national consensus; based on thousands of mosques, its cadre of imams preached against government corruption, appealing to the commercial strata marginalized by the state (who financed the organization), and to the educated unemployed and recently urbanized; the FIS's base of support was chiefly distinguished from that of the FLN by its exclusion from state patronage networks. The military's repression of the FIS after it won the 1991 elections left Algeria without an effective party system.[20]

Limited party pluralism

In the next phase of development beginning in the 1970s, the region was dominated by post-populist republics or monarchies under which a dominant president or monarch allowed limited scope for political pluralism. Such states were associated with two main types of party system, the 'dominant party system' (in which the ruling single party permits small opposition parties) and the 'palace-dominated multiparty system'.

The dominant party system was an outcome of the liberalization in the authoritarian republics beginning in the 1970s. As the populist consensus that accompanied single party rule collapsed and rulers began to economically liberalize against the resistance of statist interests while populations threatened by this turned to political Islam, regimes sought to mobilize social forces favourable to liberalization, find ways to co-opt opposition, and trade limited participation rights for public acceptance of the gradual abandonment of the populist social contract. Their strategy, a limited pluralization of the party system was, arguably, an adaptation to the ideological pluralization of the political arena.

Egypt after Nasser is the best case of the dominant party system in the Middle East. As Egypt's Nasserite consensus dissolved, the all-embracing ASU was disbanded in 1976 and some of its fragments or the remnants of pre-revolutionary parties allowed to constitute themselves as 'loyal' opposition parties – provided they refrained from 'destructive' criticism of regime policy. While the presidency remains the centre of authoritarian power and beyond accountability, and the ruling party never fails to win a large parliamentary majority, opposition parties are allowed to compete, not for governing power, but for *access* to power (e.g. parliamentary seats) and for the patronage at the command of the ruler. While the dominant government party seeks to straddle the centre of the political spectrum, opposition parties flank it on the left and right.

The ruling National Democratic Party (NDP) is a direct descendant of the ASU, incorporating the ruling alliance of senior bureaucrats, top police and army officers, businessmen, and the provincial landed notables, albeit shorn of the left-wing intellectuals and politicized officers who briefly dominated the ASU. The NDP's ideology of a mixed economy was compatible with both the public sector in which many bureaucrats and state managers had a stake and the growing role of private and foreign capitalism from which both officials and pro-regime businessmen were being enriched. The party did not determine government policy (which ignored many of its recommendations) but its parliamentary caucus was the source of a stream of initiatives and responses to government meant to defend or promote the particular interests of elements of its largely bourgeois constituency while providing its MPs access to patronage.

More an appendage of government than an autonomous political force, the party enjoyed little loyalty from its members, had few activists, hence only a primitive organization. This reflected its lack of interest in mass mobilization; if anything, its function was to enforce demobilization. As such, it had to depend on village headmen and local notables to bring out the vote; it also lacked financial resources to back its candidates who depended on personal resources to run their campaigns and on their ability to deliver government patronage to attract votes. Nevertheless, by way of the clientele networks of the notables it co-opted, the NDP brought a portion of the village and urban masses into the regime camp, denying the opposition access to them; it also nominally incorporated large numbers of government employees and, an instrument of corporatism, placed its partisans in the top posts of many of the professional and labour syndicates.

An array of opposition political parties seemed to give expression to different interests and values than those of the ruling party. More than personalistic factions, they either revived some pre-Nasser political tradition or were rooted in a major societal or issue cleavage, and the rough correspondence between their ideologies and their social bases seemed for a while to be moving Egyptian politics beyond a mere competition of patrons and *shillas* without social roots. Two liberal parties grouping landlords and wealthy professionals positioned themselves to the 'right' of the ruling party: the tiny Liberal (*Ahrar*) Party and the New Wafd, the voice of the old aristocracy excluded from power by Nasser and of the wing of the private bourgeoisie still antagonistic to the state. On the left, the National Progressive Unionist Party (NPUP) or *Tagammu* brought together, behind an ideology of nationalist populism, a coalition of Marxist and Nasserite intellectuals and trade union leaders under the left-wing ex-Free Officer, Khalid Muhyyi ad-Din. It had a small but well organized base of activists, but the regime, in intimidating trade unionists into distancing themselves from it, robbed it of its putative mass constituency and it later degenerated into a government-aligned faction opposed to political Islam. The Socialist Labour Party (SLP), a descendant of the radical nationalist pre-1952 Misr al-Fatat, began as a defender of the public sector and critical of western alignment, but, lacking a mass base, moved into close alignment with the Muslim Brotherhood under the slogan 'Islam is the solution.' The Brotherhood itself, never legalized as a party, nevertheless stood candidates as independents or under the SLP banner. Led by *'ulama* and wealthy merchants, it was silent on the regime's economic liberalization but highly critical of its western alignment. While the movement was weak among industrial workers and peasants, it was strongly attractive to more 'marginal' elements such as educated unemployed rural migrants and the traditional mass of small merchants and artisans who wanted an 'Islamic economy' that accepted private property and profit but sought to contain their inegalitarian consequences by a moral code and a welfare state. The Brotherhood was differentiated from smaller more radical Islamic groups by its willingness to proselytize peacefully within the political system.

As strategies for accessing power, opposition parties could lean either toward demonstrating loyalty to the regime in order to get patronage or toward mobilizing and representing constituencies. If they attempted the latter they could, as in the (pre-democratic) Mexican political system, become 'parties of pressure' mobilizing interests outside the ruling coalition and, as they captured popular support, forcing the dominant party to adopt parts of their programmes; such a dynamic would allow the opposition parties to influence policy and defend the interests of marginalized sectors of society. The conditions for this outcome included sufficient organizational ability on the part of the opposition parties, sufficient political freedom to access the masses, and some freedom of electoral competition.

The potential for institutionalization of such a relatively representative dominant party system peaked in the 1984 and 1987 elections which were the most open and competitive since 1952 and in which issues carried the greatest weight. In 1984 the New Wafd and the Muslim Brotherhood formed a joint ticket that captured 58 of 448 seats with 15 per cent of the vote and emerged as the main opposition forces; in 1987 the New Wafd, competing alone, got 35 seats, while the small Liberal and Labour parties, joined with the Muslim Brotherhood in the Islamic Alliance, won 60. Thus, while the government majority remained unchallengeable, it had declined and the Wafd and the Islamic movement emerged as a significant opposition presence in parliament. For opposition activists, elections gave the chance to affect public opinion and raise issues that would otherwise have remained off the public agenda. In parliament, the Liberal and Wafd parties advocated economic and political liberalization, the National Progressives defended labour and peasant rights, and the Islamicists won Islamization concessions from the secular regime.

However, the regime stopped short of allowing (and even reversed) the political freedoms needed to expand party pluralization to the level of the mass public and make the opposition parties effective parties of pressure. The government's manipulation of electoral laws, its monopoly of the broadcast media, severe restrictions put on the opposition's ability to campaign and associate, intimidation of opposition activists and the often fraudulent administration of elections by the Interior Ministry all enforced the message that the opposition would not be allowed to translate its potential support over issues into commensurate votes and seats in parliament. The low turnout for elections indicated that many Egyptians were unconvinced that voting under these conditions made any difference to political outcomes; those who did vote, behaving rationally, voted according to a candidate's perceived ability to deliver patronage, a resource largely controlled by the regime.

In this situation, the government party was able to co-opt the local notables with the best personal followings and family alliances who, knowing they had to deliver government patronage to retain their seats, were deferent towards it. Because opposition parties also needed to deliver patronage they too tended over time to mute their opposition. The one exception to the enervation of the opposition parties was the Muslim Brotherhood which alone possessed a significant cadre of activists, independent financial resources, and real organization; precisely for this reason it became the main target of government repression, suffering massive arrests of its cadres at election time, which effectively contained its electoral potential.

In general, thus, the pluralization of the party system actually reinforced the regime: as Maye Kassem persuasively argued, competitive multi-party elections assumed the function of co-opting and taming the opposition while reaffirming and expanding clientelism as the main link between government and the public. Even if some more politically conscious urban middle and working class voters sometimes voted on an issue basis, the government could offset their votes with a mass of rural votes delivered on a clientele basis. The opposition parties channelled political activity that might otherwise have taken a covert, even violent, anti-regime direction into more tame, manageable forms. Additionally, the divisions in the opposition generally allowed the regime to play off secularists against Islamists, left against right.[21]

The transformation of a single party system into a dominant party system is by no means easy or inevitable. Egypt's was the first and most durable such experiment while similar attempts in Algeria and Tunisia failed, resulting in civil war in the first and continued nearly single party rule in the second. Limited pluralism has also taken country-specific variations in Yemen and Iran. The unification of the two Yemeni single party states resulted at first in a unique cohabitation between the two ruling parties, the conservative-tribalist People's General Congress of the north and the ex-Marxist Yemen Socialist Party of the south, later joined by the Islamist Islah party; all, however, remained subordinated to the military presidency.[22] Somewhat different yet was post-revolutionary Iran where the single party, the Islamic Republican Party, never more than an umbrella for disparate groups, dissolved into several clergy-led networks each of which expressed the views of distinct societal constituencies. In this proto-multiparty system, electoral competition was real and came to turn on issues, first the struggle between populist radicals and economic pragmatists; then that between cultural conservatives and liberals. The impact of the electorate on outcomes has, however, been filtered by the 'checks and balances' of the non-elected theocratic part of the political system – the religious leader and the council of guardians which vets electoral candidates.

A second type of limited pluralism is the palace-dominated fragmented party system. The palace pluralism practised by monarchies in Morocco and, intermittently, in Jordan and Kuwait, allows multiple party competition arbitrated by a monarchy 'above' partisan politics. Parties compete for parliamentary seats but if they challenge royal authority – notably to pick and dismiss governments – the king has the option to dissolve parliament, even to close down party politics and assume 'personal rule'.

Monarchic pluralism is most authentic in Morocco. Much more even than in Egypt, the main parties have programmes, organizations and substantial constituencies. In the 1950s the Istiqlal, the mass independence party led by veteran nationalist Allal al-Fassi, had 250,000 active members, branches at the grassroots level and full time party officials; if, at its core, it was the party of the traditional urban bourgeoisie, its vague nationalist ideology allowed it to incorporate a broad societal cross-section, including the urban poor. Its main weaknesses, typical of such independence parties, was an urban centredness that left the rural (and Berber) hinterland in the hands of conservative notables who tended to support the monarchy and its inability to prevent the post-independence breakaway of many of its more radical activists and trade union cadres who formed the National Union of Popular Forces (NUPF).

Above the parties, the monarchy had a unique nationalist legitimacy while controlling the levers of state patronage and of repression (including an army disproportionately recruited from Berber tribes). The king, possessed of these resources and exploiting the Istiqlal's weaknesses, was able to avoid a choice between repression of all party pluralism and letting a majority party or coalition control the government. Rather, he was able to preserve the right to make and unmake governments while allowing enough party pluralism to satisfy participatory pressures.

The king sustained royal power by dividing and forcing parties to compete for his favour. To be played off against the urban-centred opposition parties, there was always a party of the 'king's men', recruited from the high bourgeoisie and the traditional rural Berber tribes. Ironically, the main parties fragmented precisely over whether to play the king's game, with the NUPF splitting from the Istiqlal over its refusal to play and it itself later eclipsed by breakaway elements that were willing to do so (which formed the Socialist Union of Popular Forces). Thus, Morocco's party evolution has been away from a single mass party toward increasing party fragmentation and weakness, a reflection of the declining mobilizational capacity of the parties and the divide and rule policy of the king.

Under this system, the parties do have a role in providing the ministerial elite and in mediating between the king and people. The king tolerates this limit on royal sovereignty because he found the narrowing of his support under personal rule invited instability (attempted coups), and because limited pluralism actually helped, as Zartman argued, to consolidate the regime. Their participation in the system not only co-opts the party elite but, because their inclusion requires they moderate the demands of their constituencies, it tends to weaken their societal support to the king's benefit. In Owen's view, the parties have been reduced to pressure groups for particular interests, their cohesion resting on their ability to obtain government patronage by appeasing the monarch. Yet, parties have regularly demonstrated sufficient electoral support that the king has felt obliged to include them in government or, alternatively, to take the wind out of their sails by co-opting their demands as his own; in this sense they function as 'parties of pressure' serving as crucial safety valves by ensuring some responsiveness to interests outside the establishment. Even when the parties have turned radical and resorted to strikes that have degenerated into urban insurrection over economic deprivation, they have been useful to the king in that examples are made of them: jail terms for their leaders, followed by amnesty and possibly co-optation. Thus, the Moroccan monarchy has been able to simultaneously tolerate partisan activity and remain in control of it by an assiduous exploitation of the societal cleavages expressed by the fragmented party system.[23]

In Jordan, an artificial state with little identity of its own, hence highly vulnerable to the 'transstate' feature of Arab politics, palace pluralism was more limited. Jordan produced only one purely Jordanian party of significance, the National Socialists of Sulayman Nabulsi, and it was anti-royalist. All other credible parties have been branches of transstate movements: the ba'th and communists were strong in the 1950s, and thereafter the offshoots of the Palestinian PFLP and DFLP, and the local branch of the Muslim Brotherhood have been the most durable and credible parties. Given this, the king, despite his ability to manipulate various tribal-based 'palace parties,' could not afford to permit party politics to develop unconstrained without jeopardizing the very existence of the regime. Nevertheless, Jordan has alternated between periods of limited pluralism and personal rule.[24]

Mass competitive party systems

In the Middle East's most 'advanced' and recognizably 'democratic' societies, Turkey and Israel, mass incorporating competitive party systems play central roles. The alternation in power of ruling and opposition parties is central to the formation and accountability of governments and the party configuration is crucial to their effectiveness.

Turkey's transition from a single to a two-party system in the 1950s remains the prototype for democratization in the region. Each of the two rival parties that emerged incorporated distinct social constituencies: the formerly ruling Republican People's Party (RPP) centred on retired military officers, urban bureaucrats and intellectuals, while the new opposition Democrat Party (DP), led by businessmen and rural notables, appealed to the rural majority. Competitive elections made a difference, for example, in allowing peasant voters to force governmental responsiveness to formerly neglected rural interests. Societal and parliamentary support enabled the majority DP to sustain stable government for a decade.[25]

The two main parties proved remarkably institutionalized, surviving leadership and ideological changes and forced reconstructions during periods of military intervention. The RPP survived the transition to a two-party system, a long period in opposition in the 1950s, and a transformation in its leadership to professionals and intellectuals and of its base to urban white and blue collar workers, becoming, under Bulent Ecevit, a social democratic party. The Democrat Party, although mutating into several new incarnations, notably the Justice Party (JP), could be said to have survived several leadership changes while still representing the same broad business–rural coalition.

After 1960, the two-party system evolved into a multi-party system, reflective of the deepening mobilization and polarization of society, with smaller, more radical parties emerging on the left and right and speaking for those dissatisfied by the two main centrist parties. In addition, periodic military interventions that briefly banned and forced parties to reconstitute themselves, weakened the parties. After the 1960 intervention, the Islamic National Salvation Party, mobilizing imams and religious students as grassroots activists, built an effective organization that incorporated a constituency among small businessmen and artisans, becoming the third largest party. The National Action Party, an authoritarian nationalist, pan-Turkist party with some middle class and youth support, exercised disproportionate influence owing to its pivotal role in making up centre-right coalitions in the 1970s. In this period, the JP and RPP alternated pluralities but the JP was more successful in forming governing (centre-right) coalitions. Intensified party competition and the accompanying scramble for state patronage led to ineffective coalition governments and fiscal deficits that opened the door to political instability and the 1970 and 1980 military interventions.

After the 1980 intervention, the party system became increasingly fragmented. The centre-right split into the Motherland Party (neo-liberal, Anatolian based) and the True Path party (descendant of the Justice Party). The centre-left was divided by rival personalities between the Democrat Left Party of Ecevit, Erdel Inonu's Social Democratic Populist Party, and Deniz Baykal's Republican Peoples Party. Thus was ushered in another period of weak coalition governments, increasingly discredited in the public eye, which ended in the implosion of all the parties except the Islamic Justice and Development Party (descendant of the Islamic Salvation, later the Refah Party) that decisively won the 2003 elections.[26] Its formation of a government, in the face of the Islamophobia of the military, was a test of the power of parties.

In Israel, party development took a similar course. Two strong parties, the dominant left-wing Mapai (later Labor), incorporating the trade unions, and the rightist Herut (later Likud) were initially permanent ruling and opposition parties. By the 1980s, they were alternating in power or occasionally joining in national unity governments. Simultaneously, however, the polarization of society led to fragmentation of the vote and the party system, hence a disproportionate weight acquired by small extremist parties in unstable coalition governments. The result was an ongoing paralysis in foreign policy that obstructed the prospects for Middle East peace. Party weakness was paralleled by the increasing co-optation of ex-generals into party leadership.[27] The Israeli and Turkish cases show that, as mass politicization turns into democratization, party capacity determines the effectiveness and stability of government and where it does not keep up with political mobilization, weak governance results.

It must, finally, be observed that the region's high proportion of *no-party states* arguably reflects certain of its special features, tribalism and oil. The monarchies of the Persian Gulf have dispensed with parties without suffering instability in part because tribal loyalties encapsulated individuals; but additionally because oil rentierism retarded mass mobilization and revitalized the tribes as conduits of patronage and ruling families as functional surrogates for parties.[28]

Trade Unions

The literature on Middle East labour unions is even sparser than that on parties.[29] Unions, class organizations par excellence, are often thought to be marginalized by the power of religion, tribe or ethnicity as foci of identity in Middle East societies still in the stage of early industrialization. Yet, as Beinen and Lockman argue, capitalist penetration divided a portion of the populace between capitalists and workers, and the latter organized into unions against exploitation and insecurity and on the basis of class solidarity.[30] According to Eric Davis, working class solidarity even bridged Iraq's deep ethnic–sectarian divisions for periods.[31] Organized workers made up a small part of the mass population in the Middle East, but they were concentrated in strategic sectors and were frequently the most radical social force. Even in tribal Saudi Arabia pro-Nasserite unionization among oil workers was enough of a threat to invite brutal repression. In Iran, in spite of royal repression, strikes in the oil fields were decisive in paralysing and bringing down the Shah's regime.[32] The precise fate of unions was not, however, wholly in their own hands and reflected their adaptations to the evolution of the regimes and party systems in which they operated.

Unions under early pluralism

Unions emerged on the political landscape in the early pluralist period. Even if still weak, their relatively organized and concentrated numbers made them, at a time when civil society had barely emerged, potentially important allies or opponents of political elites and parties. In Iran, Reza Shah's industrialization and Marxist organizing prepared the way for Tudeh-led unions to briefly exercise real power in the streets and factories after the Second World War. Because, according to Halpern,[33] strikes could seldom win gains (the scarcity of capital and the reserve army of unemployed dictated an unfavourable labour market) and because labour was frequently targeted for government repression, unions tended to seek their ends through politics more than collective bargaining. Thus, in newly independent Syria, the labour movement, facing strict government controls and struggling for the right to unionize without its activists being fired, had a mere 6,000 members in 1947, rising to 46,000 by 1958; it was the simultaneous rise of Ba'thist–communist influence in government and in union leadership that started the expansion of labour rights.[34]

Because capital was often foreign in this period, the working class struggle overlapped with and tended to radicalize the nationalist one. Thus, in Egypt, the 1919 revolution was a catalyst of union militancy and Wafd leaders, in the forefront of union leadership, sought to both use and contain labour militancy. In Tunisia and Morocco unions were pivotal to the independence struggle. In Iraq, railway, port and oil workers organized by communists and militant nationalists were in the vanguard of the struggle against the British and the monarchy.[35] Similarly, in Yemen, Aden port workers provided organized shock troops for the National Liberation Front.

Unions under authoritarian–corporatism

Where Labour unions were active in the nationalist movement, they became partners in governance with the ruling nationalist parties in the post-independence period. Yet, across the region, this issued in corporatist arrangements tying unions to authoritarian nationalist states which insisted that all classes had to subordinate their special interests to the national development project. Under a populist 'social contract' unions, in return for eschewing strikes and enhancing productivity, acquired privileged access to power and favourable labour legislation. Labour leaders had to walk a fine line between serving their constituency and their political masters.

As, however, statist development broke down amidst a capital accumulation failure, regimes began to renege on the populist social contract: the success of economic liberalization and revived private accumulation required that investor rights take precedence over worker entitlements, ending the coincidence of interest between regimes and unions. From the 1970s, trade unions had to struggle to keep their members' conditions from declining yet nowhere were they able to assert independence from government. Rather, the earlier populist form of inclusionary corporatism gave way to an exclusionary variety in which unions became instruments for controlling labour discontent.[36]

Several country cases illustrate the varying fates of unions under authoritarian–corporatism. Under the Syrian ba'th, the populist version of corporatism was institutionalized. Unionization, accelerating parallel to development of the public sector, reached 540,000 members in 1992, about three-quarters of them public sector workers. Ba'thist corporatism drew its initial 'populist' character from the fact that the party, seeking to mobilize popular support against the old classes it overthrew, accorded unions privileged access to power denied to the party's bourgeois rivals. But gradually, unions were transformed into corporatist transmission belts of the ba'th regime, enforcing its policies more than struggling for workers' rights; union leaders actually collaborated in suppressing strikes in the public sector.

The Syrian labour confederation became, as Perthes put it, a kind of 'chamber of the public sector,' representing its interests – in which arguably workers had a stake – in the political system, initially trying to protect it against corruption and later from the threat of privatization. After 1977, Izz ad-Din Nasser, a powerful 'Alawi syndicalist on the party regional command, developed the union into an apparatus running hospitals and clinics for its members, owning enterprises, and represented on state decision-making bodies affecting workers. Most important, its representation on the public sector manager appointment committee enabled it to vet candidates (together with the party and Industry Ministry), making managers' career prospects dependent on union goodwill; this enabled Nasser to turn the union into a font of patronage resistant to public sector rationality and reform.[37]

The Egyptian case illustrates the transition from populist to post-populist corporatism.[38] The Free Officers that made Egypt's 1952 revolution professed a corporatist view of society but corporatism can serve quite different development strategies. While the regime was still looking to encourage private and foreign capital, it was ready to repress workers (as at Kafr al-Dawwar). Once it embarked on a statist course, it was more interested in winning their support (against the capitalists it was starting to subordinate): hence progressive legislation expanded workers' rights, notably job and social security. Yet union activists were not passive in this process: they successfully demanded creation of a central union federation in the belief it would concentrate worker power (opposed by the interior ministry for precisely this reason) and they won guaranteed access to policy makers. The quid pro quo was that the union federation accept the regime's screening of its leadership candidates, tolerate repression of Marxist activists demanding union independence, and restrain, not facilitate, worker demands once favourable labour legislation had been conceded. In fact, union activism declined and strikes became relatively rare and localized. Workers accepted this in part because most identified with Nasser and his nationalist developmental project while he felt constrained to meet the expectations of his constituency.

As, however, Sadat and Mubarak shifted their political base away from labour and moved to meet the demands of private capital, relations with government changed. Spontaneous local strikes, though illegal, greatly increased as anger at withdrawals of acquired rights generated a sense of solidarity among workers. The government repressed these strikes but, to contain them, also made concessions. This tendency to prioritize containment of threats to its political legitimacy over the financial profitability of public sector firms gave union militants some clout. Moreover, the Labour federation struck alliances with public sector managers to successfully obstruct early post-Nasser attempts to privatize the public sector where job security was highly valued.

By the 1990s, however, the indebted Mubarak regime, no longer able to evade IMF pressures and consolidating its alliance with business associations, pushed ahead with privatization. The union leadership, now protected from electoral removal by the membership and either co-opted by privileges or intimidated by the deployment of security forces against recalcitrant unionists, could not resist regime pressure to accept privatization. It attempted to protect worker rights under privatization, but only by lobbying, not by trying to mobilize the union bases. Thus, even as labour's main gain under Nasser, the security of public sector employment, was being lost, the regime used its corporatist mechanisms to paralyse union resistance. Union militants, in response, began a new phase of struggle for trade union independence and the right to strike.

The Tunisian case illustrates how an autonomous trade union movement was incorporated into a populist–authoritarian regime and after a period of union–regime struggle, subjugated as an instrument of post-populist control over Labour. Tunisia's Union Générale Tunisienne du Travail (UGTT) began as an exceptionally powerful union. It was a partner of the Neo-Destour party in the nationalist struggle with a mobilizing ability not matched even by the party. In the 1950s, the UGTT had a core of experienced cadres and 150,000 members, 70 per cent of workers. It became a near co-equal of the party in government. Four-fifths of unionists also belonged to the party, so there was no clear institutional conflict of interest; indeed union leaders were frequently appointed to high state and party posts.

In the late 1950s, however, the union leader, Ahmad Ben Salah, was purged for advocating radical socialist reforms. Thereafter the union leadership sought to defend workers' specific interests in regime councils but in 1965 it was again purged for its defence of union autonomy. Nevertheless, in 1969–70, the union achieved the right to collectively bargain with the employers' organization and in 1977 it accepted a social charter under which government mediated wage demands between labour and capital. However, as government policy moved from populism to neo-liberalism, union and government became regular antagonists; union leader Habib Ashour became increasingly critical of the government and resigned from the party leadership under union rank and file pressure. In 1978, as wages failed to keep up with inflation, the left wing of the union encouraged strikes culminating in a national strike and riots put down by security forces under command of the future president, Zine al-Abidine Ben Ali; Ashour, who had failed to condemn the riots, was briefly jailed. When bread riots against reductions in subsidies erupted in 1984, Ashour was again jailed. In the 1980s, the economically liberalizing prime minister, Muhammad Mzali, seeing Ashour as his main rival, used massive police repression against the union, including a purge of militant syndicalists (replaced by moderates unwilling to confront the government) and withdrawal of the union's right to collect dues (which made it dependent on the government for its finances). Under Ben Ali, this subjugation of the union was a precondition for pushing through the labour 'reforms' needed to attract private investment.[39]

Unions under deepened pluralism

Moroccan and Turkish unions under mature pluralism did not necessarily carry greater clout than those under corporatism. In Turkey, unions, banned under the Kemalist regime, were legalized in 1947 and the dominant union federation, Turk-Is, took to bargaining for benefits with the party in power. In the 1960s, militant unionists split off from Turk-Is to form DISK (Confederation of Revolutionary Workers Unions), which spearheaded a wave of strikes and helped found a Workers Party. The response of the state was the military interventions of 1971 and 1980 which banned the Workers Party and DISK and rolled back worker rights: the adoption of an export-led growth strategy required the cheapening of labour to make Turkish exports competitive.[40]

The Union of Moroccan Labour began as one of the strongest unions in the Middle East, having 600,000 members; but splits in the political parties that the king encouraged brought similar splits in the union, shattering its solidarity. Unions retained autonomy and the right to strike and government sometimes responded to their pressures; but the unions' militancy brought periodic repression and, aware of Morocco's vast 'reserve army of unemployed', they became self-restraining in their demands.

Arguably, the effectiveness of unions in the Middle East depends less on pluralist or corporatist arrangements, since labour is readily repressed under both, than on whether the state's strategy of development is populist or neo-liberal.

Conclusion: Parties and Unions in Middle East Politics

The important role played by parties and unions in the Middle East should raise serious questions about 'exceptionalist' claims that culture deters wide-scale association there. The spread of literacy, industrialization and class formation propelled politicization and the consequent development of large-scale parties and unions, even if factional *shillas* and clientelism persisted inside formal organizations. Culture is plastic, not static, and it is, thus, political-economy factors (such as level of development, elite strategies and amount of political freedoms) that determine variations in the relative balance between impersonal (rational-legal/ideological) association and traditional forms of *'asabiya* in party and union formation.

In the early pluralist period when no class or state elite enjoyed hegemony over the political arena, ideology, expressive of group and class conflict, allowed individuals and groups to cooperate in the drive for change, and party organization associated them on a less asymmetric basis by comparison to the clientele networks of the notables. But early pluralism remained relatively limited to the upper and middle classes and seldom penetrated the rural areas.

With the rise of populist-authoritarian regimes, party organization proved an indispensable new 'political technology' in the launching of 'revolutions from above' that mobilized and organized large sectors of the middle and lower classes; authoritarian republics that did not develop an effective ruling party proved unstable, such as North Yemen and Iraq from 1958 to 1968. To be sure, party association by itself proved unable to consolidate these states and the resort of leaders to small group solidarity and clientelism as a supplementary political cement inside or parallel to formal institutions tended to curtail political life within ruling parties. However, as the case of trade unions under authoritarian corporatism showed, such tendencies did not render such institutions wholly powerless.

As populist authoritarianism gave way, dominant party systems emerged as instruments of co-optation, clientelism and of divide and rule tactics in the transition towards neo-liberal capitalism, and in certain monarchies party pluralism has played a similar role. Where democratization has advanced, as in Turkey, it depended on the emergence of a mass incorporating multi-party system and is threatened by its seeming decline.

It is, therefore, apparent that party and union development is inextricably bound up with – and cannot be ignored in any convincing analysis of – the very processes of state formation and development in the Middle East.

NOTES

1   Halpern, *Politics of Social Change*, pp. 281–3.
2   Huntington, *Political Order in Changing Societies*, p. 398.
3   Deeb, *Party Politics in Egypt*; Khoury, *The Patterns of Mass Movements*; Rudebeck, *Party and People in Tunisia*; Moore, *Tunisia since Independence*; Harik, 'The Single Party as a Subordinate Movement'.
4   Amin, *The Arab Nation*; Hussein, *The Class Struggle in Egypt*.
5   Of the major texts on Middle East politics, only Owen, *State, Power and Politics*, and Dawisha and Zartman, *Beyond Coercion*, treat parties at any length.
6   Richards and Waterbury, *A Political Economy of the Middle East*, pp. 312–18.
7   Bill and Springborg, *Politics in the Middle East*, pp. 84–105, 235.
8   A few articles have addressed the role of Islamist parties, including Azza Karam, 'Islamist Parties in the Arab world'; Robert Mortimer, 'Islam and Multi-party Politics in Algeria'; and Cecil Jolly, 'Du MTI à la Nahda'.
9   Korany, Brynen and Noble, *Political Liberalization and Democratization in the Arab World*, has no chapter on parties; Salame, *Democracy without Democrats* has a chapter on solidarity groups, but not parties; parties are only mentioned in passing in Norton, *Civil Society in the Middle East*; Abu Khalil's article, 'Change and democratization in the Arab world: the role of political parties', merely assesses the dismal climate for parties and barely mentions actual parties.
10 Goldschmidt, 'The Egyptian Nationalist Party'; Jabbur, *al-fikra al-siyasi*; Jankowski, *Egypt's Young Rebels*.

11 Yamak, *The Syrian Social Nationalist Party.*

12 Mitchell, *The Society of Muslim Brothers.*

13 Akhavi, 'Iran'; Cottam, 'Political Party development in Iran'; Nahavandi, 'L'évolution des partis politiques Iraniens'.

14 Simon, 'Iraq'.

15 AbuKhalil, 'Lebanon'; Suleiman, *Political Parties in Lebanon*; Entelis, *Pluralism and Party Transformation in Lebanon*; Yamak, 'Party Politics'.

16 Huntington, 'Social and Institutional Dynamics of One-Party Systems'.

17 Owen, *State, Power and Politics*, pp. 266–72; Harik, 'The Single Party'.

18 Owen, *State, Power and Politics*, pp. 255–66.

19 Hinnebusch, *Syria*, pp. 76–8, 80–3.

20 Kapil, 'Algeria'.

21 Kassem, *In the Guise of Democracy*; Hinnebusch, *Egyptian Politics under Sadat*, pp. 158–70, 186–222, 302–4.

22 Renaud Detalle, 'Les partis politiques au Yemen'.

23 Zartman, 'Opposition as Support of the State'; Mednikoff, 'Morocco'; Owen, *State, Power and Politics*, pp. 233–4.

24 On recent Jordanian parties, see Brigitte Curmi, 'Partis politiques en Jordanie', and Ellen Lust-Okar, 'The Decline of Jordanian Political Parties'.

25 Karpat, *Turkey's Politics*; Rustow, 'The Development of Political Parties in Turkey'.

26 Landau, 'Turkey'.

27 Roberts, *Party and Policy in Israel.*

28 Olivier De Lage, 'La vie politique en Peninsula arabique'.

29 An anthology edited by Lockman (1994) and monographs on Egypt by Beinen and Lochman (1988) and Pripstein-Posusney (1997) are the notable exceptions.

30 Beinen and Lockman, *Workers on the Nile.*

31 Davis, 'Historiography of the Iraqi Working Class'.

32 Assef Bayat, *Workers and Revolution in Iran.*

33 Halpern, *The Politics of Social Change*, pp. 335–9.

34 Longuenesse, 'La Classe Ouvrière au Proche-Orient: La Syrie'.

35 Davis, 'Historiography of the Iraqi Working Class'.

36 Pratt, *The Legacy of the Corporatist State*, p. 8, citing Huwayda 'Adli.

37 Hinnebusch, *Syria under the Ba'th*; Longuenesse; 'La Classe Ouvrière au Proche-Orient'; Perthes, *The Political Economy of Syria under Asad*, pp. 173–80.

38 Marsha Pripstein-Posusney, *Labor and the State in Egypt.*

39 Halpern, *The Politics of Social Change*, pp. 324–6; Murphy, *Economic and Political Change in Tunisia*, pp. 47–8, 52–5; Richards and Waterbury, *A Political Economy of the Middle East*, pp. 341–2; Ayubi, *Overstating the Arab State*, pp. 211–12.

40 Ahmad, 'The Development of Working Class Consciousness in Turkey'; Margulies and Yildizoglu, 'Trade Unions and Turkey's Working Class'.

FURTHER READING

Classics on Middle East parties include Deeb, *Party Politics in Egypt: The Wafd and its Rivals, 1919–39*; Rudebeck, *Party and People in Tunisia*; Devlin, *The Ba'th Party*; and Karpat, *Turkey's Politics: The Transition to a Multi-Party System*. There is practically no major current book-length study on Middle East political parties available. One survey of parties has been published but it employs no conceptual framework or comparative method and is a mere collection of country cases, although most are very competently written and provide a wealth of empirical information (Frank Tachau, *Political Parties of the Middle East and North Africa*). A special issue of *Revue des Mondes musulmans et de la Méditerranée*, 81–2, 1996, was devoted to parties, combining country cases with a thematic introduction by Pierre-Robert Baduel, 'Les partis politiques dans la gouvernementalisation de l'Etat des pays arabes', pp. 9–51. Turkey is something of an exception to the neglect of parties: see the works by Sherwood (1967–8), Turan (1988), Heper and Landau (1991) and Rubin and Heper (2002). Major studies on workers and labour unions include Martha Pripstein-Posusney, *Labor and the State in Egypt*; Zachary Lockman, *Workers and the Working Class in the Middle East*; and Ellis Goldberg, *Tinker, Tailor and Textile Worker: Class and Politics in Egypt 1930–52*.

CHAPTER EIGHTEEN

Political Life and the Military

GARETH STANSFIELD

Introduction

Middle East political life remains commonly associated with the prevalence of armed forces (of the formal and informal variety) and the involvement of them in the domestic affairs of the states which they are tasked to defend. The prevalence of military regimes and associated coups in the mid-twentieth century created a legacy that has continued into the present, affecting both the actual mechanics of contemporary Middle Eastern states, and popular perceptions as to the prominence of the military in domestic political life. Recent events in the region have done little to weaken the commonly-held assumption that the Middle East is a violent place, subject to the involvement of military forces in political affairs. Indeed, many lay observers consider this relationship to be the norm. However, the common opinion of academics tends to disagree with that of public opinion and, within the scholarly literature, it is now common to discuss the declining role of the military in the affairs of Middle Eastern states.

Whether the role of the military remains all-important as perhaps the media would have us believe, or its influence on political life has diminished as the majority of scholars would argue, is a debate that forms the focus of this chapter. I contend that the relationship between the military and political life in Middle Eastern states has changed particularly from the 1950s onwards. Perhaps this suggests that I support the arguments depicting the normalization of the military. However, 'change' does not necessarily have to mean that the influence of the military has diminished. It may instead mean that the manner in which the relationship between military and civilian political structures manifests itself has altered, becoming less obvious and brutal than it was in the mid-twentieth century. There remains an undeniable imprint of the legacy of military involvement in the affairs of state which is effectively furthering perceptions of the militarization of Middle East politics, from the impressive Soviet-style parades of Saddam's Iraq, through to the presence of conscripts guarding the streets of modern-day Damascus. However, with some notable exceptions aside, what has been the most often used indicator illustrating the dominance of the military in Middle East politics – the coup d'etat – has been in a state of numerical decline since the 1970s. With a coup now indeed being something of a rare event in the Middle East, many observers have equated this lack of overt military muscle-flexing as proof that the role of the military in political life has quantitatively and qualitatively decreased, with the army perhaps adopting a more 'normalized' position within society. This may certainly be the case in some countries – many regimes brought to power by the military, or subsequently threatened by its political aspirations, learned with unsurprising alacrity how to maintain control over their potentially rebellious military commanders. Saddam Hussein's Iraq was perhaps the most notable example of how a civilian regime brutally cowed into submission the army as a source of potential rebellion against the government of the day. In a less bloody fashion, Egypt under Hosni Mubarak presents a more acceptable model of how to preserve civilian rule and normalize the position of the military in society, in perhaps a more constructive and sustainable method than that promoted in Iraq.

Such thinking suggests that the military did not change with the times and, in effect, accepted a position of subordination within the state. To envisage the military as being tamed over the second half of the twentieth century, effectively neutralized as a domestic political force by increasingly shrewd civilian politicians, suffers from viewing the relationship between military and political leaders in a one-dimensional manner, with possible changes in the aspirations of the military leadership not being fed into the equation. While in some cases it is perhaps useful to view the role of the military in political life as being moribund, effectively tamed by the state, the Middle East is anything but monolithic in its political patterns and processes, and it is apparent that in some cases there is validity in describing the military as being satiated, content with its niche in society but maintaining influence over key affairs of state through what Ayubi described as 'the more subtle intertwinings between civil and military structures' (Ayubi, 1995: 257). Indeed, it could be argued that military-led coups were little more than the most obvious manifestation of a breakdown in the very complex relationship between officers and politicians. Therefore, the decline in the number of coups could equally, and perhaps more satisfactorily, be explained in an opposing way – that the decline of coups indicates that the aspirations of the military are being met by the civilian government, thereby negating the need for its violent replacement. If the 'intertwinings' mentioned by Ayubi remain stable and succeed in providing the military with its needs, one could expect the violent expression of the military coup to become a rarity in the political development of the country. Such stability does not logically mean that the role of the military has diminished – it implies that the relationship between military and civilian structures has altered and perhaps matured.

This chapter will analyse this basic issue of how to understand the military–civilian relationship and how it has developed across the Middle East. With the formative mid-twentieth-century period of modern Middle East politics being dominated by coups, the analysis of their causative factors has become the *idée fixe* of the majority of the literature written on the subject. Due to constraints of brevity, the traditional approach of using the military coup as an indicator of the military–political relationship will be developed as the founding point of this chapter. However, its limitations as an analytical tool employed to explain the contemporary relationship will also be assessed.

The Military Coup d'Etat

With the first wave of military coups occurring in the mid-twentieth century, it is common that most accounts choose this most volatile of periods as the starting point for analyses addressing the role of the military in political life. Some observers, however, feel that the martial proclivity of Middle Eastern society is even more deeply embedded and choose to delve earlier into history to illustrate that the association of the military with political life is not a phenomenon peculiar to the mid-twentieth century onwards. The appetite for the combative undertakings of the Arab people, for example, and the supposed martial leanings of Islam form common arguments that characterize the discourse looking at the origins of the importance of the military in the region.

The instability apparent in the mid-twentieth century, characterized by the seemingly incessant involvement of the military in the political life of many Middle Eastern countries, forms an obvious starting point. Emerging from the shadows cast by their imperial masters as newly independent states, newly formed governments found themselves often unable to unite unstable societies behind their colonialist-coloured visions of what the state should 'be'. Beyond these domestic stresses, regional and external factors also served to undermine whatever limited legitimacy the incumbent civilian governments possessed. Combined with this domestic fragility, itself pernicious enough to undermine many governments, was the catalyst of an external foe in the form of Israel. The inability of Arab governments to combat the establishment of the state of Israel, and the subsequent failure of Arab military forces in defeating their enemies (whether Israeli or western) created a wave of antagonism emerging from society against their seemingly inept political leaders. Pre-eminent among the ranks of disgruntled groups was the military itself – embarrassed in the field (armies rarely overthrow governments after victory on the battlefield after all), victims of the perceived corruption of their civilian political masters, yet organized and motivated in a manner unparalleled within the state, the military was both the victim of inept civilian leaders and the avenging agent of change (Rustow, 1963: 10–11). The result witnessed the armed forces of successive countries embarking upon coups in rapid succession to remove incumbent regimes which were often seen as corrupt, inefficient and willing to do the bidding of their colonial sponsors. Exactly why it was the military that led such rebellions will be investigated at a later point. However, even before the end of the Second World War, the prominence of the military in political life and its ability to effect change had been exposed by the instability apparent in Iraq, with the Bakr Sidqi coup in 1936 followed closely by the Rashid Ali revolt of 1941, both illustrating the unpopularity of the civilian governments put in place by the British, and the growing power and support base of the military (Batatu, 1978: 28–9; Picard, 1990: 189). These events proved to be the precursors for more sustained military intervention across the Middle East in the period following World War II. After securing independence in the immediate aftermath of the war, Syria suffered three coups in rapid succession (starting in 1949), and experienced 14 serious attempts by the military to secure power until the ascension of Hafez al-Asad in 1970 (Brooks, 1998: 13). Turkey, perhaps the most 'westward' orientated of Middle East countries next to Israel witnessed the decisive involvement of the military in the downfall of four civilian governments since 1960, whether through full-blooded coups, or through more subtle yet equally effective means (Jenkins 2001: 35). To get an indication of the regional spread of military intervention through this period, Hurewitz charts the involvement of the armed forces in the overturning of eight civilian regimes in the Middle East (including Pakistan) between 1949 and 1969 alone (Hurewitz, 1969: 108–9). The pattern therefore seems to be clear – the mid-twentieth century experienced many occurrences of armed forces in the Middle East choosing to influence the civilian political life of the countries which they were tasked with defending. To understand the processes behind the pattern, however, is a more elusive matter.

Causes of Coups

With modern Middle Eastern history being so heavily punctuated with violent transitions of power, it is perhaps understandable that the most common approach to addressing the involvement of the military in political life has been to find an explanation for why military coups occurred on such a regular basis. Earlier works in particular focused extensively upon the overt, aggressive actions of military leaders seeking a political position in Middle Eastern states by undertaking military coups against their governments. The magnitude of academic effort invested in this direction has perhaps been responsible to a great extent for the continued association of the military with political life in the region. The larger and more diffuse question regarding the position of the military in the state, and the relationship between the military and government in less stressful times has, by comparison, not received the same level of attention (Owen 2000: 199).

This focus upon the occurrence of coups has imbued upon analyses a belief that Middle East political life is inherently unstable, at the mercy of martial intervention and unable to develop in a peaceful, sustainable manner. This direction of analysis led to theories which attributed militarism in politics as peculiar to the region, emphasizing either the presumed natural penchant of Middle Eastern peoples toward martial affairs, or a structural tendency within Islam to promote the relationship between soldiers and politicians (Ayubi, 1995: 258). Halpern openly supported these ideas when he stated that '[s]oldiers have governed a majority of the Middle Eastern countries almost continuously for at least a millennium ... [t]here has never been a tradition in the Middle East of separating military from civilian authority. Quite the contrary' (Halpern 1962: 277). Hurewitz, similarly, begins his extensive analysis of the military's position in Middle East politics by investigating the legacy of Islam, lucidly tracing the military–civilian relationship throughout Islamic history. However, while having undoubted value as a historical exercise, it is perhaps weakened by the fact that many regions have a similar history of militarization, not least western Europe. Continuing the trend, Khuri and Obermeyer noted that 'the early Muslims took advantage of the military-like structural characteristics of the Arabian tribes in order to disseminate the teachings of Islam and expand its conquests' (Khuri and Obermeyer 1974: 56). The findings of this approach are therefore clear – militarism in the Middle East is a product of cultural penchants and confessional tendencies creating a political and social milieu predisposed to the involvement of the military in political life.

Rather than looking toward historical precedents, others sought answers by focusing on the social conditions affecting the Middle East and identified that the emergence of new social structures and the disintegration of traditional systems favoured the development of the army as the ruling group (Perlmutter 1969: 123). The conditions for the rise of the military in what were described as 'praetorian' states were seen to be a combination of poorly considered actions of western imperial rulers, and the perceived deterministic militarism of the Arabs and Islam. In discussing why

Israel was not a praetorian state in 1969 'in contrast to the other states in the Middle East', Perlmutter listed the following necessary conditions contributing to the rise of praetorianism: (1) an ineffective and army-sustained political and civic culture; (2) a low level of political institutionalization and lack of sustained support for political structures; (3) weak and ineffective political parties; (4) lack of common purpose and ideological consolidation; and (5) a lack or decline of professionalism because political considerations win out over those of internal organization and career concerns (Perlmutter 1969: 123–4).

In the hands of an Israeli writer, praetorianism focused on the weaknesses of Arab political culture when compared with that of Israel. Perlmutter argued that Israel had a long established civil structure; was a politically complex and institutionally structured state with highly cohesive and stratified classes; possessed universality and identity of values between civilian and military sectors, and, perhaps most pertinently for our discussion '[encouraged a] policy of depoliticization restrain[ing] the Israeli army and its officer corps from becoming a vehicle for political power' (Perlmutter 1969: 124).

However, even when praetorianism is considered from an overtly Zionist viewpoint, a clear picture is developed that depicts the military in the Arab world, at least, emerging as the strongest sector of society with its members best qualified to fill the gaps that emerged in the decision-making structures of state, whether through structural weaknesses of civic society inherited from previous regimes, or through the supposed war-like nature of Middle Eastern peoples, or perhaps reflecting the stage of political development through which certain countries were passing.

Emphasizing this latter possibility, Halpern saw the armed forces as being connected to the 'New Middle Class' of non-propertied individuals without the benefit of family connections or the ability to survive from traditional patrimony. Faced with dealing with the tensions of class differences, the 'New Middle Class' penetrated the expanding army and made it the vanguard of its cause, overpowering the ruling classes with a wave of military coups (Halpern 1962: 278–9). With reference to Iraq, Batatu supports this essentially class-based analysis, at least of the earlier coups: '[these first coups in Iraq] represented a successful, even if shortlived, break by the armed segment of the middle class in to the narrow circle of the ruling order' (Batatu, 1978: 28). With regard to events in Egypt, Harb, in a further contribution to the field, traces the high level of involvement of the military in governing the country between 1952 and 1970 and notes that 'staffing the cabinet, ministries and state machinery with military personnel was a constant practice for two reasons: the military's belief that it alone had the bureaucratic organizing skills to run the affairs of the state and assuring control over a traditionally independent bureaucracy' (Harb, 2003: 4–5).

Therefore, in addition to being ideally placed to assume power in Middle Eastern states through the general weaknesses endemic in society as depicted by the supporters of praetorianism, the military could also be considered as being the most organized group at the vanguard of social change. Ayubi discusses military intervention into political life as a result of the absence of institutional and sociological hegemony in the society, leading the military to undertake 'wars of manoeuvre' to capture the state machinery. Military regimes would then undertake radical socioeconomic reforms, as was seen in Turkey, Egypt, Syria and Iraq as a means to safeguard the position of the military regime by securing the support of the lower and middle classes, and by reducing the influence of the established classes of the *ancien régime.* The link with class-based analyses comes from the fact that it was common for many officers to hail from provincial areas rather than the landed aristocracy, thereby injecting into the debate class struggle as a motivating force behind the military's involvement in political life. Within Iraq, for example, Baram notes that, with the transformation of Iraq's economy that began in the 1930s, 'young men from small towns in the Sunni–Arab triangle (Baghdad-Mosul-Jazira), and above all, from Tikrit, started to permeate the officer corps' (Baram 2003: 94). This theory was popular, and remains so particularly among those who favour class-based analyses. However, it has also been readily criticized as being too simplistic in explaining the dynamics of the involvement of the military in politics beyond simply seizing power, particularly as new military regimes often acted according to their own peculiar interests, rather than paying heed to the aspirations of any particular social class. Indeed, while many military regimes adopted Marxist slogans to promote a support-base among the proletariat, leftist parties were persecuted as much as any other group that were deemed to be a political threat to the regime. Class-based analyses of the military's involvement in political life falter on the initial premise that the military was indeed the vanguard of the 'New Middle Class'. Owen, for example, dismisses the theory of the 'New Middle Class' by suggesting that the link between the middle classes and the military as a motivating political force was not clear cut: '[a]rmies have their own institutional imperatives which mean that their technological, educational or administrative resources are not simply available to the rest of society for whatever civilian purpose they may happen to be needed' (Owen, 2000: 198). The military therefore had its own aspirations. At times these aspirations overlapped with those of other components of society, but often they did not.

The causative factors behind the prevalence of military coups are complex and vary country-to-country in the weight attributable to the range of difference factors. However, it is perhaps misleading to consider Middle East political life of the mid-twentieth century as being unique with regard to the often violent involvement of the military. Across the globe, military coups were, if not common, then certainly not unusual at this time. What perhaps is more unusual is the manner in which Middle Eastern militaries seemingly became a secondary consideration in the affairs of state beyond the 1970s. Writing in 1974, Khuri and Obermeyer noted that '[t]he ascent of the military to power is not a uniform experience – it changes with time and social circumstances'. They went further and contended that '[t]he focus of analysis should be upon the military as a social process rather than upon the simple power politics of individual coups, attempted coups or counter coups' (Khuri and Obermeyer 1974: 55). Indeed, to view the military–political life relationship as a positive correlation between the number of coups and the dominance of the military in the state is to ignore the growth and development of Middle Eastern societies and their associated military organizations in the second half of the twentieth century.

The Decline of Coups

If the prevalence of coups was taken as the indicator of the role of the armed forces in the political life of a country, the period beginning with the 1970s would suggest that the presence of military officers within governments was at an all time low, as coups were fewer in number than at any time in the previous three decades (Bill and Springborg 1990: 247). From being, as Be'eri explains, a region suffering from the 'continuous interference and the ascendance of army officers' to, according to Brooks, a region where 'successful military coups have become virtually non-existent since the late-1970s', the Middle East has undergone a significant transformation (Be'eri 1982: 69; Brooks 1998: 13). Out of the 14 main Arab countries, only Egypt and Libya currently have leaders who are in power because they were military officers, and only two more, Sudan and Yemen are governed by what may be described as pseudo-military figures (Rubin 2002: 3). As the armed forces have become a more institutionalized and regularized feature of the political landscape of the Middle East, the manner in which the military chooses to influence the political direction of the state has become less obvious and more clinical rather than flagrant and brutal in its character. Similarly, by the 1970s, political leaders, many of them benefiting from military coups empowering them in the first place, learned how to maintain their hold on power whether through the accommodation of the military, as occurred in Egypt under Mubarak, or through the taking over of the military as occurred in Iraq under Saddam.

If we return to the earlier theories of military involvement in political life, including the perceived aggression of the Arabs and the militarism of Islam facilitating the creation of a society prone to the intervention of the military in the affairs of state, it is somewhat difficult to understand why military coups have been relatively scarce from the early 1970s onward. Has the nature of Middle Eastern society changed? Is the region no longer home to pockets of instability allowing for the emergence of organized forces capable of hijacking the levers of power within states? Or has the military changed? Has it become emasculated through the machinations of wily politicians who learned their lessons well regarding how to rise above the threat of military intervention? Or, perhaps, has the influence of the military remained as strong as ever, but has adopted less obvious routes by which to influence decision-making within the state – thereby making the falling incidences of coups somewhat secondary to our understanding of the military–state relationship?

When addressing why military coups were so prevalent in the mid-twentieth century, one is struck by the simplicity of military organization at the time. Middle Eastern armies were often the direct creations of western military missions, creating an army in the image of the occupiers (it will be interesting to see if something similar will happen in Iraq under US tutelage), with tasks limited to certain areas of national defence. This resulted in, firstly, the armed forces being contained and small with an inadequate ability to project power against the enemies of the state. The military, therefore, was a weak but compact entity. Few had air forces, navies were often more symbolic in nature than having any practical application, and it would be some years before Middle Eastern governments would begin to institutionalize internal security forces tasked with defending the governments and regimes from the societies over which they presided, including watching the actions of the military itself. It was, therefore, easy for the most organized component of society – the military – to coordinate coups and remove governments.

Times changed quickly, and to plan a coup became a much more difficult task than in the coup d'état heyday of the mid-twentieth century. Firstly, the Middle East became a major importer of arms, and now accounts for over half of all arms deliveries to the Third World (Ayubi, 1995: 260). With military expansion being readily evident, therefore, it is too simplistic to argue that the reasons for the decline of coups can be found in the declining importance of the military. Indeed, the situation would appear to be quite the opposite as the armed forces are much larger and have branched out into different sections. The Syrian army, for example, numbered only a few thousand men at the time of the first coup led by Husni Zaim, and was still only a paltry forty thousand when the Ba'athists took power in 1963 (Picard, 1990: 193). On the eve of the 1973 war with Israel, it numbered 170,000 men, while President Hafez al-Asad left the army standing at half a million strong by the end of the century (Zisser 2002: 122). Combined with this increase in overall numbers of men (and women, in Israel) serving in the military has also come the segmentization of the organization. Through linkages with the military of western countries and the Soviet Union before its demise, Middle Eastern armed forces now commonly have segmented land armies, air forces, navies (although they still remain weak), and an array of specialist outfits. They enjoy access to the latest armaments that require intensive training in order to operate the new systems, and, perhaps more than in the period of the 'prevalent coup', the military may stake a claim to being the most competent segment of society. Picard notes that, in 1985, 66 per cent of conscripts in the Egyptian army were high school graduates, with 14 per cent being university graduates (Picard, 1990: 193). If one accepts that the military forces of the Middle East follow the patterns laid down by their western instructors, it is to be expected that the proportions of educated servicemen have continued to increase. This expansion and diversification of military forces in the region would make the task of a military leader plotting to overthrow the government very difficult as he sought to ensure that he had the support of the many colleagues he would need across the variety of outfits which constitute a modern military machine. However, the relative importance of the military in society would remain as high as ever.

Compounding this first issue of the changing nature of Middle Eastern militaries, contemporary political rulers are themselves the product of the years of the military coups. Therefore, coups are now known events, ones which have certain operational needs leaving a trail of tell-tale signs for the regime's security services (of which there are often many) to predict and prevent such actions. The Middle East is now resplendent with methods aimed at limiting the possibility of a military coup being planned, and if implemented, being successful. The regime of Saddam Hussein in Iraq was perhaps the most adept at neutralizing the threat from the military. In a country which had a long history of political involvement from the armed forces, Saddam moved decisively to ensure that he would not become just another episode in the traumatized history of the state. From seizing power with the assistance of the military, the civilian Ba'ath Party succeeded in removing their partners from their power sharing positions and proceeded to pursue tactics designed to ideologically join the military with the Ba'ath Party, and also to subordinate the military leadership to their civilian masters. In both Iraq and Syria, the Ba'ath governments created comprehensive, overlapping, security networks. The armed forces, therefore, could not operate against the government secure in the knowledge that their plans remained secret. The eyes and the ears of the government were, quite literally, everywhere as many a military man was unfortunate enough to find out.

To act as an ultimate insurance policy against the military establishment, governments also sought to arm their own loyalists to act as defenders of the regime. In Saudi Arabia, the regular army was matched by the National Guard recruited from tribes deemed loyal to the regime. In Jordan, similarly, the king maintained loyalists from the tribes living in rural areas, ensuring that the urban centres could never militarily mount a challenge against the throne. In Iraq, Abdul Karim Qassim created a private army (the Republican Guard) to act as the defenders of the regime, and Saddam put an extra layer on top of this in the 1990s (the Special Republican Guard) in effect guarding against the guards, just in case. In addition to these traditional military outfits, political leaders developed complex security and surveillance networks, often tasked with watching each other rather than any other group, and the army was a focus of attention for virtually all of them. Saddam, again, perfected this security overkill, but the tactic had adherents across the whole of the region. Syria in particular strove to ensure that the ideology of the Ba'ath Party was imprinted on the military, and maintained the situation with an array of security services quite similar in structure and approach to those of their Ba'athist cousins in Iraq.

Ideas pertaining to the forced dominance of the civilians over the military have merit, if only through the graphic examples provided by the modern histories of Syria and Iraq. However, there are conceptual problems with promoting what would appear to be an overt struggle for control of the state and, if only the arguments given above are followed, a rather one-sided picture is produced that incorrectly assumes that the political culture of the military has remained static to a great extent. Even though it is an incontrovertible fact that the military organizations of Middle Eastern states have expanded over time, the underlying assumption is that the military leadership still wanted to undertake coups, yet just didn't have the opportunities as presented in the good old days of the mid-twentieth century. However, organizations grow and develop, and the military of the Middle East is no exception to the rule. Ayubi establishes the linkage between socio-economic improvements and the military by noting that 'the military elite as a whole (and not only the group that made the revolution) have often managed to benefit in socio-economic terms. The new social opportunities created for all military people may help dissuade potential aspirants from indulging in political adventure again' (Ayubi, 1995: 262).

With the impact of improving socio-economic standards in mind, a more nuanced approach would accept the fact that the reduction in the number of coups was not achieved by coercion and threats alone. The military in Egypt did not suffer the same bloody treatment as was meted out to the military in Iraq and Syria, for example. From being a dominant force during the Egyptian Revolution of 1952, the Egyptian military now occupies a 'behind the scenes' position within the political system due to a 'sidelining' process initiated by President Nasser following Egypt's defeat in the 1967 war with Israel, and continued by his successors (Harb, 2003: 1). This sidelining process was an effective combination of promoting higher levels of professionalism within the military, and enhancing the socio-economic position of the officer corps within society in exchange for support for the regime. The peaceful transition of power within Egypt from Nasser to Sadat to Mubarak is often cited as evidence of the apolitical nature of the Egyptian military. However, it should also be realized that all three presidents were/are military figures themselves and Mubarak continues to maintain strong links with his military leaders. As such, the military continues to be an unwavering support base of the regime, indicating that, while Egypt is for now a coup-free zone, the military is far from being a non-political actor. Indeed, the relationship may be one of reciprocity, with 'the regime look[ing] out for both corporate and military interests [while] the military uses its status and power to support the regime' (Harb, 2003: 9).

It is within this matrix of coercion and accommodation that perhaps we can identify the changing nature of the military's role in the political life of the state. The Middle East is not a homogeneous region and displays an array of political systems, levels of development, and political outlooks. It should therefore be expected that the position within the matrix is different for individual countries. To understand how the position of the military has developed, and why its relation with the state has altered over the last half-century, it is necessary to bring the discussion up to date with reference to the contemporary Middle East. For reasons of space, it is unfortunately not possible to provide a comprehensive account of the military–political life relationship in every state. Instead, situations and developments of particular interest and importance will be identified and assessed.

The Contemporary Situation

The continued pre-eminence of the military in the political life of Middle Eastern states is suggested simply by the sheer size of military organizations in the region. An often-used indicator employed to illustrate the importance of the military in the Middle East – defence expenditure – would suggest that the potential for the armed forces to involve themselves in affairs of state remains as high as at any time previously. The high profile of the military in the Middle East reflects the fact that the military establishment across the region remains the largest and most costly in the developing world. According to the Stockholm International Peace Research Institute (SIPRI), in 2001 the Middle East spent an estimated 6.3 per cent of Gross Domestic Product (GDP) on armed forces, nearly three times greater than the global average of 2.3 per cent. To give some idea of the high level of spending, North American expenditure was estimated at 3 per cent of GDP, and western Europe was again lower at 1.9 per cent. The size and importance of the armed forces in the Middle East in terms of the investment made into their structures would support the notion that military leaders continue to have the means to occupy a pre-eminent position in political life (Bill and Springborg, 1990: 247).

Therefore, defence expenditure remains high and the historical legacy of military intervention is obvious for all to see. It should thus not be surprising that events continue to occur that graphically illustrate the fact that the military in the Middle East has not yet totally disengaged from political life and, even though the number of coups may be declining, military organizations in the Middle East are still able to display their political muscles. In undertaking a discussion focusing on the contemporary military–civilian relationship in the region, it is necessary to introduce a classification enabling meaningful comparisons to take place. For the purposes of simplicity, and the fact that his divisions are logically based and remain analytically valid, I will employ the divisions identified by Ayubi and focus on selected countries in each group (Ayubi, 1995: 266). The first group to be addressed are the radical popular republics (Egypt, Syria, Sudan, Libya and, until recently, Iraq). The second group includes the conservative kin-based monarchies. For the purposes of this chapter, I identify a third group of non-Arab states i.e. Turkey, Iran and Israel, with a particular focus on Turkey.

Popular republics: Egypt, Syria and Iraq

I have already said a great deal about the military formations of Egypt, Syria and Iraq. Indeed, as these three countries were home to the majority of the military coups that occurred in the mid-twentieth century, it is understandable that they form a core to an analysis of the subject. However, the three cases exhibit stark differences in the contemporary setting, with Egypt an example of a state with an army seemingly adopting a normalized position; Syria is in an apparent period of uncertainty as President Bashar al-Asad seeks to secure the unreserved support of the military leadership; and Iraq with a military brutalized by the pernicious attention of the Ba'th regime of Saddam Hussein, until it was unceremoniously disbanded after the occupation of Iraq in March 2003.

Egypt remains a primary focus for observers who claim that the Middle East has left its days of military coups behind. Perhaps there is reason to be confident. Mubarak has been successful in quelling Islamist militants, and seems to be triumphant in promoting policies of economic liberalization. As stated previously, the Egyptian army is commonly considered to be the most western of Arab armies, only bettered in the region by the militaries of Turkey and Israel. Stemming from President Sadat's decision in the early 1970s to secure the patronage of the United States rather than the Soviet Union, the Egyptian military underwent a radical process of transformation. Since military aid was made available to Egypt in 1975, the US has contributed nearly $28 billion in weapons sales, training and exercises (Frisch, 2002: 97). An estimated 70 per cent of Egypt's tanks are of western design, the air force now includes the ubiquitous F-16 fighter, and the navy is equipped with British designed fast attack vessels. Exercises with the US are now institutionalised in the 'Bright Star' event that takes place diurnally. However, beyond these rather striking developments in hardware procurement and training, the comparison displays some fundamental flaws.

Firstly, the Egyptian army remains inordinately large when compared with western professional forces that are more notable by their compactness. Quoting figures from the International Institute of Strategic Studies (IISS) *Military Balance*, Brooks totals the number of active, reserve and paramilitary personnel at 934,000 in 1997, not far behind the million strong army of Saddam at that time, but equipped with modern US weaponry rather than obsolete equipment of Soviet vintage (Brooks: 1998: 42). The size and power of the Egyptian military is problematic to reconcile with the seeming position of subservience within the state. If we consider the argument outlined earlier by Harb, of the Egyptian military accepting a subordinate role in a system that safeguards its interests, but limits its direct influence in political life, a basic question arises as to how the Egyptian government can afford to accommodate such an immense military in purely economic terms (Harb, 2003: 1). This is of particular importance when we consider the continuing rise of Islamic fundamentalism in Egypt, and the potential recruiting ground a disaffected military of considerable size would undoubtedly be.

The first level of accommodation comes at the highest levels of the military establishment. The leadership of the military constitutes a privileged few in society, able to secure patronage from the president and reciprocating with loyalty of action. Secondly, rather than pursue a Western model of encouraging military staff to live in civilian areas, Egyptian military personnel are isolated in purpose built cities, primarily as a means to limit the influence of Islamist parties attempting to subvert the defenders of the realm. Lastly, and perhaps most importantly, the government made the military into an economic partner in the development of the state, including its own expansion and the construction of military cities. This development of what Ayubi termed a 'military–industrial' complex is how the military continues, in Egypt in particular, to maintain a highly influential position in the political life of the state, and how the Egyptian President continues to be able to fund a military of immense size (Ayubi, 1995: 273). In such an environment, Bill and Springborg tellingly note that 'officers do not have to be in cabinets or parliaments nor stage coups d'etat to have significant influence over important economic and political decisions' (Bill and Springborg, 2000: 268). Through this method, the military became inextricably tied at all levels to the continuing prosperity of the president and government. However, far from being a normalized apolitical institution, disengaged from political affairs of state, the military of Egypt is, in fact, a political actor of considerable magnitude. The lack of a recent military coup merely emphasizes how involved in the state the military has become.

The situation of the military in Syria is perhaps more reminiscent of the post-coup phase of the military–political life relationship, as the regime leadership strives to secure the support of the military to legitimize its own position. The death of Hafez al-Asad in 2000 merely set the situation back thirty years as the military re-appraised its position when faced with the ascendance of Hafez's (non-military) son Bashar.

The influence of the military on the political life of Syria peaked with the 'Correct-ive Revolution' of 1970 that brought Hafez al-Asad to power. The new president, as commander of the air force, had a considerable power base within the military elite, yet as president he still subordinated the military and distanced it from involvement in the affairs of state. An attempt was made to 'professionalize' the army, and it could be seen that it moved away from the previous pastime of the Syrian military – the coup d'état – to a more traditional role for a national army – external involvement in Lebanon and displaying antipathy toward Israel. The pre-eminence of Hafez al-Asad over the affairs of Syria for more than three decades would suggest that he was largely successful in alleviating the threat posed by the military. However, upon his death and the ascendancy of Bashar, many observers doubted the ability of the new leader to survive. The proven ability of Bashar's uncle, Rifaʻat, to organize opposition among the military leadership was proven as long ago as 1984, when Hafez al-Asad suffered a serious illness that brought up the issue of succession (Brooks: 1998: 59). Syria remains in transition as Bashar seeks to stamp his authority on the political system, and the military come to terms with having a new commander who may, or may not, be as forceful as his father was before him. In any case, one can again see that the military remains a potent force within the political life of Syria.

The relationship between the military and political life in Iraq has, for the time being, become a matter for the historical record as, under US occupation, the Iraqi army was disbanded in May 2003. However, Iraq is perhaps the most graphic example of the involvement of the military in the political process. The Iraqi army was first raised on January 6, 1921, even before Faisal was crowned king. It had three tasks: to defend the monarchy from well-armed tribes; to deal with the threat of rebellion, and; to contribute to nation-building via conscription and an inculcated sense of nationalism. The army did these tasks, but senior officers also developed their own vision of nationalism which would ultimately clash with their political masters

(Hashim, 2002: 12–13). British domination of Iraq radicalized the officer corps, and provided fertile ground for the military to plot their involvement in politics. The first coup of the twentieth century in the Arab Middle East occurred in 1936 in Iraq, with the military forcing seven cabinet changes between 1936 and 1941. These early coups culminated with the 1941 coup placing the pan-Arab nationalist Rashid Ali al-Gailani as Prime Minister. His subsequent pro-German position forced Britain to go to war with Iraq in May, resulting in Iraq's reoccupation. The military returned with the coup of 1958 which overthrew the monarchy and established a republic under the leadership of Brig. Gen. Abdul Karim Qassim. The final phase of military activity occurred in 1963. With the assistance of the military, the Ba'th Party mounted a coup which removed Qassim from power, only to be overthrown itself by the military in November 1963. The next five years saw Iraq's political life dominated by the military.

The survival of Saddam's regime can be understood by viewing it as a reaction to the history of involvement of the military in Iraq's political life, and to the lessons learned in 1963. The new leaders of the Ba'th, including Saddam, recognized the threat posed by the military and, when they seized power in 1968, ensured that their army co-conspirators were quickly banished from the state (Anderson and Stansfield, 2004: 550–1). From being the power behind the president in 1968, then becoming president himself in 1979, Saddam Hussein managed to survive by constructing mechanisms which nullified the ability of the military to be involved in the political process. Saddam was also successful in permeating the military with the ideology of the Ba'th Party, as he indeed did with the rest of the state, yet it was his mistrust of his military leaders that led him to establish and develop a security apparatus of Byzantine complexity combined with an Orwellian *modus operandi*. Parallel military structures were also created by the Ba'th regime with the primary task of defending it from any attempt by the military to seize power, a tactic common across many other states (Hashim, 2002: 23). As occurred in Egypt, the military became dependent in a corporate sense upon Saddam's patronage and, with Iraq's considerable economic spending power, became a large well-equipped military establishment by the 1980s.

The conservative monarchies: Saudi Arabia

These states include primarily Saudi Arabia, Kuwait, and Jordan. However, issues identified in this section may also be applicable to other Gulf monarchies. For these states, and particularly Saudi Arabia, while the presence of armed men in society has been common, especially among the tribes of Arabia, the establishment of a professional army was something which happened relatively recently in their histories.

For Saudi Arabia, the issue of the military is extremely sensitive. On the one hand, the area of the country is considerable at over 800,000 square miles, and home to the largest proven oil reserves in the world. This obviously warrants a large, or at least efficient, standing army, particularly after the events of 1990 when Iraqi forces could have marched into the Kingdom with relative ease. Saudi investments in this area would suggest that the government agrees, with spending on defence in the mid-1990s averaging around 17–18 billion dollars per annum. However, for what is a huge amount of money, representing approximately a quarter of the annual GNP for this period, the result has seen only a questionable improvement in the ability of the kingdom to defend itself. Ayubi estimated that half of Saudi defence expenditure in the mid-1990s went into constructing bases and military infrastructure, 30 per cent on training, and only 20 per cent on hardware (Ayubi, 1995: 279). This tends to indicate that the Saudis have some very big bases, with not many soldiers on them. This is particularly embarrassing when it is realized that Jordan and Syria to the north are both oil-poor yet possess military forces of significantly higher numbers and ability than their Saudi neighbours.

The fear of the Saudi government remains the security of the ruling elite and the apprehension of establishing a military force with enough power to overthrow their political masters. Such views may have been implanted by watching the wave of coups occurring in the Middle East in the mid-twentieth century, which only served to prove to the Saudi government that a large military would more than likely turn on its owner, rather than on its owner's enemies. The lack of militarization in Saudi Arabia was also a welcome development for imperial and neo-imperial powers alike. The British were certainly keen to foster the impression that large armies were problematic to its dependants in the Gulf, and the US, ever concerned about the security of Saudi Arabia and its oil supplies, preferred a situation whereby it would assist with external defensive issues, while the Saudi government remained able through loyal tribal militias to maintain its hold on power within the state, with no organized military to oppose it.

With regime security in mind, and recognizing the potential for even the emasculated Saudi army to overthrow the House of Saud, the Saudi government expanded the National Guard as a traditional, and supposedly loyal, tribal force from the 1970s onward. This, combined with financial and material inducements, forms the basis of the security structure for the royal family. Even so, only the forces of the Royal Guard and the Security Forces of the Ministry of the Interior are allowed within the confines of Riyadh – obviously, the government does not feel totally secure even with a vastly weakened military (Ayubi, 1995: 284).

Non-Arab states: Turkey

Perhaps more so than any other Middle Eastern state, the contemporary relationship between the civilian administration and the military within Turkey illustrates the continued influence of the armed forces on political direction. The Turkish state has suffered a history of military intervention during the 1960s, 1970s, 1980s and 1990s in some fashion to reshape Turkish politics, but always returning control to civilians after a short period (Sakallioglu, 2002: 189). The Turkish government claims many attributes which would suggest that civil–military relations are conducted in a manner that enshrines the separation of responsibilities. The existence of a parliament resplendent with opposition forces, an independent judiciary and a media which has at times taken a position against the armed forces may suggest that the era of direct involvement of the military in the affairs of the Turkish state, at least, are over. However, as in many other regional countries, parliament has often been ignored, the judiciary continues to be subservient to its political masters and the media is owned by oligarchic networks which are themselves tied to the military (Cizre, 2000: 23). The strength and influence of the military establishment became apparent on 28 February 1997 when it intervened in the affairs of the civilian government. Facing a resurgent Islamist tendency within the government, the military-dominated National Security Council forced the Islamist Prime Minister Necmettin Erbakan to resign.

Arguably, the military in Turkey is now more powerful than at any time in the history of the near century-old republic (Cizre, 2000: 3).

While the 'February 28 process' in Turkey indicates that the military maintains a constant vigil ensuring that the civilian structures of governance act in a manner in accordance with its own interests, there is a new momentum within Turkey to foster democratic institutions, particularly with regard to securing membership of the European Union (EU) where a government dictated to by its armed forces would not be tolerated. Furthermore, the weakening of the Kurdistan Workers' Party (PKK) of Abdullah Ocalan has removed a further pillar sanctifying the continued existence of extensive military powers within the state itself.

If there are forces working to normalize the position of the military within the Turkish state, such as the needs of the EU and the diminution of the threat from Kurdish separatists, other forces are working to promote the involvement of the military. Situations which promulgated military intervention at earlier moments in the histories of other Middle East states are now commonplace in Turkey. The unwieldy nature of Turkish democracy and its associated corruption at the highest levels has served to promote the military as the most efficient institution within the state – a situation that some theorists believe underlies military coups. Jenkins notes that 'on several occasions in recent Turkish history, political infighting has brought the machinery of government close to collapse. In such situations it has been to the military that the Turkish public has tended to turn, either to intervene directly or to provide leadership in applying pressure to the government' (Jenkins, 2001: 6). The earthquake of 1999, and the associated failure of the government to alleviate the suffering of its civilians did little to weaken these feelings of support toward the military.

As in Egypt, the Turkish military is outwardly modern, with western equipment and even an important part of NATO, yet it remains a large organization standing at nearly a million regulars and conscripts with a track record of recent involvement in the affairs of state. The problem for Turkey is to reconcile two divergent political processes – pursuance of EU membership with the maintenance of an offensive position against the forces of Islamism (which threaten the secular nature of the state) and Kurdish separatism (which threatens the integrity of the state). Combating these twin threats to the Kemalist Turkish state remains the *raison d'être* for the Turkish military, and will continue to provoke its involvement into the civilian affairs of state for some years to come. Jenkins again chillingly foretells that 'under such circumstances, the Turkish military is unlikely to be prepared to relinquish the future of the country to its civilian politicians. For the foreseeable future it is likely to remain in the political arena, not so much initiating policy as ensuring that it remains within what the military believes to be acceptable parameters' (Jenkins, 2001: 84–5).

Conclusion

More often than not, the involvement of the military in political life resulted in a change (or attempted change) of government. Indeed, few states in the region managed to achieve a peaceful transition between leaders in the mid-twentieth century. Still, it would seem that the golden age of the military coup in the Middle East has now waned. The proliferation of coups in the mid-twentieth century served to colour popular perceptions of the position of the military in the political life of the state. Indeed, many observers consider the falling occurrence of military coups as evidence of the relationship between civilian and military structures conforming to the norms of western societies. However, it does not necessarily follow that a reduction in the number of military coups equates to a reduction in the influence of the armed forces in the affairs of state. It could quite easily be considered in an opposing manner – that the military establishments have achieved a level of influence that is considered acceptable to their leaders, and an insurmountable situation to redress by civilian bodies. While it is undeniable that the absolute number of coups declined from 1980 onwards, it is apparent that those regimes which did manage to secure a peaceful transition in recent years (Egypt between Anwar Sadat and Hosni Mubarak and Syria between Hafez and Bashar al-Asad are perhaps the most obvious examples) are still far from secure: Mubarak's government, while enjoying a recipro- cal relationship with the military, remains fearful of the potential influence of Islamists over the rank-and-file, and Bashar al-Asad continues to struggle in legitimizing his presidency and securing the full support of the military leadership. The military may not be out on the street pushing its political agenda, but its role in influencing the direction of political life remains significant.

While it is understandable that such a positive link between military coups and military influence is often cited, it is problematic to accept the relationship unre- servedly. Owen clearly illustrates this problem by emphasizing that the two questions – of causative factors behind military coups and the role of the armed forces in political life – are quite separate. The focus upon the military coup aspect of military influence negates the existence of other less obvious methods by which the armed forces can exert influence over a government – 'officers in barracks can be just as influential as officers in government' after all (Owen, 2000: 198).

The case studies chosen reflect the complexity of addressing the role of the military in the political life of Middle Eastern states, yet all, to some extent, illustrate that the situation is far more obscure than simply describing the situation as 'normalizing'. The relationship between military and civilian actors has matured over a traumatic half century, with both sides establishing new roles and methods of interaction. In some countries, this has been achieved in what may be described as a sustainable 'civil' manner. Egypt, for example, continues to maintain a huge military force, yet the policy of accommodation initially implemented by President Nasser and continued by his successors has brought the military into the very heart of the state by incorpor- ating it into the economy in a highly integrated manner. Other countries, and most notably Saudi Arabia, remain in a situation of uncertainty, driven by fears surrounding the domestic security of the state, yet aware that they are fundamentally weak when compared to their neighbours. Such a situation would drive any government into the hands of a more powerful protector, as it has done in the Kingdom in its relationship with the US in recent years. Yet this only serves to fuel internal instability, further prompting the need for more domestic military forces. Turkey, perhaps, is the ultimate proof that the decline in the number of coups certainly does not equate to the decline in influence of the military in political life. In Turkey, there is an undeni- able history of the military watching the affairs of state closely, ready to pounce when a situation arises that goes against the precepts of Kemalism and/or the interests of the military. Torn between the Kemalist ideals of the modern Turkish state and the post-modern direction of EU membership resplendent with minority rights and freedom of religious expression, even within institutions of government, the

Turkish military remains a potent organization in the changing circumstances of the state.

The hidden meaning behind the quantitative decline in the number of coups occurring in the Middle East since 1970 is not, in the main, to be found in the victory of civilian leadership over the military. Instead, the quantitative decline in coups is more effectively explained by a qualitative increase in the level of effectiveness of the military in the political direction of the state. The manner in which the military chooses to express its political will has perhaps changed more than any particular demise in its weakness. Military coups may indeed be less frequent, but the role of the military in the affairs of state remains an important factor in understanding the stresses and strains that colour contemporary Middle East politics.

FURTHER READING

There are several 'classics' focusing on the relationship between the military and the political life of the state in the Middle East written from the mid-twentieth century onwards, and therefore being written often with a focus on the causative factors of 'the military coup d'état' in mind. The most prominent of these titles includes Hurewitz, *Middle East Politics: The Military Dimension*; Tarbush, *The Role of the Military in Politics: A Case Study of Iraq to 1941*; and the two volumes of Haddad, *Revolutions and Military Rule in the Middle East*. The theoretical focus of much of this early work was derived from wider-ranging works, with concepts and frameworks being adapted from the study of South American and Asian politics. Key references include Nordlinger, *Soldiers in Politics: Military Coups and Governments*; Finer, *The Man on Horseback: The Role of the Military in Politics*; and Johnson (ed.), *The Role of the Military in Under-developed Countries*. Israeli scholars have maintained a strong focus on addressing the military–political relationship within Arab states and Israel and can offer useful analyses from an involved, and at times coloured, perspective. Useful early references include Be'eri, *Arab Offices in Arab Politics and Society*; and Perlmutter, *Military and Politics in Israel: Nation-building and Role Expansion*.

Many texts which have a 'country' rather than specifically 'military' focus offer a wealth of information which merely needs to be consolidated. Iraq has a strong body of literature discussing the role of the military in politics (see Tarbush), but works such as Batatu's extensive *The Old Social Classes and the Revolutionary Movements of Iraq* is an invaluable resource. Zabih's *The Iranian Military in Revolution and War* and Perthes' *The Political Economy of Syria under Asad* perform similar tasks for Iran and Syria respectively. Studies on the military in Turkey are perhaps the most numerous in recent years, with several analytically rigorous monographs appearing, including Jenkins, *Context and Circumstance: The Turkish Military in Politics*; and Cizre, *Politics and Military in Turkey into the 21st Century*.

Recent specific works on the military–political relationship have been few and far between. Several general texts offer very good chapters/sections on the role of the military, including Ayubi, *Overstating the Arab State*; Bill and Springborg *Politics in the Middle East*; and Owen, *State, Power and Politics in the Making of the Modern Middle East*. One recent collection of essays, however, has emerged with an explicit focus on the role of the military in political life. Edited by Rubin and Keaney, their *Armed Forces in the Middle East: Politics and Strategy* attempts to bring up-to-date analyses regarding the military–political linkages in the Middle East with a series of country-based essays.

CHAPTER NINETEEN

Political Economy
From Modernization to Globalization

SIMON MURDEN

Introduction

The economic practices, institutions and relationships that exist within and between societies have always played a central role in shaping the political arrangements of human societies, including which people run political and social life and how they do it. In the study of such political economy, various derivations of Marxist thought have cast an enormous shadow. For Marx, man was an inescapably economic being and his history was a definable process of socio-economic development. The ultimate destination of Marx's theory of historical materialism has been greatly disputed, but the idea that societies go through a process of development has become a basic assumption in western or westernized political economy. What seems indisputable is that the practice of capitalism has driven the process of 'modernization' since the eighteenth century, whereby new forms of technology and organization have transformed the way that many humans live. Many societies that were dominated by an agricultural mode of production were transformed by the advent of urbanization and industrialization. Technology managed the natural environment, while the economics of production, trade and exchange became much more complex and specialized. In many places, modernization also transformed the politics of human societies. Traditional forms of social organization and governance, based on kinship or religion, gradually gave way to more rational and contractual arrangements. Socio-economic class was the dominant social form of modernization, while the territorial state was the political institution that defined modernity.

Modernization was pioneered in western Europe, but the process was to become a truly global phenomenon. Notwithstanding the disadvantages of coming late to the game of capitalism and modernization, many economic theorists and policy makers in non-European societies have assumed that sooner or later their societies would experience modernization too. While the basic trend toward modernization is apparent across the world, the way the process has developed outside Europe has been shaped by the particular conditions that apply. In the 1960s, development theorists in Latin America led the study of less developed societies by describing the problems that made modernization an especially difficult experience in their region. For Latin America, modernizing in a world dominated by western capitalists was a path to dependency and exploitation.

The road to modernization has been similarly difficult for the societies of the Middle East, especially so due to the power and distinctiveness of some cultural ideas and social structures. Modernization in the Middle East has run into, as well as merged with, entrenched forms of culture and social organization. Certainly, it is not necessary to advocate some kind of nineteenth-century Orientalism to believe that the study of political economy in the region must go beyond pure socio-economic theory towards incorporating local conditions. For instance, to reduce Islam to the role of 'super-structural' support for particular class interests does not really do the phenomenon justice. Many human beings believe in the existence of a revealed God and behave accordingly, regardless of their economic situation. The particular combination of socio-economic and cultural components in the study of political economy in the Middle East has varied over the years. During the 1970s and 1980s, studies of the region's political economy tended to prioritize the socio-economic, while since the end of the cold war, the pendulum swung back towards the cultural dimension. An eclectic approach is perhaps the best one; some political and social phenomena are principally rooted in socio-economic factors, while some are not.

The political economy of the Middle East is complex. The region is marked by great diversity. The nature of the environment, the availability of natural resources, and the presence of human capital differs widely. In common with most of the world, the Middle East has also experienced enormous changes in the last two centuries, much of which were driven by outside forces. The advent of the Industrial Revolution was largely responsible for bringing modernization – and the globalization associated with it – to the Middle East in the nineteenth and twentieth centuries. The experience was to be a difficult one for Middle Eastern peoples. By the end of the twentieth century, the great promise of modernization had petered out into pessimism as the process became associated with political and economic failure, repression, uncertainty and foreign occupation.

The Era of Modernization

The era of nineteenth and twentieth century modernization was integrally associated with the political, economic and military power of Europeans and, later, of Americans. The origins of what became the west's international pre-eminence can be traced back at least to the sixteenth century when European soldiers and entrepreneurs harnessed a number of key technologies. With their ships, maps, compasses, steel weapons and guns, Europeans forged a number of trading and colonial empires that were global in their extent. The emerging entity of the European territorial state added yet another dynamic, for its ability to monopolize political authority and mobilize resources was a telling advantage in consolidating the expansion of European power.

During the seventeenth and eighteenth centuries, Europeans skirted the heartlands of the Muslim world. The Ottoman empire remained the alien superpower on Europe's doorstep, but the powers of the great Muslim empires were ebbing. The Ottoman and Indian Mughal empires had long been highly developed states, but, partly as a consequence of this 'over-development', had crushed the dynamism of their societies. The bureaucratic–military elite of the Muslim empires could only develop the economy so far, while their system of law, taxation, regulation and frequent war-making discouraged private ownership, capital accumulation, entrepreneurship, and long-distance trade. The dominant 'mode of production' was tributary and so an independent bourgeoisie did not emerge.[1] Muslim societies had no answer to the fighting-entrepreneur of Europe or to the emerging scale of production and capital accumulation taking place there. The fatal moment could only be postponed for so long. European states and entrepreneurs forced economic concessions, but these were then used as the entry points for more direct intervention. The British moved on the Muslim states of India during the course of the eighteenth century. For the Middle East and North Africa, the year 1798, with Napoleon's fully fledged invasion of Egypt and Palestine, marked the turning point for the Ottoman empire at large.

The Europeans not only unleashed their military power in the Middle East, but also let loose their technologies, ideas and economic practices. One of the most immediate responses in the region was the imitation of Europe's technology and national institutions in Muhammad Ali's new dynasty in Egypt in the early nineteenth century. The basis for sustained success based on a European model did not exist, though, and Muhammad Ali's state-led industrialism and militarism was to quickly fade. Iniquitous commercial treaties in association with direct military pressure exposed the Egyptian state to the full blast of European competition and sharp practice. In fact, during much of the nineteenth century, the Ottoman empire as well as Egypt and Iran were subject to de-industrialization.[2] The European powers went on to practise either direct colonial subjugation or a variety of imperial management techniques. France moved on North Africa, while Britain forced entry into Egypt, the Arabian Peninsula and Sudan. With its cotton and canal, Egypt was the major prize for Britain. Britain coerced Egypt with debt and military threat until it launched a full-scale invasion and occupation of the country in 1882. The British dominated Egypt in association with a class of large landowners and merchants that were co-opted into producing commercial crops – especially cotton and wheat – for the imperial marketplace. A bourgeoisie class was in the making, but it was on the periphery of the imperial system and it was dependent on the British. In fact, the roots of the elite within Egyptian society were made increasingly shallow as the older relationship between landlord and peasant was superseded by the new relationship between local client and imperial market.

The kind of modernization that took place in the nineteenth and twentieth centuries, then, was either as a consequence of a direct European presence or undertaken as indigenous elites sought to emulate the Europeans. In the Ottoman empire, the Sultan initiated the *tanzimat* reforms, although this meant modernization was largely about expanding the capabilities of the state rather than any broader reform process. The Middle East region took on the industrial and technological side of modernity to a greater extent than the political and social revolution that was also taking place in Europe. Middle Eastern peoples acquired railways, steam ships and telegraphs, but saw little of political parties, trade unions and parliaments. With the final dissolution of the Ottoman empire at the end of the First World War, Britain and France would also carve up much of the region into a system of territorial states. Britain forged and presided over Iraq, Transjordan and Palestine, while France took on Syria and Lebanon. The states created by Britain and France faced something of a legitimacy-deficit, but the power of the territorial state was considerable and they would be lasting entities.

The *modus operandi* of the global European empires that drew the Middle East into the modern world was essentially exploitative. In such places as Egypt and Algeria, a specialization on commercial agriculture was the principal requirement in their 'international division of labour'. In Iran, Iraq and Arabia, the imperial system was more interested in the production and exportation of oil, and the management of the capital that flowed from it. A fraction of the huge profits from oil were scattered across local political systems to corrupt a sufficient number of local notables to sustain the trade on imperial terms.[3] Thus, the peoples of the Middle East experienced what was the wave of imperial globalization that swept across the world from the mid-nineteenth century. Modernization was patchy in a geographical and developmental sense, but the lives of many Middle Easterners were now bound up with economic forces that lay many miles over the horizon. For those working to supply the raw materials of global capitalism, then, globalization has long been a reality.

The Political Economy of Post-colonial Modernization

The kind of political orders left in the Middle East region by European colonial powers were unsustainable. In fact, the very process of modernization introduced by Europeans created the system of education and the institutions of modern civil society – such as political parties, labour unions and newspapers – that generated a national consciousness which was hostile to foreign powers and their local allies. Modernization also established modern armed forces and it was to be from within this institution that the principal authors of change were to come. The military was the most organized force in society. Moreover, a new cadre of army officers was to become something of a phenomenon: the son of the 'petit-bourgeois' official or trader that had graduated from the modern education system and who had found social mobility in the army. The new officer was determinedly modern and committed to a model of modernization based on ethnic nationalism and the territorial state.

Turkey pioneered the route to secular nationalism after the First World War. The state was seized by a senior officer, Mustafa Kemal, who was convinced that in order to survive in the modern world, Muslims had to be more like the Europeans. A whole range of laws was introduced to emulate Europe, including a new calendar, a new script and new rules about wearing Europeanized dress. Society was de-Islamized. A similar model emerged in Iran soon after, when a cavalry commander, Reza Khan, overthrew the Qajar monarchy. The Arab world did not go as far in rejecting traditional culture as in Turkey and Iran, but the new officers led a wave of coups d'état underpinned by a secular, socialist and nationalist ideology. The overthrow of the pro-British monarchy in Egypt in 1952 produced the iconic figure of this 'Arab revolution', Colonel Jamal Abdul Nasser. The revolution forged by these Arab modernists went on to reach its ultimate expression in the Ba'th Party (Renaissance Party) and in their seizure of Syria and Iraq in the 1960s. Only in a few places, notably Saudi Arabia and Morocco, was the tide of Arab modernism resisted. The Saudi monarchy led the traditionalist survivors because the relationship between rulers and ruled had not been so compromised by the penetration of colonial powers and because the al-Saud were fortunate to enjoy an enormous windfall from oil.

The secular modernists brought a socio-economic revolution to the Arab world. The political systems left by Britain and France were swept away, and the class of landowners and large merchants associated with the colonial powers was much reduced in size, wealth and social power. Meanwhile, Arab modernizers believed in the organizing power of the state, and used it to set about building a new social base to underpin their rule, to secure a greater independence in the world, and to engineer a better society. It would take some time for fully blown socialism to emerge, but the economic philosophy of the Arab modernizers embodied state planning, widespread public ownership, and a strategy of import substitution. Local markets were to be protected from foreign competition in order to give room for local industries to develop. If one pillar of Arab modernism was state-led developmentalism, the other was corporatizing welfarism. Millions of people were drawn into state organizations at various levels. Public-sector jobs, the provision of public education and health services, and subsidies on basic goods formed the backbone of this populist corporatism. Many benefited, but it was a coalition of army officers, bureaucrats, public-sector capitalists and employees, and the industrial labour force that was at the heart of the new ruling coalition. A social contract was struck. Development and social justice in return for acquiescence to the national project set out by the state leadership.

Populist modernization in some Arab countries initially looked quite progressive, but it was not democratic and there were contradictions that were always likely to undermine progress. Clientelism dogged political development. According to Hisham Sharabi, the Arab world suffered from the worst of both worlds: the patriarchal character of traditional Arab societies continued to manifest itself in the workings of the 'modern' Arab state.[4] The state worked on the basis of deference to the headman as well as social relations characterized by personalized politics, patronage and solidarity group hierarchies. Thus, the Arab state lacked some of the rational and contractual arrangements and individualism that existed within the fully modern states of the west. In fact, populist modernization facilitated a patriarchal authoritarianism writ large and, in some cases, it allowed a novel clan-based totalitarianism. Such state leaderships were sometimes said to enjoy a degree of autonomy from their societies, but, in most cases, patrons were as locked into these systems of rights and obligations as their clients. For Daniel Brumberg, state leaderships were far from autonomous, being

> institutionally and ideologically intertwined with key social groups whose loyalty flowed from the instrumental and thus fragile calculations of a patron–client relationship. Any bid by the regime to renege on the 'ruling bargain' that sustained this relationship was bound to provoke opposition from the popular groups whose livelihood depended on the state.[5]

In other words, there was inertia at the heart of the state, and as time would show the capacity of state leaderships to actually create and sustain new social and economic facts on the ground was perhaps less than it may have appeared.

The Failure of Populist Modernization in the Arab World

For a time, progressive modernization was accompanied by great hopes. Arab states like Algeria, Libya, Tunisia, Egypt, Yemen, Syria and Iraq appeared to achieve a new level of independence from the foreign interests and began a broader modernization process. New houses, roads, utilities, schools, hospitals and public-sector jobs improved the lot of most people.

It was all a false dawn. Populist modernization was to be a failure. Bureaucrats are rarely good entrepreneurs and the Arab bureaucrat was no exception. Public sectors quickly became bloated, weighed down by the corruption and incompetence that is such a feature of political systems run along clientelist lines. The economics of import substitution was also counter-productive in the longer term, as investment was misdirected and productive efficiency declined. At the same time, as economic development faltered, the demand for welfare was soon outstripping the resources available. States slid towards debt and balance of payments shortfalls. The oil boom of the 1970s threw many states a lifeline, but it was a temporary respite. The front line in the failure of the modernizing state was an unfolding disaster in the big cities of the Middle East. City life was too often characterised by urban sprawl, rapid population growth and rural-to-urban migration, decaying fabric and poor services. Meanwhile, the state was also failing to provide sufficient employment, even for the new high school and university graduates. By the mid-1970s, state-led development could no longer generate any real hope of progress for millions of urban dwellers.

The failure of state planning highlighted the 'distorted' nature of the moderniza- tion project in the Middle East. The region may have taken on some of the physical artefacts of modernization, but it had largely failed to develop many of the institu- tional arrangements and political and social values that made modernization work so much better in the contemporary west. The capacity of the Middle Eastern state to mobilize and properly utilize the resources at their disposal was low. In his major work, *Over-Stating the Arab State*, Nazih Ayubi mapped out the weakness of the Arab state. Arab states might be 'fierce' but the idea that they were 'strong' was a myth. Ayubi noted of Arab states that

> Although they have large bureaucracies, mighty armies and harsh prisons, they are lamentably feeble when it comes to collecting taxes, winning wars or forging a really 'hegemonic' power bloc or an ideology that can carry the state beyond the coercive and 'corporative' level and into the moral and intellectual sphere.[6]

In the Gramscian terms used by Ayubi, the soldiers, bureaucrats and state capitalists that ran the Arab state had failed to consolidate a true social hegemony. The Arab state might possess the full panoply of bureaucratic and coercive instruments, but it did not have a secure place in the minds of many of its people and so its writ did not run where its officials were absent. Far too many citizens were indifferent or even hostile to their leaders, their state, and the laws under which they lived. The inability of Middle Eastern countries to get the state fully internalized in the minds of their people or to create a hegemonic social bloc was partly a consequence of what Ayubi called their 'articulated modes of production' and associated social formations.[7] Various kinds of traditional and modern groups continued to exist and interact, but also to support alternative visions of society. Once the developmental and welfare resources of the 'populist' state were exhausted, it had very little to fall back on, apart from coercion. A crisis of social hegemony loomed.

The faltering of the big progressive modernizers left the conservative Gulf states – Saudi Arabia, Kuwait, the United Arab Emirates, Bahrain, Qatar and Oman – in the driving seat of the regional economy. The kind of modernization going on in the Gulf sheikhdoms was even more distorted, partly because it was oil that really gave life to modernization in the Gulf. During the 1970s and 1980s, the low population/high income dynamic of the Gulf states enabled rapid physical and institutional modernization. Buying in skills and labour from around the world, the landscape of the desert community was superseded by that of modern urban life: the nomad, camel and mud brick house were superseded by the high-rise dwelling, road and car, consumer goods, the nuclear family, and the clock.[8] The institutions of government were also put in place: a modern-looking bureaucracy and military, as well as systems of health and education. In the Gulf, oil meant that all this could be achieved without putting significant demands of taxation on the local population. The state was a giver and not a taker, although this meant that it was relatively autonomous and was under little popular pressure to develop more formalized systems of citizen participation.

The development philosophy of the oil sheikhdoms was also significantly different to that of the progressive modernizers. The objective of the modernization programmes in the Gulf was to consolidate traditional political and social practices and forms of organization, with family and tribal networks integrated with the emerging modern sector. Moreover, while the state dominated the commanding heights of the economy, the ruling families were committed to private-sector activities as well as strong connections with foreign business interests. Modernization and the activities of the private and foreign sectors were bound to introduce social changes, but the potentially de-stabilizing impact of these was mitigated by well-funded welfarism. The public–private link was instrumental in circulating oil revenues through society. A whole system of subsidies, contracting for the public sector, and import licensing of goods and labour co-opted support for the state and its modernization project.

The kind of modernization taking place in the Gulf was very uneven. The Gulf sheikhdoms were what Hazem Beblawi and Giacomo Luciani referred to as 'rentier states'.[9] The state presided over an economic system in which the principal motive was chasing the easy oil rents around the economy. The circulation and consumption of capital supported the traditional networks of family rule, but as a strategy for a self-sustaining capitalism, the culture of rentierism left much to be desired. The private sector was skewed towards state contracts, trading, property and stock speculation, and restrictive franchising deals. The incentive for local businessmen to work hard or to demonstrate much in the way of real entrepreneurialism was limited. Foreign managers and labourers did much of the work required for modernization. What had emerged within the Gulf societies, Nazih Ayubi observed, was a lumpen bourgeoisie.[10]

Whether the Gulf sheikhdoms could have modernization without a corresponding political and social revolution remained to be seen. Traditional elites in the Gulf, Sharif Elmusa perceived, sought to 'have technology without social change, the tree of knowledge without temptation. Faust without the Devil'.[11] In reality, the technologies of modernity are not mere 'technofacts' but also cultural instruments, offering new ways of perceiving and interacting with the world. Modernization brought a tidal wave of foreign goods and ideas. In the longer term, the model of 'traditionalist modernization' established in the Gulf might become the prescription for a rather frustrated society. Nevertheless, the passage of time seemed to suggest that traditionalist modernization in the oil sheikhdoms had quite some mileage in it. Physical modernization was achieved with a minimum of effort and relatively little instability. For a time at least, the modernization project in the Gulf was not self-sustaining, but the oil money kept it going.

Infitah

The faltering of the populist Arab states and the growing importance of the Gulf sheikhdoms led to a re-evaluation of the modernization project across the Middle East. Oil revenues were a pool of capital which all sought to tap. Direct transfers of aid and investment from the Gulf to capital-poor countries were made. Migrant labour from countries such as Egypt, Sudan, Yemen, Lebanon, Jordan and Syria also travelled to the major oil producers. The foreign exchange that migrant labour earned soon represented significant inflows of private capital into those countries, pump-priming new private-sector activity and international economic networks. The development of the new private-sector economy coincided with a fiscal crisis in many Arab states. Arab leaderships soon realized that addressing the fiscal crisis not only meant tapping into the new private sources of capital but also offloading existing public-sector obligations. In many ways, what was to happen in the Middle East from the 1970s was a prelude to the colossal revival of capitalist principles that was to sweep across the world in the 1980s and 1990s. In the Middle East, the idea of economic reform had a name: it was *infitah* or opening.

Egypt had led the charge towards populist modernization and it was the first to rethink. By the mid-1970s, the regime of Anwar Sadat was moving to ease regulations on some economic activities, encourage private and foreign investment and trade, and cut public spending. The *infitah* embodied a new alliance between the bureaucracy and private sector. The entrenched power of the socialist bureaucracy as represented by the Arab Socialist Union (ASU) was curtailed and a number of chambers of commerce and businessmen's clubs were promoted as new nodes of consultation and patronage.[12] In addition, economic reform meant that Sadat was able to access new sources of aid from the US and the Gulf. By the 1980s, the *infitah* model had been taken up, to a greater or lesser extent, in most of the Arab world. What was happening across the region was a convergence of political and economic practice. No matter their origin, whether secular populist or conservative monarchy, state leaderships were increasingly underpinned by a public–private alliance of capitalists and bureaucrats that ran a mixed economy and sought to engage with international capitalism.

The problem was that the *infitah* represented yet more distorted development. Reform was patchy and the benefits did not extend very far into society. The new markets were rigged for the benefit of an emerging class of private oligarchs and their bureaucratic allies within the state. The economics of crony capitalism were largely based on political and social criteria rather than market principles. Business ties were often cemented by personal, family and marriage alliances, while the capacity of those who were able to make profits was significantly determined by the decisions of state regulators. Such dynamics encouraged corruption. Moreover, while the state continued to dominate the commanding heights of the economy, private businesses were confined to the service sector and rentier activities, especially the speculative trading of land and consumer goods.

Infitah reforms also raised the spectre of social inequality. The new public–private elites may or may not have continued to pay lip service to old populist ideologies, but in practice they tended to aspire to western lifestyles that were far removed from the lives of ordinary people. The elite was essentially abandoning the masses to their poverty and backwardness. For far too many ordinary people, modernization meant an urban experience of underemployment, poor housing, intermittent services, second jobs and long hours commuting. The newly educated poor were a particular problem, with their social mobility blocked by fewer public-sector jobs and by a private sector monopolized by the new class of public–private oligarchs. The sense of betrayal and victimhood was particularly evident amongst the young. A youth revolt against the state, private capitalists and foreign interests was in the making. The potential of this urban rage became clear in Egypt in January 1977, when after cuts in subsidies on basic goods spontaneous rioting on a shockingly massive scale broke out across Cairo and other Egyptian cities.

The Islamic Rebellion against Secular Modernization

The social alienation taking place in the Middle Eastern city was soon to be given a voice by the forces of militant Islam. At first, state leaders like Sadat had tried to co-opt traditional social forces against the leftist opponents of *infitah*, but Islamic revivalists could not be controlled. In the 1970s and 1980s, militant Islam was not simply anti-modern. Many Islamic revivalists wanted the benefits of modernization, but only under an entirely new social contract, which recognized that Islam was a timeless truth that must be at the centre of any political and social system. The forces of secularism and unbelief – bad Muslims and infidel foreigners – must not be allowed to shape the modernization project in Muslim societies.

Within their communities, Islamists talked about things that ordinary people wanted to hear. Islamic revivalism was a populism that offered a return to the equality and mutual recognition of the believer community. In practice, Islamists often moved to fill the gaps left vacant by the state, offering local health, education, welfare and even banking services. A flow of money from the oil-rich Gulf sheikhdoms supported the Islamic sub-sector, but much of its work was conducted by a large number of local volunteers. Local doctors, lawyers, engineers and teachers fed up with the grinding inertia of the bureaucratic state were often enthusiasts for Islamic practices. Small-scale merchants and manufacturers, who were losing out to modern systems of production and retail commerce, were attracted to the Islamic alternative. Islam also struck a chord with the young urban poor who could not find fitting employment or the means to begin family life. Thus, the Islamic revival was not simply the revolt of the dispossessed. It was a broadly based coalition that was hostile to the *infitah* oligarchy. The coming together of the frustrated professional, the idle educated and the impoverished populace was a dangerous combination, and political violence was soon on its way.

In the years that followed the Islamic revival of the 1970s, the politics of many Middle Eastern countries would be utterly paralysed. Beyond the epic moment of the Iranian revolution in 1978–9, a deadlock of social forces was to develop. The Islamists were unable to finish off those that ran the secular state while the secular state was unable to finish off the Islamists. The chronic social instability that resulted, with most violence in Algeria, Egypt, Syria and Iraq, represented a tremendous block to any social or economic reform. For Fouad Ajami, Islam was a reaction to the failure of the secular Arab state to make the modern world work for Arabs but seemed unlikely to offer much solace in the long run. Ajami observed that

> Authenticity becomes a refuge when practical politics fails to deliver concrete solutions to foreign weakness, to domestic breakdown, to cultural seduction. The connection

between the Arab *thawra* [revolution] of the post-1967 years to the Saudi era of a decade later, from the Marxist–Leninist tracts to the fundamentalist exhortations, is not as tenuous as it at first seems. One leads to the other. Both are made of the same material: the desire for a quick fix, that brief moment of elation when all appears resolved before things come tumbling down.[13]

The Islamists offered an analysis of what was wrong with modernity, but it was doubtful that they could contribute much to the resolution of the crisis. By the mid-1980s, the whole modernization project was stuck amid conditions of chronic economic failure, political instability and social violence. The dilemmas of the modernization crisis were soon to get even more pronounced.

Late Twentieth-century Globalization

In the course of the 1980s, a global revolution was in the making. Many of the features of the revolution had long existed, but the coming together of a number of key factors by the end of the decade inaugurated a new era – one defined by what has become known as globalization. New technology played an important part. Transportation and communications technologies had rapidly developed after the Second World War, but it was the new microchip electronics of the 1970s and 1980s that really brought cheap and instantaneous communications over the long distances, facilitating an unknown quantity and quality of human interconnectedness across the globe. However, the full implications of the technology could not have been realized without the two great political developments of the 1980s. Firstly, the Thatcher–Reagan revolution in Britain and the United States made a liberal capitalist revivalism the new economic orthodoxy of the west. The neo-liberals sought to reduce the role of the state in economics, give markets back to private capitalists, and further deregulate international trade and exchange. Harnessing the new technologies, the significance of multi-national corporations (MNCs) and global financial networks centred on New York, London and Tokyo was thus to increase markedly. The multilateral economic institutions of the existing western system – the International Monetary Fund (IMF), the World Bank and the General Agreement on Tariffs and Trade (GATT) (later to become the World Trade Organization) were also moved to centre stage in the management of the global economy. Second, the west won the cold war. The collapse of the Soviet Union lifted the remaining internal and external restraints on western market reforms. Socio-economic stability was a lesser concern for western leaders and large parts of the world were now open for business. New markets lay for the taking, just as new ideas and technologies provided the means for taking them.

What was so radical about late twentieth century globalization was the way that global networks carried liberal ideas and practices to almost every corner of the world. The sovereignty of existing states was circumvented, with multilateral institutions challenging them from above, and MNCs and information and trade networks from below. States remained powerful actors – and the essential facilitators of global–local trading relations – but the myth of their absolute supremacy was no longer sustainable. Borders were now too permeable. The new 'terms of trade' were pressed home by key western states and multilateral institutions, but also by the power of the ideas associated with them. The western alliance was both agent and role model. Others were co-opted into the global system not only because they believed what the west wanted was probably inevitable, but also because the west's liberalism struck universal aspirations for progress. In the late twentieth century, western liberalism had a presence and plausibility which enabled westerners to penetrate and transform non-western societies in a way not seen before, not even during the age of nineteenth-century European colonialism.

The end of the cold war and the emergence of liberal globalization changed the agenda in the study of political economy. Liberal capitalism stood as a giant. Alternative explanations and prescriptions were completely overshadowed. Marx was dimmed still further. The critiques of capitalism found in development studies also seemed less realistic. Any relevant political economy was now all about the implications of engaging in the global marketplace and how to go about doing it better. For the iconic thinker of triumphant liberalism, Francis Fukuyama, the defeat of the alternatives had been inevitable. The 'liberal idea' represented the most powerful combination of political and economic forms in history: the rule of law, liberal democracy and capitalist free markets. Liberal capitalism had not only out-produced and out-competed all the alternatives during the twentieth century, but also represented the ultimate form of government. The liberal idea gave humans what they universally longed for: a reasonable degree of prosperity and the recognition of their equal worth as human beings. Indeed, in the sense that the liberal state represented the best form of government that humans could seemingly imagine, the history of political and social evolution was at an end.[14] It was now clear what real modernization must look like. Fukuyama observed that by virtue of what he called the Mechanism of Modern Natural Science,

> All countries undergoing economic modernization must increasingly resemble one another: they must unify nationally on the basis of a centralized state, urbanize, replace traditional forms of social organisation like tribe, sect and family with economically rational ones based on function and efficiency, and provide for the universal education of their citizens. Such societies have become increasingly linked with one another through global markets and the spread of a universal consumer culture.[15]

For Fukuyama, it was clear that liberal capitalism was the only system that could properly organize complex post-industrial economies. It might take time, but eventually every society on earth would have to face up to the liberal idea. In the meantime, there would be two worlds: the post-historical world and the old historical world. One was modern, one was backward, and the relationship between the two would be uneasy. Of course, the big gap in the liberal optimism represented by Fukuyama was a lack of appreciation for the problems associated with being a late modernizer and the persistent inequalities that exist within a global system dominated by western capitalists.

The Global Social Power of Liberal Capitalism and Economic Reform in the Middle East

Global liberal capitalism had global social power. Businessmen and pro-market officials in almost every country numbered amongst a globalization elite. The new elite shared common attributes due to the fact that many of its members tended to be well travelled, largely western educated and English speaking, and internationalist in aspiration. They were the kind of people that met under the auspices of the World Economic Forum in Davos, Switzerland. The globalization elite manned the emerging network of globalization economics. The global economy had its core in the US, Europe and Japan, but it flowed into public and private networks in secondary city regions. In the Middle East, there were significant pockets of globalization economics and the globalization elite in Cairo, Jeddah, Riyadh, Kuwait City, Abu Dhabi, Dubai, as well as most other capitals. The globalization elite were important in their own right in setting up deals and channelling capital into local business activities, but they were also important in establishing a mood for the adoption of the economic principles and practices of the global economy.

To bring most Middle Eastern countries within the bounds of global markets required an enormous amount of 'structural adjustment'. Western states and multilateral institutions made the reform agenda clear: the need for law and order, lower taxes, a clear regulatory code, secure property rights, a sound financial sector, reasonably free markets, stable and properly valued currencies, and an educated labour force.[16] State leaderships were the mediators between the supporters of global engagement and the still powerful national interests. While many state leaders recognized the need for macro-economic reform, any reform process would have to moderate its impact on the existing national economy as well as keep an eye on political and social stability. For many bureaucrats, public-sector managers, industrial and agricultural workers and the urban poor the benefits of economic reform were often not immediately obvious. Political concerns tended to slow economic reform to a crawl almost everywhere.

In fact, it was a growing financial crisis in the 1990s, and especially external indebtedness, that really drove structural adjustment forward. The prospect of defaulting on foreign debts forced countries like Algeria, Egypt and Jordan to enter directly into IMF and World Bank stabilization programmes (based on the quick reduction of deficits, cuts in spending, controls on credit and public-sector borrowing, rises in interest rates, and wage and price controls). The experience of IMF intervention was always difficult and the results variable. In Jordan, IMF intervention must count as something of a success story, although it took much of the 1990s for Jordan to absorb IMF-led liberalization measures and it was only after 1998 that some economic benefits were becoming clear. In Egypt, the Mubarak government often voiced its frustrations with the IMF and there were long periods when Egypt did not operate within the guidelines set down. The IMF stabilization agreement of May 1987, for instance, was substantially ignored until the IMF had to come back with a more comprehensive reform package in 1991.[17] IMF supervision helped keep Egypt afloat, but the country remained constantly balanced on the edge of an economic crisis.

An acceptance by state leaderships of the emerging global trade regime in the 1990s also embodied many dilemmas. Most Middle Eastern states queued up to jump into the new World Trade Organization (WTO) as it emerged from the final round of GATT in 1993–4. Morocco, Kuwait, Bahrain and Pakistan were signatories of the WTO. Tunisia, Egypt, Turkey, Qatar and the UAE had been members of GATT, and were on a fast track to WTO membership.[18] Oman joined in 2000. Saudi Arabia wanted to join. Iran's application to the WTO in May 2001 was blocked by the US. With a whole system of intrusive monitoring and enforcement across the breadth of economic activities, WTO membership threatened most developing states with a significant loss of authority and control in the domestic economy. Developing countries had ten years to come into full compliance with WTO rules, but even that was unlikely to prepare most for the blast of competition likely to follow. The loss of control embodied in WTO membership was only really worth contemplating if the costs could be offset by increased performance in export markets, but for most Middle Eastern countries this was far from a sure thing. Nevertheless, Middle Eastern states felt they could not be left out, although a prolonged period of haggling seemed inevitable as convergence dates loomed.

In the Gulf States, it was the WTO agenda rather than IMF intervention that nudged the states towards reform.[19] The Gulf States were committed to expanding their role in the global economy and also needed to create far more jobs for their rapidly growing populations. The days of the high income/low population dynamic were gone. As things stood in the Gulf States, foreign business activity was tightly controlled by means of restrictive laws, licensing rules and import/export controls. Foreigners were not allowed equity partnerships in many economic activities. The 'negative list' in Saudi Arabia, for instance, included oil exploration, drilling and production, insurance, real estate, investment in Mecca and Medina, telecommunications, fishing, education, sea and air transport, television, radio, electricity distribution, health, defence-related industries, and publishing. Many of these kinds of restrictions had to change. WTO membership required privatization, tax reform, opening local financial markets, redrafting business regulations, increasing official and legal transparency, and rules tightening up on the enforcement of patents and copyrights. Real reforms were now on the agenda in the Gulf, especially in some of the smaller sheikhdoms, but whether a country like Saudi Arabia could really fulfil the requirements of the WTO without fundamental political and social reform remained to be seen. When information and trade is so restricted by the state, when women cannot fully participate in economic and social life, and when temporary foreign workers do so much of the work, a more balanced and self-sustaining kind of modernization could not take place. The peoples and governments of the Gulf had yet to decide whether they really wanted to go toward truly advanced stages of modernization. Oil money continued to give the Gulf States alternatives, although diminishing ones.

The reform process would go ahead across the Middle East, but it was measured. In terms of privatization, the outright transfer of ownership from public to private sector has been rare. In Egypt, for instance, the privatization programme took over two decades to set up; it gradually moved from managerial reforms within the public sector, to contracting out some public functions to private companies, towards public–private joint ventures, and finally towards fuller privatizations. It was not until the mid-1990s that parts of the public sector were sold to local private investors in their own right. The Egyptian stock market was also revived in 1996 as privatization issues were offered. As elsewhere in the Middle East, public–private partnerships were a favoured method of upgrading key utilities, such as electric power and telecommunications. The principal beneficiaries of this incremental approach were the public–private oligarchs that were first primed by Sadat's *infitah* reforms. Beyond handy connections within the state to smooth the way, doing business in Egypt – as everywhere else in the Middle East – still meant doing battle with the rules of the state and the practices of the entrenched bureaucracy.

The Inherent Instability of Globalization in the Middle East

Late twentieth-century globalization embodied an enormous challenge to every country in the world. For those countries that possessed a reasonable degree of economic competitiveness and a system of consensual politics for managing social change, the breaking down of existing boundaries and the opening up of new markets across the world represented an enormous opportunity. The United States and United Kingdom were the chief beneficiaries. Many developing countries, including most Middle Eastern countries, lacked these competitive advantages. For these countries, globalization threatened significant risks, which could be broadly grouped in two forms.

First, there were the risks of economic reform, which almost always de-stabilized the national economy. As national regulations governing production, trade, and foreign exchange were liberalized, almost all less-developed economies experienced serious imbalances that did not necessarily correct themselves. A vicious circle was evident almost everywhere. Easing regulations led to a burst of imports, consumption and inflation which increased trade deficits and indebtedness, which led to a real or de facto devaluation in the local currency, which introduced further inflationary pressures and reduced the standard of living for many. At the same time, cuts in public spending threaten reductions in subsidies and pay cuts or lay-offs in the public sector. Fiscal and macro-economic stabilization, improvements in the supply-side of the economy, and export-led growth were supposed to be the pay-offs for reform, but they rarely helped to offset the vicious circle quickly enough. Speculative business practices within the private sector almost always worsened the problems. By the end of the 1990s, the entire developing world – from Argentina to South Korea – had gone through a period of shattering economic instability, with the Asian crash of 1997–8 being the most spectacular example of the boom and bust of economies.

Economic instability often directly caused political and social instability, as groups and classes left behind in the reform programme fought to secure their interests. Those working in the unreconstructed public sector and the welfare-reliant urban poor were the most threatened. Various kinds of political and social conflict emerged. In Morocco, Tunisia, Egypt, Jordan and other countries there were civil protests and disturbances. In the Islamic Republic of Iran, modernizers and traditionalists within the government and on the streets struggled over the country's future. In Algeria, the catastrophic failure of Chadhi Benjedid's reform programme contributed to the outbreak of a dreadful civil war. In Iraq, the failure of the reform programme in the late 1980s – and its breakdown into an imports–debts–devaluation–inflation cycle – was one of the key factors that prompted Saddam Hussein to formulate an economic policy by other means: at first, by physically coercing businessmen and then invading Kuwait. In most other places, social alienation resulted in deviant activities. Increased levels of crime and of criminal organization were a side-effect of the new globalization.

The other major cause of instability associated with the new globalization was that it came with an avalanche of global culture. The cultural milieu of globalization is a complex mix of global and local but, in the last analysis, it is western dominated and invited everyone else to integrate themselves with the amoral and the secular. Satellite television and the internet made it increasingly difficult for states to go on screening the flow of goods and images, although this did not stop Islamic states like Saudi

Arabia and Iran trying. The cultural issue was particularly stark in the Middle East because of the continuing influence of Islamic religion and culture on society. To what extent Islam represents a block to global modernity is the subject of debate, but the association of modernity and globalization with the west and its culture is problematic.[20] The value system of Islam, much less that of militant Islamism, embodies a completely different approach for understanding and appreciating the world. Islam is a vision of community and social control, while liberalism is a one of economic liberation, individual choice and the removal of constraints. Islam tends to frown on the idea of individual autonomy and consciousness. Indeed, many Islamists wanted an Islamic state that enforced illiberal injunctions on almost all matters of social life.

For Middle Easterners, the principal issue was not really whether they should engage with globalization – for they really had little choice – but how they should go about doing it. At the frontline of cultural synthesis was the culture of material satisfaction that is integral to globalization, and which cannot be dismissed as mere ephemera. Western goods, trademarks, tastes and entertainments have enormous capacity to 'crowd out' the local alternatives. In his seminal book, *Jihad vs. McWorld*, Benjamin Barber described the advance of this 'McWorld' as an utterly ubiquitous experience of American consumer icons and a landscape of shopping malls, cinemas, sports stadiums and branded restaurants. McWorld promoted the ideals of individualism, consumerism, romantic love and sex, images of youth and female liberation, and glamorized violence.[21] Barber was in no doubt that McWorld – perhaps inadvertently – had embarked on an enormous assault on the culture and social order of all societies, and, in the end, it would probably conquer them all.

Globalized modernity was also synonymous with the ideology of the market and of economic man, *homo economicus.*[22] To accept the market as a prime motivation for human behaviour has profound implications. *Homo economicus* behaves according to the logic of competition and self-interest, and in his purest form does not care about the nation, religion, or any other socio-cultural being other than to point out that they are a distortion of the rational economic order. Of course, Middle Easterners were far from discarding their socio-cultural traditions – in fact, their capitalism was still rather too socio-cultural for its own good – but some powerful contradictory impulses seemed likely to torment Muslim societies. The kind of individualism, consumerism and secular morality that underpinned globalization economics was apt to contradict the kind of social relations underwritten by kinship, duty and God. Above all, the logic and practice of *homo economicus* threatened to smash apart the existing power relations of the patriarchal structures of Muslim society by drawing women and youth into worlds of wage-earning work, leisure time and consumption. Making women and young people workers and consumers, and giving them the ability to make social and economic choices was revolutionary.

Wherever global and local models met each other, there was a complex contest for relevance. The contest was conducted at the higher levels of politics and political thinking, but also during a myriad of day-to-day experiences for millions of ordinary people. In his book *Orientalism, Postmodernism and Globalism*, Bryan Turner argued that the real threat to local cultures probably came at the level of the everyday. According to Turner,

> beliefs are adopted or rejected because they are relevant or not relevant to everyday needs and concerns. What makes religious faith or religious commitment problematic in a

globalized post-modern society is that everyday life has become part of a global system of exchange of commodities which are not easily influenced by political leaders, intellectuals or religious leaders. The corruption of pristine faith is going to be brought about by Tina Turner and Coca-Cola and not by rational arguments and reaction, inspection of presuppositions and the understanding of Western secularism.[23]

The penetration of the day-to-day was profound. While the promoters of Islam adapted to the kind of modernity that was seen in most of the twentieth century – in some cases by actually seizing the modern state – they would probably find that responding to the low-level cultural synthesis of post-modern globalization was much more problematic. The real danger for Islamists was not that Muslims would reject their heritage or oppose Islam, but that they would simply lose interest in it amid the myriad of seductive products, diverse images and lifestyle choices that they now faced during everyday life.

The Muslim Middle East met the global challenge with a combination of imitation, resistance and synthesis. The patterns of change were complex. What the cultural tussle between the global and the local in the Middle East seemed likely to do, though, was to create yet more distorted development. Islam was a factor in the political economy of some parts of the Middle East, especially where there was an Islamic state or a significant Islamic opposition. Where Islam was strong, the meshing of global and local cultures was bound to be delayed. Moreover, different people seemed likely to change at different paces. Elites seemed to be changing more quickly than the mass of ordinary people. According to Mehran Kamrava, non-western societies faced a kind of 'variable speed' westernization, with partial reconstructions of identity incrementally moving particular individuals, classes and communities through change.[24] If visions of the future differed too much, however, social stability would be threatened as would engagement with globalized modernity. The real problem in the Middle East was that most states still did not have a satisfactory way of mediating the differences and tensions brought out by globalization. The authoritarianism of both state leaderships and Islamic opposition trapped most societies in a halfway house of modernization, where it was impossible to go either forward or back, and where economic failure and chronic instability were the principal features of life.

The Future of the Middle East

Few Middle Easterners could look back on the twentieth century and not feel that something had gone wrong with the era of modernization. The outcome had been a patchwork of authoritarian states and peripheral economies that did not work very well. One or two of these states had become true tyrannies. Most Middle Eastern states were dominated by entrenched interests that depended on coercion, misdirected public spending, rent seeking, and monopolism. All authoritarian states and restrictive social systems suffer from the same socio-economic disadvantage; in the system that they preside over, far too few people are productive and they have to support far too many people that are not. The new wave of globalization modernity that emerged from the 1980s was set to further expose the inherent problems with Middle Eastern modernization. *Infitah* and globalization reorganized the ruling coalition in many failing states in order to draw on the resources of the private and foreign sectors, but this scarcely addressed the broader crisis. At the same time, the Islamic opposition was bidding for the dispossessed and frustrated, and was able to organize a sizeable constituency across the social spectrum, but Islamism did not provide a credible programme to resolve all the problems. Only in Iran did partly modernized Islamists seize the state, but soon the Islamic Republic was beset by the same kind of troubled modernization as everyone else. Islam was not necessarily anti-modern, but it did make engagement with global capitalism and culture particularly problematic. Most Muslims realized that they needed a compromise, but it was unclear how a moral competitiveness in globalized markets could be forged.

The development of liberalism and democracy had made modernity work so much better in the west, but the social constituency and cultural mood to support the meshing of liberal values and Middle Eastern culture appeared some way off at the beginning of the twenty-first century. The stunted development of liberal values in Middle Eastern society could be traced to several factors: the fact that modernity was handed to Middle Easterners by the west, the way that the region was beset by endless international conflicts, the continued strength of traditional solidarity groups and illiberal ideologies, the persistence of state leaderships who could not contemplate giving up power, and the failure of economic policy. The development of more balanced and successful economies, the emergence of an independent middle class, and a revolution in political culture was required to bridge the democracy gap of modernization in the Middle East. As things stood, most Middle Easterners were trapped between an uninspired authoritarian state and an Islamic opposition that posed more questions than it answered. Underdevelopment and poverty were a pervasive fact of life in the Middle East, and even if economic reforms led to a more successful private sector, most ordinary people could not expect a better life anytime soon. The crises of economic failure and cultural change seemed likely to rack Middle Eastern societies for the foreseeable future.

NOTES

1   Ayubi, *Overstating the Arab State*, pp. 80–2.
2   Ayubi, *Overstating the Arab State*, p. 87.
3   See Elm, *Oil, Power and Principle: Iran's Oil Nationalization and Its Aftermath*.
4   Sharabi, Hisham, *Neopatriarchy: A Theory of Distorted Change in Arab Society*.
5   Brumberg, 'Authoritarian legacies and reform strategies in the Arab world', p. 234.
6   Ayubi, *Overstating the Arab State*, xi.
7   Ayubi, *Overstating the Arab State*, pp. 26–7.
8   Elmusa, 'Faust without the devil? The interplay of technology and culture in Saudi Arabia', pp. 345–57.
9   Beblawi and Luciani, *The Rentier State*.
10 Ayubi, *Overstating the Arab State*, p. 225.
11 Elmusa, 'Faust without the devil? The interplay of technology and culture in Saudi Arabia', p. 350.
12 Ehteshami and Murphy, 'Transformation of the corporatist state in the Middle East', p. 761.
13 Ajami, *The Arab Predicament*, pp. 173–4.
14 According to Fukuyama, 'The Mechanism is, in other words, a kind of Marxist interpretation of history that leads to a completely non-Marxist conclusion. It is the desire of 'man the species-being' to produce and consume that leads him to leave the countryside

for the city, to work in large factories or large bureaucracies rather than on the land, to sell his labour to the highest bidder instead of working in the occupation of his ancestors, to acquire an education and to submit to the discipline of the clock. But, contrary to Marx, the kind of society that permits people to produce and consume the largest quantity of products on the most equal basis is not a communist one, but a capitalist society.' Fukuyama, *The End of History and the Last Man*, p. 131.

15 Fukuyama, *The End of History and the Last Man*, xiv–xv.
16 Scholte, 'Global capitalism and the state', pp. 441–2.
17 Hinnebusch, 'The politics of economic reform in Egypt', p. 161.
18 Blum, 'The Middle East adapts to GATT', pp. 2–3.
19 Mahdi, Fadhil A., 'Responses to globalization in the Gulf countries', p. 2.
20 Bill and Springborg, *Politics in the Middle East*, p. 67.
21 Barber, *Jihad vs. McWorld*, p. 81.
22 See Brohman, 'Economism and critical silences in development studies: a theoretical critique of neoliberalism', p. 298.
23 Turner, *Orientalism, Postmodernism and Globalism*, p. 10.
24 Kamrava, 'Social change', *Politics and Society in the Developing World*, pp. 110–11.

FURTHER READING

The standard texts on the era of modernization in the Middle East are *State, Power and Politics in the Making of the Modern Middle East* by Roger Owen and *The Politics of the Middle East* by James Bill and Robert Springborg. Bill and Springborg draw on the comparative politics literature to illuminate the relationship between modernization and political development. For a more detailed case study of the political economy of European imperialism, *Oil, Power and Principle* by Mostafa Elm describes British practices in Iran and the response of Iranian nationalists up to the 1950s.

Before the 1990s, the study of Middle Eastern political economy was often informed by a Marxist-influenced analysis. Examples of such an approach are the many works of Samir Amin, notably *The Arab Economy* (1982), and the edited volumes by Tim Niblock, *Iraq: The Contemporary State* and *State, Society and Economy in Saudi Arabia*. Many studies cover the failure of populist Arab nationalism, but *The Arab Predicament* by Fouad Ajami remains a landmark work. Nazih Ayubi's *Overstating the Arab State* draws on Gramsci to chart the inherent crisis in Arab modernization. The growing importance of the Gulf oil economies and the regional dynamics they established is examined in *The Rentier State* by Hazem Beblawi and Giacomo Luciani.

The era of globalization is described in a number of seminal works, notably Francis Fukuyama's *The End of History* and Benjamin Barber's *Jihad vs. McWorld*. Studying the impact of globalizing liberal capitalism has become the only game in town. The two volumes entitled *Political Liberalization and Democratization in the Arab World* edited by Baghat Korany, Rex Brynen and Paul Noble reflect the globalization perspective. In more depth, global–local dynamics are charted in works such as *Postmodernism and Islam* by Akbar S. Ahmed, *Orientalism, Postmodernism and Globalism* by Bryan S. Turner, *Islam, the Middle East and the New Global Hegemony* by Simon Murden, and *Globalization and the Politics of Development in the Middle East* by Clement Henry and Robert Springborg.

PART VII

Modern Issues and Contemporary Challenges

CHAPTER TWENTY

Islamic Urbanism, Urbanites, and the Middle Eastern City

MICHAEL E. BONINE

Studies focused on the city or its inhabitants in the Middle East over the last several decades have continued to provide new and meaningful insights, reflecting the growing sophistication of methodologies and approaches in history and the social sciences in general. From the perspective of many disciplines, there is a greater use of primary records and data as well as an increasing number of programs, institutes, and journals which focus on the city. This chapter examines the principal trends of the more recent scholarship and literature on the city in the Middle East.

The Demise – and Persistence – of the Islamic City Model

The French orientalists' background for the emergence of a model of the Islamic city has been addressed by Raymond (1994, ch. 11), who also discusses how revisionists' views began to emerge in the second half of the twentieth century. Several conferences and volumes included perspectives on the Islamic city at this time (Lapidus, 1969; Hourani and Stern, 1970; L. Carl Brown, 1973), soon followed by other edited works in the 1980s (Sergeant, 1980; Serageldin and El-Sadek, 1982; Germen, 1983; Saqqaf, 1987). This decade of focus on the (Islamic) city culminated in the research project, "Urbanism in Islam," sponsored by the Japanese Ministry of Education, Science and Culture in 1989–91, when in October 1989 over 200 participants assembled in Tokyo for the International Conference on Urbanism in Islam (Yukawa, 1989).[1]

The most critical and cogent analysis of the Islamic city remains, however, Janet Abu-Lughod's "The Islamic City – Historic Myth, Islamic Essence, and Contemporary Relevance" (1987). She indicates several strands (or *isnad*) of literature, one being the French orientalists that finalizes with von Grunebaum (Raymond, ch. 11) and another *isnad* provided by Lapidus (1967), whose work Abu-Lughod claims created generalizations about Muslim urban society based principally upon Mamluk Damascus, Cairo, and Aleppo. Whether Lapidus intended his work to be a more universal model of the Islamic city may be debatable; however, in other works he does propose that a Muslim urban society with specific characteristics and institutions only emerged by the tenth and eleventh centuries in the Middle East (Lapidus, 1969b).

It is, in fact, the institutions of Muslim society which have become the focus for many discussions of Middle Eastern urban society and hence the Islamic city. Physical characteristics, which dominated the discussions of the orientalists, have been augmented by the deepening understanding of the role and place of *shari'a* (Islamic law) and particular Muslim/Islamic institutions within Middle Eastern societies. For example, the Ottoman historian, Inalcik (1990), depicts how the Byzantine capital became an Islamic capital after 1453 by the founding of bazaars, *bedestans* (a type of closed bazaar), mosques, and *madrasas* (religious schools), as well as creating Muslim neighborhoods by importing Muslims into the city to replace the Christian Greeks and other departed groups. *Waqf* (religiously endowed property) was a key for many of the new structures, which was used particularly to support newly built *imarets*, which were complexes of mosques, *madrasas*, hospitals, hospices, fountains, libraries, and other structures. Other studies of the importance of *waqf* or the role of the *qadi* (judge) will be detailed below.

Although a discussion of the characteristics of – or the existence of – an Islamic city per se is not as central as it might have been in the 1970s and 1980s, there still have been continued major critiques and summaries of the Islamic city in the literature. A number of Japanese historians have been responsible for several edited volumes on the Islamic city (Haneda and Miura, 1994; Tsugitaka, 1997), marking the influence and legacy of the extensive Japanese project on Islamic urbanism mentioned above. That many scholars consider the concept of the Islamic city to be dead or of little use, is noted by Haneda, who stresses that "it is time urban studies in the Islamic world were given a new framework and methodological direction" (Haneda, 1994).

On the other hand, a few scholars – or professionals – continue to adhere to the idea of an Islamic city. This is particularly true for some architects or planners who have written on the city in the Middle East (but less so for the architectural/art historians). For instance, Stefano Bianca, an architect and planner who worked for over thirty-five years in consulting for urban renewal and city planning projects throughout the Middle East, in his *Urban Form in the Arab World* (2000) ascribes considerable influence to Islam for the form and function of Arab cities. He believes that the Islamic built environment is due to the "traditional Muslim philosophy of life" and hence his purpose is "to explore the inner motivations behind visual structures as the main sources of pre-formal shaping forces and morphological structuring principles" (p. 9). Seeing Islam as an all-embracing religion with a set of ritualized patterns of human behavior, comes full circle to the orientalists' viewpoint: "Islam as a religious and social order has always maintained a certain archaic simplicity. Its way of life remained faithful to the original modes of human behaviour defined by the first nucleus of the Muslim community in Medina" (p. 11). A spiritual dimension is also present for Islamic architecture and art, particularly as espoused – and influenced by – Titus Burckhardt (1976), and hence the sacred becomes part of Bianca's explanation of the Islamic built environment.

With Bianca we once again see the arguments of the French orientalists, including advocacy of the strong nomadic (and tribal) background of Middle Eastern society (which influences urban form!), the focus on the absence of formal, civic institutions, and the lack of central planning. Although these beliefs and orientalist arguments have long been discounted by historians and other scholars, the fact that his book is published by Thames & Hudson, the influential publisher of art and architecture books, is an indication that a new generation, of at least architects and city planners, will need to be alerted to the possible pitfalls of these (spiritual) causal explanations of the Islamic built environment as espoused by Bianca.

Other architects have continued to identify an Islamic or Muslim city, although they contribute perhaps more reasoned explanations for some of the patterns of the city than Bianca. Basim Hakim (1986) lays out principles and guidelines for the Islamic built environment based upon (Maliki) *shari'a*. Using the rulings of *qadis* from fourteenth-century Tunis, he proposes how the *shari'a* provided for minimum street widths and heights of buildings, screening of roofs from onlookers, eliminating protrusions into the street, ownership of shared walls between owners, regulating rainwater from one neighbor's roof to another, and regulating waste water channels and cesspools. Yet, by juxtaposing fourteenth-century Maliki law with the traditional, contemporary *medina* of Tunis, Hakim discounts, or at least clouds, the possibility of evolutionary change over the centuries, and his model for the Islamic built environment suggests the orientalists' frozen orient.

Both Bianca and Hakim represent a view prevalent among many architects and urban planners focused on the Middle East – that contemporary "modern" structures and planning are not conducive to the Islamic Middle East, and that there is a need to turn to traditional structures and principles, calling for an "Islamic renaissance". Jamel Akbar (1988), for instance, examines the patterns of responsibility, the "forms of submission" over property, and the elements of the traditional built environment of the Muslim (Islamic) city. He advocates that the typical texture of the Muslim built environment is due to principles regulating four elements: (1) *fina'* (space on the street abutting a property used exclusively by those owners); (2) dead-end streets; (3) *hima* (land which cannot be developed by individuals); and (4) public spaces such as streets and squares. Akbar received a Ph.D. in architecture in 1984 from the Massachusetts Institute of Technology, and it is, in fact, a joint program at MIT and Harvard which has been responsible for much work on Islamic urbanism and architecture during the last few decades.

In 1979 the Aga Khan Program for Islamic Architecture was established, with generous support by the Aga Khan and a collaborative effort between the MIT Department of Architecture and the Department of Fine Arts and the Graduate School of Design at Harvard; co-founded by Oleg Grabar, the first Islamic art and architecture professor to teach at Harvard (and the first Aga Khan Professor of Islamic Art and Architecture in the Fine Arts Department at Harvard), and William L. Porter, the head of MIT's Department of Architecture. Grabar created a "school" of Islamic art and architecture, with dozens of students receiving their Ph.D. working with him at Harvard, while at MIT many Ph.D. students have focused on planning and Islamic architecture. The program also created the Harvard Documentation Center for Islamic Architecture. The architecture program has sponsored exhibits and conducted many workshops, conferences, studio courses, and field studies, including, for instance, projects or studio courses in Aleppo, Cairo, Fez, Essaouira [Morocco], Bukhara, Peshawar, and Mostar [then in Yugoslavia]). The Aga Khan Program for Islamic Architecture is responsible for perhaps the leading journal in Islamic urbanism and architecture (and art), *Muqarnas: An Annual on Islamic Art and Architecture*, which began in the early 1980s.

Separate from the MIT and Harvard Aga Khan Program is the Aga Khan Award for Architecture, based in Geneva. It has supported even more workshops and publications, as well as awards for contemporary Islamic architecture and urban planning. Whether or not historians and other social scientists agree if there is an Islamic city – architects and planners have been producing what they consider is an Islamic built environment: mosques, religious schools, Islamic houses, Islamic parks, Islamic neighborhoods – and hence Islamic cities. A number of the Aga Khan Award's publications are the proceedings of conferences and provide papers and discussions about planning and architectural issues related to the Middle East (and the Muslim world) (e.g., Aga Khan Award for Architecture, 1978, 1980).

An understanding of the city in Islamic times has benefited considerably from the field of Islamic art and architecture (i.e. architectural history), a field that encompasses historical and archaeological perspectives as well. Although the focus of this work is often on the characteristics and evolution (and diffusion) of individual architectural elements and building styles, with a particular emphasis on monumental buildings, their studies nevertheless have contributed to our interpretations of the built environment in the Islamic context. The pioneering work on early Islamic (monumental) architecture of K. A. C. Creswell (1932–40) has been expanded or reinterpreted by other scholars (e.g. Ettinghausen and Grabar, 1987; Hillenbrand, 1995; Blair and Bloom, 1994). Yet, the fact that there is a multitude of articles and major treatises on Islamic or Muslim architecture provides a continuing possible credence – and quandary – for the debate and quest for the existence of an Islamic city.

Some studies (or collections) represent a number of disciplinary approaches that examine one specific (Islamic period) city. For example, a volume on medieval (ninth-century) Samarra (Robinson, 2001) resulted from a symposium held at Oxford in 1996 with specialists representing Islamic history, numismatics, archaeology, and medieval Arabic literature. Other examples include multi-disciplinary studies on San'a and Jerusalem (Serjeant and Lewcock, 1983; Auld and Hillenbrand, 2000).

Finally, it should be mentioned that (besides Jerusalem), Istanbul has perhaps the largest number of studies on a single city in the Middle East. Much of the work on Istanbul has been done by Turkish scholars (and often published only in Turkish). Kuban's history of Istanbul (1996), is a most comprehensive overview of the city, and no other city in the Middle East has been covered as comprehensively as the eight-volume encyclopedia of Istanbul (Dunden Bugune Istanbul Ansiklopaedisi, 1993–5). Published only in Turkish, these volumes have extended entries on mosques and other important buildings, neighborhoods, individuals, organizations, institutions, major events, physical features, and many other items related to the history, society and culture of Istanbul. Accompanied by a plethora of colored (and black and white) photographs and maps, Istanbul has been documented like no other city in the Middle East (or most other cities of the world, in fact).

Social and Urban Histories: The Mining of Primary Documents

One genre of studies which has emerged more strongly within the last several decades has concentrated on social urban history, a reflection of the growing interest and methodology for understanding societies and individuals in the social sciences in general. It is an attempt to understand the complexities of (urban) society as well as the role and life of the typical individual. The importance of subcommunities, social networks, and patronage relationships have helped us understand how the urban society functioned – and how individuals flourished, struggled, or just survived.

Social histories of cities in the Middle East have become possible particularly because of the extensive use of primary documents. One of the earlier and most comprehensive, monumental, works is S. D. Goitein's six volumes (1967–88) based upon the use of fragment documents from Cairo's Geniza, a storeroom attached to a synagogue for discarded writings that could not be thrown away because they might contain the name of God.[2] Goitein reconstructs the social and economic Mediterranean world of the eleventh century. Since most merchants, judges, and other individuals who wrote these documents lived in cities, particularly in Fustat (next to Cairo), these volumes provide amazing details about medieval urban society (and the documents are not limited to the Jewish population of the times).

Other documents which have provided major insights into urban society are *sijills*, the *shari'a* court records of the *qadi* or Islamic judge. Marcus's study of eighteenth-century Aleppo (1989), for example, shows how Aleppo provided and distributed its food, how taxes were collected and the city administrated, how real estate transactions worked and houses changed ownership, how merchants operated within the city, how health – and death – was dealt with in the city, and how *sharia* court decisions affected the population, and the status and role of women in the city. The use of *sijills* enables us to begin to have an in-depth understanding of this Arab, Ottoman city and its society.

The use of Ottoman archives, in fact, has transformed historical studies of the Ottoman period, and these documents have provided new primary sources for understanding the city. The study of sixteenth- and seventeenth-century cities in Anatolia by the historian Suraiya Faroqhi (1984, 1987) represents such use of extensive primary archival documents to reconstruct the economy and society of this period: how townsmen made a living, how houses were bought and sold, how retailers and merchants bought and sold their goods, and many other facets of socio-economic life. Similarly, for Ottoman Cairo, the historian Nelly Hanna, using, for example, *qadi* court records (and *waqf* records – see below), has provided several in-depth studies of the housing, merchants, and the urban history of Cairo (1983, 1984, 1991, 1998).

Waqf documents have provided yet another rich source for reconstructing urban society in the past. The use and analysis of *waqf* deeds was pioneered particularly by Ömer Lutfi Barkan (e.g. 1970) using Ottoman documents, and what has emerged with more and more studies in the last several decades is the confirmation that *waqf* was one of the fundamental institutions of the city and Muslim society in the Middle East. *Waqf* documents have enabled us to better understand property and incomes, individual obligations, economic relationships, and the support of mosques, religious schools and other institutions.

McChesney's portrayal of four hundred years in the history of the 'Alid shrine in Balk, Afghanistan (1991), provides an unusual long-term social history, and an example of how a city, Mazar-i Sharif, was created: "The transformation of the shrine from village holy site to urban conglomeration was largely dependent on the economic fortunes of the shrine, and these in turn were predicated mainly on the management of the waqf endowment" (p. ix). In another study of (mainly eighteenth-century) Ottoman Damascus, Leeuwen (1999) shows how *waqf* itself was used as an instrument of political and economic control, as well as a mainstay for the social system.

A rather unique source of primary material is related to Istanbul. At the end of the nineteenth century, foreign insurance companies came to the Ottoman capital to provide fire risk insurance for houses and office or public buildings. This was particularly prompted by a huge fire in the main foreign neighborhood of Pera (Beyoglu) in 1870 – such fires being common among the wooden houses of Istanbul.

This led to a set of fire risk cadastre maps for Istanbul being commissioned in 1904–6, drawn by the British Chase E. Goad construction engineering company. This was then followed by maps drawn by French and Germans, completed in 1919. However, a much more widespread and detailed set of maps of Istanbul was prepared from 1922 to 1945 by Jacques Pervititch, an Austrian topographer of Croatian origin. These cadastre maps, referred to as the Insurance Maps of Pervititch, provide at scales of 1:2400 and then 1:600 or 1:500 amazing detail – lot by lot, house by house (with addresses!), information about the type of housing, construction materials and techniques, as well as the land use of the empty spaces.[3] All the maps have been brought together in one publication, a rather huge volume with the maps published in color (Aya Oyak, 2000), where the assertion is made that "[they] expect the Pervititch maps to be one of the basic reference sources for empirical urban history research in the 21st century" (p. 15).

The city of Jerusalem has been the subject of thousands of works that can be characterized as biblical or religious literature, although the city is also the focus of much serious urban research as well, ranging from Mamluk architecture (Burgoyne, 1987) to historical geographic studies on nineteenth- and early twentieth-century Jerusalem (Ben-Arieh, 1984, 1986; Kark and Michal, 2001). These latter studies, in fact, represent the development of a strong field of historical (urban) geography among Israeli geographers. Another work that needs to be singled out is F. E. Peters's work on Jerusalem (1985), whose volume is a collection of first-hand accounts of the city by pilgrims, chroniclers, and various visitors over the millennia.

Peters, in fact, has written a similar work on Mecca (1994), which therefore provides us with stories and accounts of this most important city for Islam. And then, in a more intriguing book relevant to this chapter, Peters has compared Jerusalem and Mecca as a typology of the holy city (1986). He devises a set of criteria for a holy city, and, interestingly, and significantly, completely avoids the "Islamic city" debate as discussed above. Both cities are centers for pilgrimages, but not just "the mere existence of . . . holy places, but rather the presence in the city of a *sacrum* . . . [which] exercises an attraction not merely on the city's immediate hinterland but over an extended network" (p. 3, italics in original).

Form, Water and the Urban Fabric: Morphologies of the Middle Eastern City

The classic model of the Islamic city concentrated on certain physical attributes, such as the existence and location of bazaars, mosques, baths, walls, and palaces. However, a rather more sophisticated treatment of morphology has emerged within the last few decades, particularly by some architects who concentrate on the urban texture or urban fabric. This means that instead of focusing on just one building complex, the aim is to understand how the various elements, from housing to religious and commercial buildings, are arranged and how they interact and function. Space and settlement patterns become the objective of study.

One scholar who has contributed considerably to this orientation is the Italian architect Attilio Petruccioli, who founded *Environmental Design: Journal of the Islamic Environmental Design Research Centre*. This approach advocates that there is (and perhaps can be created in design) an Islamic urban fabric or cityscape. Hakim (1986) also examines the urban fabric, identifying the urban and architectural elements for what he considers an Islamic design. Geographers, particularly Germans, also have contributed to morphological studies of the Islamic city (the *orientalische Stadt*), writing detailed monographs of specific Middle Eastern cities (or regions). One of these geographers, Eugen Wirth (2000), has published an extensive two-volume work (in German) which represents a lifetime of scholarship, bringing together in one place his ideas and contributions which have been published in numerous journal articles, chapters, and books over the decades. The bazaar or *suq* often has been a principal focus of the German work as well (e.g. Gaube[4] and Wirth, 1978, 1984). Extensive maps of cities and associated monographs also have part of the monumental project, the *Tübinger Atlas des Vorderen Orients (TAVO)*.

Water and architecture have provided the theme for a number of urban studies, where the influence and design of water systems for palaces, Islamic gardens, or entire cities (including Mughal gardens in India) provide the focus (e.g. Petruccioli, 1994). Bonine (1979) has explained how traditional irrigation and canal systems (*qanats*) have influenced the structure and orientation of many traditional Iranian cities. Instead of the stereotypical chaotic irregularity, the traditional streets of many Iranian cities were rather orthogonal, following irrigation canals and pathways and roads which were determined by the slope and orthogonal field patterns.

The form of Iranian cities is only one possibility in the debate on whether or not traditional Middle Eastern (or Islamic) cities were planned – or hence unplanned. While spontaneous or "organic" city growth may occur, as in the case of Iranian cities, certain "royal" cities, ranging from Samarra and the classic Mansur's round city of Baghdad to the Moroccan palace complex and establishment of Fez Jdid (New Fez), indicate that often there was extensive planning (e.g. see Wirth, 2000). For one possible "Islamic" influence, Bonine (1990) has investigated whether the *qibla* (direction of prayer towards Mecca) had any influence on the morphology and orientation of cities in Morocco. He finds that some cities were indeed laid out in the direction of the *qibla*, which determined many street patterns and the city axis if the slope conditions allowed.

Morphological characteristics sometimes have been the principal means used to identify "regional" types of Islamic cities. The proposal by Raymond (ch. 11) of the existence of a traditional Arab–Mediterranean city is an example of this approach. Of course the classic Islamic city model was in essence mainly a description of the North African or Maghrebi city (and especially the Moroccan city). Other analyses of Muslim (period) cities which discuss, and hence somewhat create normative regional models, include, for example, works on Ottoman, Balkan, Iranian, and Central Asian cities (Bierman, et al., 1991; Todorov, 1983; Gaube, 1979; Kheirabadi, 1991; Giese, 1980).

Urbanization and Modernization: From Colonialism to the Global

The Middle East has undergone extensive urbanization and transformative changes in the twentieth century. Rural to urban migration and the simple demographics of greater number of births versus deaths have continued to increase the urban population – despite decreasing national fertility rates in the last several decades. First, it should be mentioned that historical urban development and population growth (and hence urbanization) constitute the subject of numerous studies (or are part of more comprehensive works). Examples of the latter, for instance, include two major urban histories of Cairo, one by a historian (Raymond, 2000) and another by a sociologist (Abu-Lughod, 1971), and one on Istanbul by an architect and urban historian (Kuban, 1996). Another architect, Çelik (1986), shows how Istanbul in the second half of the nineteenth century, similar to the story of Cairo, re-created many of the urban physical features of European cities (with Paris especially as the model).

The Qajar dynasty of Iran in the nineteenth century also attempted European-style planning in Tehran, modeled on Paris (and being impressed with the changes being implemented in Cairo and Istanbul). In 1867 Nasser od-Din Shah, taking advantage of widespread damage to the Qajar capital caused by recent floods, demolished the old city walls and expanded the city from three to seven and a half square miles, building a new wall and moat. New wide and straight streets were built, lined by trees and water channels (Gurney, 1992).

Other impacts of European colonialism on the city have been documented; for instance, for Alexandria (Reimer, 1997) and Morocco (Wright, 1991). In the latter work, Wright advocates that during the French protectorate of Morocco the plans and policies of the Resident-General Hubert Lyautey and the architect and urban planner Henri Prost, had a dual purpose: modernization and preservation. *Villes nouvelles* were created next to the *madinas*, especially to attract French *colons*, while the traditional *madinas* – and its culture – were to be preserved. "Their goal … was to protect certain aspects of cultural traditions while sponsoring other aspects of modernization and development, all in the interest of stabilizing colonial domination" (p. 85). Abu-Lughod (1980), in a work centered on Rabat, condemns the French policies for creating what she provocatively calls "urban apartheid" in Morocco.

General studies of urban (or population) growth and urbanization, including statistical analyses, are not common for the Middle East, although specific countries or smaller regions have been examined more frequently. Most general discussions of the population of the Middle East devote little attention to the urban population or to urbanization. One of the few books specifically on urbanization in the Middle East is the woefully out-of-date (and small) volume by Costello (1977). The continuing rapid urban growth and primacy has been more recently discussed by Bonine (1997c) in an overview of cities in the Middle East up to the mid-1990s.

Located in Tours, France, the Centre d'Etudes et de Recherches URBAMA (Urbanisation du Monde Arabe) in the last several decades has sponsored considerable field research and publications on contemporary cities in the (Arab) Middle East. These works include statistical and demographic studies, the results of field work and analyses of contemporary documents (e.g. census data), and various edited collections. The French have, in fact, funded and operated institutes in a number of cities in the Middle East, such as L'Observatoire urbain du Caire contemporain, which was established in 1984. Besides sponsoring contemporary urban research and projects in Cairo, it also publishes an informative newsletter.[5]

Migration to the city has fueled urban growth, and the study of labor migration and foreign laborers has emerged as a major theme for research. Although there are foreign migrant shepherds and agricultural laborers, particularly in the Arabian peninsula states, most jobs are in the city. In the 1970s and 1980s, Birks and Sinclair (e.g. 1980) provided detailed country case studies, as well as studies by others focused on human resources and labor issues (e.g. Serageldin et al., 1981). The Gulf states have been a particularly interesting case, where the "Petroleum Urbanization" was fueled by oil-boom revenues, including the construction of new petrochemical cities such as Jubail and Yanbu (Pampanini, 1997). In all six Arab states of the Gulf Cooperation Council (GCC) the majority of the labor force are foreigners – as well as constituting a majority of the total population in Kuwait, Qatar, and the United Arab Emirates (Bonine, 1997a). These welfare states have become dependent upon their foreign labor and attempts at Arabization of the labor force have not been very successful. Conservative social values also mean that few women participate in the labor force, even though more and more women are becoming highly educated in the Gulf (Kapiszewski, 2001).

Even the once small Saudi Arabian provincial town of 'Unayzah in the Najd has been shown to have undergone profound changes from the oil boom beginning in the 1970s. Soraya Altorki and Donald Cole, two anthropologists at the American University in Cairo, conducted field work between October 1986 and January 1987, providing a rare study of a Saudi Arabian town and its highly gender segregated society typical of the peninsula (1989). While Cole interviewed men, Altorki, as a female and Saudi national, had unusual access to the women. They document the economic and social changes and how many of these were occurring before the oil boom – yet, how the acceleration of these changes could indeed be called transformation. They indicate how the local population has evolved from being primarily domestically organized workers to wage labor and then to salaried employees, as foreigners become the unskilled and semi-skilled laborers. Yet, despite new houses, paved streets, new automobiles and other conspicuous consumption, they emphasize that "the boom ... did not solve the underlying problem of economic development – the creation of a modern productive economy capable of sustaining a high standard of living" (pp. 247–8).

Similar to the rest of the world, globalization has arrived in the Middle East, and this spread of free-market capitalism has had different results and reactions among the population, the vast majority of whom are urbanites. However, what form the impact takes on urban society is not always predictable, and there are local responses to globalization and foreign influences. Sharon Nagy (2000), an anthropologist, has shown how urban plans in Qatar were introduced by foreign consulting firms and were transformed by the local political and social situation. She indicates that a number of plans were not implemented because of the rapidity of population growth and development, while in other cases the local processes and relationships between certain ministries have promoted some plans and neglected others.

As modernization and globalization have overtaken the cities of the Middle East, the "traditional" urban fabric and buildings often have been demolished or considerably altered with urban renewal and new, grand projects, leaving little of the urban heritage and urban memory or identity for the new generations. This has led to attempts at urban conservation, to preserve not only significant buildings but also historic city centers ("saving the *madina*"). The dilemma has been how to preserve a culturally important site versus the rights, needs, and preferences of the population living in those areas. Pre-modern cityscapes and historic buildings attract tourists – and their dollars – and so the municipal (and national) governments, as well as international organizations such as UNESCO which are interested in preservation, are often in conflict with the local inhabitants. While the idea of creating a museum city (such as the Soviets did for Khiva, now in present-day Uzbekistan) is one possibility, the best solution is perhaps trying to establish a "living", vibrant old city in which the residents have a real stake. The projects to conserve the *madinas* of Fez and Aleppo are perhaps two of the best-known attempts to provide an urban design and program that would enable the residents to "re-establish an organic link with the past" and feel that they would benefit from such an endeavor (Bianca, 2000: 331). Yet, using the destruction of the urban heritage of Amman as the primary example, Al-Asad is able to lament that:

> [F]ar too many physical manifestations of the past in Amman and other cities in the Middle East have been destroyed. This destruction is part of a wider set of ruptures affecting this part of the world. These ruptures have partly resulted from the population explosions swelling its cities, which in turn are the consequences of such factors as natural population growth, migration from the countryside, policies of increased governmental centralization, and the political crises that have affected the region. These demographic explosions have destroyed feelings of identification that people had with their neighborhoods and cities ... Original inhabitants of a city such as Amman have seen their neighborhoods transformed beyond recognition. (pp. 60–1)

Cities have also had to be rebuilt because of war and civil conflict. The reconstruction of Beirut after its sectarian civil wars had damaged or destroyed much of its built environment, has provided a particular challenge to urban planners – and for government policies (Khalaf and Khoury, 1993). The old Central Business District of Beirut, in fact, was bulldozed completely, and an entirely new downtown constructed. A number of Iranian cities also had to be repaired or rebuilt after the Iran–Iraq War of 1980–8 had devastated many residences and other urban structures.[6]

Another city affected extensively by war and conflict is the holy city of Jerusalem. A magnified macrocosm of the Arab–Israeli conflict itself, the control of this symbolic city is still one of the major unresolved issues. The Israeli period, particularly after the reunification (or occupation, depending on point of view) of the city in 1967, has received considerable focus. For instance, Meron Benvenisti (1996), a former deputy mayor of Jerusalem, provides an insider's view of the politics and culture of the city, while *Living Together Separately*, by a geographer and an anthropologist (Romann and Weingrod, 1991), as the title so aptly describes, is an examination of how Jews and Muslims have separate – and separated – experiences and existences. As they summarize:

> [O]ne of the most striking features of the united city is that an Arab or Jewish identity can be and is attributed to all neighborhoods, public functions, commercial establishments, and even basic consumer goods. There is very little that appears to be neutral or that can be given a different label: practically everything is categorized as either "Jewish" or "Arab." The boundaries between group members are also tight and apparently impermeable. (p. 221)

Romann and Weingrod conducted their research in the mid-1980s, before the *intifada* that began at the end of 1987, and that uprising would have reinforced the separation of the two groups even more. And even though the Oslo Accords and the peace process then progressed in the early 1990s, that was followed by Israeli governments less willing to negotiate with the Palestinians; and then the *al-aqsa intifada* began in September 2000. At the beginning of the twenty-first century Muslims and Jews in

Jerusalem are now more suspicious and afraid of each other, and even less willing or able to interact (Dumper, 2002).

Contemporary Urban Society and Politics: Further Perspectives from Anthropology and other Social Sciences

Many of the works previously discussed focus on contemporary urban society; yet, there are other studies that are also based on another type of primary data – field research and interviews. It is particularly anthropologists who have used this methodology to provide significant insights into the lives of individuals as well as the wider society. Yet, anthropological and sociological research on society (urban or rural) is often curtailed or even prohibited by some governments in the Middle East, and so this type of investigation sometimes can be difficult or even impossible. This means that Morocco, Egypt, Yemen, Turkey, and Iran (before the Islamic Republic) have had numerous studies, while they are rare in the GCC states and almost non-existent in such states as Libya, Syria, or Iraq.

A number of monographs on specific cities are examinations of urban societies as a reflection of a national or regional pattern (Moroccan, Egyptian, Yemeni, etc.), and indicate the variety and complexity of what has often been lumped together as "Middle Eastern society" or "Muslim society." Since there is seldom the situation of having both a male and female researcher, as was the case for Altorki and Cole's study of 'Unayzah, as mentioned above, the gender of the researcher affects which members of the society he or she can interact with or interview. The degree of gender segregation also differs in various regions of the Middle East as well as for class and social levels.

Urban minorities, particularly the Jewish populations of North Africa, have received considerable attention by scholars, and the literature on minorities and Jews in the Middle East is, in fact, quite extensive (e.g. Hirschberg, 1974, 1981; Laskier, 1991; Deshen and Zemmer, 1996). As an officially recognized minority in Islam, a *dhimma* or people of the Book, Jews were protected by the state and provided important economic services, and although allowed to have their own rituals and beliefs, they always had to respect the sensibilities of the Muslims (Furman, 2000: 4). Hence Jews lived in separate neighborhoods or quarters. These living areas were somewhat imposed upon the Jewish communities, although the Jews actually preferred to be separate so that they could practice their beliefs and rituals unhindered by the Muslim majority. The *mellah*, in fact, was the name for the separate Jewish neighborhoods in most Moroccan cities. It often had straighter streets than the rest of the *madina*, and usually was next to the royal palace for protection and to be more accessible to the government for needed services (or taxes) (Brown, 1981; Miller, et al., 2001).

Besides interviews, anthropologists for many decades have incorporated considerable secondary written materials and even archival materials in their research on urban societies, and so any boundary between historian and anthropologist (and between other disciplines) is certainly a blurred one. For example, related to a work on the Jewish communities in Morocco (the anthropologist) Shlomo Deshen (1989) extensively uses collections of the legal responses of rabbis who served in the Jewish courts in the eighteenth and nineteenth centuries, and as he notes, his study "straddles two disciplines, history and social anthropology" (p. ix). Dale Eickelman's study of the city of Boujad (1976) focuses on popular Islam and how it is interpreted in new social and economic realities, and includes considerable information on the history and development of Moroccan Islam from secondary written materials. Another anthropologist, Kenneth Brown (1976), examining Salé from 1830 to 1930, uses substantial archival material from Moroccan families in that town.

Scholarship on women in Middle Eastern society has progressed considerably during the last several decades, and studies of gender relations in the city have similarly moved forward. The focus in these works is on women's experiences and their particular circumstances – or, often, their plight and problems in urban areas. There have been a number of monographs by mainly women anthropologists which concentrate specifically on women in urban areas, including, for example, works on women in Cairo, Zabid (Yemen), Khartoum, Fez, or Oman (Early, 1993; Wikan, 1980; Singerman and Hoodfar, 1996; Meneley, 1996; Cloudsley, 1984; Eickelman, 1984). Alexandria and other Egyptian urban areas have provided significant data for the medical anthropologist Marcia Inhorn's analyses of Egyptian women's reproductive behavior and crises (1994, 1996).

Social networks have become important for social scientists within the last few decades, and this is reflected in studies on urban society in the Middle East. For instance, Diane Singerman (1995) has focused on women and informal networks (and informal politics), from the household to the neighborhoods of Cairo, while Jenny White (1994) has investigated women's piecework and family workshop production in a poor rural immigrant neighborhood of Istanbul. White shows how women's work is devalued (women don't "work" even though they may spend 50 hours a week at this labor). Women labor mainly for the family and kin, and hence are poorly compensated for their toil and production.

White, in fact, has continued to maintain contacts and conduct research in the same suburb of Istanbul since the 1980s and this commuity, Ümraniye, is the foundation of her more recent book (2002), which provides insights into local (and national) politics in Turkey. She shows how social and community networks based upon personal face-to-face relationships are the key to understanding why the Islamists have been so successful in Istanbul (and elsewhere in Turkey). White stresses that the political success of the Islamists is not due to their religious message per se, but more due to "their unique organizational ability to incorporate a wide variety of local voices and desires into the national political process on a continual basis" (p. 274). In another focus on local or informal urban networks and associations, Guilain Denoeux (1993) has provided a comparative examination of urban unrest in Egypt, Iran, and Lebanon. One of his conclusions is that informal networks are the new grassroots strategy for political organization in the Middle East.

> [S]tudents of urbanization in the Third World should not overestimate the integrative qualities of urban networks, and they might wish to reassess the prevailing consensus concerning the stabilizing role that informal groups play among the urban poor. Ad hoc associations that reduce individual and societal stress by providing marginalized, alienated, or victimized populations with access to resources and sources of social solidarity can also operate as very effective structures for political mobilization against a regime. (p. 201)

Such networks might be found in informal or illegal (squatter) settlements on the margins of many cities in the Middle East. Besides White's studies mentioned above, there are other works focused on squatter settlements (or their inhabitants) in the larger cities, including Cairo, Istanbul, Ankara, Casablanca, Tunis, and Tehran, for example (Oldha, et al., 1987; El Kadi, 1987; Heper, 1978; Danielson and Keles, 1985; Khosrokhavar, 1992). In the case of many Turkish cities, the occupants of *gecekondus* or illegal settlements have been able to pressure the government for services and to obtain legal status for their land and houses in return for votes for particular political candidates and parties. In Tunis, the illegal settlements or *gourbi-villes* have been a major factor for the religious resurgence among the marginalized population (Vasile, 1997). In fact, throughout the Middle East it is often the Islamist groups who are providing actual aid and psychological support to the urban poor, as the governments are unable or unwilling to deliver the needed services.

Conclusions: The Challenge for Urban Studies

This chapter has brought out the increasingly multi-faceted and sophisticated approaches to understanding the city and its inhabitants in the Middle East. Many disciplines are involved and there are numerous ways to study or analyze these (often massive and rapidly increasing) conglomerations of people. Some focus on the architecture and the morphology or urban fabric in order to understand society in time and space. Others work with extensive archival records to recreate the past, and still others are interviewing today's urbanites, attempting to grasp the impact of globalization and the dynamic economic and social changes taking place today among the societies of the Middle East. Cities which have hundreds (and many with thousands) of years of history provide both challenges and opportunities to try and understand these past urban societies. Similarly, contemporary urban societies provide a challenge as to how to analyze (or be allowed to analyze) them.

In the 1970s, this author wrote a state-of-the-art article on urban studies in the Middle East for the *MESA Bulletin* (1976). Much more work on cities and urban societies has been done since that time, which not only is reflected in this essay, but also has been documented a decade ago in the extensive bibliography, *The Middle Eastern City and Islamic Urbanism* (Bonine, et al., 1994), which has over 7,500 entries (and needs to be updated!). As has been discussed, more use of primary sources and an emphasis on the influence of Islamic law and various institutions, such as *waqf*, have brought about much deeper understandings of how a city was organized and administered, and how the urban population coped, survived, and changed over time. The ability to manage greater amounts of material is providing new avenues for research. More nuanced understandings of gender and the role of women, and the fact that there are now more women conducting research among women and about women's issues in the Middle East, are most positive developments. The continuing accumulation of urban studies portends to provide us with many new perspectives, although because of limitations and prohibitions against certain kinds of research in some countries, certain types of studies remain very uneven geographically.

The Middle East is becoming one of the most urbanized regions of the world. And as the place where cities may have first emerged, cities and urbanites remain most fertile objectives of study. Yet we are only just beginning to understand the social histories of these cities and the dynamic changes (or resistance to change) of these contemporary urban societies. We have yet to really focus on solving the environmental and social problems of the urban areas (Bonine, 1997c), nevertheless solving the wider political problems leading to peace or a voice for the people in this region. Only when the latter begins to be accomplished will we be able to concentrate on understanding – and improving – the lives of the individual urbanite and the environments of the cities of the Middle East.

NOTES

1   A second but smaller conference was held in Tokyo the next year (1990), with proceedings published as well (Yukawa, 1994).
2   The Geneza records were known from the end of the nineteenth century and there were a few studies using them in the first half of the twentieth century. However, it is Goitein's work which has mined the most information from these documents, creating a Geneiza School, since his students have continued to use these records for other detailed analyses of society and economic conditions.
3   These insurance maps exist in several places in Turkey, including the Aya Oyak collection (an insurance company), the Ataturk Library, the German Archaeological Institute (and some at the University of Bonn in Germany), the Istanbul Chamber of Architects, and the Union of Insurance and Reinsurance Companies of Turkey. The insurance maps were utilized to project fire (and flood) risks and hence helped determine the price of coverage by insurance companies until the 1950s, after which they became less useful because of improvements against fire in the housing stock and better responses against fire by the municipality, as well as the fact that Istanbul had begun to expand considerably beyond the area of the original maps.
4   Heinz Gaube is not a geographer, but a Professor of Islamic Studies at the University of Tübingen and who was a specialist not only in Islamic Studies but also Iranian philology, art history, and archaeology.
5   Also, in Tehran there is the Institut Français de Recherche en Iran and similar French-sponsored research facilities in Istanbul and other cities in the Middle East.
6   Ahwaz, which had been virtually abandoned during the Iran–Iraq War, was largely destroyed, although other Iranian cities near the Iraqi border were also heavily damaged.

CHAPTER TWENTY-ONE

Oil and Development

PAUL STEVENS

Introduction

Throughout the twentieth century, international oil and the Middle East have been inexorably linked. The region, as an increasingly important oil producer and exporter, played and still plays a major role in influencing developments in the international oil industry. Equally, since the first oil was exported, the oil revenues and the oil operations have had a profound impact on the economic, social and political situation in both the Arab countries and the wider region. This chapter addresses these interrelated issues. We track the development of the region as a major oil exporter and its influence on developments in the wider international oil industry. Next, we consider the economic, social and political impact of the oil revenues and the industry more generally on the countries of the region.

Several qualifications are required. Constraints of space force heroic generalization. This is in a context where there were and are significant differences between the major oil exporting countries of the region. Thus much of the richness of the story is lost but hopefully those interested can pick up on this from the suggested reading listed at the end. Also, because this is aimed at a general audience, the normal academic citations and references are absent. However, the curious and the sceptical can satisfy themselves with this suggested reading although they should be warned that this is an area which suffers from a paucity of literature. Finally, the region itself is unhelpful geographically. The full story requires the inclusion of Iran which would be satisfied with the terminology of the 'Middle East'. However, the use of this term would exclude North Africa which has also played an important role in the story of both oil and development. But the term Arab world, which includes North Africa, of course excludes Iran. Thus throughout the chapter the use of the term 'region' denotes the Arab world and Iran

As the chapter will outline, it is very difficult not to conclude that the impact of oil on development in the region has been less than positive. What follows is generally a gloomy account of distortion and lost opportunities. How much of this negative picture is the result of oil is clearly a matter for debate and dispute. Without doubt, other forces have been at work ranging from a post-colonial legacy, the occupation of Palestine and a global economic system which is often cruel and unforgiving to its participants, to name but a few. However, in this chapter the emphasis is on oil as a cause for so much of the region's woes. While the story is more complex than this, such a view does fit into the more general literature on why resource abundant countries perform badly compared with those less generously endowed by nature. Thus this rather negative story is not confined to the region.

The Development of the Oil Industry

The development of the oil industry began with concession agreements. In all the countries of the region, as for the rest of the world outside of the USA, sub-soil minerals such as oil are the property of the state. In the early days of the industry, no country in the region had the technical or managerial ability to develop these oil resources. Foreign companies were required to provide the skill, capital and markets for their development. The extent to which such company involvement was part of the tools and aims of empire is much discussed in the literature, given the hegemony exercised by the major powers, specifically Britain and France. However, whatever the historical reality, within the region, the oil companies were seen to be an extension of colonial power. This fact of perception became a very important part of the story.

In the early decades of the twentieth century, there were only a small number of such companies, the so-called 'seven sisters'. To use their modern names these were BP, Chevron, Exxon, Gulf, Mobil, Shell and Texaco. Conventionally, the French company CFP is also added to make the 'eighth sister'. Collectively they became known as the majors. They operated in the region under the terms of the various concession agreements between themselves and the governments. Table 21.1 lists the early agreements. After the 1950s, for reasons to be explained, the nature of these agreements changed, moving towards joint ventures and other forms of production sharing and service contracts as newer companies entered the arena.

It was these old-style concession agreements which set the context for subsequent developments. While the details of the agreements differed there were four common features which can be identified. First, the agreements were for very long periods of time. The four concessions in Iran, Iraq, Kuwait and Saudi Arabia had an average life of 82 years. Second, the agreements covered very large tracts of territory. In the case of Iraq and Kuwait the agreements covered the whole of the country. Furthermore, unlike later agreements, these early agreements had no provision for relinquishing acreage. In effect the companies could sit on the acreage for a long time, do nothing themselves and at the same time prevent the government from doing anything. A third common feature was the financial terms. In the concessions these were a fixed royalty paid per ton of production. The final feature was the huge amount of managerial control ceded to the oil companies in the development of their concession

Table 21.1   A history of oil agreements in the Middle East

Country	Agreement	Date
Iran	D'Arcy Concession	1901
	Iranian Consortium Agreement	1954
Iraq	Turkish Petroleum Company	1911
	Iraq Petroleum Company	1928
Kuwait	Kuwait Oil Company	1933
Saudi Arabia	Socal Concession	1933

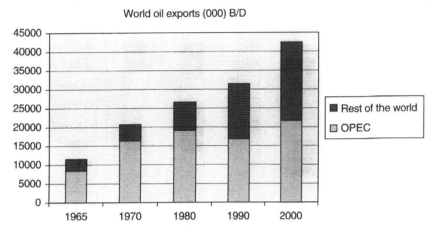

Figure 21.1   Sources of world oil exports, 1965–2000
Source: *BP Statistical Review of World Energy*

areas. Apart from requirements of 'good oil field practice' which some but not all the agreements contained, the companies had complete discretion and freedom to decide on the extent of exploration, whether discovered reserves should be developed, the level of production and how the oil should be disposed of. In effect they became a state within a state with total control over what was to become in most cases the key resource of the country. The importance of oil and oil exports flowing from these agreements grew both for the world oil markets and the countries of the region. The magnitudes are well illustrated in figures 21.1 and 21.2.

The key to this growing role of the region's oil supplies lay in changes to the pricing mechanisms for oil. Prior to 1928, the international oil industry had been characterized by intense and vicious price wars between the majors. In 1928, tired of the negative consequences of such competition, the majors negotiated the 'as-is' agreement which was intended to end price wars. A key ingredient was the 'Gulf basing point system'. Thus oil products imported anywhere in the world had a landed price as though they had been bought and shipped from the US Gulf of Mexico. This 'uniformity' was achieved by the addition of a 'phantom freight rate' which the majors then pocketed. In 1944, the British and American navies complained to their governments of this practice. The outcome was that the Iranian Abadan Refinery at the head of the Persian Gulf became a second basing point. This crucial decision effectively opened up world oil markets to lower-cost Middle East crude whose natural market was now determined by real freight costs. In 1945, the western limit of this market was the east coast of Italy. By 1949, it had extended to the east coast of the USA. The introduction of this dual basing point system began the era in which Middle East oil exports dominated world oil trade. Figure 21.2 shows the importance of the region in OPEC since the 1960s.

While these concession agreements started the process of producing and exporting oil, they also triggered a series of growing concerns from the governments of the region which were to have a profound effect on the development of the oil industry in the Middle East and the wider world.

There were two broad areas of criticism which emerged through the 1950s. The first criticism was the rigidity of the agreements. Quite simply, there was no option to

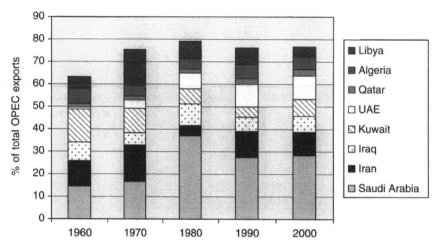

Figure 21.2   Middle East and North African share of OPEC production, 1960–2000
Source: *OPEC Statistical Bulletin*, various years

renegotiate terms despite their long life and the fact they covered so much of the available acreage. The second criticism was the issue of managerial control.

The relinquishment issue received a boost when, in 1960, Iraq implemented Law 80. This was a unilateral taking of all of the company's acreage except existing producing fields. This prompted others in the region to relinquish acreage to pre-empt a repeat performance. The consequent availability of acreage enabled newer oil companies to enter the region. These included the national oil companies of the consuming countries such as ENI, Hispanoil, Deminex and the Japanese National Oil Company and the smaller American 'independents' such as Occidental, Philips, and Amoco etc. The fact these new entrants were willing to offer not only better terms but also a much greater role for the governments, put the older-style concession agreements under ever greater pressure.

The disputes over the financial terms of the concessions rumbled on. At the start of the 1950s, following the lead set by Venezuela, the region's oil producers moved to a system of profits tax as well as royalties, based upon the setting of posted prices. The next twenty years saw a succession of disputes and negotiations over the precise terms of the fiscal take ranging from the treatment of royalties to various other accounting issues, not least the percentage of profits tax. However, the result was a growing volume of oil revenues feeding into the countries of the region.

However, such renegotiated changes, although important, failed to address the second area of criticism, the managerial freedom available to the companies. The result was that host governments continually put pressure on the companies to secure greater control over decision making. This desire for control by governments was driven by three factors.

First, they wanted to determine the rate at which the oil was developed and produced. After 1960, the posted prices (which determined tax-take) were effectively fixed following the creation of OPEC. This creation had been in response to companies' effort to lower these prices unilaterally. Thus the only mechanism to increase government revenue was to increase production. As the governments became progressively more dependent on oil revenues, this imperative grew.

Second, there was a growing view that the oil sector should play a more integrated role in the economic development of the countries, especially as a spur to industrialization which was seen as the obvious means of progress. This is discussed in more detail later. It was perceived this could be achieved more easily if governments had greater control over procurement for the industry. A related issue of control was the flaring of associated gas by the oil companies which was seen by the governments as a waste of national resources.

Finally, there was the politics. The majors were seen as tools of the former imperial powers – Britain and France or tools of the imperial power in waiting – the USA. As such, they were seen as a serious threat to sovereignty. This was at a time when the United Nations Organization among others was pushing the concept of 'permanent sovereignty over natural resources'. This argued that governments should control these resources rather than companies. Such ideas fell on very fertile soil in the countries of the region.

Thus the 1960s saw the start of a growing battle for control between the governments of the region and the majors. In an effort to move towards greater managerial control, the governments began to create their own national oil companies. This began in Iran in 1951 with the creation of the National Iranian Oil Company. By the early 1970s, every oil producing country had its own national oil company.

However, there was reluctance within the governments to nationalize. This was for two reasons. First, there was the fate of the Iranian nationalization. The ousted Dr Mossadegh, the architect of the nationalization process, faced a death sentence from the new government following the coup of 1954 designed by the British and Americans to resolve the nationalization dispute. Second, there was concern that nationalization would break up the majors' control of the international oil market leading to price weakness. During the 1960s the majors, through their joint control of Gulf oil supplies, had been able to manage the excess capacity to produce oil in such a way as to mute any downward pressure on prices. Thus the major operating companies such as the Iraq Petroleum Company (IPC), the Kuwait Petroleum Company (KPC), the Arabian American Oil company (Aramco) and the Iranian Consortium orchestrated crude supply to balance the global oil market. However, as new supplies developed in response to greater exploration and development by new companies, national oil companies and the majors; this put growing pressure on the ability of the majors to manage the excess capacity. As the decade of the 1960s progressed, the real price of oil continued to fall, aggravated especially by growing competition among the national oil companies selling crude. It was greatly feared that general nationalizations in the region would simply aggravate such price competition.

Their reluctance to nationalize created a fundamental problem for the governments because they were under growing domestic political pressure to expel the foreign oil companies, seen as tools of the former imperial powers. This clamour to nationalize reached its peak in June 1967 as a backlash against the humiliating defeat of the Arabs in the Six Day War in which both the USA and Britain were seen as being instrumental by the 'Arab Street'.

In an effort to divert pressures for outright nationalizations, Shaykh Zaki Yamani, the oil minister of Saudi Arabia developed the idea of 'participation'. This was an attempt to get the majors into alliance with the producing governments to prevent the newer oil companies undermining the price structure. This was to be done by what Sheik Yamani described as a 'catholic marriage' (i.e. indissoluble). Thus the producer governments would take an increasing equity share in the operating companies, eventually reaching the controlling figure of 51 per cent. And, at the same time, they would take equity in the downstream activities – refining and marketing – of the majors who owned the operating companies. During the course of the negotiations, this latter demand for downstream involvement was put to one side but the resulting negotiations produced 'the General Agreement on Participation' in October 1972. This gave the governments an initial 25 per cent of the operating companies rising to 51 per cent within ten years.

However, while the 'participation' saga was unfolding, the oil market was also changing. Two factors were key. First, the announcement and process of 'participation' had effectively halted investment in capacity in the Gulf by the majors in anticipation of their losing access to equity oil. Second, following lower prices plus the world economic boom associated with the 'OECD economic miracle', world oil demand in the early 1970s began to grow strongly. The result of these two factors was a rapid erosion of the excess capacity which had characterized the oil market in the 1950s and 1960s. This, coupled with the growing pressure by the producer governments for greater control of their oil resources outlined earlier, moved the world inexorably towards the first oil shock.

Since the introduction of posted prices in 1949, the price of oil had been an administered price set by the majors. They had jealously guarded their unilateral ability/right to manage this process. Although they could have set the prices at fairly high levels they chose to set them at the lower range of what would have been possible. This was to pre-empt competition from nuclear, greatly feared by the majors in the 1960s and to prevent their own governments from interfering too much in their operations in response to excessive profitability. The post-Second World War decades had seen plentiful cheap oil fuelling the 'OECD economic miracle' causing the governments to 'leave oil to the oil companies'.

In Libya, in 1970, the new revolutionary government demanded that prices be the result of a negotiated process between themselves and the companies. Their eventual success opened the door to other governments in the region to join the negotiations operating through OPEC. The result was that the price was administered by both companies and governments in a market where supplies were tightening. In October 1973, the governments decided they no longer needed the majors' involvement in price setting and unilaterally announced two large increases in oil price in October and again in December, effectively quadrupling the international price of oil. They were unaware or uninterested in the competitive implications for oil in world energy markets and were unconcerned about the reaction of consumer governments. This was the first oil shock.

The result was a huge revenue windfall for the region's oil producers together with a rethinking of the role of the oil sector which will be discussed later. Initially, Saudi Arabia had been uneasy about the magnitude of the price hike but in 1975, with the accession of King Khalid, the higher price was accepted and Saudi Arabia effectively took on a swing role to protect the existing price but, at the same time, preventing it from going higher. Meanwhile, beginning with the Algerian and Iraqi nationalizations of their operating companies in 1972, the agreement on 'participation' began to unravel as governments demanded a greater equity share faster. Thus by 1976, with the exception of Abu Dhabi and Libya, the governments in the region had taken over the upstream oil operations. Not only did they now determine price, they also determined production levels and investment in the sector.

The Iranian oil workers' strike which began in October 1978, followed by the Iranian revolution and the Iraq–Iran War, all conspired to create the second oil shock whereby the price of oil tripled. The whole process of the second shock was driven by panic and misunderstanding as consumer governments, notably the USA and Japan, urged their companies to secure oil supplies at any price. Feeding this was the fact that many appeared to expect an Islamic revolutionary 'domino effect' to bring down governments on the other side of the Persian Gulf. This added to the scramble to secure oil supplies which fed the growing upward pressures on price.

In October 1981, OPEC eventually regained control of the market with the marker crude priced at $34 per barrel. However, the consequences of the two oil shocks were now beginning to appear in the market. On the demand side, oil began to be pushed out of the global primary energy mix. On the supply side, there began a major surge in non-OPEC supply. The combination put enormous pressure on OPEC's ability to defend the unprecedented high price as it struggled with problems of both cheating on production quotas (introduced in 1982) and overestimating the call on OPEC to make the negotiations on quota division easier. Up to 1985, Saudi Arabia was willing to absorb both cheating and error but the result was a collapse in Saudi production from over 10 million barrels per day (b/d) in 1981 to some 2.5 million b/d by the summer of 1985. At that point Saudi Arabia announced a major change in policy away from balancing the market and away from administered oil prices. The result in 1986 was a major price collapse – the third oil shock – with the price falling from the high twenties to the mid-teens in terms of dollars per barrel.

The situation was rescued by a joint understanding between Saudi Arabia and Iran developed during 1986. However, one of the dimensions of this understanding was to drop administered oil prices and instead use a mixture of spot prices of a limited number of crudes – mainly WTI, Brent and Dubai. Since these prices were determined in the marketplace and increasingly in forward and futures markets, they became increasingly volatile. Much of the subsequent history of the oil markets was the story of how OPEC struggled to defend prices, sometimes successfully, sometimes less so. However, the key was Saudi Arabia's role as market stabilizer. This was achieved because Saudi Arabia was willing and able to carry significant levels of excess capacity. It could then use this to offset the sorts of market disruptions associated with the events of 1990–1 and the events of 2003. In effect, Saudi Arabia became the central banker to the international oil market. This was a unique role which no other producer was able to replicate.

In addition to their impact on the oil market, such events also created significant regional tensions. In particular, the availability of oil revenues was key to allowing Iraq and Iran to wage war during the decade of the 1980s. Thus others in the region had a strong vested interest to ensure some constraints upon those revenues. For example, it seems clear that Kuwait's cheating in the late 1980s which presaged the Iraqi invasion, was aimed at weakening oil prices in an effort to weaken both protagonists. Thus OPEC deliberations were very much influenced by regional politics. As one Latin American OPEC member once remarked to the author, 'The problem of divisions within OPEC is simple. It is our butter and their guns!'

As the 1990s progressed, the oil producer governments of the region began to look again to the international oil companies for involvement in their oil sector. This was driven by two factors – the battle for capacity and a growing suspicion in some cases of the motivations of the national oil companies. Negotiations within OPEC over quota levels were strongly influenced by capacity. In particular, it was crucial that countries did not produce below their quotas for fear of losing volume in the next negotiations. In a sense, much of the crude producing capacity in the region was a legacy of the work and investment by the majors. Over time, the large fields which dominated production in the region began to tire and require not just attention but attention based upon the latest and best technology. In many cases this required involving foreign oil companies. A second motive for opening was to provide some means against which to benchmark the performance of the national oil company. This was driven by the growing suspicion that these companies were heavily involved in rent seeking, i.e. diverting resources away from the coffers of state for their own purposes. Thus countries such as Algeria, Iran, Iraq, Kuwait and even Saudi Arabia (for gas only) began programmes to secure foreign company investment in the upstream. The record of these attempts has been mixed as often the attempted opening fell foul of domestic politics.

In the future, the central role of the region in the international oil market is unlikely to diminish, at least in the next thirty years or so. Indeed, some such as the International Energy Agency see this role increasing in importance. The logic behind this view rests on the simple fact that in 2002, according to the BP Statistical Review of World Energy 2003, over 47 per cent of world exports came from the region, which also contained over 69 per cent of proven world oil reserves. It also stems from the unique role played by Saudi Arabia in trying to stabilize the oil market. Since the events of 9/11 and the invasion of Iraq in 2003, there has been much talk of the oil importers, especially the USA, finding alternatives in places as diverse as Russia, the Caspian and sub-Saharan Africa. However, the reality is that this is a virtually irrelevant quest. The oil market is truly international. What matters is not being able to get access to oil but the price of that access. If there are problems in the region and the oil price there spikes, it spikes everywhere irrespective of source.

However, at some point in the not too distant future the world will begin to want less oil as changes in technology forced by policy drivers such as the environment and supply security move the world to other fuel sources. When that process begins, the impact of oil on the region will be a function of what is left. As the next section argues, the generally negative impact of oil does not generate optimism.

The Impact on Development

How economists define 'development' has long been a source of debate and discussion. For the oil producers of the region, the traditional definition of growth in per capita gross national income has always been of limited value. First, because as a mean average it takes no account of income distribution which is particularly relevant where large oil revenues accrue to the state. Second, because as an exhaustible resource, the oil element of 'income' can be viewed as a liquidation of assets. In such a context, wider development definitions to do with standard and quality of life take on even greater significance.

At the risk of pre-empting the discussion in this section, the record of development in the Arab world has been poor. The recent joint report by the UNDP and the Arab Fund for Economic and Social Development – the Arab Human Development Report 2002, presents a damning condemnation of development progress in the Arab world. The headings of the overview tell it all. Thus the central section is on

'Aspirations for freedom and democracy remain unfulfilled' and contains four sections – 'Development not engendered is endangered'; 'bridled minds, shackled potential'; 'as development management stumbles, economies falter'; and finally 'the curse of poverty: denying choices and opportunities, degrading lives'.

The relevance of the last two paragraphs can be seen in figure 21.3. Thus the relatively higher per capita income in the Arab world has not translated into a creditable performance as measured by the UNDP's Human Development Index. The comparison is particularly noticeable in relation to the east Asia and Pacific region. To some degree this failure in the region can be attributed to the impact of the oil sector but the nature of the transmission mechanism from oil to development failure can be difficult to disentangle. Furthermore, it is dangerous to assert that the poor development record is entirely the result of oil revenues. As the introduction suggested, other complex political and economic factors have been at work. For example, a major source of economic failure in the region has been the weakness of the private sector. To some extent this was the legacy of revolutionary change in governments whereby the new ruling elites, generally from a military background, had to destroy the political power of the old elites. The most obvious method was to destroy their economic power. Thereafter, in the best traditions of predatory states, economic power was vested exclusively in the state via its ruling elite, to the exclusion of others. Thus what follows is only part of a very complex story.

An aspect which must be emphasized is the crucial importance of oil and gas exports throughout the region. There is a tendency to focus attention only on the regional OPEC members but the majority of other Arab countries are also highly dependent upon oil export revenues. Such countries include Egypt, Syria, Oman, Yemen and Bahrain. The picture is graphically illustrated in figure 21.4. Iraq is excluded for lack of data but effectively the majority of Iraqi merchandise exports since the 1980s have consisted of oil and oil products adding it to the list of oil dependent countries of the region. This section attempts to consider the impact of oil on development in the region in terms of three factors – oil revenue impacts, the

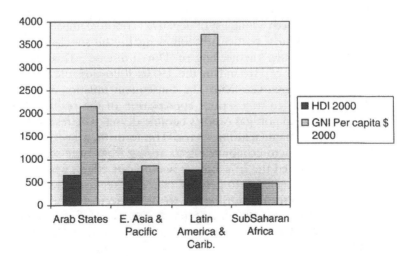

Figure 21.3   Per capita income and development: a regional comparison, 2000
Source: *World Bank Development Indicators* 2002

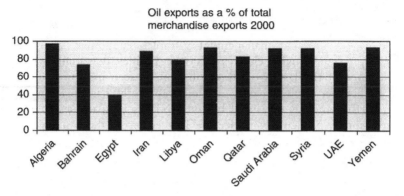

Figure 21.4   Oil dependence in the Middle East and North Africa
For Egypt and Qatar the data is for 2001; for Libya and Yemen 1998; for Kuwait 1999
Source: *World Bank Development Indicators*

forward linkages from the oil sector to the rest of the economy and the backward linkages from the sector.

The impact of oil revenues

The oil revenue impact needs to be considered in terms of its economic impact and its socio-political impact since both are keys to development. The patterns of revenue flow for the region's OPEC members are shown in figure 21.5. Without doubt, some benefits have accrued to the Arab oil exporters from the inflow of revenue. In many cases, it was the revenues which built the infrastructure of the economies. To be sure, during the process, much was wasted and much was quite inappropriate to the needs of the economy but certainly in the Gulf Cooperation Council (GCC) countries, without oil revenues there would be very little by way of basic infrastructure. Similarly, the oil revenues in many countries helped create a welfare state which undoubtedly benefited the bulk of the population with the provision of health, education and other basic services.

However, there has also been a long list of negative economic impacts arising from the influx of large oil revenues, particularly following the oil shocks of the 1970s. First, there is the impact under the heading of 'Dutch disease'. This was originally named after the experience of Holland in the 1970s following the discovery and development of the Groningen Gas field. The consequent inflation and changes to the nominal exchange rate led to a serious appreciation of the real exchange rate. Imports became cheaper and non-gas exports became dearer. The result was a major contraction in the Dutch manufacturing sector. The term then became used more widely for other negative macro-economic effects arising from large-scale oil and gas export projects. This included the so-called 'crowding out effect' whereby the successful hydrocarbon sector manages to get first call on other scarce resources in the economy thereby limiting their contribution to other sectors. For much of the region, the sector which suffered the greatest damage from these effects was agriculture, although as suggested earlier often the failure of this sector was also associated with earlier land reforms aimed at undermining the economic power of the ruling elites displaced by the new rulers. Since the majority of the population tended to live and work in rural areas, this clearly had negative effects for the bulk of the population.

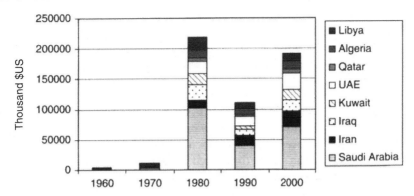

Figure 21.5 Oil export revenues in the region, 1960–2000
Source: *OPEC Statistical Bulletin*, various years

Second, the revenues tended to lead to too much state intervention in the economy. In part this was simply because, as the owner of the oil and gas, the revenues in the first instance accrued to the state and they were responsible for dissemination. In many cases, it was also driven by an ideological belief in the role of the state in an economy. However, the presence of large oil revenues made the dream of state intervention a more realistic possibility.

Two particular areas of such intervention were damaging. First, were attempts by governments to pick 'economic winners', usually in the form of large-scale heavy industry. In order to protect them from their own inefficiencies, often under the guise of the 'infant industry' argument, this required trade barriers and other forms of protection which insulated much of the economy from the necessary pressures of competition. Thus these 'winners' in most cases turned out to be inefficient, uncompetitive losers. They absorbed ever greater resources generating little by way of real wealth. Furthermore they never seemed to grow out of their 'infant' status, thereby reducing the need for protection. Indeed, to the contrary, they tended to create powerful political lobby support which allowed them to maintain and often strengthen the extent of their protection. The second area of intervention was a tendency to introduce subsidies on a variety of basic goods and services. To be fair this was seen as a way of dispersing some benefits from oil to the mass of the population where there were many barriers to alternative, more efficient means to disperse the wealth. However, such subsidies encouraged rapid and wasteful consumption of the services and embodied gross inefficiencies in the recipients and suppliers of subsidized inputs.

The final negative economic impact arose from the fact that large oil revenues enabled government to embark on very misguided spending programmes. Part of this misguided spending was to do with expenditure and investment in the economy referred to in the previous paragraphs. Another obvious area was in spending on the military although to be fair, faced with the threat posed by Israel, it can be argued there was little choice for the frontline states other than to divert resources into military preparedness. Also, the presence of so much money tended to feed conflict as differing parties used the oil revenues to fund their ideology at the expense of the ideology of others. Thus many civil wars and disorders in the region had 'foreign' paymasters to thank for the funds which fed the conflicts and kept them going.

In addition to the economic impacts from oil revenues, there were also serious socio-political effects, all of which, without exception, were negative.

The first most obvious point is that large-scale oil revenues entrenched regimes in the region. The revenues represented resources which could be used either to buy off opposition or to secure the means to suppress it. Thus incompetent and corrupt government was able to survive for much longer than would otherwise have been the case. Related to this was the fact that easy access to oil and gas revenues meant that governments did not need to try and raise revenue by other means. This lack of a fiscal link carried with it several implications. It meant there was little or no need for the governments to consult those they ruled. Imposing taxation forces people into demanding a greater say on who rules them and in demanding greater transparency and greater accountability in that rule. While it is true that many of the most successful economies since the 1970s have not been democracies, nonetheless, if economic progress is not the only criterion, then democracy in whatever form it may take does matter. The lack of a fiscal link also tends to weaken the requirement of due diligence in decision making. It also means the state has little or no interest in promoting taxpayers, which would form the backbone of any private sector activity in the economy.

Second, the presence of oil revenues tended to lead to the creation of rentier societies. Put simply, these are societies where there is a serious disconnect between effort and reward. As a result, productivity by nationals tends to be low. One consequence is a much greater reliance upon expatriate workers which characterizes the GCC countries. In turn, for a number of countries, most notably Saudi Arabia, this greatly aggravates unemployment among nationals simply because they are regarded by their own private sectors as expensive, unproductive, and difficult to get rid of, and their educational background is often unsuited to modern employment. Thus for example in Saudi Arabia, only around 5 per cent of the private sector workforce consists of Saudi nationals in a situation where the demographic pressures are adding large numbers to the job market.

Third, the oil revenues have speeded up the process of mass access to various forms of communications and mass media. One result has been a strong demonstration effect as people have seen what happens elsewhere. This raised expectations which in turn encouraged ill-thought-out spending plans often based upon competition with immediate neighbours rather than what was appropriate. This compounded the problems arising from the misguided spending programmes discussed earlier. Also, when these expectations were dashed, as they frequently were, this fed growing discontent into the domestic political context. In turn this contributed to the perception of the region as being politically unstable, which inhibited inward investment as can be seen from figure 21.6. This further isolated the economies of the region from the global economy. Also, since many of the countries of the region were basing their development strategy on inward investment, this further undermined their economic progress.

Fourth, the influx of revenues encouraged rent seeking and corruption. Both rent seeking and corruption are prevalent in all countries and both absorb resources which should be used to improve the well-being of society. The only difference is that the former is regarded as normal behaviour and the latter is regarded as illegal although the distinction is often blurred. It is important however to keep a perspective on the impact of such behaviour on development. Absorbing resources in these ways may or

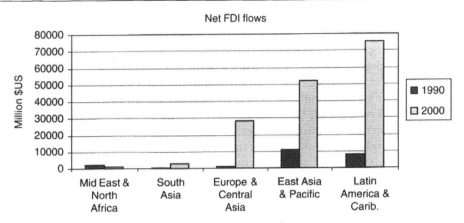

Figure 21.6 Foreign direct investment: a regional comparison
Source: *MEES*, 46 (23), 2003, paper by Sami Haddad

may not promote development. For example, arguably one of the most successful economies in history – the USA between 1865 and 1928 – was extremely corrupt both in politics and in business, courtesy of the 'robber barons'. Similarly, in more modern times both Italy and Japan are generally viewed as political systems imbued with high levels of corruption and yet these too have been successful economies. The key is what happens to the captured resources. If they are invested domestically this promotes economic growth, although there may be undesirable effects on income distribution. If they are lost in conspicuous consumption or foreign bank accounts, the economy loses. It is more likely that resources captured by politicians and bureaucrats would be used in such a way than re-invested domestically.

Working on the assumption that such behaviour is undesirable, large-scale oil revenues seriously aggravate the problem. Most obviously they make the target pot larger, thus increasing the rewards for rent seeking and corruption. An infamous New York gangster once asked 'why did he rob so many banks?' replied 'because that is where the money is!' Large oil revenues also tend to weaken the requirement and urges for due diligence. Put simply, if there seems to be plenty, diverting resources seems to matter less. Furthermore, since corruption occurs at the interface between the government and the private sector, the greater the role of government in an economy as a result of oil revenues, the greater the scope for corruption. Finally it becomes a self-feeding process. The larger the rent captured, the more resources available for the creation of rent-seeking opportunities.

Finally, and arguably most importantly in terms of the negative socio-political effects, the oil revenues strengthened the tendency of the region to produce 'predatory states' as opposed to 'developmental states'. A 'developmental state' has two elements – an ideological component and a structural component. The ideological component is when the ruling elite adopt 'developmentalism' as their prime objective. Thus their legitimacy is derived from the ability to deliver economic development, implying both growth and poverty reduction. These elites then establish a form of ideological hegemony – via the ballot box or less desirable means – over the rest of the society. The structural component involves the capacity to implement policies 'sagaciously and effectively' which will deliver development. Apart from the obvious technical capabilities this also requires a strong state which can resist pressure from strong, short-sighted private interests and/or some form of 'social anchor' which restrains any temptation to use its autonomy in a predatory manner. The difference between a 'developmental' and a 'predatory' state is often very thin.

A 'predatory state' by contrast is simply where the ruling elite are 'takers' rather than 'makers'. Thus their only interest is to plunder the society and they are sufficiently powerful or there are insufficient constraints to prevent them from doing so. A key part of the analysis must be the realization that a 'developmental state' can still fail. While the 'right' ideology might be there, and the limits of predation in place, the capacity of the state to implement effective policies might not be enough to manage certain problems. Such problems may be driven by exogenous shocks, mistakes or just good old-fashioned bad luck.

Large-scale oil revenues encourage 'predatory states' by a number of mechanisms. First, as with rent seeking and corruption, they make the pot larger and therefore more attractive to 'take'. The more there is to steal the greater the temptation to do so. Second, the oil revenues generate resources to suppress opposition to the predation either by the use of force or by simply buying off potential problems. Finally, often the major powers, dependent upon oil, will provide support and legitimacy for predatory regimes in an effort to ensure the continued flow of oil, thereby protecting them both from internal problems and threats from neighbours. Saddam's Iraq provided a classic example.

Thus for all these reasons, the impact of large windfall oil revenues on the region has not been helpful in terms of development. Rather, the experience provides a salutary lesson of the dangers of what has been termed in the literature 'resource curse'.

The impact of forward linkages

For oil and gas projects, the forward linkages relate to the provision of energy and chemical feedstock inputs into the rest of the economy. For the region this linkage has been central to the story of oil and development. For good or ill, successive governments have seen the oil sector as the engine for progress through industrialization.

The real trigger to these developments came in the early 1970s and arose from several factors. During the 1960s, the concept of 'unbalanced growth' became popular among many development economists. This emerged as a reaction to concepts of 'balanced growth' which had been much discussed in the 1950s. The 'balanced growth' school argued a poor economy should develop with all sectors growing in line to avoid wasteful under or over capacity. To achieve this of course required government to coordinate growth through a series of plans. However, many viewed this as unrealistic. If an economy had the resources for all sectors to grow smoothly and the managerial competence to do so, it would hardly be a poor developing economy in the first place. Rather, the idea was to have a 'leading development sector'. This would actually unbalance the other sectors of the economy leading in many cases to shortage which in turn would provide unmistakable price signals to the decision makers who were seen to be the real scarce resource. This idea, similar to the 'big push' school of development which had been popular immediately post-Second World War, began to catch the attention of policy planners in the developing world including that region. In such a context the oil sector was seen as the obvious candidate to lift the rest of the economy 'up by its bootstraps'.

As explained, during 1972–6, in most of the region, the governments had taken over control of oil production from the majors. This carried two implications. First, it meant that the producer governments had the option to determine where refineries were to be located. Previously, the major oil companies as disposers of the crude had that choice and they had built the majority of the refinery capacity in the 1950s and 1960s in the marketplace – namely western Europe and Japan. Now that location choice fell to the regions' oil exporters as disposers of the crude. Second, for a number of years there had been a growing dispute between the majors and the governments over associated gas. This gas, produced as a by-product of crude oil, had previously been flared on the grounds that for the companies there was no viable alternative economic use. Governments, however, had strongly objected to what they saw as a waste of their natural resources. Once they took over control of operations they could decide what to do with the associated gas. They all began investing in infrastructure to collect the gas which meant they then had to find a use for it. This process of gaining access to gas was reinforced as many of the newer companies exploring, in many cases, began to find gas rather than oil. Egypt provides a classic example of this. It seemed patently obvious that a major use for the gas was as a feedstock for petrochemical plants.

Finally, the first oil shock meant that oil exporting governments suddenly had what seemed like unlimited resources with which to fund the building of the necessary infrastructure and plant to develop major refining and petrochemical capabilities. The result of these factors was many plans to build large-scale export refineries and petrochemical complexes. The refinery plans were the first to run into trouble. Prior to the first oil shock, the international oil industry had taken the view that the strong growth in oil demand during the 'OECD economic miracle' of the 1960s would continue forever. During the 1960s this had led to global oil demand growing around 8–10 per cent per annum. As a result they had been building large amounts of new refinery capacity. Much of this was planned and initiated in the early 1970s. However, the quadrupling of the oil price in 1973 coupled with the consequent global recession meant that oil demand actually fell just as much of this new capacity emerged onstream. The resultant refinery over-capacity effectively wiped out any profitability in refining. The prospect of adding greatly to this over-capacity forced most governments in the region to reconsider their plans and in the event, only Saudi Arabia went ahead with new export refinery capacity.

However, this was far from the end of the story. The national oil companies, especially Kuwait, longed for downstream involvement. As a result, in the 1980s when the international oil companies began to sell off refineries and marketing networks, many were bought by the Arab oil producers following the lead of the Venezuelans. However, the motives for these investments were debatable. The official explanation was that securing downstream outlets for crude oil – implicit in such investments – was a means of locking in volume at a time when OPEC members were facing increasing competition from non-OPEC. However, an alternative explanation was that the national oil companies saw investments abroad as a way of deepening the information asymmetries which already existed between themselves and their controlling principals. The principal was normally the finance ministry since in most cases the oil ministry had effectively been captured by the national company. It was the information asymmetries which enabled the companies to capture rent for their own use. The result was a growing unease over the behaviour of the national oil companies. As explained, it was this which contributed to the growing pressure in many countries to re-open the upstream oil sector to the international oil companies. Allowing in these companies would provide a form of benchmarking by which the performance of the national oil company could be assessed.

Unlike the majority of the plans for refinery capacity, the petrochemical plans remained and were implemented. Many countries spent much to develop new petrochemical complexes in order to use the associated gas as feedstock. As with the downstream investment the wisdom of such moves has been widely debated. For many in the region, the development of the petrochemical sector is seen as a source of achievement. Certainly the figures of expanded capacity for basic petrochemicals are impressive. By 2001 according to the *Oil and Gas Journal* (23 April 2001) the Middle East had 7 per cent of the world's capacity to produce ethylene, one of the key petrochemical building-blocks, representing an increase of 30.5 per cent over 2000. However, a more hard headed approach does raise questions. Huge amounts of money were invested in both the infrastructure and the plant. On a purely accounting basis it is doubtful if these were justified. For example, the development of the petrochemical complex at Jubail in Saudi Arabia cost some $21 billion for the infrastructure, and many regard this official figure as a considerable understatement. In addition, the actual plant cost a further $17 billion. In terms of broader development targets, the argument about the benefits of the sector is less clear. In terms of generating employment the impact has been minimal simply because petrochemicals are not at all labour intensive. However, in terms of broadening the productive base there has been an impact and several countries have moved in to the secondary and tertiary phases of petrochemical production based upon the earlier investments. This is when the basic petrochemical products are converted into manufactured plastic items. However, these cases are usually associated with large-scale subsidies.

Two competing explanations are generally offered to explain why these investments generally have proved less effective in the development process than hoped for by their supporters. The first is that they faced serious discrimination from the importing countries of the OECD, especially the European Union. Thus various trade barriers were erected against petrochemical imports from the region. In part, this was justified by the importers on the grounds that the gas feedstock price was too low. In fact this was a debatable argument given the low opportunity cost of the gas, i.e. there was virtually no viable alternative use. A stronger argument was the subsidies offered to the capital and the utility supplies.

The second argument why the experience was of limited help in promoting development is that the investments were made by governments trying to pick 'winners' and, as explained earlier, this has not been successful in the region. The reality is almost certainly a combination of both explanations. However, the fact remains that the viability of the petrochemical sector without subsidy, originally on capital and now on utilities, must be seriously in doubt. To the extent that the gas is now finding alternative export uses, this argument becomes stronger since these alternatives significantly increase the opportunity cost of the gas which should be reflected in the basic feedstock price.

The impact of backward linkages

The backward linkages from the oil sector refer to those inputs into the sector from the local economy. The greater these linkages, then the more successful oil has been as a 'leading development sector'. Such linkages range from employment opportunities to the input of equipment. Arguably, for many of the GCC countries it is these backward linkages which led to the present economic basis of the countries. This is simply because before oil, there was very little alternative economic activity apart from some re-exports and pearling. A classic example of developing such linkages (and a model for other countries about to become major oil exporters) was Operation Bultiste in Saudi Arabia. In the early 1950s, when Aramco began serious operations, it became apparent that for every dollar spent on producing crude oil, two dollars had to be spent on flying in the most basic of supplies and equipment. To try to develop a local capability, Aramco identified some of the brightest of its Saudi employees. It then provided capital and training for them to leave Aramco and set up their own businesses to service Aramco's needs. The result was effectively the economic development of the kingdom's eastern province.

In terms of employment, the quantitative effect has been limited simply because oil is a capital rather than labour intensive activity. However, in many countries of the region the oil industry has been instrumental in developing a highly skilled cadre of workers in terms of both technical and commercial competencies. Perhaps the best example was in Iraq until the excesses of Saddam's regime led to a large-scale diaspora.

Conclusions

Without doubt, the Middle East has played a crucial role in the development of the international oil industry in the twentieth century. Indeed, the region was instrumental in making it the 'century of oil'. However, this failed to translate into real sustainable development in the region. Indeed, sadly, the region confirms some of the worst experiences of 'resource curse'. Furthermore it is difficult to see how this dilemma can be resolved in the region. Before the necessary reforms to the economic system can take place to create a more liberal economic environment with a vibrant private sector to promote development, there must be serious and fundamental political reform. To use the language of Gorbachev's Russia, there can be no *perestroika* (economic liberalization) without *glasnost* (political liberalization). The problem has been and remains that large-scale oil revenues provide support to existing regimes. This support has been reinforced by external powers because of their key status as oil suppliers to the world's markets. This entrenches the regimes and makes changing them far more difficult without a major upheaval of the sort seen in Eastern Europe which led to the collapse of communism. Thus 'glasnost' seems further away than ever and with it any real prospect of economic development to improve the lot of ordinary citizens in the region.

FURTHER READING

Resource course: general

Auty, R. (ed.) (2002) *Resource Abundance and Economic Development*, Oxford University Press, Oxford.

Meyer, J., Chambers, B. and Farooq, A. (eds.) (1999) *Development Policies in Natural Resource Economies*, Edward Elgar, Cheltenham.

Stevens, P. (2003) 'Resource impact: curse or blessing? – A literature survey', *Journal of Energy Literature*, 9(1).

The international oil industry

Hartshorn, J. (1993) *Oil Trade: Politics and Prospects*, Cambridge University Press, Cambridge.

Sampson, A. (1975) *The Seven Sisters: The Great Oil Companies and the World They Made*, Hodder and Stoughton, London.

Stocking, G. W. (1970) *Middle East Oil*, Vanderbilt University Press, Nashville.

Yergin, D. (1991) *The Prize*, Simon & Schuster, New York.

Oil and development in the Arab world

Beblawi, H. and Luciani, G. (eds.) (1987) *The Rentier State*, Croom Helm, London.

Eden, D. G. (1979) *Oil and Development in the Middle East*, Praeger, New York.

Kubursi, A. A. (1984) *Oil, Industrialization and Development in the Arab Gulf States*, Croom Helm, London.

Mabro, R. (1980) *Oil Revenues and the Cost of Social and Economic Development in Energy in the Arab World*, Vol. 1, *Kuwait*, AFESD and OAPEC.

Mabro, R. and Monroe, E. (1974) 'Arab wealth from oil: problems of its investment', *International Affairs*, January.

Mkandawire, T. (2001) 'Thinking about developmental states in Africa', *Cambridge Journal of Economics*, 25.

Niblock, T. and Wilson, R. (eds.) (1999) *The Political Economy of the Middle East*, Cambridge University Press, Cambridge.

Rumaihi, M. (1986) *Beyond Oil*, Al Saqi Books, London.

Stevens, P. (1986) 'The impact of oil on the role of the state in economic development: a case study of the Arab world', *Arab Affairs*, 1(1).

UNDP and the Arab Fund for Economic and Social Development (2002) *The Arab Human Development Report*, UNDP, New York.

CHAPTER TWENTY-TWO

Modernizing Women in the Middle East

VALENTINE M. MOGHADAM

In many ways, the period since the 1980s has not been kind to the women of the Middle East. Economic stagnation in a post-oil boom era, the spread of patriarchal Islamist movements, the persistence of the authoritarian state, the non-resolution of the Palestinian–Israeli conflict, and the US invasion and occupation of Iraq have all left their mark on the legal status, economic well-being, and security of Middle Eastern women. And yet, despite these travails, and to a certain extent because of them, women in the Middle East and North Africa have developed strategies for survival and empowerment and have evolved in ways that shatter every stereotype that has represented them as victimized, passive, and traditional. They are building strong women's organizations, conducting research, demanding equal citizenship, and networking internationally. In the process, they are changing the nature of the public sphere and helping to build civil society in their countries.

This chapter examines some of the main developments that have affected Middle Eastern women in recent decades and in which they have been involved. It begins with an overview of the characteristics of the population of Middle Eastern women and proceeds to discuss those economic and political processes that have had the greatest impact on them. It ends with an elaboration of the growing women's movement and its principal demands.

Characteristics, Defining Features, and Variations

Since the 1980s, the subject of women in the Middle East has been tied to the larger issue of Islamic revival, also known as fundamentalism or political Islam or Islamism. The rise of Islamist movements in the Middle East has reinforced stereotypes about the region, in particular the idea that Islam is ubiquitous in the culture and politics of the region, that tradition is tenacious, that the clergy have the highest authority, and that women's status is everywhere low. How do we begin to assess the status of women in the Middle East? For some, one must begin with Islam – and Islam is either deemed to be responsible for women's second-class citizenship and male domination or is regarded as the source of women's rights and empowerment. In either case, it is the status of women *in Islam* that is being scrutinized, rather than the social status of groups of women in actually existing Middle Eastern societies.

The focus on the status of women *in Islam* may be important to theologians and to believing women, but it does little to satisfy historical, social science, or feminist inquiry. For one thing, Islam is experienced, practiced, and interpreted quite differently over time and space. The Tunisian sociologist Abdelwahab Bouhdiba (1985) convincingly showed that although the Islamic community may consider itself unified, Islam is fundamentally "plastic," inasmuch as there are various Islams – Tunisian, Iranian, Malay, Afghan, Saudi Arabian, Senegalese, and so on. In order to understand the social implications of Islam, therefore, it is necessary to look at the broader sociopolitical and economic order within which it is exercised. Similarly, in order to understand the social positions of Middle Eastern women, one needs to examine the sociopolitical and economic environment within which they are situated. Whether the Qur'an's message regarding women is inherently conservative and hostile or egalitarian and emancipatory is not irrelevant to social scientific, historical, or feminist inquiry, but it is less central or problematical than it is often made out to be. Certainly Islam as a religion is not the defining factor in shaping women's lives in Middle Eastern societies. Instead, we need to examine economic and political factors, including social-structural characteristics.

Women in the Middle East constitute a diverse and heterogeneous population, and their social positions within and across countries vary by social class, ethnicity, age, education, and urban/rural location. Other important factors that shape women's legal status and social positions are the country's social structure and stage of development, as well as the nature of the state and its economic, social, and cultural policies. There is no archetypal Middle Eastern woman, but rather women inserted in quite diverse socioeconomic and cultural arrangements. The fertility behavior and needs of a poor peasant woman are quite different from those of a professional woman or a wealthy urbanite. The educated Saudi woman who has no need for employment and is chauffeured by a Sri Lankan migrant worker has little in common with the educated Moroccan woman who needs to work to augment the family income and also acquires status with a professional position. There is some overlap in cultural conceptions of gender in Morocco and Saudi Arabia, but there are also profound dissimilarities (and driving is only one of the more trivial ones). Saudi Arabia is far more conservative than Morocco in terms of what is considered appropriate for women. Women are likewise divided ideologically and politically. Some women activists have aligned themselves with liberal, social democratic, or communist organizations; others have lent their support to Islamist/fundamentalist groups. Some women reject religion as patriarchal; others wish to reclaim religion for themselves or to identify feminine aspects of it. Some women reject traditions and time-honored customs; others find identity, solace, and strength in them. More research is needed to determine whether social background shapes and can predict political and ideological affiliation, but in general women's social positions have implications for their consciousness and activism.

Economically, the countries of the region comprise oil economies poor in other resources, including population (Kuwait, Libya, Oman, Qatar, Saudi Arabia, United Arab Emirates [UAE]); mixed oil economies (Algeria, Iraq, Iran, Egypt, Tunisia, Syria); and non-oil economies (Israel, Jordan, Morocco, Sudan, Turkey, Yemen). The countries are further divided into the city-states (such as Qatar and the UAE); the "desert states" (for example, Libya and Saudi Arabia); and the "normal states" (Iran, Egypt, Syria, Turkey). The latter have a more diversified structure, and their resources include oil, agricultural land, and large populations. Some of the countries are rich in capital and import labor (Kuwait, Libya, Saudi Arabia), while others are poor in capital or are middle-income countries that export labor (Algeria, Egypt, Morocco, Tunisia, Turkey, Yemen). Some countries have more-developed class structures than others; the size and significance of the industrial working class and of the modern middle class, for example, vary across the region. There are differences in the development of skills ("human capital formation"), in the depth and scope of industrialization, in the development of infrastructure, in standards of living and welfare, and in the size of the female labor force.

Politically, the state types range from theocratic monarchy (Saudi Arabia) to secular republican (Turkey). Several Gulf states have no constitutions; until 1992, the Kingdom of Saudi Arabia had no formal constitution apart from the Qur'an and the Sharia, the Islamic legal code. Many states in the Middle East have experienced legitimacy problems, which became acute in the 1980s. Political scientists have used various terms to describe the states in the Middle East: "authoritarian–socialist" (for Algeria, Iraq, Syria), "radical Islamist" (for Iran and Libya), "patriarchal–conservative" (for Jordan, Morocco, Saudi Arabia), and "authoritarian–privatizing" (for Egypt, Tunisia, Turkey). Most of these states have strong capitalistic features while some retain feudalistic features. The term "neopatriarchal state," adopted from Hisham Sharabi (1988), is a useful umbrella label for the various state types in the Middle East, especially in terms of its implications for women. In the neopatriarchal state, unlike liberal or social democratic societies, religion is bound to power and state authority; moreover, the family, rather than the individual, constitutes the universal building block of the community. The neopatriarchal state and the patriarchal family reflect and reinforce each other. Of course, in some cases, modernizing or revolutionary states have undermined patriarchal structures, or attempted to do so, through legislation aimed at weakening traditional rural landlord structures or the power of tribes. But most states have been ambivalent about transforming women and the family. They have sought the apparently contradictory goals of economic development and strengthening of the family. The latter objective is often a bargain struck with more conservative social elements, such as religious leaders or traditional local communities. For Sharabi, "the most advanced and functional aspect of the neopatriarchal state … is its internal security apparatus, the *mukhabarat* … In social practice ordinary citizens not only are arbitrarily deprived of some of their basic rights but are the virtual prisoners of the state, the objects of its capricious and ever-present violence … It is in many ways no more than a modernized version of the traditional patriarchal sultanate" (Sharabi, 1988: 145). The 1990s saw the beginnings of political liberalization or quasi-democratization in a number of countries (notably Turkey) and the emergence of vibrant democracy movements in others (notably Iran). But Middle Eastern states remain authoritarian and citizen participation limited (Richards and Waterbury, 1996; Henry and Springborg, 2001). This sometimes adversely affects the operations of women's organizations.

Across the countries one observes a variable mix of religion and politics. Although Turkey is the only country in the region with a constitutional separation of religion and the state, Islam is not a state religion in Syria, whose constitution provides that "freedom of religion shall be preserved, and the state shall respect all religions and guarantee freedom of worship to all, provided that public order is not endangered." The constitution also guarantees women "every opportunity to participate effectively and completely in political, social, economic, and cultural life." In Syria, as in many countries in the region, urban women, especially those who are educated and professional, enjoy a degree of freedom comparable to their counterparts in, for example, Latin American countries. But it is difficult to reconcile women's rights with Islamic law (Sharia), which remains unfavorable to women with regard to marriage, divorce, and inheritance. Most of the countries in the region are governed to some degree by the Sharia. This is especially the case in the area of family law, although in some countries (e.g., Saudi Arabia, the Islamic Republic of Iran) the penal code is also based on Islamic law. (In the Jewish state of Israel, family law is based on the Halacha and supervised by the rabbinate.) Tunisia modernized its family law immediately after independence, and further reforms were adopted in 1993. Turkey's family law was not based on Islam but was quite conservative nonetheless, until the women's movement forced changes in 2001. Elsewhere, family laws based on Islamic texts continue to govern the personal and family status of women, and hence confer on them second-class citizenship.

The economic and political diversity in the region results in intra-regional differentiation in gender norms, as measured by differences in women's legal status, education levels, fertility trends, employment patterns, and political participation. For example, gender segregation in public is the norm and the law in Saudi Arabia but not in Lebanon, Jordan, Morocco, Tunisia, or Syria. Following the Iranian Revolution, the new authorities prohibited abortion, discouraged contraception, and lowered the age of marriage for girls to puberty. Not surprisingly, fertility rates soared in the 1980s (though they dropped in the late 1990s after a policy change). But in Tunisia contraceptive use was widespread in the 1980s and the average age of marriage for women was 25 and today is 27. Turkish women were given the right to vote in 1934, and in the 1950s and 1960s women began to occupy a large share of high-status occupations such as law, medicine, and university appointments. Women's participation in government as key decision-makers and as members of parliament varies across the region. In almost all the countries, women vote, run for parliament, and are appointed to governmental positions. In 2000, about 25 percent of judges in Algeria and Tunisia were women, whereas some other countries still banned women from judicial positions.

Despite this diversity, there are some common characteristics that are particularly noticeable when comparisons are made with women in some other regions. These common features are relatively high (though declining) fertility rates, gender gaps in literacy, relatively limited access to paid employment, and under-representation in the political system (see tables 22.1 and 22.2). Although a growing number of countries in the region are now predominantly urbanized, there remain sizeable rural populations in countries such as Egypt, Syria, Yemen, Turkey, and Iran. As a result of these large rural populations, the age at first marriage remains relatively low and the fertility of women in the Middle East tends to be higher on average than other countries at similar stages of development (UNDP, 2002; Moghadam, 2003: 133–4). Moreover, women in nearly all the countries of the region experience second-class citizenship due to certain provisions in Muslim family law and patriarchal cultural practices and norms.

The persistence of a patriarchal system that favors men is partly the result of the influence of Islamist movements since the early 1980s. The relatively limited access to paid employment is largely a function of the capital-intensive, male-intensive nature of the regional oil economy, as well as the existence of relatively high wages for men during the oil boom years (from roughly 1960 to the mid-1980s). Women in the

Table 22.1 Female economic activity rates, by region, 2000

Region	Rate (%)	Index (1990 = 100)	As % of male rate
Arab states[a]	32.9	117	41
East Asia and the Pacific	68.9	99	82
Latin America and the Caribbean	42.0	108	51
South Asia	43.3	106	51
Sub-Saharan Africa	62.3	99	73
Central and Eastern Europe and the CIS (former Soviet Union)	57.8	99	81

[a]The category Arab states excludes Iran and Turkey.
Source: UNDP, *Human Development Report 2002*, table 25, p. 237

Middle East have always been involved in political movements (e.g., independence, national liberation, socialist, and feminist movements) but their presence in formal political structures (e.g., political parties, parliaments, governments) has been more recent and remains limited. Except in Turkey, where women were given the right to vote in 1930, other countries granted women voting rights in the 1950s (Egypt, Lebanon, Syria, Tunisia), the 1960s (Algeria, Iran, Libya, Morocco, the former People's Democratic Republic of Yemen), or even later (Iraq). Their limited political participation, therefore, has partly to do with the relative novelty of elections, partly to do with the experience of colonialism, and partly to do with the patriarchal gender system. Although women are found in the rank-and-file and leadership of political parties (e.g., Algeria, Morocco, Tunisia, Turkey), nowhere have they reached a "critical mass," and their appointment to party or government positions has been largely a form of tokenism. Women are certainly elected to parliament, but their share of parliamentary seats in 1999 ranged from a mere 1 percent in Morocco to 10 percent in Syria; Israel's proportion of women was 12 percent. (By contrast, Vietnam and Argentina had about a 27 percent female share in parliament.)

It should be noted that in response to the rise of Islamism, and in order to address the problem of second-class citizenship and economic marginalization, women in the Middle East have formed a dynamic women's movement that seeks to challenge patriarchal gender arrangements, expand women's civil, political, and social rights, and empower women economically and politically. Women's organizations are keen to increase women's political participation, encouraging women to run in national elections, supporting women's involvement in local elections, and insisting that more women be appointed to ministerial and sub-ministerial positions. The hope is that women politicians would be more likely to draft or support legislation that would improve the status of women in family law and labor law. Barriers to women's participation in formal politics remain formidable, but at the start of the new millennium, there were some encouraging developments. For example, the establishment of a gender quota system in Morocco resulted in a 10.8 percent female share in the November 2002 parliamentary elections. And in the summer of 2002, President Bouteflika of Algeria appointed an unprecedented five women to cabinet posts.

These positive developments have come about partly as a result of changes in the characteristics of the female population. Rising educational attainment and smaller family size has freed up women's time for civic and political engagement. Fertility rates are high in the poorest and most conservative countries: six births per woman in

Table 22.2 Women's political participation: MENA in comparative perspective

Country	% parliamentary seats in single or lower level chamber occupied by women			% Women in decision-making positions in government			
				Ministerial level		Sub-ministerial level	
	1987	1995	1999	1994	1998	1994	1998
MENA							
Algeria	2	7	3	4	0	8	10
Bahrain	—	—	—	0	0	0	1
Egypt	4	2	2	4	6	0	4
Iran	1	3	5	0	0	1	1
Iraq	13	11	6	0	0	0	0
Israel	8	9	12	4	0	5	9
Jordan	0	1	0	3	2	0	0
Kuwait	0	0	0	0	0	0	7
Lebanon	—	2	2	0	0	0	0
Libya	—	—	—	0	0	2	4
Morocco	0	1	1	0	0	0	8
Oman	—	—	—	0	0	2	4
Qatar	—	—	—	0	0	3	0
Saudi Arabia	—	—	—	0	0	0	0
Sudan	8	8	5	0	0	0	0
Syria	9	10	10	7	8	0	0
Tunisia	6	7	7	4	3	14	10
Turkey	1	2	4	5	5	0	17
UAE	0	0	0	0	0	0	0
Yemen	—	1	1	0	0	0	0
Other							
Argentina	5	22	28	0	8	3	9
Brazil	5	7	6	5	4	11	13
Chile	—	8	11	13	13	0	8
China	21	21	22	6	—	4	—
Cuba	34	23	28	0	5	9	11
Malaysia	5	8	8	7	16	0	13
Mexico	11	14	17	5	5	5	7
Philippines	9	9	12	8	10	11	19
South Africa	2	25	30	6	—	2	—
Venezuela	4	6	13	11	3	0	7
Viet Nam	18	18	26	5	0	0	5

Short rule indicates data not available.
Source: *The World's Women 2000*, Table 6A

Saudi Arabia, Yemen, and Palestine (the West Bank and Gaza) – and in the latter, adolescent fertility rates are also very high. But fertility is declining dramatically elsewhere; it ranges from 2.2–2.7 births per woman in Iran, Tunisia, Turkey, and Lebanon. Almost everywhere, women with higher education have the lowest fertility rates. Indeed, educational attainment is growing among women in the Middle East, while the gender gaps are narrowing. Although illiteracy is common among women in the older age groups and universal schooling has yet to be achieved in some of the poorer countries (notably Yemen), enrollment rates for girls at the primary and secondary school levels are rising and nearly at a par with boys. Some countries have made tremendous progress since the early 1980s. For example, in 1980 the expected years of schooling for girls in Oman and Saudi Arabia was only two and five years, respectively, but by 1997 it had increased to nine years, according to World Bank figures (World Bank, 2000). In Iran and the United Arab Emirates, girls can expect to complete at least eleven years of schooling. We know less about the quality of education that women receive, although some research shows that government cutbacks have resulted in crowded classrooms, fewer qualified teachers, and poor instructional materials in the state-owned schools, at least in many of the Arab countries (UNDP, 2002).

Most significantly, women in the Middle East are more likely to enroll in universities than they were in the past. In 2003, more than 50 percent of college students in Bahrain, Iran, Jordan, Kuwait, Lebanon, Qatar, and Saudi Arabia were women; in Libya, Morocco, Palestine, and Tunisia, more than 40 percent of college students were women. Young women have been entering into higher education fields of study such as engineering, medicine, law, commerce, and finance, and they are increasingly graduating with degrees in mathematics and computer sciences. In Turkey, the proportion of women in universities almost doubled, from 19 to 37 percent, between 1968 and 1990. But it increased even faster in engineering (7 to 22 percent), in mathematics and natural sciences (22 to 46 percent), and in agriculture and forestry (10 to 33 percent). In 1994–5, Turkish women were awarded 45 percent of the undergraduate and 33 percent of the postgraduate degrees in mathematics and computer science. Egypt has a high proportion (30 percent) of women engineering students at the university level (ILO, 1997; Moghadam, 1998, ch. 2). In the early 1990s, the percentage of business administration students at the third level who were women was 70 percent in Bahrain, 39 percent in Jordan and Tunisia, and 35 percent in Turkey. Countries with respectable percentages of women receiving first university degrees in mathematics and computer sciences in 1994–5 included Iran (33 percent), Jordan (45 percent), Saudi Arabia (28 percent), Tunisia (22 percent), and Turkey (45 percent). Women are also a larger proportion of graduates in media and information fields. This is especially true in Algeria, Egypt, Lebanon, and Tunisia, where they are the majority, and in Iran and Jordan, where women are 34–40 percent of graduates in third-level mass communications and documentation studies (UN, 2000: chart 4.13, p. 97).

Rising educational attainment as well as declining household budgets in a post-oil boom era has led to growing involvement of women in the formal and informal sectors of the economy, and their share of the labor force increased between 1980 and 1997. This is particularly true of countries such as Jordan, Kuwait, Oman, Saudi Arabia, and the UAE, where women's participation in the labor force was previously negligible and the economies relied almost entirely on foreign contract labor. The 1990s saw increases in women's employment in Turkey, Egypt, Iran, and Algeria, largely in the teaching and health professions, to a lesser extent in sales and services. Improved enumeration techniques also yielded higher percentages of women in agriculture, as well as in urban informal occupations. In Egypt, Jordan, Iran, and Turkey, the growth of women-owned businesses and especially of non-governmental organizations (NGOs) has been a noticeable trend. Women's involvement in manufacturing is found in almost all the large countries, but it is greatest in Tunisia and Morocco. As in other regions of the world economy, however, much of the work available to working-class women is irregular and ill-paid, while even middle-class women in the civil service have seen the real value of their salaries deteriorate considerably. An elite corps of professional women is found in both public and private sectors, but their numbers in the highest administrative and managerial categories are small. In most countries of the region, unemployment rates are high, and they are disproportionately high for women (Moghadam, 2002; Moghadam, 2003, ch. 2; CAWTAR, 2002).

The growing mass of educated and employed Middle Eastern women has taken part in national-level movements and is increasingly aware of international or global developments. The UN Decade for Women (1975–85), four UN world conferences on women, the UN's Convention on the Elimination of All Forms of Discrimination Against Women, and the global women's rights agenda all have influenced domestic politics and discourses in the Middle East. Women's organizations increasingly look to the UN's women's rights agenda for legitimacy and support. We will return to the women's rights movement later in the chapter, but first it may be helpful to examine some of the other ways that women have been involved in and affected by economic and political developments. In particular, we will examine forms of migration; revolutions, wars, and political conflicts; and Islamist movements and the question of veiling.

Social Changes and Women in the Middle East

Women have been involved in and affected by various types of population movements, including rural–urban migration, international labor migration, and forced exile. Although urbanization and rural–urban migration initially result in women's economic marginalization and domesticity, at later stages women's life-options increase and they have greater access to education, employment, and social services. This is as true of the Middle East as it is of any other region. In almost all the large cities, a certain "housewife-ization" occurred in the 1950s and 1960s as rural women migrated to the cities and male kin obtained jobs in the growing services and manufacturing sectors. But as daughters attained schooling, their aspirations and their activities expanded. At the same time, and beginning in the 1960s, oil-fueled development encouraged labor migration from labor-surplus and capital-poor economies to capital-rich and labor-deficit oil economies. There was substantial Tunisian migrant labor in Libya, Egyptian and Palestinian migrant labor in the Gulf emirates, and Yemeni labor in Saudi Arabia. This migration affected, among other things, the structure of populations, the composition of the households, and the economies of both sending and receiving countries. Many of the oil-rich Gulf states came to have large populations of non-citizens, and female-headed households proliferated in the labor-sending countries. During the years of the oil boom, roughly until the mid-1980s, workers' remittances were an important factor in not only the welfare of families and households but also in the fortunes of economies such as those of Jordan and Egypt. Other forms of labor migration that were not tied to oil involved population movements to Europe, principally by North Africans and Turks. Historically, North Africans have migrated to the cities of France, although large populations of Moroccans have settled in Belgium, the Netherlands, and Spain as well. And in the late 1980s Italy became another destination for North African migrant workers. Turkish "guest workers" became an important source of labor to (West) German capital as early as the 1950s.

In a third form of population movement with gender implications, political conflict creates streams of refugees, exiles, asylum-seekers, and emigrants. The creation of the state of Israel and subsequent conflicts with Arabs and Palestinians produced countless Palestinian refugees and emigrants, while the 1953 Shah–CIA coup d'état in Iran, the aftermath of the 1979 Islamic Revolution, and the Iran–Iraq War resulted in several waves of Iranian exiles, emigrants, and asylum-seekers, most of whom have been residing in Europe and North America. Emigration and the diasporic condition almost always result in changes in attitudes and behavior, but whether these changes improve or worsen women's lot depends on many intervening factors. In the refugee camps on the Algeria–Morocco border, where 160,000 Sahrawis have lived since the 1980s, the women who make up three-quarters of the adult population have played a central role in running the camps from the time of their arrival. They set up committees for health, education, local production, social affairs, and provisions distribution (O'Connell, 1993). Janet Bauer (1991) informed us that among Algerian Muslim immigrants in France, women have a strong role in maintaining religious rituals and symbolic meanings that are important in preserving cultural identity and adaptation. The same is true for many Turkish residents in Germany.

The situation for Iranian refugees, exiles, and immigrants seems to differ, however, as they may be ambivalent about the very traditions and religious rituals from which individuals are said to seek comfort in times of crisis or change. Socioeconomic status and political ideology may also explain differences between Algerian, Turkish, and Iranian immigrants. In her study of Iranian immigrants in France, Vida Nassehy-Behnam (1991) stated: "Since the initiation of 'theocracy,' Iranian emigration in general has been partly motivated by the pervasiveness of a religious ideology which impinges so dramatically upon individual lifestyles." She then offers two categories of Iranian emigrants: (1) political emigrants, that is, those whose exodus began in February 1979, including monarchists, nationalists, communists, and the Iranian Mojahedin; and (2) sociocultural emigrants, defined as those Iranians who were not politically active but left the country out of fear over an uncertain future for their children and/or because of the morose atmosphere that prevailed in Iran, especially for women and youth. In their study of Iranian exiles and immigrants in Los Angeles, Bozorgmehr and Sabagh (1991) showed that some 65 percent of immigrants and 49 percent of exiles had four or more years of college. These findings for Iranians stand in contrast to the figures for many other migration streams in the United States. Another difference between Iranian exiles, refugees, and immigrants and those of North Africa and Turkey is the greater preponderance of religious minorities – Christians, Jews and Baha'is – among Iranians. Such minorities are especially prevalent within the Iranian exile group in Los Angeles. Bozorgmehr and Sabagh offered these religious patterns as an explanation for why the Iranian exiles they surveyed perceived less prejudice than other immigrant groups, which may contain a larger share of Muslims.

These factors – socioeconomic status, education, and political ideology – shape the experience of women exiles, immigrants, and refugees. Bauer noted that although women in Middle Eastern societies are rarely described as migrating alone, many Iranian women do go into exile alone. The women she interviewed in Germany typically had been involved in secular left-wing political and feminist activities in

Iran; many had high school or college educations. She explained: "Some married young in traditional marriages; others were single or divorced. Some were working class; others middle or upper middle class … but most of those I interviewed did come into exile with some ideas about increasing personal autonomy and choice" (Bauer, 1991: 93).

Can there be emancipation through emigration? Bauer noted the growing feminist consciousness of Iranian exiles and wrote that among those she interviewed, there was a general feeling that the traumatic events of 1979–82 had initiated cross-class feminist cooperation among women and rising consciousness among all Iranians on the issue of gender relations. She added that larger political goals may be lost, however, as people put aside notions of socialist revolution, social transformation, and political activity and wrap themselves in introspection and their individual lives. Although this was true for the early 1990s, a repoliticization occurred in the latter part of the 1990s, in tandem with the emergence of a movement for political reform within Iran. Expatriate Iranians have regained their political identity and aspirations, with different perspectives on the reform movement, "Islamic feminism," prospects for "Islamic democracy," secularism, and other political alternatives.

Like other regions, the Middle East has had its share of revolutions, wars, civil conflicts, and political movements, all of which have produced dramatic changes that affect women and men profoundly, if differently. Revolutions are a special case of political and social change that usually result in strong states that can carry out reforms and political change, including change in the status of women. A case in point is the People's Democratic Republic of Yemen, once known as the Cuba of the Middle East, which in the 1970s sought to release women from patriarchal kin control, integrate them into economic and political activities, and establish a progressive family code. By contrast, the Iranian Revolution produced an Islamic Republic, which in the 1980s instituted gender segregation, veiling, and Islamic laws and norms, including a Muslim family law that reinstated polygamy and unilateral male divorce and emphasized women's wifely duties and childbearing responsibilities. The evolution and complex longer-term outcomes of these two separate revolutionary experiments provide rich material for scholars of revolution, the state, and social change. The PDRY, or South Yemen, merged with the more conservative North Yemen in 1990, and the process of unification resulted in the revision of the family code, a diminishment of women's rights, and the elimination of the official discourse of women's emancipation. In the second half of the 1990s, the Islamic Republic of Iran faced the emergence of a movement for political reform, along with movements of women, youth, and intellectuals from Iran's large middle class that appeared to defy the clerical authorities and reject many of the state's laws and norms.

Modernizing revolutionary states have been crucial agents in the advancement of women by enacting changes in family law, providing education and employment, and encouraging women's participation in public life. This occurred in Egypt during the rule of Gamal Abdel Nasser, where a kind of "state feminism" emerged (Hatem, 1994). The Iraqi Ba'th regime in its radical phase (1960s and 1970s) undertook social transformation by introducing a land reform program that changed the conditions of the peasantry and by establishing a welfare state for the urban working classes and the poor. In its drive against illiteracy and for free education, the Ba'thist revolution produced one of the best-educated intelligentsias in the Arab world. Even a hostile study of Iraq (Al-Khalil, 1991) credited the regime with giving women the right to

Plate 22.1   Queen Rania of Jordan: representative of a new generation of Arab women
Source: © *AlHayat* Newspaper, London

have careers and participate in civic activities. This does, of course, raise questions about the impact on women of the Iran–Iraq War, the 1991 Gulf War and the subsequent sanctions regime. Over the years, the paucity of information has made a serious study impossible, but the available evidence suggests that the combination of wars, international sanctions, and Saddam Hussein's own flawed policies and priorities resulted in the deterioration of women's status and conditions in Iraq. Conditions probably worsened immediately after the American invasion and occupation of 2003. The destruction of the country's social and physical infrastructure, the collapse of the state, the emergence of looting and lawlessness, and the iron fist of an occupying power is likely to have heightened women's sense of insecurity and disempowerment.

Political conflict or war can certainly wreak havoc on societies and on the population of women, as has been the case with the Arab–Israeli wars, the Iran–Iraq War, the

Lebanese civil war, the 1991 Gulf War, and the Algerian civil conflict. But paradoxically, it can also bring about a heightened sense of gender awareness and political activism on the part of women. In some cases, an unexpected outcome of economic crisis caused by war could be higher education and employment opportunities for women. A study conducted by a professor of education at a Lebanese university suggests that following the Lebanese civil war, Lebanese parents felt more strongly that educating their daughters was a good investment and that higher education represented a financial asset. In addition to offering good work opportunities and qualifications for a "better" husband, a degree acts as a safety net should a woman's marriage fail or should she remain single. Moreover, the long civil war in Lebanon produced a remarkable body of literature with strong themes of social and gender consciousness. Miriam Cooke's analysis of the war writings of the "Beirut Decentrists" in the late 1970s and early 1980s showed the emergence of a feminist school of women writers (Cooke, 1986).

The Iran–Iraq War of 1980–8 certainly allowed the Islamic state in Iran to strengthen itself, to impose its will upon the population, and to compel women to conform to its rules on veiling and segregation. However, a study of women's employment patterns in post-revolutionary Iran in 1986 by the present author found that notwithstanding the exhortations of Islamist ideologues, women had not been driven out of the workforce and their participation in government employment had slightly increased relative to 1976 (Moghadam 1988). This I attributed to the imperatives of the wartime economy, the human resource needs of the expanding state apparatus, and women's resistance to subordination. A more recent study confirmed this hypothesis. Maryam Poya (1999) found that the mobilization of men at the war front and the requirements of gender segregation had resulted in an increased need for female teachers and nurses. In Iraq, too, the mobilization of female labor accelerated during the war with Iran, though this was apparently coupled with the contradictory exhortation to produce more children (Lorenz, 1991).

One result of the war in both countries was the ever-increasing allocation of central government expenditure to defense, at the expense of health, education, and services. Also, during the war, women in Iran were constantly harassed by zealots if they did not adhere strictly to Islamic dress and manner. Those women who complained about hijab or resisted by showing a little hair or wearing bright-colored socks were admonished to "feel shame before the corpses of the martyrs of Karbala" – a reference to an incident in religious history as well as to the fallen soldiers in the battle with Iraq. However, an unintended consequence of the war was to override early ideological objections to female employment in the civil service. As the state apparatus proliferated, and as a large proportion of the male population was concentrated at the war front, women found opportunities for employment in the government sector that Islamist ideologues had earlier denied them. Eventually, the war had a deteriorating effect on employment for both men and women. Yet in the 1990s the Iranian authorities encouraged women to take up fields of study and employment they deemed both socially necessary and appropriate for women, especially medicine and teaching. Meanwhile, Iranian women themselves began to issue calls for the modernization of family law, more employment opportunities, and greater political participation.

The most obvious case of the impact of political conflict is that of the Palestinians, whose expulsion by Zionists or flight from their villages during periods of strife caused changes in rural Palestinian life and the structure of the family (Nakhleh and Zureik, 1980; Abdo, 1987). In some ways, the prolonged uprising, which organized and mobilized so many Palestinians, had a positive impact on women's roles, inasmuch as women were able to participate politically in what was once the most secular and democratic movement in the Arab world. Internationally, the best known Palestinian women have been the guerrilla fighter Leila Khaled and the diplomat and English professor Hanan Ashrawi – two contrasting examples of roles available to Palestinian women in their movement. In the 1970s Palestinian women's political activity and participation in resistance groups expanded, whether in Lebanon, the West Bank, Gaza, in universities, or in refugee camps. During the first intifada, Palestinian women organized themselves into impressive independent political groups and economic cooperatives. A feminist consciousness became more visible among Palestinian women, and some Palestinian women writers, such as Samira Azzam and Fadwa Tuqan, combined a critique of patriarchal structures and a fervent nationalism to produce compelling work.

At the same time, the Palestinian movement has exalted women as mothers and as mothers of martyrs. This emphasis on their reproductive role has created a tension on which a number of authors have commented (Peteet, 1993; Abdo, 1995; Rubenberg, 2001). During the latter part of the 1980s, another trend emerged among the Palestinians, especially in the impoverished Gaza Strip: Islamist vigilantes who insisted that women cover themselves when appearing in public. The frustrations of daily life, the indignities of occupation, and the inability of the secular and democratic project to materialize may explain this shift. What began as a sophisticated women's movement in the early 1990s that sought feminist interventions in the areas of constitution-writing and social policy experienced setbacks toward the end of the decade, as the West Bank and Gaza faced Islamization and continued Israeli occupation (Hammami and Johnson, 1999). As noted by Zahira Kamal, a leading figure in the women's movement, "Palestinian women are prisoners of a concept of 'women and the intifada' " (Kamal, 1998: 88).

Algerian women have been involved twice in conflicts which have profoundly affected them: the war of liberation in the 1950s and early 1960s and the civil conflict between Islamists and the state in the 1990s. But whereas their earlier participation was conducted within a nationalist frame, the later struggle was framed as feminist, modernist, and anti-fundamentalist (Cherifati-Merabtine, 1994; Moghadam 2001). In the Islamist terror campaign that followed the military's decision to prevent the Front Islamique du Salut from taking over the government after their electoral victory in 1991, numerous women and girls were raped or killed, and a number of women activists were assassinated. Nonetheless, Algerian women formed many new women's organizations and developed a critique of both state autocracy and political Islam. Throughout the decade, they championed modernity and individual rights while also holding on to the socialist legacy of equality of citizens. They were critical of past practice, which subsumed the woman question under national liberation and the building of Algerian-style socialism. The ideological and cultural divide between Islamist and non-Islamist women activists was enormous; feminists distinguished "women of the modernist trend" from the women of the Islamist movement. According to one such activist-theorist, Doria Cherifati-Merabtine, the modernist women's movement was comprised mainly of older university women from the first post-independence generation of intellectuals. She observed that these women "have learned, at their expense, that no change is possible if the outlook on woman and her place within society does not evolve." And although these modernist women "carry generous ideas and an egalitarian project of society," their experience leads them to "put the recognition of the Woman-Individual on the agenda" (Cherifati-Merabtine, 1994).

The rise of Islamic fundamentalism has had significant effects on women throughout the Middle East. Women themselves have been divided for and against these movements. Fundamentalism reflected the contradictions of modernization, the difficult transition to modernity underway in the region, and the conflict between traditional and modern norms, relations, and institutions. Islamic fundamentalist movements emerged as the global economic policy environment shifted from Keynesian to neoliberal, as talks on a new international economic order (NIEO) collapsed, and as world communism went into decline. Also relevant in their emergence were the important cultural changes taking place globally and within countries, including the internationalization of western popular culture and changes in gender relations, the structure of the family, and the position of women. The Iranian Revolution of 1978–9, which produced the Islamic Republic of Iran, had a demonstration effect throughout the Middle East. It appeared to many dissidents and religious radicals that a project for the Islamization of state and society could prevail, and that this would be the solution to economic, political, and cultural crises.

There have been important differences among Islamist movements; some have sought state power or have used violence while others have been satisfied to influence public policies or take part in governance non-violently. In most cases, however, Islamist movements have been preoccupied with cultural identity and authenticity, and this has had implications for women's autonomy and range of choices. Women's crucial role in the socialization of the next generation makes them symbols of cultural values and traditions, and thus they are expected to behave and dress in prescribed ways. Some Muslim women regard this role as an exalted one, and they gladly assume it, becoming active participants, though rarely ideologues, in Islamist movements. Other women find it an onerous burden; they resent restrictions on their individuality, mobility, and personal freedoms. In some countries, the nonconformist women pursue education, employment, and foreign travel to the extent that they can, joining women's associations or political organizations in opposition to Islamist movements. In Algeria, as we saw, the Islamist movement spurred a militant feminist movement, something that did not exist before. In other countries, nonconformist women face legal restrictions on dress, occupation, travel, and encounters with men outside their own families. Their response can take the form of resentful acquiescence, passive resistance, or self-exile. This response was especially strong among middle-class Iranian women during the 1980s, although in the 1990s women began to challenge the gender system and patriarchal Islamist norms more directly.

The rise of fundamentalism also generated polemics surrounding hijab (modest Islamic dress for women) in every country. During the era of early modernization and nation-building, national progress and the emancipation of women were considered synonymous. This viewpoint entailed discouragement of the veil and encouragement of schooling for girls. The veil was associated with national backwardness, as well as female illiteracy and subjugation. But a paradox of the 1980s was that more and more educated women, even working women (especially in Egypt), took to the veil. Scholars within Middle East women's studies tackled the conundrum in different ways. Some emphasized the personal choice and enhanced opportunities that veiling represented, especially for the women of the lower middle class and conservative families (El-Guindy, 1981; MacLeod, 1991; Hoodfar, 1991). Others stressed its link to the appeal of fundamentalism and religious identity among women (Badran, 1994; Toprak, 1994). Yet others pointed out that veiling was compulsory in some countries (notably Saudi Arabia and the Islamic Republic of Iran) and that elsewhere one could discern strong social pressures on women to veil and thus achieve respectability. What is more, such social pressures often took the form of harassment and intimidation by self-styled enforcers (males) of correct religious behavior and public morality (Najmabadi, 1991; Tohidi, 1994; Moghadam, 2001). The case of Turkey, however, differs from the other cases discussed above, in that its main Islamic political party not only has not engaged in harassment of non-veiled women (which in any event would be very difficult, given the tradition of secular republicanism and the power of the military), but has emphasized human rights and personal choice in Turkish women's decision to veil or not to veil.

Women's Movements in the Middle East

The structural features of the region – authoritarian states, oil-based (or "rentier") economies, and the strength of Islamist forces – make the struggle for civil, political, and social rights distinctive and difficult. In particular, the movement for women's citizenship and for the establishment of civil society has had to contend with patriarchal Islamist movements, neopatriarchal states, and religious-based family laws – a rather formidable combination of forces. It is all the more remarkable, therefore, that women's institutionalized second-class citizenship is being challenged by women's organizations throughout the region, using a variety of legal and discursive strategies. In general, feminists and the women's organizations are quietly rebelling against women's location in the private domain and men's control of the public domain. In particular, they are calling for: (1) the modernization of family laws, (2) the criminalization of domestic violence and other forms of violence against women, (3) women's right to retain their own nationality and to pass it on to their children (a demand mainly of Arab women), and (4) greater access to employment and participation in political decision-making. They are also pointing out that existing family laws are at odds with the universal standards of equality and nondiscrimination embodied in international instruments such as the Convention on the Elimination of All Forms of Discrimination Against Women. In many Middle Eastern countries, women's rights organizations are comprised of highly educated women with employment experience and international connections. What is more, the nature of women's organizations has changed, and their activities have become more deliberate, self-conscious, and political. The fact that these organizations exist at all is a sign of important demographic changes, of women's increasing access to the public sphere, and of the gradual process of political liberalization in the region. What is especially noteworthy is that the women's organizations are working to change the nature of that public sphere, to enhance the rights of women in the private sphere, to advance democratization, and to build civil society.

The global women's rights agenda and the UN conferences of the 1990s – especially the 1994 International Conference on Population and Development, which took place in Cairo, and the 1995 Beijing Conference – created a favorable opportunity structure that allowed for the proliferation of women's organizations and women-led NGOs in the Middle East. Whereas the 1950s to 1970s saw women involved almost exclusively in either official women's organizations or charitable associations, the 1990s saw the expansion of many types of women's organizations. At the same time, increasing state conservatism in some countries forced women's organizations and feminist leaders to assume a more independent stance than before. Indeed, one observer has noted the shift from "state feminism to civil society feminism" in the Middle East.[1]

In analyzing the proliferation of women's organizations during the 1990s, seven types of women's organizations may be identified. These are service organizations, worker-based organizations, professional associations, women-in-development (WID) NGOs, research centers and women's studies institutes, women's auxiliaries of political parties, and women's rights or feminist organizations. All are contributing to the development of civil society in the region, although the feminist organizations are perhaps doing so most consciously – a point also made by other feminist observers (Guenena and Wassef, 1999; Sadiqi, 1999; Al-Ali, 2000). The WID NGOs have an important function in fulfilling the development objectives of civil society: decentralized, participatory, and grassroots use of resources. For example, in Bahrain, "women's voluntary associations have come to form an integral part of civil society," which is responsible for "initiating all organizations for the handicapped as well as institutions for modern education" (Fakhro, 1997: 2). In Iran, too, women have formed a large number of NGOs that provide social services, address the problems of Afghan refugee women and girls, and educate the public on the environment. Groups focusing on women workers are few, but are likely to grow as more women enter the workforce. One such group, the Palestinian Working Women Society, was formed to improve conditions of women workers and raise their awareness about labor rights and trade unions. Besides national groupings, there are region-wide organizations and networks within which women are active, such as the Arab Women's Solidarity Association, the Arab Human Rights Organization, the Maghreb–Mashrek Gender Link Information Project (GLIP), and transnational feminist networks such as Women Living Under Muslim Laws, the Sisterhood is Global Institute, and the Women's Learning Partnership.

The women's rights or feminist organizations appear to be the most significant contributors to citizenship and civil society. These organizations target women's subordinate status within family law, women's low participation in formal politics, and violence against women. Members of such organizations, such as the Lebanese League for Women's Rights, often run (successfully or otherwise) for political office.[2] Beirut is home to the Women's Court: the Permanent Arab Court to Resist Violence Against Women, which launched highly visible campaigns in 1995, 1998, and 2000. Women's rights and feminist organizations seem to be most numerous in North Africa, where they formed the Collectif 95 Maghreb Egalité, which was the major organizer behind the "Muslim Women's Parliament" at the NGO Forum that preceded the fourth UN world conference on women, in Beijing in September 1995. In preparing for the post-Beijing follow-up, the Collectif 2000 formulated an alternative "egalitarian family code" and promoted women's political participation. Social rights were also placed on the agenda of women's advancement. In Morocco in 1995, women's groups convened a roundtable on the rights of workers, to explore the ways in which a revised labor code could better address women's conditions, include domestic workers in the definition of wage-workers and the delineation of rights and benefits, set the minimum work age at 15, and provide workers on maternity leave with full salary and a job-back guarantee.[3] In 2000 controversy emerged over the proposed national plan for women's development. An ambitious document to extend education, employment, and political participation to Moroccan women, the plan came under attack by conservative Islamic forces, especially because the reform of family law was inscribed in the plan. In response, Moroccan feminists took to the streets in support of the plan, while the government of Prime Minister Youssefi sought to institute a "social dialogue" to promote the plan. However, in the face of overwhelming opposition from Islamist forces, in 2002 the government had to withdraw the plan. But victory came in October 2003, when Morocco's young king issued a royal decree supporting reform of the family law, and the parliament adopted it in January 2004.

Another way that MENA women have been contributing to civil society is through literary efforts, including the publication of books, journals, and films. Morocco's Edition le Fennec has produced numerous books on women's rights issues as well as many literary works by women, while l'Union de l'Action Féminin produces the monthly *8 Mars*. The very lively women's press in Iran – a stand-in for an organized women's movement – is considered popular and audacious. It includes *Zanan* (*Women*), *Zan-e Rouz* (*Today's Woman*), *Hoghough-e Zanan* (*Women's Rights*), and *Jens-e Dovvom* (*Second Sex*). Shahla Lahiji's Roshangaran Press has published important feminist works as well as historical studies, while the new Cultural Center of Women organized by Noushin Ahmadi-Khorassani and others produces feminist analyses, calendars, compendiums, and the journal *Jens-e Dovvom*. Feminist newspapers are produced in Turkey, and the Women's Library in Istanbul contains research and documentation on women and gender issues. Mention should also be made of the first Arab Women's Book Fair, held in Cairo in November 1995 and organized by Noor, a women's publishing house in Cairo. *Al-Raida*, a quarterly feminist journal of the Institute for Women's Studies in the Arab World, of the Lebanese American University, has had issues since 1976 on topics such as women in Arab cinema, women and the war in Lebanon, women and work, and violence against women.

Demographic, political, and economic changes are the internal factors behind the growth of women's organizations, but global effects have been important as well. The role of the UN and its world conferences has been especially important. Women's organizations from the Arab countries first met at a regional meeting – sponsored by the UN's regional commission for West Asia (ESCWA) as part of UN preparations for the Beijing Conference – which took place in early November 1994 in Amman, Jordan. The two-week deliberations resulted in a document entitled "Work Program for the Non-Government Organizations in the Arab Region." That document summarized women's conditions in Arab countries as follows: (1) Women suffer a lack of employment rights and undue burdens caused by economic crisis and structural adjustment policies. (2) The absence of democracy and civil rights harms women especially. (3) There is inequality between men and women in authority and decision-making. (4) Women suffer from violence, including "honor crimes." The solutions offered were comprehensive. The document called for the immediate ratification and implementation of the Convention on the Elimination of All Forms of Discrimination against Women, and a revision of all national laws that discriminate against women. It called for legal literacy and free legal services for women, the promotion of women judges, "revision and modernization of the legislation related to women's status in the family," the insertion of the rights of the wife in the marriage contract, and "the amendment of nationality laws so that children can join their mothers and enjoy their nationalities."[4]

With the exception of the call for nationality rights, these demands are similar to those made by feminists and the women's organizations in Iran and Turkey. Turkish feminists have long made domestic violence and street harassment of women major targets of their collective action; they have also been involved in peace actions (Tekeli, 1986; Arat, 1999). Iranian secular feminists and Islamic feminists alike actively promote women's rights in both the women's press and in the intellectual press to which they have contributed. Their primary concern is to enhance women's (civil) rights in the family, particularly with respect to marriage, divorce, and child custody. Azam Taleghani's attempt to run for president in 1997 also raised the important question of political rights for women; in the 2001 presidential elections, some forty women tried to run for the presidency, though all were disqualified. It is not irrelevant to note that the dramatic fertility decline in Iran – now close to two children per woman – frees women's time for participation in public affairs.

The engagement of women's rights activists with the state is illustrative of an approach that may be called "critical realist." That is, feminists are critical of the neopatriarchal nature of the state and the way that it reinforces their subordinate status, and they are aware that the authoritarian Middle Eastern state limits the political participation of citizens, including women's rights activists. The Egyptian state, for example, closed down the Arab Women's Solidarity Association for its criticism of Egypt's role in the 1991 Gulf War; imprisoned and prosecuted the sociology professor and human rights activist Saad eddin Ibrahim in 2000–2; and in June 2003 refused to grant a license that would enable the New Woman Research Group to function as an NGO. But Middle Eastern feminists are also aware that the state is an unavoidable institutional actor. They therefore make claims on the state for the improvement of their legal status and social positions, or they insist that the state live up to commitments and implement the conventions that it has signed – notably, the Convention on the Elimination of All Forms of Discrimination Against Women.

Conclusions

The turbulence and dramatic changes of recent decades have affected Middle Eastern women in different ways, but they have hardly been passive onlookers. Instead, they have actively taken part in movements for social and political change – revolution, national liberation, human rights, women's rights, and democratization. Women also have been actively involved for and against Islamist/fundamentalist movements. Islamist women are discernible by their dress, the Islamic hijab. Anti-fundamentalist women are likewise discernible by their dress, which is western, and by their liberal or left-wing political views. In between are Muslim women who may or may not veil but are dismayed by women's second-class citizenship. Women also have been involved in and affected by economic development and economic stagnation. Whether as rural workers, managers of households, factory workers, service workers, street vendors, teachers, nurses, or professionals, Middle Eastern women have contributed to economic production and social reproduction – though their contributions are not always acknowledged, valued, or remunerated. At times they have been disproportionately affected by economic difficulties.

The discussion above has indicated that change in the Middle East and its impact on women has been neither linear nor uniform but contradictory and paradoxical, though there have been some predictable patterns, trends, and outcomes. In particular, the discussion has drawn attention to the potentially revolutionary role of middle-class Middle Eastern women, especially secular feminists and Muslim feminists. These women are not simply acting out roles prescribed for them by religion, by culture, or by neopatriarchal states; they are questioning their roles and status, calling for greater rights, participating in movements, and taking sides in ideological battles. In particular, they are at the center of the new social movements for democratization, civil society, and citizenship – however difficult and limited these have been thus far.

NOTES

1 Author's interview with Shaha Riza, Middle East Gender Unit, the World Bank, May 1, 2000.
2 In the summer of 2000, nine Lebanese women ran for parliamentary seats in a campaign organized by the National Committee to Follow-up Women's Issues and the Lebanese Women's Council.
3 "Roundtable on the Rights of Female Wage-earners: Need for Joint Action", in *Exaequo*, Information Bulletin published by the Directorate of Multilateral Cooperation, Rabat, no. 1, August 1995, p. 3.
4 The right of women to retain their own nationality after marriage to a foreigner is a right that European women won in stages. Feminists first tried to win nationality rights for women through the League of Nations-sponsored Women's Consultative Committee on Nationality in the 1930s. It should also be noted that Article 9 of the Convention on the Elimination of All Forms of Discrimination Against Women requires States Parties to grant women equal rights with respect to their nationality and to the nationality of their children. Many Middle Eastern countries that have signed the Convention entered reservations to this article.

FURTHER READING

The following texts offer the best introduction to the subject of Middle Eastern women both in its historical and contemporary dimensions: Leila Ahmed, *Women and Gender in Islam: Historical Roots of a Modern Debate*, Yale University Press, 1993; Nikki Keddie and Beth Baron, *Women in Middle Eastern History*, Yale, 1991; Valentine M. Moghadam, *Modernizing Women*, 2nd edn., Lynne Rienner, Boulder and London, 2003.

See also the following titles: Suha Abdel Kader, *Egyptian Women in a Changing Society 1899–1987*, Boulder, Lynne Rienner, 1987; Haleh Afshar (ed.), *Women and Politics in the Third World*, London, Routledge, 1996; Nadje Al-Ali, *Secularism, Gender and the State: The Egyptian Women's Movement*, Cambridge, Cambridge University Press, 2000; Sadekka Arebi, *Women and Words in Saudi Arabia*, New York, Columbia University Press, 1994; Yael Azmon, and Dafna N. Izraeli (eds.), *Women in Israel*, Transactions Publishers, New Brunswick and London, 1993; Beth Baron, *The Women's Awakening in Egypt*, New Haven, Yale University Press, 1994; Camillia Fawzi El-Solh, and Judy Mabro, *Muslim Women's Choices: Religious Beliefs and Social Reality*, Berg Publishers, 1994, offer various interpretations of the history and status of women in Middle East Societies.

Chapter Twenty-Three

Politics and Religion

BEVERLEY MILTON-EDWARDS

And if you rule between people then rule with justice.
Sura al-Maʾidah:42, The Qurʾan

Introduction

The notion in the modern age that religion should shape or influence politics is, in some ways, increasingly moribund – an old-fashioned idea that belongs in the past. Yet, the debate about modern politics in the Middle East is still shaped, and some would argue, also stymied by the historic relationship between faith and politics. This essay will reflect the ways in which traditional religion formed a part of established political and other institutions in the Middle East. I will contend that this relationship was altered and even dislocated entirely with the advent of the modernity project. Indeed by the early twentieth century the force of the modernization project and the modernity discourse appeared to signal the eclipse of faith from the political and public realm. In reality this was not always the case. It is my contention that because faith had been deeply embedded in the established institutions of Middle Eastern empires and states as well as social structures, it proved less easy to eject it under the modernization process. Although many nationalist movements and new political orders attempted to exclude religion, others were compelled to engage in a reform, reinterpretation and rehabilitation of faith into institutions and social structures into the modern nation-state entities that today characterize the Middle East. This process, in turn, was disrupted by the religious revivalism wave that appeared on the horizon of the political landscape in the Middle East from the 1970s onwards. Revivalism or resurgence of all things religious emerged as a challenge to secular and national ideologies and projects. It has gained some ground at the expense of secular nationalism articulated in a variety of locales across the region as the new populism of the closing decades of the twentieth century.

Religion remains an important marker of identity in a variety of ways to the Muslims, Jews and Christians of the modern Middle East. Their sense of identity, however, is not fixed but changed and altered by a continual process of striving to find a 'fit' with the modernity process. Faith appears to matter as a symbol of that which is defined and understood as tradition in contrast to the modern. Yet, the process of striving and transformation, defence and subsequent reaction began in the eighteenth century when as a result of the colonial project, spearheaded by European states, reform was thrust upon a region defined as mostly Muslim. In the face of continued European expansion into the region the Muslim rulers there appeared increasingly impotent. This process of emasculation is symbolized by Napoleon's capture and occupation of Egypt in 1798. Rodenbeck describes the difference in the public and private motives for Napoleon's daring act. In public he came 'as a servant of Allah and of the Ottoman sultan. His mission was to punish the wicked Mamluks and rescue Egypt from their grasp' ... [In private] 'Of course, there were other more practical reasons: the economic potential of Egypt and the weakness of its Ottoman masters; Napoleon's megalomania and his romantic visions of the East; his wish to threaten Britain's hold in India'.[1] The modernity project was thrust upon the region as part of the baggage of occupation and dominance. Further decline somehow appeared inevitable and further inroads by the colonizers resulted in the near termination of Muslim governance. Societal upheaval, political change, economic turmoil and indebtedness combined with the ascendancy of an alien culture culminated in the exclusion of faith (other than in symbolic form) from the public arena. The sense of disruption to the geographic and spiritual centre of Islam was immense and intense, giving rise to tensions, conflicts and resistance centred on dimensions of faith and rule in the Middle East. The Muslim response to these changes has been multi-faceted, symbolizing a palpable internal discourse that has taken place for more than a century about Muslim options in the modern world. Some have proposed a path of retreat and violent resistance, others have argued for an embrace of the modernity project as a Muslim project. The debate has been both institutionally and society based, it has always centred on power and its control in the modern age. Its elite and populist dimensions have underscored the continuing perceived relevance of the religious voice in the debate about governance, power and political systems in the majority of the region's modern Muslim majority nation states. Yet in other ways this debate has also reverberated among other traditional faith groups of the region including Jews and Christians.

Jews, even following the exodus from the Holy Land, have remained a part of the religious landscape of the region. Jewish minority populations in Iraq, Yemen, Syria, Egypt and other parts of the region were significant in their contribution to the development of Muslim majority societies and institutions. In the Ottoman period, for example, despite their status as *dhimmis* and the obligation to pay a poll tax known as *jizya*, Jews and Christians, according to Hourani, 'enjoyed a special position ... and had their own legal systems of personal law ... in this way, the non-Muslims were integrated into the body politic.'[2] The establishment of the state of Israel in 1948 in fulfilment of the secular Zionist project ended this episode in the history of faith and state in the region. Under the terms of the Zionist project Israel was founded as a secular state for Jews. Nevertheless, the religious identity of Israel's Jewish citizens has been increasingly ascendant in determining internal political dimensions to governance and the national project. Faith in politics, whether at the micro-level of Shabbat keeping or the macro level of the religious imperative behind some elements of the national settler movement in the Palestinian territories, remains a feature of power in modern-day Israel.

Christian minorities in the region remain, but grow smaller and less significant than in past centuries. Although initial beneficiaries of the missionary schooling that was part of the baggage of the European interlude in the region they too remained perceived as part of the native peoples of the region that were to be dominated politically and economically by European states. Instead of realizing their potential as important interlocutors between the Muslim majority and European colonizers their significance diminished in the wake of the modernity project that transformed state and nation in the region. As a subject people many Christian intellectuals and elites strove alongside their Muslim brothers and sisters to achieve self-determination and independence. Intellectuals from Christian backgrounds played an important part in shaping emerging nationalist and socialist discourse that would run counter to the tradition of faith in politics. The Christian population of the region, however, remains in decline with no more than 12 million remaining in the region. How Christians faced the quandaries of the modernity project in relation to politics and governance has been important in explaining, for example, the powerful and yet destructive political dynamic of contemporary Lebanon as a multi-confessional state. In Egypt, the Coptic community has been pulled into political battles as targets of fundamentalist radical Islamist fanatics with disturbing consequences for the future of plural societies and sectarian polities in the region.

Faith and State

The contribution of Muslims in the political life of a community is understood as fundamental to the faith itself. Although primarily a religious leader, when the Prophet Muhammad established a community and form of statehood in the city of Medina, Islam was also understood as being defined in relation to temporal as well as spiritual power. Hence Muhammad established a set of norms for governance that would inspire and shape the temporal realms that were established, according to the faith, by his successors. The extension of Muslim governance was, therefore, tied to the expansion of the faith across continents and cultures. Expansion of Islam as a political force was, therefore, often closely tied to the establishment of the faith in other domains. In this way faith and state were a demonstrable reality with faith embedded in established institutions and social structures. It is argued that governance was made manifest in this manner because of the unitary nature of the faith. Islam, it is explained, is a faith system that centres on the concept of faith and politics as fused and permanently intertwined. The ways in which faith informs and colours governance and politics are myriad and although it is true that faith was embedded in the state, states that claimed to rule in the name of Islam were often very different in tone and emphasis. Rulers across Muslim domains did not interpret the rule of Islam in the same ways. Instead, they attached more or less emphasis to some dimensions of Islamic governance than others. The Muslim jurists were also there to legitimate distinctions that were drawn between politics and faith by the rulers. The realm of the *shari'a* was thus circumscribed by some jurists in the Sunni tradition leaving rulers a certain degree of autonomy or room for manoeuvre. Ibn al-Muqaffa' asserts the need for the provision for discretionary power of the ruler over the laws of Islam, 'Therefore, he concluded the caliph was free to determine and codify the sunna as he thought fit. The plea of Ibn al-Muqaffa' for state control over law (and, incidentally, over religion, too) was in full accord with the tendencies prevailing at the very beginning of the 'Abbasid era. But this was merely a passing phase, and orthodox Islam refused to be drawn into too close a connexion with the state', claims Schacht.[3] Additionally, other cultural traditions and religious influences impacted on the method of interpretation that emerged in local contexts. Attempts to codify the laws of governance within Islam did take place but not in a consistent fashion. This resulted in literatures produced by jurists dealing with the issue of governance and authority. Qadis and jurists such as al-Marwardi and Ibn Taymiyyah did address such matters underscoring the obligation to rule justly in the name of Islam. In this way the political was addressed by the legal obligations inherent in the *shari'a*. The development of such normative thinking grew out of the experiences of intense disruption that characterized early political challenges that arose within the Islamic fold following the death of the Prophet. Internal tension, battle and schism characterized the period described by Lambton as the 'Great Fitna' betraying the extent of civil strife that had taken grip in the early Islamic period.[4]

This tension was partly settled through the development of a discourse that commended order at the expense of justice – if carried out in the name of Islam. Hence the import of faith on the political level, as al-Marwardi asserted, 'for without governance, disorder and barbaric behaviour would arise amongst the wanton and lawless. As ... al-Awfah al-Awdi has said ... "There is no benefit to a leaderless people when disorder reigns, and they will never have a leader if the ignorant among them leads" '.[5] Faith and state did appear to be important but because it was able to remain responsive, dynamic and reflexive of societal dynamic for many centuries.

Islam Entrenched

In this way, throughout the history of Islam, faith was tied into the institutions of the state through law, through the status of the clerical elite, the jurists and qadis, the waqf endowments and patronage of the ruling elite. Islam emerged in an institutionalized form in distinction to the manifestation of its more populist forms in the multitude of Muslim domains that stretched across not just regions but continents. This perspective of an inextricable tie between religion and politics has, however, been challenged by Eickelman and Piscatori, who contend that, historically, such a linkage was just not present. 'The presuppostion of the union of religion and politics', they argue, 'is unhelpful for three reasons.'[6] Such views play a part in: 'exaggerating the uniqueness of Muslim politics, [they] inadvertently perpetuat[ed] "Orientalist" assumptions' and, finally, 'contribut[ed] to the view that Muslim politics is a seamless web.'[7] The religion, therefore, traditionally affected or altered the nature of the political dynamic in Muslim states but not in a necessarily consistent and orthodox fashion. Additionally, the convention of interpretation (*ijtihad*) and innovation (*tajdid*), combined or coupled with doctrinal and schismatic difference produced a range of forms of governance. The Kharjite revolt alone succeeded in altering forever the dynamic within Sunni Islam in relation to leadership, governance and the faithful followers of Islam. This epoch, with others that followed, provided examples of numerous encounters and revelations of the faith that influenced followers. This encouraged different paths to governance. Indeed, from the seventh century onwards Islam, as established through successive dynasties, under the Umayyads, 'Abbasids, Mamluks, Safavids and Ottomans secured faith by incorporating many styles of leadership and system; from reformist to fundamentalist, scripturalist to interpretative, benign to despotic, liberal to conservative. The religion acted as a cornerstone (often aligned to military, economic or strategic strength as well) to political systems that were widespread and varied.

The impact of the political on the religious and vice versa resulted in a complicated history where the political hue of Islam assumed greater importance, often in response to a challenge or contest for authority, yet none of this was unusual. The history of Islam and, therefore, of political Islam, is one of dynamism. Islam's faithful have confronted unjust authority. Vibrant, and responsive to the passage of time, the followers of Islam have played a part in the generation, change and reform of political systems throughout the Middle East and beyond. Political Muslims have been rulers, the ruled, in government and in opposition, claiming legitimacy in the name of the faith, as well as contesting and protesting it.

Modernity and Exclusion

At the beginning of the twentieth century the scope of the Ottoman empire encompassed the territories of the present-day Middle East. Ottoman power had been maintained for more than four centuries. The impact of European intrusion, however, was already apparent in the weakening defences and grasp by the Ottoman structures of governance on its subjects and there was evidence of a dissipating attachment to Islam at societal levels. The traditions of Islam symbolized by the Ottoman ruler were under assault. The sultan, symbol of Islamic authority, guardian of the most holy sites in Islam, and upholder of the laws of Islam, had his legitimacy undermined from within as well as without. The battle for the survival of the established traditions of Islam would take place on many fronts. Primarily, though, Islam remained part of the institutions of Ottoman rule through the maintenance of the *shari'a*. The courts of Islamic law were central to Ottoman governance and tied all Muslim citizens of the empire to the principles and tenets of Islam. Non-Muslim minorities were permitted their own religious courts and subject to the payment of *jizya* were not made subject to the authority of *shari'a* law. The importance of a developed legal system and judicial processes founded on Islamic law promoted the establishment of religious figures into an elite cadre that upheld and legitimated the rule of the sultan. Islam was effectively tied into the state and accorded the same status as other institutions. The importance of these officials to the hegemonic nature of the state in a vast empire governing a diverse population should not be underestimated. Hourani contends that in creating an official clerical class (*'ulama*) in 'parallel with the political, politico-military and bureaucratic corps; there was an equivalence ... These official *'ulama* played an important part in the administration of empire.'[8] Yet the commitment to *shari'a* was not exclusive to the *'ulama* and the sultan contributed to the legal norms by issuing his own edicts and rules (*kanun* or *firman*) that were administered and upheld by the religious elite. Nevertheless it was increasingly difficult to defend Islam from the growing pretensions to power that were resurgent from within the territorial fold of the empire. When aligned with European military clout, such as that exhibited by the Sharif of Mecca in launching his jihad against the Ottoman authorities during the First World War, there was little the Ottoman authorities could do to counter the claim to raise the banner of Islam in the name of Muslim freedom and liberty. Even within the heart of the empire conspiracy and plots to overthrow the existing order emerged in the form of new nationalisms. The most potent threat of all came from within, and Kemal Ataturk's new Turkish nationalism symbolized it.

Ataturk's nationalism reflected an attempt at the comprehensive exclusion of Islam as part of the modernity project in the Middle East. The nationalist project as outlined by Ataturk severed the link between faith and state that had, in many ways, defined the Ottoman political project. On organizing the resistance in 1919 and promoting the movement for independence the republican cause in Turkey was successful. In 1922 the sultanate was abolished, by 1924 the caliph was deposed and Ataturk and his followers introduced a raft of legislative changes that would result in Islam being removed from definitions of statehood in Turkey. This process was part of a comprehensive secularization of the state and its institutions and included replacing *shari'a* with civil laws, the prohibition of the fez, the replacement of the Islamic calendar with a Gregorian one, and the removal of Islam from the Turkish constitution. Islamic schools and sufi orders were closed down. The Republican People's Party, established by Ataturk, signalled the depth of political as well as social revolution that was being embarked on. The assault on Islam as a public and political institution could not have been more comprehensive, yet Turkey would remain the only locale in the Middle East throughout the twentieth century where such wholesale transformation, as part of the modernity project, was achieved.

Whither Faith?

Thus the emergence of modern nation states; their establishment as a set of institutions often autonomous and independent from faith, and in particular Islam, was made manifest in the Middle East in a process that was inextricably linked to the fuzzy border between colonial control and post-independence governance. It is my contention, however, that in relation to faith there was no uniform pattern of state or nation building that saw religion completely divorced from politics or power. Rather, what appears to emerge is a spectrum of statehood in which there is evidence of states at one end where religion was eschewed and at the other end where religion appears to signify and define the state. In between there is evidence of an uneasy alliance between politics and religion. In sum then we might speak of three broad manifestations: the first manifestation relates to the majority of states within the region where an uneasy relationship between faith ascendant and secularism challenged emerges and the nation project is cast into a state of confusion. The second is a smaller minority of states that claim Islamic credentials and include Saudi Arabia and theocratic Iran. Finally there is Turkey where religion was rejected and the secular state was constructed as part of Ataturk's project. Even today, however, the doors to this secular bastion are being hammered by ascendant Islamists making their claim to power. In many respects then the notion that was established in the early to mid-twentieth century of secular statehood in Muslim societies has been significantly eroded by religious revivalism and its challenge to the hegemonic intentions of the secularists. This has resulted not just in an assault on the symbols of secularism in society (closing down bars, keeping religious holy days, segregating the sexes) but on the institutions of state and nation. In the majority of states, as I have already noted, the symbols of faith were regularly employed by those engaged in the secular nation-building and state-building project to establish national hegemony, nation-ness and community. In this respect the symbols of faith were incorporated and used as an important legitimating agent of new identities and states. Flags, muftis, rabbis, religious symbols, priests, religious parties, religious ministries, religious law and courts, prayer, broadcasting, were all evidence of the import attached to religious imagery or sacred symbols in the construction of national identities across the Middle East. In Israel the establishment of a secular democratic state in 1948 has not precluded the growing power of religious leaders in mainstream politics, nor their alliances with the state in legitimating decisions that give religious rather than secular character to the Jewish state. In Israel there has been a significant play-off between the religious and political elite, particularly in terms of major issues such as national identity and citizenship. In Saudi Arabia, the al-Sa'ud family not only derives its legitimacy to rule the country from its traditionally close links with the Wahhabi movement but faith lies at the heart of the shaping of the state and national identity. Traditional, conservative and fundamentalist, the al-Sa'ud elite has shaped the state according to its interpretation of the principles of Islam. Yet it has also had to contend with internal Islamist dissension. Social and religious conservatism in the Kingdom defined as Islamic has led to a challenge aimed at the elite. External factors, including the ascendancy of Ayatollah Khomeini in Iran in 1979, a deepening of economic relations between Saudi Arabia and the economies of the west, led to criticism and agitation in radical circles in the Kingdom. Their ire was not only directed at the monarchy but at the perception of encroaching westernization in Saudi Arabia. From the margins the radicals gradually impacted on popular society and the state compounded matters by entering into a competition for influence at this level. From the margins discourse took place in mosques and through the dissemination of new literatures and even protests against the state. The state continued to respond by upping the ante on its sole claim to religious credentials while at the same time attempting to rein in the radicals where possible. The responsibility for religious behaviours has been reappropriated by the state in an attempt to underscore its religious character. In particular the religious police (*mutawwa*) has been increasingly incorporated into the institutions of the state and its powers of enforcement of social-religious behaviours has been increased. In this way the monarchy must be seen as the ultimate upholder of Islamic values. It is obliged to incorporate Islam in more than just a symbolic manner and demonstrate to significant elements of society that it will preserve this identity in the face of the cultural threat posed by westernization. Religion then has to continue as the fundamental core of the state and its ruling elite. In the creation of the 'imagined communities' that lay at the heart of modern nation and state building in the Middle East, religion, therefore, has been consistently employed as a means of establishing legitimacy and a sense of continuity amid the upheavals, reaction to and even as part of the modernization process.

   The global political changes of the early twentieth century had appeared to weaken the place of religion in institutions of the state and political systems in the region. The security and continuity of Islam, for example, appeared to be undermined as western political ideas filtered throughout the region and were manifest in a rainbow of nationalisms. The imported and adopted ideologies of the west appeared to challenge the traditional orthodoxy of Islam to its very core. The tradition of western political thought that had been established over many centuries promoted the secularization of society; this meant that the bonds between faith and politics would have to be broken. Yet as Bouchlaka remarks, 'while the secular elite sought to achieve a radical rupture with the socio-cultural traditions of Islamic society ... it is quite misleading to attempt a reading of modern Islamic society on the basis of the movement of elites and their strategies without contemplating the rhythm and language of their society as a whole'.[9] The concept of rule by the people for the people (with Allah absent from the arrangement) coupled with the endorsement of capitalist and other economic agendas, clashed jarringly with the norms of rule and governance traditionally associated with Islam in the Middle East. Secularism and nationalism represented the demotion of Islam and its clerical elite. Muslim thinkers responded by calling for reform, and set about the modernization of Islam with an increasing sense of urgency.

Reform

It is the case that in the majority of modern Muslim societies in the Middle East an uneasy and, as yet still unresolved, interface between faith and politics has emerged. This new dynamic between faith and politics is partly explicable by the response of the Islamic elite to the challenges posed by the ideologies of nationalism and secularism that gripped the Middle East in the first half of the twentieth century. An aspect of the response is symbolized by the emergence of modernist or reformist thinkers who, Mousalli argues, 'have found that Islam must accommodate modernity and modernity must accommodate Islam'.[10] The modernist trend was never limited to one geographic or schismatic domain but reflected the growth of a new generation of thinkers spearheaded by figures like al-Afghani, 'Abduh, Rashid Rida, and Ali Shariati. The impact of their ideas, discourses, and engagements in the political arena contributed to the emergence of a core of thinkers in Egypt, Lebanon, Syria, Iran and so forth who advocated that Islam and modernity could be reconciled. They were considered revolutionaries and subversives of their time, a group who posed a potent threat to the nationalist regimes that were being established in their midst. Indeed, the very notion of Islamic modernism as opposed to traditionalism was in itself revolutionary and acted as a catalyst for change in a number of political arenas.

These thinkers recognized the importance of the relationship between the new state system that was emerging and subsequently evolving in the Middle East and Islam. In this respect Esposito contends that, 'Unlike conservative Muslims, however, Islamic modernists asserted the need to revive the Muslim community through a process of reinterpretation or reformulation of their Islamic heritage in light of the contemporary world.'[11] They attempted to establish new discourses within Islamic circles where modernity could not only be accommodated but made relevant. This created many problems and led to the recognition of issues centred on the reconcilability of the principles of new nationalisms with modern Islam. The dilemma for such thinkers was how to present Islam as relevant without undermining the core principles that appeared to shape it. For at the heart of modernity lay secularism and this inevitably meant the diminishment of Islam. This problem was dealt with by successive generations of thinkers and ideologues who either took modernity and looked for a fit within Islam or vice versa. Islamization of the motifs of new political discourses was often the result.

Although thinkers like al-Afghani, 'Abduh, Rida, al-Banna or Shariati share commonalities, their ideas reflected the differing approaches they took to the modernist project, its impact on the political establishment and the emergence of a new Islamic project that would change the face of Islamism in the region forever. Such thinkers were representative of both the establishment and anti-establishment elements who sought to break or make anew their bonds with the state in its contemporary guise.

Al-Afghani, for example, was a significant activist. He was not content to merely pontificate from the minaret but to engage in shaping new approaches to help Muslims deal with the impact of modernization. This process of dealing with modernity was, for these thinkers, sullied by its hitch to the colonial project in the Middle East. In opposing colonialisms and resisting the domination of one people over another, were the Islamists then condemned to damn modernity as well? Al-Afghani did attempt to promote a discourse of faith that was made relevant to modern politics and the state. He argued that Islam and its followers were capable of meeting the modernity project head on. Kedourie, however, believes that al-Afghani failed in his task: 'he cultivated a reputation of Islamic zeal, while he was in fact a secret unbeliever'.[12] Yet, Kedourie underestimates the impact of al-Afghani's conceptualization of the modern Muslim project. For al-Afghani was contending that nationalism was not the only route out of oppression, subjugation and dependence. He promoted Islam as a means of rising above the petty politics of the modern nation-state. He believed that Islam should be established as the most meaningful dimension of modern identity. Thus for al-Afghani the stained past and waning of Islam was explicable only by recognizing that the time for change and a return to the faith had come.

"Abduh as the torch-bearer of al-Afghani took this new message of revitalised and relevant Islam back into the establishment and institutions of Islam. Portrayed as a "rationalist who influenced and inspired not only a whole school of thinkers and reformers ... but a number of non-Egyptians and even non-Muslims as well".' Abduh progressed the Islamist project by attempting to demonstrate its value to emerging nationalist and anti-colonial discourses.[13] He sought to achieve this by exercising influence through the important social networks that still provided a foundation to Muslim identity in the region. In this way he sought to work within the system rather than agitate for its overthrow by revolutionary means. He sought to re-evaluate power relations as much from below as above and address the modernity project with the same focus as the modernizers themselves. He did not shy away from hot political issues such as women's rights and emancipation. Instead he forwarded new interpretations and discourses of Islam that were genuinely reformist in principle and outlook. This bottom-up approach impacted on the state through the adoption of particular policies that demonstrated a reconciliation between state power and faith in the modern era. Jawad, for example, argues that 'Abduh's position on legal reform regarding the rights of women in divorce were directly responsible for positive changes in the field of divorce and the courts in Tunisia.[14] 'Abduh's new direction was a straightforward outcome of modernist debate on faith and politics. It formed part of the attempt to return to the fundamentals, to cast aside ornamented traditions and folkish practices to a new Islam that was as dynamic and modern as its ideological and cultural and economic opponents. This development also signalled a departure from the image of the old theologians tied to the past to a new generation who were open to departing from customary approaches to faith in application – in certain cases. Herein lies the major weakness of the reformist process, and one that has drawn criticism from many quarters. For it is contended that the reformist process did not symbolize a wholesale or comprehensive reform of Islam or embracing of the modernity project. Rather, it was a piecemeal attempt to claim modernity for Islam and ensure the preservation of the place of the faith in the centre of the political as well as private domains of modern states.

'Abduh's successor, Rashid Rida epitomized the more assertive and scripturalist approach to the modernist project. His *salafi* beliefs invoked a reaction against the secular project in its societal rather than political form. Al-Azmeh has argued that as such this dimension of reformism attended to society first and not the political framework or structures of the states. Al-Azmeh states that 'reformism engaged in theorising the reconstitution of civil society in terms of itself rather than in terms of politics'. It was the mark of Rida's project.[15] Rida succeeded in influencing a new generation of Muslims who would become not just social reformers but political reformers and revolutionaries as well. For in his work Rida consistently reflected on an engagement with a changing political reality that was shaped by colonialism and demanded a response to it. In this way his work reflected the decline of Islam and the challenge of secular nationalist discourse. He acknowledged the Islamist project must also address the contest for power at the level of state as well as society. A revitalized faith community would be better able to withstand the slings and arrows of the contest ahead if it were cohesive and animated by a fundamental interpretation of Islam. In this way, Rida contended that Islam would not only match but counter the secular project and naturally lead to the restoration of the true faith at the centre of the political sphere and its institutions of governance. In Rida's arrangement of power the *'ulama* would be restored to their place of natural authority, alongside the caliph at the heart of the state. From this point the *shari'a* would be restored and the power and dynamism of Islam as a competitor in the emerging global system of nation-states would be assured.

For the reformist project was not solely concerned with modernity and its accommodation but the place of a revitalized Islam in competition for power against it. For these thinkers, and others, like Shariati, the modernist project was not to be unquestioningly accepted and slavishly followed. These thinkers attempted to open new debates within Islam and offer a critique of dimensions of the modernist project. As Ali Shariati notes,

> I hope soon to see the day when the present state of affairs, which is colored by pessimism, cursing and evil-teaching perpetuated among Muslims by the enemies of Islam in order to instigate trouble between them so that they can forget the real enemy, will be transformed ... all Muslims should follow the true Islamic teachings and enjoy friendship and understanding ... our professors along with the 'ulama, our illiterate believers along with the intellectuals, ... our modernized along with the traditionalists ... will all be able to sit together and defend each other in a united struggle against the plots facing Muslims. It will also be the day when Muslims enhance their knowledge of true Islam.[16]

Although it is the case that the early reformists did not necessarily ignite the passions of the populist mass with talk of revolution and firebrand politics, their ideas, discourse and ideologies did give inspiration to the wider region-wide movement by Islamists to contest and challenge state power and the project of secular nationalism in a variety of domains that had a distinctly populist appeal.

Successor populist organizations, or movements such as the Muslim Brotherhood, played a part in generating new dimensions in the contest between Islam and nationalism, faith and the attempt by national elites to exclude it from political domains, in the twentieth century. Zubaida claims that the Muslim Brotherhood, has 'in one form or another, been the most prominent fundamentalist current in

Sunni Islam'.[17] Hassan al-Banna and fellow traveller Sayyid Qutb contributed to the shaping of a discourse that promoted the revival of Islam in all aspects of the public and societal domain as a challenge to secular nationalism, westernism and the colonial experience. Hassan al-Banna not only established the roots of a region-wide network for Islamic revivalism but, as Mousalli reminds us, he 'opened up the theoretical possibility of harmonizing Western political thought with the Islamic. Unlike al-Mawdudi and Sayyid Qutb, who radicalized the doctrine of *hakimiyya* [divine rule], he transformed it into a human act'.[18]

The Brotherhood network posed a serious challenge to the concerted effort by the leaders of the post-revolutionary secular regimes of the Middle East to give no more than a passing nod to Islam in symbolic form. For in their efforts to remove Islam from the centre and place it and its adherents on the margins a reaction was deep and widespread. The concept behind the Muslim Brotherhood was to advance the notion of the import of Islam at every level of society as well as politically. In this way Islam was promoted as an alternative agenda to that of secular nationalism.

Thinking and discourse within and on the fringes of the movement was disrupted by the departure of al-Banna – as a result of bloody assassination at the hands of the agents of the Egyptian state – and the ascendance of Sayyid Qutb. Throughout the 1950s and 1960s much internal debate and discourse then centred on future directions and the political challenges ahead. The establishment of a populist base, with Brotherhood activities centred on social reform, welfare, education and the improvement of people's living and social conditions, meant that the movement could withstand the winds of dissent that emerged from Qutb and his followers. Not only that, but the Brotherhood demonstrated that they could act as a substitute for the failed state that emerged from the nationalist socialist experiments embarked upon by Nasser and his successors. The importance of such activities and networks should not be underestimated, for as Kepel (1994) alleges, 'these networks play an essential part in assimilating those elements of the population who aspired to taste the fruits of modernity and prosperity but could not get them'.[19]

Qutbian discourse transcended the primary need for networks of socially active Muslims engaged with society. Sayyid Qutb espoused an alternate perspective that reflected on the internal state of Arab society and politics as well as external relations with other actors in the international order. As Ayubi contends, 'Qutbian discourse ... tends to influence people's thought and action in a psychologically tense way that creates in the individual not the ability to reconstruct reality but rather the dream of breaking with that reality.'[20] Qutb's ideas not only influenced the political dynamic of Nasserist Egypt, leading to him being considered a major threat and thus imprisoned and executed by the authorities but he influenced others who fell under the radical mantle. These groups promoted a significant alteration in the path of Islamic politics; driving it into a revolutionary phase. Revolution would be wrought from within through the employment of the strategy of jihad. Qutb's analysis of society and the political system fixed on the deterioration of such polities when placed under secular rule. Such societies, he contended, were characterized by disorder, lax morals, loss of spiritual fundamentals which he labelled as *jahiliyya*. Qutb asserted that the only path out of such disorder was radical. He promoted jihad as the means for emancipation. As such he declared, 'The truth of the faith is not fully established until a jihad is undertaken on its behalf among the people ... a struggle to remove them from this state (*jahiliyya*).'[21] This call was not so much an assault on the west as on the new secular post-revolutionary political orders of the Middle East that had emerged from the ashes of colonial rule and the rise of nationalist movements for independence. Qutb's number one target were Arab leaders who, in his view, had turned their back on Islam and thus damned the societies they led to Godless disorder. The old Muslim fear of disorder 'fitna' appears to be equated with nationalist and secularist discourse and Qutb, like al-Ghazali and Ibn Taymiyyah before him, is radicalized by the consequences of such rule. For Qutb in such a state of emergency, the gradualist approach, as advocated by al-Banna, was just not possible. A wholesale change was advocated as the order of the day. For Qutb the leaders of Islam must spearhead and lead the change from below. Change was an obligation and the establishment of a political order could only be achieved if Islam were at the centre of such efforts. But with Islam placed back in the centre the contest with secular nationalist and other alternatives would be inevitable for Qutb's vision of political order allowed little room for the 'apostates'. This established a new tension between Islam revived and radical and the prevailing political order in the majority of post-independence states in the Middle East. The legitimacy of the state was contested by those who adhered to such principles and ideas. In the wake of Qutb's death his ideas lived on and were spread across the Middle East and beyond by young adherents of Islam revived. The radicalism which eventually characterized Qutb became the starting point of many radical groups. As Esposito asserts, however, the import of Qutbian discourse can be observed in two ways, 'evolution, a process which emphasises revolutionary change from below, and revolution, the violent overthrow of established systems of government'.[22] In the main, however, Qutb's influence was detected as revolutionary and violent. He has been seen as the inspiration behind the radical fringe in Egypt, Palestine, Afghanistan, and Algeria. Without doubt he advocated a return of Islam from the margins of society and politics back to the centre of modern Middle Eastern political entities in the contemporary era. This implies that he brooked no compromise with the forces of secularism.

Contest from the Margins

The resurgence and revival of faith in the 1970s has traditionally been tied to explanations of the 'watershed defeat' of the Arabs against Israel in the Six Day War of 1967 and the emergence of a 'crisis of identity' in Muslim majority states in the region. Indeed it is contended that from this point a new political epoch and a challenge to the discourses of nationalism and secularism arose in the heartlands of the Middle East. Chief among these responses was an increasing belief in Arab circles that the loss of Islam as core to Arab identity and politics explained the decline, defeat and subjugation of modern Arab states to the power of the west as symbolized by the state of Israel. Additionally it should be noted that in Israel the victory achieved in the war of 1967 against the Arabs underscored the impression in some quarters that the divinely ordained messianic project to establish Eretz Israel (Greater Israel) was within striking distance if Jews settled occupied Arab lands and confirmed their claim to statehood. Elemental to such thinking was a sense of empowerment that bestirred in fundamentalist circles within Judaism. Returning to Islam, Esposito contends that the new discourse reflected an increasingly common experience befalling Muslim societies in the region. Citizens of such societies were left with a 'sense that existing political, economic and social systems had failed; a disenchantment with, and at the time a rejection of the West ... the conviction that Islam provides a self-sufficient ideology for state and society, a valid alternative to secular nationalism, socialism and capitalism'.[23] One outcome of such processes was the further development of political activism in the name of Islam. The re-emergence of Islam as a powerful political and social force was utilized by both state and non-state actors alike. The subsequent relevancy of Islam to many political processes, the varying interpretations of its ideologues, thinkers and the formation of many new movements for change became increasingly salient and noticeable. A fresh cohort of political actors materialized to challenge and counter-challenge the claims to legitimacy previously held by the secularists and nationalists.

Some controversy has ensued over the naming of the phenomenon that emerged in the latter half of the twentieth century that was indicative of the new ways in which an interface between faith and politics was established. Labelling the new phenomenon has had important implications for state responses and strategic dynamics of the international political order. The imprint of Islam on the political has been variously termed as 'Islamic fundamentalism', 'Islamism', and 'political Islam'. These definitions signal the subjectivity that has entered the domain of historiography of contemporary Islamism. Fundamentalist Islam is defined by Beinin and Stork as a phenomenon that may be 'compared to politically activist, socially conservative movements mobilized by revivalist Christian, Jewish and Hindu identities'[24] Yet, as these authors acknowledge, such a definition fixes, limits and reduces Islam in its political guise. As such it fails to allow room for Islam in all its political guises. Nazih Ayubi contends that employing the label of political Islam 'tend(s) to emphasise the political nature of Islam and to [acknowledge that its supporters] engage ... in direct anti-state activities'.[25] Additionally the phenomenon has been associated with the radical prefix and defined as part of a wider terrorist phenomenon that is perceived as shaping Islam in its contemporary manifestation. The radical end of the spectrum is construed as front-line Islamism; its youthful, radical, violent vanguard nature is interpreted as revealing the true nature of Islam as a revealed historical phenomenon. Additionally Islamism manifest in modern state form is assumed to be indicative of the anti-democratic, despotic tradition made real in the modern age as a counterpoint to everything that the secular modern and progressive philosophies of the western domain represent. Hence, Islam (even in state form) is condemned to the margins and perceived and associated with an existential threat to an international order shaped by western norms and values. Somehow, in a mirroring or repeat of past historical epochs writers such as Bernard Lewis contend that from the margins, 'the Muslim world is again seized by an intense – and violent – resentment of the West. Suddenly America has become the arch-enemy, the incarnation of evil, the diabolic opponent of all that is good, and specifically for Muslims, of Islam'.[26]

The contention that Islam from the margins has become intimately associated not only with the politics of revolution but violence as well has dominated much contemporary historiography of the many hundreds of societies, movements, associations, and parties that have arisen within the fold of political Islam. The image that predominates Western media depictions of the phenomenon is thus a reductive stereotype of bearded fanatics brandishing their RPGs and surrounded by an enraged ragged mob chanting 'Death to America', 'Death to Israel'. Their backdrop is almost any domain of the modern Middle East. While it is true that Islam can be represented in this way and that there are radicals who exhibit such behaviours and hostilities the issue here lies with their representativeness and legitimacy of their cause and support. It also belies the real breadth of the Islamist spectrum even when viewed on the margins.

In one sense the initial successes of the battles from the margin gave impetus to the contention that Islam ascendant would reclaim the modern nation state and make it its own again. The revolution in Iran in 1979 and the establishment of a new state order based on clerical rule from Tehran sounded alarm bells in many failing nationalist regimes across the Middle East, as well as beyond. The majority of emerging assessments of the revolution attributed its import in terms of the violent and authoritarian character of Islam in its modern guise. The revolution, like so many other actions or activities promoted by Islamists, was seldom interpreted as legitimate. The demand to oppose despotic and authoritarian rule, illegitimate foreign occupation, injustice and human rights abuses were largely ignored when espoused by Islamists and their supporters. Although the state was failing, Islamist intervention in Muslim states across the region was treated with suspicion and outright hostility. Community mindedness was interpreted as conspiracy and evidence of the deeply embedded and malign transnational networks that supported the fanatic agendas of modern Muslims.

In Egypt, Jordan, Lebanon, Saudi Arabia, Algeria, Tunisia, Syria, Kuwait and even Israel, however, Islamism could be identified in each context in many guises. While it is true that conflict and associated violence often came to dominate relations between Islamists and the state, there were only a handful of examples where Islamists formed organizations or movements for specifically violent purposes. In as much as a clash took place, it centred at the intellectual level on the contest between Islam and nationalism rather than nation and nation-state. In Algeria the Islamist movement was an established part of the political culture and had played its part in the movement for independence from the French. The establishment of the post-independence state then was in part a process wrought by the efforts of Algerian Islamists alongside their counterparts. They were state-focused and realized the parameters of power as set by the FLN. In one sense then Algerian Islamists recognized their place on the margins of the new state, yet through its re-Islamization agenda Islamists established deep connections with elements of an increasingly frustrated popular mass. Indeed as the mass experienced greater distance from the state, its elite and power and so then the populace of the margins expanded to the benefit of the Islamists. The emergence of a politically mobilized movement, FIS, drew on the extensive social networks that had been established throughout the 1980s. These networks were an important substitute for a weakening and failing state and as such established political credit among the populace that could be drawn on at a future date. The public riots of 1988 signalled the point at which the political credit and credence would come into play against the state in a contest for legitimacy. The vanguard of the new alliance of groupings was predominantly young and radical; the old guard were largely absent and radical challenge was the order of the day. Seeking to exploit the opportunity for change that presented itself in the political liberalization efforts of the state the challenge was mounted in an all-out contest for political power. Any opportunity for power-sharing would be stillborn in the turmoil that followed. The serious civil conflict that gripped the country after the early 1990s was perceived as inspired by Islamist violence. The interface between religion and politics exploded in such a spectacular fashion that the country has been dragged under by conflict. An authoritarian secular regime was engaged in a conflict against populist elements led, in large part, by a loose coalition of Islamist elements drawn from the margins of Algerian political society. Political liberalization failed in Algeria and in part Islam was blamed. Yet the battle for power in Algeria was triggered by an economic crisis that hit society at the lowest levels. FIS converted popular credit into support in elections. In 1992 fearing further electoral inroads and a loss of power the state elite moved to preserve itself, suspending elections, declaring a state of emergency and allowing the military to effectively seize control. In the conflict that followed both sides have emerged with their hands sullied with the blood of innocents. The attempt to exclude religion from state power wracked the country with instability, disorder and chaos. In the bid for power Islamist groups encountered a state elite prepared to despatch a national army to preserve the power of the regime. The struggle for a new political order was effectively stalled, yet the ambition for power remains.

Religion and politics has been focused on the state and the power that accrues to it. In the twentieth century religious elements have found themselves in contest with state elites when they represent a secular conception of power that is designed to exclude. In some states religious parties and interest groups have found themselves accommodated by the state as part of a bargain to establish the legitimacy of certain national political projects that are otherwise contested. This does not present the dilemma for Islamists that might previously have been assumed. For as Piscatori reminds us, there is evidence of an emerging consensus within many Islamist circles of an acceptance of the modern nation-state and thus a distinction between the sacred and profane realms. Indeed, Piscatori contends that Islam has added credence and legitimacy to the nationalist project in the region, 'it became an intermediary, in territorial terms, between the larger Islamic community (*umma*) and the smaller nation'.[27] There is certainly enough evidence to contend that throughout the twentieth century the interface between religion and politics in the Middle East has been re-cast in a tense but ultimately new way. Accommodation, whether voluntary or forced, has emerged in a series of new discourses that focus on the function of religion in nation-states. Many modern religious movements have emerged with distinctively nationalist and political hues. Many conflicts have been labelled as religious as a means of generating new forms of support and legitimacy for contests of power that have taken place within states and between states in the region. Religious practice and observance may have gone into decline in the earlier part of the twentieth century but the latter part has been characterized by a growth in state-sanctioned and non-state-sanctioned observance in all faith groups in the Middle East. For some minority groups faith revival is tied to sheer survival as demographics, economic factors and conflicts drive emigration and migration within and from the region.

To portray faith politics, as I have described it, through the headlines and not the stories behind the headlines is to give a false impression of the places in the political spectrum that religion in the Middle East occupies. Within the broad spectrum of faith and politics, religio-nationalism, Islamism, right-wing messianism and liberation theologies are but part of the story. And it is my contention that such representations of faith and politics do not, as others have claimed, represent 'the gospel for the youth, inaugurating a new era' in the history of religion and politics in the Middle East in which religion will dominate the state.[28] For tied to the spiritual impulse that is seen as motivating contemporary forays into the political is evidence of a tie to temporal concerns as well. The issue here is whether in the battle for power religious elements will always seek theocratic establishments or other arrangements in the Middle East.

It may appear that I have been disingenuous in avoiding a primary discussion of the apparent link between religion and violence carried out in the name of faith in the Middle East but my purpose here was to demonstrate the intimate link that has always been apparent between faith and politics and not the disruption of the link that the secular nationalist project seemed to create. For it is the disruption of this relationship that in part explains the presence of violence in the encounter between religion and politics in the contemporary era. I do not believe that there is anything innate to the faiths of the region, and Islam in particular, that compels its adherents to violence and conflict. In being perceived as a fundamental element of the colonial project in the Middle East, secularism was always going to be an enemy to faith communities. Unless it was employed in its symbolic form to add legitimacy to particular state projects the modernization project appeared to push faith to the fringes. This reveals a deep tension between such concepts and their adherents and makes any attempt at synthesis all the harder. As Hourani is quoted as asserting, 'In trying to explain the history of the Middle East in modern times we should always be aware of two interlocking rhythms of change: that which reforming governments and thinkers and external forces tried to impose upon society, and that which a great stable society with a long and continuous tradition of thought and of life in common was producing from within itself, partly by its own internal movement, and partly in reaction to forces coming from outside.'[29] As Hourani indicates, faith based interactions and interventions in the politics of the Middle East are a reflection of the continuous and responding internal patterns and traditions that characterize politics. The advent of secularism as part of the colonial, modernization and western project may have disrupted such patterns but a variety of religious movements, from the National Religious Party in Israel to the Shi'a clerical elite of Lebanon have demonstrated that they have now gained ground in terms of populist politics at the expense of those that champion secular nationalist ideologies. What remains strikingly absent from many internal discourses in any of the intellectual camps of the region is a focus on the politics of power-sharing and accommodation in which the zero-sum game currently played by both sides is thrown out and political problems are met through the reform of political systems that are genuinely based on the principles of representation, principles of popular mandates and power-sharing. National unity dialogue in the West Bank and Gaza Strip between Palestinian nationalists and Islamists floundered on the reluctance by both sides to accommodate and accept the popular power and legitimacy of the other. The same, I believe, is the case in Iran where the zero-sum game is currently played out in the emerging conflict between reformers and conservatives. Accommodation is possible. There is evidence of this in the case of Hizb Allah in Lebanon. This resistance movement, founded on radical Shi'a revolutionary principles has undergone an ideological evolution in respect of its lived experiences not only as part of the national resistance project against the Israeli occupation, but perhaps just as importantly, as a political player in Lebanon's highly confessional and consociational state. In this imperfect democracy Hizb Allah – as a Lebanese political player – has demonstrated that faith is an important player in the political life of modern nation-states.

The expression of faith, attachment and observance of its tenets is traditionally tied to the history of the Middle East and religion revived remains an expression of the

character of politics in the contemporary history of the region. The unresolved
tension between the sacred and the profane will continue to animate the patterns of
politics that shape the region in the twenty-first century.

NOTES

1   Rodenbeck, *Cairo, the City Victorious*, pp. 151–2.
2   Hourani, *A History of the Arab Peoples*, p. 220.
3   J. Schacht, *Cambridge Encyclopedia*, p. 543.
4   Lambton, *State and Government*, p. 16.
5   al-Marwardi, *al-Ahkam*, p. 20.
6   Eickelman and Piscatori, *Muslim Politics*, p. 56.
7   Ibid. p. 56.
8   Hourani, ibid., p. 223.
9   Bouchlaka, 'Secularism', p. 23.
10 Mousalli, *Moderate and Radical Islamic*, p. 181.
11 Esposito, *Islam and Politics*, p. 47.
12 Kedourie, *Politics in the Middle East*, p. 82.
13 Ayubi, *Political Islam*, p. 57.
14 Jawad, *The Rights of Women*, p. 77.
15 al-Azmeh, *Islams*, p. 65.
16 Shariati, *Message*, p. 1.
17 Zubaida, *Islam*, p. 47.
18 Mousalli, *Moderate and Radical Islam*, p. 129.
19 Kepel, *The Revenge*, p. 24.
20 Ayubi, *Political Islam*, p. 141.
21 Qutb, *Milestones*, pp. 8–9.
22 Esposito, *The Islamic Threat*, p. 129.
23 Esposito, *The Islamic Threat*, p. 17.
24 Beinin and Stork, *Political Islam*, p. 3.
25 Ayubi, *Political Islam*, p. 69.
26 Lewis, *Roots of Muslim Rage*, p. 53.
27 Piscatori, *Islam*, p. 77.
28 Rapoport, 'Fear and trembling', p. 663.
29 Hourani, 'How should we', p. 129.

FURTHER READING

A great variety of sources covering the topics of religion and politics in the Middle East have
been published since the early 1980s. Some of the most comprehensive and sensitive histories
of the region to include reflection on faith are that of Albert Hourani in a *History of the Arab
Peoples* and Steven R. Humphreys, in *Islamic History*, Princeton, Princeton University Press,
1991. For a reflection on the tensions between modernity as a secular project and the
challenges posed to faith, and Islam in particular, the work of Fred Halliday, *Islam and the
Myth of Confrontation: Religion and Politics in the Middle East*, London, I. B. Tauris, 1996,
and Bassam Tibi, *Arab Nationalism: Between Islam and the Nation-State*, Houndmills, Palgrave, 1997, add important depth and dimension to current debates and scholarship. The work
of Esposito and Kepel is commended for the multi-dimensional insight it attempts to generate
when assessing the importance of the phenomenon of Islamic revivalism and its political
dimensions within the Middle East (Esposito, John L., *Unholy War: Terror in the Name of
Islam*, Oxford and New York, Oxford University Press, 2002; Kepel, Gilles, *Jihad: The Trail of*

Political Islam, Cambridge, MA, Belknap Press of Harvard University Press, 2002). Olivier Roy offers a hypothesis that Islamists have largely failed in their task in *The Failure of Political Islam*, tr. Carol Volk, Cambridge, MA, Harvard University Press, 1994. This should be compared with Said Amir Arjomand, *From Nationalism to Revolutionary Islam*, Albany, State University of New York Press, 1984, and Youssef M. Choueiri, *Islamic Fundamentalism*, London and Washington, 2001. Butterworth and Zartman reflect on Islam as people-centred rather than fixed on the institutions of the state and reflect on how the nineteenth- and twentieth-century faith mobilized communities in a number of ways: Butterworth, Charles E. and Zartman, I. William, *Between State and Islam*, Cambridge, Cambridge University Press, 2001.

CHAPTER TWENTY-FOUR

Ethnonational Minorities in the Middle East
Berbers, Kurds, and Palestinians

LISE STORM

One of the fundamental issues in understanding the Middle East – past and present – is to recognize the diverse nature of the countries in the region. Far from being a homogeneous region, the Middle East is a patchwork of peoples and religions giving home to numerous minorities. Among the ethno-national and religious minorities, the minorities most frequently studied are the Berbers, Kurds, Turkmen, Armenians, Palestinians, Circassians, Assyrians, Copts, Jews, Hindus, Druze, Alawis, Yezidis, Zoroastrians, Baha'is, Orthodox Christians, Roman Catholics, and Protestants.

This chapter focuses on minorities in the contemporary Middle East with particular emphasis on state–minority relations and minority mobilization. The chapter begins with a brief introduction to the study of minorities in general as well as in the Middle East, and then proceeds to outline the theoretical model behind the analysis. The core of the chapter focuses on state–minority relations and minority mobilization in the Middle East, showing how factors such as state policies, the strength of group identity, the degree of group cohesion, the political environment, state violence, external support, and the international status of the 'host' state, have affected minority mobilization among a number of select minorities in the Middle East.

What a Minority Is ... and Is Not

Despite the fact that the plight of minorities has been studied for decades there continues to be disagreement over how to define minorities. Among the different minorities living in the world today, the ethnic minority is the most widely recognized. In the field of minority studies there has been a preoccupation with the ethnic minority to such an extent that some scholars have come to state that 'the most relevant axis separating minorities from others in modern society is the ethnic one'.[1]

The majority of scholars centring their attention on the ethnic dimension of the minority issue, however, tend to have a rather broad definition of what constitutes an ethnic group. One of the more prominent authorities on the subject, Donald Horowitz, defines an ethnic group as a unit with an idea of a common origin, which recruits members primarily through kinship (but transcends face-to-face interactions), and which has a notion of distinctiveness (regardless of whether this notion consists of a number of unique cultural traits). In Horowitz's own words, 'so conceived, ethnicity easily embraces groups differentiated by color, language, and religion; it covers "tribes", "races", "nationalities", and castes'.[2]

The virtue of Horowitz's definition of ethnic group – the fact that it is broad and inclusive – is at the same time its biggest weakness. By grouping together minorities defined by unique cultural traits such as colour, language and religion, comparison under one umbrella is facilitated, but if the purpose is to compare, for instance, a minority defined by a unique religion with a minority defined by another unique religion, it would be more suitable to compare these two minorities under the umbrella 'religious minority' rather than 'ethnic minority' since religious affiliation is the defining characteristic of the two minorities and hence the point of focus.

Various scholars in the field of minority studies operate with several categories of minorities. Among them, Ted Gurr and Barbara Harff single out five types of minorities under an 'ethnic group' umbrella: ethnonationalists, indigenous peoples, communal contenders, ethnoclasses, and religious minorities.[3]

- *Ethnonationalists* are defined as ethnic groups that are relatively large and regionally concentrated (but do not necessarily live within the boundaries of a single state). Ethnonationalists strive towards greater autonomy or independence.
- *Indigenous peoples* are the descendants of the original inhabitants of conquered or colonized regions. The primary aim of this type of minority is to regain control over their traditional lands and resources and to protect their languages and ways of life.
- The boundary between ethnonationalists and *communal contenders* is blurred. The main point of difference is the fact that communal contenders aim their efforts at achieving greater power-sharing within the central government within the 'host' state rather than secession.
- *Ethnoclasses* are ethnic groups that resemble classes. These groups are ethnically or culturally distinct, they occupy distinct social strata, and they have specialized economic roles in society. Ethnoclasses resemble communal contenders in that they seek to improve their status within the political system of the 'host' state (although the aim is usually improved economic opportunities, equal political rights, or better public services rather than power-sharing).
- *Religious minorities* are groups that are religiously distinct. The aims of religious minorities differ somewhat due to the fact that this type of minority usually bases its demands on religious issues coupled with issues regarding nationality or class.

Although Gurr and Harff's approach opens the way for more nuanced comparisons, I prefer the slightly different approach by Kumaraswamy. Where Gurr and Harff in their categorization tend to focus on the aims of minorities – such as secession, autonomy, power-sharing and equal opportunities – Kumaraswamy centres his categories on characteristics relating to the minorities' unique traits. Working on the Middle East, Kumaraswamy operates with five broad categories:[4]

- *Religious minorities*: Examples are the Jews and Christian dominations such as Copts, Greek Orthodox, Greek Catholic, Maronites, Latins and Protestants
- *Ethnic/national minorities*: Such as the Kurds, Druze, Armenians, Circassians, Assyrians, southern Sudanese, Berbers, Turkmen and Palestinians in Israel

- *Heterodox Islamic minorities:* Such as for example the Alawis, Druze, Ismailis, and Baha'is
- *Political minorities:* Among them the Shia[5] in Saudi Arabia and the Sunni in Iran
- *Majoritarian minorities:* The Shia in Bahrain and Iraq, the Sunni in Syria, and Palestinians in Jordan

For scholars working on minorities in the Middle East, this typology is a step forward from Hourani's original categorization of minorities in the Middle East, as groups that are not Sunni and/or Arab.[6] Whereas Hourani's definition excludes from the list of minority groups the Sunni Arabs in Iran and Oman, and the Palestinians living in Israel, these minorities are all covered by Kumaraswamy's typology.

In this chapter, minorities will be defined along the lines of Kumaraswamy's typology, although with the following amendments:

1. The category 'heterodox Islamic minorities' will be incorporated into that of 'religious minorities', since the defining characteristic of heterodox Islamic minorities is religious.
2. 'Majoritarian minorities' will be included in the category of 'political minorities', due to the fact that the defining characteristic of 'majoritarian minorities' is that these groups are excluded from power or discriminated against politically although they form the numerical majority.[7]

This leaves one with three categories of minorities: religious, ethnonational, and political minorities.

The Mobilization of Minorities

When analysing minority mobilization in the Middle East one encounters the problem that the framework for undertaking such an analysis is underdeveloped. Of the limited number of models available, the most comprehensive – and the most widely used theoretically and empirically – is that by Ted Gurr and Barbara Harff as presented in their influential *Ethnic Conflict in World Politics.*[8]

Gurr and Harff's model seeks to provide extensive explanatory power by focusing on a broad range of factors. The authors contend that seven factors (the degree of group discrimination, strength of group identity, degree of ethnic group cohesion, type of political environment, severity of governmental violence, external support, and the international status of the regime) and their interrelations influence the probability of the occurrence of minority mobilization.[9] The relationship between the seven factors and the extent of minority mobilization (in the form of ethnopolitical violence) is depicted in figure 24.1.

Although having stated that I recognize three different categories of minorities – religious, ethnonational and political – the analysis of the plight of minorities in the Middle East has in this chapter been limited to the study of ethnonational minorities, in an effort to give a more in-depth analysis of the selected minorities rather than simply a survey of minorities in the Middle East. The focus of the analysis will be on three minorities that have played a significant role in the political development of their 'host' states throughout modern history: the Berbers in Algeria and Morocco; the Kurds in Iran, Iraq, Syria and Turkey; and the Palestinians in the West Bank and

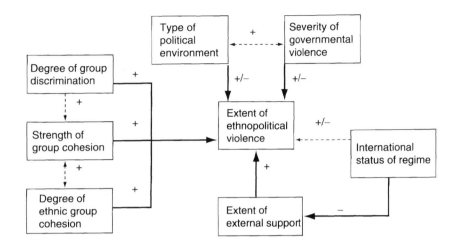

_____ Relations for which hypotheses are developed in Gurr and Harff's analytical framework

------- Relations for which hypotheses are not developed in the analytical framework

Figure 24.1 Gurr and Harff's framework for explaining ethnopolitical violence
Gurr and Harff (1994, p. 86). For an earlier and broader-ranging version of the model, see Ted Gurr, 'Why minorities rebel: explaining ethnopolitical protest and rebellion', in Ted Gurr (ed.), *Minorities at Risk* (Washington, DC, United States Institute of Peace Press, 1993), p. 125.

Gaza, Jordan and Lebanon. By limiting the study to these three minorities, Horowitz's *Ethnic Groups in Conflict* could have been used as the framework for analysis. However, Horowitz centres his attention on only two factors – relative group position and relative regional position – significantly limiting the scope of the analysis when compared to the model provided by Gurr and Harff.[10] Although Horowitz's framework would have allowed me to pay more attention to detail, having already significantly limited the scope of my analysis by focusing only on a very small number of cases, I shall adopt Gurr and Harff's model which enables me to study more factors. This combination, I hope, should allow me to produce a study that pays attention to detail and variety at the same time.

Who Are the Berbers?

The origin of the Berbers has been somewhat disputed; some scholars have in the past described the Berbers as descendants of the Canaanites, the Phoenicians, the Celts, the Basques and the Caucasians. However, today there seems to be general agreement that the Berbers are the descendants of the original indigenous Capsian tribes of North Africa.[11]

Throughout history the Berber community in North Africa has played a powerful role, sometimes even as rulers of the region. Berber rule in North Africa dates as far back as 200 BCE, when the Berbers governed the ancient states of Numidia and Mauretania. Berber influence in the region declined somewhat after the Islamic conquest in the seventh century, largely due to the intense arabization campaign carried out by the Islamic conquerors. However, by the tenth century the Berbers regained some of their lost power after having supported the Fatimids in their conquest of North Africa. When the Fatimids eventually withdrew, the region suffered decades of tribal wars, which finally came to an end in the eleventh century when the Berbers regained control of the region and established the Almoravid – and later the Almohad – dynasties. When the Almohad dynasty began to disintegrate in the middle of the thirteenth century, so did the power of the Berber and Berber consciousness. From the mid-thirteenth century and onwards, the Berbers living outside the region's mountainous areas became gradually more arabized, resulting in the decline of Berber identity.

Today the Berbers inhabit vast areas across North Africa, including parts of Algeria, Mauritania, Morocco, Tunisia, Libya, Mali and Niger. As is evident from table 24.1, Algeria and Morocco have the highest concentration of Berbers, with the Berber community amounting to an estimated 37 per cent of the population in Morocco and 25 per cent of the Algerian population.[12]

In Morocco, the country with the highest concentration of Berbers, the Berbers are geographically concentrated in three regions, each with its own Berber dialect. The northern and north-eastern Rif mountains and some adjacent valleys are populated by Tarifit-speakers, Tamazight-speakers live in the mountains and valleys of the Middle Atlas region, and the Tashelhit-speakers (alternatively, Shluh-speakers) populate the High Atlas and the anti-Atlas mountains in south-western Morocco.[13]

In Algeria, the Berber population is largely concentrated in Kabylia, the Aurès, the Mzab Valley in northern Sahara and the Ahaggar and Ajjer mountains. Some smaller Berber communities can be found in parts of western Algeria and in the Sahara.[14] The vast majority of Algerian Berbers speak the Berber Tamazight language, although a minority north of the Aurès Mountains speak Shawiya, and the Tuareg speak their own Tamarshak dialects.[15]

The different Berber dialects are all part of the Afro-Asiatic language group, which comprises the Semitic languages as well as Ancient Egyptian. Although the Berber dialects vary to a great extent, they are all clearly recognizable as one language. Because the Berber dialects are hardly spoken by anyone outside the Berber community, they constitute a unique characteristic that has served as a means to knit the community closer together resulting in a fairly strong group identity. Not surprisingly, it is also the Tamazight language that has become the main focal point in the current revival of Berber consciousness.[16]

Table 24.1 Berber demography

Country	Berber population	Berber concentration (%)
Algeria	7,620,000	25
Libya	150,000	5
Mali	450,000	6
Morocco	29,347,000	37
Niger	650,000	10
Tunisia	200,000	3
Total	38,417,000	—

Sources: Amy Pate, 'Berbers in Algeria' and 'Berbers in Morocco', *Minorities at Risk*, 2001; and Trevor Mostyn and Albert Hourani (eds), *The Cambridge Encyclopedia of the Middle East and North Africa* (Cambridge: Cambridge University Press, 1988), p. 29

Apart from the Tuareg who are pastoral, the life of most Berbers is centred on the village and the tribe. Berber society is highly tribal and segmentary in its organization; several Berber tribes exist, and each tribe can be divided into sub-groups, which in turn can be divided into further sub-groups, the fragmentation continuing until reaching the small fraction of the nuclear family. However, due to the high fluidity of the Berber tribal system, people within a tribe are not necessarily united by blood line; in fact, some tribes are solely based on the fact that they occupy the same territory.[17]

The Berber tribal system is highly egalitarian in nature. Despite its tribal nature, there is no centralized authority within the tribal system, leaving each tribal unit – from the nuclear family and upwards – free to act as if it were in fact fully autonomous. Society in Berber communities is based on a complex system of balance of power, in which the underlying principle is that for every action there will in general be a reaction from an opposing unit. Despite 'coalition' building among the Berber tribes, leading to the formation of so-called Berber confederations, this underlying principle of responsibility and consequence has so far kept Berber society from degenerating into anarchy.[18]

The Berbers in Algeria

Algeria's Berber population was among the strongest supporters of Algerian independence, playing a central role in the revolt against French rule. The first revolts against the French took place in the Berber-dominated region of Kabylia in 1945, as did the 1954 revolt which later spread throughout the country.[19]

Despite the strength of the Berber community in Algeria, due to the Berber elite's dominant position within the Algerian nationalist movement, the Berber elite never succeeded in developing strong ties to the Berber community during the period of struggle for independence, primarily because issues such as independence and personal relations were placed before Berber–Arab issues.[20]

After independence the Berber community grew increasingly wary of the new political leadership of Ahmed Ben Bella and Houari Boumedienne, leading to the establishment of the Berber-dominated party Forces des Fronts Socialistes (FFS) in 1963 under the leadership of Hocine Ait Ahmed, one of the most prominent figures in the independence movement. The main objective of the FFS was to increase Berber influence within the central government, demanding greater participation and integration in newly independent Algeria. Despite the fact that the FFS only attempted to increase Berber representation and that the party only enjoyed support from parts of Algeria's Berber population, influential members of the regime – including Berbers – saw the party as a serious threat to the integrity of the Algerian state. As a result, in 1964 Ait Ahmed was arrested, leading to the collapse of the Berber movement in Algeria.[21]

During the 1960s the Berbers in Algeria suffered harsh repression by the regime. Berbers were prohibited from expressing their culture and speaking Tamazight, giving Berber names to children was banned, and the Berber-dominated areas were overlooked by the government with regard to socio-economic development.[22] The harsh repression led to increased group cohesion among the country's Berber population, eventually resulting in initially peaceful expressions of dissatisfaction by the Berber community by the early 1970s.

As the repression continued a Berber movement, the Berber Cultural Movement (MCB), began to take form among Berber students in Algeria, enjoying support from Berber intellectuals in France. The MCB demanded an end to compulsory arabization in Algeria, calling for official recognition of the Berber language and culture, including the teaching of both in the educational system, and the introduction of democracy in the country.[23]

In 1980 disaffected Berbers and the Algerian authorities clashed during the so-called 'Berber Spring', in which angry Berbers took to the streets in Algiers and Tizi Ouzou to protest against the government's ban on a lecture by a famous Berber writer and anthropologist at Tizi-Ouzou University. The confrontation lasted five days, leading to the death of between thirty and fifty persons, hundreds of wounded civilians and mass arrests.[24]

The nullification of the electoral process and the banning of the victorious Front Islamique du Salut (FIS) in 1991 changed the nature of the Berber struggle in Algeria. After 1991 Algeria's Berbers found themselves in a situation where they were caught between two struggling groups, none of which seemed inclined to support the Berbers in their quest for increased rights and recognition and, hence, none of which enjoyed support among the Berber community. During the 1990s the Berbers in Algeria condemned the FIS and its violent methods, while at the same time demonstrating against the regime due to its reluctance to recognize their language and culture.[25] By 2004, despite a constitutional amendment in 1996 acknowledging Berber identity as part of Algeria's common heritage, Tamazight has still not been recognized as the country's second language, and the teaching of the Tamazight language and Berber culture in the educational system is still highly limited.

The Berbers in Morocco

Despite the rather strong Berber group identity, the Moroccan Berbers have lived more or less peacefully within the state of Morocco since independence, apart from a few violent protests rooted primarily in the Rif region. Since the 1980s, however, Berber display of dissatisfaction with the regime has primarily taken the form of verbal protest centred on demands for public recognition and protection of the Berber culture and language.

Much of the Berber disaffection has been routed through the Mouvement Populaire, a political party established in 1959 representing mainly the Berber and rural segments of the Moroccan population. Influential circles within Moroccan political life are strongly against the Berber cultural movement, among them are the influential independence party Istiqlal and Shaykh 'Abd al-Salam Yasin's outlawed Islamist party Harakat al 'Adl wal-Ihsan. In recent years, however, the Berber have come to find growing support among the more progressive political parties such as l'Union Socialiste des Forces Populaires, which seeks to improve the status of civil society and introduce democracy to Morocco, as well as from the king himself, who seeks to counterbalance the growing influence of the Islamist movement.[26]

Despite the existence of political channels such as the MP and the USFP, much of the Berber dissatisfaction with the regime has been routed through grassroots organizations such as the Charter of Agadir and Tillelli. The Charter of Agadir was established in 1991 by six cultural associations – later joined by five others – in an effort to counter arabization and the subsequent marginalization of the Berber culture and language, by introducing constitutional guarantees regarding the establishment of Tamazight as an official language, as well as guarantees concerning the use of the Berber language and cultures in cultural and educational activities, in teaching programmes, and in the written, audio and visual mass media.[27]

When these demands were not met, frustration spread among the Berber population resulting in growing activities among the Berber cultural associations. In 1994 a group of Berber activists publicly addressed the then Prime Minister Mohammed Karim Lamrani during 1 May demonstrations, demanding official recognition of Tamazight. The regime responded by arresting seven members of Tillelli, a Berber cultural association, charging them with disturbing public order and threatening the sanctity of the state. Four of the seven activists were eventually released, while the remaining three were sentenced to imprisonment and hefty fines. This harsh response by the regime was met with widespread public antipathy, and with more than four hundred Moroccan lawyers volunteering to defend the activists, their sentences and fines were reduced, making the activists free men only a little more than two months after they were first arrested.[28]

The increasing demands for the recognition of the Berber culture and language of the 1990s coupled with the growing strength of the Islamist opposition resulted in the introduction of audio and visual news broadcasts in the three main Moroccan Tamazight dialects in August 1994. In addition to these improvements, King Hassan also made a move to improve the status of Tamazight in educational activities, by issuing a royal decree in 1995 authorizing the necessary changes to the curriculum to permit the teaching of Tamazight in schools. In 2001 King Mohammed VI established an institute dedicated to the promotion and protection of the Berber language and culture – the Royal Institute of Amazigh Culture – giving in to some of the Berber demands, but the royal decree of 1995 paving the way for the teaching of Tamazight in schools has not yet been implemented.[29]

Who Are the Kurds?

The Kurds are a culturally distinct people, whose ancestors have inhabited the area north and east of the Tigris and Euphrates river basins. Although there is difference in opinion as to the ethnic origins of the Kurds, the majority of scholars tend to agree that the Kurds originate from the Medes.[30]

The current Kurdish population can be traced back to the people who lived in the region more than two thousand years ago.[31] However, despite having populated the area for more than two millennia, the Kurds have had to make do with varying degrees of autonomy within other states and empires, never having succeeded in forming their own state. The struggle for political power in the form of autonomy or independence has dominated the political history of the Kurds. During a period of four hundred years, from the beginning of the sixteenth to the end of the nineteenth century, Kurdish tribal leaders led several rebellions against the Ottoman rulers in an effort to establish Kurdish rule in the principalities primarily inhabited by Kurds.[32]

In the early sixteenth century the Kurdish tribal chiefs proved successful in their efforts, striking a deal with the Ottoman rulers that effectively awarded autonomous status to sixteen Kurdish principalities in return for Kurdish military support for the empire. This system of indirect rule lasted until the early nineteenth century, when it came to an abrupt end when the Ottoman empire re-established direct control over the Kurdish principalities in an effort to strengthen Ottoman identity throughout the empire. With the increased tightening of Ottoman rule, the Kurds initiated a new series of more than fifty rebellions, but none of them led to the reestablishment of Kurdish autonomy.[33]

After the defeat of Ottoman Turkey in the First World War, the so-called Sykes–Picot Agreement of May 1916 proposed the division of the Kurdish areas between Britain, France and Russia, leaving the Kurds uncertain about their future status. At first the British, who controlled most of the territory, were determined to establish a Kurdish state, an idea that enjoyed some American support. The Treaty of Sèvres of 1920, which provided the legal framework for the creation of a Kurdish state, was never implemented, however, and with the adoption and implementation of the Lausanne Treaty in 1923, the Kurdish areas became officially divided between the states of Iran, Iraq, Syria and Turkey.[34]

Today the Kurdish people are the largest people in the world without their own state. Approximately 26,910,000 Kurds are spread all over the world today, the vast majority living in the Middle East, although large Kurdish communities can also be found in Armenia, Azerbaijan and Germany (see table 24.2).

Despite being an ethnically distinct group, populating the same territory and sharing the same history, the Kurds are a highly fragmented ethnic group, not just due to the fact that they are divided between several countries, which has meant a break in the shared history, but also largely because of the existence of several Kurdish dialects, all very different from each other. The two dominant Kurdish dialects are Kurmanji and Sorani. Kurmanji is spoken northwards from Mosul and Urumiya as far as the former Soviet Union, whereas Sorani is spoken southwards from Urumiya to Khanaqin on both sides of the Iran–Iraq border. In Iran, the Kurds mainly speak Sorani or one of the sub-dialects of Leki, Gurani and Kermanshahi; in Iraq the Kurds are divided between Kurmanji and Sorani; whereas in Turkey all Kurds speak Kurmanji, apart from the Zaza-speakers of the Dersim region.[35]

The use of the Kurdish language from country to country varies somewhat, however. In Turkey the Kurdish language was officially banned until 2002, and although restrictions still exist today, Kurdish can be heard in the public space. Because of the previous severe penalties on the use of the Kurdish language, many Kurds in Turkey do not speak Kurdish. In Iran, Iraq and Syria, on the other hand, most Kurds are bilingual, speaking both Kurdish and Farsi in Iran and Kurdish and Arabic in Iraq and Syria. However, since the creation of the Kurdish autonomous region in northern Iraq in the aftermath of the Second Gulf War, the linguistic map among the Kurds in Iraq is beginning to change, with the generation growing up in the 1990s only mastering Kurdish and not Arabic.[36]

Although the Kurds adhere to several different faiths – among them Shi'ism, *Ahl-i Haqq* and Yezidism – the vast majority are Sunni Muslims like their compatriots in Turkey, Iraq and Syria. In Iran, the fact that the Kurds are mainly Sunni sets them further apart from the overwhelmingly Shi'i Iranians. However, the Sunni Kurds in Iran, Iraq, Syria and Turkey differ from most of their Sunni brothers in that they often adhere to one of two religious brotherhoods, the Naqshbandiyya and the Qadiriyya, due to tribal ties.[37]

Although Kurdish society has been largely detribalized during the past decades, particularly in Turkey, and despite the fact that many Kurds are effectively non-tribal,

Table 24.2 Kurdish demography

Country	Kurdish population	Kurdish concentration (%)
Iran	6,600,000	12
Iraq	4,400,000	23
Syria	1,160,000	9
Turkey	13,650,000	24
Other countries	1,100,000	—
Total	26,910,000	—

Sources: Ted Gurr and Barbara Harff, *Ethnic Conflict in World Politics* (Boulder: Westview Press, 1994), p. 32; and David McDowall, *A Modern History of the Kurds* (London: I. B. Tauris, 1997 revised and updated paperback edition), pp. 3–4

Kurdish society in each of the four countries is still affected by tribal culture to some extent, especially in Iraq. The Kurdish tribes, consisting of clans, lineages and households, are bound together by different factors such as blood and geographic proximity, and to an increasing extent also by political affiliation. In many areas the tribes have lost their position as the primary social and economic unit, but in the more secluded rural areas they continue to remain highly important. Interestingly, the tribes in Iraq seem to have undergone something of a political revival since the beginning of the 1990s, with the Kurdish tribes in the autonomous region in northern Iraq commanding large armies and vast amounts of the resources of the Kurdish regional government.[38]

The Kurds in Iran

Despite repression by the Iranian regime since the division of the Kurds at the beginning of the 1920s, the Kurds in Iran did only rebel twice during the 1920s and 1930s, and in both cases Kurdish tribal chiefs who were driven by the desire for power rather than nationalist sentiments led the rebellion.[39]

By the end of the 1930s the Kurds had been effectively subjugated due to Reza Shah's policy of homogenization, which involved the attempted introduction of a single unifying language as well as the imposition of a uniform dress code on urban, agrarian and pastoral peoples. With regard to the Kurds, who were seen as a potential destabilizing factor in Iranian society, the policy of homogenization went further, however. During the late 1920s and the early 1930s, a large number of Kurdish tribal chiefs were detained by the regime, other tribal chiefs had their land confiscated – usually without compensation – and the Kurdish population was forcibly displaced from its tribal homelands to other parts of Iran.[40]

The harsh repression of the Kurds during the 1920s and 1930s led to growing Kurdish dissatisfaction with the regime and an emergent Kurdish nationalism in Iran. With the abdication of Reza Shah following British and Soviet occupation of western Iran in August 1941, the aspirations of the Kurds grew stronger, leading to several Kurdish rebellions and eventually to the formation of the first Kurdish party in Iran, the Komala-i Jiyanawi Kurdistan in 1942 and later the Kurdistan Democratic Party–Iran, which absorbed the membership of Komala in 1945. The whole affair culminated in the proclamation of the Mahabad Republic by the Iranian Kurds in January 1946.[41]

The Mahabad Republic proved remarkably short lived, however. Less than a year after its formation, the Mahabad Republic collapsed after Iranian troops invaded without meeting any resistance. In the years following the Mahabad Republic, repression of the Kurds in Iran increased markedly, beginning with the execution of the Kurdish leaders involved in the formation of the Mahabad Republic, and later the prohibition on the use of the Kurdish language in the realms of publishing and teaching.[42]

As a result of harsh repression, the emerging Kurdish nationalist movement remained quiet until the demise of the Pahlavis in 1979. With the weakness of the new Islamic regime of Ayatollah Khomeini, the Kurds in Iran saw an opportunity to achieve what they had been dreaming of for decades: Kurdish autonomy for Iranian Kurdistan. During 1979 the Kurds and the Iranian regime held a number of meetings regarding local autonomy for the Kurds, but a final agreement was never reached, and the Kurds grew increasingly frustrated. As a result, in the period from late 1979 until 1984 the relations between the Kurds and the Iranian regime were dominated by a cycle of warfare and subsequent negotiations. By the end of 1984 the Kurds had once again come under Iranian control, and their position was only to weaken further in the following years. In 1989 the leader of the dominant Kurdish party in Iran, Dr Abdul-Rahman Qassemlou of the Kurdistan Democratic Party–Iran, was assassinated in Vienna where he was scheduled to meet Iranian government officials for negotiations over Kurdish accommodation.[43]

With the assassination of Qassemlou and other Kurdish leaders in the late 1980s the Kurdish nationalist movement was effectively stifled, something it does not seem to have recovered from even today. Although the Kurdish parties in Iran remain weak, the opposition to the regime and the wish for autonomy are still as pertinent as ever among the Kurdish population and the Kurdish political elite, leaving a huge gulf between the Kurdish population and the Iranian regime.[44]

The Kurds in Iraq

Being linguistically, racially and culturally different, coupled with geographic concentration in the four northern governorates of Dohuk, Erbil, Suleimaniyah and Darbandikhan, severe government repression, and a long sense of shared history, have contributed to strong group coherence and secessionist aspirations among the Kurds. Ever since the creation of the state of Iraq in 1920 and the accession of King Faisal I in 1921, the Kurds have sought to gain autonomy within the entity of the Iraqi state.[45] Despite promises of the creation of a Kurdish autonomous entity with the future option of independence in the Sèvres Treaty of 1920, and British promises of the right to govern their own areas in 1922, the Kurds in Iraq never achieved autonomy.[46]

With the rise of Kurdish nationalism in Iran and the subsequent formation of the short-lived Mahabad Republic on Iranian territory in 1946, a coherent Kurdish nationalist movement also began to take form in Iraq under the leadership of Mullah Mustafa Barzani. In 1970, with the Iraqi regime severely weakened by the past years' high frequency of military coups and Kurdish rebellions, the Iraqi government found itself in a position where it was forced to negotiate with the rebellious Kurds. The negotiations, headed by the Iraqi vice-president Saddam Hussein and the leader of the Kurdistan Democratic Party, Mullah Mustafa Barzani, resulted in the signing of what came to be known as the March Agreement, granting the Kurds de facto autonomy throughout the Kurdish-dominated regions.[47]

Although the Iraqi regime began the implementation of the agreement, mistrust dominated the relationship between the Kurds and the regime. The Kurds feared that the Iraqi government would not keep its promises and added additional demands to the agreement, while the Iraqi regime grew simultaneously distrustful of the Kurds, fearing that they were trying to take over Kirkuk as well as cooperating with the Iranians. As a result of the tense relations coupled with the lack of US support for the Kurds, the agreement fell apart during the early 1970s.[48] In the following years, throughout the 1970s and 1980s, state repression of the Kurds grew steadily under the so-called Anfal campaigns under which as many as an estimated 100,000 civilian Kurds lost their lives.[49]

During the last weeks of the Second Gulf War (1991), the Kurds rebelled *en masse* against the Iraqi regime, trying to regain lost territory and demanding autonomy for the Kurdish-dominated northern governorates. The uprising was brutally put down by the Iraqi government forces, and the world watched as Kurds fled into the mountains to escape death. In the wake of the massive suffering (famously documented by CNN) the international community – under the leadership of Britain, the United States and France (France later pulled out) – established a so-called safe haven for the Kurds above the thirty-sixth parallel in northern Iraq. Following the establishment of the safe haven and the subsequent failure of the talks between the Kurds and the Iraqi regime, the regime withdrew all its officials from the Kurdish controlled north in October 1991, effectively leaving the region in a power vacuum. To fill this vacuum the Kurds held parliamentary elections in May 1992, creating the first Kurdish parliament in history.[50]

Despite the outbreak of civil war between the two dominant Kurdish parties, the Kurdistan Democratic Party (KDP) and the Patriotic Union of Kurdistan (PUK) in 1994–6, the Kurds have lived in peace with each other since the signing of peace agreements between the two parties in Washington in 1998 and 1999. Although two parliaments currently rule in the Kurdish autonomous region, the parties share several unified policies (including foreign policy and the policy towards the state of Iraq), and they share the same overall goal of Kurdish autonomy within a future federal Iraqi state. This demand is largely supported by the Kurdish population of which, however, the most part seems to prefer the more radical goal of the establishment of a fully independent Kurdish state in northern Iraq.[51]

In an effort to increase their chances of gaining autonomy or independence the Iraqi Kurds actively supported the American invasion of Iraq in March 2003. So far, however, the Kurds have not received any guarantees from the American administration indicating that the United States would support Kurdish autonomy.[52] Rather than supporting the Kurds in their quest for autonomy, the American administration's strong emphasis on the role of the Iraqi Governing Council (IGC) and the forthcoming Transitional National Assembly (TNA) seems to indicate that US priority at the moment is to secure the unity of the Iraqi state. Although the Kurdish leaders have from time to time voiced their dissatisfaction with the contemporary Iraqi administration and the outline of the draft constitution, they have kept their four seats in the IGC as well as their five ministerial posts.

The Kurds in Turkey

The Kurds in Turkey – the largest Kurdish community anywhere in the world – is the group of Kurds that have suffered the most since the official division of the Kurds in

1923. Although some Kurds seem to have been in favour of the creation of a Turkish state at the beginning of the 1920s, their opinions soon changed with the abolition of the caliphate in 1924, in which it became clear that the Turkish regime had no intention of accepting dual identities.[53]

In an effort to escape Turkish rule, the Kurds in Turkey rebelled several times during the 1920s under the leadership of different Kurdish tribal chiefs who were eager to increase their personal power. Despite several victorious battles, the Kurds were eventually defeated by the end of 1932 after a series of mass executions and deportations carried out by the Turkish regime in the early 1930s. In an effort to enhance the sense of Turkishness and to keep the country's several minorities under control, the regime adopted a new law granting the state the power to displace forcibly members of those minorities that were considered in need of assimilation. In addition, the law granted the state the power to dissolve all villages or urban quarters where Turkish was not the mother tongue, and prohibited the formation of associations whose membership was not made up of a majority of Turkish-speakers. Although the law was never implemented nationally due to its immense scope, it was applied locally in Kurdish-dominated cities such as Van, Bitlis and Siirt.[54]

Kurdish opposition to the law was most strongly voiced in the Dersim province, which had traditionally been opposed to Turkish rule. In 1935 the Turkish regime announced its intention to establish control of the province via the use of military force coupled with administrative reorganization. Getting the Dersim province under control proved harder than first expected due to the fierce resistance to the Turkish troops from the Kurdish population. However, by the end of 1938 the Turkish authorities had achieved their goal, albeit at the expense of tens of thousands of lives.[55]

Despite the subjugation of the Kurds all over Turkey from 1938 onwards, Turkish repression of the Kurds continued. Although Kurds were allowed to participate in the country's political process by joining the already established Turkish parties, the Kurds and many other minorities were prohibited from forming their own political parties and organizations. Moreover, the ban on the use of the Kurdish language as well as the use of words referring to the Kurds, such as 'Kurd' and 'Kurdistan' remained in place, effectively reducing the proportion of Kurds able to speak their own mother tongue.

Fuelled by the failure of the Kurdish parties established in the 1960s and the 1970s coupled with the growing resentment among the Kurds due to harsh repression and economic neglect of the Kurdish-dominated provinces in south-eastern Turkey which had led to severe poverty among the Kurdish population, the militant Kurdistan Workers' Party (PKK) emerged in the early 1970s under the leadership of Abdullah Öcalan. During the 1980s, with the aim of securing independence for the Kurdish-dominated areas in south-eastern Turkey, the PKK launched several violent attacks against Turkish armed forces and other targets within Turkey, causing the loss of life of thousands of Turks and Kurds over the years. In 1991 and 1992 the PKK escalated the attacks, leading to armed response by the Turkish military. During the 1990s the PKK and the Turkish armed forces clashed on numerous occasions in south-eastern Turkey in what strongly resembled outright war.[56]

After Turkey gained support from the Iraqi Kurds in their fight against the PKK, the PKK found itself under attack from several fronts, eventually resulting in the party assuming – at least on the surface – a more conciliatory attitude by adopting a unilateral ceasefire and altering its party programme demands from independence to autonomy and democracy.[57]

With the arrest of Öcalan in 1999, the PKK was severely weakened; something the party does not seem to have recovered from yet. The PKK is no longer a major actor in Turkish politics. Although some Turkish Kurds undoubtedly would like to see the return of a strong PKK, the majority of the Kurds in Turkey did not support the PKK during its heyday and do not wish to see its return, preferring peaceful politics to armed rebellion. Although political parties based on ethnicity or religion are still prohibited in Turkey, de facto but unofficially Kurdish parties do exist and contest the elections, albeit under harassment and discrimination.[58] In recent years, with Turkey's attempt to join the European Union as a full member, the condition of the Kurds has improved. In 2002 the Turkish parliament paved the way for the legalization of the Kurdish language, allowing the use of Kurdish in public, including in teaching and the media. Although Kurdish is now more widely used as a result of the new law, several restrictions remain in place with regard to when, where and how much the language can be used.[59] Taking into account that the European Union is aware of the fact that these restrictions remain in place, coupled with Turkey's desire to join the Union fully, there is optimism that the last restrictions on the use of the Kurdish language will disappear in the near future.

The Kurds in Syria

The majority of the Kurds in Syria are originally Turkish Kurds, who left Turkey in the 1920s in order to escape the harsh repression of the Kurds in that country. These Kurds were later joined in Syria by a new large group that drifted out of Turkey throughout the interwar period during which the Turkish campaign to assimilate its Kurdish population was at it highest.[60]

Compared with their Kurdish compatriots living in Iran, Iraq and Turkey, the Kurds in Syria have been remarkably quiet. Although large segments of the Kurds in Syria offered their support to the Kurds rebelling in Turkey and Iraq during the 1920s, 1930s and 1940s, the Kurds in Syria never rebelled themselves.[61] Some scholars suggest that the Kurds in Syria have lived a relatively peaceful existence because they only make up a small minority. However, the fact that the Kurds in Syria suffered harsh repression and persecution in the 1960s and 1970s – when thousands of Kurds were forcibly displaced and an estimated 120,000 Kurds were stripped of their Syrian citizenship – may also help explain their quietist behaviour.[62]

During the 1980s and 1990s the Kurds in Syria seem to have begun to change their tactics, however. In 1986 members of the Kurdish community and Syrian police clashed during celebrations of the Kurdish festival Newroz. Similarly, Kurds and the Syrian authorities came to blows in 1992, when Kurds marked the thirtieth anniversary of the census that stripped so many of them of their Syrian citizenship. In spring 2004, frustration over the continued repression of the Kurds coupled with Arab–Kurdish differences over the war in Iraq, fuelled unrest among the Kurds in Syria. As in 1986 and 1992 the violent clashes between members of the Kurdish community and the Syrian authorities resulted in mass arrests and the death of several Kurds.[63]

Who Are the Palestinians?

The majority of Palestinians are the descendants of the original Canaanite inhabitants of the region, something most of the definitions of Palestinians today fail to acknowledge. These contemporary definitions trace the origins of the Palestinians not back to the Canaanites, but stress instead the bonds between the Palestinians and the mainly Arabic-speaking people inhabiting the region in the centuries immediately preceding the British Mandate of 1919.

Despite the fact that the words 'Palestine' and 'Palestinian' have been used since the days of Herodotus, Palestinian national identity did not begin to take form until the nineteenth century; until then the main points of reference with regard to group coherence in Palestinian society had been the units of the tribe, the clan, and the family. With the concept of nationalism in the ascendant in Europe, the demise of the Ottoman Empire and the French conquest of Syria, the Palestinians came to see themselves increasingly as Palestinians, demanding the recognition of Palestine and Palestinian identity.[64]

With the end of the British Mandate in 1948, Palestine was to be divided into two independent states – one Jewish and one Arab. However, the failure of the Arab armies to carry out a well-coordinated plan, coupled with the aggressive policies of the newly formed Zionist armed groups, forced many Palestinians to flee the area, seeking refuge mainly in the neighbouring countries of Lebanon, Syria and Jordan. With the creation of the state of Israel in 1948, the number of Palestinian refugees escalated. By late 1948 an estimated 800,000 Palestinians had left their homes in the search for security, ending up in makeshift refugee camps in the West Bank and Gaza, as well as in neighbouring Lebanon, Syria and Jordan.[65]

With the conflict still unresolved today, the vast majority of the Palestinians who were expelled or fled their homes in the 1940s have still not been able to return; instead they have been joined by thousands more over the years. Today the Palestinian people are spread all over the world, although the majority continue to live in the West Bank and Gaza or in other countries of the Middle East (see table 24.3).

Traditionally, Palestinian society has been agricultural, with the majority of the population living and working in the rural areas. However, with increased reliance on cash crops and the sale of land to Jewish immigrants in the 1930s, Palestinian society began to change rapidly. Due to lack of work in the countryside, large segments of the Palestinian population were forced to relocate from the countryside to the urban centres in search of work. However, the Palestinian urban centres were unable to cope with the sudden increase in population and sharp increase in demand for work, leading to poor living conditions and high unemployment. Urbanization – and unemployment – further increased with the Six Day War in 1967 and the subsequent Israeli occupation of the West Bank and Gaza coupled with the Israeli policy of economic annexation and land confiscation. As a result, a vast number of Palestinians had no other choice but to seek work inside Israel, something that has become an increasing problem over the years as Israel has tightened its border policy.[66]

The Palestinians in the West Bank and Gaza

The Palestinians living in the Occupied Territories of the West Bank and Gaza share a strong sense of community, partly due to the fact that they differ ethnically and

Table 24.3 Palestinian demography

Country	Palestinian population	Palestinian concentration (%)
West Bank and Gaza	3,298,951	—
Jordan	2,626,000	48
Lebanon	463,000	12
Syria	411,000	2
Israel	1,012,741	17
Other countries	1,167,000	—
Total	8,978,692	—

Sources: The Palestinian Academic Society for the Study of International Affairs. See the internet at http:// www.passia.org/index_pfacts.htm. See also Philip Mattar, *The Encyclopedia of the Palestinians* (New York: Facts on File, 2000); and the CIA World Factbook 2003 at http://www.cia.gov/cia/publications/factbook/index.html

religiously from their Israeli occupiers – the Palestinians are Arabic-speakers and mainly Muslim in contrast to the Hebrew-speaking, predominantly Jewish Israelis – but more importantly because the Palestinians in the Occupied Territories share the same troubled history. Having been denied their own state with the adoption of the Balfour Declaration of November 1917 and the imminent creation of the British Mandate, the Palestinians rose against their occupiers during the so-called *intifada* of 1919, which escalated into large-scale violent clashes between Jews and Palestinians in 1929 and 1936.

Fuelled by frustration among the Palestinian people over continued military presence in the West Bank and Gaza, Palestinian grassroots organizations and their support base began to grow rapidly during the 1980s, culminating in a new eruption or *intifada* in 1987. This *intifada* took most political leaders – including the leadership of the PLO – by surprise. Although the PLO had not been the initiator of the *intifada,* the organization soon emerged as the leader of the uprising. By officially recognizing the right of the state of Israel to exist, advocating a two-state solution to the conflict, while simultaneously supporting UN resolutions 242 and 338, the Palestinians transformed their policy into a negotiating strategy with a unified leadership and a clear goal recognized as legitimate by several heads of state and large segments of the population in countries across the globe.[67]

The unification of the Palestinian leadership and the *intifada* resulted in the initiation of a peace process between the Palestinians and the Israeli government. For a number of years things progressed slowly, but with the victory of the Israeli Labour Party in the 1992 elections, things took a turn for the better for the Palestinians in the Occupied Territories. While embarking on secret negotiations with the Palestine Liberation Organization (PLO) in Oslo, the new Israeli Prime Minister, Yitzhak Rabin, also placed a temporary ban on further Jewish settlements in the West Bank and Gaza. By September 1993 the negotiations led to an agreement on the eventual establishment of Palestinian self-rule in the West Bank and Gaza.[68]

According to the agreement (the so-called Israel–PLO Declaration of Principles on Interim Self-Government Agreements), Israel was to transfer certain powers and responsibilities to the Palestinian Authority, including legislative powers which were to be awarded to the Palestinian Legislative Council elected in January 1996. The transfer of powers took place in a number of sequences subsequent to various agreements between Israel and the PLO. In May 1994, shortly after the Israel–PLO Cairo Agreement[69] some transfer of power and responsibilities for Gaza and Jericho did take place, and finally, following the Israel–PLO September 1995 Interim Agreement,[70] the Israel–PLO January 1997 Protocol Concerning Redeployment in Hebron,[71] the Israel–PLO October 1998 Wye River Memorandum,[72] and the Sharm el-Sheikh Agreement of September 1999,[73] power and responsibilities were transferred to Gaza, the Jericho Area and additional areas of the West Bank.

In 2000, however, violence erupted once again. With the new *intifada* ongoing, the suffering of the Palestinians in the Occupied Territories has escalated once more. Most Palestinians today live in relatively poor circumstances, enduring high unemployment coupled with rising birth rates and deteriorating public health conditions. Adding to the distress of poverty, the Israeli military presence in the West Bank and Gaza is approaching the level it had during full occupation. Recent responses by the Israeli government to the escalating violent Palestinian protests against Israeli military presence and continuing mushrooming of Jewish settlements in the West Bank and Gaza, have included the commencement of the construction of a concrete wall – with a planned total length of 230 miles – with the official purpose of protecting Israeli citizens from attacks by their Palestinian neighbours.[74]

The building of the wall – which leaves 274,000 Palestinians trapped either inside the wall or between the wall and the 1949 Armistice Line[75] – has further exacerbated the already existing economic exclusion of the Palestinians, strengthening border control and making it increasingly difficult for Palestinians to enter Israel where many Palestinians work.[76] At present, with targeted killings, summary arrests and confiscations by the Israeli military still taking place, and escalating suicide bombings by the Palestinians, reconciliation between the two parties seems unlikely, leaving the future of the Palestinians in the Occupied Territories looking bleak.

The Palestinians in Jordan

Although the Second Palestinian Congress called for the union of Palestine and Transjordan and recognized Abdallah as the King of all Palestine in Jericho, December 1948, disagreements between Palestinians and the Jordanian establishment soon erupted after the annexation of the West Bank by Jordan in 1950, as the Jordanian leadership embarked on a campaign to create a unifying Jordanian national identity. As a result of the heated relationship between the Palestinians and the Jordanian authorities – partly because of the discrimination against the Palestinians in Jordan but also because of Jordanian satisfaction with the post-1948 situation – a frustrated Palestinian assassinated King Abdallah in Jerusalem in 1951. Following the assassination of Abdallah, the Jordanian leadership grew increasingly wary of the Palestinian community in the country, fearing that the Palestinians might attempt to take over power. Accordingly, the regime increased its repression of the Palestinian community, leading eventually to the ten-day 'Black September' civil war between the PLO and the Jordanian army in 1970.[77]

The civil war between the Jordanian authorities and the Palestinian community further increased the gulf of distrust between the two. As a result, in the aftermath of the civil war, the Palestinians – who had in the past held a large percentage of all posts – were removed from the bureaucracy and the army, significantly reducing their political influence.[78] Moreover, in another effort to strengthen Jordanian national consciousness and assimilate the Palestinian community in Jordan, the regime began to promote Hashemite Arabism. When the attempt to assimilate the Palestinians proved unsuccessful, the regime changed tactics in 1972, proposing first a federation and later a confederation between Jordan and a future Palestinian state.[79]

Despite the fact that the Jordanian plan to create a 'United Arab Kingdom' resembled an offer of Palestinian autonomy within a Jordanian state rather than a federation between two equal entities, the plan was rejected by Israel. In addition, many Arab leaders also rejected the plan, although for opposite reasons to those of the Israelis. Consequently the plan was eventually shelved.[80]

In the aftermath of the Oslo accords of 1993, the Jordanian regime became increasingly anxious that the prospects of a Palestinian state in the West Bank and Gaza would lead to unrest among the Palestinians in the Jordanian East Bank. In order to curb dissent, King Hussein spoke repeatedly to the Jordanian public addressing 'all the people of Jordan' who were 'members of one family' regardless of descent and origin, and warning that anyone who tried to interfere with the Jordanian national unity would become an enemy of the state.[81]

Despite King Hussein's fears, there have been no recent Palestinian rebellions in the country. Rather, the growing Jordanian right-wing nationalist movement has proved to be much more of an obstacle to peace and harmony in the country, demanding under the slogan of 'Jordan for Jordanians' the disenfranchisement of Palestinians in Jordan, and the return of Jordan's Palestinian population to the territories assigned to the Palestinian Authority in the West Bank and Gaza.[82]

The Palestinians in Lebanon

Up until 1968 the Palestinians in Lebanon were politically unorganized. However, the Six Day War of 1967 and the subsequent influx of large groups of Palestinian refugees into Lebanon resulted in the sudden growth of several Palestinian underground organizations. To the frustration of the Israeli and Lebanese authorities these organizations came to enjoy increasing support among the Palestinians in Lebanon, leading eventually to violent clashes between Lebanese security forces and Palestinians in the refugee camps. Due to strong support for the Palestinian cause among large segments of Lebanon's Muslim population as well as from the leaders of several Arab states, in 1969 the Lebanese authorities gave in to the pressure, signing the so-called Cairo Agreement with the Palestine Liberation Organization (PLO), enabling the PLO and other Palestinian organizations to operate freely within certain areas of Lebanon.[83]

In the years leading up to the civil war (1975–90), and to a lesser extent during the civil war itself, the Palestinians in Lebanon found themselves at the centre of the political agenda as the Maronite community grew increasingly wary of their presence in the country. At the beginning of the civil war the PLO's armed militia largely refrained from taking part, but as the conflict escalated and attacks on Palestinian refugee camps increased, the more radical fractions of the PLO gradually became more involved in the fighting.[84]

Although the civil war formally came to an end after the Arab summit meeting in Riyadh on 16–18 October 1976, fighting between Israeli-backed Christian militias on the one side and the Lebanese National Movement and the PLO, on the other, continued in the southern parts of Lebanon in 1977. As a result of sustained PLO presence in the south, from where the organization launched several attacks on Israeli targets, Israel invaded southern Lebanon in March 1978. After the adoption of UN Security Council Resolutions 425 and 426, Israel withdrew from the area, handing over control of most of the border region to the UN Interim Force in Lebanon later that year. Moreover, Israel created, funded and armed a local militia to act as its proxy. This militia, known as the South Lebanese Army (SLA) acted as a buffer between the Israeli army which continued to occupy a strip of Lebanese territory north of its border, and Lebanese resistance forces. The peace proved short lived, however. As the conflict between the PLO and Israel continued to escalate, Israel invaded Lebanon again in July 1982 with the aim of destroying the PLO, massacring more than 20,000 Lebanese and Palestinian civilians at Sabra and Shatila.[85]

Since 1982 the freedom and mobility of Palestinians in Lebanon have become severely restricted: Palestinians are being prevented from taking up various forms of work, they are being prohibited from organizing politically and culturally, reconstruction of the refugee camps has been restricted, severe travel restrictions have been introduced, and they live under constant surveillance.[86] In 1992, as a result of the increased repression of the Palestinian people in Lebanon, the Palestinian political organizations present in the country publicly demanded respect for the civil and political rights of the Palestinians. When these demands were not met by the Lebanese authorities, the Palestinian organizations put forward another memorandum in 1994, calling upon the prime minister to ensure the protection of the Palestinians' basic political and civil rights.[87]

In recent years, despite improved social and political conditions among the general Lebanese population, the Palestinians in Lebanon have not experienced any significant improvements in their conditions. Because of the continued restrictions with regard to work in particular, tens of thousands of Palestinians in Lebanon have found themselves forced to renounce their Palestinian nationality and apply for Lebanese citizenship in an effort to be able to obtain work and improve the living conditions for their families.[88]

Conclusion and Perspectives

Despite the increased focus on the plight and rights of minorities since the end of the Second World War and the collapse of the Soviet Union, and the subsequent adoption of various covenants and treaties protecting the rights of the individual and minorities, minorities continue to be harshly persecuted in most countries in the contemporary Middle East regardless of their size, strength and demands.

To the question as to why the minorities in the Middle East continue to be persecuted, one can give the same answer as one would have given before the Second World War: because of their minority status. Albert Hourani, writing on minorities in the Middle East in the period from the First to the Second World War, concluded that,

> The problem of minorities in its present form springs from the fact that majority and minorities do not fully form a community with one another...

and that,

> people are still held back by historic memories and traditional loyalties from entering the new world of thought and action towards which events are driving them. As

a consequence, everything is disturbed and transitional in Arab life and society. Nationalism is still entangled with religious conceptions. Social customs are still only half-westernized, although (and this increases complexity) certain of the minorities are further on the road to Westernization than the majority. The effort to build up modern governments and administrations is still far from reaching its end: the consequence is a general instability of political life, of which the unsatisfactory relationship between governments and minorities is only a particular aspect.[89]

In the contemporary Middle East, majority and minorities do still not fully form a community with one another: nationalism continues to be entangled with religious conceptions, and the vast majority of the political regimes in the region remain far from democratic. The fact that most Middle Eastern regimes have either come to power via the use of force or have sustained their political power by the same means is one of the major reasons why minorities continue to suffer such harsh repression in the Middle East. Because these regimes lack political legitimacy – legitimacy that would have been bestowed on them had they gained power as a result of free and fair democratic elections – the political establishments find themselves in a situation where they fear anything different and potentially challenging, particularly minorities.

For fear of losing their grip on power, most Middle Eastern regimes operate a complex system of pacts and coercion, awarding an important position to one group in order to counterbalance another, the favoured group always fully aware that it risks losing its privileged position to another group if it grows too strong and potentially threatening. In other words, influential positions and political power are kept in the hands of those thought to be loyal to the regime, meaning that when loyalties change but regimes persist, powerful positions change hands from those formerly loyal to those now loyal.

Due to the fact that power is kept within closed circles, power-sharing arrangements involving the devolution of power to geographically concentrated minorities on a regional basis have never been seen as an option for solving minority conflict (apart from the Palestine/Israel case in which all Middle Eastern regimes support the Palestinians in their demand for an independent state). Power-sharing is in general seen as a threat to the stability of the regime and, in many instances also, to the security of the state. Many Middle Eastern regimes have stayed in power for considerable periods of time despite their lack of political legitimacy, largely due to corruption and coercion. Unless these regimes are forced to change their power basis from bribes and coercion to popular support, resulting in a political system in which power is distributed according to vote share rather than loyalty, there is little hope that the minorities of the Middle East will ever have the chance of obtaining more than a few trivial rights or political positions in the name of bribery.

NOTES

1 Ben-Dor, Gabriel, 'Minorities in the Middle East: Theory and Practice', in Ofra Bengio and Gabriel Ben-Dor (eds.), *Minorities and the State in the Arab World* (Boulder: Lynne Rienner, 1999), p. 1.

2 Horowitz, Donald, *Ethnic Groups in Conflict* (Berkeley: University of California Press, 1985), p. 53.

3   Gurr, Ted, and Barbara Harff, *Ethnic Conflict in World Politics* (Boulder: Westview Press, 1994), pp. 18–26.

4   Kumaraswamy, P. R., 'Problems of Studying Minorities in the Middle East', *Alternatives Journal: Turkish Journal of International Relations,* 2 (2), 2003, pp. 246–7.

5   In this chapter, the word Shia is used as a noun, whereas the term Shi'i is used as an adjective.

6   Hourani, Albert, *Minorities in the Arab World* (London: Oxford University Press, 1947), p. 1.

7   Had the purpose of the chapter not been to analyse state–minority relations and minority mobilization, I would have included an additional category: 'numerical minorities'. The citizens of the United Arab Emirates (and, until recently, the citizens of Kuwait), form a numerical minority in their own country. However, although they are the numerical minority this group is not discriminated against due to the fact that it is itself the state.

8   Gurr and Harff (1994), p. 86. For indicators of each of the seven factors see Gurr and Harff (1994), pp. 87–92 and 119–20.

9   Gurr and Harff (1994), p. 120.

10   Horowitz (1985), p. 235.

11   Camps, Gabriel, 'L'origine des Berbères', in Ernest Gellner (ed.), *Islam et société: anthropologie du Maghreb* (Paris: CNRS, 1981), pp. 9–33.

12   Pate, Amy, 'Berbers in Algeria', *Minorities at Risk,* 2001a; Pate, Amy, 'Berbers in Morocco', *Minorities at Risk,* 2001b; and Trevor Mostyn and Albert Hourani (eds.), *The Cambridge Encyclopedia of the Middle East and North Africa* (Cambridge: Cambridge University Press, 1988), p. 29.

13   Maddy-Weitzman, Bruce, 'Berbers, "Berberism," and the State in North Africa', in Moshe Ma'oz and Gabriel Sheffer (eds.), *Middle Eastern Minorities and Diasporas* (Brighton: Sussex Academic Press, 2002), pp. 157–8. See also Pate (2001b).

14   Maddy-Weitzman, Bruce, 'The Berber Question in Algeria: Nationalism in the Making?', in Bengio and Ben-Dor (1999), pp. 33–4; and Mostyn and Hourani (1988), p. 302.

15   Mostyn and Hourani (1988), p. 29; and Brett, Michael, and Elizabeth Fentress, *The Berbers* (Oxford: Blackwell Publishers, 1997), p. 3.

16   Harff, Barbara, 'Minorities, Rebellion, and Repression in North Africa and the Middle East', in Gurr (1993), p. 230. See also Pate (2001a and 2001b); and Brett and Fentress (1997), p. 3.

17   Brett and Fentress (1997), p. 231.

18   Brett and Fentress (1997), p. 232 and 252.

19   Maddy-Weitzman (1999), p. 36.

20   Maddy-Weitzman (1999), p. 37.

21   Brett and Fentress (1997), pp. 196–7 and 272; and Maddy-Weitzman (1999), pp. 37–8. See also, Micaud, Charles, 'Conclusion', in Ernest Gellner and Charles Micaud, *Arabs and Berbers: From Tribe to Nation in North Africa* (London: Heath and Company, 1972), p. 436.

22   Maddy-Weitzman (1999), p. 38; and Brett and Fentress (1997), p. 274.

23   Pate (2001a). See also, Silverstein, Paul, 'Realizing Myth: Berbers in France and Algeria', *Middle East Report,* 26 (3), 1996, pp. 11–12.

24   Maddy-Weitzman (1999), p. 40; and Silverstein (1996), p. 11.

25   Maddy-Weitzman (1999), pp. 41–7; and Silverstein (1996), pp. 13–14.

26   Maddy-Weitzman (2002), pp. 159–63.

27   Layachi, Azzedine, *Civil Society and Democratization in Morocco* (Cairo: Ibn Khaldun Center, 1995), p. 139; and Maddy-Weitzman (2002), p. 161. NB! Similar demands were raised in the 1960s and 1970s but were not met. See Harff (1993), p. 232.

28   US Department of State, 'Morocco Human Rights Practices 1994'. See the internet at   http://dosfan.lib.uic.edu/ERC/democracy/1994_hrp_report/94hrp_report_nea/

Morocco.html; TAMAZGHA, 'The Amazight Issue in Morocco', UN Economic and Social Council, International Convention on the Elimination of All Forms of Racial Discrimination (ICERD), 62nd Session of the Commission for the Elimination of Racial Discrimination, Geneva, 3–21 March 2003; and Maddy-Weitzman (2002), p. 161.

29 Laskier, Michael, 'A Difficult Inheritance: Moroccan Society Under King Muhammad VI', *Middle East Review of International Affairs,* 7 (3), 2003, pp. 15–16; Maddy-Weitzman (2002), p. 162; and Pate (2001).

30 Van Bruinessen, Martin, *Agha, Shaikh and State: The Social and Political Structures of Kurdistan* (London: Zed Books, 1992), pp. 115–16; and Gurr and Harff (1994), p. 30.

31 The term 'Kurdistan' denoting this region was, however, first used in the twelfth century. See David McDowall, *A Modern History of the Kurds* (London: I. B. Tauris, 1997), p. 6.

32 McDowall (1997); and Gurr and Harff (1994), pp. 32–7.

33 McDowall (1997); and Gurr and Harff (1994), pp. 32–7.

34 McDowall (1997); and Gurr and Harff (1994), pp. 32–7.

35 Mostyn and Hourani (1988), p. 464.

36 Stansfield, Gareth, 'Governing Kurdistan', in Brendan O'Leary, John McGarry, and Khaled Saleh (eds.), *The Future of Kurdistan in Iraq* (Philadelphia, PA: University of Pennsylvania Press, forthcoming 2004).

37 Mostyn and Hourani (1988), p. 464.

38 Ciment, James, *The Kurds: State and Minority in Turkey, Iraq and Iran* (New York: Facts on File, Inc., 1996), pp. 75–105.

39 Gurr and Harff (1994), p. 39; and McDowall (1997), pp. 214–28.

40 McDowall (1997), pp. 223–6.

41 McDowall (1997), pp. 231–48.

42 Gurr and Harff (1994), p. 40.

43 Gurr and Harff (1994), p. 40.

44 McDowall (1997), pp. 274–9; and Ciment (1996), pp. 152–5.

45 In fact, Kurdish rebellions can be traced all the way back until 1878. These early rebellions were primarily of tribal character, however. See, Gareth Stansfield, *Iraqi Kurdistan: Political Development and Emergent Democracy* (London: RoutledgeCurzon, 2003), p. 61.

46 Ma'oz, Moshe, 'Ethnic and Religious Conflict in Iraq', in Ma'oz and Sheffer (2002), p. 185.

47 Bengio, Ofra, 'The Case of Iraq', in Ofra Bengio and Gabriel Ben-Dor (eds.), *Minorities and the State in the Arab World* (Boulder: Lynne Rienner, 1999), pp. 152–3.

48 Stansfield (2003), pp. 75–6.

49 Stansfield (2003), p. 90; and McDowall, David, *A Modern History of the Kurds* (London: I. B. Tauris, 1997), pp. 357–60.

50 McDowall (1997), pp. 379–80; and Stansfield (2003), p. 96.

51 Stansfield (forthcoming 2004).

52 Anderson, Liam, and Gareth Stansfield, *The Future of Iraq: Dictatorship, Democracy, or Division?* (New York: Palgrave Macmillan, 2004), p. 235.

53 Gurr and Harff (1994), p. 37.

54 McDowall (1997), pp. 206–7.

55 McDowall (1997), pp. 208–9.

56 Gurr and Harff (1994), p. 39.

57 Ciment (1996), pp. 143–4.

58 US Department of State, 'Country Reports on Human Rights Practices: Turkey, 2002'. See the internet at http://www.state.gov/g/drl/rls/hrrpt/2002/18396.htm.

59 US Department of State, 'Country Reports on Human Rights Practices: Turkey, 2002'. See the internet at http://www.state.gov/g/drl/rls/hrrpt/2002/18396.htm. See also,

Human Rights Watch, 'Turkey 2003: Human Rights Developments', at http://www.hrw.org/wr2k3/europe13.html.

60 Hazen, William, 'Minorities in Assimilation: The Kurds of Iran, Iraq, Syria, and Turkey', in R. D. McLaurin (ed.), *The Political Role of Minority Groups in the Middle East* (New York: Praeger Publishers, 1979), pp. 51–3; and Mostyn and Hourani (1988), p. 467.

61 Hazen (1979), pp. 58–60 and 67.

62 Human Rights Watch, 'Syria: The Silenced Kurds', *Human Rights Watch*, 8(4), October 1996; Hazen (1979), p. 67; and Mostyn and Hourani (1988), p. 467.

63 Amnesty International, 'Syria: Mass arrests of Syrian Kurds and fear of torture and other ill-treatment', *Amnesty International*, Press release MDE 24/020/2004, 16 March 2004.

64 Khalidi, Rashid, *Palestinian Identity: The Construction of Modern National Consciousness* (New York: Columbia University Press, 1997); and Muslih, Muhammad, 'Arab Politics and the Rise of Palestinian Nationalism,' *Journal of Palestine Studies*, 16(4), 1987, pp. 77–94.

65 See Save the Children online at http://www.savethechildren.org.uk/eyetoeye/info/refugees.html.

66 See Mostyn and Hourani (1988), pp. 468–72. NB! For the Palestinians living in refugee camps the situation has been somewhat different. The majority of these Palestinians are either unemployed or work in workshops in the camps set up by the International Red Cross and the United Nations Relief and Works Agency.

67 UN resolution 242 calls for Israel to withdraw from the territories occupied in the June 1967 war, while UN resolution 338 calls for a cease-fire to halt the October 1973 war and for the implementation of resolution 242. For the full text of the resolutions, see the *United Nations* on the Internet at http://ods-dds-ny.un.org/doc/RESOLUTION/GEN/NR0/240/94/IMG/NR024094.pdf?OpenElement and http://ods-dds-ny.un.org/doc/RESOLUTION/GEN/NR0/288/65/IMG/NR028865.pdf?OpenElement.

68 For the full text of the agreement, see *Le Monde Diplomatique* on the internet at http://mondediplo.com/focus/mideast/r1280.

69 For the full text of the agreement, see *Le Monde Diplomatique* on the internet at http://mondediplo.com/focus/mideast/a2315.

70 For the full text of the agreement, see *Le Monde Diplomatique* on the internet at http://mondediplo.com/focus/mideast/a2316.

71 For the full text of the agreement, see *Le Monde Diplomatique* on the internet at http://mondediplo.com/focus/mideast/a2317.

72 For the full text of the agreement, see *Le Monde Diplomatique* on the internet at http://mondediplo.com/focus/mideast/a2318.

73 For the full text of the agreement, see *Le Monde Diplomatique* on the internet at http://mondediplo.com/focus/mideast/a2319.

74 McGreal, Chris, 'Israeli Wall to encircle Palestine', *Guardian*, 18 March 2003.

75 Huggler, Justin, 'UN report attacks Israel's "separation fence" ', *New Zealand Herald*, 13 November 2003.

76 Ramadan, Saud, 'Analysis: World will judge Israel's wall', *Washington Times*, 24 February 2004.

77 Susser, Asher, 'The Palestinians in Jordan: Demographic Majority, Political Minority', in Bengio and Ben-Dor (1999), pp. 96–7; and Israeli, Raphael, *Palestinians Between Israel and Jordan* (New York: Praeger Publishers, 1991), pp. 5–6.

78 Israeli (1991), p. 7; Susser (1999), p. 98.

79 Susser (1999), p. 101.

80 Susser (1999), p. 101; Israeli (1991), p. 108.

81 Susser (1999), p. 102.

82 Susser (1999), p. 102.

83 Mostyn and Hourani (1988), p. 372; Peteet, Julie, 'From Refugees to Minority: Palestinians in Post-War Lebanon', *Middle East Report*, vol. 26, no. 3, 1996, p. 28.
84 Mostyn and Hourani (1988), pp. 372–3.
85 Mostyn and Hourani (1988), p. 373.
86 Peteet (1996), p. 29.
87 Peteet (1996), p. 29.
88 Peteet (1996), p. 29; and Peleg, Gil, 'Palestinians in Lebanon', *Minorities at Risk*, 2002. See the internet at http://www.cidcm.umd.edu/inscr/mar/data/lebpal.htm.
89 Hourani (1947), p. 109.

FURTHER READING

For the best works on minorities in general see Ted Gurr's *Minorities at Risk* (Washington, DC: United States Institute of Peace Press, 1993), and Ted Gurr and Barbara Harff's *Ethnic Conflict in World Politics* (Boulder: Westview Press, 1994). Donald Horowitz's *Ethnic Groups in Conflict* (Berkeley: University of California Press, 1985) is another excellent book on the subject, the book is much more comprehensive than the two books previously mentioned, but the theoretical framework is less explicit. On political rights of minorities in the contemporary Western world – issues that are likely to become relevant to minorities in the Middle East in the near future – look no further than Will Kymlicka's *Politics in the Vernacular: Nationalism, Multiculturalism, and Citizenship* (Oxford: Oxford University Press, 2001). With regard to minorities in the Middle East, Albert Hourani's *Minorities in the Arab World* (London: Oxford University Press, 1947) is an absolute must, as are *Middle Eastern Minorities and Diasporas* by Moshe Ma'oz and Gabriel Scheffer (Brighton: Sussex Academic Press, 2002) and *Minorities and the State in the Arab World* by Ofra Bengio and Gabriel Ben-Dor (Boulder: Lynne Rienner, 1999).

CHAPTER TWENTY-FIVE

Civil Society in the Middle East

TIM NIBLOCK

Introduction

Some writers have questioned the utility of the concept 'civil society'. Roger Owen, for example, contends that the notion has 'failed to generate the type of questions and hypotheses which encourage new and innovative lines of social enquiry ... it lacks rigour, explanatory power and so the ability to provide guidance about either present-day socio-political dynamics or future trends'.[1]

In some respects, this scepticism is justified. As will be shown later, the concept has been subject to many different definitions and interpretations, which spread confusion when the term is used loosely. It is also true that the empirical study of civil associations does not lead on to many useful generalizations about the dynamics shaping contemporary developments – whether in the Arab world or elsewhere.

Some of the contentions which have been made about civil society's role in laying the basis for democratization, moreover, have been misleading. The idea that civil society is the critical factor for democratic change came to the fore in the late 1980s, as an explanation for the rapid disintegration of the communist regimes of eastern Europe. Some eastern European intellectuals contended that the changes were a natural outcome of a prior burgeoning of civil society within the states concerned. In fact, this interpretation was largely incorrect. With the exception of the (important) case of Poland – where the combined activities of the Solidarity union and the Catholic church did have a substantial impact on events – the collapse of communism stemmed mainly from other factors. Of central importance were the economic and legitimacy crises with which the communist regimes were confronted, which led on to a loss of self-confidence at the heart of the regimes. This spread from the Soviet Union to countries dependent on Soviet support, and opened the way for political change. What was initially seen by the regimes as a measure of limited political reform soon revealed the narrow basis on which the regimes were based.

There are, however, four respects in which the concept of civil society has been useful in the study of Middle Eastern politics and history. First, empirical studies of civil associations in Middle Eastern states do generate insights into how individual political systems function, even though no generalizable conclusions across different states may follow. Second, classifying Middle Eastern states according to the scope, which they provide for civil society provides a useful perspective on the linkages between political structure and civil freedoms. Third, whatever the merits or demerits of the concept, it now forms part of the discourse on political change, within Middle Eastern states themselves. In the words of Eva Bellin:

> 'Civil society' (that is, *al-mujtama' al-madani*) has entered the discourse of the Arab world and become a central concept in current Arab debate over the direction of politics in the region. State officials use it to promote their projects of mobilisation and 'modernisation'; Islamists use it to angle for a legal share of public space; and independent activists and intellectuals use it to expand the boundaries of individual liberty.[2]

Fourth, the concept forms the fulcrum of an important debate which has developed on the differences (real or supposed) between Islamic and western societies. The central issue is whether the values of civil society are inherently western, and alien to Islamic societies. The debate over whether civil society has existed, does exist, or could exist in the Middle East has, in many ways, been more revealing and thought-provoking than has the empirical study of civil society organizations. It has been akin to the debate on Orientalism, which dominated Middle Eastern studies for much of the late 1970s and 1980s. In that debate also, researchers were forced to examine the assumptions from which they started, the values which underpinned their work, and the coherence of their mindsets. Substantial differences in the way in which the region is seen, and in the values and assumptions which observers use when analysing developments in the region, then, are revealed in the debate about civil society.

This chapter will give attention both to the theoretical debate and to the empirical experience. On the empirical side, emphasis will be given to classifying states according to the scope of civil society which they allow, and explaining how this relates to political structure. We begin with the theoretical debate.

The Theoretical Debate: Gellner and Mardin

Most contemporary theorists of civil society have a common starting point. There is a general acceptance that the critical sphere of civil society consists of the space between citizens and the state. Civil society, therefore, is composed of the associations and organizations whose primary objective it is to promote or represent the views and interests, or organize the activities, of different groups of citizens. The bodies concerned have to be autonomous of the state. At the same time, however, they need to be operating within a context where the state safeguards their freedom of operation – preferably within a clearly articulated legal framework, but at least in a manner where their autonomy is assured. The associations themselves, moreover, need to act in a manner where they respect each other's right to operate. Saad Eddin Ibrahim sums up these various strands as follows:

> civil society is composed of non-state actors or non-governmental organisations – e.g. political parties, trade unions, professional organisations, community development associations, and other interest groups. Normatively, civil society implies values and behavioural codes of tolerating, if not accepting, the different 'others' and a tacit or explicit commitment to the peaceful management of differences among individuals and collectivities sharing the same public space – i.e. the polity.[3]

Beyond this common basis, however, there are differences. Some writers limit the kinds of association which count as part of civil society, excluding those which are based on 'primordial units'. Esmail, writing from this perspective, lists 'the family, the kin-group, the neighbourhood, the tribe, the ethnic or religious community' as comprising prim-ordial groupings which do not in themselves count as part of civil society.[4]

In the context of the Middle East, these exclusions are highly important. It could be contended, indeed, that the strongest social institutions which inhabit the area between citizen and state in the Middle East have traditionally been those based on clan/tribal groupings or on religious communities. If these are included in the definition of civil society, then Middle Eastern civil society has been relatively strong (at least in some countries, at some times); if they are excluded, the social institutions and organizations which remain are not nearly as significant – and Middle Eastern civil society has been weak.

The contention that the Middle East (or more specifically Muslim countries) has traditionally lacked the kind of civil associations which constitute civil society, and therefore forms a difficult terrain for the development of civil society today, has been given weight by the academic prominence of some of those who have espoused the view. Of particular significance here are the writings of the sociologist Ernest Gellner and the historian Serif Mardin. Their views are presented in this section, with counter-arguments being examined in that which follows. Both of them lay emphasis on the uniqueness of the western cultural tradition, differentiating this tradition from all other traditions, but both give emphasis to the contrast with Islamic societies.

To Gellner, the concept of civil society cannot rest simply with the notion of a 'set of diverse non-government institutions, which is strong enough to counterbalance the state.'[5] He points out that traditional agrarian-based societies are 'well endowed in highly structured and partly or wholly autonomous communities', but that these communities themselves 'maintain their cohesion, internal discipline and solidarity by a heavy ritual underscoring of social roles and obligations . . . generally conceived in kin terms'.[6] He contends that in such situations 'discipline is enforced by a prolifer-ation of minor punishable transgressions, the avoidance of which puts a burden on each individual and keeps him in awe of the social order as a whole'.[7] In other words, tribal and religious communal organization is not a genuine part of civil society: the oppression of kings is simply displaced (or complemented) by the 'dictatorship of cousins'. The individual remains 'caged' within a system of oppression, without the rights which freedom requires. Gellner contends, therefore, that the existence of autonomous social organization cannot constitute the only criterion for civil society.

The most basic requirement for civil society, Gellner maintains, is that individuals are 'modular'. Similar to an item in a set of modular furniture, the individual must be able to join up with (or leave) whatever units of society are open to membership. In practical terms, people must be free to join or leave societies and associations at will, unbound by any understandings of relationship or blood:

> Modular man can combine into effective associations and institutions without these being total, many-stranded, underwritten by ritual, and made stable through being linked to a whole set of relationships, all of these then being tied in with each other and so immobilised. He can combine into specific-purpose, *ad hoc*, limited associations, without binding himself by some blood ritual. He can leave an association when he comes to disagree with its policy without being open to the charge of treason.[8]

Civil society to Gellner, then, is a 'cluster of institutions and associations strong enough to prevent tyranny, but which are, nevertheless, entered freely rather than imposed by birth or by awesome ritual'.[9]

A society of this nature needs a certain commonality of values and practices. Modularity requires that people are substitutable: one man must be able to fill the slot previously left by another. There are, of course, differences among people, but there needs to be an underlying cultural homogeneity: 'the communication symbols employed by the new occupant of the slot must be culture-compatible with those of his new neighbours'.[10] Modularity in fact 'makes not only for civil, but also for nationalist society', because modular man is only substitutable within the cultural boundaries of the 'idiom in which he has been trained to communicate, to emit and to receive messages'.[11] People have, moreover, to be trained to behave in this way, within the context of what Gellner calls a 'High Culture'.

> It can only be done by means of formal education, transmitting to its wards the standardised, codified rules of a culture that, precisely in virtue of this codification and its inherent links to specialised educational institutions, is a *High* Culture.[12]

To Gellner, the civil society that emerged in the west was, in these respects, very different from Islamic society. The religious conflicts of the sixteenth and seventeenth centuries in Europe led to a stalemate, which was resolved through widespread secularization. Societies developed which were plural, yet united around a core of common secular values. In the Islamic world, the Islamic *umma* and its religious orthodoxy remained dominant, preventing trends towards secularism and reinforcing loyalties that were communal in character. 'Modular man' is, in this perspective, not the common pattern of humanity in the Islamic world, and the region is not well suited to civil society. This explains, in Gellner's view, the difficulty which civil society has had in taking hold in Islamic countries.

The writing of Şerif Mardin is yet more insistent on the cultural uniqueness of the west's experience of civil society. Mardin refers to civil society as a 'western dream', which is part of the social history of Western Europe. He explains this as follows:

> The dream itself, the ability to dream the dream, is the expression of a unique premise concerning the components of a social system, a premise that also assumed more precise outlines within modern European history. That postulate is the idea that social relations are both sustained and energised by autonomous, secular collectives with legal personality operating within a frame of rationalised and self-referential law.[13]

He locates the origins of the dream in the medieval European town, where the concept and practice of an autonomous sphere of activity was developed, being carried forward by the growing bourgeoisie and finding expression in the 'increasingly well-established idea that political rights and obligations stemmed from property'.[14] This led on to the political philosophical movements of the seventeenth, eighteenth and nineteenth centuries, which created the theories of civil society found in Locke, Hegel and others. These theories became integral to western social attitudes and beliefs.

The dream, and the turning of the dream into reality, is in Mardin's view unique to the west:

> A characteristic of the transformation of the Western dream into reality is that this metamorphosis is limited to the West. Civil society, for example, does not translate into Islamic terms. Civility, which is a latent content of civil society, does, but these two are not interchangeable terms.[15]

He contends that the 'Muslim dream of society' was very different. Set within the context of political obligations that are laid down by the Qur'an and the interpretations of Qur'anic commentators, the 'Muslim dream shifted to the ideal of a social equilibrium created under the aegis of a just prince'.[16] Whereas western ideas focused on the legal rights and obligations of individuals, therefore, Muslim ideas focused on social cohesion. Among the characteristics of Muslim societies, which followed from this, were that 'the cracks of a compromised, unrealised system of justice' were filled in by the charismatic authority of the leader, and that emphasis was placed on justice rather than freedom. Instead of the patchwork of voluntary associations found in European cities, Islamic cities were segmented on the basis of 'religious communities and groups belonging to different legal schools, guilds, fraternities lineage groups and ethnic communities'. There was no hegemony of the bourgeoisie, which could erase the differences between segmentary groupings.[17]

The perspective, which Mardin puts forward on the prospects for civil society in the Islamic world, then, is not bright. While Muslim states may acquire some of the institutional trappings of civil society, he contends, the underlying reality is very different: 'the dream of Western society has not become the dream of Muslim societies and this incongruity is part of the difficulty of the latter experience'.[18]

The Theoretical Debate: Asserting Middle Eastern Civil Society

The perceptions of Gellner and Mardin are no doubt valuable, and it is true that the emphasis in Islamic societies has been more on collective rights than individual rights. The pessimistic conclusions, which they draw with regard to the future of civil society in the Islamic world, however, are questionable. The western intellectual tradition has not always been dominated by a dream of individual human rights guaranteed by impartial and secular law. For significant parts of the twentieth century the political dreams of large numbers of Europeans were centred on ideologies of social cohesion: fascism and National Socialism on the right (cohesion around a national cause and leader), and communism on the left (creating social cohesion on the basis of a classless society). The victory of liberalism did not seem inevitable in the middle decades of the century. Nor, as will be shown later, has the concept of individual freedom been totally absent from Islamic societies. The contest between promoting social cohesion and defending individual rights, then, exists within both western and Islamic societies. It does not constitute a simple dividing line between the two.

Reference to a 'western dream' of civil society, moreover, carries a sense of unreality in those parts of the world which have undergone bitter experiences under the colonial rule of western powers. A dream of civil freedom, which applies only in the colonial power's home territory (or only among its own people), and is dismissive of the rights of others beyond its borders, betrays the universalistic values that are usually attributed to liberalism.

If civil society is valued for the limit which it imposes on the arbitrary power of government, moreover, there seems no reason to exclude primordial religious and communal associations. These groupings, based on tribe or religion, clearly do help to limit the power of governments, constituting a sphere of activity that is independent of governmental control. The strength of religious and tribal allegiances, indeed, gives associations of this kind a form of protection, which other civil associations may lack. While the latter depend primarily on legal structures to defend their autonomy, in other words, the former have the protection of effective power. Governments will be reluctant to confront them, recognizing their ability to mobilize substantial sections of the population in their support. Many of the political problems facing the governments of developing countries after independence, in fact, arose precisely from the strength of communal associations. The state-socialist single party states which dominated much of the developing world in the 1960s and early 1970s sought to suppress religious and tribal allegiances precisely because of their strength – and their resultant ability to frustrate governmental plans to transform society and economy, and create a new order.

Nor is it clear that religious and tribal associations simply transfer oppression from the state to the religious/tribal leaderships. The perception that tribal and religious communal organization constitutes a cage within which individuals are trapped and controlled by traditional leaders should not necessarily be accepted. It neglects the extent to which individuals choose to use these organizations to defend their own individual and communal interests. Western capitalism, moreover, produces forms of caging which also restrict individual freedom of action, based on economic need. No doubt there are issues of individual freedom which arise in communal organizations, as there are in some civil associations based on non-communal interests,[19] but a blanket refusal to consider religious and tribal associations as part of civil society is not warranted. There is good reason, therefore, to bring this form of association into the scope of what constitutes civil society.

The political implications of Gellner's contentions on 'modular man', moreover, need to be considered. If civil society does indeed require that society be composed of 'modular men and women', with a strong degree of cultural homogeneity, the political prescriptions for the non-western world are bleak. Two alternative prescriptions would seem to follow. One would be to recognize the impossibility of building civil society outside of the western world, abandoning attempts to do so. This, however, runs counter to practical experience. Non-modular societies have played host to western-style civil society in a number of non-western countries, in the Indian sub-continent, Latin America, South-East Asia and elsewhere. Or else, Islamic and other non-western societies could be re-constructed, such that individuals are induced to adopt secular values, with nationalist rather than communal affiliations, and fitting into the modular pattern.[20] There is, however, something dated about such a prescription. The project of re-constituting society around a secular and nationalist set of values was characteristic of the Arab state-socialist regimes of the 1960s. The ideology of the Ba'thist regime in Iraq after 1968, for example, emphasized strongly the re-making of society on a basis of 'modern' and nationalist values.[21] No doubt Gellner himself would not have favoured this prescription.

Finally, and perhaps most important, the practical experience has been that, when the opportunity for civil organization is given to populations in the Middle East, civil associations spring up quickly and prolifically. The notion is clearly not alien to the peoples of the region. Evidence of this will be presented in the sections which follow.

An Overview of the Development of Civil Society in the Middle East

In keeping with the points made in the last section, the definition of civil society used in this overview will not exclude primordial groupings (above the level of the family). Civil associations based on religious or tribal affiliations, therefore, will be brought into the discussion.

Pre-modern Islamic societies in the Middle East functioned within a framework where the powers of government were limited by the autonomous roles of different groupings in society. The rights of the different groupings were recognized and generally respected by those who wielded political authority. While the latter authority derived its legitimacy from 'a combination of conquest and/or religious sources', as Saad Eddin Ibrahim has said, there was nonetheless a public space 'shared by *ulama*, merchants, guilds, Sufi orders, and sects (*millat*s)'.[22] Outside of the urban areas, the public space was occupied largely by peasants and tribes. There, the influence exerted by the political authority was frequently very limited: 'other collectivities, especially the tribes, were quite autonomous from, if not outright defiant of the central authority'.[23]

Even in the urban areas, the power of the political authority was limited:

> various groups coexisted and interacted with a great deal of autonomy. Guilds, religious sects, and ethnic groups ran most of their own internal affairs through elected or appointed leaders. The latter were accountable to both the political authority and their own communities.[24]

Under this system, social provision and the regulation of personal status matters was mostly left to the communal organizations, such that the societies 'not only knew the equivalent of civil formations but also survived through them. Individuals relied on these formations for identity and much of their basic needs'.[25] This form of civil association, therefore, was both strong and relatively autonomous – probably more so than the civil associations which existed in European cities at this time.

Western economic and political penetration into the Islamic world changed the character of civil society in the Middle East. The period of western rule did not, however, obliterate all aspects of the pre-existing civil society. Many of the traditional elements of society remained in being, and communal organizations continued to play a role. Their ability to resist the power of the state no doubt lessened, and in some cases they became little more than branches of the colonial state's administrative apparatus, but mostly they retained an element of autonomy of the state. The new middle class which developed as a result of western penetration, moreover, created new associations framed around professional, labour and political interests. Political parties, sometimes in alliance with traditional communal groupings, mobilized the population against the colonial powers and in favour of independence.[26]

The period which immediately followed independence in most Middle Eastern countries saw civil associations continuing on much the same basis as before. Governments were now led by the political leaders who had waged the struggle for independence. Increasingly, however, the political system came under strain. Social and economic change was bringing to the fore social forces whose interests demanded a radical transformation of society. The prominent role in civil society played by communal leaders, backed by the religious and tribal allegiances, and often limited the ability or willingness of governments to respond to the demands of the educated middle class, industrial workers and students.

The state-socialist or populist regimes which came to power in much of the Arab world in the 1950s and 1960s narrowed substantially the scope for civil society. Under these regimes there was an implicit social contract between the mass of the population and the ruling regimes: the state would seek the rapid development of the economy and consolidate national independence, and the population would remain politically quiescent. The right to autonomous political or civil action was not part of the equation. Civil organization outside of the umbrella of the state was either prohibited or severely restricted. Religious, ethnic and tribal allegiances persisted – despite the efforts of the regimes – but they were driven underground. They tended to re-surface with renewed vigour once regimes began to liberalize.

It is worth noting, however, that state-socialist regimes did not dispense with social organization itself. On the contrary, they were active in arranging the population into unions of many kinds: trade unions, professional unions, youth federations, women's federations etc. Although these unions were controlled by the government, and therefore did not constitute part of civil society, they were nonetheless socially significant. Their objective, as far as the state was concerned, was in part one of control; but they were also intended to undermine the traditionalist communal groupings and to unify sectors of the population on a 'modern' basis – around common economic, social and professional interests.[27] The paradox was that the state's role in promoting the organizations undermined their ability to defend these interests. Some were, nonetheless, strong enough to survive in the more liberal political environments which followed state socialism, and to play an autonomous role.

The period since the 1970s has seen a move towards political and economic liberalization, although not necessarily to democratization, in the Middle East. Over these years there has been a substantial increase in the number of civil associations. Regimes have themselves had an interest in promoting this development: the state no longer has the resources to fulfil the welfare provisions inherent in the state-socialist social contract, such that it needs to rely on the involvement of non-government organizations to provide assistance to the impoverished parts of the population; the economic hardships imposed on substantial parts of the population in the early stages of economic liberalization make it desirable to provide 'safety-valves' – channels through which frustration can be expressed; the forging of new links with the western world is facilitated if the political and social structures have some resonance with western forms; and political leaderships have needed to develop new areas of political support, especially among middle-class circles with an established commitment to autonomous civil organization.

There has been a growing realization among regimes, moreover, that the suppression of civil society associations may not be an effective means to restrict the circulation of information critical of the government. Middle Eastern populations today are increasingly informing themselves through satellite television and the Internet.[28] Associations which are banned can publicize their views through these means. The publicity which a group gains by being subject to a ban may in practice enable it to obtain better access to the international media. The international dimension of a civil association's activities, indeed, has in some cases become the lifeblood that keeps it in being. Attempts to ban satellite dishes have been made, but with the exception of Iraq have been of limited effect.

Saad Eddin Ibrahim reports that the number of Arab NGOs grew from less than 20,000 in the mid-1960s to about 70,000 in the late 1980s.[29] It seems likely that the number has increased steadily since then, although probably not at the same pace. There is certainly pressure coming from the societies concerned for civil associations to be given more scope and freedom, and it is significant that this pressure comes from all parts of the political spectrum – from Islamist, through liberal to communist.

Middle Eastern society, then, has been consistently grappling with civil organization since the early part of the twentieth century. When populations have had the opportunity to form civil associations, they have generally done so with enthusiasm. The reciprocity between freedom to express one's own opinion and willingness to allow others the same privilege remains problematic, but the Middle East is not alone in that respect.

Religious Dimensions of Civil Society in the Middle East

Religious-based civil associations have constituted a vital – perhaps the most vital – element in Middle Eastern civil society. It is, therefore, important to consider how such associations have developed in recent years, and how they have affected the wider social and political system. Of particular significance in the latter regard is whether they have helped to strengthen agendas of democratization.

The role of the Islamic religious infrastructure in shaping the values of people in the region (non-Muslim as well as Muslim) has clearly been crucial since classical times. In playing this role Islamic leaders have operated from a basis of considerable autonomy. Their independence of the temporal rulers has conveyed to the population the consciousness of an independent civil society – perhaps possessing more legitimacy than that of the temporal rulers. Much of the discourse coming from this quarter, indeed, has stressed the significance of civil society and the need for an autonomous sphere of religious jurisprudence. Ahmad Moussali points out that the development of jurisprudence in the Islamic world was the consequence of social interaction between scholars and segments of society, and that right up to the collapse of the Ottoman empire 'the *ulama* proved resistant to absorption or disintegration'. The historical role of the scholars' institution, he says 'has always been as intermediaries between the state and segments of civil society'.[30]

The religious-based associations which impinge most directly on the development of civil society in the contemporary Middle East are those seeking to change or improve social and political conditions: voluntary aid and welfare associations, and movements which have been formed to promote an Islamic (or specific form of Islamic) social, economic and/or political agenda. Mosques and churches do, of course, take part in some of these activities themselves. In the less urbanized societies, religious communal leaders have sometimes created political movements or parties to defend or promote the interests of their community. In Sudan, for example, the leadership of the Mahdist Ansar religious order became leaders of the Umma Party prior to independence, and have retained that position ever since.[31]

Religious-based voluntary associations and political/social movements have grown steadily both in number and strength since the early 1970s. The phenomenon of Islamism is discussed elsewhere in this book and will not be covered here. The increased activity of Islamic voluntary associations is often linked to the general trend of growing Islamism, but it draws sustenance from wider social and economic developments in the region. On the one hand, the funding to finance these associations has been more plentiful than in the past. The rise in oil prices in the decade of the 1970s, and the economic surplus which this generated in oil-producing countries, together with the spread of Islamic banks and investment companies, put Islamic non-governmental organizations (and political movements) in a strong position to raise new funding.

On the other hand, the social needs to which such associations cater have become ever more acute. Programmes of economic liberalization, adopted under pressure from the International Monetary Fund and other international financial institutions, have reduced or eliminated food subsidies, cut welfare provision for the poorer parts of society, and slimmed down the state sector with a consequent loss of jobs.[32] There has, therefore, been an increased need for welfare provision from the non-state sector. Civil associations with religious affiliations or connections have been the major ones to step into this gap. While it is the Islamic associations which have attracted most attention (and have had the most resources), Christian associations have also been very active, as have Jewish associations within Israel. The strength of the civil associations in this field has often been enhanced by their multiple roles. Proselytizing bodies and political movements, for example, have been instrumental in providing welfare, as well as carrying out their specific religious and political missions. In Egypt the Muslim Brotherhood established, and continues to liaise closely with, many of the major Islamic organizations providing welfare.

The significance of religious-based civil society for agendas of democratization is complex. Strong civil associations in this sphere clearly do strengthen the overall civil sphere, buttressing the power of society relative to that of the state. Whether this necessarily strengthens the basis for democratization, however, may depend on practical circumstances. The case of Iran is instructive. It was religious civil organization, allied to the bazaar, which provided the dynamic behind the Iranian revolution. Through this alliance the Shah was overthrown and replaced initially by a liberal parliamentary regime. This Islamic-based revolution can, indeed, be seen as one of the most striking examples in the late twentieth century of civil society bringing about radical political change. Political change in Iran was, in this respect, unlike change in Eastern Europe and the former Soviet Union, Latin America and southern Africa. There, as noted above, political change was rather more dependent on a combination of economic failure, regime loss of self-confidence, and external pressure. In Iran the central moving force was, without doubt, civil society. Yet the initial multi-party democratic structures which were put in place immediately after the revolution did not last long (albeit re-emerging in a rather different form in the 1990s). It is, however, debatable whether this was due to the inherent nature of the Islamist forces which gained power or to the international and regional responses to the revolution. Among the regional responses was the initiation of the Iran–Iraq War.

The experience with Islamist civil associations elsewhere in the Middle East, as regards their impact on democratization processes, has also been nuanced. Islamist movements have often been prominent in raising human rights issues and calling for democratic change. Sometimes, indeed, they have been more strident in pressing for democratic change than have non-religious political parties. Among those which have stressed democratic and human rights agendas have been the Tunisian al-Nahda movement led by Rashid al-Ghannushi, the Muslim Brotherhood in Egypt, the Islamic Salvation Front (FIS) in Algeria, the Movement for Justice and Development

Party in Morocco, the Islamic Justice and Development Party in Turkey (and its predecessor, the Welfare Party), the National Islamic Front in Sudan and the Muslim Brotherhood in Jordan. In some cases, such parties – most notably in Turkey, but also to some extent in Morocco and Jordan – have shown that they can operate effectively within a parliamentary setting. In so doing they have strengthened the democratic credentials of the political system. Yet there are also cases where the record is less positive. The Sudanese National Islamic Front (NIF), which operated effectively within the parliamentary system which existed in Sudan between 1986 and 1989, was the moving force behind the military coup which ended that liberal democratic experience and introduced a military-backed regime. The prominence in international Islamist circles of Hassan al-Turabi, the NIF leader, gave a particular significance to this experience. There are, moreover, Islamist movements which are explicitly opposed to liberal democracy (mostly those identifying with 'radical Islam'), or else promote an exclusionary version of democracy limited to parties accepting a particular interpretation of Islamic principle.

Socio-economic Dimensions of Civil Society in the Middle East

Literature on civil society tends to assume that socio-economic development relates positively to civil society: the higher the level of socio-economic development, the more likely it is that civil society will be well advanced.[33] This does not, however, provide a useful insight into the dynamics of civil society in the Middle East.

If socio-economic development is measured by the UNDP's Human Development Index a complex pattern emerges. The Index presents composite figures on human development in all countries, based on statistics which cover life expectancy at birth, adult literacy rate, enrolment in education, and GDP per capita. In the 2003 Index, based on figures from 2001, Israel gains the top ranking among the countries of the Middle East. It is ranked as 22 in the international order of best performance in human development. The Middle Eastern countries which follow, in order of good performance, can be grouped into three categories: the Gulf Arab oil-producing countries and Libya (Bahrain at 37,[34] Qatar 44, Kuwait 46, UAE 48, Libya 61, Saudi Arabia 73, Oman 79); the bulk of the remaining countries (Lebanon 83, Jordan 90, Tunisia 91, Turkey 96, Iran 106, Algeria 107, Syria 110, Egypt 120, and Morocco 126); and the three poorest countries (Sudan 138, Yemen 148, and Mauretania 154).[35] The position of Israel at the top of the list may suggest a link between socio-economic development and civil society, as Israel does have a strong civil society, with a wide range of civil associations which operate within a clear legal structure. The rest of the list, however, does not bear witness to any such linkage.

Even if only modern-sector civil associations are counted, no clear correlation between the level of socio-economic development and civil society activity emerges. Such associations have probably been as active in Yemen, and at times in Sudan, as they have been in the Gulf Arab oil-producing countries. Turkey, and to a lesser extent Egypt and Iran, despite being ranked relatively low in the overall index, have hosted significant numbers of active and powerful civil associations. The legal framework within which civil associations operate, moreover, is considerably stronger in Turkey and Egypt than it is, for example, in Saudi Arabia.

Two factors do seem to carry some significance. The first is population size. Those countries with substantial populations do tend to have the more active and powerful civil associations, Israel excepted. The critical factor here, presumably, is that civil associations require sufficient numbers of committed and like-minded people willing to exert their efforts in the field concerned. Egypt, Iran and Turkey, for example, have the largest populations in the region and some strong modern-sector civil associations. The populations of the Arab states of the Gulf are simply not sufficient to support these kinds of associations. Second, civil associations are most active in countries with a substantial manufacturing sector. The Middle Eastern countries whose manufactured exports account for more than 50 per cent of total exports are Israel (94 per cent), Lebanon (69 per cent), Jordan (66 per cent), Tunisia (77 per cent), Turkey (82 per cent), Morocco (64 per cent).[36] These tend to be the states where modern-sector civil associations are strongest, and where there is a legal framework to protect them.

State and Civil Society: Classifying Middle Eastern Countries

To identify the political dynamics which foster or discourage civil society in the Middle East it is necessary first to classify the countries concerned according to the character and strength of their civil societies. It should then be possible to examine what (if any) political characteristics are shared by the countries within each category.

The most fundamental factor used here to differentiate countries is whether the state concerned is willing to allow organizations critical of key aspects of government policy to operate. It is contended that the willingness to allow such organizations to operate indicates an acceptance of the limitations on governmental power, and an acknowledgement that the state must work together with civil society. Such willingness, moreover, needs to be backed by the civil associations having effective legal protection. It is contended that a willingness to allow such organizations to operate indicates a basic acceptance of the limited character of governmental power, and an acceptance that the state needs to work together with civil society. Usually the ability of opposition civil associations to operate freely does require a robust framework of law to protect them. A civil association linked to a powerful social grouping (perhaps a tribal confederation or religious movement), however, could enjoy effective protection through this alternative channel.

An assessment of the character and strength of civil society, paying particular attention to the freedom to operate civil associations critical of key aspects of government policy, is inevitably relativist. It depends on what aspects of government activity are regarded as 'key', and on the degree of freedom which the associations enjoy. This dimension of relativism, however, is an essential part of the picture: the assessment of the strength of civil society does depend on judgement. Even in western democratic systems civil associations operate within bounds.

The only Middle Eastern countries which are not covered in the classification which follows are Algeria, the Palestinian territories, Sudan and Mauritania. Instabilities and/or regime changes in those areas make it difficult to draw long-lasting conclusions.

Civil societies with civil associations which campaign against key elements of government policy exist

The Middle Eastern states which fall into this category are Israel, Jordan, Lebanon, Morocco and Turkey. All have a range of political parties, which operate within guaranteed legal frameworks. The parties have competed in elections which have been described as free by international observers, and some in each country have campaigned for governmental change. All of the countries mentioned also have a reasonable number of other civil associations, covering different spheres of social life. While there continue to be human rights abuses in all of these countries, the impact of this on civil associations is lessened by governmental measures aimed at restricting the abuse.

The above comments are not intended to suggest that any of the above countries mirror western democratic experience. Writers have pointed to the 'non-liberal representative democracy' in Israel,[37] the 'authoritarian secularism' which (at least until recently) existed in Turkey,[38] and the 'managed liberalisation' in Jordan.[39] Civil society, however, must not be seen as an all-or-nothing concept.

In the three categories of states which follow, civil associations critical of key government policies either do not exist or else operate under significant restriction and harassment.

Civil societies with civil society associations critical of key elements of government policy, but operating under heavy restriction

Egypt, Kuwait, Tunisia and Yemen all fall into this category. Civil associations critical of the government are under severe pressure from the government, denied legal status and perhaps being undermined through the creation of government-controlled organizations in the same field of activity. Leaders of such associations are subject to periodic arrest and imprisonment. Generalized human rights abuse exists, moreover, weakening the confidence of civil associations to pursue activities of which the state may disapprove. All of these countries, nonetheless, have a wide range of civil society associations in the social sphere.

In Egypt, Tunisia and Yemen the opposition political parties which exist are subject to government-instigated vote rigging at elections, and governmental attempts to discredit, divide or possibly co-opt them. This has been the experience of such parties as the Socialist Labour Party and the Progressive Unionist Patriotic Rally in Egypt, the Yemeni Socialist Party, and the Democratic Socialist Movement in Tunisia. Some political movements which appear to enjoy widespread support, moreover, are not allowed to register as parties or compete openly in the political system. Among these are the Muslim Brotherhood and the Communist Party in Egypt, those Yemeni political movements which had fought for separation in the 1994 civil war, and the al-Nahda party in Tunisia.[40]

In Kuwait no formal political parties compete in the parliamentary elections, but the informal political groupings which do compete are nonetheless well defined and protected by their linkage to significant groupings in Kuwaiti society. The informality of this system, the presence of traditionalist groupings owing loyalty to the ruling family, and the country's substantial resources which can be used to buy off discontent, have enabled the Kuwaiti government to avoid overt and harsh political measures against potential opponents. At times when political opposition has become substantial, the parliamentary system has been suspended (as in 1976 and 1986).[41]

In all four countries, strong civil associations exist in fields which do not impinge on government policy: self-help groups of many different kinds, associations with charitable purposes, literary and artistic societies etc. Chambers of commerce and industrial and financial pressure groups play significant roles. Associations which concern themselves with human rights issues, however, find themselves subject to the same restrictions and limitations as opposition political parties.

Civil societies with substantial civil associations, but in specific areas where the state permits such activity

The two main countries which fall into this bracket are Saudi Arabia and Iran. Both of them have, in different ways and to different extents, strong civil associations. These civil associations, however, only exist within closely defined spheres.

The case of Saudi Arabia raises a difficulty in determining what should count as civil society. The state was founded, and continues to be based, on an alliance between the temporal rulers (the Al Sa'ud) and the religious hierarchy which promotes the teaching of Muhammad 'Abd al-Wahhab. The religious hierarchy is clearly inter-twined with the state. Yet there are some respects in which the state is not the dominant side in this relationship. The great vitality of religious life in Saudi Arabia, and the extent to which large numbers of people take more heed of advice from religious leaders than of instructions from the government, means that religious leaders can and do limit and constrain governmental policy. The religious leaders closest to the state, moreover, are subject to pressure from others who have no dependence on the state. Pressure from below keeps the central religious leadership from betraying Wahhabist principles. The history of the third Saudi state (from 1902) bears witness to many incidents where governments have had to change or adapt policies in response to pressures from Islamic bodies within the country.[42]

Outside of the official religious hierarchy, moreover, there is in Saudi Arabia a large number of Islamic associations (charitable bodies, and groupings for the promotion of Islamic belief and practice within and outside the country), which depend on the spontaneous support and enthusiasm of the associations' members. Financial support may come from private individuals, Islamic banks and commercial undertakings. On occasion this informal religious sector has given rise to movements which have come into conflict with the government. During and after the First Gulf War, radical Islamists took a lead in mobilizing opinion against the presence of US troops in the country and calling for political reform. Some of the leaders of this grouping were imprisoned, while others fled into exile and organized politically from abroad.[43] Some Islamists moved outside the realm of civil society, aligning themselves with Usama bin Ladin and employ-ing violent means to change the situation within and outside the country.

In addition to the religious sphere of civil society in Saudi Arabia, there is also the tribal dimension. While tribal identity has become less significant over the years, it remains sufficiently strong to give tribal leaders an autonomous social role. They still need to be consulted and conciliated by the government, creating a constraint on governmental actions.

In Iran, the form of civil society organization is more modern, in so far as it involves political parties and associations based on economic, professional and social interests. Yet these organizations must all operate within the framework of the ideology of the Islamic revolution. Debates in the parliament, and the elections to parliament, have been marked by a seriousness of discussion and vitality of debate, which have been absent from many other parliaments of the region. Yet the candidature of all those who seek to contest parliamentary seats (at the time of writing) has to be approved by the Council of Guardians. Associations such as women's groups have been very successful in confronting the government on a wide range of issues, but such action can only be effectively pursued within the context of Islamic law.[44]

Countries with limited civil associations

Two different kinds of state exist within this category. The first comprises states which are antipathetic to the existence of civil associations outside of the control of the state – even where these pursue straightforward functional roles which have no political overtones. While this was a common pattern in the Middle East from the late 1950s to the early 1970s, the only countries which still retain this approach are Syria and Libya (and Iraq prior to the fall of the Ba'thist regime). Even in these countries, some civil associations do exist outside of the control of the state, typically religious charities and chambers of commerce. As noted above, the absence of independent civil associations does not imply an absence of popular organization. On the contrary, these countries (Ba'thist Syria and Iraq in particular) have strong organizations which purport to represent sections of the population, albeit under state control. Some of these organizations (such as the peasant and trade unions in Syria) may be sufficiently strong to survive a change of regime and establish an autonomous role in a subsequent regime.[45]

The second kind of state referred to here is the smaller oil-producing states of the Gulf, with the exception of Kuwait. Bahrain, Qatar, the United Arab Emirates and Oman do allow a reasonable array of civil associations to operate, especially in areas which do not concern political or human-rights issues. The small size of the local populations, the limited role that the foreign communities who form the majority of the population can play in social organization, and the nature of the rentier state (where populations look to government to solve their economic problems) ensures that civil associations enjoy small memberships and play a limited role. Chambers of Commerce and religious associations tend to be the most active elements in civil society.[46]

Explaining the Political Dynamics Underpinning Development towards Civil Society

On the basis of the above classification, one significant factor differentiating the political dynamics of those countries where civil society is relatively strong, from those where it is less strong, may be suggested. Civil society organization develops most effectively in political systems where those who exercise executive power are ultimately prepared to relinquish it. This generalization no doubt applies to non-Middle Eastern states also, but it will be contended here that it is of particular value in assessing the civil society prospects of Middle Eastern countries.

Preparedness to relinquish power is not equivalent to an acceptance of liberal democracy. To suggest that liberal democracy is a requirement for vibrant western-style civil society is certainly realistic. This does not, however, provide a useful indicator of how civil society can develop in a range of societies which do not conform to western democratic norms. The criterion of 'preparedness to relinquish power' can be used to identify those state systems which are most likely to foster civil society.

Those who exercise executive power, and who may fall from power, do not necessarily hold the ultimate political authority. The top-most political authority, thus, may lie elsewhere and may not itself be subject to removal – as is the case in the Jordanian and

Moroccan monarchies. It may in fact be the presence of a guarantor of the continuity of the state which makes possible some alternation in those who exercise executive power. A change in government will in this case not threaten the state's coherence or survival. A cabinet of ministers which knows that its tenure in government is limited will have an incentive to work with society, rather than against it.

The political systems in all of the states in the first category above allow for alternation of those in executive power. Some consideration will now be given to the factors which have made this possible in each case. In Israel, the state draws its strength from a perception of its political Zionist mission, catering for the interests of the international Jewish community as well as its own citizens. An open civil society, at least covering the Jewish parts of the population, is a requirement for such a mission, and the alternation of those in power is a necessary concomitant.

In Turkey, civil society has developed strongly within a system where the army acts as a guarantor of the secular Turkish state. Elections have been possible, political parties have operated, and those in power have been voted out of power. Historically, however, progress in this direction has depended on the military's confidence that the core character of the state would be retained. The Islamic Justice and Progress Party was able to come to power in Turkey in 2001 precisely because the previous governmental elite was confident that the army would prevent the new government from changing the nature of the Turkish state.

In Morocco and Jordan, the monarchs have, as suggested above, constituted the critical guarantors. A wide range of civil society associations (including political parties and organizations covering sensitive human rights concerns) have been able to operate. In both cases, however, a key distinction is made between criticism of the government, which is permitted, and criticism of the monarch, which is not.

In Lebanon, the dynamic comes more from an external guarantor. Syria, while not permitting pluralism at home, has effectively maintained a social and political pluralism within Lebanon. Prior to the civil war, the Lebanese state was overshadowed by the country's civil society – groupings based on confessional allegiances. It was, indeed, the inability of the state to control the clashes between these powerful groupings – increasingly operating outside of the penumbra of civil power – which laid the basis for the civil war. Since the Ta'if Agreement of 1992, which brought the civil war to an end, Syria has presided over a new balance in Lebanese society. Strong civil associations operate in an uneasy balance, constrained by Syria's overriding regional power.

The contrast with countries in the second category is instructive. In Egypt, Tunisia and Yemen, the presidents head the executive arm of government, and are directly involved in policy-making. In Kuwait, the role of prime minister is filled by a senior member of the ruling family. In all these cases, therefore, criticism of the government cannot be distinguished from criticism of the president or ruling family. There is no space between the highest political authority and those who exercise executive power. In all four cases, criticism of the governmental leadership automatically becomes criticism of the state leadership, leading on (if it is heavy enough) to political crisis. The room for civil associations critical of government policy is narrowed.

The prospects of strengthening civil societies in the Middle East, therefore, depend critically on the political structures in place. A focus on democracy may be less relevant than ensuring that processes are available whereby those exercising executive power can and will relinquish it.

NOTES

1   Owen, 'Rethinking the Civil Society Approach'. Also see Kumar, 'Civil Society: an Enquiry'; Bryant, 'Social Self-Organisation, Civility and Sociology'; and Hall, 'In Search of Civil Society', p. 3.
2   Bellin, 'Civil Society in Formation: Tunisia', p. 121.
3   Ibrahim, 'Civil Society and Prospects for Democratization', p. 28.
4   Esmail, 'Self, Society, Civility and Islam', p. 61.
5   Gellner, 'The Importance of Being Modular', p. 32.
6   Ibid., p. 33.
7   Ibid., p. 33.
8   Ibid., pp. 41–2.
9   Ibid., p. 42.
10 Ibid., p. 43.
11 Ibid., p. 43.
12 Ibid., p. 44.
13 Mardin, 'Civil Society in Islam', p. 278.
14 Ibid., p. 281.
15 Ibid., p. 279.
16 Ibid., p. 285.
17 Ibid., p. 286.
18 Ibid., p. 295.
19 Civil associations which campaign against abortion, for example, are advocating the restriction of a civil liberty, whether justified or not. Communist and fascist parties operating in liberal democracies, moreover, have sometimes advocated restricting the range of political competition.
20 The alternative to this would be to argue simply that civil society, given its western roots, should not be promoted outside of the western world. For such an approach see Seligman, *The Idea of Civil Society.*
21 See Al-Khalil, *Republic of Fear*, pp. 73–109.
22 Ibrahim, 'Civil Society and Prospects for Democratization', p. 30.
23 Ibid., pp. 30–1.
24 Ibid., p. 31.
25 Ibid., p. 32.
26 Ibid., pp. 36–7.
27 For a good description of how this operated in Syria, see Hinnebusch, Raymond, 'State, Civil Society and Political Change', pp. 220–3.
28 Opposition movements have clearly been very aware of this, as is shown by the large number of sophisticated web-sites offered by Middle Eastern political organizations. Islamist groupings have been particularly active in this. With regard to satellite television, the widespread viewing of channels such as Al-Jazira and Al-Arabiyyah (and to a lesser extent western channels) has forced the governmental media to be more open – if only so as to be able to deny allegations made by the opposition.
29 Ibrahim, 'Civil Society and Prospects for Democratization', p. 39.
30 The emphasis which Islamic thinkers, both classical and modern, have themselves placed on civil society is described well by Ahmed Moussali in his article 'Modern Islamic Fundamentalist Discourses', pp. 79–119.
31 Niblock, *Class and Power*, chs. 5 and 6. Also Lesch, 'The Destruction of Civil Society in the Sudan', pp. 154–9.

32 For a general perspective on the interactions between economic liberalization and civil society, see Kleinberg and Clark, *Economic Liberalization, Democratization and Civil Society in the Developing World* (Macmillan, Basingstoke, 2000).

33 Some useful perspectives on this can be found in Mouzelis, 'Modernity, Late Development and Civil Society', pp. 224–49.

34 Bahrain's high ranking is worthy of note. The contribution of oil exports to the Bahraini GNP is lower than that in any of the other countries in this category. The Human Development Index, therefore, does not simply reflect the advantages which flow from oil production. The inclusion of Libya in this category of countries with relatively high indices is also significant, given that the figures were based on data from 2001, when Libya had just emerged from eight years of UN sanctions.

35 United Nations Development Programme, pp. 241–4.

36 United Nations Development Programme, pp. 286–9.

37 Doron, 'Two Civil Societies and one State', p. 193.

38 Gole, 'Authoritarian Secularism and Islamist Politics', p. 20.

39 Brand, 'In the Beginning was the State: the Quest for Civil Society in Jordan', p. 184.

40 For the information on Egyptian, Tunisian and Yemeni parties see Carapico, *Civil Society in Yemen*, pp. 170–211; Bellin, 'Civil Society in Formation: Tunisia', pp. 120–47; and Al-Sayyid, 'A Civil Society in Egypt', pp. 269–94.

41 See Hicks and al-Najjar, 'The Utility of Tradition: Civil Society in Kuwait', pp. 186–213. Whether suspension remains a viable option in Kuwait is debatable. The 1991 Gulf War, and the western claim that the war was being fought, in part, to uphold the values of democracy, makes the United States sensitive to allegations of non-democratic practice in Kuwait. The government is thus subject to more significant external pressure than may exist elsewhere.

42 Niblock, *State, Society and Economy*, pp. 75–105.

43 Among the internal leaders who were imprisoned were Salman al-Auda, Safar al-Hawali and Nasir al-Omar. They remained in prison for some five years. Among those who left, and organized opposition from abroad, were Muhammad al-Mas'ari and Sa'd al-Faqih.

44 Kazemi, 'Civil Society and Iranian Politics', pp. 119–52.

45 Hinnebusch, 'State, Society and Political Change', pp. 214–42.

46 Crystal, J., 'Civil Society in the Arabian Gulf', in Norton, J. (ed.), vol. 2, pp. 259–86.

FURTHER READING

The two volumes edited by Augustus Richard Norton, under the title *Civil Society in the Middle East*, have played a particularly significant role in the development of studies in this field. They contribute substantially by their theoretical perspectives, but also through the country studies of individual states. Although published in 1996, the work retains much of its relevance today. A more recent (2002) collection, that edited by Amyn Sajoo and entitled *Civil Society in the Muslim World*, covers more of the critique which there has been about the application of civil society concepts to the Muslim world. Much of the emphasis of this work, however, is on areas outside of the Middle Eastern heartland. Among the book-length country studies of civil society have been M. Kamali's *Revolutionary Iran: Civil Society and the State in the Modernization Process*, and Sheila Carapico's *Civil Society in Yemen: The Political Economy of Activism in Modern Arabia*. The wider, and very extensive, literature on civil society in general provides insights which are of considerable importance to the Middle East. Among these, of particular note is John Keane's *Civil Society: Old Images, New Visions*.

CHAPTER TWENTY-SIX

The States-system in the Middle East
Origins, Development, and Prospects

SIMON BROMLEY

Introduction

Ever since the extension of the European states-system to the region and the development of industrial capitalism in north-west Europe, the identification of a group of countries as constituting the Middle East has been one made by powers *outside* the region; it has not, for the large part, been a term of identification used within it. As the historian Bernard Lewis has pointed out: '[u]nlike India, China or Europe, the Middle East has no collective identity. The pattern, from the earliest times to the present day, has been one of diversity – in religion, in language, in culture, and above all in self-perception' (1998, p.133). This may be an overstatement, but it does capture an important truth. Muslims have shared and contested the Middle East with Jews and Christians (to speak only of the major monotheisms); Arabs have coexisted with Persians, Turks, Kurds and Berbers (among others); and social identities have ranged from the religious, to the linguistic and ethnic, to the (national) territorial, to the secular political.

In the days of the British empire, the British referred to the 'Near East' as those countries that were strategically important in protecting the economic and military links to India and thence to the Far East – what are nowadays, Turkey, Iran, Egypt, Jordan, Palestine and Israel, Iraq, Lebanon, Syria, Saudi Arabia, Yemen and the Gulf States. In Arabic, the term Mashriq refers to the countries of the Arab East – that is, the British 'Near East' minus its two non-Arab but Islamic states, Turkey and Iran, and minus the Jewish state established in 1948, Israel – and the Maghrib refers to the Arab states of North Africa – Libya, Tunisia, Morocco, Algeria, and Mauritania. Nowadays, the dominant outside power in the region, the United States, defines the Middle East as part of south-west Asia for the purposes of geostrategic and military planning, a region spreading from the Arab east through Iran to Afghanistan, Pakistan and the largely Muslim successor states to the former Soviet Union in Central Asia.

Politically and developmentally speaking Israel is set apart from the rest of the region, but geopolitically its conflicts with the Palestinians and the wider Arab world (and, more recently, Iran) impact on both sides of that antagonism. Turkey and Iran, by contrast, share many development issues with the core Arab states, and the fortunes of the latter and Iran (as well as some of the Maghrib countries – Algeria and Libya) have been strongly conditioned by oil-based development. Politically and economically, the core regional interactions are among these states, and not with the wider west Asian or African Arab countries. Thus, in what follows, I will mainly concentrate on what the British used to call the Near East, although I will occasionally pay attention to the Maghrib as well. I will not, however, consider Israel, except where it impacts on developments in the surrounding region.

The unifying theme of the origins, development and prospects of the states-system in the Middle East is, I will argue, that of empire. The *origins* of the contemporary states-system in the Middle East are to be found in the geopolitical settlement that followed the conclusion of the First World War. That war was, inter alia, a conflict between rival European imperialisms; a geopolitical moment that saw the liquidation of the Tsarist, Austro-Hungarian and Ottoman empires as actors in the European geopolitical drama; and a turning point that foreshadowed the politics of anti-colonial, nationalist assertion in the non-European world. It was also a conflict that marked a shift in world politics from an era dominated by Europe and its empires to one in which the global rivalry between capitalism and communism, the United States and the Soviet Union, provided the dominant forcefield of international alignments. The post-colonial *development* of the Middle East was thus worked out in a context of retreating European imperial power and advancing superpower involvement. And it is against that backdrop that the politics – national, regional and international – of the newly independent states of the Middle East during the twentieth century have to be understood. Finally, now that communism no longer competes as a global, ideological rival to liberal-democratic capitalism, and in the wake of the dissolution of the Soviet Union as a global power, the United States holds sway over the *prospects* for the states-system in the Middle East as never before. The future development of Middle East states and their place in the states-system – both regional and global – will depend critically on relations with an international order in which the United States exercises unrivalled power.

In what follows, I begin by looking at the origins of the modern Middle East states-system, seeing this as the outcome of the internal collapse and external destruction of the Ottoman empire in the face of the economic and geopolitical competition generated by the development of industrial capitalism and national states in Europe. Looking at the states-system of the region today, it is easy to forget that before, during and even shortly after the First World War, the idea that the Ottoman empire, which nominally controlled most of the Middle East (excepting the interior of the Arabian peninsula and Iran), should or could be replaced by a set of independent states was treated with derision in the capitals of the major European powers. Nor did the idea of independent statehood make any more sense to the subject peoples of the Ottoman empire. It was only with the disintegration of the empire and the subsequent birth of *Turkish* reform nationalism in the years immediately before the First World War that a future for the Arab provinces outside the caliphate became thinkable.

In fact, it is only a small exaggeration to say that the victorious European allies in the First World War, the British and French, stumbled into creating a states-system in the region for want of a better alternative, not out of belief or design. As David Fromkin has argued, 'having destroyed the old order in the region, and having deployed troops, armoured cars, and military aircraft everywhere from Egypt to

Iraq, *British policy-makers imposed a settlement upon the Middle East in 1922 in which, for the most part, they themselves no longer believed'* (1991, p. 562). As we will see, there is much more to say than this, since social forces and political actors in the region also played an important role in these developments. But it is right to stress that, in so far as they shaped the politics and geopolitics of the region, the European powers did so for their own reasons with indecent haste and with little or no attention to the political realities on the ground.

After examining the origins of the states-system in the Middle East, I turn to a consideration of the main patterns of state formation and political development in the era of independence. State formations, and the subsequent patterns of political development, have been shaped by the social structure inherited at independence, international factors – deriving from the international economy and the role of outside powers – and the resources available to the state, especially oil and external military support. In considering the politics and geopolitics of the states-system in the Middle East I also look at the question of Middle East unity: Is there a (potential) unity to the states-system in the region given either by Islam or Arabism?

Finally, I briefly consider the prospects for states and the states-system in the Middle East. Following the end of the Cold War and the removal of the Soviet Union/Russia as a major external power in the region, the dominant issues are those of development – political and economic – in an increasingly interdependent world in which the United States exercises an immense influence. Can the states of the region, individually and collectively, muster the necessary legitimacy to pursue the kinds of reform needed for development? And what role will outside powers – above all, the United States – play in the future politics of the states-system in the Middle East?

The Making of the Modern Middle East

At the zenith of its power and wealth under the rule of Suleiman the Magnificent (1520–66), the Ottoman empire comprised most of what is now known as the Middle East (excepting the interior of the Arabian peninsula and Iran), virtually all of North Africa along the Mediterranean coast, Greece and Turkey, together with most of the Balkans, the Crimea, Georgia and Armenia. Around the same time, the Mughal empire was consolidated in India (1556–1606) and the Safavid empire was established in Iran (1587–1629). These Muslim empires found themselves in competition and conflict with the Christian empires of Europe as well as with one another. The Ottomans were regularly at war with European powers (including Russia), only finally being evicted from European geopolitical competition by defeat at Vienna in 1683. Shi'ite Persians and Sunni Turks fought repeatedly from the late sixteenth through to the mid-seventeenth centuries. As well as facing significant external challenges, the Muslim empires were confronted by internal peasant risings and bids for autonomy by local magnates. Indeed, as early as 1607, the English ambassador to the Ottoman empire remarked that the latter was 'in great decline, almost ruined', and internal order was only restored in the second half of the seventeenth century.

The Muslim empires were unable to compete with the power and wealth generated by the increasingly capitalist, industrial and national states of Europe. During the eighteenth and nineteenth centuries there was what amounted to a 'general crisis' of the Muslim empires (Bayly, 1989). The Mughal and Safavid empires were destroyed by 'tribal breakouts', India falling to outright colonial conquest by the British, while Persia maintained an uneasy independence in the face of Russian and British pressure. In Qajar Iran (1779–1924) central power was never restored, such that formal political independence coexisted with informal domination by Britain and Russia. Meanwhile, in the Ottoman domains the authority of the Porte was challenged by the rise of provincial rulers: military pashas in Egypt and Syria, *derebeys* (valley lords) in Anatolia, *ayans* (domestic notables) in Rumelia and *Wahhabi* tribal forces in Arabia.

At the Treaty of Kutchuk Kainardji (1774), the Russians established rights of protection over the Christian Holy places in the empire, the Porte's Orthodox Christian subjects and thus their considerable economic activities. The English had already established similar rights for their nationals and co-religionists in the seventeenth century. By these and other means, European powers exercised considerable influence within the empire. What was known in Europe as the Eastern Question (conventionally dated from 1774 to 1923) – i.e. the question of what would replace the Ottoman empire and how – was prompted by this internal enfeeblement of the Muslim empires, especially of the Ottoman domains, combined with the external pressures arising from the economic and geopolitical expansion of the European powers and their non-European empires. For as Tsar Nicholas said in 1853, Europe had a 'sick man, seriously ill ... on its hands': from this time on (if not before), the consensus of opinion among ruling circles in Europe 'was that Islam was hopelessly sterile and stationary, that its devotees had walled themselves up in a mental prison from which they could neither escape nor be rescued' (Kiernan, 1969, p. 140). Or, as Lord Clarendon put it: 'the only way to improve [the Ottomans], is to improve them off the face of the earth' (quoted in Kedourie, 1987, p. 15).

Thus, the context of the Eastern Question – and hence the pattern of state formation in the Middle East that followed – was given by the process of Ottoman decline on the one hand and the expansion of European capitalism on the other. But the fortunes of north-western Europe and the lands of the Porte were not simply uneven – embracing the dynamism of industrial capitalism and national states in the one and pre-capitalist stagnation and imperial rule in the other. They were also combined. The dynamics of capitalist and colonial expansion throughout the Muslim land empires in general, and in the Middle East in particular, were shaped by the general crises of these empires, and this expansion complemented the hold that capitalism had already established on the Atlantic seaboard. Equally, internal responses and attempts at reform within the Muslim world played an active role in shaping its pattern of incorporation into the world market and states-system dominated by the Europeans.

Malcolm Yapp has pointed out that what Europeans tended to see 'as an affair of diplomacy conducted in the chancelleries of Europe' – namely, the Eastern Question – was, in the Middle East, 'a bloody battle for land' (1987, p. 16). At the centre of this latter struggle was the means by which property relations and forms of rule in the Middle East were recomposed by, as well as incorporated into, the capitalist world market and states-system. For this long process of decline and incorporation was precisely the epoch in which, first, the distinction was forged between the 'developed' and the 'developing' world and, secondly, the capitalist world market and a small number of rapidly industrializing states established their global dominance. From this point onwards, political and economic development in the region was dependent in the sense that it occurred in conditions of subordination to the European world and its (American) offshoots.

In order to pursue these themes, the rest of this section will examine the nature of the Ottoman empire and the other parts of the Middle East prior to the major expansion of European power in the eighteenth and nineteenth centuries. Having established the broad contours of these societies, I turn to the expansion of European capitalism and states, and the internal responses in Turkey and Egypt. Against this background, I then look at the role of the 'peace-making' at the conclusion of the First World War in the formation of several key states.

State, economy and society in the Middle East

Before the advent of capitalist modernity and the era of independent states, broadly speaking three kinds of society were present in the Middle East: the Ottoman heartlands, areas dominated by tribal nomadism and the Safavid empire. To understand the differences between these and their implications for subsequent development, we need to note that in societies dominated by peasant agriculture (and greater or lesser elements of tribal nomadism) there have been a variety of ways by which ruling classes extracted an economic surplus in order to support their rule and luxury consumption. Broadly speaking, we can distinguish 'tributary' from 'feudal' arrangements. Under tributary arrangements, a centralized and unified state-class secured political–military rights to tax an independent peasantry, whereas feudalism involved a decentralized and fragmented landlord class extracting rents from a dependent peasantry.

The Ottoman empire exhibited marked tributary, rather than feudal, tendencies. Following the decline of the Persian rule of the Abbasid caliphate (750–1258), Arab tribes and Turkish cavalry established Seljuq rule in Iraq, Syria and Iran, and then confronted, and successfully contested, a declining Byzantium. Internally stagnating and stretched by war, Byzantium suffered a major defeat at the hands of the Seljuq Turks at Manzikert (1071) and called for assistance from the West. However, the counter-offensive launched from Vienna – involving the participation of the Franks, the Normans and the Italian city-states – failed, and the Ottoman armies inflicted crushing defeats on feudal Europe at Nicopolis (1396) and Varna (1444). Following repeated Mongol invasions, and after decades of cavalry warfare, the Osmanli sultanate consolidated its rule as Turkish armies went from strength to strength. Constantinople (Istanbul) fell in 1453, much of the Balkans followed, as did large swathes of the Middle East in the sixteenth century. Perhaps the most powerful empire of its time, under the rule of Suleiman, the Ottoman empire enjoyed revenues twice those of Charles V in the West.

The character of the Turkish conquests gave rise to a particular pattern of economic and political-military power, as Chris Wickham has pointed out:

> [much of the Islamic world] had one socio-political feature in common ... unlike in the Roman and Chinese empires, where a roughly homogeneous aristocratic class participated in the profits of both state and landlordship, in most of these 'Islamic' states a state class clearly stood in opposition to an aristocratic class of local landowners. There was certainly overlap, but the two were socially and often ethnically distinguishable, and frequently antagonistic in ideology, as well as their economic base. (1985, p. 176)

Indeed, in the Ottoman case a particularly pure form of tributary state and economy was consolidated between ca. 1280 and 1453. With the exception of *waqf* (or religious) lands, all land was the patrimony of the sultan. Both Islamic law and Ottoman practice classed land as belonging to the state (*miri*). Peasant families with rights of access and use to the land, organized into wider village communities, constituted the main units of production and consumption. Peasants farmed the land and paid taxes to the state. The sultan's 'household' – this was a form of patriarchal or patrimonial authority in which there was no separation between family and state authority – was staffed by ex-Christian 'slaves' taken as tribute and by the Islamic stratum of *sipahi* cavalry who were, in turn, urban-based and dependent on the *timars* (benefices) granted by the sultan in return for military service. (As the cavalry later gave way to a salaried army, so the benefices became tax farms.) The use of the term 'slave', used in relation to servile forces, in the Islamic world has often been misunderstood. The term 'was a loose one, denoting dependants with a total and exclusive loyalty; collectively they formed the ruler's "family" ' (Kiernan, 1980, p. 238); and 'the sultan's slaves ... commanded armies, governed provinces, and controlled the central administrations. Used of these ... such words as the Arabic *mamluk* and Turkish *kul*, though technically meaning "slave", carried a connotation not of enslavement or servility but of power and dominance' (Lewis, 1988, p. 65).

In contrast to the classic case of European feudalism, *timars* were neither heritable, nor did they bring rights of jurisdiction over the peasantry, and the revenues attached to them were set by the sultan's treasury. These arrangements pertained mostly in the empire's Anatolian (Turkish) and Rumelian (Balkan) core. In some other regions such as Egypt, Iraq and Arabia, there were no *timar* lands; instead these were garrisoned by janissary troops and paid taxes directly to the treasury. Profits from guild regulation of markets and customs dues also went to the urban-based intermediaries of the state.

But what was the social position and role of the Sunni *ulema*? Dating from the Abbasid period (750–1258), *madrasa* (theological and legal colleges), endowments and fees constituted the clergy as a major group of surplus takers and this enabled them to extend their functions to charity, education, justice and informal social and political leadership. The new Turkish conquerors, of nomadic stock and backed by slave armies, originally had little or no experience of sedentary agriculture and imperial administration. Thus the *ulema* were in a position to organize significant elements of society but they could not suppress banditry and parasitic disorder, while the new overlords could provide order but could not rule. The happy synthesis formed by this conjunction has been well summarized by Ira Lapidus:

> Faced with military elites unfamiliar with local traditions, the 'ulema' emerged, on the basis of religious prestige and educational and judicial authority as a new communal notability. The 'ulema' married into established merchant, administrative, and land-owning families, and merged with the older local elites to form a new upper class defined by religious qualifications. The 'ulema' assumed the functions as well as the status of the former elites. They took charge of local taxation, irrigation, judicial and police affairs, and often became scribes and officials in the Saljuq succession states ... While conquerors and regimes came and went, Islam became ever more firmly and widely entrenched as the basis of social and political order. (1988, pp. 176, 180)

Thus, it was the social distance between the tributary appropriation of the Turkish state class and the extant local nobility which allowed the consolidation of the religious classes. In the Ottoman case, imperial Turkish overlords, whether state officials or military personnel, resided in towns and lived off the land, often failing to learn the language of the local nobility and peasantry. As Max Weber pointed out, this meant that imperial rule relied on the tacit cooperation of urban forces, especially the merchants and the *ulema*. Like the *ulema*, merchants required overlords: to maintain order; to sustain networks of trade and finance; and, often, to be their largest customers. Over time, the imperial rule of the Ottomans established a high degree of state control over both the Sunni *ulema* and the merchants.

Formally speaking, the official corps of Sunni theologians, judges and teachers came to run parallel to the tributary structure. This religious hierarchy performed important administrative functions and filled the leading civil and judicial posts of the state. In the provinces, personnel recruited from the *ulema* formed the basis of administration. At the head of the *ulema* stood the *Sheikh-ul-Islam*, the supreme religious leader who interpreted the *shari'a* for the faithful. Islamic doctrine and law provided the ideology of the Osmanli empire.

However, there were areas that did not produce an agrarian surplus sufficient to resource urban-based, military power. This was the kind of social world described by Ibn Khaldun in *The Muqaddimah* (1377). In these regions, the tributary state was unable to control the rural areas, essentially because of the greater weight of pastoral nomadism with its mobile means of production, armed populations and absence of urban growth. Tribal pastoralism did not permit any significant material development or any lasting and widespread social stratification or political authority within the community. The tribal nobility was not reproduced by regulated intermarriage and it had no power to tax, control or command. In these regions, Islam was popular (Sufi), or folk Islam, focused on loyalty to the hierarchical authority established by religious leaders; it was less scriptural, less rule-bound and less egalitarian than orthodox Sunni Islam.

Finally, there was Shi'i Persia. The theological basis of the Shi'i *ulema*, originally articulated at a time when temporal political power resided with Sunni Muslims, lies in the notion that they are the collective deputies of the Occulted Imam (Momen, 1989). After the Safavid conquest of Iran, however, Shi'ism was proclaimed the religion of the state. The latter was composed of a tributary structure similar to that on Ottoman lands, though the control of the central state was weaker to the extent that its army was composed of tribal levies. This reflected the greater presence of tribal nomadism, and thus tribal organization, as well as effective landlord control, within post-Mongol Iran. While the empire lasted, the Shi'i *ulema* supported Safavid power against the Ottomans and the Safavids deferred to the *ulema* on a range of issues. Lapidus argues that by the late Safavid period, 'Shi'ism had duplicated the whole complex of religious sensibility already found within Sunnism. It thus became a comprehensive alternative vision of Islam' (1988, p. 299). Overall, especially in post-Safavid Iran (including the rule of the Qajars, 1779–1924), the Shi'i *ulema* constituted a powerful grouping of surplus takers that was able to establish a much greater degree of independence from central tributary structures than the Sunni *ulema* in Ottoman domains.

In sum, on the eve of incorporation in the capitalist world market and major geopolitical entanglements with European powers, it is possible to distinguish a range of different kinds of society in the Middle East, in each of which the articulation of Islam took its own distinctive form. The first of these was the core of the Ottoman empire, encamped in urban areas linked to sedentary agriculture, where Sunni Islam was geared towards the provision of administration and justice. The second consisted of those regions of the Ottoman domain where the centre's writ was more attenuated, either as a result of stronger tribal organization or because of logistical distance from the Anatolian core, where Islam largely meant Sufi orders or the folk Islam of tribes. And finally, there was Shi'i Persia (Iran), where a form of Islam doctrinally distinct from the Sunni mainstream played a variety of social roles in relation to shifting historical alignments of political power.

Before I turn to the expansion of European power and the incorporation of the Middle East into the capitalist world market and the European-dominated states-system, it is important to draw attention to two points that are important for what follows. In the first place, the economic system of the Ottoman and Safavid empires was relatively static. Any dynamic that the Ottoman empire possessed was based on perpetual military conquest: the Ottoman polity was a 'plunder machine' (Jones, 1981). Once external expansion was blocked, 'the natural tendency of the system', says Perry Anderson, 'was always to degenerate into parasitic tax-farming' (1974a, p. 500). Similarly, pastoral nomadism was by its very nature a relatively static form of social order. Even if tribal conflict precipitated the temporary emergence of a confederation, the paucity of the available surplus meant that state formation was unthinkable: rather than fighting wars, nomads pursued feuds. Where tribal cohesion survived it proved to be destructive of development as such, for in so far as nomads accumulated surpluses at all this was by means of parasitic plunder from sedentary agriculture or from the siphoning off of tribute from trade routes (Anderson, 1974b; Moghadam, 1988). This economic stagnation meant that incorporation into the world market occurred on highly unequal terms.

Second, notice that Islam, considered as a form of religious identification and symbolic culture, varied in its social location and institutional role. Sunni Islam equally buttressed Ottoman power and tended to the needs of the rural population. Shi'i doctrine seemed equally compatible with acephalous tribal organization, support for the Safavid tributary state and the independent organization of the *ulema* in post-Safavid Iran. As a set of institutions – the *ulema*, mosques, the *madrasa*, *shari'a* law and *qadi* justice – the role of Islam also varied depending on its relation to the state and social forces. In the urban centres of the Ottoman lands the Sunni *ulema* were organized in parallel to the tributary structure of the state; for the mass of the population 'folk' Islam, or in the Iranian case the Shi'ite *ulema*, were socially and materially independent of the state. To describe the Middle East in terms of Muslim societies is, therefore, of little help in analysing how Islam operated socially and institutionally.

Economic incorporation and internal reform

The growing economic presence of Europeans in the Middle East was accompanied by a formidable deployment of military power, especially after the creation of the 'second' British Empire following the Treaty of Paris (1763) and the Napoleonic invasion of Egypt (1798). Beginning with Mahmoud II (1809–33), the Porte responded to these challenges with a series of vigorous attempts at internal reform as forces within the Ottoman empire sought to overhaul its military and economic capabilities. Despite a number of reform initiatives – most notably during the Tanzimat era (1839–76) – the Ottomans were unable to resist the centrifugal forces from within and the growing pressure for change from without. The ambitions of Muhammad Ali in Egypt (1805–48) only compounded the fragmentation of Ottoman rule.

Even before the European encroachments of the eighteenth century, Ottoman power was fragmenting. Tax-farms were originally civilian and non-hereditary posts but by the late seventeenth century they began to develop their own armies and de facto control. This resulted in local conflicts between warring magnates. As Wickham argues, the struggle continued:

> with a continual struggle between state and notables as to how far private property law should be accepted, and whom it should benefit; but even the weakened (and commercially undermined) Ottoman state of the late nineteenth century could at least hold notables to a standoff until World War I ... Real local independence was ... only possible by usurping the powers of *central* government – and, in Muhammad Ali's Egypt, actually using them more effectively. (1985, p. 181)

Rulers in Turkey and Egypt sought to modernize their armies by adopting weaponry and tactics from the West and replacing mercenaries by conscripts, and this required increased taxes. The attempt to raise revenue by abolishing tax farming, appointing salaried officials and regularizing legal administration exacerbated conflicts between the central administration and local elites. As long as the centre held (in the Ottoman core until the First World War and in Egypt from 1805 to 1848), the resulting loss of local power – as what had become virtual fiefs were replaced by salaried officials – had the effect of drawing the state into a closer infrastructural role, strengthening rural security and thereby laying a basis for sustained economic progress. In Turkey military reorganization was a result of European pressure, whereas in Egypt it was motivated by a desire for independence from the Ottoman centre. In both cases, however, it was the need of the state for revenues which laid the grounds for the formation of a settled, agrarian capitalist class, rather than pressure from landed and commercial elements. In the Turkish case the central tributary apparatus remained strong and no real landed class emerged, but in Egypt a class of big landowners did develop, and they came to monopolize political power. The onerous loans contracted to finance modernization had the effect, secondly, of leading to growing financial penetration by the West. Before long the failure of the reforms to generate sufficient growth and revenue resulted in the bankruptcy of the state (1875 in Turkey and 1876 in Egypt), followed by the direct European supervision of the public finances. In the case of Egypt, European influence produced the Urabist revolt and this, combined with its strategic position vis-à-vis British routes to India, led to outright occupation by the British in 1882.

European economic influence in the Middle East expanded throughout the nineteenth century through: the imposition of free trade and the intrusion of foreign currencies; the development of consular or mixed courts administering European legal codes for their nationals operating commercially; foreign control over public revenue and expenditure, or direct occupation; and foreign merchants who came to control large parts of commerce and finance (and even some cotton production and export). Underpinning these forms of influence were the *capitulations* which had been traded by the Porte for diplomatic support. These latter take their name from the Latin, *capitula*, the chapter headings of the texts of commercial agreements between the Porte and foreign merchants. Originally struck at a time of Ottoman strength, these agreements allowed merchants a high degree of autonomy in the empire. However, as the balance of economic power shifted in Europe's favour, they became a powerful means of incorporation into the world market. While the Ottoman core continued to be dominated by peasant production and Turkish landlords, elsewhere there were dramatic changes. The result, as Charles Issawi has argued, was that:

> In Iraq and Syria the settlement of titles was carried out in conditions that transferred huge amounts of tribal and village lands to sheiks and other notables; in Egypt Muhammad Ali laid the basis of a large landlord class; and in North Africa a large proportion of the land was acquired, mainly by expropriation or chicanery, by European settlers. ... By 1914, Europeans held all the commanding heights of the economy except for land-ownership in the Middle East, and the minority groups [Greeks, Jews, Armenians, Syro-Lebanese Christians for example] occupied the middle and some of the lower slopes. (1982, pp. 4, 9)

So, as Roger Owen, concludes: 'In the course of the 19th century the Middle East was integrated, as a producer of primary products and market for manufactured goods and colonial produce, in the international network of trade' (1981, p. 29). Increased economic integration with Europe drove many indigenous manufacturers out of business and encouraged the expansion of cash crops. As a result, economic activity concentrated on the building of infrastructure and the provision of irrigation. In the case of the former, port cities formed major points of growth; as to the latter, the bulk of agricultural expansion was extensive in character. Most of the increased rural surplus did not feed back into further agricultural improvement. Rather, it was either consumed by or channelled into the emerging client–patron political activity of the urban notability.

The First World War and the formation of Middle East states

While the rivalries that provided the conditions for the First World War were first and foremost European, the Middle East played an important role in the global conflict. After the demonstration of Russian weakness in the war against Japan (1904–5), the French and the British forged the Entente Cordiale based upon reciprocal support in Morocco and Egypt, respectively. In 1907, Russia and Britain came to a similar deal in relation to Iran, Afghanistan and the Far East (this formed the Triple Entente), securing British interests in the Gulf. Once struck, these alliances set the framework for war. The crumbling authority of the Ottoman empire and the tensions thereby created in the Balkans provided the fuse: the Russians supported the Balkan League against Turkey and contested the role of Austria-Hungary; only Germany could guarantee the position of Austria-Hungary; the Franco-Russian alliance strengthened as German power increased; and Britain was threatened by German expansion. The fact that the Entente powers (above all Russia) constituted the greatest threat to the Ottomans and refused the empire an entente made it all but certain that the Turks would enter the conflict on the side of the Central Powers. The conduct of the war brought economic ruin to large parts of the empire and military attrition further eroded central control.

To understand what followed it is necessary to appreciate British war aims: to limit German power in Europe *and* to defend the British empire. This meant that while Germany was the adversary in Europe, Russia was a potential challenger in Asia. Yet Russia was for the moment an ally against Germany. How, then, could Germany be defeated without also bringing about an expansion of Russian power? It was originally in answer to this question that the importance of military operations in the Middle East was recognized. Lord Kitchener, whose entire career had been devoted to the military administration of the British empire and who had served in the Sudan, India and Egypt, argued that Russia had to be kept in the war until Germany was vanquished, and that afterwards the Muslim caliphate should be transferred to Arabia which Britain could then control with its naval power. The logic of Kitchener's overall strategy has been outlined by Fromkin thus:

> The War Minister's plan was for Britain to take possession of Alexandretta [now Iskenderum in Turkey], the great natural port on the Asian mainland opposite Cyprus, and to construct a railroad from it to the Mesopotamian provinces (now in Iraq), of which Britain would also take possession. It was generally believed (though not yet proven) that the Mesopotamian provinces contained large oil reserves which were deemed important by Churchill and the Admiralty. It was believed, too, by Kitchener and others, that the ancient Mesopotamian lands watered by the Tigris and the Euphrates rivers could be developed so as to produce agricultural riches; but in Kitchener's view the principal advantages of his proposal were strategic. The British railroad from the Mediterranean to the head of the Persian Gulf would enable troops to move to and from India rapidly. The broad swath of British-owned territory it would traverse would provide a shield for the Persian Gulf, as well as a road to India. (1991, pp. 140–1)

In view of these developments, Britain's aims came to include the removal of Ottoman claims to sovereignty over Cyprus and Egypt, an extension of its position in the south of Iran to include the neutral zone, and Iraq, together with support of it to the west, namely Palestine. France's main territorial claim was for Syria and Lebanon, where French colonialists identified themselves as the protectors of the Maronite community. During the war Anglo-French competition over territory and oil had been partly resolved through the Sykes–Picot Agreement of 1916 to divide the Arab provinces. Britain's positions in Iraq, Egypt, the Gulf, Arabia and Iran were kept off the agenda at Versailles, and Clemenceau and Lloyd George agreed that Palestine should come under British control. This left only the fate of Lebanon and Syria to be determined. A final settlement of Allied rivalries was made at the San Remo conference in 1920, where it was agreed that France would take Syria and Lebanon, that Britain would control Iraq, Transjordan and Palestine, and that Iraqi oil would be shared.

The other major Allied power, the United States, had only limited interests in the Middle East before the First World War. But in 1919 the State Department began to prosecute US interests with vigour, essentially because of oil. As William Stivers has shown, the US oil companies 'were in the vanguard of U.S. penetration into the Middle East' (1982, p. 110). However, the United States did not seek to supplant Anglo-French power. On the contrary, US 'jackal diplomacy' favoured the retention of European hegemony over the region. As Fromkin explains:

both the State Department and the oil companies were in favour of British hegemony in the area. The oil companies were prepared to engage in exploration, development, and production only in areas governed by what they regarded as stable and responsible regimes ... many officials ... expressed dismay at the thought that Britain and France might relinquish control of their Middle Eastern conquests, and ... expressed fear for the fate of American interests should they do so. (1991, p. 535)

The central question for the British was how to achieve their objectives at low cost. This became pressing as popular resistance soon threatened the British position. Uprisings took place in Egypt during the winter of 1918–19; Afghanistan revolted in the spring of 1919; Ibn Saud and Hussain crossed swords in Arabia from the spring of 1919; the Kemalist revolt in Turkey began in early 1920 and in the summer Greek forces invaded with British backing; Arab nationalists confronted French power in Syria in the spring and summer of 1920; and in the summer of 1920 there were tribal revolts in Iraq.

Iraq played a central role in British strategy for the Middle East because (together with Transjordan, Palestine and Egypt) it connected the eastern Mediterranean to the Gulf and hence to India. As well as being a key crossing for transport routes and having considerable capacity for food crop and cotton production, the control of northern Iraq was seen as essential for the control of the south, which in turn was necessary for the military defence of Anglo-Persian's oil fields in Iran. In addition, in time of war the Iraqi oil fields would be vital to naval power in the region. Accordingly, Britain wanted the oil-bearing region of Mosul to be incorporated into Iraq so that its revenues could finance the proposed Iraqi administration. France and the United States accepted, in return for shares in the new oil concession.

The solution (agreed under Churchill's leadership at the Cairo Conference in March 1921) was to install Faisal as head of an Arab government in Iraq, to deploy air power for the purposes of tribal pacification and to increase the subsidy paid to Ibn Saud in Arabia. In Iraq a client government was established in which the British maintained effective control over military, fiscal and judicial administration. The revitalized Turkish Petroleum Company operated the Mosul and Basra fields, now with US and French participation. The revenues from Mosul oil financed the state and tribal revolts were pacified by the vicious but low-cost use of air power. In October 1922 the Anglo-Iraqi Treaty largely replaced the Mandate, but these new arrangements still maintained British control over finance, administration and defence and foreign policy.

Something similar occurred in Egypt. This time a nationalist revolt in 1919 resulted in a reassessment of imperial strategy by the British. In February 1922 the protectorate was renounced, but control over defence and foreign policy, the security of the Suez Canal, the government of the Sudan and the future of the capitulations remained in British hands.

By 1914 Ottoman influence in Arabia had ended. Ibn Saud increased his power aided by British subsidy and weapons. However, the role of Hussain as ruler of the Hejaz and thus controller of the pilgrimage, and as head of the Hashemites (his sons Faisal and Abdullah ruled Iraq and Transjordan, respectively), constituted a threat to the authority of the Saudis. By 1924 Hussain had been defeated militarily by Ibn Saud and the Ikhwan. Thereafter, Ibn Saud signed the Treaty of Jedda with the British in 1927 and then used the provision of mechanized weaponry by the latter to suppress the Ikhwan. Founded on the Wahhabi–Saudi movement and alliance, the Kingdom of Saudi Arabia was thus established in 1932. Somewhat earlier, in 1899, what was to become Kuwait came under British control, as Britain agreed to become the patrons of the locally dominant al-Sabah family. This arrangement was formalized in the Anglo-Ottoman agreement of 1913. After the war, acting on 'behalf' of Kuwait, Sir Percy Cox managed to get Ibn Saud to abandon his claim for much of the Basra vilayet in what was now Iraq in return for a large part of Kuwaiti territory on the Gulf.

On the other shore of the Gulf, in Iran, things had evolved rather differently to events in the Ottoman lands. From the end of the eighteenth century, Iran was ruled by the Qajars, a noble class of Turkish tribal origin which had defeated the Zand dynasty of southern Iran. The central state was weak and the nobility was powerful. In 1906 a constitutional revolution took place. Largely confined to Tehran, the deadlock between the Qajar government and the Majlis was ended by the shah's coup in 1908. Acting against the liberal movement, Britain went along with Russian support for the shah. Then in July 1909 the constitutional forces were bolstered by the support of two provincial groups: the anti-landlord movement in Gilan, led by Caucassian revolutionaries, and the Bakhtiyari tribal nomads. Still no real government or state was consolidated. Finally, Russian troops intervened to end the constitutionalist experiment for good in 1911.

This fragmented society had been reduced to the status of a semi-colony by the incursions of Russia in the north and Britain in the south, including the flouting of its wartime neutrality. An arrangement had been formalized by the Anglo-Russian convention of 1907 'which divided Iran into three respective spheres of influence; Russian in the north, British – with the oil concession area – in the south, and neutral in the middle' (Halliday, 1974, p. 467). After the war Reza Khan's coup of 21 February 1921 laid the basis for a process of state formation. This was now supported by many forces because of fears of communism and for Iran's independence. After abolishing the Qajar dynasty, Reza Khan crowned himself Reza Pahlavi Shah in 1925.

Finally, what became of the core of the Ottoman empire itself? In 1908 the Young Turk movement of junior army officers and bureaucrats seized power. The Committee of Union and Progress finally ended the ensuing uncertainty in a coup of 23 January 1913. The CUP continued the Ottomanist formula for reform: a secular system of law and education, a liberal constitution, a strengthened army and administration and more emphasis on economic development. But given secessionist movements in the Balkans operating under the protection of Christian powers and dependent incorporation in the world market under the aegis of a non-Muslim bourgeoisie, the Turkish national movement assumed a dictatorial and Muslim-nationalist form, as Ottoman identity proved incapable of providing a unifying framework for programmes of renewal. Ottomanism had become simply the formula for disintegration, the Sunni *ulema* a bulwark of reaction. It was from this matrix that the Turkish Republic was forged by Mustafa Kemal after the war.

Immediately after the war the Allies were originally determined to maintain control of Turkey and to this end occupied Istanbul in March 1920. The new Soviet state began supporting Kemal in 1919 and renewed their commitment after deteriorating relations with the British in 1921. By the spring of 1922 the (British-backed) Greek forces had been routed. Kemal had emerged victorious in the civil war as early as the end of 1920. Nonetheless, it was to take until January 1921 for Mustafa Kemal to persuade the Grand National Assembly that sovereignty resided in the 'nation'.

The sultanate was abolished in November 1922 and Turkey became a republican state.

These, in brief outline, are the origins of some of the more important of the contemporary Middle East states. I now consider how this pattern of development and history of state formation influenced the politics of the region under more or less independent rule.

Political Independence, Modernization and Development

The sources for state formation in the Middle East – roughly summarized in Table 26.1 – have had a profound effect on subsequent patterns of political development. Strategies of political development in the states of the Middle East have reflected patterns of social structure inherited at independence, the role of international factors – deriving from the international economy and the role of outside powers – and the resources available to the state, especially the role of oil. While there are some common patterns of political development, especially in the more populous states, it is important to study the variations. These are related to a number of features, including most importantly: (1) the relation of the state to the landed classes, the peasantry and to tribes on the one hand, and to the European colonial powers on the other; (2) the relation of the post-independence state to the world market and states-system; (3) the impact of large oil rents on the path of political development; and (4) the social location of Islam within the broader pattern of change in these societies.

Based on these kinds of considerations, it is possible, broadly speaking, to identify three models of political development in the twentieth century (see Gerber, 1987; Bromley, 1994, 1997). There are, first, the revolutionary nationalist, socially modernizing and politically authoritarian regimes of Egypt, Iraq and Syria, which followed, in different circumstances, the import-substituting industrialization originally pursued by Turkey (and to a lesser extent Iran) in the years between the First and Second World Wars. These regimes all pursued state-led, national and protectionist models of development. All have been characterized by authoritarian political systems.

Within this broad category of authoritarian state-led development, there have been important variations. In the first place, different social structures and different relations to external powers characterized the Arab states (Egypt, Iraq and Syria), on the one hand, and Turkey and Iran, on the other. In the Arab states, urban-based landowners had large holdings alongside a dependent peasantry, while in Turkey and Iran land ownership was more dispersed and fragmented. Also, the Arab states experienced a greater degree of European colonial control and influence, and effective independence came later, after the Second World War. One result of this different social structure and history was that, while Turkey and Iran underwent essentially nationalist *coup d'états* directed against weakened tributary states and religious establishments, the Arab states experienced military-led 'revolutions from above' directed against domestic landed classes and foreign influence. And, second, some of these states – notably, Iraq and Iran – became major oil producers, especially after the 1960s and 1970s, while Turkey, Egypt and Syria did not. The development of the oil sector meant that the state could rely on externally generated rents to finance its own activities and as a source of foreign exchange for the national economy. This rentier model of development had a range of wider implications for the state and society as a whole.

Table 26.1 Formative influences on Middle East state formation

	Social structure	Role of external powers	Major oil producer
Turkey	Small- and medium-scale land-owning class; and merchant class	Independent of direct or indirect control of a European power; informal US influence after 1945	No
Iran	Small- and medium-scale land-owning class; nomadic tribes; strong urban merchants; and strong independent *ulema*	Indirect influence of Britain and Russia in nineteenth and twentieth centuries; informal US influence 1953–79	Yes
Egypt	Presence of strong, urban-based landowning and merchant class	Part of Ottoman empire in nineteenth century; British protectorate 1914–22; informal British influence until 1952; US influence after 1971	No, but significant rentier earnings after mid-1970s
Syria	Presence of strong, urban-based landowning and especially merchant class	Part of Ottoman empire in nineteenth century; French protectorate 1920–43, some autonomy from 1930; independent; allied to Soviet Union after early 1970s until 1991	No, but significant rentier earnings after mid-1970s
Iraq	Presence of strong, urban-based landowning and merchant class	Part of Ottoman empire in nineteenth century; British influence 1918–58; formally independent from 1932; allied to Soviet Union after early 1970s until 1991	Yes
Jordan	Small- and medium-scale land-owning class; merchant class; and nomadic tribes	Part of Ottoman empire in nineteenth century; British control; independent but informal British influence, 1922–58	No
Lebanon	Large Christian population, presence of urban merchant class; small- and medium-scale landowning class	Part of Ottoman empire in nineteenth century; French influence; protectorate 1920–43; independent; 1975 civil war followed by Syrian influence	No
Saudi Arabia	Nomadic tribal forms; trade-based merchants; powerful *ulema* allied to ruling family	Informal British influence in the nineteenth and early twentieth centuries; US influence after 1945	Yes
Kuwait	Strong, trade-based merchant class; tribes	Informal British influence in nineteenth century; 1899–1971 informal British influence; independent since 1961; US influence after 1971	Yes

The second model of political development characterized the small states such as Jordan and Lebanon, which lacked either large-scale land ownership or oil wealth, where the state played a more limited role in development, neither expropriating a land-owning class, nor controlling access to oil revenues, and a more pluralistic mobilization of resources and politics has been the result. Though neither state has established proper democratic rule on a stable basis, both have some experience of partial democracy, Jordan through a monarchical system and Lebanon by means of consociationalism.

And finally, there have been the pure 'rentier' states of Saudi Arabia and the Gulf States such as Kuwait, which lacked landed classes, indeed lacked any significant productive socio-economic forces, prior to the formation of the modern state, and developed almost solely based on oil rents and more or less direct external support. The limited social basis of these regimes and the fact that the state appropriates virtually all its resources from external sources has meant that there has been very little scope for the emergence of independent organization in either the economic or the political sphere. Ruling tribes have been turned into monarchies and authoritarian monarchical rule is the norm.

In Turkey, the powers of foreign and minority interests were broken by the Kemalist national movement. The absence of any significant landed class and the dependent position of the *ulema*, together with the absence of colonial rule, facilitated a rapid and successful consolidation of state power in the circumstances created by the First World War. Turkey was the first state in the region to undertake an active national, state-led model of development. It did so in a generally supportive international context: first, in the inter-war years, Turkey received diplomatic support from Britain as a barrier to Soviet influence, and the state-led development that began in the 1930s coincided with a more general drift towards economic autarchy; and, second, during the Cold War, Turkey benefited from economic and military assistance from the United States and its project of import-substituting industrialization was able to take advantage of the global economic upturn of the long-boom of the 1950s–70s.

By contrast, both the Egyptian (1952) and Iraqi (1958) revolutions were anti-imperialist in orientation, and were defined against the interests of the dominant imperialist powers in the region, Britain and the United States. Both states rejected strategic alliances with the west, maintained hostile relations with Israel, courted relations with the Soviet Union and attempted to play an independent role in the regional politics of the Arab world. Syria followed a similar path in many respects. Egypt was able to gain international assistance from both sides in the Cold War, but was economically disadvantaged by the events of 1956 – the nationalization of the Suez Canal and the subsequent Anglo-French and Israeli military operations against Egypt – and suffered a major political setback with the 1967 Arab–Israeli War and the subsequent ascendancy of the conservative oil states in the Gulf and Saudi Arabia. Egypt's hesitant economic liberalization in the 1970s, the *infitah* (opening), was undertaken before its import substitution had produced any genuine industrial deepening, and Egypt has thus far been unable to replicate Turkey's limited successes in this area. However, the turn to the West after 1973 did help Egypt to become a major recipient of US aid. Iraq's formative years, those of the rise of the Ba'th after 1968, were those of rapidly rising oil prices. These made significant additions to the resources available to the state and enabled the regime both to consolidate its repressive apparatus to an enormous degree and to become a major distributor of economic and social largesse. After the early 1970s, Iraq (like Syria also) allied itself with the Soviet Union.

After the initial consolidation of Ibn Saud's rule (in the late 1920s and early 1930s) with British backing, the external environment of Saudi development was determined by a pattern of integration into the world market through a single commodity, oil, and by an increasingly strong strategic alliance with the United States. Although not without tensions, this relationship was founded on common interests based on an exchange of oil for security, especially after 1967 and the political and military defeat of radical nationalist forces in the Arab world.

In Iran, after a coup in 1953, liberal nationalist and communist forces were weakened and placed on the defensive, and the power of the shah increased as a result of rising oil revenues and the economic, military and security assistance of the United States. This meant that, in marked contrast to the Egyptian and Iraqi cases, the programme of pre-emptive land reform and state-led industrialization was initiated from within the regime, was pro- rather than anti-imperialist; and during the attempted augmentation of state power under the shah in the 1960s and 1970s, Iran was the major regional ally of the United States along with Saudi Arabia.

The size and influence of oil and strategic rents differed widely across the states of the Middle East. Saudi Arabia and the Gulf States (Oman, Kuwait, Qatar, Bahrain, and the United Arab Emirates) lie at one end of the spectrum, with huge levels of oil reserves and production in comparison to their populations and the non-oil sectors of their economies. These are unambiguously rentier economies and rentier states, with oil incomes accounting for around two-thirds to three-quarters of GNP, and oil (as well as oil-financed overseas investments) providing virtually all of the states' revenues. At the other end of the spectrum lies Turkey, which has no oil, but nevertheless gains some rents from transit fees. In addition, Turkey derived significant strategic rents in the form of US aid because of its role in the Cold War and benefited from the post-war boom in Western Europe via workers' remittances, mainly from (West) Germany. Until the 1980s, Egypt had no petroleum production, and although oil and gas now provide a major source of foreign exchange, this does not make Egypt a rentier economy or state. But a high level of US assistance after 1973, aid from the Arab oil states, transit fees, earnings from the Suez Canal, tourism and workers' remittances have all made Egypt highly dependent on external sources of income for foreign exchange.

Iran, Iraq and Algeria are intermediate and more complex cases. According to Karshenas (1990), in Iran the share of oil revenues in total government income was about 50 per cent in the period 1963–7, rising to over 75 per cent in the period 1973–7. In the latter period, oil income accounted for slightly less than one-third of GNP and for between 80 and 90 per cent of its foreign exchange earnings. Thus while it is accurate to refer to a rentier state in Iran during the 1970s, this is not an accurate characterization of the Iranian *economy* as a whole, but rather of the latter's ability to generate foreign exchange. In Iraq, oil accounted for about 30 per cent of GNP prior to the 1973/4 price rises and this figure rose to over 60 per cent in the mid-1970s, with oil income already providing more than one-half of total state revenues in the mid-1960s. By the late 1970s, virtually all of Iraq's foreign exchange was earned by oil exports. This was also the case in Algeria (if one adds earning from exports of natural gas).

Where they existed, breaking the power of the notables – that is, the landed classes allied to the Western imperial powers – was a precondition for launching encompassing strategies of national development after independence. The absence of such a class in Turkey meant that state-led industrialization faced no such obstacles. In Egypt and Iraq, by contrast, 'land reform was the handmaiden of state-led industrialization strategies' (Richards and Waterbury, 1990, p. 151). Though unavowed, the Turkish model was the basic paradigm for these states. In the process, reformers expropriated their political enemies: the new professional middle class and military groups displaced the old order linked to foreign, external control over the economy and foreign policy. In Iran, land reform was pre-emptive and was not directed against foreign control since Iranian landlords had not aligned with the imperial powers. In marked contrast, in the oil-rich states of Saudi Arabia and the Gulf, oil provided the basis for a rather different path of socio-economic transformation, dependent on the West not just for the import of capital goods but for skilled labour power and security as well.

Against this background, some analysts have distinguished 'conservative' and 'radical' regimes based on the model of state-led development adopted (Richards and Waterbury, 1990). In the conservative, state-capitalist variant, the state seeks to mobilize resources and provide the infrastructure for capitalist development while transferring its own surpluses to the private sector – the cases of Turkey since 1950, Iran between 1963 and 1979, Egypt since 1973, Saudi Arabia in the 1980s and 1990s. A second type exists where the state retains the surpluses on its own operations, captures a large share of those in the remaining private sector and then attempts to secure for the state more or less complete control over resource mobilization, if not state control over all property – Turkey hesitantly in the 1930s, Egypt nominally after 1961, Iran for a while after the 1979 revolution, and Iraq from 1963 to 2003. It is worth noting that oil states are to be found in both camps, and the main impetus behind moves towards the radical variant appears to have had more to do with the degree of difficulty, and hence the level of social conflict involved, in consolidating state power than with the ideological orientation of, or the resources available to, the regime. In short, the radical model has been very largely a response to weak and contested political legitimacy. Where the processes of establishing the legitimacy of the state and the regime were protracted or violent, then the role of the state assumed a greater presence throughout society, including the economy.

Another distinction that is often drawn concerns the political form of the regime (see, especially, Ayubi, 1995). On the one side, there are the monarchies – such as Jordan, Saudi Arabia, the Gulf states, and Morocco. And on the other, there are the nominally republican systems of Syria, Egypt, Iraq and the like. Turkey is a restricted democracy (its scope limited by a military-dominated national security council) and Iran a clerical dictatorship with significant elements of popular participation. But, in practice, these distinctions count for less than might appear, and one certainly cannot conclude that the republican regimes are in some sense more developed than the monarchies – whatever their ideological proclamations to the contrary. The reason for this is that across the Arab Middle East – that is, Turkey and Iran aside – sectarian, tribal and family patrimonialism has 'blurred the distinction between monarchies and republics' (Hinnebusch, 2002, p. 12).

Finally, the social location of Islam varied widely. In Turkey, the Sunni *ulema* was highly dependent on the tributary power of the Ottoman state which it served, and it was also therefore bound up with the discrediting of that experience. This left it more or less defenceless against a militantly secularist pattern of social development. Not-withstanding the attempts by the military in the 1970s and 1980s to mobilize Islam against the secular left, Islamist forces remain under state control and do not pose a challenge to state power. In Egypt, the lack of any clear association between Islam and decline (imperialist control being a much more cogent target), in combination with the importance of Islam to Arabic culture, led to a weaker attack on the institutions of Islam, though here too religious institutions – of urban, Sunni Islam and of Sufi orders – were brought under state control. However, the autonomy allowed to Islamic organizations under Sadat (again as a means of combating the left), together with the absence of competitive, secular politics and the depth of the Egyptian economic crisis in the 1980s, produced organized Islamic forces which by building alternative forms of welfare and employment posed a serious challenge to state power in many regions during the 1990s. In Iraq, the ethnic and religious heterogeneity, combined with the minority status of the Sunni Arab elite, resulted in a strongly secular ideology of state development, stressing Arab nationalist ideology. Any op-position from religious forces has either been co-opted into the clientelist network of the state or faced savage repression. In Saudi Arabia, there is yet another pattern: modernization was *with* rather than *against* Islam, and this produced a traditional political order buttressed by the Sunni *ulema*. And finally, in Iran after the secular, nationalist rule of the shah, the independence of the Shi'ite *ulema* from the state, together with the depth of their penetration of social and material reproduction in the traditional economy and society, contributed to the Islamic character of the revolu-tion of 1979 and Khomeini's populism.

The search for legitimacy

Across the Middle East as a whole, socio-economic development was impressive in the 1960s and 1970s, thereafter falling off as the quick returns to domestic capital accumulation diminished, and as the worldwide economic slowdown, whose effects were delayed by the cushioning effects of oil rents, belatedly made its impact felt from the mid-1980s onwards. The early 1980s saw higher growth based on oil rents, but by the end of the decade war, falling real oil prices, rising debts and internal difficul-ties of public sector performance restricted the opportunities for growth. Outside of the oil sector, the overall performance was not impressive: the region was character-ized by rising food imports, as agricultural output failed to keep pace with population growth; and the manufacturing sector accounted for a mere 15 per cent of GNP by the mid-1980s, with the Middle East accounting for a small and declining share of world exports and foreign investment. The comparative economic performance of the Middle East in the 1990s continued to deteriorate.

Disappointing though the economic development of the region has been, it is arguably politics rather than economics that explains this state of affairs, for it can be argued that the single biggest problem for the states of the Middle East remains the difficulty of establishing durable and effective forms of political authority that are capable of commanding the mass loyalties of their populations and pursuing encom-passing strategies of social and economic transformation. At the time of writing, there is not a single state in the region that can be said to enjoy a settled legitimacy among its population, let alone secure guarantees of individual civil and political rights and democratic means of effecting a change in government.

There are at least three somewhat separate questions to unpack in this context. In the first place, the task of state formation, of constructing states that can make an effective claim to sovereign authority over their territories and establish the recognition of that claim by other, similarly constituted, states, has been a difficult and protracted process. Since independence, the states of the region have struggled not only to impose domestic authority but also to manage peaceful and cooperative relations with one another. While the levels of military control of domestic politics and of inter-state conflict were not substantially higher in the Middle East than in other regions of the developing world during the period from the 1950s to the 1970s, thereafter the fortunes of the region have steadily diverged from the limited trend towards greater civilian control of the state and more democratic politics in many other regions.

As oil revenues rose in the 1970s and 1980s, the share of military expenditure in GDP in the Middle East was very nearly twice that of the next most militarized region (the Warsaw Pact countries) and over three times the world average. Across the region, the exigencies of rapidly consolidating state power in a threatening inter-state environment, fostering industrialization from a subordinate position in the international division of labour and forging a social basis for the new, post-independence regimes all conspired to augment the power of the military within the state. Outside powers, especially the United States and, until the end of the Cold War, the Soviet Union, played a key facilitating role in this process. As Charles Tilly noted:

> With fair consistency, the US acted to protect Israel, to crack Arab unity, to foster oil-producing collaborators who would undercut OPEC unity, to sell American weapons to reliable clients, and in the process to establish the legitimacy of its own military presence in the Middle East. The United States did not act alone ... [Between 1960 and 1986] world-wide military expenditure, in constant dollars, rose about 40 percent, in the Middle East it sextupled; military expenditure rose less rapidly than national income in most of the world, but increased from 5.6 to an exhausting 18.1 percent of GNP in the Middle East. With help and encouragement from the United States, Israel pumped up its military expenditures from 2.9 to 19.2 percent of GNP, Saudi Arabia from 5.7 to 22.7 percent, Iran from 4.5 to 20 percent, Iraq from 8.7 to a debilitating 32 percent. (1991, p. 40)

It is important to notice, however, that this cannot be attributed solely or even primarily to the Arab–Israeli conflict. The biggest military spenders – Iran, Saudi Arabia and Iraq – are those with the most access to oil rents, not the so-called frontline states in the Arab–Israeli conflict, that is, Egypt, Jordan and Syria. Moreover, the largest conflicts in the region – measured either in human or economic terms – have been those between Iraq and Iran (1980–8) and those arising from intra-Arab and Arab–Western rivalries – Iraq-Kuwait–United States (1990–1, 2003). (With the exception of the war that founded the state of Israel, the Arab–Israeli wars have been relatively minor in terms of casualties and force deployments.) The crippling weight of the military in the political economy of the region is not only a massive dead-loss for economic and social development but it has also served to buttress an authoritarian, national security model of politics in even the most successful of countries such as Turkey and Egypt.

Secondly, even where the sovereign authority of the state has been established, where the stateness or statehood of the political system is reasonably secure, political regimes in the Middle East have displayed strong elements of what Linz and Stepan have called sultanism:

> In sultanism, the private and public are fused, there is a strong tendency toward familial power and dynastic succession, there is no distinction between a state career and personal service to the ruler, and, most of all, the ruler acts only according to his own unchecked discretion, with no larger, impersonal goals. (1996, p. 52)

To be sure, sultanism has been combined with more conventional forms of authoritarianism, and, in a few cases, with elements of democracy. Nevertheless, sultanism is an important feature of politics in the Middle East, and it has proved to be a significant obstacle to both political and socio-economic development. Regimes with a strong element of sultanism have proved to be prey to the idiosyncracies of rulers and their cliques, often beholden to narrow factional interests, and generally unresponsive to broad national interests in development. What is equally striking has been the limited movement away from sultanism and authoritarianism towards democracy – Turkey excepted. What Samuel Huntington (1991) described as the Third Wave of democratization, beginning in southern Europe in the mid-1970s before spreading to Latin America and parts of southeast Asia and thence to the former communist world, has had very little impact on the Middle East (Bromley, 1997). In fact, there is not a single state in the region that could be classified, without substantial qualification, as democratic on any reasonable definition of that much-contested term.

Turkey is something of an exception to this generalization and there have been some recent interesting movements of reform in Iran as well. Since the military coup of 1980, Turkey has held regular elections, though certain parties and politicians have been banned from participation and the military retain an effective veto over the political process, including helping to bring down a democratically elected government in 1997. However, Turkey's desire for membership of the European Union (alongside internal struggles for human rights and democratic reforms) has improved the prospects for democratic government. In Iran, a young and increasingly articulate population coexists with an elderly (male) clerical oligarchy and the political system is divided between an elected component and a self-perpetuating religious elite, with the latter currently controlling the key aspects of state power.

And, thirdly, the fact that the states of the region have been not only authoritarian but also, to a greater or lesser extent, sultanistic, has meant that they have displayed only limited developmental tendencies. Notwithstanding impressive contributions to the development of physical and social infrastructure and, in some cases, significant resource mobilization for capital accumulation, no state in the region has approximated the developmental achievements of East Asia (Issawi, 1995). Turkey, Egypt and Iran all have significant achievements to their credit in specific sectors and in some periods of their development but not even these countries begin to compare with the likes of South Korea and Taiwan, or even with Malaysia and Thailand among more recent developers.

The reasons for these problems of state formation, and of arbitrary and unresponsive regimes, remain the subject of sharp disagreement among analysts of Middle East political economy. A recent report from the Arab Fund for Economic and Social Development argued that:

the region [that is, the Arab Middle East] is hampered by three key deficits that can be considered defining features:

- the freedom deficit;
- the women's empowerment deficit;
- the human capabilities/knowledge deficit relative to income. (UNDP, 2002, p. 27)

There is widespread agreement that modern states operating according to norms of democratic politics, albeit sensitive to the religious sensibilities of their peoples; that regimes committed to a degree of social inclusiveness, especially in relation to gender; that government responsiveness to the aspirations of their populations, especially their political demands; and that encompassing models of development geared to systematic and credible economic reform and a determined attempt to develop human resources and the conditions for sustainable livelihoods – that all of these have been relatively absent. Turkey and Iran fare better in these areas but neither is a secure, stable democracy and both face considerable challenges in developing the capabilities of their people.

The regional states-system: unity or rivalry?

The most common candidate for the regional identity of the Middle East is, of course, Islam. Even if one limits the region to its Arab states, the cultural core of Arabic civilization apart from the language is still Islam. Prior to the Renaissance, the Reformation and the scientific and technological revolution of the seventeenth century in Europe, Islamic civilization had some claim to be 'the greatest, most advanced, and most open civilization in human history' (Lewis, 2002, p. 159). How, then, can we account for what Bernard Lewis has called the 'eclipse' of this once great civilization? Why has it apparently had such great difficulty accommodating to the demands of a modern world that has been made global by the power and example of the west? This is not the place to review the complex history of interaction between the Islamic societies of the Middle East and the forces and institutions of modernity but it is worth noting a surprising convergence of opinion amongst analysts both inside and outside the region.

Written by Arab and Muslim scholars, the Report of the Arab Fund for Economic and Social Development quoted above essentially argues that the root cause of the region's relative lack of development has been a multifaceted denial of freedom and a failure to address the individual and collective prerequisites of resources and opportunities needed to expand human capabilities. Drawing on Amartya Sen's *Development As Freedom* (1999), the Report argues that freedoms are not only important in their own right but also because of their instrumental value in promoting development. Similarly, the historian Bernard Lewis concludes his discussion of *What Went Wrong?*, by saying:

it is precisely the lack of freedom – freedom of the mind from constraint and indoctrination, to question and inquire and speak; freedom of the economy from corrupt and pervasive mismanagement; freedom of women from male oppression; freedom of citizens from tyranny – that underlies so many of the troubles of the Muslim world. (2002, p. 159).

Where the authors of the Report and historians such as Lewis part company is in their assessment of the causes of this pervasive lack of freedom, since for the latter it is precisely what unites the Middle East and once made it such a great civilization that now accounts for its misfortunes. To invert a well-known slogan of Islamist political groupings ('Islam is the way'), for Lewis, Islam has become the problem.

Thus, Bernard Lewis argues that Islam has failed to follow the path of secularization pioneered in the west. This involved two transformations: first, faith became a matter of private, not public, belief, such that *public identity* became predominantly *national*, not religious; and second, the source of political authority, the basis of *sovereignty*, was transferred from God to *the people*. According to Lewis, 'both of these ideas were alien to Islam, but in the course of the nineteenth century they became more familiar, and in the twentieth they became dominant among the Westernized intelligentsia who, for a while, ruled many if not most Muslim states' (2002, p. 106). Secularism in the Middle East thus meant not a separation of religion and the state and a privatization of religious belief, but, rather, an attempt by modernizing states to control the political expression of religion. On this account, the problems of political development stem primarily from the difficulty of establishing the national state as the primary focus of political loyalty and identity in competition with Islamic loyalties and identities. The modern politics of the Middle East has been, according to a similar analysis produced by Elie Kedourie, a 'tormented endeavour to discard the old ways' (1992, p. 346).

If one asks why Islam has presented such an obstacle to the construction of secular, popular forms of national loyalty and identity, the answer, according to Lewis, is that, unlike Christianity, Islam represents a *fusion* of religious and political authority; it provides the basis for an extensive politico-legal order as well as a moral code (see also Lewis, 2003). Lewis illustrates this as follows: Christianity teaches its followers what is right and wrong, good and evil, but the Qur'an enjoins believers to '*command* good and *forbid* evil' (my emphasis). That is to say, there is no equivalent in Islam to Christ's teaching to 'render unto Caesar what is Caesar's'. Moreover:

> Islam is not so much a matter of orthodoxy as of orthopraxy ... What Islam has generally asked of its believers is not textual accuracy in belief, but loyalty to the community and its constituted leader ... [Islam establishes a] boundary – not between orthodoxy and heterodoxy, which is relatively unimportant, but between Islam and apostasy ... And apostasy, according to all schools of Muslim jurisprudence, is a capital offence. (1998, p. 126).

Others have argued that what a given religion amounts to politically speaking is socially contingent on the contexts in which it operates and the interests that it expresses; and that, while the lexicon and idiom of politics in the Middle East is often 'Islamic', it can be understood in essentially secular terms (Zubaida, 1993 and 2003). On this account, it is *the context of authoritarian politics* – explicable in terms of such factors as the presence of rentier states, arbitrary colonial state formation, inter-state conflict and the like – *that produces authoritarian and patriarchal interpretations of Islam*. But whatever the reason, it remains the case that secular political power, which derives its authority from a nationally defined people, and which is oriented towards regulating a complex modern society based on open inquiry and high levels of personal freedom, is a standing challenge to the currently dominant interpretations of Islam and, in particular, to the demand for rule according to Islamic law, the *shari'a*.

In Iran, the secular project was pursued so vehemently under the shah (1953–79) that it provoked an event unique in modern history, that is, a social revolution carried out under the leadership of religious forces, resulting in the construction of a hybrid revolutionary and theocratic regime. And in Turkey, the paradigm example of 'secularism' in the Middle East, the country whose political and economic development has most closely sought to emulate that of the west, there has been a gradual reassertion of the role of Islam in public life, notwithstanding the role of the armed forces as the self-appointed guardians of a secular constitution. In Algeria, religious-political opposition to the nominally secular and socialist regime that gained independence from France has resulted in a violent civil war. In Saudi Arabia, the monarchical regime of the House of Saud has relied on religious support to legitimate its rule but now faces religiously inspired challenges to its legitimacy. In Syria and Egypt, secular regimes, backed by the armed forces, remain in power but they face considerable, if varying, degrees of domestic opposition. Until the second US-led war against Iraq in 2003, Iraq was also a secular, military regime. Viewing these and similar developments, authors such as Lewis and Kedourie reckon that the project of state secularism has failed.

The result of that failure, they argue, is a general spread of pan-Islamic challenges to the authority of particular states and regimes. Analysing the significance of this challenge is complicated by the fact that many regimes have used state-controlled religion as an ideological weapon, especially against the secular left – communists and liberals. The result, as Lewis says, is that there are two sorts of pan-Islamic politics:

> One is political in inspiration, sometimes diplomatic in method, and usually conservative in policy. The other is popular, usually radical, often subversive. Both at times enjoy governmental support, the one by patriarchal, the other by revolutionary regimes. Both also receive significant financial support from private individuals, mainly in Arabia and the Gulf, who combine new wealth with old aspirations. There is of course no clear differentiation, since governments try to exploit popular movements elsewhere, while popular movements seek to influence or even control government. (1998, p. 143)

But if the analyses of Lewis and Kedourie are correct, if the fusion of religion and politics, of faith and power, in Islam is fundamentally inimical to the forms of modern freedom that are essential to contemporary political and economic development, then any unity founded on Islamic principles is unlikely to offer the region much hope. Even if Sami Zubaida and others are correct to insist that how Islam is interpreted in the political field is contested and depends upon context and interests, rather than texts, the currently dominant forms of Islam are repressive and backward-looking. In any case, such pan-Islamic unity as there is has, thus far, been primarily informal rather than formal, and lacking in institutionalization rather than organized.

In reality, such organization of regional cooperation for development as there is – and it must be said that it is extremely limited – has been pan-Arab, not pan-Islamic. (After all, a majority of the world's Muslims do not live in the Middle East.) Among the Arab countries of the Middle East, a common language and culture might form a basis for integration. And, at the level of the movement of people and ideas, this is undoubtedly true. Moreover, pan-Arabism has played an important ideological role both within particular Arab countries and as an ideology of inter-state manoeuvre. But it is a mistake to posit an Arab identity in opposition to other national forms of identification. Arab nationalist movements have in fact been *weakest* in those places with the most *homogeneous* Arab populations – Egypt and Saudi Arabia – and *strongest among minorities in the ethnically and religiously most heterogeneous states* – Syria and Iraq.

Nevertheless, there are a number of Arab organizations, usually under the auspices of the Arab League, which was founded in 1945 in the days when pan-Arab aspirations were real competitors to the weakly developed national loyalties of the newly emerging states. The Arab League has a Council and General Secretariat and there is a Council of Joint Arab Defence as well as an Economic and Social Council. These councils meet to coordinate policies; to propose common projects; to reach unified Arab positions in international negotiations (for example, on conventions on the environment, human rights); and to discuss candidates as Arab representatives in important international institutions such as the United Nations Security Council and other UN organizations. The annual Summit of Arab heads of state has also become an institutional feature denoting a potential drive for closer economic and cultural ties (Choueiri, 2000, pp. 107–8).

But all of this has produced very little, if any, change on the ground in terms of economic integration and political unity. Inter-Arab trade accounts for 7–10 per cent of total Arab trade, and this figure has not changed since the 1950s. Foreign investment originating in Arab countries goes overwhelmingly to the high-income industrial countries. Politically, Arab states have failed to take unified positions on matters of international concern, even on the Arab–Israeli conflict. As the Report of the Arab Fund for Economic and Social Development lamented, 'Arab countries continue to face the outside world and the challenges posed by the region itself, individually and alone' (UNDP, 2002, p. 121).

Taking a somewhat wider focus and including Turkey and Iran in the Middle East region does not improve the picture. Iran and Turkey are not members of any of the Arab regional organizations (though Turkey is part of the EU–Med initiative) and Turkey is, in fact, more closely linked to the west than to the rest of the Middle East. It is a long-standing and important member of the west's principal military organization, the North Atlantic Treaty Organization (NATO), and a member of the Organization for Economic Cooperation and Development, an organization whose members include mainly the high-income industrialized countries. Despite significant elements of a common Islamic culture, Iran is divided from the Arab world by language, by doctrinal differences within Islam – the majority of Iranian Muslims are Shi'a whereas the majority in the Arab world are Sunni – and, above all, by geopolitical differences over the strategic management of the Gulf and by political differences since the rise to power of a revolutionary Islamic regime in Tehran in 1979. Moreover, both Turkey and Iran see their futures as much in relation to future developments in Central Asia as in connection to the Middle East.

The Prospects for Middle East States in the Global Order

Considered as a region, the Middle East does not act with one voice in the world of international politics, though individual countries play a role on particular issues. The most important way in which the region's development impacts on the global agenda is through the political economy of oil. The Middle East is home to around 65–70 per cent of the world's oil reserves and thus constitutes a vital interest for the

THE STATES-SYSTEM IN THE MIDDLE EAST

high-income industrialized countries and rapidly industrializing countries such as China and India. Middle East states form the core of the Organization of Petroleum Exporting Countries, the body that attempts to control levels of oil output in relation to market demand in order to maximize their long-run revenues. On occasion (in 1973/4 and again in the late 1970s), OPEC has been in conflict with the major oil-importing countries over the price and security of supply of oil. And many oil-producing countries in the region are reluctant to open their oil sectors fully to Western companies and competitive pressures. Most states regard the control established after the nationalization of Western companies in the 1970s as a form of economic sovereignty to be safeguarded.

The dominance of oil in the region's political economy affects not only the oil-producing states. This is so for two reasons. First, to a limited but still significant extent the rents of the oil states have been recycled to the non-oil Arab states through the remittances of migrant workers, through transit fees for pipelines and shipments and through aid. Second, because of oil the region has assumed a wider geopolitical significance in international politics and is thus the recipient of very large location, or strategic, rents in the form of aid and military assistance. Hazem Beblawi thus concluded that

> the oil phenomenon has cut across the whole of the Arab world, oil rich and oil poor. Arab oil states have played a major role in propagating a new pattern of behaviour, i.e. the rentier pattern ... The impact of oil has been so pre-eminent that it is not unrealistic to refer to the present era of Arab history as the oil era, where the oil disease has contaminated all of the Arab world. (1990, p. 98)

Similar arguments were advanced in relation to Pahlavi Iran during the 1960s and 1970s and apply equally to the regime that has been in power since the revolution of 1979.

In addition to the specific features of rentier economies and states – that is, economies where the national income or the generation of foreign exchange is dominated by oil rents and states where the bulk of the revenue derives from oil – the presence of oil in the Middle East has had two further effects. It has attracted the interests of outside powers, and with them the provision of support for friendly regimes. And the regional role of the United States in particular has served to contain or frustrate radical movements in the region that might have threatened the west's access to oil on favourable terms. Defence of the *status quo*, in which the distribution of oil reserves in relation to population (particularly marked in Saudi Arabia and the Gulf states) favours the west and in which no power – regional or other – is in a position to oppose US policies of openness to the world market, has been the main aim of US foreign policy in the region. At the same time, the threats to these arrangements posed by radical nationalist forces (Nasser's Egypt in the 1950s and 1960s, Saddam's Iraq until 2003, and Khomeini's Iran in the 1980s and 1990s) have resulted in equally solid support for Israel. In turn, the continued reproduction of the Arab–Israeli conflict and the availability of rentier incomes have conspired to make the Middle East the most armed region of the world, and has thereby bolstered the presence of military and authoritarian forces in the region's polities. Whether the second US-led war against Iraq of 2003 proves to be a turning point, or simply a repetition, in this vicious cycle remains to be seen.

Oil aside, the most extensive linkage of the regional to wider global agendas is through the European Union's 'Euro-Mediterranean Partnership Initiative' and Turkey's longstanding commercial agreements, including a customs union, with the EU. Turkey aims for membership of the EU and the formal position is that this remains a long-run potential, but there is considerable doubt within the Union – openly expressed in Greece, Germany, France and Italy – that it could ever qualify for accession. And even if Turkey did meet the objective criteria for membership, many still doubt that it could join, partly because its size would imply a considerable shift of power within the governance of the EU and partly on the grounds that culturally speaking Turkey is not a European country. The United States has consistently maintained that Turkey should become a member of the EU, in order to bind it firmly into the Western political and economic camp. Turkey's role in Central Asia after the Cold War is, as far as the United States is concerned, an important balance to Iranian and Russian influence as well as a southern anchor for NATO.

At the same time, the European Union has pursued an ambitious regional cooperation agreement – centred on the creation of a free-trade area between the EU and the Mediterranean countries running from Morocco to Turkey – since the EU–Med summit in Barcelona in 1995. It embraces twelve Mediterranean countries: Algeria, Cyprus, Egypt, Israel, Jordan, Lebanon, Malta, Morocco, Syria, Tunisia, Turkey and the Palestinian territories. The agenda extends beyond economic relations and includes measures to enhance regional security and the strengthening of cultural and educational ties. The core, however, is the drive for freer trade and investment links and this requires the EU to negotiate separate accession agreements with the twelve Mediterranean states and for the latter to negotiate similar arrangements with one another. In 2001, for example, the EU signed a 'Partnership Agreement' aimed at freeing trade (with significant exceptions in the agricultural sector) with Egypt, which in turn had concluded agreements with Lebanon, Syria, Morocco, Tunisia, Libya, Iraq and Jordan. While the original grand scheme of an EU–Mediterranean free trade area is unlikely to be realized any time soon, it has served to institutionalize a degree of cooperation on trade and aspects of development. To this end, the process also established biennial summits to monitor progress.

The United States has voiced its concerns that the EU–Mediterranean initiative should not operate at the expense of other countries and in 1999 formally served notice that it would not relinquish commercial opportunities to the EU or others. Given that the EU aims to make its agreements WTO/GATT compatible, this is unlikely to involve significant conflict (except perhaps over agriculture) as both the EU and the US are pushing for freer trade and investment in the region. Indeed, immediately after the second US-led war against Iraq in 2003, President Bush announced a proposal for a free-trade agreement between the Middle East and the United States and committed to assisting the states of the region to join the WTO process. To be sure, the process is immeasurably complicated by the wider Middle East 'Peace Process', in which the United States, Russia and the United Nations also have a role to play alongside the EU.

Thus far, as we have seen, the states of the region have been unable to establish sufficient domestic legitimacy and sufficient trust in one another to reduce levels of inter-state rivalry, and this has limited projects of regional integration. In turn, this has resulted in the countries of the region responding to global political agendas largely on their own, independently of coordinated regional initiatives. Such limited regional coordination as there has been has largely been imposed by external actors, such as the European Union through its Mediterranean initiative. More encompassing organizations or policies of regional economic and political cooperation have not yet taken root in the Middle East, thereby limiting the bargaining power of the region's states in international diplomacy and negotiations.

The Middle East is in many respects an artificial region. It lacks a clear cultural or political identity, and the levels of economic integration within it are very low. Every country in the region relates much more to the world outside the region than it does to its neighbours. The region has been unable to organize its affairs and define its voice in terms of a single, or even a dominant, inter-governmental organization. There are, at root, two reasons for this. First, the states of the region and the regimes that preside over them have, for reasons of colonial history and for reasons of the authoritarian political consequences of oil-based development, had great difficulty in establishing legitimacy. Rule has been authoritarian, often capricious and, above all, ineffective in securing broad-based socio-economic development. Inter-state rivalries and conflicts, which in turn distort developmental priorities, are, to a very considerable extent, a function of these underlying domestic insecurities. And, second, mainly because of oil and partly because of Israel, the region attracts the attention and intervention of the major powers, above all the United States. For complex (and sometimes unintended) reasons, Western strategy has historically contributed substantially to reinforcing authoritarian rule and to exacerbating levels of militarization in the region.

Taken together, domestic insecurities and external intervention, the problems of state formation and regime legitimacy, and of oil-based political and military aggrandizement of the state, have produced regional rivalries rather than integration. The strategy of the Bush administration that has gradually unfolded since the events of September 11, 2001, and especially in the wake of the war against Iraq in 2003 and the tentative renewal of the Israel–Palestine 'Peace Process', is presented as a bold attempt to break decisively with this pattern of development. Whether that is what the United States has in mind for the region – and it now enjoys a degree of influence unparalleled since the days of European colonial control – remains to be seen as do the prospects for success of any project to reorder the region from the outside.

If the United States is seriously committed to a politics of regime building in Iraq, and if this can be accomplished on a representative and inclusive basis, the impact on other states in the region might be dramatic. Immediately after the end of the war against Iraq, opposition groups and advocates of reform in Syria and Iran were arguing that the only way of confronting the new-found US power in the region was by means of internal reform. Similar pressures are bound to spread to Egypt and Saudi Arabia. And if either Iran or Egypt, or both, were to move in the direction of freer societies, more representative politics and continued economic reform – both have significant elements of popular participation, the basis for an independent legal system, a track-record of serious, if limited, economic reform and considerable reserves of national legitimacy – this would have a major stimulus across the region. Alternatively, the United States might lose interest in its grand designs for Iraq, or events in Iraq may simply destabilize the wider regional balance, perhaps bringing Turkish intervention in the north over the Kurdish issue, instability to Saudi Arabia as a result of popular revolt and uncertainty over the political direction of the Iraqi Shiʻa and their relations with Iran. In that event, the prospects for regional development would evaporate in the face of a protracted period of civil strife and regional conflict.

Only time will tell how these alternative pressures work themselves out. The grounds for optimism are, in my view, slim but twofold: first and most importantly, that many people in the region, including many elites, recognize that the old order is no longer sustainable; and, second, that having committed itself to a new order in Iraq, the United States would face a massive loss of global credibility – not to mention a host of *future* problems – were it to leave the region worse than it found it prior to military intervention.

FURTHER READING

Two introductory and comprehensive studies, Carl L. Brown, *International Politics and the Middle East: Old Rules, Dangerous Game*, Princeton University Press, 1984, and Raymond Hinnebusch, *The International Politics of the Middle East*, Manchester University Press, 2003, offer complementary interpretations of the Middle Eastern state-system in its historical and cultural contexts. Tareq Y. Ismael, *International Relations of the Contemporary Middle East: A Study of World Politics*, Syracuse, New York, Syracuse University Press, 1986, is a good introduction to the Middle East in its international linkages. The general issue of state formation in the Middle East is discussed in Simon Bromley, *Rethinking Middle East Politics*, Polity Press, Oxford, 1994, while Adeed Dawisha, *Egypt in the Arab World: The Elements of Foreign Policy*, Wiley, New York, 1976, explores the function of domestic and regional issues in the formation and pursuit of the foreign policies of a pivotal Middle Eastern state.

The Arab–Israeli conflict and its regional and international ramifications are treated in Kirstin Schulze, *The Arab–Israel Conflict*, Longman, London, 1999, and in Charles D. Smith, *Palestine and the Arab–Israeli Conflict*, St. Martin's Press, New York, 1996.

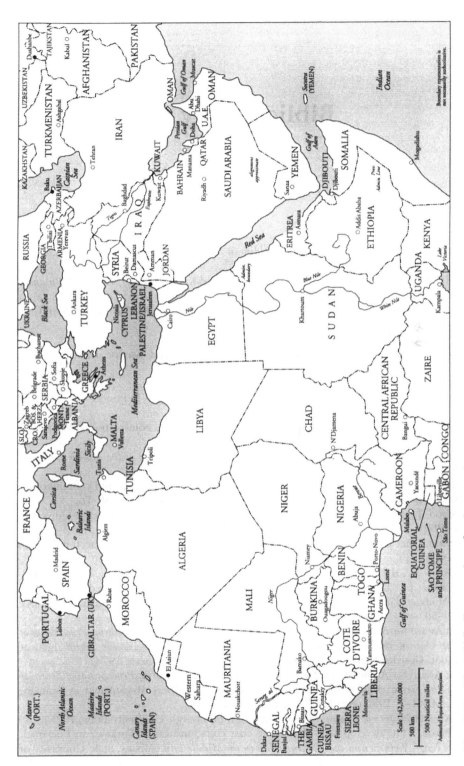

Map 26.1 The Middle East: a region of nation-states?

Bibliography

Abbott, Nabia, *The Qurrah papyri from Aphrodito in the Oriental Institute* (Chicago, University of Chicago Press, 1938).

'Abd al-Ḥamid b. Yaḥyā al-Kātib, "Risāla," in Muḥammad Kurd 'Alī (ed.), *Rasā'il al-Bulaghā'* (Cairo, 1946), pp. 173–210.

Abdo-Zubi, Nahla, *Family, Women and Social Change in the Middle East: The Palestinian Case* (Toronto, Canadian Scholars' Press, 1987).

'Abdul-Raziq, 'Ali, *al-Islam wa-usul al-hukm* (Cairo, 1925).

Abrahamian, Ervand, "The 1953 coup in Iran," *Science and Society*, 65 (2), 2001, pp. 182–215.

Abrahamian, Ervand, *Khomeinism* (London: I. B. Tauris, 1993).

Abrahamian, Ervand, *Iran Between Two Revolutions* (Princeton, NJ, Princeton University Press, 1982).

AbuKhalil, "Change and democratization in the Arab world: the role of political parties," *Third World Quarterly*, 18 (1), 1997, pp. 149–64.

AbuKhalil, As'ad, "Lebanon," in Frank Tachau (ed.), *Political Parties of the Middle East and North Africa* (London, Mansell, 1994), pp. 297–368.

Abu-Lughod, Janet L., "The Islamic city – historic myth, Islamic essence, and contemporary relevance," *International Journal of Middle East Studies*, 19, 1987, pp. 155–76.

Abu-Lughod, Janet L., *Rabat: Urban Apartheid in Morocco* (Princeton, Princeton University Press, 1980).

Abu-Lughod, Janet L., *Cairo: 1001 Years of the City Victorious* (Princeton, Princeton University Press, 1971).

Abun-Nasr, J. M., *A History of the Maghrib in the Islamic Period* (Cambridge, 1987).

Adams, Charles J., "The hermeneutics of Henry Corbin," in Richard Martin (ed.), *Approaches to the Study of Islam in Religious Studies* (University of Arizona Press, Tucson, 1985), pp. 129–50.

Aga Khan Award for Architecture, *Toward an Architecture in the Spirit of Islam: Proceedings of Seminar One in the Series, Architectural Transformations in the Islamic World*, held at Aiglemont, Gouvieux, France, April 1978 (Aga Khan Awards, Geneva, 1978).

Aga Khan Award for Architecture, *Places of Public Gathering in Islam: Proceedings of Seminar Five in the Series, Architectural Transformations in the Islamic World*, held in Amman, Jordan, May 4–7, 1980 (Aga Khan Awards, Geneva, 1980).

Ahmad, Aziz, *A History of Islamic Sicily* (Edinburgh, Edinburgh University Press, 1975).

Ahmad, Feroz, "The development of working class consciousness in Turkey," in Lockman, Zachary (ed.), *Workers and the Working Class in the Middle East* (Albany, State University of New York Press 1994), pp. 133–64.

Ahmad, Feroz, *The Young Turks: The Committee of Union and Progress in Turkish Politics, 1908–1914* (Oxford, Clarendon Press, 1969).

Ahmed, Akbar S., *Post-Modernism and Islam: Predicament and Promise* (London, Routledge, 1992).

Ahmed, Akbar S. and Donnan, Hastings (eds.), *Islam, Globalization and Postmodernity* (London: Routledge, 1994).

Ahrweiler, Hélène, "L'Asie Mineure et les invasions arabes (VIIe–IXe siècles)," *Revue Historique*, 227, 1962.

Ajami, Fouad, *The Arab Predicament: Arab Political Thought and Practice Since 1967* (Cambridge, Cambridge University Press, 1992).

Ajami, Fouad, *The Vanished Imam: Musa al-Sadr and the Shi'a of Lebanon* (Cornell University Press, Ithaca, 1986).

Akbar, Jamel, *Crisis in the Built Environment: The Case of the Muslim City* (Singapore, Concept Media, 1988).

Akbayar, Nuri, *Beikta: Past and Present* (Beikta Municipality, Economic and Social History Foundation of Turkey, Istanbul, 1998).

Akçura, Yusuf, *Üç Tarz-ı Siyaset* (Ankara, Türk Tarih Kurumu Yayınları, 1976).

Akhavi, Shahrough, "Iran," in Frank Tachau (ed.), *Political Parties of the Middle East and North Africa* (London: Mansell, 1994), pp. 133–73.

Akhavi, Shahrough, "The role of the clergy in Iranian politics, 1949–1954," in J. A. Bill and W. M. Roger Lewis (eds.), *Musaddiq, Iranian Nationalism and Oil* (I. B. Tauris, London, 1988), pp. 91–117.

Akhavi, Shahrough, *Religion and Politics in Contemporary Iran: Clergy–State Relations in the Pahlavi Period* (Albany, State University of New York Press, 1980).

Aktar, Ayhan, *Varlik Vergisi ve "Türkleştirme" Politikaları, İletişim Yayınları 599- Tarih Dizisi 4* (Istanbul, Iletişim Yayınları, 2000).

Al-Ali, Nadje, *Secularism, Gender and the State: The Egyptian Women's Movement* (Cambridge, Cambridge University Press, 2000).

Ale-Ahmad, Jalal, *Plagued by the West*, tr. P. Sprachman (New York, 1981).

Algar, Hamid, "The Revolt of Āghā Khān Maīallatī and the Transference of the Ismaʿīlī Imamate to India", *Studia Islamica*, 29 (1969), pp. 55–81.

Algar, Hamid, *Religion and State in Iran, 1785–1906: The Role of the Ulama in the Qajar Period* (Berkeley, University of California Press, 1969).

Aliev, Ahmed, "Zametki o sufiiskom ordene sukhravardiia," *Islam v istorii narodov Vostoka* (Moscow, Nauka, 1981), pp. 154–9.

Alp, Tekin, *Kemalizm* (İstanbul, Istanbul Cumhuriyet Matbaasi, 1936).

Altorki, Soraya, and Donald P. Cole, *Arabian Oasis City: The Transformation of 'Unayzah* (Austin, University of Texas Press, 1989).

Amanat, Abbas, *Pivot of the Universe: Nasir al-Din Shah Qajar and the Iranian Monarchy 1831–1896* (Berkeley and Los Angeles, University of California Press, 1997).

Amanat, Abbas, *Resurrection and Renewal: The Making of the Bābī Movement in Iran, 1844–1850* (Ithaca: Cornell University Press, 1989).

Amanat, Abbas, "In between madrasa and marketplace: the designation of clerical leadership in Modern Shi'ism," in S. A. Arjomand (ed.), *Authority and Political Culture in Shi'ism* (New York: SUNY, 1988), pp. 98–132.

Amin, Samir, *The Arab Economy* (1982).

Amin, Samir, *Iraq: The Contemporary State.*

Amin, Samir, *The Arab Nation*, tr. M. Pallis (London, Zed Press, 1978).

Amir-Moezzi, Mohammad Ali, *The Divine Guide in Early Shi'ism: The Sources of Esotericism in Islam*, tr. D. Streight (New York, State University of New York Press, 1994).

Amnesty International, "Syria: mass arrests of Syrian Kurds and fear of torture and other ill-treatment," *Amnesty International*, press release MDE 24/020/2004, 16 March 2004.

Anawati, Georges and Louis Gardet, *Mystique musulmane: aspects et tendences, experiences et techniques* (Paris, J. Vrin, 1976).

Anderson, Benedict, *Imagined Communities* (London and New York, Verso, 1993).

Anderson, Liam and Gareth Stansfield, *The Future of Iraq: Dictatorship, Democracy or Division?* (New York, Palgrave Macmillan, 2004).

Anderson, Lisa, *The State and Social Transformation in Tunisia and Libya, 1830–1980* (Princeton NJ, Princeton University Press, 1986).

Anderson, M. S. (ed.), *The Great Powers and the Near East 1774–1923* (London, Edward Arnold, 1970).

Anderson, P., *Lineages of the Absolutist State* (London, New Left Books, 1974a).

Anderson, P., *Passages from Antiquity to Feudalism* (London, New Left Books, 1974b).

Andrews, Peter Alford (ed.), *Ethnic Groups in the Republic of Turkey* (Wiesbaden, Ludwig Reichert Verlag, 1989).

Aneer, G., *Imam Ruhullah Khumaini, Sah Muhammad Riza Pahlavi and the Religious Traditions of Iran* (Stockholm, 1985).

Andrae, Tor, *In the Garden of Myrtles: Studies in early Islamic Mysticism*, tr. B. Sharpe (New York, State University of New York Press, Albany, 1987).

Andrae, Tor, *Islamische Mystiker*, tr. H. C. Crede (Stuttgart, W. Kohlhammer, 1960).

Anon, *The Life of the Reverend Humphrey Prideaux, D.D., Dean of Norwich* (London, 1748).

Ansari, A. M., *Modern Iran since 1921: The Pahlavis and After* (London, Longman, 2003).

Antonius, George, *The Arab Awakening* (London, 1938).

Arat, Yesim, "Democracy and women in Turkey: in defense of liberalism," in Nitza Berkovitch and Valentine M. Moghadam (eds.), *Social Politics: International Studies in Gender, State, and Society*, Special Issue on Middle East Politics: *Feminist Challenges*, 6 (3), 1999, pp. 370–87.

Arberry, Arthur J., *Revelation and Reason in Islam* (London, G. Allen, 1957).

Arberry, Arthur J., *Sufism: An Account of the Mystics of Islam* (New York, Harper and Row, 1950).

Arberry, Arthur J., *An Introduction to the History of Sufism* (London, Longman and Green, 1943).

'Arīb b. Sa'd al-Qurṭubī, *Ṣillat Ta'rīkh al-Ṭabarī* (Leiden, 1897). (Edited by M. J. de Goeje).

Arnold, T. W., *The Preaching of Islam* (Lahore, Ashraf Press, 1968).

Arjomand, Said Amir, "Shi'ite jurisprudence and constitution making in the Islamic Republic of Iran," in M. Marty and R. S. Appleby (eds.), *Fundamentalisms and the State: Remaking Polities, Economies and Militance* (Chicago, University of Chicago Press, 1993), pp. 88–109.

Arjomand, Said Amir, *The Shadow of God and the Hidden Imam: Religion, Political Order and Societal Change in Shi'ite Iran from the Beginning to 1890* (Chicago, University of Chicago Press, 1984).

Arjomand, Said Amir, *From Nationalism to Revolutionary Islam* (Albany, State University of New York Press, 1984).

Arjomand, Said Amir, *Authority and Political Culture in Shi'ism* (Albany, State University of New York Press, 1980).

Al-Asad, Mohammad, "Ruptures in the evolution of the Middle Eastern city: Amman," in Michael E. Bonine (ed.), *Population, Poverty, and Politics in Middle East Cities* (Gainesville, University Press of Florida, 1997), pp. 46–63.

Ashtiany, J., *Abbasid Belles-lettres* (Cambridge, 1990).

Al-Askar, Abdullah, *Al-Yamama in the Early Islamic Era* (Reading, Itacha Press, 2002).

Aslanapa, Oktay, *Turkish Art and Architecture* (New York, Praeger, 1971).

Al-Aswad, Ibrahim, *Al-Rihla al-Imbraturiyya fī'l-Mamalik al-'Uthmaniyya* (Ba'abda, al-Matba'a al-'Uthmaniyya, 1898).

Ataman, Mühittin, "Özal leadership and restructuring of Turkish ethnic policy in the 1980s," *Middle Eastern Studies*, 38 (4), 2002.

Atatürk, Mustafa Kemal, *Nutuk* (Ankara, Kültür Bakanliği Yayınları, 1980).

Auld, S. and Robert Hillenbrand (eds.), *Ottoman Jerusalem: The Living City* (London, Altajir World of Islam Trust, 2000).

Auty R. (ed.), *Resource Abundance and Economic Development* (Oxford, Oxford University Press, 2002).

Avineri, Schlomo, *The Making of Modern Zionism* (New York, Basic Books, 1981).

Avishai, Bernard, *The Tragedy of Zionism: Revolution and Democracy in the Land of Israel* (New York, Farrar Straus Giroux, 1985).

Ayalon, David, *Outsiders in the Lands of Islam: Mamlūks, Mongols and Eunuchs* (London, Variorum Reprints, 1988).

Ayalon, David, *The Mamlūk Military Society* (London, Variorum Reprints, 1979).

Ayalon, David, *Studies on the Mamlūks (1250–1517)* (London, Variorum Reprints, 1977).

Ayalon, David, *Gunpowder and Firearms in the Mamlūk Kingdom* (London, Vallentine, Mitchell, 1956).

Ayalon, David, *Islam and the Abode of War* (London, Variorum Reprints, 1944).

Ayubi, Nazih, *Over-Stating the Arab State: Politics and Society in the Middle East* (London, I. B. Tauris, 1995).

Ayubi, Nazih, "Withered socialism or whether socialism? The radical Arab states as populist-corporatist regimes," *Third World Quarterly*, 13 (1), 1992, pp. 89–105.

Ayubi, Nazih, *Political Islam: Religion and Politics in the Arab World* (London, Routledge, 1991).

Al-Azdī: al-Azdī, Abū Zakarīyā Yazīd b. Muḥammad, *Ta'rīkh al-Mawṣil*, ed. 'Alī Ḥabība (Cairo, 1967).

Aziz, Talib, "Fadlallah and the remaking of the Marja'iya'," in Linda Walbridge (ed.), *The Most Learned of the Shī'a* (New York: Oxford University Press, 2001), pp. 205–15.

Al-Azmeh, Aziz, *Muslim Kingship* (London, I. B. Tauris, 1997 and 2001).

Al-Azmeh, Aziz, *Islams and Modernities* (London, Verso, 1993).

Babaie, Susan, Kathryn Babayan, Ina Baghdiantz-McCabe, and Massumeh Ferhad, *Slaves of the Shah: New Elites of Safavid Iran* (2003).

Babajanov, Bakhtiiar, "Dukchi-ishan", *Islam na territorii byvshei Rossiiskoi imperii*, Part 2 (Vostochnaia literature, Moscow, 1999), pp. 35–7.

Babayan, Kathryn, *Mystics, Monarchs and Messiah: Cultural Landscape of Early Modern Iran* (Cambridge, MA: Harvard University Press, 2002).

Babayan, Kathryn, "Sufis, Dervishes and Mullas: the controversies over spiritual and temporal dominion in seventeenth-century Iran," in C. Melville (ed.), *Safavid Persia: The History and Politics of an Islamic Society* (I. B. Tauris, Cambridge, 1996), pp. 117–38.

Badran, Margot, "Gender activism: feminists and Islamists in Egypt," in V. M. Moghadam (ed.), *Identity Politics and Women: Cultural Reassertions and Feminisms in International Perspective* (Boulder, CO, Westview, 1994), pp. 202–27.

Bakhash, S., *Iran: Monarchy, Bureaucracy & Reform under the Qajars: 1858–1896* (London, Ithaca Press, 1978).

Balādhurī, Ahmad ibn Jābir, "Ansāb al-ashrāf," in W. Ahlwardt (ed.), *Anonyme Arabische Chronik Band XI* (Leipzig, 1883).

Al-Balādhurī, Aḥmad b. Yaḥyā, *Futūh al-Buldān* ed. M. J. de Goeje (Leiden, 1968).

Baldick, Julian, *Mystical Islam: An Introduction to Sufism* (I. B. Tauris, London, 1989).

Baldick, Julian, "Massignon: man of opposites," *Religious Studies*, 23, 1987, pp. 29–39.

Baram, Amatzia, "Saddam's power structure: the Tikritis before, during and after the war," in Toby Dodge and Steven Simon (eds.), *Iraq at the Crossroads: State and Society in the Shadow of Regime Change* (International Institute of Strategic Studies (IISS), Adelphi Paper 354, Oxford, Oxford University Press/IISS), pp. 93–114.

Barber, Benjamin, *Jihad vs. McWorld: How Globalism and Tribalism Are Reshaping the World* (New York, Ballantine Books, 1996).

Barbir, Karl, *Ottoman Rule in Damascus, 1708–1758* (1980).

Barkan, Ömer L., *Süleymaniye Cami ve Imareti Inaati (1550–1557)*, vol. 1 (Ankara, Türk Tarih Kurumu Basimevi, 1972).

Barkan, Ömer Lutfi and Ekrem Hakki Ayverdi, *Istanbul Vakiflari Tahrir Defteri: 953 (1546) Tarihli* (Istanbul, Baha Matbaasi, 1970).

Barkey, Henri J. and Graham E. Fuller, *Turkey's Kurdish Question* (New York, Rowman & Littlefield, 1998).

Barkey, Karen, *Bandits and Bureaucrats: The Ottoman route to state centralization* (1997).

Barnett, Michael N., *Dialogues in Arab Politics* (New York, Columbia University Press, 1998).

Barthold, Vasilii, "Pamiati Zhukovskogo," in V. Barthold, *Sochineniia*, vol. 9, Moscow, Vostochnaia literature, 1963), pp. 699–703.

Barthold, Vasilii, *Sochineniia* (9 vols, Moscow, Vostochnaia literature, 1963).

Bartlett, Robert, *The Making of Europe* (Princeton, Princeton University Press, 1993).

Bashear, Suliman, *Arabs and Others in Early Islam* (Princeton, Darwin Press, 1997).

Bashir, Shahzad, *Messianic Hopes and Mystical Visions: The Nurbakhshiya between Medieval and Modern Islam* (Colombia, SC, University of South Carolina Press, 2003).

Basilov, Vladimir, *Kul't sviatykh v islame* (Moscow, Nauka, 1970).

Batatu, Hanna, *The Old Social Classes and the Revolutionary Movements of Iraq: A Study of Iraq's Old Landed Classes and Its Communists, Ba'thists and Free Officers* (Princeton NJ, Princeton University Press, 1978).

Bates, Michael, "The coinage of Syria under the Umayyads, 692–750 A.D.," in M. A. Bakhit and Robert Schick (eds.), *The Fourth International Conference on the History of Bilād al-Shām during the Umayyad Period* (Amman, Jordan University, 1989), vol. 2, pp. 195–228.

Bates, Michael, "History, geography, and numismatics in the first century of Islamic coinage," *Revue Suisse de Numismatique*, 65, 1986, pp. 231–62.

Batunskii, "Iz istorii zapadnoevropeiskogo vostokovedeniia perioda imperializma (K. Bekker)," *Nauchnye trudy i soobscheniia AN Uzbekskoi SSR*, Tashkent, 2 (1961), pp. 314–23.

Bauer, Janet, "A long way home: Islam in the adaptation of Iranian women refugees in Turkey and West Germany," in Asghar Fathi (ed.), *Iranian Refugees and Exiles Since Khomeini* (Costa Mesa, CA, Mazda Publishers, 1991), pp. 77–101.

Bayat, Assef, *Workers and Revolution in Iran: A Third World Experience of Workers' Control* (London, Zed Books, 1987).

Bayhom-Daou, Tamima, "The imam's knowledge and the Quran according to al-Faḍl b. Shādhān al-Nīsābūrī (d. 260 A.H./874 A.D.)," *Bulletin of the School of Oriental and African Studies*, vol. 64, 2001, pp. 188–207.

Bayly, C., *Imperial Meridian* (London, Longman, 1989).

De Beaureceuil, Serge Laugier, *Khwadja 'Abdullah Ansari (396–481 H./1006–1089); mystique hanbalite* (Beirut, Imprimerie Catholique, 1965).

Beblawi, Hazem and Giacomo Luciani, *The Rentier State* (London, Croom Helm, 1987).

Beblawi, Hazem, "The rentier state in the Arab world," *Arab Studies Quarterly*, 9 (4), 1987, pp. 383–98.

Beck, Lois and Nikki Keddie (eds.), *Women in the Muslim World* (Cambridge, MA, Harvard University Press, 1978).

Becker, Carl Heinrich, "Die Ausbreitung der Araber im Mittelmeergebiet," in Carl Heinrich Becker, *Islamstudien* 1 (Leipzig, Quelle und Meyer, 1924), pp. 66–145.

Becker, Carl Heinrich, "The expansion of the Saracens," in H. M. Gwatkin (ed.), *The Cambridge Mediaeval History* (Cambridge, Cambridge University Press, 1913), 1st edn, vol. 2, pp. 329–90.

Becker, Carl Heinrich, "Der Islam als Problem," *Der Islam*, vol. 1, 1910, pp. 1–21.

Beeman, W., "What is Iranian national character?" *Iranian Studies*, 9, 1976, pp. 22–48.

Be'eri, Eliezer, "The waning of the military coup in Arab politics," *Middle Eastern Studies*, 18 (1), 1982.

Be'eri, Eliezer, *Arab Offices in Arab Politics and Society* (London, Praeger, 1969).

Behnam, R., *Cultural Foundations of Iranian Politics* (Utah, 1986).

Behren-Abouseif, *Islamic Architecture in Cairo: An Introduction* (Leiden, E. J. Brill, 1989).

Beinin, Joel, and Stork, J. (eds.), *Political Islam: Essays from Middle East Report* (London, I. B. Tauris, 1997).

Beinin, Joel and Zachary Lockman, *Workers on the Nile: Nationalism, Communism, Islam and the Egyptian Working Class* (Princeton NJ, Princeton University Press, 1987).

Bel, A., *La religion musulmane en Berbérie*, vol. 1 (Paris, 1938).

Bell, Richard and W. Montgomery Watt, *Introduction to the Qur'an* (Edinburgh, Edinburgh University Press, 1970).

Bellin, E., "Civil society in formation: Tunisia," in Augustus Richard Norton (ed.), *Civil Society in the Middle East* (Leiden, E. J. Brill, 1996), vol. 1, pp. 120–47.

Belyaev, E. A., *Arabs, Islam and the Arab Caliphate in the Early Middle Ages* (New York, Frederick A. Praeger, 1969).

Ben-Arieh, Yehoshua, *Jerusalem in the 19th Century: Emergence of the New City* (Jerusalem, Yad Izhad Ben Zvi Institute, 1986).

Ben-Arieh, Yehoshua, *Jerusalem in the 19th Century: The Old City* (Jerusalem, Yad Izhad Ben Zvi Institute, 1984).

Ben-Dor, Gabriel, "Minorities in the Middle East: theory and practice," in Ofra Bengio and Gabriel Ben-Dor (eds.), *Minorities and the State in the Arab World* (Boulder, CO, Lynne Rienner, 1999), pp. 1–28.

Bengio, Ofra and Gabriel Ben-Dor (eds.), *Minorities and the State in the Arab World* (Boulder, CO, Lynne Rienner, 1999).

Bengio, Ofra, "The case of Iraq," in Ofra Bengio and Gabriel Ben-Dor (eds.), *Minorities and the State in the Arab World* (Boulder, CO, Lynne Rienner, 1999), pp. 149–69.

Benvenisti, Meron, *City of Stone: The Hidden History of Jerusalem* (Berkeley, University of California Press, 1996).

Berg, Herbert, *Method and Theory in the Study of Islamic Origins* (Leiden, E. J. Brill, 2003).

Berger, Peter, "Motif messianique et processus social dans le Bahaisme," *Archives de Sociologie des Religions*, 4, 1957, pp. 93–107.

Berkes, Niyazi, *The Development of Secularism in Turkey* (Montreal, McGill University Press, 1964).

Berkey, Jonathan, *The Formation of Islam: Religion and Society in the Near East, 600–1800* (Cambridge, Cambridge University Press, 2003).

Berque, Jacques, *Ulémas, fondateurs, insurgés du Maghreb: XVIIe siècle* (Paris, Sindbad, 1982).

Berque, Jacques, *L'Intérieur du Maghreb* (Paris, 1978).

Betts, Robert, *The Druze* (New Haven, Yale University Press, 1988).

Bianca, Stefano, *Urban Form in the Arab World: Past and Present* (New York, Thames & Hudson, 2000).

Bianca, Stefano, *Hofhaus und Paradiesgarten: Architektur und Lebensformen in der islamischen Welt* (Munich, C. H. Beck, 1991).

Bianca, Stefano, *Architektur und Lebensform im islamischen Stadtwesen* (Zürich: Verlag für Architektur Artemis, Studiopaperback, 1975).

Bierman, Irene A., Rifa'at A. Abou-El-Haj, and Donald Presiosi (eds.), *The Ottoman City and Its Parts: Urban Structure and Social Order* (New York, Aristide D. Caratzas, 1991).

Bill, James and Robert Springborg, *Politics in the Middle East* (New York, HarperCollins, 1990).

Bill, James, and W. R. Louis (eds.), *Musaddiq, Iranian Nationalism and Oil* (London, I. B. Tauris, 1988).

Bill, James and Carl Leiden, *Politics in the Middle East* (Boston, Little, Brown and Co., 1979).

Birks, J. S. and Sinclair, C. A., *International Migration and Development in the Arab Region* (Geneva, International Labour Office, 1980).

Bisheh, Ghazi (ed.), *Studies in the History and Archaeology of Jordan* (Amman, Department of Antiquities, 1995).

Blair, Sheila S., and Jonathan M. Bloom, *The Art and Architecture of Islam: 1250–1800* (New Haven, Yale University Press, Pelican History of Art, 1994).

Blaisdell, Donald C., *European Financial Control in the Ottoman Empire: A Study of the Establishment, Activities, and Significance of the Administration of the Ottoman Public Debt* (New York, AMS Press, 1966).

Blank, Jonah, *Mullas on the Mainframe: Islam and Modernity among the Daudi Bohras* (Chicago, University of Chicago Press, 2001).

Blum, Charlotte, "The Middle East adapts to GATT," *Middle East Economic Digest*, March 10, 1995, pp. 2–3.

Blay-Abramski, Irit Irene, "From Damascus to Baghdad: the Abbasid Administrative System as a Product of the Umayyad Heritage" *(41/661–320–932*, dissertation, Princeton, 1982).

Bonine, Michael E. (ed.), *Population, Poverty and Politics in Middle East Cities* (University Press of Florida, Gainesville, 1997).

Bonine, Michael E., Eckart Ehlers, Thomas Krafft, and Georg Stöber (eds.), *The Middle Eastern City and Islamic Urbanism: An Annotated Bibliography of Western Literature* (Bonn, Ferd. Dümmlers Verlag, Bonner Geographische Abhandlungen, no. 91, 1994).

Bonine, Michael E., "Cities of the Middle East and North Africa," in Stanley D. Brunn and Jack F. Williams (eds.), *Cities of the World: World Regional Urban Development* (New York, HarperCollins College Publishers, 1993), pp. 305–49.

Bonine, Michael E., "The sacred direction and city structure: a preliminary analysis of Islamic cities of Morocco," *Muqarnas, An Annual on Islamic Art and Architecture*, 7, 1990, pp. 50–72.

Bonine, Michael E., "Oil and urban development in the Middle East," *The Korean Journal of the Middle East Studies*, 10, 1989, pp. 11–23.

Bonine, Michael E., "Islam and commerce: Waqf and the bazaar of Yazd, Iran," *Erdkunde*, 41 (3), 1987, pp. 182–96.

Bonine, Michael E. and Rainer Cordes, "Oil urbanization: Zum Entwicklungsprozess eines neuen Typs orientalischer Städte," *Geographische Rundschau*, 35 (9), 1983, pp. 461–2, 465.

Bonine, Michael E., "The morphogenesis of Iranian cities," *Annals of the Association of American Geographers*, 69 (2), 1979, pp. 208–24.

Bonine, Michael E., "Urban studies in the Middle East," *Middle East Studies Association Bulletin*, 10 (3), 1976, pp. 1–37.

Bonine, Michael E., "Population growth, the labor market, and Gulf security," in David E. Long and Christian Koch (eds.), *Gulf Security in the Twenty-First Century* (London, I. B. Tauris), pp. 226–64, 309–10.

Bonner, Michael, *Aristocratic Violence and Holy War: Studies in the Jihad and the Arab-Byzantine Frontier* (New Haven, American Oriental Society, 1996).

Bora, Tanıl, " 'Ekalliyet Yılanları': Türk Milliyetçiliği Ve Azınlıklar," in Tanıl Bora (ed.), *Milliyetçilik* (İstanbul, İletişim Yayınları, 2002).

Van den Bos, Matthijs, *Mystical Regimes: Sufism and the State in Iran from the Qajar Era to the Islamic Republic* (Leiden, E. J. Brill, 2002).

Bosworth, Clifford Edmund, "The coming of Islam to Afghanistan," in Yohannan Friedman (ed.), *Islam in Asia, I: South Asia* (Jerusalem: Magnes Press, 1984), pp. 1–22.

Botiveau, Bernard, *Loi islamique et droit dans les sociétés arabes* (Paris, Éditions Karthala, 1993).

Botman, Selma, *Egypt from Independence to Revolution, 1919–1952* (Syracuse, Syracuse University Press, 1991).

Botman, Selma, *The Rise of Egyptian Communism 1939–1970* (Syracuse, NY, Syracuse University Press, 1988).

Bouchlaka, R., "Secularism, despotism and democracy: the legacy of imperialism," in A. el-Affendi (ed.), *Rethinking Islam and Modernity, Essays in Honour of Fathi Osman* (Leicester, Islamic Foundation, 1991).

Bouhdiba, Abdelwahab, *Sexuality in Islam* (London, Routledge and Kegan Paul, 1985).

Bouhdiba, Abdelwahab, and D. Chevallier (eds.), *La ville arabe dans l'Islam* (Tunis, 1982).

Bousquet, G.-H., "Oberservations sur la nature et causes de la conquête arabe," *Studia Islamica*, 6, 1956, pp. 37–52.

Bousquet, G.-H., "Quelques remarques critiques et sociologiques sur la conquête arabe et les théories émises à ce sujet," *Studi Orientalistici in Onore de Giorgio Levi della Vida* (Rome, Istituto per l'Oriente, 1956), pp. 52–60.

Böwering, Gerhard, *Minor Qur'an Commentary of Abu 'Abd al-Rahman al-Sulami (d. 412/ 1021)* (Beirut, Dar al-Mashriq, 1995).

Böwering, Gerhard, *The Mystical Vision of Existence in Classical Islam: The Qur'anic Hermeneutics of the Sufi Sahl al-Tustari (d. 283/896)* (Berlin, de Gruyter, 1980).

Bowersock, Glynn W. (ed.), *Late Antiquity: A Guide to the Postclassical World* (Cambridge, MA, Harvard University Press, 1999).

Bowersock, Glynn W., *Hellenism in Late Antiquity* (Ann Arbor: University of Michigan Press, 1996).

Bowring, John, *Report on the Commercial Statistics of Syria* (New York: Arno Press, 1973).

Bozorgmehr, Mehdi and Georges Sabagh, "Iranian exiles and immigrants in Los Angeles," in Asghar Fathi (ed.), *Iranian Refugees and Exiles since Khomeini* (Costa Mesa, CA, Mazda Publishers, 1991), pp. 121–44.

Brand, L., "In the beginning was the state: the quest for civil society in Jordan," in Augustus Richard Norton (ed.), *Civil Society in the Middle East* (Leiden, Brill, 1996), vol. 1, pp. 167–85.

Braudel, Fernand, *La Méditerranée et le Monde Méditerranéen à l'Epoque de Philippe II* (Paris, 1949); 2 vols., translated into English by Sian Reymolds as *The Mediterranean and the Mediterranean World in the Reign of Philip II* (New York, Harper and Row, 1972).

Brenner, Michael, *Zionism: A Brief History*, tr. S. Frisch (Princeton, Markus Wiener, 2003).

Brett, Michael, *The Rise of the Fatimids* (Leiden, 2001).

Brett, Michael, *Ibn Khaldun and the Medieval Maghrib* (Aldershot, 1999).

Brett, Michael and Elizabeth Fentress, *The Berbers* (Oxford, Blackwell Publishers, 1996).

Breuilly, John, *Nationalism and the State* (Manchester, Manchester University Press, 1993).

Brignon, J. et al. *Histoire du Maroc* (Paris, 1967).

Brohman, John, "Economism and critical silences in development studies: a theoretical critique of neoliberalism," *Third World Quarterly*, 16 (2), 1995, pp. 297–318.

Bromley, Simon, "Middle East exceptionalism: myth or reality?" in D. Potter et al. (eds.), *Democratization* (Cambridge, Polity Press, 1997).

Bromley, Simon, *Rethinking Middle East Politics* (Cambridge, Polity Press, 1994).

Brooks, E., "The Arab occupation of Crete," *English Historical Review*, 28, 1913, pp. 431–43.

Brooks, Risa, *Political–Military Relations and the Stability of Arab Regimes* (International Institute of Strategic Studies (IISS), Adelphi Paper 324, Oxford, Oxford University Press for the IISS, 1998).

Brosselard, Charles, *Les Khouan: de la constitution des ordres religieux musulmans en Algérie* (Paris, Challamel, 1859).

Brown, Daniel, *A New Introduction to Islam* (Malden, MA, Blackwell, 2003).

Brown, John P. (ed.), *The Darvishes or Oriental Spiritualism* (Frank Cass, London, 1968).

Brown, Kenneth L., "Mellah and Medina: a Moroccan city and its Jewish quarter," in S. Moraq et al. (eds.), *Studies in Judaism and Islam* (Jerusalem, Magnes Press, 1981), pp. 253–81.

Brown, Kenneth L., *People of Salé: Tradition and Change in a Moroccan City, 1830–1930* (Manchester University Press, Manchester, 1976).

Brown, L. Carl (ed.), *From Madina to Metropolis: Heritage and Change in the Near Eastern City* (Princeton, Darwin Press, 1973).

Brown, Peter, *The World of Late Antiquity. From Marcus Aurelius to Muhammad* (London, Thames and Hudson, 1971).

Browne, Edward, *Literary History of Persia* (2 vols, London, T. F. Unwin, 1902–6).

Van Bruinessen, Martin, *Agha, Shaikh and State: The Social and Political Structures of Kurdistan* (London, Zed Books, 1992).

Brummett, Palmira, *Ottoman Seapower and Levantine Diplomacy* (1994).

Brunschvig, R., *La Berbérie orientale sous les Hafsides*, 2 vols. (Paris: 1940–7).

Bryant, "Social self-organisation, civility and sociology: a comment on Kumar's 'Civil Society'," *British Journal of Sociology*, 44 (3), 1993, pp. 397–401.

Brynen, Rex, Bahgat Korany, and Paul Noble (eds.), *Political Liberalisation & Democratization in the Arab World, Volume 2: Comparative Experiences* (Boulder, CO, Lynne Rienner 1998).

Brynen, Rex, Bahgat Korany, and Paul Noble (eds.), *Political Liberalisation & Democratization in the Arab World, Volume 1: Theoretical Perspectives* (Boulder, CO, Lynne Rienner Publishers, 1995).

Buckley, R., "The early Shiite Ghulah," *Journal of Semitic Studies*, 42, 1997, pp. 301–25.

Budeiri, Musa, *The Palestine Communist Party 1919–1948* (London, Ithaca Press, 1979).

Buehler, Arthur F., Ekrem Isin, and Tierry Zarcone (eds.), *The Qadiriyya* (inaugural issue of *Journal of the History of Sufism*) (Paris and Istanbul, Simurgh Publications, 2000).

Buehler, Arthur F., *Sufi Heirs of the Prophet: The Indian Naqshbandiyya and the Rise of the Mediating Sufi Shaykh* (Columbia, SC, University of South Carolina Press, 1998).

Bulliet, Richard W., *Islam: The View from the Edge* (New York, Columbia University Press, 1994).

Bulliet, Richard W., *Conversion to Islam in the Medieval Period* (Cambridge, MA, Harvard University Press, 1979).

Burckhardt, Titus, *Art of Islam: Language and Meaning* (London, World of Islam Festival, 1976).

Burgoyne, Michael Hamilton, *Mamluk Jerusalem: An Architectural Study* (Essex, Scorpion Publishing, on behalf of the British School of Archaeology in Jerusalem by the World of Islam Festival Trust, 1987).

Burke, Edmund, "The sociology of Islam: the French tradition," in Malcolm Kerr (ed.), *Islamic Studies: A Tradition and Its Problems* (Malibu, CA, Undena Publications, 1980), pp. 73–88.

Burman, Thomas E., *Religious Polemic and the Intellectual History of the Mozarabs, c.1050–1200* (Leiden, E. J. Brill, 1994).

Butler, Alfred J., *The Arab Conquest of Egypt and the Last Thirty Years of the Roman Dominion* (Oxford, Clarendon Press, 1978).

Butterworth, Charles E. and I. William Zartman, *Between State and Islam* (Cambridge, Cambridge University Press, 2001).

Cahen, Claude, *Pre-Ottoman Turkey: A General Survey of the Material and Spiritual Cultures and History, c. 1071–1330*, tr. J. Jones-Williams (New York, Taplinger Pub. Co., 1968).

Cahen, Claude, "Fiscalité, Propriété, Antagonismes sociaux en Haute-Mésopotamie au temps des premiers 'Abbasides d'apres Denys de Tell-Mahré," *Arabica*, 1, 1954, pp. 136–52.

Cahen, C., *The Formation of Turkey: The Seljukid Sultanate of Rum: Eleventh to Fourteenth Century*, ed. and tr. P. M. Holt (Harlow, 2001).

Caillé, Jacques, *La ville de Rabat jusqu'au Protectorat français* (Paris, 1949).

Calder, Norman, *Studies in Early Muslim Jurisprudence* (Oxford, Clarendon Press, 1993).

Calder, Norman, "Doubt and prerogative: the emergence of an Imami Shī'ī theory of *ijtihād*," *Studia Islamica*, 70, 1989, pp. 57–78.

Calder, Norman, "*Khums* in Imāmī Shī'ī jurisprudence from the tenth to the sixteenth century AD," *Bulletin of the School of Oriental and African Studies*, 45 (1), 1982, pp. 39–47.

Calder, Norman, "Accommodation and revolution in Imami Shi'i jurisprudence: Khumayni and the classical tradition," *Middle Eastern Studies*, 18 (1), 1982, pp. 2–20.

Calder, Norman, "*Zakāt* in Imāmī Shīʿī Jurisprudence from the Tenth to the Sixteenth Century AD," *Bulletin of the School of Oriental and African Studies*, 44 (1), 1981, pp. 469–80.

Calmard, Jean, "Marʿashīs," *EI*, 6, pp. 510–18.

Cambridge History of Africa, vols. 3 (1977) and 4 (1975) (Cambridge).

The Cambridge History of Iran, Vol. 5, *The Saljuk and Mongol Periods*, ed. J. A. Boyle (Cambridge, 1968); Vol. 6, *The Timurid and Safavid Periods*.

Cameron, Averil, *The Mediterranean World in Late Antiquity: AD 395–600* (London, Routledge, 1993).

Cameron, Averil, "The eastern provinces in the 7th century A.D. Hellenism and the emergence of Islam," in S. Said (ed.), *Hellenismos. Quelques Jalons pour une Histoire de l'Identité Grecque* (Leiden, E. J. Brill, 1991).

Camps, Gabriel, "L'origine des Berbères," in Ernest Gellner (ed.), *Islam et société : anthropologie du Maghreb* (Paris, CNRS, 1981), pp. 9–33.

Canard, Marius, "L'expansion arabe: le problème militaire," *L'Occident et l'Islam nell'Alto Medioevo 1* (Spoleto, 1965), pp. 37–63.

Canard, Marius, "Les expeditions des Arabes contre Constantinople dans l'histoire et dans la légende," *Journal Asiatique*, 208, 1926, pp. 61–121.

Canefe, Nergis, "Turkish nationalism and ethno-symbolic analysis: the rules of exception," *Nations and Nationalism*, 8 (2), 2002.

Canfield, Robert (ed.), *Turko-Persia in Historical Perspective* (1991).

Carapico, S., *Civil Society in Yemen* (Cambridge, Cambridge University Press, 1998).

Cattan, Henry, *The Palestine Question* (London, Croom Helm, 1988).

CAWTAR, *Globalization and Gender: Economic Participation of Arab Women* (Tunis, CAWTAR Arab Women's Development Report, 2001).

Çelik, Zeynep, *The Making of Istanbul: Portrait of an Ottoman City in the Nineteenth Century* (Seattle, University of Washington Press, 1986).

Chamberlain, M., "The Ayyubids and the crusader era," in C. Petty (ed.), *The Cambridge History of Egypt*, vol. 1 (Cambridge, 1998).

Chamberlain, Michael, *Knowledge and Social Practice in Medieval Damascus, 1190–1350* (Cambridge, Cambridge University Press, 1994).

Chambert-Loir, Henri and Claude Guilliot (eds.), *Le culte des saints dans le monde Musulmane* (Paris, École française d'Extrême-Orient, 1995).

Chehabi, H. E., *Iranian Politics and Religious Modernism; the Liberation Movement of Iran under the Shah and Khomeini* (Ithaca, NY, Cornell University Press, 1990).

Cherifati-Merabtine, Doria, "Algeria at a crossroads: national liberation, Islamization, and women," in V. M. Moghadam (ed.), *Gender and National Identity: Women and Politics in Muslim Societies* (London, Zed Books, 1994).

Chittick, William C., *Sufism: A Short Introduction* (Oxford, Oneworld, 2000).

Chittick, William C., *The Self-Disclosure of God: Principles of Ibn al-ʿArabi's cosmology* (Albany, State University of New York Press, 1998).

Chittick, William C., *Faith and Practice in Islam: Three Thirteenth-century Sufi Texts* (Albany, State University of New York Press, 1992).

Chittick, William C., *The Sufi Path of Knowledge: Ibn al-ʿArabi's metaphysics of imagination* (Albany, State University of New York Press, 1989).

Chodkiewicz, Michel, *The Seal of the Saints: Prophethood and sainthood in the doctrine of Ibn ʿArabi*, tr. L. Sherrard (Cambridge, Islamic Texts Society, 1993).

Chodkiewicz, Michel, *Le sceau des saints: prophétie et sainteté dans la doctrine d'Ibn Arabi* (Paris, Gallimard, 1986).

Choueiri, Youssef M., *Modern Arab Historiography* (London, Routledge Curzon, 2003).

Choueiri, Youssef M., *Arab Nationalism: A History* (Oxford, Blackwell, 2000).

Choueiri, Youssef M., *Islamic Fundamentalism* (Boston, Twayne Publishers, 1990, 2003).

CIA World Factbook 2003. See the internet at: http://www.cia.gov/cia/publications/factbook/index.html.

Ciment, James, *The Kurds: State and Minority in Turkey, Iraq and Iran* (New York, Facts on File, 1996).

Cizre, Umit, *Politics and Military in Turkey into the 21st Century* (European University Institute (EUI) Working Paper RSC 2000/24. San Domenico di Fiesole, Italy, EUI, 2000).

Clapham, Christopher, *Third World Politics: An Introduction* (London, Croom Helm, 1985.)

Clarke, James J., *Oriental Enlightenment: The Encounter between Asian and Western Thought* (London and New York, Routledge, 1997).

Clarke, John I., "Contemporary urban growth," in Gerald H. Blake and Richard I. Lawless (eds.), *The Changing Middle Eastern City* (Totowa, NJ, Barnes & Noble, 1980), pp. 34–53.

Clarke, John I. and W. B. Fisher (eds.), *Populations of the Middle East and North Africa: A Geographical Approach* (London, University of London Press, 1972).

Cloudsley, Anne, *Women of Omdurman: Life, Love and the Cult of Virginity* (New York, St. Martin's Press, 1984).

Cohen, J.-L. et al. (eds.), *Algier. Paysage urbain et architecture* (Paris, 2003).

Cohen, Mitchell, *Zion and State: Nation, Class and the Shaping of Modern Israel* (Oxford, Basil Blackwell, 1987).

Cole, Juan, "Shaykh Ahmad al-Ahsa'i on the sources of religious authority," in Linda Walbridge (ed.), *The Most Learned of the Shi'a* (New York, Oxford University Press, 2001), pp. 82–93.

Collins, Roger, *The Arab Conquest of Spain, 710–797* (Oxford, Basil Blackwell, 1989).

Commins, David Dean, *Islamic Reform: Politics and Social Change in Late Ottoman Syria* (New York, Oxford University Press, 1990).

Conrad, Lawrence I., "Futūh," in Julie S. Meisami and Paul Starkey (eds.), *Encyclopedia of Arabic Literature* (London, Routledge, 1998), pp. 237–40.

Conrad, Lawrence I., "Recovering lost texts: some methodological issues," *Journal of the American Oriental Society*, 113, 1993, pp. 258–63.

Cook, Michael, *Commanding Right and Forbidding Wrong in Islamic Thought* (Cambridge, Cambridge University Press, 2000).

Cook, Michael, *The Koran: A Very Short Introduction* (Oxford, Oxford University Press, 2000).

Cook, Michael, *Muhammad* (Oxford, Oxford University Press, 1983).

Cook, Michael and Patricia Crone, *Hagarism, The Making of the Islamic World* (Cambridge, Cambridge University Press, 1977).

Cooke, Miriam, *War's Other Voices: Women Writers on the Lebanese Civil War* (Cambridge, Cambridge University Press, 1986).

Cooperson, Michael, "Ibn Hanbal and Bishr al-Hafi: A case study in biographical tradition," *Studia Islamica*, 86, 1997, pp. 71–102.

Corbin, Henry, *En Islam iranien, aspects spirituels e philosophiques*, 4 vols. (Paris, Gallimard, 1971–2).

Corbin, Henry, *Creative Imagination in the Sufism of Ibn 'Arabi*, tr. R. Manheim (Princeton, NJ, Princeton University Press, 1969).

Corbin, Henry, *Histoire de la philosophie islamique* (Paris: Gallimard, 1964).

Cornell, V. J., *Realm of the Saint: Power and Authority in Moroccan Sufism* (Austin, 1998).

Coulson, Noel J., *A History of Islamic Law* (Edinburgh, Edinburgh University Press, 1964).

Coulson, Noel J., "Bayt al-Māl," *Encyclopedia of Islam* (Leiden, E. J. Brill, 1960–).

Costello, Vincent F., *Urbanization in the Middle East* (Cambridge, Cambridge University Press, 1977).

Cottam, R. "Political party development in Iran," *Iranian Studies*, 1 (3), 1968, pp. 82–95.

Cottam, R., *Nationalism in Iran* (Pittsburgh, 1964).

Crapanzano, Vincent, *The Hamadsha: A Study in Moroccan Ethnopsychiatry* (Berkeley, University of California Press, 1973).

Creswell, K. A. C., *Early Muslim Architecture: Umayyads, Early Abbasids and Tulunids*, 2 vols (Oxford, Clarendon Press, 1932–40).

Crone, Patricia and Fritz Zimmermann (eds.), *The Epistle of Sālim ibn Dhakwān* (Oxford, Oxford University Press, 2001).

Crone, Patricia, *Roman, Provincial and Islamic Law: The Origins of the Islamic Patronate* (Cambridge, Cambridge University Press, 1987).

Crone Patricia, *Meccan Trade and the Rise of Islam* (Princeton, NJ, Princeton University Press, 1987).

Crone, Patricia and Martin Hinds, *God's Caliph* (Cambridge, Cambridge University Press, 1986).

Crone, Patricia, *Slaves on Horses: The Evolution of the Islamic Polity* (Cambridge, Cambridge University Press, 1980).

Crystal, Jill, "Civil society in the Arabian Gulf," in Augustus Richard Norton (ed.), *Civil Society in the Middle East* (Leiden, E. J. Brill, 1996), vol. 2, pp. 259–86.

Cuneo, P., *Storia dell'urbanistica. Il mondo islamico* (Rome, 1986).

Curmi, Brigitte, "Parties politiques en Jordanie: au Coeur des soubresauts du Moyen-Orient," *Revue des Mondes musulmans et de la Méditerranée*, 81–2, 1996, pp. 231–56.

Daftary, Farhad, *The Ismāʿīlīs: Their History and Their Doctrines* (Cambridge, Cambridge University Press, 1990).

Dağı, İhsan D., *Batılılaşma Korkusu* (Ankara, Liberte Yayınları, 2003).

Dahan-Kalev, Henriette, "The 'other' in Zionism: the case of the Mizrahim," *Palestine and Israel Journal*, 8 (1), 2001.

Dallal, Ahmad, "Ghazali and the perils of interpretation," *Journal of the American Oriental Society*, 122 (4), 2002, pp. 773–87.

Damghani, Ahmad, "Persian contributions to Sufi literature in Arabic," in Leonard Lewisohn (ed.), *Classical Persian Sufism: from its origins to Rumi* (London and New York, Khaniqahi Nimatullahi Publications, 1993), pp. 33–58.

Daniel, Elton L., *The Political History of Khurasan under Abbasid Rule, 747–820* (Minneapolis and Chicago, Bibliotheca Islamica, 1979).

Danielson, Michael N. and Kele, Ruen, *The Politics of Rapid Urbanization: Government and Growth in Modern Turkey* (New York, Holmes & Meier, 1985).

Daoulatli, A., *Tunis sous les Hafsides* (Tunis, 1976).

Darling, Linda, *Revenue Raising and Legitimacy* (1997).

Darrag, Ahmad, *L'Egypte sous le Regne de Barsbay 825–841/1422–1438* (Damascus, Institut Français de Damas, 1961).

Daryaee, Touraj, "The collapse of the Sasanian power in Fārs/Persis," *Nāme-ye Irān-e Bāstān*, 2, 2002, pp. 1–18.

Davis, Eric, "History for the many or history for the few? The historiography of the Iraqi working class," in Lockman, Zachary (ed.), *Workers and the Working Class in the Middle East* (Albany, State University of New York Press, 1994), pp. 271–302.

Davis, Uri, *Israel: An Apartheid State* (London, Zed Books, 1987).

Dawisha, Adeed, *Arab Nationalism in the Twentieth Century* (Princeton, NJ, Princeton University Press, 2003).

Dawisha, Adeed and I. William Zartman, *Beyond Coercion: The Durability of the Arab State* (London, Croom Helm, 1988).

Dawn, C. Ernest, *From Ottomanism to Arabism: Essays on the Origins of Arab Nationalism* (Urbana, IL., University of Illinois Press, 1973).

Décobert, Christian, *Le mendicant et le combattant. L'institution de l'Islam* (Paris, Éditions du Seuil, 1991).

Deeb, Marius, *Party Politics in Egypt: The Wafd and its Rivals, 1919–39* (London, Ithaca Press, 1979).

De Jong, Frederick and Bernd Radtke (eds.), *Islamic Mysticism Contested: Thirteen Centuries of Confrontations and Polemic* (Leiden, E. J. Brill, 1999).

De Lage, Olivier, "La vie politique en Peninsula arabique: Qatar, Emirates arabes unies, Bahrein," *Revue des Mondes musulmans et de la Méditerranée*, 81–2, 1996, pp. 319–29.

Denoeux, Guilain, *Urban Unrest in the Middle East: A Comparative Study of Informal Networks in Egypt, Iran, and Lebanon* (Albany, State University of New York Press, 1993).

Depont, Octave and Xavier Coppolani, *Les confréries religieuses musulmanes. Publié sous le patronage de M. Jules Cambons, gouverneur générale de l'Algérie* (Paris, Jourdan, 1897).

Deshen, Shlomo, *The Mellah Society: Jewish Community Life in Sherifian Morocco* (Chicago, Chicago University Press, 1989).

Deshen, Shlomo, and Walter Zenner (eds.), *Jews among Muslims: Communities in the Pre-colonial Middle East* (London, Macmillan, 1996).

Detalle, Renaud "Les parties politiques au Yemen: paysage après le bataille," *Revue des Mondes musulmans et de la Méditerranée*, 81–2, 1996, pp. 341–96.

Deverdun, G. *Marrakech des origines à 1912* (Rabat, 1959).

Devlin, John, *The Ba'th Party: A History from its Origins to 1966* (Stanford, CA, Hoover Institution Press, 1976).

Dilthey, Wilhelm, *Introduction to the Human Sciences*, tr. Ramon J. Betanzos (Detroit, Wayne State University Press, 1988).

Al-Dīnawarī, Abū Ḥanīfa Aḥmad b. Dāwūd, *Al-Akhbār al-Ṭiwāl* (ed. V. Guirgass and I. I. Krachkovskii) (Leiden, 1912).

Division for the Advancement of Women (UN), "International standards of equality and religious freedom: implications for the status of women," in Moghadam (ed.), *Identity Politics and Women* (1994).

Djaït, Hichem, *Al-Kūfa, Naissance de la ville islamique* (Paris, G.-P. Maisonneuve et Larose, 1986).

Donner, Fred McGraw, "From believers to Muslims: confessional self-identity in the early Islamic community," *Al-Abḥāth*, 51, 9–53, 2003.

Donner, Fred McGraw, "Orientalists and the rise of Islam," in Sami Khasawnih (ed.), *Orientalism: Dialogue of Cultures. Proceedings of a Conference held in 'Amman, Jordan, 22–24 October 2002* (Amman, University of Jordan, 2004) pp. 57–84.

Donner, Fred McGraw, *Narratives of Islamic Origins. The Beginnings of Islamic Historical Writing* (Princeton, NJ, Darwin Press, 1998).

Donner, Fred McGraw, "Centralized authority and military autonomy in the early Islamic conquests," in Averil Cameron (ed.), *The Byzantine Early Islamic Near East, III: States, Resources, and Armies* (Princeton: Darwin Press, 1995), pp. 337–60.

Donner, Fred McGraw, "The growth of military institutions in the early caliphate and their relation to civilian authority," in monograph supplementing the journal *Al-Qantara*, 14, 1993, pp. 311–26.

Donner, Fred McGraw, "The formation of the Islamic state," *Journal of the American Oriental Society*, 106, 1986, pp. 283–96.

Donner, Fred McGraw, *The Early Islamic Conquests* (Princeton, NJ, Princeton University Press, 1981).

Doron, Gideon, "Two civil societies and one state," in Augustus Richard Norton (ed.), *Civil Society in the Middle East* (Leiden, E. J. Brill, 1996), vol. 2, pp. 193–220.

Dorsky, Susan, *Women of 'Amran: A Middle Eastern Ethnographic Study* (Salt Lake City, University of Utah Press, 1986).

Douglas, J. Leigh, *The Free Yemeni Movement, 1935–1962* (Syracuse, NY, Syracuse University Press, 1987).

Doumato, Eleanor Abdella and Marsha Pripstein Posusney (eds.), *Women and Globalization in the Arab Middle East: Gender, Economy and Society* (Boulder, CO, Lynne Rienner, 2003).

Dozy, Reinhart, *Essay sur l'histoire de l'Islamisme,* tr. V. Chauvin (Leiden, E. J. Brill, 1979).

Dresch, Paul, *A History of Modern Yemen* (Cambridge, Cambridge University Press, 2001).

Dsuqi, 'Asim, *Mujtama' 'ulama' al-Azhar, 1895–1961* (Cairo, Dar al-Thaqafa al-Jadida, 1980).

Duka, Theodore, "The influence of Buddhism upon Islam," *Journal for the Royal Asiatic Society,* 1904, pp. 125–41.

Dumper, Michael, *The Politics of Sacred Space: The Old City of Jerusalem in the Middle East Conflict* (Boulder, CO, Lynne Rienner, 2002).

Dünden Bugüne Istanbul Ansiklopaedisi (From Yesterday to Today: The Encyclopedia of Istanbul), 8 vols (Türkiye Ekonomik ve Toplumsal Tarih Vakfi, Istanbul, 1993–5).

Dunlop, D.M., *The History of the Jewish Khazars* (Princeton, 1954).

Al-Duri, A. A., *The Historical Formation of the Arab Nation,* tr. Lawrence I. Conrad (London, Croom Helm, 1987).

Duveyrier, Henri, *La confrérie musulmane de Sidi Mohammed ben 'Ali es-Senousi et son domaine géographique en l'année 1300 de l'hégire* (Paris, Société géographique, 1883).

Early, Evelyn A., *Baladi Women: Playing with an Egg and a Stone* (Boulder, CO, Lynne Rienner, 1993)

Eaton, Richard, *The Sufis 1300–1700: Social Roles of Sufis in medieval India* (Princeton, NJ, Princeton University Press, 1977).

Eden, D. G., *Oil and Development in the Middle East* (New York, Praeger, 1979).

Ehteshami, Anoushiravan and Murphy, Emma, "Transformation of the corporatist state in the Middle East," *Third World Quarterly,* 17 (4), 1996, pp. 753–72.

Eickelman, Dale F., *The Middle East and Central Asia: An Anthropological Approach* (Upper Saddle River, NJ, Prentice Hall, 1998).

Eickelman, Dale F., *Knowledge and Power in Morocco* (Princeton, Princeton University Press, 1985).

Eickelman, Dale F., *Moroccan Islam: Tradition and Society in a Pilgrimage Center* (Austin, University of Texas Press, 1976).

Eickeman, Christine, *Women and Community in Oman* (New York, New York University Press, 1984).

Eisenstadt, S. N., *Israeli Society* (London, Weidenfeld and Nicolson, 1967).

Eldem, Edhem, Daniel Goffman, and Bruce Masters, *The Ottoman City between East and West* (1999).

El Kadi, Galila, *L'urbanisation spontanée au Caire* (Tours, Centre d' Etudes et de Recherches URBAMA, no. 18, 1987).

Elm, Mostafa, *Oil, Power and Principle: Iran's Oil Nationalization and its Aftermath* (New York, Syracuse University Press, 1992).

Elmusa, Sharif S., "Faust without the devil? The interplay of technology and culture in Saudi Arabia," *Middle East Journal,* 51 (3), 1997, pp. 345–57.

Emerson, Rupert, *From Empire to Nation: The Rise to Self-Assertion of Asian and African Peoples* (Cambridge, Harvard University Press, 1960).

Enayat, Hamid, "Iran: Khumayni's concept of the 'Guardianship of the Jurist'," in J. Piscatori (ed.), *Islam and the Political Process* (Cambridge, Cambridge University Press, 1982), pp. 160–80.

Encyclopaedia of Islam (Leiden, E. J. Brill, 1960–2004), 2nd edn, vols. 1–11, plus supplements.

Encyclopedia of Islam (Leiden, E. J. Brill, 1913–64), 1st edn, vols. 1–8, plus supplement.

Entelis, John, *Pluralism and Party Transformation in Lebanon: al-Kataib, 1936–1970* (Leiden, E. J. Brill, 1975).

Ephrat, Daphna, *A Learned Society in a Period of Transition. The Sunni "ulama" of eleventh-century Baghdad* (New York, State University of New York Press, 2000).

Ernst, Carl, *The Shambhala Guide to Sufism* (Boston and London, Shambhala, 1997).

Ernst, Carl, *Ruzbihan Baqli: Mystical Experience and the Rhetoric of Sainthood in Persian Sufism* (Surrey, Curzon, 1996).

Ernst, Carl, "Traditionalism, the perennial philosophy, and Islamic studies," *Middle East Studies Association Bulletin*, 28 (2), 1994, pp. 176–81.

Ernst, Carl, *Words of Ecstasy in Sufism* (Albany, NY, State University of New York Press, 1985).

Escallier, Robert, *Citadins et espace urbain au Maroc* (Tours, Centre d'Etudes et de Recherches URBAMA, Université de Tours, Fascicule de Recherches no. 8, 1984, 2 vols.).

Esmail, Aziz, "Self, society, civility and Islam," in Amyn Sajoo (ed.), *Civil Society in the Muslim World* (London, I. B. Tauris, 2002), pp. 61–94.

Esposito, John L., *Unholy War: Terror in the Name of Islam* (Oxford and New York, Oxford University Press, 2002).

Esposito, John L. and Michael Watson (eds.), *Religion and Global Order* (Cardiff, University of Wales Press, 2000).

Esposito, John L., *The Islamic Threat: Myth or Reality?* (Oxford, Oxford University Press, 1992).

Esposito, John L., *Islam: The Straight Path* (New York, Oxford University Press, 1988).

Esposito, John L., *Islam and Politics* (New York, Syracuse University Press, 1984).

Van Ess, J., "From Wellhausen to Becker: the emergence of *Kulturgeschichte* in Islamic studies," in Malcolm Kerr (ed.), *Islamic Studies: A Tradition and Its Problems* (Malibu, CA, Undena, 1980), pp. 27–51.

Van Ess, J., *Frühe muʿtazilitische Häresiographie; zwei Werke des Nāshiʾ al-Akbar (gest. 293H.)* (Wiesbaden and Beirut, Franz Steiner Verlag, 1971).

Ettinghausen, Richard and Oleg Grabar, *The Art and Architecture of Islam: 650–1250* (New York, Viking Penguin, Pelican History of Art, 1987).

Evron, Boas, *Jewish State or Israeli Nation?* (Bloomington and Indianapolis, Indiana University Press, 1995)

Ewing, Katherine Pratt, *Arguing Sainthood: Modernity, Psychoanalysis, and Islam* (Durham, NC, Duke University Press, 1997).

Faghfoory, M., "Ulama–state relations in Iran: 1921–1941," *International Journal of Middle East Studies*, 19, 1987, pp. 413–32.

Fakhro, Mounira, "Civil society and non-governmental organizations in the Middle East: reflections on the Gulf," *The Middle East Women's Studies Review*, 11 (4), 1997, pp. 1–3.

Faksh, M., "The Alawi community of Syria: a new dominant political force," *Middle Eastern Studies*, 20 (2), 1984, pp. 133–53.

Farah, Tawfic (ed.), *Pan-Arabism and Arab Nationalism: The Continuing Debate* (Boulder, CO, Westview Press, 1987).

Faroqhi, Suraiya, "Social life in cities," in Halil Inalcik (ed.), *An Economic and Social History of the Ottoman Empire: 1300–1914* (Cambridge, Cambridge University Press, 1994), pp. 576–608.

Faroqhi, Suraiya, *Men of Modest Substance: House Owners and House Property in Seventeenth-century Ankara and Kayseri* (Cambridge, Cambridge University Press, 1987).

Faroqhi, Suraiya, *Towns and Townsmen of Ottoman Anatolia: Trade, Crafts and Food Production in a Urban Setting 1520–1650* (Cambridge, Cambridge University Press, 1984).

Farouk-Sluglett, Marion and Peter Sluglett, *Iraq since 1958: From Revolution to Dictatorship* (London, I. B. Tauris, 2003).

Fathi, Asghar (ed.), *Iranian Refugees and Exiles Since Khomeini* (Costa Mesa, CA, Mazda Publishers, 1991).

Fawaz, Leila Tarazi, *An Occasion for War: Civil Conflict in Lebanon and Damascus in 1860* (Oxford and London, Centre for Lebanese Studies and I. B. Tauris, 1994).

Fawaz, Leila Tarazi, *Merchants and Migrants in Nineteenth-century Beirut* (Cambridge, Cambridge University Press, 1983).

Fernandez, Leonor, *The Evolution of a Sufi Institution in Mamluk Egypt: The khanqah* (Berlin, K. Schwartz, 1988).

Fernea, Elizabeth Warnock (ed.), *Women and the Family in the Middle East: New Voices of Change* (Austin, University of Texas Press, 1985).

Fernea, Elizabeth Warnock, and Basima Bezirgan (eds.), *Middle Eastern Women Speak* (Austin, University of Texas Press, 1977).

Finer, Samuel E., *The Man on Horseback: The Role of the Military in Politics* (Boulder, CO, Westview Press, 1988).

Finkelstein, Norman, *The Holocaust Industry: Reflections in the Exploitation of Jewish Suffering* (London, Verso, 2000).

Firestone, Reuven, *Jihad: The Origin of Holy War in Islam* (New York, Oxford University Press, 1999).

Fischbach, Michael, *State, Society and Land in Jordan* (Leiden, E. J. Brill, 2000).

Fischer, Michael, "Imam Khomeini: four levels of understanding," in John Esposito (ed.), *Voices of Resurgent Islam* (New York and Oxford, Oxford University Press, 1983), pp. 150–74.

Flapan, Simha, *The Birth of Israel: Myths and Realities* (New York, Pantheon, 1987).

Flapan, Simha, *Zionism and the Palestinians* (London, Croom Helm, 1979).

Fleischer, Cornell, *Bureaucrat and Intellectual in the Ottoman Empire* (Princeton, 1986).

Fletcher, Joseph, *Studies on Chinese and Islamic Inner Asia* (Aldershot, Variorum, 1995).

Floor, Willem, *A Fiscal History of Iran in the Safavid and Qajar Periods* (1998)

Foucault, Michel, "The history of sexuality," in William McNeill and Karen S. Feldman (eds.), *Continental Philosophy: An Anthology* (Oxford, Blackwell, 1998), pp. 381–90.

Foucault, Michel, *The Order of Things: An Archeology of the Human Sciences* (London, Vintage Books, 1994).

Foucault, Michel, *Histoire de la sexualité*, 2 vols. (Paris, Gallimard, 1976).

Fraser, T. G., *The Arab–Israeli Conflict* (Basingstoke, Macmillan, 1995).

Freeman-Grenville, C. P., *The Muslim and Christian Calendars* (London, Oxford University Press, 1963).

Frick, Heinrich, *Ghazalis Selbstbiographie: Ein Vergleich mit Augustins Konfessionen* (Leipzig, J. C. Hinrichs, 1919).

Friedman, Yohannan, "A contribution to the early history of Islam in India," in M. Rosen-Ayalon (ed.), *Studies in Memory of Gaston Wiet* (Jerusalem, Institute of Asian and African Studies, Hebrew University of Jerusalem, 1977), pp. 309–33.

Frisch, Hillel, "Guns and butter in the Egyptian army," in Barry Rubin and Thomas A. Keaney (eds.), *Armed Forces in the Middle East: Politics and Strategy* (BESA Studies in International Security, London, Frank Cass, 2002), pp. 93–112.

Fromkin, D., *A Peace To End All Peace* (Harmondsworth, Penguin, 1991).

Fück, J. W., "Islam as an historical problem in European historiography since 1800," in Bernard Lewis and P. M. Holt (eds.), *Historians of the Middle East* (Oxford, Oxford University Press, 1962).

Fukuyama, Francis, *The End of History and the Last Man* (London, Penguin Books, 1992).

Furman, Uriah, "Minorities in contemporary Islamist discourse," *Middle Eastern Studies*, 36 (4), 2000, pp. 1–20.

Gaborieau, Marc, Alexandre Popovic, and Thierry Zarcone (eds.), *Naqshbandis: cheminements et situation actuelle d'un ordre mystique musulman : actes de la Table ronde de Sèvres 2–4 mai 1985* (Istanbul and Paris, Éditions Isis., 1990).

Gabrieli, Francesco, "Muhammad ibn al-Qāsim al-Thaqafi and the Arab Conquest of Sind," *East and West*, 15, 1965, pp. 281–95.

Gairdner, William, *Al-Ghazzali's Mishkat al-anwar: The Niche for Lights* (London, Royal Asiatic Society, 1915).

Garcin de Tassy, Joseph, *La poésie philosophique et religieuse chez les persans* (Paris, Benjamin Duprat, 1860).

Garcin, J. C. et al. (eds), *Etats, sociétés et cultures du Monde Musulman médiéval, Xe–XVe siècle* (Paris, 1995, 2000).

Gaube, Heinz and Eugen Wirth, *Aleppo: Historische und geographische Beiträge zur baulichen Gestaltung, zur sozialen Organisation und zur wirtschaftlichen Dynamik einer vorderasiatischen Fernhandelsmetrople* (Dr. Ludwig Reichert, Beihefte zum Tübinger Atlas des Vorderen Orients, Reihe B [Geisteswissenschaften] Nr. 58, Wiesbaden, 1984).

Gaube, Heinz, *Iranian Cities* (New York, New York University Press, 1979).

Gaube, Heinz, and Eugen Wirth, *Der Basar von Isfahan* (Dr. Ludwig Reichert, Beihefte zum Tübinger Atlas des Vorderen Orients, Reihe B [Geisteswissenschaften] Nr. 22, Wiesbaden, 1978).

Geertz, Clifford, *Islam Observed: Religious Development in Morocco and Indonesia* (New Haven, Yale University Press, 1968).

Geiger, Abraham, *Was hat Mohammed aus dem Judenthume aufgenommen?* (Bonn, 1832) (English translation, *Judaism and Islam*, Madras, 1898).

Geiling, S., "The Marja'iyya in Iran and the nomination of Khamenei in December, 1994," *Middle Eastern Studies*, 33 (4), 1997, pp. 777–88.

Gelber, Nathan M., *Zur Vorgeschichte des Politischen Zionismus* (Vienna, Phaidon-Verlag, 1927).

Gellner, Ernest, "The importance of being modular," in John Hall (ed.), *Civil Society: Theory, History, Comparison* (Cambridge, Polity Press, 1995), pp. 32–55.

Gellner, Ernest, *Postmodernism, Reason and Religion* (London, Routledge, 1992).

Gellner, Ernest, *Nations and Nationalism* (Oxford, Blackwell, 1984).

Gellner, Ernest, (ed.), *Islam et société: anthropologie du Maghreb* (Paris, CNRS, 1981).

Gellner, Ernest and Charles Micaud, *Arabs and Berbers: From Tribe to Nation in North Africa* (London, Heath and Company, 1972).

Gerber, H., *The Social Origins of the Modern Middle East* (Boulder, CO, Lynne Rienner, 1987).

Germen, Aydin (ed.), *Islamic Architecture and Urbanism*. Selected Papers from a Symposium Organized by the College of Architecture and Planning, 5–10 January 1980 (Dammam, King Faisal University, 1983).

Gershoni, Israel and James P. Jankowski, *Redefining the Egyptian Nation, 1930–1945* (New York, Cambridge University Press, 1995).

Ghods, M. Reza, "Iranian nationalism and Reza Shah," *Middle Eastern Studies*, 27 (1), 1991, pp. 35–45.

Gibb, Sir Hamilton A. R., *The Arab Conquests of Central Asia* (London, Royal Asiatic Society, 1923).

Giddens, Anthony, *The Nation-State and Violence* (Berkeley, University of California Press, 1985).

Giese, Ernst, "Aufbau, Entwicklung und Genese der islamisch-orentalischen Stadt in Sowjet-Mittelasien," *Erdkunde*, 24, 1980, pp. 46–60.

Gillard, David, *The Struggle for Asia 1828–1914: A Study in British and Russian Imperialism* (London, Methuen, 1977).

Gilsenan, Michael, "Trajectories of contemporary Sufism," in Ernst Gellner (ed.), *Islamic Dilemmas: Reformers, Nationalists and Industrialization* (Berlin and New York, Mouton Publishers, 1985), pp. 187–98.

Gilsenan, Michael, *Saint and Sufi in Modern Egypt: An essay in the sociology of religion* (Oxford, Clarendon Press, 1973).

Glassen, Erika, *Die frühen Safawiden nach Qazi Ahmad Qumi* (Freiburg, Schwarz, 1970).

Gleave, Robert, "*Jihād* and the Religious Legitimacy of the Early Qajar State," in Robert Gleave (ed.), *Religion and Society in Qajar Iran* (London, RoutledgeCurzon, 2005).

Gleave, Robert, "Political aspects of modern Shi'i legal discussions: Khumayni and Khu'i on *ijtihad* and *qada*," in B. Robinson (ed.), *Shaping the Current Islamic Reformation* (London, Frank Cass, 2002), pp. 96–116.

Goffman, Daniel, *The Ottoman Empire and Early Modern Europe* (2002).

Goitein, S. D., *A Mediterranean Society: The Jewish Communities of the Arab World as Portrayed in the Documents of the Cairo Geniza*, 5 vols (Berkeley, University of California Press, 1967–88).

Gökalp, Ziya, *Türkçülüğün Esasları* (Istanbul, Kum Saati Yayİnlarİ, 2001).

Goldschmidt, Arthur, "The Egyptian Nationalist Party: 1892–1919," in P. M Holt (ed.), *Political and Social Change in Modern Egypt* (London, Oxford University Press, 1968).

Goldziher, Ignaz, *Introduction to Islamic Theology and Law*, tr. Andras and Ruth Hamori (Princeton, NJ, Princeton University Press, 1981).

Goldziher, Ignaz, *Muhammedanische Studien* (Halle, Max Niemayer, 1890), vol. 2; English translation, *Muslim Studies* (London: George Allen and Unwin, 1971, vol. 2).

Goldziher, Ignaz, *Die Richtungen der islamischen Koranauslegung* (Leiden, E. J. Brill, 1920).

Gole, Nilufer, "Authoritarian secularism and Islamist politics: the case of Turkey," in Augustus Richard Norton (ed.), *Civil Society in the Middle East* (Leiden, E. J. Brill, 1996), vol. 2, pp. 17–44.

Golombek, Lisa and Donald Wilber, *The Timurid Architecture of Iran and Turan*, 2 vols (Princeton, Princeton University Press, Princeton Monographs in Art and Archaeology, 1988).

Goodwin, Godfrey, *A History of Ottoman Architecture* (New York, Thames and Hudson, 1971).

Gordon, M., *The Breaking of a Thousand Swords* (Albany, 2001).

Goria, Wade, *Sovereignty and Leadership in Lebanon, 1943–1976* (London, Ithaca Press, 1986).

Green, Arnold H., *The Tunisian Ulama, 1873–1915: Social Structure and Response to Ideological Currents* (Leiden, E. J. Brill, 1978).

Gril, Denis, "Le personnage coranique de de Pharaon d'après l'interprétation d'Ibn 'Arabi," *Annales Islamologiques*, 14, 1978, pp. 37–57.

Gril, Denis, "Le commentaire du verset de la lumière d'après l'interprétation d'Ibn 'Arabi," *Bulletin d'études orientales de l'Institut Français de Damas*, 29, 1977, pp. 179–87.

Grötzbach, Erwin, *Städte und Basare in Afghanistan: Eine stadtgeographische Untersuchung* (Dr. Ludwig Reichert, Beihefte zum Tübinger Atlas des Vorderen Orients, Reihe B [Geisteswissenschaften] Nr. 16, Wiesbaden, 1979).

Von Grunebaum, Gustav, *Classical Islam: A History 600–1258*, tr. Kathrine Watson (Chicago, Aldine Publications, 1970).

Von Grunebaum, Gustav, "The nature of Arab unity before Islam," *Arabica*, 10, 1963, pp. 5–23.

Guenena, Nemat, and Nadia Wassef, *Unfulfilled Promises: Women's Rights in Egypt* (Cairo and New York, Population Council, 1999).

Guillaume, Alfred, *The Life of Muhammad* (Oxford, Oxford University Press, 1955); (translation of Ibn Ishāq, Sīrat rasūl allāh).

El-Guindy, Fadwa. "Veiling *intifah* with Muslim ethic: Egypt's contemporary Islamic movement," *Social Problems*, 8, 1981, pp. 465–85.

Gurr, Ted and Barbara Harff, *Ethnic Conflict in World Politics* (Boulder, CO, Westview Press, 1994).

Gurr, Ted, "Why minorities rebel: explaining ethnopolitical protest and rebellion," in Ted Gurr (ed.), *Minorities at Risk* (Washington, DC, United States Institute of Peace Press, 1993), pp. 123–38.

Gurr, Ted (ed.), *Minorities at Risk* (Washington, DC, United States Institute of Peace Press, 1993).

Gurney, John D., "The transformation of Tehran in the later nineteenth century," in Chahryar Adle and Bernard Hourcade (eds.), *Téhéran capitale bicentenaire* (Paris and Tehran, Institut Français de Recherche en Iran, Bibliotheque Iranienne 37, 1992).

Gwatkin, H. M. (ed.), *The Cambridge Mediaeval History* (Cambridge, Cambridge University Press, 1913).

Habermas, Jürgen, *The Postnational Constellation* (Oxford, Polity Press, 2001).

Haddad, G. M., *Revolutions and Military Rule in the Middle East: The Arab States (Part 2): Egypt, the Sudan, Yemen and Libya* (New York, 1973).

Haddad, G. M., *Revolutions and Military Rule in the Middle East: The Arab States (Part 1): Iraq, Syria, Lebanon and Jordan* (New York, 1971).

Haim, Sylvia G., "Alfieri and al-Kawakibi," *Oriente Moderno*, 34, 1954, pp. 321–34.

Hakim, Basim Selim, *Arabic–Islamic Cities: Building and Planning Principles* (London, KPI, 1986).

Hale, William, *Turkish Foreign Policy 1774–2000* (Portland, OR, Frank Cass, 2002).

Hale, William, *Turkish Politics and the Military* (London, Routledge, 1994).

Hall, John, "In search of civil society," in John Hall (ed.), *Civil Society: Theory, History, Comparison* (Cambridge, Polity Press, 1995), pp. 1–31.

Hallaq, Wael B., *Authority, Continuity and Change in Islamic Law* (Cambridge, Cambridge University Press, 2001).

Halliday, Fred, *Islam and the Myth of Confrontation: Religion and Politics in the Middle East* (London, I. B. Tauris, 1996).

Halliday, Fred, *Arabia Without Sultans* (Harmondsworth, Penguin, 1974).

Halm, Heinz, *The Empire of the Mahdi* (Leiden, 1996).

Halm, Heinz, *Shiism*, tr. J. Watson (Edinburgh, Edinburgh University Press, 1991).

Halpern, Manfred, *The Politics of Social Change in the Middle East and North Africa* (Princeton, Princeton University Press, 1963).

Halpern, Manfred, "Middle Eastern armies and the new middle class," in John Johnson (ed.), *The Role of the Military in Under-Developed Countries* (Princeton, NJ, Princeton University Press, 1962), pp. 277–316.

Hammami, Rema and Penny Johnson, "Equality with a difference: gender and citizenship in transition Palestine," *Social Politics*, 6 (3), 1999, pp. 314–43.

Hammer-Purgstall, Josef, *Das arabische hohe Lied der Liebe* (Vienna: Kaiserl. königl. Hof- und staatsdruckerei, 1854).

Hammoudi, Abdellah, *Master and Disciple: The Cultural Foundations of Moroccan Authoritarianism* (Chicago, Chicago University Press, 1997).

Haneda, Masashi, "Introduction: an interpretation of the concept of the 'Islamic City'," in Masashi Haneda and Toru Miura (eds.), *Islamic Urban Studies* (London, Kegan Paul, 1994), pp. 1–10.

Haneda, Masashi and Toru Miura (eds.), *Islamic Urban Studies: Historical Review and Perspectives* (London, Kegan Paul, 1994).

Hanna, Nelly, *Making Big Money in 1600: The Life and Times of Isam'il Abu Taqiyya, Egyptian Merchant* (Syracuse, Syracuse University Press, 1998).

Hanna, Nelly, *Habiter au Caire: La maison moyenne et ses habitants aux XVIIe et XVIIIe siècles* (Cairo, Institut Français d'Archéologie Orientale, *Etudes urbaines*, 2, 1991).

Hanna, Nelly, *Construction Work in Ottoman Cairo (1517–1789)* (Cairo, Institut Français d'Archéologie Orientale, supple. aux *Annales Islamoloqiques*, no. 4, 1984).

Hanna, Nelly, *Urban History of Bulaq in the Mamluk and Ottoman Periods* (Cairo, Institut Français d'Archéologie Orientale, suppl. aux *Annales Islamoloqiques*, no. 3, 1983).

Hanna, Sami, and George H. Gardner, *Arab Socialism: A Documentary Survey* (Leiden, E. J. Brill, 1969).

Harb, Imad, "The Egyptian military in politics: disengagement or accommodation?" *The Middle East Journal*, 57 (2), 2003, pp. 269–91.

Harff, Barbara, "Minorities, rebellion, and repression in North Africa and the Middle East," in Ted Gurr (ed.), *Minorities at Risk* (Washington, DC, United States Institute of Peace Press, 1993), pp. 217–51.

Harik, Iliya, "The single party as a subordinate movement: the case of Egypt," *World Politics,* 26 (1), 1973.

Harris, Rabia, *The Risalah: Principles of Sufism* (Chicago, IL, Great Books of the Islamic World, Kazi Publications, 2002).

Hartmann, Richard, "Zur Frage nach der Herkunft und den Anfängen des Sufitums," *Der Islam,* 6, 1916, pp. 31–70.

Hartmann, Richard, *Al-Kuschairi's Darstellung des Sufitums* (Berlin, Mayer & Müller, 1914).

Hartshorn J., *Oil Trade: Politics and Prospects* (Cambridge, Cambridge University Press, 1993).

Hasan, Ahmad Husayn, *al-Jama'at al-siyasiyya al-islamiyya wa-l-mujtama' al-madani* (Cairo, al-Dar al-Thaqafiyya li-l-Nashr, 2000).

Hasan, S. A., "A survey of the expansion of Islam into Central Asia during the Umayyad Caliphate," *Islamic Culture* 48, 1974, pp. 177–86.

Hasan, S. A., "A survey of the expansion of Islam into Central Asia during the Umayyad Caliphate," *Islamic Culture,* 47, 1973, pp. 1–13.

Hasan, S. A., "A survey of the expansion of Islam into Central Asia during the Umayyad Caliphate," *Islamic Culture,* 45, 1971, pp. 95–113.

Hasan, S. A., "A survey of the expansion of Islam into Central Asia during the Umayyad Caliphate," *Islamic Culture* 44, 1970, pp. 165–76.

Hashim, Ahmed, "Saddam Husayn and Civil–Military Relations in Iraq: the quest for legitimacy and power," *The Middle East Journal,* 57 (1), 2002, p. 9.

Hatem, Mervat, "The paradoxes of state feminism," in Barbara Nelson and Najma Chaudhury (eds.), *Women and Politics Worldwide* (New Haven, CT, Yale University Press).

Hathaway, Jane, *Politics of Households in Ottoman Egypt* (1997).

Hawting, Gerald, *The First Dynasty of Islam. The Umayyad Caliphate Ad 661–750* (London, Routledge, 2000).

Hawting, Gerald, *The Idea of Idolatry and the Emergence of Islam* (Cambridge, Cambridge University Press, 1999).

Hayes, Carlton, "The historical evolution of modern nationalism," in R. R. Smith (New York, 1931).

Hayes, Carlton, *Essays on Nationalism* (London, Macmillan, 1926).

Haykel, Bernard, *Revival and Reform in Islam: The Legacy of Muhammad Al-Shawkani* (Cambridge, Cambridge University Press, 2003).

Hazen, William, "Minorities in assimilation: the Kurds of Iran, Iraq, Syria, and Turkey," in R. D. McLaurin (ed.), *The Political Role of Minority Groups in the Middle East* (New York, Praeger Publishers, 1979), pp. 49–75.

Hazony, Yoram, *The Jewish State: The Struggle for Israel's Soul* (New York, Basic Books, 2001).

Heck, Gene, "Gold mining in Arabia and the rise of the Islamic state," *Journal of the Economic and Social History of the Orient,* 42, 1999, pp. 364–95.

Henry, Clement, and Robert Springborg, *Globalization and the Politics of Development in the Middle East* (Cambridge, Cambridge University Press, 2001).

Heper, Martin, and Jacob Landau (eds.), *Political Parties and Democracy in Turkey* (London, I. B. Tauris, 1991).

Heper, Metin, and Ahmet Evin (eds.), *State, Democracy and the Military in Turkey in the 1980s* (Berlin, Walter de Gruyter, 1988).

Heper, Metin, *Gecekondu Policy in Turkey: An Evaluation with a Case Study of Rumelihisarüstü Squatter Area in Istanbul* (Istanbul, Boaziçi University Press, 1978).

Herzl, T., *The Complete Diaries of Theodore Herzl* (New York, Herzl Press and Thomas Yoseloff, 1956).

Hess, A. C., *The Forgotten Frontier* (Chicago and London, 1978).

Heyd, Uriel, "The Ottoman 'Ulema and westernization in the time of Selim III and Mahmud II," in Heyd (ed.), *Studies in Islamic History* (Jerusalem, 1961), pp. 63–96.

Hicks, N., and G. al-Najjar, "The utility of tradition: civil society in Kuwait," in Augustus Richard Norton (ed.), *Civil Society in the Middle East* (Leiden, E. J. Brill, 1996), vol. 1, pp. 186–213.

Higgot, Richard, and Nicola Phillips, "Challenging triumphalism and convergence: the limits of global liberalization in Asia and Latin America," *Review of International Studies* 26 (3), 2000, pp. 359–79.

Higgot, Richard, and Nicola Phillips, "Contested globalization: the changing context and normative changes," *Review of International Studies*, 26, special issue, December 2000, pp. 131–53.

Al-Hilāl b. al-Muḥassin al-Ṣābī, al-Wuzarā' (Cairo, 1958); (ed. 'Abd al-Sattār Aḥmad Farrāj).

Hillenbrand, C., *The Crusades: Islamic Perspectives* (Edinburgh, 1999).

Hillenbrand, Robert, *Islamic Architecture: Form, Function and Meaning* (New York, Columbia University Press, 1994).

Hinds, Martin, "Küfan political alignments and their background in the mid-seventh century AD," in J. Bacharach et al. (eds.), *Studies in Early Islamic History* (Princeton NJ, Darwin Press, 1996), pp. 1–28.

Hinds, Martin, "The murder of the Caliph 'Uthmān," in J. Bacharach et al. (eds.), *Studies in Early Islamic History* (Princeton, NJ, Darwin Press, 1996), pp. 29–55.

Hinds, Martin, "The Ṣiffīn arbitration agreement," in J. Bacharach et al. (eds.), *Studies in Early Islamic History* (Princeton, NJ, Darwin Press, 1996), pp. 56–96.

Hinds, Martin, "The banners and battle cries of the Arabs at Ṣiffīn (AD 657)," in J. Bacharach et al. (eds.), *Studies in Early Islamic History* (Princeton, NJ, Darwin Press, 1996), pp. 97–142.

Hinds, Martin, "A letter from the Governor of Egypt concerning Egyptian–Nubian relations," in J. Bacharach et al. (eds.), *Studies in Early Islamic History* (Princeton, NJ, Darwin Press, 1996), pp. 160–87.

Hinds, Martin and Hamdi Sakkout, "A letter from the Governor of Egypt to the King of Nubia and Muqurra concerning Egyptian–Nubian relations in 141/758," in Wadād al-Qāḍī (ed.), *Studia Arabica et Islamica. Festschrift for Ihsān 'Abbās on his Sixtieth Birthday* (Beirut, American University of Beirut, 1981), pp. 209–29.

Hinnebusch, Raymond, "Introduction: the analytical framework," in R. Hinnebusch and A. Ehteshami (eds.), *The Foreign Policies of Middle East States* (Boulder, CO, Lynne Rienner, 2002).

Hinnebusch, Raymond, *Syria: Revolution from Above* (London, Routledge, 2001).

Hinnebusch, Raymond, "State, civil society and political change in Syria," in Augustus Richard Norton (ed.), *Civil Society in the Middle East* (Leiden, E. J. Brill, 1996), vol. 1, pp. 214–42.

Hinnebusch, Raymond, "State and civil society in Syria," *Middle East Journal*, 47 (2), 1993, pp. 243–57.

Hinnebusch, Raymond, "The politics of economic reform in Egypt," *Third World Quarterly*, 14 (1), 1993, pp. 159–71.

Hinnebusch, Raymond, "Political parties in the Arab state: Libya, Syria, Egypt," in Adeed Dawisha and I. William Zartman (eds.), *Beyond Coercion: The Durability of the Arab State* (London: Croom Helm for Istituto Affari Internazionali, 1988), pp. 35–60.

Hinnebusch, Raymond, *Egyptian Politics under Sadat* (Boulder, CO, Lynne Rienner, 1988).

Hinnebusch, Raymond, "Syria under the Ba'th: social ideology, policy, and practice," in Laurence O. Michalak and Jeswald Salacuse (eds.), *Social Legislation in the Contemporary Middle East* (Berkley, Institute of International Studies, 1986).

Hirschberg, H. Z., *A History of the Jews in North Africa, Vol 2: From the Ottoman Conquests to the Present Time* (Leiden, E. J. Brill, 1981).

Hirschberg, H. Z., *A History of the Jews in North Africa, Vol 1: From Antiquity to the Sixteenth Century* (Leiden, E. J. Brill, 1974).

Hobsbawm, Eric, *Nations and Nationalism since 1780: Programme, Myth, Reality* (Cambridge, Cambridge University Press, 1990).

Hodgson, Marshall G. S., *The Venture of Islam*, vol. 3 (Chicago, Chicago University Press, 1974).

Hoffman, Valerie, *Sufism, Mystics, and Saints in Modern Egypt* (Columbia, SC, University of South Carolina Press, 1995).

Holt, Peter M., *The Age of the Crusades* (London, Longman, 1986).

Holt, Peter M., *Egypt and the Fertile Crescent, 1516–1922: A Political History* (Ithaca, Cornell University Press, 1985).

Homerin, Emile, *From Arab Poet to Muslim Saint* (Columbia, SC, University of South Carolina Press, 1994).

Homerin, Emile, "Ibn Taimiyah's 'al-Sufiyah wa-l-fuqara'," *Arabica*, 32 (2), 1985, pp. 219–44.

Honarmand, M., *Pahlavism - Maktab-e No* (Tehran, Ordibehesht 1345, April/May 1966).

Hoodfar, Homa, "Return to the veil: personal strategy and public participation in Egypt," in Nanneke Redclift and M. Thea Sinclair (eds.), *Working Women: International Perspectives on Labour and Gender Ideology* (London and New York, Routledge, 1991), pp. 104–24.

Hopkins, J. F. P., *Medieval Muslim Government in Barbary* (London, 1958).

Horne, Alistair, *A Savage War of Peace: Algeria, 1954–1962* (London, Macmillan, 1977).

Horowitz, Donald, *Ethnic Groups in Conflict* (Berkeley, University of California Press, 1985).

Horowitz, D., and Moshe Lissak, *Origins of the Israeli Polity: Palestine Under the Mandate*, tr. Charles Hoffman (Chicago, University of Chicago Press, 1978).

Horten, Max, *Indische Strömungen in der islamischen Mystik*, 2 vols. (Heidelberg and Leipzig, O. Harrassowitz, 1927–8).

Hourani, Albert, *A History of the Arab Peoples* (Cambridge: Belknap Press of Harvard University Press, 1991).

Hourani, Albert, "How we should write the history of the Middle East," *International Journal of Middle East Studies*, 23, 1991.

Hourani, Albert, *Arabic Thought in the Liberal Age, 1798–1939* (Cambridge, Cambridge University Press, 1983).

Hourani, Albert, and S. M. Stern (eds.), *The Islamic City: A Colloquium* (Oxford, Bruno Cassirer, 1970).

Hourani, Albert, *Syria and Lebanon: A Political Essay* (London, Oxford University Press, 1947).

Hoyland, Robert, *Arabia and the Arabs: From the Bronze Age to the Coming of Islam* (London: Routledge, 2001).

Hoyland, Robert, *Seeing Islam as Others Saw It* (Princeton, NJ, Darwin Press, 1997).

Huggler, Justin, "UN report attacks Israel's 'separation fence'," *The New Zealand Herald*, 13 November, 2003.

Human Rights Watch, "Turkey 2003: human rights developments," at http://www.hrw.org/wr2k3/europe13.html.

Human Rights Watch, "Syria: the silenced Kurds," *Human Rights Watch*, 8 (4), 1996.

Humphreys, Steven R., *Islamic History* (Princeton, Princeton University Press, 1991).

Huntington, Samuel, *The Third Wave* (Norman, University of Oklahoma Press, 1991).

Huntington, Samuel, "Social and institutional dynamics of one-party systems," in Louis J. Cantori (ed.), *Comparative Political Systems* (Boston, Holbrook Press, 1974), pp. 323–70.

Huntington, Samuel, *Political Order in Changing Societies* (New Haven, Yale University Press, 1968).

Hurewitz, J. C., *Middle East Politics: The Military Dimension* (London, Praeger for the Council on Foreign Relations, 1969).

Hurgronje, Christiaan Snouck, *Het Mekaansche feest* (Leiden, E. J. Brill 1880).

Hurgronje, Christiaan Snouck, "Islam," in *Selected Works of C. Snouck Hurgonje* (Leiden, E. J. Brill, 1957), pp. 1–108.

Hussein, Mahmoud, *Class Conflict in Egypt* (New York, Monthly Review Press, 1973).

Ibn al-Athīr, *'Izz al-Dīn, Al-Kāmil f ī 'l-Ta'rīkh*, ed. C. J. Tornberg (Beirut, 1982).

Ibn Ḥawqal, *Abū'l-Qāsim, Kitāb Ṣūrat al-Arḍ*, ed. J. H. Kramers (Leiden, 1939).

Ibn Iyās, *Journal d'un Bourgeois du Caire*, 2 vols., tr. and annotated by Gaston Wiet (Paris: Libraire Armand Colin, 1955/1960).

Ibn Isḥāq, Muhammad, *Sīrat rasūl allāh*, 2 vols., ed. F. Wüstenfeld (Göttingen, Dieterich, 1858–1860).

Ibn al-Kalbi, Hisham b. Muhammad, *Jamharat al-Nasab* (Beirut, 1986).

Ibn Khaldun, *The Muqaddimah: an Introduction to History*, 3 vols., tr. F. Rosenthal (Princeton and London, 1967).

Ibn Khayyāṭ, *Khalīfa, Ta'rīkh*, ed. Akram Āiyā' al-'Umarī (Beirut, 1977).

Ibn Miskawayh, Abū 'Alı Aḥmad b. Muḥammad, "Tajārib al-Umam," in H. F. Amedroz, *The Experiences of the Nations* (London, 1920–1).

Ibn al-Muqaffa', *Risāla f ī l-Ṣaḥāba*, ed. C. Pellat (1976).

Ibn Sallām, Abū 'Ubayd al-Qāsim, *Kitāb al-Amwāl*, (ed. Muhammad Khalıl Harās (Beirut, 1988).

Ibn Ṭayfūr, Aḥmad b. Abī Ṭahir, *Kitāb Baghdad*, ed. H. Keller (Leipzig, 1908).

Ibrahim, S. E., "Civil society and prospects for democratization in the Arab world," in Augustus Richard Norton (ed.), *Civil Society in the Middle East* (Leiden, Brill, 1996), vol. 1, pp. 23–51.

Idris, H. R., *La Berbérie orientale sous les Zirides*, 2 vols. (Paris, 1962).

Ilbert, Robert, *Alexandrie 1830–1930: Histoire d'une communauté citadine*, 2 vols (Cairo, Institut Français d'Archéologie Orientale, 1996).

Imber, Colin, *The Ottoman Empire, 1300–1650* (New York, Palgrave Macmillan, 2002).

Imber, Colin, *Ebu's-su'ud: The Islamic Legal Tradition* (Edinburgh, Edinburgh University Press, 1997).

Imber, Colin, "The persecution of the Ottoman Shi'ites according to the Muhimme Deferleri 1565–1585," *Der Islam*, 56 (2), 1979, pp. 245–73.

Inalcik, Halil, *The Ottoman Empire: The Classical Age, 1300–1600* (Phoenix, 1994).

Inalcik, Halil, and Donald Quatert (eds.), *An Economic and Social History of the Ottoman Empire* (Cambridge, Cambridge University Press, 1994).

Inalcik, Halil, "Istanbul: an Islamic city," *Journal of Islamic Studies*, 1, 1990, pp. 1–23.

Inalcik, Halil, "Arab–Turkish relations in historical perspective (1260–1914)," *Studies in Turkish–Arab Relations*, Annual I, Istanbul, 1986, pp. 148–57.

Inalcik, Halil, "Suleiman the lawgiver and Ottoman law," *Archivum Ottomanicum*, 1, 1969, pp. 105–38.

Inalcik, Halil, "Ottoman methods of conquest," *Studia Islamica*, 2, 1954, pp. 102–29.

Inalcik, Halil, "Istanbul," *Encyclopedia of Islam*, 4, pp. 224–48.

Inhorn, Marcia C., "Population, poverty, and gender politics: motherhood pressures and marital crises in the lives of poor urban Egyptian women," in Michael E. Bonine (ed.), *Population, Poverty and Politics in Middle East Cities* (Gainesville, University Press of Florida, 1997), pp. 169–207.

Inhorn, Marcia C., *Infertility and Patriarchy: The Cultural Politics of Gender and Family Life in Egypt* (Philadelphia, University of Pennsylvania Press, 1996).

Inhorn, Marcia C., *Quest for Conception: Gender, Infertility, and Egyptian Medical Tradition* (Philadelphia, University of Pennsylvania Press, 1994).

International Labour Office, *Breaking Through the Glass Ceiling: Women in Management* (Geneva, ILO, 1997).

Irwin, R., *Islamic Art* (London, 1997).

Al-Iṣfahānī, Abū'l-Faraj, *'Alī b. al-Ḥusayn, Maqātil al-Ṭālibiyīn*, ed. Aḥmad Ṣaqr (Cairo, 1949).

Al-Iṣfahānī, Abū'l-Faraj, *'Alī b. al-Ḥusayn, Kitāb al-Aghānī*, ed. Muhammad Hatim (Cairo, 1963).

Ismatov, Bobomurod, *Panteisticheskaia filosofskaia traditsiia v persidsko-tadzhikskoi Poezii IX–XV vv.* (Donish, Dushanbe, 1986).

Israeli, Raphael, *Palestinians between Israel and Jordan* (New York, Praeger Publishers, 1991).

Issawi, Charles, *The Middle East Economy* (Princeton: Markus Wiener, 1995).

Issawi, Charles, *An Economic History of the Middle East and North Africa* (New York, Columbia University Press, 1982).

Al-Iṣtakhrī, Abū Isḥāq Ibrāhim b. Muḥammad, *Kitāb Masālik wa'l-Mamālik*, ed. M. J. de Goeje (Leiden, 1927).

Istanbul, a quarterly magazine, no. 1, 1992–no. 47, 2003.

Jabbur, George, *Al-fikra al-siyasi al-mu'asir fi Suriya* (London, Riad El-Rayyes, 1987).

Jackson, Peter, and Laurence Lockhart (eds.), *Cambridge History of Iran, Vol VI: The Timurid and Safavid Periods* (Cambridge, Cambridge University Press, 1986).

Al-Jāḥiẓ', 'Amrāb. Baḥr, "Manāqib al-Turk," in G. van Vloten (ed.), *Tria Opuscula Auctore Abu Othman Amr ibn Bahr al-Djahiz Basrensi* (Leiden, 1968), pp. 1–56.

Al-Jāḥiẓ', 'Amrāb. Baḥr, *Al-Bayān wa'l-Tabyīn* (Cairo, 1926–7).

Al-Jahshiyārī, Muḥammad b., *'Abdūs, Kitāb al-Wuzarā*, ed. M. al-Saqqā et al. (Cairo, 1938).

Jandora, John W., *The March from Medina. A Revisionist Study of the Arab Conquests* (Clifton, Kingston Press, 1990).

Jankowski, James, *Egypt's Young Rebels, "Young Egypt": 1933–1952* (Stanford, CA, Hoover Institution Press, 1975).

Jarry, Jacques, "L'Égypte et l'invasion musulmane," *Annales Islamologiques*, 6, 1966, pp. 1–29.

Jawad, H., *The Rights of Women in Islam: An Authentic Approach* (Basingstoke, Macmillan, 1998).

Jelavich, Barbara, *History of the Balkans: Eighteenth and Nineteenth Centuries* (Cambridge, Cambridge University Press, 1983).

Jenkins, Gareth, *Context and Circumstance: The Turkish Military in Politics* (International Institute of Strategic Studies (IISS) Adelphi Paper 337, Oxford, Oxford University Press for the IISS, 2001).

Johnson, Michael, *Class and Client in Beirut: the Sunni Muslim Community and the Lebanese State 1840–1985* (London, Ithaca Press, 1986).

Jolly, Cecil, "Du MTI à la Nahda [en Tunisie]," *Cahiers de l'Orient*, 38, 1995, pp. 19–40.

Jones, E., *The European Miracle* (Cambridge, Cambridge University Press, 1981).

Julien, Charles-André, *Le Maroc face aux impérialismes: 1415–1956* (Paris, Editions Jeune Afrique, 1978).

Julien, Charles-André, *History of North Africa from the Arab Conquest to 1830* (London, 1970).

Juynboll, Gautier, *Muslim Tradition: Studies in Chronology, Provenance and Authorship of Early ḥadīth* (Cambridge, Cambridge University Press, 1983).

Kably, M., *Société. pouvoir et religion au Maroc à la fin du Moyen Age* (Paris, 1986).

Kadıoğlu, Ayşe, "The paradox of Turkish nationalism and the construction of official identity," *Middle Eastern Studies,* 32 (2), 1996.

Kaegi, Walter E., *Byzantium and the Age of the Caliphates* (London, Longman, 1986).

Kafadar, Cemal, "Les Troubles Monétaires de la fin du XVIe Siècle et la Prise de Conscience Ottomane du Déclin," *Annales* 2, 1991, pp. 381–400.

Kafadar, Cemal, *Between Two Worlds: The Construction of the Ottoman State* (Berkeley, University of California Press, 1986).

Kamal, Zahira, "The development of the Palestinian women's movement in the occupied territories: twenty years after the Israeli occupation," in Suha Sabbagh (ed.), *Palestinian*

Women of Gaza and the West Bank (Bloomington, Indiana University Press, 1998), pp. 78–88.

Kamrava, Mehran, *Politics and Society in the Developing World* (London, Routledge, 2000).

Kapil, Arun, "Algeria," in Frank Tachau (ed.), *Political Parties of the Middle East and North Africa* (London, Mansell, 1994), pp. 1–68.

Kapiszewski, Andrzej, *Nationals and Expatriates: Population and Labour Dilemmas of the Gulf Cooperation Council States* (Ithaca Press, Reading, 2001).

Karam, Azza, "Islamist parties in the Arab world: ambiguities, contradictions and perseverance," *Democratization*, 4 (4), 1997, pp. 157–79.

Kark, Ruth, and Michal Oren-Nordheim, *Jerusalem and its Environs: Quarters, Neighborhoods, Villages, 1800–1948* (Jerusalem, Hebrew University Press and Magnes Press, 2001).

Karpat, Kemal, *The Gecekondu: Rural Migration and Urbanization* (Cambridge, Cambridge University Press, 1976).

Karpat, Kemal, *Turkey's Politics: The Transition to a Multi-Party System* (Princeton, NJ, Princeton University Press, 1959).

Karshenas, M., *Oil, State and Industrialisation in Iran* (Cambridge, Cambridge University Press, 1990).

Kassem, Maye, *In the Guise of Democracy: Governance in Contemporary Egypt* (Reading, Ithaca Press, 1999).

Katouzian, H., "Nationalist trends in Iran, 1921–1926," *International Journal of Middle East Studies*, 10, 1979, pp. 533–51.

Katz, Steven (ed.), *Mysticism and Language* (Oxford, Oxford University Press, 1992).

Al-Kawakibi, *Oriente Moderno*, 34, 1954, pp. 335–7.

Al-Kawakibi, 'Abd al-Rahman, *Taba'i' al-istibdad* (Cairo, 1931).

Kayyali, A. W. (ed.), *Zionism, Imperialism and Racism* (London, Croom Helm, 1979).

Kayali, Hasan, *Arabs and Young Turks: Ottomanism, Arabism and Islamism in the Ottoman Empire 1908–1918* (Berkeley and Los Angeles, University of California Press, 1997).

Kazemi, Farhad, "Civil society and Iranian politics," in Augustus Richard Norton (ed.), *Civil Society in the Middle East* (Leiden, E. J. Brill, 1996), vol. 2, pp. 119–52.

Kazziha, W., *Revolutionary Transformation in the Arab World* (London, 1975).

Keddie, Nikki R., *Qajar Iran and the Rise of Reza Khan, 1796–1925* (Costa Mesa, CA, Mazda Publishers, 1999).

Keddie, Nikki R., *Religion and Politics in Iran: Shi'ism from Quietism to Revolution* (New Haven, Yale University Press, 1983).

Keddie, Nikki R., *Roots of Revolution, an Interpretative History of Modern Iran* (New Haven and London, Yale University Press, 1981).

Kedourie, Elie, *Politics in the Middle East* (Oxford: Oxford University Press, 1992).

Kedourie, Elie, *England and the Middle East* (London: Mansell Publishing, 1987).

Kedourie, Elie, *Nationalism* (London: Hutchinson, 1966).

Kelman, Herbert, "Israel in transition from Zionism to post-Zionism," *The Annals of the American Academy*, 555, 1998.

Kennedy, Hugh, *The Armies of the Caliphs* (London, 2001).

Kennedy, Hugh, *The Prophet and the Age of the Caliphates. The Islamic Near East from the Sixth to the Eleventh Century* (London, Longman, 1986).

Kennedy, Hugh, *Muslim Spain and Portugal* (London, 1986).

Kepel, Gilles, *Jihad: the Trail of Political Islam* (Cambridge, MA, Belknap Press of Harvard University Press, 2002).

Kepel, Gilles, *The Revenge of God* (Cambridge, Polity Press, 1994).

Kepel, Gilles, *Muslim Extremism in Egypt* (Berkeley, University of California Press, 1985).

Keshavarz, Fatemeh, *Reading Mystical Lyric: The case of Jalal al-Din Rumi* (Columbia, SC, University of South Carolina Press, 1998).

Keyder, Çağlar, *State and Class in Turkey: a Study in Capitalist Development* (London, Verso, 1987).

Khadduri, Majid, *Independent Iraq 1932–1958: A Study in Iraqi Politics until the Revolution of 1958* (London, Oxford University Press, 1960).

Khalaf, Samir, and Philip Khoury (eds.), *Recovering Beirut: Urban Design and Post-War Reconstruction* (Leiden, E. J. Brill, 1993).

Khalidi, Rashid, "Concluding remarks," in Méouchy and Sluglett (eds.), *The British and French Mandates in Comparative Perspective/Les mandats français et anglais dans une perspective comparative* (Leiden, E. J. Brill, 2004).

Khalidi, Rashid, *Palestinian Identity: The Construction of Modern National Consciousness* (New York, Columbia University Press, 1997).

Khalidi, Rashid et al. (eds.), *The Origins of Arab Nationalism* (New York, Columbia University Press, 1991).

Khalidi, Tarif, *Classical Arab Islam* (Princeton, Darwin Press, 1985).

Khalidi, Walid, *Palestine Reborn* (London and New York, I. B. Tauris, 1992).

Al-Khalil, Samir, "Iraq and its future," *New York Review of Books* (April 11), 1991, p. 12.

Al-Khalil, Samir, *Republic of Fear* (London, Hutchinson Radius, 1989).

Khanykov, Nikolai, *O miuridakh i miurudizme* (an offprint of a journal article; no date or place of publication (Library of the Institute for Oriental Studies, St. Petersburg Branch).

Al-Khatib, Muhyyi al-Din, *al-M'utamar al-'arabi al-awwal* (Cairo, 1913).

Kheirabadi, Masoud, *Iranian Cities: Formation and Development* (Austin: University of Texas Press, 1991).

Khomeini, R., "The granting of capitulatory rights to the US," reproduced in H Algar (ed.), *Islam & Revolution: Writings and Declarations of Imam Khomeini* (Berkeley: Mizan Press, 1981).

Khosrokhavar, Farhad, "Nouvelle banlieue et marginalité: la cité Taleghani à Khak-e Sefid," in C. Adle and B. Hourcade (eds.), *Téhéran Capitale bicentenaire* (Paris and Tehran, Institut Français de Recherche en Iran, Bibliothèque Iranienne, 37, 1992), pp. 307–27.

Khoury, Dina Rizk, *State and Provincial Society in the Ottoman Empire: Mosul, 1540–1834* (1998).

Khoury, Enver, *The Patterns of Mass Movements in Arab Revolutionary-Progressive States* (The Hague, Mouton, 1970).

Khoury, Philip S., *Syria and the French Mandate: the Politics of Arab Nationalism, 1920–1946* (Princeton, NJ, Princeton University Press, 1987).

Khoury, Philip S., *Urban Notables and Arab Nationalism: The Politics of Damascus 1860–1920* (Cambridge, Cambridge University Press, 1983).

Khuri, Fuad I., and Gerald Obermeyer, "The social bases for military intervention in the Middle East," in Catherine McArdle Kelleher (ed.), *Political-Military Systems: Comparative Perspectives* (SAGE Research Progress Series on War, Revolution, and Peacekeeping, vol. 4. London: Sage, 1974), pp. 55–86.

Kiernan, V., *State and Society in Europe 1550–1650* (Oxford, Basil Blackwell, 1980).

Kiernan, V., *The Lords of Humankind* (London, Century Hutchinson, 1969).

Kili, Suna, "Kemalism in contemporary Turkey," *International Political Science Review,* 1 (3), 1980.

Kimmerling, Baruch, and Joel S. Migdal, *Palestinians: The Making of a People* (New York, Macmillan, 1993).

Kinberg, Leah, "What Is Meant by *zuhd*?," *Studia Islamica,* 41, 1985, pp. 24–44.

Al-Kindī, Muḥammad b. Yusūf, *Kitāb al-Wulāt*, ed. R. Guest (London, 1912).

Kirişçi, Kemal, and Gareth M. Winrow, *The Kurdish Question and Turkey: An Example of a Trans-State Ethnic Conflict* (Portland, OR, Frank Cass, 2003).

Kleinberg, R., and A. Clark (eds.), *Economic Liberalization, Democratization and Civil Society in the Developing World* (Basingstoke: Macmillan, 2000).

Knapp, Wilfrid, *North West Africa: A Political and Economy Survey* (Oxford, Oxford University Press, 1977).

Knysh, Alexander, "A clear and present danger: 'Wahhabism' as a rhetorical foil," *Die Welt des Islams*, 44 (2), 2004, pp. 3–26.

Knysh, Alexander, "Sufism as an explanatory paradigm: the issue of the motivations of Sufi resistance movements in Western and Russian scholarship," *Die Welt des Islams*, 42 (2), 2002, pp. 139–73.

Knysh, Alexander, "Review of Mojaddedi's 'The Biographical Tradition in Sufism'," *Bulletin of the School of Oriental and African Studies*, 65 (3), 2002, pp. 576–8.

Knysh, Alexander, "Review of Chittick's '*Sufism: A Short Intorduction*'," *Islam and Christian-Muslim Relations*, 13 (2), 2002, pp. 231–2.

Knysh, Alexander, "The *Tariqa* on a landcruiser: the resurgence of Sufism in Yemen," *Middle East Journal*, 3, 2001, pp. 399–414.

Knysh, Alexander, *Islamic Mysticism: A Short History* (Leiden, E. J. Brill, 2000).

Knysh, Alexander, "Review of Elizabeth Sirriyeh's 'Sufis and Anti-Sufis'," *Middle East Journal*, 54 (2), 2000, pp. 322–4.

Knysh, Alexander, "Review of Leonard Lewisohn, '*The Legacy of Mediaeval Persian Sufism*'," *Journal of the Royal Asiatic Society*, 9 (3), 1999, pp. 434–8.

Knysh, Alexander, *Ibn 'Arabi in the Later Islamic Tradition: The Making of a Polemical Image in Medieval Islam* (Albany, State University of New York Press, 1999).

Knysh, Alexander, "Review of Stepaniants' 'Sufi Wisdom'," *Journal of Religion*, 75 (4), 1995, pp. 606–7.

Knysh, Alexander, "Sufizm," in Stanislav Prozorov (ed.), *Islam: istoriograficheskie ocherki* (Moscow, Nauka, 1991), pp. 109–207.

Koçak, Cemil, "Kemalist Milliyetçiliğin Bulanık Suları," in Tanıl Bora (ed.), *Milliyetçilik* (İstanbul, İletişim Yayınları, 2002).

Kohlberg, Etan, "Shurayh," *Encyclopedia of Islam*.

Kohlberg, Etan, "From Imāmiyya to Ithnā-'Ashariyya," *Bulletin of the School of Oriental and African Studies*, 39, 1976, pp. 521–43.

Kohn, Hans, *A History of Nationalism in the East* (New York, Harcourt Brace, 1929).

Köksal, Duygu, "Fine-tuning nationalism: critical perspectives from republican literature in Turkey," *Turkish Studies*, 2 (2), 2001.

Kopp, Horst and Eugen Wirth, *Beiträge zur Stadtgeographie von Sana'a* (Dr. Ludwig Reichert, Beihefte zum Tübinger Atlas des Vordern Orients, Reihe B [Geisteswissenschaften] Nr. 95, Wiesbaden, 1990).

Korany, Bahgat, Rex Brynen, and Pau Noble (eds.), *Political Liberalization and Democratization in the Arab World* (Boulder, CO, Lynne Rienner, 1995).

Kornberg, Jacques, *Theodor Herzl: From Assimilation to Zionism* (Bloomington and Indianapolis, Indiana University Press, 1993).

Korotaev, Andrey, Vladimir Klimenko, and Dimitry Proussakov, "Origins of Islam: Political-Anthropological and Environmental Contexts," *Acta Orientalia*, 52, 1999, pp. 243–76.

Kraemer, C. J., Jr. (ed.), *Excavations at Nessana, III: Non-Literary Papyri* (Princeton, Princeton University Press, 1958).

Von Kremer, Alfred, *Geschichte der herrschenden Ideen des Islams* (Leipzig, F. A. Brockhaus, 1868).

Krymskii, Agafangel, "Sufizm," *Entsiklopedicheskii slovar'*, ed. Izd. F. A. Brokgauz i I. A. Efron, vol. 32, (St. Petersburg, 1901), pp. 129–34.

Krymskii, Agafangel, "Ocherk razvitiia sufizma (tasawwuf) do kontsa III v. gidzhry," *Drevnosti vostochny. Trudy Vostochnoi komissii Imp. Moskovskogo arkheologicheskogo obschestva*, 2 (1), 1896, pp. 28–73.

Kuban, Doan, *Istanbul: An Urban History: Byzantion, Constantinopolis, Istanbul* (Istanbul, Economic and Social History Foundation of Turkey, 1996).

Kubiak, Wladyslaw B., *Al-Fustāt, Its Foundation and Early Urban Development* (Cairo, American University Cairo, 1987).

Kubursi, A. A., *Oil, Industrialization and Development in the Arab Gulf States* (Croom Helm, London, 1984).

Kumar, "Civil society: an enquiry into the usefulness of an historical term," *British Journal of Sociology*, 44 (3), 1993, pp. 375–95.

Kumaraswamy, P. R., "Problems of studying minorities in the Middle East," in *Alternatives: Turkish Journal of International Relations*, 2 (2), 2003, pp. 244–64.

Kunt, M., and C. Woodhead (eds.), *Suleiman the Magnificent and His Age* (London and New York, 1995).

Kunt, M., *The Sultan's Servants* (Columbia University Press, 1983).

Kushner, David, *The Rise of Turkish Nationalism 1876–1908* (London, Frank Cass, 1977).

Labat, Séverine, *Les islamistes algériens* (Paris, Seuil, 1995).

Lacoste, Y., *Ibn Khaldun: The Birth of History and the Past of the Third World* (London, 1984).

Lambton, A., *State and Government in Medieval Islam: An introduction to the study of Islamic Political Theory: The Jurists* (Oxford, Oxford University Press, 1981).

Lammens, Henri, "La république marchande de la Mecque vers l'an 600 de notre ère," *Bulletin de l'Instiut Égyptien*, 5th series, 4, 1910, pp. 23–54.

Landau, Jacob, *Pan-Turkism: From Irredentism to Cooperation* (Bloomington, Indiana University Press, 1995).

Landau, Jacob, "Turkey," in Frank Tachau (ed.), *Political Parties of the Middle East and North Africa* (London, Mansell, 1994), pp. 549–610.

Lapidus, Ira M., *A History of Islamic Societies* (Cambridge, 1988).

Lapidus, Ira M. (ed.), *Middle Eastern Cities: A Symposium on Ancient, Islamic, and Contemporary Middle Eastern Urbanism* (Berkeley, University of California Press, 1969).

Lapidus, Ira M., "Muslim cities and Islamic societies," in Ira M. Lapidus, *Middle Eastern Cities: A Symposium on Ancient, Islamic, and Contemporary Middle Eastern Urbanism* (Berkeley, University of California Press, 1969), pp. 47–79.

Lapidus, Ira M., *Muslim Cities in the Later Middle Ages* (Cambridge, MA, Harvard University Press, 1967).

Laqueur, Walter *A History of Zionism* (New York, Schocken, 1989).

Laroui, Abdallah, *Les origines sociales et culturelles du nationalisme marocain, 1830–1912*, (Paris, Maspero, 1977).

Laroui, Abdallah, *The History of the Maghrib: an Interpretative Essay* (Princeton, 1977).

Laskier, Michael, "A difficult inheritance: Moroccan society under King Muhammad VI," *Middle East Review of International Affairs*, 7 (3), 2003, pp. 1–20.

Laskier, Michael M., *North African Jewry in the 20th Century: The Jews of Morocco, Tunisia, and Algeria* (New York, New York University Press, 1991).

Laurent, Joseph, *L'Arménie entre Byzance et l'Islam depuis da conquête arabe jusqu'en 886*, 2nd edn., revised and enlarged by Marius Canard (Lisbon: Librairie Bertrand, 1980).

Layachi, Azzedine, *Civil Society and Democratization in Morocco* (Cairo, Ibn Khaldun Center, 1995).

Leatherdale, Clive, *Britain and Saudi Arabia, 1925–1939: The Imperial Oasis* (London, Frank Cass, 1983).

Lecam, J., *Les Sarrazins dans le haut moyen-âge français* (Paris: G. P. Maisonneuve 1965).

Van Leeuwen, Richard, *Waqfs and Urban Structures: The Case of Ottoman Damascus* (Leiden, E. J. Brill, Studies in Islamic Law and Society 11, 1999).

Le Monde Diplomatique on the internet at http://mondediplo.com/focus/mideast/a2315.

Le Monde Diplomatique on the internet at http://mondediplo.com/focus/mideast/a2316.

Le Monde Diplomatique on the internet at http://mondediplo.com/focus/mideast/a2317.

Le Monde Diplomatique on the internet at http://mondediplo.com/focus/mideast/a2318.

Le Monde Diplomatique on the internet at http://mondediplo.com/focus/mideast/a2319.

Le Monde Diplomatique on the internet at http://mondediplo.com/focus/mideast/r1280.

Lesch, Ann Mosely, "The destruction of civil society in the Sudan," in Augustus Richard Norton (ed.), *Civil Society in the Middle East* (Leiden, E. J. Brill, 1996), vol. 2, pp. 153–92.

Lespès, René, *Alger, étude de géographie et d'histoire urbaine* (Paris, 1930).

Le Tourneau, Roger, *The Almohad Movement in North Africa* (Princeton, 1969).

Le Tourneau, Roger, *L'Evolution politique de l'Afrique de Nord musulmane, 1920–1961* (Paris, A. Colin, 1962).

Le Tourneau, Roger, *Fez in the Age of the Marinids* (Norman, 1961).

Le Tourneau, Roger, *Fes avant le protectorat: étude économique et sociale d'une ville de l'Occident musulman* (Casablanca, 1949).

Levanoni, Amalia, *A Turning-point in Mamlūk History* (Leiden, E. J. Brill, 1995).

Lévi-Provençal, Evariste, *Histoire de l'Espagne Musulmane*, 3 vols. (Paris, G. P. Maisonneuve, 1950–3).

Levin, N. Gordon, *The Zionist Movement in Palestine and World Politics 1880–1918* (London, D. C. Heath and Co., 1974).

Levtzion, Nehamia (ed.), *Conversion to Islam* (New York, Holmes and Meier, 1979).

Lewis, Bernard, *The Crisis of Islam* (London, Weidenfeld and Nicolson, 2003).

Lewis, Bernard, *The Emergence of Modern Turkey* (New York and Oxford, Oxford University Press, 2002).

Lewis, Bernard, *What Went Wrong?* (London, Weidenfeld and Nicolson, 2002).

Lewis, Bernard, *The Multiple Identities of the Middle East* (London, Methuen, 1998).

Lewis, Bernard, *The Middle East: a Brief History of the last 2,000 Years* (New York, Scribner, 1995).

Lewis, Bernard, "Some oberservations on the significance of heresy in the history of Islam," *Studia Islamica*, 1, 1953, pp. 43–63.

Lewisohn, Leonard (ed.), *Classical Persian Sufism: From its origins to Rumi* (London and New York: Khaniqahi Nimatullahi Publications, 1992).

Lewisohn, Leonard (ed.), *The Legacy of Medieval Persian Sufism* (London and New York: Khaniqahi Nimatullahi Publications, 1992).

Lifchez, Raymond, *The Dervish Lodge: Architecture, Art, and Sufism in Ottoman Turkey* (Berkeley, University of California Press, 1992).

Linz, Juan, and Alfred Stepan, *Problems of Democratic Transition and Consolidation* (Baltimore, Johns Hopkins University Press, 1996).

Litvak, Meir, *Shi'i Scholars in Nineteenth-Century Iraq: the 'ulama' of Najaf and Karbala'* (New York, Cambridge University Press, 1998).

Lockman, Zachary, *Comrades and Enemies: Arab and Jewish Workers in Palestine 1906–1948* (Berkeley and Los Angeles, University of California Press, 1996).

Lockman, Zachary, *Workers and the Working Class in the Middle East* (Albany, State University of New York Press, 1994).

Loeb, Laurence D., *Outcaste: Jewish Life in Southern Iran* (New York, Gordon and Breach, 1977).

Longuenesse, Elizabeth, "La Classe Ouvrière au Proche-Orient: La Syrie." *Pensée*, n. 197, February 1978, 12–132.

Lorenz, Andrea W., "Ishtar was a woman," *Ms.* (May–June 1991), pp. 14–15.

Louis, Wm. Roger, "British imperialism and the end of the Palestine Mandate," in W. Roger Louis and Robert W. Stookey (eds.), *The End of the Palestine Mandate* (Austin, TX, 1986).

Louis, Wm. Roger, *The British Empire in the Middle East 1945–1951: Arab Nationalism, the United States and Postwar Imperialism* (London, Oxford University Press, 1984).

Luizard, Pierre-Jean, *La formation de l'Iraq contemporain* (Paris, CNRS Éditions, 1991).

Lust-Okar, Ellen, "The decline of Jordanian political parties: myth or reality?" *International Journal of Middle East Studies*, 33 (4), 2001, pp. 545–71.

Mabro R., *Oil Revenues and the Cost of Social and Economic Development in Energy in the Arab World. Volume 1, Kuwait AFESD and OAPEC* (1980)

Mabro, R., and E. Monroe, "Arab wealth from oil: problems of its investment," *International Affairs*, January 1974.

Macdonald, Duncan, *The Religious Attitude and Life in Islam* (Chicago, University of Chicago Press, 1909).

Macdonald, Duncan, *Development of Muslim Theology, Jurisprudence and Constitutional Theory* (New York, C. Scribner's Sons, 1903).

MacLeod, Arlene Elowe, *Accommodating Protest: Working Women, the New Veiling, and Change in Cairo* (New York, Columbia University Press, 1991).

Maddy-Weitzman, Bruce, "Berbers, 'Berberism,' and the state in North Africa," in Moshe Ma'oz and Gabriel Sheffer (eds.), *Middle Eastern Minorities and Diasporas* (Brighton, Sussex Academic Press, 2002), pp. 153–78.

Maddy-Weitzman, Bruce, "The Berber question in Algeria: nationalism in the making?", in Bengio and Ben-Dor (1999), pp. 31–52.

Madelung, Wilferd, "Shī'ism in the age of the Rightly Guided Caliphs," in *Shī'ite Heritage: Essays on Classical and Modern Traditions*, ed. L. Clarke (Global Publications, Binghamton, 2001) pp. 9–19.

Madelung, Wilferd, *The Succession to Muhammad* (Cambridge, Cambridge University Press, 1997).

Madelung, Wilferd, "The Fatimids and the Qarmaṭīs of Baḥrayn," in Farhad Daftary (ed.), *Mediaval Isma'ili History and Thought* (Cambridge, Cambridge University Press, 1996), pp. 21–74.

Madelung, Wilferd, *Religious Trends in Early Islamic Iran* (Albany, NY, State University of New York Press, 1988).

Madelung, Wilferd, *Arabic Texts Concerning the History of the Zaydi Imams* (Wiesbaden and Beirut, Franz Steiner Verlag, 1987).

Madelung, Wilferd, "Authority in Twelver Shiism in the absence of the imam," in *La Notion d'autorité au Moyen Age: Islam, Byzance, Occident* (Paris: Presses Universitaires de France, 1982), pp. 163–73.

Madelung, Wilferd, "The minor dynasties of northern Iran," in R. N. Frye (ed.), *The Cambridge History of Islam*, vol. 4 (Cambridge, Cambridge University Press, 1975), pp. 198–249.

Madelung, Wilferd, *Der Imam al-Qāsim bin Ibrāhīm und die Glaubenslehre der Zaiditen* (Berlin, De Gruyter, 1965).

Madelung, Wilferd, "Fatimiden und Baḥrainqarmaṭen," *Der Islam*, 34, 1959, pp. 34–88.

Madelung, Wilferd and Paul Walker, *The Advent of the Fatimids* (London, I. B. Tauris, 2000).

"Madrasa," *Encyclopedia of Islam*, 2nd edn.

Mahdi, Fadhil A., "Responses to globalization in the Gulf countries" (paper presented to the Conference on Globalisation and the Gulf, July 2–4, 2001, Institute of Arab and Islamic Studies, University of Exeter, United Kingdom).

Majd, Mohammad Gholi, *Resistance to the Shah Landowners and the Ulama in Iran* (Gainesville, University Press of Florida, 2000).

Makdisi, George, "Hanbalite Islam," in Merlin Swartz (ed.), *Studies on Islam* (Oxford, Oxford University Press, 1981), pp. 216–74.

Makdisi, George, *The Rise of Colleges, Institutions of Learning in Islam and the West* (Edinburgh, Edinburgh University Press, 1981).

Makdisi, George, "The Hanbali School and Sufism," *Humaniora Islamica*, 2, 1974, pp. 61–72.

Malcolm, John, *The History of Persia from the Most Early Period to the Present Time*, 2 vols. (London, John Murray, 1815).

Mallat, Chibli, *The Renewal of Islamic Law* (Cambridge, Cambridge University Press, 1993).

Manandean, H., "Les invasions arabes en Arménie (Notes Chronologiques)," *Byzantion*, 18, 1948, pp. 163–95.

Mantran, R. (ed.), *Histoire de l'empire ottoman* (Paris, 1989).

Ma'oz, Moshe, and Gabriel Sheffer (eds.), *Middle Eastern Minorities and Diasporas* (Brighton, Sussex Academic Press, 2002).

Ma'oz, Moshe, "Ethnic and religious conflict in Iraq," in Moshe Ma'oz and Gabriel Sheffer (eds.), *Middle Eastern Minorities and Diasporas* (Brighton: Sussex Academic Press, 2002), pp. 179–92.

Al-Maqqari, *The History of the Mohammedan Dynasties of Spain* (London, 2002).

Al-Maqrīzī, Aḥmad b. 'Alī, Itti'ā' al-'unafā', ed. J. al-Shayyal and Muhammad Ahmad (Cairo, 1969–73).

Marcus, Abraham, *The Middle East on the Eve of Modernity: Aleppo in the Eighteenth Century* (New York, Columbia University Press, 1989).

Mardin, Şerif, "Civil Society in Islam," in John Hall (ed.), *Civil Society: Theory, History, Comparison* (Cambridge, Polity Press, 1995), pp. 278–300.

Margulies, Ronnie and Yildizoglu, Ergin, "Trade unions and Turkey's working class," *Middle East Report*, 14 (2), 1984, pp. 15–30, 31.

Al-Marrākushi, Ahmad b., *Muḥammad, Al-Bayān al-Mughrib*, ed. E. Levi-Provençal and G. S. Colin (Leiden, 1948).

Martin, Vanessa, "Khumaini, knowledge and the political process," *Muslim World*, 87 (1997), pp. 1–16.

Martin, Vanessa, *Islam and Modernism: The Iranian Revolution of 1906* (London, I. B. Tauris, 1989).

Marsot, Afaf [Lutfi al-Sayyid], *Egypt's Liberal Experiment, 1922–1936* (Berkeley and Los Angeles, University of California Press, 1977).

Massignon, Louis, *Essay on the Origins of the Technical Language of Islamic Mysticism by Louis Massignon* (Notre Dame, IN, University of Notre Dame Press, 1997).

Massignon, Louis, *The Passion of Husain b. Mansur al-Hallaj: Mystic and martyr of Islam*, tr. Herbert Mason (Princeton, NJ, Princeton University Press, 1982).

Massignon, Louis, *Essai sur les origines du lexique technique de la mystique musulmane*, 2nd edn. (Paris, P. Geuthner, 1954).

Masters, Bruce, *Christians and Jews in the Ottoman Arab World: The Roots of Sectarianism* (Cambridge, Cambridge University Press, 2001).

Masters, Bruce, "The 1850 'Events' in Aleppo: an aftershock of Syria's incorporation in the capitalist world system," *International Journal of Middle Eastern Studies*, 22, 1990, pp. 3–20.

Masters, Bruce, *The Origins of Western Economic Dominance in the Middle East: Mercantilism and the Islamic Economy in Aleppo, 1600–1750* (New York, New York University Press, 1988).

Al-Mas'ūdī, 'Alī b. al-Ḥusayn, *al-Tanbīh wa'l-Ishrāf* (Beirut, 1981).

Al-Mas'ūdī, 'Alī b. al-Ḥusayn, *Murūj al-Dhahab*, ed. C. Pellat (Beirut, 1966–79).

Mattar, Philip, *The Encyclopedia of the Palestinians* (New York, Facts on File, 2000).

Matthee, Rudolph, *Politics of Trade in Safavid Iran: Silk for Silver, 1600–1730* (Cambridge, Cambridge University Press, 2000).

Maury, B., A. Raymond, J. Revault, and M. Zakariya, *Palais et maisons du Caire. Époque Ottomane* (Paris, 1983).

McCarthy, Justin, *The Population of Palestine; Population History and Statistics of the late Ottoman Period and the Mandate* (New York, Columbia University Press, 1990).

McChesney, R. D., *Waqf in Central Asia: Four Hundred Years in the History of a Muslim Shrine, 1480–1889* (Princeton, NJ, Princeton University Press, 1991).

McDowall, David, *A Modern History of the Kurds* (London, I. B. Tauris, 1997).

McDowall, David, *The Palestinians: The Road to Nationhood* (London, Minority Rights Group, 1994).

McGreal, Chris, "Israeli wall to encircle Palestine," *Guardian*, March 18, 2003.

McLaurin, R. D. (ed.), *The Political Role of Minority Groups in the Middle East* (New York, Praeger Publishers, 1979).

Mednicoff, David M, "Morocco," in Frank Tachau (ed.), *Political Parties of the Middle East and North Africa* (London, Mansell, 1994), pp. 133–73.

Meier, Fritz, *Essays on Islamic Piety and Mysticism* (Leiden, E. J. Brill, 1999).

Meier, Fritz, "Khurasan and the end of classical Sufism," *Essays on Islamic Piety and Mysticism* (Leiden, E. J. Brill, 1999), pp. 189–218.

Meier, Fritz, *Baha'-i Walad. Grundzüge seines lebens und seine mystik* (Leiden, E. J. Brill, 1989).

Meier, Fritz, *Abu Sa'id-i Abu l-Hayr (357–440–967–1049). Wirklichkeit und legende* (Leiden, E. J. Brill, 1976).

Meier, Fritz, "Soufisme et déclin culturel dans l'histoire de l'Islam," *Actes du Symposium organisé par R. Brunschvig et G. E. von Grunebaum avec le concours de A. Abel [et al.] Sous les auspices des universités de Bordeaux et de Chicago* (Paris, Editions Besson Chantemerle, 1957).

Meisami, Julie S. and Paul Starkey (eds.), *Encyclopedia of Arabic Literature* (London, Routledge, 1998).

Melchert, Christopher, "The Hanabila and the early Sufis," *Arabica*, 48, 2001, pp. 352–67.

Melchert, Christopher, *The Formation of the Sunni Schools of Law, 9th–10th century* CE (Leiden, E. J. Brill, 1997).

Melville, Charles, *Safavid Persia: The History and Politics of an Islamic Society* (1996).

Melville, Charles, "Sarbadarids," *Encyclopaedia of Islam* (1960–), pp. 47–9.

Meneley, Anne, *Tournaments of Value: Sociability and Hierarchy in a Yemeni Town* (Toronto, University of Toronto Press, 1996).

Méouchy, Nadine, and Peter Sluglett (eds.), *The British and French Mandates in Comparative Perspective/ Les mandats français et anglais dans une perspective comparative* (Leiden, E. J. Brill, 2004).

Meriwether, Margaret L., *The Kin Who Count: Family and Society in Ottoman Aleppo, 1770–1840* (Austin, University of Texas Press, 1999).

Mernissi, Fatima, *Dreams of Trespass: Tales of a Harem Girlhood* (Addison-Wesley, Reading, MA, 1994).

Mervin, Sabrina, *Un réformisme chiite* (Paris, Beirut, Damascus: Karthala, Cermoc, Ifead, 2000).

Merza, A. K., "Economic reforms in major Arab oil-producing countries," paper presented to the Conference on Globalization and the Gulf, July 2–4, 2001, Institute of Arab and Islamic Studies, University of Exeter, United Kingdom, 21 pp.

Messick, Brinkley, *The Calligraphic State. Textual Domination and History in a Muslim Society* (Berkeley, University of California Press, 1993).

Meyer J., B. Chambers and A. Farooq (eds.), *Development Policies in Natural Resource Economies* (Cheltenham, Edward Elgar, 1999).

Micaud, Charles, "Conclusion," in Ernest Gellner and Charles Micaud, *Arabs and Berbers: From Tribe to Nation in North Africa* (London, Heath and Company, 1972), pp. 431–8.

Mikhailov, Fiodor, "Religioznye vozzreniia turkmen zakaspiiskoi oblasti," in Vladimir Nalivkin (ed.), *Sbornik materialov po musul'manstvu*, vol. 2, Pozenoer (St. Petersburg, Tashkent, 1900), pp. 85–103.

Miller, Rory, "Informal empire in Latin America," in Robin W. Winks (ed.), *The Oxford History of the British Empire*, vol. 5, Historiography (Oxford, Oxford University Press, 1999), pp. 437–49.

Miller, Susan Gibson, Attilio Petruccioli, and Mauro Bertagnin, "Inscribing minority space in the Islamic city: the Jewish quarter of Fez (1438–1912)," *Journal of the Society of Architectural Historians*, 60, 3 (2001), pp. 310–27.

Minganga, Alfons, *Sources Syriaques* I (Leipzig: Otto Harrassowitz for Imprimerie des Pères Dominicains à Mossoul, 1907–1908).

Minorsky, Vladimir, "The poetry of Shāh Ismāʿīl I," *Bulletin of the School of Oriental Studies,* 10 (1938–42), pp. 1006–53.

Mirza Kazem-Bek, Aleksandr, *Izbrannye sochineninia* (Elm, Baku, 1985).

Mitchell, Richard P., *The Society of the Muslim Brothers* (London, Oxford University Press, 1969).

Mkandawire, T. (2001), "Thinking about developmental states in Africa," *Cambridge Journal of Economics,* 25.

Moaddel, Mansoor, *Class, Politics, and Ideology in the Iranian Revolution* (New York, Columbia University Press, 1993).

Moghadam, Valentine M., *Modernizing Women: Gender and Social Change in the Middle East* (Boulder, CO, Lynne Rienner, 2003).

Moghadam, Valentine M, "Enhancing women's participation in the Middle East and North Africa," in Heba Handoussa and Zafiris Tzanatos (eds.), *Employment Creation and Social Protection* (Washington, DC, and Cairo, World Bank and American University in Cairo Press, 2002).

Moghadam, Valentine M., "Organizing women: the new women's movement in Algeria," *Cultural Dynamics,* 13 (2), 2001, pp. 131–54.

Moghadam, F., "Nomadic invasions and the development of productive forces: an historical study of Iran (1000–1800)," *Science and Society,* 52 (4), 1988.

Moghadam, Valentine M., "Women, work and ideology in the Islamic republic," *International Journal of Middle East Studies,* 20 (2), 1988, pp. 221–43.

Mojaddedi, Jawid A., *The Biographical Tradition in Sufism: The* tabaqat *Genre from al-Sulami to Jami* (Surrey, Curzon, 2001).

Molé, Marijan, *Les mystiques musulmans* (Paris, Presses Universitaires de France, 1965).

Molé, Marijan, "Les Kubrawiya entre sunnisme et chiisme au VIIIe et IXe siècles de l'hégire," *Revue des études islamiques,* 29 (1961), pp. 61–142.

Momen, Moojan, "Authority and opposition in Twelver Shiʾism," in R. Burrell (ed.), *Islamic Fundamentalism* (London, Royal Asiatic Society, 1989).

Momen, Moojan, *An Introduction to Shiʾi Islam* (New Haven, Yale University Press, 1985).

Moore, Clement Henry, "Political parties," in I. William Zartman and William Mark Habeeb (eds.), *Polity and Society in Contemporary North Africa* (Boulder, CO, Westview Press, 1993), pp. 42–67.

Moore, Clement Henry, *Tunisia since Independence: The Dynamics of One-party Government* (Berkeley, University of California Press, 1965).

Moore, R. I., *The First European Revolution, c. 970–1215* (Oxford, Blackwell, 2000).

Moosa, Matti, *Extremist Shiʿites: The Ghulat Sects* (State of New York University Press, New York, 1988).

Morgan, D., *Medieval Persia, 1040–1787* (London: 1988).

Morgan, D., *The Mongols* (Oxford, 1986).

Morgan, D., "Re-thinking Safavid Shiʾism," in L. Lewisohn and D. Morgan (eds.), *The Heritage of Sufism* (Oxford, One World, 1999), vol. 3, pp. 19–27.

Morgan, Robin, "Women in the intifada," in Suha Sabbagh (ed.), *Palestinian Women of Gaza and the West Bank* (Bloomington, Indiana University Press, 1998).

Morony, Michael G., "The late Sasanian economic impact on the Arabian peninsula," *Nāme-ye Irān-e Bāstān,* 1 (2), 2001–2, pp. 25–37.

Morony, Michael G., "Arab conquest of Iran," *Encyclopedia Iranica,* 2, 1987, pp. 203–10.

Morony, Michael G., *Iraq after the Muslim Conquests* (Princeton, NJ, Princeton University Press, 1984).

Morris, Benny, *Righteous Victims: A History of the Zionist–Arab Conflict, 1881–2001* (New York, Vintage Books, 2001).

Morris, Benny, *The Birth of the Palestinian Refugee Problem, 1947–49* (Cambridge, Cambridge University Press, 1987).

Morris, James W., "Situating Islamic 'mysticism': between written traditions and popular spirituality," in Robert A. Herrera (ed.), *Mystics of the Book: Themes, Topics, and Topologies* (New York, Peter Lang, 1993), pp. 293–334.

Morris, James W., "Ibn 'Arabi and his interpreters: part 1: recent French translations," *Journal of the American Oriental Society*, 106, 3 (1986), pp. 539–64; "Part 2: influences and interpretations," *ibid.*, 106, 4 (1986), pp. 733–56; "Part 3: influences and interpretations (conclusion)," 107, 1 (1987), pp. 101–20.

Morris, James W., *The Wisdom of the Throne: An Introduction to the Philosophy of Mulla Sadra* (Princeton, NJ, Princeton University Press, 1981).

Mortimer, Robert, "Islam and multi-party politics in Algeria," *Middle East Journal*, 1991, 45 (4), pp. 575–93.

Mostyn, Trevor, and Albert Hourani (eds.), *The Cambridge Encyclopedia of the Middle East and North Africa* (Cambridge, Cambridge University Press, 1988).

Motzki, Harald (ed.), *Hadith: Origins and Developments* (Aldershot, Ashgate, 2003).

Motzki, Harald, *The Origins of Islamic Jurisprudence: Meccan Fiqh Before the Classical Schools* (2002).

Motzki, Harald (ed.), *The Biography of Muhammad: The Issue of the Sources* (Leiden, E. J. Brill, 2000).

Mousalli, A. S., *Moderate and Radical Islamic Fundamentalism, The Quest for Modernity, Legitimacy and the Islamic State* (Gainesville, University Press of Florida, 1999).

Moussali, Ahmed, "Modern Islamic fundamentalist discourses," in Augustus Richard Norton (ed.), *Civil Society in the Middle East* (Leiden, E. J. Brill, 1996), vol. 1, pp. 79–119.

Mouzelis, N., "Modernity, late development and civil society," in John Hall (ed.), *Civil Society: Theory, History, Comparison* (Cambridge, Polity Press, 1995), pp. 224–49.

Moynihan, Elizabeth B., *Paradise as a Garden: In Persia and Mughal India* (New York, George Braziller, 1979).

Mubarak, Zaki, *Al-Tasawwuf al-islami fi 'l-adab wa 'l-akhlaq* (Beirut, Dar al-Jil, 1975).

Muir, Sir William, *The Caliphate: Its Rise, Decline, and Fall* (Beirut, Khayats, 1963).

Munson, Henry, *Religion and Power in Morocco* (New Haven, CT, and London: Yale University Press, 1993).

Murden, Simon, *Islam, the Middle East and the New Global Hegemony* (Boulder, CO, Lynne Rienner, 2002).

Murphy, Emma, *Economic and Political Change in Tunisia: From Bourguiba to Ben Ali* (Basingstoke, Macmillan, 1999).

Muslih, Muhammad, "Arab politics and the rise of Palestinian nationalism," *Journal of Palestine Studies*, 16 (4), 1987, pp. 77–94.

Nagy, Sharon, "Dressing up downtown: urban development and government public image in Qatar," *City and Society*, 12 (1), 2000, pp. 125–47.

Nahavandi, Firouzeh, "L'évolution des partis politiques Iraniens, 1948–78," *Civilisations*, 34 (1–2), 1984, 323–64.

Najmabadi, Afsaneh, "Hazards of modernity and morality: women, state and ideology in contemporary Iran," in Deniz Kandiyoti (ed.), *Women, Islam, and the State* (London, Macmillan, 1991), pp. 48–76.

Nakash, Yitzhak, *The Shi'is of Iraq* (Princeton, NJ, Princeton University Press, 1994).

Nakhleh, Khalil and Elia Zureik (eds.), *The Sociology of the Palestinians* (New York, St. Martin's Press, 1980).

Nalivkin, Vladimir, "Ocherk blagotvoritel'nosti u osedlykh tuzemtsev Turkestanskogo kraia," in Vladimir Nalivkin (ed.), *Sbornik materialov po musul'manstvu*, vol. 2 (Pozenoer, St. Petersburg, Tashkent, 1900), pp. 138–47.

Nasr, Seyyed Hossein, "The rise and development of Persian Sufism," Leonard Lewisohn (ed.), *Classical Persian Sufism: From Its Origins to Rumi* (London and New York, Khaniqahi Nimatullahi Publications, 1993).

Nasr, Seyyed Hossein, "Persian Sufi literature: its spiritual and cultural significance," in Leonard Lewisohn (ed.), *Classical Persian Sufism: From Its Origins to Rumi* (London and New York: Khaniqahi Nimatullahi Publications, 1992), pp. 1–10.

Nassehy-Behnam, Vida, "Iranian immigrants in France," pp. 102–19 in Fathi (1991).

Nawid, Senzil K., *Religious Response to Social Change in Afghanistan, 1919–29: King Aman-Allah and the Afghan Ulama* (Costa Mesa, CA, Mazda Publishers, 1999).

De Neveu, Édouard, *Les khouan, ordres religieux chez les musulmanes* (Paris, 1846).

Niblock T. and R. Wilson (eds.), *The Political Economy of the Middle East* (Cambridge, Cambridge University Press, 1999).

Niblock, Tim, *Class and Power in Sudan* (London, Macmillan, 1987).

Niblock, Tim, *State, Society and Economy in Saudi Arabia* (London, Croom Helm, 1982).

Nicholson, Reynold, *Selected Poems from Divan-i Shams-i Tabriz* (Cambridge, Cambridge University Press, 1952).

Nicholson, Reynold, *The Idea of Personality in Sufism* (Cambridge: Cambridge University Press, 1923).

Nicholson, Reynold (ed.), *The Kitab al-luma fi'l-tasawwuf of Abu Nasr 'Abdallah . . . al-Sarraj al-Tusi* (Leiden and London, E. J. Brill and Luzac, 1914).

Nicholson, Reynold, *The Mystics of Islam* (London, George Bell and Sons, 1914).

Nicholson, Reynold, "A historical inquiry concerning the origin and development of Sufism," *Journal of the Royal Asiatic Society* (1906), pp. 303–48.

Nöldeke, Theodor, "Arabs (Ancient)," in James Hastings et al. (eds.), *Encyclopaedia of Religion and Ethics* (Edinburgh, T. & T. Clark, 1908–26).

Nordlinger, Eric A., *Soldiers in Politics: Military Coups and Governments* (Englewood Cliffs, NJ, Prentice-Hall, 1977).

Norris, H. T., *The Berbers in Arabic Literature* (London and New York, 1982)

North, Albrecht, "Zum Verhältnis von Kalifaler Zentralgewalt und Provinzen in umayad-discher Zeit. Die 'Sulh' "Anwa' Traditionen für Aegypten und den Iraq," *Die Welt des Islams* 14, 1973, pp. 150–62.

North, Albrecht, and Lawrence I. Conrad, *The Early Arabic Historical Tradition: A Source-Critical Study* (Princeton, NJ, Darwin Press, 1994).

Norththrup, Linda S., *From Slave to Sultan* (Stuttgart, Franz Steiner Verlag, 1998).

Norton, Augustus Richard, *Civil Society in the Middle East* (Leiden, E. J. Brill, 1995).

Nwyia, Paul, *Exégèse coranique et langage mystique: Nouvel essai sur le lexique technique des mystiques musulmans* (Beirut, Dar el-Machreq, 1970).

Nwyia, Paul, "Le tafsir mystique attribué à Ğa'far Sadiq," *Mélanges de l'Université St. Joseph*, 43 (1968), pp. 182–230.

Nyberg, Henrik, *Kleinere Schriften des Ibn Arabi* (Leiden, E. J. Brill, 1919).

Obermann, Julian, *Die religiose und philosophische Subjektivismus Ghazzali's* (Vienna, W. Brau-müller, 1921).

O'Brien, Donal B. Cruise, *Charisma and Brotherhood in African Islam* (Oxford, Clarendon Press, 1988).

O'Brien, Donal B. Cruise, *The Mourides of Senegal: The Political and Economic Organization of an Islamic Brotherhood* (Oxford, Clarendon Press, 1971).

O'Connell, Helen, *Women and the Family* (London, Zed Books, 1993).

O'Fahey, Rex S., *Enigmatic Saint: Ahmad ibn Idris and the Idrisi Tradition* (Evanston, IL, Northwestern University Press, 1990).

Oldham, Linda, Haguer El Haddi, and Hussein Tamaa, *Informal Communities in Cairo: The Basis of a Typology* (Cairo, American University in Cairo Press, 1987).

Omran, Adbel R. and Farzaneh Roudi, "The Middle East population puzzle," *Population Bulletin*, 48 (1), 1993.

O_uz, Burhan, *Bizans'tan Günümüze Istanbul Sulari* (Aralk, Istanbul, 1998).

Owen, R., *State, Power and Politics in the Making of the Modern Middle East*, 2nd edn (London, Routledge, 2000).

Owen, R., "Rethinking the civil society approach to the Middle East: the informal economy as a possible alternative," in John Gelvin (ed.), *The Civil Society Debate in Middle Eastern Studies* (Berkeley, UCLA Press, 1999), pp. 34–48.

Owen, R., *The Middle East in the World Economy 1800–1914* (London, Methuen, 1981).

Owen, R., "The role of the army in Middle East politics: a critique of existing analyses," in *Review of Middle East Studies* 3 (London: Ithaca Press, 1978), pp. 63–81.

Oyak, Aya, *Jacques Pervititch Sigorta Haritalarinada / Istanbul in the Insurance Maps of Jacques Pervititch* (Aya Oyak Insurance Group, Prepared by the History Foundation of Turkey [English text and Turkish text], Istanbul, n.d., ca. 2000).

Özdalga Elisabeth (ed.), *Naqshbandis in Western and Central Asia: change and continuity*, papers read at a conference held at the Swedish Research Institute in Istanbul, June 9–11, 1997 (Surrey, Curzon Press, 1999).

Pahlavi, M. R., *Be Sooye Tamadun-e Bozorg* (Tehran, undated).

Palestinian Academic Society for the Study of International Affairs. See the internet at http://www.passia.org/index_pfacts.htm.

Palmer, Edward, *Oriental Mysticism: A Treatise on Sufistic and Unitarian Theosophy of the Persians* (London, Frank Cass, 1969).

Pampanini, Andrea H., *Cities from the Arabian Desert: The Building of Jubail and Yanbu in Saudi Arabia* (Westport, CT, Praeger, 1997).

Panzac, D. (ed.), *Les villes dans l'empire ottoman*, Paris, 2 vols (Paris, 1991–4).

Pappé, Ilan, *The Israel/Palestine Question* (London, Routledge, 1999).

Pappé, Ilan, *Britain and the Arab–Israeli Conflict, 1948–51* (London, Macmillan, 1988).

Paret, Rudi, *The Study of Arabic and Islam at German Universities* (Wiesbaden, F. Steiner, 1968).

Patai, Raphael (ed.), *The Complete Diaries of Theodore Herzl*, 5 vols., tr. Harry Zohn (New York: Herzl Press, 1960).

Pate, Amy, "Berbers in Algeria," *Minorities at Risk*, 2001a. See the internet at http://www.cidcm.umd.edu/inscr/mar/data/algberb.htm.

Pate, Amy, "Berbers in Morocco", *Minorities at Risk*, 2001b. See the internet at http://www.cidcm.umd.edu/inscr/mar/data/morberb.htm.

Pedersen, Johannes, "Zum Problem der islamischen Mystik," *Orientalistische Literaturzeitung*, 34 (1931), pp. 198–204.

Peirce, Leslie, *The Imperial Harem* (Berkeley, CA, University of California Press, 1993).

Peleg, Gil, "Palestinians in Lebanon," *Minorities at Risk*, 2002. See the internet at http://www.cidcm.umd.edu/inscr/mar/data/lebpal.htm.

Pellat, Charles, *Le milieu basrien et la formation de Gāhiz* (Paris, AdrieMaisonneuve, 1953).

Perlmutter, Amos, *Military and Politics in Israel: Nation-Building and Role Expansion* (London, Frank Cass, 1969).

Perry, John R., *Karim Khan Zand: A History of Iran, 1747–1779* (Chicago, Chicago University Press, 1979).

Perthes, Volker, *The Political Economy of Syria Under Asad* (London, I. B. Tauris, 1995).

Peteet, Julie, "From refugees to minority: Palestinians in post-war Lebanon," *Middle East Report*, 26 (3), 1996, pp. 27–30.

Peteet, Julie, "Authenticity and gender: the presentation of culture," in Judith Tucker (ed.), *Arab Women: Old Boundaries, New Frontiers* (Bloomington, Indiana University Press, 1993).

Peters, F. E., *Mecca: A Literary History of the Muslim Holy Land* (Princeton, NJ, Princeton University Press, 1994).

Peters, F. E., *Jerusalem and Mecca: The Typology of the Holy City in the Near East* (New York, New York University Press, 1986).

Peters, F. E., *Jerusalem: The Holy City in the Eyes of Chronicles, Visitors, Pilgrims, and Prophets from the Days of Abraham to the Beginnings of Modern Times* (Princeton, NJ, Princeton University Press, 1985).

Petruccioli, Attilio (ed.), *Bukhara: The Myth and the Architecture* (Cambridge, MA, Aga Khan Program for Islamic Architecture, 1999).

Petruccioli, Attilio (ed.), *Rethinking the XIXth Century City* (Cambridge, MA, Aga Khan Program for Islamic Architecture, 1998).

Petruccioli, Attilio (ed.), *Il giardino islamico: Architettura, natura, paesaggio* (Electa, Milan, 1994).

Philipp, Thomas, *Acre: The Rise and Fall of a Palestinian City, 1730–1831* (New York, Columbia University Press, 2002).

Picard, Elizabeth, "Arab military in politics: from revolutionary plot to authoritarian state," in Giacomo Luciano, *The Arab State* (Berkeley, CA, University of California Press, 1990), pp. 189–219.

Piscatori, J., *Islam in a World of Nation States* (Cambridge, Cambridge University Press, 1986).

Popovic, Alexandre (ed.), *Bektachiyya: Études sur l'ordre mystique des Bektachis et les groupes relevant de Hadji Bektach* (Paris and Istanbul, Les Editions Isis, 1995).

Popovic, Alexandre, and Gilles Veinstein (eds.), *Les Voies d'Allah: les ordres mystiques dans l'islam des origines à aujourd'hui* (Paris, Fayard, 1996).

Posusney, Marsha Pripstein and Eleanor Abdella Doumato, "Introduction: the mixed blessing of globalization," in Eleanor Abdella Doumato and Marsha Pripstein Posusney (eds.), *Women and Globalization in the Arab Middle East: Gender, Economy, and Society* (Boulder, CO, Lynne Rienner, 2003), pp. 1–22.

Poulton, Hugh, *Top Hat, Grey Wolf and Crescent: Turkish Nationalism and the Turkish Republic* (London: Hurst and Co., 1997).

Powers, D. S., *Law, Society and Culture in the Maghrib, 1300–1500* (Cambridge, 2002).

Poya, Maryam, *Women, Work and Islamism: Ideology and Resistance in Iran* (London, Zed Books, 1999).

Pozdnev, Piotr, *Dervishi v musul'manskom mire* (Orenburg, 1886).

Prior, Michael, *Zionism and the State of Israel: A Moral Inquiry* (London and New York, Routledge, 1999).

Pratt, Nicola, *The Legacy of the Corporatist State: Explaining Worker's Responses to Economic Liberalization in Egypt* (Durham, Centre for Middle East and Islamic Studies, Durham Middle East Paper, no. 60, 1998).

Pripstein-Posusney, Marsha, *Labor and the State in Egypt: Workers, Unions and Economic Restructuring* (New York, Columbia University Press, 1997).

Prochaska, David, *Making Algeria French: colonialism in Bône, 1870–1920* (Cambridge, Cambridge University Press, 1990).

Puin, G.-R., "Observations on early Qur'an manuscripts in Ṣanʿāʾ, " in Wild, Stefan (ed.), *The Qur'an as Text* (Leiden: Brill, 1996).

Puin, G.-R., "Der Dīwān von ʿUmar ibn al-Hattāb. Ein Beitrag zur frühislamischen Verwaltungsgeschichte" (dissertation, Bonn, 1970).

Al-Qalqashandī, *La Syrie a l'Epoque des Mamelouks* (Paris, Librairie Orientaliste Paul Geuthner, 1923).

Qasatli, Nuʾman, *Al-Rawda al-Ghannaʾ ʿDimashq al-Fayhaʾ* (Beirut, 1876) reprinted (Beirut, Dar al-Raʾid al-ʿArabi, 1981).

Al-Qasimi, Shaykh Sultan Muhammad, *The Myth of Arab Piracy in the Gulf* (London, Croom Helm, 1986).

Qudāma b. Ja'far, *al-Kharāj wa Ṣinā 'at al-Kitāba*, ed. Muḥammad Ḥusayn al-Zubaydī (Baghdad, 1981).

Qudāma b. Ja'far, *Kitāb al-Kharāj* (Leiden and London, 1965).

Qutb, S., *Milestones* (Kuwait: Holy Koran Publishing, 1988).

Radtke, Bernd, "Theosophie (*Hikma*) and Philosophie (*Falsafa*): Ein Beitrag zur Frage der *hikmat al-mashriq/al-ishraq*," *Asiatische Studien*, 42 (2), 1988, pp. 156–74.

Radtke, Bernd, "Theologen und Mystiker in Hurasan und Transoxanien," *Zietschrift der Deutschen Morgenländischen Gesellschaft*, 136 (2), 1986, pp. 536–69.

Radtke, Bernd, *Al-Hakim al-Tirmidi: Ein islamischer Theosoph des 3./9. Jahrhunderts* (Freiburg, Schwarz, 1980).

Rafeq, Abdul-Karim, "Coexistence and integration among the religious communities in Ottoman Syria," in *Islam in the Middle Eastern Studies: Muslims and Minorities* (Osaka, Japan Center for Area Studies, 2003), pp. 97–131.

Rafeq, Abdul-Karim, "Damascus and the pilgrim caravan," in Leila Tarazi Fawaz and C. A. Bayly (eds.), *Modernity and Culture: From the Mediterranean to the Indian Ocean* (New York, Columbia University Press, 2002), pp. 130–43.

Rafeq, Abdul-Karim, "Craft organization, work ethics, and the strains of change in Ottoman Syria," *Journal of the American Oriental Society*, 111 (3), 1991, pp. 495–511.

Rafeq, Abdul-Karim, "New light on the transportation of the Damascene pilgrimage during the Ottoman period," in Robert Olson (ed.), *Islamic and Middle Eastern Societies*, (Battelboro, VT, Amana Books, 1987), pp. 127–36.

Rafeq, Abdul-Karim, "The social and economic structure of Bab al-Musalla (al-Midan), Damascus, 1825–1875," in George N. Atiyeh and Ibrahim M. Oweiss (eds.), *Arab Civilization: Challenges and Responses: Studies in Honor of Constantine K. Zurayk* (Albany, State University of New York Press, 1988).

Rafeq, Abdul-Karim, "The impact of Europe on a traditional economy: the case of Damascus, 1840–1870," in Jean-Louis Bacqué-Grammont et Paul Dumont (eds.), *Economie et Sociétés dans l'Empire Ottoman (fin du XVIIIe–début du XXe Siècle* (Paris, Centre National de la Recherche Scientifique, 1983), pp. 419–32.

Rafeq, Abdul-Karim, *The Province of Damascus, 1723–1783* (Beirut, Khayats, 1970).

Rahman, Fazlur, *Islam* (London, Weidenfeld & Nicolson, 1966).

Ramadan, Saud, "Analysis: world will judge Israel's wall," *Washington Times*, February 24, 2004.

Rapoport, D., "Fear and trembling: terrorism in three religious traditions," *American Political Science Review*, 78, 1984, pp. 662–84.

Al-Rasheed, Madawi, *A History of Saudi Arabia* (Cambridge, Cambridge University Press, 2002).

Rashid, Ahmed, *Taliban* (New Haven, CT, Yale University Press, 2000).

Rashwan, Malik Muhammad Ahmad, *'Ulama' al-Azhar bayna Bunabart wa-Muhammad 'Ali (1212–1258) (1798–1840)* (Cairo, Matba'at al-Amanah, 1989).

Raymond, André, *Arab Cities in the Ottoman Period* (Aldershot, 2002).

Raymond, André, "Islamic city, Arab city: orientalist myths and recent views," *British Journal of Middle Eastern Studies*, 21 (1), 1994, pp. 3–18.

Raymond, André, *Cairo*, tr. Willard Wood (Cambridge, MA, Harvard University Press, 2000; orig. pub. Le Caire, Librairie Arthème Fayard, 1993).

Raymond, André, *The Great Arab Cities in the 16th–18th Centuries. An Introduction* (New York, 1984).

Raymond, André, *Artisans et Commerçants au Caire au XVIIIe Siècle*, 2 vols. (Damascus, Institut Français de Damas, 1973, 1974).

Reimer, Michael J., *Colonial Bridgehead: Government and Society in Alexandria, 1807–1882* (Cairo, American University in Cairo Press, 1997).

Reinert, Benedict, *Die Lehre vom tawakkul in der klassischen Sufik* (Berlin, de Gruyter, 1968).

Reissner, Johannes, *Ideologie und Politik der Muslimbrüder Syriens: von den Wahlen 1947 bis zum Verbot unter Adib as-Sisakli 1952* (Freiburg, Klaus Schwarz, 1980).

Repp, R. C., *The Müfti of Istanbul: A Study in the Development of the Ottoman Learned Hierarchy* (London, 1986).

Revue du Monde Musulman et de la Méditerranée (REMMM), formerly *Revue de l'Occident Musulman et de la Méditerranée (ROMM)*.

Richards, Alan and John Waterbury, *A Political Economy of the Middle East* (Boulder, CO, Westview Press, 1996).

Richards, D. S. (ed.), *Islamic Civilization, 950–1150: A colloquium published under the auspices of the Near Eastern History Group, The University of Pennsylvania* (London, Cassirer, 1973).

Riley-Smith, J., *The Crusades: A Short History* (New Haven, 1987).

Rinn, Louis, *Marabouts et Khouan. Étude sur l'Islam en Algérie* (Paris, A. Jourdan, 1884).

Rippin, Andrew (ed.), *The Qur'an: formative interpretation* (Aldershot, Ashgate, 1999).

Rippin, Andrew, *Muslims, Their Religious Beliefs and Practices, Vol. 1. The Formative Period* (London, Routledge, 1993).

Ritter, Hellmut, *The Ocean of the Soul: Men, the world and God in the stories of Farid al-Din 'Attar* (Leiden, E. J. Brill, 2003).

Rizvi, Athar Abbas, *A History of Sufism in India*, 2 vols (New Delhi, Munshiram Manoharlal, 1978).

Roberts, Samuel J., *Party and Policy in Israel* (Boulder, CO, Westview Press, 1990).

Robinson, Chase, *Islamic Historiography* (Cambridge, Cambridge University Press, 2002).

Robinson, Chase, *A Medieval Islamic City Reconsidered: An Interdisciplinary Approach to Samarra* (Oxford, Oxford University Press, 2001).

Robinson, Chase, *Multidisciplinary Approaches to Samarra* (Oxford, 2000).

Robinson, Francis, *Atlas of Islamic History from 1500* (facts on file Inc., 1983).

Rodenbeck, M., *Cairo, the City Victorious* (London, Picador, 1998).

Rodinson, Maxime, *The Arabs* (Chicago, The University of Chicago Press, 1981).

Rodinson, Maxime, *Israel: A Colonial-Settler State* (New York, Pathfinder Press, 1973).

Rodinson, Maxime, *Islam et capitalisme* (Paris, Seuil, 1966).

Ro'i, Yaacov, *Islam in the Soviet Union: From the Second World War to Gorbachev* (New York, Columbia University Press, 2000).

Romann, Michael and Alex Weingrod, *Living Together Separately: Arabs and Jews in Contemporary Jerusalem* (Princeton, NJ, Princeton University Press, 1991).

Rossi, Ettore, "Una traduzione turca dell' opera '*Della Tirannide*' di V. Alfieri Probabilmente conosciuta da al-Zu'aytir, Akram, 'al-mu'tamar al-islami," *Al-Hayat* (London, June 20, 1994).

Rostow, Dankwart A., "The military in Middle Eastern society and politics," in Sydney N. Fisher (ed.), *The Military in the Middle East* (Columbus, Ohio State University Press, 1963), pp. 3–20.

Roy, Olivier, "The crisis of religious legitimacy in Iran," *Middle Eastern Studies*, 53 (2), 1999, pp. 201–16.

Roy, Olivier, *The Failure of Political Islam* (Cambridge, MA, Harvard University Press, 1994).

Rubenberg, Cheryl, *Palestinian Women: Patriarchy and Resistance in the West Bank* (Boulder, CO, Lynne Rienner, 2001).

Rubin, Barry, "The military in contemporary Middle East politics," in Rubin and Keaney (eds.), *Armed Forces in the Middle East* (London, Frank Cass, 2002), pp. 1–22.

Rubin, Barry, "The military in contemporary Middle East politics," *Middle East Review of International Affairs* (MERIA), 5 (1), 2001.

Rubin, Barry, *The Arab States and the Palestine Conflict* (Syracuse, NY, Syracuse University Press, 1981).

Rubin, Barry and Metin Heper, *Political Parties in Turkey* (London, Frank Cass, 2002).

Rubin, Barry and Thomas A. Keaney (eds.), *Armed Forces in the Middle East: Politics and Strategy*. BESA Studies in International Security (London, Frank Cass, 2002).

Rubin, Uri, *The Eye of the Beholder: The Life of Muhammad as Viewed by the Early Muslims* (Princeton, NJ, Darwin Press, 1995).

Rubin, Uri, "The life of Muhammad and the Islamic self-image," in Motzki (ed.), *Issue of the Sources*, pp. 3–17.

Rückert, Friedrich, *Sieben Bücher morgenländischer Sagen und Geschichten* (Stuttgart, S. G. Liesching, 1837).

Rudebeck, Lars, *Party and People in Tunisia* (New York, Praeger, 1969).

Rumaihi, M., *Beyond Oil* (London, Saqi Books, 1986).

Rustow, D. A., "The development of political parties in Turkey," in Joseph LaPalombara and Myron Weiner (eds.), *Political Culture and Political Development* (Princeton, NJ, Princeton University Press, 1966).

Ruthven, Malise, *Islam in the World* (Oxford, Oxford University Press, 1997).

Rzakulizade, S. D., *Panteizm v Azerbaidzhane v X–XII vv.* (Baku: Elm, 1982).

Saadaoui, A., *Tunis ville ottomane* (Tunis, 2001).

Sachar, Howard M., *A History of Israel: From the Rise of Zionism to Our Time* (Oxford: Basil Blackwell, 1977).

Sachedina, Abdulaziz, *The Just Ruler (al-sulṭān al-ʿādil) in Shīʿite Islam* (Oxford, Oxford University Press, 1988).

De Sacy, Antoine Silvestre (ed.), *Pend-naméh, le livre des conseils de Férid-Eddin Attar* (Paris, Chez Debure frères, 1819).

Sadiqi, Fatima, "Aspects of Moroccan feminism," in Fatima Sadiqi et al. (eds.), *Mouvements Féministes: Origines et Orientations* (Fez, Centre d'Etudes et de Recherches sur la Femme, 1999), pp. 195–214.

Said, Edward, *Orientalism* (Harmondsworth, Penguin, 1989).

Sajoo, Amyn, *Civil Society in the Muslim World* (London, I.B. Tauris, 2002).

Sakallioglu, Umit Cizre, "The military and politics: a Turkish dilemma," in Barry Rubin and Thomas A. Keaney (eds.), *Armed Forces in the Middle East: Politics and Strategy*, BESA Studies in International Security (London: Frank Cass, 2002), pp. 189–205.

Salame, Ghassan, *Democracy Without Democrats?* (London, I. B. Tauris, 1994).

Salibi, Kamal, *A House of Many Mansions: The History of Lebanon Reconsidered* (London, I. B. Tauris, 1988).

Salim, Mohammad A., "A critical approach to Sufism," *University Studies, Karachi*, 4 (2), 1967, pp. 55–81.

Sampson, A., *The Seven Sisters: The Great Oil Companies and the World They Made* (London: Hodder and Stoughton, 1975).

Saqqaf, Abdulaziz Y. (ed.), *The Middle East City: Ancient Traditions Confront a Modern World* (New York, Paragon House, 1987).

Sarkis, Khalil, *Rihlat al-Imbratur Ghallium al-Thani Imbratur Almanya wa-Qarinatuhu ila Filastin wa-Suriyya* (Damascus, Dar al-Farabi, 1977).

Saul, Samir, *La France et L'Egypte de 1882 à 1914: Intérêts économiques et implications politiques* (Paris, Comité pour l'histoire économique et financière de la France, Ministère de l'Économie, des Finances et de l'Industrie, 1997).

Sauvaget, Jean, "Equisse d'une histoire de la ville de Damas," *REI*, 4, 1934.

Savage, Elizabeth, *A Gateway to Hell, A Gateway to Paradise. The North African Response to the Arab Conquest* (Princeton, Darwin Press, 1997).

Save the Children online at http://www.savethechildren.org.uk/eyetoeye/info/refugees.html.

Savory, R., "Orthodoxy and aberrancy in Ithna Ashari Shi'i tradition," in W. Hallaq and D. Little (eds.), *Islamic Studies Presented to Charles J Adams* (Leiden, E. J. Brill, 1991), pp. 169–82.

Sayigh, Yezid, *Armed Struggle and the Search for State: The Palestinian National Movement, 1949–1993* (Oxford, Clarendon Press, 1997).

Al-Sayyid, Marsot, "A civil society in Egypt," in Augustus Richard Norton (ed.), *Civil Society in the Middle East* (Leiden, E. J. Brill, 1996), vol. 1, pp. 269–94.

Al-Sayyid, Marsot, Afaf Lutfi, *Egypt in the Reign of Muhammad Ali* (Cambridge, Cambridge University Press, 1984).

Scarcia, Gianroberto, "Iran ed eresia musulmana nel penso del Corbin," *Studi e materiali di storia della religione*, Napoli, 29, 1958, pp. 113–27.

Schacht, Joseph, "Law and justice," in *Cambridge Encyclopaedia of Islam* (Cambridge, Cambridge University Press, 1989).

Schacht, Joseph, *Introduction to Islamic law* (Oxford, Oxford University Press, 1964).

Schacht, Joseph, *The Origins of Muhammadan Jurisprudence* (Oxford, Clarendon Press, 1950).

Schenker, Hillel, "The making of T'kuma: an interview with Yigal Eilam," *Palestine and Israel Journal*, 5 (2), 1998.

Sherwood, W. B., "The rise of the justice party in Turkey," *World Politics*, 20, 1967–8, pp. 54–65.

Schimmel, Annemarie, *A Two-Colored Brocade: The Imagery of Persian Poetry* (Chapel Hill, University of North Carolina Press, 1992).

Schimmel, Annemarie, *As Through a Veil: Mystical Poetry in Islam* (New York, Columbia University Press, 1982).

Schimmel, Annemarie, *Mystical Dimensions of Islam* (Chapel Hill, University of North Carolina, 1975).

Schirazi, Asghar, *The Constitution of Iran: Politics and the State in the Islamic Republic* (London, I. B. Tauris, 1997).

Schmucker, Werner, *Untersuchungen zu einigen wichtigen Bodenrechtlichen Konsequenzen der islamichen Eroberungsbewegung* (Bonn, Selbstverlag des orientalischen Seminars der Universität, 1972).

Schoeler, Gregor, "Foundations for a new biography of Muhammad: the production and evaluation of the corpus of traditions from 'Urwah b. al-Zubayr," in Berg (ed.), *Method and Theory*, pp. 21–8.

Scholem, Gershom, *Major Trends in Jewish Mysticism* (New York, Schocken Books, 1988).

Scholte, Jan Aart, "Global capitalism and the state," *International Affairs*, 73 (3), 1997, pp. 427–52.

Schroeter, Daniel J., "Jewish quarters in the Arab–Islamic cities of the Ottoman empire," in Avigdor Levy (ed.), *The Jews of the Ottoman Empire* (Princeton, Darwin Press, 1994) pp. 287–300.

Schroeter, Daniel J., "Trade as a mediator in Muslim–Jewish relations: southwestern Morocco in the 19th century," in Mark R. Cohen and A. Udovitch (eds.), *Jews among Arabs: Contacts and Boundaries* (Princeton, Darwin Press, 1989), pp. 113–40.

Schweid, "Jewishness and Israeliness," *Palestine and Israel Journal*, 8 (4), 2001, and 9 (1), 2002.

Seale, Patrick, *The Struggle for Syria: A Study of Post-war Arab Politics 1945–1958* (London, Oxford University Press, 1965).

Sears, Stuart D., "A Monetary History of Iraq and Iran, ca. CE 500–750" (dissertation, University of Chicago, 1997).

Sedgwick, Mark J., *Sufism: The Essentials* (Cairo, American University of Cairo Press, 2000).

Segev, Tom, *Elvis in Jerusalem: Post-Zionism and the Americanization of Israel* (New York, Metropolitan Books, 2001).

Segev, Tom, *One Palestine Complete: Jews and Arabs Under the British Mandate* (London, Little, Brown and Co., 2000).

Segre, Claudio G., *The Fourth Shore: the Italian Colonization of Libya* (Chicago, University of Chicago Press, 1974).

Seligman, A., *The Idea of Civil Society* (New York, Free Press, 1992).

Sen, A., *Development As Freedom* (Oxford, Oxford University Press, 1999).

Serageldin, Ismail, James Socknat, J. Stace Birks, and Clive Sinclair, "Some issues related to labor migration in the Middle East and North Africa," *The Middle East Journal*, 38 (4), 1984, pp. 615–42.

Serageldin, Ismail, and Smair El-Sadek (eds.), *The Arab City: Its Character and Islamic Cultural Heritage* (Proceedings of the Symposium, held in Medina, Kingdom of Saudi Arabia, February 28–March 5, 1981 (Riyadh, Arab Urban Development Institute, 1982).

Serageldin, Ismail, James Socknat, Stace Birks, Bob Li and Clive Sinclair, *Manpower and International Labor Migration in the Middle East and North Africa* (Washington, DC: The World Bank, 1981).

Serjeant, R. B. (ed.), *The Islamic City* (Selected Papers from the Colloquium held at the Middle East Centre, Faculty of Oriental Studies, Cambridge, United Kingdom, July 19–23, 1976 (Paris, UNESCO, 1980).

Serjeant, R. B. and Ronald Lewcock (eds.), *San'a: An Arabian Islamic City* (London, World of Islam Festival Trust, 1983).

Setton, K. (ed.), *History of the Crusades* (Madison, 1955–75).

Shaban, M. A., *Islamic History, A.D. 600–750 (A.H. 132): A New Interpretation* (Cambridge, Cambridge University Press, 1971).

Sharabi, Hisham, *Neopatriarchy: A Theory of Distorted Change in Arab Society* (Oxford, Oxford University Press, 1988).

Sharara, Waddah, *al-Umma al-qaliqa* (Beirut: Dar al-Nahar, 1996).

Sharara, Waddah, *Dawlat "Hizbu-l-lah": Lubnan majtama'-an Islami-yyan* (Beirut, Dar al-Nahar, 1996).

Shariati, A., *Message to the Enlightened Thinkers*, at http://www.shariati.com/

Shatzmiller, M., *The Berbers and the Islamic State* (Princeton, 2000).

Sherbiny, Naiem A., "Expatriate labor flows to the Arab oil countries in the 1980s," *The Middle East Journal*, 38 (4), 1984, pp. 643–67.

Sherbiny, Naiem A. and Ismail Serageldin, "Expatriate labor and economic growth: Saudi demand for Egyptian labor," in Malcolm H. Kerr and El Sayed Yassin (eds.), *Rich and Poor States in the Middle East: Egypt and the New Arab Order* (Boulder, Westview Press, 1982).

Shmidt, Aleksandr, '*Abd al-Wahhab ash-Sharanii (+973/1565) i ego kniga* Razsypanykh zhemcuzhin (St. Petersburg, Tipografiia Imperatorskoi akademii nauk, 1914).

Shindler, Colin, *Israel, Likud and the Zionist Dream* (London, I. B. Tauris, 1995).

Shkodra, Zija, "Les Esnaf ou Corporations dans la Vie Urbaine Balkanique des XVII–XVIIIe Siècle," *Studia Albanica*, 2, 1985, pp. 47–76.

Shkodra, Zija, *Esnafet Shqipatre* (Tirane, 1973).

Shlaim, Avi, *Collusion Across the Jordan: King Abdullah, the Zionist Movement and the Partition of Palestine* (Oxford, Clarendon Press, 1988).

Shoufani, Elias S., *Al-Riddah and the Muslim Conquest of Arabia* (Beirut, Arab Institute for Research and Publishing, and Toronto, University of Toronto Press, 1972).

Shuval, T., *La ville d'Alger vers la fin du XVIIIème siècle* (Paris, 1998).

Signoles, Pierre (ed.), *Petites villes et villes moyennes dans le Monde Arabe* (Tours, Centre d'Etudes et de Recherches URBAMA, Université de Tours, Fascicule de Recherches, nos. 16 and 17, 1986).

Signoles, Pierre, *L'espace tunisien: Capitale et Etat-Région* (Tours: Centre d'Etudes et de Recherches URBAMA, Université de Tours, Fascicule de Recherches, nos. 14 and 15, 1985).

Silberstein, Laurence J., *The Postzionism Debates: Knowledge and Power in Israeli Culture* (New York, Routledge, 1999).

Silverstein, Paul, "Realizing myth: Berbers in France and Algeria," *Middle East Report*, 26 (3), 1996, pp. 11–15.

Simon, Reeva, "Iraq," in Frank Tachau (ed.), *Political Parties of the Middle East and North Africa* (London, Mansell, 1994), pp. 174–97.

Simon, Robert, "Muhammad and the Jihād," *Acta Orientalia*, 52, 1999, pp. 235–42.

Simonsen, Jørgen Bæk, *Studies in the Genesis and Early Development of the Caliphal Taxation System* (Copenhagen, Akademisk Forlag, 1988).

Singer, Amy, *Palestinian Peasants and Ottoman Officials* (1994).

Singerman, Diane and Homa Hoodfar (eds.), *Development, Change, and Gender in Cairo* (Bloomington, Indiana University Press, 1996).

Singerman, Diane, *Avenues of Participation: Family, politics, and Networks in Urban Quarters of Cairo* (Princeton, Princeton University Press, 1995).

Sirriyeh, Elizabeth, *Sufis and Anti-Sufis: The defence, rethinking and rejection of Sufism in the modern world* (Richmond, Surrey, Curzon, 1999).

Skinner, Quentin, *The Foundations of Modern Political Thought* (Cambridge, Cambridge University Press, 1978).

Sluglett, Peter, "La monarchie dans le monde arabe: mythes et réalités," in Rémy Leveau and Abdellah Hammoudi (éds.), *Monarchies Arabes: Transitions et dérives dynastiques* (Paris, La documentation Française, 2002), pp. 143–58.

Sluglett, Peter, "Formal and informal empire in the Middle East," in Robin W. Winks (ed.), *The Oxford History of the British Empire, vol. V: Historiography* (Oxford, Oxford University Press, 1999), pp. 416–36.

Sluglett, Peter and Marion Farouk-Sluglett, "The precarious monarchy: Britain, Ibn Sa'ud, and the establishment of the kingdom of Hijaz, Najd and dependencies, 1925–1932," in T. Niblock (ed.), *State, Society and Economy in Saudi Arabia* (London, Croom Helm, 1982), pp. 36–57.

Sluglett, Peter, *Britain in Iraq 1914–1932* (London, Ithaca Press, 1976).

Smith, Anthony D., *The Ethnic Origins of Nations* (Oxford, Blackwell, 1988).

Smith, Margaret, *Studies in Early Islamic Mysticism in the Near and Middle East* (Oxford, Oneworld, 1995).

Smith, Margaret, *The Sufi Path of Love* (London, Luzac, 1954).

Snouck-Hurgronje, Christiaan, *Verspreide Geschriften/Gesammelte Schriften*, 5 vols. (Bonn and Leipzig, K. Schroeder, 1923–7).

Soudavar, "The early Safavids and their cultural interactions with surrounding states," in N. Keddie and R. Mathee (eds.), *Iran & the Surrounding World* (Seattle, University of Washington Press, 2002).

Sourdel, Dominique, *Medieval Islam* (London and Boston, Routledge and Kegan Paul, 1983).

Spuler, Bertold, *Iran in früh-islamischer Zeit* (Wiesbaden, Franz Steiner, 1952).

Stansfield, Gareth, *Iraqi Kurdistan: Political development and emergent democracy* (London, Routledge Curzon, 2003).

Stein, Kenneth, *The Land Question in Palestine 1917–1939* (Chapel Hill, NC, 1984).

Stein, Leonard, *Zionism* (London, Ernest Benn, 1925).

Stern, S. M., "The early Ismā'īlī missionaries in north-western Persia and in Khurāsān and Transoxania," *Bulletin of the School of Oriental and African Studies*, 23, 1960, pp. 56–90.

Stevens and Elmissiri (eds.), *Israel and South Africa: The Progression of a Relationship* (New Brunswick, North American Inc., 1977).

Stevens, P., "Resource impact: curse or blessing? A literature survey," *The Journal of Energy Literature*, 9 (1), 2003.

Stevens, P., "The impact of oil on the role of the state in economic development: a case study of the Arab world," *Arab Affairs*, 1 (1), 1986.

Stevenson, Thomas B., *Social Change in a Yemeni Highlands Town* (Salt Lake City, University of Utah Press, 1985).

Stivers, W., *Supremacy and Oil* (Ithaca, NY, Cornell University Press, 1982).

Stocking, G. W., *Middle East Oil* (Nashville, Vanderbilt University Press, 1970).

Suleiman, Michael, *Political Parties in Lebanon: the Challenge of a Fragmented Political Culture* (Ithaca, NY, Cornell University Press, 1967).

Susser, Asher, "The Palestinians in Jordan: demographic majority, political minority," in Bengio and Ben-Dor (1999), pp. 91–109.

Al-Ṣūlī, Abū Bakr Muḥammad b. Yaḥyā, *Kitāb al-Awrāq*, ed. A. Khalidov (St Petersburg, 1998).

Sviri, Sara, *The Taste of Hidden Things: Images on the Sufi Path* (Inverness, CA: The Golden Sufi Center, 1997).

Swedenburg, Ted, *Memories of Revolt: The 1936–1939 Rebellion and the Palestinian National Past* (Minneapolis, University of Minnesota Press, 2003).

Al-Tabarī, Muhammad ibn Jarīr, *Ta'rīkh al-rusul wa l-mulūk* (Leiden, E. J. Brill, 1879–1901).

Tachau Frank (ed.), *Political Parties of the Middle East and North Africa* (London, Mansell, 1994).

Tadjikova, K., "Osobennosti sufizma v sredenvekovom Kazakhztane," *Izvestiia Akademii nauk KazSSR*, 2, 1978, pp. 57–62.

Taha, ʿAbdulwahid Dhanun, *The Muslim Conquest and Settlement of North Africa and Spain* (London, Routledge, 1989).

Al-Tahtawi, Rifaʿa Rifʿat, *Takhlis al-ibriz ila talkhis bariz* (Cairo, 1973).

Al-Tahtawi, Rifaʿa Rifʿat, *Anwar Tawfiq al-jalil* (Cairo, 1285/1868).

TAMAZGHA, "The Amazight issue in Morocco," UN Economic and Social Council, International Convention on the Elimination of All Forms of Racial Discrimination (ICERD), 62nd Session of the Commission for the Elimination of Racial Discrimination, Geneva, 3–21 March, 2003.

Tarbush, Mohammad A., *The Role of the Military in Politics: A Case Study of Iraq to 1941* (London and New York, KPI, 1985).

Tekeli, Sirin, "Emergence of the feminist movement in Turkey," in Drude Dahlerup (ed.), *The New Women's Movement: Feminism and Political Power in Europe and the USA* (London, Sage, 1986), pp. 179–99.

Terrasse, H., *Histoire du Maroc* (Paris, 1949).

Terry, Janice, *Cornerstone of Egyptian Political Power: The Wafd 1919–1952* (London, Third World Centre, 1982).

Tholuck, Friedrich, *Blütensammlung aus der morgenlandischen Mystik* (Berlin, Ferdinand-Dimmler, 1825).

Thompson, Elizabeth, *Colonial Citizens: Republican Rights, Paternal Privileges and Gender in French Syria and Lebanon* (New York, Columbia University Press, 1999).

Thorau, Peter, *The Lion of Egypt* (London, Longman, 1987).

Tibi, Bassam, *Arab Nationalism: Between Islam and the Nation-State* (Basingstoke, Hampshire and London, Macmillan Press, 1997).

Tibi, Bassam, *Arab Nationalism: A Critical Inquiry* (New York, St. Martin's Press, 1990).

Tilman Nagel, "Das Kalifat der Abbasiden," in U. Haarmann (ed.), *Geschichte der arabischen Welt* (Munich, Verlag C. H. Beck, 1987), pp. 110–65.

Tilly, Charles, "War and state power," *Middle East Report*, 171, 1991.

Todorov, Nikolai, *The Balkan City: 1400–1900* (Seattle, University of Washington Press, 1983).

Tohidi, Nayereh, "Modernity, Islamization, and women in Iran," in V. M. Moghadam (ed.), *Gender and National Identity: Women and Politics in Muslim Societies* (London, Zed Books, 1994), pp. 110–47.

Toprak, Binnaz, "Women and fundamentalism: the case of Turkey," in Moghadam (ed.), *Identity Politics and Women* (1994), pp. 293–306.

Toprak, Binnaz, "The religious right," in Irvin C. Schick and Ertugrul Ahmet Tonak (eds.), *Turkey in Transition: New Perspectives* (New York, Oxford University Press, 1987).

Triaud, Jean-Louis, *La légende noire de la Sanusiyya: une confrérie musulmane et saharienne sous le regard français (1840–1930)* (Paris, Editions de Maison des sciences de l'homme, 1995).

Tsugitaka, Sato (ed.), *Islamic Urbanism in Human History: Political Power and Social Networks* (London, Kegan Paul, 1997).

Turan, Ilter, "Political parties and the party system in post-1983 Turkey," in M. Heper and A. Evin (eds.), *State, Democracy and the Military: Turkey in the 1980s* (Berlin, Walter de Gruyter, 1988).

Turnbull, C. M., "Formal and informal empire in east Asia," in Robin W. Winks (ed.), *The Oxford History of the British Empire, vol. V: Historiography* (Oxford, Oxford University Press, 1999), pp. 379–402.

Turner, Bryan, *Orientalism, Postmodernism and Globalism* (London, Routledge, 1994).

Turner, Bryan, "Towards an economic model of virtuoso religion," in Ernst Gellner (ed.), *Islamic Dilemmas: Reformers, Nationalists and Industrialization* (Berlin and New York, Mouton Publishers, 1985), pp. 49–72.

Turner, Victor, *The Ritual Process* (Chicago, Aldine, 1969).

" 'Ulama'," *Encyclopedia of Islam*, 2nd edn.

Ülken, Hilmi, "L'école wudjudite et son influence sur la pensée torque," *Wiener Zeitschrift für Kunde des Morgenlandes*, 62, 1969, pp. 193–208.

United Nations (UN), *The World's Women 2000: Trends and Statistics* (New York, UN, 2000).

United Nations on the internet at http://ods-dds-ny.un.org/doc/RESOLUTION/GEN/NR0/240/94/IMG/NR024094.pdf?OpenElement.

United Nations on the internet at http://ods-dds-ny.un.org/doc/RESOLUTION/GEN/NR0/288/65/IMG/NR028865.pdf?OpenElement.

United Nations Development Programme (UNDP), *Human Development Report* (Oxford, Oxford University Press, 2003).

UNDP and the Arab Fund for Economic and Social Development, *The Arab Human Development Report* (New York, UNDP, 2002).

"Urban Fabric," *Special Issue of Environmental Design: Journal of the Islamic Environmental Design Research Centre*, 1989.

US Department of State, "Country reports on human rights practices: Turkey, 2002." See the internet at http://www.state.gov/g/drl/rls/hrrpt/2002/18396.htm.

US Department of State, "Morocco: human rights practices 1994." See the internet at http://dosfan.lib.uic.edu/ERC/democracy/1994_hrp_report/94hrp_report_nea/Morocco.html.

Veselovskii, Nikolai, "Pamiatnik Khodzhi Akhrara v Samarkande," *Vostochnye zametki. Sbornik stateii i issledovanii professorov i prepodavatelei vostochnyakh iazykov Imperatorskogo St Peterburgskogo universiteta* (St. Petersburg, St. Petersburg University, 1895), pp. 321–35.

Vasile, Elizabeth, "Devotion as distinction, piety as power: religious revival and the transformation of space in the illegal settlements of Tunis", in Michael E. Bonine (ed.), *Population, Poverty, and Politics in Middle East Cities* (Gainesville, University Press of Florida, 1997), pp. 113–40.

Vatikiotis, P. J., *Conflict in the Middle East* (London, George Allen & Unwin, 1971).

Vaziri, M., *Iran as Imagined Nation* (London, Paragon House, 1993).

Vernon Schubel, *Religious Performance in Contemporary Islam: Shi'i Devotional Rituals in South Asia* (Columbia, University of South Carolina Press, 1993).

Vikør, Knut, *Sufi and Scholar on the Desert Edge: Muhammad b. 'Ali al-Sanusi and his Brotherhood* (London, Hurst and Company, 1995).

Vowinckel, K., *Translation of Geschichte der nationalen Bewegung im Orient* (K. Vowinckel, Berlin, 1928).

Vryonis, Speros, *The Decline of Medieval Hellenism in Asia Minor and the Process of Islamization from the Eleventh through the Fifteenth Century* (Berkeley, University of California Press, 1986).

Walbridge, Linda S., *The Most Learned of the Shi'a: the institution of Marja' taqlid* (New York, Oxford University Press, 2001).

Walker, P., *Exploring an Islamic Empire* (London, 2001).

Wansbrough, John, *Quranic Studies* (London, Oxford University Press, 1977).

Wansbrough, John, "Res ipsa loquitur: history and mimesis," in Berg (ed.), *Method and Theory*, pp. 3–19.

Waardenburg, Jean-Jacques, *L'Islam dans le miroir de l'Occident* (Paris and The Hague, Mouton, 1963).

al-Wakil, 'Abd al-Rahman, *Hadhihi hiya al-sufiyya* (Cairo, Matba'at al-Sunna al-Muhammadiyya, 1955).

Watenpaugh, Keith, "Towards a new category of colonial theory: colonial cooperation and the Survivors' Bargain. The case of the post-genocide Armenian community of Syria," in Nadine Méouchy, and Peter Sluglett (eds.), *The British and French Mandates in Comparative Perspective/Les mandats français et anglais dans une perspective comparative* (Leiden, E. J. Brill, 2004), pp. 597–623.

"Water and architecture," *Special Issue of Environmental Design: Journal of the Islamic Environmental Design Research Centre*, 1985.

Watt, W. M., *The Formative Period of Islamic Thought* (Edinburgh, Edinburgh University Press, 1973).

Watt, W. M., *Muhammad. Prophet and Statesman* (Oxford, Oxford University Press, 1961).

Watt, W. M., *Muhammad at Mecca* (Oxford, Oxford University Press, 1953).

Waugh, Earle, *The Munshidin of Egypt: Their world and their song* (Columbia, SC, University of South Carolina Press, 1989).

Weeks, John R., "The demography of Islamic nations," *Population Bulletin*, 43 (4), 1988.

Wellhausen, Julius, *Das arabische Reich und sein Sturz* (Berlin, Georg Reimer, 1902).

Wellhausen, Julius, *Reste arabischen Heidentums* (Berlin, 1897).

Wensinck, Arent Jan, *Bar Hebraeus's Book of the Dove Together with Some Chapters from his Ethikon* (Leiden: E. J. Brill, 1919).

Wensinck, Arent Jan, *Mohammed en de Joden te Medina* (Leiden, E. J. Brill, 1908).

Wheeler, Brannon M., *Applying the Canon in Islam: The Authorization and Maintenance of Interpretive Reasoning in Hanafi Scholarship* (Albany, State University of New York Press, 1996).

Whitcomb, Donald S., "The Misr of Ayla: new evidence for the early Islamic city," in G. Bisheh (ed.), *Studies in History and Archaeology of Jordan 5: Art and Technology through the Ages* (Amman: Department of Antiquities, 1995), pp. 277–88.

White, Jenny B., *Islamist Mobilization in Turkey: A Study in Vernacular Politics* (Seattle, University of Washington Press, 2002).

White, Jenny B., *Money Makes Us Relatives: Women's Labor in Urban Turkey* (Austin, University of Texas Press, 1994).

Whitelam, Keith, *The Invention of Ancient Israel* (London, KPI, 1997).

Wickham, C., "The uniqueness of the east," *Journal of Peasant Studies*, 12 (2–3), 1985.

Wilbur, D., *Reza Shah Pahlavi: The Resurrection and Reconstruction of Iran* (New York, 1975).

Wiley, Joyce N., *The Islamic Movement of Iraqi Shi'as* (Boulder and London: Lynne Rienner, 1992).

Williams, L. F. Rushbrook (ed.), *Sufi Studies: East and West* (New York, E. P. Dutton and Co., 1973).

Wikan, Unni, *Life among the Poor in Cairo* (London, Tavistock Publications, 1980).

Winter, Michael, *Society and Religion in early Ottoman Egypt: Studies in the writings of 'Abd al-Wahhab al-Sha'rani* (New Brunswick, NJ, Transaction Books, 1982).

Wirth, Eugen, *Die orientalische Stadt im islamischen Vorderasien und Nordafrika* (Mainz, Verlag Philipp von Zabern, 2000).

Wittek, Paul, *The Rise of the Ottoman Empire* (New York, Burt Franklin, 1971).

Wood, Alfred C., *A History of the Levant Company* (New York, Barnes and Noble, 1964).

World Bank, *World Development Indicators 2000* (World Bank, 2000).

Wright, Gwendolyn, *The Politics of Design in French Colonial Urbanism* (Chicago, Chicago University Press, 1991).

Yamak, Labib Zuwiyya, "Party politics in the Lebanese political system," in Leonard Binder (ed.), *Politics in Lebanon* (New York, John Wiley, 1966), pp. 143–66.

Yamak, Labib Zuwiyya, *The Syrian Social Nationalist Party: An Ideological Analysis* (Cambridge, MA, Harvard Center for Middle Eastern Studies, 1966).

Al-Yaʻqūbī, Aḥmad b. Abī Yaʻqūb, *Kitāb al-Buldān*, ed. M. J. de Goeje (Leiden, 1892).

Al-Yaʻqūbī, Aḥmad b. Abī Yaʻqūb, *Taʼrīkh*, ed. M. Houtsma (Leiden, 1883).

Yāqūt, Yaʻqūb b. ʻAbd Allāh, *Muʻjam al-Buldān*, ed. F. Wustenfeld (Leipzig, 1886).

Yergin, D., *The Prize* (New York, Simon & Schuster, 1991).

Yukawa, Takashi (ed.), *Urbanism in Islam* (The Proceedings of the 2nd International Conference on Urbanism in Islam (ICUIT II), Nov. 27–9, 1990. Research Project "Urbanism in Islam" and the Middle Eastern Culture Center in Japan, Tokyo, 1994).

Yukawa, Takashi (ed.), *Urbanism in Islam* (The Proceedings of the International Conference on Urbanism in Islam (ICUIT), Oct. 22–8, 1989. Research Project "Urbanism in Islam" and the Middle Eastern Culture Center in Japan, Tokyo, 1989).

Abū Yūsuf Yaʻqūb b. Ibrāhīm al-Anbārī, *Kitab al-Kharāj* (Leiden and London, 1969).

Zabih, Sepehr, *The Iranian Military in Revolution and War* (London, Routledge, 1988).

Zachariadou, E. (ed.), *The Ottoman Emirate* (1993)

Zaehner, Robert, *Hindu and Muslim Mysticism* (London: University of London, Athlone Press, 1960).

Zaman, Muhammad Qasim, *The Ulama in Contemporary Islam: custodians of change* (Princeton: Princeton University Press, 2002).

Zaman, Muhammad Qasim, *Religion and Politics Under the Early ʻAbbasids: the emergence of the proto-Sunni elite* (Leiden, E. J. Brill, 1997).

De Zambaur, E., *Manuel de généalogie et de chronologie pour l'histoire de l'Islam* (Hannover, Heinz Lafaire, 1927).

Zamir, Meir, *Lebanon's Quest: The Road to Statehood 1926–1939* (London, I. B. Tauris, 1997).

Zamir, Meir, *The Formation of Modern Lebanon* (Ithaca, NY, Cornell University Press, 1985).

Zarrīnkūb, ʻAbd al-Husayn, "Persian Sufism in its historical perspective," *Iranian Studies*, 3 (3–4), 1970, pp. 136–220.

Zarrīnkūb, ʻAbd al-Husayn, "The Arab conquest of Iran and its aftermath," *Cambridge History of Iran*, 4 (Cambridge, Cambridge University Press), pp. 1–56.

Zartman, I. William, "Opposition as support of the state," in Dawisha and Zartman (eds.), *Beyond Coercion* (1988), pp. 61–87.

Ze'evi, Dror, *An Ottoman Century: The District of Jerusalem in the 1600s* (1996).

Zeghal, Malika, *Gardiens de l'Islam: les oulémas d'Al Azhar dans l'Égypte contemporaine* (Paris, Presses de la fondation nationale des sciences politiques, 1996).

Zeine, N. Zeine, *Arab–Turkish Relations and the Emergence of Arab Nationalism* (Beirut, Khayat's, 1958).

Zhukovskii, Valentin (ed.), *Raskrytie skrytogo za zavesoi* (Kashf al-mahdzhub) Abu 'l-Khasana Ibn Osmana al-Dzhullabi al-Khudzhviri (Leningrad, Izdatel'stvo Leningradskogo gosudarstvennogo universiteta, 1926).

Zilfi, Madeline C., *The Politics of Piety: The Ottoman ulema in the Postclassical Age (1600–1800)*, (Minneapolis, MN, Bibliotheca Islamica, 1988).

Zisser, Eyal, "The Syrian army on the domestic and external fronts," in Barry Rubin and Thomas A. Keaney (eds.), *Armed Forces in the Middle East: Politics and Strategy* (BESA Studies in International Security, London, Frank Cass, 2002).

Zohny, Ahmed T., "Towards an apolitical role for the Egyptian military in the management of development," *Orient*, 28 (4), 1987.

Zu'aytir, Akram, *Mudhakkirat: Bawakir al-Nidal*, vol. 1 (Beirut, al-Mu'assasa al-'Arabiyya li-al-Dirasat, 1994).

Zubaida, Sami, *Law and Power in Islam* (London, I. B. Tauris, 2003).

Zubaida, Sami, "The nation-state and religious community in the Middle East," in Thomas Scheffler (ed.), *Religion Between Violence and Reconciliation* (Ergon Verlag/Orient Institut, 2002), pp. 457–70.

Zubaida, Sami, *Islam, the People and the State* (London, I. B. Tauris, 1993).

Zürcher, Erik J., *Turkey: A Modern History* (London, I. B. Tauris, 1998).

Zureik, Aisha Harb, *The Effect of War on University Education* (project discussed in *Al-Raida*, Beirut University College, 9 (52), 1991).

Index

Note: 'n.' after a page reference indicates the number of a note on that page.

Printed in the USA/Agawam, MA
December 7, 2010

555449.017